THE SCOUTING REPORT: 1993

Produced by STATS, Inc.
(Sports Team Analysis and Tracking Systems, Inc.)

John Dewan, Editor
Don Zminda, Associate Editor

Statistics by STATS, Inc.

HarperPerennial
A Division of HarperCollins*Publishers*

The player photographs which appear in THE SCOUTING REPORT: 1993 were furnished individually by the 28 teams that comprise Major League Baseball. Their cooperation is gratefully acknowledged: Baltimore Orioles, Boston Red Sox, California Angels, Chicago White Sox, Cleveland Indians, Detroit Tigers, Kansas City Royals, Milwaukee Brewers, Minnesota Twins, New York Yankees, Oakland A's, Seattle Mariners, Texas Rangers, Toronto Blue Jays, Atlanta Braves, Chicago Cubs, Cincinnati Reds, Colorado Rockies, Florida Marlins, Houston Astros, Los Angeles Dodgers, Montreal Expos, New York Mets/Mark Levine, Philadelphia Phillies, Pittsburgh Pirates, St. Louis Cardinals, San Diego Padres and San Francisco Giants. Special thanks to the Louisville Redbirds and Stan Denny.

FIRST EDITION

Designed by STATS, Inc.

ISSN 0743-1309

ISBN 0-06-273192-0

93 94 RRD 3 2 1

Table of Contents

Acknowledgments

It seems that this section of the book gets longer every year. The staff at STATS Inc. has grown and many of them have focused their talents toward producing this book. So there are quite a few people to thank for their talents, efforts and expertise, without which this book would not be the same.

Don Zminda, has been my associate editor for the last four years. It is a role that draws upon his numerous talents. He coordinates all the scouts. He is the first editor of all the reports and as such must bring consistency to scouting reports written by many talented but diverse analysts. He is also the author of the minor league prospect reports. Once again this book is a tribute to his many talents. As always, it was a pleasure to work with you Don.

Dr. Richard Cramer, founder and Chairman of the Board of STATS, Inc., is the person most responsible for the computer systems which are used by STATS' reporters to score every play and to chart the direction and distance of each ball put into play. From this information Dick developed the batting and pitching charts which appear in this book. This information comes out of the same STATS system used by TV broadcasters, newspapers and Major League teams for inside information. Thanks to Dick for making this all possible.

In his second year as production assistant for this book, Ross Schaufelberger has done a tremendous job and has been indispensable. He was copy editor, assistant statistical editor and coordinator of the production of this book. Thanks for another great job.

Steve Moyer as statistical editor was the eagle eye this year, reviewing each and every statistic for accuracy and relevance. This job drew upon his extensive baseball background to verify and enhance statistics on 28 teams.

Thanks to Pat Quinn who took over many of the typesetting tasks this year and readily became an expert at it.

If you enjoy the rankings which appear for each player, as I do, please join me in thanking Chuck Miller and Bob Mecca who worked at producing this section.

Thanks to Michael Coulter who was the new assistant copy editor this year. Michael also worked on acquiring the player photos which appear in the book.

Thanks to Bud Podrazik who performed the layout of the photos and the charts, and to Alissa Hudson who assisted in the photo collection. I also gratefully acknowledge all the teams who have provided these photos.

My appreciation goes to the rest of the STATS' staff who kept the office rolling and who are also, in one way or another, responsible for all the statistical information which you find in this book: Arthur Ashley, Vice President, Sue Dewan Vice President, Jules Aquino, Rob McQuown, Marge Morra, Jim Musso, Suzette Neily, David Pinto, Debra Pokres, and Allan Spear.

It would be difficult to produce the Stars, Bums and Sleepers of 1993 without the insight of Bill James' formula for projecting player performance. Thanks Bill.

The terrific statistics you find within this book would not be possible without the STATS, Inc. reporters who covered every game throughout the 1992 season. Thanks.

Thanks to our editor at HarperCollins, Robert Wilson.

And a special thanks to my wife, Sue, and my two-year-old son, Jason. They put up with a part-time husband and father whenever these book deadlines consume so much of my time.

— John Dewan

The Scouting Staff

A baseball scout is a careful observer with years of proven experience and an eye for detail -- someone who can tell you who's good, and who isn't. Our own scouts fit that definition very well. **The Scouting Report** writing staff consists of both beat reporters and STATS employees who cover major league games on a regular basis, and they know their stuff. We feel justifiably proud of their work, and we'd like to recognize them for their outstanding efforts.

The scouting reports in this book were written by the following people, in conjunction with our editors:

Baltimore Orioles	Kent Baker *Baltimore Morning Sun*
Boston Red Sox	Peter Gammons *ESPN/The Boston Globe*
California Angels	Dave King and Don Zminda *STATS, Inc.*
Chicago White Sox	Don Zminda *STATS, Inc.*
Cleveland Indians	Paul Hoynes *Cleveland Plain Dealer*
Detroit Tigers	Chuck Miller and Don Zminda *STATS, Inc.*
Kansas City Royals	Marc Bowman *STATS, Inc.*
Milwaukee Brewers	Matt Greenberger *STATS, Inc.*
Minnesota Twins	Dennis Brackin *Minneapolis Star-Tribune*
New York Yankees	John Benson *Diamond Analytics*
Oakland Athletics	Carrie Muskat *United Press International*
Seattle Mariners	Steve Kolk *STATS, Inc.*
Texas Rangers	Don Zminda *STATS, Inc.*
Toronto Blue Jays	Howard Sinker *Minneapolis Star-Tribune*
Atlanta Braves	Steve Moyer *STATS, Inc.*
Chicago Cubs	Ross Schaufelberger *STATS, Inc.*
Cincinnati Reds	Peter Pascarelli *ESPN/The Sporting News*
Colorado Rockies	Matt Greenberger *STATS, Inc.*
Florida Marlins	Matt Greenberger *STATS, Inc.*
Houston Astros	Joe Heiling *Beaumont Enterprise & Journal*
Los Angeles Dodgers	Don Hartack *STATS, Inc.*
Montreal Expos	Marco Bresba *STATS, Inc.*
New York Mets	John Benson *Diamond Analytics*
Philadelphia Phillies	Peter Pascarelli *ESPN/The Sporting News*
Pittsburgh Pirates	John Perrotto *Beaver County Times*
St. Louis Cardinals	Matt Greenberger *STATS, Inc.*
San Diego Padres	Peter Pascarelli *ESPN/The Sporting News*
San Francisco Giants	Peter Pascarelli *ESPN/The Sporting News*

The minor league prospect reports were written by Don Zminda.

This is STATS' fourth edition of **The Scouting Report,** and we'd like to recognize the hearty breed of writers who have worked on all four editions of the book: Kent Baker, John Benson, Marc Bowman, Dennis Brackin, Joe Heiling, Paul Hoynes, John Perrotto and Howard Sinker. Thanks to everyone who helped put together these books, but most especially you gentlemen.

On a personal level, I'd like to thank Ross Schaufelberger, whose attention to detail is a major reason this book is a quality product; Peter Gammons and Peter Pascarelli, for helping give this book their own touch of class; Steve Moyer, for his expertise on minor league prospects; Dick Cramer and John and Sue Dewan, for making STATS the state of the art in sports statistics; and my wife Sharon, for her patience and support always, but especially at Scouting Report time.

— Don Zminda

Introduction

A year ago, not many fans, even the readers of the top baseball publications, knew much about an unimposing righthander who had spent 1991 working for the Pirates' AA farm club at Carolina. Readers of **The Scouting Report**, however, knew that Tim Wakefield was a knuckleballer who "could have a very productive (and lengthy) career." And last fall Wakefield was starring for the Pirates.

A year ago, not many people outside of Cleveland knew very much about the Tribe's quiet young second baseman. Readers of **The Scouting Report**, however, knew that we had Carlos Baerga tabbed as a "future All-Star." And last July, the future arrived for Baerga at the midsummer classic in San Diego.

A year ago, not even the New York Mets themselves considered a tall, skinny righthander from one of their Class A clubs to be much of a pitching prospect. Readers of **The Scouting Report**, however, knew about Jose Martinez' "long shot" potential and "awesome stats." And last fall the Mets were as despondent over losing Martinez in the expansion draft as the Florida Marlins were elated to get him with an early pick.

We could go on, but we think you get the picture. **The Scouting Report** long ago earned its stripes as an analyst of major league talent, but we're not about to start resting on our laurels. Every year we try to turn out the best, most complete version of **The Scouting Report** yet, and we think we've succeeded once again. Our pool of top scouts is outstanding, as usual, and includes the likes of Peter Gammons and Peter Pascarelli.

We try to add something new each year, like last year's popular "prospects page": that's where **Scouting Report** readers first learned about Wakefield and Martinez, and also about such then-obscure players as the Padres' Frank Seminara and the Braves' Javier Lopez. This year, hot off the expansion draft, we offer complete sections on the new Florida Marlins and Colorado Rockies -- both the well-known names like Bryan Harvey, and the lesser ones like Eric Wedge.

Without a doubt, this is our most comprehensive edition yet, including reports on over 825 major- and minor-league players. Along with those lively, well-written reports, we give you a mountain of useful, easy-to-understand data. This includes hitting and pitching charts based on the 1992 season. The hitting charts show you graphically where each player hits the ball, while the pitching charts measure the effectiveness of every pitcher (in four different situations) in performing his most basic task -- throwing a strike. Take a look at some of the players we have labelled as having "pinpoint control", like Bob Tewksbury, and you'll immediately realize the secret to their success.

Returning for a third year is the popular section entitled "Stars, Bums and Sleepers." In this section, a fantasy/rotisserie smorgasbord, you'll get a feel for what to expect from each player in 1993: whether they will improve, decline, remain consistent, even come out of nowhere to surprise. If you had looked through this section last season, you'd have noticed that we expected that Cal Ripken and Devon White would drop in production (they did), and that Reggie Sanders and Leo Gomez were "sleepers" (they were).

The Prospect Pages

For the second straight season, **The Scouting Report** presents a "prospects page" for each team, including the new Marlins and Rockies. For each club, we've chosen five outstanding minor-league players -- many of them ready to make a major-league impact in 1993 and almost all expected to make an impact within two or three years. We try to avoid the hype, and instead identify the guys who will be helping their club in the next few years.

As a useful guide, we include "major league equivalencies" for the position players who played at the AA or AAA level in 1992. The MLE is a tool, adjusted for league and ball park, devised by Bill James to indicate how a minor-league hitter would do at the major-league level based on his minor-league stats. Is this system necessary? Of course it's necessary; some minor leaguers compile their stats in a hitters' paradise like Albuquerque (team batting average .297), while others struggle in a pitchers' yard like Pawtucket (team batting average .247). Does the system work? Of course it works; the James system was pointing out how Dodger and Brewer hitting prospects were overrated -- while Red Sox and Blue Jay prospects were underrated -- several years ago.

Along with the five prospects for each team, we include an organization overview. Some clubs are simply better at developing talent than others; just ask the fans of the Atlanta Braves (good) or the New York Yankees (extremely bad).

The Players

For each major-league team, we have reports on anywhere from 22 to 27 major league players. Most include a full page of scouting information, but four to six players from each club receive half-page reports. We try to make each club as up-to-date for 1993 as possible -- that's why we have sections on the Marlins and Rockies. But because of our deadline, players who moved to new clubs after November 24 will be listed with their old organizations.

The Scouting Report Page

The Scouting Report page for primary players has two columns. The left column provides an in-depth report by an expert scout/analyst who covers the teams on a daily basis. The right column contains statistical information. Starting at the top of the column it lists:

Position: The first position shown is the player's most common position in 1992. If a position player played at any other positions in 10 or more games, those positions are shown also. For pitchers, SP stands for starting pitcher and RP for relief pitcher. A second pitching position is shown if a starting pitcher relieved at least four times or a relief pitcher started at least twice.

Bats and Throws: L=left-handed, R=right-handed, B=both (switch-hitter).

Opening Day Age: This is the player's age on April 5, 1993.

Born: Birth date and place.

ML Seasons: This number indicates the number of different major league seasons in which this player has actually appeared. For example, if a player was called up to play in September in each of the last three seasons, the number shown would be three (3). Note that this is different from the term Major League Service, which only counts the actual number of days a player appears on a major league roster.

Overall Statistics: These are traditional statistics for the player's 1992 season and his career through 1992.

Pitcher Strike Charts

The pitcher strike charts answer the question "How Often Does He Throw Strikes?" The charts are constructed based on the most extreme pitchers at throwing strikes in baseball. Our data shows that, depending on the pitcher and the situation, pitchers will toss a strike between 40 and 80 percent of the time. Therefore we've constructed the chart to represent the 40-80% range of throwing strikes.

Here are some ground rules: When you read your USA Today box score or hear an announcer state that a pitcher has thrown 97 pitches, 62 of them for strikes, the strike count includes swinging strikes, taken strikes, foul balls **and** balls hit in play. Even though not all balls hit into play are strikes, the theory is that most of them are, and the ones that aren't would be difficult to judge. Our charts reflect this. The charts are then broken into four categories. **All Pitches** is straight forward, as is **First Pitch.** We define **Ahead** as being any time there are more strikes than balls in the count (0-1, 0-2, 1-2). **Behind** includes counts with more balls than strikes (1-0, 2-0, 3-0, 2-1, 3-1, 3-2).

League averages are shown in each chart. Here are the 1992 league averages:

Strike Percentage by League — 1992

	American	National
All Pitches	61.4%	63.1%
First Pitch	55.5%	57.9%
Ahead in the Count	56.1%	58.7%
Behind in the Count	68.7%	69.4%

You'll notice the National League throws a slightly higher percentage of strikes in all cases for the third straight year.

Hitting Diagrams

The hitting diagrams shown in these reports are the most advanced of their kind in baseball. For every game and every ball hit into play last year (both hits and outs), STATS' trained reporters entered data into the STATS computer. They kept track of the kind of batted ball -- ground ball, fly ball, pop-up, line drive or bunt, as well as the distance of each ball. Direction is kept by dividing the field into 26 "wedges" angling out from home plate. Distance is measured in 10-foot increments from home plate.

Below are switch-hitting Atlanta outfielder Otis Nixon's 1992 hitting diagrams. One chart shows where Nixon hit the ball against left-handed pitchers (i.e. when he was batting right-handed); the other shows him against righties (batting lefty).

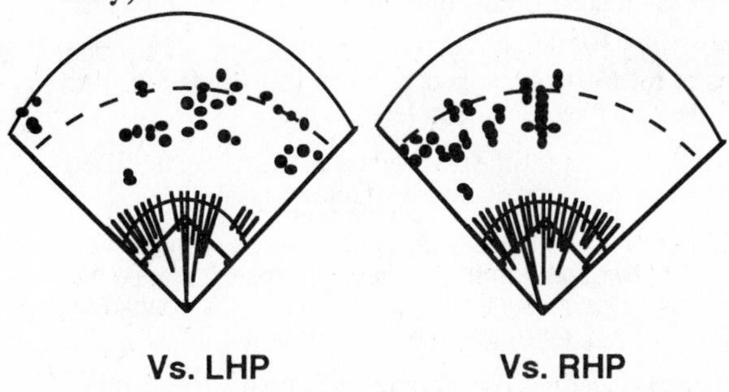

Vs. LHP Vs. RHP

In the diagrams, ground balls and short line drives are shown by the various length lines in the infield: the longer the line, the more ground balls and liners were hit in that direction. Let's assume Atlanta is playing the World Champion Toronto Blue Jays. It can be seen that when he's facing a lefty, Nixon hits most of his grounders up the middle or to the left side. So if southpaw Jimmy Key is pitching, the Jays would be advised to play first baseman John Olerud well off the line, position second baseman Roberto Alomar closer to second, station shortstop Manuel Lee normally, and put third baseman Kelly Gruber closer to the shortstop hole than usual. If a righty, say Jack Morris, is pitching, however, Nixon uses the whole field a little more, though he still tends to go the opposite way. So the infielders should play him a little more straightaway than they would with Key pitching.

In the outfield, batted balls are shown by dots. The dotted line in the outfield is 300 feet away from home plate, indicating how deep an outfield normally plays. By examining the diagram, it is clear that Nixon usually hits the ball to the middle of the diamond or to the opposite field if a lefty is working, and he doesn't hit it very far. If Key is on the mound, left fielder Candy Maldonado and center fielder Devon White should be bunched toward the middle, and right fielder Joe Carter should be straightaway, all playing shallow. But against righties, Neixon almost always hits the ball to the middle or left side, and again shallow; he hardly ever pulls. So with Morris working, the outfield should play him like they would a right-handed pull hitter, only shallower; all three outfielders can swing over to the left.

Technical Information on the Diagrams

A lot of experimentation went into producing these charts. When we first started, we tried to show every single batted ball that was hit into play by each player. We found that the charts became very cluttered for everyday players. We began experimenting with trying to show only the most meaningful information. When all was said and done, here's what we ended up with:

a. Pop-ups and bunts are excluded. We excluded pop-ups because 95% of these are caught regardless of how fielders are positioned. We excluded bunts because defensing a bunt is a whole different strategy that is primarily used on a select number of players and situations.

b. Ground balls under 50 feet are excluded. These are swinging bunts and are somewhat rare. We exclude them because they don't provide a true indication of the direction of a batted ball reaching an infielder or going through the infield.

c. For everyday players, we excluded what we call isolated points in the outfield. If a player hit only one ball in a given area of the field with no other batted balls in the vicinity all season, we exclude it from the chart. We felt that one ball does not give a true indication of a tendency. This rule did not apply to balls hit farther than 380 feet; all batted balls over 380 feet are shown. See Cecil Fielder for many examples.

d. Similarly, for players who play infrequently, we expanded the data sample to create a larger pattern of dots in the outfield when he tended to hit in a given area more frequently.

e. For ground balls over 50 feet, we excluded only the rare isolated ground ball. For most players, almost all of their ground balls are shown.

Other notes of interest:

The field itself is drawn to precise scale, with the outfield fence reaching 400 feet in centerfield and 330 feet down the lines. Keep in mind that parks are configured differently so that a dot that is shown inside of the diagram might actually have been a home run. Similarly, a dot outside the fence in the diagram might actually have been in play.

Liners under 170 feet are part of the infield. We give responsibility for short line drives to the infielders.

No distinction is made between hits and outs.

1992 Situational Stats

There are eight situational breakdowns for every primary player. **Home** and **Road** show performance between playing in his home park versus on the road. **Day** and **Night** show performance in day games versus night games. For hitters, **LHP** and **RHP** show the player's performance versus left-handed pitchers and right-handed pitchers, respectively. For pitchers, **LHB** and **RHB** show how the opposition batters hit against that pitcher based on the side of the plate from which they hit. **Sc Pos** stands for Scoring Position. It shows batting performance when hitting with runners in scoring position. For pitchers, **Sc Pos** shows the opposition's batting statistics when there are men in scoring position against that pitcher.

The definition we use for **Clutch** here can be simply restated as the late innings of a close game. For those of you interested in the exact definition, clutch is when it is the seventh inning or later and the batting team is up by one run, tied, or has the tying run on base, at bat, or on deck. You'll notice a similarity to the save definition. This is intentional; it allows our definition of Clutch to be consistent with a very well-known statistic, the save.

1992 Rankings

This section shows how the player ranked against the league, against his teammates, and by position in significant categories. Thanks to the power of the STATS computer, we not only include traditional categories, but also the less traditional categories as shown in the Major League Leaders section of this book. The Definitions and Qualifications section below provides some details on these lesser known categories. Due to space considerations, when a player ranked high in numerous categories, we omitted some of the less interesting rankings.

Major League Leaders

The chapter immediately following this introduction is a complete listing of Major League Leaders. The top three players in each category are shown for each league separately. You'll notice a STATS flavor to these leaders. Not only do we show the leaders for the common categories like batting average, home runs and ERA, but you'll also find less traditional categories like steals of third and pitches thrown.

Definitions and Qualifications

The following are definitions and qualifications for the Major League Leaders and Rankings.

Definitions:

Times on Base -- Hits plus walks plus hit by pitch.

Groundball/Flyball Ratio -- The ratio of all ground balls hit to fly balls and pop-ups hit. Bunts and line drives are excluded completely.

Runs scored per time reached base -- This is calculated by dividing Runs Scored by Times on Base.

Clutch -- This category shows a player's batting average in the late innings of close games: the seventh inning or later with the batting team ahead by one, tied, or has the tying run on base, at bat, or on deck.

Bases Loaded -- This category shows a player's batting average in bases loaded situations.

GDP per GDP situation -- A GDP situation exists any time there is a man on first with less than two outs. This statistic measures how often a player grounds into a double play in that situation.

Percentage of Pitches Taken -- This tells you how often a player lets a pitch go by without swinging.

Percentage of Swings Put into Play -- This tells you how often a player hits the ball into fair territory when he swings.

Run Support per Nine Innings -- This indicates how many runs are scored for a pitcher by his team while he was pitching translated into a per nine inning figure.

Baserunners per Nine Innings -- These are the hits, walks and hit batsmen allowed per nine innings.

Strikeout/Walk Ratio -- This is simply a pitcher's strikeouts divided by his walks allowed.

Stolen Base Percentage Allowed -- This figure indicates how successful opposing baseunners are when attempting a stolen base. It's stolen bases divided by stolen base attempts.

Save Percentage -- This is saves divided by save opportunities. Save opportunities include saves plus blown saves.

Blown Saves -- A blown save is given any time a pitcher comes into a game where a save situation is in place and he loses the lead.

Holds -- A hold is given to a pitcher when he comes into the game in a save situation, but is removed before the end of the game while maintaining his team's lead. The pitcher must retire at least one batter to get a hold.

Percentage of Inherited Runners Scored -- When a pitcher comes into a game with men already on base, these runners are called inherited runners. This statistic measures the percentage of these inherited runners that the relief pitcher allows to score.

First Batter Efficiency -- This statistic tells you the batting average allowed by a relief pitcher to the first batter he faces.

Qualifications:

In order to be ranked, a player had to qualify with a minimum number of opportunities. The qualifications are as follows:

Batters

Batting average, slugging percentage, on-base average, home run frequency, ground ball/fly ball ratio, runs scored per time reached base and pitches seen per plate appearance -- 502 plate appearances

Percentage of pitches taken, lowest percentage of swings that missed and percentage of swings put into play -- 1500 pitches seen

Percentage of extra bases taken as a runner -- 15 opportunities to advance

Stolen base percentage -- 20 stolen base attempts

Runners in scoring position -- 100 plate appearances with runners in scoring position

Clutch -- 50 plate appearances in the clutch

Bases loaded -- 10 plate appearances with the bases loaded

GDP per GDP situation -- 50 plate appearances with a man on first and less than two outs

Vs LHP -- 125 plate appearances against left-handed pitchers

Vs RHP -- 377 plate appearances against right-handed pitchers

BA at home -- 251 plate appearances at home

BA on the road -- 251 plate appearances on the road

Leadoff on-base average -- 150 plate appearances in the number-one spot in the batting order

Cleanup slugging percentage - 150 plate appearances in the number-four spot in the batting order

BA on 3-1 count -- 10 plate appearances putting the ball into play or walking on a 3-1 count

BA with 2 strikes -- 100 plate appearances with 2 strikes

BA on 0-2 count -- 20 plate appearances putting the ball into play or striking out on a 0-2 count

BA on 3-2 count -- 20 plate appearances with a 3-2 count

Pitchers

Earned run average, run support per nine innings, baserunners per nine innings, batting average allowed, on-base average allowed, slugging percentage allowed, home runs per nine innings, strikeouts per nine innings, strikeout/walk ratio, stolen base percentage allowed, GDPs per nine innings, pitches thrown per batter and groundball/flyball ratio off -- 162 innings pitched

Winning percentage -- 15 decisions

GDPs induced per GDP situation -- pitchers facing 30 batters in GDP situations

Save Percentage -- 20 save opportunities

Percentage of inherited runners scoring -- 30 inherited runners

First batter efficiency -- 40 games in relief

BA allowed, runners in scoring position -- pitchers facing 150 batters with men in scoring position

ERA at home -- 81 innings pitched at home

ERA on the road -- 81 innings pitched on the road

Vs LHB -- 125 left-handed batters faced

Vs RHB -- 377 right-handed batters faced

Relief Pitchers

ERA, batting average allowed, baserunners per 9 innings, strikeouts per 9 innings -- 54 innings in relief

Fielders

Percentage caught stealing by catchers -- catchers with 75 stolen base attempts against them

Fielding percentage -- 100 games at a position; 30 chances for pitchers

Major League Leaders

1992 American League Leaders

Batters

Batting Average
Edgar Martinez .343
Kirby Puckett .329
Frank Thomas .323

Home Runs
Juan Gonzalez 43
Mark McGwire 42
Cecil Fielder 35

Runs Batted In
Cecil Fielder 124
Joe Carter 119
Frank Thomas 115

Games Played
Cal Ripken 162
Carlos Baerga 161
Travis Fryman 161

At Bats
Travis Fryman 659
Carlos Baerga 657
Mike Devereaux 653

Runs Scored
Tony Phillips 114
Frank Thomas 108
Roberto Alomar 105

Hits
Kirby Puckett 210
Carlos Baerga 205
Paul Molitor 195

Singles
Carlos Baerga 152
Chuck Knoblauch 151
Kirby Puckett 149

Doubles
Frank Thomas 46
Edgar Martinez 46
Don Mattingly 40
Robin Yount 40

Triples
Lance Johnson 12
Mike Devereaux 11
Brady Anderson 10

Stolen Bases
Kenny Lofton 66
Pat Listach 54
Brady Anderson 53

Caught Stealing
Luis Polonia 21
Pat Listach 18
Chad Curtis 18

Walks
Frank Thomas 122
Mickey Tettleton 122
Tony Phillips 114

Intentional Walks
Wade Boggs 19
Mickey Tettleton 18
Ken Griffey Jr 15

Hit by Pitch
Mike Macfarlane 15
Shane Mack 15
Keith Miller 14

Strikeouts
Dean Palmer 154
Cecil Fielder 151
Jay Buhner 146

Ground into Double Play
George Bell 29
Tino Martinez 24
Gregg Jefferies 24

Sacrifice Bunts
Jerry Browne 16
Mike Bordick 14
Tony Pena 13

Sacrifice Flies
Joe Carter 13
Chuck Knoblauch 12
Robin Yount 12

Batter Plate Appearances
Brady Anderson 749
Tony Phillips 733
Travis Fryman 721

Times on Base
Frank Thomas 312
Tony Phillips 282
Brady Anderson 276

Total Bases
Kirby Puckett 313
Joe Carter 310
Juan Gonzalez 309

Slugging Percentage
Mark McGwire .585
Edgar Martinez .544
Frank Thomas .536

Slugging off LHP
Paul Molitor .659
Frank Thomas .650
Ken Griffey Jr .624

Slugging off RHP
Juan Gonzalez .561
Edgar Martinez .532
Mark McGwire .527

Cleanup Slugging
Mark McGwire .591
Juan Gonzalez .546
Danny Tartabull .491

On-Base Average
Frank Thomas .439
Danny Tartabull .409
Roberto Alomar .405

OBA off LHP
Danny Tartabull .494
Kenny Lofton .466
Paul Molitor .464

OBA off RHP
Frank Thomas .433
Chili Davis .408
Shane Mack .403

Leadoff OBA
Rickey Henderson .426
Brian Downing .414
Paul Molitor .383

HR Frequency - AB/HR
Mark McGwire 11.1
Juan Gonzalez 13.6
Mickey Tettleton 16.4

Groundball/Flyball Ratio
Steve Sax 2.6
Luis Polonia 2.5
Lance Johnson 2.3

Runs/Time Reached Base
Devon White 46.5%
Joe Carter 46.0
Greg Vaughn 43.0

SB Success %
Henry Cotto 92.0%
Devon White 90.2
Tim Raines 88.2

Steals of third
Luis Polonia 12
Roberto Alomar 12
Pat Listach 9
Lance Johnson 9
Rickey Henderson 9

BA Scoring Position
Lou Whitaker .369
Tim Raines .361
Luis Sojo .356

BA Late & Close
Jerry Browne .465
Roberto Alomar .430
Edgar Martinez .390

BA Bases Loaded
Mel Hall .667
Chili Davis .625
Brian Harper .571

GDP/GDP Situation
Keith Miller 1.9%
Kevin Maas 1.9%
Brady Anderson 1.9

BA vs LH Pitchers
Paul Molitor .424
Edgar Martinez .376
Carlos Baerga .375

BA vs RH Pitchers
Edgar Martinez .331
Kirby Puckett .329
Shane Mack .320

BA at Home
Roberto Alomar .354
Carlos Baerga .353
Kirby Puckett .348

BA on the Road
Edgar Martinez .373
Frank Thomas .342
Paul Molitor .334

BA on 3-1 Count
Jack Daugherty .750
Mike Stanley .714
Pat Listach .667

BA With 2 Strikes
Brian Harper .289
Edgar Martinez .279
Paul Molitor .266

BA on 0-2 Count
Paul Molitor .360
Chuck Knoblauch .351
Jerry Browne .333

BA on 3-2 Count
Jeff Kent .454
Mike Gallego .438
Walt Weiss .405

Pitches Seen
Brady Anderson 2,976
Tony Phillips 2,898
Frank Thomas 2,840

Pitches Seen per PA
Mickey Tettleton 4.22
Jose Canseco 4.19
Danny Tartabull 4.14

% Pitches Taken
Lance Blankenship 69.3%
Rickey Henderson 69.1
Brian Downing 65.8

% of Swings that Missed

Wade Boggs	**4.2%**
Lance Johnson	7.2
Jody Reed	7.6

% Swings Put Into Play

Jody Reed	**64.4%**
Gregg Jefferies	62.6
Wade Boggs	59.6

Bunts in Play

Kenny Lofton	**73**
Pat Listach	46
Brian McRae	42

Pitchers

Earned Run Average

Roger Clemens	**2.41**
Kevin Appier	2.46
Mike Mussina	2.54

Wins

Kevin Brown	**21**
Jack Morris	**21**
Jack McDowell	20

Losses

Erik Hanson	**17**
Melido Perez	16
Jack Armstrong	15
Jim Abbott	15
Rick Sutcliffe	15

Win-Loss Percentage

Mike Mussina	**.783**
Jack Morris	.778
Juan Guzman	.762

Games Pitched

Kenny Rogers	**81**
Duane Ward	79
Steve Olin	72

Games Started

Mike Moore	**36**
Rick Sutcliffe	**36**
Kevin Brown	35
Bill Wegman	35
Frank Viola	35
Ben McDonald	35

Complete Games

Jack McDowell	**13**
Kevin Brown	11
Roger Clemens	11

Shutouts

Roger Clemens	**5**
Mike Mussina	4
Dave Fleming	4

Games Finished

Dennis Eckersley	**65**
Jeff Montgomery	62
Steve Olin	62

Innings Pitched

Kevin Brown	**265.2**
Bill Wegman	261.2
Jack McDowell	260.2

Hits Allowed

Kevin Brown	**262**
Bill Wegman	251
Rick Sutcliffe	251

Batters Faced

Kevin Brown	**1,108**
Bill Wegman	1,079
Jack McDowell	1,079

Runs Allowed

Rick Sutcliffe	**123**
Kevin Brown	117
Scott Sanderson	116
Kirk McCaskill	116

Earned Runs Allowed

Rick Sutcliffe	**118**
Jack Morris	108
Bill Gullickson	107
Ben McDonald	107

Home Runs Allowed

Bill Gullickson	**35**
Ben McDonald	32
Dennis Cook	29

Walks Allowed

Randy Johnson	**144**
Bobby Witt	114
Mike Moore	103

Hit Batters

Randy Johnson	**18**
Nolan Ryan	12
Kevin Brown	10
Jack Morris	10
Todd Stottlemyre	10

Strikeouts

Randy Johnson	**241**
Melido Perez	218
Roger Clemens	208

Wild Pitches

Mike Moore	**22**
Juan Guzman	14
Jeff Parrett	13
Ron Darling	13
Melido Perez	13
Randy Johnson	13

Balks

Dennis Cook	**5**
John Dopson	3
Rich Monteleone	3
Jack Armstrong	3

Run Support per 9 IP

Scott Sanderson	**6.2**
Kevin Tapani	6.1
Jack Morris	6.0

Baserunners per 9 IP

Mike Mussina	**9.8**
Roger Clemens	10.0
Kevin Appier	10.2

Batting Average Allowed

Randy Johnson	**.206**
Juan Guzman	.207
Kevin Appier	.217

Slugging Pct Allowed

Juan Guzman	**.275**
Randy Johnson	.307
Roger Clemens	.308

On-Base Average Allowed

Mike Mussina	**.278**
Roger Clemens	.279
Kevin Appier	.281

Home Runs per 9 IP

Juan Guzman	**.299**
Kevin Brown	.373
Charles Nagy	.393

Strikeouts per 9 IP

Randy Johnson	**10.3**
Juan Guzman	8.2
Melido Perez	7.9

Strikeout/Walk Ratio

Roger Clemens	**3.4**
Charles Nagy	3.0
Kevin Tapani	2.9

Stolen Bases Allowed

Randy Johnson	**42**
Jack McDowell	29
Scott Kamieniecki	29

Caught Stealing Off

Melido Perez	**18**
Chuck Finley	**18**
John Smiley	16
Jack McDowell	16
Randy Johnson	16
Jack Morris	16

SB% Allowed

Kevin Brown	**36.8%**
Ron Darling	43.5
Charles Nagy	44.4

GDPs induced

Charles Nagy	**34**
Scott Erickson	31
Frank Viola	29

GDPs Induced per 9 IP

Scott Erickson	**1.3**
Chuck Finley	1.2
Charles Nagy	1.2

GDPs Induced/GDP Situation

Vince Horsman	**27.3%**
John Doherty	23.2
Dave Otto	21.9

Grd/Fly Ratio Off

Greg Hibbard	**2.5**
Scott Erickson	2.5
Charles Nagy	2.4

BA Allowed Scoring Position

Kevin Appier	**.167**
Mike Mussina	.175
Greg Harris	.193

Pitches Thrown

Jack McDowell	**3,994**
Bill Wegman	3,876
Roger Clemens	3,821

Pitches Thrown per Batter

Bill Gullickson	**3.29**
Greg Hibbard	3.33
Chris Bosio	3.33

Pickoff Throws

Kirk McCaskill	**334**
Jim Abbott	266
Mark Langston	262

ERA at Home

Bill Wegman	**2.26**
Julio Valera	2.34
Charles Nagy	2.34

ERA on the Road

Roger Clemens	**1.90**
Jim Abbott	2.33
Kevin Appier	2.33

BA Off by LH Batters

Jimmy Key	**.176**
Rusty Meacham	.188
Cal Eldred	.188

BA Off by RH Batters

Randy Johnson	**.208**
Kirk McCaskill	.209
Dave Stewart	.217

Relievers

Relief ERA

Jeff Russell	**1.63**
Roberto Hernandez	1.65
Derek Lilliquist	1.75

Relief Wins

Rusty Meacham	**10**
Eric Plunk	9
Alan Mills	9
Jeff Parrett	9

Relief Losses

Greg Harris	**8**
Jeff Nelson	7
Scott Radinsky	7
Mike Schooler	7

Saves

Dennis Eckersley	**51**
Rick Aguilera	41
Jeff Montgomery	39

Blown Saves

Jeff Russell	**9**
Jeff Nelson	8
Jeff Reardon	8
Scott Radinsky	8
Gregg Olson	8

Save Opportunities

Dennis Eckersley	**54**
Rick Aguilera	48
Jeff Montgomery	46

Save Percentage

Dennis Eckersley	**94.4%**
Tom Henke	91.9
Doug Henry	87.9

Holds

Duane Ward	**25**
Jeff Parrett	19
Greg Harris	19
Mark Guthrie	19

Relief Innings

Todd Frohwirth	**106.0**
Rusty Meacham	101.2
Duane Ward	101.1

Relief BA Allowed

Roberto Hernandez	**.180**
Mike Fetters	.185
Derek Lilliquist	.187

Runners/9 IP Relievers

Dennis Eckersley	**8.3**
Derek Lilliquist	8.6
Roberto Hernandez	8.7

Relief Strikeouts/9 IP

Dennis Eckersley	**10.5**
Duane Ward	9.1
Mark Guthrie	9.1

% Inherited Runners Scored

Dennis Eckersley	**6.5%**
Steve Frey	10.0
Dennis Powell	12.0

First Batter Efficiency

Dennis Powell	**.100**
Jim Austin	.135
Jeff Montgomery	.143

Fielding

Errors by Pitcher

Melido Perez	**10**
Kevin Brown	8
Matt Young	6

Errors by Catcher

Ivan Rodriguez	**15**
Brian Harper	13
Terry Steinbach	10

Errors by First Base

Mo Vaughn	**15**
Frank Thomas	13
Wally Joyner	10
Cecil Fielder	10

Errors by Second Base

Steve Sax	**20**
Carlos Baerga	19
Jody Reed	14

Errors by Third Base

Gregg Jefferies	**26**
Robin Ventura	23
Dean Palmer	22

Errors by Shortstop

Gary DiSarcina	**25**
Mark Lewis	**25**
Pat Listach	24

Errors by Left Field

Kevin Reimer	**11**
Brady Anderson	7
Glenallen Hill	6
Candy Maldonado	6

Errors by Center Field

Juan Gonzalez	**8**
Kenny Lofton	**8**
Devon White	7
Willie Wilson	7

Errors by Right Field

Joe Carter	**8**
Mark Whiten	7
Ruben Sierra	7

% CS off Catchers

Ivan Rodriguez	**51.8%**
Sandy Alomar Jr	44.9
Terry Steinbach	43.8

1992 National League Leaders

Batters

Batting Average

Gary Sheffield	**.330**
Andy Van Slyke	.324
John Kruk	.324

Home Runs

Fred McGriff	**35**
Barry Bonds	34
Gary Sheffield	33

Runs Batted In

Darren Daulton	**109**
Terry Pendleton	105
Fred McGriff	104

Games Played

Craig Biggio	**162**
Steve Finley	**162**
Jeff Bagwell	**162**

At Bats

Marquis Grissom	**653**
Terry Pendleton	640
Jay Bell	632

Runs Scored

Barry Bonds	**109**
Dave Hollins	104
Andy Van Slyke	103

Hits

Andy Van Slyke	**199**
Terry Pendleton	**199**
Ryne Sandberg	186

Singles

Brett Butler	**143**
Terry Pendleton	138
Mark Grace	134

Doubles

Andy Van Slyke	**45**
Ray Lankford	40
Mariano Duncan	40
Will Clark	40

Triples

Deion Sanders	**14**
Steve Finley	13
Andy Van Slyke	12

Stolen Bases

Marquis Grissom	**78**
Delino DeShields	46
Steve Finley	44
Bip Roberts	44

Caught Stealing

Ray Lankford	**24**
Brett Butler	21
Tony Fernandez	20

Walks

Barry Bonds	**127**
Fred McGriff	96
Brett Butler	95

Intentional Walks

Barry Bonds	**32**
Will Clark	23
Fred McGriff	23

Hit by Pitch

Dave Hollins	**19**
Jeff Bagwell	12
Ruben Amaro	9

Strikeouts

Ray Lankford	**147**
Dave Hollins	110
Matt D. Williams	109

Ground into Double Play

Darrin Jackson	**21**
Gary Sheffield	19
Jeff Bagwell	17

Sacrifice Bunts

Brett Butler	**24**
Jay Bell	19
Steve Finley	16

Sacrifice Flies

Jeff Bagwell	**13**
Will Clark	11
Andy Van Slyke	9

Batter Plate Appearances

Craig Biggio	**721**
Jay Bell	712
Marquis Grissom	707

Times on Base

Barry Bonds	**279**
Craig Biggio	271
Brett Butler	269

Total Bases

Gary Sheffield	**323**
Ryne Sandberg	312
Andy Van Slyke	310

Slugging Percentage

Barry Bonds	**.624**
Gary Sheffield	.580
Fred McGriff	.556

Slugging off LHP

Gary Sheffield	**.640**
Dave Hollins	.620
Barry Bonds	.599

Slugging off RHP

Fred McGriff	**.558**
Gary Sheffield	.549
Andy Van Slyke	.545

Cleanup SLG

Barry Bonds	**.684**
Fred McGriff	.557
Larry Walker	.510

On-Base Average

Barry Bonds	**.456**
John Kruk	.423
Brett Butler	.413

OBA off LHP

Barry Bonds	**.445**
Barry Larkin	.443
Gary Sheffield	.420

OBA off RHP

Brett Butler	**.420**
Bip Roberts	.416
Andy Van Slyke	.411

Leadoff OBA

Bip Roberts	**.396**
Craig Biggio	.378
Ray Lankford	.375

HR Frequency - AB/HR

Barry Bonds	**13.9**
Fred McGriff	15.2
Gary Sheffield	16.9

Groundball/Flyball Ratio

Willie McGee	**3.6**
Otis Nixon	3.0
Ozzie Smith	2.5

Runs/Time Reached Base

Otis Nixon	**45.7%**
Marquis Grissom	43.6
Terry Pendleton	41.5

SB Success %

Eric Davis	**95.0%**
Mariano Duncan	88.5
Marquis Grissom	85.7

Steals of third

Marquis Grissom	**24**
Craig Biggio	12
Jose Offerman	8
Brett Butler	8

BA Scoring Position

Terry Pendleton	**.391**
Barry Larkin	.340
Gary Sheffield	.339

BA Late & Close

Lenny Dykstra	**.414**
Gary Sheffield	.410
Glenn Braggs	.388

BA Bases Loaded

Eddie Murray	**.667**
Eric Karros	.625
Chico Walker	.600

GDP/GDP Situation

Dave Justice	**0.9%**
Mitch Webster	1.8
Darren Daulton	2.4

BA vs LH Pitchers

Felix Jose	**.374**
Ricky Jordan	.371
Gary Sheffield	.365

BA vs RH Pitchers

Andy Van Slyke	**.345**
Bip Roberts	.340
Mark Grace	.323

BA at Home

Gary Sheffield	**.365**
Bip Roberts	.353
Barry Bonds	.338

BA on the Road

John Kruk	**.340**
Mark Grace	.330
Andy Van Slyke	.328

BA on 3-1 Count

Fred McGriff	**.800**
Bret Barberie	.750
Barry Bonds	.625

BA With 2 Strikes

Ozzie Smith	**.303**
Lenny Dykstra	.299
Tony Gwynn	.291

BA on 0-2 Count

Luis Salazar	**.350**
Ozzie Smith	.333
Gary Sheffield	.314

BA on 3-2 Count

Tony Gwynn	**.438**
Willie McGee	.419
Lenny Dykstra	.389

Pitches Seen

Craig Biggio	**2,758**
Brett Butler	2,743
Ray Lankford	2,697

Pitches Seen per PA

Brett Butler	**4.06**
Todd Zeile	3.98
Delino DeShields	3.96

% Pitches Taken

Dave Magadan	**63.5%**
Barry Bonds	63.3
Spike Owen	62.7

% of Swings that Missed

Tony Gwynn	**6.5%**
Ozzie Smith	8.6
Brett Butler	8.9

% Swings Put Into Play

Tony Gwynn	**62.3%**
Mark Lemke	60.0
Mark Grace	57.2

Bunts in Play

Brett Butler	**97**
Otis Nixon	45
Steve Finley	40

Pitchers

Earned Run Average

Bill Swift	**2.08**
Bob Tewksbury	2.16
Greg Maddux	2.18

Wins

Tom Glavine	**20**
Greg Maddux	**20**
Dennis Martinez	16
Mike Morgan	16
Bob Tewksbury	16
Ken Hill	16

Losses

Tom Candiotti	**15**
Orel Hershiser	**15**
Andy Benes	14
Anthony Young	14
Tim Belcher	14
Kyle Abbott	14
Trevor Wilson	14

Win-Loss Percentage

Bob Tewksbury	**.762**
Tom Glavine	.714
Charlie Leibrandt	.682

Games Pitched

Joe Boever	**81**
Doug Jones	80
Mike Perez	77
Xavier Hernandez	77

Games Started

Steve Avery	**35**
John Smoltz	**35**
Greg Maddux	**35**

Complete Games

Terry Mulholland	**12**
Doug Drabek	10
Curt Schilling	10

Shutouts

David Cone	**5**
Tom Glavine	**5**
Bruce Hurst	4
Doug Drabek	4
Greg Maddux	4
Curt Schilling	4
Pedro Astacio	4

Games Finished

Doug Jones	**70**
John Wetteland	58
Randy Myers	57

Innings Pitched

Greg Maddux	**268.0**
Doug Drabek	256.2
John Smoltz	246.2

Hits Allowed

Andy Benes	**230**
Terry Mulholland	227
Randy Tomlin	226

Batters Faced

Greg Maddux	**1,061**
Doug Drabek	1,021
John Smoltz	1,021

Runs Allowed

Tim Belcher	**104**
Orel Hershiser	101
Terry Mulholland	101

Earned Runs Allowed

Tim Belcher	**99**
Terry Mulholland	97
Bruce Hurst	93

Home Runs Allowed

Bud Black	**23**
Bruce Hurst	22
Omar Olivares	20
Kyle Abbott	20

Walks Allowed

David Cone	**82**
Bobby Ojeda	81
John Smoltz	80
Tim Belcher	80

Hit Batters

Greg Maddux	**14**
David Cone	9
Dennis Martinez	9
Mark Gardner	9

Strikeouts

John Smoltz	**215**
David Cone	214
Greg Maddux	199

Wild Pitches

John Smoltz	**17**
Dwayne Henry	12
Ken Hill	11
Frank Castillo	11
Mike Morgan	11
Doug Drabek	11

Balks

Trevor Wilson	**7**
Bud Black	**7**
Ken Hill	4
Bob Scanlan	4
Darryl Kile	4

Run Support per 9 IP

Tom Glavine	**5.3**
Terry Mulholland	5.0
Greg Swindell	4.9

Baserunners per 9 IP

Curt Schilling	**8.9**
Bob Tewksbury	9.3
Greg Maddux	9.6

Batting Average Allowed

Curt Schilling	**.201**
Greg Maddux	.210
Sid Fernandez	.210

Slugging Pct Allowed

Greg Maddux	**.280**
Dennis Martinez	.287
Curt Schilling	.288

On-Base Average Allowed

Curt Schilling	**.254**
Bob Tewksbury	.265
Dennis Martinez	.271

Home Runs per 9 IP

Greg Maddux	**.235**
Tom Glavine	.240
Danny Jackson	.268

Strikeouts per 9 IP

David Cone	**9.8**
Sid Fernandez	8.1
John Smoltz	7.8

Strikeout/Walk Ratio

Bob Tewksbury	**4.6**
Jose Rijo	3.9
Rheal Cormier	3.5

Stolen Bases Allowed

Steve Avery	**42**
David Cone	34
Ken Hill	30
Tom Candiotti	30

Caught Stealing Off

Dennis Martinez	**17**
Charlie Leibrandt	16
Bobby Ojeda	15

SB% Allowed

Terry Mulholland	**28.6%**
Bud Black	33.3
Tim Belcher	35.3

GDPs induced

Mike Morgan	**29**
Randy Tomlin	27
Bill Swift	26

GDPs Induced per 9 IP

Bill Swift	**1.4**
Randy Tomlin	1.2
Mike Morgan	1.1

GDPs Induced/GDP Situation

Bill Sampen	**23.9%**
Zane Smith	23.5
Gil Heredia	21.2

Grd/Fly Ratio Off

Bill Swift	**2.6**
Greg Maddux	2.6
Mike Morgan	2.5

BA Allowed Scoring Position

Curt Schilling	**.176**
Doug Drabek	.177
David Cone	.180

Pitches Thrown

John Smoltz	**3,768**
Greg Maddux	3,726
Doug Drabek	3,699

Pitches Thrown per Batter

Bob Tewksbury	**3.14**
Craig Lefferts	3.29
Orel Hershiser	3.33

Pickoff Throws

Charlie Leibrandt	**257**
Chris Nabholz	250
Tom Glavine	247

ERA at Home

Mike Morgan	**1.38**
Bob Tewksbury	1.52
Greg Maddux	1.91

ERA on the Road

Ken Hill	**2.33**
Jose Rijo	2.43
Greg Maddux	2.47

BA Off by LH Batters

Todd Worrell	**.174**
Rod Beck	.178
Rob Dibble	.180

BA Off by RH Batters

Greg Maddux	**.176**
Doug Drabek	.189
John Smoltz	.191

Relievers

Relief ERA

Mel Rojas	**1.43**
Rod Beck	1.76
Jose Melendez	1.81

Relief Wins

Doug Jones	**11**
Scott Bankhead	10
Xavier Hernandez	9
Mike Perez	9

Relief Losses

Roger McDowell	**10**
Jeff Innis	9
Lee Smith	9

Saves

Lee Smith	**43**
Randy Myers	38
John Wetteland	37

Blown Saves

John Wetteland	**9**
Norm Charlton	8
Roger McDowell	8
Lee Smith	8
Randy Myers	8

Save Opportunities

Lee Smith	**51**
Randy Myers	46
John Wetteland	46

Save Percentage

Doug Jones	**85.7%**
Lee Smith	84.3
Rob Dibble	83.3

Holds

Todd Worrell	**25**
Paul Assenmacher	20
Jeff Innis	16
Marvin Freeman	16

Relief Innings

Doug Jones	**111.2**
Joe Boever	111.1
Xavier Hernandez	111.0

Relief BA Allowed

Rod Beck	**.190**
Rob Dibble	.193
Todd Worrell	.198

Runners/9 IP Relievers

Rod Beck	**7.7**
Doug Jones	9.5
Mel Rojas	9.6

Relief Strikeouts/9 IP

Rob Dibble	**14.1**
John Wetteland	10.7
Norm Charlton	10.0

% Inherited Runners Scored

Al Osuna	**15.0%**
Joe Boever	16.4
Mel Rojas	17.2

First Batter Efficiency

Bryan Hickerson	**.113**
Denny Neagle	.133
Paul Assenmacher	.143

Fielding

Errors by Pitcher

Danny Jackson	**8**
Dwight Gooden	6
Greg W. Harris	5
Darryl Kile	5

Errors by Catcher

Benito Santiago	**12**
Darren Daulton	11
Mike Scioscia	9

Errors by First Base

Eddie Murray	**12**
Fred McGriff	**12**
Will Clark	10
Sid Bream	10

Errors by Second Base

Kurt Stillwell	**16**
Robby Thompson	15
Delino DeShields	15

Errors by Third Base

Matt D. Williams	**23**
Terry Pendleton	19
Dave Hollins	18

Errors by Shortstop

Jose Offerman	**42**
Jay Bell	22
Rafael Belliard	14

Errors by Left Field

Bernard Gilkey	**5**
Derrick May	**5**
Oscar Azocar	4
Ron Gant	4
Eric Davis	4

Errors by Center Field

Marquis Grissom	**7**
Sammy Sosa	6
Reggie Sanders	6

Errors by Right Field

Dave Justice	**8**
Willie McGee	6
Felix Jose	6

% CS off Catchers

Kirt Manwaring	**50.5%**
Joe Girardi	41.0
Greg Olson	39.1

Stars, Bums and Sleepers — Who's Who in 1993

The science of predicting the rise and fall of baseball players may be a lot of things, but one thing it isn't is EXACT. Our skepticism always leads us to the following question: "Why predict at all?" And our curiosity (and chutzpah) invariably leads us to answer: "Because it's fun, and we might learn something along the way."

What STATS has done in this section and in parts of its other publications is to try and stoke the fires of baseball debate and conversation, things that baseball fans enjoy most. That is not to say these predictions are light-hearted. Research by Bill James and John Dewan has created a system that puts an objective stamp on a player's ability. This system was used, along with the subjective advice of our scouts and staff experts, to create the following easy-to-use summarized prognostications, called "Stars, Bums, and Sleepers," and last year it proved to work quite well in delivering some useful hints.

For fantasy players who want a reliable gauge of a player abilities, we have created this section. For those fans who want to look at some reasoned evaluations that will stir up some good baseball talk, we have created this section. And for those fans who want someone to tell them to bet their salary that Gary Sheffield will hit .330 with 33 home runs . . . well, there's always Las Vegas. Have fun!

How To Use This Section

Every position is broken into four groups: Expect A Better Year in '93, Look for Consistency, Production Will Drop and 1993 Sleepers. Here's the key point to remember when looking at the first three of these categories. **A player is put into one of these three groups based on his 1992 performance.** For example, Darren Daulton is shown in the category Production Will Drop. That means that you probably shouldn't expect him to hit .270 again, especially in conjunction with 27 homers and 109 RBI. However, we still believe that Daulton could have one of the better years among all catchers in baseball, as he did in 1992. A year in which he knocks out 17 homers, drives in 70 runs and walks 78 times would be amongst the best numbers put up by any major-league catcher in '93, but they would still pale in comparison to the numbers he put up in 1992.

We do things a little differently in the section entitled 1993 Sleepers, but we continue to do them well. Last year in the sleepers section you would have players like Reggie Sanders, Leo Gomez, Dean Palmer, Pedro Munoz, Mike Mussina, Rod Beck, Roberto Hernandez, Doug Henry, and Doug Jones. You can bet (not literally, of course) that many of this year's crop of sleepers will wake up the baseball world. The numbers we show in this section are each player's combined minor- and major-league performance for 1992. The idea here is to show what this player is **capable** of doing. We've tried to factor projected playing time into the equation as this book went to press in late 1992, but you'll get a better idea as the season starts as to who's playing and who's not.

Finally, within each grouping (for example, left fielders listed under Expect A Better Year) we've ranked the players based on our own expectations of performance from best performance to worst.

Taking this example, we rank Ron Gant ahead of Greg Vaughn and Eric Davis. But we leave it up to you to decide (or you can ask us for more info) as to how much more Ron Gant's offense will improve compared to Candy Maldonado's anticipated decline.

How We Developed This Section

We broke down all 660+ regular major-league players in this book into their most common position played in 1992. We then looked at every player in two basic ways: statistical analysis and subjective rating.

For our statistical model, we looked at historical patterns of performance to help us project performance for each player. Here are some of the factors that we plugged into our computer:

Career trends -- A player should not be judged simply based on his most recent year of performance, although the tendency for most fans (and many "experts") is to do just that. While it is possible that a player who had a good year in relation to the rest of his career has suddenly become a better ballplayer, it's much more likely that it was simply a good year. Meaning, of course, that it's likely he'll come down to a more normal performance the following year. While it is possible for a .276 career hitter like Andy Van Slyke to hit .324 again, it's much more likely he'll come back down to the .270 range that he's established for his career. The same is true about a bad season for most players. If his playing time does not get severely cut, a player with a bad season will usually rebound.

Player Age -- The best age for a position player in baseball is 26 or 27. Based on historical studies, this is the age when hitters have their best years. So, the rule of thumb is that if a batter is less than 26, you can expect some improvement over the level of play he's established so far in his career. If a batter is over 27, you can expect some decrease in his playing performance from **the level of play he has established in recent years and over his career.** The age when a pitcher reaches his peak is somewhat more nebulous. While it isn't possible to pinpoint a specific peak age like can be done for hitters, we are able to blend in many factors based on a pitcher's career that give us an accurate indicator of those whose potential is rising or falling.

Minor League Performance -- In his book ***The Bill James Abstract***, Bill has found that minor league performance, when properly adjusted, is just as reliable in predicting major league performance as is prior major league performance. Therefore, we've looked at minor league performance here to help us project 1993, especially for the players we called "Sleepers."

We then added our own subjective considerations:

Playing Time -- When considering how good a player will be in a given year, you first have to determine how often he'll get a chance to play. This we've done by evaluating players compared to their teammates. Do your own research this spring to find out more about a team's plans for a player if you're not sure -- and don't forget to take into account a player's injury-prone nature.

Pitchers' Inconsistency -- For every five hitters you can name as being reasonably consistent from year to year, there is probably only one pitcher who can compare in consistency. Some of the most consistently tough pitchers in baseball over the past several years (Chuck Finley, Dwight Gooden, Bret Saberhagen) can suddenly have a stinker. We used many subjective considerations in devising our pitcher evaluations.

Catcher

Expect A Better Year in '93

	1992 Statistics			
	Avg.	HR	RBI	SB
B.J. Surhoff	.252	4	62	14
Chris Hoiles	.274	20	40	0
Mike Macfarlane	.234	17	48	1
Ivan Rodriguez	.260	8	37	0
Matt Nokes	.224	22	59	0
Benito Santiago	.253	11	44	2
Sandy Alomar Jr	.251	2	26	3
Eddie Taubensee	.222	5	28	2
Greg Myers	.231	1	13	0
Rick Wilkins	.270	8	22	0
Todd Hundley	.209	7	32	3
Brent Mayne	.225	0	18	0
Joe Girardi	.270	1	12	0
Lenny Webster	.280	1	13	0

Look for Consistency

	1992 Statistics			
	Avg.	HR	RBI	SB
Tom Pagnozzi	.249	7	44	2
Mike LaValliere	.256	2	29	0
Lance Parrish	.233	12	32	1
Tony Pena	.241	1	38	3
Ron Karkovice	.237	13	50	10
Damon Berryhill	.228	10	43	0
Carlton Fisk	.219	5	26	4
Greg Olson	.238	3	27	2
Mike Stanley	.249	8	27	0

Production Will Drop

	1992 Statistics			
	Avg.	HR	RBI	SB
Mickey Tettleton	.238	32	83	0
Darren Daulton	.270	27	109	11
Brian Harper	.307	9	73	0
Terry Steinbach	.279	12	53	2
Pat Borders	.242	13	53	1
Joe Oliver	.270	10	57	2
Don Slaught	.345	4	37	2
Dave Valle	.240	9	30	0
Kirt Manwaring	.244	4	26	2

1993 Sleepers

	1992 Statistics (includes minor leagues)			
	Avg.	HR	RBI	SB
Mike Piazza	.335	24	97	1
Dave Nilsson	.282	7	64	12
Dan Walters	.310	6	47	1
Jesse Levis	.351	7	47	1
Steve Decker	.272	8	75	2

First Base

Expect A Better Year in '93

	1992 Statistics			
	Avg.	HR	RBI	SB
Cecil Fielder	.244	35	124	0
Will Clark	.300	16	73	12
Rafael Palmeiro	.268	22	85	2
John Olerud	.284	16	66	1
Wally Joyner	.269	9	66	11
Tino Martinez	.257	16	66	2
Kent Hrbek	.244	15	58	5
Paul Sorrento	.269	18	60	0
Andres Galarraga	.243	10	39	5
Brian Hunter	.239	14	41	1
Lee Stevens	.221	7	37	1
Scott Cooper	.276	5	33	1
Ricky Jordan	.304	4	34	3

Look for Consistency

	1992 Statistics			
	Avg.	HR	RBI	SB
Frank Thomas	.323	24	115	6
Fred McGriff	.286	35	104	8
Jeff Bagwell	.273	18	96	10
Mark Grace	.307	9	79	6
Eddie Murray	.261	16	93	4
Eric Karros	.257	20	88	2
Randy Milligan	.240	11	53	0
Orlando Merced	.247	6	60	5

Production Will Drop

	1992 Statistics			
	Avg.	HR	RBI	SB
Mark McGwire	.268	42	104	0
John Kruk	.323	10	70	3
Don Mattingly	.287	14	86	3
Sid Bream	.261	10	61	6
Pete O'Brien	.222	14	52	2
Gene Larkin	.246	6	42	7

1993 Sleepers

	1992 Statistics (includes minor leagues)			
	Avg.	HR	RBI	SB
John Jaha	.290	20	79	16
Hal Morris	.269	6	53	6
Mo Vaughn	.248	19	85	4
Reggie Jefferson	.319	12	50	1
Greg Colbrunn	.289	13	66	4
Terry Jorgensen	.297	14	76	3
Pedro Guerrero	.229	4	23	2

Second Base

Expect A Better Year in '93

	1992 Statistics			
	Avg.	HR	RBI	SB
Harold Reynolds	.247	3	33	15
Steve Sax	.236	4	47	30
Mark Lemke	.227	6	26	0
Jose Lind	.235	0	39	3
Pat Kelly	.226	7	27	8
Kurt Stillwell	.227	2	24	4
Joey Cora	.246	0	9	10
Tim Teufel	.224	6	25	2

Look for Consistency

	1992 Statistics			
	Avg.	HR	RBI	SB
Roberto Alomar	.310	8	76	49
Chuck Knoblauch	.297	2	56	34
Delino DeShields	.292	7	56	46
Craig Biggio	.277	6	39	38
Jody Reed	.247	3	40	7
Robby Thompson	.260	14	49	5
Mickey Morandini	.265	3	30	8
Lenny Harris	.271	0	30	19
Keith Miller	.284	4	38	16
Billy Ripken	.230	4	36	2
Luis Alicea	.245	2	32	2
Willie Randolph	.252	2	15	1

Production Will Drop

	1992 Statistics			
	Avg.	HR	RBI	SB
Ryne Sandberg	.304	26	87	17
Carlos Baerga	.312	20	105	10
Lou Whitaker	.278	19	71	6
Tony Phillips	.276	10	64	12
Mike Bordick	.300	3	48	12
Scott Fletcher	.275	3	51	17
Billy Doran	.235	8	47	7
Lance Blankenship	.241	3	34	21
Luis Sojo	.272	7	43	7
Mike Sharperson	.300	3	36	2
Jeff Treadway	.222	0	5	1

1993 Sleepers

	1992 Statistics (includes minor leagues)			
	Avg.	HR	RBI	SB
Geronimo Pena	.286	10	43	17
Juan Samuel	.272	0	23	8
Jeff Frye	.284	3	40	12
Bret Boone	.287	17	88	18
Carlos Garcia	.295	13	74	21
Tim Naehring	.241	5	19	1
Mike Gallego	.251	3	16	1
Jose Oquendo	.274	0	10	0
Eric Young	.315	4	60	34

Third Base

Expect A Better Year in '93

	1992 Statistics			
	Avg.	HR	RBI	SB
Wade Boggs	.259	7	50	1
Leo Gomez	.265	17	64	2
Matt D. Williams	.227	20	66	7
Todd Zeile	.257	7	48	7
Chris Sabo	.244	12	43	4
Jeff Kent	.239	11	50	2
Dave Magadan	.283	3	28	1
Jeff King	.231	14	65	4
Kelly Gruber	.229	11	43	7
Jerry Browne	.287	3	40	3
Dave Hansen	.214	6	22	0

Look for Consistency

	1992 Statistics			
	Avg.	HR	RBI	SB
Gregg Jefferies	.285	10	75	19
Robin Ventura	.282	16	93	2
Dean Palmer	.229	26	72	10
Kevin Seitzer	.270	5	71	13
Steve Buechele	.261	9	64	1
Charlie Hayes	.257	18	66	3
Tim Wallach	.223	9	59	2
Scott Livingstone	.282	4	46	1
Brook Jacoby	.261	4	36	0
Gary Gaetti	.226	12	48	3

Production Will Drop

	1992 Statistics			
	Avg.	HR	RBI	SB
Gary Sheffield	.330	33	100	5
Edgar Martinez	.343	18	73	14
Dave Hollins	.270	27	93	9
Terry Pendleton	.311	21	105	5
Ken Caminiti	.294	13	62	10
Rene Gonzales	.277	7	38	7
Scott Leius	.249	2	35	6

1993 Sleepers

	1992 Statistics (includes minor leagues)			
	Avg.	HR	RBI	SB
Hensley Meulens	.278	27	101	15
Sean Berry	.292	22	81	8
Bret Barberie	.253	4	32	9
Kevin Young	.318	8	69	19
Mike Pagliarulo	.200	0	11	2

Shortstop

Expect A Better Year in '93

	1992 Statistics			
	Avg.	HR	RBI	SB
Cal Ripken	.251	14	72	4
Shawon Dunston	.315	0	2	2
Ozzie Guillen	.200	0	7	1
Jeff Blauser	.262	14	46	5
Alan Trammell	.275	1	11	2
Jose Offerman	.260	1	30	23
Bill Spiers	.313	0	2	1
Craig Grebeck	.268	3	35	0
Mark Lewis	.264	5	30	4

Look for Consistency

	1992 Statistics			
	Avg.	HR	RBI	SB
Travis Fryman	.266	20	96	8
Barry Larkin	.304	12	78	15
Jay Bell	.264	9	55	7
Tony Fernandez	.275	4	37	20
Manuel Lee	.263	3	39	6
Dick Schofield	.206	4	36	11
Greg Gagne	.246	7	39	6
Felix Fermin	.270	0	13	0
Gary DiSarcina	.247	3	42	9
Dave Howard	.224	1	18	3

Production Will Drop

	1992 Statistics			
	Avg.	HR	RBI	SB
Pat Listach	.290	1	47	54
Ozzie Smith	.295	0	31	43
Omar Vizquel	.294	0	21	15
Spike Owen	.269	7	40	9
Jeff Huson	.261	4	24	18
Randy Velarde	.272	7	46	7
Andy Stankiewicz	.268	2	25	9

1993 Sleepers

	1992 Statistics (includes minor leagues)			
	Avg.	HR	RBI	SB
Wil Cordero	.309	8	35	6
John Valentin	.266	14	54	2
Royce Clayton	.230	7	42	23
Juan Bell	.213	4	31	9

Left Field

Expect A Better Year in '93

	1992 Statistics			
	Avg.	HR	RBI	SB
Ron Gant	.259	17	80	32
Mike Greenwell	.233	2	18	2
Kevin Mitchell	.286	9	67	0
Greg Vaughn	.228	23	78	15
Kevin Reimer	.267	16	58	2
Kevin McReynolds	.247	13	49	7
Luis Gonzalez	.243	10	55	7
Eric Davis	.228	5	32	19
Milt Thompson	.293	4	17	18
Greg Briley	.275	5	12	9
Lonnie Smith	.247	6	33	4

Look for Consistency

	1992 Statistics			
	Avg.	HR	RBI	SB
Barry Bonds	.311	34	103	39
Rickey Henderson	.283	15	46	48
Luis Polonia	.286	0	35	51
Moises Alou	.282	9	56	16
Daryl Boston	.249	11	35	12
Pete Incaviglia	.266	11	44	2
Jerald Clark	.242	12	58	3
Thomas Howard	.277	2	32	15

Production Will Drop

	1992 Statistics			
	Avg.	HR	RBI	SB
Shane Mack	.315	16	75	26
Tim Raines	.294	7	54	45
Brady Anderson	.271	21	80	53
Bip Roberts	.323	4	45	44
Candy Maldonado	.272	20	66	2
Bernard Gilkey	.302	7	43	18
Mariano Duncan	.267	8	50	23
Glenallen Hill	.241	18	49	9
Dan Gladden	.254	7	42	4
Kevin Bass	.269	9	39	14

1993 Sleepers

	1992 Statistics (includes minor leagues)			
	Avg.	HR	RBI	SB
Ivan Calderon	.245	3	26	1
Derek Bell	.242	2	19	10
Jeff Conine	.293	20	81	4
Derrick May	.281	10	53	5
Vince Coleman	.283	2	23	27
Monty Fariss	.261	12	59	5

Center Field

Expect A Better Year in '93

	1992 Statistics			
	Avg.	HR	RBI	SB
Reggie Sanders	.270	12	36	16
Howard Johnson	.223	7	43	22
Ellis Burks	.255	8	30	5
Lenny Dykstra	.301	6	39	30
Brian McRae	.223	4	52	18
Milt Cuyler	.241	3	28	8
Dave Martinez	.254	3	31	12
Dwight Smith	.276	3	24	9

Look for Consistency

	1992 Statistics			
	Avg.	HR	RBI	SB
Ken Griffey Jr	.308	27	103	10
Juan Gonzalez	.260	43	109	0
Roberto Kelly	.272	10	66	28
Ray Lankford	.293	20	86	42
Devon White	.248	17	60	37
Lance Johnson	.279	3	47	41
Junior Felix	.246	9	72	8
Mike Felder	.286	4	23	14

Production Will Drop

	1992 Statistics			
	Avg.	HR	RBI	SB
Kirby Puckett	.329	19	110	17
Andy Van Slyke	.324	14	89	12
Marquis Grissom	.276	14	66	78
Mike Devereaux	.276	24	107	10
Kenny Lofton	.285	5	42	66
Brett Butler	.309	3	39	41
Steve Finley	.292	5	55	44
Robin Yount	.264	8	77	15
Darrin Jackson	.249	17	70	14
Otis Nixon	.294	2	22	41
Willie Wilson	.270	0	37	28
Bob Zupcic	.276	3	43	2
Stan Javier	.249	1	29	18

1993 Sleepers

	1992 Statistics (includes minor leagues)			
	Avg.	HR	RBI	SB
Deion Sanders	.304	8	28	26
Bernie Williams	.295	13	76	27
Sammy Sosa	.263	8	26	20
Ryan Thompson	.270	17	56	12

Right Field

Expect A Better Year in '93

	1992 Statistics			
	Avg.	HR	RBI	SB
Ruben Sierra	.278	17	87	14
Jose Canseco	.244	26	87	6
Bobby Bonilla	.249	19	70	4
Jay Buhner	.243	25	79	0
Paul O'Neill	.246	14	66	6
Chad Curtis	.259	10	46	43
Mark Whiten	.254	9	43	16
Pedro Munoz	.270	12	71	4
Chito Martinez	.268	5	25	0
Darryl Strawberry	.237	5	25	3
Dale Murphy	.161	2	7	0
Wes Chamberlain	.258	9	41	4
Alex Cole	.255	0	15	16

Look for Consistency

	1992 Statistics			
	Avg.	HR	RBI	SB
Danny Tartabull	.266	25	85	2
Dave Justice	.256	21	72	2
Tony Gwynn	.317	6	41	3
Eric Anthony	.239	19	80	5
Willie McGee	.297	1	36	13
Joe Orsulak	.289	4	39	5
Dante Bichette	.287	5	41	18
Jim Eisenreich	.269	2	28	11
Dan Pasqua	.211	6	33	0

Production Will Drop

	1992 Statistics			
	Avg.	HR	RBI	SB
Joe Carter	.264	34	119	12
Larry Walker	.301	23	93	18
Felix Jose	.295	14	75	28
Andre Dawson	.277	22	90	6
Darryl Hamilton	.298	5	62	41
Rob Deer	.247	32	64	4
Tom Brunansky	.266	15	74	2
Cory Snyder	.269	14	57	4
Ruben Amaro	.219	7	34	11
Mitch Webster	.267	6	35	11

1993 Sleepers

	1992 Statistics (includes minor leagues)			
	Avg.	HR	RBI	SB
Tim Salmon	.320	31	111	10
Phil Plantier	.265	12	44	2
Jesse Barfield	.155	3	9	1
Luis Mercedes	.294	3	33	35
Kevin Koslofski	.291	7	45	10

Designated Hitter

Expect A Better Year in '93

	1992 Statistics			
	Avg.	HR	RBI	SB
Julio Franco	.234	2	8	1
Kevin Maas	.248	11	35	3
Jack Clark	.210	5	33	1

Look for Consistency

	1992 Statistics			
	Avg.	HR	RBI	SB
Albert Belle	.260	34	112	8
George Bell	.255	25	112	5
Chili Davis	.288	12	66	4
Harold Baines	.253	16	76	1

Production Will Drop

	1992 Statistics			
	Avg.	HR	RBI	SB
Paul Molitor	.320	12	89	31
Dave Winfield	.290	26	108	2
George Brett	.285	7	61	8
Glenn Davis	.276	13	48	1

1993 Sleepers

	1992 Statistics (includes minor leagues)			
	Avg.	HR	RBI	SB
Bo Jackson	.000	0	0	0

Starting Pitchers

Expect A Better Year in '93

	1992 Statistics				
	W	L	ERA	Sv	BR/9
Zane Smith	8	8	3.06	0	10.15
Steve Avery	11	11	3.20	0	11.05
Tom Candiotti	11	15	3.00	0	10.74
Jim Abbott	7	15	2.77	0	11.94
Bret Saberhagen	3	5	3.50	0	10.60
Nolan Ryan	5	9	3.72	0	12.53
Frank Seminara	9	4	3.68	0	13.19
Greg W. Harris	4	8	4.12	0	11.44
Ramon Martinez	8	11	4.00	0	12.84
Pete Harnisch	9	10	3.70	0	10.93
Chuck Finley	7	12	3.96	0	13.79
Joe Hesketh	8	9	4.36	1	13.44
Jose DeLeon	2	8	4.37	0	12.35
Scott Sanderson	12	11	4.93	0	13.41
Erik Hanson	8	17	4.82	0	13.16
Jack Armstrong	6	15	4.64	0	13.28
Luis Aquino	3	6	4.52	0	13.57
Kyle Abbott	1	14	5.13	0	13.03
Eric King	4	6	5.22	1	13.50
Tom Browning	6	5	5.07	0	14.28
Pat Rapp	0	2	7.20	0	13.50
Ryan Bowen	0	7	10.96	0	21.39

Look for Consistency

	1992 Statistics				
	W	L	ERA	Sv	BR/9
Curt Schilling	14	11	2.35	2	8.95
Roger Clemens	18	11	2.41	0	10.00
Dennis Martinez	16	11	2.47	0	9.58
Mike Mussina	18	5	2.54	0	9.78
Sid Fernandez	14	11	2.73	0	9.77
Jose Rijo	15	10	2.56	0	9.90
Kevin Appier	15	8	2.46	0	10.24
Tom Glavine	20	8	2.76	0	10.76
Doug Drabek	15	11	2.77	0	9.75
Juan Guzman	16	5	2.64	0	10.36
Mike Morgan	16	8	2.55	0	10.69
John Smoltz	15	12	2.85	0	10.62
John Smiley	16	9	3.21	0	10.31
David Cone	17	10	2.81	0	11.68
Jack McDowell	20	10	3.18	0	11.36
Melido Perez	13	16	2.87	0	11.27
Bill Wegman	13	14	3.20	0	10.83
Chris Bosio	16	6	3.62	0	10.54
Bill Swift	10	4	2.08	1	10.38
Charlie Leibrandt	15	7	3.36	0	11.10
Mark Portugal	6	3	2.66	0	10.48
Andy Benes	13	14	3.35	0	11.52
Jimmy Key	13	13	3.53	0	11.13
Randy Tomlin	14	9	3.41	0	11.77
Frank Castillo	10	11	3.46	0	10.87
Frank Viola	13	12	3.44	0	11.72
Mark Langston	13	14	3.66	0	11.24
Bob Welch	11	7	3.27	0	11.57
Terry Mulholland	13	11	3.81	0	10.85
Kevin Tapani	16	11	3.97	0	11.41
Chris Nabholz	11	12	3.32	0	11.77
Tim Belcher	15	14	3.91	0	11.23
Scott Erickson	13	12	3.40	0	12.23
Tim Wakefield	8	1	2.15	0	10.96
Ben Rivera	7	4	3.07	0	11.35
Kevin Gross	8	13	3.17	0	11.52
Jose Guzman	16	11	3.66	0	12.29
Bruce Hurst	14	9	3.85	0	11.35
Rheal Cormier	10	10	3.68	0	11.23
Dave Stewart	12	10	3.66	0	11.83
Bobby Ojeda	6	9	3.63	0	13.58
Arthur Rhodes	7	5	3.63	0	12.02
Mike Bielecki	2	4	2.57	0	11.71
Craig Lefferts	14	12	3.76	0	11.69
John Burkett	13	9	3.84	0	11.53
Donovan Osborne	11	9	3.77	0	11.72
Dwight Gooden	10	13	3.67	0	11.80
Orel Hershiser	10	15	3.67	0	12.22
Bill Gullickson	14	13	4.34	0	11.29
Ben McDonald	13	13	4.24	0	11.74
Omar Olivares	9	9	3.84	0	11.70
Jim Deshaies	4	7	3.28	0	11.81
Randy Johnson	12	14	3.77	0	13.52
Bud Black	10	12	3.97	0	12.10
Pete Schourek	6	8	3.64	0	12.11
Charlie Hough	7	12	3.93	0	11.89
Mike Moore	17	12	4.12	0	13.72
Kirk McCaskill	12	13	4.18	0	12.66
Mark Gardner	12	10	4.36	0	12.42
Kelly Downs	6	7	3.37	0	13.34

Dennis Cook	5	7	3.82	0	11.85
Hipolito Pichardo	9	6	3.95	0	12.53
Todd Stottlemyre	12	11	4.50	0	12.83
Alex Fernandez	8	11	4.27	0	12.33
Greg Hibbard	10	7	4.40	1	12.84
Butch Henry	6	9	4.02	0	12.33
Bill Krueger	10	8	4.53	0	12.39
Ricky Bones	9	10	4.57	0	12.45
Trevor Wilson	8	14	4.21	0	12.97
Chris Hammond	7	10	4.21	0	12.64
Frank Tanana	13	11	4.39	0	13.74
Chris Haney	4	6	4.61	0	11.81
Bert Blyleven	8	12	4.74	0	12.45
Darryl Kile	5	10	3.95	0	13.72
Scott Kamieniecki	6	14	4.36	0	13.02
Bobby Witt	10	14	4.29	0	13.94
Mark Clark	3	10	4.45	0	12.15
Jose Mesa	7	12	4.59	0	13.61
Mike Gardiner	4	10	4.75	0	12.81
Shawn Boskie	5	11	5.01	0	13.35
Tim Leary	8	10	5.36	0	14.49
Joe Slusarski	5	5	5.45	0	13.97
Bob Milacki	6	8	5.84	1	14.47
Scott Scudder	6	10	5.28	0	15.77
Willie Banks	4	4	5.70	0	15.08
Scott Aldred	3	8	6.78	0	16.06

Production Will Drop

1992 Statistics

	W	L	ERA	Sv	BR/9
Greg Maddux	20	11	2.18	0	9.57
Bob Tewksbury	16	5	2.16	0	9.27
Cal Eldred	11	2	1.79	0	9.06
Ken Hill	16	9	2.68	0	10.94
Pete Smith	7	0	2.05	0	10.37
Charles Nagy	17	10	2.96	0	10.86
Greg Swindell	12	8	2.70	0	10.66

Jaime Navarro	17	11	3.33	0	10.76
Kevin Brown	21	11	3.32	0	11.79
Jack Morris	21	6	4.04	0	11.67
Dave Fleming	17	10	3.39	0	11.39
Bob Walk	10	6	3.20	2	12.07
Pedro Astacio	5	5	1.98	0	11.20
Brian Barnes	6	6	2.97	0	11.34
Ron Darling	15	10	3.66	0	11.95
Jimmy Jones	10	6	4.07	0	11.56
Mark Gubicza	7	6	3.72	0	11.88
Julio Valera	8	11	3.73	0	12.16
Rick Sutcliffe	16	15	4.47	0	12.59
Rick Reed	3	7	3.68	0	11.66
Danny Jackson	8	13	3.84	0	13.05
Brian Williams	7	6	3.92	0	12.52
Dave Haas	5	3	3.94	0	12.41
John Dopson	7	11	4.08	0	12.67
Brian Fisher	4	3	4.53	1	12.61

1993 Sleepers

1992 Statistics
(includes minor leagues)

	W	L	ERA	Sv	BR/9
Tim Pugh	16	11	3.35	0	12.52
Sam Militello	15	5	2.64	0	10.64
Mike Trombley	13	10	3.58	0	11.67
Andy Ashby	1	6	5.40	0	12.99
Bob Wickman	18	6	3.21	0	11.46
Mike Harkey	5	2	3.46	0	12.38
Joe Magrane	4	7	4.30	0	14.46
Scott Chiamparino	3	7	2.53	0	10.41
Roger Pavlik	11	9	3.41	0	12.42
Dave Stieb	5	7	4.71	0	13.05
Pat Mahomes	12	9	4.04	1	12.50
Tommy Greene	5	4	4.70	0	13.70
Pat Combs	6	8	4.14	0	12.31

Relief Pitchers

Expect A Better Year in '93

1992 Statistics

	W	L	ERA	Sv	BR/9
Gregg Olson	1	5	2.05	36	10.27
Rob Dibble	3	5	3.07	25	10.36
Carl Willis	7	3	2.72	1	9.53
Bryan Harvey	0	4	2.83	13	10.36
Mike Henneman	2	6	3.96	24	11.06
Doug Henry	1	4	4.02	29	12.18
Jeff Brantley	7	7	2.95	7	11.29
Mark Guthrie	2	3	2.88	5	9.84
Mark Wohlers	1	2	2.55	4	10.95
Jeff Fassero	8	7	2.84	1	12.29
Alejandro Pena	1	6	4.07	15	11.36
Kent Mercker	3	2	3.42	6	11.72
Mike Stanton	5	4	4.10	8	11.45
Mark Eichhorn	4	4	3.08	2	11.60
Kenny Rogers	3	6	3.09	6	12.13
Mike Jackson	6	6	3.73	2	12.40
Rick Honeycutt	1	4	3.69	3	12.46
Paul Assenmacher	4	4	4.10	8	13.37
Bryn Smith	4	2	4.64	0	11.81
Bobby Thigpen	1	3	4.75	22	15.38
Roger McDowell	6	10	4.09	14	15.71
Mike Schooler	2	7	4.70	13	13.94
Tom Gordon	6	10	4.59	0	13.39
Bob MacDonald	1	0	4.37	0	12.74
Mike Timlin	0	2	4.12	1	13.60
Edwin Nunez	1	3	4.85	3	13.20
David Wells	7	9	5.40	2	13.65
Chuck Crim	7	6	5.17	1	13.97
Ken Patterson	2	3	3.89	0	14.90
Tim Burke	3	4	4.15	0	14.75
Dave Righetti	2	7	5.06	3	13.21
Mike Boddicker	1	4	4.98	3	14.23
Greg Cadaret	4	8	4.25	1	15.63
Barry Jones	7	6	5.68	1	15.76
Les Lancaster	3	4	6.33	0	16.10
Russ Springer	0	0	6.19	0	16.31
Terry Mathews	2	4	5.95	0	17.01
Brian Bohanon	1	1	6.31	0	16.36
Lee Guetterman	4	5	7.09	2	16.36
Mark Davis	2	3	7.13	0	18.00

Look for Consistency

1992 Statistics

	W	L	ERA	Sv	BR/9
Dennis Eckersley	7	1	1.91	51	8.32
Rick Aguilera	2	6	2.84	41	10.53
Tom Henke	3	2	2.26	34	10.02
Lee Smith	4	9	3.12	43	10.56
Steve Farr	2	2	1.56	30	9.52

Jeff Montgomery	1	6	2.18	39	9.91
John Franco	6	2	1.64	15	9.55
Duane Ward	7	4	1.95	12	10.30
Jeff Reardon	5	2	3.41	30	12.10
Norm Charlton	4	2	2.99	26	11.95
Rod Beck	3	3	1.76	17	7.73
Roberto Hernandez	7	3	1.65	12	8.75
Steve Olin	8	5	2.34	29	11.31
John Wetteland	4	4	2.92	37	11.23
Stan Belinda	6	4	3.15	18	10.98
Todd Worrell	5	3	2.11	3	9.98
Bob Scanlan	3	6	2.89	14	11.03
Randy Myers	3	6	4.29	38	13.44
Joe Boever	3	6	2.51	2	12.29
Mike Maddux	2	2	2.37	5	10.73
Ted Power	3	3	2.54	6	11.51
Jim Gott	3	3	2.45	6	11.66
Todd Frohwirth	4	3	2.46	4	11.97
Scott Radinsky	3	7	2.73	15	13.65
Jose Melendez	6	7	2.92	0	10.58
Mitch Williams	5	8	3.78	29	15.44
Bryan Hickerson	5	3	3.09	0	9.89
Greg Harris	4	9	2.51	4	12.20
Dan Plesac	5	4	2.96	1	11.62
John Candelaria	2	5	2.84	5	11.72
Jesse Orosco	3	1	3.23	1	10.85
Anthony Young	2	14	4.17	15	12.35
Roger Mason	5	7	4.09	8	11.97
Dwayne Henry	3	3	3.33	0	11.19
Danny Darwin	9	9	3.96	3	12.11
Steve Frey	4	2	3.57	4	12.51
John Doherty	7	4	3.88	3	12.41
Tony Fossas	1	2	2.43	2	13.96
Mike Hartley	7	6	3.44	0	12.93
Jeff Robinson	4	3	3.00	1	13.62
Todd Burns	3	5	3.84	1	11.62
Jim Bullinger	2	8	4.66	7	13.76
Bob McClure	2	2	3.17	0	13.17
Wally Whitehurst	3	9	3.62	0	12.62
Mark Leiter	8	5	4.18	0	13.02
Gene Harris	0	2	4.15	0	11.57
Russ Swan	3	10	4.74	9	13.11
Jeremy Hernandez	1	4	4.17	1	12.52
Al Osuna	6	3	4.23	0	13.28
Donn Pall	5	2	4.93	1	13.32
Steve Wilson	2	5	4.18	0	14.04
Scott Ruskin	4	3	5.03	0	12.91
Wilson Alvarez	5	3	5.20	1	15.43
Dave Burba	2	7	4.97	0	14.39
Cliff Brantley	2	6	4.60	0	15.68
Mike Magnante	4	9	4.94	0	15.31
Pat Hentgen	5	2	5.36	0	14.48
Paul Gibson	0	1	5.23	0	13.79
Rich DeLucia	3	6	5.49	1	14.74
Calvin Jones	3	5	5.69	0	14.45
Dave Weathers	0	0	8.10	0	18.90

Production Will Drop

	1992 Statistics				
	W	L	ERA	Sv	BR/9
Doug Jones	11	8	1.85	36	9.51
Jeff Russell	4	3	1.63	30	11.13

Mel Rojas	7	1	1.43	10	9.57
Derek Lilliquist	5	3	1.75	6	8.61
Xavier Hernandez	9	1	2.11	7	10.22
Mike Fetters	5	1	1.87	2	9.91
Mike Perez	9	3	1.84	0	9.97
Terry Leach	6	5	1.95	0	9.90
Rusty Meacham	10	4	2.74	2	9.74
Darren Holmes	4	4	2.55	6	10.20
Jim Austin	5	2	1.85	0	11.11
Joe Grahe	5	6	3.52	21	12.36
Sergio Valdez	0	2	2.41	0	8.92
Rich Rodriguez	6	3	2.37	0	10.48
Alan Mills	10	4	2.61	2	11.58
Bob Patterson	6	3	2.92	9	11.41
Jim Corsi	4	2	1.43	0	12.68
Cris Carpenter	5	4	2.97	1	10.23
Scott Bankhead	10	4	2.93	1	11.33
John Kiely	4	2	2.13	0	11.78
Jeff Parrett	9	1	3.02	0	11.44
Tom Edens	6	3	2.83	3	12.14
Rich Monteleone	7	3	3.30	0	10.59
Storm Davis	7	3	3.43	4	11.79
Jeff Innis	6	9	2.86	1	12.99
Gary Wayne	3	3	2.63	0	12.75
Vince Horsman	2	1	2.49	1	12.46
Steve Foster	1	1	2.88	2	11.70
Marvin Freeman	7	5	3.22	3	12.73
Eric Plunk	9	6	3.64	4	12.43
Mike Munoz	1	2	3.00	2	12.94
John Habyan	5	6	3.84	7	13.25
Chuck McElroy	4	7	3.55	6	13.34
Willie Blair	5	7	4.00	0	11.56
Kevin Wickander	2	0	3.07	1	15.59
Rob Murphy	3	1	4.04	0	12.45
Paul Abbott	0	0	3.27	0	14.73
Denny Neagle	4	6	4.48	2	13.14
Dennis Powell	4	2	4.58	0	12.79
Danny Cox	5	3	4.60	3	13.36
Tim Scott	4	1	5.26	0	14.58
Kevin Campbell	2	3	5.12	1	15.37
Kevin Ritz	2	5	5.60	0	15.12
Daryl Irvine	3	4	6.11	0	15.11

1993 Sleepers

	1992 Statistics (includes minor leagues)				
	W	L	ERA	Sv	BR/9
Dave Nied	17	9	2.64	0	9.71
Jay Howell	1	4	2.73	4	12.44
Steve Reed	2	1	2.14	43	8.68
Kent Bottenfield	13	10	3.22	1	11.55
Matt Whiteside	2	2	1.97	33	10.11
Larry Andersen	1	2	3.14	2	9.21
Keith Shepherd	4	5	2.48	9	9.16
Paul Quantrill	8	11	3.80	1	12.72
Steve Shifflett	4	6	2.16	14	11.20
Jeff Nelson	2	7	3.30	6	12.97
Bill Sampen	2	7	3.35	0	13.08
Mike Butcher	7	4	3.16	4	13.89
Kurt Knudsen	5	4	4.00	6	12.67
Kip Gross	7	6	3.63	8	12.06

American League Players

BRADY ANDERSON

Position: LF
Bats: L **Throws:** L
Ht: 6' 1" **Wt:** 185

Opening Day Age: 29
Born: 1/18/64 in Silver Spring, MD
ML Seasons: 5

Overall Statistics

	G	AB	R	H	D	T	HR	RBI	SB	BB	SO	AVG
1992	159	623	100	169	28	10	21	80	53	98	98	.271
Career	549	1704	239	406	70	21	31	168	106	233	308	.238

Where He Hits the Ball

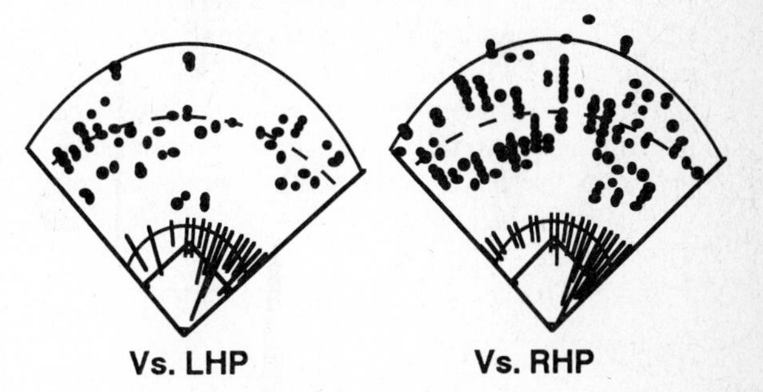

1992 Situational Stats

	AB	H	HR	RBI	AVG		AB	H	HR	RBI	AVG
Home	313	82	15	46	.262	LHP	190	43	5	26	.226
Road	310	87	6	34	.281	RHP	433	126	16	54	.291
Day	185	53	5	19	.286	Sc Pos	134	39	4	59	.291
Night	438	116	16	61	.265	Clutch	89	27	1	9	.303

1992 Rankings (American League)

- 1st in pitches seen (2,976) and plate appearances (749)
- 3rd in triples (10), stolen bases (53), times on base (276) and least GDPs per GDP situation (1.9%)
- Led the Orioles in runs scored (100), sacrifice bunts (10), sacrifice flies (9), stolen bases, caught stealing (16), intentional walks (14), hit by pitch (9), strikeouts (98), pitches seen, plate appearances and stolen base percentage (76.8%)
- Led AL left fielders in at-bats (623), triples, total bases (280), sacrifice flies, stolen bases, walks (98), intentional walks, pitches seen, plate appearances and games played

HITTING:

Brady Anderson became the offensive catalyst of the Orioles last season. He finally had the kind of season the O's expected when they acquired him from Boston in midseason 1988. Anderson batted .271, a career high by 40 points, and drove in 80 runs, nearly tripling his previous best of 27. After totaling 10 homers in four years, he walloped 21. With a .373 on-base average, Anderson gave the team its first bona fide leadoff man since Al Bumbry a decade ago.

With better body control, quicker bat speed and a limited amount of external tinkering, Anderson achieved major league stardom at last. He scored 100 runs -- only six Orioles have ever done that -- walked 98 times and totaled 59 extra-base hits in a pretty good imitation of the best of Rickey Henderson. With his 80 RBI, Anderson fell just short of Harvey Kuenn's 1956 record of 85 RBI by a number-one batter. He is a solid fastball hitter who can also adjust to breaking stuff. Left-handers still give him trouble, but not enough to keep him out of the lineup.

BASERUNNING:

Anderson put his speed to good use, easily leading the team with 53 stolen bases in 69 attempts. He has learned how to read pitchers' moves better and is generally on his own unless manager John Oates gives him a stop sign. He accelerates well on the basepaths and his speed usually covers an occasional overly-daring move.

FIELDING:

With a flair for the spectacular, Anderson is equally at home diving for the sinking liner or banging into the wall to bring back a potential home run. He outraces a lot of drives in the gaps and moves well both toward the line and the middle. His arm isn't the strongest, but it's adequate.

OVERALL:

A late bloomer, Anderson made the All-Star team last season and, for the first time, goes to spring training assured of a regular job. Now that he has arrived, his dedication should keep him on top.

GLENN DAVIS

Position: DH
Bats: R **Throws:** R
Ht: 6' 3" **Wt:** 211

Opening Day Age: 32
Born: 3/28/61 in Jacksonville, FL
ML Seasons: 9

Overall Statistics

	G	AB	R	H	D	T	HR	RBI	SB	BB	SO	AVG
1992	106	398	46	110	15	2	13	48	1	37	65	.276
Career	985	3606	502	945	174	13	189	594	28	363	584	.262

Where He Hits the Ball

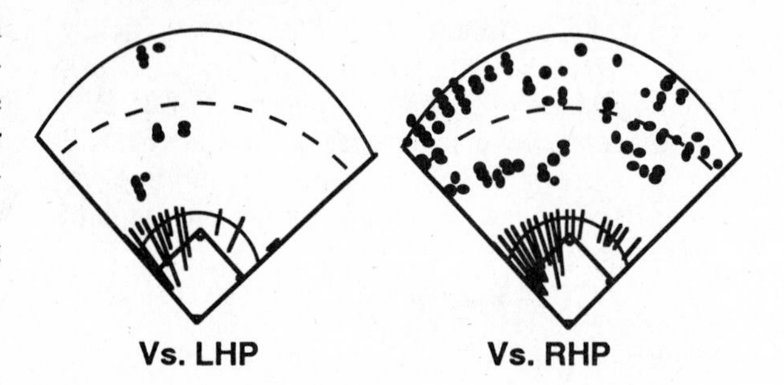

1992 Situational Stats

	AB	H	HR	RBI	AVG		AB	H	HR	RBI	AVG
Home	200	58	5	15	.290	LHP	107	27	4	18	.252
Road	198	52	8	33	.263	RHP	291	83	9	30	.285
Day	101	25	1	8	.248	Sc Pos	99	25	1	31	.253
Night	297	85	12	40	.286	Clutch	54	10	2	3	.185

1992 Rankings (American League)

- Did not rank near the top or bottom in any category

HITTING:

It took Glenn Davis virtually all of 1992 to find his swing, but it looked as if he may have finally done so. The only trouble is, it was not his home run swing. Davis batted a career-high .276 last year, and he hit .290 after the All-Star break. But the former Astro wound up with only 13 homers and 48 RBI, a far cry from the 30-homer, 90-RBI seasons the Orioles envisioned when they traded three good young players for him two years ago.

Davis had one hot streak in the middle of the season when his average climbed to .307. Otherwise, he struggled to regain the power stroke that made him one of the most feared sluggers in the National League. For the most part, his two Oriole years have been clouded by a series of injuries, disappointments and a minimal return on Baltimore's $7 million investment. Davis has totaled only 23 homers in two Oriole seasons, while missing long stretches with back and shoulder problems that have threatened his career. Understandably, he has become the object of criticism. The fans are still waiting for the consistent long swing and rocket shots that are his trademark.

BASERUNNING:

Not one to make many attempted steals, Davis is nonetheless a good, smart baserunner for his size. He is aggressive and doesn't hurt a team with stupid mistakes.

FIELDING:

Davis was restricted almost exclusively to designated hitting last season, first because a shoulder injury made it difficult to throw and second because manager John Oates didn't want to fiddle with him when he was hitting well. But he has worked hard at defense and made himself a better than average first baseman.

OVERALL:

Keeping Davis on the field is the Orioles' major priority. Only then will they learn how much his physical ailments have cost him. In two seasons, he has 23 homers and 76 RBI over 574 Oriole at-bats. If he can pack those numbers into one season, a lot of the criticism will die down.

PITCHING:

A new-old environment helped Storm Davis rebound from two dreary seasons in Kansas City. Returning to Baltimore, the city where he had once been "a young Jim Palmer," Davis had a respectable year while working mostly out of the bullpen. The veteran's 7-3 record marked his first winning season since 1989; his 3.43 ERA was his lowest since 1984, when he was in his first tour of duty with the Orioles. The righthander was a completely different pitcher from 1991, when he had gone 3-9 with a 4.96 ERA for the Royals.

Davis is no longer the phenom whose first major-league complete game in 1982 brought a crucial victory over Milwaukee in a game the Orioles had to win. Though he won 19 games for the Athletics as recently as 1989, his fastball doesn't have the pop it once did. These days he must rely more on placement than on sheer power. Davis also has an arch problem in his left heel that sometimes limits his work.

In addition to the fastball, Davis throws a forkball, curve and slider, and is versatile enough to be used as a starter, middle man or finisher. Davis made two starts last year and also had four saves. He improved his performance against lefthanders in 1992, holding them to a .241 average.

HOLDING RUNNERS AND FIELDING:

Davis is a hard pitcher for runners to read and he knows how to hold them close. He was often a victim of weak-throwing catchers last year, however, and permitted nine steals in 11 attempts. He fields commendably enough and is always aware of game situations.

OVERALL:

The days of projected superstardom have long passed, but Davis had a nice comeback in 1992 and understands his role. After two years of frustration with the Royals, he is willing to take the ball in whatever situation his team needs him. He had free agent "repeater rights" last winter, so his team might not necessarily be Baltimore.

STORM DAVIS

Position: RP
Bats: R **Throws:** R
Ht: 6' 4" **Wt:** 225

Opening Day Age: 31
Born: 12/26/61 in Dallas, TX
ML Seasons: 11

Overall Statistics

	W	L	ERA	G	GS	Sv	IP	H	R	BB	SO	HR
1992	7	3	3.43	48	2	4	89.1	79	35	36	53	5
Career	109	84	3.98	364	231	7	1634.2	1663	786	605	937	124

How Often He Throws Strikes

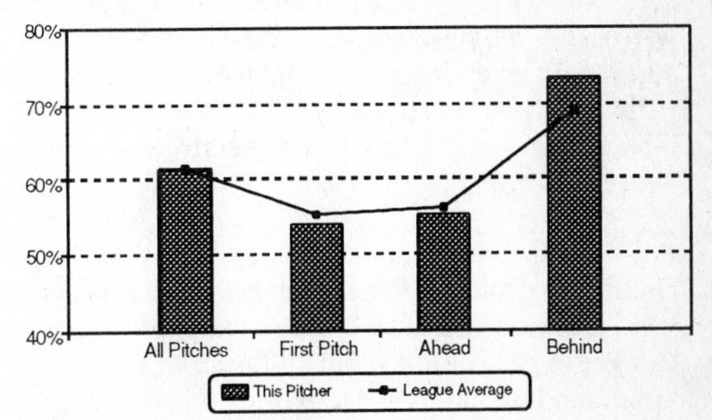

1992 Situational Stats

	W	L	ERA	Sv	IP		AB	H	HR	RBI	AVG
Home	5	1	2.85	1	47.1	LHB	137	33	2	15	.241
Road	2	2	4.07	3	42.0	RHB	187	46	3	23	.246
Day	3	3	4.46	0	34.1	Sc Pos	90	24	2	34	.267
Night	4	0	2.78	4	55.0	Clutch	113	25	2	11	.221

1992 Rankings (American League)

- 6th in relief wins (7)
- 9th in lowest percentage of inherited runners scored (21.6%)
- Led the Orioles in first batter efficiency (.200)

HITTING:

In the course of one season, Mike Devereaux developed from a good, solid ballplayer into a viable MVP candidate. While batting second for the majority of the 1992 campaign, Devereaux led the Orioles with career highs of 24 homers, 107 RBI and 180 hits. He produced mightily in the clutch, driving in 86 runs in 179 at-bats with men in scoring position. Devereaux also recorded some of the best numbers for hitting with the bases loaded (.520 average, 38 RBI) since such statistics were first kept in 1975. He was poison to left-handed pitching, batting .351.

Once a pretty wild swinger, Devereaux cut down on the habit of trying to pull everything last year. He went to right-center field more often and was not nearly as susceptible to the breaking pitch away. As Devereaux matured, he became a more patient hitter. As a result, he was fooled less often than in the past. He cut down his strikeouts last year from 115 to 94.

BASERUNNING:

Batting in front of the power guys most of the year, Devereaux's steal chances were limited. He can get in gear quickly, but still hasn't fully mastered reading pitchers' moves. He was caught stealing nearly 50 percent of the time he attempted to steal last year.

FIELDING:

Devereaux is a competent outfielder who gets an outstanding jump on fly balls and uses his speed to great advantage. He makes some brilliant catches, but occasionally has a problem dropping the ball after a long run. Opponents will take liberties on his arm, which is poor for a center fielder.

OVERALL:

After shifting from leadoff, Devereaux may have found a home in the number-two spot in the batting order. He is not a classic hit-and-run man, but he cut down on his strikeouts and made more contact. When he did that, good things usually happened. Now he has to show he can make them happen again.

MIKE DEVEREAUX

Position: CF
Bats: R **Throws:** R
Ht: 6' 0" **Wt:** 195

Opening Day Age: 30
Born: 4/10/63 in Casper, WY
ML Seasons: 6

Overall Statistics

	G	AB	R	H	D	T	HR	RBI	SB	BB	SO	AVG
1992	156	653	76	180	29	11	24	107	10	44	94	.276
Career	584	2116	272	547	92	25	63	267	64	160	337	.259

Where He Hits the Ball

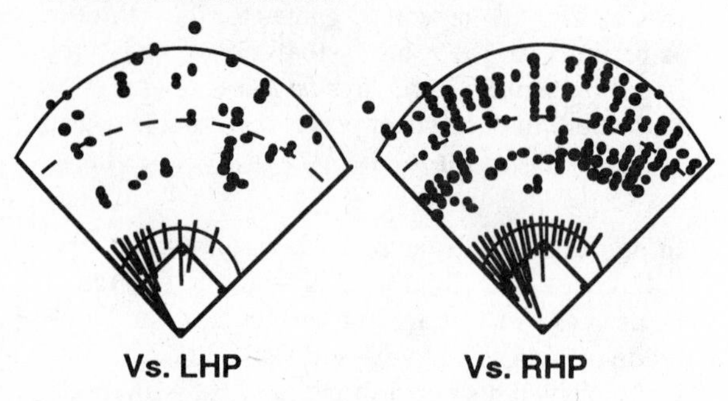

1992 Situational Stats

	AB	H	HR	RBI	AVG		AB	H	HR	RBI	AVG
Home	334	86	14	54	.257	LHP	168	59	9	29	.351
Road	319	94	10	53	.295	RHP	485	121	15	78	.249
Day	187	36	3	15	.193	Sc Pos	179	51	7	86	.285
Night	466	144	21	92	.309	Clutch	98	21	6	21	.214

1992 Rankings (American League)

- → 2nd in triples (11)
- → 3rd in at-bats (653)
- → 4th in pitches seen (2,782)
- → 5th in total bases (303) and slugging percentage vs. left-handed pitchers (.589)
- → Led the Orioles in batting average (.276), home runs (24), at-bats, hits (180), singles (116), doubles (29), triples, total bases, RBI (107), sacrifice flies (9), slugging percentage (.464), HR frequency (27 ABs per HR), batting average with the bases loaded (.520), batting average vs. left-handed pitchers (.351), slugging percentage vs. left-handed pitchers, batting average on the road (.295) and batting average with two strikes (.254)

TODD FROHWIRTH

Position: RP
Bats: R **Throws:** R
Ht: 6' 4" **Wt:** 205

Opening Day Age: 30
Born: 9/28/62 in Milwaukee, WI
ML Seasons: 6

PITCHING:

Proving that his first American League season was no fluke, down-under specialist Todd Frohwirth was effective again in 1992. Frohwirth couldn't quite match his 1991 campaign, when he posted a 1.87 ERA for the Orioles and allowed only 64 hits in 96.1 innings. But the righty's ERA was once again excellent at 2.46, and he recorded 15 holds while appearing in a career-high 65 games.

Frohwirth's unorthodox submarine delivery makes him tough to hit because hitters seldom see his style. From his unusual angle he throws a sinking fastball, a change and a "slurve"-type slider which has a flat break. Frohwirth wore down slightly at year's end after leading the league in relief innings most of the year. He also tended to be a little streaky. But, overall, his stuff was once again poison to opposing hitters.

Frohwirth accumulated four saves last year, but he is primarily a middle reliever and set-up man for Gregg Olson. His main problem as a closer is that he lacks the velocity to blow hitters away. Frohwirth fanned only 58 men 106 innings last year. He's usually much tougher on right-handed hitters than lefties because of the movement on his stuff, though that wasn't the case in 1992.

HOLDING RUNNERS AND FIELDING:

Frohwirth is hampered in that he throws fielded ground balls sidearm -- like he pitches. That makes him a little slow pulling the trigger, but he is balanced and accurate. The problem is similar with his delivery to the plate: a slight delay in getting off the pitch. Therefore, runners take some liberties, but he has improved.

OVERALL:

A man with a wry sense of humor, Frohwirth is popular among his teammates and his success has made him a valuable member of the bullpen. With his good control and ability to keep the ball in the park (just 12 home runs allowed in 289 career innings), his importance can't be discounted.

Overall Statistics

	W	L	ERA	G	GS	Sv	IP	H	R	BB	SO	HR
1992	4	3	2.46	65	0	4	106.0	97	33	41	58	4
Career	14	9	2.71	188	0	7	289.0	248	96	107	195	12

How Often He Throws Strikes

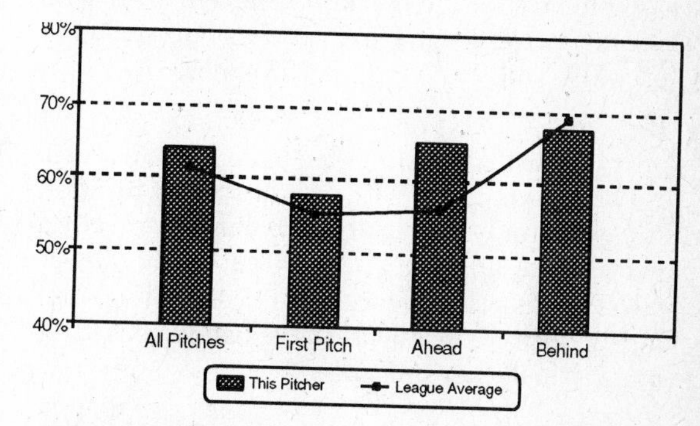

1992 Situational Stats

	W	L	ERA	Sv	IP		AB	H	HR	RBI	AVG
Home	2	1	1.84	2	58.2	LHB	142	35	1	15	.246
Road	2	2	3.23	2	47.1	RHB	250	62	3	37	.248
Day	1	1	4.97	0	29.0	Sc Pos	136	37	2	46	.272
Night	3	2	1.52	4	77.0	Clutch	155	35	1	25	.226

1992 Rankings (American League)

- 1st in relief innings (106)
- 9th in holds (15) and highest percentage of inherited runners scored (40.6%)
- Led the Orioles in games pitched (65), holds, most GDPs induced per GDP situation (17.1%) and relief innings

HITTING:

There don't appear to be any more trips to Rochester in Leo Gomez' future. The young third sacker made the Orioles' Opening Day roster in 1991, then had to be sent down to AAA after a month when he didn't hit. Gomez stuck around all year in 1992 and turned in a 17-homer, 64-RBI campaign. Though he hasn't had a 500 at-bat season yet, he's totaled 33 homers in two years.

Although he raised his batting average by 32 points last year, Gomez still lacks consistency and tends to be streaky. After hitting .288 before the All-Star break last year, he hit only .237 afterward. He compensated for the lower batting average with a power surge, however, hitting 11 of his 17 homers after the break. A selective hitter who doesn't swing at many bad pitches, Gomez drew 63 walks while fanning only 78 times.

If there was one problem with Gomez' play last year, it was that he struggled in clutch situations. He batted only .225 with men in scoring position last year, and .221 in the late innings of close games. The Orioles kept him out of the power slots in their batting order, never batting him higher than sixth all year. He batted most frequently in the seventh spot.

BASERUNNING:

No opposing pitcher shudders with Gomez at first. He represents little threat to steal and usually needs the ball to be put in play before getting underway. He's also very susceptible to the double play when at bat.

FIELDING:

Sheer hard work has turned Gomez from a shaky glove man into a steady, sometimes spectacular one. He has always had a strong and true arm, but he has improved dramatically in his movement to both sides. Although his error total has risen, that is partially because he is getting to more balls.

OVERALL:

Although room for progress exists, Gomez has firmly implanted himself in the Orioles' plans. He has an excellent work ethic and is making strides as a hitter. He provides run-producing potential at the lower end of the batting order.

LEO GOMEZ

Position: 3B
Bats: R **Throws:** R
Ht: 6' 0" **Wt:** 180

Opening Day Age: 26
Born: 3/2/67 in Canovanas, Puerto Rico
ML Seasons: 3

Overall Statistics

	G	AB	R	H	D	T	HR	RBI	SB	BB	SO	AVG
1992	137	468	62	124	24	0	17	64	2	63	78	.265
Career	267	898	105	224	41	2	33	110	3	111	167	.249

Where He Hits the Ball

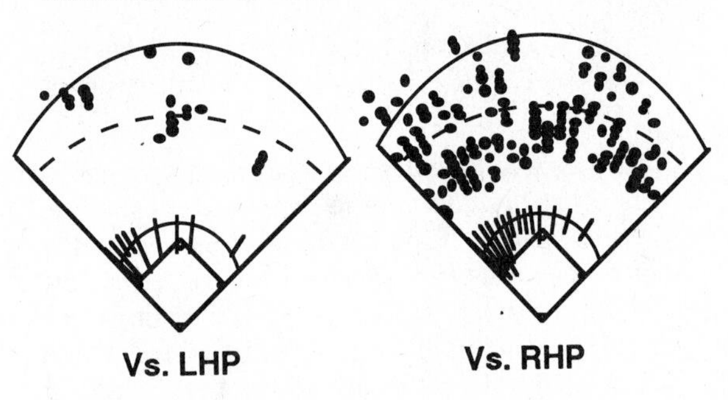

1992 Situational Stats

	AB	H	HR	RBI	AVG		AB	H	HR	RBI	AVG
Home	226	59	6	25	.261	LHP	104	26	4	17	.250
Road	242	65	11	39	.269	RHP	364	98	13	47	.269
Day	143	37	6	19	.259	Sc Pos	120	27	5	47	.225
Night	325	87	11	45	.268	Clutch	68	15	4	10	.221

1992 Rankings (American League)

- ➡ 3rd in lowest groundball/flyball ratio (.58)
- ➡ Led AL third basemen in hit by pitch (8)

CHRIS HOILES

Position: C
Bats: R **Throws:** R
Ht: 6' 0" **Wt:** 206

Opening Day Age: 28
Born: 3/20/65 in Bowling Green, OH
ML Seasons: 4

HITTING:

On the way to a 30-plus home-run season, Chris Hoiles was sabotaged last June when hit on the wrist by a Tim Leary pitch. Hoiles missed almost two months before finally returning in mid-August. Yet he still finished with 20 homers, third on the Oriole team, in only 310 at-bats. He seemed to show few ill effects from the injury, hitting six home runs in 117 ABs after his return.

A strong player who generates a lot of pop, Hoiles has power to all sections of the field. He hits long, soaring fly balls that often become classic home runs. Though he belted only 10 doubles and a single triple, Hoiles topped the Oriole team with a .506 slugging percentage.

Hoiles' drawbacks in 1992 included only 40 RBI and a .205 average with men in scoring position. Against lefties, he hit four homers, but drove in only five runs all season. All but three of his homers last year were solo shots. On the other hand, Hoiles has matured into a more patient hitter (55 walks, a .384 on-base average) and has shown more ability to go with the pitch than in the past.

BASERUNNING:

No warning flags are flown with Hoiles on the bases. He is a typical catcher: slow. Hoiles was 0-for-2 in stolen base attempts and is a station-to-station runner who benefits from hit-and-run plays.

FIELDING:

Hoiles has developed into a respectable major-league catcher who calls a decent game. His movement has improved, and he blocks errant pitches well. But last year he regressed in the throwing department, throwing out only 16 of 103 runners (15.5 percent). He'll have to improve this part of his game.

OVERALL:

Two seasons ago, Hoiles polished his defense; last season, he upgraded his power and intensity on offense. Now he needs to put the two together. The All-Star potential is there, but he'll have to improve his performance with men on base. He'll also have to work on his throwing.

Overall Statistics

	G	AB	R	H	D	T	HR	RBI	SB	BB	SO	AVG
1992	96	310	49	85	10	1	20	40	0	55	60	.274
Career	232	723	92	181	29	1	32	78	0	90	136	.250

Where He Hits the Ball

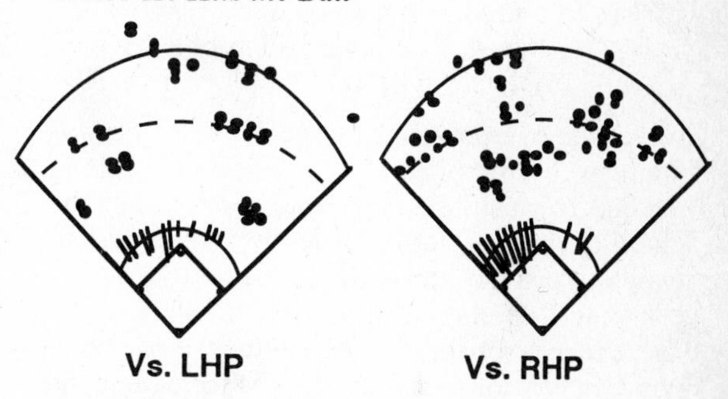

1992 Situational Stats

	AB	H	HR	RBI	AVG		AB	H	HR	RBI	AVG
Home	164	45	8	20	.274	LHP	80	23	4	5	.287
Road	146	40	12	20	.274	RHP	230	62	16	35	.270
Day	89	24	9	12	.270	Sc Pos	73	15	3	23	.205
Night	221	61	11	28	.276	Clutch	44	9	3	8	.205

1992 Rankings (American League)

- 1st in lowest percentage of runners caught stealing as a catcher (15.5%)
- 2nd highest fielding percentage at catcher (.994)

PITCHING:

The Orioles acquired Craig Lefferts and put him directly into a highly pressurized situation last year. They received mixed results. Needing a left-handed starter, the O's won a late-season bidding contest for Lefferts, who was pitching for San Diego and eligible for free agency at the end of the year. But the veteran produced only a single victory for Baltimore over the last month.

After being thrust into the heat of a pennant race, the converted reliever had won 13 games for the Padres before the August 31 deal. However, Lefferts was only 1-3 as an Oriole with a 4.09 ERA. He was very tough on lefthanders (.182) while in a Baltimore uniform, but with the pitch he uses to neutralize righties -- a tricky screwball -- not functioning well, he had problems with them (.276).

Never the overpowering type even when he was younger, Lefferts has always relied on keeping the ball down and staying ahead in the count. His inability to do either consistently prompted San Diego to convert him from a reliever to a starter last year. Lefferts goes after hitters with a sinker and slider (probably his best pitch), along with pinpoint control. But when he gets the ball up, he falls into trouble.

HOLDING RUNNERS AND FIELDING:

Lefferts is a heady veteran who has a fine move to first. He does his best to keep runners honest, but a slow delivery hinders him, and last year opponents swiped 20 bases in 30 attempts against him. His experience serves him well defensively.

OVERALL:

Lefferts is a difficult player to gauge based on a short trial. He flourished as a National League starter but was only so-so after the trade. It's likely that late-season fatigue was a factor, and he also needed to adjust to the hitters in a new league. Lefferts' arsenal is not what it once was, but the Orioles are hurting for a left-handed starter. He could fill the bill -- if they can re-sign him.

CRAIG LEFFERTS

Position: SP
Bats: L **Throws:** L
Ht: 6' 1" **Wt:** 210

Opening Day Age: 35
Born: 9/29/57 in Munich, West Germany
ML Seasons: 10

Overall Statistics

	W	L	ERA	G	GS	Sv	IP	H	R	BB	SO	HR
1992	14	12	3.76	32	32	0	196.1	214	95	41	104	19
Career	54	62	3.17	614	37	100	1027.2	956	413	282	634	96

How Often He Throws Strikes

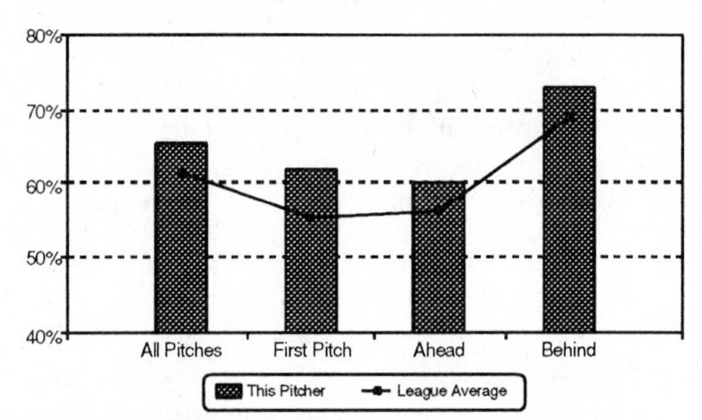

1992 Situational Stats

	W	L	ERA	Sv	IP		AB	H	HR	RBI	AVG
Home	7	6	3.67	0	95.2	LHB	123	30	2	13	.244
Road	7	6	3.84	0	100.2	RHB	636	184	17	67	.289
Day	4	3	3.08	0	64.1	Sc Pos	158	44	2	54	.278
Night	10	9	4.09	0	132.0	Clutch	52	15	1	3	.288

1992 Rankings (American League)

→ Did not rank near the top or bottom in any category

PITCHING:

The numbers weren't that flashy, but Ben McDonald made strong progress last season. Despite a .500 record (13-13) and 4.24 ERA, the big righty became a much more complete pitcher. McDonald, whose ERA at the All-Star break was an unsightly 5.00, posted a 3.39 mark during the second half.

The key to McDonald's late surge was the addition of a slider that he could employ on nights when his big overhand curve couldn't find the plate. Previously, McDonald was a one-dimensional pitcher who had to rely almost exclusively on his 90-plus fastball when the curve went south. McDonald also throws a change-up, but uses it very judiciously.

A stricter training regimen the previous winter helped McDonald avoid the series of injuries that had plagued him in his early years. He made 35 starts, one less than his total for the previous two seasons combined. But he was a hard-luck pitcher who received little batting support late in the season (nine runs over an eight-start span). He also made too many fat pitches. McDonald's 32 homers allowed were only three short of the club record. Most of his problems came at Camden Yards; at the O's new home his ERA was 4.90, with 21 gopher balls in 18 starts.

HOLDING RUNNERS AND FIELDING:

McDonald still needs refinement in keeping runners close. His high leg kick and delivery time are minuses, and a big reason why he allowed 20 steals in 28 attempts last year. McDonald has good lateral movement off the mound and the quick reactions of the basketball player he once was.

OVERALL:

Nobody is ready to ship McDonald to the Hall of Fame now after those glorious predictions when he was the first player picked in the 1989 draft. He is only two games over .500 in his career, but there are signs that he is maturing and on the verge of finally fulfilling his promise. Being relieved of the responsibility of being the Orioles' lead pitcher seemed to relax him last year.

BEN McDONALD

Position: SP
Bats: R **Throws:** R
Ht: 6' 7" **Wt:** 214

Opening Day Age: 25
Born: 11/24/67 in Baton Rouge, LA
ML Seasons: 4

Overall Statistics

	W	L	ERA	G	GS	Sv	IP	H	R	BB	SO	HR
1992	13	13	4.24	35	35	0	227.0	213	113	74	158	32
Career	28	26	4.02	83	71	0	479.1	435	227	156	311	59

How Often He Throws Strikes

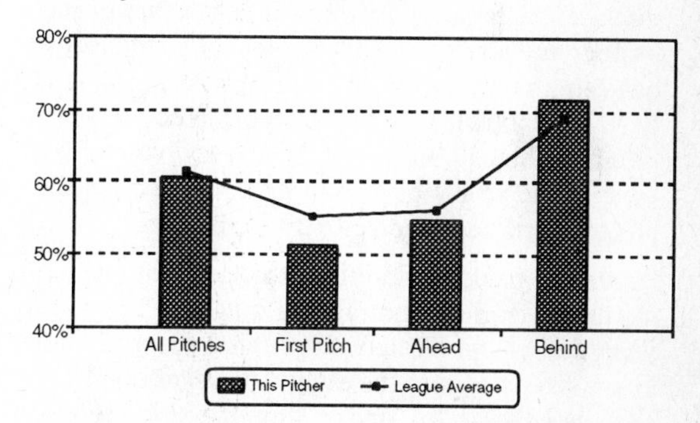

1992 Situational Stats

	W	L	ERA	Sv	IP		AB	H	HR	RBI	AVG
Home	5	8	4.90	0	117.2	LHB	405	95	14	41	.235
Road	8	5	3.54	0	109.1	RHB	458	118	18	59	.258
Day	3	5	4.79	0	67.2	Sc Pos	179	51	7	66	.285
Night	10	8	4.01	0	159.1	Clutch	58	16	3	10	.276

1992 Rankings (American League)

- 1st in fielding percentage at pitcher (1.000)
- 2nd in home runs allowed (32) and worst ERA at home (4.90)
- 3rd in games started (35)
- 4th most home runs allowed per 9 innings (1.27)
- Led the Orioles in home runs allowed, walks allowed (74), hit batsmen (9), strikeouts (158), balks (2), highest groundball/flyball ratio (1.07) and strikeouts per 9 innings (6.3)

PITCHING:

To Bob Milacki's credit, he took a mid-season demotion to Triple-A Rochester last year with equanimity. He worked his way back up and pitched creditably down the stretch after going 5-7 with a 6.34 ERA in his first stint. But Milacki, who was 1-1 after his return from the minors, was still a long way from the form he showed as a rookie surprise in 1989. During that memorable year, his 243 innings and 14-12 record helped keep the Orioles in the pennant race all season. Since then, Milacki has gone 21-25 over three seasons, and has yet to get his ERA below the 4.00 mark.

Milacki has an extremely diverse repertoire of pitches. He throws two kinds of fastballs, a curve, a slider and an excellent straight change that often has hitters way out in front. The key has always been his control. When he's ahead in counts, he's tough. When he's behind, he's very vulnerable because he won't blow away the opposition and has to sacrifice some velocity for control.

In years past, Milacki's troubles sometimes stemmed from a shortage of run support. Last year, though, he created a lot of his own problems. He gave up a lot of runs early; hitters tattooed him at a .347 clip in his first inning of work. He also yielded 16 homers, 140 hits and 44 walks in only 115.2 innings.

HOLDING RUNNERS AND FIELDING:

The ball-strike count has a direct bearing on Milacki's facility at holding runners. When the count favors him, he is solid and concentrates better. But if he is in that unfavorable groove, he is less effective, and last year that was usually the case; he permitted 11 steals in 12 attempts. For his size, Milacki comports himself well defensively.

OVERALL:

Milacki carried a sizable contract after winning his arbitration case last year; unfortunately, his production was not commensurate with his salary. When he's right, Milacki is a complete pitcher, but his consistency has waned. His future with Baltimore is anything but secure.

BOB MILACKI

Position: SP
Bats: R **Throws:** R
Ht: 6' 4" **Wt:** 232

Opening Day Age: 28
Born: 7/28/64 in Trenton, NJ
ML Seasons: 5

Overall Statistics

	W	L	ERA	G	GS	Sv	IP	H	R	BB	SO	HR
1992	6	8	5.84	23	20	1	115.2	140	78	44	51	16
Career	37	37	4.19	121	109	1	703.0	700	344	255	350	73

How Often He Throws Strikes

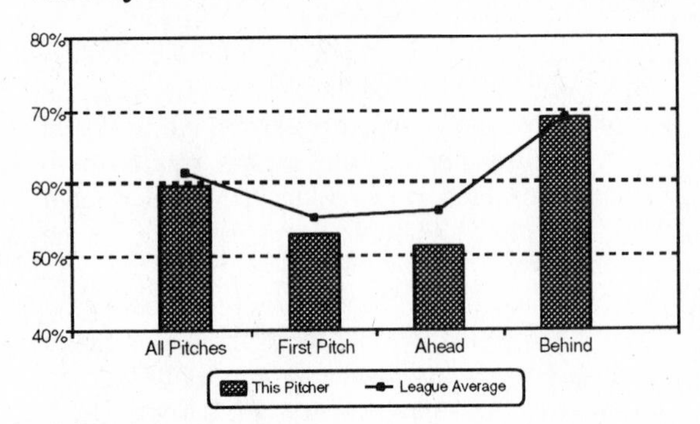

1992 Situational Stats

	W	L	ERA	Sv	IP		AB	H	HR	RBI	AVG
Home	4	4	6.00	0	60.0	LHB	211	55	6	24	.261
Road	2	4	5.66	1	55.2	RHB	261	85	10	47	.326
Day	2	1	5.20	1	36.1	Sc Pos	130	37	3	52	.285
Night	4	7	6.13	0	79.1	Clutch	18	6	3	4	.333

1992 Rankings (American League)

- Led the Orioles in wild pitches (7)

RANDY MILLIGAN

Position: 1B
Bats: R **Throws:** R
Ht: 6' 1" **Wt:** 234

Opening Day Age: 31
Born: 11/27/61 in San Diego, CA
ML Seasons: 6

HITTING:

The most selective Oriole at the plate, Randy Milligan has a tremendous batting eye. He topped the club last year with 106 walks, and his .383 on-base percentage was only a point behind Chris Hoiles for the team lead. But Milligan is a big man at 6-1 and 234, and he's a first baseman. The Orioles expect homers and runs batted in from that position, and last year Milligan didn't give it to them. The Orioles left him unprotected going into the expansion draft.

Over the last three years, Milligan has seen his home run total decline from 20 to 16 to 11. He drove in only 53 runs in 1992, and his .240 batting average was his worst figure since coming to Baltimore in 1989. As usual, Milligan had no trouble getting on base, but he's stopped supplying the sock expected of a hitter in the middle of the lineup. People are now saying he takes too many pitches.

Milligan is also a very streaky ballplayer. He gets into a groove briefly, then falls back out of it. Last year his monthly averages were .213, .306, .247, .222, .287 and .158 -- all over the map. Milligan was also troubled at Camden Yards, hitting a minuscule .193 there despite banging the first grand slam in the new park.

BASERUNNING:

Known as "Moose," Milligan is not a base stealer. He made only one attempt in 1992 and failed. His last successful steal was in 1990. But once he gets his momentum going, he has surprising speed and uses it wisely.

FIELDING:

With Glenn Davis relegated to a DH role for most of 1992 due to a sore shoulder, Milligan was commendable enough in the field. He made only seven errors. But he is not unduly polished and makes an occasional mental gaffe.

OVERALL:

The Orioles would like to see Milligan hike his power figures and perhaps be a little less picky at the plate. He doesn't hurt the offense by walking, but he could help it more with additional extra-base hits. A positive influence in the clubhouse, he is among the most popular players on the team.

Overall Statistics

	G	AB	R	H	D	T	HR	RBI	SB	BB	SO	AVG
1992	137	462	71	111	21	1	11	53	0	106	81	.240
Career	554	1755	258	450	86	9	62	236	16	373	357	.256

Where He Hits the Ball

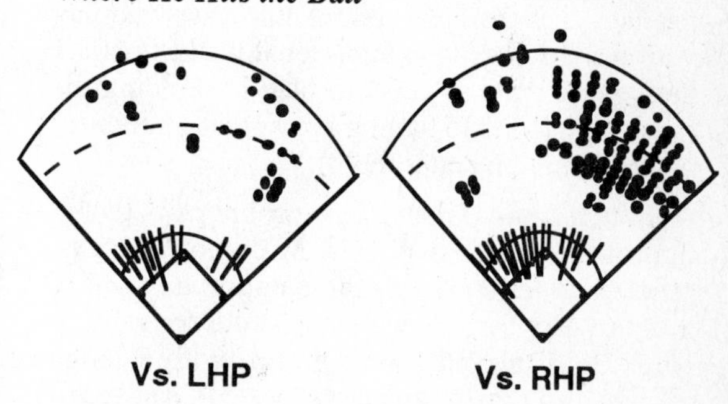

1992 Situational Stats

	AB	H	HR	RBI	AVG		AB	H	HR	RBI	AVG
Home	233	45	7	26	.193	LHP	107	30	3	14	.280
Road	229	66	4	27	.288	RHP	355	81	8	39	.228
Day	140	38	1	16	.271	Sc Pos	119	26	3	42	.218
Night	322	73	10	37	.227	Clutch	75	15	2	8	.200

1992 Rankings (American League)

- 1st in lowest batting average at home (.193)
- 4th in walks (106), most pitches seen per plate appearance (4.07) and on-base percentage vs. left-handed pitchers (.462)
- Led the Orioles in walks, GDPs (15), on-base percentage (.383), most pitches seen per plate appearance and on-base percentage vs. left-handed pitchers
- Led AL first basemen in pitches seen per plate appearance and on-base percentage vs. left-handed pitchers

PITCHING:

There is no doubt Alan Mills was the most pleasant surprise on the Oriole pitching staff last year. Acquired from the Yankees in a little-noticed spring training deal for two minor leaguers, Mills proceeded to dazzle the opposition for much of the year. At the All-Star break, Mills had a 7-1 record and a minuscule ERA of 1.36. He cooled off after that, in part because of a tender arm, but his final figures (10-4, 2.61) were extremely respectable.

A longtime Yankee farmhand, Mills had a history of walking too many batters. In 58 lifetime innings with the Yanks, he'd walked 41, and the Yanks finally concluded he was a fringe major leaguer . . . if that. His control still wasn't perfect with the Orioles (44 unintentional walks in 103.1 innings). But Mills compensated by holding the opposition to a .215 batting average. With runners on, he was even better (.198).

Although some minor elbow problems bothered him during the second half, Mills notched nine relief victories and made three important starts at a time when the O's were desperate for starting help. He displayed a strong arm, with a tough slider and good velocity on his fastball. Righthanders hit just .191 against him and he was equally productive at home and away. His walk-strikeout ratio (54-60) still needs improvement and he sometimes makes careless pitches.

HOLDING RUNNERS AND FIELDING:

Mills has superb athletic talent and can bound off the mound or react to the line drive with the best of them. He needs some polish at holding runners, but is working on it. Pitching only a little over 100 innings last year, he allowed 12 steals in 16 attempts -- an unacceptable rate.

OVERALL:

If he can make progress at controlling both his excitability and his pitches, Mills has a good future. He has the versatility to pitch in long, middle or short relief and can also start. Only 26, he was a major find for the Orioles at a relatively minor price.

ALAN MILLS

Position: RP/SP
Bats: B **Throws:** R
Ht: 6' 1" **Wt:** 190
Opening Day Age: 26
Born: 10/18/66 in Lakeland, FL
ML Seasons: 3

Overall Statistics

	W	L	ERA	G	GS	Sv	IP	H	R	BB	SO	HR
1992	10	4	2.61	35	3	2	103.1	78	33	54	60	5
Career	12	10	3.18	77	5	2	161.1	142	63	95	95	10

How Often He Throws Strikes

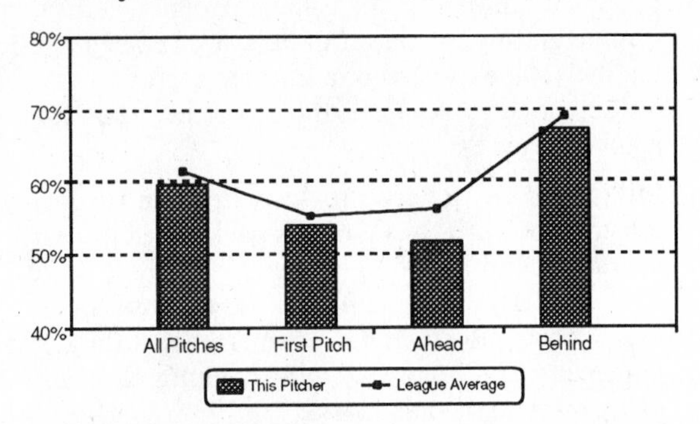

1992 Situational Stats

	W	L	ERA	Sv	IP		AB	H	HR	RBI	AVG
Home	5	2	2.54	2	49.2	LHB	168	41	2	17	.244
Road	5	2	2.68	0	53.2	RHB	194	37	3	20	.191
Day	2	2	4.14	0	37.0	Sc Pos	109	21	2	32	.193
Night	8	2	1.76	2	66.1	Clutch	104	19	0	7	.183

1992 Rankings (American League)

- 2nd in relief wins (9)
- 6th in lowest batting average allowed in relief (.198)
- 8th in relief innings (90)
- Led the Orioles in relief wins and lowest batting average allowed in relief

CY YOUNG STUFF

PITCHING:

Mike Mussina is the genuine article. In 1992, his first full major league season, Mussina blossomed into an All-Star pitcher, a big-game pitcher and a remarkably consistent pitcher. He ranked fourth in the American League in wins, first in winning percentage and third in ERA. Watching him pitch last season, it was hard to believe the youngster was only 23 years old.

The first Oriole in 10 years to lead the majors in winning percentage (.783), Mussina topped the staff with 241 innings and comported himself exceptionally well in the heat of a pennant race. Here's the mark of a clutch pitcher: after September 1, Mussina was 5-0 with a 1.56 ERA. And another: with runners in scoring position last year, Mussina held the opponents to a .175 batting average.

Extremely coachable, Mussina is an intelligent pitcher who oozes confidence and competitiveness. He should, because he has a major-league arsenal. His control is almost always impeccable and he knows how to use the strike zone. With two kinds of fastballs, a knuckle curve that is difficult to pick up, a conventional curve, straight change-up and occasional slider, this youngster has it all. He is exceptionally tough on lefties, holding them to a .220 average with a single homer and 17 RBI in 422 at-bats last year.

HOLDING RUNNERS AND FIELDING:

Very quick to the plate and well-schooled, Mussina is excellent at holding baserunners. Though Oriole catcher Chris Hoiles had problems throwing out runners last year, Mussina permitted only nine steals in 18 attempts. A fundamentally sound fielder who transmits intensity, he is always aware of the game situation.

OVERALL:

Favorable comparisons between Mussina and Jim Palmer, the greatest Oriole pitcher ever, are already cropping up. Mussina might have won the Cy Young Award but for some blown saves last year. He's a good candidate to do it soon, barring injury. He is talented, wise beyond his years and has an uncommon desire to excel.

MIKE MUSSINA

Position: SP
Bats: R **Throws:** R
Ht: 6' 2" **Wt:** 182

Opening Day Age: 24
Born: 12/8/68 in Williamsport, PA
ML Seasons: 2

Overall Statistics

	W	L	ERA	G	GS	Sv	IP	H	R	BB	SO	HR
1992	18	5	2.54	32	32	0	241.0	212	70	48	130	16
Career	22	10	2.63	44	44	0	328.2	289	101	69	182	23

How Often He Throws Strikes

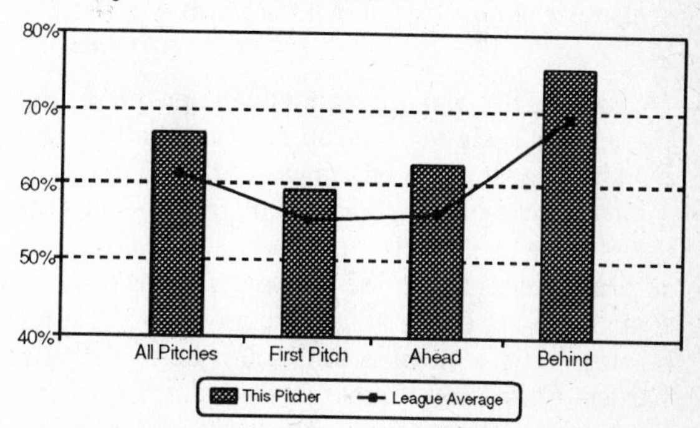

1992 Situational Stats

	W	L	ERA	Sv	IP		AB	H	HR	RBI	AVG
Home	7	3	2.65	0	115.2	LHB	422	93	1	17	.220
Road	11	2	2.44	0	125.1	RHB	466	119	15	48	.255
Day	3	2	3.33	0	51.1	Sc Pos	154	27	1	39	.175
Night	15	3	2.33	0	189.2	Clutch	82	21	1	7	.256

1992 Rankings (American League)

- 1st in winning percentage (.783), lowest on-base percentage allowed (.278) and least baserunners allowed per 9 innings (9.8)
- 2nd in shutouts (4) and lowest batting average allowed with runners in scoring position (.175)
- 3rd in ERA (2.54) and lowest groundball/flyball ratio (0.9)
- Led the Orioles in ERA, wins (18), complete games (8), shutouts, innings pitched (241), runners caught stealing (9), winning percentage, strikeout/walk ratio (2.7), lowest batting average allowed (.239), lowest slugging percentage allowed (.348) and lowest stolen base percentage allowed (50.0%),

STOPPER

GREGG OLSON

Position: RP
Bats: R **Throws:** R
Ht: 6' 4" **Wt:** 206

Opening Day Age: 26
Born: 10/11/66 in Omaha, NE
ML Seasons: 5

PITCHING:

Gregg Olson used to come into save situations and blow people away with his 90-plus fastball and a devastating curveball that dropped away like magic. Now, Olson has to pitch more and fire away less. The results are still plenty good. The young righty recorded 36 saves last year, his third straight 30-save season. His 2.05 ERA was the second lowest of his impressive career.

No longer a mere power pitcher, Olson has added a sinking fastball to his equipment and become more refined. He retains his quest for perfection, mandatory for a closer, but is now more under control after a blown save. With maturation, Olson finally realizes he is always under a microscope. He doesn't let that bother him like it once did.

As usual, Olson had a somewhat checkered season in 1992. He went through a brief fallow period in August when others were utilized to finish games. But overall he was still mighty. Olson's 36 saves were one short of his own club record, and his conversion rate of 82 per cent was very good. Olson is not exactly automatic any more, but he is close. His control is still solid, he is still the hardest Oriole to hit and there is minimal difference in his effectiveness against lefties or righties.

HOLDING RUNNERS AND FIELDING:

The byword in these areas is work. Olson has improved slightly in checking runners, but still has a long way to go. Last year he permitted 10 steals in 10 attempts, though weak-throwing catchers didn't help him. Defense is also sometimes a problem for him. He rushes throws at times and occasionally is out of position.

OVERALL:

Olson is now more inclined to pinpoint location rather than raw power to dispatch opponents. He has also taken a more realistic approach to his rare failures, understanding that even Dennis Eckersley, the best there is, loses one once in a while. A star closer for the last four years who's still only 26, he's likely to get even better.

Overall Statistics

	W	L	ERA	G	GS	Sv	IP	H	R	BB	SO	HR
1992	1	5	2.05	60	0	36	61.1	46	14	24	58	3
Career	17	19	2.36	270	0	131	305.1	244	83	140	303	9

How Often He Throws Strikes

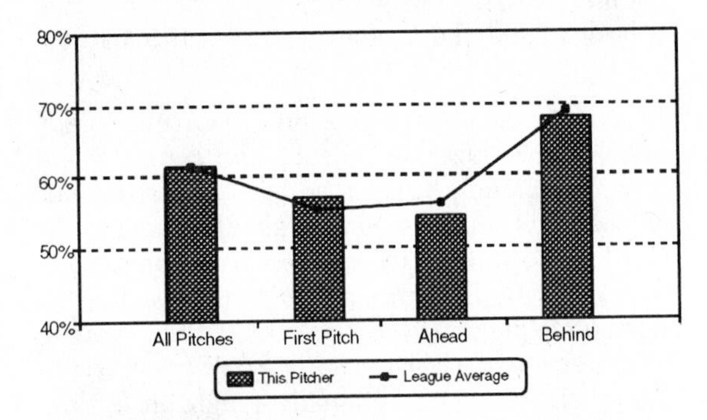

1992 Situational Stats

	W	L	ERA	Sv	IP		AB	H	HR	RBI	AVG
Home	1	1	1.38	17	32.2	LHB	113	22	0	8	.195
Road	0	4	2.83	19	28.2	RHB	105	24	3	9	.229
Day	0	3	2.86	10	22.0	Sc Pos	63	11	0	13	.175
Night	1	2	1.60	26	39.1	Clutch	162	37	3	17	.228

1992 Rankings (American League)

- ➡ 2nd in blown saves (8)
- ➡ 4th in saves (36) and save opportunities (44)
- ➡ 5th in games finished (56), lowest percentage of inherited runners scored (16.1%) and strikeouts per 9 innings in relief (8.5)
- ➡ Led the Orioles in saves, games finished, save opportunities, save percentage (81.8%), blown saves, lowest percentage of inherited runners scored, relief ERA (2.05), least runners allowed per 9 innings in relief (10.3) and strikeouts per 9 innings in relief

HITTING:

A master craftsman at the plate, Joe Orsulak is one of those guys who could hit falling out of bed. In five seasons with the Orioles, Orsulak has batted .288, .285, .269, .278 and .289. He's led the Orioles in hitting during three of the five seasons, including 1992. He has the ninth best career average (.281) in Oriole history.

Though his final figures wound up right around where usually are, Orsulak had a very streaky season in 1992. He got off to a horrible start and was batting only .216 on June 1. Then he caught fire, batting a torrid .366 in June and July. Orsulak cooled off in August (.273), then slumped near the end of the season after spraining his left thumb. He batted .218 after September 1, spoiling his chance to hit .300 for the first time in seven seasons.

The lefty swinger has his own style, putting the ball in play and forcing the defense to perform. He has excellent bat control and can turn on the inside pitch or flick at outside offerings and send them the opposite way. He concentrates hard, uses the entire field and rarely gets fooled. Orsulak played against all kinds of pitching last year and held his own against lefties (.250).

BASERUNNING:

Orsulak picks his spots to steal because he has lost a step. He rarely makes baserunning mistakes and employs his remaining speed to advantage. He's aggressive when he has to be.

FIELDING:

Opposing runners were less inclined to run on Orsulak's arm last season after his astonishing 22 assists in 1991. He commanded respect from all but the fastest runners. He is a down-in-the-trenches outfielder who will daringly go after shots to the wall or sinking liners.

OVERALL:

A blue-collar player who does his job without much fanfare, Orsulak is a fan favorite. He always winds up with extensive playing time, even though his power and speed have waned. That playing time might not be with the Orioles in 1993 as Orsulak was a free agent.

JOE ORSULAK

Position: RF/LF
Bats: L **Throws:** L
Ht: 6' 1" **Wt:** 210

Opening Day Age: 30
Born: 5/31/62 in Glen Ridge, NJ
ML Seasons: 9

Overall Statistics

	G	AB	R	H	D	T	HR	RBI	SB	BB	SO	AVG
1992	117	391	45	113	18	3	4	39	5	28	34	.289
Career	930	2935	384	817	131	29	37	265	82	221	266	.278

Where He Hits the Ball

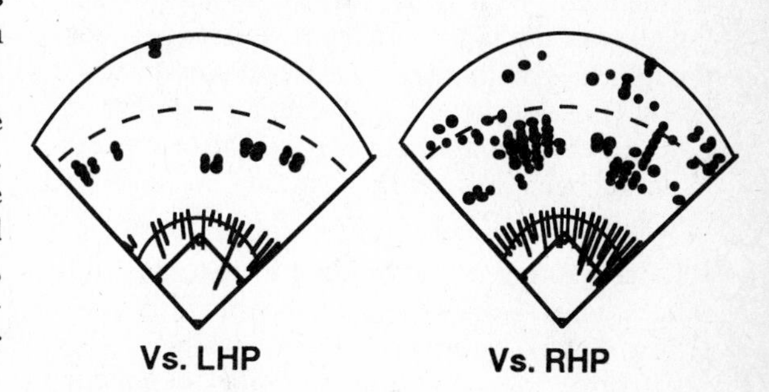

1992 Situational Stats

	AB	H	HR	RBI	AVG		AB	H	HR	RBI	AVG
Home	180	50	2	18	.278	LHP	80	20	0	11	.250
Road	211	63	2	21	.299	RHP	311	93	4	28	.299
Day	116	34	0	6	.293	Sc Pos	85	26	2	36	.306
Night	275	79	4	33	.287	Clutch	65	21	1	3	.323

1992 Rankings (American League)

- 5th in least GDPs per GDP situation (3.2%)
- Led the Orioles in batting average with runners in scoring position (.306) and batting average in the clutch (.323)
- Led AL right fielders in least GDPs per GDP situation

ARTHUR RHODES

Position: SP
Bats: L **Throws:** L
Ht: 6' 2" **Wt:** 204

Opening Day Age: 23
Born: 10/24/69 in Waco, TX
ML Seasons: 2

PITCHING:

The Orioles were trying to play it cozy with young Arthur Rhodes, preferring not to rush him to the big leagues until they were sure of his readiness. But last summer, injuries and staff ineffectiveness forced them to call Rhodes up from Triple-A Rochester in July. The results were quite satisfying. Rhodes exceeded all expectations by immediately giving the team four straight outstanding starts and going on to win seven games. Rhodes was a much more mature pitcher than he'd been in 1991, when he was 0-3 with an 8.00 ERA in an eight-start trial.

Like many young lefthanders, Rhodes has fought control problems throughout most of his career. In 36 innings with the O's in '91, he fanned 23 -- but allowed the same number of walks. Last year, though, he compiled a 2-to-1 strikeout-to-walk ratio (77 strikeouts, 38 walks) and showed poise beyond what management believed he possessed. With runners in scoring position, he held the opposition to a .217 average.

Rhodes' velocity is outstanding -- up to the mid-90's at times -- and he's capable of blowing away hitters. Lately, he has added a quick slider to his repertoire that gives hitters more to ponder. Rhodes' poise under pressure was evident by a 3-1 record and 1.73 ERA on the road, all in meaningful games.

HOLDING RUNNERS AND FIELDING:

A lefthander with a quick move to the plate, Rhodes helps himself in holding baserunners. Last year he permitted only four steals in eight attempts -- outstanding for a power pitcher who doesn't have a big gun behind the plate. Defensively, he employs his athletic skills well and doesn't hurt himself with silly mistakes.

OVERALL:

Hailed as the second coming of Vida Blue, Rhodes has made tremendous strides in one year. He got himself and his pitches under control and made an impact that will give him a leg up in a bid for the rotation next year. If he continues to restrict the number of runners he allows, Rhodes has a bright future. His raw talent is unquestioned.

Overall Statistics

	W	L	ERA	G	GS	Sv	IP	H	R	BB	SO	HR
1992	7	5	3.63	15	15	0	94.1	87	39	38	77	6
Career	7	8	4.83	23	23	0	130.1	134	74	61	100	10

How Often He Throws Strikes

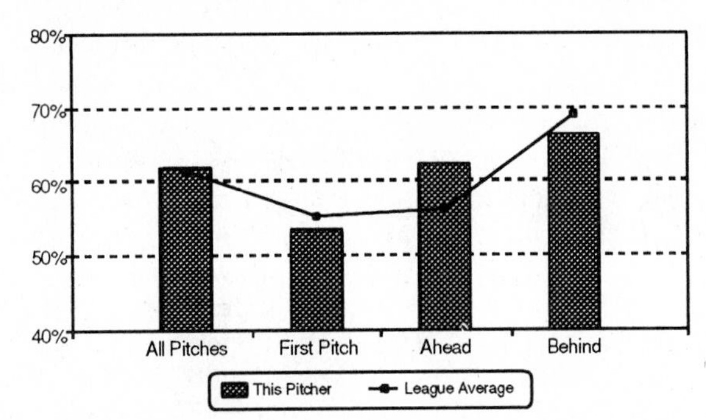

1992 Situational Stats

	W	L	ERA	Sv	IP		AB	H	HR	RBI	AVG
Home	4	4	4.81	0	58.0	LHB	40	10	0	2	.250
Road	3	1	1.73	0	36.1	RHB	308	77	6	28	.250
Day	1	1	3.29	0	13.2	Sc Pos	83	18	1	23	.217
Night	6	4	3.68	0	80.2	Clutch	16	8	0	5	.500

1992 Rankings (American League)

- Did not rank near the top or bottom in any category

HITTING:

Billy Ripken responded to a semi-platoon situation with a so-so 1992 season. Forced to share time with Mark McLemore, Ripken batted a modest .230, slumped in the stretch and did a lot of experimenting with his stance and approach. Nothing helped much. He had only one month over .245 -- July, when he batted .286. With brother Cal Junior also slumping and dad Cal Senior fired as the O's third base coach at the end of the year, it must have been a very depressing season for the Ripken family.

The youngest Ripken has had a couple of seasons over .290, but shouldn't be expected to hit that way every year. In truth, his .291 average in 1990 was probably an aberration. In four of the last five seasons, Ripken has batted below .240. He hasn't been helped by nagging injuries, the result of playing very hard.

Ripken usually hits eight or ninth and is a good hit-and-run man at the bottom of the order. He is also an adept bunter, tying for the team lead in sacrifices with 10. But he had only 19 extra-base hits and was again susceptible to high pitches and breaking balls. He still has a tendency to try to pull the ball like a power hitter, which he most definitely is not.

BASERUNNING:

Not especially fast for a middle infielder, Ripken is fundamentally sound on the bases. Injuries have often slowed him and he is not a legitimate base stealer, with only two swipes in 1992.

FIELDING:

This is where Ripken shines. A hard-nosed hustler, he scratches and claws and isn't timid about hanging in there on double play pivots. He throws across his body skillfully, goes back on the pop-up nicely and ranges to both sides well. He committed only four errors in 1992.

OVERALL:

A solid glove was not enough to keep Ripken from sharing time with Mark McLemore last year. Ripken was exposed in the expansion draft, but drew no interest. The Orioles were shopping the market for a free agent at his position.

BILLY RIPKEN

Position: 2B
Bats: R **Throws:** R
Ht: 6' 1" **Wt:** 186

Opening Day Age: 28
Born: 12/16/64 in Havre de Grace, MD
ML Seasons: 6

Overall Statistics

	G	AB	R	H	D	T	HR	RBI	SB	BB	SO	AVG
1992	111	330	35	76	15	0	4	36	2	18	26	.230
Career	667	2087	217	510	92	5	13	168	20	137	239	.244

Where He Hits the Ball

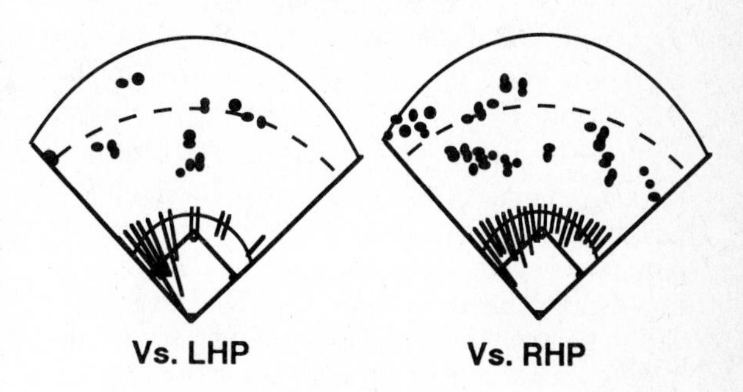

1992 Situational Stats

	AB	H	HR	RBI	AVG		AB	H	HR	RBI	AVG
Home	149	38	3	22	.255	LHP	109	25	0	9	.229
Road	181	38	1	14	.210	RHP	221	51	4	27	.231
Day	92	20	2	10	.217	Sc Pos	87	23	1	30	.264
Night	238	56	2	26	.235	Clutch	24	5	1	5	.208

1992 Rankings (American League)

- 2nd highest fielding percentage at second base (.993)
- Led the Orioles in sacrifice bunts (10) and bunts in play (18)

HALL OF FAMER

HITTING:

Cal Ripken went from the penthouse to the outhouse last season. Ripken followed a Most Valuable Player year with a mystifying backslide that included a 73-game drought without a homer, the longest of his outstanding career. He wound up with a .251 average and a career worst 72 RBI. After hitting 20-plus homers and driving in 80 or more runs for ten straight seasons, Ripken reached neither figure in 1992.

Ripken's crouching stance and approach stayed consistent, but his production drooped badly. No one seemed to have the answer. He was shifted out of the third spot to fourth and fifth in the batting order. He was also rested a little more often late in games. But nothing seemed to help. Ripken never did adjust to Camden Yards, batting only .237 with five homers and 23 RBI in the Orioles' new home. His road figures -- .265, nine, 49 -- were much closer to his usual standard.

Ripken admitted that concerns about signing a new contract were distracting during the season. After the negotiations concluded in a $30.5 million windfall he had a solid finish. Ripken continued to be a tough out, fanning only 50 times and batting .276 with men in scoring position.

BASERUNNING:

Ripken has average speed, but outstanding knowledge of when to take an extra base. He steals only a few bases each year (four in 1992). However, foolish mistakes are alien to him. He is rarely thrown out taking liberties.

FIELDING:

Ripken won his second straight Gold Glove last year. Despite sacrificing some range because of his size, he is uncanny about where to play hitters. He'll make bullet throws to first when necessary. Twelve errors was relatively high for him, but very respectable overall.

OVERALL:

Now that he is secure in his Oriole uniform for five more years, look for Ripken to rebound offensively. In 1993, manager John Oates plans to give him more late-game breathers, although his pursuit of Lou Gehrig's consecutive-game streak will continue.

CAL RIPKEN

Position: SS
Bats: R **Throws:** R
Ht: 6' 4" **Wt:** 224

Opening Day Age: 32
Born: 8/24/60 in Havre de Grace, MD
ML Seasons: 12

Overall Statistics

	G	AB	R	H	D	T	HR	RBI	SB	BB	SO	AVG
1992	162	637	73	160	29	1	14	72	4	64	50	.251
Career	1800	6942	1043	1922	369	34	273	1014	32	752	797	.277

Where He Hits the Ball

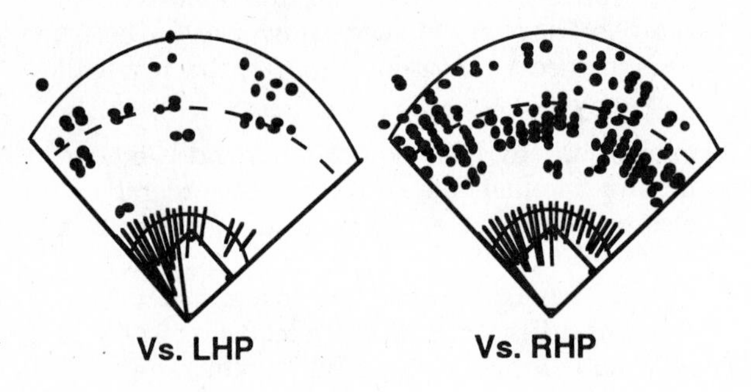

1992 Situational Stats

	AB	H	HR	RBI	AVG		AB	H	HR	RBI	AVG
Home	312	74	5	23	.237	LHP	165	38	2	13	.230
Road	325	86	9	49	.265	RHP	472	122	12	59	.258
Day	198	53	5	25	.268	Sc Pos	145	40	4	57	.276
Night	439	107	9	47	.244	Clutch	77	19	0	9	.247

1992 Rankings (American League)

- 1st in games played (162)
- 4th in intentional walks (14)
- 5th in plate appearances (715)
- Led the Orioles in singles (116), doubles (29), intentional walks, games played, highest groundball/flyball ratio (1.22), batting average on 0-2 count (.273), lowest percentage of swings that missed (10.1%) and highest percentage of swings put into play (54.6%)
- Led AL shortstops in sacrifice flies (7), walks (64), intentional walks, hit by pitch (7), times on base (231) and games played

DAVID SEGUI

Position: 1B/RF
Bats: B **Throws:** L
Ht: 6' 1" **Wt:** 200

Opening Day Age: 26
Born: 7/19/66 in Kansas City, KS
ML Seasons: 3

HITTING:

A lack of playing time has become a detriment to David Segui, a switch-hitter with an impressive minor league batting record. In three seasons with the Orioles, Segui has never batted more than 212 times in a season, and as a result his bat work has suffered. The youngster batted only .233 in 1992, a career low.

The Orioles realize that Segui has the talent to do a lot better than that, which is why he was the O's only expansion protection at first base. It's been difficult for him to keep sharp because he has a lot of movement in his swing and needs to play to perfect it. To his credit, Segui is not a complainer and waits his turn. He's proven useful as a pinch-hitter, last year going 4-for-11 (.364).

Segui is not a home run hitter and has to spray the ball around to be effective. He does have some doubles power to the gaps, and he possesses a good batting eye. His ability to switch-hit makes him a valuable man to have on the bench and forces the opposing manager to re-think pitching changes. He'll usually make contact.

BASERUNNING:

Segui is yet another average runner on a rather slow team. He isn't daring or pell-mell and stays within his capabilities. Segui had only one stolen base attempt last year and made it.

FIELDING:

Slick beyond his years, Segui is frequently used for late-inning defense in place of Randy Milligan at first. He reacts swiftly, moves well in both directions and handles throws nicely. Occasionally, he goes to the outfield where he has progressed after an adjustment period. His arm is below average.

OVERALL:

Rust is Segui's primary enemy. He has shown an ability to hit in the clutch and there's little doubt that he could hit for a decent average if given more regular work. His career might be better served elsewhere, some place where his line-drive bat could be utilized more regularly. With the Orioles there are just too many players ahead of him.

Overall Statistics

	G	AB	R	H	D	T	HR	RBI	SB	BB	SO	AVG
1992	115	189	21	44	9	0	1	17	1	20	23	.233
Career	241	524	50	133	23	0	5	54	2	43	57	.254

Where He Hits the Ball

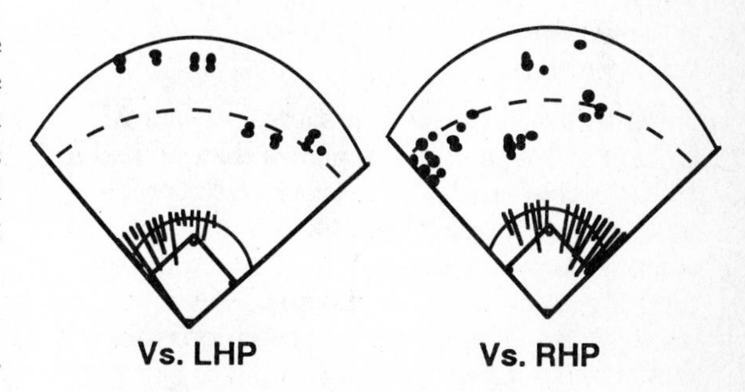

1992 Situational Stats

	AB	H	HR	RBI	AVG		AB	H	HR	RBI	AVG
Home	75	16	1	11	.213	LHP	78	16	0	9	.205
Road	114	28	0	6	.246	RHP	111	28	1	8	.252
Day	68	15	0	5	.221	Sc Pos	59	13	0	15	.220
Night	121	29	1	12	.240	Clutch	33	9	0	1	.273

1992 Rankings (American League)

→ Did not rank near the top or bottom in any category

RICK SUTCLIFFE

Position: SP
Bats: L **Throws:** R
Ht: 6' 7" **Wt:** 215

Opening Day Age: 36
Born: 6/21/56 in Independence, MO
ML Seasons: 16

PITCHING:

A tough competitor who became the big brother and prodder of the Orioles' pitching staff, Rick Sutcliffe gave Baltimore all he had last season. Always focused and a shining example to the young starting staff, his presence was indispensable. So were his 16 wins, though Sutcliffe had his ups and downs over the course of the long season.

Sutcliffe works with tremendous intensity and expects no less from his peers. At times, especially when he didn't win in July, Sutcliffe had very little. He has lost velocity on his fastball after two years of arm problems and had a lot to prove to the Cubs, who let him go, and to himself. To compensate for lesser stuff at his age, he approached every game as if it were the last in the World Series.

Sutcliffe led the majors in starts, pitched 237.1 innings and won 10 more games than he had in 1990-91 combined. Consistency was a problem, as he never had two good months in a row, but even in his bad stretches, he continued to battle. Sutcliffe throws the conventional four pitches (fastball, curve, slider, change) and looks for the groundball out.

HOLDING RUNNERS AND FIELDING:

A wily veteran, Sutcliffe moves quickly to first, but a slow delivery hurts him. Last year he permitted 22 steals in 27 attempts, which is very bad. At age 36, he has slowed down in the field, but overall is above average because of his experience.

OVERALL:

Sutcliffe entered the winter desiring to remain in Baltimore, and got his wish by signing a one-year deal worth $2 million, not unreasonable for what he provides the team. Sutcliffe is a rock for the pitching staff, a gamer who's a role model for their blossoming young pitchers. How much does he have left? Sutcliffe is hittable these days and must depend on control and command. But his presence in the clubhouse cannot be measured by statistics.

Overall Statistics

	W	L	ERA	G	GS	Sv	IP	H	R	BB	SO	HR
1992	16	15	4.47	36	36	0	237.1	251	123	74	109	20
Career	155	125	3.90	412	350	6	2464.1	2357	1159	975	1573	202

How Often He Throws Strikes

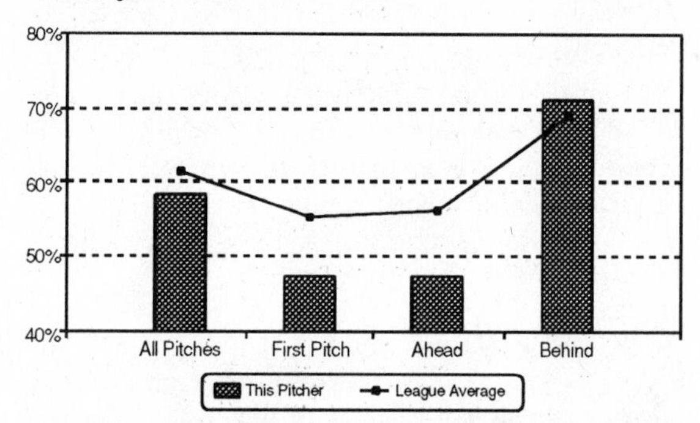

1992 Situational Stats

	W	L	ERA	Sv	IP		AB	H	HR	RBI	AVG
Home	9	8	4.17	0	131.2	LHB	431	114	13	49	.265
Road	7	7	4.85	0	105.2	RHB	489	137	7	50	.280
Day	3	6	3.69	0	70.2	Sc Pos	207	52	8	81	.251
Night	13	9	4.81	0	166.2	Clutch	101	25	2	8	.248

1992 Rankings (American League)

- → 1st in games started (36)
- → 2nd in hits allowed (251)
- → 3rd in losses (15)
- → 4th in batters faced (1,018)
- → Led the Orioles in losses, games started, hits allowed, batters faced, walks allowed (74), wild pitches (7), balks (2), pitches thrown (3,803), pickoff throws (213), stolen bases allowed (22), GDPs induced (20) and GDPs induced per 9 innings (.76)

HITTING:

Veteran minor leaguer Jeff Tackett spent eight years in the bush leagues, the last three at AAA Rochester, before he finally reached the promised land with the Orioles in 1991. Now that he's arrived, Tackett doesn't seem in any hurry to leave. Chris Hoiles' broken wrist gave the catcher a chance to show his stuff for an exteded period last year, and Tackett played very well. He performed far better than his .240 average indicated.

For a player who once went 1,211 minor-league at-bats without a home run, Tackett had a veritable explosion last summer. He connected five times in his first 20 games as a part-timer and suddenly felt comfortable as a hitter. Still only 27, he has just learned how to hit and use his natural strength. Tackett had a penchant for changing his position in the batter's box in the minors, but settling on one stance helped him.

Tackett did nice work against lefties last year, hitting .288, with four of his five homers, in only 52 at-bats. Righties bothered him (.220), however, and brought his average down after Hoiles was hurt.

BASERUNNING:

Tackett once stole 16 bases in the minors, but that was back in 1986, when he was 20. Years of squatting behind the plate have left him with catcher's speed, which is to say little. He has never stolen a base in the majors and probably won't be asked to unless he's on the back end of a double steal.

FIELDING:

This is Tackett's forte. Always a solid receiver, he threw out 34 percent on steal attempts, more than double Hoiles' rate. Another season of learning the hitters will help him because his techniques are excellent and his arm is a cannon.

OVERALL:

Tackett survived the expansion draft and will probably return as the Orioles' backup to Chris Hoiles. He is ideal in this role and a valuable guy to have around as a spot starter vs. lefties.

JEFF TACKETT

Position: C
Bats: R **Throws:** R
Ht: 6' 2" **Wt:** 206

Opening Day Age: 27
Born: 12/1/65 in Fresno, CA
ML Seasons: 2

Overall Statistics

	G	AB	R	H	D	T	HR	RBI	SB	BB	SO	AVG
1992	65	179	21	43	8	1	5	24	0	17	28	.240
Career	71	187	22	44	8	1	5	24	0	19	30	.235

Where He Hits the Ball

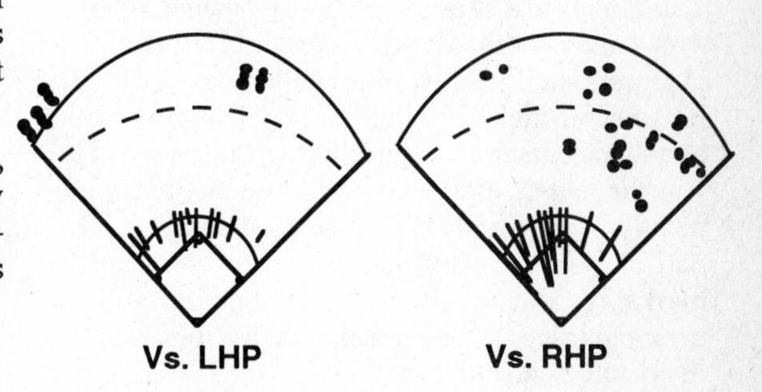

1992 Situational Stats

	AB	H	HR	RBI	AVG		AB	H	HR	RBI	AVG
Home	87	22	4	16	.253	LHP	52	15	4	7	.288
Road	92	21	1	8	.228	RHP	127	28	1	17	.220
Day	59	10	1	5	.169	Sc Pos	50	11	1	19	.220
Night	120	33	4	19	.275	Clutch	21	5	1	5	.238

1992 Rankings (American League)

- Did not rank near the top or bottom in any category

TIM HULETT

Position: 3B/DH
Bats: R **Throws:** R
Ht: 6' 0" **Wt:** 199

Opening Day Age: 33
Born: 1/12/60 in Springfield, IL
ML Seasons: 9

Overall Statistics

	G	AB	R	H	D	T	HR	RBI	SB	BB	SO	AVG
1992	57	142	11	41	7	2	2	21	0	10	31	.289
Career	595	1765	194	428	73	12	44	182	13	110	355	.242

HITTING, FIELDING, BASERUNNING:

Tim Hulett is a superb utility player who always keeps himself ready. Last year, his fourth in a Baltimore uniform, was probably his best. Hulett hit a career-high .289 in a limited role, 51 points above his career average entering the season. He was the team's top batter with runners in scoring position (.417) and played strong defense at second and third during his infrequent starts. Remarkably, Hulett did this while dealing with a personal tragedy, the mid-season death of his son in an auto accident.

Hulett has very good pop for an infielder. In 1986, his only year as an everyday player, he belted 17 homers for the White Sox. He's somewhat of a wild swinger, not walking much and striking out frequently. Hulett hangs in there against both kinds of pitching, last year batting .294 vs. lefties and .284 vs. righties. Though third base and second are his primary positions, he can also fill in at shortstop. Hulett is no gazelle on the basepaths, but he is smart and resourceful. He's not a basestealer, with only one successful swipe since 1986.

OVERALL

A personal favorite of manager John Oates, Hulett has a low-key personality which blends in nicely with the Baltimore team fabric. He's a useful player who is extremely conscientious and hits well off the bench.

CHITO MARTINEZ

Position: RF
Bats: L **Throws:** L
Ht: 5'10" **Wt:** 182

Opening Day Age: 27
Born: 12/19/65 in Belize, Central America
ML Seasons: 2

Overall Statistics

	G	AB	R	H	D	T	HR	RBI	SB	BB	SO	AVG
1992	83	198	26	53	10	1	5	25	0	31	47	.268
Career	150	414	58	111	22	2	18	58	1	42	98	.268

HITTING, FIELDING, BASERUNNING:

A sensation in 1991, when he came out of nowhere to hit 13 homers in only 216 at-bats as an Oriole rookie, Chito Martinez proved only human in 1992. Martinez was again a useful performer, hitting .268 and posting a fine on-base percentage of .366. But while logging about the same number of at-bats as in '91 (198), he hit only five home runs.

All season long Martinez never regained the devastating power stroke that marked his entrance into the majors. A lack of playing time was one problem. When going well, Martinez has a lightning-like bat and precision timing. But when he isn't playing, he requires time to regain that groove. Locked in a pennant race, the Orioles couldn't afford to be very patient with him. He was nonetheless a very serviceable bench player.

Martinez is only an average outfielder at best, frequently taking bad angles and getting fooled on fly balls. His top asset is a strong arm. He has decent speed, but rarely uses it. He did not record a steal in 1992.

OVERALL:

Martinez had three straight 20-home run seasons in the minors, so he figures to regain some of his home run stroke. Even if he doesn't, though, he'll be a valuable bench player if he displays the varied offensive skills he has shown in his brief major league career. The right field job may be his for the taking this spring.

MARK McLEMORE

Position: 2B/DH
Bats: B **Throws:** R
Ht: 5'11" **Wt:** 195

Opening Day Age: 28
Born: 10/4/64 in San Diego, CA
ML Seasons: 7

Overall Statistics

	G	AB	R	H	D	T	HR	RBI	SB	BB	SO	AVG
1992	101	228	40	56	7	2	0	27	11	21	26	.246
Career	402	1122	163	257	37	8	5	102	56	112	175	.229

HITTING, FIELDING, BASERUNNING:

Some clutch hits early in the 1992 season affixed Mark McLemore in the Orioles' scheme. McLemore wound up sharing second base with Billy Ripken, and though his .246 batting average was nothing to brag about, he outhit Ripken by 16 points. The figure marked a career high for the infielder, who had previously flubbed chances with the Angels, Indians and Astros. McLemore entered the season with a .225 lifetime average over six seasons.

With the Orioles, McLemore displayed solid plate coverage, a line-drive swing and the ability to use the whole field. He was one of the team's top pinch hitters and finished second on the club with 11 stolen bases in restricted action. McLemore applied himself well after his floundering career was resurrected. He is not as flashy as Ripken defensively, but he hustles and is better than adequate. With men in scoring position, McLemore hit .307 and collected 26 of his 27 RBI.

OVERALL:

McLemore's success off the bench and in part-time duty made him a player the Orioles would hate to lose. He offers a lot of qualities the team badly needs, especially speed and an ability to hit in the clutch. He made the most of another major-league opportunity. If he sticks with the O's this year, and the O's don't sign a free agent for second base, he could end up with a lot of playing time.

LUIS MERCEDES

Position: RF
Bats: R **Throws:** R
Ht: 6' 3" **Wt:** 193

Opening Day Age: 25
Born: 2/20/68 in San Pedro de Macoris, Dominican Republic
ML Seasons: 2

Overall Statistics

	G	AB	R	H	D	T	HR	RBI	SB	BB	SO	AVG
1992	23	50	7	7	2	0	0	4	0	8	9	.140
Career	42	104	17	18	4	0	0	6	0	12	18	.173

HITTING, FIELDING, BASERUNNING:

Highly touted prospect Luis Mercedes didn't get much of a chance to show his stuff to the Orioles last season. Expected to start the season as the Orioles' left fielder, Mercedes was left in the lurch when the O's gave Brady Anderson one last chance. Mercedes did get 50 scattered at-bats with Baltimore, but his seven hits and .140 average were hardly indicative of his ability.

Mercedes spent most of the year at AAA Rochester where he hit .313 and missed winning the International League batting title by a fraction of a point. The youngster had batted .334 at Rochester in 1991, so it's obvious he can hit. He's a line-drive, singles hitter who sprays the ball to all fields. Patience and confidence are his virtues at the plate. He isn't afraid to take a walk.

Mercedes was third in the International League in stolen bases with 35, but he sometimes approaches baserunning with fearless, and foolish, abandon. A converted infielder, he can use his speed to advantage in the outfield. He still makes some judgement errors afield, but they are usually from overeagerness. He needs more polish.

OVERALL:

Mercedes has had a checkered past, one which includes several fights in the minors. That reputation stands in his way, and now Anderson does also. But the Orioles realize his value and protected him from expansion. Mercedes is a possible DH, and a trade is not out of the question.

ORGANIZATION OVERVIEW:

The Orioles are one of those "low budget" clubs which feels unable to toss around free agent money. Unlike teams which pay mere lip service to the concept, the O's seem committed to player development. They've been willing to put youngsters in key positions -- Leo Gomez, Chris Hoiles, Mike Mussina, Greg Olson, Ben McDonald -- and suffer through youthful growing pains. Those pains paid off in 1992; now, as with several other clubs, it'll be interesting to see whether the contending O's are as patient toward their youth as the struggling O's were.

MANNY ALEXANDER

Position: SS **Opening Day Age:** 22
Bats: R **Throws:** R **Born:** 3/20/71 in San Pedro De Macoris, DR
Ht: 5' 10" **Wt:** 160

Recent Statistics

	G	AB	R	H	D	T	HR	RBI	SB	BB	SO	AVG
92 AA Hagerstown	127	499	70	129	23	8	2	41	43	25	64	.259
92 AAA Rochester	6	24	3	7	1	0	0	3	2	1	3	.292
92 AL Baltimore	4	5	1	1	0	0	0	0	0	0	3	.200
92 MLE	133	503	59	116	19	5	1	35	30	17	70	.231

At some time after Cal Ripken has played his 3,000th consecutive game, the Orioles will begin their search for a new shortstop. Or so it seems. Manny Alexander is only 22 years old, and he seems patient and promising enough to take over for Cal Jr. someday. One more product of the shortstop factory in San Pedro de Marcoris, D.R., Alexander appears to have the defensive goods and he can run like a tropical wind. The question is whether he'll hit; thus far he hasn't. But Alexander's very young. They'll be watching him this year at AAA Rochester.

DAMON J. BUFORD

Position: OF **Opening Day Age:** 22
Bats: R **Throws:** R **Born:** 6/12/70 in Baltimore, MD
Ht: 5' 11" **Wt:** 165

Recent Statistics

	G	AB	R	H	D	T	HR	RBI	SB	BB	SO	AVG
91 A Frederick	133	505	71	138	25	6	8	54	50	51	92	.273
92 AA Hagerstown	101	373	53	89	17	3	1	30	41	42	63	.239
92 AAA Rochester	45	155	29	44	10	2	1	12	23	14	23	.284
92 MLE	146	507	65	112	22	3	0	33	42	39	89	.221

If Cal Jr. had broken in when Don Buford was still in the Oriole lineup, how fitting it would have been if he had had a pop-fly collision with Don's son Damon. Just a slight exaggeration there, as the elder Buford retired in 1972 . . . but son Damon may well play with Cal. Like Alexander, Buford is 22, can run (64 steals last year), and appears to have the defensive goods. Since he hit .284 in 155 at-bats at AAA Rochester, he may have the offensive goods as well. He'll probably get a full year at AAA in 1993.

JOHN P. O'DONOGHUE

Position: P **Opening Day Age:** 23
Bats: L **Throws:** L **Born:** 5/26/69 in Wilmington, DE
Ht: 6' 6" **Wt:** 198

Recent Statistics

	W	L	ERA	G	GS	Sv	IP	H	R	BB	SO	HR
91 A Frederick	7	8	2.90	22	21	0	133.2	131	55	50	128	6
92 AA Hagerstown	7	4	2.24	17	16	0	112.1	78	37	40	87	6
92 AAA Rochester	5	4	3.23	13	10	0	69.2	60	31	19	47	5

Nepotism department: you can't play for the O's unless your father did, too. Like Don Buford, O'Donoghue's dad John Sr. played for the O's in 1968 (along with numerous other clubs). Like his dad, John Jr. is a left-handed pitcher and not the hardest thrower in the world. But the 6-foot-6 O'Donoghue, an undrafted free agent, has moved rapidly through the Oriole system. The O's are looking for left-handers and it would be no shock to find the younger O'Donoghue in the big leagues very soon.

BRAD L. PENNINGTON

Position: P **Opening Day Age:** 23
Bats: L **Throws:** L **Born:** 4/14/69 in Salem, IN
Ht: 6' 5" **Wt:** 205

Recent Statistics

	W	L	ERA	G	GS	Sv	IP	H	R	BB	SO	HR
91 A Kane County	0	2	5.87	23	0	4	23.0	16	17	25	43	1
91 A Frederick	1	4	3.92	36	0	13	43.2	32	23	44	58	4
92 A Frederick	1	0	2.00	8	0	2	9.0	5	3	4	16	0
92 AA Hagerstown	1	2	2.54	19	0	7	28.1	20	9	17	33	0
92 AAA Rochester	1	3	2.08	29	0	5	39.0	12	10	33	56	2

Speaking of left-handed pitchers, the Orioles are going to be taking a long look at Brad Pennington this spring. A southpaw with some serious heat, Pennington has fanned 429 men in 313.1 pro innings . . . but he's also walked 318 and his lifetime record is 10-27. Was HIS dad Steve Dalkowski? Pennington had a 2.08 ERA at Rochester last year. And that makes him a serious prospect for 1993.

MARK E. SMITH

Position: OF **Opening Day Age:** 22
Bats: R **Throws:** R **Born:** 5/7/70 in Pasadena, CA
Ht: 6' 3" **Wt:** 205

Recent Statistics

	G	AB	R	H	D	T	HR	RBI	SB	BB	SO	AVG
91 A Frederick	38	148	20	37	5	1	4	29	1	9	24	.250
92 AA Hagerstown	128	472	51	136	32	6	4	62	15	45	55	.288
92 MLE	128	452	41	116	26	4	3	50	10	31	57	.257

The ninth player chosen in the 1991 draft, Smith was a collegiate star in the excellent program at USC. In his first full year of professional baseball, Smith didn't have too many problems at AA Hagerstown; he showed a quick line drive bat and some speed, with 15 steals in 20 attempts. The Orioles have regarded the 205-pounder as a power prospect, but thus far he hasn't shown that. He'll probably need to, as his glove is nothing special.

HITTING:

In March, Wade Boggs's agent called the Red Sox' two-year $9.2M offer "an insult," and so it was decided that Boggs would play out the season and become a free agent. In the process, Boggs turned 34 and hit .259. It was the first time he'd batted under .300 as a professional since he hit .263 at Elmira in 1976, when Jimmy Carter was president and Elvis was alive.

What happened? Boggs pointed to weather, the pressure of the contract, poor batting orders, problems with his eyes. . . After coming into the year with a .381 lifetime average in Fenway, .310 on the road, he was so messed up that he batted .243 at home, .274 on the road. After entering the season a career .364 against righthanders and .304 against lefties, he batted .253 against righties and .272 against lefties.

Was Boggs frozen by the pressure of the contract last year, or did he start to decline physically? Some point to his feet. When Boggs was in his prime he was like a great tennis player at the plate, bouncing back and forth on the balls of his feet, volleying off two-strike pitches until he found something he liked. The last couple of years he has seemed far more flat-footed both at bat and in the field.

BASERUNNING:

Really all you can say about Boggs as a basestealer is that he's consistent. He's never stolen more than three bases in a season, and the last time he got that high was 1984. He's as conservative as they come running the bases.

FIELDING:

Even if Boggs' defensive range has slipped, he is still a premier defensive third baseman. Few third basemen can start the 5-4-3 double play or do the 360 after backhanding balls the way Boggs can.

OVERALL:

Boggs is not washed up. He still doesn't swing and miss (fewer than anyone in baseball), so his hand-eye skill isn't gone. He may not drive the ball through the gaps the way he once did, but someday we'll sit back and wonder how he could ever have batted .198 in a month (August), or .243 for a season in Fenway Park.

WADE BOGGS

Position: 3B/DH
Bats: L **Throws:** R
Ht: 6' 2" **Wt:** 197

Opening Day Age: 34
Born: 6/15/58 in Omaha, NE
ML Seasons: 11

Overall Statistics

	G	AB	R	H	D	T	HR	RBI	SB	BB	SO	AVG
1992	143	514	62	133	22	4	7	50	1	74	31	.259
Career	1625	6213	1067	2098	422	47	85	687	16	1004	470	.338

Where He Hits the Ball

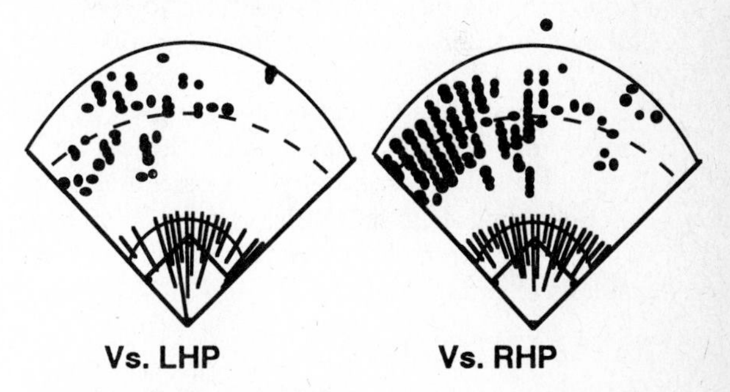

1992 Situational Stats

	AB	H	HR	RBI	AVG		AB	H	HR	RBI	AVG
Home	251	61	4	26	.243	LHP	158	43	1	21	.272
Road	263	72	3	24	.274	RHP	356	90	6	29	.253
Day	193	50	1	12	.259	Sc Pos	106	33	2	44	.311
Night	321	83	6	38	.259	Clutch	90	29	0	10	.322

1992 Rankings (American League)

- 1st in intentional walks (19) and lowest percentage of swings that missed (4.1%)
- 3rd in highest percentage of swings put into play (59.6%)
- Led the Red Sox in triples (4), walks (74), intentional walks, hit by pitch (4), times on base (211), games played (143), highest groundball/flyball ratio (1.88), batting average with runners in scoring position (.311), batting average vs. right-handed pitchers (.253), slugging percentage vs. right-handed pitchers (.354), on-base percentage vs. right-handed pitchers (.364), batting average on the road (.274) and percentage of swings that missed

TOM BRUNANSKY

Position: RF/1B/DH
Bats: R **Throws:** R
Ht: 6' 4" **Wt:** 220

Opening Day Age: 32
Born: 8/20/60 in Covina, CA
ML Seasons: 12

HITTING:

The entire 1992 Red Sox season could be summarized with this: Tom Brunansky won the team's triple crown, leading them in batting (.266), homers (15) and RBI (74). When October came, management announced that it had declined to pick up the option on Brunansky's contract for 1993. So after hitting as high as .260 for the first time in almost a decade and reaching a career high of 31 doubles, Brunansky found himself out on the market at age 32.

While Brunansky struggled the last month with only one homer and a .222 average, he had a solid season moving back and forth between first base and right field. His 1992 rise from .229 to .266 came from his diligence in learning to take the ball away and hit it to right field with runners on base. He also learned to become more patient (four pitches per plate appearance, eighth in the league) and foul off tough pitches he couldn't handle. He still is essentially a guess hitter who can be retired with fastballs. But he hammers mistake breaking balls and guesses right on fastballs in certain situations.

BASERUNNING:

A smart baserunner, Brunansky runs everything out as hard as he can; in fact, a half-dozen of his doubles in Fenway were the result of him busting as hard as he could from the first step out of the batters box. However, Red Sox-itis has affected him -- he's 8-for-25 stealing in a Boston uniform.

FIELDING:

Brunansky lost a step or two in the outfield two years ago, but any sign of age stopped there. He is still an extremely sound fundamental player: he plays hitters well, runs the proper angles in right, and gets himself into position to throw.

OVERALL:

Twins General Manager Andy MacPhail once said that the worst trade he ever made was sending Brunansky to the Cardinals for Tommy Herr in 1988. "Not so much for production, but for character," says MacPhail. Considering MacPhail's record of two World Championships in five years in Minnesota, his comment says something about Tom Brunansky and his overall worth to a team.

Overall Statistics

	G	AB	R	H	D	T	HR	RBI	SB	BB	SO	AVG
1992	138	458	47	122	31	3	15	74	2	66	96	.266
Career	1656	5860	760	1454	287	29	255	856	66	721	1071	.248

Where He Hits the Ball

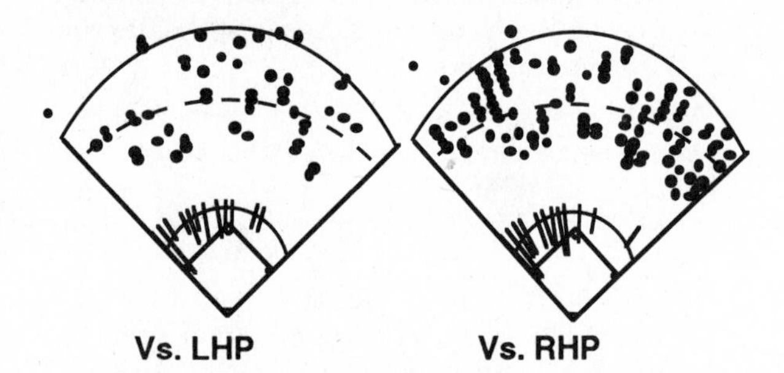

1992 Situational Stats

	AB	H	HR	RBI	AVG		AB	H	HR	RBI	AVG
Home	217	70	10	47	.323	LHP	132	30	6	20	.227
Road	241	52	5	27	.216	RHP	326	92	9	54	.282
Day	159	40	6	26	.252	Sc Pos	115	31	4	58	.270
Night	299	82	9	48	.274	Clutch	90	26	4	23	.289

1992 Rankings (American League)

- 1st in least runs scored per time reached base (.25)
- 3rd in worst batting average on the road (.216)
- 5th in lowest batting average vs. left-handed pitchers (.227) and highest batting average at home (.323)
- Led the Red Sox in batting average (.266), home runs (15), doubles (31), total bases (204), RBI (74), sacrifice flies (7), strikeouts (96), slugging percentage (.445), on-base average (.354), HR frequency (30.5 ABs per HR), most pitches seen per plate appearance (4.00) and batng average on an 0-2 count (.269)

HITTING:

When Ken Brett was a young pitching phenom for Boston in 1970, he put a sign up in the bathroom of his Commonwealth Avenue apartment. It read: "The Worst Curse in Life is Unlimited Potential." "I know what he meant," says Ellis Burks. Back in 1988, Burks was 23 and Boston's next great star. He batted .294, knocked in 92 runs, stole 25 bases and played a brilliant center field. Five years later, after shoulder, knee and back problems, his career is very much in doubt.

Burks is a quiet, shy, exceedingly nice person, but he is laid back in a city that runs at 78 RPM and whose fans and media are, to be kind, r-o-u-g-h. Burks has shied away from the limelight, never seeming at ease. However, the biggest factor in his decline has been his injuries. Last year's .255 average, with eight homers and 30 RBI in 66 games, indicates that he just wasn't right. He has trouble turning on fastballs the way he once did, and has not been able to drive balls all over the field. Last year he had so much trouble pulling the trigger that he hit only .197 against lefties; he'd hit .299 against them in his career.

BASERUNNING:

Burks has lost so much confidence in his ability to steal bases that in the last three years he has stolen 20 bases and been thrown out 24 times. This is quite a slide for a man who in his first three seasons was 73-for-93.

FIELDING:

Early in his career, Burks played extremely shallow, broke back well and dove for everything. But ever since he hurt his shoulder diving for a ball, he's been much more cautious, and has had trouble throwing in cold weather. Chronic knee problems have affected the break he once had in the outfield, and he has eventually started playing deep to compensate.

OVERALL:

After being left unprotected in the expansion draft -- and then not being selected -- perhaps the best thing for Burks is to move on to another city where he won't be analyzed and psychoanalyzed. In Boston, things have never seemed right. Most of all, Burks needs to be healthy.

ELLIS BURKS

Position: CF
Bats: R **Throws:** R
Ht: 6' 2" **Wt:** 205

Opening Day Age: 28
Born: 9/11/64 in Vicksburg, MS
ML Seasons: 6

Overall Statistics

	G	AB	R	H	D	T	HR	RBI	SB	BB	SO	AVG
1992	66	235	35	60	8	3	8	30	5	25	48	.255
Career	722	2794	440	785	160	27	93	387	93	251	450	.281

Where He Hits the Ball

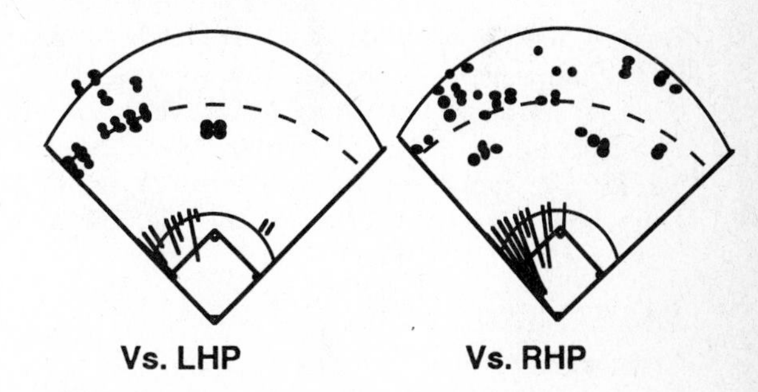

1992 Situational Stats

	AB	H	HR	RBI	AVG		AB	H	HR	RBI	AVG
Home	108	25	4	18	.231	LHP	66	13	3	8	.197
Road	127	35	4	12	.276	RHP	169	47	5	22	.278
Day	90	20	2	8	.222	Sc Pos	65	13	2	20	.200
Night	145	40	6	22	.276	Clutch	50	12	2	8	.240

1992 Rankings (American League)

- Did not rank near the top or bottom in any category

JACK CLARK

Position: DH/1B
Bats: R **Throws:** R
Ht: 6' 3" **Wt:** 210

Opening Day Age: 37
Born: 11/10/55 in New Brighton, PA
ML Seasons: 18

Overall Statistics

	G	AB	R	H	D	T	HR	RBI	SB	BB	SO	AVG
1992	81	257	32	54	11	0	5	33	1	56	87	.210
Career	1994	6847	1118	1826	332	39	340	1180	77	1262	1441	.267

Where He Hits the Ball

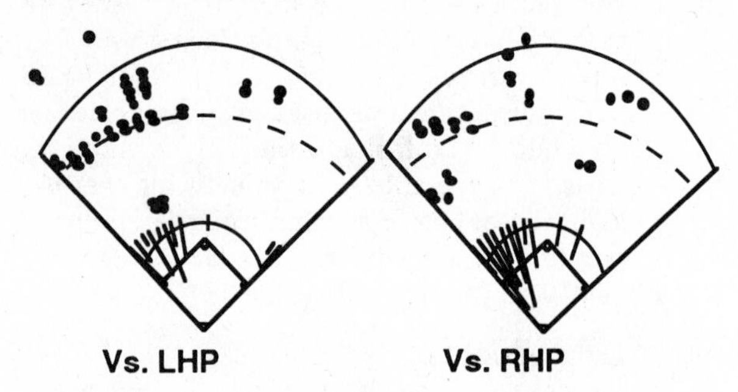

1992 Situational Stats

	AB	H	HR	RBI	AVG		AB	H	HR	RBI	AVG
Home	116	30	0	10	.259	LHP	95	28	2	14	.295
Road	141	24	5	23	.170	RHP	162	26	3	19	.160
Day	72	19	3	14	.264	Sc Pos	73	14	2	29	.192
Night	185	35	2	19	.189	Clutch	62	11	0	6	.177

1992 Rankings (American League)

- 3rd in worst batting average with two strikes (.123)
- 4th in worst batting average on an 0-2 count (.045)
- Led the Red Sox in least GDPs per GDP situation (5.5%), batting average vs. left-handed pitchers (.295) and on-base average vs. left-handed pitchers (.460)

HITTING:

At this point, you don't even want to know where all his money went. There were all the cars, the restaurant, hundreds of thousands of dollars to credit cards and Nordstrom's. Yes, Jack Clark was flat broke. And if that weren't bad enough, his mother became very ill and nearly died. Then his shoulder went so bad on him that when the season mercifully ended, he was considering surgery. Sometimes money just ain't enough.

Off-field problems don't even begin to address the fall of Jack Clark the player. After all, he batted .210 with five homers and 33 RBI. He did not hit *one home run* in Fenway Park, and did nothing better along that vein on the road, hitting .170. He knocked in nine runs after the All-Star Break. The Red Sox tried to get out of the last year of his three year, $8.7M deal by working this trade: Clark and Matt Young to Milwaukee for Ron Robinson and Franklin Stubbs; the Brewers would have sent Clark to California for Junior Felix and released Young. Problem is, Jackie Autry said thanks, but no thanks.

BASERUNNING:

Clark is your typical Red Sox baserunner. He's a 56 percent stealer in his career, and was a mighty 1-for-2 in 1992. He hasn't had more than one triple in a season since 1986.

FIELDING:

Clark is pretty much exclusively a DH these days. He played 13 games at first base, fielding .992 and making only one error. He also batted .317 when used as a first sacker. Nonetheless, he's a liability in the field.

OVERALL:

If healthy -- and Clark never was one for doing much off-season work -- he should be able to hit for power again and at least do damage against lefthanders by pulling the fastball. He will forever wave at right-handed breaking balls in the dirt. He may also need to get out of Boston, where he is booed when he pulls his car onto Boylston Street, two blocks from Fenway.

STAFF ACE

ROGER CLEMENS

Position: SP
Bats: R **Throws:** R
Ht: 6' 4" **Wt:** 220

Opening Day Age: 30
Born: 8/4/62 in Dayton, OH
ML Seasons: 9

PITCHING:

Roger Clemens's 1992 season was proof that there is no such thing as a purely individual award. 1992 was one of the four years in the last seven in which he did not win the Cy Young Award, yet there never was much better proof that a pitcher's performance and record cannot be separated from that of his team. The Red Sox blew five Clemens leads; if they had held three of the five, he would have finished with 21 wins instead of his 18-11 record. That would have tied for the league lead and probably won him the award.

Last season was only different in that Clemens wilted in September. He pulled a groin muscle from all the grueling innings he worked in 0-0, 1-0, 2-1 games. Yet, in the year in which he turned 30, this was really no different a season than any of the last seven except '86, when he magically went 24-4, carried Boston to the World Series and won the MVP and Cy Young awards.

Clemens is to pitching what Lombardi's Packers were to football: hard-nosed, in-your-face, basic power. He isn't the hardest thrower in the game, but he will maintain that 91-94 MPH fastball for nine innings. He doesn't have three above-average pitches like a John Smoltz or Juan Guzman, but he always works to find complimentary pitches within each game; sometimes the slider, sometimes his curveball, sometimes he goes fastball-forkball. Most of all, he is a world-class fastball artist.

HOLDING RUNNERS AND FIELDING:

Over the years, Clemens has worked on every element of his game. Where once he was easy to run on, now, between his slide-step and countless throws to first base, he has become more difficult to steal against. He's a competent fielder.

OVERALL:

Clemens is power, and he is a grinder. His indefatigable work habits, diligence and preparation -- right down to his notebooks on umpires -- should keep him in annual contention for the Cy Young Award for another five years. Whether or not he wants to do that in Boston is another story.

Overall Statistics

	W	L	ERA	G	GS	Sv	IP	H	R	BB	SO	HR
1992	18	11	2.41	32	32	0	246.2	203	80	62	208	11
Career	152	72	2.80	273	272	0	2031.0	1703	708	552	1873	128

How Often He Throws Strikes

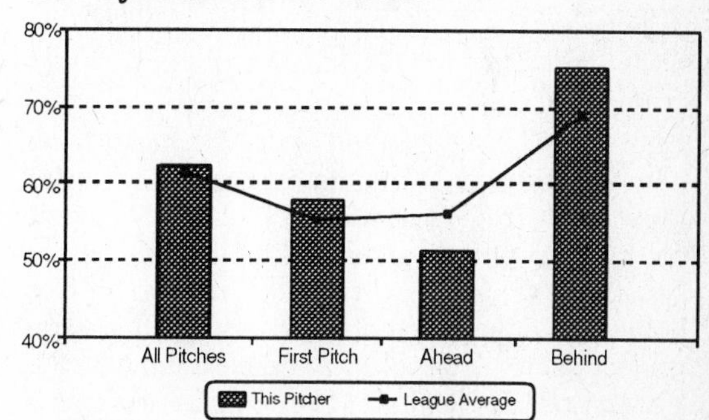

1992 Situational Stats

	W	L	ERA	Sv	IP		AB	H	HR	RBI	AVG
Home	8	6	2.88	0	128.1	LHB	447	101	6	27	.226
Road	10	5	1.90	0	118.1	RHB	460	102	5	43	.222
Day	5	4	2.16	0	79.1	Sc Pos	209	42	0	52	.201
Night	13	7	2.53	0	167.1	Clutch	98	21	0	5	.214

1992 Rankings (American League)

- 1st in ERA (2.41), shutouts (5), strikeout/walk ratio (3.4) and ERA on the road (1.90)
- 2nd in complete games (11), lowest on-base average allowed (.279) and least baserunners allowed per 9 innings (10.0)
- 3rd in strikeouts (208), pitches thrown (3,821), lowest slugging percentage allowed (.308) and most pitches thrown per batter (3.86)
- Led the Red Sox in ERA, wins (18), complete games, shutouts, innings pitched (246.2), hit batsmen (9), pitches thrown, pickoff throws (259), winning percentage (.621) and strikeout/walk ratio

SCOTT COOPER

Position: 1B/3B
Bats: L **Throws:** R
Ht: 6' 3" **Wt:** 205

Opening Day Age: 25
Born: 10/13/67 in St. Louis, MO
ML Seasons: 3

HITTING:

Midway through the 1992 season, the consensus among the Red Sox coaching staff was that Scott Cooper had a salami bat. He hit the ball, but it never went anywhere. All considered, the coaches wondered why the Red Sox had so built him up so much that they considered Jeff Bagwell a lesser prospect and gave him to Houston for Larry Andersen.

The Red Sox kept talking about all the teams that wanted Cooper, but the only offer they got in the spring was from the Cubs. For Les Lancaster. The day after Boston rejected the deal, Lancaster was released. Oh yes. Bagwell's numbers in the Astrodome would have led the Red Sox in batting, slugging, on-base percentage, hits, doubles, triples, homers, RBI, extra-base hits, runs and stolen bases.

But while Cooper had to bounce back and forth between third and first, he eventually began to grow on the Red Sox. Cooper took advantage of his playing time, started looking for pitches in situations, worked on driving the ball and hit five homers. Cooper's numbers over a full season project out to 42 doubles, 10 homers and 66 RBI. He won't be carried to Cooperstown in a rickshaw with those figures, but they are acceptable.

BASERUNNING:

Cooper is, like his team, slow. Even in the minors, he never stole more than three bases in a season. But that kind of speed is nothing new in this organization.

FIELDING:

The first thing one notices about Cooper defensively is his rocket arm. He has solid hands and charges balls well. His problem as a rookie was backhanding balls. If he still has a problem with his backhand, then he needs to play every day to determine whether or not he can work it out.

OVERALL:

Cooper proved as a rookie that he deserves a chance to play every day. He looks like he can be a .270-10-70 player. He's apt to be a solid clutch hitter who doesn't make All-Star teams but earns a healthy living. He was protected by the Red Sox going into the expansion draft as a hedge against losing Boggs.

Overall Statistics

	G	AB	R	H	D	T	HR	RBI	SB	BB	SO	AVG
1992	123	337	34	93	21	0	5	33	1	37	33	.276
Career	139	373	40	109	25	2	5	40	1	39	36	.292

Where He Hits the Ball

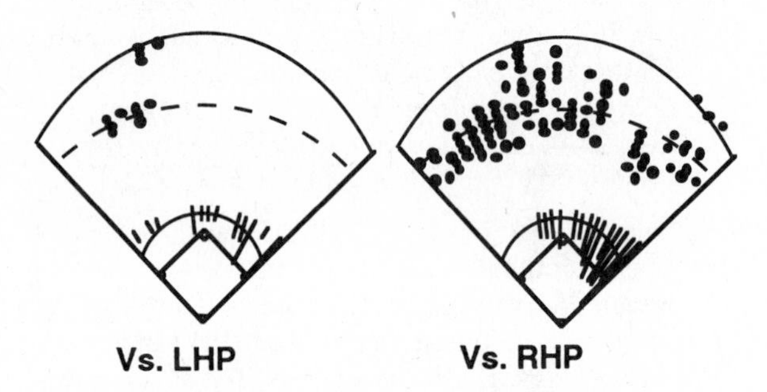

1992 Situational Stats

	AB	H	HR	RBI	AVG		AB	H	HR	RBI	AVG
Home	155	45	2	10	.290	LHP	41	11	1	5	.268
Road	182	48	3	23	.264	RHP	296	82	4	28	.277
Day	105	33	2	12	.314	Sc Pos	72	20	0	28	.278
Night	232	60	3	21	.259	Clutch	76	24	0	9	.316

1992 Rankings (American League)

→ Did not rank near the top or bottom in any category

PITCHING:

The Red Sox are convinced that Danny Darwin is their third starter. "With Clemens, Viola and Darwin, we have as good a big three as there is in the game," said General Manager Lou Gorman at the end of last season. Coming off an unfortunate '91 season in which he got hurt and ended up having shoulder surgery, Darwin bounced back throwing as hard as ever. Twice he went into the sixth inning with no-hitters.

But there is still one undeniable statistic that Gorman and the Red Sox ignore: Darwin, 37, has never won 10 games in one season as a starter. In fact, in 1992, his 4-5, 3.53 record as a starter brought his career American League record as a starter to 48-70. It's also been six years since he last started more than 20 games, and over the last five seasons has won 20 of 48 starts. His Houston manager, Art Howe, maintained that even during his 1990 season when he won the National League ERA title, Darwin tired after a dozen starts.

Darwin is still primarily a power pitcher, relying on a fastball, slider and an increasingly effective forkball that's helped him both as a starter and against left-handed hitters. He slings the ball with a three-quarters delivery that can intimidate right-handed batters (who batted .238 against him, lefties .281). He throws right around 90 MPH, and because he throws so many strikes and challenges hitters (a 124-53 strikeout-walk ratio), he tends to give up some long homers.

HOLDING RUNNERS AND FIELDING:

Darwin is a good fielder. He is average at preventing steals because he has a slow delivery, but he works hard at holding runners. He permitted only 14 steals last year.

OVERALL:

Darwin will go into the season as Boston's third starter, which come late June may or may not hold up, especially at age 37. But even if the tall, slender righthander cannot hold up as a starter for six months, he will be a vital contributor in one form or another.

DANNY DARWIN

Position: RP/SP
Bats: R **Throws:** R
Ht: 6' 3" **Wt:** 195

Opening Day Age: 37
Born: 10/25/55 in Bonham, TX
ML Seasons: 15

Overall Statistics

	W	L	ERA	G	GS	Sv	IP	H	R	BB	SO	HR
1992	9	9	3.96	51	15	3	161.1	159	76	53	124	11
Career	123	124	3.49	551	235	32	2142.2	2006	935	649	1431	187

How Often He Throws Strikes

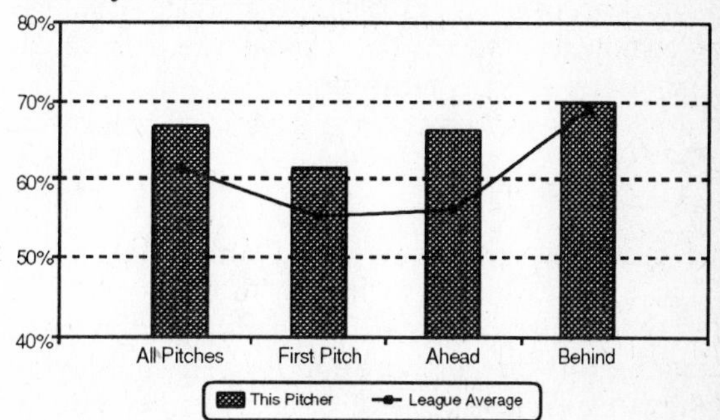

1992 Situational Stats

	W	L	ERA	Sv	IP		AB	H	HR	RBI	AVG
Home	6	4	4.26	1	76.0	LHB	274	77	1	31	.281
Road	3	5	3.69	2	85.1	RHB	344	82	10	39	.238
Day	3	1	2.01	1	67.0	Sc Pos	174	41	3	55	.236
Night	6	8	5.34	2	94.1	Clutch	144	36	3	16	.250

1992 Rankings (American League)

- 4th in highest batting average allowed in relief (.279)
- 6th in highest ERA in relief (4.80)
- Led the Red Sox in strikeouts per 9 innings in relief (7.1)

PITCHING:

Before last season, the last time John Dopson had won a big-league game was 1989. After being acquired by the Red Sox from Montreal with Luis Rivera for Spike Owen, he was 12-8 that season and established himself as a potential third or fourth starter. But the next spring Dopson hurt his arm, was winless in only four starts and spent the entire 1991 season recovering from elbow surgery.

The Red Sox didn't know what to expect when Dopson came to spring training last year, but he appeared to be all the way back when he moved into the rotation in May. He was 6-4 at the All-Star Break and seemed to be on his way to a 12-15 win season. But Dopson simply stopped winning, and now the Red Sox don't know which direction his career is going as he turns 30 in July. Was his 1-7, 4.73 second half a sign of his future, or was he simply not ready for the grind of 25-30 starts after surgery?

Dopson has good stuff, a hard-boring sinker and nasty slider that he mixes with an occasional forkball. But he has to dominate with his best stuff at all times, because thus far he hasn't shown he can win close games. There is a lot that can go wrong with him on the mound, principally because he isn't a particularly good athlete. His delivery can get out of sync between innings, and thus he can throw three perfect innings, then go hog-wild in the fourth.

HOLDING RUNNERS AND FIELDING:

Dopson doesn't help himself with the little things in pitching, so he can be beaten by his weaknesses: fielding (he can be bunted on easily), holding runners and covering first. He permitted 17 steals in 24 attempts last year.

OVERALL:

Dopson has been knocked for a lack of drive and intensity, which affects his conditioning as well as his fielding. And some question his toughness. But after coming back from arm problems, he will get every opportunity to prove that his 12-8 season in '89 was more of a reflection of his career than the last three have been.

JOHN DOPSON

Position: SP
Bats: L **Throws:** R
Ht: 6' 4" **Wt:** 235

Opening Day Age: 29
Born: 7/14/63 in Baltimore, MD
ML Seasons: 6

Overall Statistics

	W	L	ERA	G	GS	Sv	IP	H	R	BB	SO	HR
1992	7	11	4.08	25	25	0	141.1	159	78	38	55	17
Career	22	32	3.84	89	86	0	511.0	515	257	179	264	52

How Often He Throws Strikes

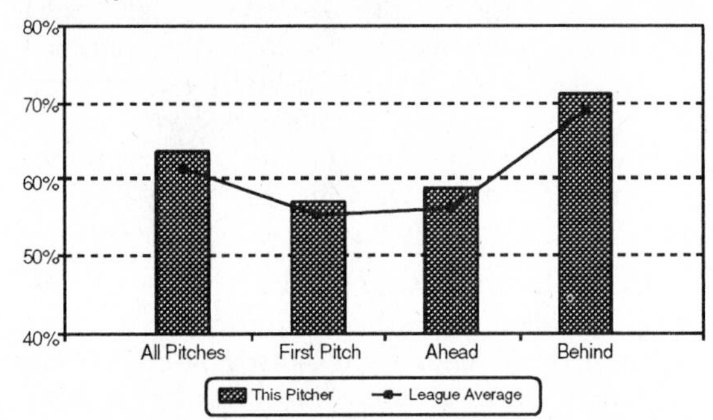

1992 Situational Stats

	W	L	ERA	Sv	IP		AB	H	HR	RBI	AVG
Home	5	5	2.69	0	83.2	LHB	257	71	5	23	.276
Road	2	6	6.09	0	57.2	RHB	297	88	12	39	.296
Day	3	2	3.71	0	43.2	Sc Pos	132	36	2	40	.273
Night	4	9	4.24	0	97.2	Clutch	36	16	2	7	.444

1992 Rankings (American League)

- 2nd in balks (3)
- 6th in ERA at home (2.69)
- Led the Red Sox in home runs allowed (17), balks, highest percentage of GDPs induced per GDP situation (17.2%) and ERA at home

PITCHING:

Tony Fossas is a specialist. Use him for one or two left-handed batters, and he is one of the premier relief pitchers in the American League. Leave him out there too long to face too many right-handed batters... "I'll admit that then I have some problems," says the 35-year old lefthander. "But I can pitch every day if they give me the chance." Specialist? Tony Fossas is the definition: 60 appearances, 29.2 innings.

Last season, Fossas wasn't used consistently and didn't pitch as well as he had in 1991, when he held first batters to a .130 average and held leads 29 of 33 times. For some reason found inexplicable by his teammates, manager Butch Hobson and pitching coach Rich Gale lost confidence in Fossas, but the fact remains that he maintained a 2.43 ERA. The entire Boston bullpen fell apart after June 1; that certainly affected Fossas, whose role was less important than it would have been had the team had more leads to protect.

Still, Fossas faced 59 left-handed batters. He allowed only 15 to reach base, three by walk. In Fenway Park, perhaps the best left-handed hitters' park in baseball, he had a 1.40 ERA. Lefthanders batted .214 and slugged .321 against him, strong figures for any lefty pitcher, and he managed two saves. Because he is so well conditioned, he is able to pitch every day.

HOLDING RUNNERS AND FIELDING:

Quick to the plate, Fossas is difficult to run on. He permitted only four steals last year. He is also a good fielder.

OVERALL:

If you're looking for a full-time lefthanded reliever who gets out everyone -- a Randy Myers or Mitch Williams, Mike Stanton or Scott Radinsky -- Fossas isn't your guy. But if you're looking for a left-handed specialist, especially on a strong team with a deep bullpen, then Fossas is a very useful pitcher. If the Red Sox don't want him and throw him out in the street, as Joe Tex would say, some other team will want him.

TONY FOSSAS

Position: RP
Bats: L **Throws:** L
Ht: 6' 0" **Wt:** 187

Opening Day Age: 35
Born: 9/23/57 in Havana, Cuba
ML Seasons: 5

Overall Statistics

	W	L	ERA	G	GS	Sv	IP	H	R	BB	SO	HR
1992	1	2	2.43	60	0	2	29.2	31	9	14	19	1
Career	8	9	3.84	212	0	4	182.2	192	89	76	114	12

How Often He Throws Strikes

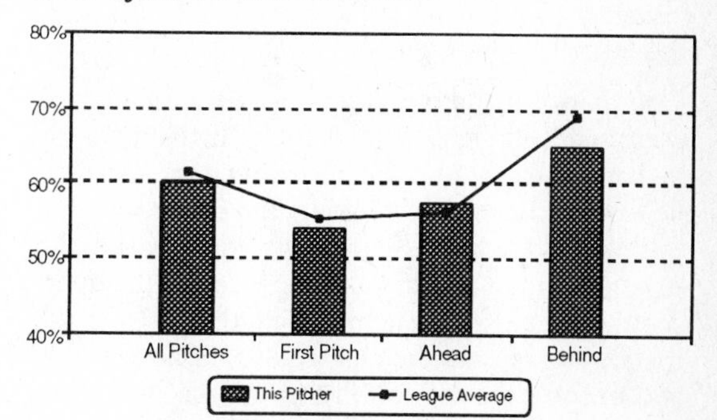

1992 Situational Stats

	W	L	ERA	Sv	IP		AB	H	HR	RBI	AVG
Home	1	2	1.40	1	19.1	LHB	56	12	0	9	.214
Road	0	0	4.35	1	10.1	RHB	55	19	1	15	.345
Day	0	2	3.12	1	8.2	Sc Pos	54	16	0	23	.296
Night	1	0	2.14	1	21.0	Clutch	44	13	0	9	.295

1992 Rankings (American League)

→ Did not rank near the top or bottom in any category

PITCHING:

If you look at the cold, hard stats, you figure Mike Gardiner has little future. He is 27 and in a little over two major-league seasons has made 43 starts for the Red Sox, going 11-21 with a 5.23 ERA. After finishing 1992 with a 2-8 record and a 4.82 ERA in 18 starts, he enters 1993 with his career at the crossroads.

There are two reasons that Gardiner's problems in the majors have been frustrating. The first is that he has been extremely successful in the minors. The other part of the frustration is that he has better stuff than they credited him for in the Mariner organization; his fastball is above-average, albeit straight, and at times he has shown a tight slider, a change and a slow curveball, although the latter has often gotten him in trouble.

One theory is that Gardiner has yet to gain self-confidence in the majors. Another is that because he has yet to get his change-up over consistently, he runs into trouble after going flat-out for several innings. "It could be that confidence and the change-up go hand in hand," says one AL superscout. "If he'll stop pitching with the pedal to the metal, he may get the change over, start to relax and become a solid fourth starter who gives you 225 innings."

HOLDING RUNNERS AND FIELDING:

Gardiner does a fine job of holding runners, permitting only three steals in five attempts last year. He's a decent fielder with that tough hockey mentality; twice he's been smoked in the leg by vicious line drives through the middle, and not only has he shaken them off, but refused to even rub the wounds.

OVERALL:

With the Red Sox staff built around Clemens and Viola, Gardiner didn't get much chance to work in the regular rotation last year. When he did, he didn't pitch very well. But given his heart, if Gardiner can come up with a solid, consistent offspeed pitch, he could be a surprise to the Boston -- or another -- staff in 1993.

MIKE GARDINER

Position: SP/RP
Bats: R **Throws:** R
Ht: 6' 0" **Wt:** 200

Opening Day Age: 27
Born: 10/19/65 in Sarnia, Ontario, Canada
ML Seasons: 3

Overall Statistics

	W	L	ERA	G	GS	Sv	IP	H	R	BB	SO	HR
1992	4	10	4.75	28	18	0	130.2	126	78	58	79	12
Career	13	22	5.07	55	43	0	273.1	288	174	110	176	31

How Often He Throws Strikes

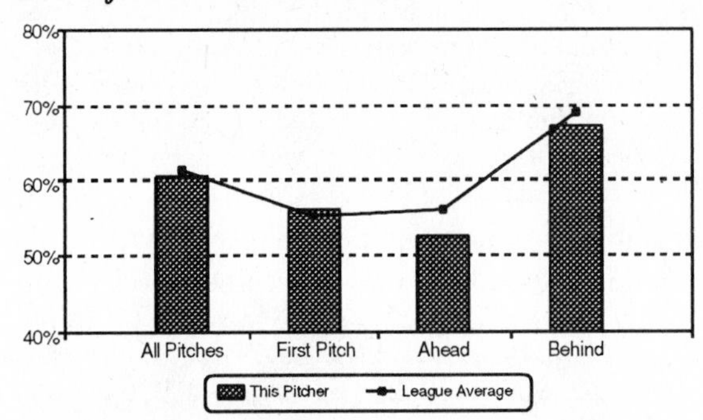

1992 Situational Stats

	W	L	ERA	Sv	IP		AB	H	HR	RBI	AVG
Home	2	1	4.41	0	51.0	LHB	221	57	3	23	.258
Road	2	9	4.97	0	79.2	RHB	277	69	9	41	.249
Day	1	5	6.53	0	40.0	Sc Pos	115	32	2	45	.278
Night	3	5	3.97	0	90.2	Clutch	31	9	0	3	.290

1992 Rankings (American League)

- Did not rank near the top or bottom in any category

HITTING:

Think back to the player Mike Greenwell looked like he might become at the end of the 1988 season, when he was 25. He had just come off seasons in which he'd batted .328 and .325. In 1987, he hit 19 homers and knocked in 89 runs in just 412 at-bats, and followed it up with an '88 year in which he hit 22 homers and 69 extra-base hits and had 119 RBI. Lou Piniella called him "one of the five best in the game."

But Greenwell hasn't hit 15 homers in a season since. In fact, he hit 11 combined in 1991-92. For two years, Greenwell had been troubled by ankle, knee and elbow problems. He tried all sorts of shoes and claimed that because of the ankle he had to hit off his front foot. He usually looked as if he were a batting flamingo, lurching forward every time anyone threw him an offspeed pitch. Then last spring his elbow got so bad that he finally had to have an operation, which effectively cut his season by two-thirds and ended his misery, especially the misery of constant booing.

BASERUNNING:

Greenwell likes to be aggressive on the bases, and in the four years prior to '92 he averaged 13 steals a year. Injured in 1992, he swiped only two. Sometimes his managers would have liked to have a remote control device to keep him from running into outs, but on the Red Sox any speed or daring is refreshing.

FIELDING:

Greenwell has been able to get by in Fenway because covering left field in Fenway is like playing your living room. But on the road, Greenwell has serious deficiencies in terms of range, reading balls and playing angles. His arm is also very weak. He is an adventure.

OVERALL:

Greenwell may never be the player the Red Sox once thought he would be, so they constructed their team of the '90s without him, which is hardly a team at all. But if Greenwell is healthy, he is a hitter, he plays hard, and, at his wildest, he keeps both teams in the game simultaneously.

MIKE GREENWELL

Position: LF
Bats: L **Throws:** R
Ht: 6' 0" **Wt:** 205

Opening Day Age: 29
Born: 7/18/63 in Louisville, KY
ML Seasons: 8

Overall Statistics

	G	AB	R	H	D	T	HR	RBI	SB	BB	SO	AVG
1992	49	180	16	42	2	0	2	18	2	18	19	.233
Career	831	2980	418	912	167	26	84	489	60	312	230	.306

Where He Hits the Ball

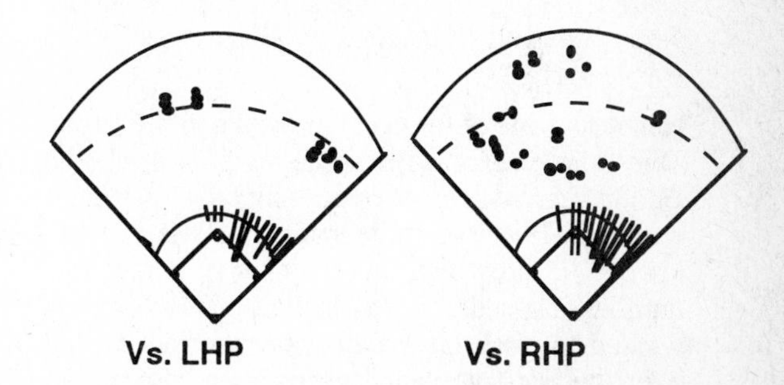

1992 Situational Stats

	AB	H	HR	RBI	AVG		AB	H	HR	RBI	AVG
Home	83	19	0	8	.229	LHP	58	13	0	5	.224
Road	97	23	2	10	.237	RHP	122	29	2	13	.238
Day	74	17	1	8	.230	Sc Pos	51	9	0	13	.176
Night	106	25	1	10	.236	Clutch	38	15	0	4	.395

1992 Rankings (American League)

- 8th in batting average on a 3-1 count (.571)

PITCHING:

Greg A. Harris is 37 years old, is 63-75 over his career, is on his seventh team and only once in his career has had as many as a dozen saves (20, in 1986 for Texas). But the slight, curveballing veteran has cut himself a niche as one of the most valuable utility pitchers in the game, sort of the Mariano Duncan of the bullpen.

Harris is one of the best middle relievers in the game. But if a team needs him to rush in and start, he can do that too. And while he is certainly not a closer in the true sense, he can occasionally close. As the clubs filed recommendations for the All-Star team last June, Red Sox manager Butch Hobson pushed for Harris. When the trading deadline neared in August, the one Boston player about whom General Manager Lou Gorman had calls was Harris.

Harris has one of the best curveballs in the game. Over the years, with some help from Mike Boddicker and from an opportunity to experiment with it in 1990 (when he made 30 starts), he has learned to throw it from a number of angles at a number of speeds. Harris is ambidextrous and has wanted to pitch left-handed, but the fact is that over the last five years lefties have batted .225 (.211 last season), righties .248 against him. The knock against Harris over the years is that he shouldn't be asked to close too often: he tends to start nibbling with his curveball, missing, complaining about umpires and blowing leads.

HOLDING RUNNERS AND FIELDING:

With one of the trickiest moves in the game for a righthander, Harris certainly doesn't need to go left-handed to hold runners. Last year he permitted only three steals with six runners caught stealing. He's also a fine fielder.

OVERALL:

The one thing Boston worried about last fall was that Harris' second half performance (2-5, 3.72, as opposed to 2-4, 1.52 in the first half) might be an indication that he is feeling his age. But his conditioning and curveball style should belie those worries.

GREG HARRIS

Position: RP
Bats: B **Throws:** R
Ht: 6' 0" **Wt:** 175

Opening Day Age: 37
Born: 11/2/55 in Lynwood, CA
ML Seasons: 12

Overall Statistics

	W	L	ERA	G	GS	Sv	IP	H	R	BB	SO	HR
1992	4	9	2.51	70	2	4	107.2	82	38	60	73	6
Career	63	75	3.55	540	98	44	1256.0	1125	567	550	943	107

How Often He Throws Strikes

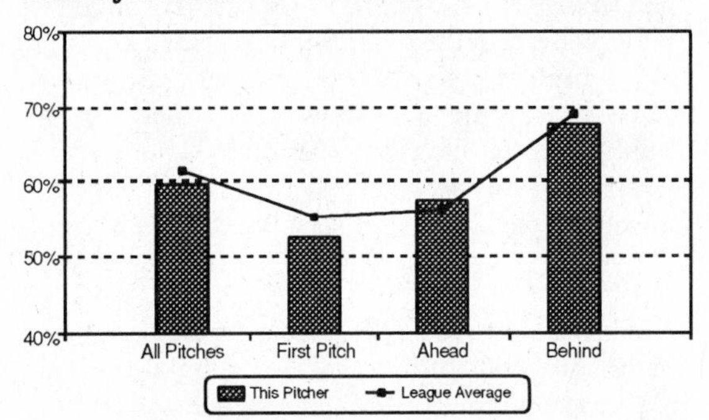

1992 Situational Stats

	W	L	ERA	Sv	IP		AB	H	HR	RBI	AVG
Home	3	1	2.79	3	58.0	LHB	142	30	2	14	.211
Road	1	8	2.17	1	49.2	RHB	240	52	4	26	.217
Day	3	4	3.43	2	39.1	Sc Pos	119	23	1	34	.193
Night	1	5	1.98	2	68.1	Clutch	164	34	2	12	.207

1992 Rankings (American League)

- 1st in relief losses (8)
- 2nd in holds (19)
- 3rd in lowest batting average allowed with runners in scoring position (.193)
- 5th in games pitched (70)
- Led the Red Sox in games pitched, holds, lowest batting average allowed vs. left-handed batters (.211), first batter efficiency (.172), lowest batting average allowed with runners in scoring position, lowest percentage of inherited runners scored (24.7%), ERA in relief (2.66), relief losses, relief innings (94.2), lowest batting average allowed in relief (.219) and least baserunners per 9 innings in relief (12.5)

HITTING:

Asking a Red Sox fan what the highlight of the 1992 season is a little like asking George McGovern what state he most enjoyed carrying in 1972. Regardless, ask a thousand, and you will get the same answer a thousand times over. It was the night of August 3 against the Toronto Blue Jays, and Billy Hatcher did something so rare in Fenway Park that some fans weren't even certain what had happened. On that night, Hatcher noticed that Toronto's Juan Guzman wasn't even bothering to look him back to third, so he took off for the plate and stole home. Fenway erupted, was electric for three nights, and made the Tom Bolton-Hatcher trade worthwhile for that golden moment.

At 32, Hatcher isn't a full-time player, and he batted only .238 for Boston. He certainly isn't a full-time leadoff hitter, as his five-year leadoff on-base percentage is .289. He did for the Red Sox what he's done for every team he's played on. He gave them a jump-start with speed, clutch hitting (.321 late and close), hustle and a huge dose of character. But because his contract called for $2M in 1993, the Red Sox didn't pick up the option, choosing instead to attempt to re-sign him for half the money.

BASERUNNING:

Hatcher's steals have dwindled from 30 to 11 to 4 the last three years, but he can score from first in any ballpark on a double, has terrific running instincts and is daring.

FIELDING

Hatcher is fine in left field because of his speed, hustle and knowledge of the game, but he isn't a center fielder. His throwing arm is average at best.

OVERALL:

Hatcher had always been labelled a turf player, but his numbers are virtually identical on turf and grass the last few years. He's a fastball, front-foot hitter who gets up to the plate and hacks. Most of all, he's one of the genuinely good people in the game, which is why Hobson asked the front office to bring him back in '93.

BILLY HATCHER

Position: LF/CF
Bats: R **Throws:** R
Ht: 5'10" **Wt:** 190

Opening Day Age: 32
Born: 10/4/60 in Williams, AZ
ML Seasons: 9

Overall Statistics

	G	AB	R	H	D	T	HR	RBI	SB	BB	SO	AVG
1992	118	409	47	102	19	2	3	33	4	22	52	.249
Career	1004	3521	474	926	171	25	42	311	196	221	401	.263

Where He Hits the Ball

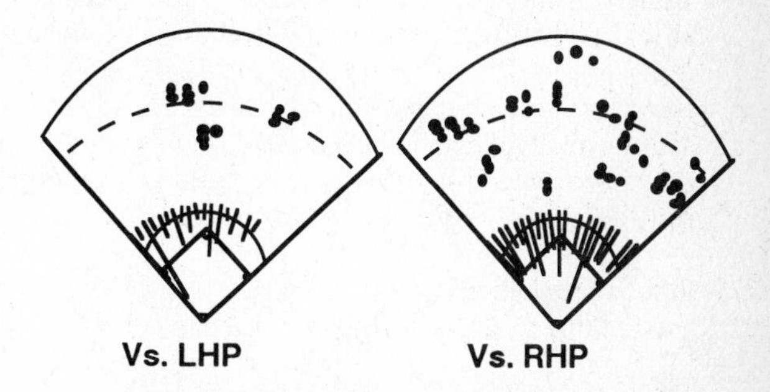

1992 Situational Stats

	AB	H	HR	RBI	AVG		AB	H	HR	RBI	AVG
Home	191	52	1	17	.272	LHP	141	34	2	7	.241
Road	218	50	2	16	.229	RHP	268	68	1	26	.254
Day	121	29	1	11	.240	Sc Pos	103	26	0	27	.252
Night	288	73	2	22	.253	Clutch	81	26	1	8	.321

1992 Rankings (American League)

- 1st in lowest leadoff on-base percentage (.247)
- 6th in batting average in the clutch (.350)
- Led the Red Sox in batting average in the clutch
- Led AL left fielders in batting average in the clutch

PITCHING:

In 1991, Joe Hesketh was 12-4 for the Red Sox and was one of the most effective lefthanders in the league in the second half. He was rewarded with a contract worth two years and an option at $1.5 million per season. Cynics questioned the club's decision to throw so much in the 33-year-old lefthander's basket, pointing out that with his slight (6'2", 173 pounds) frame, he might have trouble holding up over an entire season. After all, argued those cynics, when did Joe Hesketh ever pitch enough innings to qualify for the ERA title? Never.

That distinction still holds. After two decent months, Hesketh wore down and was eventually yanked from the rotation, finishing the season with 25 starts and 148.2 innings (his 153.1 the previous year was his most since 1985). When he is strong, Hesketh has good, solid stuff. He has an average fastball that he runs and sinks and a nasty, sharp-breaking slider that usually ends up in the dirt as righties swing over it. Some felt that in his second year as a starter in the American League that batters better laid off his slider, but it breaks so hard that when he is right, no one can lay off it.

HOLDING RUNNERS AND FIELDING:

Hesketh's tricky motion usually keeps baserunners close, but not in 1992. He permitted 17 steals in 21 attempts, though three of the caught stealings were on Hesketh pickoffs. Ordinarily a good fielder, he committed four errors last year and fielded .875.

OVERALL:

There is a strong possibility that if Hesketh is still with Boston he will pitch his way back into the rotation and again give them three solid months. After that, if he cannot hold up, it will be back to the bullpen. Or, then again, maybe they can use Hesketh as a starter until July 1, then put Danny Darwin into the rotation at that point for the rest of the season. In those 32-35 starts, they might get a 15-18 game winner.

JOE HESKETH

Position: SP/RP
Bats: L **Throws:** L
Ht: 6' 2" **Wt:** 173

Opening Day Age: 34
Born: 2/15/59 in Lackawanna, NY
ML Seasons: 9

Overall Statistics

	W	L	ERA	G	GS	Sv	IP	H	R	BB	SO	HR
1992	8	9	4.36	30	25	1	148.2	162	84	58	104	15
Career	49	38	3.63	286	89	20	794.1	768	364	303	609	72

How Often He Throws Strikes

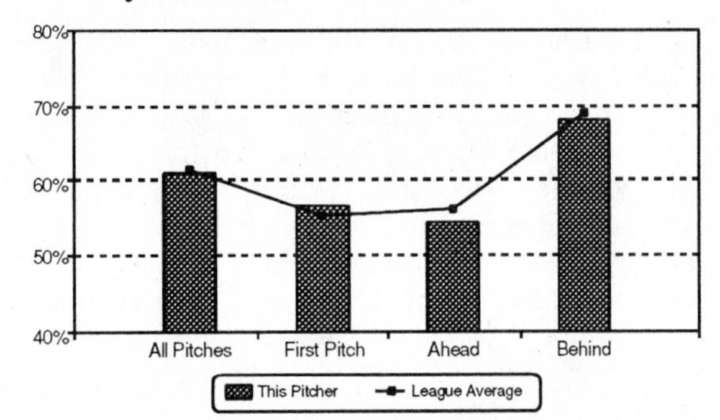

1992 Situational Stats

	W	L	ERA	Sv	IP		AB	H	HR	RBI	AVG
Home	4	4	4.50	0	66.0	LHB	98	25	2	13	.255
Road	4	5	4.25	1	82.2	RHB	490	137	13	56	.280
Day	5	2	3.04	0	56.1	Sc Pos	141	37	3	51	.262
Night	3	7	5.17	1	92.1	Clutch	27	7	1	2	.259

1992 Rankings (American League)

- 2nd in worst fielding percentage at pitcher (.875)
- 7th in highest batting average allowed vs. right-handed batters (.280)

HITTING:

Tony Pena may be 35 celsius, but when the 1992 season was over, the first thing the Red Sox ownership did was convince Pena and his agent Tom Reich to sign a one year extension. "Our pitching staff's ERA was the one thing that was representative," said GM Lou Gorman of the second-best mark in the league (3.58). "And Pena had a lot to do with that ERA." With Pena behind the plate, the Red Sox staff ERA was 3.49. With John Marzano, Eric Wedge and whoknowswho? back there, the staff ERA was 3.87.

Pena can also still hit a little. After working hard with batting coach Rick Burleson for two months, Pena made adjustments, batted .262 after July and believes he may be able to hit that high again. He cut down on his wild, swing-from-the-derriere style. Now Pena is in a stance that looks as if he's sitting in a choir stall, has gone to a lighter bat and makes better, more consistent contact.

BASERUNNING:

Pena still has some speed and last year stole three bases in five attempts. After grounding into 23 double plays in both 1990 and '91, he worked harder at getting out of the box more quickly last year and reduced that figure to 11.

FIELDING:

There are many who don't like some of Pena's catching habits. He likes to sit on the ground, which the Cardinals people stopped because they felt it restricted him on pitches that sail up and out of the strike zone, and on bunts and pop-ups. But Pena has been catching that way since he was a kid on the streets of Santiago, D.R., and no one in Boston is going to ask him to change.

OVERALL:

Pena isn't with the Red Sox for his offensive production; he's there to handle and catch a veteran pitching staff with Roger Clemens and a lot of offspeed throwers. He still does that very well. So what if he was there in Santiago to greet Columbus.

TONY PENA

Position: C
Bats: R **Throws:** R
Ht: 6' 0" **Wt:** 185

Opening Day Age: 35
Born: 6/4/57 in Monte Cristi, Dominican Republic
ML Seasons: 13

Overall Statistics

	G	AB	R	H	D	T	HR	RBI	SB	BB	SO	AVG
1992	133	410	39	99	21	1	1	38	3	24	61	.241
Career	1624	5550	584	1481	256	26	95	614	78	382	704	.267

Where He Hits the Ball

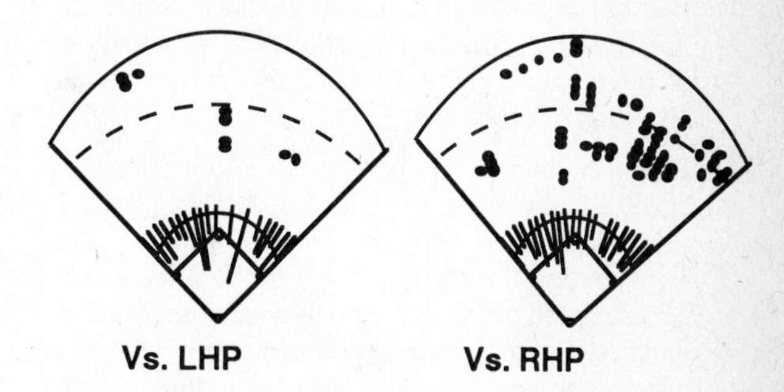

1992 Situational Stats

	AB	H	HR	RBI	AVG		AB	H	HR	RBI	AVG
Home	203	56	1	20	.276	LHP	111	28	1	11	.252
Road	207	43	0	18	.208	RHP	299	71	0	27	.237
Day	118	35	0	15	.297	Sc Pos	111	27	0	34	.243
Night	292	64	1	23	.219	Clutch	79	24	1	6	.304

1992 Rankings (American League)

- 3rd in sacrifice bunts (13)
- Led the Red Sox in sacrifice bunts, batting average with the bases loaded (.545) and bunts in play (18)
- Led AL catchers in sacrifice bunts, batting average on a 3-2 count (.308) and bunts in play

HITTING:

Of all the problems that Butch Hobson encountered as a rookie manager, none was more perplexing than those of Phil Plantier. At Pawtucket, Plantier and Hobson had been close. Hobson's ability to discipline, motivate and relate to younger players in the minor leagues had earned him the job when the Red Sox fired the popular Joe Morgan. But in his rookie season, Hobson found himself in conflict with Plantier.

Plantier was bitter about being singled out and sent to the minor leagues. He and Hobson had a blow-up in Baltimore when Plantier failed to show up for early hitting. By the time the season was over, the Red Sox didn't know which direction Plantier's career would take. In 1991, when Plantier came to Boston and clocked 11 homers in 148 at-bats, the Red Sox believed they had one of the league's rising sluggers. But in '92 he had all kinds of problems.

Plantier's odd shift in personality and work habits could be written off as a quick dose of big league-itis, but anyone who promised so much has at least earned the right to have the whole experience written off as the maturing process. Plantier insisted that part of his problem stemmed from an off-season elbow operation from which there were complications and from which he didn't fully recover.

BASERUNNING:

Like most Red Sox players, Plantier has below-average speed and is a conservative baserunner. He stole only two bases last year in five attempts.

FIELDING:

With the Red Sox, Plantier has been a left fielder asked to play right. He has below average range at either position, but could learn to handle left adequately. His arm is below average.

OVERALL:

While Plantier has a modest 18 homers in 512 major league at-bats, there have been glimpses of 30-home run power. The bat speed is there. If Plantier is healthy, his head is focused and he can communicate with new hitting coach Mike Easler, some of that potential will resurface.

PHIL PLANTIER

Position: RF/LF/DH
Bats: L **Throws:** R
Ht: 5'11" **Wt:** 195

Opening Day Age: 24
Born: 1/27/69 in Manchester, NH
ML Seasons: 3

Overall Statistics

	G	AB	R	H	D	T	HR	RBI	SB	BB	SO	AVG
1992	108	349	46	86	19	0	7	30	2	44	83	.246
Career	175	512	74	137	27	1	18	68	3	71	127	.268

Where He Hits the Ball

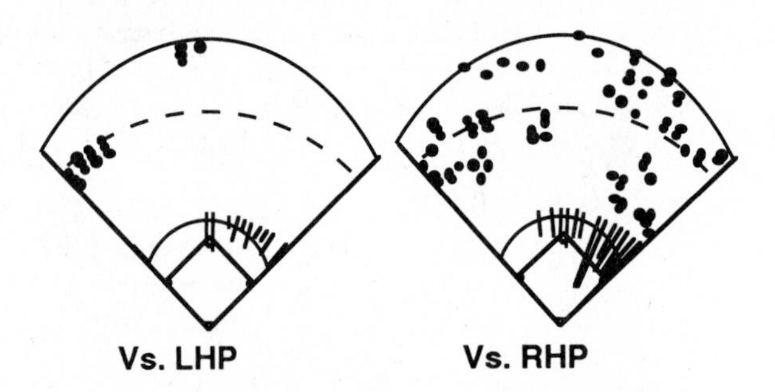

1992 Situational Stats

	AB	H	HR	RBI	AVG		AB	H	HR	RBI	AVG
Home	201	54	5	23	.269	LHP	71	11	0	1	.155
Road	148	32	2	7	.216	RHP	278	75	7	29	.270
Day	138	32	4	13	.232	Sc Pos	90	15	1	21	.167
Night	211	54	3	17	.256	Clutch	71	18	1	6	.254

1992 Rankings (American League)

- 3rd in lowest batting average with runners in scoring position (.167)
- 7th in batting average on a 3-1 count (.571)
- Led the Red Sox in batting average on a 3-1 count, highest percentage of strikes taken (23.1%) and outfield assists (6)
- Led AL right fielders in batting average on a 3-1 count

HITTING:

It was obvious by midseason last year that Luis Rivera was not Butch Hobson's shortstop of choice. John Valentin was promoted and, along with Scott Cooper and Bob Zupcic, got the chance to see if any of Hobson's Pawtucket graduates could create some future prospects for the last-place Red Sox. Meanwhile, Rivera effectively was pushed off to the side. He batted only 35 times after a July slump in which he hit only .121, and finished the season at .215.

No one ever claimed that Rivera was a great player, but there was a reason that the Royals tried so hard to acquire him during the season. The year before, when Joe Morgan singled him out for criticism on a play Morgan later admitted he misread, Rivera's peers rose to his defense against the manager.

Rivera is essentially a bail hitter who likes to pull off and swing hard at the fastball on the inner half of the plate. He worked hard in clutch situations to take fastballs and push them to right field. Because he has so much trouble with breaking balls and the pitch away, his five-year average with runners in scoring position (.228) and late and close situations (.191) are pretty dreadful.

BASERUNNING:

Rivera doesn't run particularly well, although he is smart on the bases. He's little threat to steal, with four swipes each of the last three years and a career success rate of 50 percent.

FIELDING:

Rivera will occasionally mess up routine plays, and when he plays too often he tends to get tired and make errors in bunches. His range is average, and he has good hands and an accurate arm when focused.

OVERALL:

The chances are good that the Red Sox will set Rivera free and play Valentin full-time now that Rivera is up in the seven-figure world. Some other team can likely get a gamer pretty cheap. Rivera can hit some fastballs, catches the ball most of the time, plays hard and is good for the ballclub.

LUIS RIVERA

Position: SS
Bats: R **Throws:** R
Ht: 5'10" **Wt:** 175

Opening Day Age: 29
Born: 1/3/64 in Cidra, Puerto Rico
ML Seasons: 7

Overall Statistics

	G	AB	R	H	D	T	HR	RBI	SB	BB	SO	AVG
1992	102	288	17	62	11	1	0	29	4	26	56	.215
Career	638	1940	209	452	100	9	24	187	18	148	370	.233

Where He Hits the Ball

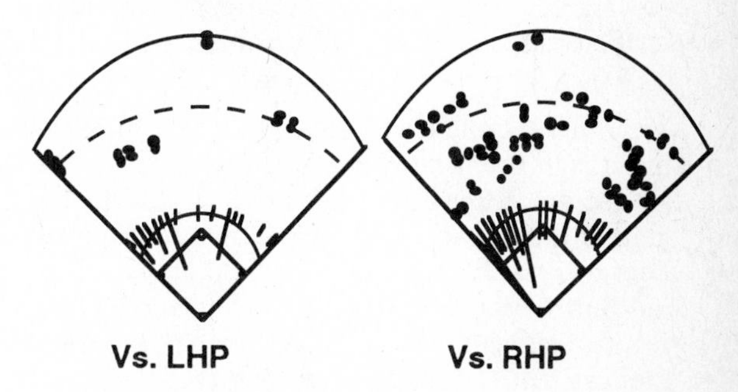

1992 Situational Stats

	AB	H	HR	RBI	AVG		AB	H	HR	RBI	AVG
Home	127	22	0	14	.173	LHP	78	14	0	7	.179
Road	161	40	0	15	.248	RHP	210	48	0	22	.229
Day	93	25	0	11	.269	Sc Pos	87	23	0	28	.264
Night	195	37	0	18	.190	Clutch	53	7	0	3	.132

1992 Rankings (American League)

- → 1st in lowest batting average with the bases loaded (.000)
- → 2nd in lowest batting average in the clutch (.132)

MO VAUGHN

Position: 1B/DH
Bats: L **Throws:** R
Ht: 6' 1" **Wt:** 230

Opening Day Age: 25
Born: 12/15/67 in Norwalk, CT
ML Seasons: 2

HITTING:

Mo Vaughn, The Hit Dog, was another young Red Sox player who started the 1992 season with great expectations but suffered through disappointments and frustrations. Like Phil Plantier, Vaughn was sent to the minors, had several run-ins with Butch Hobson and had his attitude questioned. And while his .257-8-37 second half stats brought his numbers close to respectability -- hey, on this team, Vaughn's 13 homers placed him second -- he will go to spring training not knowing where his career is going.

It was thought that Mo could be a masher, a power hitter to all fields who could knock in runs. Vaughn expected to walk in and be an impact player, and when things went wrong, he became confused. His problems with Hobson got so bad they ended up in a widely-reported fight.

Vaughn had trouble with fastballs in on him, as he has a significant hitch in his swing. Because he gets so much topspin, he has trouble consistently getting the ball in the air with enough power at Fenway, which may be a little deep for him as a pull hitter. But in the final half he made adjustments and went back to taking the ball out over the plate and driving it to left field.

BASERUNNING:

Vaughn is a more adventurous baserunner than most of his Red Sox teammates. Despite his size he attempted six steals last year; he was safe only three times, however.

FIELDING:

Vaughn led all AL first basemen in errors despite playing less than half a full-season's total at the position. He had trouble with his footwork, which caused him to lose sight -- and plain miss -- throws below his knees and above his cap bill. But while Vaughn is huge, he is a pretty good athlete with light feet, so he can improve.

OVERALL:

Will Vaughn be a .300 hitter with 30 homers? Probably not. But he showed enough in terms of adjustments to think he can hit a whole lot better than he did in his first full season.

Overall Statistics

	G	AB	R	H	D	T	HR	RBI	SB	BB	SO	AVG
1992	113	355	42	83	16	2	13	57	3	47	67	.234
Career	187	574	63	140	28	2	17	89	5	73	110	.244

Where He Hits the Ball

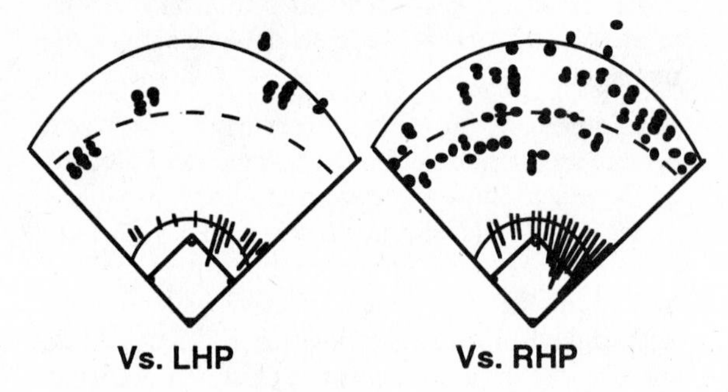

1992 Situational Stats

	AB	H	HR	RBI	AVG		AB	H	HR	RBI	AVG
Home	202	53	8	37	.262	LHP	79	15	5	14	.190
Road	153	30	5	20	.196	RHP	276	68	8	43	.246
Day	122	29	5	19	.238	Sc Pos	100	22	4	44	.220
Night	233	54	8	38	.232	Clutch	70	18	1	8	.257

1992 Rankings (American League)

➡ Led AL first basemen in errors (15)

WORKHORSE

FRANK VIOLA

Position: SP
Bats: L **Throws:** L
Ht: 6' 4" **Wt:** 210

Opening Day Age: 32
Born: 4/19/60 in East Meadow, NY
ML Seasons: 11

PITCHING:

In the final week of the season with the Red Sox playing in Toronto, Boston was so strapped for pitching that Butch Hobson decided to start Matt Young. General Manager Lou Gorman, respecting that the Brewers were still very much in the race, called Hobson and asked him to consider using Frank Viola on three days rest. Viola jumped at the idea, took a no-hitter into the ninth and pitched a 1-0 one-hitter over David Cone.

So, maybe Viola isn't quite the pitcher he was when he was 24-7 and won the Cy Young Award in 1988. Granted, he's 59-56 since, 26-27 the last two seasons for second-division Met and Red Sox teams. But basically he did precisely what the Red Sox signed him to do in 1992. He was second in the league in starts (35), he gave them 238 innings and pitched well enough to win another four or five games; unfortunately for Viola, he received 3.63 runs a start, the second-worst support in the league. One concern is that he continued to be a first-half pitcher; over the past five seasons Viola is 52-24, 2.81 before the break, 31-39, 3.81 afterward.

Viola at 33 hasn't changed much. He's basically a fastball/change-up pitcher, and there probably isn't a better change-up around than his circle variety; it dead-fishes away from right-handed batters. He also still has the solid breaking ball for lefthanders, so unlike many premier change-up pitchers, he is still tough on left-handed hitters (.211). He uses his change-up well in specific counts, and induced the third-most GDPs in the league with 29.

HOLDING RUNNERS AND FIELDING:

Viola, who utilizes a slide step, holds runners well enough that he allowed only 12 steals in his 36 starts. He is also a fine defensive player; his 47 assists last year led all American League pitchers.

OVERALL:

There's no reason to believe that Viola will change in the near future. If the Red Sox improve their defense and offense, he will add four-six wins with his annual 235-250 innings.

Overall Statistics

	W	L	ERA	G	GS	Sv	IP	H	R	BB	SO	HR
1992	13	12	3.44	35	35	0	238.0	214	99	89	121	13
Career	163	137	3.70	377	376	0	2577.0	2550	1171	751	1722	271

How Often He Throws Strikes

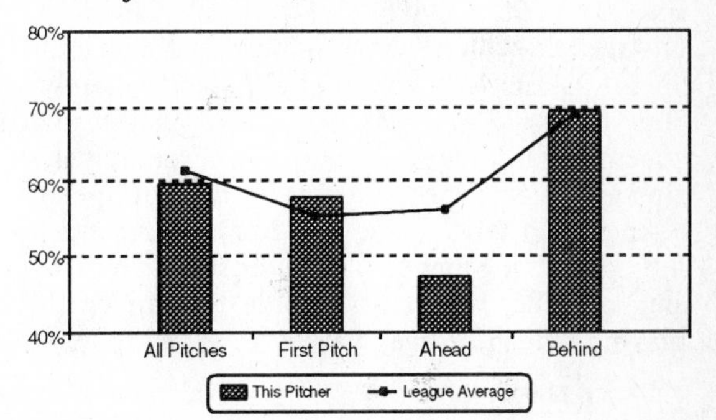

1992 Situational Stats

	W	L	ERA	Sv	IP		AB	H	HR	RBI	AVG
Home	8	7	4.08	0	117.0	LHB	109	23	1	11	.211
Road	5	5	2.83	0	121.0	RHB	777	191	12	77	.246
Day	6	5	3.24	0	83.1	Sc Pos	193	48	4	73	.249
Night	7	7	3.55	0	154.2	Clutch	121	23	2	8	.190

1992 Rankings (American League)

- → 2nd in least run support per 9 innings (3.6)
- → 3rd in games started (35) and GDPs induced (29)
- → 4th in pitches thrown (3,807)
- → 5th in balks (2), lowest slugging percentage allowed (.331) and most GDPs induced per 9 innings (1.1)
- → Led the Red Sox in losses (12), games started, hits allowed (214), batters faced (999), walks allowed (89), wild pitches (12), GDPs induced, least pitches thrown per batter (3.81) and most GDPs induced per 9 innings

HITTING:

In a year of disappointments at Fenway Park, Bob Zupcic was the exception. In 1989 and 1990, Zupcic batted .217 and .213 at AA New Britain. But in 1991 at AAA Pawtucket, he turned it around, going from .188 in July to bat .300 the remainder of the season. When '92 was over he'd hit .276 in Boston. Zupcic didn't exactly tear down the Back Bay with his power, totalling three homers and 43 RBI in 392 at-bats. But after five years that seemed destined for Omaha, Zupcic established himself as a legitimate major-league player and was protected from expansion.

To his credit, Zupcic shortened up and simply hit the ball up the middle with runners in scoring position (.295, .324 late and close). But after hitting .328 with all three homers and slugging .474 in the first half, he was pitched far differently after the All-Star break. Instead of the steady stream of fastballs most newcomers see, Zupcic started getting breaking balls and offspeed pitches, and thus far he has had a tough time hitting anything that breaks. In the second half he slugged .286, which isn't going to earn much playing time in Fenway Park.

BASERUNNING:

Zupcic has only average speed but has good running instincts and rare Red Sox aggressiveness. He stole only two bases last year, but had four straight seasons stealing in double figures while in the minors.

FIELDING:

Zupcic is a solid defensive outfielder with an above-average arm. He is ideally suited to right field, especially since he has the athletic ability to get to the line and come up throwing, but ended up having to play center in '92. While he was certainly Boston's best center fielder, he doesn't have the kind of speed and range that would put him in the top class.

OVERALL:

The Red Sox believe that Zupcic will eventually develop 12-15 home run power (he hit 18 in '91 at Pawtucket, albeit in a bandbox). He will be interesting to watch, because he has good work habits and has shown the ability to improve. By how much is the next question.

BOB ZUPCIC

Position: CF/LF/RF
Bats: R **Throws:** R
Ht: 6' 4" **Wt:** 220

Opening Day Age: 26
Born: 8/18/66 in Pittsburgh, PA
ML Seasons: 2

Overall Statistics

	G	AB	R	H	D	T	HR	RBI	SB	BB	SO	AVG
1992	124	392	46	108	19	1	3	43	2	25	60	.276
Career	142	417	49	112	19	1	4	46	2	26	66	.269

Where He Hits the Ball

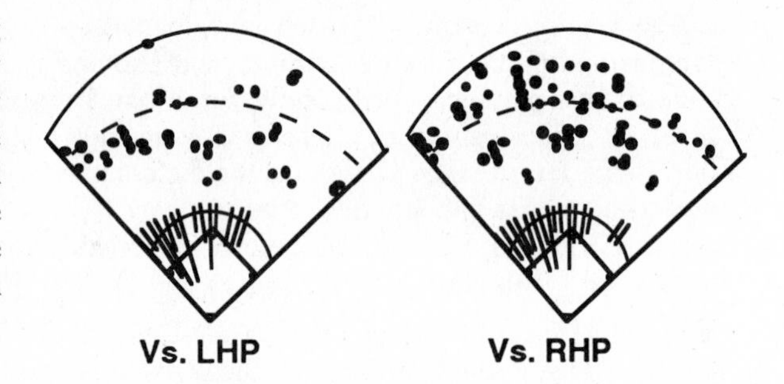

1992 Situational Stats

	AB	H	HR	RBI	AVG		AB	H	HR	RBI	AVG
Home	189	50	3	25	.265	LHP	133	39	0	15	.293
Road	203	58	0	18	.286	RHP	259	69	3	28	.266
Day	133	38	1	14	.286	Sc Pos	95	28	2	40	.295
Night	259	70	2	29	.270	Clutch	68	22	2	16	.324

1992 Rankings (American League)

- Led the Red Sox in hit by pitch (4)

DARYL IRVINE

Position: RP
Bats: R **Throws:** R
Ht: 6' 3" **Wt:** 195

Opening Day Age: 28
Born: 11/15/64 in Harrisonburg, VA
ML Seasons: 3

Overall Statistics

	W	L	ERA	G	GS	Sv	IP	H	R	BB	SO	HR
1992	3	4	6.11	21	0	0	28.0	31	20	14	10	1
Career	4	5	5.68	41	0	0	63.1	71	43	33	27	3

PITCHING, FIELDING & HOLDING RUNNERS:

Maybe it's the potholes on route 95 between Pawtucket and Boston, maybe it's the alignment of the planets. Darryl Irvine keeps running up great minor league numbers, but when he gets to the Red Sox, the roof falls in. Three straight years he's been called up leading the Pawtucket club in saves, and each time he has had dreadful problems, as his stairway ERA (4.67, 6.00, 6.11) demonstrates.

Irvine is a hard sinker-slider pitcher whose best running fastball usually ends up out of the strike zone. The problem is that in the majors, batters have laid off his sinker and forced him to come up -- which, with a straight fastball, has caused him problems. In his 63.1 career innings, he's had 33 walks and 27 strikeouts. He also hasn't thrown his slider consistently for strikes; that's one reason righthanders (.302) hit him better than lefties (.267), who basically try to pull his sinker. Irvine played errorless ball last year and is quite good at holding runners. He's allowed only one steal in his major-league career.

OVERALL:

Irvine has been through a series of arm problems in the minors and battled back. He's never gained confidence in the majors, but it could be that somewhere, somehow he will get another chance, get his sinker over and be a solid middle reliever. The ability is there.

TIM NAEHRING

Position: SS/2B
Bats: R **Throws:** R
Ht: 6' 2" **Wt:** 190

Opening Day Age: 26
Born: 2/1/67 in Cincinnati, OH
ML Seasons: 3

Overall Statistics

	G	AB	R	H	D	T	HR	RBI	SB	BB	SO	AVG
1992	72	186	12	43	8	0	3	14	0	18	31	.231
Career	116	326	23	72	15	0	5	29	0	32	61	.221

HITTING, FIELDING, BASERUNNING:

Only recently considered Boston's shortstop of the future, Tim Naehring has become their utility infielder of the present. Naehring's career was derailed in 1991 by back problems which eventually required major surgery. Part of a a buttock muscle had to be transplanted to his back, and one immediate result was that his buttocks tightened up on him at times. Although he recovered well enough to resume his major-league career last year, he wasn't the same player.

Naehring got into 72 games for the Sox last year, and the good news was that the back held up; he did, however, miss about six weeks with a sprained right wrist. The youngster did a good job in the field while playing second, short, and third. He committed only three errors and displayed decent range at each position. He never had much speed, so that wasn't a problem.

Naehring's bat work, however, was a source of concern. He displayed little of his old power and was hitting only .191 when he had to go on the disabled list. He looked a lot better after his September return, hitting .340 in 50 at-bats.

OVERALL:

Naehring's September surge renewed hopes that he may finally have regained his pre-injury bat skills. With the departure of Jody Reed, the second base job is open for Naehring to take this spring.

PAUL QUANTRILL

Position: RP
Bats: L **Throws:** R
Ht: 6' 1" **Wt:** 175

Opening Day Age: 24
Born: 11/3/68 in London, Ontario, Canada
ML Seasons: 1

Overall Statistics

	W	L	ERA	G	GS	Sv	IP	H	R	BB	SO	HR
1992	2	3	2.19	27	0	1	49.1	55	18	15	24	1
Career	2	3	2.19	27	0	1	49.1	55	18	15	24	1

PITCHING, FIELDING & HOLDING RUNNERS:

When the Red Sox were putting together their expansion list, Paul Quantrill's name was right there behind Clemens and Viola with the sure things. He's a tough, hard-running sinkerballer from Ontario who will start '93 as Boston's top set-up man, but could well end up their closer. He doesn't have the one overpowering or trick pitch that characterizes closers. But in that role, makeup is often more important than raw stuff, and this kid is a hard-nosed competitor with that great hockey background.

Quantrill had been a starter in the minors and was off to a bad start (6-8, 4.46) with AAA Pawtucket before being asked to make some mechanical changes. He got himself straightened out and pitched well in Boston. He ended up with a 2.19 ERA, and while he had problems getting both his slider (righties hit .305, lefties .260) and offspeed pitches over, he should make that progression this year. He did a good job of holding runners, and his hockey training ought to help his defense, though he made two errors last year.

OVERALL:

Quantrill is never going to have great numbers because his rubber arm makes him the one guy on the staff the manager can always abuse when he's got no one left. But he definitely can pitch.

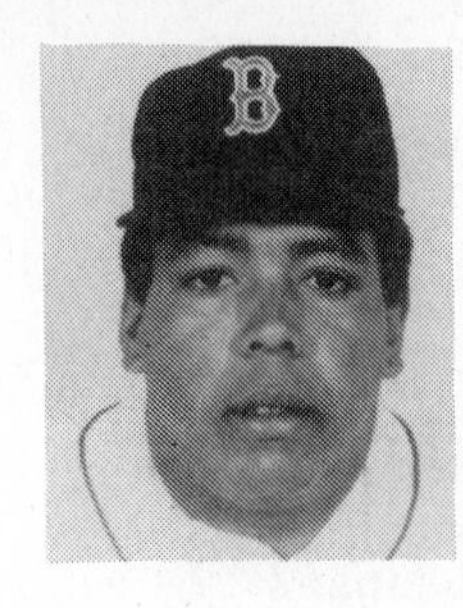

CARLOS QUINTANA

Position: 1B/RF
Bats: R **Throws:** R
Ht: 6' 2" **Wt:** 220

Opening Day Age: 27
Born: 8/26/65 in Estado Miranda, Venezuela
ML Seasons: 4

Overall Statistics

	G	AB	R	H	D	T	HR	RBI	SB	BB	SO	AVG
1992		Did Not Play										
Career	337	1073	132	306	54	1	18	146	2	122	155	.285

HITTING, FIELDING, BASERUNNING:

Right before spring training, Carlos Quintana was seriously injured in a bizarre automobile accident back home in Venezuela. When the season was over, not only hadn't he played at all, he still hadn't regained feeling in his thumb. The Red Sox, who protected him for the expansion draft, hope they get him back in 1993, because his was a major loss as they took their dive into last place in the American League East.

Quintana was missed first and foremost because in 1991 he made himself into an outstanding defensive first baseman. He has terrific hands, stretches well, gives a good target and improved his footwork to become a key to their infield. Without him, first base defense was a major problem.

But since the Sox had the worst offense in the division, they surely missed his bat also. Quintana had made himself one of the better situational hitters in the league. Normally a right-center field hitter, he had made considerable progress looking for breaking balls or guessing first pitch fastballs and driving them to left and left-center. The Red Sox feel that he could become a 15-18 homer, 80-95 RBI man who is tough in the clutch. He's very slow.

OVERALL:

Not only is recovery from injury a concern, but the Red Sox also are concerned about Quintana's weight. He could grow as large as El Salvador.

JOHN VALENTIN

Position: SS
Bats: R **Throws:** R
Ht: 6' 0" **Wt:** 170

Opening Day Age: 26
Born: 2/18/67 in Mineola, NY
ML Seasons: 1

Overall Statistics

	G	AB	R	H	D	T	HR	RBI	SB	BB	SO	AVG
1992	58	185	21	51	13	0	5	25	1	20	17	.276
Career	58	185	21	51	13	0	5	25	1	20	17	.276

HITTING, FIELDING, BASERUNNING:

Last winter, John Valentin was added to the Red Sox 40-man roster as an afterthought; in fact, at one point it appeared that Double-A shortstop Jimmy Byrd would be the final addition to the roster. After all, Valentin was 25, and his climb through the minors included numbers like .246, .218, .198 . . .

But three weeks into spring training, the kid from Jersey City had opened eyes with his hands and strong, accurate arm. He went back to AAA Pawtucket to open the season and showed power (nine homers in 331 at-bats). He was soon recalled. After a solid 58-game, 185 at-bat stint in which he batted .276 with five homers and a .427 slugging percentage, he goes into 1993 as Boston's regular shortstop.

Whether or not Valentin will hit for average once he's been around the league a couple of times and sees a lot of offspeed pitches remains to be seen. But he does appear to be a shortstop with average range, good hands, a strong arm and the ability to make the dazzling play. His problem is that sometimes he gets a little too fancy and his manager has to get on him. His speed is only average.

OVERALL:

Valentin might hit 12-15 homers in the right season if he doesn't get picked apart by breaking stuff. He's a good athlete, and good athletes usually make adjustments.

HERM WINNINGHAM

Position: LF/CF
Bats: L **Throws:** R
Ht: 5'11" **Wt:** 190

Opening Day Age: 31
Born: 12/1/61 in Orangeburg, SC
ML Seasons: 9

Overall Statistics

	G	AB	R	H	D	T	HR	RBI	SB	BB	SO	AVG
1992	105	234	27	55	8	1	1	14	6	10	53	.235
Career	868	1888	212	452	69	26	19	147	105	157	417	.239

HITTING, FIELDING, BASERUNNING:

Herm Winningham did precisely what the Red Sox acquired him to do last year. He filled in as a fifth outfielder, played solid defense, did a decent (.244) job against right-handed pitching and provided character. Basically, a fifth outfielder is supposed to be ever-ready and be a good guy on the club, and they don't come any better in terms of character than Herm Winningham.

The knee operation Winningham had in Cincinnati has reduced his speed, so that while in his Met and Expo days he was a threat to steal (he stole 29 for the '87 Expos), now he's just an average runner and basestealer (6-of-11). Nevertheless, he has good instincts and seldom makes mistakes on the basepaths. He is a first-ball fastball hitter without much power who just tries to put the ball in play. He's also become a valuable pinch hitter, which might make him more suited to the National League.

OVERALL:

Although he's only a .239 lifetime hitter, Winningham has the skills of a useful bench player. He remains capable of playing all three outfield positions. While his arm is a bit weak for right, the free agent will likely find a job somewhere for two reasons: he is a true center fielder and managers want him around.

ORGANIZATION OVERVIEW:

The Red Sox farm system used to be considered underrated. Now it's thought to be overrated after the 1992 flops of Mo Vaughn and Phil Plantier, among others. Under Lou Gorman, the Sox have concentrated on developing their best players, slowly if need be, and the heck with those minor-league winning percentages. Fine and good, as long as those prospects eventually develop. Last year they didn't, but one bad year shouldn't be enough to question the whole enterprise. Should it?

GREG BLOSSER

Position: OF **Opening Day Age:** 21
Bats: L **Throws:** L **Born:** 6/26/71 in Bradenton, FL
Ht: 6' 3" **Wt:** 200

Recent Statistics

	G	AB	R	H	D	T	HR	RBI	SB	BB	SO	AVG
91 AA New Britain	134	452	48	98	21	3	8	46	9	63	114	.217
92 AA New Britain	129	434	59	105	23	4	22	71	0	64	122	.242
92 AAA Pawtucket	1	0	1	0	0	0	0	0	0	1	0	.000
92 MLE	130	430	50	101	24	2	18	60	0	46	133	.235

The Red Sox' number-one draft choice out of high school in 1989, Blosser is not yet 22 years old. But last year he belted 22 home runs at AA New Britain, stamping him as a definite power prospect. Thus far Blosser hasn't hit for average (.217 and .242 in two seasons at New Britain), and he looks like a 120-strikeout guy, though he's also walked a respectable number of times. Blosser doesn't have much speed or a great arm, so his bat is going to make or break him. Boston will be patient with him; they may need to be.

JEFF McNEELY

Position: OF **Opening Day Age:** 23
Bats: R **Throws:** R **Born:** 10/18/69 in Monroe, NC
Ht: 6' 2" **Wt:** 190

Recent Statistics

	G	AB	R	H	D	T	HR	RBI	SB	BB	SO	AVG
91 A Lynchburg	106	382	58	123	16	5	4	38	38	74	74	.322
92 AA New Britain	85	261	30	57	8	4	2	11	10	26	78	.218
92 MLE	85	256	25	52	8	2	1	9	6	18	86	.203

Considered one of the top prospects in baseball, Jeff McNeely suffered through a miserable, injury-riddled campaign in 1992. After hitting .313 and .322 at the Class A level in 1990-91, McNeely ran into a stone wall at AA New Britain, suffering through assorted ailments and batting only .218. McNeely has tremendous athletic skills with great speed and outstanding outfield range, and the Red Sox aren't going to give up on him after one bad season. But like a lot of their top prospects, McNeely seemed truly jinxed last year.

FRANK RODRIGUEZ

Position: P-SS **Opening Day Age:** 20
Bats: R **Throws:** R **Born:** 12/11/72 in Brooklyn, NY
Ht: 6' 0" **Wt:** 175

Recent Statistics

	W	L	ERA	G	GS	Sv	IP	H	R	BB	SO	HR
92 A Lynchburg	12	7	3.09	25	25	0	148.2	125	56	65	129	11

Is he a pitcher or a shortstop? One of the most talked-about prospects in baseball, Rodriguez has been successful at both spots in his young career. Last year the Sox finally convinced Rodriguez that his future was on the mound (at least they thought so), and the youngster had great velocity while going 12-7 for Class A Lynchburg. For Rodriguez, it never seems easy though. By year's end some people were grumbling that Rodriguez "pitches like a shortstop," and he had a statutory rape charge hanging over his head. The Boston talk shows must love this guy.

KEN RYAN

Position: P **Opening Day Age:** 24
Bats: R **Throws:** R **Born:** 10/24/68 in Pawtucket, RI
Ht: 6' 3" **Wt:** 200

Recent Statistics

	W	L	ERA	G	GS	Sv	IP	H	R	BB	SO	HR
92 AA New Britain	1	4	1.95	44	0	22	50.2	44	17	24	51	0
92 AAA Pawtucket	2	0	2.08	9	0	7	8.2	6	2	4	6	1
92 AL Boston	0	0	6.43	7	0	1	7.0	4	5	5	5	2

The Red Sox' need for a closer might be a golden opportunity for Ken Ryan this year. They'd love him to succeed; a local boy, Ryan was born in Pawtucket, RI and grew up in Seekonk, MA. An undrafted free agent, Ryan struggled as a starter but started developing quickly when shifted to the bullpen in 1991. He has good makeup and a 90 MPH fastball, ideal for late relief. The Sox protected him in the expansion draft, and he may make their roster this spring.

AARON H. SELE

Position: P **Opening Day Age:** 22
Bats: R **Throws:** R **Born:** 6/25/70 in Golden Valley, MN
Ht: 6' 5" **Wt:** 205

Recent Statistics

	W	L	ERA	G	GS	Sv	IP	H	R	BB	SO	HR
91 A Winter Havn	3	6	4.96	13	11	1	69.0	65	42	32	51	2
92 A Lynchburg	13	5	2.91	20	19	0	127.0	104	51	46	112	5
92 AA New Britain	2	1	6.27	7	6	0	33.0	43	29	15	29	2

Boston's number-one pick in 1991, Sele was a college ace at Washington State University. In only a year and a half of professional ball, the righty has created a strong impression. Though he's a big man, Sele is not overpowering; his best pitch is a curveball, and he's already got a varied repertoire. He's not afraid to pitch inside, with 25 hit batters in 229 professional innings. He should be at AA, maybe AAA this year, but if he's going to make the majors it should be fairly soon.

PITCHING:

Jim Abbott has emerged as the Angels' best starting pitcher, finishing last year with a 2.77 ERA (fifth best in the American League) and his third straight 200-inning season. Why, then, was his record 7-15? Lack of support was the only reason. Abbott's 2.64 runs received per nine innings was the least in the major leagues (the other three members of the Angels rotation, Chuck Finley, Mark Langston and Julio Valera, also placed among the worst six in the AL). Consistently good whether he won or not, Abbott never had a monthly ERA higher than 3.57.

Like his colleague Chuck Finley, Abbott doesn't really rely on one pitch, although his fastball can be dominant at times. The key to his success is often his curveball, which he throws slightly more often than his slider. Two things changed Abbott's career a couple of years ago: throwing with confidence when behind in the count and recapturing the inside part of the plate. He keeps the ball low in the strike zone and gets lots of groundball outs.

Although '92 was an exception, Abbott has often struggled early in the year. His lifetime record in April is 2-10. Possessing good mechanics, he has remained relatively injury-free, although he landed himself on the disabled list in July when he strained his rib cage.

HOLDING RUNNERS AND FIELDING:

The one-handed Abbott had some troubles with line drives in '92, but remains a very effective fielder. He did not commit an error last season. Once very poor at holding runners, he allowed only 14 steals in 27 attempts last year, an excellent ratio.

OVERALL:

The Angels have three good lefty starters, and there has been talk that Abbott, the lowest-salaried and thus easiest to deal, will be traded. If so, they will lose not only their best pitcher, but a fan-pleasing, charismatic young man who is the prize of the Angels' player development/scouting staff. Many feel that Abbott's best days, and possibly a Cy Young Award, are ahead of him.

JIM ABBOTT

Position: SP
Bats: L **Throws:** L
Ht: 6' 3" **Wt:** 210

Opening Day Age: 25
Born: 9/19/67 in Flint, MI
ML Seasons: 4

Overall Statistics

	W	L	ERA	G	GS	Sv	IP	H	R	BB	SO	HR
1992	7	15	2.77	29	29	0	211.0	208	73	68	130	12
Career	47	52	3.49	125	125	0	847.0	866	369	287	508	55

How Often He Throws Strikes

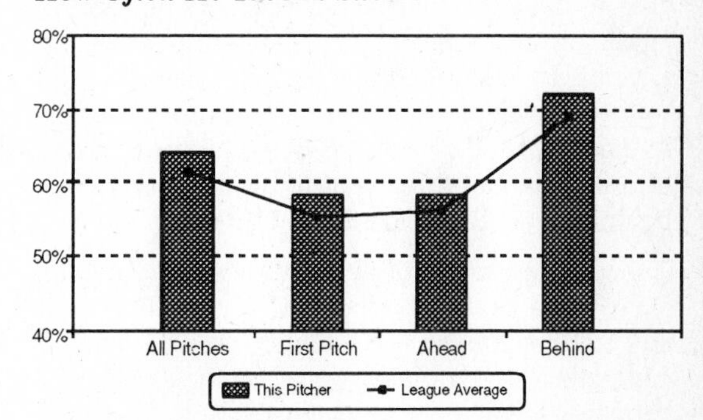

1992 Situational Stats

	W	L	ERA	Sv	IP		AB	H	HR	RBI	AVG
Home	2	8	3.32	0	95.0	LHB	128	35	0	9	.273
Road	5	7	2.33	0	116.0	RHB	662	173	12	57	.261
Day	1	3	2.11	0	47.0	Sc Pos	169	43	4	53	.254
Night	6	12	2.96	0	164.0	Clutch	91	33	3	11	.363

1992 Rankings (American League)

- 1st in least run support per 9 innings (2.6)
- 2nd in pickoff throws (266), ERA on the road (2.32) and pickoffs (10)
- 3rd in losses (15) and worst winning percentage (.318)
- Led the Angels in ERA (2.77), losses, pickoff throws, highest groundball/flyball ratio (1.8), lowest stolen base percentage allowed (51.8%), least pitches thrown per batter (3.54), least home runs allowed per 9 innings (.51) and ERA on the road

BERT BLYLEVEN

Position: SP
Bats: R **Throws:** R
Ht: 6' 3" **Wt:** 220

Opening Day Age: 42
Born: 4/6/51 in Zeist, Holland
ML Seasons: 22

PITCHING:

Not many people would have disagreed with the idea that Bert Blyleven's 279th win on July 20th, 1990 would be his last. After all, an ensuing injury to his right shoulder (requiring two operations) left Blyleven inactive for almost two full seasons. But he defied the odds and returned to pick up win number 280 on May 30th of 1992. Blyleven managed to start 24 games last year, picking up eight wins in his renewed quest for 300. For the most part he struggled, however, as his 4.74 ERA would suggest.

Blyleven pitched at least six innings in 13 of his 24 starts, but only once past the seventh. He was easy to hit, as opponents batted .285 against him. Blyleven compensated by displaying excellent control. He permitted just 29 free passes in 133 innings while striking out 70. With those 70 strikeouts, Blyleven passed Tom Seaver to move into the number-three spot in all-time strikeouts behind Nolan Ryan and Steve Carlton.

The next generation of pitchers may be calling the curveball a Blyleven, since nobody has thrown it any better in his era. He will mix in an occasional cut fastball, but it relies greatly on the element of surprise. Righthanders had no problem against Blyleven whatever the pitch -- .308 batting average with a .487 slugging percentage.

HOLDING RUNNERS AND FIELDING:

Blyleven does all the things expected of him: he backs up plays, covers first well and puts his glove up when the ball is hit right at him. Other than that, he isn't going to help himself much in the field. Ten of 14 runners who attempted to steal against him were successful, not a good ratio, but not much of a problem either.

OVERALL:

Blyleven will be 42 come April and most teams just won't be interested in him, given his mediocre numbers. However, the Angels have been burned by giving up on aging veterans like Dave Winfield and Brian Downing. They may provide Blyleven with one more chance to pick up the 13 wins he needs for 300.

Overall Statistics

	W	L	ERA	G	GS	Sv	IP	H	R	BB	SO	HR
1992	8	12	4.74	25	24	0	133.0	150	76	29	70	17
Career	287	250	3.31	692	685	0	4969.1	4632	2029	1322	3701	430

How Often He Throws Strikes

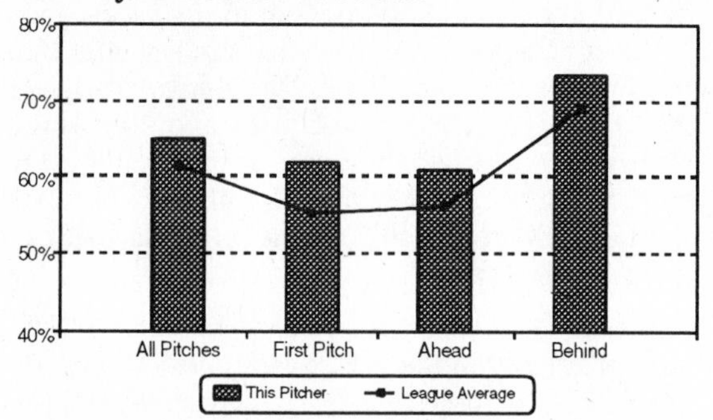

1992 Situational Stats

	W	L	ERA	Sv	IP		AB	H	HR	RBI	AVG
Home	4	6	4.31	0	64.2	LHB	253	66	6	26	.261
Road	4	6	5.14	0	68.1	RHB	273	84	11	45	.308
Day	2	3	7.76	0	31.1	Sc Pos	130	45	3	55	.346
Night	6	9	3.81	0	101.2	Clutch	22	7	0	2	.318

1992 Rankings (American League)

- Led the Angels in balks (1)

CHUCK CRIM

Position: RP
Bats: R **Throws:** R
Ht: 6' 0" **Wt:** 185

Opening Day Age: 31
Born: 7/23/61 in Van Nuys, CA
ML Seasons: 6

PITCHING:

Very little has gone right in recent years for Chuck Crim, once one of the most durable and effective relievers in baseball. After posting a 2.83 ERA in 76 games for the Brewers in 1989, Crim has lost more and more effectiveness with each passing season. The righthander is not a big man at six feet and 185 pounds, yet he averaged almost 70 appearances a season from 1988 through 1991. Crim led the American League in games pitched in both 1988 and 1989, and it's possible he's become a victim of overwork.

The Angels thought a change of scenery might help Crim last year, and they traded pitchers Mike Fetters and Glenn Carter to Milwaukee to obtain him. Unfortunately, Crim was worse than ever last year. His 5.17 ERA last year was the worst of his six major league seasons. Once again used almost exclusively in a middle relief role, he consistently got hammered.

Crim has never been a strikeout pitcher, instead rising to prominence as a sinkerballer who could induce the double play. He's still a groundball pitcher, but no longer an effective one. While he doesn't yield many walks, Crim often falls behind in the count, and that's when he gets into trouble. Last year opponents batted .362 when he was behind in the count, .210 when he got ahead. Serving up a lot of fat pitches, he permitted 11 homers in only 87 innings. Crim had particular problems with right-handed hitters, who batted .328 with nine homers against him last year.

HOLDING RUNNERS AND FIELDING:

Crim has improved as a fielder over the years, but can be erratic with his throwing. Crim's stolen bases allowed declined greatly in 1992. He has had problems with people running on him in the past, but not in 1992.

OVERALL:

After his poor season last year, Crim wouldn't seem to have much of a future with the Angels. However, he is signed through 1993, and he's hardly old at 31. He'll probably get another chance to revive his sagging career -- either with California, or somewhere else.

Overall Statistics

	W	L	ERA	G	GS	Sv	IP	H	R	BB	SO	HR
1992	7	6	5.17	57	0	1	87.0	100	56	29	30	11
Career	40	37	3.71	389	5	43	616.2	645	287	180	281	60

How Often He Throws Strikes

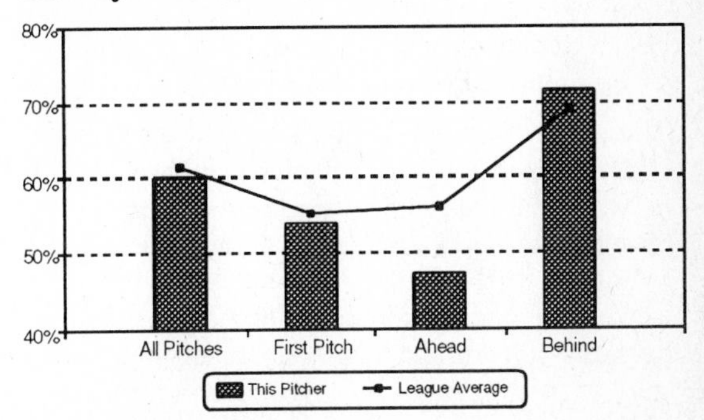

1992 Situational Stats

	W	L	ERA	Sv	IP		AB	H	HR	RBI	AVG
Home	4	1	5.31	0	40.2	LHB	137	33	2	21	.241
Road	3	5	5.05	1	46.1	RHB	204	67	9	44	.328
Day	2	3	6.00	0	21.0	Sc Pos	102	35	3	54	.343
Night	5	3	4.91	1	66.0	Clutch	88	28	5	18	.318

1992 Rankings (American League)

- 2nd in highest batting average allowed in relief (.293)
- 3rd highest ERA in relief (5.17) and lowest strikeouts per 9 innings in relief (3.1)
- 4th in most runners allowed per 9 innings in relief (14.0)
- Led the Angels in games pitched (57), hit batsmen (6), holds (8), lowest batting average allowed to left-handed batters (.241), relief wins (7), relief losses (6) and relief innings (87)

OVERLOOKED

CHAD CURTIS

Position: RF/LF/CF
Bats: R **Throws:** R
Ht: 5'10" **Wt:** 180

Opening Day Age: 24
Born: 11/6/68 in Marion, IN
ML Seasons: 1

HITTING:

A long shot who wasn't drafted until the 45th round in 1989, Chad Curtis hustled his way onto the Angel roster last spring, and quickly into the hearts of their fans. After years of bringing up rookies who ended up as flops, they weren't about to complain that Curtis batted only .259 in his first season.

Though his average was on the mediocre side, Curtis displayed a number of assets last season. The rookie showed surprisingly good judgement at the plate, walking 51 times in 441 at-bats while recording just 71 strikeouts. His power was deceiving; though Curtis is only 5'10" and 180 pounds, he turns on the ball well, and surprised a lot of people by hitting 10 home runs. A ground-ball hitter, he was able to use his outstanding speed to leg out a lot of hits.

There were some holes in his game, to be sure. Curtis likes to look for a pitch he can handle, and he was far better when ahead in the count (.360) than behind in it (.226). Like a lot of rookies, he struggled in the clutch, batting only .226 with runners in scoring position. On the whole, however, his performance was very satisfying.

BASERUNNING:

Extremely fast, Curtis has stolen as many as 63 bases in a season. His 43 steals as an Angel rookie ranked eighth in the American League, and he should get better with experience. Curtis is extremely aggressive and will take the extra base with consistency.

FIELDING:

Curtis led the American League in outfield assists with 16, but his arm is not all that powerful. He's a converted third baseman, and his strong points are accuracy and the ability to get rid of the ball quickly. He played all three outfield positions last year, but his future appears to be in left field. Curtis' great speed should help him there.

OVERALL:

Curtis was probably the Angels' most successful newcomer since Wally Joyner. With his assets -- a little power, great speed, a terrific work ethic -- he appears to have a solid future.

Overall Statistics

	G	AB	R	H	D	T	HR	RBI	SB	BB	SO	AVG
1992	139	441	59	114	16	2	10	46	43	51	71	.259
Career	139	441	59	114	16	2	10	46	43	51	71	.259

Where He Hits the Ball

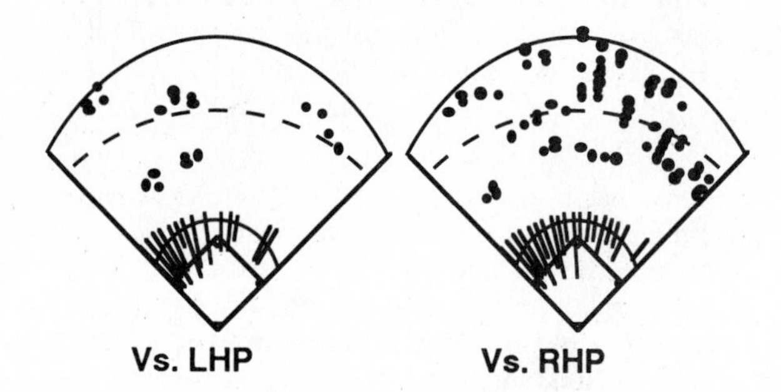

1992 Situational Stats

	AB	H	HR	RBI	AVG		AB	H	HR	RBI	AVG
Home	201	53	5	20	.264	LHP	122	33	6	22	.270
Road	240	61	5	26	.254	RHP	319	81	4	24	.254
Day	111	24	3	11	.216	Sc Pos	106	24	4	38	.226
Night	330	90	7	35	.273	Clutch	76	18	2	5	.237

1992 Rankings (American League)

- 1st in outfield assists (16)
- 2nd in caught stealing (18)
- Led the Angels in walks (51), slugging percentage (.372), on-base average (.341), HR frequency (44.1 ABs per HR), pitches seen per plate appearance (3.71), batting average with the bases loaded (.444), slugging percentage vs. left-handed pitchers (.484), on-base average vs. left-handed pitchers (.393), highest percentage of pitches taken (55.8%) and outfield assists
- Led AL right fielders in stolen bases (43), caught stealing, batting average on an 0-2 count (.278), steals of third (6) and outfield assists

GARY DiSARCINA

Position: SS
Bats: R **Throws:** R
Ht: 6' 1" **Wt:** 178

Opening Day Age: 25
Born: 11/19/67 in Malden, MA
ML Seasons: 4

HITTING:

DiSarcina symbolized the Angels' commitment to youth last year. Handed the shortstop job, the youngster wound up playing 157 games, most for any American League shortstop this side of Cal Ripken. In the end, DiSarcina's season was good enough to offer hope, but not good enough to forget about some concerns with his bat.

Right now, DiSarcina's biggest problem at the plate is his lack of patience. Like a lot of young hitters who love the fastball, he likes to jump on the first pitch, and he had good results when he put it in play (.327 last year). But doing that, he fell behind on a lot of counts, and then he was in trouble (.190). As one would expect from a rookie, DiSarcina also walked infrequently: just 20 times in over 550 plate appearances for an on-base percentage of just .283.

DiSarcina is a slap hitter who likes the ball out over the plate. He had problems in the clutch last year, hitting only .229 with runners in scoring position and a horrible .132 (12-for-91) in the late innings of close games.

BASERUNNING:

DiSarcina once stole 16 bases at Edmonton, but his speed is not exceptional. He legged out only 19 doubles and had no triples last year; he also grounded into 15 double plays. He swiped nine of 16 in '92 and has the potential to do a little, though not a lot, better.

FIELDING:

Although DiSarcina tied for the league lead in shortstop errors, the Angels liked his glove work. His range is better than average (he was second in the majors in assists) and he turns the double play sharply. His hands are soft and his instincts equal to or better than Dick Schofield's.

OVERALL:

DiSarcina had a decent enough rookie year, but he'll need to improve if he wants to be more than just an average player. His defense should keep him in the lineup for awhile; his bat work, though, needs a lot of polish. By protecting DiSarcina in the expansion draft, the Angels showed their expectations that he will improve.

Overall Statistics

	G	AB	R	H	D	T	HR	RBI	SB	BB	SO	AVG
1992	157	518	48	128	19	0	3	42	9	20	50	.247
Career	195	632	61	148	22	1	3	45	10	26	64	.234

Where He Hits the Ball

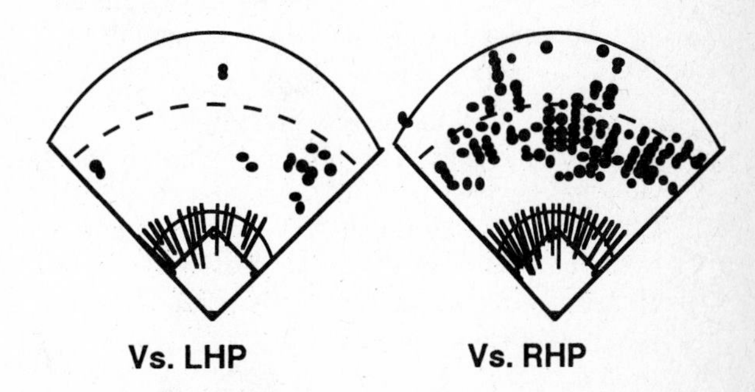

1992 Situational Stats

	AB	H	HR	RBI	AVG		AB	H	HR	RBI	AVG
Home	251	59	2	25	.235	LHP	114	26	0	4	.228
Road	267	69	1	17	.258	RHP	404	102	3	38	.252
Day	144	35	2	12	.243	Sc Pos	118	27	0	36	.229
Night	374	93	1	30	.249	Clutch	91	12	1	7	.132

1992 Rankings (American League)

- 1st in lowest slugging percentage (.301), lowest on-base percentage (.283) and lowest batting average in the clutch (.132)
- 2nd in least pitches seen per plate appearance (3.12)
- Led the Angels in hit by pitch (7), games played (157) and highest percentage of swings put into play (55.1%)
- Led AL shortstops in hit by pitch, GDPs (15), errors (25) and highest percentage of swings put into play

HITTING:

As a selection in the 30th round of the draft, which Damion Easley was, the odds against appearing in the big leagues are pretty high. Those odds for him become even higher considering his team has a high-priced free agent (Gary Gaetti) at his position. So don't pinch Easley and ruin his unlikely trip to Anaheim Stadium.

Easley played pretty well when called up to replace the injured Rene Gonzales last August 12. But after a good start, he struggled. Like several of his teammates, Easley has a poor grasp of the strike zone, walking just eight times in 165 plate appearances while striking out 26 times. He is a dead fastball hitter: he batted .333 on the first pitch and .447 (17-for-38) when ahead in the count, but only .140 (7-for-50) when behind.

Those numbers raise the question of whether Easley can hit major league breaking stuff well enough to make it. The jury is definitely out. Easley has never batted .300 at any level, even in hit-happy Edmonton. He has little home run power. He's not much of a groundball hitter, so he isn't taking full advantage of his speed. In the NBA, they'd call him a "project."

BASERUNNING:

Easley was successful in a decent, but not awe-inspiring, nine of 14 stolen base attempts. He should do better with his great speed. Easley has the potential to swipe 30 or more.

FIELDING:

Easley is a fine athlete, but has yet to settle at one position. Originally a center fielder, he was shifted to shortstop with good results. But with Gary DiSarcina blocking the way, the Angels moved Easley to third, and again he played well. He is blessed with great reaction speed and a fine arm.

OVERALL:

Easley did reasonably well in his Angel trial last year. However, he is powerless at a traditionally power-laden position. There are also huge questions about his ability to hit for average. However, the Angels protected him in the expansion draft; they hope he can be their regular third baseman.

DAMION EASLEY

Position: 3B
Bats: R **Throws:** R
Ht: 5'11" **Wt:** 155

Opening Day Age: 23
Born: 11/11/69 in New York, NY
ML Seasons: 1

Overall Statistics

	G	AB	R	H	D	T	HR	RBI	SB	BB	SO	AVG
1992	47	151	14	39	5	0	1	12	9	8	26	.258
Career	47	151	14	39	5	0	1	12	9	8	26	.258

Where He Hits the Ball

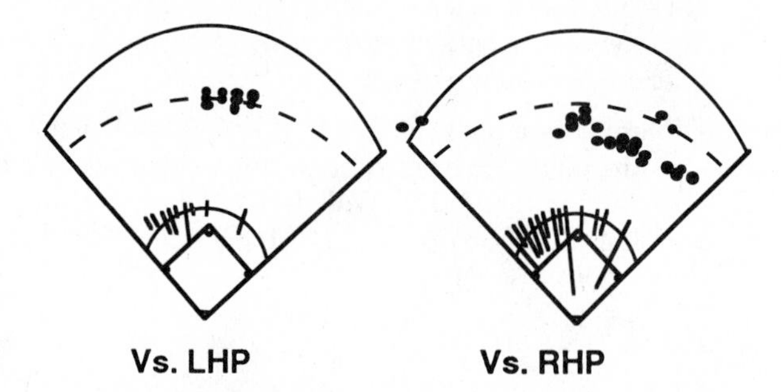

1992 Situational Stats

	AB	H	HR	RBI	AVG		AB	H	HR	RBI	AVG
Home	67	18	1	6	.269	LHP	36	10	0	3	.278
Road	84	21	0	6	.250	RHP	115	29	1	9	.252
Day	36	6	1	4	.167	Sc Pos	34	9	1	12	.265
Night	115	33	0	8	.287	Clutch	34	8	1	4	.235

1992 Rankings (American League)

→ Did not rank near the top or bottom in any category

PITCHING:

An All-Star pitcher who'd gone 52-27 from 1989 through 1991, Chuck Finley had a tough, injury-racked season in 1992. The lefthander needed a good second half (5-3, 2.74 ERA) to boost his final figures to 7-12, 3.96. However, Finley pitched a lot better than his record indicates. Lack of support plagued him. Even with all his early struggles, Finley's final ERA was only marginally higher than in 1991 (3.80), when he went 18-9.

At the start of the season, Finley was out with a toe injury which was exceptionally slow to heal. When he returned to the rotation in late April, it was obvious he was still hurting. At the All-Star break he was 2-9 with a 5.44 ERA, but by then he was returning to health. His monthly ERAs from May onward show his progress: 6.12, 5.35, 3.67, 2.87, 2.42. By season's end, he was obviously the Finley of old.

Finley doesn't have one best pitch. He's able to get people out with either his fastball, curve, slider, split-finger or change-up. He will throw any of them at any time. Control is sometimes a problem for Finley, who was among the league leaders with 98 walks allowed. A big man at 6'6" and 214 pounds, he needs to push off on his left foot to get good velocity. When the big toe on that foot was hurting, he wasn't the same pitcher.

FIELDING AND HOLDING RUNNERS:

Finley has always had a lot of baserunners attempting to run on him. But in '92, as with the past couple years, they had only marginal success. Last year 18 of the 39 who tried were tossed out -- a solid mark. On defense, Finley is erratic, with good range but questionable judgment and an erratic throwing arm.

OVERALL:

With three lefty starters, the Angels have considered trading Finley, but his big, long-term contract (through 1995) makes him difficult to deal. If he stays with California, there's no reason why he can't be a big winner again. When healthy, he's one of the best lefties in the AL.

CHUCK FINLEY

Position: SP
Bats: L **Throws:** L
Ht: 6' 6" **Wt:** 214

Opening Day Age: 30
Born: 11/26/62 in Monroe, LA
ML Seasons: 7

Overall Statistics

	W	L	ERA	G	GS	Sv	IP	H	R	BB	SO	HR
1992	7	12	3.96	31	31	0	204.1	212	99	98	124	24
Career	73	62	3.45	217	160	0	1198.2	1131	508	510	839	101

How Often He Throws Strikes

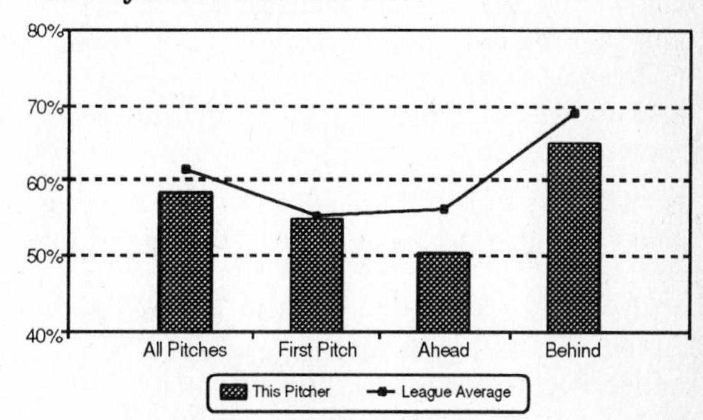

1992 Situational Stats

	W	L	ERA	Sv	IP		AB	H	HR	RBI	AVG
Home	3	5	3.93	0	105.1	LHB	87	35	1	9	.402
Road	4	7	4.00	0	99.0	RHB	675	177	23	79	.262
Day	1	3	5.04	0	64.1	Sc Pos	198	44	5	62	.222
Night	6	9	3.47	0	140.0	Clutch	62	15	2	6	.242

1992 Rankings (American League)

- 1st in runners caught stealing (18) and highest on-base percentage allowed (.359)
- 2nd in most baserunners allowed per 9 innings (13.8) and most GDPs induced per 9 innings (1.2)
- 3rd highest batting average allowed (.278)
- Led the Angels in hits allowed (212), home runs allowed (24), walks allowed (98), wild pitches (6), stolen bases allowed (21), runners caught stealing, GDPs induced (28), most GDPs induced per 9 innings, most GDPs induced per GDP situation (17.1%) and lowest batting average allowed with runners in scoring position (.225)

PITCHING:

After a poor year for the Expos in 1991, Steve Frey resurrected himself with a solid season for the 1992 Angels. The 5'9" lefthander, who followed his former Montreal manager Buck Rodgers to Anaheim, adapted to the American League strike zone very well. Frey posted a 3.57 ERA along with some other impressive figures while appearing in 51 games.

Frey began the season as a set-up man under Rodgers, but his role changed after the bus wreck that sidelined his boss. Replacement manager John Wathan used Frey as more of a long reliever. Once Rodgers returned on August 28, Frey went back to a set-up/closer role and gave up just one run in his last 10 appearances. Tough in the clutch, Frey held opponents to a .127 average (7-for-55) with runners in scoring position. He also allowed only five of 50 inherited runners to score, the second-best ratio in the majors.

Frey throws a fastball, curve, slider and an occasional change-up. He relies almost entirely on the curve -- a hard breaking pitch that is murder on lefthanders. They hit just .189 against Frey, though five of the six homers he allowed were to lefties. Righties had success waiting on the curveball and working deeper into the count. His control is good; his walk totals are inflated by the fact that he seems to lose batters on purpose rather than grooving his less-than-impressive fastball.

FIELDING AND HOLDING RUNNERS:

Frey is a very good fielder and helps himself out a lot with the glove. He allowed only three steals in six attempts, but his move is not considered good. As a lefty, he could help himself by developing the move further.

OVERALL:

Frey's career seems in good hands with Rodgers, who appears to know how to handle him effectively. But it is worth noting that Frey is on the frail side, and has had problems remaining effective over long stretches. He had a 1.44 ERA before the break last year, 8.36 afterward.

STEVE FREY

Position: RP
Bats: R **Throws:** L
Ht: 5' 9" **Wt:** 170

Opening Day Age: 29
Born: 7/29/63 in Southampton, PA
ML Seasons: 4

Overall Statistics

	W	L	ERA	G	GS	Sv	IP	H	R	BB	SO	HR
1992	4	2	3.57	51	0	4	45.1	39	18	22	24	6
Career	15	7	3.67	153	0	14	162.0	155	79	85	89	17

How Often He Throws Strikes

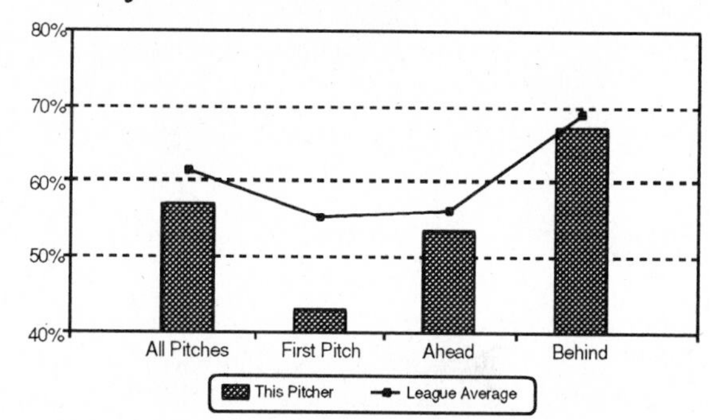

1992 Situational Stats

	W	L	ERA	Sv	IP		AB	H	HR	RBI	AVG
Home	2	1	3.00	2	21.0	LHB	53	10	5	8	.189
Road	2	1	4.07	2	24.1	RHB	111	29	1	9	.261
Day	3	0	2.55	3	17.2	Sc Pos	55	7	1	10	.127
Night	1	2	4.23	1	27.2	Clutch	77	18	1	5	.234

1992 Rankings (American League)

- 2nd in lowest percentage of inherited runners scored (10.0%)
- Led the Angels in first batter efficiency (.233) and lowest percentage of inherited runners scored

GARY GAETTI

Position: 3B/1B/DH
Bats: R **Throws:** R
Ht: 6' 0" **Wt:** 200

Opening Day Age: 34
Born: 8/19/58 in Centralia, IL
ML Seasons: 12

HITTING:

After two seasons, the Angels' Gary Gaetti experiment ranks up there with "Ishtar" and "Heaven's Gate" as a Southern California debacle. Though Gaetti managed to lead the Angels with 12 home runs last year, that was the second- lowest total of his career. His .226 average and 48 RBI were career lows. Things got so bad last year that Gaetti's disappointing 1991 figures (.246-18-66) began to look positively Cooperstown-like.

Gaetti did nothing right at the plate in 1992. He seemed uncomfortable in the batter's box and unsure of the strike zone. He walked just 21 times in 486 plate appearances. Gaetti likes the fastball and will jump on it, but with increasingly meager results. He hit only .224 when he put the first pitch in play last year, about 80 points below the major league average.

Gaetti used to handle righthanders pretty well, but he now seems overmatched against them (.217 last year). His .250 average against lefties was a result of a dead-pull attitude. Against righties, Gaetti will stay back on the ball but no longer has the required bat speed.

BASERUNNING:

Gary Gaetti once stole as many as 14 stolen bases in a season, but those days are long gone. He swiped only three last year, his lowest total in 10 years. To be fair, Gaetti is still mobile up the first base line, especially as third basemen go. He grounded into just nine double plays.

FIELDING:

A four-time Gold Glove winner at third (1986-89) Gaetti no longer fields his position very well. His range is now only a little above average, if that, and his fielding average last year (.926) was a career low by plenty. The Angels finally shifted him to first base, a position he is still learning.

OVERALL:

By all accounts, Gary Gaetti is a heck of a guy. But his baseball skills are leaving him the way most people leave a dentist's office. He's signed through 1994, meaning the Angels will probably keep him around, but Gaetti's future is in serious doubt.

Overall Statistics

	G	AB	R	H	D	T	HR	RBI	SB	BB	SO	AVG
1992	130	456	41	103	13	2	12	48	3	21	79	.226
Career	1643	6031	745	1523	287	28	231	872	82	412	1060	.253

Where He Hits the Ball

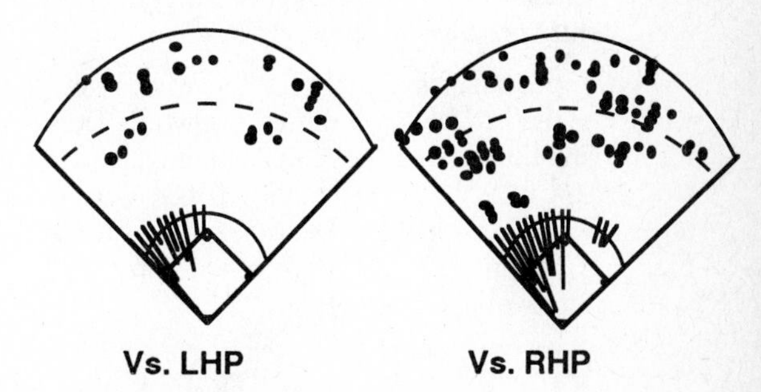

1992 Situational Stats

	AB	H	HR	RBI	AVG		AB	H	HR	RBI	AVG
Home	231	60	8	30	.260	LHP	124	31	5	15	.250
Road	225	43	4	18	.191	RHP	332	72	7	33	.217
Day	129	28	4	26	.217	Sc Pos	112	28	3	35	.250
Night	327	75	8	22	.229	Clutch	87	20	1	10	.230

1992 Rankings (American League)

- 1st in lowest cleanup slugging percentage (.324) and lowest percentage of pitches taken (40.4%)
- Led the Angels in home runs (12), errors at first base (5) and errors at third base (17)

RENE GONZALES

Position: 3B/1B/2B
Bats: R **Throws:** R
Ht: 6' 3" **Wt:** 195

Opening Day Age: 31
Born: 9/3/61 in Austin, TX
ML Seasons: 8

Overall Statistics

	G	AB	R	H	D	T	HR	RBI	SB	BB	SO	AVG
1992	104	329	47	91	17	1	7	38	7	41	46	.277
Career	482	1069	125	249	36	3	13	91	16	97	167	.233

Where He Hits the Ball

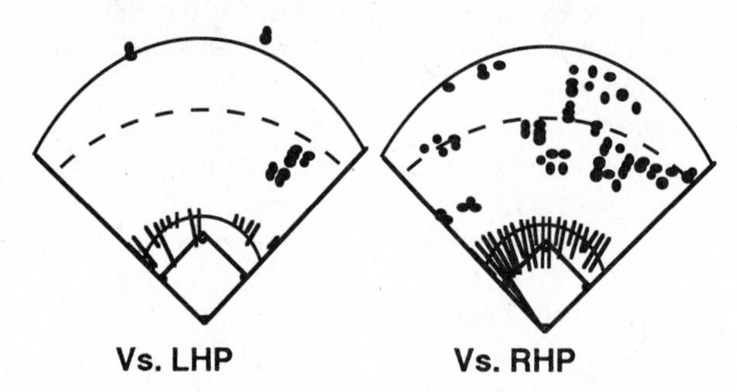

1992 Situational Stats

	AB	H	HR	RBI	AVG		AB	H	HR	RBI	AVG
Home	168	50	6	24	.298	LHP	71	19	3	11	.268
Road	161	41	1	14	.255	RHP	258	72	4	27	.279
Day	106	28	2	13	.264	Sc Pos	65	21	3	33	.323
Night	223	63	5	25	.283	Clutch	52	10	1	6	.192

1992 Rankings (American League)

- 1st in most GDPs per GDP situation (25.4%)
- Led the Angels in GDPs (17) and highest batting average on a 3-2 count (.276)

HITTING:

Before he went down for the season in August with a broken forearm, Rene Gonzales was one of the surprise stories of 1992. Gonzales hit more home runs (seven) in his 329 at-bats last year than he had in his previous seven seasons in the majors combined (six). His .277 average was 63 points higher than his career average. And he remained hot until the premature end to his season.

Prior to last season, Gonzales had only seen significant time with a wretched 1988 Baltimore Oriole squad, when he hit .215 with two homers in 237 at-bats. After being released by the Blue Jays after the '91 season, Gonzales bulked up in the off-season with buddy (and fellow surprise) Brady Anderson. The result was the Angels' most consistently productive player of 1992.

Everything Gonzales did right last year was new. He drove the ball better and used the whole field for the first time. He displayed excellent power to straight-away left and up the alleys. A line drive hitter, Gonzales suddenly found a way to hit the breaking ball in '92. He made more consistent contact and walked more often.

BASERUNNING:

Not a fast man, Gonzales relies on surprise to steal a base, which he did seven times in 11 attempts last year. However, he gets out of the box slowly. He was worst in the majors in grounding into double plays per double play situation.

FIELDING:

Even at his hottest, neither Buck Rodgers nor John Wathan appeared to know where to play Gonzales. His best position is probably third base, which he played adequately in '92. He is a smart fielder with better range to his left. Overall, his range isn't great and he can make throwing errors in bunches. He played decently at second and first base.

OVERALL:

To say Gonzales surprised last year is a huge understatement. He'll have to show he can do it again, and his position in the field is a question mark. Third base is his best, but second or even first base are possibilities. As a free agent, his versatility could help a team.

PITCHING:

Joe Grahe saved his career by the greatest of fortunes. After starting the 1992 season in the Angels' rotation, Grahe was bombed repeatedly (2-3, 5.90) and sent to the minors in early May. It was the third straight year he had flubbed a shot at a starting role, and some people thought he'd never get another one.

Then fate intervened, in the form of a mishap to another pitcher. Angel relief ace Bryan Harvey hurt his elbow, and eventually was lost for the season. Recalled to the big club, Grahe was sent to the bullpen. Then, given a save opportunity on June 11 against Chicago, he converted. That was just the beginning. By the end of the season, Grahe would convert 21 of 24 opportunities and become a certified finisher in his own right. As a reliever, Grahe's ERA was 1.80, and he allowed just 40 hits and 57 baserunners in 55 innings. Only three of the 18 runners that he inherited came around to score -- an outstanding number.

Grahe has traditionally relied on three pitches -- fastball, curve and slider -- along with an occasional change-up. He got into trouble by throwing the fastball exclusively when behind in the count. As a reliever, though, he began getting his curveball over and spotting his pitches perfectly. While some believed Grahe returned with more heat on the fastball, the difference was probably mastery of the curve.

HOLDING RUNNERS AND FIELDING:

Grahe is a good fielder and is getting better at holding runners. Five of the 12 who tried to run against him last year were caught. He no longer loses concentration with men on base -- another big reason for his success as a reliever.

OVERALL:

Grahe's future, so bleak early in 1992, now appears much brighter. But one area of concern is his low strikeout total. He fanned only 22 men in his 55 relief innings last year, and there are very few successful relievers with those kind of numbers. Will he continue to succeed as a closer, or is he better suited for a set-up role? It's an open question.

JOE GRAHE

Position: RP/SP
Bats: R **Throws:** R
Ht: 6' 0" **Wt:** 200

Opening Day Age: 25
Born: 8/14/67 in West Palm Beach, FL
ML Seasons: 3

Overall Statistics

	W	L	ERA	G	GS	Sv	IP	H	R	BB	SO	HR
1992	5	6	3.52	46	7	21	94.2	85	37	39	39	5
Career	11	17	4.27	72	25	21	211.0	220	110	95	104	10

How Often He Throws Strikes

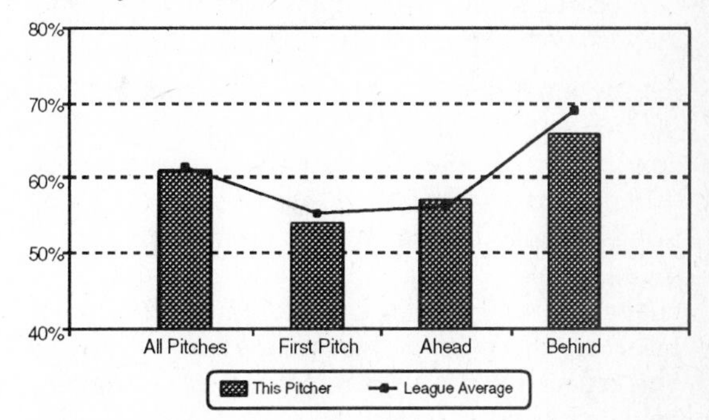

1992 Situational Stats

	W	L	ERA	Sv	IP		AB	H	HR	RBI	AVG
Home	2	4	3.94	14	45.2	LHB	157	45	1	14	.287
Road	3	2	3.12	7	49.0	RHB	189	40	4	23	.212
Day	2	2	2.88	8	34.1	Sc Pos	89	22	2	32	.247
Night	3	4	3.88	13	60.1	Clutch	150	30	2	12	.200

1992 Rankings (American League)

- 4th in highest save percentage (87.5%) and lowest relief ERA (1.80)
- 5th in least baserunners allowed per 9 innings in relief (9.7)
- 6th in least strikeouts per 9 innings in relief (3.6)
- Led the Angels in saves (21), games finished (31), hit batsmen (6), save opportunities (24), save percentage, relief ERA, lowest batting average allowed in relief (.205) and least baserunners allowed per 9 innings in relief

PITCHING:

Mark Langston followed up his Cy Young-level 1991 season with a solid, if unspectacular, 1992. He came out of the gate by winning five of his first six decisions. He finished by winning just two games after August 12, but was pitching better than he did early in the season. Closing the season in his usual strong fashion, Langston posted a 2.69 ERA after August 1.

The oft-maligned lefthander has now reached the 220-inning mark for seven consecutive years, and is a safe bet to do so again in 1993. Langston's pitching style has never changed: power most of the way, mixed in with a respectable breaking ball. He has had trouble with control in the past, but has reduced his walk total from 112 in '89 to 104, 96 and 74 the last three years.

As his innings totals suggest, Langston has remained virtually injury-free over his career. Despite throwing over 11,000 pitches over the past three years, his fastball has lost very little. Langston also has an excellent curveball with a nice, quick break, a good slider, and a fine change-up which he masks with good arm speed. His stuff is effective against all kinds of hitters, but especially deadly against lefties. Langston held left-handed hitters to a .173 average last year, and a .199 mark over the last five.

FIELDING AND HOLDING RUNNERS:

Langston remains among the top fielding pitchers in the American League. His delivery and follow-through help him come off the mound in a good fielding position. He has historically had good success holding runners, but struggled a bit in this area last year. He permitted 21 steals in 31 attempts last year.

OVERALL:

At 32, Langston is one of the few pitchers in baseball capable of shouldering a big workload year after year without breaking down. Though his strikeout totals have been declining since he fanned 262 batters for the '87 Mariners, he remains a power pitcher, and an extremely effective one. If the Angels ever improve their offense, Langston is a good candidate to win 20 games.

MARK LANGSTON

Position: SP
Bats: R **Throws:** L
Ht: 6' 2" **Wt:** 184

Opening Day Age: 32
Born: 8/20/60 in San Diego, CA
ML Seasons: 9

Overall Statistics

	W	L	ERA	G	GS	Sv	IP	H	R	BB	SO	HR
1992	13	14	3.66	32	32	0	229.0	206	103	74	174	14
Career	128	115	3.75	299	296	0	2072.2	1817	965	942	1805	203

How Often He Throws Strikes

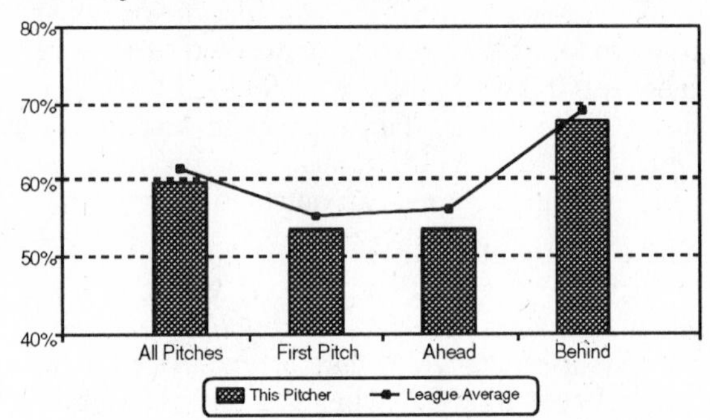

1992 Situational Stats

	W	L	ERA	Sv	IP		AB	H	HR	RBI	AVG
Home	9	7	3.61	0	132.0	LHB	110	19	2	12	.173
Road	4	7	3.71	0	97.0	RHB	742	187	12	71	.252
Day	3	1	3.70	0	56.0	Sc Pos	170	48	2	64	.282
Night	10	13	3.64	0	173.0	Clutch	115	24	2	9	.209

1992 Rankings (American League)

- 1st in pickoffs (11)
- 3rd in pickoff throws (262) and lowest run support per 9 innings (3.7)
- Led the Angels in wins (13), games started (32), complete games (9), shutouts (2), innings pitched (229), batters faced (941), hit batsmen (6), strikeouts (174), pitches thrown (3,456), stolen bases allowed (21), winning percentage (.481), highest strikeout/walk ratio (2.4), lowest batting average allowed (.242), lowest slugging percentage allowed (.343), lowest on-base percentage allowed (.305), least baserunners allowed per 9 innings (11.2) and strikeouts per 9 innings (6.8)

HITTING:

The Angels acquired Toronto's Greg Myers, along with Rob Ducey, in a midseason trade for reliever Mark Eichhorn. The idea was to shore up a weak offense by adding a left-handed bat behind the plate. Unfortunately, Myers quickly came up injured. He arrived on July 31 and, after eight games in August with California, went out for the season with bone chips in his right wrist. He had only 78 at-bats all year, hitting only .231 with a single home run.

When healthy, Myers is strictly used against right-handed pitchers; he has never started a game versus a lefthander, and is 11-for-66, .167, against southpaws over the last five years. He was an effective platoon player for the Blue Jays in 1991, batting .262 with eight homers in only 309 at-bats.

Although the Angels saw very little of him, Myers has good power to right field and can hit the breaking ball, though he is primarily a fastball hitter. He stands well off the plate and has never been hit by a pitch during his major league career. Myers doesn't walk much, and he's always been prone to the double play ball, though he grounded into only two last year.

BASERUNNING:

Myers has never stolen a base in the major leagues, but he's attempted only two. As his double play figures show (31 in 690 at-bats), he's very slow. However, he hustles on the basepaths and has just enough to take the extra base.

FIELDING:

Behind the plate is a problem area. While Myers cut down on his errors in '92, people run on him without fear. He is slow to come out of his crouch and his arm isn't very strong. He does not have a reputation for calling a particularly good game behind the plate.

OVERALL:

The Angels' catching situation is a mess. As it stands, Myers has the best bat of the lot and may end up as part of a platoon -- the most ambitious role he could hope for, given his struggles against lefthanders. Myers was available in the expansion draft, but was not selected, while counterpart John Orton was protected by the Angels.

GREG MYERS

Position: C
Bats: L **Throws:** R
Ht: 6' 2" **Wt:** 205

Opening Day Age: 26
Born: 4/14/66 in Riverside, CA
ML Seasons: 5

Overall Statistics

	G	AB	R	H	D	T	HR	RBI	SB	BB	SO	AVG
1992	30	78	4	18	7	0	1	13	0	5	11	.231
Career	248	690	63	164	38	1	14	72	0	50	101	.238

Where He Hits the Ball

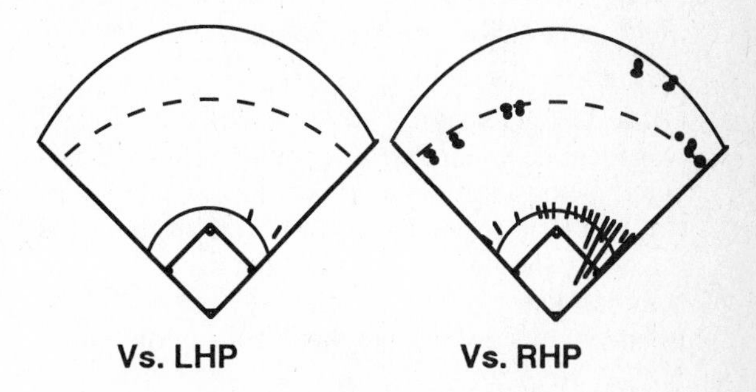

1992 Situational Stats

	AB	H	HR	RBI	AVG		AB	H	HR	RBI	AVG
Home	32	9	0	6	.281	LHP	5	0	0	0	.000
Road	46	9	1	7	.196	RHP	73	18	1	13	.247
Day	20	5	0	5	.250	Sc Pos	22	6	1	12	.273
Night	58	13	1	8	.224	Clutch	11	3	0	3	.273

1992 Rankings (American League)

- Did not rank near the top or bottom in any category

JOHN ORTON

Position: C
Bats: R **Throws:** R
Ht: 6' 1" **Wt:** 192

Opening Day Age: 27
Born: 12/8/65 in Santa Cruz, CA
ML Seasons: 4

Overall Statistics

	G	AB	R	H	D	T	HR	RBI	SB	BB	SO	AVG
1992	43	114	11	25	3	0	2	12	1	7	32	.219
Career	119	306	30	62	13	0	3	25	1	24	97	.203

Where He Hits the Ball

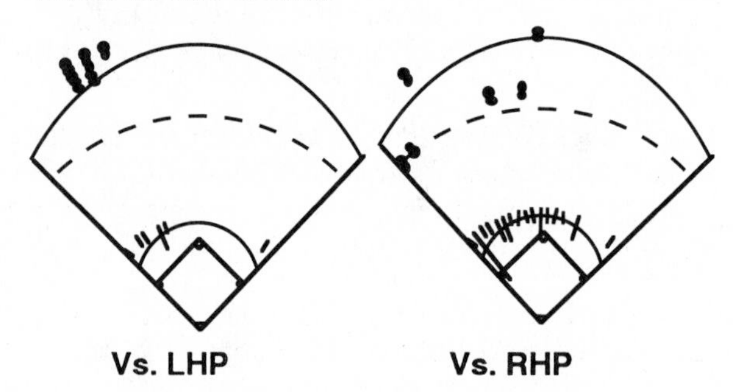

1992 Situational Stats

	AB	H	HR	RBI	AVG		AB	H	HR	RBI	AVG
Home	71	16	1	6	.225	LHP	25	3	1	5	.120
Road	43	9	1	6	.209	RHP	89	22	1	7	.247
Day	29	5	0	4	.172	Sc Pos	25	6	1	11	.240
Night	85	20	2	8	.235	Clutch	9	1	0	0	.111

1992 Rankings (American League)

- Did not rank near the top or bottom in any category

HITTING:

The Angels have been waiting for John Orton to develop since they drafted him in the first round in 1987. The wait was supposed to be over last year when the club let go of Lance Parrish in June to open up some playing time for the young catcher. Unfortunately, Orton didn't seize the opportunity, battling injury and hitting only .219.

Orton's average was a career high, which says something about the way he's struggled with the bat. Though he's not a power hitter (three homers in 306 lifetime at-bats), he's struck out in about one-third of his career at-bats. Attempts to shorten his swing have failed, and he looks as if every curveball is the first one he's overseen. Along with his low average, he doesn't walk much; his career on-base average is a terrible .269.

Orton began last year at AAA Edmonton, then was recalled when Parrish got hurt in June. Basically handed the starting position at that point (Parrish was soon released), Orton strained his throwing shoulder in early July and went on the disabled list. He hit a little better after returning in late August (.250), but that's not saying much.

BASERUNNING:

Not horribly slow, Orton stole his first major league base in 1992 (he was also caught once). His speed is not bad once he gets going, and he's a threat to move from first to third on a single.

FIELDING:

This is Orton's forte. He possesses a cannon arm, although he only threw out 12 of 34 opposing runners last year, and he also has a reputation for calling an excellent game behind the plate. He did make five errors, however, and still rushes his throws a bit. Nonetheless, he is easily the best of the Angels' defensive backstops.

OVERALL:

The Angels aren't exactly overloaded with great catchers, so Orton should get his best opportunity to play next year. But the attitude at Anaheim Stadium has changed from anticipation to impatience. He's running out of chances, but the Angels will give him at least one more shot. He was on their expansion protection list.

HITTING:

Luis Polonia has developed into a respectable leadoff batter who could provide real spark to a good offense. Unfortunately for him, the Angel offense doesn't quite meet that description. California's poor 1992 season was hardly the fault of Polonia, who led the league's worst attack in both batting (.286) and runs scored (83).

A lefthander who gave up switch-hitting several years ago, Polonia's biggest drawback is his inability to hit lefties (.227 last year). This is nothing new, and the Angels sometimes sit himdown with a southpaw pitching. Against either righties or lefties, Polonia is a slap hitter with negligible power. He has learned to hit down on the ball and is the beneficiary of many infield hits.

Polonia has never walked much, which is the main reason he can't be rated among the top leadoff men. He has improved significantly, however. He's walked 52 and 45 times the last two seasons, after totaling only 50 bases on balls in 1989-90 combined.

BASERUNNING:

Polonia has become a prolific basestealer over the last two seasons, swiping 48 and then 51 last season. But he still gets caught stealing too much -- a league-high 21 times last year. Polonia's follies on the basepaths used to make him an American League rival to Lonnie Smith, but he's improved in that area of his game.

FIELDING:

Polonia is still a poor fielder. His arm is weak, and his range in left field has never improved from his rookie year. His adventures in the outfield still rival Disneyland as the most exciting attraction in Anaheim. With Curtis, Felix and Salmon on hand to man the outfield, Polonia might be used more as a designated hitter. He seems to like the job, batting .314 in 188 at-bats as a DH last year.

OVERALL:

Polonia was surprisingly left unprotected in the expansion draft. The Angels took a gamble that his high salary would discourage a draft pick, and won. Polonia fought off numerous injuries in '92 and has become a real fan favorite. Polonia still has some rough edges, but California is more than happy with him.

LUIS POLONIA

Position: LF/DH
Bats: L **Throws:** L
Ht: 5' 8" **Wt:** 150

Opening Day Age: 28
Born: 10/12/64 in Santiago City, Dominican Republic
ML Seasons: 6

Overall Statistics

	G	AB	R	H	D	T	HR	RBI	SB	BB	SO	AVG
1992	149	577	83	165	17	4	0	35	51	45	64	.286
Career	753	2740	426	818	96	41	13	242	195	200	329	.299

Where He Hits the Ball

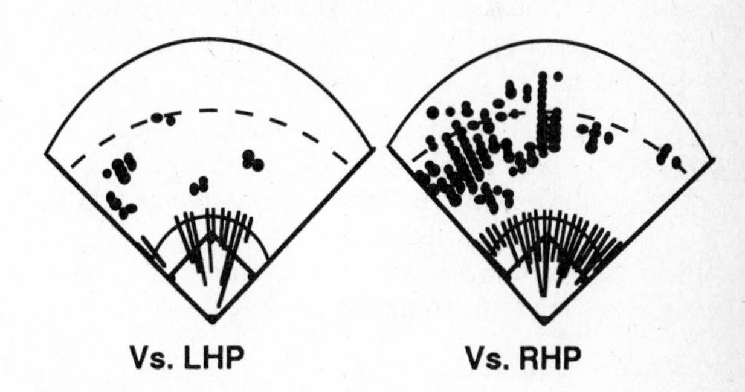

1992 Situational Stats

	AB	H	HR	RBI	AVG		AB	H	HR	RBI	AVG
Home	266	76	0	19	.286	LHP	132	30	0	5	.227
Road	311	89	0	16	.286	RHP	445	135	0	30	.303
Day	167	47	0	9	.281	Sc Pos	99	30	0	35	.303
Night	410	118	0	26	.288	Clutch	87	25	0	8	.287

1992 Rankings (American League)

- 1st in caught stealing (21), lowest HR frequency (577 ABs with 0 HR) and steals of third (12)
- 2nd in highest groundball/flyball ratio (2.51), lowest slugging percentage vs. left-handed pitchers (.250) and picked off base (5)
- Led the Angels in batting average (.286), at-bats (577), runs scored (83), hits (165), singles (144), total bases (190), sacrifice bunts (8), stolen bases (51), caught stealing, intentional walks (6), times on base (211), GDPs (17), pitches seen (2,117), plate appearances (635), highest groundball/flyball ratio, stolen base percentage (70.8%), bunts in play (24) and steals of third

TOP PROSPECT

TIM SALMON

Position: RF
Bats: R **Throws:** R
Ht: 6' 3" **Wt:** 210

Opening Day Age: 24
Born: 8/24/68 in Long Beach, CA
ML Seasons: 1

HITTING:

Who came the closest to a triple crown last season? Gary Sheffield? Not even close. It was Angel super-prospect Tim Salmon, who finished just four batting points away from taking the honor at AAA Edmonton. The Baseball America Minor League Player of the Year has been the recipient of a careful eye from the parent club. California constantly fought the temptation to call up the youngster while the team languished in the second division for the entire year.

Salmon was finally recalled while the Angels were on the road. He made his home debut on the same day that manager Buck Rodgers returned to the team, keeping the media fanfare to a dull roar. Salmon soon hit a 15th inning home run to beat the Cleveland Indians and was hitting respectably until a wrist injury slowed him. He finished the season batting .177 in 79 at-bats.

Analyzing Salmon based on his big league experience is very tough. He looked overmatched at times -- he's always had enormous strikeout totals -- but he also showed a powerful swing. Salmon has always been a patient hitter; he had 102 walks (majors and minors) in '92.

BASERUNNING:

Salmon stole a high of 12 bases at AA Midland in 1991, but is not much of a threat to run. At 6-3, 210, he takes a while to get going, but still has the legs to run out the occasional double or triple.

FIELDING:

Salmon looked uncomfortable in right field and made two errors in very limited time. However, he's regarded as a fine outfielder with a good arm and surprising range for a big man.

OVERALL

A late bloomer, Salmon didn't post home run totals in double figures until 1991, a season in which he hit only .245 at the AA level. He's come a long way in a short time, and will have to handle the pressure that goes with being one of the top prospects in baseball. The ability appears to be there and the Angels are counting on him.

Overall Statistics

	G	AB	R	H	D	T	HR	RBI	SB	BB	SO	AVG
1992	23	79	8	14	1	0	2	6	1	11	23	.177
Career	23	79	8	14	1	0	2	6	1	11	23	.177

Where He Hits the Ball

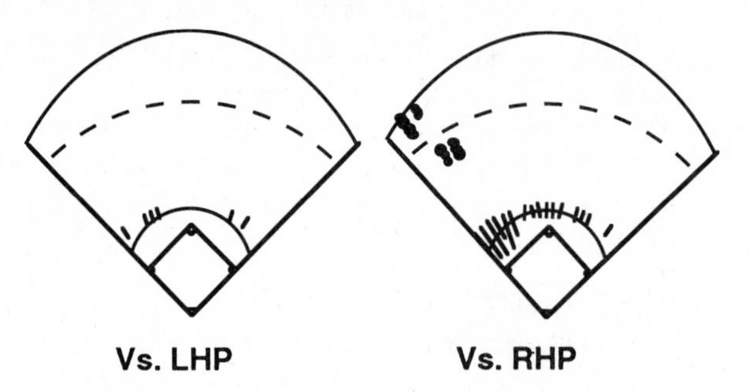

1992 Situational Stats

	AB	H	HR	RBI	AVG		AB	H	HR	RBI	AVG
Home	32	7	1	2	.219	LHP	13	3	1	2	.231
Road	47	7	1	4	.149	RHP	66	11	1	4	.167
Day	8	2	1	3	.250	Sc Pos	21	4	0	4	.190
Night	71	12	1	3	.169	Clutch	19	2	1	2	.105

1992 Rankings (American League)

- Did not rank near the top or bottom in any category

LUIS SOJO

Position: 2B
Bats: R **Throws:** R
Ht: 5'11" **Wt:** 174

Opening Day Age: 27
Born: 1/3/66 in Barquisimeto, Venezuela
ML Seasons: 3

Overall Statistics

	G	AB	R	H	D	T	HR	RBI	SB	BB	SO	AVG
1992	106	368	37	100	12	3	7	43	7	14	24	.272
Career	252	812	89	212	29	4	11	72	12	33	55	.261

Where He Hits the Ball

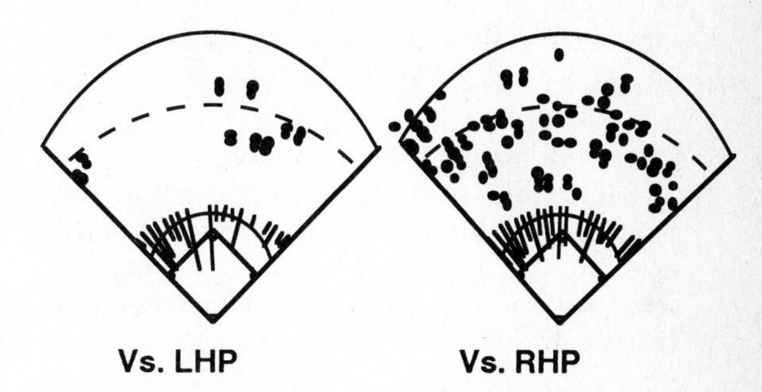

1992 Situational Stats

	AB	H	HR	RBI	AVG		AB	H	HR	RBI	AVG
Home	186	50	2	25	.269	LHP	95	21	0	6	.221
Road	182	50	5	18	.275	RHP	273	79	7	37	.289
Day	106	32	4	17	.302	Sc Pos	90	32	2	38	.356
Night	262	68	3	26	.260	Clutch	64	21	2	10	.328

1992 Rankings (American League)

- 3rd in batting average with runners in scoring position (.356)
- 4th in most GDPs per GDP situation (20.9%) and highest batting average on an 0-2 count (.323)
- Led the Angels in batting average with runners in scoring position (.356), batting average in the clutch (.328) and batting average on an 0-2 count

HITTING:

Luis Sojo started the 1992 season in a place he didn't want to be: at AAA Edmonton. For a while, the young infielder had to bide his time while Bobby Rose and then Rene Gonzales got chances at the Angels' second base job. But after the bus wreck in May which injured several Angel players, including Rose, Sojo was called up and never went back down.

The second sacker batted .272 last year, third-best on the Angels and a career high. In three major league seasons, Sojo has raised his average steadily (.225, .258, .272) while improving in other areas as well. Although he's only 5'11" and 174 pounds, Sojo is stronger than he looks. He had seven homers and 43 RBI in only 368 at-bats last year, and he should be able to reach double figures if given the playing time. He also performed very well in the clutch last year, hitting .356 with runners in scoring position.

Sojo's main weakness is lack of patience. He drew only 14 walks last year, and even in the minors, he never had more than 35. However, he's hardly a wild swinger; he struck out only 24 times last year. Sojo's also one of the best bunters around, extremely dependable in sacrifice situations.

BASERUNNING:

Sojo is not a good basestealer. He stole seven last year -- but in 18 attempts, a terrible percentage. He is not all that fast, but he's wise on the basepaths and will hustle out some doubles and triples.

FIELDING:

Sojo's fielding took a major step forward in '92. He made just seven errors for a .985 fielding percentage. His range is among the best in the American League and he could eventually win a Gold Glove, especially if he improves his steadiness to his left.

OVERALL:

Sojo's '92 season represented a major improvement and gives him the inside track on the starting position for 1993. He'll have to continue to play well to fend off Rene Gonzales because the Angels can't afford many good glove/no stick players.

LEE STEVENS

Position: 1B
Bats: L **Throws:** L
Ht: 6' 4" **Wt:** 219

Opening Day Age: 25
Born: 7/10/67 in Kansas City, MO
ML Seasons: 3

Overall Statistics

	G	AB	R	H	D	T	HR	RBI	SB	BB	SO	AVG
1992	106	312	25	69	19	0	7	37	1	29	64	.221
Career	191	618	61	139	36	0	14	78	3	57	151	.225

Where He Hits the Ball

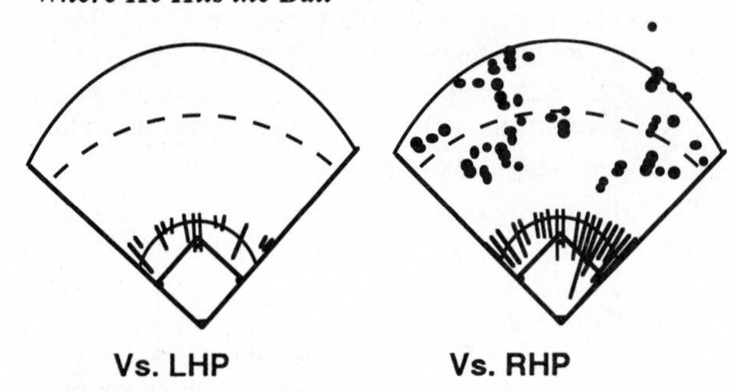

1992 Situational Stats

	AB	H	HR	RBI	AVG		AB	H	HR	RBI	AVG
Home	169	31	2	21	.183	LHP	44	7	0	5	.159
Road	143	38	5	16	.266	RHP	268	62	7	32	.231
Day	90	23	3	11	.256	Sc Pos	72	18	2	29	.250
Night	222	46	4	26	.207	Clutch	51	13	0	3	.255

1992 Rankings (American League)

- 5th in highest batting average on an 0-2 count (.320)
- Led the Angels in intentional walks (6)
- Led AL first basemen in highest batting average on an 0-2 count

HITTING:

A first-round draft choice who starred at each level of the Angels' minor league system, Lee Stevens was a major disappointment last year. Handed the first base job when Wally Joyner departed via free agency, Stevens batted only .221 in his first season in Anaheim. He aroused hopes when he hit .357 while playing part-time in August, but then was the same old struggling Stevens the rest of the year (.222).

Stevens was expected to provide power last year, and messed himself up. He hit six homers in 191 at-bats before the All-Star break, but his average was only .199. After the break Stevens cut down on his swing, and the result was a better average (.256). But he hit only one second-half home run. One could hardly say he was making progress.

As a major leaguer, Stevens has yet to show that he can hit the breaking ball. He is still not good at going with the pitch and often swings on top of the ball. He also seems to have lost his discipline. After compiling good base on balls totals during his minor league career, he had only 23 unintentional walks last season while fanning 64 times in 312 at-bats.

BASERUNNING:

Stevens is not a good baserunner, and is absolutely no threat to run. In a Buck Rodgers type of offense, this may end up hurting him. He is only 3-for-10 stealing in his major league career.

FIELDING:

Stevens improved greatly last year at first base. He does not show the greatest reaction moving toward the line, but is solid once he gets to the ball and has a strong arm. A converted outfielder, he figures to get even better.

OVERALL:

Once the Angels' most heralded prospect, Stevens found his reputation tarnished by his poor season in 1992. Although he was exposed to expansion, the two new teams were not interested. Returning to Anaheim, he'll probably get another chance to prove himself. The Angels desperately need offensive improvement at first base.

PITCHING:

In the midst of an Angel season which saw their team bus wrecked, their manager sidelined and their winning percentage sink, Julio Valera was one of the bright spots. The former Met prospect didn't overwhelm people after coming over in a mid-April trade for Dick Schofield. But Valera turned in a nice, steady effort, posting a fine 3.73 ERA and an 8-11 record that suffered from lack of run support.

Still only 24, Valera was once considered one of the top pitching prospects in the Met system. New York thought so highly of Valera that they brought him up in the heat of the 1990 pennant race to start a crucial game against the Pirates. Valera failed that trial, but probably never would have left New York if it hadn't been for some well-publicized weight problems. Listed at 215 pounds, Valera ballooned to 250-plus in the spring of '91, and that soured New York on his work ethic. The trade may have been a wake-up call, as Valera was slimmer and more dedicated last year.

After one start and a couple of relief appearances following the deal, Valera pushed the struggling Joe Grahe out of the rotation and soon pitched a complete-game five-hitter against the Yankees to solidify his spot. Though a big man, Valera lacks a dominating fastball. His best pitch is an exploding slider, which he uses primarily when ahead in the count. To improve more overall, Valera must learn to keep the slider down and over the plate as a reliable out pitch.

FIELDING AND HOLDING RUNNERS:

Valera tends to be slow to the plate and has a hard time holding runners. Sometimes he forgets about baserunners, and his throws to first are often erratic. He fields his position reasonably well, however.

OVERALL:

The Angels have had trouble developing right-handed pitchers, so Valera's rotation spot seems to be fairly secure. With the trade of one of their three ace lefties almost certain, Valera figures to begin the '93 season as the squad's number-three starter.

JULIO VALERA

Position: SP
Bats: R **Throws:** R
Ht: 6' 2" **Wt:** 215

Opening Day Age: 24
Born: 10/13/68 in San Sebastian, Puerto Rico
ML Seasons: 3

Overall Statistics

	W	L	ERA	G	GS	Sv	IP	H	R	BB	SO	HR
1992	8	11	3.73	30	28	0	188.0	188	82	64	113	15
Career	9	12	3.90	35	31	0	203.0	209	93	75	120	16

How Often He Throws Strikes

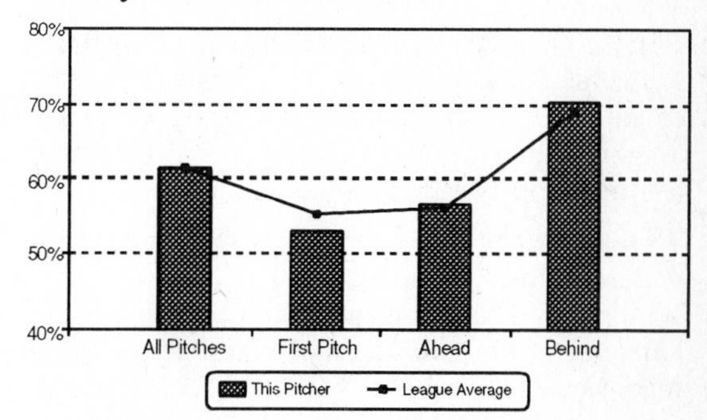

1992 Situational Stats

	W	L	ERA	Sv	IP		AB	H	HR	RBI	AVG
Home	6	3	2.34	0	96.0	LHB	336	98	4	26	.292
Road	2	8	5.18	0	92.0	RHB	382	90	11	43	.236
Day	3	3	2.98	0	60.1	Sc Pos	170	39	1	45	.229
Night	5	8	4.09	0	127.2	Clutch	47	14	0	5	.298

1992 Rankings (American League)

- 2nd in lowest ERA at home (2.34) and highest ERA on the road (5.18)
- 6th in lowest run support per 9 innings (3.9)
- 8th in shutouts (2) and highest stolen base percentage allowed (77.8%)
- Led the Angels in shutouts, highest run support per 9 innings, ERA at home and lowest batting average allowed vs. right-handed hitters (.236)

MIKE BUTCHER

Position: RP
Bats: R **Throws:** R
Ht: 6' 1" **Wt:** 200

Opening Day Age: 27
Born: 5/10/65 in Davenport, IA
ML Seasons: 1

Overall Statistics

	W	L	ERA	G	GS	Sv	IP	H	R	BB	SO	HR
1992	2	2	3.25	19	0	0	27.2	29	11	13	24	3
Career	2	2	3.25	19	0	0	27.2	29	11	13	24	3

PITCHING, FIELDING & HOLDING RUNNERS:

Former Royals prospect Mike Butcher may have saved his career with a fairly impressive showing as an Angel rookie last year. Working out of the Angel bullpen, Butcher recorded a 3.25 ERA and averaged nearly a strikeout an inning.

To say Butcher was a surprise would be a major understatement. Released by the Royals in mid-season 1988, the righthander had spent three seasons at the Angels' AA Midland farm club, recording ERAs of 6.55, 6.21, and 5.22. Butcher is not the hardest thrower in the world, but his pitches have excellent movement and he's always recorded a lot of strikeouts. His problem has been control: he's walked a lot of batters, and has been hurt by falling behind in the count often.

With the Angels, Butcher's control was sharper, though still not great. He did not allow a run over his first 9.2 innings in the bigs, but then struggled a bit as teams got a second look. He doesn't have a quick delivery to the plate and had some trouble with runners stealing bases on him. He played errorless ball last year for the Angels.

OVERALL:

Nearly 28, Butcher is one of those guys who received a lot of chances because he had a lively arm. He is expected to recover completely from postseason arthroscopic surgery. If he can continue to get the ball over the plate consistently, he has an opportunity to succeed with the Angels.

ROB DUCEY

Position: LF
Bats: L **Throws:** R
Ht: 6' 2" **Wt:** 180

Opening Day Age: 27
Born: 5/24/65 in Toronto, Ontario, Canada
ML Seasons: 6

Overall Statistics

	G	AB	R	H	D	T	HR	RBI	SB	BB	SO	AVG
1992	54	80	7	15	4	0	0	2	2	5	22	.188
Career	214	379	54	89	20	3	2	32	10	40	105	.235

HITTING, FIELDING, BASERUNNING:

Toronto native Rob Ducey should have been a natural with the Blue Jays, who have hungered for Canadian players. But though Ducey spent five seasons at the AAA level, usually compiling good numbers, he never got an extended chance with the big club. Ducey thought he might get that chance when the Jays traded him to the Angels, along with Greg Myers, for Mark Eichhorn last July. Guess again. Ducey wound up getting only 80 at-bats combined with the two teams last year (59 with California). He batted only .188, and never got the opportunity to find his stroke. In six major league seasons, Ducey's has a total of 379 at-bats.

Nearly 28, Ducey has a line drive stroke and the power to hit 10 homers or so. He's patient and can draw some walks, but strikeouts have been his big problem. In those 379 ABs he's fanned 105 times. He has good, though not great, speed, and can steal a few bases. His defense is outstanding enough to keep him employed at least on the substitute level for many teams.

OVERALL:

Ducey could be a fifth outfielder on some teams, but probably not with the Angels. He is too much like many other players on the Angels: blessed with the ability to play, but without the ability to excel. The Angels requested waivers on him after the season, enabling him to become a free agent if so desired.

MIKE FITZGERALD

Position: C
Bats: R **Throws:** R
Ht: 5'11" **Wt:** 190

Opening Day Age: 32
Born: 7/13/60 in Long Beach, CA
ML Seasons: 10

Overall Statistics

	G	AB	R	H	D	T	HR	RBI	SB	BB	SO	AVG
1992	95	189	19	40	2	0	6	17	2	22	34	.212
Career	848	2316	220	545	95	9	48	293	31	292	432	.235

HITTING, FIELDING, BASERUNNING:

A favorite of Angel manager Buck Rodgers, Mike Fitzgerald came to California from Montreal, where he had been one of Rodgers' catchers for several seasons. While Rodgers missed most of the 1992 season recovering from his bus crash injury, Fitzgerald wound up getting into 95 games. The veteran receiver batted only .212, but proved a useful player.

A decent hitter during most of his Montreal days, Fitzgerald has always had a little pop in his bat. He showed that trait with the Angels, hitting six home runs in 189 at-bats. He has also had a knack for hitting well in clutch situations, and he didn't disappoint, hitting .255 with runners in scoring position last year -- 43 points above his season average. Fitzgerald also did nice work against lefties, batting .304 in 69 at-bats.

Fitzgerald needs to hit, because his catching skills are not overwhelming. Rodgers likes the way he handles pitchers, but his weak arm is a problem. Fitzgerald is fairly fast for a catcher and has stolen 14 bases in the last three years.

OVERALL:

A free agent, Fitzgerald might be back if the Angels can't settle on a catcher. They could probably do worse, especially if Fitzgerald's low batting average (25 points worse than his previous career rate) was due to an adjustment to the American League.

RON TINGLEY

Position: C
Bats: R **Throws:** R
Ht: 6' 2" **Wt:** 194

Opening Day Age: 33
Born: 5/27/59 in Presque Isle, ME
ML Seasons: 6

Overall Statistics

	G	AB	R	H	D	T	HR	RBI	SB	BB	SO	AVG
1992	71	127	15	25	2	1	3	8	0	13	35	.197
Career	142	292	27	55	9	1	5	23	1	25	85	.188

HITTING, FIELDING, BASERUNNING:

The quintessential backup receiver, Ron Tingley has seldom been a regular in the minor leagues, much less the majors. So by Tingley standards, 1992 was a career year. The veteran got into 71 games with the Angels last season, his second-highest total as a professional. Of course, he was his usual self with the bat, hitting .197, so California was wise enough to limit him to 127 at- bats. Even that total was a major-league high for Tingley.

By this point, everybody knows that Tingley will never hit; his lifetime average is below .200, and he never did too much with the bat even in the minors. He will hit an occasional long one (three homers last year), and he's a good bunter. But that's about it. Quite obviously, Tingley has been kept around because of his defense, which is excellent. He handles pitchers very well, but his main asset is his arm -- he threw out 45 percent of the runners who tried to steal off him in '92. He's a very slow runner.

OVERALL:

Tingley has been in the Angel organization since 1989, though mostly as an anonymous member. He will be 34 in May, so he probably won't last too much longer. However, his arm and pitch-calling skills are good enough to allow him to stick somewhere for another year or two.

ORGANIZATION OVERVIEW:

Those old free-spending days seem to be over for the California Angels. Jackie Autry, the owner's wife, is now controlling the purse strings, and for the past few years she's had the Cowboy's wallet on a diet. (Think Gene still has a few bills stuffed in his cowboy boots, in case Gary Gaetti starts feeling unloved?) One result is that the Angels have started bringing up some of their prospects; they've also shown a little patience with them, and that always helps. Not all the moves have worked out. The Halos have found that big numbers at Edmonton don't always mean a guy can hit in the majors, but they're learning. If Whitey Herzog stays around, California should start making some progress.

KEVIN FLORA

Position: 2B
Bats: R **Throws:** R
Ht: 6' 0" **Wt:** 180
Opening Day Age: 23
Born: 6/10/69 in Fontana, CA

Recent Statistics

	G	AB	R	H	D	T	HR	RBI	SB	BB	SO	AVG
91 AA Midland	124	484	97	138	14	15	12	67	40	37	92	.285
92 AAA Edmonton	52	170	35	55	8	4	3	19	9	29	25	.324

A former second-round draft pick, Flora was off to a terrific start at AAA Edmonton (.324) when he sprained his ankle and went out for the year. Flora has good speed (40 steals in 1991) and the tools to master second base; thus far he's been a little rough defensively, but he's a converted shortstop and still learning. Since Flora was protected by the Angels for the expansion draft, he could be in Anaheim before the 1992 season ends.

HILLY HATHAWAY

Position: P
Bats: L **Throws:** L
Ht: 6' 4" **Wt:** 185
Opening Day Age: 23
Born: 9/12/69 in Jacksonville, FL

Recent Statistics

	W	L	ERA	G	GS	Sv	IP	H	R	BB	SO	HR
92 A Palm Sprngs	2	1	1.50	3	3	0	24.0	25	5	3	17	1
92 AA Midland	7	2	3.21	14	14	0	95.1	90	39	10	69	2
92 AL California	0	0	7.94	2	1	0	5.2	8	5	3	1	1

Hillary Houston Hathaway -- now there's a name. The lefthander was a 35th-round draft choice in 1989, and he wasn't rated one of the club's top prospects a year ago. But Hathaway went 7-2, 3.21 at AA Midland this year, and even got into two games with the Angels. Though Hathaway isn't overpowering, he has excellent command of his pitches. The Angels were so impressed with his work that they chose to protect him, and not Bryan Harvey, in the expansion draft.

TROY E. PERCIVAL

Position: P
Bats: R **Throws:** R
Ht: 6' 3" **Wt:** 215
Opening Day Age: 23
Born: 8/9/69 in Riverside, CA

Recent Statistics

	W	L	ERA	G	GS	Sv	IP	H	R	BB	SO	HR
91 A Boise	2	0	1.41	28	0	12	38.1	23	7	18	63	0
92 A Palm Sprngs	1	1	5.06	11	0	2	10.2	6	7	8	16	0
92 AA Midland	3	0	2.37	20	0	5	19.0	18	5	11	21	1

What an interesting prospect. The Angels drafted Percival as a catcher in 1990, but when he didn't hit, they tried him on the mound and discovered that he had a 95+ MPH fastball. In two seasons in the Angel system, Percival has struck out 100 men in 68 innings while reaching the AA level. He's also had some arm problems, but they don't seem to be serious. People are already projecting him as the Angels' closer now that Bryan Harvey is gone. If his arm is all right, Percival could well become a star reliever.

EDDIE PEREZ

Position: 1B
Bats: R **Throws:** R
Ht: 6' 4" **Wt:** 215
Opening Day Age: 23
Born: 9/11/69 in Cincinnati, OH

Recent Statistics

	G	AB	R	H	D	T	HR	RBI	SB	BB	SO	AVG
91 A Boise	46	160	35	46	13	0	1	22	12	19	39	.287
92 A Palm Sprngs	54	204	37	64	8	4	3	35	14	23	33	.314
92 AA Midland	62	235	27	54	8	1	3	23	19	22	49	.230
92 MLE	62	221	16	40	5	0	1	13	9	10	52	.181

The son of the new Reds manager, young Perez is a big man whom the Angels drafted in the first round in 1991. Despite his size, he has fine speed, with 45 steals in 58 career attempts, and the versatility to play first, third or the outfield. He has a good throwing arm as well. Perez hit well in the low minors but struggled at AA Midland last year. Thus far he hasn't hit for power; at the positions he plays, he'll have to start in order to be considered a top prospect.

RON WATSON

Position: P
Bats: L **Throws:** R
Ht: 6' 6" **Wt:** 250
Opening Day Age: 24
Born: 9/12/68 in Newton, MA

Recent Statistics

	W	L	ERA	G	GS	Sv	IP	H	R	BB	SO	HR
91 A Boise	0	1	6.23	18	3	0	26.0	35	28	15	27	1
92 A Quad City	8	5	1.29	40	0	10	70.0	43	20	42	69	2

A lowly 39th-round draft pick in 1990, Watson, like Hathaway, advanced so far in 1992 that the Angels risked losing Bryan Harvey to protect him in the expansion draft. The righty reliever had a 1.29 ERA, 10 saves and 69 strikeouts in 70 innings for Class A Quad City. That impressed the Angels, but apparently didn't impress Midwest League managers; they left him off the list of the league's top prospects.

WILSON ALVAREZ

Position: RP/SP
Bats: L **Throws:** L
Ht: 6' 1" **Wt:** 175

Opening Day Age: 23
Born: 3/24/70 in Maracaibo, Venezuela
ML Seasons: 3

PITCHING:

No one connected with the White Sox will ever forget Wilson Alvarez' Sox debut: a stunning no-hitter against the Orioles in 1991. That game -- only his second major league start -- was an indication of exactly how much potential Alvarez has. But after shouldering a very heavy workload in 1991, the prized prospect was kept under wraps for most of the 1992 season.

Between the majors, minors and winter league action, Alvarez worked close to 300 innings in '91 -- a lot of usage for anyone, but especially for a pitcher who was then only 21 years old. The Sox deliberately took it easy with Alvarez last year, giving him only 100 innings of work. While they were disappointed with his 5.20 ERA, they knew they weren't really using him enough to keep him sharp.

Alvarez has a world of stuff, and his problem is simple: he needs to throw strikes. His fastball is plenty good and he also throws a decent slider, but Alvarez' premier pitch is a sharp-breaking curveball. Even in the minors, he often had problems getting the curve over the plate. Used the way he was last year -- sporadically -- he found the task impossible. Sixty-five walks (in 100.1 innings) were one result; so were numerous fat pitches served up when he was desperate to throw a strike. A lot of those juicy offerings wound up over the fence (12 HRs).

HOLDING RUNNERS AND FIELDING:

Alvarez has an improving move to first. He keeps runners close to the bag, and last year stealers were only 9-for-17 against him. He is not yet a good fielder, though; he leaves himself in poor position to field balls hit up the middle, and he committed two errors in only 20 chances last year.

OVERALL:

With the loss of Greg Hibbard in the expansion draft, Alvarez is the only left-handed starter remaining on the staff. Alvarez figures to get regular work this year, and that should help him refine his control. But as a probable contender, the White Sox won't be able to just leave the youngster in the rotation until he finds himself. If Alvarez has problems winning, a return to the minors is possible.

Overall Statistics

	W	L	ERA	G	GS	Sv	IP	H	R	BB	SO	HR
1992	5	3	5.20	34	9	1	100.1	103	64	65	66	12
Career	8	6	4.77	45	19	1	156.2	153	93	96	98	23

How Often He Throws Strikes

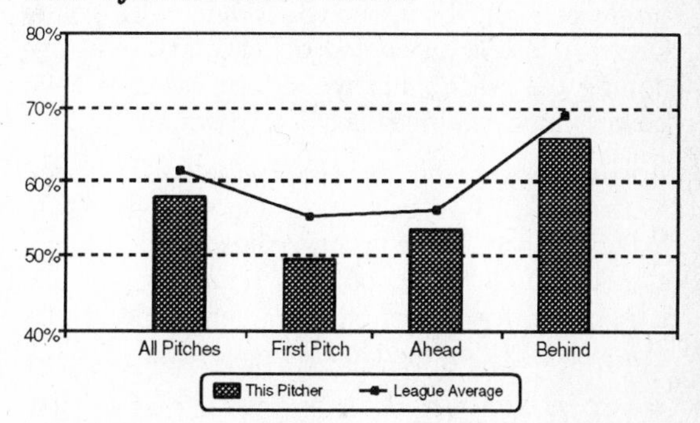

1992 Situational Stats

	W	L	ERA	Sv	IP		AB	H	HR	RBI	AVG
Home	2	1	5.56	0	45.1	LHB	89	20	0	11	.225
Road	3	2	4.91	1	55.0	RHB	290	83	12	47	.286
Day	0	2	4.70	0	23.0	Sc Pos	107	27	4	47	.252
Night	5	1	5.35	1	77.1	Clutch	32	12	1	5	.375

1992 Rankings (American League)

- Did not rank near the top or bottom in any category

HITTING:

George Bell moved crosstown last spring in a headline-grabbing trade between the two Chicago ball clubs. The Cubs got Sammy Sosa, a possible star of the future; the Sox received Bell, who continues to be a star of the present. The veteran slugger hit 25 homers and drove in 112 runs for the Sox, the second-highest total of his career.

While his final figures were satisfying, Bell had something of an up-and-down season. After batting .356 in April, he went 165 at-bats without hitting a home run between May 5th and June 22nd. Then, forced to wear a knee brace because of an injury, Bell found that he had to shorten his stride. Presto -- he was off on a torrid streak which produced eight homers and 33 RBI in an 18-game stretch. Bell soon cooled off (eventually abandoning the brace), but wound up with his best power numbers since his MVP season of 1987.

A wild swinger who loves the fastball and seldom walks (his .294 on-base percentage was anemic), Bell has always been prone to those hot-and-cold streaks. He'll make some of the ugliest swings imaginable for weeks on end, then come to life and start carrying the club.

BASERUNNING:

Bell once stole 21 bases in a season, but with his bad knees, he's now often removed for a pinch runner. He did steal five bases in seven attempts last year, but also grounded into a league-high 29 double plays.

FIELDING:

Bell is an error-prone outfielder with a weak arm, so the Sox used him mainly as a DH last year. The plan for 1993 is to play him in the field more, since it seems to help his hitting by keeping his mind in the game. Though Bell didn't complain about DH duty, he batted .247 in that role, .333 when used as an outfielder.

OVERALL:

An intense, combative player, Bell is one of those guys people either love or hate. The Cubs seemed anxious to get rid of him; the Sox considered him a positive influence. Driving in 112 runs, of course, is a great way to win respect.

GEORGE BELL

Position: DH/LF
Bats: R **Throws:** R
Ht: 6' 1" **Wt:** 202

Opening Day Age: 33
Born: 10/21/59 in San Pedro de Macoris, Dominican Republic
ML Seasons: 11

Overall Statistics

	G	AB	R	H	D	T	HR	RBI	SB	BB	SO	AVG
1992	155	627	74	160	27	0	25	112	5	31	97	.255
Career	1485	5713	778	1613	291	32	252	938	66	318	722	.282

Where He Hits the Ball

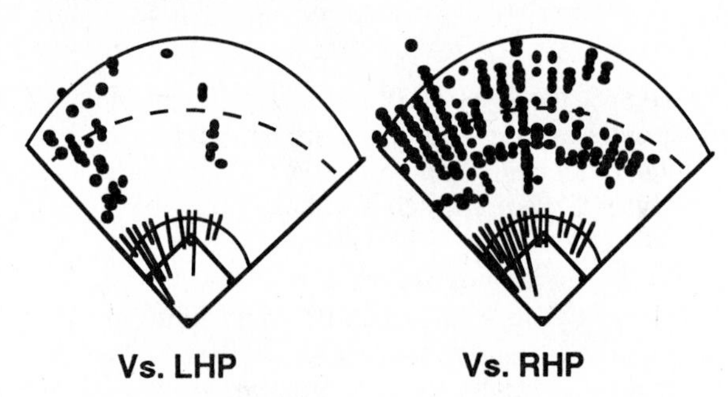

1992 Situational Stats

	AB	H	HR	RBI	AVG		AB	H	HR	RBI	AVG
Home	326	85	16	63	.261	LHP	142	44	7	28	.310
Road	301	75	9	49	.249	RHP	485	116	18	84	.239
Day	142	35	5	19	.246	Sc Pos	212	62	10	88	.292
Night	485	125	20	93	.258	Clutch	99	23	2	7	.232

1992 Rankings (American League)

- 1st in GDPs (29)
- 2nd in lowest on-base average vs. right-handed pitchers (.276)
- 4th in RBI (112)
- Led the White Sox in home runs (25), at-bats (627), hit by pitch (6), strikeouts (97), GDPs and batting average on a 3-1 count (.545)
- Led designated hitters in at-bats, RBIs, hit by pitch, GDPs and batting average on a 3-1 count

ALEX FERNANDEZ

Position: SP
Bats: R **Throws:** R
Ht: 6' 1" **Wt:** 205

Opening Day Age: 23
Born: 8/13/69 in Miami Beach, FL
ML Seasons: 3

PITCHING:

Twice chosen as a number-one draft pick (by the Brewers in 1988 and the White Sox in 1990), Alex Fernandez has been touted by some as the "next Tom Seaver." Yet after two and a half seasons working for a contending club, Fernandez has a won-lost record of 22-29. He has yet to win in double figures or even post a winning season. People are starting to ask what's wrong with the young righthander, who's still only 23.

It sure isn't his stuff. Fernandez possesses a 90 MPH fastball, a rapidly improving curve, an above-average slider, and a change-up which can freeze hitters. Yet last year he permitted five runs or more 11 times in 29 starts; for purposes of comparison, Jack McDowell allowed five or more runs only four times in 34 starts.

That leads people to question Fernandez' head. Some say the cocky youngster won't respond to coaching. Others claim he's reluctant to pitch inside, especially to righthanders. Too often Fernandez simply aims his fastball -- instead of just letting loose -- and ends up tossing it right down the middle for a three-run homer. The White Sox finally tried a little "reality therapy" with Fernandez last year, shipping him to AAA Vancouver in midseason. When he returned he was the same old exasperating Alex -- pitching poorly, yet wondering aloud why the club had sent him down in the first place.

HOLDING RUNNERS AND FIELDING:

Fernandez is an above-average fielder, but needs to work on holding baserunners. He regressed in that department last year, allowing 15 steals in 19 attempts.

OVERALL:

The White Sox have been looking for a number-two starter behind Jack McDowell, and they've hoped Fernandez would assume the role. That's a heavy burden for any pitcher, and perhaps too much for the youthful Fernandez, who started only eight minor league games before arriving in Chicago in 1990. Fernandez is plenty young enough to become a winning major league pitcher . . . but he'll have to start showing some maturity pretty soon.

Overall Statistics

	W	L	ERA	G	GS	Sv	IP	H	R	BB	SO	HR
1992	8	11	4.27	29	29	0	187.2	199	100	50	95	21
Career	22	29	4.28	76	74	0	467.0	474	240	172	301	43

How Often He Throws Strikes

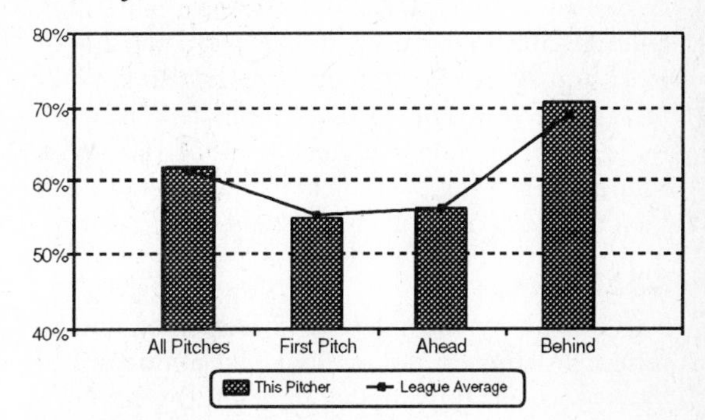

1992 Situational Stats

	W	L	ERA	Sv	IP		AB	H	HR	RBI	AVG
Home	4	7	4.39	0	110.2	LHB	351	88	9	49	.251
Road	4	4	4.09	0	77.0	RHB	385	111	12	38	.288
Day	0	1	6.04	0	28.1	Sc Pos	177	47	3	63	.266
Night	8	10	3.95	0	159.1	Clutch	76	20	3	5	.263

1992 Rankings (American League)

- 2nd highest batting average allowed vs. right-handed batters (.288)
- 5th highest ERA at home (4.39)
- 6th in highest batting average allowed (.270) and stolen base percentage allowed (78.9%)
- Led the White Sox in shutouts (2), home runs allowed (21) and hit batsmen (8)

CARLTON FISK

Position: C
Bats: R **Throws:** R
Ht: 6' 2" **Wt:** 223

Opening Day Age: 45
Born: 12/26/47 in
Bellows Falls, VT
ML Seasons: 23

Overall Statistics

	G	AB	R	H	D	T	HR	RBI	SB	BB	SO	AVG
1992	62	188	12	43	4	1	3	21	3	23	38	.229
Career	2474	8703	1274	2346	421	47	375	1326	128	847	1375	.270

Where He Hits the Ball

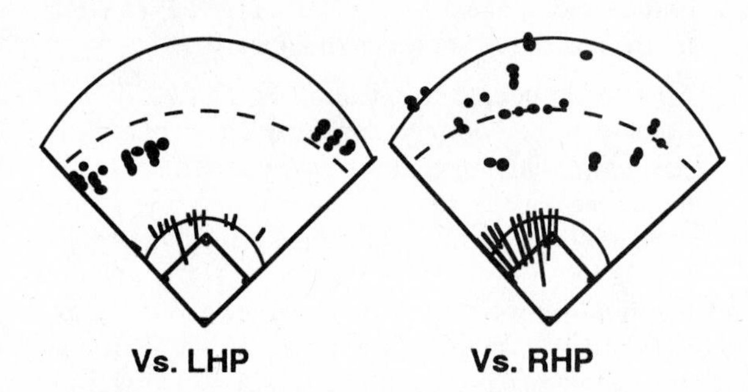

Vs. LHP Vs. RHP

1992 Situational Stats

	AB	H	HR	RBI	AVG		AB	H	HR	RBI	AVG
Home	79	18	2	7	.228	LHP	49	10	0	0	.204
Road	109	25	1	14	.229	RHP	139	33	3	21	.237
Day	53	10	0	2	.189	Sc Pos	47	10	0	17	.213
Night	135	33	3	19	.244	Clutch	33	11	0	7	.333

1992 Rankings (American League)

- ➡ 1st in lowest batting average on a 3-1 count (.000)

HITTING:

After fooling Father Time for over a decade, Carlton Fisk found the magic gone in 1992. A nagging foot injury kept Fisk out of the Sox lineup until June, and when he returned he never really got his bat going. Playing in only 62 games, Fisk batted .229, the second-lowest full-season average of his career. After reaching double figures in homers 19 times in the previous 20 years, he managed only three round-trippers in '92. Just eight of his 43 hits went for extra bases.

Fisk used to be a great fastball hitter, but at his advanced age, he's getting overpowered more and more often. These days a pitcher with a good heater will go right after him, making him prove he can get around on it. Fisk remains a pull hitter, and with his uppercut swing, he's still capable of reaching the fences on occasion. But those moments are now increasingly rare, and he's no longer the legendary clutch hitter of old. With runners in scoring position and two outs last year, Fisk recorded only one hit in 26 at-bats.

BASERUNNING:

Fisk has always been a smart baserunner, and he remains one even though he's lost almost all of his speed. Picking his spots carefully, he stole three bases in three attempts last year, becoming one of the oldest players ever to record a steal. Over the last four years, he's 12-for-16 in stolen base attempts.

FIELDING:

Fisk has always been prized for his ability to handle pitchers. His "sermons on the mound" to young pitchers are legendary. He still throws out a respectable number of baserunners, but lack of mobility is now a problem for him. It's one reason he isn't asked to handle knuckleballer Charlie Hough.

OVERALL:

At age 45, Fisk needs to catch only a handful of games (25) to break Bob Boone's career record for games caught (2,225). Though he was unsigned at season's end, the White Sox seemed interested in letting him break the record in a Sox uniform. Even in a backup role, he has considerable value.

CRAIG GREBECK

Position: SS
Bats: R **Throws:** R
Ht: 5' 7" **Wt:** 160

Opening Day Age: 28
Born: 12/29/64 in Johnstown, PA
ML Seasons: 3

Overall Statistics

	G	AB	R	H	D	T	HR	RBI	SB	BB	SO	AVG
1992	88	287	24	77	21	2	3	35	0	30	34	.268
Career	254	630	68	160	40	6	10	75	1	76	98	.254

Where He Hits the Ball

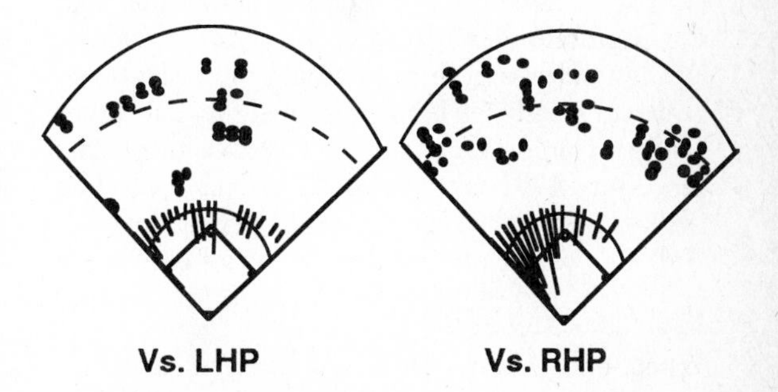

1992 Situational Stats

	AB	H	HR	RBI	AVG		AB	H	HR	RBI	AVG
Home	134	36	2	23	.269	LHP	86	25	0	9	.291
Road	153	41	1	12	.268	RHP	201	52	3	26	.259
Day	72	16	0	11	.222	Sc Pos	68	18	0	27	.265
Night	215	61	3	24	.284	Clutch	60	12	0	6	.200

1992 Rankings (American League)

- 8th lowest batting average on a 3-2 count (.094)

HITTING:

Sometimes satisfaction gets mixed with frustration, and in that regard, Craig Grebeck had a career year in 1992. In the off-season, Grebeck was looking forward to being the White Sox second baseman (satisfaction). Then the Sox went out and traded for Steve Sax (frustration). Before Grebeck could settle back into a utility role, Ozzie Guillen suffered a year-ending knee injury, and Grebeck became the Sox shortstop. He handled the job in superb fashion, hitting a solid .268 and fielding steadily (satisfaction). But in August, Grebeck suffered a season-ending injury himself, a freakish broken right foot (frustration). What's a fellow to think?

Grebeck ought to simply feel satisfied. Though he's only 5-7 and 160 pounds, the little man can swing a potent bat -- he's probably the best fastball hitter on the Sox team. Over a third of his hits went for extra bases last year, including 21 doubles in only 287 at-bats. His average improved each month before the injury: .217 April, .257 May, .266 June, .308 July. He was tough in the clutch, batting .297 with runners on base.

BASERUNNING:

Grebeck's aggressiveness on the bases is reflected in his high doubles total -- he's fearless about pursuing the extra sack. That aggressiveness did not pay off in stolen bases last year. Grebeck is a sub-50 percent stealer in his professional career, and a terrible one-for-seven in the majors.

FIELDING:

Some people expected the Sox to deal for a shortstop when Guillen went down, but the club had confidence in Grebeck. It paid off. The youngster displayed both sure hands (only eight errors) and more-than-adequate range. He's just as good at second, maybe even better.

OVERALL:

Grebeck's presence gives the Sox some margin for error in 1993. If Guillen isn't ready this spring, Grebeck is the obvious alternative. But he could also wind up as the second baseman if Sax is traded or continues to slump. Even if both are back in the lineup, Grebeck figures to log a lot of playing time.

HITTING:

Ozzie Guillen's 1992 season came to an abrupt conclusion last April 21 when he was injured in an outfield collision with teammate Tim Raines. Guillen suffered torn ligaments in his right knee, and after undergoing surgery, spent the rest of the season in rehab. Though Craig Grebeck did a fine job until he himself was injured, the White Sox were never quite the same without their spirited shortstop. Enormously popular as well as talented, Guillen is often considered the heart and soul of the Chicago team.

A dependable slap hitter, Guillen almost always hits in the .260-.270 range, above average for a shortstop. He likes the high fastball and handles the bat extremely well, spraying the ball around the diamond. He's also a very adept bunter. Guillen suffers from an extreme lack of power, however -- only ten homers in an eight year career -- and an almost legendary lack of discipline. His pre-injury 1992 numbers -- 40 at-bats, only one walk -- were only slightly below average for him. Guillen's career on-base average is a lowly .287.

BASERUNNING:

When completely healthy, Guillen is a smart, aggressive baserunner with excellent speed. He's also an aggressive base stealer, but his judgement often deserts him. Guillen's career stolen base average is only a little over 60 percent, too low a mark. It remains to be seen how much the injury will affect his speed.

FIELDING:

Guillen won a Gold Glove in 1990, and at his best he was good enough to earn several more. His range was outstanding, he was excellent on the double play, and his arm, though not the strongest around, was more than adequate. But once again, he'll have to prove he's completely healthy before the White Sox can relax.

OVERALL:

The enthusiastic Guillen has worked hard to get himself back in shape, and he's expected to recover from his injuries as shown by his protection from expansion. Ligament damage is always serious, however, and the White Sox will be watching him closely this spring. They need him badly.

OZZIE GUILLEN

Position: SS
Bats: L **Throws:** R
Ht: 5'11" **Wt:** 150

Opening Day Age: 29
Born: 1/20/64 in Oculare del Tuy, Venezuela
ML Seasons: 8

Overall Statistics

	G	AB	R	H	D	T	HR	RBI	SB	BB	SO	AVG
1992	12	40	5	8	4	0	0	7	1	1	5	.200
Career	1095	3841	432	1021	143	42	10	338	136	124	308	.266

Where He Hits the Ball

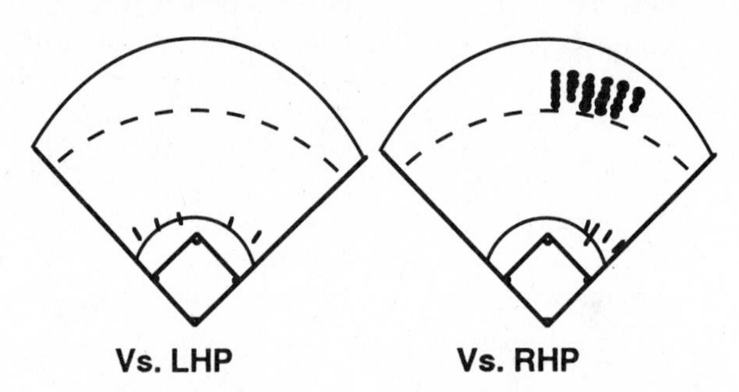

1992 Situational Stats

	AB	H	HR	RBI	AVG		AB	H	HR	RBI	AVG
Home	17	3	0	2	.176	LHP	19	3	0	1	.158
Road	23	5	0	5	.217	RHP	21	5	0	6	.238
Day	10	2	0	3	.200	Sc Pos	15	6	0	7	.400
Night	30	6	0	4	.200	Clutch	8	0	0	0	.000

1992 Rankings (American League)

- Did not rank near the top or bottom in any category

OVERLOOKED

PITCHING:

No pitcher on the White Sox -- and few pitchers in baseball -- made greater strides toward stardom than Roberto Hernandez last year. When the season began, Hernandez was the tenth or eleventh pitcher on the roster, and he was twice dispatched to AAA Vancouver. By year's end Hernandez was sporting a staff-low 1.65 ERA, and he was sharing the closer's role with Scott Radinsky. He converted 10 of his last 11 save opportunities. Hernandez' late-season work was so effective that he basically turned Bobby Thigpen, the 57-save man, into a little-used mop-up pitcher.

What makes the story even more remarkable is that Hernandez was only one year removed from major surgery. While pitching for Vancouver early in '91, he began suffering from numbness in his pitching hand. Blood clots were discovered, and doctors needed to transfer veins from his inner thigh to his right forearm. Immensely strong at 6-4 and 220 pounds, Hernandez recovered so quickly that he was pitching in Chicago by September. By the end of 1992, the injury was all but forgotten.

Though he seemingly came out of nowhere last year, Hernandez, at 28, is no kid. Born in Puerto Rico, he grew up in the States and was the Angels' Number One draft choice in 1986 out of the University of South Carolina (Aiken). His early minor league work was disappointing, and the Sox obtained him in a 1989 minor league deal. He throws a hard, sinking fastball, along with a good slider, and he's capable of dominating hitters. Hernandez averaged nearly a strikeout an inning last year while holding batters to a .180 average.

HOLDING RUNNERS AND FIELDING:

Though a power pitcher, Hernandez does a good job of holding runners, who were only 4-for-8 on steal attempts last year. He reacts well defensively and can handle his position.

OVERALL:

The White Sox were enormously impressed with Hernandez' work last year. He might well be their closer this year; at the least, he's slated for a major relief role.

ROBERTO HERNANDEZ

Position: RP
Bats: R **Throws:** R
Ht: 6' 4" **Wt:** 220

Opening Day Age: 28
Born: 11/11/64 in Santurce, Puerto Rico
ML Seasons: 2

Overall Statistics

	W	L	ERA	G	GS	Sv	IP	H	R	BB	SO	HR
1992	7	3	1.65	43	0	12	71.0	45	15	20	68	4
Career	8	3	2.72	52	3	12	86.0	63	30	27	74	5

How Often He Throws Strikes

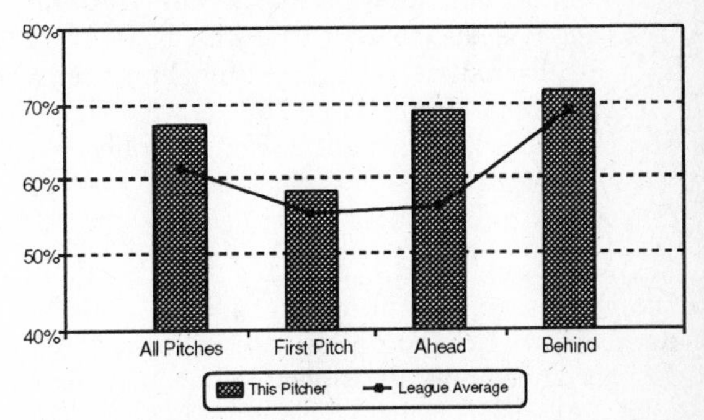

1992 Situational Stats

	W	L	ERA	Sv	IP		AB	H	HR	RBI	AVG
Home	5	1	0.44	6	40.2	LHB	107	20	1	13	.187
Road	2	2	3.26	6	30.1	RHB	143	25	3	11	.175
Day	2	1	2.89	2	18.2	Sc Pos	64	11	1	20	.172
Night	5	2	1.20	10	52.1	Clutch	162	31	2	19	.191

1992 Rankings (American League)

- 1st in lowest batting average allowed in relief (.180)
- 2nd in relief ERA (1.65)
- 3rd in least baserunners allowed per 9 innings in relief (8.7)
- 4th in most strikeouts per 9 innings in relief (8.6)
- Led the White Sox in relief ERA, relief wins (7), lowest batting average allowed in relief, least baserunners allowed per 9 innings in relief and most strikeouts per 9 innings in relief

PITCHING:

"The Chuckster," Charlie Hough, suffered through an exasperating season in 1992. Hough, who began the season with 195 career victories, found nailing down number 200 was about as elusive as one of his knuckleballs. Hough notched his 199th victory on June 28 against the Yankees, but his 200th didn't come until almost six weeks later, on August 5 vs. the Twins. It wasn't that Hough was pitching poorly; it was that his hitters and (especially) his bullpen seemed to be conspiring against him. Much of Hough's season was like that. His 7-12 record belied some very good pitching.

Hough will turn 45 before the 1993 season, but that's not terribly old for a knuckleballer. At the same age Phil Niekro went 16-8 with a 3.08 ERA for the 1984 Yankees, and Hoyt Wilhelm posted a 1.72 ERA for the 1968 White Sox. As with Niekro and Wilhelm, the knuckler is Hough's only real weapon; he uses his "batting practice" fastball only as a surprise attack.

While Hough's ERA declined for the third straight season, one disturbing sign in his 1992 numbers was the drop in his strikeout total. Hough fanned only 76 batters, by far his lowest total since he became a starter in 1982. Is the knuckler losing its dance?

HOLDING RUNNERS AND FIELDING:

Hough doesn't look like much of an athlete, but he's surprisingly agile around the mound. He probably gets off the mound to cover first better than any other pitcher on the White Sox staff. He has a quick pickoff move and makes endless throws to first, but the knuckler makes him easy to steal on. Runners were 17-for-20 in stolen bases with Hough pitching last year.

OVERALL:

Hough had a 4.69 ERA after the break last year, and for a time the Sox took him out of their rotation. The club has talked about moving a younger pitcher into his starting spot, so the free agent may be throwing his knuckler for another team this year. A respected veteran and all-around good guy, he should be able to latch on with someone.

CHARLIE HOUGH

Position: SP
Bats: R **Throws:** R
Ht: 6' 2" **Wt:** 190

Opening Day Age: 45
Born: 1/5/48 in Honolulu, HI
ML Seasons: 23

Overall Statistics

	W	L	ERA	G	GS	Sv	IP	H	R	BB	SO	HR
1992	7	12	3.93	27	27	0	176.1	160	88	66	76	19
Career	202	191	3.67	803	385	61	3482.1	2963	1624	1542	2171	346

How Often He Throws Strikes

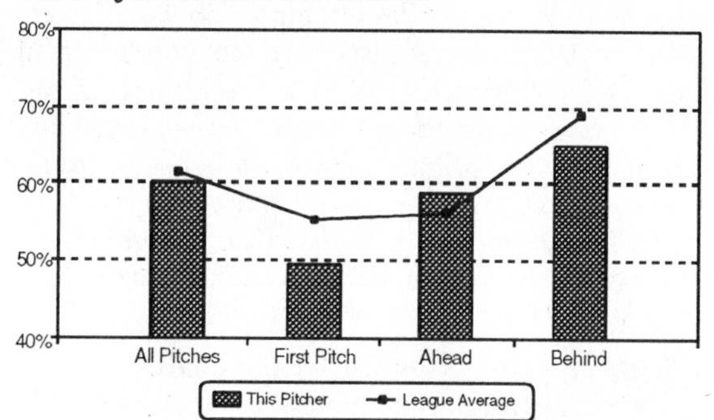

1992 Situational Stats

	W	L	ERA	Sv	IP		AB	H	HR	RBI	AVG
Home	6	4	3.49	0	100.2	LHB	267	63	7	22	.236
Road	1	8	4.52	0	75.2	RHB	403	97	12	52	.241
Day	1	1	3.45	0	44.1	Sc Pos	137	36	4	52	.263
Night	6	11	4.09	0	132.0	Clutch	64	17	3	9	.266

1992 Rankings (American League)

- 2nd highest stolen base percentage allowed (85.0%)
- 4th lowest run support per 9 innings (3.7)
- 5th lowest winning percentage (.368), lowest strikeout/walk ratio (1.2) and least strikeouts per 9 innings (3.9)
- Led the White Sox in wild pitches (10), lowest batting average allowed (.239) and lowest batting average allowed vs. left-handed batters (.236)

LANCE JOHNSON

Position: CF
Bats: L **Throws:** L
Ht: 5'11" **Wt:** 160

Opening Day Age: 29
Born: 7/6/63 in Cincinnati, OH
ML Seasons: 6

Overall Statistics

	G	AB	R	H	D	T	HR	RBI	SB	BB	SO	AVG
1992	157	567	67	158	15	12	3	47	41	34	33	.279
Career	584	2059	258	563	61	38	4	176	131	120	177	.273

Where He Hits the Ball

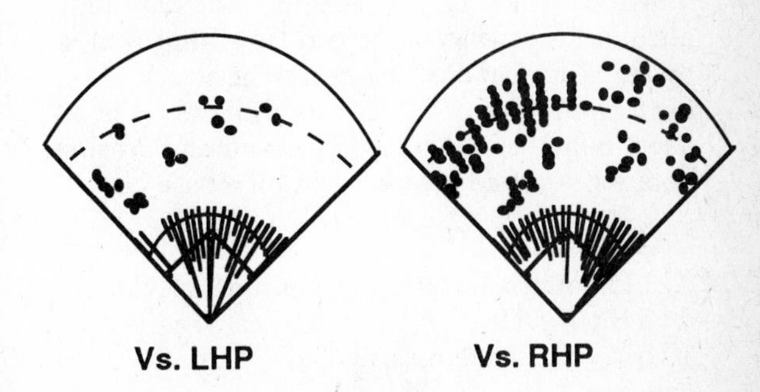

1992 Situational Stats

	AB	H	HR	RBI	AVG		AB	H	HR	RBI	AVG
Home	274	72	2	25	.263	LHP	158	42	0	14	.266
Road	293	86	1	22	.294	RHP	409	116	3	33	.284
Day	138	43	0	5	.312	Sc Pos	142	39	0	43	.275
Night	429	115	3	42	.268	Clutch	94	21	0	5	.223

1992 Rankings (American League)

- 1st in triples (12) and least pitches seen per plate appearance (3.04)
- 2nd lowest percentage of swings that missed (7.2%)
- 3rd in highest groundball/flyball ratio (2.3) and steals of third (9)
- Led the White Sox in singles (128), triples, caught stealing (14), lowest percentage of swings that missed and steals of third
- Led AL center fielders in triples, caught stealing, GDPs, groundball/flyball ratio, batting average on a 3-2 count (.333) and steals of third

HITTING:

Lance Johnson was a consistent .300 hitter in the minor leagues, and for much of the 1992 season, he seemed intent on reaching the charmed circle again. Johnson reeled off a major league-high 25-game hitting streak in July and early August, raising his average to .305. Unfortunately, he quickly fell to earth, going just two for his next 33, and wound up right at his normal .270- .280 level. In three seasons as a Sox regular, Johnson has batted .285, .274 and last year's .279.

Johnson has outstanding speed, and he takes full advantage of it as a hitter. He likes high pitches, both fastballs and breaking stuff, and tries to chop them into the ground in order to use his speed. At 160 pounds he doesn't have much power, but he'll surprise people on occasion. While he has only four career homers -- three of them last year -- Johnson has led the league in triples each of the last two seasons.

With his great bat control and ability to make contact (only 33 strikeouts last year), Johnson would seem like an ideal top-of-the-order hitter. The problem is that he lacks patience, shown by his meager total of 34 walks last season. The Sox have used him mostly in the seventh and eighth spots in the order.

BASERUNNING:

As he learns American League pitchers, Johnson continues to improve as a basestealer. His 41 steals last year were a career high, and his success rate (75 percent in '92) is also improving.

FIELDING:

Called "One Dog" for his ability to track down flies, Johnson is a Gold Glove-caliber center fielder. He has marvelous range and instincts for the ball. His throwing arm is below average, but Johnson compensates by charging balls well and getting rid of them quickly.

OVERALL:

Johnson's great defense is so crucial to the White Sox that he doesn't have to hit a lot to stay in the lineup. He'd be more valuable if he could learn a little discipline, but at his current level he's a major asset to the club.

RON KARKOVICE

Position: C
Bats: R **Throws:** R
Ht: 6' 1" **Wt:** 215

Opening Day Age: 29
Born: 8/8/63 in Union, NJ
ML Seasons: 7

Overall Statistics

	G	AB	R	H	D	T	HR	RBI	SB	BB	SO	AVG
1992	123	342	39	81	12	1	13	50	10	30	89	.237
Career	459	1171	145	265	55	3	36	145	20	94	346	.226

Where He Hits the Ball

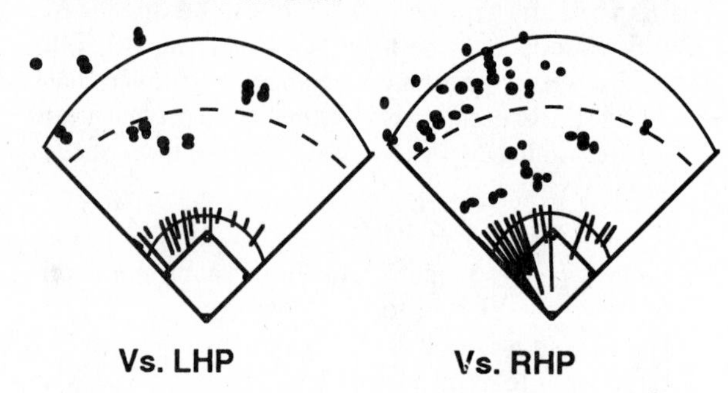

1992 Situational Stats

	AB	H	HR	RBI	AVG		AB	H	HR	RBI	AVG
Home	171	39	5	18	.228	LHP	107	24	4	15	.224
Road	171	42	8	32	.246	RHP	235	57	9	35	.243
Day	76	16	3	11	.211	Sc Pos	90	24	2	34	.267
Night	266	65	10	39	.244	Clutch	54	11	1	4	.204

1992 Rankings (American League)

- → 7th lowest batting average with 2 strikes (.134)
- → Led the White Sox in batting average on an 0-2 count (.240)

HITTING:

Carlton Fisk's nagging foot injury gave Ron Karkovice a golden opportunity last year -- a chance to show his stuff as the everyday White Sox receiver. Karkovice failed to take full advantage, and entered September with a .209 average. It wasn't until the final month, long after Fisk had returned, that Karkovice finally got untracked. In his last 26 games the stocky catcher drove in 20 runs and batted .318, with six home runs. He wound up with 13 homers and 50 RBI, both career highs, in only 342 at-bats.

Karkovice has a short, powerful stroke, and he can hit a fastball a long way. He's always had a tendency to chase breaking pitches in the dirt, however, which is why he's hit over .250 only once in his seven-year career. He's improved in recent years, but even last season he struck out in over one-fourth of his at-bats. Karkovice is an adept bunter and will lay one down on occasion both for sacrifice purposes and for a base hit.

BASERUNNING:

At 215 pounds, Karkovice looks the typical plodding catcher. He's anything but. Last year he stole 10 bases in 14 attempts, and he's 20 for 26 in his career.

FIELDING:

Karkovice's rifle arm is what brought him to the major leagues. Until last year, he'd tossed out nearly 50 percent of his opposing base stealers. Karkovice's total declined to the 30 percent range in 1992, but Sox pitchers have to share some of the blame. He continues to improve as a handler of pitchers, and he catches the knuckleball as well as anyone around. Last year Sox pitchers had a better ERA with Karkovice catching (3.77) than they did with Fisk (3.98).

OVERALL:

Fisk still figures to be around in 1993, so Karkovice will once more have to battle for playing time. His defense is so solid that it can compensate for most of his offensive shortcomings. But he'll have to avoid the kind of long slump he suffered in '92 if he wants the Sox to make a complete commitment to him.

TERRY LEACH

Position: RP
Bats: R **Throws:** R
Ht: 6' 0" **Wt:** 190

Opening Day Age: 39
Born: 3/13/54 in Selma, AL
ML Seasons: 10

PITCHING:

Usually not the type to make a quick impression, Terry Leach did just that with the White Sox in 1992. A last-minute addition to the Sox staff at the end of spring training, Leach started the season as a long reliever. But before long he was one of the club's most important relievers, routinely answering the call in tight situations. Though he never got a save opportunity, Leach posted a brilliant 1.95 ERA, the lowest of his ten-year career. It was a very satisfying season for the veteran righty, who'd been cast adrift last winter by the World Champion Twins.

Now 39, Leach seems in no hurry to leave the majors. That makes sense, since it took him long enough to get there. Leach didn't pitch his first major league game until he was 27, and didn't arrive to stay until 1987, when he was 33. A classic submariner, Leach didn't throw very hard even when he was young. With his sweeping underhand motion, he gets lots of groundball outs, and he's always been much more effective against righties than vs. lefties. Leach held righthanders to a .187 average last year, and lefties to a .263 mark. His improvement against lefthanders was marked; in 1991, southpaw swingers had lit him up for a .367 average.

Leach's .215 opponent batting average last year was fairly amazing, since it's the sort of mark usually posted only by pitchers who strike out a lot of hitters. That's not Leach, who fanned only 22 men in 73.2 innings.

HOLDING RUNNERS AND FIELDING:

Fairly easy to steal on because of his slow, awkward delivery, Leach did well to allow only seven steals in 10 attempts last year. His motion makes it difficult to field balls hit back at him, though he does his best.

OVERALL:

Submarine pitchers often have a long shelf life -- just look at Ted Abernathy and Kent Tekulve. After his work in 1992, Leach seems assured of a job this year. It'll be a shock, though, if he posts figures similar to those of '92.

Overall Statistics

	W	L	ERA	G	GS	Sv	IP	H	R	BB	SO	HR
1992	6	5	1.95	51	0	0	73.2	57	17	20	22	2
Career	38	27	3.16	362	21	9	683.2	673	274	195	328	38

How Often He Throws Strikes

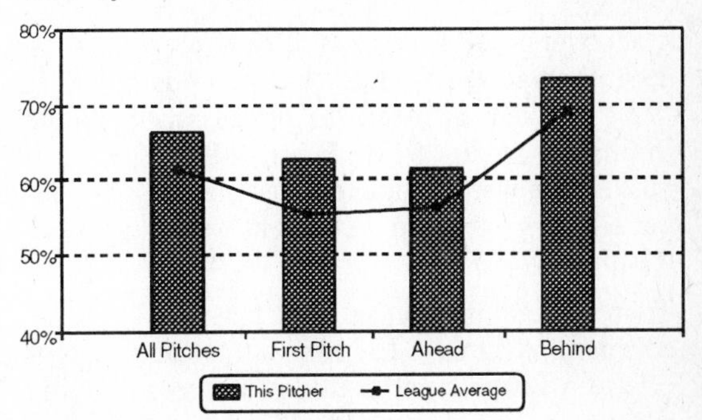

1992 Situational Stats

	W	L	ERA	Sv	IP		AB	H	HR	RBI	AVG
Home	3	0	0.84	0	32.0	LHB	99	26	0	6	.263
Road	3	5	2.81	0	41.2	RHB	166	31	2	17	.187
Day	0	2	2.16	0	8.1	Sc Pos	65	13	1	20	.200
Night	6	3	1.93	0	65.1	Clutch	114	31	1	9	.272

1992 Rankings (American League)

- 1st in least strikeouts per 9 innings in relief (2.7)
- 5th in first batter efficiency (.170)
- Led the White Sox in first batter efficiency and innings pitched in relief (73.2)

KIRK McCASKILL

Position: SP
Bats: R **Throws:** R
Ht: 6' 1" **Wt:** 205
Opening Day Age: 32
Born: 4/9/61 in Kapuskasing, Ontario, Canada
ML Seasons: 8

PITCHING:

When the White Sox signed ex-Angel Kirk McCaskill before the start of the 1992 season, they knew they hadn't acquired another Roger Clemens. What they expected from McCaskill was a dependable righty who would give them 175 or more innings of work, win about half his decisions, and post an ERA around the 4.00 level. Solid innings, in other words.

McCaskill gave them that and more, not that he was brilliant. After going 10-19 in 1991, McCaskill went 12-13 in 1992. The better record was partially due to pitching for a better club. But he gave the club 34 starts, a career high; 209 innings, his best total since 1989; 109 strikeouts, his most since '86; and a 4.18 ERA, an improvement over his 1991 mark of 4.26. After permitting 19 homers in 1991, McCaskill yielded only 11 in '92. He also allowed far fewer hits per nine innings than in '91 (8.3 vs. 9.8). McCaskill proved he was completely recovered from the bone-chip surgery he underwent before the 1991 campaign.

There's nothing unusual about McCaskill's assortment of pitches. He throws the standard repertoire -- fastball, curve, slider, change -- relying more on movement and changing speeds than on velocity. He has excellent arm action on his change, which is probably his best pitch, and the downward movement on his pitches gets him a lot of groundball outs. Control was sometimes a problem for him last year, as he allowed a career-high 95 walks.

HOLDING RUNNERS AND FIELDING:

McCaskill has a good, tricky move to first, one of the best in the league among righthanders. Though he allowed a lot of baserunners, he permitted only 12 steals in 21 attempts, an excellent ratio. A former hockey player, he's a great all-around athlete who fields his position very well.

OVERALL:

McCaskill proved once again last year that he's a solid fourth or fifth starter, and the White Sox were reasonably pleased with his efforts. They wouldn't mind seeing the same McCaskill who went 17-10 for the 1986 Angels, but they're not really expecting much more than he provided in 1992.

Overall Statistics

	W	L	ERA	G	GS	Sv	IP	H	R	BB	SO	HR
1992	12	13	4.18	34	34	0	209.0	193	116	95	109	11
Career	90	87	3.91	226	223	0	1430.0	1384	692	543	823	120

How Often He Throws Strikes

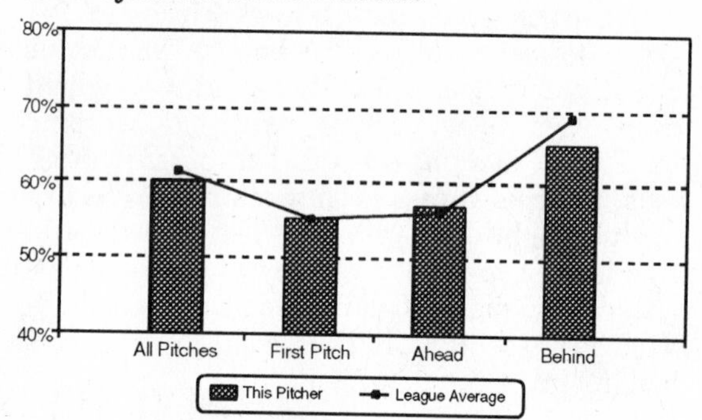

1992 Situational Stats

	W	L	ERA	Sv	IP		AB	H	HR	RBI	AVG
Home	6	7	3.54	0	109.1	LHB	379	106	6	50	.280
Road	6	6	4.88	0	99.2	RHB	417	87	5	49	.209
Day	3	2	2.92	0	52.1	Sc Pos	171	51	3	83	.298
Night	9	11	4.60	0	156.2	Clutch	51	13	1	6	.255

1992 Rankings (American League)

- 1st in pickoff throws (334)
- 2nd in lowest batting average allowed vs. right-handed batters (.209)
- 4th lowest strikeout/walk ratio (1.1)
- Led the White Sox in losses (13), games started (34), walks (95), balks (2), pickoff throws, lowest slugging percentage allowed (.343), lowest stolen base percentage allowed (57.1%), least home runs allowed per 9 innings (0.5) and lowest batting average allowed vs. right-handed batters (.209)

CY YOUNG STUFF

JACK McDOWELL

Position: SP
Bats: R **Throws:** R
Ht: 6' 5" **Wt:** 180

Opening Day Age: 27
Born: 1/16/66 in Van Nuys, CA
ML Seasons: 5

PITCHING:

The White Sox' unquestioned staff ace, Jack McDowell reached the 20-victory plateau for the first time in his career last season. Over the last three seasons, McDowell has improved his won-lost record each year, from 14-9 to 17-10 to last year's 20-10. Meanwhile his ERA has dropped from 3.82 to 3.41 to 3.18. The tall righthander continues to improve, and he'll only be 27 years old this year.

Though he won 20 games and led the majors in complete games for the second straight year, McDowell had some frustrating moments late in '92. He notched his 20th win on September 8, with nearly four weeks left in the season, but failed to win again. In his last five starts McDowell pitched into the eighth inning or better each time while posting a 3.27 ERA, but came away without a victory. In those five starts, his teammates scored only 13 runs for him.

McDowell throws a 90 MPH fastball and a fine curve, but in recent years he has relied increasingly on his great split-fingered fastball, a pitch which almost looks like a curveball. He used to throw a slider, but after hanging it too often, junked it in favor of the splitter. The pitch has become his best weapon.

HOLDING RUNNERS AND FIELDING:

McDowell has a fine pickoff move, nabbing seven runners last year. He's the established master of the fake-to-third, throw-to-first move. He's a power pitcher with a high leg kick, however, and runners will take off on him. McDowell was in the top three in both stolen bases allowed (29) and runners caught stealing (16) last year. He's an excellent fielder with good reactions on balls hit back to him. McDowell committed two errors in 1992, a high total for him.

OVERALL:

At his age, with a track-record of improvement while playing for a winning team, McDowell would seem to be in line for a Cy Young Award soon. As one of the game's "ultimate competitors," he just wants to keep getting better.

Overall Statistics

	W	L	ERA	G	GS	Sv	IP	H	R	BB	SO	HR
1992	20	10	3.18	34	34	0	260.2	247	95	75	178	21
Career	59	39	3.49	132	132	0	906.0	811	376	308	633	73

How Often He Throws Strikes

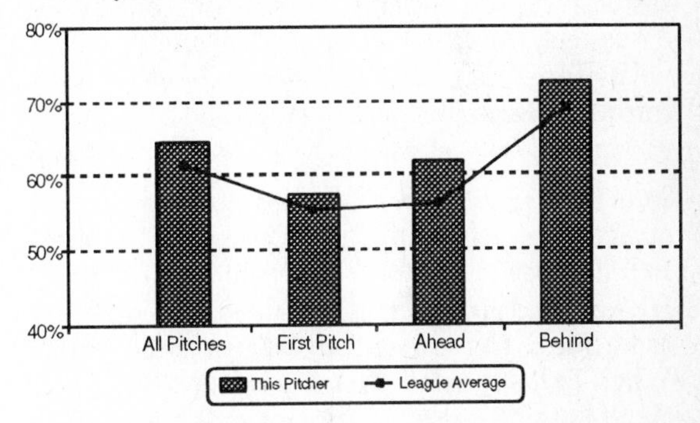

1992 Situational Stats

	W	L	ERA	Sv	IP		AB	H	HR	RBI	AVG
Home	9	5	2.77	0	120.1	LHB	486	128	13	46	.263
Road	11	5	3.53	0	140.1	RHB	497	119	8	44	.239
Day	6	3	3.35	0	86.0	Sc Pos	208	46	6	67	.221
Night	14	7	3.09	0	174.2	Clutch	101	22	0	7	.218

1992 Rankings (American League)

- 1st in complete games (13) and pitches thrown (3,994)
- 2nd in batters faced (1,079) and stolen bases allowed (29)
- 3rd in wins (20), innings pitched (260.2), runners caught stealing (16) and least GDPs induced per 9 innings (0.4)
- Led the White Sox in ERA (3.18), wins, games started (34), complete games, innings pitched, hits allowed, batters faced, home runs allowed (21), strikeouts, pitches thrown, stolen bases allowed, runners caught stealing, winning percentage, highest strikeout/walk ratio (2.4), and lowest batting average allowed with runners in scoring position (.221)

DONN PALL

Position: RP
Bats: R **Throws:** R
Ht: 6' 1" **Wt:** 183

Opening Day Age: 31
Born: 1/11/62 in Chicago, IL
ML Seasons: 5

PITCHING:

After having the best season of his major league career in 1991, Donn Pall had his worst campaign in 1992. Pall's ERA more than doubled, from 2.41 to 4.93. While he worked two more innings (73.0) than he did in '91, Pall appeared in only 39 games, his lowest total since his mid-year debut in 1988. After the All-Star break he saw action in only 15 contests, and it was fairly obvious that manager Gene Lamont had lost confidence in him.

Pall reported no arm problems, so that can be discounted as a possible explanation. His control remained excellent, with only 19 unintentional walks in those 73 innings. Loss of velocity on his fastball was one explanation, as Pall fanned only 27 batters. But then Pall, who relies mostly on his split-fingered pitch, has never been a hard thrower. He continued to get a good number of groundball outs, as always.

In truth, Pall may have been a victim of circumstances as much as anything. Under Jeff Torborg, Pall had been a middle reliever and set-up man. He was used in important situations, but carefully, as he doesn't have the strongest arm in the world. When Pall struggled after a good start last year, Gene Lamont began to give his old assignments to Terry Leach. Pall became a long reliever, a new role for him. The three- and four-inning stints he was often asked to work may not have been the proper way to use his type of arm.

HOLDING RUNNERS AND FIELDING:

Pall has done a good job of holding runners in the past, but his pitching problems seemed to distract him last year. He permitted ten steals in 11 attempts -- very poor considering his low total of innings. He continued to field his position in good fashion, particularly in starting double plays.

OVERALL:

The White Sox have a number of righty relief possibilities for 1993, and Pall will have to scramble for a position. He's capable of a rebound, but only if used in a way which suits his arm.

Overall Statistics

	W	L	ERA	G	GS	Sv	IP	H	R	BB	SO	HR
1992	5	2	4.93	39	0	1	73.0	79	43	27	27	9
Career	19	16	3.49	216	0	9	335.2	330	144	98	180	33

How Often He Throws Strikes

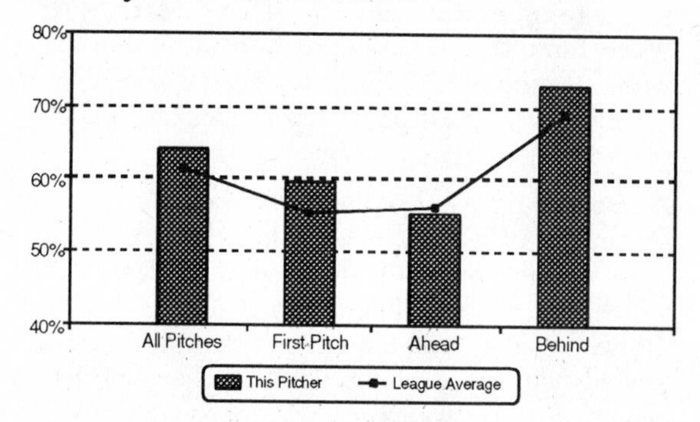

1992 Situational Stats

	W	L	ERA	Sv	IP		AB	H	HR	RBI	AVG
Home	4	0	5.26	1	39.1	LHB	103	30	2	13	.291
Road	1	2	4.54	0	33.2	RHB	187	49	7	30	.262
Day	4	1	3.58	0	32.2	Sc Pos	75	22	4	35	.293
Night	1	1	6.02	1	40.1	Clutch	78	21	0	6	.269

1992 Rankings (American League)

- 4th in highest ERA in relief (4.93) and least strikeouts per nine innings in relief (3.3)
- 5th in balks (2)
- Led the White Sox in balks and most GDPs induced per GDP situation (16.1%)

PITCHING:

Bobby Thigpen's 1992 problems gave Scott Radinsky a midseason chance at the job he's been yearning for -- the White Sox closer role. Though Radinsky was pitching solidly, manager Gene Lamont made a September switch, giving most of the late-inning jobs to another up-and-comer, Roberto Hernandez. With two talented young relievers, the manager wanted to see what each could do.

Radinsky got his chance shortly after the All-Star break, when Thigpen was struggling. During a month-long period between July 22 and August 22, Radinsky pitched in 14 games, and didn't allow an earned run in 13 of them. He recorded 10 saves in 12 opportunities over that span. Though Radinsky wound up going two months without allowing an earned run, Lamont gave most of the last-month save opportunities to Hernandez, who was just as hot. Two bad outings in the final week lifted Radinsky's ERA to a still-respectable 2.73.

There are several reasons why Lamont might have reservations about Radinsky as a full-time closer. One is that the southpaw's stuff -- mainly a 90+ MPH fastball and a good curve -- was a lot more effective against lefty swingers than versus righties last year. Control is another problem: Radinsky yielded about one unintentional walk per two innings pitched last year. He also had eight blown saves, though half of them came in a three-week stretch when he was still backing up Thigpen.

HOLDING RUNNERS AND FIELDING:

Radinsky seems like the kind of fastball pitcher runners could take advantage of, but that isn't the case. He has a good move to first, and in each of the last two seasons, he's permitted only one stolen base. He's only an average fielder, but he's never made an error in his three major-league seasons.

OVERALL:

Though he wasn't perfect last year, Radinsky showed he could finish games effectively when given the top job. He might get a longer look this year, possibly in a left/right tandem with Hernandez.

SCOTT RADINSKY

Position: RP
Bats: L **Throws:** L
Ht: 6' 3" **Wt:** 190

Opening Day Age: 25
Born: 3/3/68 in Glendale, CA
ML Seasons: 3

Overall Statistics

	W	L	ERA	G	GS	Sv	IP	H	R	BB	SO	HR
1992	3	7	2.73	68	0	15	59.1	54	21	34	48	3
Career	14	13	3.05	197	0	27	183.0	154	68	93	143	8

How Often He Throws Strikes

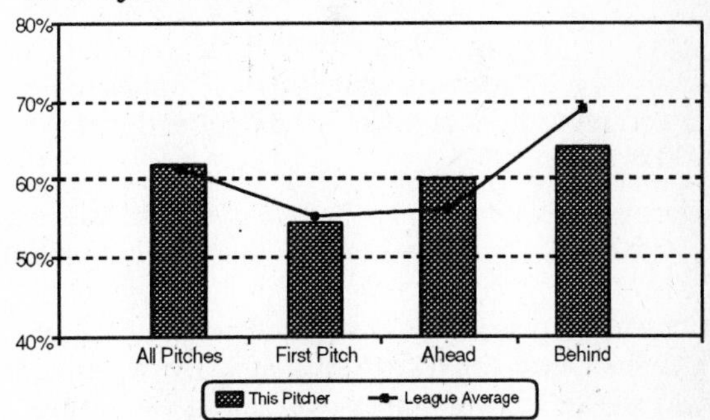

1992 Situational Stats

	W	L	ERA	Sv	IP		AB	H	HR	RBI	AVG
Home	3	2	1.17	9	30.2	LHB	66	12	2	8	.182
Road	0	5	4.40	6	28.2	RHB	156	42	1	26	.269
Day	1	2	2.70	3	20.0	Sc Pos	77	18	1	27	.234
Night	2	5	2.75	12	39.1	Clutch	160	37	3	21	.231

1992 Rankings (American League)

- 1st in lowest save percentage (65.2%)
- 2nd in blown saves (8) and relief losses (7)
- 5th most baserunners allowed per 9 innings in relief (11.7)
- Led the White Sox in games pitched (68), holds (16), blown saves and relief losses

CLUTCH HITTER

TIM RAINES

Position: LF/DH
Bats: B **Throws:** R
Ht: 5' 8" **Wt:** 185

Opening Day Age: 33
Born: 9/16/59 in Sanford, FL
ML Seasons: 14

HITTING:

Listening to some of the Chicago call-in radio shows, one might conclude that trading for Tim Raines was the worst mistake the White Sox ever made. Never mind that Raines batted .294 last year (.346 after the All-Star break). Or that he scored 102 runs, sixth-most in the league. Or that he stole 45 bases. Raines was supposed to bring a pennant to Chicago, and he hasn't been able to do that.

What he has given the club is exactly what it wanted from him: speed and on-base ability at the top of the batting order. He's shown surprising power at times, especially from the left side, and he's performed well in the clutch (.361 with runners in scoring position last year). Pitchers respect him, trying to keep the ball high and away from him. A very disciplined hitter, Raines will lay off most of those pitches and frequently draws walks (81 in 1992).

One reason some Chicagoans are down on Raines is that he has gotten off to slow starts in both his White Sox seasons. Nagging injuries, notably hamstring problems, have hindered him. Last year he didn't catch fire until late July, when he was shifted to the number-two spot in the batting order. From then on he was outstanding, hitting .391 after August.

BASERUNNING:

One of the best basestealers ever, Raines hasn't lost much at age 33. He was 45 for 51 (88 percent) last year, and his career success rate of 85 percent is the best in major-league history for more than 500 attempts.

FIELDING:

Raines has had some fielding lapses during his two Chicago seasons. He often misjudges fly balls, and his arm, despite decent assist totals, is not strong. However, his great speed permits him to outrun many of his mistakes, and he gets to many balls other fielders could never reach.

OVERALL:

When the 1992 season ended, there was considerable debate in Chicago circles about whether Raines would be protected in the expansion draft. He was protected, and he figures to remain one of the great table setters in the game.

Overall Statistics

	G	AB	R	H	D	T	HR	RBI	SB	BB	SO	AVG
1992	144	551	102	162	22	9	7	54	45	81	48	.294
Career	1704	6465	1138	1923	315	96	108	656	730	939	679	.297

Where He Hits the Ball

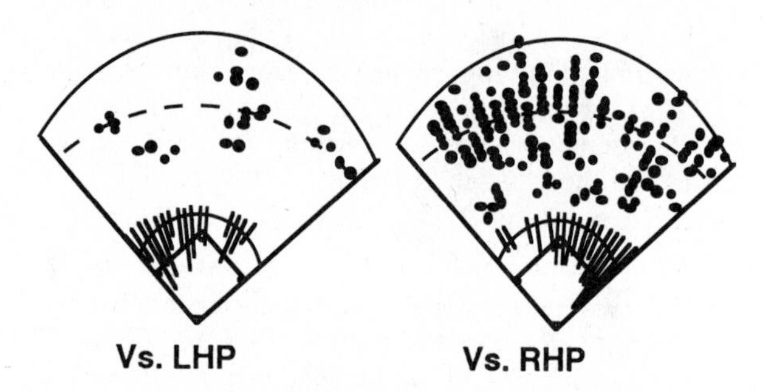

1992 Situational Stats

	AB	H	HR	RBI	AVG		AB	H	HR	RBI	AVG
Home	263	84	4	24	.319	LHP	135	34	0	11	.252
Road	288	78	3	30	.271	RHP	416	128	7	43	.308
Day	116	27	1	11	.233	Sc Pos	108	39	1	45	.361
Night	435	135	6	43	.310	Clutch	87	25	3	11	.287

1992 Rankings (American League)

- → 2nd highest batting average with runners in scoring position (.361)
- → 3rd highest stolen base percentage (88.2%)
- → 4th in triples (9) and bunts in play (39)
- → Led the White Sox in stolen bases (45), stolen base percentage, least GDPs in GDP situations (5.1%), batting average with runners in scoring position, batting average at home (.319), bunts in play and outfield assists (12)
- → Led AL left fielders in runs scored (102), batting average with runners in scoring position, batting average at home, fielding percentage (.994), bunts in play and lowest percentage of swings that missed (8.6%)

HITTING:

The off-season acquisition of Steve Sax from the Yankees was supposed to be one of the final pieces in the White Sox pennant puzzle. It wasn't meant to be, both for Sax and the White Sox. The club finished a disappointing third, and one of the reasons was that Sax batted a career-low .236.

Never shy about expressing his opinions, Sax often noted that he was hitting into tough luck last year. He was careful to add that he was having a bad year. Both observations have merit. One of the most extreme groundball hitters in the major leagues, he often hit the ball hard, but right at somebody.

However, it isn't just bad luck when your average drops 68 points in one year (from .304 to .236), as Sax' did in 1992. At 33, his bat speed has slowed a little, and he can no longer turn on a fastball like he used to. Sax is smart enough to make the adjustments needed to survive. He needs to hit for a high average, as he's never had a lot of discipline (43 walks last year).

BASERUNNING:

Sax has always been considered an outstanding baserunner, and he was exactly that for White Sox. Sax stole 30 bases in 42 attempts in 1992; it was the seventh straight time he's swiped 30 or more, and the tenth time in his career. His success rate (71 percent last year) has always been excellent.

FIELDING:

Gene Lamont noted that Sax seemed to take his hitting problems into the field last year, which is a fair assessment. After several steady seasons, Sax committed 20 errors last year, the most in the majors at his position. He showed neither great range nor the ability to turn the double play. Of course, working with several different shortstops didn't help him.

OVERALL:

Sax is a high-strung sort -- some would call him a whiner -- and his temperament seemed ill-suited to the Chicago team last year. Neither expansion team was interested in his fat contract when the Sox left him unprotected. Still, if he could hit .290 again, the Second City would probably find his act a lot more acceptable.

STEVE SAX

Position: 2B
Bats: R **Throws:** R
Ht: 5'11" **Wt:** 188

Opening Day Age: 33
Born: 1/29/60 in Sacramento, CA
ML Seasons: 12

Overall Statistics

	G	AB	R	H	D	T	HR	RBI	SB	BB	SO	AVG
1992	143	567	74	134	26	4	4	47	30	43	42	.236
Career	1705	6797	891	1915	273	46	53	541	437	548	576	.282

Where He Hits the Ball

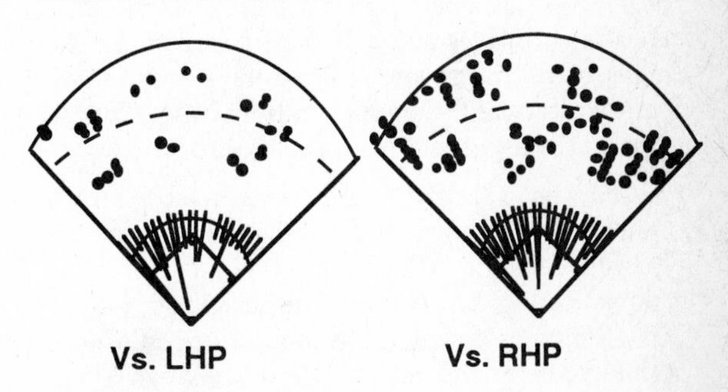

1992 Situational Stats

	AB	H	HR	RBI	AVG		AB	H	HR	RBI	AVG
Home	292	66	1	21	.226	LHP	157	36	1	7	.229
Road	275	68	3	26	.247	RHP	410	98	3	40	.239
Day	128	33	0	11	.258	Sc Pos	122	25	2	44	.205
Night	439	101	4	36	.230	Clutch	89	18	0	7	.202

1992 Rankings (American League)

- 1st in groundball/flyball ratio (2.6)
- 2nd lowest leadoff on-base average (.289)
- 3rd lowest slugging percentage vs. left handed pitchers (.299) and lowest batting average at home (.226)
- Led the White Sox in sacrifice bunts(12), groundball/flyball ratio and highest percentage of swings put into play (58.9%)
- Led AL second basemen in grounders hit, groundball/flyball ratio and errors (20)

PITCHING:

Late in the 1992 campaign, Bobby Thigpen reached a career milestone. By notching his 200th career save on September 20 against the Indians, Thigpen, at 29, became the youngest reliever ever to reach the 200 mark. If the celebration was a little muted, one could understand. By that point of the season, Thigpen was a little-used third option on the Sox closer list, ranking well behind Scott Radinsky and Roberto Hernandez.

Only two years after shattering the single-season save record by recording 57, Thigpen suffered through the worst season of his major-league career. His 22 saves were his lowest total since he became the club's full-time closer in 1988. His 4.75 was a career high by nearly a run. After posting 19 saves and a 3.25 ERA before the All-Star break, he recorded only three with a 7.58 mark afterward. Opposing hitters lit up Thigpen for a .321 average during the second half.

What went wrong? Thigpen's arm wasn't hurting, but there was little question that his fastball was losing velocity. After fanning 34 men in 36 innings during the first half, he struck out only 11 in 19 innings during the second. Thigpen's heater finally seemed to revive late in the year, after a period of relative inactivity, so perhaps the problem was simply a tired arm. Like most closers, Thigpen needs the fastball to succeed. His other main pitch, a slider, is not a great weapon.

HOLDING RUNNERS AND FIELDING:

A good athlete who played the outfield during his college days at Mississippi State, Thigpen has always fielded his position very well. His move to first has never been outstanding, but he seems to be improving in that department. After allowing eight stolen bases in 1991, Thigpen permitted only three (in three attempts) in '92.

OVERALL:

Thigpen's future with the White Sox appears clouded. No club needs three closers, and both Radinsky and Hernandez pitched better than Thigpen last year. Thigpen's arm appears to be sound, and he'd undoubtedly attract a lot of interest on the trading block despite not being selected in the expansion draft.

BOBBY THIGPEN

Position: RP
Bats: R **Throws:** R
Ht: 6' 3" **Wt:** 195

Opening Day Age: 29
Born: 7/17/63 in Tallahassee, FL
ML Seasons: 7

Overall Statistics

	W	L	ERA	G	GS	Sv	IP	H	R	BB	SO	HR
1992	1	3	4.75	55	0	22	55.0	58	29	33	45	4
Career	28	33	3.09	399	0	200	507.0	451	190	212	343	46

How Often He Throws Strikes

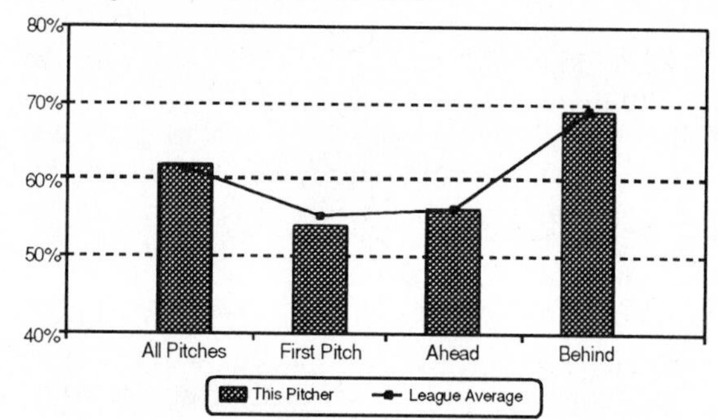

1992 Situational Stats

	W	L	ERA	Sv	IP		AB	H	HR	RBI	AVG
Home	1	2	3.77	9	28.2	LHB	80	27	1	12	.338
Road	0	1	5.81	13	26.1	RHB	131	31	3	23	.237
Day	0	3	6.64	10	20.1	Sc Pos	72	19	1	31	.264
Night	1	0	3.63	12	34.2	Clutch	143	36	2	26	.252

1992 Rankings (American League)

- 2nd lowest save percentage (75.9%) and most runners allowed per 9 innings in relief (15.4)
- 5th highest batting average allowed in relief (.275)
- Led the White Sox in saves (22), games finished (40), save opportunities (29), save percentage and lowest percentage of inherited runners scored (30.8%)

FUTURE MVP?

HITTING:

Not yet 25, Frank Thomas has become the greatest offensive force in the American League. Last year, in only his second full season, he ranked first in on-base average (.439), third in slugging (.536), second in runs scored (108), third in RBI (115), and in the top three in a number of other categories (see chart). No other player in the league comes close to matching the breadth of Thomas' offensive skills.

The only complaint one could make about Thomas' 1992 season concerned his drop in home runs, from 32 to 24. Thomas stands well off the plate in Lau/Hriniak fashion, and as a result pitchers have begun to work him low and outside a lot. Thomas has such great extension and bat speed that he can pull such pitches on a line into the left field corner -- resulting in more doubles (a league-leading 46), but fewer homers. If he stood closer to the plate, Thomas might hit a few more dingers, but the Sox are reluctant to tinker with success. Nor do they worry when people complain that Thomas "only swings at strikes." Didn't they say the same thing about Ted Williams?

BASERUNNING:

At 6-5 and 240 pounds, Thomas isn't going to break any speed records. He's not at all slow, however, and he's a pretty smart baserunner. He commits an occasional baserunning gaffe, but last year he stole six bases in nine attempts -- very good for such a huge man.

FIELDING:

A shoulder injury forced Thomas to work as a DH in 1991. Playing full-time at first in '92, he had a lot of problems. Thomas' 13 errors were second only to Mo Vaughn's 15, and he often looked awkward and unsure of himself. He needs to do better, but there's no reason why he can't improve.

OVERALL:

Late last season, Thomas was lobbying himself for the MVP Award, and only the Sox' disappointing season kept him from winning it. Thomas figures to be a serious candidate for years to come, regardless of how his teammates perform.

FRANK THOMAS

Position: 1B
Bats: R **Throws:** R
Ht: 6' 5" **Wt:** 240

Opening Day Age: 24
Born: 5/27/68 in Columbus, GA
ML Seasons: 3

Overall Statistics

	G	AB	R	H	D	T	HR	RBI	SB	BB	SO	AVG
1992	160	573	108	185	46	2	24	115	6	122	88	.323
Career	378	1323	251	426	88	7	63	255	7	304	254	.322

Where He Hits the Ball

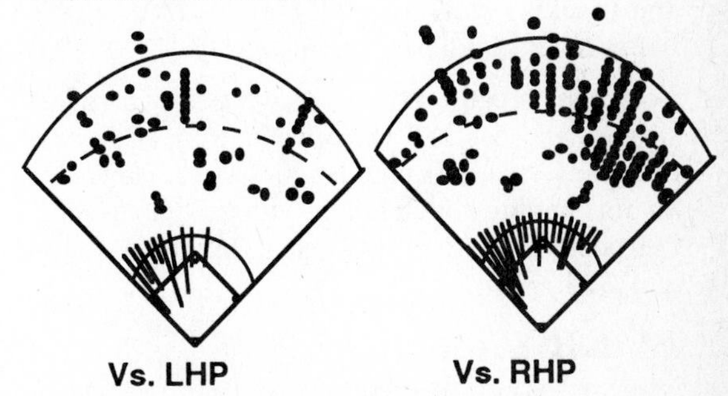

1992 Situational Stats

	AB	H	HR	RBI	AVG		AB	H	HR	RBI	AVG
Home	292	89	10	54	.305	LHP	140	50	8	26	.357
Road	281	96	14	61	.342	RHP	433	135	16	89	.312
Day	151	45	7	34	.298	Sc Pos	174	54	5	84	.310
Night	422	140	17	81	.332	Clutch	108	32	4	23	.296

1992 Rankings (American League)

- 1st in doubles (46), walks (122), times on base (312), on-base average (.439) and on-base percentage vs. right-handed pitchers (.433)
- 2nd in runs scored (108), slugging percentage vs. left handed pitchers (.650), batting average on the road (.342), errors at first base (13) and lowest fielding percentage at first base (.992)
- Led the White Sox in batting average (.323), runs scored, hits (185), doubles, total bases (307), RBI (115), sacrifice flies (11), walks, times on base, pitches seen (2,840), plate appearances (711), games played (160), slugging percentage and on-base average

GREAT RANGE

ROBIN VENTURA

Position: 3B
Bats: L **Throws:** R
Ht: 6' 1" **Wt:** 192

Opening Day Age: 25
Born: 7/14/67 in Santa Maria, CA
ML Seasons: 4

HITTING:

After his breakthrough 1991 campaign (23 homers, 100 RBI), Robin Ventura was expected to produce more of the same in '92. Though his home run total dropped a little to 16, Ventura came through in fine fashion. The third baseman drove home 93 runs and scored 85 while batting a solid .282. He is one of the finest young players in the American League.

Though he can turn on a fastball and drive it out of the park, Ventura is primarily a line drive hitter with power to all fields. His home run decline wasn't due to loss of power; Ventura belted 38 doubles, an increase of 13 over the previous season. Pitchers often will often throw him fastballs and breaking stuff low and outside, figuring it's better to let him go the opposite way.

Ventura is a patient hitter, drawing 93 walks last season, and has had more walks than strikeouts each season of his major league career. He is also an outstanding clutch hitter: with runners in scoring position the last two years, he's bafted .333 and .324.

BASERUNNING:

Ventura has below-average speed, and he's one of those guys you'd like to nail to first base: in his career, he's stolen only five bases in 17 attempts. When not trying to steal he's a fine baserunner, and will take the extra sack whenever his legs permit it.

FIELDING:

Ventura won a Gold Glove in 1991, and though he committed 23 errors in 1992, the Sox were campaigning for him to win another. He has great range and instincts for the position; he led all major league third sackers in both putouts and assists. The Sox feel that many of Ventura's errors last year were due to Frank Thomas' problems scooping up throws.

OVERALL:

A legendary batting star at Oklahoma State University, Ventura has yet to bat .300 in the majors. It could happen this year, with just a little more consistency. One bad month (.185 batting average in July) was all that kept Ventura from the charmed circle last year.

Overall Statistics

	G	AB	R	H	D	T	HR	RBI	SB	BB	SO	AVG
1992	157	592	85	167	38	1	16	93	2	93	71	.282
Career	480	1736	230	470	83	3	44	254	5	236	197	.271

Where He Hits the Ball

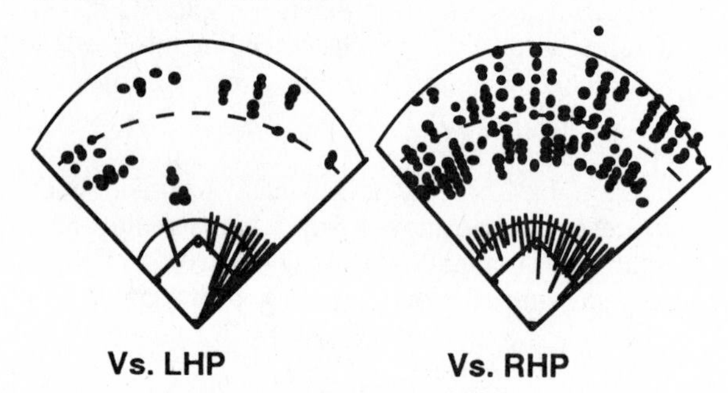

1992 Situational Stats

	AB	H	HR	RBI	AVG		AB	H	HR	RBI	AVG
Home	285	84	7	50	.295	LHP	182	47	2	28	.258
Road	307	83	9	43	.270	RHP	410	120	14	65	.293
Day	150	56	7	28	.373	Sc Pos	148	48	3	69	.324
Night	442	111	9	65	.251	Clutch	100	26	2	12	.260

1992 Rankings (American League)

- 2nd most errors at third base (23)
- 6th in doubles (38) and highest on-base percentage vs. right-handed pitchers (.387)
- Led the White Sox in intentional walks (9) and batting average with two strikes (.235)
- Led AL third basemen in RBIs (93), walks (93), times on base (260), pitches seen (2,664), plate appearances (694), games played (157) and batting average with runners in scoring position (.324)

SHAWN ABNER

Position: RF/LF/CF
Bats: R **Throws:** R
Ht: 6' 1" **Wt:** 194

Opening Day Age: 26
Born: 6/17/66 in Hamilton, OH
ML Seasons: 6

Overall Statistics

	G	AB	R	H	D	T	HR	RBI	SB	BB	SO	AVG
1992	97	208	21	58	10	1	1	16	1	12	35	.279
Career	392	840	89	191	39	4	11	71	6	43	153	.227

HITTING, FIELDING, BASERUNNING:

When the White Sox recalled Shawn Abner from their AAA Vancouver farm club early last year, expectations were modest. The first player chosen in the 1984 amateur draft, Abner had been a career disappointment, batting only .210 over parts of five major league seasons. Abner surprised people by hitting .279 and winding up as a semi-regular in right field.

Abner is a studious player, and he quickly absorbed the lessons of the Hriniak school of hitting: head still, hands held high and well back, release the top hand after swinging through the ball. It helped him make more consistent hard contact, and improved his work against right-handed breaking pitches. Platooned early, Abner wound up batting .314 against righties. He still didn't hit with much power, and he lacks discipline, with only 12 walks in over 200 at-bats. Though he possesses good speed, Abner is no basestealer, with only one steal in three attempts last year. He is, however, a fine outfielder with a good arm. He has a special knack for making sliding catches on sinking liners.

OVERALL:

Abner did a nice job for the Sox last year, but he figures to spend more time on the bench in 1993. He lacks power, and the Sox are desperate for some pop from the right field position. However, Abner has the skills to be a very valuable reserve.

JOEY CORA

Position: 2B/DH
Bats: B **Throws:** R
Ht: 5' 8" **Wt:** 152

Opening Day Age: 27
Born: 5/14/65 in Caguas, Puerto Rico
ML Seasons: 5

Overall Statistics

	G	AB	R	H	D	T	HR	RBI	SB	BB	SO	AVG
1992	68	122	27	30	7	1	0	9	10	22	13	.246
Career	308	710	104	175	20	6	0	43	45	77	69	.246

HITTING, FIELDING, BASERUNNING:

A disappointment when tried as a regular in 1991, Joey Cora was a success as a utility player in 1992. Despite infrequent stints in the White Sox lineup, Cora raised his overall average five points to .246. After banging only five extra-base hits in 228 at-bats in '91, he had eight extra-base knocks in 122 ABs in '92. Cora's biggest advance was in the discipline department. He drew 22 walks, two more than his 1991 figure despite his lower at-bat total. Cora's on-base average was a very fine .371.

Cora has the variety of skills that make for a good utility man. He's versatile and can do a respectable defensive job at second, short and third. Second base is his best position; after having some problems there in 1991, he fielded .984 there last year and showed good range. A switch-hitter, he's a plate-crowder who frequently gets hit by pitches, and he's done competent work from both sides. He hits the curveball fairly well, and he almost always makes contact (only 13 strikeouts last year). Cora is an excellent baserunner, swiping 10 sacks in 13 attempts. He was frequently used as George Bell's "legs" in the late innings.

OVERALL:

Cora is not yet 28, and except for a half season in '91, he hasn't had an extended opportunity to win a full-time job. With the White Sox, he probably won't get that chance. With someone else, he just might.

MICHAEL HUFF

Position: RF
Bats: R **Throws:** R
Ht: 6' 1" **Wt:** 180

Opening Day Age: 29
Born: 8/11/63 in Honolulu, HI
ML Seasons: 3

Overall Statistics

	G	AB	R	H	D	T	HR	RBI	SB	BB	SO	AVG
1992	60	115	13	24	5	0	0	8	1	10	24	.209
Career	174	383	59	90	16	2	4	35	15	50	78	.235

HITTING, FIELDING, BASERUNNING:

A pleasant surprise as a reserve outfielder in 1991, Michael Huff missed much of the '92 season when he fractured his left shoulder making a diving catch in Seattle. Huff was on the shelf from mid-June until September 1, and he couldn't get untracked after his return. Huff went 6-for-41 over the last month, reducing his final average to .209.

The White Sox feel that his 1992 numbers aren't a fair assessment of Huff's skills. He was a steady .300 hitter in the minors, and he hit .251 for the Indians and White Sox in 1991. A groundball hitter who likes to go the other way, Huff does not have a lot of power. He is, however, a patient hitter, and will usually draw an above-average number of walks. When healthy he's an excellent basestealer, but the injury shut down that part of his game last year. Huff is a fine, speedy outfielder with good range and a strong arm. He can handle all three outfield positions.

OVERALL:

Not projected as a regular with the White Sox, Huff would possibly get a more extended chance with a weaker club. However, he is now 29 years old, a little long in the tooth to be considered a "prospect." He has value as a reserve, however, and can probably stick in the majors in that role.

DAN PASQUA

Position: RF
Bats: L **Throws:** L
Ht: 6' 0" **Wt:** 203

Opening Day Age: 31
Born: 10/17/61 in Yonkers, NY
ML Seasons: 8

Overall Statistics

	G	AB	R	H	D	T	HR	RBI	SB	BB	SO	AVG
1992	93	265	26	56	16	1	6	33	0	36	57	.211
Career	816	2421	317	597	117	14	110	366	5	309	582	.247

HITTING, FIELDING, BASERUNNING:

A useful platoon player during four previous seasons with the White Sox, Dan Pasqua had a terrible 1992. After averaging 16 homers per year from 1988 to 1991, Pasqua managed only six round-trippers, the lowest total of his career. Pasqua's .211 average and 33 RBI were his lowest figures since his 60-game debut with the 1985 Yankees.

A flyball hitter with good discipline, Pasqua will occasionally chase a bad breaking pitch; he can handle the fastball, and even last year, pitchers were reluctant to challenge him on a consistent basis. He simply wasn't hitting, either for average or power. And Pasqua needs to hit, because he lacks other skills: his outfield arm and range are below average (though he does have sure hands), and his speed is nonexistent. One main problem for Pasqua was that he wasn't completely healthy for much of last year. A torn right hamstring forced him on the shelf in June, and, after returning a month later, he quickly suffered a recurrence of the injury.

OVERALL:

At 31, Pasqua is young enough to come back after his dismaying 1992 season. He is signed through 1994, and the Sox figure to give him another chance. He'll have to hit a lot better than he did in '92, however, if he wants to see much playing time.

CHICAGO WHITE SOX MINOR LEAGUE PROSPECTS

ORGANIZATION OVERVIEW:

The White Sox have become known as a club which drafts very well, thanks to the four-year bonanza which netted Jack McDowell, Robin Ventura, Frank Thomas and Alex Fernandez -- all number-one Sox draft choices from 1987 through 1990. The man who orchestrated those picks, general manager Larry Himes, now has the same job with the Cubs. It's too early to fairly assess the current Ron Schueler regime. Right now the White Sox system is loaded with good pitching prospects; hitters are scarce. As a losing club, the Sox were patient with their youngsters. It remains to be seen how indulgent the Schueler regime will be now that the club seems to be only a couple of players away from a division title.

JASON P. BERE

Position: P **Opening Day Age:** 21
Bats: R **Throws:** R **Born:** 5/26/71 in
Ht: 6' 3" **Wt:** 192 Cambridge, MA

Recent Statistics

	W	L	ERA	G	GS	Sv	IP	H	R	BB	SO	HR
91 A South Bend	9	12	2.87	27	27	0	163.0	116	66	100	158	8
92 A Sarasota	7	2	2.41	18	18	0	116.0	84	35	34	106	3
92 AA Birmingham	4	4	3.00	8	8	0	54.0	44	22	20	45	1
92 AAA Vancouver	0	0	0.00	1	0	0	1.0	2	0	0	2	0

A lowly 36th-round draft choice in 1990, Bere has come a long way in a short time. When the '92 season started, he was pitching at Class A Sarasota; when the season ended, he was a mainstay at AA Birmingham, and the Sox protected him in the expansion draft. Imposing at 6'3", Bere throws hard; he's allowed only 271 hits in 370 minor league innings, with 349 strikeouts. His control, a problem in 1991, improved last year. Bere figures to start 1993 at AAA but could be with the big club before year's end.

RODNEY E. BOLTON

Position: P **Opening Day Age:** 24
Bats: R **Throws:** R **Born:** 9/23/68 in
Ht: 6' 2" **Wt:** 190 Chattanooga, TN

Recent Statistics

	W	L	ERA	G	GS	Sv	IP	H	R	BB	SO	HR
91 A Sarasota	7	6	1.91	15	15	0	103.2	81	29	23	77	2
91 AA Birmingham	8	4	1.62	12	12	0	89.0	73	26	21	57	3
92 AAA Vancouver	11	9	2.93	27	27	0	187.1	174	72	59	111	9

Bolton hasn't had to come as far as Bere, but it's close -- he was a 13th-round pick in the same 1990 draft. Bolton spent the '92 campaign at AAA Vancouver and had another winning season. Thus far in his career, he's 36-21 with a 2.12 ERA. He throws strikes, and he's said to have a top-quality slider. Bolton has never stayed long at any minor league level, and might not have to spend another year in AAA. He could make the club outright this spring.

BRIAN DRAHMAN

Position: P **Opening Day Age:** 26
Bats: R **Throws:** R **Born:** 11/7/66 in
Ht: 6' 3" **Wt:** 205 Kenton, KY

Recent Statistics

	W	L	ERA	G	GS	Sv	IP	H	R	BB	SO	HR
92 AAA Vancouver	2	4	2.01	48	0	30	58.1	44	16	31	34	5
92 AL Chicago	0	0	2.57	5	0	0	7.0	6	3	2	1	0

Thus far in his career, Brian Drahman's main claim to fame is that he was traded even-up for a 200-game winner, Jerry Reuss. That was at the end of Reuss' career; Drahman hopes he's at the beginning of his. Last year Drahman notched a record 30 saves at AAA Vancouver, with a 2.01 ERA. His problems are simple: he doesn't throw as hard as the classic late relievers, and the Sox have a lot of pitchers in his way. Expansion was made for men like this.

LARRY W. THOMAS

Position: P **Opening Day Age:** 23
Bats: R **Throws:** L **Born:** 10/25/69 in
Ht: 6' 1" **Wt:** 190 Miami, FL

Recent Statistics

	W	L	ERA	G	GS	Sv	IP	H	R	BB	SO	HR
91 A Utica	1	3	1.47	11	10	0	73.1	55	22	25	61	2
91 AA Birmingham	0	0	3.00	2	0	0	6.0	6	3	4	2	0
92 A Sarasota	5	0	1.62	8	8	0	55.2	44	14	7	50	1
92 AA Birmingham	8	6	1.94	17	17	0	120.2	102	32	30	72	4

The White Sox' second round pick in 1991, Thomas will inevitably be compared with Scott Ruffcorn, the Sox' first pick that year. Both began last year at Class A Sarasota, but it was Thomas who moved up to AA Birmingham after a 5-0 start. Ruffcorn probably throws a little harder, but they don't draft junkballers in the second round. Since Thomas has a lifetime ERA of 1.76 thus far, it's probably safe to call him a prospect.

BRANDON L. WILSON

Position: SS **Opening Day Age:** 24
Bats: R **Throws:** R **Born:** 2/26/69 in
Ht: 6' 1" **Wt:** 175 Owensboro, KY

Recent Statistics

	G	AB	R	H	D	T	HR	RBI	SB	BB	SO	AVG
91 A South Bend	125	463	75	145	18	6	2	49	41	61	70	.313
91 AA Birmingham	2	10	3	4	1	0	0	2	0	0	2	.400
92 A Sarasota	103	399	68	118	22	6	4	54	30	45	64	.296
92 AA Birmingham	27	107	10	29	4	0	0	4	5	4	16	.271

If Ozzie Guillen can't come back this year, the White Sox seem well protected at shortstop. They have Craig Grebeck at the major-league level and now Wilson, who has solidified his rating as one of the brightest prospects in their system. Wilson doesn't have dazzling range, but he's a very steady shortstop, he can run (35 steals last year), he has a good batting eye, and he can hit (.294 career minor-league average). He's still probably a year away from the majors.

SANDY ALOMAR JR

Position: C
Bats: R **Throws:** R
Ht: 6' 5" **Wt:** 215

Opening Day Age: 26
Born: 6/18/66 in Salinas, Puerto Rico
ML Seasons: 5

Overall Statistics

	G	AB	R	H	D	T	HR	RBI	SB	BB	SO	AVG
1992	89	299	22	75	16	0	2	26	3	13	32	.251
Career	280	948	93	248	52	2	12	105	7	49	106	.262

Where He Hits the Ball

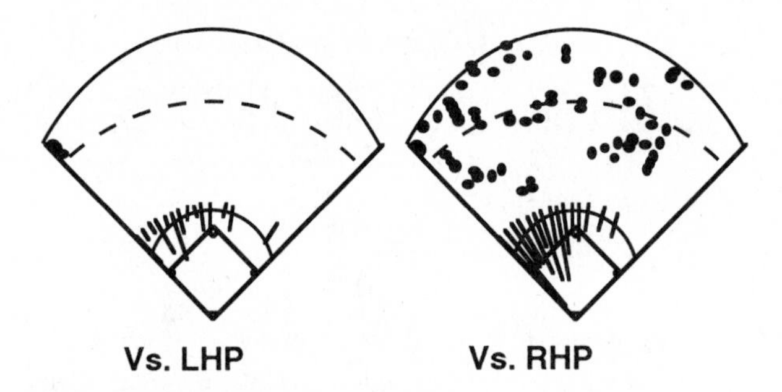

1992 Situational Stats

	AB	H	HR	RBI	AVG		AB	H	HR	RBI	AVG
Home	158	41	1	15	.259	LHP	58	11	0	3	.190
Road	141	34	1	11	.241	RHP	241	64	2	23	.266
Day	73	16	0	4	.219	Sc Pos	65	15	1	24	.231
Night	226	59	2	22	.261	Clutch	64	17	0	7	.266

1992 Rankings (American League)

- 2nd in highest percentage of runners caught stealing as a catcher (44.9%)
- 7th in lowest batting average on a 0-2 count (.050)

HITTING:

In 1990, Sandy Alomar Jr. hit .290 and won the American League Rookie of the Year award. Since then, he's spent too much time in the trainer's room. Over the past two seasons, Alomar has had only 483 at-bats while battling an assortment of injuries. Over that time, he's batted just .238 with two homers and 33 RBI -- about half the production he achieved in 1990.

Last year a variety of injuries -- split webbing on his right hand, sore right hand, knee, thigh and a broken cheekbone -- cost Alomar playing time. His season ended for all intents and purposes when he strained cartilage in his right knee sliding into third base on August 16. In the last two years, Alomar has played in only 140 games.

Alomar was scheduled to play winter ball in Puerto Rico after last season to get more at-bats. When healthy, he is a singles hitter despite his good size - -- 6-5 and 215 pounds. He can hit behind the runner, bunt, hit-and-run and hit in the clutch. Last year, though, he hit only .231 with runners in scoring position. He'll need a lot of at-bats to rediscover that disciplined stroke.

BASERUNNING:

Alomar runs well for a catcher and might steal three to four bases a year. He can go from first to third and slides hard. A hard slide caused the injury to his right knee.

FIELDING:

In spite of his injuries, Alomar remains one of the best defensive catchers in the AL. He's quick behind the plate and no one blocks balls in the dirt better. After straining the rotator cuff in his right shoulder in 1991, Alomar re-strengthened it through weight training and threw well to all bases last year.

OVERALL:

The Indians need a healthy Alomar to be a contender -- they're a better team when he's behind the plate. His pitch selection is improving, but sometimes he lets pitchers shake him off too much. In 1990, Alomar was a team leader as a rookie. He needs to play a full season to re-assume that role.

CARLOS BAERGA

Position: 2B
Bats: B **Throws:** R
Ht: 5'11" **Wt:** 185

Opening Day Age: 24
Born: 11/4/68 in San Juan, Puerto Rico
ML Seasons: 3

Overall Statistics

	G	AB	R	H	D	T	HR	RBI	SB	BB	SO	AVG
1992	161	657	92	205	32	1	20	105	10	35	76	.312
Career	427	1562	218	457	77	5	38	221	13	99	207	.293

Where He Hits the Ball

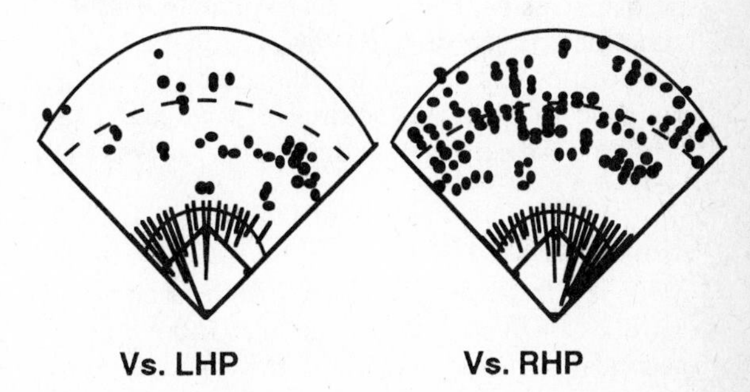

1992 Situational Stats

	AB	H	HR	RBI	AVG		AB	H	HR	RBI	AVG
Home	329	116	9	50	.353	LHP	168	63	4	35	.375
Road	328	89	11	55	.271	RHP	489	142	16	70	.290
Day	217	70	5	33	.323	Sc Pos	182	56	5	81	.308
Night	440	135	15	72	.307	Clutch	126	40	2	13	.317

1992 Rankings (American League)

- 1st in singles (152)
- 2nd in at-bats (657), hits (205), games played (161) and highest batting average at home (.353)
- 3rd in highest batting average vs. left-handed pitchers (.375)
- Led the Indians in batting average (.312), at-bats, hits, singles, doubles (32), total bases (299), sacrifice flies (9), intentional walks (10), hit by pitch (13), times on base (253), most pitches seen (2,373), plate appearances (716), games played, batting average vs. left-handed pitchers, batting average vs. right-handed pitchers (.290) and slugging percentage vs. left-handed pitchers (.500)

HITTING:

A couple of years ago Rich Dauer, then a coach for the Indians, took one look at Carlos Baerga and said, "He could be a batting champion." The switch-hitting Baerga has done nothing to refute those words. Last year he became the first American League second baseman ever to hit at least .300 with 200 hits, 20 homers and 100 RBI in the same season. He did all that as a 23 year old playing his first full season at second base.

A line drive hitter, Baerga never hit more than 12 homers in a season before last year. He's a sucker for high fastballs, but not many other pitches give him problems. Baerga has the ability to turn on low breaking balls -- especially batting left-handed -- and drive them a long way.

Baerga is not a patient hitter. He had the second most at-bats (657) in the big leagues last year, but walked only 35 times, 10 of them intentional. But when a player gets 205 hits, the second-most in baseball, and hits .308 with runners in scoring position, patience is nit-picking.

BASERUNNING:

Baerga's body looks like a big block of ice. He's about 5'11" and weighs 185 pounds. A body like that shouldn't be able to run, but Baerga can. He stole 10 bases in 12 attempts last year. He goes from first to third well and slides hard.

FIELDING:

Not just a hitter, Baerga has good range, especially going behind second base, and a strong arm that allows him to play a very deep second base. The Indians led the majors with 176 double plays and it was mostly due to Baerga's fearless work on the pivot at second.

OVERALL:

Baerga wants to be the best second baseman in baseball. It's not just talk. He's missed only five games in two years and worked to avoid the hamstring pulls that bothered him in 1990 and 1991. His teammates took to calling him "The Franchise" last season. They weren't kidding.

IN HIS PRIME

HITTING:

Albert Belle is an aggressive hitter who tries to do one thing with almost every pitch thrown his way -- pull it to left field and hit a home run. Hitting coach Jose Morales works with him constantly to be more patient and hit the pitch where it is thrown. Sometimes the advice works for a while, but more often it fades away. Given Belle's production over the last two seasons -- 62 home runs, 207 RBI -- it's doubtful he's going to change.

Belle almost never misses a mistake pitch. Hang a breaking ball over the plate or get a fastball up in the strike zone and he'll hit it a long way. He drove in a career-high 112 runs last year, but the number could have been even higher. Because he is so aggressive, Belle is easy to pitch to in clutch situations. He hit only .239 with runners in scoring position last year, and still guessed too much. He'd go to the plate looking for one pitch, and when he saw it he'd swing even if it wasn't a strike.

BASERUNNING:

Belle is a frustrating player to watch. If he draws a walk, it will sometimes take him more than 20 seconds to reach first base. But he does have decent speed -- he stole eight bases in 10 attempts -- and above-average baserunning instincts. He goes from first to third well.

FIELDING:

Before the All-Star break last year, manager Mike Hargrove used Belle almost strictly as a DH. Belle felt he was too young for that role. He tended to hit better when he played left field, even though he is an average fielder at best. He looks awkward running after fly balls, but usually makes the catch. His throwing arm is below average.

OVERALL:

Belle behaved himself for the most part last year after a troublesome 1991. He feuded with Hargrove off and on, but usually managed to stay in the lineup. When Belle does that, he's always going to drive in runs.

ALBERT BELLE

Position: DH/LF
Bats: R **Throws:** R
Ht: 6' 2" **Wt:** 200

Opening Day Age: 26
Born: 8/25/66 in Shreveport, LA
ML Seasons: 4

Overall Statistics

	G	AB	R	H	D	T	HR	RBI	SB	BB	SO	AVG
1992	153	585	81	152	23	1	34	112	8	52	128	.260
Career	347	1287	164	335	62	7	70	247	13	90	288	.260

Where He Hits the Ball

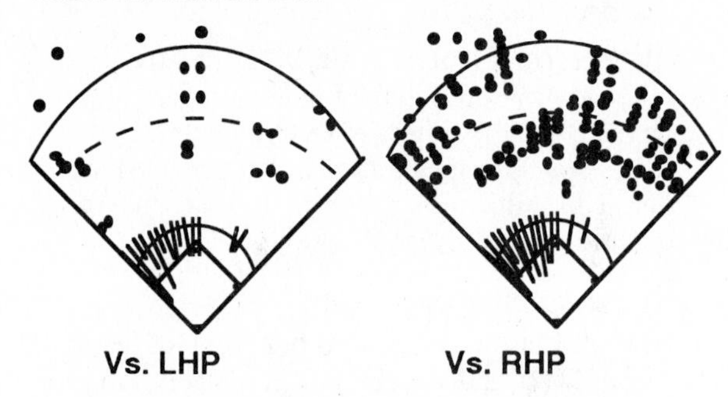

1992 Situational Stats

	AB	H	HR	RBI	AVG		AB	H	HR	RBI	AVG
Home	285	76	15	63	.267	LHP	138	35	8	27	.254
Road	300	76	19	49	.253	RHP	447	117	26	85	.262
Day	191	47	6	31	.246	Sc Pos	155	37	12	81	.239
Night	394	105	28	81	.266	Clutch	106	25	5	23	.236

1992 Rankings (American League)

- ➟ 4th in home runs (34) and RBI (112)
- ➟ 7th in HR frequency (17.2 ABs per HR)
- ➟ 9th in strikeouts (128) and GDPs (18)
- ➟ 10th in slugging percentage (.477)
- ➟ Led the Indians in home runs, RBI, strikeouts, GDPs, slugging percentage and HR frequency
- ➟ Led designated hitters in home runs, RBI, strikeouts and HR frequency

PITCHING:

If the Indians had a solid pitching staff, Dennis Cook would be the perfect long reliever. He keeps his team close, will throw inside and can pitch effectively in chunks of five and six innings. Last season, however, the Indians didn't have a solid staff, forcing Cook to do a lot more starting than relieving. It didn't turn out to be all bad though. Cook had a respectable record, winning five games and posting a decent 3.82 ERA.

Cook developed a cut fastball during the season to go along with his forkball, slider and regular heater. It gave the lefthander an out pitch against both right-handed and left-handed batters. With hitters looking inside for his cutter, Cook was able to pitch to the outside part of the plate more effectively. While the cut fastball was a big pitch for Cook, his heater is still his best pitch. It's not overpowering, but when Cook is able to put it in the right spots, he not only can be effective, he can win.

Cook's location isn't bad, but when he makes a mistake it's hard to miss. He allowed 29 homers last year, and since 1990 he's given up 49. In his 25 starts, he'd usually give up at least one homer in the first three innings and then settle down.

HOLDING RUNNERS AND FIELDING:

Cook has a tricky move to first. Maybe too tricky: he led the American League with five balks last year. Much of that had to do with AL umpires getting their first look at his move. Except for these balks, he shut down the running game, allowing only eight steals in 18 attempts. He's a decent fielder.

OVERALL:

Cook did just what the Indians expected last year. He pitched well as both a starter and reliever. He's smart, intense and usually finds a way to keep his club in a ballgame. If he's the Tribe's fourth or fifth starter this year, it wouldn't be a terrible thing.

DENNIS COOK

Position: SP/RP
Bats: L **Throws:** L
Ht: 6' 3" **Wt:** 185

Opening Day Age: 30
Born: 10/4/62 in Lamarque, TX
ML Seasons: 5

Overall Statistics

	W	L	ERA	G	GS	Sv	IP	H	R	BB	SO	HR
1992	5	7	3.82	32	25	0	158.0	156	79	50	96	29
Career	24	20	3.66	126	64	1	474.2	442	223	162	248	68

How Often He Throws Strikes

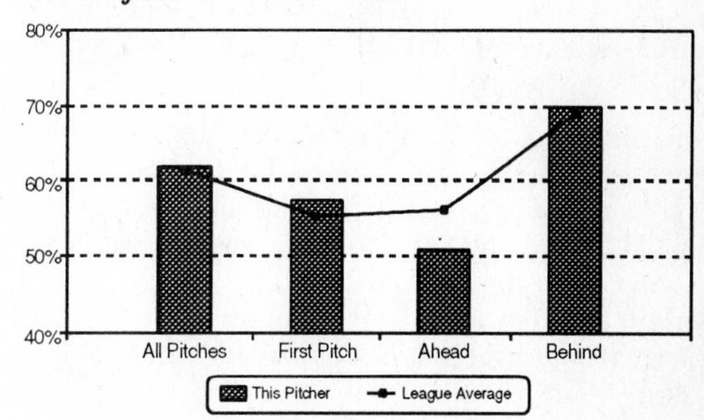

1992 Situational Stats

	W	L	ERA	Sv	IP		AB	H	HR	RBI	AVG
Home	4	3	4.04	0	91.1	LHB	98	23	4	12	.235
Road	1	4	3.51	0	66.2	RHB	513	133	25	64	.259
Day	2	3	3.99	0	70.0	Sc Pos	129	33	5	41	.256
Night	3	4	3.68	0	88.0	Clutch	31	6	1	2	.194

1992 Rankings (American League)

- 1st in balks (5)
- 3rd in home runs allowed (29)
- 10th in highest ERA at home (4.04)
- Led the Indians home runs allowed, balks and lowest batting average allowed vs. right-handed batters (.259)

FELIX FERMIN

Position: SS/3B
Bats: R **Throws:** R
Ht: 5'11" **Wt:** 170

Opening Day Age: 29
Born: 10/9/63 in Mao, Valverde, Dominican Republic
ML Seasons: 6

Overall Statistics

	G	AB	R	H	D	T	HR	RBI	SB	BB	SO	AVG
1992	79	215	27	58	7	2	0	13	0	18	10	.270
Career	578	1692	169	431	42	9	1	111	17	123	105	.255

Where He Hits the Ball

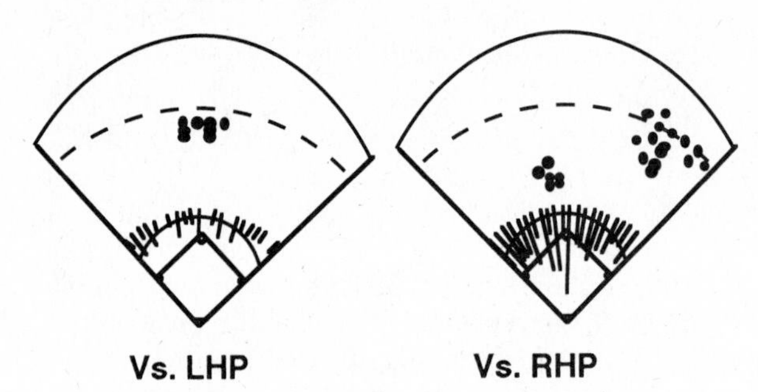

1992 Situational Stats

	AB	H	HR	RBI	AVG		AB	H	HR	RBI	AVG
Home	102	30	0	7	.294	LHP	42	14	0	4	.333
Road	113	28	0	6	.248	RHP	173	44	0	9	.254
Day	87	25	0	5	.287	Sc Pos	49	14	0	13	.286
Night	128	33	0	8	.258	Clutch	37	8	0	1	.216

1992 Rankings (American League)

- 1st in lowest batting average on a 3-1 count (.000)

HITTING:

Felix Fermin doesn't try to fool anybody when it comes to hitting. How can someone who has hit one home run in 1,692 big-league at-bats fool anybody? Fermin simply does what he's always done -- make contact, advance runners with sacrifice bunts, hit behind runners and work the hit-and-run. The shortstop batted .270 last year, the third straight year he'd improved his average. But as usual, he was strictly a singles hitter, with only nine extra-base blows.

The Indians benched Fermin for most of last season because they were intent on giving the starting shortstop job to Mark Lewis. Yet in the last month of the season when they were trying to win as many games as possible to bury their 105-loss season of 1991, they turned to Fermin and he responded.

Fermin chokes up on the bat and splits his hands while swinging. He likes to hit fastballs from center field to the right field line and rarely pulls a pitch. This makes him fairly easy to defense, with opposing outfielders shifting toward the right field line and playing shallow. An excellent contact hitter, he's struck out only 37 times in his last 639 at-bats.

BASERUNNING:

Fermin runs hard but not fast. He's aggressive, always looking to take an extra base on a single, and goes from first to third well. Due to a weak 59 percent career basestealing success ratio entering the 1992 season, he did not make an attempt all year.

FIELDING:

Fermin is one of the most underrated shortstops in the American League. He has fine range to his left and right and a surprisingly strong throwing arm. He is an aggressive fielder, always charging hard for groundballs hit in front of him.

OVERALL:

Cleveland kept Fermin as an insurance policy last year in case Lewis failed. He kept his mouth shut and went along with the plan. Although some in the Indians' front office think they should stick with Fermin as the starter, he'll likely see the same or less playing time for the Tribe in '93.

HITTING:

Glenallen Hill is an exciting hitter because of his awesome power. In 369 at-bats last year, he hit a career-high 18 homers with 16 doubles and one triple. A total of 39 percent of his hits went for extra bases.

Unfortunately, Hill has flaws in his swing. Breaking balls down and away give him problems. He tends to step in the bucket during his swing and sometimes looks so mechanical it's tempting to look for bolts in his neck. But when Hill keeps his swing short and compact, he has as much power as any Indian including Albert Belle. He is not a patient hitter, however. He struck out 73 times last year while drawing only 20 walks -- a big reason he hit only .241.

Hill's main problem since coming to Cleveland from Toronto in 1991 hasn't been pitches or pitchers. It's been staying healthy. Hill suffered a pulled groin muscle at the end of spring training that cost him to miss April and most of May. Near the end of the season he injured his back and missed a chance to reach 20 homers. He suffered a back injury in 1991 that limited him to only 37 games with the Indians.

BASERUNNING:

Hill is a fast baserunner. He can beat out infield hits and get from first to third quickly. At one point last year, he stole three straight bases, but his judgement and timing weren't good. In 15 attempts, Hill was thrown out six times.

FIELDING:

Hill can play all three outfield positions although he saw most of his action in left last year. He goes into the gaps well, but has trouble charging grounders, causing a few of his six errors last year. His arm is average and can be run on.

OVERALL:

If Hill stayed healthy, it would be interesting to see what he could do in 500 at-bats. However, that possibility may only come with a different team. If Belle is the starting left fielder this year, Hill will again get less playing time. He's already voiced his displeasure over that possibility and could be traded for a pitcher.

GLENALLEN HILL

Position: LF/DH
Bats: R **Throws:** R
Ht: 6' 2" **Wt:** 210

Opening Day Age: 28
Born: 3/22/65 in Santa Cruz, CA
ML Seasons: 4

Overall Statistics

	G	AB	R	H	D	T	HR	RBI	SB	BB	SO	AVG
1992	102	369	38	89	16	1	18	49	9	20	73	.241
Career	277	902	118	221	35	6	39	113	25	64	201	.245

Where He Hits the Ball

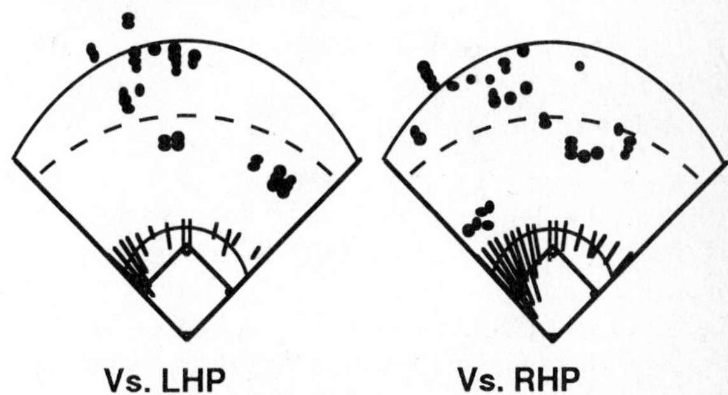

1992 Situational Stats

	AB	H	HR	RBI	AVG		AB	H	HR	RBI	AVG
Home	179	46	7	24	.257	LHP	105	28	7	18	.267
Road	190	43	11	25	.226	RHP	264	61	11	31	.231
Day	108	24	1	7	.222	Sc Pos	86	21	3	31	.244
Night	261	65	17	42	.249	Clutch	80	16	7	13	.200

1992 Rankings (American League)

- Did not rank near the top or bottom in any category

THOMAS HOWARD

Position: LF/CF/RF
Bats: B **Throws:** R
Ht: 6' 2" **Wt:** 205

Opening Day Age: 28
Born: 12/11/64 in Middletown, OH
ML Seasons: 3

Overall Statistics

	G	AB	R	H	D	T	HR	RBI	SB	BB	SO	AVG
1992	122	361	37	100	15	2	2	32	15	17	60	.277
Career	248	686	71	182	29	5	6	54	25	41	128	.265

Where He Hits the Ball

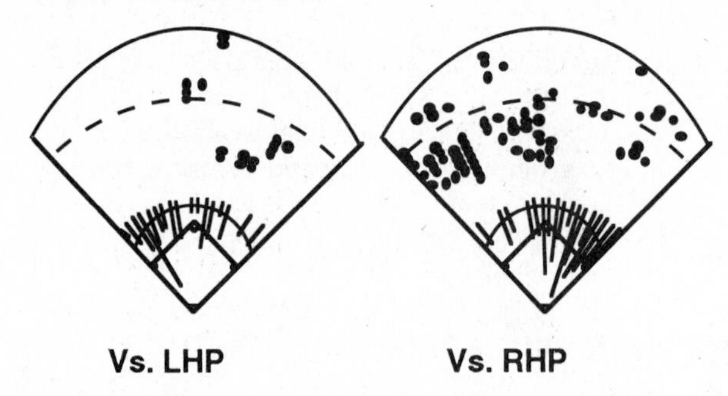

1992 Situational Stats

	AB	H	HR	RBI	AVG		AB	H	HR	RBI	AVG
Home	181	49	1	18	.271	LHP	104	30	2	11	.288
Road	180	51	1	14	.283	RHP	257	70	0	21	.272
Day	125	35	1	8	.280	Sc Pos	85	26	0	27	.306
Night	236	65	1	24	.275	Clutch	75	21	1	9	.280

1992 Rankings (American League)

- 10th in lowest stolen base percentage (65.2%)
- Led the Indians in sacrifice bunts (10) and least GDPs per GDP situation (6.8%)

HITTING:

In San Diego, Thomas Howard and former manager Greg Riddoch clashed. So when the Indians needed an outfielder in mid-April because of an injury to Glenallen Hill, the Padres accepted two minor leaguers for the switch-hitting former number-one draft pick.

The trade gave Howard's career a boost. He played all three outfield positions and immediately started hitting. By April 30, he was hitting .353. By June 9 he was still hitting .319 and playing almost every day. Howard didn't show much power but hit to all fields and batted .306 with runners in scoring position. He hit .288 against lefthanders and .272 against righthanders. American League pitchers found out quickly he could hit a fastball, but Howard continued to hit even when they started throwing more curveballs, sliders and forkballs.

Howard spent much of the season near the .300 mark, but when his average dropped in September his playing time was cut. Hill was getting the call in left field during the last month of the season, and there was speculation that the Indians didn't play Howard because they didn't want him to get too much exposure before the expansion draft. The Indians denied that.

BASERUNNING:

Howard runs the bases well. He stole a career-high 15 bases for the Tribe last year, though he was also caught stealing eight times. He should be able to improve with experience.

FIELDING:

Howard was the Indians' most consistent outfielder. His best positions are left and center field, but he played some innings in right as well. He goes back on balls well and seldom gets fooled. When he makes a mistake, he admits it. He has a good throwing arm but had to protect it somewhat after suffering a separated right shoulder in a collision at first base on May 2.

OVERALL:

Before the expansion draft, the Indians didn't know whether to protect Howard or Hill, so they kept both. Howard is the ideal fourth outfielder. He can run, play good defense, switch-hit and come off the bench.

MARK LEWIS

Position: SS
Bats: R **Throws:** R
Ht: 6' 1" **Wt:** 190

Opening Day Age: 23
Born: 11/30/69 in Hamilton, OH
ML Seasons: 2

Overall Statistics

	G	AB	R	H	D	T	HR	RBI	SB	BB	SO	AVG
1992	122	413	44	109	21	0	5	30	4	25	69	.264
Career	206	727	73	192	36	1	5	60	6	40	114	.264

Where He Hits the Ball

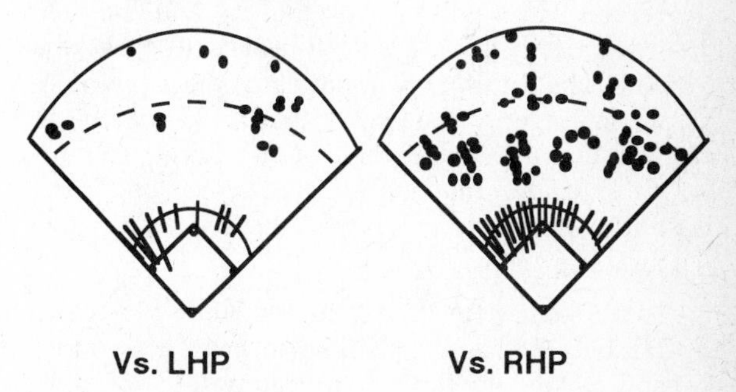

1992 Situational Stats

	AB	H	HR	RBI	AVG		AB	H	HR	RBI	AVG
Home	195	54	2	17	.277	LHP	97	28	2	10	.289
Road	218	55	3	13	.252	RHP	316	81	3	20	.256
Day	110	29	0	5	.264	Sc Pos	83	16	0	22	.193
Night	303	80	5	25	.264	Clutch	75	15	0	3	.200

1992 Rankings (American League)

- 6th in lowest batting average with the bases loaded (.077)
- Led AL shortstops in errors (25)

HITTING:

On a team full of young players with bright talent, Mark Lewis should be one of the brightest. Instead, Lewis' first full year in the big leagues stood out only because it was so dull. More questions than answers were raised about the Indians' number-one pick in 1988 and many of them dealing with Lewis' hitting.

The youngster went to spring training reportedly locked in a battle with Felix Fermin for the shortstop's job. But the contest was a joke. The Indians handed the job to Lewis on a silver platter. He was supposed to be a shortstop whose offense would make up for his average defensive skills. Last year, however, he was mostly an easy out with the bat.

Lewis doesn't generate much bat movement before the pitcher delivers the ball. The Indians have been trying to give him a cocking mechanism for the last few years so he can generate better bat speed. However, he hasn't been able to make the adjustment. There are some who believe Lewis is too stubborn to really try.

BASERUNNING:

Lewis runs every ground ball out hard. However, he's not a great basestealer. He stole four bases in nine attempts last year and had mediocre success rates in the minors.

FIELDING:

Lewis has good range to his right, but almost none going behind second base. Eventually, the Indians had Lewis cheat toward second and he started reaching more ground balls. He has a strong but erratic arm. His ball sails, especially if he doesn't set his feet to throw. Lewis went through a 20-game stretch (April 24-May 23) in which he made 15 errors. He settled down thereafter but still committed 26 miscues overall.

OVERALL:

Lewis suffered from a peptic ulcer last year. He came to spring training at a pudgy 210 pounds, but by the All-Star break was down to an unhealthy-looking 185. There were times he looked almost emaciated. Undoubtedly, this condition affected his play. It appears the Indians are committed to him for this season and will be looking for improvement.

DEREK LILLIQUIST

Position: RP
Bats: L **Throws:** L
Ht: 6' 0" **Wt:** 214

Opening Day Age: 27
Born: 2/20/66 in Winter Park, FL
ML Seasons: 4

Overall Statistics

	W	L	ERA	G	GS	Sv	IP	H	R	BB	SO	HR
1992	5	3	1.75	71	0	6	61.2	39	13	18	47	5
Career	18	26	4.23	137	50	6	363.2	402	188	98	196	40

How Often He Throws Strikes

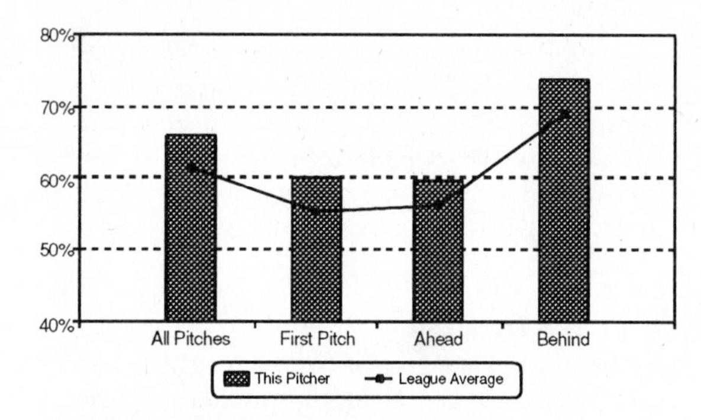

1992 Situational Stats

	W	L	ERA	Sv	IP		AB	H	HR	RBI	AVG
Home	2	2	2.25	5	32.0	LHB	90	18	1	7	.200
Road	3	1	1.21	1	29.2	RHB	119	21	4	11	.176
Day	2	1	2.66	3	20.1	Sc Pos	59	10	1	13	.169
Night	3	2	1.31	3	41.1	Clutch	130	30	3	13	.231

1992 Rankings (American League)

- 2nd in least baserunners per 9 innings in relief (8.6)
- 3rd in relief ERA (1.75) and lowest batting average allowed in relief (.187)
- 4th in games pitched (71)
- 9th in holds (15)
- Led the Indians in holds, lowest batting average allowed in relief with runners in scoring position (.169), lowest percentage of inherited runners scored (22.2%), relief ERA, lowest relief batting average allowed, least baserunners allowed per 9 innings in relief and most strikeouts per 9 innings in relief (6.9)

PITCHING:

A good thing happened to lefthander Derek Lilliquist in Puerto Rico between the 1991 and 1992 seasons. He rediscovered his old pitching motion while playing winter ball. It was the same motion Lilliquist had used at the University of Georgia -- before all the professional gurus tried to shape it more to their liking. The Indians reaped the rewards. Lilliquist had a career year in 1992: 71 appearances (the most by a Tribe left-hander since Sid Monge made 76 in 1979), a 1.75 ERA, and six saves, the first six of his career.

Lilliquist had pitched himself out of the National League by way of Atlanta and San Diego, and the Indians claimed him on waivers after the 1991 season. He went to spring training and emerged from a field of several lefthanders to make the club. His role was well-defined: enter a game in the late innings to face a tough left-handed hitter with the score tied or the Indians leading. Lilliquist expanded the role by proving he could get righthanders out, too. Lefties hit .200 and righties just .176 against him.

Lilliquist is a finesse pitcher with good location. His best pitch is a fastball but he has a good slider and change-up as well. He rarely throws a ball over the fat part of the plate. A starter through most of his career, Lilliquist loved pitching in relief. His arm bounced back well, although he had to learn how to pace himself warming up in the bullpen.

HOLDING RUNNERS AND FIELDING.

Lilliquist never seemed to worry much about baserunners last year. He went right after the batter but still allowed only four stolen bases. He didn't make an error in 71 appearances.

OVERALL:

The Indians would love to see Lilliquist do exactly what he did last year -- carry a tie or lead to the Tribe closer, or close the game himself. He went from the waiver wire to one of the league's best lefty middle relievers. Although he was left unprotected in the expansion draft, it was said to be related to his pending arbitration, not because of his ability.

GREAT SPEED

HITTING:

The Indians had an idea what Kenny Lofton could do as a baserunner and center fielder when they acquired him from Houston before the start of the 1992 season. They had no idea how he'd do offensively as their leadoff hitter. Now they, and the American League, do. Lofton finished second in the AL Rookie of the Year voting.

Lofton gave the Indians the kind of production from the leadoff spot they hadn't had since before Brett Butler fled Cleveland after the 1987 season. He showed maturity by taking pitcher after pitcher deep into the count. He showed patience by striking out only 54 times and drawing 68 walks in 576 at-bats. He showed toughness by playing the second half with a broken hamate bone in his right hand.

The left-handed hitting Lofton has outstanding speed and beat out 32 bunt hits last year. He is a line drive hitter who mostly hits the ball from left-center to center field. Lofton is a fastball hitter, but will bloop a change-up or breaking ball over the shortstop's head into left center. He hit .325 with runners in scoring position last year.

BASERUNNING:

Lofton stole 66 bases last year to lead the American League. He was the first rookie to do so since Luis Aparicio in 1956. Lofton's speed is special. He can beat out grounders to short and second and routinely stole second base on pitchouts. On April 26 against Milwaukee, Lofton became the first Indian since 1981 to make a straight steal of home.

FIELDING:

As dominant as Lofton was on the bases, he was even better playing center field. He seemed to make two to three highlight film catches a week. His speed allowed him to make diving catches on balls over the infielders' heads and to catch long drives into the gaps. He had a better arm than anyone expected, trying Mark Whiten for the club lead with 14 assists.

OVERALL:

Lofton is a key player in general manager John Hart's plan to rebuild the Indians. The calendar said 1992 was Lofton's rookie year, but from day one he never played like one.

KENNY LOFTON

Position: CF
Bats: L **Throws:** L
Ht: 6' 0" **Wt:** 180

Opening Day Age: 25
Born: 5/31/67 in East Chicago, IN
ML Seasons: 2

Overall Statistics

	G	AB	R	H	D	T	HR	RBI	SB	BB	SO	AVG
1992	148	576	96	164	15	8	5	42	66	68	54	.285
Career	168	650	105	179	16	8	5	42	68	73	73	.275

Where He Hits the Ball

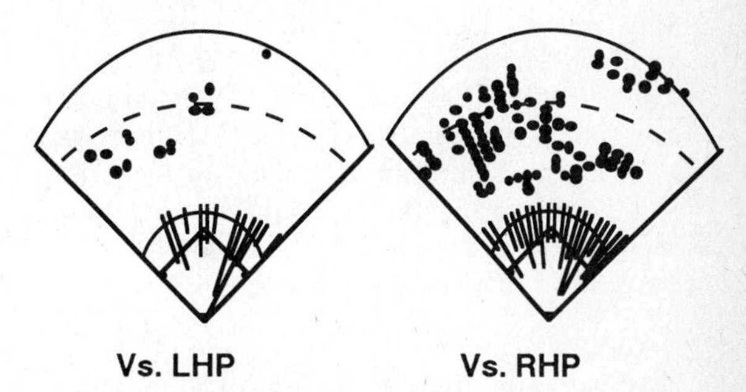

1992 Situational Stats

	AB	H	HR	RBI	AVG		AB	H	HR	RBI	AVG
Home	277	81	3	22	.292	LHP	122	45	0	12	.369
Road	299	83	2	20	.278	RHP	454	119	5	30	.262
Day	185	54	1	10	.292	Sc Pos	114	37	2	37	.325
Night	391	110	4	32	.281	Clutch	102	23	1	5	.225

1992 Rankings (American League)

- 1st in stolen bases (66) and bunts in play (73)
- 2nd in on-base percentage vs. left-handed pitchers (.466)
- Led the Indians in runs scored (96), triples (8), stolen bases, caught stealing (12), on-base percentage (.362), highest groundball/flyball ratio (2.1), stolen base percentage (84.6%), batting average with runners in scoring position (.325), on-base percentage vs. left-handed pitchers, batting average on the road (.278), bunts in play, highest percentage of pitches taken (60.9%), lowest percentage of swings that missed (8.4%), highest percentage of swings put into play (58.0%) and steals of third (6)

CARLOS MARTINEZ

Position: 1B/3B
Bats: R **Throws:** R
Ht: 6' 5" **Wt:** 175

Opening Day Age: 27
Born: 8/11/65 in La Guaira, Venezuela
ML Seasons: 5

HITTING:

Last year did not start well for Carlos Martinez. In January, he underwent surgery for a herniated disk. It was thought the 6-5, 175-pound Martinez might be out for the year. But he returned to the big leagues in time to remind all interested parties that he is still an intriguing hitter.

Martinez is every inch hitter. Fastballs, breaking balls, it doesn't matter: he hits them all. He often gives away the first two strikes in an at-bat with wild-looking swings. He seems to concentrate better that way, but also gives away a lot of at-bats. His style also prevents him from walking much (only seven times last year).

The Indians didn't recall Martinez last year until May 29. By the All-Star break, he had batted only 65 times. But then he got lucky. On August 30, manager Mike Hargrove started him at third base to get some punch into the offense. Martinez, who hadn't played third since 1989 with the White Sox, went 3-for-5 with two home runs. He started nearly every game for the rest of the season and drove in 27 runs in 33 games.

BASERUNNING:

Martinez might be the funniest-looking man in baseball when he runs the bases. He's all arms and legs to begin with, and when he pumps all four limbs up and down in a frantic effort to get to first base, it is a sight to behold. He's no threat to steal.

FIELDING:

Martinez doesn't play first or third well enough to be a regular, but he surprised the Indians' coaching staff with his play at third. His size and rubber-band type body would appear to work against him at the hot corner, but he has good reactions. His arm, once very strong, is now average.

OVERALL:

Although there is a chance he may be traded, Martinez should be back with the Indians this year in a valuable reserve role. His bat will assure him of steady work, if not a starting role.

Overall Statistics

	G	AB	R	H	D	T	HR	RBI	SB	BB	SO	AVG
1992	69	228	23	60	9	1	5	35	1	7	21	.263
Career	359	1162	112	308	52	6	19	121	9	48	173	.265

Where He Hits the Ball

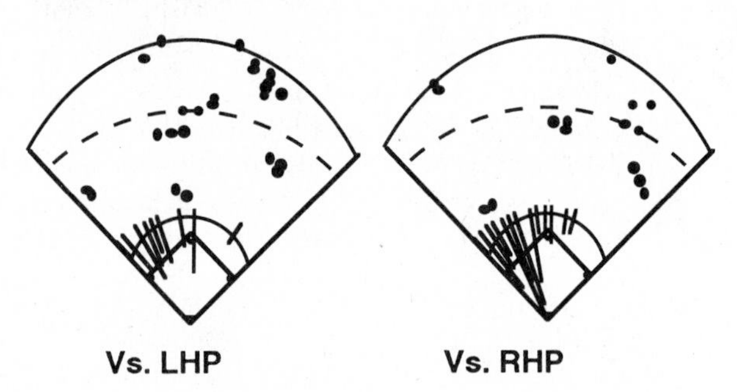

1992 Situational Stats

	AB	H	HR	RBI	AVG		AB	H	HR	RBI	AVG
Home	99	30	2	18	.303	LHP	96	25	1	14	.260
Road	129	30	3	17	.233	RHP	132	35	4	21	.265
Day	75	20	4	14	.267	Sc Pos	64	16	2	32	.250
Night	153	40	1	21	.261	Clutch	42	10	1	10	.238

1992 Rankings (American League)

- Did not rank near the top or bottom in any category

PITCHING:

The Indians did some recycling with Jose Mesa last season. Thought to be damaged beyond repair in Baltimore, they acquired him for a minor-league outfielder at the All-Star break. Most people didn't expect much, but Mesa, who'd gone 3-8 with 5.19 ERA for the Orioles, improved those figures to 4-4 and 4.16 for the Indians.

Pitching coach Rick Adair went to work with Mesa immediately after the trade. First he convinced him to hold his glove differently during his delivery. Mesa had been holding it straight up like Roger Clemens. Adair felt that was preventing Mesa from keeping the ball down in the strike zone. So Mesa turned his left wrist slightly, yielding more impressive results. He still had control problems, but his fastball stayed down in the zone.

Adair also asked him to sharpen his slider and curveball. He took away Mesa's slow curveball and gave him a sharper and harder slider and curve in its place. Finally, and perhaps most importantly, the Indians let Mesa take a regular turn in the rotation. He'd been getting irregular work as Baltimore's fifth starter but took a regular turn with the Indians. He made 15 starts for Cleveland and 10 were quality, though he had trouble getting past the seventh inning. After the season the Indians sent Mesa to the Florida Instructional League to learn a new pitch -- the split-fingered fastball. His best pitch by far is still his 88-94 MPH fastball.

HOLDING RUNNERS AND FIELDING:

Mesa is not the best fielder. He made two errors in 28 appearances last year. He has a decent move to first base and pays attention to baserunners; however, he permitted 14 steals in 22 attempts last year.

OVERALL:

The Indians may have gotten lucky with Mesa. He felt the Orioles had lost confidence in him because he walked too many batters. But when the Indians kept him in the rotation on a regular basis, he responded. He could be a third, fourth or fifth starter for the Tribe this year. He was one of only four pitchers protected by the Tribe for the expansion draft.

JOSE MESA

Position: SP
Bats: R **Throws:** R
Ht: 6' 3" **Wt:** 222

Opening Day Age: 26
Born: 5/22/66 in Azua, Dominican Republic
ML Seasons: 4

Overall Statistics

	W	L	ERA	G	GS	Sv	IP	H	R	BB	SO	HR
1992	7	12	4.59	28	27	0	160.2	169	86	70	62	14
Career	17	28	5.09	64	62	0	362.1	395	215	174	167	34

How Often He Throws Strikes

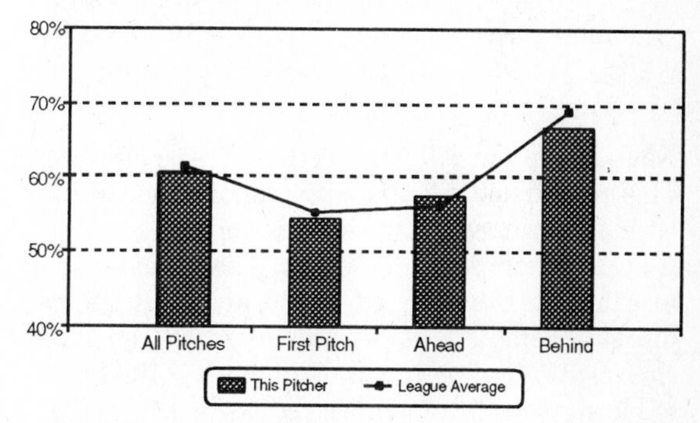

1992 Situational Stats

	W	L	ERA	Sv	IP		AB	H	HR	RBI	AVG
Home	2	5	4.40	0	77.2	LHB	328	100	8	33	.305
Road	5	7	4.77	0	83.0	RHB	291	69	6	36	.237
Day	1	8	5.99	0	73.2	Sc Pos	151	45	3	55	.298
Night	6	4	3.41	0	87.0	Clutch	37	11	1	3	.297

1992 Rankings (American League)

- 5th in lowest winning percentage (.368)
- 7th in highest batting average allowed with runners in scoring position (.298)
- 8th in highest ERA on the road (4.77)
- 10th in highest batting average allowed vs. left-handed batters (.305)

STAFF ACE

CHARLES NAGY

Position: SP
Bats: L **Throws:** R
Ht: 6' 3" **Wt:** 200

Opening Day Age: 25
Born: 5/5/67 in Fairfield, CT
ML Seasons: 3

PITCHING:

In spring training the Indians looked at their roster and saw they didn't have anyone who resembled a number-one starter. Greg Swindell and Tom Candiotti had been traded, and they didn't know enough about newly-acquired Jack Armstrong and Scott Scudder, so they gave the job with hesitation to Charles Nagy. Nagy, with equal hesitation, accepted. All Nagy did was win 17 games, the most by a Tribe righthander since Bert Blyleven won 19 in 1984. He pitched 252 innings, the most since Candiotti pitched 252.1 innings in 1986.

Nagy has one good pitch, a sinking fastball, and one great pitch, his slider. He throws the sinker a lot with runners on base and it produced double play after double play last year. The nasty slider is his strikeout pitch. He also throws a split-fingered fastball and a change-up.

Nagy made the All-Star team last year with an 11-4 record and a 2.40 earned run average at the break. Then he went into a slump, going 2-6 in his first nine starts after the break. The main reason was fatigue. Between August 2 and August 25, he threw 4 complete games in five starts, and his shoulder became sore. So the Indians started giving him five and sometimes six days rest between starts. Nagy responded by winning four of his last five outings. Another key to his late-season revival was that Nagy again started throwing his slider to left-handed batters. He'd thrown it often in the first half but for some reason stopped doing it after the break.

HOLDING RUNNERS AND FIELDING:

Nagy might be the best fielding pitcher on the Indians. He's excellent at handling hard grounders back to the mound. Nagy also holds runners very well, permitting only 12 steals in 27 attempts last year.

OVERALL:

Only a second-half slump prevented Nagy from winning 20 games last year. He established himself quickly as the team's ace. At 25, it's a role he should hold for a long time. He's rarely missed a start since turning pro in 1989.

Overall Statistics

	W	L	ERA	G	GS	Sv	IP	H	R	BB	SO	HR
1992	17	10	2.96	33	33	0	252.0	245	91	57	169	11
Career	29	29	3.71	75	74	0	509.0	531	225	144	304	33

How Often He Throws Strikes

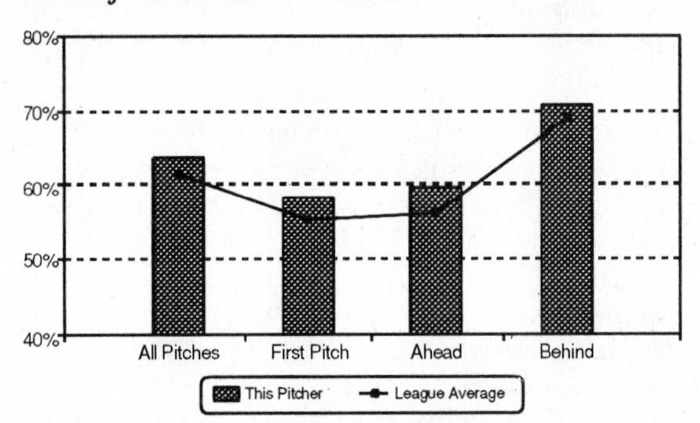

1992 Situational Stats

	W	L	ERA	Sv	IP		AB	H	HR	RBI	AVG
Home	8	4	2.34	0	134.1	LHB	424	106	5	38	.250
Road	9	6	3.67	0	117.2	RHB	520	139	6	41	.267
Day	4	4	3.29	0	82.0	Sc Pos	207	56	2	68	.271
Night	13	6	2.81	0	170.0	Clutch	100	32	1	4	.320

1992 Rankings (American League)

- 1st in GDPs induced (34)
- 2nd in highest strikeout/walk ratio (3.0)
- 3rd in highest groundball/flyball ratio allowed (2.4), lowest stolen base percentage allowed (44.4%), least home runs allowed per 9 innings (.39), most GDPs induced per 9 innings (1.2) and ERA at home (2.35)
- Led the Indians in ERA (2.96), wins (17), games started (33), complete games (10), shutouts (3), innings pitched (252), hits allowed (245), batters faced (1,018), strikeouts (169), wild pitches (7), most pitches thrown (3,606), most runners caught stealing (15), GDPs induced, winning percentage (.630) and highest strikeout/walk ratio

PITCHING:

For the first time over a full season in his career, Steve Olin got a legitimate chance at being a number-one closer. Although his role was somewhat blurred because of manager Mike Hargrove's closer-by-committee plan, the submarining right-hander saved 29 games in 36 chances. Olin allowed only 11 of 49 inherited runners to score and retired 51 of 72 first batters. He held the opposition to a .184 average with runners in scoring position.

Like some righty submariners, Olin has problems against left-handed hitters, causing Hargrove to use others to close games. Lefty swingers hit .324 against Olin last year after hitting .330 in 1991. Hargrove's use of other pitchers seemed to ease the pressure on the versatile Olin, who can pitch in a set-up role and even go three or four innings in tie ballgames.

Olin's best pitch is a sinking fastball. It produces a lot of ground balls, and since he was usually pitching with runners on base, a lot of double plays. It also helped produce eight opponent home runs when he got it up in the strike zone. He'd permitted only two gopher balls in 1991. Olin also throws a slider, the pitch he tries to jam lefthanders with, and a change-up that former submariner Dan Quisenberry taught him.

HOLDING RUNNERS AND FIELDING:

Olin doesn't worry much about baserunners; what closer does? But he does a fine job of holding them, allowing only two steals in six attempts last year. Olin didn't make an error in 20 total chances last year. He is an expert at starting the 1-6-3 double play.

OVERALL:

The Indians said they were going to build their bullpen around Olin and they did. There were stretches when he seemed to be a bit forgotten, but he received plenty of work overall, appearing in 72 games and pitching 88.1 innings. Olin might never become the kind of stopper who saves 40 games a year, but he is effective in most closing situations.

STEVE OLIN

Position: RP
Bats: R **Throws:** R
Ht: 6' 2" **Wt:** 190

Opening Day Age: 27
Born: 10/4/65 in Portland, OR
ML Seasons: 4

Overall Statistics

	W	L	ERA	G	GS	Sv	IP	H	R	BB	SO	HR
1992	8	5	2.34	72	0	29	88.1	80	25	27	47	8
Career	16	19	3.10	195	1	48	273.0	272	108	90	173	14

How Often He Throws Strikes

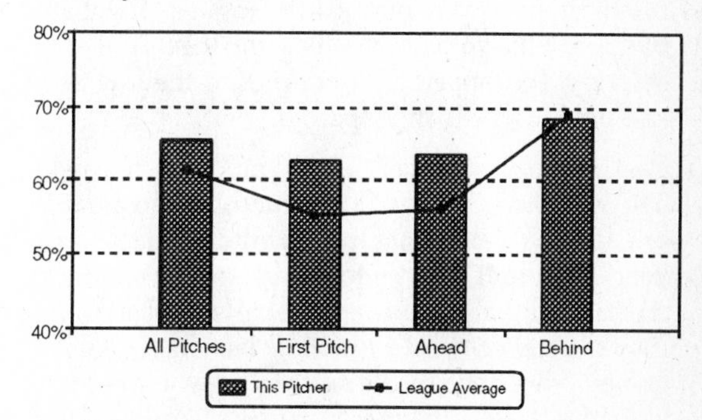

1992 Situational Stats

	W	L	ERA	Sv	IP		AB	H	HR	RBI	AVG
Home	4	3	4.37	13	45.1	LHB	145	47	1	12	.324
Road	4	2	0.21	16	43.0	RHB	176	33	7	20	.188
Day	3	1	3.56	10	30.1	Sc Pos	87	16	1	20	.184
Night	5	4	1.71	19	58.0	Clutch	212	52	6	25	.245

1992 Rankings (American League)

- 2nd in games finished (62)
- 3rd in games pitched (72)
- 5th in most GDPs induced per GDP situation (20.8%) and relief wins (8)
- 6th in blown saves (7) and highest batting average allowed vs. left-handed batters (.324)
- 7th in save opportunities (36)
- 8th in saves (29)
- 9th in relief innings (88.1)
- Led the Indians in games pitched, saves, games finished, hit batsmen (4), save opportunities, save percentage (80.6%) and blown saves

PITCHING:

Eric Plunk may have turned his career around last year. Plunk was released late in spring training by Toronto. The Indians signed him to a minor-league contract because they lacked a hard thrower in their big-league bullpen. Plunk spent a month at AA Canton-Akron but before long held a featured role with the Tribe. The righthander reached career highs in both wins (nine) and games pitched (58).

The reports on Plunk from 1991 were not good. He'd run into problems with his delivery while pitching for the New York Yankees. The 6-5 righthander had a history of control problems but has always been able to throw his fastball over 90 MPH. It kept him in the big leagues. But then Plunk lost his velocity while trying to simplify his delivery. It dropped from 90-plus to the low 80s, and put his career in jeopardy.

Last season, however, Plunk adjusted his new delivery and his velocity returned. So did a hard-breaking curveball that locked hitters' knees. Last year he didn't try to fool anybody. He threw mostly fastballs, hard curveballs and sliders. Plunk excelled while pitching late in tied/close games. It was one of the reasons he won a career-high nine games, the most wins by a Tribe reliever since Dan Spillner won 12 in 1982.

HOLDING RUNNERS AND FIELDING:

Plunk does a decent job of holding runners. He isn't a particularly sharp fielder, however. In his second appearance last year, Plunk escaped serious injury when Pedro Munoz of the Twins hit him in the right eye with a line drive. Plunk's glasses helped protect him.

OVERALL:

Plunk picked a good time to set career highs in several categories. He became a free agent at the end of 1992 and stirred some interest, but the Tribe quickly signed him to a two-year deal. They re-signed him so eagerly because he was their only hard-throwing righthander in the bullpen.

ERIC PLUNK

Position: RP
Bats: R **Throws:** R
Ht: 6' 5" **Wt:** 217

Opening Day Age: 29
Born: 9/3/63 in Wilmington, CA
ML Seasons: 7

Overall Statistics

	W	L	ERA	G	GS	Sv	IP	H	R	BB	SO	HR
1992	9	6	3.64	58	0	4	71.2	61	31	38	50	5
Career	40	35	4.06	305	41	12	653.2	573	325	410	572	67

How Often He Throws Strikes

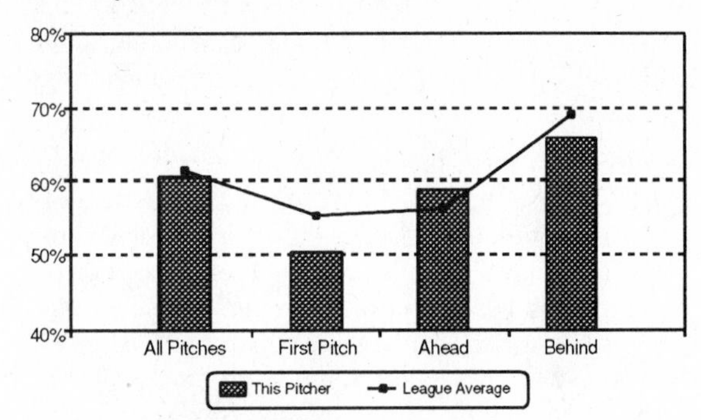

1992 Situational Stats

	W	L	ERA	Sv	IP		AB	H	HR	RBI	AVG
Home	6	3	4.10	2	37.1	LHB	118	28	1	9	.237
Road	3	3	3.15	2	34.1	RHB	148	33	4	22	.223
Day	4	2	2.42	1	22.1	Sc Pos	73	17	2	26	.233
Night	5	4	4.20	3	49.1	Clutch	165	33	5	17	.200

1992 Rankings (American League)

- 2nd in relief wins (9)
- 5th in relief losses (6)
- 10th in first batter efficiency (.180)
- Led the Indians in first batter efficiency, relief wins and relief losses

PITCHING:

It's hard to call the Indians fortunate when they haven't been a contender since 1959. But the Tribe did catch a break last season when it signed three scrap-heap pitchers -- Derek Lilliquist, Eric Plunk and Ted Power. The trio helped to give the Indians one of their best bullpens in years. Power may have been the biggest surprise of all. At age 37, the veteran righty posted a 2.54 ERA, the lowest of his long career.

Released by Cincinnati late in spring training, Power appeared in two of the Tribe's last three exhibition games on a trial basis and made the club. He proved a perfect fit for the youngest team in the American League. His experience settled the bullpen -- and his pitching didn't hurt either. Power pitched long relief, set-up and even closed, saving six games while leading Tribe relievers with 99.1 innings pitch. Power allowed only 25-of-84 inherited runners to score and seemed to thrive on the tension of pitching with runners on base.

Power surprised the Tribe's coaching staff by frequently breaking 90 MPH with his fastball. He specialized in keeping the ball down and producing big double plays on ground balls. Power also developed a cut fastball he used to throw to both right- and left-handed batters; it became his second-best pitch. He also throws a slider, curveball and change-up.

HOLDING RUNNERS AND FIELDING:

Power is diligent about trying to hold runners. He'll make repeated throws to first to keep them close, but without success. He permitted eight steals in 11 attempts last year. Power is a good fielder and didn't make an error last year.

OVERALL:

Power turned out to be the old hand the Indians needed. More importantly, he enjoyed his role. The team thought so highly of him that they re-signed him for 1993 before he was able to file for free agency. Power was the best kind of veteran -- producing on the field and in the clubhouse.

TED POWER

Position: RP
Bats: R **Throws:** R
Ht: 6' 4" **Wt:** 220

Opening Day Age: 38
Born: 1/31/55 in Guthrie, OK
ML Seasons: 12

Overall Statistics

	W	L	ERA	G	GS	Sv	IP	H	R	BB	SO	HR
1992	3	3	2.54	64	0	6	99.1	88	33	35	51	7
Career	66	65	3.94	519	85	57	1114.1	1102	540	435	674	94

How Often He Throws Strikes

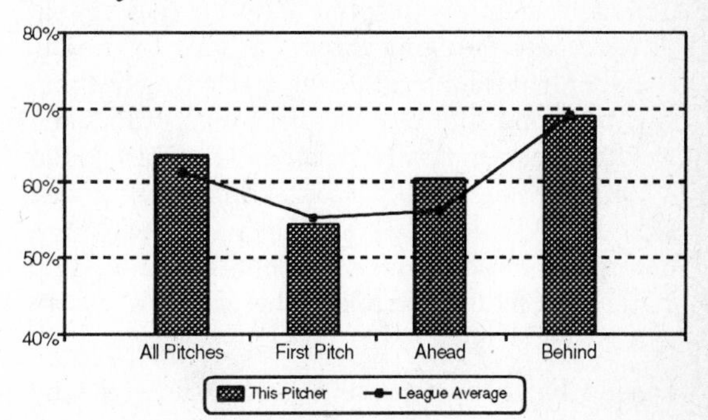

1992 Situational Stats

	W	L	ERA	Sv	IP		AB	H	HR	RBI	AVG
Home	2	1	1.64	3	55.0	LHB	133	30	1	9	.226
Road	1	2	3.65	3	44.1	RHB	222	58	6	42	.261
Day	0	2	2.29	2	39.1	Sc Pos	114	23	3	43	.202
Night	3	1	2.70	4	60.0	Clutch	151	36	2	20	.238

1992 Rankings (American League)

- 4th in relief innings (99.1)
- 9th in least strikeouts per 9 innings in relief (4.6)
- Led the Indians in hit batsmen (4), lowest batting average allowed vs. left-handed batters (.226), lowest batting average allowed with runners on (.213) and relief innings

PITCHING:

The Indians gave Scott Scudder the second chance he didn't get in Cincinnati. They handed him a spot in the rotation last year and let him pitch. But Scudder's right arm didn't cooperate. The young righthander strained the triceps muscle in his right arm just before the All-Star break. Scudder went on the disabled list after a July 29 start against Milwaukee and didn't return until September. He made two more starts but both were cut short because of the injury. For the season, Scudder went only 6-10 for his new club with a career-high 5.28 ERA.

It was a season of change and pain for Scudder. Pitching coach Rick Adair tried to remake Scudder's delivery in spring training, feeling that Scudder was throwing across his body too much. Scudder had trouble adjusting and spring training was one long film clip of full counts, walks and wild pitches. Gradually, Adair and Scudder found a delivery they could work with. During one stretch in the first half, Scudder went 4-3 in a nine-game stretch with seven quality starts. Two starts later, though, he injured himself in a victory against Oakland.

During his good stretch, Scudder showed why scouts always liked his arm when he was with Cincinnati. His fastball was in the high 80s/low 90s and he was throwing his curveball and slider for strikes. Adair says Scudder had the best curveball on the staff. Yet Scudder's control would vanish as quickly as it appeared.

HOLDING RUNNERS AND FIELDING:

Scudder does not hold runners well. His delivery to the plate is slow and he doesn't give his catcher a chance to throw anybody out. He's a decent fielder, however.

OVERALL:

The Indians put Scudder on a weight-training program during the off-season. He'd never lifted weights before, but the Indians wanted him to get stronger to help him avoid injury. If Scudder stays healthy, he could be the Tribe's number-two or three starter this year. But the question marks are still there; he was left exposed by the Indians (and then not selected) in the expansion draft.

SCOTT SCUDDER

Position: SP
Bats: R **Throws:** R
Ht: 6' 2" **Wt:** 185

Opening Day Age: 25
Born: 2/14/68 in Paris, TX
ML Seasons: 4

Overall Statistics

	W	L	ERA	G	GS	Sv	IP	H	R	BB	SO	HR
1992	6	10	5.28	23	22	0	109.0	134	80	55	66	10
Career	21	33	4.76	94	63	1	382.1	390	227	202	225	42

How Often He Throws Strikes

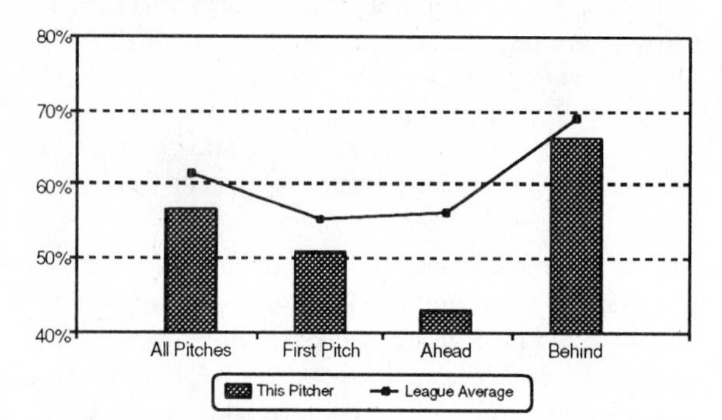

1992 Situational Stats

	W	L	ERA	Sv	IP		AB	H	HR	RBI	AVG
Home	2	5	5.06	0	53.1	LHB	251	75	5	36	.299
Road	4	5	5.50	0	55.2	RHB	191	59	5	21	.309
Day	3	2	4.13	0	48.0	Sc Pos	119	35	3	45	.294
Night	3	8	6.20	0	61.0	Clutch	31	15	0	4	.484

1992 Rankings (American League)

- 8th in lowest winning percentage (.375)
- Led the Indians in wild pitches (7)

HITTING:

When first baseman Paul Sorrento came to the Indians from Minnesota late in spring training for two minor-league pitchers, most people considered it a "so what?" deal. With the Twins, Sorrento had played in the shadow of Kent Hrbek, batting .222 over 189 at-bats in parts of three different seasons. But given a chance by Cleveland, Sorrento proved he could hit with good power. The lefty swinger batted .269 with 18 homers and 60 RBI in 140 games for the Indians.

Sorrento, a left-handed hitter, spent most of the season in the number-five spot. Since he showed a weakness against lefties (.156), Sorrento spent the year platooning with Carlos Martinez and Reggie Jefferson. It proved a good arrangement, as all three players were productive.

Sorrento was not a patient hitter early in the season. Lunging at numerous pitches, he was hitting just .217 on June 4. But hitting coach Jose Morales talked to him about keeping his weight back and waiting for his pitch, and the message made an impression; Sorrento hit .296 the rest of the season. He pulled most of his home runs to right field, but also hit breaking balls and tailing fastballs hard to left center, where the majority of his hits went.

BASERUNNING:

Sorrento is one of the slowest Indians. He has only one stolen base in the major leagues and was 0-for-3 in 1992. His baserunning instincts aren't good either.

FIELDING:

Sorrento's play at first base, particularly scooping low throws out of the dirt, was pitiful at the start of the year. He had an excuse since he was a converted outfielder. But through his own hard work and that of infield coach Ron Clark, he improved greatly. Sorrento does a nice job handling line drives and hard-hit grounders.

OVERALL:

A spare part with the Twins but an expansion protection with the Indians, Sorrento was acquired because Jefferson injured his elbow in spring training. With Sorrento proving he can hit and Jefferson set to be back at full strength, the Indians' offense is stronger for the depth.

PAUL SORRENTO

Position: 1B/DH
Bats: L **Throws:** R
Ht: 6' 2" **Wt:** 223

Opening Day Age: 27
Born: 11/17/65 in Somerville, MA
ML Seasons: 4

Overall Statistics

	G	AB	R	H	D	T	HR	RBI	SB	BB	SO	AVG
1992	140	458	52	123	24	1	18	60	0	51	89	.269
Career	221	647	71	165	30	2	27	87	1	72	135	.255

Where He Hits the Ball

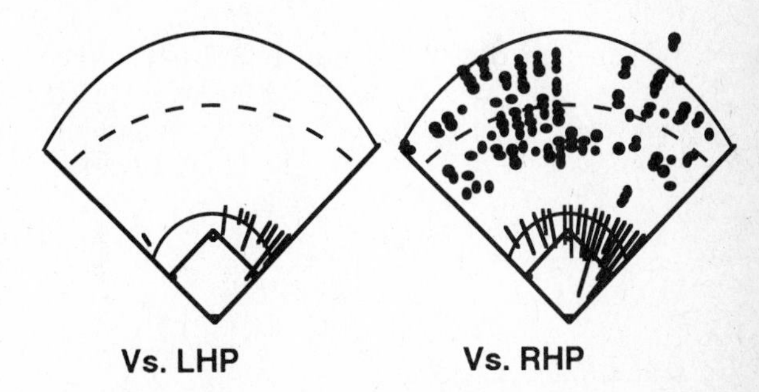

1992 Situational Stats

	AB	H	HR	RBI	AVG		AB	H	HR	RBI	AVG
Home	226	65	11	31	.288	LHP	45	7	0	4	.156
Road	232	58	7	29	.250	RHP	413	116	18	56	.281
Day	159	46	9	22	.289	Sc Pos	115	25	4	43	.217
Night	299	77	9	38	.258	Clutch	89	22	4	14	.247

1992 Rankings (American League)

- 3rd in lowest batting average with the bases loaded (.063)
- 4th in lowest batting average on an 0-2 count (.045)
- 10th in slugging percentage vs. right-handed pitchers (.472)
- Led the Indians in slugging percentage vs. right-handed pitchers and on-base percentage vs. right-handed pitchers (.351)

STRONG ARM

MARK WHITEN

Position: RF
Bats: B **Throws:** R
Ht: 6' 3" **Wt:** 215

Opening Day Age: 26
Born: 11/25/66 in Pensacola, FL
ML Seasons: 3

HITTING:

Mark Whiten is built like a linebacker, but last season he hit like a utility infielder. The switch-hitter looked overmatched from both sides of the plate and had trouble getting the ball out of the infield during the last weeks of the season. Whiten batted only .228 after September 1 with one extra-base hit in 101 at-bats.

The Indians sent Whiten to their Florida Instructional League team after the season to try and improve his stance and swing. They especially wanted him to improve his power from the left side; he batted .244 lefty with only six home runs and 35 RBI in 381 at-bats. They aren't as worried about his right-handed swing: he batted .283 right-handed.

Whiten is a decent low-ball hitter, but he has trouble with fastballs up in the strike zone. He pops them up or can't catch up to them and hits harmless infield grounders. The Indians worked with Whiten to get a better timing mechanism on his swing before the pitch arrives, but he's stubborn. To his credit, he's a patient hitter, and led the team with 72 walks.

BASERUNNING:

Though not a good basestealer (16-for-28 last year), Whiten is the best pure baserunner on the Indians, including Kenny Lofton. The Indians have a run-and-bunt play where the runner on first takes off on the pitch, touches second and keeps going to third on the bunt. Whiten ran it perfectly last year.

FIELDING:

Whiten has one of the strongest right field arms in the American League. When he picks up a ball, baserunners freeze. But he made seven errors last year, many of them by failing to field groundball hits. The accuracy of his throws and hustle on defense faded late in the year.

OVERALL:

Whiten is a fine athlete. He can do everything on a baseball field . . . except hit consistently. The Indians seem willing to wait at least one more year to see if that part of his game can catch up to his athletic skills.

Overall Statistics

	G	AB	R	H	D	T	HR	RBI	SB	BB	SO	AVG
1992	148	508	73	129	19	4	9	43	16	72	102	.254
Career	297	1003	131	252	38	12	20	95	22	109	201	.251

Where He Hits the Ball

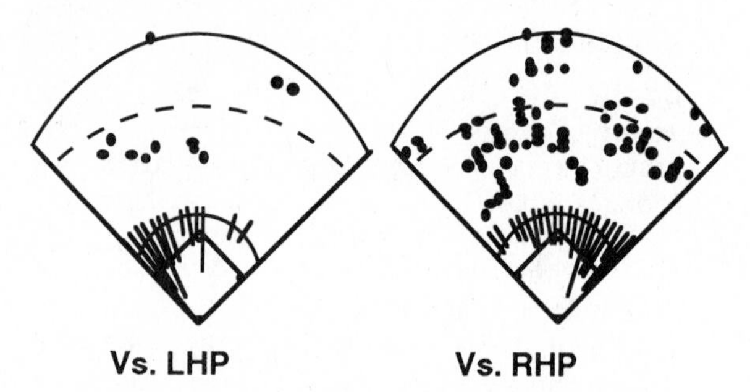

Vs. LHP   Vs. RHP

1992 Situational Stats

	AB	H	HR	RBI	AVG		AB	H	HR	RBI	AVG
Home	260	70	6	25	.269	LHP	127	36	3	8	.283
Road	248	59	3	18	.238	RHP	381	93	6	35	.244
Day	159	45	2	10	.283	Sc Pos	112	24	3	33	.214
Night	349	84	7	33	.241	Clutch	91	22	3	10	.242

1992 Rankings (American League)

- 6th in lowest stolen base percentage (57.1%)
- 10th in highest groundball/flyball ratio (1.8)
- Led the Indians in caught stealing (12), walks (72), intentional walks (10) and most pitches seen per plate appearance (3.76)

PITCHING:

Kevin Wickander made it back to the big leagues for almost a full season last year. That was a victory in itself, considering the twists and turns the lefthander's career has taken. In 1990, Wickander made the Indians' Opening Day roster but slipped and fell on a concrete walkway at Anaheim Stadium on May 30, fracturing his left elbow. The injury ended his season. In 1991 he pitched only 37 innings in the minors because he underwent treatment at the Cleveland Clinic for a drinking problem.

Wickander started last season at AAA Colorado Springs but joined the Indians in early May. He was used mostly to get one or two left-handed hitters out late in a ballgame. His best pitch is a cut fastball that looks like a slider. He throws the cutter with either a big break or a small break, and it is especially effective against left-handed hitters. Wickander also throws a regular fastball and a curveball.

Wickander's major problem has been lack of control. Though he had a 3.07 ERA last year, he yielded 28 walks in 41 innings. He also had trouble retiring the first batter he faced. Fifty percent (22-of-44) of first batters faced reached base. In August and September, Wickander appeared to be pitching scared when brought into tight situations. It was one of the reason he pitched in only 21 games after July 18.

HOLDING RUNNERS AND FIELDING:

Wickander is a good fielder and he pays attention to runners on base. When he first came up, he used to sprint off the mound and back up first base on infield grounders. He doesn't do that any more.

OVERALL:

Last season's success should help the hyper Wickander. He made it back to the big leagues after two career-threatening falls. What he has to do now is relax, realize he can pitch in the big leagues and stop waiting for someone to send him back to the minors. He has excellent movement on all his pitches; what he needs now is confidence.

KEVIN WICKANDER

Position: RP
Bats: L **Throws:** L
Ht: 6' 2" **Wt:** 202

Opening Day Age: 28
Born: 1/4/65 in Fort Dodge, IA
ML Seasons: 3

Overall Statistics

	W	L	ERA	G	GS	Sv	IP	H	R	BB	SO	HR
1992	2	0	3.07	44	0	1	41.0	39	14	28	38	1
Career	2	1	3.21	56	0	1	56.0	59	21	34	48	1

How Often He Throws Strikes

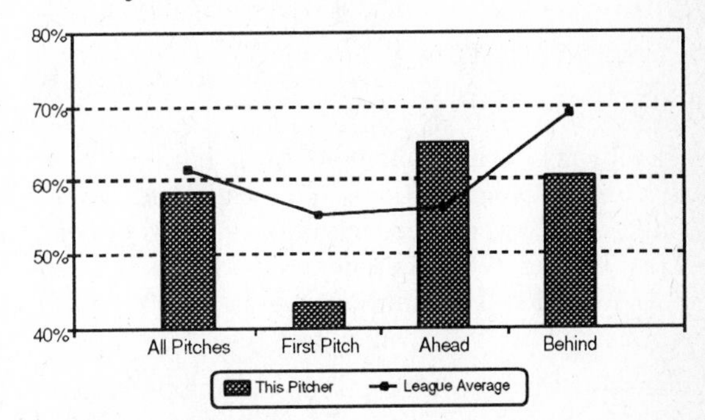

1992 Situational Stats

	W	L	ERA	Sv	IP		AB	H	HR	RBI	AVG
Home	1	0	1.47	0	18.1	LHB	54	15	0	6	.278
Road	1	0	4.37	1	22.2	RHB	96	24	1	8	.250
Day	0	0	1.23	0	7.1	Sc Pos	54	10	0	12	.185
Night	2	0	3.48	1	33.2	Clutch	44	13	0	6	.295

1992 Rankings (American League)

- 1st in worst first batter efficiency (.444)
- Led the Indians in hit batsmen (4)

BROOK JACOBY

Position: 3B
Bats: R **Throws:** R
Ht: 5'11" **Wt:** 195

Opening Day Age: 33
Born: 11/23/59 in Philadelphia, PA
ML Seasons: 11

Overall Statistics

	G	AB	R	H	D	T	HR	RBI	SB	BB	SO	AVG
1992	120	291	30	76	7	0	4	36	0	28	54	.261
Career	1311	4520	535	1220	204	24	120	545	16	439	764	.270

HITTING, FIELDING, BASERUNNING:

Brook Jacoby is no longer the player who hit 69 home runs between 1985 and 1987. He has lost bat speed, and a sore right elbow has limited his ability to extend his arms on pitches. But instead Jacoby has learned to be a finesse hitter. He's become adept at blooping curveballs and sliders into right field and concentrates on making contract instead of hitting homers. Good fastballs up and in will still get him out, but he hit .306 with runners in scoring position last year.

Jacoby, traded to Oakland during the 1991 season, returned to Cleveland as an insurance policy. The policy paid off when rookie third baseman Jim Thome hurt his right wrist in spring training. Jacoby became the everyday third baseman, fielded his position well, and was hitting .280 at the All-Star break. His playing time was cut in the second half, but he still played fine late-inning defense. His throws have lost some zip, but he makes up for it with accuracy and a quick release. He's never had much speed and did not steal a base last year.

OVERALL:

Jacoby did just what he was signed to do. He played good defense, helped settle a young team in the clubhouse and hit .387 (12-for-31) coming off the bench. But the Tribe may be out of room. The Indians had an option on Jacoby for 1993, but they allowed him to test his free market value.

REGGIE JEFFERSON

Position: 1B
Bats: B **Throws:** L
Ht: 6' 4" **Wt:** 210

Opening Day Age: 24
Born: 9/25/68 in Tallahassee, FL
ML Seasons: 2

Overall Statistics

	G	AB	R	H	D	T	HR	RBI	SB	BB	SO	AVG
1992	24	89	8	30	6	2	1	6	0	1	17	.337
Career	55	197	19	51	9	2	4	19	0	5	41	.259

HITTING, FIELDING, BASERUNNING:

Reggie Jefferson did not enjoy 1992. He missed all of spring training, and a chance to be the Tribe's Opening Day first baseman because of a pulled ligament in his left elbow. When he did make it back to Cleveland, he was unexpectedly sent back to Class AAA when the Indians acquired Jose Mesa over the All-Star break.

When Jefferson was finally brought back on Sept. 17, he made up for lost time. He hit .377 (23-for-61) in the final 15 games of the season. Jefferson, a switch-hitter, had a much more compact swing that helps him hit to all fields with extra-base power. He drew only one walk in 89 at-bats, but that was probably because he was trying to make an impression.

Jefferson even looked more confident at first base. He handled grounders better and made better throws to second base and home plate. He is not a fast man on the bases and has been bothered by hamstring pulls in the past.

OVERALL:

Jefferson fumed when the Indians sent him down at the All-Star break. He eventually bolted Class AAA Colorado Springs just before the start of the Pacific Coast League playoffs. After spending three days at home, he rejoined the club and helped them win the PCL championship. He also helped ensure his future with the Tribe. He was one of their 15 expansion draft protections.

JESSE LEVIS

Position: C
Bats: L **Throws:** R
Ht: 5' 9" **Wt:** 180

Opening Day Age: 24
Born: 4/14/68 in Philadelphia, PA
ML Seasons: 1

Overall Statistics

	G	AB	R	H	D	T	HR	RBI	SB	BB	SO	AVG
1992	28	43	2	12	4	0	1	3	0	0	5	.279
Career	28	43	2	12	4	0	1	3	0	0	5	.279

HITTING, FIELDING, BASERUNNING:

Jesse Levis is a pint-sized catcher (5'9"), but the guy can hit. Plus he's left-handed, which makes him that much more valuable. Between trips to the big leagues, Levis hit .364 (92-for-253) with six homers and 44 RBI at Class AAA Colorado Springs. He has some trouble with breaking balls, but not significantly. He'll hit to left center and can also pull the ball with power. He's a patient hitter and has had more walks than strikeouts during each of the last three seasons.

Levis needs work on his game behind the plate. He needs to improve at calling pitches, and his throwing arm is only average. He tossed out only two of nine opposing basestealers last year. Levis also could use improvement in blocking the plate, although that aspect of his game improved as the season went along. Like most catchers, Levis doesn't run well.

OVERALL:

The Indians are grooming Levis to be the ideal backup catcher in the big leagues. They need him, too, because of the injury problems starter Sandy Alomar Jr. has experienced over the last two years. He survived the expansion draft and should get some playing time in Cleveland this year.

JUNIOR ORTIZ

Position: C
Bats: R **Throws:** R
Ht: 5'11" **Wt:** 185

Opening Day Age: 33
Born: 10/24/59 in Humacao, Puerto Rico
ML Seasons: 11

Overall Statistics

	G	AB	R	H	D	T	HR	RBI	SB	BB	SO	AVG
1992	86	244	20	61	7	0	0	24	1	12	23	.250
Career	625	1569	120	408	56	4	5	157	7	105	185	.260

HITTING, FIELDING, BASERUNNING:

The Indians signed catcher Junior Ortiz to a Class AAA contract last winter, slating him to back up Sandy Alomar Jr. -- particularly necessary if Joel Skinner couldn't come back from shoulder surgery. So what happened? Ortiz set career highs in at-bats and runs batted in because Alomar was beset by injuries and Skinner never returned. Ortiz is a contact hitter who can work the hit-and-run. He hit .299 with runners in scoring position (.306 with two outs) last year.

Defensively Ortiz caught in 86 games, the most in his 11 big-league seasons. He eventually ran out of gas and had trouble with wild pitches and blocking balls in the dirt. He showed a pretty strong arm, even though he cut down only 30 percent of the potential basestealers he faced (25-for-84). Ortiz, who had trouble blocking the plate early in the year, became a stone wall as the season went on. He might be the slowest runner on the club. He's stolen only seven bases in 24 attempts during his career.

OVERALL:

Ortiz bailed the Indians out of big-time catching trouble last year. He did a good job behind the plate and supplied more offense than they had expected. Regardless, he filed for free agency at the end of the year, and it was unlikely that he'd return.

ORGANIZATION OVERVIEW:

Cleveland -- Land of Opportunity. No club has embraced the "go with youth" philosophy more than the Indians have over the last couple of years. Not that they had a lot of choice; since Cleveland couldn't afford veteran players with big salaries, they were forced to dump them in exchange for younger and cheaper ones. Done right, this method can work. The trick is to get the **right** kids and nurture them. Like the Pirate teams of the mid-to-late eighties, the Indians appear to be doing just that.

MIKE CHRISTOPHER

Position: P **Opening Day Age:** 29
Bats: R **Throws:** R **Born:** 11/3/63 in Petersburg, VA
Ht: 6' 5" **Wt:** 205

Recent Statistics

	W	L	ERA	G	GS	Sv	IP	H	R	BB	SO	HR
92 AAA Colo Sprngs	4	4	2.91	49	0	26	58.2	59	21	13	39	2
92 AL Cleveland	0	0	3.00	10	0	0	18.0	17	8	10	13	2

Land of Opportunity? Mike Christopher sure hopes so. The righty reliever has been pitching at the AAA level since 1989 for three organizations: the Yankees, Dodgers and now Indians. Christopher's not the hardest thrower around but he must be doing something right. He's recorded sub-3.00 ERAs in places like Albuquerque and Colorado Springs, where pitchers normally get hammered. And in 13 major league games, he has an ERA of 2.45. The Mike Perez of 1993? Christopher can surely help somebody this expansion year.

ALAN EMBREE

Position: P **Opening Day Age:** 23
Bats: L **Throws:** L **Born:** 1/23/70 in Vancouver, WA
Ht: 6' 2" **Wt:** 185

Recent Statistics

	W	L	ERA	G	GS	Sv	IP	H	R	BB	SO	HR
92 A Kinston	10	5	3.30	15	15	0	101.0	89	48	32	115	10
92 AA Canton-Akron	7	2	2.28	12	12	0	79.0	61	24	28	56	2
92 AL Cleveland	0	2	7.00	4	4	0	18.0	19	14	8	12	3

Cleveland's hurting for a lefty starter, and they're pretty excited about Embree, even though he spent half of 1992 at the Class A level. Embree was rated the number-two prospect in the Carolina League and was reputed to be the hardest thrower in the circuit. Moved up to AA Canton-Akron, he was, if anything, even better. Embree struggled in four late-season starts with the Indians, so he could start 1993 at the AAA level. He shouldn't be there for very long; the Tribe made him one of only four pitchers protected in the expansion draft.

WAYNE KIRBY

Position: OF **Opening Day Age:** 29
Bats: L **Throws:** R **Born:** 1/22/64 in Williamsburg, VA
Ht: 5' 11" **Wt:** 185

Recent Statistics

	G	AB	R	H	D	T	HR	RBI	SB	BB	SO	AVG
92 AAA Colo Sprngs	123	470	101	162	18	16	11	74	51	36	28	.345
92 AL Cleveland	21	18	9	3	1	0	1	1	0	3	2	.167
92 MLE	123	441	65	133	15	8	7	48	31	23	29	.302

Like Christopher, Kirby is an older guy (29), who was trapped for years in the Dodger system, but he has posted some intriguing minor league numbers. In 1992 the outfielder hit .345 at Colorado Springs, the second time he's hit over .340 at the AAA level. He doesn't have a lot of power, but he does possess excellent speed, with 51 stolen bases last year. If nothing else, Kirby seems a cinch to be a useful player on somebody's bench this year. He may be a little more than that.

DAVE MLICKI

Position: P **Opening Day Age:** 24
Bats: R **Throws:** R **Born:** 6/8/68 in Cleveland, OH
Ht: 6' 4" **Wt:** 185

Recent Statistics

	W	L	ERA	G	GS	Sv	IP	H	R	BB	SO	HR
92 AA Canton-Akron	11	9	3.60	27	27	0	172.2	143	77	80	146	8
92 AL Cleveland	0	2	4.98	4	4	0	21.2	23	14	16	16	3

Like Embree, Mlicki pitched at the AA level in 1992, and also finished the year in the Tribe rotation. Mlicki was also winless, which didn't discourage Cleveland much. Mlicki doesn't throw nearly as hard as Embree; his best pitch is a slider, and he's had some control problems. In his four starts with the Indians, he allowed 23 hits and 16 walks in 16.2 innings. That makes him even more likely than Embree to open 1993 in AAA. But he should be pitching in Cleveland some time this year.

JIM THOME

Position: 3B **Opening Day Age:** 22
Bats: L **Throws:** R **Born:** 8/27/70 in Peoria, IL
Ht: 6' 3" **Wt:** 200

Recent Statistics

	G	AB	R	H	D	T	HR	RBI	SB	BB	SO	AVG
92 AA Canton-Akron	30	107	16	36	9	2	1	14	0	24	30	.336
92 AAA Colo Sprngs	12	48	11	15	4	1	2	14	0	6	16	.313
92 AL Cleveland	40	117	8	24	3	1	2	12	2	10	34	.205

One of the foundations of the Tribe youth movement, Thome was supposed to be the Indians' third baseman last year. For a while he was, but Thome was bothered by a sore shoulder, and when he was healthy enough to play, he didn't hit. Thome batted only .205 in 40 games for the Indians, but he showed he was still a prospect by hitting well over .300 in stints at Canton and Colorado Springs. Defensively, he appears to have the goods. Still only 22, Thome should get a chance to redeem himself this season.

MARK CARREON

Position: LF/RF/DH
Bats: R **Throws:** L
Ht: 6' 0" **Wt:** 195

Opening Day Age: 29
Born: 7/9/63 in Chicago, IL
ML Seasons: 6

Overall Statistics

	G	AB	R	H	D	T	HR	RBI	SB	BB	SO	AVG
1992	101	336	34	78	11	1	10	41	3	22	57	.232
Career	373	932	107	240	37	1	31	106	8	64	131	.258

Where He Hits the Ball

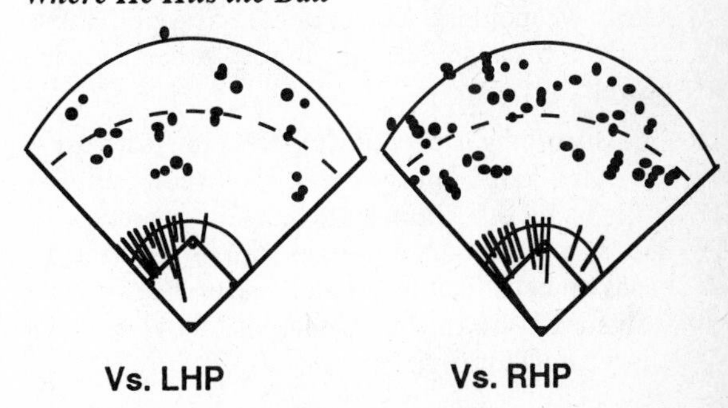

Vs. LHP   Vs. RHP

1992 Situational Stats

	AB	H	HR	RBI	AVG		AB	H	HR	RBI	AVG
Home	151	32	5	19	.212	LHP	111	22	2	8	.198
Road	185	46	5	22	.249	RHP	225	56	8	33	.249
Day	136	32	4	15	.235	Sc Pos	90	18	2	29	.200
Night	200	46	6	26	.230	Clutch	45	12	1	5	.267

1992 Rankings (American League)

- → 8th in highest batting average on an 0-2 count (.304)
- → 9th lowest batting average with runners in scoring position (.200)
- → 10th highest batting average with 2 strikes (.253)
- → Led the Tigers in highest batting average on an 0-2 count and highest batting average with 2 strikes
- → Led AL left fielders in highest batting average on an 0-2 count

HITTING:

A valuable bench player with the Mets for several seasons, Mark Carreon seemed a good bet to succeed when the Tigers obtained him before the start of the 1992 season. With the Mets, Carreon had shown a knack for pinch-hitting, filling in and keeping his bat sharp while being limited to 200 at-bats or so. Tiger manager Sparky Anderson has spent his career getting the maximum out of players just like him.

The trade may work yet, but Carreon was a disappointment in 1992. He did log a career-high 336 at-bats, but that was due mostly to injuries suffered by Rob Deer and Dan Gladden. He showed a little pop with 10 homers and 41 RBI, but his batting average was the lowest of his career at .232. A righty swinger, Carreon was useless in a platoon role, as he batted only .198 vs. lefties. He hit .200 with runners in scoring position.

Some of Carreon's problems may have been due to adjusting to a new league. He's an anxious swinger who takes a good cut while seldom walking, and he may have been swinging at too many bad pitches while trying to hit the longball. He was also bothered by a pulled stomach muscle which caused him to miss three weeks.

BASERUNNING:

Carreon had eight consecutive seasons (1981-1988) in the Mets farm system with double-figure stolen bases, but he's never shown a hint of that in the majors. Carreon stole three bases in four attempts last year, the best performance of his major league career.

FIELDING:

Carreon can play all three outfield positions, but none of them very well. He has bad range and a weak arm, and he can make an adventure out of catching an easy fly ball.

OVERALL:

Carreon struggled last year, but there's no reason why he can't become a useful bench player again. With good health and a season of adjustment to the American League under his belt, he ought to be a lot better this year.

MILT CUYLER

Position: CF
Bats: B **Throws:** R
Ht: 5'10" **Wt:** 185

Opening Day Age: 24
Born: 10/7/68 in Macon, GA
ML Seasons: 3

HITTING:

Milt Cuyler's rookie performance in 1991 -- 77 runs scored, 41 steals, a .257 average -- gave promise for a bright future. The Tigers expected better things from their 23-year-old center fielder last year, but Cuyler suffered through a difficult second season. The switch-hitter batted only .241 before going out for the year on July 25 with a strained right knee.

As a hitter, Cuyler's main asset is his great speed; "My game is centered around my legs," he says simply. He hits the ball on the ground in order to leg out as many singles as possible, and he's also an extremely adept drag bunter. Cuyler's knee bothered him all last year, and as a result he was nearly weaponless. Cuyler needs to beat out those singles, because he has almost no extra-base power.

One disturbing aspect of Cuyler's play last year -- unrelated to his injury -- was his loss of patience at the plate. In the minors he had always recorded decent walk totals, and as a rookie he drew 52 bases on balls. But in his half season last year, he walked only 10 times. One hopes that was only a one-year aberration.

BASERUNNING:

Forget Cuyler's 1992 figures. He stole only eight bases in 13 attempts, but that was because his knee problem shut down his running game. He swiped 41 as a rookie, and can do even better than that.

FIELDING:

Cuyler shows promise of becoming one of the great center fielders. He had over 400 putouts as a 1991 rookie, and was on his way to topping that when he was injured last year. He plays shallow and can track down any fly ball. However, his arm is on the weak side.

OVERALL:

Cuyler's numbers were disappointing last year, but his bad knee was the big reason. He's expected to return to health this year; if he's at full speed, he should be a much better player. The Tigers protected him from expansion, so they hope so.

Overall Statistics

	G	AB	R	H	D	T	HR	RBI	SB	BB	SO	AVG
1992	89	291	39	70	11	1	3	28	8	10	62	.241
Career	262	817	124	205	29	9	6	69	50	67	164	.251

Where He Hits the Ball

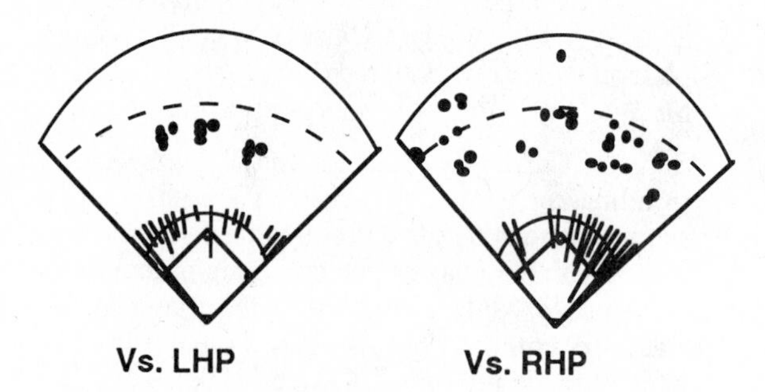

1992 Situational Stats

	AB	H	HR	RBI	AVG		AB	H	HR	RBI	AVG
Home	148	29	1	9	.196	LHP	86	25	2	8	.291
Road	143	41	2	19	.287	RHP	205	45	1	20	.220
Day	103	25	0	9	.243	Sc Pos	74	21	2	27	.284
Night	188	45	3	19	.239	Clutch	37	6	0	0	.162

1992 Rankings (American League)

- 1st in lowest batting average on an 0-2 count (.000)
- 5th in bunts in play (29)
- Led the Tigers in sacrifice bunts (8) and bunts in play
- Led AL center fielders in sacrifice bunts and least GDPs per GDP situation (6.7%)

ROB DEER

Position: RF
Bats: R **Throws:** R
Ht: 6' 3" **Wt:** 225

Opening Day Age: 32
Born: 9/29/60 in Orange, CA
ML Seasons: 9

Overall Statistics

	G	AB	R	H	D	T	HR	RBI	SB	BB	SO	AVG
1992	110	393	66	97	20	1	32	64	4	51	131	.247
Career	1002	3365	503	746	128	12	205	536	38	503	1210	.222

Where He Hits the Ball

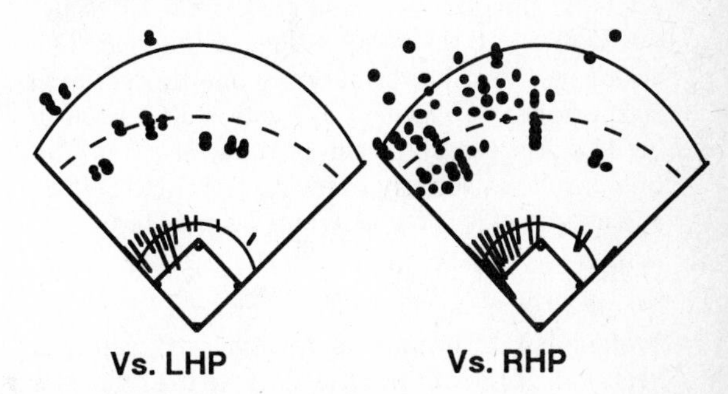

1992 Situational Stats

	AB	H	HR	RBI	AVG		AB	H	HR	RBI	AVG
Home	173	44	13	28	.254	LHP	99	29	14	21	.293
Road	220	53	19	36	.241	RHP	294	68	18	43	.231
Day	129	30	12	25	.233	Sc Pos	99	21	5	32	.212
Night	264	67	20	39	.254	Clutch	65	17	5	9	.262

1992 Rankings (American League)

- 1st in lowest percentage of swings put into play (29.8%)
- 2nd in highest percentage of swings that missed (32.2%)
- 6th in home runs (32)
- 8th in strikeouts (131)
- 9th in lowest batting average with the bases loaded (.091)

HITTING:

After a 1991 season which was history-making in the wrong sense, Rob Deer entered 1992 with his major league career in jeopardy. Deer had belted 25 homers in '91, but his .179 average was a 20th-century low for players with at least 400 at-bats. The big outfielder came back strongly from that disaster, hitting 32 homers while batting a very-respectable .247. Both figures were the second best of his nine-year career. Even more remarkably, Deer hit his homers in only 393 at-bats; he spent two long stints on the disabled list during the season.

There's never been any question that Deer can hit with great power. He's hit at least 23 homers during each of his seven full seasons in the majors. He's averaged 28 dingers per year over that span despite the fact that he's never had a 500 at-bat season. He loves the fastball, particularly the high hard one, and with his big uppercut swing, he finds it almost impossible to stop his swing once he commits himself. As a result Deer has fanned in over one-third of his major league at-bats, and continued to do so even in 1992, a great season for him. Luckily, Deer also draws an above-average number of walks. Last year his on-base percentage was .337 -- nearly 100 points above his batting average.

BASERUNNING:

Deer has only average speed and keeps excess baserunning to a minimum. He did steal four bases in six attempts last year, however. He's an aggressive baserunner, and good at breaking up the double play.

FIELDING:

What Deer may lack in speed, he makes up for by knowing where to play hitters. He is an above-average right fielder who has the strongest throwing arm on the Tiger team.

OVERALL:

Deer is a unique player. He's known primarily for homering and striking out, but he has stuck around in the majors because he can get on base as well as slug. If he stays at his '93 level and stays healthy, he should finally get a 500 at-bat season, which could produce some interesting numbers.

PITCHING:

When the struggling Tigers put out a "calling all pitchers" alert last year, righthander John Doherty was one of several youngsters to get his first major league opportunity. Used as both a reliever and as a starter, Doherty made the most of his chance. His 7-4 record was one of the few winning marks on the team, and his 3.88 ERA was the third-lowest on the Tiger staff.

Doherty had been a reliever throughout his minor league career, so it was no surprise that he began last year in the Tiger bullpen. He pitched pretty well in that role, recording three saves and ten holds, though his ERA was a bit on the high side at 4.12. But with the club hurting for starting pitchers, Sparky Anderson pulled a switch and put Doherty in the rotation late in the year. The youngster, who had made only one professional start prior to 1992, went 5-2 with a 3.67 ERA in his 11 starts. Not surprisingly, durability was a bit of a problem. Doherty threw no complete games, and averaged less than six innings per start.

Doherty relies on a good sinking fastball that produces a steady stream of ground balls. He averaged 3.02 grounders for every flyball last year, one of the highest ratios in the majors. He's tough to take out of the yard (only four home runs). He needs good control to succeed. He had that good control in 1992. Doherty averaged only 1.9 walks per nine innings last year.

HOLDING RUNNERS AND FIELDING:

As a rookie, Doherty did a fine job of controlling the running game. He allowed only four steals in eight attempts, an outstanding ratio. Defensively, he's very quick off the mound, ranking sixth among major league pitchers last year with four double plays.

OVERALL:

Doherty's in a good position. Groundball pitchers like him often thrive at Tiger Stadium, with its long infield grass. He's also shown he can succeed both as a starter and as a reliever. He should get lots of work this year.

JOHN DOHERTY

Position: RP/SP
Bats: R **Throws:** R
Ht: 6' 4" **Wt:** 200

Opening Day Age: 25
Born: 6/11/67 in Bronx, NY
ML Seasons: 1

Overall Statistics

	W	L	ERA	G	GS	Sv	IP	H	R	BB	SO	HR
1992	7	4	3.88	47	11	3	116.0	131	61	25	37	4
Career	7	4	3.88	47	11	3	116.0	131	61	25	37	4

How Often He Throws Strikes

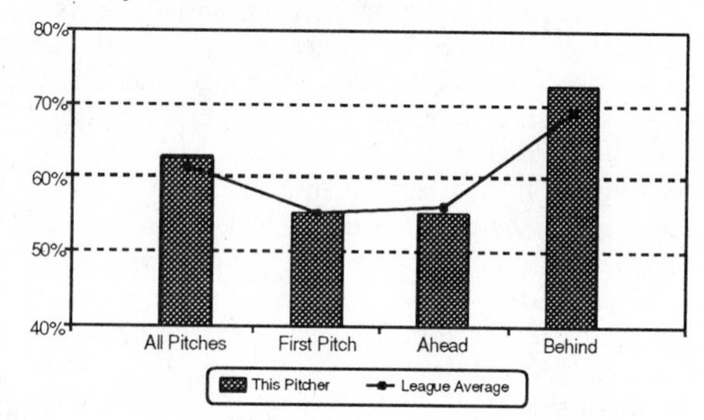

1992 Situational Stats

	W	L	ERA	Sv	IP		AB	H	HR	RBI	AVG
Home	5	1	3.83	1	56.1	LHB	200	48	1	26	.240
Road	2	3	3.92	2	59.2	RHB	257	83	3	25	.323
Day	2	2	2.10	1	34.1	Sc Pos	116	33	1	44	.284
Night	5	2	4.63	2	81.2	Clutch	59	23	1	7	.390

1992 Rankings (American League)

- 2nd in most GDPs induced per GDP situation (23.2%)
- 5th in least strikeouts per 9 innings in relief (3.5)
- 9th in highest relief ERA (4.12)
- Led the Tigers in GDPs induced (22), most GDPs induced per GDP situation and lowest batting average allowed vs. left-handed batters (.240)

CECIL FIELDER

Position: 1B/DH
Bats: R **Throws:** R
Ht: 6' 3" **Wt:** 250

Opening Day Age: 29
Born: 9/21/63 in Los Angeles, CA
ML Seasons: 7

HITTING:

Cecil Fielder is shaped like Babe Ruth, and he's certainly hit his share of Ruthian homers. So it seemed appropriate that Fielder matched one of Ruth's most cherished records last season. By driving in a major-league high 124 runs, Fielder became the only player besides Ruth (1919-21) to lead both leagues in RBI for three consecutive seasons. Over the past three years, the massive first baseman has plated 389 runners -- an average of almost 130 per year.

Fielder had a remarkably consistent season in 1992. He hit .244 with 18 homers before the All-Star break, .245 with 17 home runs afterward. Not at all a "Tiger Stadium hitter," he hit 18 home runs at home, 17 on the road. He hit between six and eight homers in every month except May, when he managed only one.

Like most big sluggers, Fielder likes the ball away from him -- especially low and away -- where he can extend his arms. Usually he'll pull the ball, but Fielder hits a good number of homers to the opposite field. He loves to uncork his mighty swing on a fastball, and he strikes out a prodigious number of times (151 last year).

BASERUNNING:

Can we say Fielder is slow? Well, he's never stolen a base in the majors, and he's played 377 consecutive games without even attempting one. His career high in triples is one, and he's gone 347 contests since his last three-bagger. We can probably say he's slow.

FIELDING:

Though a huge man, Fielder is surprisingly agile around the first base bag. He has soft hands and can scoop up low throws. However, his arm is not good, and his size hampers him when he has to lumber after a pop fly.

OVERALL:

After three seasons in Detroit, Fielder has achieved the status of a legend. As the cleanup man and focal point of a potent offense, he's a definite threat to win yet another RBI crown this year. All he needs to do is stay healthy, and maintain some modest control of his weight.

Overall Statistics

	G	AB	R	H	D	T	HR	RBI	SB	BB	SO	AVG
1992	155	594	80	145	22	0	35	124	0	73	151	.244
Career	696	2297	353	590	91	3	161	473	0	287	628	.257

Where He Hits the Ball

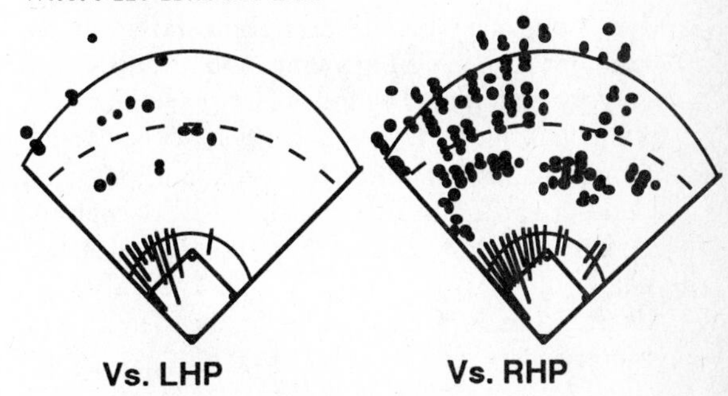

1992 Situational Stats

	AB	H	HR	RBI	AVG		AB	H	HR	RBI	AVG
Home	296	76	18	68	.257	LHP	134	31	9	31	.231
Road	298	69	17	56	.232	RHP	460	114	26	93	.248
Day	201	52	16	51	.259	Sc Pos	182	48	10	82	.264
Night	393	93	19	73	.237	Clutch	83	29	5	20	.349

1992 Rankings (American League)

- 1st in RBI (124)
- 2nd in strikeouts (151)
- 3rd in home runs (35) and highest percentage of swings that missed (30.9%)
- 4th in highest batting average on a 3-1 count (.615) and lowest percentage of swings put into play (34.9%)
- Led the Tigers in home runs, RBI, sacrifice flies (7), strikeouts, GDPs (14), highest batting average in the clutch (.349), highest batting average on a 3-1 count and highest slugging percentage vs. right-handed pitchers (.454)
- Led AL first basemen in RBI, strikeouts and highest batting average on a 3-1 count

FUTURE MVP?

HITTING:

After only two full seasons in the majors, Tiger shortstop Travis Fryman is being talked about as a major star -- the next Cal Ripken, people are saying. And why not? In 1991, Fryman posted figures (21 homers, 91 RBI) that were decidedly Ripken-like. The youngster, only 23 last year, followed up with 20 homers and 96 RBI in 1992.

Like Ripken, Fryman started out predominantly as a third baseman. In Fryman's case, it was because a great veteran, Alan Trammell, was manning his natural position. But when Trammell fractured his ankle last May, Fryman got a chance to play short. He made the most of it, missing only one game all last season.

The young slugger still has some holes in his game. Fryman has a big swing, and he strikes out at a very high rate (144 times last year). His walk total is still pretty low (40 in 1991, 45 last year). Primarily a fastball hitter, he needs to improve on breaking stuff, and he's still too pull-conscious. Fryman also wore out in the second half of last year, hitting only .235 with seven homers after the All-Star break. But, of course, he's still very young.

BASERUNNING:

A big man, Fryman has good speed. He'll never be a big basestealer, but he's stolen a respectable 20 bases in 29 attempts over the last two years. Fryman gets out of the box quickly and is an aggressive baserunner, though he sometimes makes youthful mistakes.

FIELDING:

Tall and rangy, Fryman fits the Ripken mold at shortstop: he has a strong arm, and he can cover more ground than one might think. He's good on the double play as well. But Fryman committed 20 errors at short last year, and needs to cut down on his careless throws. He's better at shortstop than at third.

OVERALL:

Fryman has enormous potential, and seems destined to get even better. His weaknesses -- strike zone judgement, stamina, defensive miscues -- are all correctable. With Trammell's return this year, he may be back at third. He'll certainly be playing somewhere.

TRAVIS FRYMAN

Position: SS/3B
Bats: R **Throws:** R
Ht: 6' 1" **Wt:** 194

Opening Day Age: 24
Born: 3/25/69 in Lexington, KY
ML Seasons: 3

Overall Statistics

	G	AB	R	H	D	T	HR	RBI	SB	BB	SO	AVG
1992	161	659	87	175	31	4	20	96	8	45	144	.266
Career	376	1448	184	388	78	8	50	214	23	102	344	.268

Where He Hits the Ball

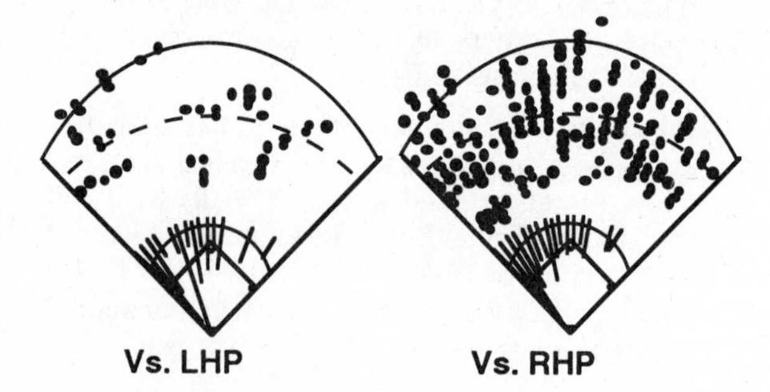

Vs. LHP Vs. RHP

1992 Situational Stats

	AB	H	HR	RBI	AVG		AB	H	HR	RBI	AVG
Home	319	74	9	40	.232	LHP	158	45	7	31	.285
Road	340	101	11	56	.297	RHP	501	130	13	65	.259
Day	219	58	5	28	.265	Sc Pos	194	52	3	72	.268
Night	440	117	15	68	.266	Clutch	85	17	4	13	.200

1992 Rankings (American League)

- 1st in at-bats (659)
- 2nd in games played (161)
- 3rd in plate appearances (721)
- Led the Tigers in at-bats, hits (175), triples (4), total bases (274), hit by pitch (6), games played, highest batting average vs. left-handed pitchers (.285) and highest batting average on the road (.297)
- Led AL shortstops in home runs (20), at-bats, hits, doubles (31), total bases, RBI (96), strikeouts (144), pitches seen (2,744), plate appearances, slugging percentage (.416), HR frequency (33.0 ABs per HR) and batting average with the bases loaded (.467)

HITTING:

After racing home with the winning run in the 1991 World Series, Dan Gladden found the Twins curiously lukewarm about signing him to another contract. So in the off-season Gladden raced all the way to Detroit, signing with the Tigers as a free agent. Unfortunately, the story didn't have a happy ending. Gladden did raise his average by seven points to .254, but in other ways the 35 year old's skills continued to erode.

Things just didn't work out for Gladden last year. Always a streaky hitter, he got off to a bad start, batting only .188 in April. He was snapping out of it when he fractured his left thumb on May 12; he wound up missing a month. After his return he swung a hot bat for a short while. But from July 1 until the end of the season, Gladden batted only .231.

Gladden has always been a first ball-fastball hitter, and he continued to hit that way for Detroit. As usual, he didn't walk much (30 times all year), nor hit for much power (seven homers). Gladden has become more of a flyball hitter in recent years, but that didn't help him at Tiger Stadium. He hit .226 at home, .275 outside Detroit.

BASERUNNING:

After stealing 20 or more bases for seven straight years from 1984 through 1990, Gladden dropped to 15 in 1991 and managed just four steals last year. At 35, he appears to be losing his speed, though he remains aggressive running the bases.

FIELDING:

Gladden's no longer fast enough to be an every-day center fielder, but he can fill in once in a while. In left, his breakneck style allows him to get to a lot of balls. He has an adequate arm for left.

OVERALL:

There always seems to be room on a Sparky Anderson roster for a scrappy player not blessed with God-given talent. Gladden was that player in 1992. Everything he accomplishes, he works for. Unfortunately, the calendar is turning and Gladden's days as a full-timer are running out.

DAN GLADDEN

Position: LF/CF
Bats: R **Throws:** R
Ht: 5'11" **Wt:** 184

Opening Day Age: 35
Born: 7/7/57 in San Jose, CA
ML Seasons: 10

Overall Statistics

	G	AB	R	H	D	T	HR	RBI	SB	BB	SO	AVG
1992	113	417	57	106	20	1	7	42	4	30	64	.254
Career	1106	4145	611	1120	187	38	61	390	214	316	575	.270

Where He Hits the Ball

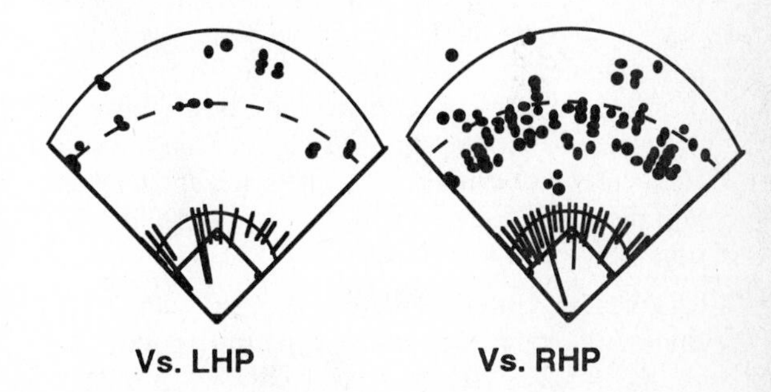

1992 Situational Stats

	AB	H	HR	RBI	AVG		AB	H	HR	RBI	AVG
Home	177	40	3	18	.226	LHP	124	35	4	18	.282
Road	240	66	4	24	.275	RHP	293	71	3	24	.242
Day	136	35	1	8	.257	Sc Pos	114	30	4	38	.263
Night	281	71	6	34	.253	Clutch	65	22	1	8	.338

1992 Rankings (American League)

- 10th in highest batting average in the clutch (.338)
- Led the Tigers in outfield assists (9)

PITCHING:

A surprise 20-game winner in 1991, Bill Gullickson entered the last two months of '92 on pace to reach the milestone for the second straight season. Unfortunately, his last 10 starts sealed his fate. Gullickson had a 13-7 record on August 7, but won only one game the rest of way. After August he really fell apart, going 0-5 with a 7.79 ERA. Even so, he led the Tigers in wins (14), innings pitched (221.2) and games started (34) for the season.

Gullickson's late-season fade was puzzling, since his stuff appeared to be about the same as ever: easy to hit, in other words. In his early days with Montreal, Gullickson was a power pitcher capable of fanning 18 Cubs in one game. But these days he throws the ball over the plate and dares hitters to hit it, which they do. He is strictly an offspeed pitcher -- fastball, slider, curve -- but not the sinkerballer you might imagine. Gullickson frequently works up in the strike zone, and he gets hurt plenty by the longball. He permitted 35 home runs last year, most in baseball.

The key to Gullickson's success, as with most finesse pitchers, is control. He permitted only 50 walks in 221.2 innings last year, an excellent ratio. He was also helped once again by the Tiger attack. Detroit provided Gullickson with 5.32 runs per game in offense, pretty close to the 5.81 he received in 1991.

HOLDING RUNNERS AND FIELDING:

Gullickson allows a lot of baserunners, so it's not surprising he permits a high total of stolen bases: 20 in 28 attempts last year. His pickoff move is actually pretty good and he keeps the runners guessing. His glove work is above average. He committed only one error and took part in three double plays.

OVERALL:

Though his late-season collapse gave the Tigers reason to be concerned, Gullickson remained the workhorse of a young, inexperienced staff. A free agent, he's probably more valuable to Detroit than he would be to most other clubs. If his salary demands are reasonable, he'll probably be back.

BILL GULLICKSON

Position: SP
Bats: R **Throws:** R
Ht: 6' 3" **Wt:** 225

Opening Day Age: 34
Born: 2/20/59 in Marshall, MN
ML Seasons: 12

Overall Statistics

	W	L	ERA	G	GS	Sv	IP	H	R	BB	SO	HR
1992	14	13	4.34	34	34	0	221.2	228	109	50	64	35
Career	145	122	3.73	349	343	0	2285.0	2317	1043	553	1144	230

How Often He Throws Strikes

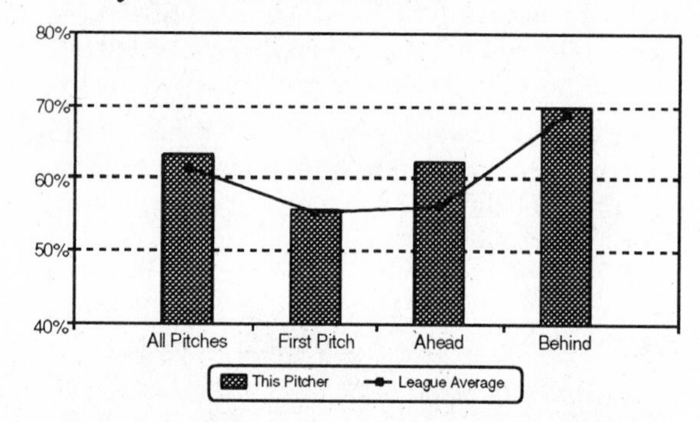

1992 Situational Stats

	W	L	ERA	Sv	IP		AB	H	HR	RBI	AVG
Home	6	9	4.28	0	130.1	LHB	414	116	18	52	.280
Road	8	4	4.43	0	91.1	RHB	439	112	17	46	.255
Day	3	6	4.72	0	74.1	Sc Pos	162	43	6	56	.265
Night	11	7	4.15	0	147.1	Clutch	78	24	4	9	.308

1992 Rankings (American League)

- 1st in home runs allowed (35), least pitches thrown per batter (3.30) and least strikeouts per 9 innings (2.6)
- 2nd in most home runs allowed per 9 innings (1.4)
- 3rd in highest slugging percentage allowed (.447)
- Led the Tigers in ERA (4.34), wins (14), losses (13), games started (34), complete games (4), shutouts (1), innings pitched (221.2), hits allowed (228), batters faced (919), home runs allowed, highest strikeout/walk ratio (1.3), lowest on-base percentage allowed (.305) and least pitches thrown per batter

DAVE HAAS

Position: SP
Bats: R **Throws:** R
Ht: 6' 1" **Wt:** 200

Opening Day Age: 27
Born: 10/19/65 in Independence, MO
ML Seasons: 2

PITCHING:

With the Tigers in desperate need of pitching help, David Haas was one of several hurlers who got an extended look last year. Haas, who spent most of the year at AAA Toledo, didn't arrive until August, but made a name for himself pretty quickly. The righthander went 5-3 in 11 starts, and his 3.94 ERA was very good by current Detroit standards.

When Tiger people talk about Haas, they don't mention an overpowering fastball or dazzling breaking stuff. They talk about his tenacity. "David takes the ball," said outgoing player development director Joe McDonald last year. "He sticks things out and gives you the very best that he has." The Tigers were especially impressed by the way Haas battled back from a brief, shaky stint with the Tigers in 1991. Used as a reliever in 11 games, he'd walked over a batter an inning while being shelled for a 6.75 ERA that year.

Haas' control was a whole lot sharper in a starting role last season. He walked only 16 men in 61.2 innings. But with his less-than-overwhelming stuff, he paid a price for throwing strikes. Haas allowed well over a hit an inning last year, and he surrendered eight home run balls. He also fanned far fewer hitters than he had during most of his professional career, less than one every two innings.

HOLDING RUNNERS AND FIELDING:

Haas has good defensive instincts and handles his 200-pound frame well around the mound. He did a fine job of holding runners last year. Only two men tried to steal on Haas, one successfully.

OVERALL:

Haas pitched pretty well in his two-month stint with Detroit last year, earning an expansion protection, but the jury's still out on whether he can continue to be successful. During his minor-league career, he had problems putting good years back-to-back, and he had only one good year once he moved past the Class A level. He'll continue to battle hitters, but his stuff may only take him so far.

Overall Statistics

	W	L	ERA	G	GS	Sv	IP	H	R	BB	SO	HR
1992	5	3	3.94	12	11	0	61.2	68	30	16	29	8
Career	6	3	4.35	23	11	0	72.1	76	38	28	35	9

How Often He Throws Strikes

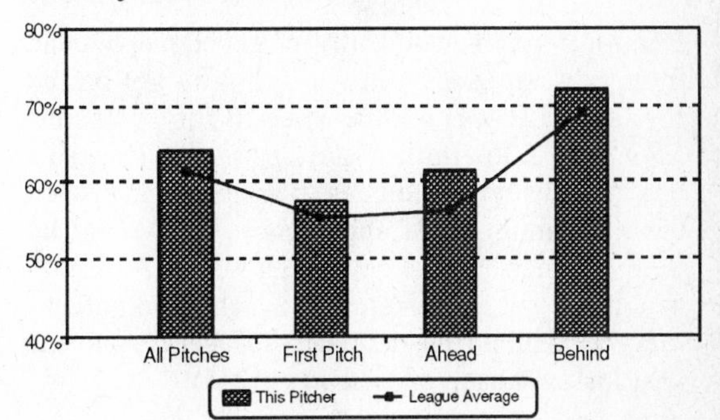

1992 Situational Stats

	W	L	ERA	Sv	IP		AB	H	HR	RBI	AVG
Home	2	1	4.65	0	31.0	LHB	116	33	3	9	.284
Road	3	2	3.23	0	30.2	RHB	130	35	5	20	.269
Day	1	1	5.65	0	14.1	Sc Pos	60	16	1	20	.267
Night	4	2	3.42	0	47.1	Clutch	3	0	0	0	.000

1992 Rankings (American League)

➟ Led the Tigers in shutouts (1)

PITCHING:

Sparky Anderson had a plan for his relief ace, Mike Henneman, last year. For several years Henneman had done fine work out of the Tiger bullpen -- so fine that Sparky often couldn't resist using him as early as the seventh inning. The problem was that Henneman's arm couldn't handle the load. While he continued to pitch 60 games or more a year, he often had bouts of ineffectiveness due to a tender arm, along with occasional stints on the disabled list.

Last year, the Anderson plan was to reserve Henneman for the ninth inning, like Dennis Eckersley. As Sparky's brainstorms go, this one worked about as well as the time he moved Lou Whitaker off second base to make room for Chris Pittaro. Henneman dutifully averaged just over an inning an appearance in April, but he got pasted for a 6.23 ERA. He did so again in July, when his ERA was 7.36. Tender arm or not, Henneman's best months were the ones in which he averaged the most innings per appearance. He wound up with a career-high 24 saves, but his ERA of 3.96 was his worst ever. Henneman, who had entered the year with a lifetime record of 49-21, had the first losing season of his career (2-6).

As usual, Henneman relied mostly on his split-fingered fastball, a pitch which gets him a lot of groundball outs. His fastball and slider are also serviceable pitches, but the splitter is his money pitch. He seems to need a little while to find his rhythm, which is probably why the one-inning experiment didn't work.

HOLDING RUNNERS AND FIELDING:

Henneman has quick reflexes and is very good at fielding his position. He controls the running game pretty well, mostly with a quick delivery to home plate.

OVERALL:

The Tigers have a bit of a dilemma with Henneman. He's their best reliever, but his stuff and arm seem better suited to set-up work than closing. He can handle the finisher's role, as long as they accept his limitations.

MIKE HENNEMAN

Position: RP
Bats: R **Throws:** R
Ht: 6' 4" **Wt:** 205

Opening Day Age: 31
Born: 12/11/61 in St. Charles, MO
ML Seasons: 6

Overall Statistics

	W	L	ERA	G	GS	Sv	IP	H	R	BB	SO	HR
1992	2	6	3.96	60	0	24	77.1	75	36	20	58	6
Career	51	27	3.05	369	0	104	534.0	488	206	192	371	31

How Often He Throws Strikes

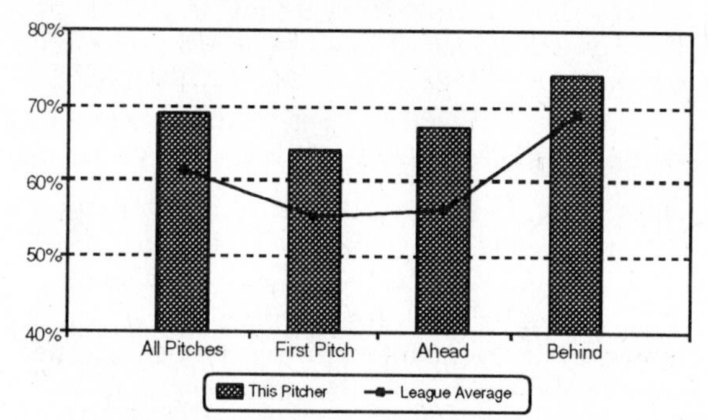

1992 Situational Stats

	W	L	ERA	Sv	IP		AB	H	HR	RBI	AVG
Home	1	4	3.19	14	42.1	LHB	144	40	2	18	.278
Road	1	2	4.89	10	35.0	RHB	149	35	4	17	.235
Day	1	1	1.37	6	26.1	Sc Pos	65	19	2	30	.292
Night	1	5	5.29	18	51.0	Clutch	171	46	4	26	.269

1992 Rankings (American League)

- 5th in save percentage (85.7%) and relief losses (6)
- 7th in games finished (53)
- Led the Tigers in saves (24), games finished, save opportunities (28), save percentage, blown saves (4), relief losses, least runners allowed per 9 innings in relief (11.1) and most strikeouts per 9 innings in relief (6.8)

PITCHING:

Something of a late bloomer, John Kiely was an undrafted free agent who didn't pitch professionally until he was 23. Kiely finally reached the majors in 1991, when he was nearly 27, and the results were hardly impressive: seven games, a 14.85 ERA. But the righthander is a scrapper, and he fought his way back to the majors last year. Judging by his work -- a 2.13 ERA -- he might be around to stay.

Kiely began last season at AAA Toledo, and as usual, he pitched very well, with a 2.84 ERA. It was the fourth straight year he'd posted a minor league ERA under 3.00, and the pitching-poor Tigers eventually recalled him. From the beginning, he looked like he belonged. Used in middle relief, Kiely didn't post a save, but he did record seven holds in a little more than half a season of work. He held the opposition to a .224 average, and a .188 mark with runners in scoring position. He proved durable, which is important in the Sparky Anderson scheme. Used in back-to-back games on 10 occasions, his ERA with no days rest was 1.10.

No fireballer, Kiely is a sidearmer who relies on a sinking fastball and breaking stuff. With his motion, he would appear to be tough on right-handed hitters, but last year he was better against lefties (.179) than righties (.259). He didn't record many strikeouts last year (18 in 55 innings), but he did notch a high number of groundball outs.

HOLDING RUNNERS AND FIELDING:

Kiely is a very good fielder with quick reactions. He didn't make an error last year, and he started three double plays. He also knows how to hold baserunners; in his 55 innings, he permitted only two stolen bases.

OVERALL:

No youngster, Kiely wasn't in awe of major league hitters last year. He's not a hard thrower, so he'll need good location if he wants to succeed. Judging by his record, there seems no reason to doubt him.

JOHN KIELY

Position: RP
Bats: R **Throws:** R
Ht: 6' 3" **Wt:** 210

Opening Day Age: 28
Born: 10/4/64 in Boston, MA
ML Seasons: 2

Overall Statistics

	W	L	ERA	G	GS	Sv	IP	H	R	BB	SO	HR
1992	4	2	2.13	39	0	0	55.0	44	14	28	18	2
Career	4	3	3.50	46	0	0	61.2	57	25	37	19	2

How Often He Throws Strikes

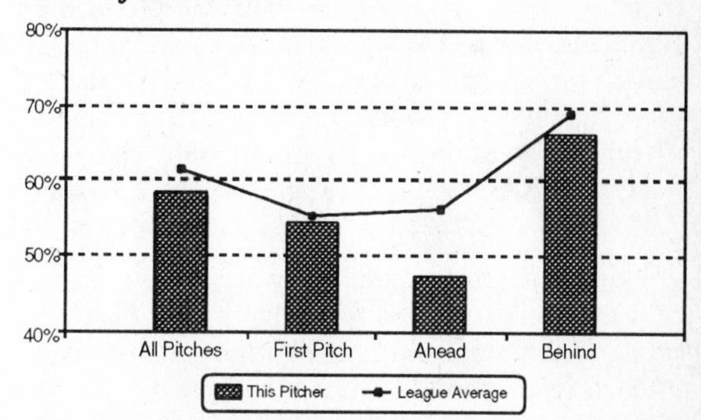

1992 Situational Stats

	W	L	ERA	Sv	IP		AB	H	HR	RBI	AVG
Home	3	0	1.00	0	27.0	LHB	84	15	0	7	.179
Road	1	2	3.21	0	28.0	RHB	112	29	2	16	.259
Day	2	0	0.78	0	23.0	Sc Pos	69	13	0	21	.188
Night	2	2	3.09	0	32.0	Clutch	56	14	2	9	.250

1992 Rankings (American League)

- 2nd in least strikeouts per 9 innings in relief (2.9)
- Led the Tigers in relief ERA (2.13) and lowest batting average allowed in relief (.224)

PITCHING:

Kurt Knudsen has had a tough time earning respect, even though he's had success at almost every level of his professional career. A ninth-round draft choice out of the University of Miami in 1988, Knudsen moved steadily up the Tiger system, posting great ERAs and sensational strikeout figures (295 in 270.2 minor league innings). But because he lacked a blazing fastball, he's never been considered a top prospect, even in his own organization.

Knudsen finally earned some of that respect in 1992, when he reached the major league level for the first time. Though a late-season fade lifted his ERA to 4.58, he pitched much better than that for most of the season. At the All-Star break the righthander was 2-0 with two saves and a 2.72 ERA. Just when he seemed to have it made, though, Knudsen ran into problems. He got hammered but good during the second half. His post All-Star ERA was 6.55; after August 1 it was 7.92.

Knudsen's high strikeout totals are more a result of deception than velocity. He has a nice, moving fastball, thrown from a tricky motion, and the pitch is very hard for hitters to pick up. Even during his disastrous second half he fanned 32 men in 34.1 innings. But Knudsen works up in the strike zone -- he's an extreme flyball pitcher -- and hitters learned to make him throw strikes. Walks plagued him (41 in 70.2 innings), and he was hurt by the home run ball once he fell behind in the count.

HOLDING RUNNERS AND FIELDING:

Knudsen appears to be a good fielder. He played errorless ball last year and started two double plays. He knows how to hold runners also. He allowed only six steals in 11 attempts while recording a pickoff.

OVERALL:

Despite his second half fade, the Tigers liked what they saw of Knudsen last year, enough to make him one of their 15 protected players in the expansion draft. There's no reason that he can't continue to strike out hitters at the major-league level. But to succeed, he'll have to throw quality strikes more consistently than he did in 1992.

KURT KNUDSEN

Position: RP
Bats: R **Throws:** R
Ht: 6' 3" **Wt:** 200

Opening Day Age: 26
Born: 2/20/67 in Arlington Heights, IL
ML Seasons: 1

Overall Statistics

	W	L	ERA	G	GS	Sv	IP	H	R	BB	SO	HR
1992	2	3	4.58	48	1	5	70.2	70	39	41	51	9
Career	2	3	4.58	48	1	5	70.2	70	39	41	51	9

How Often He Throws Strikes

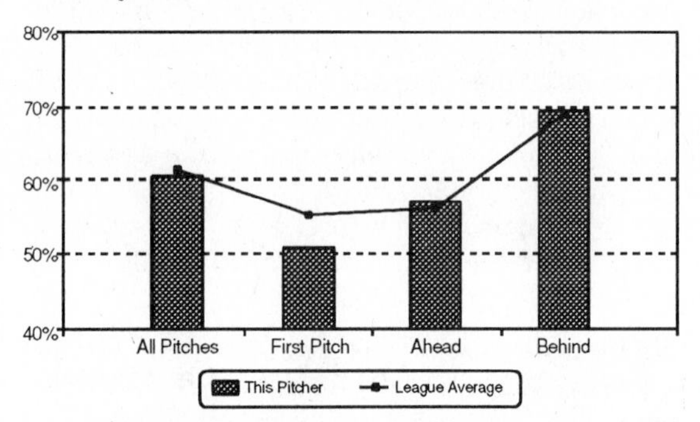

1992 Situational Stats

	W	L	ERA	Sv	IP		AB	H	HR	RBI	AVG
Home	2	1	3.93	1	36.2	LHB	109	29	4	17	.266
Road	0	2	5.29	4	34.0	RHB	156	41	5	26	.263
Day	0	1	5.09	0	23.0	Sc Pos	89	20	0	29	.225
Night	2	2	4.34	5	47.2	Clutch	96	27	3	14	.281

1992 Rankings (American League)

- 6th in most baserunners allowed per 9 innings in relief (13.6)
- 10th in highest relief ERA (4.06) and highest batting average allowed in relief (.258)
- Led the Tigers in first batter efficiency (.195)

PITCHING:

On the Tigers, any pitcher under 35 years old who wins more games than he loses is bound to cause some excitement. In Mark Leiter, Detroit knows it hasn't uncovered the next Denny McLain. But they're pleased that the big righthander has gone 17-12 over the last two seasons, posting two straight winning years. On the Tiger staff, that's a major accomplishment.

Leiter has succeeded while handling a very difficult role: he's a swingman, either starting or relieving depending on his club's need. Last year Leiter started 14 games and relieved in 21. He was more effective as a relief man in 1992 (2.65 ERA vs. 4.94 as a starter), but during his career he's pitched reasonably well in both roles. He missed a month due last year due to a strained groin muscle, but was able to avoid his former arm problems. Leiter was able to bounce back well from the injury, posting a 2.32 ERA after the All-Star break.

Leiter's best pitch is an above-average fastball which he throws from a three-quarters motion. It's not an overpowering, 90 MPH pitch but it has good movement, and he's able to work up in the strike zone and record a respectable number of strikeouts. He also throws a slider and changeup, but those are only average pitches. Leiter's stuff has usually been much more effective against right-handed hitters (.248 opponents' average last year) than vs. lefties (.312).

HOLDING RUNNERS AND FIELDING:

Leiter has a good move for a righthander. He holds runners close, records some pickoffs, and has allowed only 16 steals in 32 attempts during his career. He's only an average fielder at best.

OVERALL:

Nearly 30, Leiter finally seems over the shoulder problems which caused him to miss three full seasons while in the Oriole system. He's no world-beater, but for two years he's handled the difficult starter/reliever role. The Tigers are happy with his efforts and will be counting on him this year.

MARK LEITER

Position: RP/SP
Bats: R **Throws:** R
Ht: 6' 3" **Wt:** 210

Opening Day Age: 30
Born: 4/13/63 in Joliet, IL
ML Seasons: 3

Overall Statistics

	W	L	ERA	G	GS	Sv	IP	H	R	BB	SO	HR
1992	8	5	4.18	35	14	0	112.0	116	57	43	75	9
Career	18	13	4.45	81	32	1	273.0	274	143	102	199	30

How Often He Throws Strikes

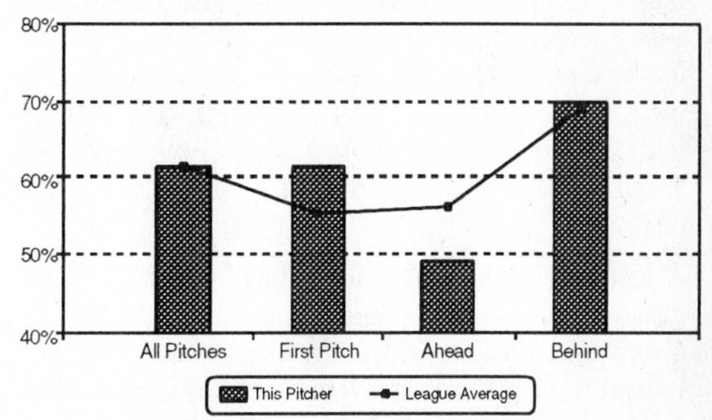

1992 Situational Stats

	W	L	ERA	Sv	IP		AB	H	HR	RBI	AVG
Home	4	3	4.28	0	61.0	LHB	189	59	4	26	.312
Road	4	2	4.06	0	51.0	RHB	230	57	5	21	.248
Day	2	1	6.30	0	30.0	Sc Pos	98	27	0	34	.276
Night	6	4	3.40	0	82.0	Clutch	49	7	1	5	.143

1992 Rankings (American League)

- 9th in highest batting average allowed vs. left-handed batters (.312)

HITTING:

When Scott Livingstone came up to the Tigers in the middle of 1991, he impressed everyone by batting .291. Nonetheless, Livingstone figured to spend 1992 as a utility player. Alan Trammell was set as the Tiger shortstop, and third base belonged to Travis Fryman. But when Trammell went out for the year with a fractured ankle, Livingstone wound up getting into 117 games. Once more the youngster did a fine job, batting a solid .282.

As an offensive force at third base, Livingstone isn't going to make anyone forget Mike Schmidt. He had one 14-homer season in the minors, but that was his only year in double figures. His major league totals -- six homers in 481 lifetime at-bats -- suggest he might be able to hit 10 or so. Primarily he's a line drive hitter, and a good contact man, with only 36 strikeouts last year. He hasn't walked much on the big-league level, but he showed a respectable amount of patience in the minors.

A lefty swinger, Livingstone has been platooned thus far in his major-league career. His 1992 figures against lefties -- .289 in 45 at-bats -- suggest he can handle them, however. He handles the bat very well, and he's a decent bunter and hit-and-run man. Once a pull hitter, he's learned to use the whole field.

BASERUNNING:

Livingstone doesn't have a lot of speed, and he's not much of a threat to steal. He stole only one base in four attempts last year, a typical performance for him. He's a fairly intelligent baserunner, though.

FIELDING:

Livingstone is not the Gold Glove type at third base, but he's good enough. His range and hands are above average, and his arm is fairly strong. He can handle the position.

OVERALL:

Considered hot-tempered early in his career, Livingstone has matured. He sat patiently waiting for his chance last year, and when he got it, he made the most of it. If Trammell is healthy, Livingstone may start this year on the bench, but he figures to see plenty of action. The Tigers showed their confidence by protecting him from expansion.

SCOTT LIVINGSTONE

Position: 3B
Bats: L **Throws:** R
Ht: 6' 0" **Wt:** 198

Opening Day Age: 27
Born: 7/15/65 in Dallas, TX
ML Seasons: 2

Overall Statistics

	G	AB	R	H	D	T	HR	RBI	SB	BB	SO	AVG
1992	117	354	43	100	21	0	4	46	1	21	36	.282
Career	161	481	62	137	26	0	6	57	3	31	61	.285

Where He Hits the Ball

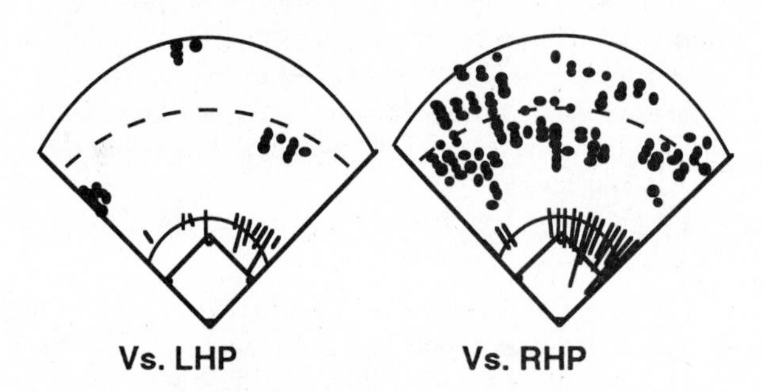

1992 Situational Stats

	AB	H	HR	RBI	AVG		AB	H	HR	RBI	AVG
Home	175	40	2	26	.229	LHP	45	13	1	7	.289
Road	179	60	2	20	.335	RHP	309	87	3	39	.282
Day	120	34	1	17	.283	Sc Pos	93	25	2	43	.269
Night	234	66	3	29	.282	Clutch	45	10	1	8	.222

1992 Rankings (American League)

- Led the Tigers in highest batting average with the bases loaded (.500) and highest batting average on a 3-2 count (.269)

MIKE MUNOZ

Position: RP
Bats: L **Throws:** L
Ht: 6' 2" **Wt:** 200

Opening Day Age: 27
Born: 7/12/65 in Baldwin Park, CA
ML Seasons: 4

PITCHING:

When the Tigers decided not to bring back Jerry Don Gleaton last year, there was an obvious need for a lefty in their bullpen. Former Dodger farmhand Mike Munoz was one of several southpaws vying for the role last spring, but he was hardly Sparky Anderson's first choice. Munoz had pitched for the Tigers at the tail end of 1991, and his work (9.64 ERA in six games) had hardly been impressive. Fortunately, Munoz pitched fairly well in camp, clinching a roster spot with some good work at the end of spring training. The lean southpaw continued to pitch sharply all year. Munoz turned in a 3.00 ERA, second-lowest on the club, while working in a staff-high 65 games.

Munoz' main job last year was simple: come in and retire left-handed hitters. He did it very well, holding lefty swingers to a .192 average. Munoz was a lot less impressive against righties (.283), but that didn't hurt him much, since a high percentage of the batters he faced were lefties. His 65 appearances totaled only 48 innings. Munoz showed off a nice moving fastball last year, and an excellent slider. His pitches sink, helping him record many groundball outs. Though Munoz was used mainly as a set-up man, he was tough in the clutch. He allowed only 11 of 55 inherited runners to score and held the opposition to a .161 average with runners in scoring position. He also recorded 15 holds, the ninth-highest total in the league.

HOLDING RUNNERS AND FIELDING:

Munoz played flawless defense in '92 in 20 chances, and he appears to be a good fielder. He holds runners fairly well, allowing only three stolen bases last year.

OVERALL:

One of those guys who pitched pretty well for years in the minors without ever getting a real major-league chance, Munoz made the most of his opportunity last year, and earned an expansion protection by the Tigers. He lacks a closer's heat (only 23 strikeouts in 48 innings last year), but he should again be valuable in a set-up role -- especially against lefties.

Overall Statistics

	W	L	ERA	G	GS	Sv	IP	H	R	BB	SO	HR
1992	1	2	3.00	65	0	2	48.0	44	16	25	23	3
Career	1	3	4.52	82	0	2	65.2	69	33	35	31	4

How Often He Throws Strikes

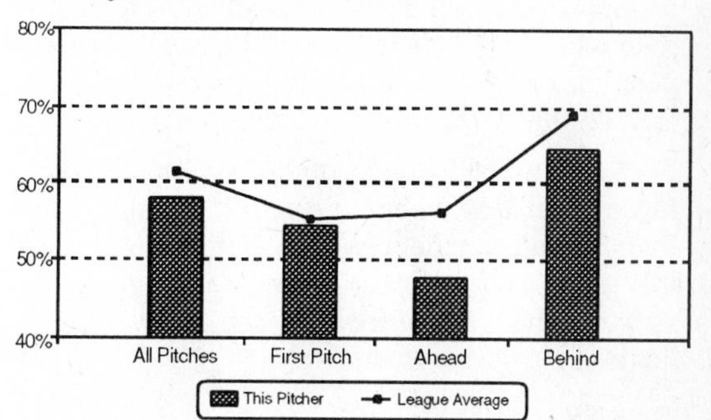

1992 Situational Stats

	W	L	ERA	Sv	IP		AB	H	HR	RBI	AVG
Home	0	2	3.68	0	22.0	LHB	73	14	0	4	.192
Road	1	0	2.42	2	26.0	RHB	106	30	3	14	.283
Day	1	0	3.77	0	14.1	Sc Pos	56	9	0	15	.161
Night	0	2	2.67	2	33.2	Clutch	55	12	2	9	.218

1992 Rankings (American League)

- 8th in lowest percentage of inherited runners scored (20.0%)
- 9th in holds (15)
- Led the Tigers in games pitched (65), holds and lowest percentage of inherited runners scored

TONY PHILLIPS

Position: 2B/3B/LF/CF/RF/DH
Bats: B **Throws:** R
Ht: 5'10" **Wt:** 175

Opening Day Age: 33
Born: 4/25/59 in Atlanta, GA
ML Seasons: 11

HITTING:

Tony Phillips is a guy you can't keep out of the lineup or off the bases. Phillips missed only three games last year while leading the American League in runs scored with 114. In his third season with Detroit, the switch-hitter continued to do a little of everything: get on base, score runs, hit for a little power, play everywhere on the diamond. No wonder Sparky Anderson considered him indispensable.

Phillips was a very consistent hitter in 1992. He hit .273 at home, .278 on the road; .270 against lefties, .278 against righties; .276 with the bases empty, .274 with runners on, .271 in the late innings of close games. About the only problem he had was handling a designated hitter role. The man who can handle any position can't handle a position on the bench: Phillips batted .209 as a DH, .290 when used in the field.

Formerly a very streaky hitter, Phillips became more consistent when he stopped laying off the high fastballs pitchers fed him. Phillips now takes that pitch and basically swings at nothing but strikes, which is the main reason his walk total has risen to such a high level.

BASERUNNING:

Not exactly your base-stealing leadoff man, Phillips stole 12 bases last year while being caught 10 times. He's not really slow, however, and legged out a career-high 32 doubles in '92. He's an extremely aggressive baserunner.

FIELDING:

A utility-man extraordinaire defensively, Phillips played 57 games at second base, 35 in right field, 24 in center, 20 at third, 14 in left and one at shortstop. He committed 11 errors, not bad for someone wearing so many different gloves. Second base is probably his best position. He has fine range there, along with the ability to turn the double play.

OVERALL:

A manager's dream, Phillips can play every day at a different position and always help the team's chances of winning. If he were several years younger and had more speed in his legs, he'd be considered one of the game's best players. Many people consider him in that class anyway.

Overall Statistics

	G	AB	R	H	D	T	HR	RBI	SB	BB	SO	AVG
1992	159	606	114	167	32	3	10	64	12	114	93	.276
Career	1292	4331	652	1120	190	37	68	450	97	634	763	.259

Where He Hits the Ball

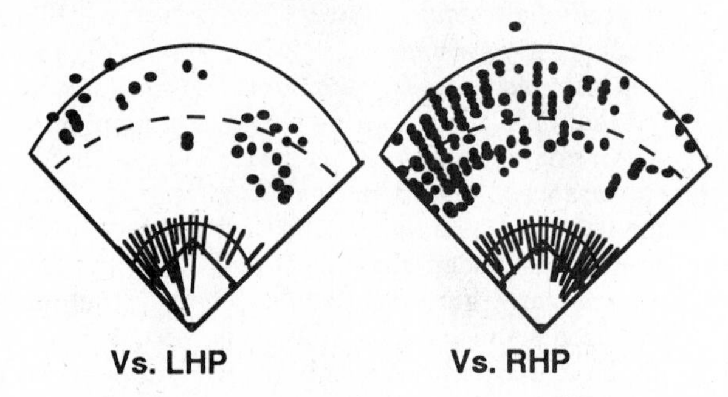

1992 Situational Stats

	AB	H	HR	RBI	AVG		AB	H	HR	RBI	AVG
Home	289	79	3	31	.273	LHP	174	47	5	23	.270
Road	317	88	7	33	.278	RHP	432	120	5	41	.278
Day	200	51	4	19	.255	Sc Pos	124	38	3	55	.306
Night	406	116	6	45	.286	Clutch	85	23	2	15	.271

1992 Rankings (American League)

- 1st in runs scored (114)
- 2nd in times on base (282), pitches seen (2,898) and plate appearances (733)
- 3rd in walks (114)
- Led the Tigers in runs scored, singles (122), doubles (32), sacrifice flies (7), caught stealing (10), times on base, pitches seen, plate appearances, on-base percentage (.387), highest groundball/flyball ratio (1.65), stolen base percentage (54.5%), highest batting average vs. right-handed pitchers (.278), highest on-base percentage vs. left-handed pitchers (.401) and highest on-base percentage vs. right-handed pitchers (.382)

FRANK TANANA

Position: SP
Bats: L **Throws:** L
Ht: 6' 3" **Wt:** 200

Opening Day Age: 39
Born: 7/3/53 in Detroit, MI
ML Seasons: 20

PITCHING:

Even though Frank Tanana led the Tiger staff in strikeouts in 1992, he hasn't exactly returned to the flame-throwing days of his California youth. Tanana led soft-tossing Detroit with the modest total of 91 punch-outs, the first time in ten years he was under the century mark. Even so, Tanana remained an effective pitcher. The 39-year-old lefty was second to Bill Gullickson on the Tigers in innings pitched, games started and wins. Winning 13 contests, Tanana was the only other Tiger beside Gullickson who reached double-figures in wins and had more than 30 games started.

Tanana's pitching style hasn't changed since the early 1980s, when arm problems forced him to re-invent himself as a finesse pitcher. His best pitch remains a curveball with excellent rotation, which he throws at various speeds. Second best is a good straight change he masks with excellent arm speed, and he also has a less-than-dazzling fastball. Mixed in with his other pitches, the Tanana heater is more effective than it has any right to be.

Tanana's stuff has always been more effective against left-handed hitters, and that was true again in 1992. He held lefty swingers to a .225 average and just two of the 22 overall home runs he surrendered. Tanana has many more problems with righties, who get a better look at his breaking stuff. Usually the possessor of very good control, Tanana allowed a career-high 90 walks last year. It's one reason his ERA rose from 3.69 to 4.39.

HOLDING RUNNERS AND FIELDING:

Only three pitchers in baseball caught more runners off base last year than Tanana, who had 10. Still, he allowed more stolen bases (21) in 1992 than he did in 1991 (17). He's always been considered a good fielder, though he committed two errors last year.

OVERALL:

Detroit native Tanana is a free agent after the 1992 season, but seems a good bet to return to the Tigers. He's durable, has plenty of experience getting batters out and keeps his ERA under 5.00. That combination makes him one of Detroit's best pitchers.

Overall Statistics

	W	L	ERA	G	GS	Sv	IP	H	R	BB	SO	HR
1992	13	11	4.39	32	31	0	186.2	188	102	90	91	22
Career	233	219	3.62	606	584	1	3984.0	3847	1800	1200	2657	420

How Often He Throws Strikes

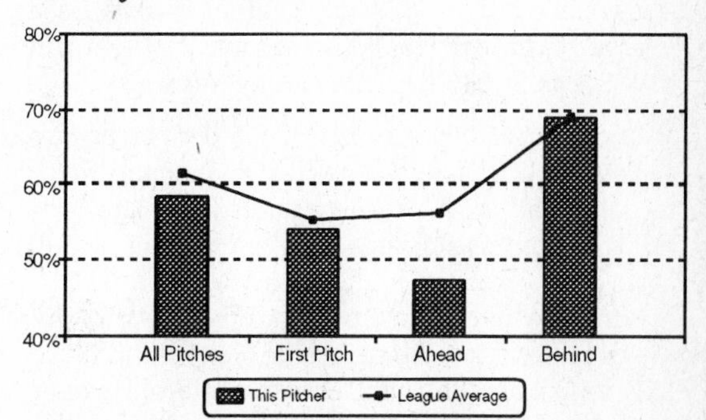

1992 Situational Stats

	W	L	ERA	Sv	IP		AB	H	HR	RBI	AVG
Home	7	5	4.98	0	77.2	LHB	102	23	2	10	.225
Road	6	6	3.96	0	109.0	RHB	602	165	20	78	.274
Day	4	4	4.28	0	69.1	Sc Pos	156	35	3	60	.224
Night	9	7	4.45	0	117.1	Clutch	46	10	2	4	.217

1992 Rankings (American League)

- 1st in lowest strikeout/walk ratio (1.0)
- 2nd in pickoffs (10)
- 3rd in highest on-base percentage allowed (.351) and most baserunners allowed per 9 innings (13.7)
- Led the Tigers in walks allowed (90), hit batsmen (7), strikeouts (91), wild pitches (11), balks (1), pitches thrown (3,152), pick-off throws (200), stolen bases allowed (21), baserunners caught stealing (11), winning percentage (.542), lowest batting average allowed (.267), lowest slugging percentage allowed (.415) and lowest stolen base percentage allowed (65.6%)

MICKEY TETTLETON

Position: C/DH
Bats: B **Throws:** R
Ht: 6' 2" **Wt:** 212

Opening Day Age: 32
Born: 9/16/60 in Oklahoma City, OK
ML Seasons: 9

HITTING:

One of the Tigers' trio of 30-home run men, Mickey Tettleton achieved a new career high by belting 32 out of the park last year. Tettleton's numbers were only slightly spoiled by a second-half slump (.221 after the All-Star break) which dropped his final average to .238. Any manager would gladly take a catcher who can hit 30 homers and drive in 80 runs; Tettleton's done that each of the last two years.

An extremely patient hitter, Tettleton makes up for a low average with his ability to draw walks. Last year he walked 122 times, tying Frank Thomas for the American League lead. It was the third straight season he'd reached the century mark. Due to his patience, Tettleton's on-base average last year was an excellent .379 -- a full 141 points higher than his batting average.

While Tettleton walks a lot, the hard swinger also strikes out a lot -- 137 times last year. Pitchers try to get ahead on the count against him, knowing he'll seldom swing at a first pitch. He's a pull hitter who likes the high pitch when batting righty, the low pitch when batting lefty. Tettleton hit much better from the right side last year (.274 to .226 lefty), but that's not a career pattern. He does considerable damage from each side.

BASERUNNING:

The element of surprise doesn't work in stealing bases if you don't have any speed. Tettleton didn't outrun anyone in 1992; he was caught all six times he tried to steal. He's not a dumb baserunner, just slow.

FIELDING:

Frequently criticized for his fielding, Tettleton proved that he could still gun down opposing baserunners, throwing out 35 percent of those trying to steal on him last year. He's an adequate catcher and handler of pitchers.

OVERALL:

A throwback, hard-working player, Tettleton has become one of the most explosive offensive catchers in the game. At 32, he may need more rest from the rigors of catching in order to keep his hitting sharp. Given that, he should remain a very productive player.

Overall Statistics

	G	AB	R	H	D	T	HR	RBI	SB	BB	SO	AVG
1992	157	525	82	125	25	0	32	83	0	122	137	.238
Career	932	2873	416	693	121	8	137	406	18	538	811	.241

Where He Hits the Ball

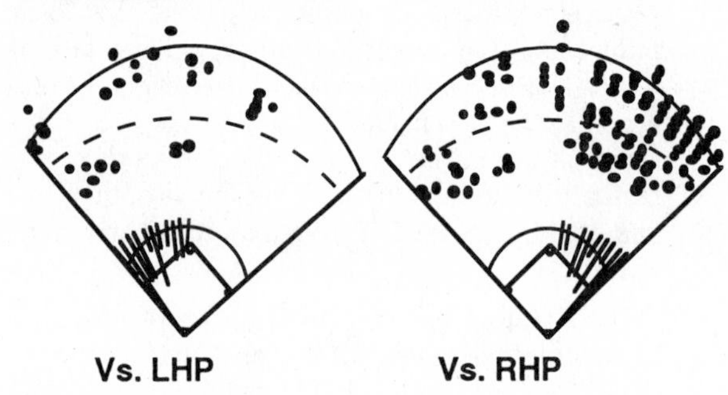

1992 Situational Stats

	AB	H	HR	RBI	AVG		AB	H	HR	RBI	AVG
Home	255	69	18	41	.271	LHP	135	37	8	23	.274
Road	270	56	14	42	.207	RHP	390	88	24	60	.226
Day	160	40	11	29	.250	Sc Pos	133	29	10	58	.218
Night	365	85	21	54	.233	Clutch	74	19	5	8	.257

1992 Rankings (American League)

- 1st in walks (122) and most pitches seen per plate appearance (4.22)
- 2nd in intentional walks (18) and lowest batting average on the road (.207)
- 3rd in HR frequency (16.4 ABs per HR)
- Led the Tigers in walks, intentional walks, slugging percentage (.469), HR frequency, most pitches seen per plate appearance, least GDPs per GDP situation (4.1%), highest slugging percentage vs. left-handed pitchers (.511) and highest percentage of pitches taken (64.9%)
- Led AL catchers in home runs (32), at-bats (525), runs scored (82), total bases (246), RBI (83), walks and intentional walks

ALAN TRAMMELL

Position: SS
Bats: R **Throws:** R
Ht: 6' 0" **Wt:** 185

Opening Day Age: 35
Born: 2/21/58 in Garden Grove, CA
ML Seasons: 16

HITTING:

At age 35, Alan Trammell is struggling to rebound from two straight injury-riddled seasons. In 1991, Trammell was limited to 101 games because of knee and ankle injuries. It was even worse in 1992. Trammell got into only 29 games before fracturing his right ankle May 15th in Kansas City. He never returned.

Before the fracture, Trammell was on his way to rebounding from a sub-par 1991 season. He had a .275 average in 102 at-bats when the injury struck. Trammell was also pelting lefties to the tune of .357 with a .500 slugging percentage.

In recent years, injuries have become a constant source of trouble for the veteran shortstop. Over the last five seasons, he's played more than 130 games only once (1990). When healthy, Trammell still possesses a nice, quick bat, with the ability to hit the ball with power to all fields. He's particularly strong on inside pitches. Trammell has excellent plate discipline, with the ability to draw a respectable number of walks. He's never struck out more than 71 times in a season.

BASERUNNING:

Trammell can still leg out the extra-base hit and can steal in double figures when his health permits. He was successful on two of his four steal attempts in 1992. No one knows how he'll return from his ankle injury, but it certainly can't add any speed to his 35-year-old legs.

FIELDING:

One of the best defensive shortstops of our time, Trammell still has above-average range and doesn't make many errors. Some of this is due to having spent 15 years with the same double play partner, but he'd be a good one with any second baseman. But his injury may prove his defensive downfall.

OVERALL:

Trammell has a lot to prove coming back in 1993. While expected to be re-signed, the free agent must show that he's healthy enough to help the team, and will have to deal with Travis Fryman, who's taken over his position. A hard worker, Trammell will undoubtedly force some playing time for himself if he's injury-free.

Overall Statistics

	G	AB	R	H	D	T	HR	RBI	SB	BB	SO	AVG
1992	29	102	11	28	7	1	1	11	2	15	4	.275
Career	1965	7179	1077	2050	356	51	162	876	212	759	755	.286

Where He Hits the Ball

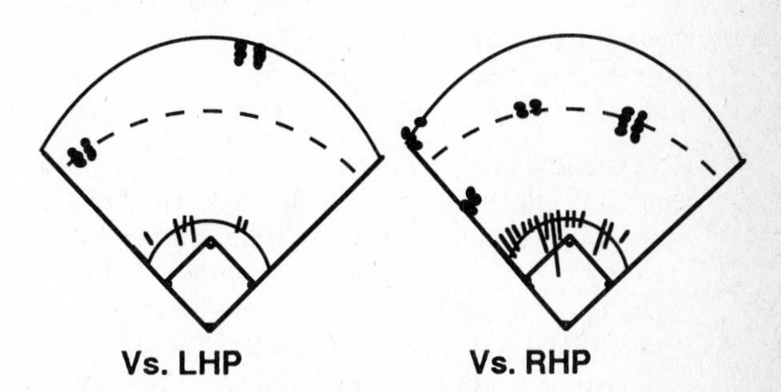

1992 Situational Stats

	AB	H	HR	RBI	AVG		AB	H	HR	RBI	AVG
Home	48	11	0	3	.229	LHP	28	10	0	6	.357
Road	54	17	1	8	.315	RHP	74	18	1	5	.243
Day	43	8	0	3	.186	Sc Pos	22	10	0	10	.455
Night	59	20	1	8	.339	Clutch	14	2	0	1	.143

1992 Rankings (American League)

- 6th in highest batting average on a 3-1 count (.600)

HITTING:

Still a productive player as he nears his 36th birthday, Sweet Lou Whitaker reached several career milestones in 1992. Whitaker recorded both his 2,000th hit and 200th home run, becoming one of the few second basemen to reach both totals. He also recorded his 1,000th career walk while remaining under 1,000 strikeouts. Whitaker's 1992 figures -- 19 homers, 71 RBI, .278 average, .386 on-base average -- were the envy of most younger players, particularly middle infielders.

Advancing age has limited Whitaker to less than 140 games in each of the past three seasons, but it hasn't limited his hitting abilities. Long noted for his problems against lefthanders, Whitaker pasted them at a .355 clip with a .548 slugging average last year. He hit .320 at Tiger Stadium, and batted .369 with runners in scoring position.

An excellent contact hitter who struck out only 46 times, Whitaker usually batted second behind Tony Phillips in the Tigers offense. Both players are very patient hitters, and their numerous bases on balls -- 114 for Phillips, 81 for Whitaker -- set up continual RBI opportunities for Cecil Fielder and company. Once a pronounced pull hitter, Whitaker has learned to go with the pitch. He can hit with power to all fields.

BASERUNNING:

Whitaker once had excellent speed, but his stolen base numbers have dropped in recent years. He hasn't stolen more than eight sacks since 1987. He's certainly lost a step or two, but he still runs the bases intelligently.

FIELDING:

Whitaker has always been known for his excellent defense. Though his range has declined, it's still more than adequate, and he committed only nine errors last year. He'll stand in and take the heat on a double play. His one weakness has always been fielding pop-ups.

OVERALL:

A Tiger Stadium fixture since 1977, Whitaker seems to have plenty of good playing days left, but as a free agent, they may not be with the Tigers. He showed few signs of slowing down in 92 and there's no reason to think he'll do so in 93.

LOU WHITAKER

Position: 2B
Bats: L **Throws:** R
Ht: 5'11" **Wt:** 180

Opening Day Age: 35
Born: 5/12/57 in New York, NY
ML Seasons: 16

Overall Statistics

	G	AB	R	H	D	T	HR	RBI	SB	BB	SO	AVG
1992	130	453	77	126	26	0	19	71	6	81	46	.278
Career	2095	7616	1211	2088	353	62	209	930	134	1047	965	.274

Where He Hits the Ball

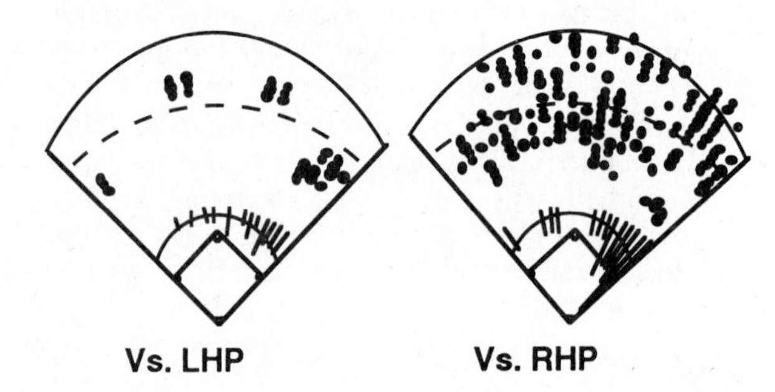

1992 Situational Stats

	AB	H	HR	RBI	AVG		AB	H	HR	RBI	AVG
Home	228	73	11	37	.320	LHP	62	22	2	15	.355
Road	225	53	8	34	.236	RHP	391	104	17	56	.266
Day	149	42	4	19	.282	Sc Pos	111	41	6	55	.369
Night	304	84	15	52	.276	Clutch	67	18	3	11	.269

1992 Rankings (American League)

- 1st in highest batting average with runners in scoring position (.369)
- 6th in highest batting average at home (.320)
- Led the Tigers in batting average (.278), highest batting average with runners in scoring position, highest batting average at home, lowest percentage of swings that missed (11.5%), highest percentage of swings put into play (50.2%) and steals of third (3)
- Led AL second basemen in slugging percentage (.461), HR frequency (23.8 ABs per HR), highest batting average with runners in scoring position and highest slugging percentage vs. right-handed pitchers (.448)

ERIC KING

Position: SP
Bats: R **Throws:** R
Ht: 6' 2" **Wt:** 218

Opening Day Age: 29
Born: 4/10/64 in Oxnard, CA
ML Seasons: 7

Overall Statistics

	W	L	ERA	G	GS	Sv	IP	H	R	BB	SO	HR
1992	4	6	5.22	17	14	1	79.1	90	47	28	45	12
Career	52	45	3.97	203	113	16	863.1	814	407	333	459	73

PITCHING, FIELDING & HOLDING RUNNERS:

Eric King broke in with the Tigers with an 11-4 record in 1986, but soon became known more for his temperament than for his pitching. King eventually moved on, first to the White Sox and then the Indians. When he signed a free agent contract with the Tigers before the '92 season, his stormy past was forgotten. The Tigers needed a pitcher, and King needed another chance.

It would be nice if this story had a happy ending, but King's 1992 season was a total disaster. He missed almost half the season with an inflamed rotator cuff, and when he was able to take the mound, he got shelled. King's 5.22 ERA was a career high, and he served up 12 home run balls in only 79.1 innings.

King has pitched better than that for most of his career. He has two variations on his fastball, plus a good curve, and he's posted ERAs of 3.51 or better four times in seven seasons. His arm is not strong, though, and he frequently breaks down. He's never pitched more than 159.1 innings in a season. He fields his position fairly well, but had trouble holding runners last year.

OVERALL:

King is a free agent after the '92 season, and at 29, could draw some interest from clubs that need pitching -- including Detroit. His arm problems will undoubtedly lower his asking price, however.

CHAD KREUTER

Position: C
Bats: B **Throws:** R
Ht: 6' 2" **Wt:** 190

Opening Day Age: 28
Born: 8/26/64 in Greenbrae, CA
ML Seasons: 5

Overall Statistics

	G	AB	R	H	D	T	HR	RBI	SB	BB	SO	AVG
1992	67	190	22	48	9	0	2	16	0	20	38	.253
Career	195	425	43	87	15	1	8	32	0	62	101	.205

HITTING, FIELDING, BASERUNNING:

When the Tigers were looking for a backup catcher last year, they took a chance on switch-hitter Chad Kreuter. To be frank, not a lot was expected from him. In 235 scattered at-bats over four seasons for the Rangers, Kreuter had hit only .166. But he proved to be a big surprise. Kreuter batted a solid .253, performing so effectively that he got into 67 games while backing up Mickey Tettleton.

Converted into a switch-hitting role fairly late in his career, Kreuter suddenly began to hit well from the left side for the first time ever, batting .290 last year left-handed. Curiously, he struggled from his natural side (.182). He also cut down on his swing after previously trying to hit for pure power. While his homer total declined to two, his batting average soared. Kreuter continued to be a patient hitter, drawing 20 walks last year. He's also a good bunter.

The Tigers obtained Kreuter mostly for his defense. He didn't disappoint. His mechanics were sound, and he tossed out an impressive 46 percent of the runners who tried to steal on him. He's very slow, and no threat to steal.

OVERALL:

Kreuter revived his career last year and was surprisingly one of three Tigers' catchers who were expansion protections. Every team needs a player who can spell their everyday catcher. If the 28 year old can continue to produce on a part-time basis, he could help the Tigers for several more years.

LES LANCASTER

Position: RP
Bats: R **Throws:** R
Ht: 6' 2" **Wt:** 200

Opening Day Age: 30
Born: 4/21/62 in Dallas, TX
ML Seasons: 6

Overall Statistics

	W	L	ERA	G	GS	Sv	IP	H	R	BB	SO	HR
1992	3	4	6.33	41	1	0	86.2	101	66	51	35	11
Career	37	27	4.16	273	39	22	642.1	659	321	240	372	55

PITCHING, FIELDING & HOLDING RUNNERS:

After five pretty good seasons with the Cubs (34-23 record), Les Lancaster left Chicago last year, partly due to financial considerations. He quickly signed with Detroit, a club which certainly needed pitching. Alas, Lancaster proved to be one more Tiger pitcher with an inflated earned run average. The righthander's 6.33 ERA was the second-highest on a terrible staff.

Lancaster's whole season was pretty much batting practice for American League hitters. He gave up 101 hits in only 86.2 innings, including 32 for extra bases. He walked 51 men and struck out only 35. Left-handed hitters raked him for a .358 average. By the All-Star break, Lancaster had become a little-used mop-up man.

Lancaster's performance was baffling, because he'd had success both starting and relieving (mostly the latter) with the Cubs. He throws both a standard and cut fastball, a good slider, and a serviceable curve and change. Last year he looked like he'd lost velocity on the fastball, and he got lit up. Lancaster is an above-average fielder, and he has a fine move to first.

OVERALL:

After the way Lancaster pitched in 1992, the Tigers didn't consider re-signing him to be a top priority. He's young enough to bounce back; this time around he probably won't be so tough in salary negotiations.

GARY PETTIS

Position: CF
Bats: B **Throws:** R
Ht: 6' 1" **Wt:** 160

Opening Day Age: 35
Born: 4/3/58 in Oakland, CA
ML Seasons: 11

Overall Statistics

	G	AB	R	H	D	T	HR	RBI	SB	BB	SO	AVG
1992	78	159	27	32	5	3	1	12	14	29	45	.201
Career	1183	3629	568	855	109	49	21	259	354	521	958	.236

HITTING, FIELDING, BASERUNNING:

Once considered one of baseball's premier center fielders, Gary Pettis is trying to hang on at age 35. Pettis began last year with the Rangers, but even a guaranteed $1.05 million contract couldn't prevent his release at the end of spring training; the Rangers preferred John Cangelosi. Pettis quickly signed with San Diego, backing up Darrin Jackson, but was released once again. He found himself swallowing his pride and returning to the Tigers' minor leagues.

Pettis finally came back up with Detroit, who needed an outfielder when Milt Cuyler was injured in July. Playing semi-regularly for the remainder of the year, he hit only .202 in 48 games but he did end up leading the team in stolen bases with 13. Drawing a good number of walks, he posted a decent .338 on-base percentage in a Tiger uniform. As usual, he was plagued by strikeouts (45 in 159 at-bats for the year). Still very fast, Pettis remains an excellent fielder who's range is still greatly above the league average. He doesn't have an incredibly strong arm, but it's adequate for center.

OVERALL:

Pettis is a free agent and once more he'll be scrambling to find a job. He could hook on with a club which needs a veteran with speed and defensive ability. Re-signing with Detroit is a possibility.

DETROIT TIGERS MINOR LEAGUE PROSPECTS

ORGANIZATION OVERVIEW:

Now that the Tigers have changed ownership, it'll be interesting to see what happens with their player development system. During the Tom Monaghan years, Detroit stuck mostly with the Whitaker/Trammell/Morris group which had come up together in the late seventies. As for prospects, the Tigers' eye for talent was demonstrated in such Sparky Anderson gems as, "Mike Laga will make us forget every power hitter who ever lived." Will the move from Domino's to Little Caeser's change all that? If you order one prospect, will you get two (with extra toppings)? We'll find out over the next few years.

RICO BROGNA

Position: 1B **Opening Day Age:** 22
Bats: L **Throws:** L **Born:** 4/18/70 in Turner Falls, MA
Ht: 6' 2" **Wt:** 202

Recent Statistics

	G	AB	R	H	D	T	HR	RBI	SB	BB	SO	AVG
92 AAA Toledo	121	387	45	101	19	4	10	58	1	31	85	.261
92 AL Detroit	9	26	3	5	1	0	1	3	0	3	5	.192
92 MLE	121	378	41	92	16	2	10	53	0	28	91	.243

Considered the top hitting prospect in the Detroit organization, Brogna has been developing, but slowly. In 1991, he couldn't cut it at the AAA level and had to be sent back to AA London. Brogna looked a lot better last year, hitting .261 at Toledo and showing some power with 10 homers. He belted another one in a 26 at-bat trial with the Tigers. Brogna won't be 23 until after the season starts, and it's possible he'll be sent back to AAA this season. He still needs a lot of polish.

IVAN CRUZ

Position: 1B **Opening Day Age:** 24
Bats: L **Throws:** L **Born:** 5/3/68 in Fajardo, PR
Ht: 6' 3" **Wt:** 210

Recent Statistics

	G	AB	R	H	D	T	HR	RBI	SB	BB	SO	AVG
91 AAA Toledo	8	29	2	4	0	0	1	4	0	2	12	.138
91 AA London	121	443	45	110	21	0	9	47	3	36	74	.248
92 AA London	134	524	71	143	25	1	14	104	1	37	102	.273
92 MLE	134	510	63	129	21	0	14	93	0	28	112	.253

Another first sacker in the considerable shadow of Cecil Fielder, Cruz has usually been one step behind Brogna. He may not be any more. Cruz spent 1992 at London, and had his best year yet with 14 homers and 104 RBI. He needs work on his strike zone judgement, but he's considered a better power prospect than Brogna, who's about two years younger. The Tigers will probably go with one of these guys, but not both. After Cruz' fine season in '92, he and Brogna are neck-and-neck.

GREG GOHR

Position: P **Opening Day Age:** 25
Bats: R **Throws:** R **Born:** 10/29/67 in Santa Clara, CA
Ht: 6' 3" **Wt:** 205

Recent Statistics

	W	L	ERA	G	GS	Sv	IP	H	R	BB	SO	HR
91 AA London	0	0	0.00	2	2	0	11.0	9	0	2	10	0
91 AAA Toledo	10	8	4.61	26	26	0	148.1	125	86	66	96	11
92 AAA Toledo	8	10	3.99	22	20	0	130.2	124	65	46	94	9

The Tigers don't need first basemen, they need pitchers, and Gohr is still one of their major hopes. Gohr, who was 10-8 at Toledo in '91, was 8-10 for the Mud Hens last year. But he made progress in other areas, lowering his ERA from 4.61 to 3.99 and improving his control, which has been a problem. A big man at 6'3" and 205 pounds, Gohr is one of the hardest throwers in an organization with a crying need for power pitchers. Unless Sparky is still committed to Walt Terrell, this could be Gohr's year.

SHAWN HARE

Position: OF **Opening Day Age:** 26
Bats: L **Throws:** L **Born:** 3/26/67 in St. Louis, MO
Ht: 6' 2" **Wt:** 190

Recent Statistics

	G	AB	R	H	D	T	HR	RBI	SB	BB	SO	AVG
92 AAA Toledo	57	203	31	67	12	2	5	34	6	31	28	.330
92 AL Detroit	15	26	0	3	1	0	0	5	0	2	4	.115

Detroit has the tortoise (Fielder) -- now they can add the Hare. One of those undrafted free agents whom it takes a while to notice, Hare has finally forced his way into the Tigers' plans by hitting .310 and .330 the last two years at Toledo. In his brief shot with the Tigers last year he hit .115, but a knee injury slowed him down. He has decent power, good strike zone judgement and a nice left-handed bat. If healthy, he should play in the majors this year.

RICH ROWLAND

Position: C **Opening Day Age:** 26
Bats: R **Throws:** R **Born:** 2/25/67 in Cloverdale, CA
Ht: 6' 1" **Wt:** 210

Recent Statistics

	G	AB	R	H	D	T	HR	RBI	SB	BB	SO	AVG
92 AAA Toledo	136	473	75	111	19	1	25	82	9	56	112	.235
92 AL Detroit	6	14	2	3	0	0	0	0	0	3	3	.214
92 MLE	136	464	68	102	16	0	24	75	7	51	121	.220

Going into spring training last year, Rowland seemed a good bet to be Tettleton's backup. Instead the Tigers sent him back to Toledo, and that may have been a break both for him and the team. Rowland had a big year for the Mud Hens (25 homers with 82 RBI). His average was on the low side (.235), but it's not bothersome because Rowland is a fine defensive receiver. Now people aren't talking about Rowland as a backup any more. Since he was protected from expansion along with Kreuter and Tettleton, Rowland might well be trade bait.

STAFF ACE

PITCHING:

When Kevin Appier met with Royals' manager Hal McRae in spring training last year, he told McRae that he was ready to replace the traded Bret Saberhagen as Kansas City's ace starter. Indeed he was. Appier fulfilled all expectations, and then some, with a season that ranked among baseball's very best. His 2.46 ERA was second in the league only to Roger Clemens (2.41), and his 15-8 record could have been even better with reasonable run support early in the season.

Royals bats provided just four runs in Appier's first four starts, causing him to post an 0-2 record despite a 1.27 ERA. The support improved later, and Appier went 12-1 in 17 starts from May through July. Appier was remarkably consistent in 1992, throwing seven or more innings in 20 of 30 starts.

Appier throws his best pitch, a running fastball, well enough to blow away good fastball hitters and hard enough to get away with pitching up in the strike zone. Appier also throws a hard slider, but his curve is just for show; he won't throw breaking balls where they can be hit. Batters often swing under his rising fastball or over his slider. Appier wants to win or lose with his best pitches. In 1991 he learned to trust his hard stuff and adopted an aggressive philosophy. He seemed to tell batters: here it comes, hit it if you can.

HOLDING RUNNERS AND FIELDING:

Appier isn't a good fielder; an exaggerated delivery leaves him out of position to field grounders. His throws to bases are erratic and he's slow to cover bunts. Appier has a good pickoff move, but his round-house delivery gives baserunners a big jump off first.

OVERALL:

Appier realized his vast potential with a marvelous 1992 campaign. While it's difficult to imagine him topping his recent performance, he should again be among the league's best starters. He's expected to be fully recovered from tendinitis in his rotator cuff which caused him to miss most of the last month of '92, although he was not progressing all that well early in the winter.

KEVIN APPIER

Position: SP
Bats: R **Throws:** R
Ht: 6' 2" **Wt:** 200

Opening Day Age: 25
Born: 12/6/67 in Lancaster, CA
ML Seasons: 4

Overall Statistics

	W	L	ERA	G	GS	Sv	IP	H	R	BB	SO	HR
1992	15	8	2.46	30	30	0	208.1	167	59	68	150	10
Career	41	30	3.10	102	90	0	623.1	585	245	195	445	39

How Often He Throws Strikes

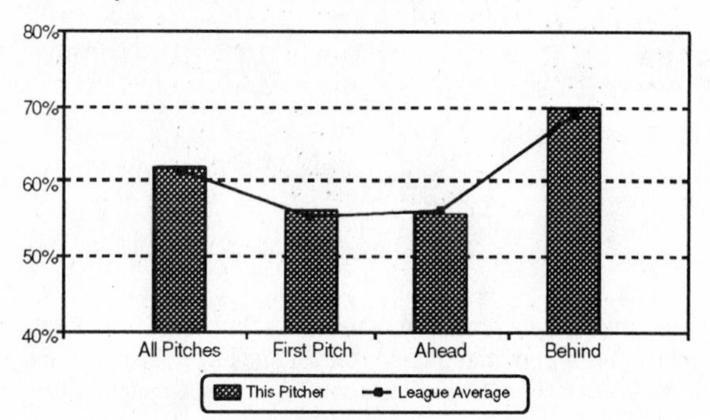

1992 Situational Stats

	W	L	ERA	Sv	IP		AB	H	HR	RBI	AVG
Home	8	5	2.60	0	104.0	LHB	370	76	7	29	.205
Road	7	3	2.33	0	104.1	RHB	401	91	3	24	.227
Day	5	0	1.96	0	41.1	Sc Pos	180	30	2	39	.167
Night	10	8	2.59	0	167.0	Clutch	91	10	2	7	.110

1992 Rankings (American League)

- 1st in lowest batting average allowed with runners in scoring position (.167)
- 2nd in ERA (2.46)
- 3rd in lowest batting average allowed (.217), lowest on-base percentage allowed (.281), least baserunners allowed per 9 innings (10.2) and lowest ERA on the road (2.33)
- Led the Royals in ERA, wins (15), games started (30), complete games (3), innings pitched (208.1), hits allowed (167), batters faced (852), home runs allowed (10), walks allowed (68), strikeouts (150), most pitches thrown (3,199), pickoff throws (156), stolen bases allowed (18), runners caught stealing (9) and winning percentage (.652)

PITCHING:

After losing half the 1992 season due to a strained right shoulder and a sore rib cage, Luis Aquino returned last summer to grab a spot in the Kansas City rotation. Aquino's absence had left the Royals auditioning replacements. They went through Mike Boddicker, Tom Gordon, Mike Magnante, Rick Reed and Hipolito Pichardo. None had pitched as well as Aquino had over the past few seasons. The righthander entered the season with a 3.45 career ERA and a 20-14 lifetime record.

After his mid-July return, Aquino didn't perform up to his past level. He gave the Royals dependable five- or six-inning starts every fifth turn, but had trouble going much farther than that. He wound up 3-5 with a 4.08 ERA as a starter. His velocity was clearly lacking, and he recorded just 11 strikeouts in 67.2 innings last year.

Since he's not overpowering even when completely healthy, Aquino needs to work both sides of the plate, varying his pitches and staying away from the hitting zones. He spots his fastball, mixing it with sliders, curves and change-ups. He's rarely wild, usually walking batters only when he tires. Lefties continued to plague Aquino last year, hitting .314 and slugging .424. An early fatigue candidate, he went more than six innings just twice in 1992, but hurled at least five innings in 10 of 13 starts.

HOLDING RUNNERS AND FIELDING:

Aquino depends upon a smooth, steady delivery, and baserunners sometimes upset his rhythm. His move to first is below average, but his short, compact delivery gives catchers a chance to catch basestealers. Aquino has worked hard to improve his fielding and is no longer a defensive liability.

OVERALL:

Consistent outings are Aquino's trademark; he allowed more than four runs in only his last start. He'll never be a big winner or throw lots of innings, but he can regularly deliver five good innings each start or pitch effective long relief. With his arm presumably healthy, he should have more stamina and velocity than in 1992.

LUIS AQUINO

Position: SP
Bats: R **Throws:** R
Ht: 6' 1" **Wt:** 195

Opening Day Age: 27
Born: 5/19/65 in Rio Piedras, Puerto Rico
ML Seasons: 6

Overall Statistics

	W	L	ERA	G	GS	Sv	IP	H	R	BB	SO	HR
1992	3	6	4.52	15	13	0	67.2	81	35	20	11	5
Career	23	20	3.60	121	55	3	474.2	487	212	149	203	30

How Often He Throws Strikes

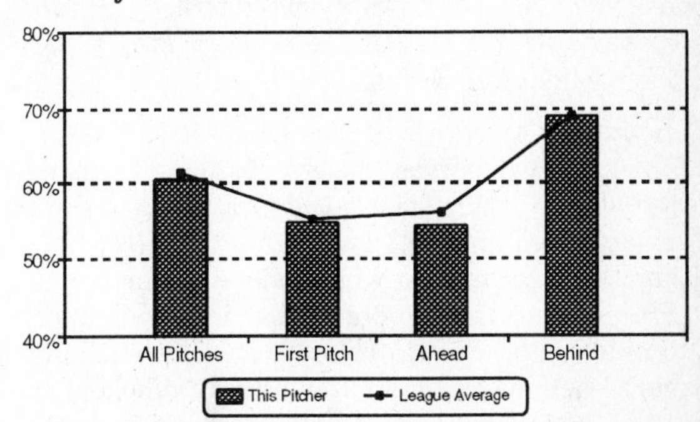

1992 Situational Stats

	W	L	ERA	Sv	IP		AB	H	HR	RBI	AVG
Home	2	2	4.02	0	31.1	LHB	118	37	2	12	.314
Road	1	4	4.95	0	36.1	RHB	149	44	3	17	.295
Day	0	0	6.75	0	4.0	Sc Pos	58	18	1	23	.310
Night	3	6	4.38	0	63.2	Clutch	12	5	0	1	.417

1992 Rankings (American League)

- 8th in highest batting average allowed vs. left-handed batters (.314)

PITCHING:

Mike Boddicker suffered his worst year ever in 1992, failing for the first time in a decade to record a double-digit win total. Boddicker had trouble from the outset and barely managed his only victory of the season in September shortly before finishing out the year on the disabled list. It was his second time on the shelf in 1992, definitely a year to forget.

After two losing starts to begin the season, Boddicker was relegated to the Royals' bullpen. Although he didn't care for the demotion, he pitched fairly well in relief. As a starter, he was 0-4 with a 6.69 ERA, and had serious control difficulties, walking 16 in 39 innings. In relief, he collected his lone victory, and posted a more respectable 3.59 ERA. Boddicker also saved three games in three chances.

Boddicker's always been a junkballer who ties hitters up with curves, change-ups and screwballs thrown at varying speeds and locations. He stays away from hitters' sweet spots and won't challenge them even when behind in the count. Free-swingers have more trouble with Boddicker; if hitters show enough patience they'll eventually get something to hit or a free pass. Boddicker has always struggled against lefties, and 1992 was no exception. They racked him for a .292 average, while righthanders hit .249. Boddicker usually hits lots of batters; he led the Royals for the second straight year, plunking eight in only 86.2 innings in 1992.

HOLDING RUNNERS AND FIELDING:

Still a slick fielder, Boddicker slowed a step in 1992 but remains among the team's better fielding pitchers. He throws to first frequently and has a good, quick move. But perhaps distracted by his pitching problems last year, he allowed 13 steals in 15 attempts.

OVERALL:

At 35, Boddicker is very close to the trail's end. He's not fooling hitters anymore, his role with the Royals is unclear, and he's no longer having much fun. Boddicker is signed for another year, but he was contemplating retirement after his disappointing 1992 season. If he decides to return, he will primarily pitch long relief.

MIKE BODDICKER

Position: RP/SP
Bats: R **Throws:** R
Ht: 5'11" **Wt:** 185

Opening Day Age: 35
Born: 8/23/57 in Cedar Rapids, IA
ML Seasons: 13

Overall Statistics

	W	L	ERA	G	GS	Sv	IP	H	R	BB	SO	HR
1992	1	4	4.98	29	8	3	86.2	92	50	37	47	5
Career	131	111	3.75	332	299	3	2069.2	2005	957	706	1306	182

How Often He Throws Strikes

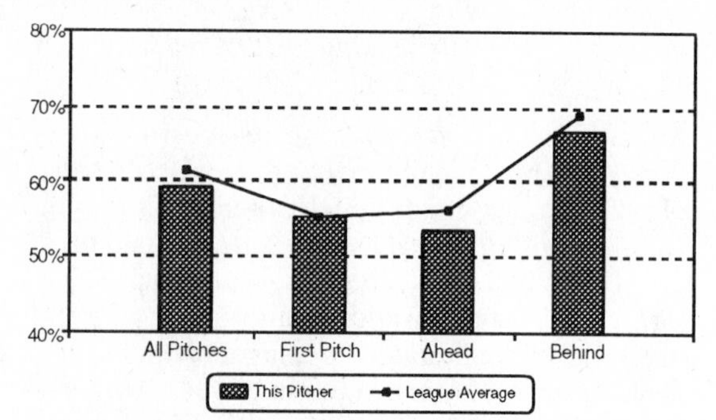

1992 Situational Stats

	W	L	ERA	Sv	IP		AB	H	HR	RBI	AVG
Home	1	2	5.70	0	36.1	LHB	168	49	2	25	.292
Road	0	2	4.47	3	50.1	RHB	173	43	3	28	.249
Day	0	1	2.57	2	28.0	Sc Pos	118	34	3	50	.288
Night	1	3	6.14	1	58.2	Clutch	24	7	1	4	.292

1992 Rankings (American League)

→ Led the Royals in hit batsmen (8)

HITTING:

At age 39, George Brett had an extremely satisfying 1992 season. Brett rebounded from his worst year (.255) to stay injury-free for only the second time since 1985. He led the Royals in several categories and capped things off with a four-hit night on September 30, the last of which being the 3000th hit of his memorable career. Brett had so much fun that, though expected to retire, he decided to come back for another season.

Normally a patient hitter, Brett dramatically widened his strike zone while pursuing the 3000-hit milestone. Early on, he often chased pitches he would have otherwise taken. Brett was hitting .182 in early May, which was one reason why the Royals began the season 1-16. Characteristically, Brett warmed when the weather did. He batted .301 with 40 extra-base hits over the final five months.

Brett still has one of the sweetest swings in the game, and he'll drive the ball with power to all fields. While his aggressive approach in 1992 kept his on-base average down (.330), it didn't diminish his offensive value much. He remained among the team's best clutch hitters, hitting .285 with runners in scoring position. Age, though, may finally be overtaking Brett; he was often overmatched by fastballs last year.

BASERUNNING:

Brett's aggressiveness carried over to the basepaths in 1992. He swiped eight bases, but it took him 14 tries. Age and knee injuries have drained his speed, but he knows when to gamble on the bases. Despite occasional risky baserunning, Brett was rarely caught stretching hits.

FIELDING:

Clearly, Brett is now a liability in the field. He has no range and a below-average arm. In limited first base duty in 1992, Brett played as conservatively as possible, always taking the sure out and never gambling. Brett is -- and should be -- a DH.

OVERALL:

Brett's 3000-hit chase helped Royals' fans forget an otherwise dismal year. Even when he was talking of retirement, there was no question the Royals wanted him back. They are delighted he is returning.

GEORGE BRETT

Position: DH/1B
Bats: L **Throws:** R
Ht: 6' 0" **Wt:** 205

Opening Day Age: 39
Born: 5/15/53 in Glendale, WV
ML Seasons: 20

Overall Statistics

	G	AB	R	H	D	T	HR	RBI	SB	BB	SO	AVG
1992	152	592	55	169	35	5	7	61	8	35	69	.285
Career	2562	9789	1514	3005	634	134	298	1520	194	1057	841	.307

Where He Hits the Ball

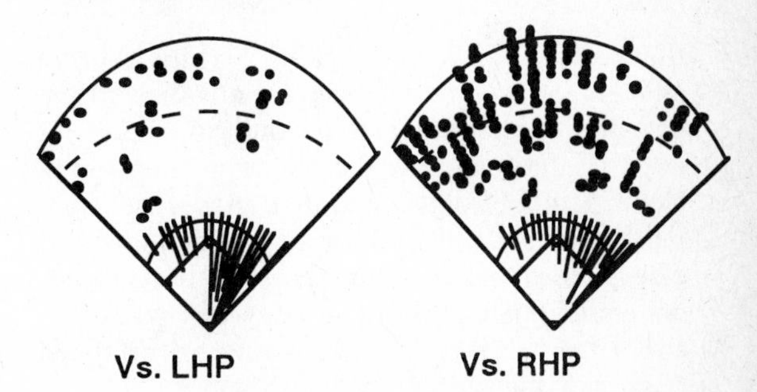

1992 Situational Stats

	AB	H	HR	RBI	AVG		AB	H	HR	RBI	AVG
Home	312	90	1	35	.288	LHP	184	51	0	20	.277
Road	280	79	6	26	.282	RHP	408	118	7	41	.289
Day	139	43	2	20	.309	Sc Pos	130	37	2	50	.285
Night	453	126	5	41	.278	Clutch	97	22	4	14	.227

1992 Rankings (American League)

- 2nd in least runs scored per time reached base (.26)
- 4th in least pitches seen per plate appearance (3.26)
- 7th in lowest percentage of pitches taken (45.7%)
- Led the Royals in batting average (.285), triples (5), intentional walks (6), games played (152), highest batting average on the road (.282) and highest batting average with 2 strikes (.254)
- Led designated hitters in caught stealing (6) and hit by pitch (6)

HITTING:

Injuries and reduced playing time eroded Jim Eisenreich's usually steady performance last season. His .269 average and 18 extra-base hits were a considerable comedown for a player who'd averaged .290 with 39 extra-base hits over three previous full seasons.

Eisenreich also had trouble repeating his fine 1991 clutch hitting. He batted only .196 with runners in scoring position in 1992 and collected just 28 RBI, down from his previous three-year 52-RBI average. Eisenreich struggled versus left-handers for the first time. After posting a .290 average against lefties before 1992, he batted .240 against southpaws last year, a sign that they are now overpowering him.

Eisenreich is a very aggressive hitter, often swinging at the first offering. He always puts the ball in play and rarely strikes out. Pitchers don't have to throw strikes; he'll swing at anything close. Hitting from an upright stance, Eisenreich pulls low inside pitches for singles and hits outside pitches to left-center for extra bases. Fireballers who jam him can induce weak grounders and flies. Eisenreich waits well on offspeed pitches and feasts on low fastballs.

BASERUNNING:

Eisenreich benefitted from aggressive Royals' baserunning in 1992. After yearly declines in steals and attempts, Eisenreich once again returned to double digits in thefts; his 65% success rate almost matches his career rate. Eisenreich still ran into some outs on the bases, but was a more effective baserunner in 1992.

FIELDING:

A mediocre outfielder, Eisenreich's arm is average at best and despite good speed, he has below-average range. A fair center or right field substitute, Eisenreich is best suited to left. Eisenreich hits the cut-off man and hustles on every play; he committed just one error in 1992.

OVERALL:

A free agent, Eisenreich felt the Royals were phasing him out last year. Despite his weaker numbers in 1992, he remains a steady fourth outfielder and left-handed pinch hitter. He shouldn't have much trouble finding a job.

JIM EISENREICH

Position: RF/LF
Bats: L **Throws:** L
Ht: 5'11" **Wt:** 200

Opening Day Age: 33
Born: 4/18/59 in St. Cloud, MN
ML Seasons: 9

Overall Statistics

	G	AB	R	H	D	T	HR	RBI	SB	BB	SO	AVG
1992	113	353	31	95	13	3	2	28	11	24	36	.269
Career	698	2144	251	594	121	23	25	237	67	150	228	.277

Where He Hits the Ball

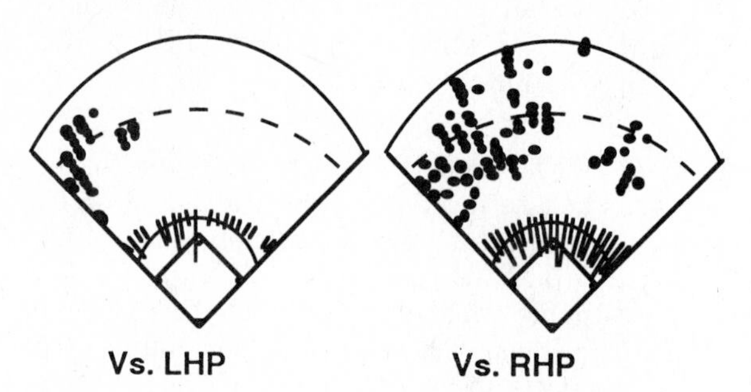

1992 Situational Stats

	AB	H	HR	RBI	AVG		AB	H	HR	RBI	AVG
Home	160	39	1	13	.244	LHP	75	18	0	7	.240
Road	193	56	1	15	.290	RHP	278	77	2	21	.277
Day	94	27	1	10	.287	Sc Pos	97	19	0	25	.196
Night	259	68	1	18	.263	Clutch	79	22	1	5	.278

1992 Rankings (American League)

- 7th in lowest batting average with runners in scoring position (.196)

PITCHING:

On the bubble after a 9-14 season in 1991, Tom Gordon earned a Royals' starting spot with a fine spring training performance. But Gordon then reversed all his good work with nine unimpressive starts. After his record reached 0-5, Gordon received a demotion to the bullpen. It was probably the best thing to happen to him all year.

While starting, Gordon did practically everything wrong: walking too many batters, allowing costly extra-base hits, surrendering leads. Most of his starts were disappointing and several were disastrous; Gordon's starting ERA was 6.08. Although Gordon made it known that he didn't like the bullpen, he was far more effective in long relief.

After running his personal losing streak to ten games with a loss in his first relief appearance, then getting shelled in his next outing, Gordon settled down to carry a 2.61 ERA over his next 28 appearances. His relief success was attributable to much better control. Gordon walked 4.8 per nine innings when starting, but 3.7 when relieving. Likewise, Gordon's strikeouts jumped from 6.3 per nine innings as a starter to 8.4 in relief.

A nasty curve is still Gordon's out pitch, but he threw more fastballs in 1992. Gordon's fastball had more pop last year and he used it well in relief; it made his curve even more difficult to hit. Both pitches were particularly effective against right-handed hitters, who batted .235 vs. Gordon. Lefties hit .287.

HOLDING RUNNERS AND FIELDING:

Gordon owns a good pickoff move and his whirling motion is difficult for baserunners to read. He has allowed basestealers only a 48 percent success rate since 1990. Gordon's concentration lapses sometimes affect his fielding, but he continues to improve with the glove.

OVERALL:

Perennially bursting with potential, Gordon has been a perennial disappointment. After seeming to find himself in the bullpen last year -- despite his distaste for the role -- he wound up on the shelf with tendinitis in his rotator cuff. His undefined role and personal conflicts with manager Hal McRae still didn't dissuade the Royals from protecting the 25 year old from expansion, however.

TOM GORDON

Position: RP/SP
Bats: R **Throws:** R
Ht: 5' 9" **Wt:** 180

Opening Day Age: 25
Born: 11/18/67 in Sebring, FL
ML Seasons: 5

Overall Statistics

	W	L	ERA	G	GS	Sv	IP	H	R	BB	SO	HR
1992	6	10	4.59	40	11	0	117.2	116	67	55	98	9
Career	44	46	3.93	171	75	2	649.2	575	318	334	611	53

How Often He Throws Strikes

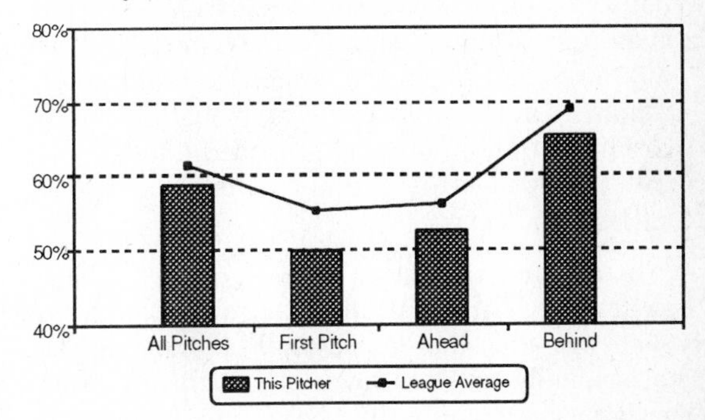

1992 Situational Stats

	W	L	ERA	Sv	IP		AB	H	HR	RBI	AVG
Home	5	4	3.36	0	59.0	LHB	202	58	3	27	.287
Road	1	6	5.83	0	58.2	RHB	247	58	6	36	.235
Day	2	6	3.60	0	45.0	Sc Pos	128	37	1	48	.289
Night	4	4	5.20	0	72.2	Clutch	57	18	2	10	.316

1992 Rankings (American League)

- 5th in balks (2)
- 6th in most strikeouts per 9 innings in relief (8.4)
- 8th in lowest winning percentage (.375)
- 9th in highest batting average allowed with runners in scoring position (.289)
- Led the Royals in losses (10), wild pitches (5), balks, and most strikeouts per 9 innings in relief

PITCHING:

After a long, slow period of recovery from rotator cuff surgery in August of 1990, Mark Gubicza finally seemed fully healthy last year. Concerns about Gubicza's arm strength proved unfounded as he turned in progressively better performances. He even threw consecutive complete game victories in mid-May, including his first shutout since 1989. But Gubicza had spotty results thereafter before missing the second half of the year with a stiff shoulder.

While he was healthy, Gubicza turned in a half-season of pitching at a level quite consistent with previous yearly performances. His 3.72 ERA, 2.9 walks and 6.5 strikeouts per nine innings, and 6.1 innings per start were all on a par with his career averages. Gubicza was almost the same pitcher he was three years ago, but without quite as much stamina. Unlike previous years, though, Gubicza had more trouble with right-handed hitters, who batted .290 against him compared to .228 for lefties.

When healthy, Gubicza's best pitch is a hard slider, and his fastball is good enough to challenge even the best fastball hitters. Gubicza occasionally got into trouble by being too fine early in the count, falling behind, and having to throw the ball in the hitters' zone. Yet, Gubicza was still tough in tight situations last year; he could usually get a strikeout when he needed it.

HOLDING RUNNERS AND FIELDING:

With a big leg kick and a slow delivery, Gubicza doesn't hold baserunners close. However, he will throw frequently to first, and last year he allowed only four steals in eight attempts. Although he's not among the team's best fielders, Gubicza has improved with the glove and has shown better composure in recent years.

OVERALL:

Gubicza made tremendous strides last year before suffering another flare-up in his shoulder. He hasn't thrown more than 133 innings in any season since 1989, and it's hard to count on him for 1993. But the Royals need a regular starter, and signed the free agent righty to a $1.25 million one-year deal in late November.

MARK GUBICZA

Position: SP
Bats: R **Throws:** R
Ht: 6' 5" **Wt:** 225

Opening Day Age: 30
Born: 8/14/62 in Philadelphia, PA
ML Seasons: 9

Overall Statistics

	W	L	ERA	G	GS	Sv	IP	H	R	BB	SO	HR
1992	7	6	3.72	18	18	0	111.1	110	47	36	81	8
Career	104	92	3.75	259	247	0	1651.2	1586	748	618	1091	97

How Often He Throws Strikes

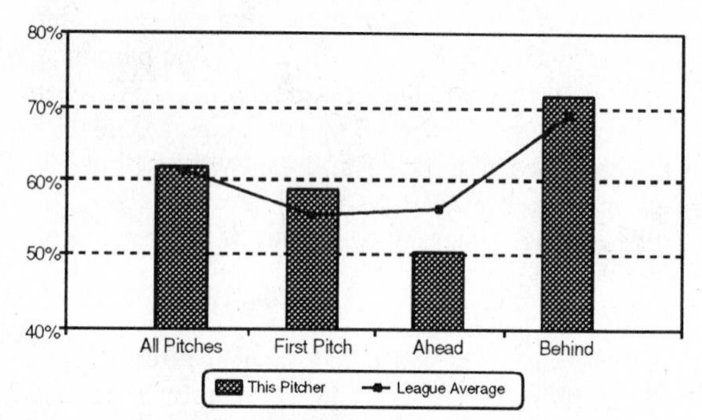

1992 Situational Stats

	W	L	ERA	Sv	IP		AB	H	HR	RBI	AVG
Home	5	2	2.88	0	68.2	LHB	215	49	5	22	.228
Road	2	4	5.06	0	42.2	RHB	210	61	3	22	.290
Day	1	3	4.13	0	32.2	Sc Pos	95	29	2	37	.305
Night	6	3	3.55	0	78.2	Clutch	40	10	2	7	.250

1992 Rankings (American League)

- Led the Royals in shutouts (1) and wild pitches (5)

CHRIS HANEY

Position: SP
Bats: L **Throws:** L
Ht: 6' 3" **Wt:** 185

Opening Day Age: 24
Born: 11/16/68 in Baltimore, MD
ML Seasons: 2

PITCHING:

Lefthander Chris Haney split 1992 between Montreal and Kansas City, coming to the Royals via a trade late in August. Haney's split seasons were mirror images of one another; he was occasionally brilliant and frequently spotty as a fifth starter for both clubs. The 24-year-old Haney spent only two years in the minors before 1992, and his lack of experience showed. He tossed shutouts for both teams, amidst frequent below-average starts.

Haney was exclusively a starter for Kansas City and took his turn in the rotation every fifth game. Regular work suited him; his best starts came after five days rest, and he posted a respectable 3.86 ERA for the Royals. However, Haney was prone to the gopher ball, allowing 11 homers in 80 innings last year. When he kept the ball in the park, he was usually able to pitch out of difficult jams.

Haney throws several pitches well, though none has yet emerged as an out pitch. His curve has bite and his fastball, while not explosively fast, is good enough to challenge most hitters. Haney's control with each pitch is the key to his success. He spots them on the corners and mixes them effectively. Excluding one abysmal start against Minnesota, Haney walked no more than three in any appearance. He also fanned more than twice as many batters as he walked.

HOLDING RUNNERS AND FIELDING:

Haney has an above-average move to first and will throw frequently to cut into a runner's lead. American League runners were cautious with Haney in 1992 -- they couldn't quite read his move yet. He's an average fielder.

OVERALL:

Haney has the makings of a good lefty starter. His sporadic major league performances thus far are the mark of a young pitcher trying to get good stuff under control. He has a lot of talent, and careful handling by the Royals could bring solid results this season and in years to follow.

Overall Statistics

	W	L	ERA	G	GS	Sv	IP	H	R	BB	SO	HR
1992	4	6	4.61	16	13	0	80.0	75	43	26	54	11
Career	7	13	4.32	32	29	0	164.2	169	92	69	105	17

How Often He Throws Strikes

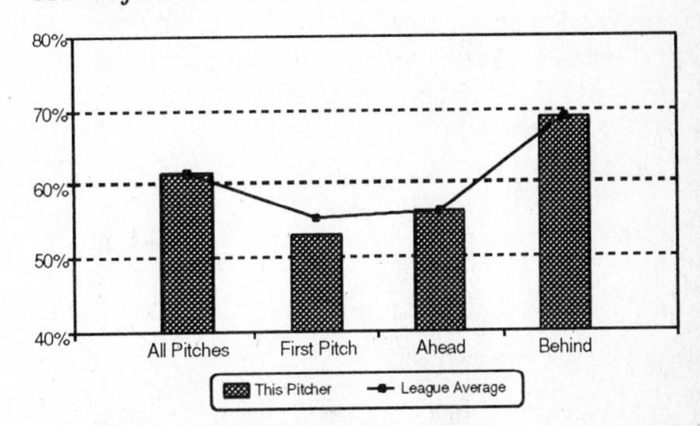

1992 Situational Stats

	W	L	ERA	Sv	IP		AB	H	HR	RBI	AVG
Home	2	4	5.91	0	42.2	LHB	66	17	2	12	.258
Road	2	2	3.13	0	37.1	RHB	237	58	9	30	.245
Day	2	2	4.09	0	22.0	Sc Pos	64	15	2	30	.234
Night	2	4	4.81	0	58.0	Clutch	6	1	1	1	.167

1992 Rankings (American League)

- 7th in least GDPs induced per GDP situation (.03)

DAVE HOWARD

Position: SS
Bats: B **Throws:** R
Ht: 6' 0" **Wt:** 165

Opening Day Age: 26
Born: 2/26/67 in Sarasota, FL
ML Seasons: 2

Overall Statistics

	G	AB	R	H	D	T	HR	RBI	SB	BB	SO	AVG
1992	74	219	19	49	6	2	1	18	3	15	43	.224
Career	168	455	39	100	13	2	2	35	6	31	88	.220

Where He Hits the Ball

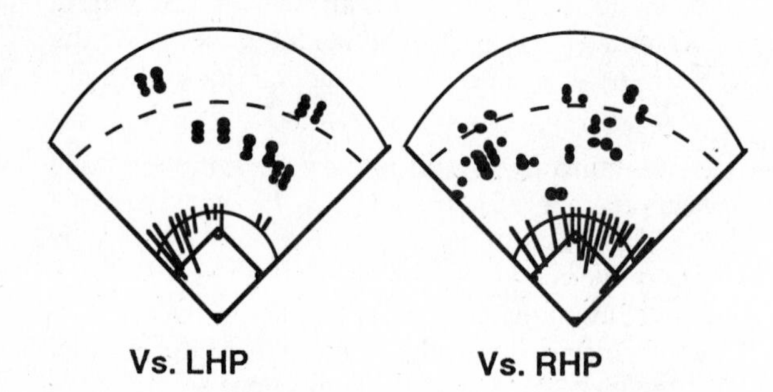

1992 Situational Stats

	AB	H	HR	RBI	AVG		AB	H	HR	RBI	AVG
Home	122	29	1	14	.238	LHP	72	15	0	2	.208
Road	97	20	0	4	.206	RHP	147	34	1	16	.231
Day	43	13	0	4	.302	Sc Pos	53	13	1	17	.245
Night	176	36	1	14	.205	Clutch	37	9	1	4	.243

1992 Rankings (American League)

- 7th in highest batting average on a 3-2 count (.368)
- Led the Royals in sacrifice bunts (8) and highest batting average on a 3-2 count

HITTING:

Although David Howard made some offensive progress in 1992, he's still among the Royals' weaker hitters. In two seasons with Kansas City, Howard has batted only .216 and .224. After six professional seasons, his highest average has been .250 with AA Memphis in 1990. Other than that, he's never batted higher than .236.

Early back problems had Howard hitting .067 last season, but he returned from the disabled list with a hot bat. Howard drove in several key runs and hit .342 during August, raising his average to .250. He eventually cooled off, leaving him with a slightly improved season overall.

Howard lacks both power and a good batting eye. He'll go with the pitch or shorten up to punch at two-strike offerings. Howard is one of the team's few good bunters, collecting eight sacrifice hits in 1992. Switch-hitting helps him avoid being jammed; he fares about equally from either side. At his best, Howard will fight off the better pitches before slapping an opposite-field hit. At his worst, he's an automatic out who's blown away by fastballs and flails at bad breaking balls.

BASERUNNING:

Not blindingly fast, Howard runs the bases tentatively, erring on the side of caution. He didn't take as many bases as he could have last year. He's stolen as many as 15 bases in the minors, but with the Royals his few steal attempts have usually occurred on hit-and-run plays.

FIELDING:

Howard's early season back trouble caused him some fielding difficulties, but his defense sparkled upon his return from AAA Omaha. He has good range, a strong, accurate arm, and his double play pivot has improved. Howard avoided youthful mistakes, and finished the year with a 30-game errorless streak.

OVERALL:

Howard resembles the little Dutch boy with his thumb in the dike. Sandwiched between defensive liabilities Gregg Jefferies and Keith Miller, he holds the opponent offense to a trickle instead of a flood. The Royals need Howard's steady shortstop play, and protected him from expansion despite his weak hitting.

FUTURE ALL-STAR

GREGG JEFFERIES

Position: 3B
Bats: B **Throws:** R
Ht: 5'10" **Wt:** 185

Opening Day Age: 25
Born: 8/1/67 in Burlingame, CA
ML Seasons: 6

Overall Statistics

	G	AB	R	H	D	T	HR	RBI	SB	BB	SO	AVG
1992	152	604	66	172	36	3	10	75	19	43	29	.285
Career	617	2317	312	644	132	12	52	280	82	183	163	.278

Where He Hits the Ball

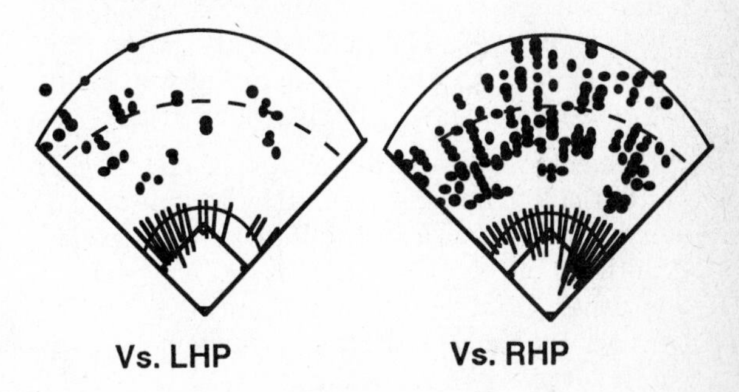

Vs. LHP Vs. RHP

1992 Situational Stats

	AB	H	HR	RBI	AVG		AB	H	HR	RBI	AVG
Home	280	81	3	37	.289	LHP	179	46	3	12	.257
Road	324	91	7	38	.281	RHP	425	126	7	63	.296
Day	151	48	4	16	.318	Sc Pos	154	39	3	61	.253
Night	453	124	6	59	.274	Clutch	110	31	1	14	.282

1992 Rankings (American League)

- 2nd in GDPs (24) and highest percentage of swings put into play (62.6%)
- 5th in lowest percentage of swings that missed (8.0%)
- Led the Royals in at-bats (604), runs scored (66), hits (172), singles (123), doubles (36), total bases (244), RBI (75), sacrifice flies (9), stolen bases (19), caught stealing (9), times on base (216), GDPs, most pitches seen (2,263), plate appearances (657), games played (152), highest slugging percentage (.404), HR frequency (60.4 ABs per HR), highest batting average vs. right-handed pitchers (.296), highest batting average on an 0-2 count (.222) and highest slugging percentage vs. right-handed pitchers (.421)

HITTING:

The Royals' major off-season acquisition, Gregg Jefferies reversed an early slump to lead his new team in many offensive categories last year. Jefferies was among the Kansas City leaders in batting average, runs scored, doubles, extra-base hits, on-base percentage, stolen bases . . . and errors. The switch-hitter batted .285, the best of his four full major league seasons.

A notoriously slow starter -- his lifetime average in April is .208 -- Jefferies saw his average sink to .205 in mid-May. But he got his act together and hit a hundred points higher (.305) the rest of the way. In his last 482 at-bats, Jefferies collected 68 RBI, despite often hitting first or second.

An aggressive fastball hitter, Jefferies will swing at the first pitch that he sees to his liking. His quick hands and well-refined swing from both sides of the plate let him handle any kind of pitch. Mainly a pull hitter until he has two strikes, Jefferies slaps outside pitches the other way for singles. He's better from the left side, batting .296 last year with most of his extra-base hits.

BASERUNNING:

Jefferies has enjoyed great success as a basestealer -- so good that his 68 percent success rate in 1992 was the worst of his career. He figures to improve as he learns American League pitchers. Jefferies runs aggressively, never missing chances to take extra bases. He's just as dangerous on the bases as he is at the plate.

FIELDING:

Although he wasn't as bad as his reputation suggested, Jefferies still led the Royals in errors by a wide margin. At times, he looked positively awful at third base. He has sufficient range and a strong arm, but simply fails to make plays consistently.

OVERALL:

Still considered by some to be a potential superstar, Jefferies had a fine first season in the American League. The Royals will look for him to assume the club's offensive leadership from George Brett, while working on his defense. It's hard to believe he's still only 25 years old.

WALLY JOYNER

Position: 1B
Bats: L **Throws:** L
Ht: 6' 2" **Wt:** 205

Opening Day Age: 30
Born: 6/16/62 in Atlanta, GA
ML Seasons: 7

Overall Statistics

	G	AB	R	H	D	T	HR	RBI	SB	BB	SO	AVG
1992	149	572	66	154	36	2	9	66	11	55	50	.269
Career	995	3780	521	1079	206	13	123	584	39	378	381	.285

Where He Hits the Ball

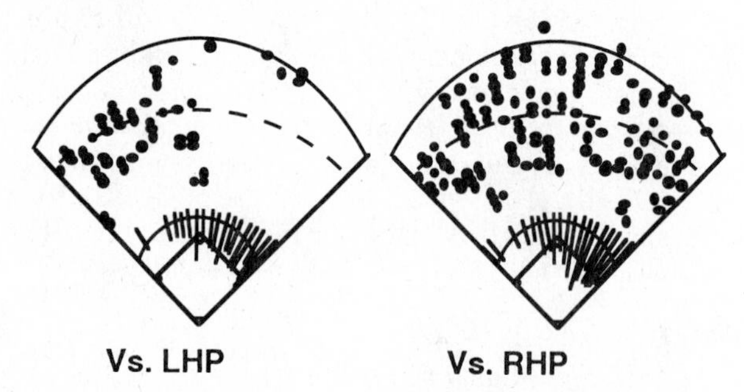

1992 Situational Stats

	AB	H	HR	RBI	AVG		AB	H	HR	RBI	AVG
Home	282	75	1	29	.266	LHP	192	46	2	20	.240
Road	290	79	8	37	.272	RHP	380	108	7	46	.284
Day	141	35	3	17	.248	Sc Pos	141	40	3	52	.284
Night	431	119	6	49	.276	Clutch	105	25	3	12	.238

1992 Rankings (American League)

- 6th in GDPs (19)
- 8th in doubles (36)
- 10th in least pitches seen per plate appearance (3.37) and most GDPs per GDP situation (17.8%)
- Led the Royals in runs scored (66), doubles, on-base percentage (.336), on-base percentage vs. right-handed pitchers (.352) and steals of third (4)
- Led AL first basemen in stolen bases (11) and steals of third

HITTING:

Wally Joyner had enjoyed great Royals Stadium success prior to his free agent signing. He was a career .380 hitter in Kansas City, so expectations were high that he would at least partially make up for the free agent loss of Danny Tartabull. Unfortunately, Joyner produced his worst season ever. He batted only .266 with a single homer at Royals Stadium, and .269 with nine dingers overall.

Joyner's season was strikingly similar to his previous-worst campaign in 1990, when he played only 83 games before suffering a stress fracture in his right knee. In 1990, Joyner batted .268, with an on-base average of .350 and a slugging average of .394. In 1992 his figures were .269, .336 and .386. The only difference was that Joyner was healthy in 1992. His nine homers and 66 RBI were among the Royals' leaders, but well below his pre-92 averages of 19 HRs and 86 RBI.

A patient hitter who will wait for his pitch, Joyner is difficult to fan as evidenced by his low total of only 50 strikeouts last year. With his quick hands, he fights off two-strike pitches until he gets one to drive. However, all too frequently in 1992, Joyner got himself out by over-swinging at more difficult pitches early in the count.

BASERUNNING:

Joyner has always been a moderately successful basestealer, and in 1992 set new career bests in both steals (11) and attempts (16). He ran more aggressively than in past years, but with only moderate success.

FIELDING:

Joyner's good fielding reputation is well deserved. When he was slowed by injury, he entered two consecutive tight ninth-inning games for defensive purposes; both times he made diving, game-saving catches. He has fine range and soft hands, and his ability to scoop low throws saves his fellow infielders numerous errors.

OVERALL:

The Royals must think a lot of Joyner. Despite his off year, they shoved aside the organization's best prospect, first baseman Jeff Conine, signing Joyner to a multi-year contract midway through 1992. Joyner, they hope, will rebound and carry a large portion of the Royals' 1993 offense.

KEVIN KOSLOFSKI

Position: RF/LF/CF
Bats: L **Throws:** R
Ht: 5' 8" **Wt:** 165

Opening Day Age: 26
Born: 9/24/66 in Decatur, IL
ML Seasons: 1

HITTING:

What diminutive Kevin Koslofski lacks in height (5'8"), he more than makes up for with tenacity and energy. Koslofski took a long time to blossom, spending six seasons below AA ball. But he followed a fine 1991 campaign at AA (Memphis) and AAA (Omaha) with a good first half last year at Omaha, earning his major league promotion after 824 minor-league games. After a hot start, he batted .248 in a Royal uniform.

A slashing, spray hitter, Koslofski has his best success with fastballs high and away, slapping singles to left. His power down the right field line is a recent phenomenon -- just one home run in his first four minor league seasons (924 at-bats). Koslofski inexplicably accounted for three of four Royals homers during a three-week stretch.

Koslofski had shown good patience in the minors, averaging a walk per nine plate appearances, but became aggressive once recalled. This helped him enjoy immediate success while he was getting the usual rookie treatment of one fastball after another. Word travelled quickly, though, and Koslofski stopped seeing first-pitch fastballs. After a .421 start, his average tumbled as he chased breaking balls out of the strike zone.

BASERUNNING:

Koslofski possesses good speed but doesn't always use it wisely. He misjudged some outfield arms early after his recall, and hasn't been a successful minor-league basestealer since A-ball. Before Koslofski becomes a good baserunner, he must show restraint while learning the league's pitchers and outfielders.

FIELDING:

Although he's still learning how to position himself, Koslofski has shown good range at all outfield positions. He's fast and has a fine arm, with 12 outfield assists in the minors in 1991. He should improve as he adjusts to major league hitters and parks.

OVERALL:

There's a lot to like about Koslofski. An energetic offensive player who can play any outfield position, he will fight for a backup or platoon outfield role with the 1993 Royals. There's room on the Royals' roster for a winner like this youngster.

Overall Statistics

	G	AB	R	H	D	T	HR	RBI	SB	BB	SO	AVG
1992	55	133	20	33	0	2	3	13	2	12	23	.248
Career	55	133	20	33	0	2	3	13	2	12	23	.248

Where He Hits the Ball

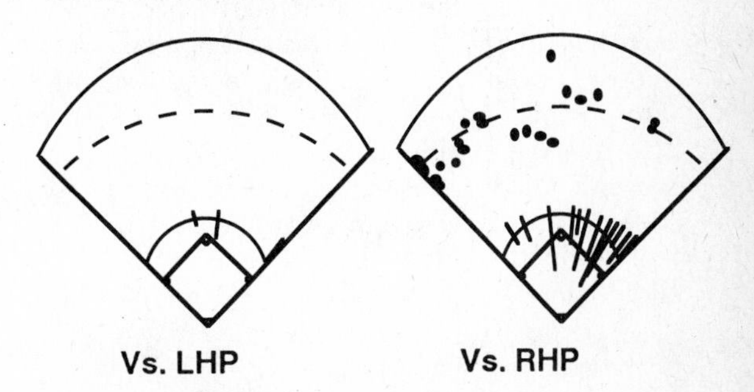

1992 Situational Stats

	AB	H	HR	RBI	AVG		AB	H	HR	RBI	AVG
Home	82	16	1	8	.195	LHP	14	6	0	1	.429
Road	51	17	2	5	.333	RHP	119	27	3	12	.227
Day	38	17	1	5	.447	Sc Pos	35	7	0	10	.200
Night	95	16	2	8	.168	Clutch	22	5	1	2	.227

1992 Rankings (American League)

- Did not rank near the top or bottom in any category

GREAT RANGE

JOSE LIND

Position: 2B
Bats: R **Throws:** R
Ht: 5'11" **Wt:** 170

Opening Day Age: 28
Born: 5/1/64 in Toabaja, Puerto Rico
ML Seasons: 6

HITTING:

Jose Lind's final half-inning as a member of the Pittsburgh Pirates will always be the ultimate nightmare for Pirate fans. The usually sure-handed Lind booted David Justice's grounder to open the floodgates in a last-gasp, pennant-losing collapse in Game 7 of the National League playoffs. But it was Lind's salary, not his error, which prompted the Pirates to trade him to Kansas City last fall. Lind was already a $2 million player, and figured to earn even more in salary arbitration. The Bucs thought that was too much to pay a .235 hitter.

Lind's trademark has never been hitting. But last season, his production dropped to alarming levels. Along with the low average, he had no homers and 39 RBI. The homer and RBI totals were his worst ever, and the batting average was only three points above his 1989 career low. Lind's .265 average in 1991 had been the highest full-season mark of his career. However, his progress stalled. He refuses to turn on any pitches, continually trying to go the other way even on balls he should drive.

BASERUNNING:

Lind's extraordinary athletic skills do not translate to the basepaths. He is an ordinary baserunner whose stolen base total dipped to a career-low three last season.

FIELDING:

His costly Game 7 error notwithstanding, Lind is a terrific defensive second baseman who finally unseated Ryne Sandberg to win a Gold Glove last year. He ranges far to his left or right to steal hits and uses his vertical leap to snare line drives headed to the gap. He also has a good arm and turns the double play well. He is to second base what Ozzie Smith is to shortstop.

OVERALL:

Though Lind is an acrobat in the field, he is a one-dimensional player. The budget-conscious Pirates felt his performance didn't measure up to his salary, and that's why they traded him. The Royals can pay the freight . . . but they'll expect more for their bucks than a .235 average.

Overall Statistics

	G	AB	R	H	D	T	HR	RBI	SB	BB	SO	AVG
1992	135	468	38	110	14	1	0	39	3	26	29	.235
Career	779	2816	292	717	111	23	8	249	50	180	288	.255

Where He Hits the Ball

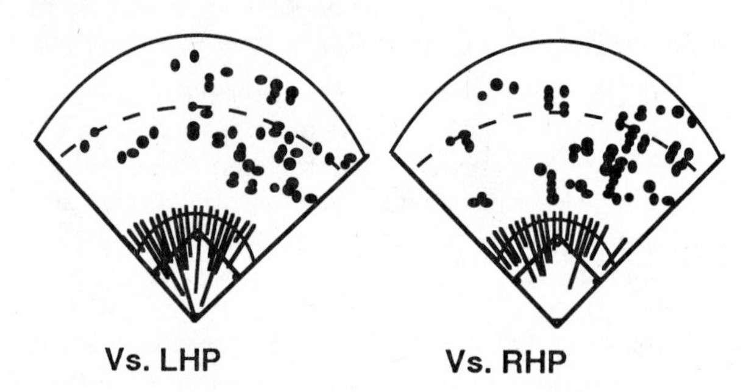

1992 Situational Stats

	AB	H	HR	RBI	AVG		AB	H	HR	RBI	AVG
Home	229	58	0	24	.253	LHP	177	42	0	14	.237
Road	239	52	0	15	.218	RHP	291	68	0	25	.234
Day	114	18	0	5	.158	Sc Pos	136	35	0	38	.257
Night	354	92	0	34	.260	Clutch	90	26	0	9	.289

1992 Rankings (National League)

- 1st in lowest slugging percentage (.269), highest fielding percentage at second base (.992) and lowest HR frequency (468 ABs with 0 HR)
- 2nd in lowest on-base percentage (.275)
- 3rd in lowest slugging percentage vs. left-handed pitchers (.282)
- Led the Pirates in GDPs (14), highest groundball/flyball ratio (1.7), lowest percentage of swings that missed (10.3%) and highest percentage of swings put into play (51.0%)
- Led NL second basemen in intentional walks (12), GDPs, fielding percentage and lowest percentage of swings that missed

MIKE MACFARLANE

Position: C/DH
Bats: R **Throws:** R
Ht: 6' 1" **Wt:** 205

Opening Day Age: 29
Born: 4/12/64 in Stockton, CA
ML Seasons: 6

HITTING:

The Royals needed power from Mike Macfarlane in 1992, and he delivered some sock to their lineup. He collected more extra-base hits (48) than singles (46), and his career-high 17 homers led the Royals. But Macfarlane batted only .234. He was a miserable clutch hitter, batting just .126 with runners in scoring position.

Severely crowding the plate, Macfarlane tries to pull everything down the line. He prefers fastballs out over the plate and struggles against inside breaking pitches. Pitchers discovered last year that he could be jammed inside. With pitchers throwing inside and Macfarlane refusing to modify his plate-hugging stance, he led the league in getting hit by pitches getting plunked 15 times.

Macfarlane struggles against right-handed pitchers; he batted .220 and fanned almost once every four at-bats. His upper-cut swing produces many fly balls, helping him avoid double play grounders despite his poor speed. Macfarlane grounded into eight DPs in 1992, not bad for a catcher.

BASERUNNING:

Usually a conservative baserunner, Macfarlane occasionally gambles on extra bases. He runs like he's pulling a sled, though, and often runs into unnecessary outs. Macfarlane's one-for-six stolen base success rate accurately reflects his basestealing acumen.

FIELDING:

The Royals' problems holding baserunners must partly be laid at Macfarlane's feet. He permitted 67 steals in 90 attempts and had so much trouble with opposition basestealers that he stopped throwing to second altogether with a runner at third. The Royals were often burned on double steals as well. An average fielder, Macfarlane is very good at blocking the plate.

OVERALL:

Incumbent catcher Macfarlane is under pressure from Brent Mayne. In 1993, the Royals will weigh Macfarlane's power against Mayne's defense. If lefty Mayne's hitting improves, Macfarlane could find himself in a platoon. The Royals have tried trading catchers in previous off-seasons and may try again, this time with Macfarlane as bait.

Overall Statistics

	G	AB	R	H	D	T	HR	RBI	SB	BB	SO	AVG
1992	129	402	51	94	28	3	17	48	1	30	89	.234
Career	484	1456	160	365	92	9	42	195	3	102	276	.251

Where He Hits the Ball

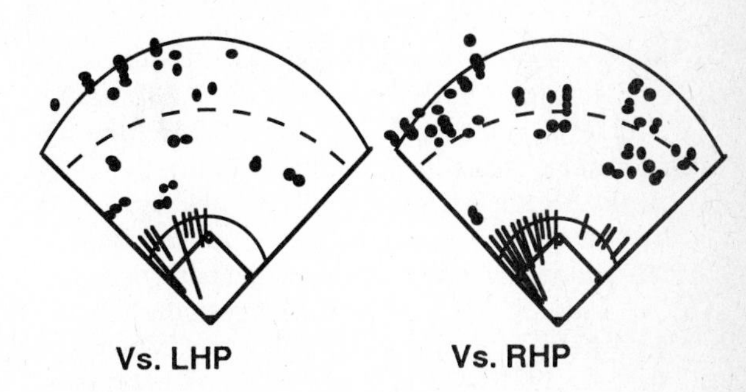

1992 Situational Stats

	AB	H	HR	RBI	AVG		AB	H	HR	RBI	AVG
Home	184	44	7	21	.239	LHP	138	36	7	18	.261
Road	218	50	10	27	.229	RHP	264	58	10	30	.220
Day	85	18	4	7	.212	Sc Pos	95	12	2	25	.126
Night	317	76	13	41	.240	Clutch	74	18	4	11	.243

1992 Rankings (American League)

- 1st in hit by pitch (15), lowest batting average with runners in scoring position (.126) and lowest batting average with the bases loaded (.000)
- 8th lowest batting average with 2 strikes (.135)
- Led the Royals in home runs (17), hit by pitch and strikeouts (89)
- Led AL catchers in doubles (28), triples (3) and hit by pitch

BRIAN McRAE

Position: CF
Bats: B **Throws:** R
Ht: 6' 0" **Wt:** 185

Opening Day Age: 25
Born: 8/27/67 in Bradenton, FL
ML Seasons: 3

Overall Statistics

	G	AB	R	H	D	T	HR	RBI	SB	BB	SO	AVG
1992	149	533	63	119	23	5	4	52	18	42	88	.223
Career	347	1330	170	331	59	17	14	139	42	75	216	.249

Where He Hits the Ball

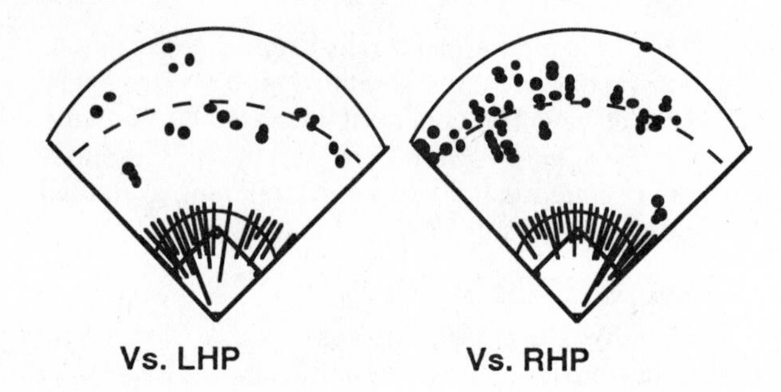

1992 Situational Stats

	AB	H	HR	RBI	AVG		AB	H	HR	RBI	AVG
Home	257	63	2	34	.245	LHP	163	38	3	20	.233
Road	276	56	2	18	.203	RHP	370	81	1	32	.219
Day	128	21	1	10	.164	Sc Pos	131	31	2	44	.237
Night	405	98	3	42	.242	Clutch	100	21	0	13	.210

1992 Rankings (American League)

- 1st in lowest batting average (.223), lowest batting average vs. right-handed pitchers (.219), lowest slugging percentage vs. right-handed pitchers (.284) and lowest batting average on the road (.203)
- 2nd in lowest slugging percentage (.308) and lowest on-base percentage (.285)
- 3rd in lowest on-base percentage vs. right-handed pitchers (.287) and bunts in play (42)
- Led the Royals in triples (5), highest groundball/flyball ratio (2.0), stolen base percentage (78.3%), most pitches seen per plate appearance (3.69), highest batting average with the bases loaded (.286), bunts in play and outfield assists (8)

HITTING:

Instead of making youthful progress, Brian McRae took a giant step backwards with a very disappointing 1992 campaign. McRae batted only .223 last year, and his career seems headed in the wrong direction. In three seasons with the Royals, the switch-hitter has batted .286, .261 and .223. McRae was the worst hitting full-time player in the major leagues last year.

In 1992, McRae was overmatched by fastballs and lunged at bad breaking balls; he was off-balance most of the year. He showed more patience by drawing a career-best 42 walks, but he wasn't much use at the top of the order. Often used as a number-two hitter last year, McRae batted .175 in the role.

McRae has had most of his success as a right-handed hitter. In his career he's hit .282 righty, .232 lefty, but last year he hit only .233 from the right side. That still was better than his .219 lefty mark. McRae's closed right-handed stance lets him hang in better against inside pitches. Batting left-handed, he opens up more and bails out early on inside pitches. Righthanders get him hacking wildly at low outside pitches, then bust him inside with fastballs, producing weak flies or easy grounders.

BASERUNNING:

Although McRae's stolen base figures were good, 18 steals in 23 tries, he committed several costly baserunning errors in 1992. He made poor choices when gambling for extra bases, often making third outs while leaving good hitters at the plate. McRae must display better game sense.

FIELDING:

McRae remains a very good center fielder. He uses his great speed to track down everything hit to Royals Stadium's spacious outfield. He lacks a good arm, however, and runners often advance on relatively shallow flies. Nevertheless, McRae's a defensive asset.

OVERALL:

McRae needs to get his career turned around in a hurry. He'll get another full season to prove his worth, as bad teams like the Royals often have few options. He's still young (25), but must improve rapidly to remain a full-time player.

HITTING:

Kevin McReynolds' first American League season was disappointing as he adjusted to the pitching and was twice sidelined with injuries. The resulting season was remarkably similar to predecessor Kirk Gibson's 1991 performance. McReynolds' 13 homers and 49 RBI were among the team's best, as were Gibson's 16 HR and 55 RBI, but his .247 average, like Gibson's .236, was below expectations. Gibson left the Royals before the '92 season, and retired before it was halfway over. McReynolds intends to stick around.

A relaxed stance and controlled swing allows McReynolds to handle any pitch. He pulls inside pitches down the line for extra bases or slaps outside pitches to right for singles. McReynolds hits behind runners and can go deep occasionally.

Usually patient, McReynolds took a strike before swinging in 1992. He walked more often than striking out, and his .357 on-base average led the Royals. Usually a dangerous clutch hitter, McReynolds struggled last year, hitting .224 with runners in scoring position. Unlike previous seasons, he ripped lefties, batting .345 and slugging .575 while hitting only .204 versus righthanders.

BASERUNNING:

Like Gibson, McReynolds knows when to take extra bases and steals with uncanny success. He succeeded in seven of eight attempts in 1992 and is 72-for-89 since 1987. He runs selectively and successfully, rarely making unnecessary outs on the bases.

FIELDING:

At least McReynolds' fielding was an improvement over Gibson's. He caught some early criticism for his nonchalant approach when chasing shallow flies, as he doesn't go all out unless the ball can be caught. McReynolds displays decent range and a respectable arm.

OVERALL:

Soft-spoken McReynolds wasn't held accountable for the Royals' dismal season like Gibson was in 1991. He's well liked by teammates, and he'll get another chance to produce in 1993. McReynolds survived the expansion draft and the Royals see him as a run-producing outfielder batting in a power spot in their order.

KEVIN McREYNOLDS

Position: LF/RF
Bats: R **Throws:** R
Ht: 6' 1" **Wt:** 215

Opening Day Age: 33
Born: 10/16/59 in Little Rock, AR
ML Seasons: 10

Overall Statistics

	G	AB	R	H	D	T	HR	RBI	SB	BB	SO	AVG
1992	109	373	45	92	25	0	13	49	7	67	48	.247
Career	1341	4892	660	1307	251	29	196	744	89	465	617	.267

Where He Hits the Ball

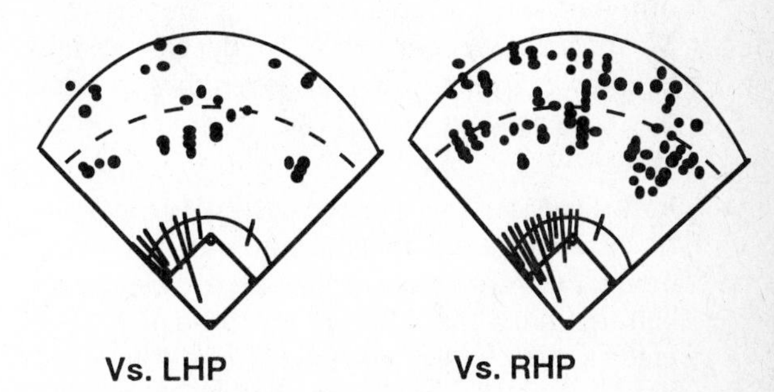

1992 Situational Stats

	AB	H	HR	RBI	AVG		AB	H	HR	RBI	AVG
Home	186	47	4	17	.253	LHP	113	39	5	22	.345
Road	187	45	9	32	.241	RHP	260	53	8	27	.204
Day	82	19	4	11	.232	Sc Pos	85	19	1	29	.224
Night	291	73	9	38	.251	Clutch	72	17	4	8	.236

1992 Rankings (American League)

- 5th in highest on-base percentage vs. left-handed pitchers (.461)
- 6th in highest slugging percentage vs. left-handed pitchers (.575)
- 8th in highest batting average vs. left-handed pitchers (.345)
- 9th in highest percentage of pitches taken (63.8%)
- Led the Royals in walks (67), batting average vs. left-handed pitchers, batting average on a 3-1 count (.417), slugging percentage vs. left-handed pitchers, on-base percentage vs. left-handed pitchers and highest percentage of pitches taken

PITCHING:

Rusty Meacham earned a spot on the Royals' roster last year with an impressive spring training performance, then went on to become the team's best set-up man. As Meacham turned in one good outing after another, his ERA dipped to 0.42 and he got even more steady work, appearing in more games than any Royals pitcher except closer Jeff Montgomery. Meacham was ineffective only in September (7.53 ERA) after posting a 1.84 ERA through his first 52 games.

A minor league starter in the Detroit system, Meacham throws a number of different pitches and has good control with all. He won't show the same batter the same pitch, and will throw each to different spots. Good location is important to Meacham's success, since he doesn't usually overpower hitters. Meacham sometimes surprises them, though; his string-bean frame belies a decent fastball.

Rail-thin Meacham is one of the quickest workers in baseball. He's in constant motion on the mound, always toeing the rubber or tossing the ball around while he waits for the batter to get ready. Once a batter gets settled in, he'd better not blink, because Meacham delivers the ball immediately. His go-go style has batters itching to get at him, but his good control of a wide repertoire often leaves them frustrated. Opponents hit .233 against Meacham last year.

HOLDING RUNNERS AND FIELDING:

Meacham has a quick delivery and throws strikes, giving his catcher a chance to nail runners trying to steal. He has an average move to first, but it is difficult for baserunners to time. Meacham is an occasionally shaky fielder, not always showing the best judgement on where to throw.

OVERALL:

The "Meacham and Montgomery Bullpen Show" was a hit for Kansas City in 1992, and it should continue this year. Although Meacham was originally groomed as a starter in the Tigers organization, he's probably not cut out for either a starting or closing role. For now the Royals are satisfied with steady, stifling set-up work from Meacham.

RUSTY MEACHAM

Position: RP
Bats: R **Throws:** R
Ht: 6' 2" **Wt:** 165

Opening Day Age: 25
Born: 1/27/68 in Stuart, FL
ML Seasons: 2

Overall Statistics

	W	L	ERA	G	GS	Sv	IP	H	R	BB	SO	HR
1992	10	4	2.74	64	0	2	101.2	88	39	21	64	5
Career	12	5	3.27	74	4	2	129.1	123	56	32	78	9

How Often He Throws Strikes

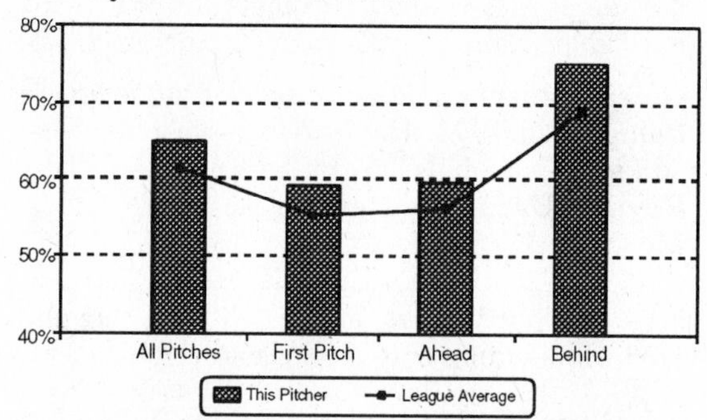

1992 Situational Stats

	W	L	ERA	Sv	IP		AB	H	HR	RBI	AVG
Home	6	0	3.81	1	54.1	LHB	144	27	1	15	.188
Road	4	4	1.52	1	47.1	RHB	234	61	4	32	.261
Day	1	0	2.16	0	16.2	Sc Pos	109	24	1	40	.220
Night	9	4	2.86	2	85.0	Clutch	194	46	3	16	.237

1992 Rankings (American League)

- 1st in relief wins (10)
- 2nd in lowest batting average allowed vs. left-handed batters (.188) and most relief innings (101.2)
- 6th in least baserunners allowed per 9 innings in relief (9.7)
- 9th in holds (15)
- Led the Royals in holds, lowest batting average allowed vs. left-handed batters, lowest percentage of inherited runners scored (30.9%), relief wins, relief innings and least baserunners allowed per 9 innings in relief

KEITH MILLER

Position: 2B/LF
Bats: R **Throws:** R
Ht: 5'11" **Wt:** 185

Opening Day Age: 29
Born: 6/12/63 in Midland, MI
ML Seasons: 6

HITTING:

When the Royals traded Bret Saberhagen to the Mets in December 1991, Keith Miller was ranked well behind Gregg Jefferies and Kevin McReynolds among the players Kansas City obtained. But the Royals gave Miller an opportunity for regular play, and he responded with career bests in all offensive categories. Miller wound up batting .284, well ahead of McReynolds (.247) and only a point behind Jefferies. He proved valuable to the weak Royals lineup, usually hitting first or second and setting the table for the Royals' RBI men.

Miller aggressively attacks every hittable pitch, smashing them back up the middle. The free-swinging Miller approaches the plate looking for fastballs and has more trouble with finesse pitchers who nibble at the corners. A fine bunter, Miller collected 7 bunt hits in 1992.

With his ability to make contact and hit behind runners, Miller is a hit-and-run trigger man. He was among the Royals' best clutch hitters, batting .341 with runners in scoring position. His slashing, gap-hitting style fits well in spacious Royals Stadium where he batted .301.

BASERUNNING:

Miller is all hustle, rarely escaping play with a clean uniform. He always looks to take extra bases whenever possible, and sometimes even when it's impossible. He runs into more outs than any other Royals player and must temper his aggressive edge with better savvy.

FIELDING:

Quickly proving he was lost in left field, Miller moved to second base late in April. He showed good range, but couldn't always make the necessary plays around the bag. A better fielder than his "bad glove" reputation suggested, Miller steadily improved his play, making just three errors in his last 35 games at second base.

OVERALL:

Every team needs hard-nosed guys like Miller to spark the offense. He doesn't help the Royals porous defense. However, the team can live with spotty glove work if Miller continues to contribute at the plate. With the acquisition of Jose Lind, he'll likely play both outfield and infield in '93.

Overall Statistics

	G	AB	R	H	D	T	HR	RBI	SB	BB	SO	AVG
1992	106	416	57	118	24	4	4	38	16	31	46	.284
Career	414	1188	178	322	64	8	11	86	60	90	179	.271

Where He Hits the Ball

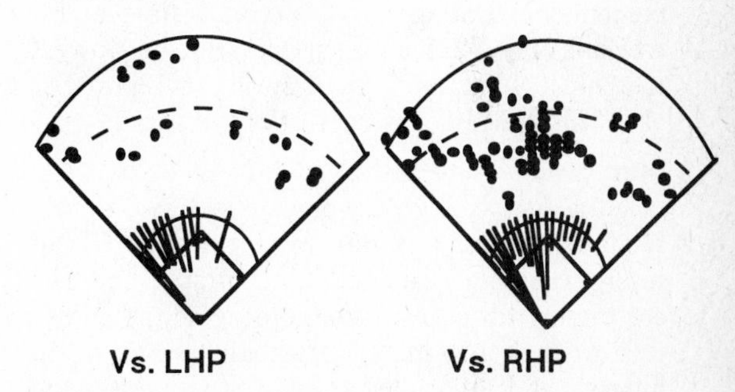

1992 Situational Stats

	AB	H	HR	RBI	AVG		AB	H	HR	RBI	AVG
Home	183	55	1	17	.301	LHP	120	32	0	10	.267
Road	233	63	3	21	.270	RHP	296	86	4	28	.291
Day	108	18	0	5	.167	Sc Pos	88	30	0	32	.341
Night	308	100	4	33	.325	Clutch	70	21	1	7	.300

1992 Rankings (American League)

- 3rd in hit by pitch (14)
- 6th in highest batting average with runners in scoring position (.341)
- 10th in lowest batting average on a 3-1 count (.100)
- Led the Royals least GDPs per GDP situation (1.9%) and highest batting average with runners in scoring position
- Led AL second basemen in hit by pitch and least GDPs per GDP situation

JEFF MONTGOMERY

Position: RP
Bats: R **Throws:** R
Ht: 5'11" **Wt:** 180

Opening Day Age: 31
Born: 1/7/62 in Wellston, OH
ML Seasons: 6

PITCHING:

Jeff Montgomery put it all together in 1992 to become one of the American League's most successful closers. Picking up where he left off in the second half of 1991, Montgomery set a career high with 39 saves, blew just seven chances all year, and lowered his 1991 ERA by 72 points. Working his way steadily to the top, Montgomery has improved his save total each of the last four seasons (18, 24, 33, 39).

Better early-season handling allowed Montgomery to remain effective wire to wire last year. He was exclusively a ninth-inning pitcher throughout most of the season and finished games in all but three of his 65 appearances -- one of the highest percentages among major league relievers. He worked only 82.2 innings last year, his lowest total since 1988, and was as strong in September (1.80 ERA) as he was the rest of the year.

Montgomery lives and dies with a great live fastball thrown with good velocity and movement. He will occasionally mix in breaking balls, but rarely where they can be hit; his offspeed pitches are merely for show. Montgomery's most effective pitch is a high, tight fastball thrown in on hitters' hands. It's a particularly effective weapon against righthanders, whom Montgomery has held to a .206 average over the last five seasons. For a hard thrower, Montgomery has fine control, allowing about one walk per three innings pitched. He also strikes out nearly three batters for every walk issued.

HOLDING RUNNERS AND FIELDING:

Montgomery holds runners quite well, primarily because he throws hard and stays ahead of hitters. He has an average move to first, but always gives catchers good pitches to handle. Montgomery throws well to all bases and has become a better fielder in recent years.

OVERALL:

Among baseball's best stoppers, Montgomery is the Royals bullpen anchor. His stability allows the other relievers to settle into defined set-up roles, thereby making the rest of the bullpen better. Still in his prime, Montgomery should be a dependable closer for several years to come.

Overall Statistics

	W	L	ERA	G	GS	Sv	IP	H	R	BB	SO	HR
1992	1	6	2.18	65	0	39	82.2	61	23	27	69	5
Career	27	22	2.57	327	1	115	441.0	370	147	153	394	28

How Often He Throws Strikes

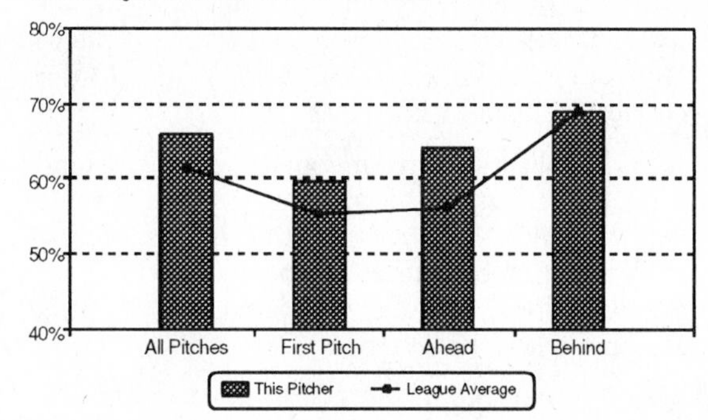

1992 Situational Stats

	W	L	ERA	Sv	IP		AB	H	HR	RBI	AVG
Home	1	4	1.85	24	48.2	LHB	146	30	2	11	.205
Road	0	2	2.65	15	34.0	RHB	151	31	3	18	.205
Day	0	3	3.44	7	18.1	Sc Pos	68	13	1	23	.191
Night	1	3	1.82	32	64.1	Clutch	209	51	4	24	.244

1992 Rankings (American League)

- 2nd in games finished (62)
- 3rd in saves (39), save opportunities (46) and first batter efficiency (.143)
- 5th in relief losses (6)
- 6th in blown saves (7)
- Led the Royals in games pitched (65), saves, games finished, save opportunities, save percentage (84.8%), blown saves, first batter efficiency, relief ERA (2.18), relief losses (6) and lowest batting average allowed in relief (.205)

PITCHING:

Hipolito Pichardo was an unlikely minor league candidate to solve the Royals' rotation woes last year. In four seasons in the Kansas City system, Pichardo had posted a 9-21 record, though his ERA was a fine 3.60. He had never pitched above the AA level, but Pichardo emerged to become an effective Royals starter, going 9-6 in 24 starts.

Pichardo was called up early last year when Luis Aquino became injured. He took over a starting role after pitching in the bullpen for a month. He won immediately, shutting out Chicago for five innings. Pichardo sputtered through some below-average starts before putting it all together with a one-hitter against Boston.

The lanky Pichardo is all arms and legs as he delivers the ball, resembling Pascual Perez in stature and delivery. He works quickly and throws fastballs, sliders and change-ups, but is most effective with sinking fastballs. His sinker has good movement and induces grounders, and Pichardo led the Royals staff with fifteen ground-ball double plays. Using good movement and staying close to the plate, Pichardo gets outs with pitches that aren't strikes. The pitches are too close to take, but difficult to drive; batters find themselves lunging after balls that are down and out of the strike zone. When Pichardo struggles, it's usually because his sinker comes in too straight.

HOLDING RUNNERS AND FIELDING:

Pichardo's delivery would seem to be difficult for baserunners to read, as he has a big wind-up with arms and legs flying everywhere. But he permitted 11 steals in 14 attempts last year. He doesn't hurt himself with the glove.

OVERALL:

Pichardo's rookie success gives him an edge toward a starting role in 1993. However, he'll need to show more stamina than he had in 1992, when he averaged only a little over five innings per start. Part of the Royals' youth movement, the 23-year-old Pichardo's development into a quality starter is imperative if the club is to succeed in the near future.

HIPOLITO PICHARDO

Position: SP/RP
Bats: R **Throws:** R
Ht: 6' 1" **Wt:** 160

Opening Day Age: 23
Born: 8/22/69 in Esperanza, Domican Republic
ML Seasons: 1

Overall Statistics

	W	L	ERA	G	GS	Sv	IP	H	R	BB	SO	HR
1992	9	6	3.95	31	24	0	143.2	148	71	49	59	9
Career	9	6	3.95	31	24	0	143.2	148	71	49	59	9

How Often He Throws Strikes

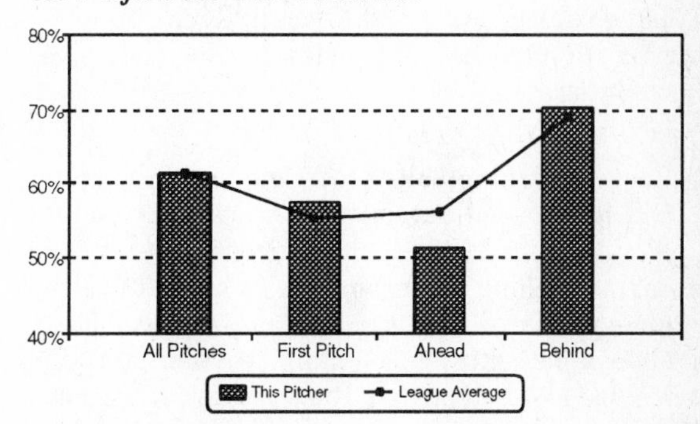

1992 Situational Stats

	W	L	ERA	Sv	IP		AB	H	HR	RBI	AVG
Home	5	2	3.94	0	75.1	LHB	244	70	3	25	.287
Road	4	4	3.95	0	68.1	RHB	310	78	6	30	.252
Day	2	1	6.31	0	35.2	Sc Pos	140	40	3	45	.286
Night	7	5	3.17	0	108.0	Clutch	9	3	0	0	.333

1992 Rankings (American League)

- 10th in highest batting average allowed with runners in scoring position (.286)
- Led the Royals in shutouts (1) and GDPs induced (15)

RICK REED

Position: SP
Bats: R **Throws:** R
Ht: 6' 0" **Wt:** 195

Opening Day Age: 28
Born: 8/16/64 in Huntington, WV
ML Seasons: 5

PITCHING:

As he has done throughout his short major-league career, Rick Reed pitched just well enough to lose in 1992. Although he kept his games close, Reed usually surrendered the tying or winning run just before departing. Minimal offensive support usually left Reed with little margin for error. Between a relief win in his season debut and a year-ending shutout, Reed went 1-7 with a 4.36 ERA.

Reed has marginal stuff. He spots his fastball on the corners, keeps his breaking pitches down in the strike zone and tries to fool free-swingers with his change-up. He doesn't overpower hitters and stays away from their hitting zones. Reed generally has good control -- he walked more than two in just one of 18 starts -- but the walks usually came back to haunt him. Overall, Reed permitted only 17 unintentional walks in 100.1 innings, while striking out nearly three times that many (49).

Reed's breaking balls produce many grounders, and he escaped several tight spots with double play balls in 1992. Thus he needs good infield defense behind him to win. He's strictly a five-inning pitcher. Excepting his lone shutout, Reed always ran into sixth-inning trouble. A right-handed low-ball pitcher, Reed had surprising success against lefties, limiting them to a .201 average. But righthanders walloped Reed, batting .326 and slugging .450. Reed's left-right differential was the largest on the Royals' staff.

HOLDING RUNNERS AND FIELDING:

With a good, consistent move to first, Reed holds baserunners well. He works hard at all aspects of the game, but is an unspectacular fielder. However, Reed doesn't hurt himself with the glove. He handles bunts well, throws accurately to all bases and shows good judgement in the field.

OVERALL:

Despite his record, Reed's job as a starter must be considered a limited success. He can succeed in a similar role with strong bullpen help and more run support than he had in 1992. Reed is better than his career 7-14 mark would indicate. He'll fight for a fifth-starter role next year.

Overall Statistics

	W	L	ERA	G	GS	Sv	IP	H	R	BB	SO	HR
1992	3	7	3.68	19	18	0	100.1	105	47	20	49	10
Career	7	14	4.40	50	36	1	225.0	247	124	46	118	23

How Often He Throws Strikes

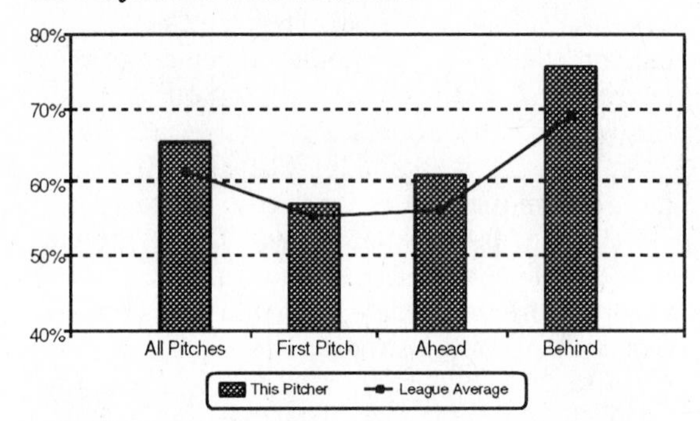

1992 Situational Stats

	W	L	ERA	Sv	IP		AB	H	HR	RBI	AVG
Home	1	2	4.53	0	43.2	LHB	169	34	5	18	.201
Road	2	5	3.02	0	56.2	RHB	218	71	5	20	.326
Day	1	2	2.35	0	23.0	Sc Pos	84	20	0	22	.238
Night	2	5	4.07	0	77.1	Clutch	6	4	1	3	.667

1992 Rankings (American League)

- 5th in lowest batting average allowed vs. left-handed batters (.201)
- Led the Royals in shutouts (1) and home runs allowed (10)

JUAN SAMUEL

Position: 2B/RF
Bats: R **Throws:** R
Ht: 5'11" **Wt:** 183

Opening Day Age: 32
Born: 12/9/60 in San Pedro de Macoris, Dominican Republic
ML Seasons: 10

HITTING:

A major star just a few years ago, Juan Samuel now finds himself drifting from team to team. Having worn out his welcome with the Dodgers after two and a half seasons, Samuel caught on last August with the Royals, who needed a second baseman to temporarily replace the injured Keith Miller. He did well enough to find work as a part-time outfielder when Miller returned, batting .284 in a Royal uniform. Kansas City liked Samuel's work, but not his salary. They declined to pick up the option on his $2.3 million contract, making him a free agent.

One of baseball's most aggressive free-swingers, Samuel always strikes out frequently while drawing few walks. He had 49 whiffs in 224 at-bats in 1992, compared to just 10 unintentional walks. He will swing at anything, but is primarily a fastball hitter. Pitchers know strikes aren't required to dispose of him. He'll chase high fastballs or breaking balls down and out of reach. Samuel swings and misses at as high a rate as any other major leaguer. When he does make contact, he'll usually hit the ball hard somewhere.

BASERUNNING:

Samuel is still a good baserunner, though hardly the man who stole 72 bases in 87 attempts back in 1984. He swiped six in seven tries for the Royals, and eight of 11 overall. Samuel possesses good speed and runs the bases aggressively.

FIELDING:

Never considered a good fielder, Samuel was positively awful in 1992. He was among the National League's worst infielders and continued that pace with six errors in just 27 games afield for the Royals. He has good range at second base, but regularly fails to make routine plays. As an outfielder, Samuel seems lost, never knowing which way to run.

OVERALL:

Samuel had a good attitude about his off-season situation; he understands that he'll have trouble being a regular again. Wherever he plays in 1993, he'll have a reduced role, and a greatly reduced salary. In that capacity he can help a club.

Overall Statistics

	G	AB	R	H	D	T	HR	RBI	SB	BB	SO	AVG
1992	76	224	22	61	8	4	0	23	8	14	49	.272
Career	1310	5146	718	1338	243	85	128	574	349	346	1208	.260

Where He Hits the Ball

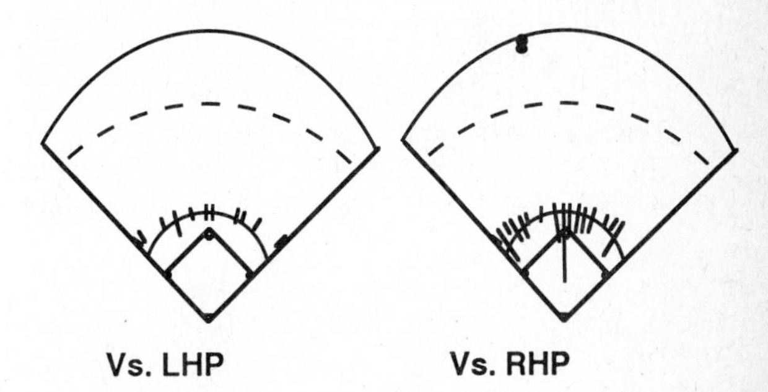

1992 Situational Stats

	AB	H	HR	RBI	AVG		AB	H	HR	RBI	AVG
Home	105	31	0	15	.295	LHP	104	30	0	9	.288
Road	119	30	0	8	.252	RHP	120	31	0	14	.258
Day	56	19	0	7	.339	Sc Pos	57	14	0	23	.246
Night	168	42	0	16	.250	Clutch	40	16	0	5	.400

1992 Rankings (American League)

- Did not rank near the top or bottom in any category

MIKE MAGNANTE

Position: RP/SP
Bats: L **Throws:** L
Ht: 6' 1" **Wt:** 180

Opening Day Age: 27
Born: 6/17/65 in Glendale, CA
ML Seasons: 2

Overall Statistics

	W	L	ERA	G	GS	Sv	IP	H	R	BB	SO	HR
1992	4	9	4.94	44	12	0	89.1	115	53	35	31	5
Career	4	10	3.99	82	12	0	144.1	170	72	58	73	8

PITCHING, FIELDING & HOLDING RUNNERS:

A victim of the sophomore slump, Mike Magnante saw his ERA more than double last year. As a rookie in 1991, the lefthander had posted a 2.45 ERA while working exclusively out of the Royal bullpen. Last year Magnante both started and relieved, but struggled to a 4.94 mark.

Magnante failed in his two-month trial as a starter, posting a 5.43 ERA in 12 starts. He posted slightly better results in the bullpen (4.15) although in his last 25 relief appearances, he allowed 12 runs. His relief work wasn't enough to salvage his season and Magnante finished with the team's worst opponent batting average, .325, and a 4.94 ERA.

Magnante's easy motion hides a decent fastball which he sets up with breaking balls away. However, too often in 1992 his breaking pitches missed and he grooved hittable fastballs. Magnante's a fine fielder and holds runners well. Despite wearing a leg brace for much of his major-league career, Magnante's quick to field bunts and softly-hit grounders.

OVERALL:

Destined again for the bullpen in 1993, Magnante would seem to have an advantage by being left-handed. But, he'll have to do better against lefty hitters, who batted .375 against him in 1992. His versatility gives Magnante a greater opportunity to succeed, but he must do more with his opportunities before the Royals give him an important role.

BRENT MAYNE

Position: C
Bats: L **Throws:** R
Ht: 6' 1" **Wt:** 190

Opening Day Age: 24
Born: 4/19/68 in Loma Linda, CA
ML Seasons: 3

Overall Statistics

	G	AB	R	H	D	T	HR	RBI	SB	BB	SO	AVG
1992	82	213	16	48	10	0	0	18	0	11	26	.225
Career	172	457	40	109	18	0	3	50	2	37	71	.239

HITTING, FIELDING, BASERUNNING:

Irregular play left Brent Mayne with a down year in 1992. Mayne had shown promise by batting .251 in 231 at-bats as a Royal rookie in 1991. But last year the lefty swinger slumped to a .225 mark, going homerless in 213 ABs.

Inactivity hampered Mayne last year. He started only about twice per week, entering most games as a late-inning substitute. Mayne's trouble hitting left-handed pitching (.136 last year) precludes more regular play. He managed just three hits against lefties last year -- one more than in 1991. He's a career .114 hitter against lefthanders compared to .252 against righthanders. Mayne is a singles hitter who's often over-matched by fastballs and lacks selectivity.

Mayne has better defensive skills than counterpart Mike Macfarlane. He blocks the plate well and has a strong, though occasionally erratic, arm. He's versatile enough to play third base, but is below average at that position. Mayne's a terrible baserunner. He runs tentatively and has little speed; he has two career steals in 11 tries.

OVERALL:

Lefty-hitting Mayne can be a good complement to right-handed Macfarlane. Mayne plays better defense and the Royals hope some good clutch hitting portends better hitting overall. He's just 25 and will start 1993 with a backup catching role. Look for Mayne's role to gain importance as the Royals build on youth.

BILL SAMPEN

Position: RP
Bats: R **Throws:** R
Ht: 6' 2" **Wt:** 195

Opening Day Age: 30
Born: 1/18/63 in Lincoln, IL
ML Seasons: 3

Overall Statistics

	W	L	ERA	G	GS	Sv	IP	H	R	BB	SO	HR
1992	1	6	3.25	52	2	0	83.0	83	32	32	37	4
Career	22	18	3.42	154	14	2	265.2	273	115	111	158	24

PITCHING, FIELDING & HOLDING RUNNERS:

Bill Sampen's luck caught up with him in 1992. In '91, Sampen had gone 9-5 for the Expos despite a mediocre 4.00 ERA. But last year, while splitting time between Montreal and Kansas City, Sampen's 1-6 record belied a fine 3.25 ERA. He didn't collect his lone victory of the year until August, shortly before he was traded to the Royals.

Sampen throws a decent fastball and a marginal slider, but needs to keep the ball down to succeed. Last year he did this better than ever before, allowing only four homers in 83 innings after surrendering 20 in 182.2 previous career innings. Mainly a reliever with both his major league clubs, Sampen seems to lack the stamina or repertoire to succeed as a starting pitcher. He lost both of his 1992 starts, posting a 6.75 ERA compared to a 2.88 relief mark. He does not have a good pickoff move, which is a major problem for a pitcher allowing a good number of baserunners. In 265.2 career innings, Sampen's permitted a whopping 48 steals in 61 attempts. He fields his position well.

OVERALL:

Sampen is one of several righthanders who'll battle for long relief roles with the Royals in 1993. The keys for him are to get his breaking ball over the plate and keep all his pitches down. If he can do that, he'll help the club this year.

STEVE SHIFFLETT

Position: RP
Bats: R **Throws:** R
Ht: 6' 1" **Wt:** 200

Opening Day Age: 27
Born: 1/5/66 in Kansas City, MO
ML Seasons: 1

Overall Statistics

	W	L	ERA	G	GS	Sv	IP	H	R	BB	SO	HR
1992	1	4	2.60	34	0	0	52.0	55	15	17	25	6
Career	1	4	2.60	34	0	0	52.0	55	15	17	25	6

PITCHING, FIELDING & HOLDING RUNNERS:

Steady minor league progress earned Kansas City native Steve Shifflett a major league recall last July. Shifflett succeeded immediately, allowing no runs in his first five appearances. He wound up pitching in 34 games, finishing 15 of them, and posting a fine 2.60 ERA. Between AAA Omaha and Kansas City, the busy righthander worked in 66 contests.

Shifflett throws a fastball, slider and change-up, but primarily relies on his good sinking fastball. When his stuff is working, he'll get a lot of groundball outs, but when he isn't sharp he can get hurt; he allowed six home runs in only 52 innings last year. Shifflett has the most trouble when his fastball comes in flat. Lefties feasted on sitting-duck fastballs from Shifflett last year, collecting eight of the 15 extra-base hits he allowed and slugging .494 against him. His pickoff move is unremarkable and he is an average fielder. He permitted three steals in four attempts last year.

OVERALL:

Shifflett is another righthander in the Royals' crowded bullpen. He's one of the younger members of the bullpen, though, and his steady minor-league progress may give him an edge against the journeymen he'll be fighting for a spot relief role in 1993. If Shifflett doesn't win a job in spring training, he'll likely be an early recall this year.

ORGANIZATION OVERVIEW:

Once one of the dominant franchises in baseball, the Royals have become a dull, losing organization over the last few seasons. Whither Kansas City? They got burned in the free agent market when they signed the Davises (Mark and Storm), so they don't do much of that sort of thing any more; they've tried blockbuster trading (Saberhagen to the Mets), but that hasn't worked yet either. The old heroes have gone or are going downhill, and they don't seem to know how to replace them. The Royals still develop some good prospects, but where are the franchise players?

BOB HAMELIN

Position: DH
Bats: L **Throws:** L
Ht: 6' 0" **Wt:** 230
Opening Day Age: 25
Born: 11/29/67 in Elizabeth, NJ

Recent Statistics

	G	AB	R	H	D	T	HR	RBI	SB	BB	SO	AVG
91 AAA Omaha	37	127	13	24	3	1	4	19	0	16	32	.189
92 A Baseball Cy	11	44	7	12	0	1	1	6	0	2	11	.273
92 AA Memphis	35	120	23	40	8	0	6	22	0	26	17	.333
92 AAA Omaha	27	95	9	19	3	1	5	15	0	14	15	.200
92 MLE	62	207	26	51	9	0	7	30	0	29	33	.246

Bob Hamelin could probably fit into Steve Balboni's old uniform, and if healthy, he could be a fair approximation of the old Royal hero: low average, high power, no speed. Hamelin, who hits from the left side, has excellent discipline -- and an aching back which is wrecking his career. In five years in the minors, Hamelin has only 1,103 at-bats, about two seasons worth; his average per "season" is 29 homers, 100 RBI, 114 walks. He's said to be finally healthy, and if he is, he could help somebody this year.

PHIL HIATT

Position: 3B
Bats: R **Throws:** R
Ht: 6' 3" **Wt:** 187
Opening Day Age: 23
Born: 5/1/69 in Pensacola, FL

Recent Statistics

	G	AB	R	H	D	T	HR	RBI	SB	BB	SO	AVG
91 A Baseball Cy	81	315	41	94	21	6	5	33	28	22	70	.298
91 AA Memphis	56	206	29	47	7	1	6	33	6	9	63	.228
92 AA Memphis	129	487	71	119	20	5	27	83	5	25	157	.244
92 AAA Omaha	5	14	3	3	0	0	2	4	1	2	3	.214
92 MLE	134	485	60	106	19	4	19	71	3	18	173	.219

Considered a power-hitting prospect, Hiatt proved it last year by hitting 29 homers with 87 RBI at AA Memphis and AAA Omaha. He also hit .244, and struck out 162 times while walking only 27 times, so you could say there's a few holes in his swing. He stole 34 bases in 1991 but was only 6-for-16 in '92. And his defense has been a little shaky, though he does have a good arm. He figures to start this year at Omaha; since the Royals need power, he could be up soon.

DANNY MICELI

Position: P
Bats: R **Throws:** R
Ht: 6' 1" **Wt:** 185
Opening Day Age: 22
Born: 9/9/70 in Newark, NJ

Recent Statistics

	W	L	ERA	G	GS	Sv	IP	H	R	BB	SO	HR
91 A Eugene	0	1	2.14	25	0	10	33.2	18	8	18	43	1
92 A Appleton	1	1	1.93	23	0	9	23.1	12	6	4	44	0
92 AA Memphis	3	0	1.91	32	0	4	37.2	20	10	13	46	5

Yet another undrafted free agent who came on in a hurry, Miceli moved from Appleton in the low-Class A Midwest League to AA Memphis of the Southern League last year without missing a beat. The reliever had ERAs below 2.00 at each spot with outstanding strikeout totals: 44 Ks in 23.1 innings at Appleton, 46 in 37.2 innings at Memphis. His control is good, and he's only 22. Keep an eye on him this year.

HARVEY PULLIAM

Position: OF
Bats: R **Throws:** R
Ht: 6' 0" **Wt:** 210
Opening Day Age: 25
Born: 10/20/67 in San Francisco, CA

Recent Statistics

	G	AB	R	H	D	T	HR	RBI	SB	BB	SO	AVG
92 AAA Omaha	100	359	55	97	12	2	16	60	4	32	53	.270
92 AL Kansas City	4	5	2	1	1	0	0	0	0	1	3	.200
92 MLE	100	346	44	84	11	1	10	48	2	25	55	.243

A 210-pound outfielder, Pulliam has some power, shown by his 16 homers in 359 at-bats at Omaha last year. With the Royals he's hit three more in 38 career AB. He doesn't run particularly well and is no better than average on defense, but Pulliam could probably provide a little punch off somebody's bench. With expansion, players like him often get a chance.

TIM SPEHR

Position: C
Bats: R **Throws:** R
Ht: 6' 2" **Wt:** 205
Opening Day Age: 26
Born: 7/2/66 in Excelsior Springs, MO

Recent Statistics

	G	AB	R	H	D	T	HR	RBI	SB	BB	SO	AVG
91 AAA Omaha	72	215	27	59	14	2	6	26	3	25	48	.274
92 AAA Omaha	109	336	48	85	22	0	15	42	4	61	89	.253
92 MLE	109	324	38	73	20	0	10	33	2	49	93	.225

The Royals haven't had a dominant catcher in several years, so Spehr figures to be in the hunt for playing time with Mike Macfarlane and Brent Mayne this season. Spehr is considered an excellent defensive catcher and was chosen as the American Association's best-fielding backstop in last year's Baseball America poll. His hitting improved greatly last year: 22 doubles, 15 homers and 61 walks in only 336 at-bats at AAA Omaha. He has a good chance of making the Royals roster this year.

JAMES AUSTIN

Position: RP
Bats: R **Throws:** R
Ht: 6' 2" **Wt:** 200

Opening Day Age: 29
Born: 12/7/63 in Farmville, VA
ML Seasons: 2

PITCHING:

The Brewers restocked their bullpen for the 1992 campaign, and one important addition was James Austin, a 28-year-old rookie. A righthander who had quietly and methodically worked his way up the Brewers' ladder after coming over in a 1989 trade with San Diego, Austin proved to be a major surprise. His 1.85 ERA was bettered only by Cal Eldred on the Milwaukee staff.

Austin had actually made the big club in 1991 after posting a 2.45 ERA in 44 innings in the rarified air of Denver. However, chronic neck problems shelved him after just five ineffective appearances (8.31 ERA). The same problems kept him out of spring training in 1990, but he pitched that season at AA El Paso and completed the transition from starter to reliever. His main weapon is a great slider that is effective up in the strike zone. The pitch yields many fly balls, but also misses for a high number of walks. Austin gave up 26 unintentional walks in his 58.1 innings, a high ratio.

Austin, who finished fifth in the league in relief ERA, gave up half of his 12 earned runs in just two games, and didn't allow a single earned run in August and September. During a stretch from early August to mid-September, he didn't allow a hit or walk in 10 of 12 games. After the All-Star break, his era was just 1.09. He was deadly when he got two strikes on hitters, holding them to a .067 average.

HOLDING RUNNERS AND FIELDING:

Austin holds runners well, and of the six runners who attempted to steal, four were caught. As a flyball pitcher, he doesn't get many chances afield, delivering a couple of assists and putouts last year and committing no errors.

OVERALL:

Obviously, any pitcher who walks as many hitters as Austin is pitching on thin ice. Still, he's pitched well for three years now and his slider is potent. The Brewers will certainly be counting on him in 1993.

Overall Statistics

	W	L	ERA	G	GS	Sv	IP	H	R	BB	SO	HR
1992	5	2	1.85	47	0	0	58.1	38	13	32	30	2
Career	5	2	2.69	52	0	0	67.0	46	21	43	33	3

How Often He Throws Strikes

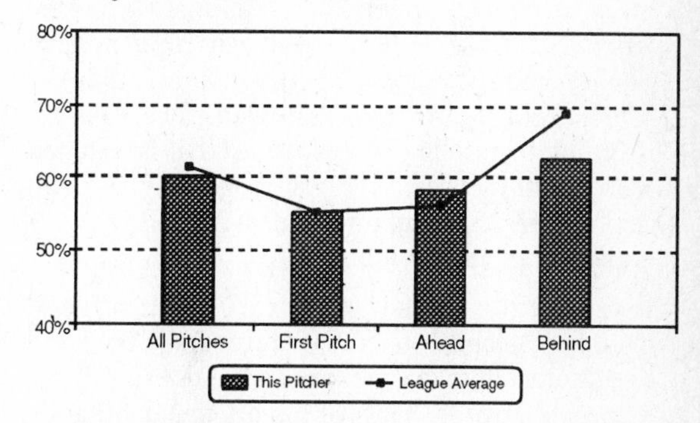

1992 Situational Stats

	W	L	ERA	Sv	IP		AB	H	HR	RBI	AVG
Home	2	1	1.11	0	32.1	LHB	82	18	0	5	.220
Road	3	1	2.77	0	26.0	RHB	117	20	2	11	.171
Day	1	1	4.67	0	17.1	Sc Pos	61	11	1	15	.180
Night	4	1	0.66	0	41.0	Clutch	51	9	0	7	.176

1992 Rankings (American League)

- 2nd in first batter efficiency (.135)
- 4th in lowest batting average allowed in relief (.191)
- 5th in lowest relief ERA (1.85)
- 10th in least strikeouts per 9 innings in relief (4.6)
- Led the Brewers in first batter efficiency and relief ERA

RICKY BONES

Position: SP
Bats: R **Throws:** R
Ht: 6' 0" **Wt:** 190

Opening Day Age: 24
Born: 4/7/69 in Salinas, Puerto Rico
ML Seasons: 2

PITCHING:

Ricky Bones came to the Brewers as part of the Gary Sheffield trade, along with Jose Valentin and promising outfielder Matt Mieske. His pitching was lackluster, and it's likely that he remained in the rotation only because of the injury absence of Ron Robinson and Teddy Higuera. Bones was 9-10 in a starting role, and his 4.76 starter's ERA (4.57 overall) attest to his difficulties.

Bones gave up more than a hit per inning for the sixth time in seven professional seasons, and his usual 2-to-1 strikeout-to-walk ratio took a turn for the worse. His opposing-hitter stats look quite similar to what Ruben Sierra did last year, but with more power. Though he worked only 163.1 innings, Bones gave up 27 home runs. He led the league in home runs allowed per nine innings pitched and trailed only Scott Sanderson in highest slugging percentage allowed. The one redeeming feature in his season was that he pitched well down the stretch. From August 18 through September 25, Bones posted a 2.40 ERA over eight games and 45 innings.

Bones throws a variety of breaking pitches, and even his fastball comes in two flavors, a riser and a splitter, neither overpowering. He doesn't throw a straight change. Each of his pitches is hittable, and he grooves an enormous number of them, regardless of the count.

HOLDING BASERUNNERS AND FIELDING:

Bones is good on comebackers, but he's doesn't display much range and made two errors. Perhaps his no-brain fielding is due to his youth and his struggles on the mound. He also did a poor job holding baserunners. Only two of his 15 base thieves were nabbed.

OVERALL:

Bones has managed to win games throughout his career (his record as a professional is 67-52) despite giving up home runs, more hits than innings pitched, and posting high ERAs. He has to make the obvious improvements -- find an out pitch and cut down the home runs -- to improve his stock, but he's shown enough to earn another shot in 1993. He's still only 24.

Overall Statistics

	W	L	ERA	G	GS	Sv	IP	H	R	BB	SO	HR
1992	9	10	4.57	31	28	0	163.1	169	90	48	65	27
Career	13	16	4.64	42	39	0	217.1	226	123	66	96	30

How Often He Throws Strikes

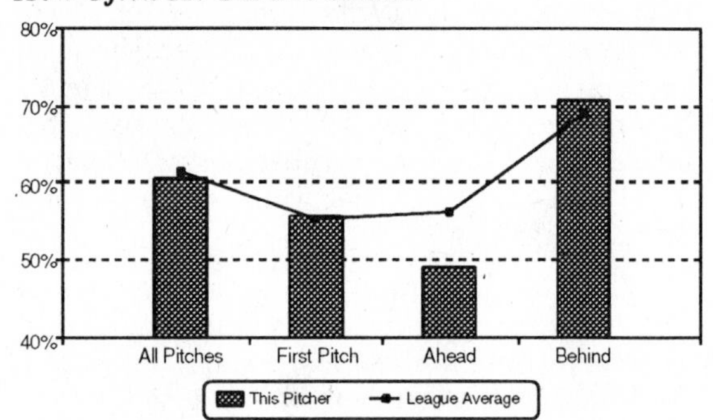

1992 Situational Stats

	W	L	ERA	Sv	IP		AB	H	HR	RBI	AVG
Home	6	4	3.25	0	99.2	LHB	302	81	9	22	.268
Road	3	6	6.64	0	63.2	RHB	339	88	18	52	.260
Day	4	2	4.02	0	62.2	Sc Pos	122	27	3	43	.221
Night	5	8	4.92	0	100.2	Clutch	39	8	2	2	.205

1992 Rankings (American League)

- 1st in highest stolen base percentage allowed (86.7%) and most home runs allowed per 9 innings (1.5)
- 2nd in highest slugging percentage allowed (.448)
- 3rd in least strikeouts per 9 innings (3.6)
- 4th in highest ERA (4.57)
- 5th in balks (2)
- 6th in home runs allowed (27) and hit batsmen (9)
- Led the Brewers in hit batsmen and balks

PINPOINT CONTROL

PITCHING:

The Brewers' ace by default, Chris Bosio had his first season without being disabled since 1989. Bosio did have his injury woes. He missed a couple of starts due to knee and back problems and suffered from a planter's wart on his right foot in April. But he started 33 games, matching his career high, and his .727 winning percentage was a personal-best and fourth in the league last year.

Bosio is a finesse pitcher with a change-up that makes his fastball look more explosive. His control has always been excellent, but in 1991 his strikeout-to-walk ratio dropped to 2-to-1 from his established rate of 3-to-1. That trend continued through the first two months of 1992, and Bosio struggled at the .500 level with an ERA over 5.00 through May. From June on, he cut his walks in half and posted an ERA of 2.82. During an eight-game stretch from June to August, he walked only one batter.

Bosio has often put himself at risk by trying to avoid the walk, resulting in too many easy strikes. In 1992 he did give up a career high 21 homers, but permitted less than one hit per inning. He's had great success inducing the double play. With excellent run support, he reeled off a team record 10 straight wins in the second half (soon tied by Cal Eldred).

HOLDING BASERUNNERS AND FIELDING:

Bosio doesn't have much range, but he covers first well and doesn't make errors. His awareness led to five double plays, second only to Frank Viola among American League pitchers. Bosio's a tempting man to run on, with 19 would-be stealers, but he helped his catchers nab seven of them.

OVERALL:

The Brewers would have loved to keep Bosio, but the free agent signed a big-bucks contract with Seattle. He is not a calm presence on a team, and he had one memorable exchange on the mound with Phil Garner last year. Bosio probably can't wait to meet Lou Piniella.

CHRIS BOSIO

Position: SP
Bats: R **Throws:** R
Ht: 6' 3" **Wt:** 225

Opening Day Age: 30
Born: 4/3/63 in Carmichael, CA
ML Seasons: 7

Overall Statistics

	W	L	ERA	G	GS	Sv	IP	H	R	BB	SO	HR
1992	16	6	3.62	33	33	0	231.1	223	100	44	120	21
Career	67	62	3.76	212	163	8	1190.0	1184	546	289	749	107

How Often He Throws Strikes

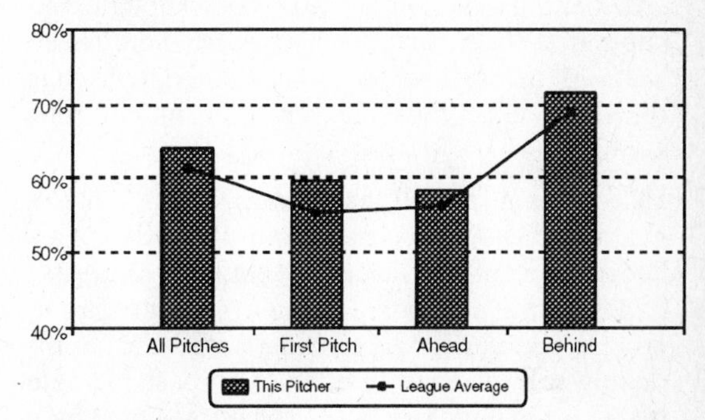

1992 Situational Stats

	W	L	ERA	Sv	IP		AB	H	HR	RBI	AVG
Home	9	3	3.03	0	127.2	LHB	421	115	10	39	.273
Road	7	3	4.34	0	103.2	RHB	457	108	11	49	.236
Day	5	2	3.84	0	68.0	Sc Pos	174	43	6	65	.247
Night	11	4	3.53	0	163.1	Clutch	92	24	0	5	.261

1992 Rankings (American League)

- 3rd in least pitches thrown per batter (3.33)
- 4th in winning percentage (.727) and strikeout/walk ratio (2.7)
- 5th in balks (2)
- Led the Brewers in wild pitches (8), balks, GDPs induced (25), winning percentage, strikeout/walk ratio, lowest on-base percentage allowed (.291), least pitches thrown per batter, least baserunners allowed per 9 innings (10.5), most run support per 9 innings (5.2), most GDPs induced per 9 innings (.97), most strikeouts per 9 innings (4.7) and lowest batting average allowed with runners in scoring position (.247)

CAL ELDRED

Position: SP
Bats: R **Throws:** R
Ht: 6' 4" **Wt:** 215

Opening Day Age: 25
Born: 11/24/67 in Cedar Rapids, IA
ML Seasons: 2

PITCHING:

After being shipped back to Denver to start the 1992 season, Cal Eldred said "I'm extremely frustrated. I'm tired of being patient." He responded by going 10-6 with a an ERA of 3.00 in offense-happy Denver. Recalled on July 15, Eldred spent the rest of the season taking out his frustrations on American League hitters. He went 11-2 with a 1.79 ERA in his half-season with the Brewers, nearly pitching Milwaukee to a division title.

Eldred's 10 consecutive victories tied a Brewer record, set five days before by Chris Bosio -- although Eldred's string was accomplished in 10 consecutive starts. He held opposing hitters to a .207 batting average for the season. Though well supported (6.55 runs per game), he didn't need the help; in his 11 victories he allowed three runs once, two runs twice, one run twice, and no runs six times.

Eldred has a fastball that pushes 90 MPH and a sharp curve. As he's moved up the ladder he's become less of a strikeout pitcher, though he still had 5.6 strikeouts per nine innings for the Brewers. He continually keeps hitters off-balance, inducing soft outs and limiting extra-base hits. He mixes up his pitches, but is sometimes hurt by a tendency to go for the kill too quickly when he gets ahead of the batter.

HOLDING RUNNERS AND FIELDING:

A big guy and somewhat deliberate in his motion, Eldred is vulnerable to the steal, allowing eight thefts in 12 attempts. Experience can probably help him in that area. His fielding is hard to judge since he hasn't pitched all that much, but he covers first well and made just one error.

OVERALL:

Eldred's numbers are so overpowering that they are suspect, since his stuff does not anything like a Ryan fastball or a Koufax curve. He could be for real; in 1992 he was 2-0 with a no-decision in the three games in which he faced a team for the second time. Eldred's nickname is "Cornfield" because he's tall and lives in Urbana, Iowa, close to the Field of Dreams. It seems appropriate, given his storybook arrival in 1992.

Overall Statistics

	W	L	ERA	G	GS	Sv	IP	H	R	BB	SO	HR
1992	11	2	1.79	14	14	0	100.1	76	21	23	62	4
Career	13	2	2.17	17	17	0	116.1	96	30	29	72	6

How Often He Throws Strikes

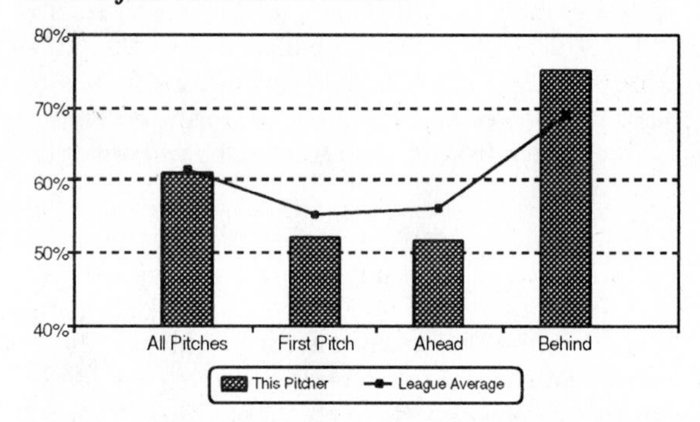

1992 Situational Stats

	W	L	ERA	Sv	IP		AB	H	HR	RBI	AVG
Home	7	0	0.76	0	59.0	LHB	154	29	2	4	.188
Road	4	2	3.27	0	41.1	RHB	213	47	2	10	.221
Day	4	2	2.40	0	41.1	Sc Pos	67	7	0	7	.104
Night	7	0	1.37	0	59.0	Clutch	48	10	0	3	.208

1992 Rankings (American League)

- 3rd in lowest batting average allowed vs. left-handed batters (.188)
- Led the Brewers in lowest batting average allowed vs. left-handed batters

PITCHING:

Former number-one Angel pick Mike Fetters never had a losing record as he worked his way towards the majors as a starter. A surplus of California starters forced him to make the transition to the bullpen in the majors as a somewhat immature 25-year-old. In 1990 he was rocked coming out of the pen, and he spent time in the majors and the minors in 1991, showing no improvement. The Angels traded him to Milwaukee for Chuck Crim in December of 1991. The Brewers didn't expect a lot, but they wound up with a rock-solid middle reliever with a 1.87 ERA.

Fetters has a standard fastball-curve-slider repertoire, keeping the ball down, and forces batters to hit the ball on the ground. Manager Phil Garner brought him along slowly, rarely working him more than two innings and being careful about resting him between outings. Fetters responded by allowing one earned run in his first 20 games.

Fetters also stopped grooving the first pitch while developing his killer instinct; he got to two strikes on nearly half the batters he faced, after which he allowed them only an .098 average. He was sixth in relief ERA (pen mate Jim Austin was fifth), and was second in lowest relief batting average allowed (.185). His 2.97 second-half ERA looks bad only when compared to the 0.84 ERA he posted in the first half. The other side of the trade, Chuck Crim, had an ERA of 5.17 in 1992.

HOLDING RUNNERS AND FIELDING:

Fetters holds runners well, and they don't often attempt to steal. He also tends to be right around the plate, putting his catchers in good position to throw. Of the seven runners who attempted to steal against him, three were caught. He fields his position well.

OVERALL:

The Brewers are loaded with sensational right-handed middle relief even after losing Darren Holmes to expansion. Though Fetters allows few baserunners, he is still unlikely to be promoted to closer if Doug Henry continues his erratic work. Whatever his role, he seems capable of putting together another strong season.

MIKE FETTERS

Position: RP
Bats: R **Throws:** R
Ht: 6' 4" **Wt:** 212

Opening Day Age: 28
Born: 12/19/64 in Van Nuys, CA
ML Seasons: 4

Overall Statistics

	W	L	ERA	G	GS	Sv	IP	H	R	BB	SO	HR
1992	5	1	1.87	50	0	2	62.2	38	15	24	43	3
Career	8	7	3.58	96	6	3	178.1	173	81	73	106	17

How Often He Throws Strikes

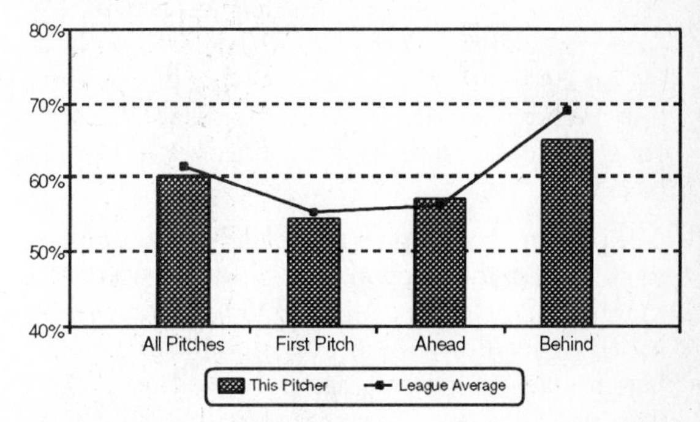

1992 Situational Stats

	W	L	ERA	Sv	IP		AB	H	HR	RBI	AVG
Home	2	0	0.63	1	28.2	LHB	71	16	1	8	.225
Road	3	1	2.91	1	34.0	RHB	134	22	2	18	.164
Day	2	0	3.71	0	17.0	Sc Pos	67	15	1	24	.224
Night	3	1	1.18	2	45.2	Clutch	89	13	1	12	.146

1992 Rankings (American League)

- 2nd in lowest batting average allowed in relief (.185)
- 6th in lowest relief ERA (1.87)
- 10th in most GDPs induced per GDP situation (18.2%) and least baserunners allowed per 9 innings in relief (9.9)
- Led the Brewers in most GDPs induced per GDP situation, lowest batting average allowed in relief and least baserunners allowed per 9 innings in relief

SCOTT FLETCHER

Position: 2B/SS
Bats: R **Throws:** R
Ht: 5'11" **Wt:** 173

Opening Day Age: 34
Born: 7/30/58 in Fort Walton Beach, FL
ML Seasons: 12

HITTING:

The Brewers were pleased with the 1991 performance of Jim Gantner, but with Gantner then 38 years old, they decided to sign veteran Scott Fletcher as insurance. Fletcher had been released by the White Sox partly due to their trade for Steve Sax, but mostly because of his own sliding performance. He had batted just .206 in 1991, though his defensive play remained steady. After a solid spring, Fletcher made the Milwaukee club, eventually won the second base job, and went on to hit .275, his best season since 1988.

Fletcher rebounded at the plate by becoming more aggressive. In 1991 he was tentative, and pitchers easily got ahead of him in the count. In 1992 he came out swinging and jumped on the first-pitch strikes that pitchers were feeding him. He hit .344 in April and .298 in May in part-time duty. When Gantner went on the disabled list in June, Fletcher pretty much took over at second base.

The pitchers got tougher and Fletcher didn't hit as well during the second half. But he was very tough in the clutch, hitting .336 with runners in scoring position, good for eighth-best in the league. He hit lefties amazingly well at .308. It was a solid professional season.

BASERUNNING:

Fletcher's 27 stolen base attempts last year were a career high, as were his 17 steals. He clearly caught Garner's running fever. He runs well, and his 53 runs scored were impressive for a 33-year-old batting mostly in the number nine spot.

FIELDING:

Fletcher is a defensive standout at second base, with good range, sure hands and a fine arm. He is very good on the double play, and his experience helped Pat Listach. His play at shortstop is not nearly as strong. He made five errors there in just 22 games.

OVERALL:

The Brewers had numerous middle-infield possibilities, and free agent Fletcher wound up signing with Boston. He outplayed Jody Reed last year; now he'll be taking Reed's place.

Overall Statistics

	G	AB	R	H	D	T	HR	RBI	SB	BB	SO	AVG
1992	123	386	53	106	18	3	3	51	17	30	33	.275
Career	1361	4411	557	1155	193	31	25	437	74	442	465	.262

Where He Hits the Ball

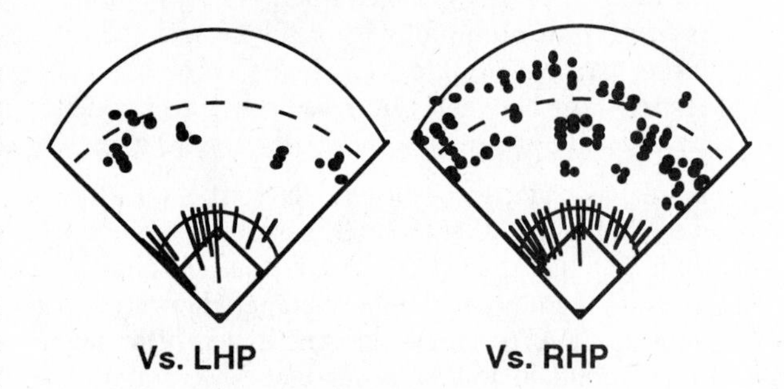

1992 Situational Stats

	AB	H	HR	RBI	AVG		AB	H	HR	RBI	AVG
Home	175	55	2	26	.314	LHP	104	32	0	13	.308
Road	211	51	1	25	.242	RHP	282	74	3	38	.262
Day	109	31	0	10	.284	Sc Pos	107	36	2	47	.336
Night	277	75	3	41	.271	Clutch	63	18	1	14	.286

1992 Rankings (American League)

- 7th in lowest stolen base percentage (63.0%)
- 8th in batting average with runners in scoring position (.336)
- Led the Brewers in hit by pitch (7), batting average with runners in scoring position and batting average with the bases loaded (.500)

HITTING:

Darryl Hamilton is a typical Brewer hitter, and somewhat like one of their pitchers: good control and finesse, but no power. Hamilton hits everything on the ground, rarely strikes out, walks a little, and is fast. The lefty swinger hit and fielded his way to everyday status in 1991. Though he had problems with lefties last year, Hamilton continued to be a very steady player. Over the last three seasons, he's batted .295, .311 and .298. Slowed by a strained quadriceps injury that put him on the disabled list in May, he batted .313 after his return.

Hamilton hit his usual high average, trailed only Paul Molitor on the club in on-base percentage, and in late-and-close situations was dominant, hitting .362 with a .522 slugging average. But he batted just .247 against lefties, which was a return to earth after the .276 mark he recorded in 1991. Manager Phil Garner used Hamilton wisely, giving him over four times as many at-bats against the righties he handles so well. He got 27 extra-base hits against righties and only four against lefthanders.

BASERUNNING:

The injury didn't affect Hamilton's speed. He was 9-for-11 as a base thief before he went on the DL. Hamilton was a speedster in the minors and Garner gave everyone the green light, so Hamilton ran 55 times total on the year. In the first half he was a spectacular 20-of-24, but he slipped after the break and was only 10-for-17 in September/October.

FIELDING:

Hamilton got most of his playing time in right field, sharing time with Dante Bichette. Though Bichette is the one with the rocket arm, Hamilton had eight assists in right to Dante's six, in fewer innings. He has great range at all three outfield positions and made no errors.

OVERALL:

Despite his problems with southpaws, Hamilton has proven his worth. With his speed and on-base ability, he should be able to score close to 100 runs given good health. His problem doing so with the Brewers is that they have lacked the big boppers to drive him in.

DARRYL HAMILTON

Position: RF/LF/CF
Bats: L **Throws:** R
Ht: 6' 1" **Wt:** 180

Opening Day Age: 28
Born: 12/3/64 in Baton Rouge, LA
ML Seasons: 4

Overall Statistics

	G	AB	R	H	D	T	HR	RBI	SB	BB	SO	AVG
1992	128	470	67	140	19	7	5	62	41	45	42	.298
Career	383	1134	172	331	43	13	8	148	74	99	101	.292

Where He Hits the Ball

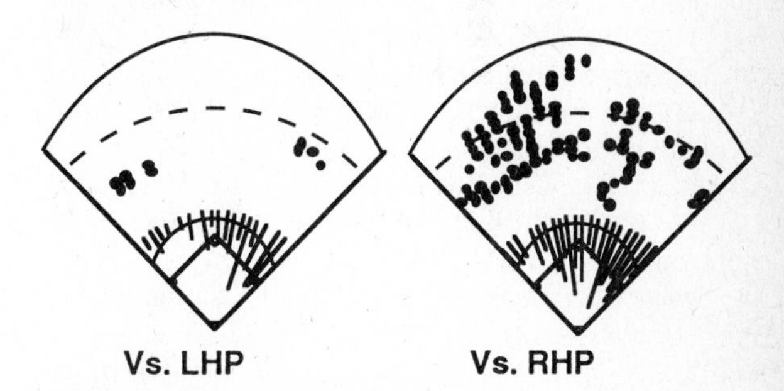

1992 Situational Stats

	AB	H	HR	RBI	AVG		AB	H	HR	RBI	AVG
Home	233	67	1	30	.288	LHP	89	22	0	13	.247
Road	237	73	4	32	.308	RHP	381	118	5	49	.310
Day	145	33	2	20	.228	Sc Pos	136	40	1	56	.294
Night	325	107	3	42	.329	Clutch	69	25	1	8	.362

1992 Rankings (American League)

- 4th in batting average in the clutch (.362)
- 6th in caught stealing (14)
- Led the Brewers in triples (7), batting average in the clutch, batting average vs. right-handed pitchers (.310), slugging percentage vs. right-handed pitchers (.423), highest percentage of pitches taken (59.4%) and outfield assists (8)
- Led AL right fielders in batting average (.298), singles (109), triples, highest groundball/flyball ratio (2.1), stolen base percentage (74.6%), batting average in the clutch, batting average vs. right-handed pitchers, on-base percentage vs. right-handed pitchers (.363), batting average with 2 strikes (.245) and bunts in play (19)

DOUG HENRY

Position: RP
Bats: R **Throws:** R
Ht: 6' 4" **Wt:** 185

Opening Day Age: 29
Born: 12/10/63 in Sacramento, CA
ML Seasons: 2

PITCHING:

If the sign of a true pitcher is his ability to succeed even when he doesn't have his best stuff, then Doug Henry is a pitcher's pitcher. Henry posted a 5.63 ERA in April, but saved 4 games in five chances. In July his ERA was 4.35, and he saved seven of eight. In August his ERA was an unbelievable 10.22 -- yet he saved five games in six opportunities. Between these bouts of shaky pitching were flashes of brilliance, like the 14-game stretch from May 27 through the end of June when he gave up a single run. For the year Henry had a high 4.02 ERA but posted 29 saves in 33 opportunities.

Although Henry's performance slipped across the board from 1991, his biggest problems were when he came into a game with runners on. Pitching from the stretch obviously bothers him, and only four relievers allowed a higher batting average with runners in scoring position than his .386 mark. Right-handed hitters really knocked him on the ropes in 1992. He allowed a .292 average to righties with a .493 slugging percentage. Henry was effective against lefties (.208), though he put too many on base.

A power pitcher who throws a fastball, forkball and slider, Henry trailed only Dennis Eckersley and Tom Henke among AL pitchers in save percentage at 88 percent. In his 68 appearances, tied for sixth in the league, the Brewers were 47-21. Like Eddie Stanky, all he does is beat you.

HOLDING RUNNERS AND FIELDING:

Henry holds runners well, or perhaps they simply waited for the hits and walks he was allowing. Either way, he limited runners to four steals in seven attempts last year. He made no errors, started two double plays, and generally fielded well.

OVERALL:

Given the excellence of the other righthanders in the Brewer pen, it is possible that Henry will be closing games on probation status in the spring of 1993. But he has certainly demonstrated a closer's mentality, and his career 44 saves in 49 chances are eloquent on his behalf.

Overall Statistics

	W	L	ERA	G	GS	Sv	IP	H	R	BB	SO	HR
1992	1	4	4.02	68	0	29	65.0	64	34	24	52	6
Career	3	5	2.94	100	0	44	101.0	80	38	38	80	7

How Often He Throws Strikes

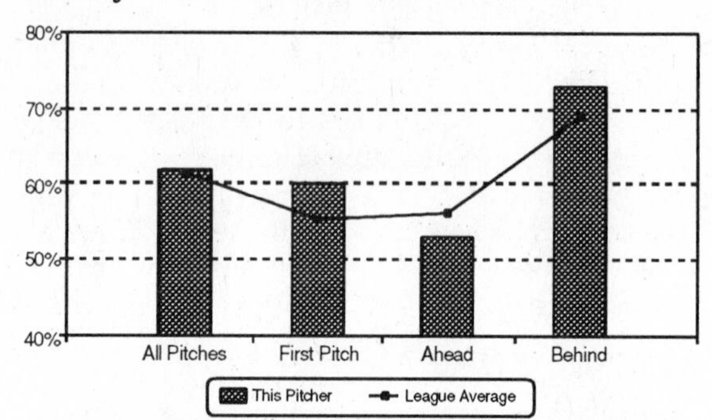

1992 Situational Stats

	W	L	ERA	Sv	IP		AB	H	HR	RBI	AVG
Home	0	1	2.72	19	36.1	LHB	106	22	1	12	.208
Road	1	3	5.65	10	28.2	RHB	144	42	5	28	.292
Day	0	0	1.59	12	22.2	Sc Pos	57	22	4	35	.386
Night	1	4	5.31	17	42.1	Clutch	141	35	1	22	.248

1992 Rankings (American League)

- → 3rd in highest save percentage (87.9%)
- → 5th in games finished (56)
- → 7th in games pitched (68)
- → 8th in saves (29)
- → 10th in save opportunities (33)
- → Led the Brewers in games pitched, saves, games finished, save opportunities, save percentage, blown saves (4), relief innings (65) and most strikeouts per 9 innings in relief (7.2)

JOHN JAHA

Position: 1B
Bats: R **Throws:** R
Ht: 6' 1" **Wt:** 195

Opening Day Age: 26
Born: 5/27/66 in Portland, OR
ML Seasons: 1

HITTING:

After a year in AA ball in 1991 in which he garnered nearly every major award, John Jaha moved up to AAA Denver in 1992. His stay was short but spectacular -- but the same can't be said about Jaha's performance for the Brewers after his midseason recall. The youngster batted .226 with only two homers in 133 at-bats for Milwaukee.

Denver's mountain air was great to Jaha. He hit a 515-foot home run and was named the best hitting prospect in AAA ball by Baseball America. After 79 games his numbers were .321-18-69 with 50 walks. He strikes out often as a function of his tremendous power, but has twice drawn more than 100 walks in a minor league season and has a career minor league on-base average of .428.

Jaha had a difficult adjustment to the major leagues. He was called up in July and struggled, particularly against lefties. After an initial bout of free-swinging, he began to get more patient, which at first helped his batting line. However, then he began taking too many pitches and falling behind in the count. He went into a slump and was played sparingly in September.

BASERUNNING:

Jaha was the 11th Brewer to steal at least 10 bases, tying a record set by the 1901 Phillies. More impressive, he was a perfect 10-for-10. If his minor league record is any indicator, 10 steals is about his limit, but with Garner setting the pace, Jaha may add a new dimension to his offensive arsenal.

FIELDING:

Jaha is an experienced first baseman after his long minor-league career. He didn't make an error in his 38 appearances, and his putouts, assists and double plays were about average.

OVERALL:

Jaha was old for a rookie at age 27, and therefore needs to produce immediately. The Brewers may be wary, because his two huge minor-league seasons were compiled in situations where offense is greatly inflated. That being said, he is certainly a major-league hitter who should show a good eye and power, though not like he had in Denver and El Paso. Jaha was an expansion protection.

Overall Statistics

	G	AB	R	H	D	T	HR	RBI	SB	BB	SO	AVG
1992	47	133	17	30	3	1	2	10	10	12	30	.226
Career	47	133	17	30	3	1	2	10	10	12	30	.226

Where He Hits the Ball

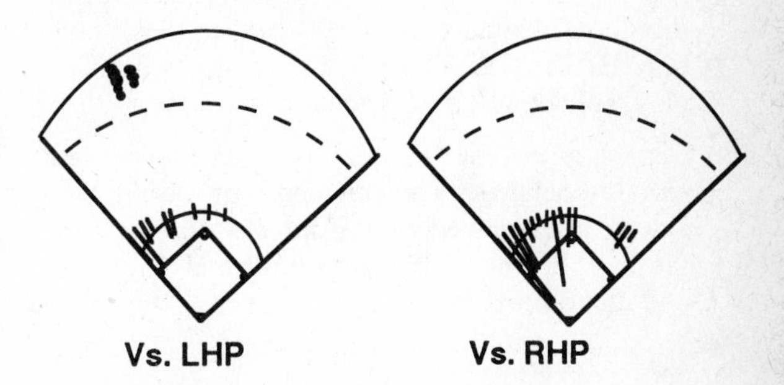

1992 Situational Stats

	AB	H	HR	RBI	AVG		AB	H	HR	RBI	AVG
Home	87	19	1	5	.218	LHP	46	8	1	5	.174
Road	46	11	1	5	.239	RHP	87	22	1	5	.253
Day	43	5	1	4	.116	Sc Pos	27	6	0	8	.222
Night	90	25	1	6	.278	Clutch	19	6	0	1	.316

1992 Rankings (American League)

- Did not rank near the top or bottom in any category

PAT LISTACH

Position: SS
Bats: B **Throws:** R
Ht: 5' 9" **Wt:** 170

Opening Day Age: 25
Born: 9/12/67 in Natchitoches, LA
ML Seasons: 1

Overall Statistics

	G	AB	R	H	D	T	HR	RBI	SB	BB	SO	AVG
1992	149	579	93	168	19	6	1	47	54	55	124	.290
Career	149	579	93	168	19	6	1	47	54	55	124	.290

Where He Hits the Ball

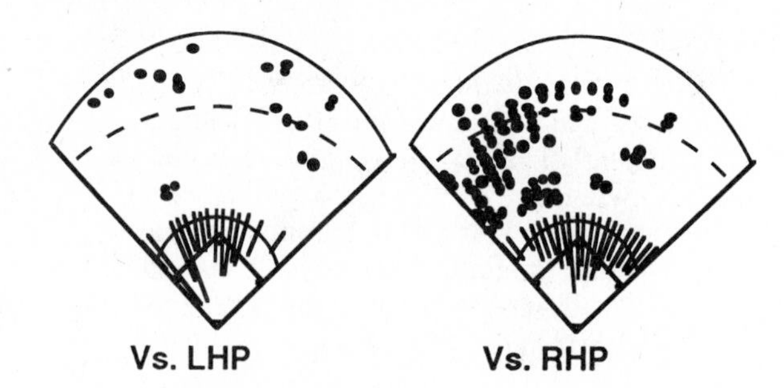

1992 Situational Stats

	AB	H	HR	RBI	AVG		AB	H	HR	RBI	AVG
Home	267	67	0	26	.251	LHP	148	51	1	18	.345
Road	312	101	1	21	.324	RHP	431	117	0	29	.271
Day	177	53	0	17	.299	Sc Pos	145	38	0	41	.262
Night	402	115	1	30	.286	Clutch	89	31	0	12	.348

1992 Rankings (American League)

- 2nd in stolen bases (54), caught stealing (18) and bunts in play (46)
- 3rd in lowest HR frequency (579 ABs per HR), highest batting average on a 3-1 count (.667) and steals of third (9)
- 4th in sacrifice bunts (12) and least GDPs per GDP situation (3.0%)
- Led the Brewers in runs scored (93), singles (142), sacrifice bunts, stolen bases, caught stealing, strikeouts (124), most pitches seen (2,597), highest groundball/flyball ratio (2.1), most pitches seen per plate appearance (4.00), least GDPs per GDP situation, bunts in play and steals of third

HITTING:

There was no clue that Pat Listach would even play at the major league level in 1992, much less succeed. But Listach surprised everyone, taking the place of the injured Bill Spiers and batting a professional-high .290 in the heat of a pennant race. The youngster was rewarded with the American League Rookie of the Year award.

A switch-hitter, Listach has no power from the left side and posted a slugging average below his on-base average batting lefty. But he displayed offensive positives in every other area. He took over the leadoff position and led the team in runs scored and stolen bases. Listach knows how to use his talents, hitting almost everything on the ground. Despite this tendency, he grounded into just three double plays in 99 double play situation. He handles the bat well, putting 46 bunts in play, collecting 12 sacrifice hits.

Listach also took a leadership role, displaying a certain cockiness. He went through a brief June slump, but bounced back. And with the game on the line, he was at his best, hitting .348 in late-and-close situations.

BASERUNNING:

Listach likes to run; in 1990 in Stockton he stole 78 bases in 106 attempts. His success rate with the Brewers slipped as the season went on, perhaps from fatigue, but he broke Paul Molitor's Brewer record for steals in a season, and was second in the American League. He's a smart baserunner as well.

FIELDING:

Listach showed terrific range at shortstop, helping give some spark to an unsettled infield. He also made 24 errors, one of the worst marks in the league, but that's the way it is with young shortstops. He turns the double play well. Listach has probably pushed Spiers to second base.

OVERALL:

If Bill Spiers plays as well as he did in 1991, he and Listach should make up one of the league's most potent keystone combinations. The one most surprising area of Listach's 1992 performance was his high batting average. But even if he slips to his usual .250, with his positives he's definitely a major leaguer.

HITTING:

How great is Paul Molitor? After turning in a stellar season in 1991, he quietly produced at nearly that tremendous level in 1992. He led the Brewers in batting, on-base average, and slugging, and remained injury-free at age 35. He's always been rough on lefties, but 1992 was overwhelming -- he pounded southpaws for a .424 average and slugged -- brace yourself -- .659. His other totals suffered from his team's offensive shortcomings, but his 89 RBI still led the team.

Molitor is a free swinger, but in the past two years he's learned to take a walk. He drew 12 intentional walks as the opposition took advantage of Greg Vaughn's problems behind him in the order. His old nickname, "The Igniter" is more appropriate than ever; he can make an offense go. Molitor is a competitor and would like to win. He talks annually about retiring, but the Brewers have developed a habit of strong finishes and the annual wait-til-next-year hopes that come with them, so he's hung around.

BASERUNNING:

Still quick at age 36, Molitor is a great baserunner. His 31 steals were his most since 1988, and his 84 percent success rate placed him seventh in the American League. He still beats out singles in the hole and takes the extra base.

FIELDING:

The most interesting thing about Molitor's fielding is his hitting. While playing first base, for the second straight year, he has hit like a storybook first baseman. In 194 at-bats while playing first he hit .371 and slugged .541. He can field, but the Brewers have learned to keep him out of harm's way.

OVERALL:

Molitor has had a career obscured by injuries, but his durability in the last few seasons has been excellent. He's put up great major-league career totals, stealing 412 bases and hitting 405 doubles with a career batting average of over .300. He seems a lock for 2,500 or more hits. A free agent, Molitor was thought to be headed either back to Milwaukee or to his Twin Cities birthplace. One of the main factors is to be where he can go out a winner.

PAUL MOLITOR

Position: DH/1B
Bats: R **Throws:** R
Ht: 6' 0" **Wt:** 185
Opening Day Age: 36
Born: 8/22/56 in St. Paul, MN
ML Seasons: 15

Overall Statistics

	G	AB	R	H	D	T	HR	RBI	SB	BB	SO	AVG
1992	158	609	89	195	36	7	12	89	31	73	66	.320
Career	1856	7520	1275	2281	405	86	160	790	412	755	882	.303

Where He Hits the Ball

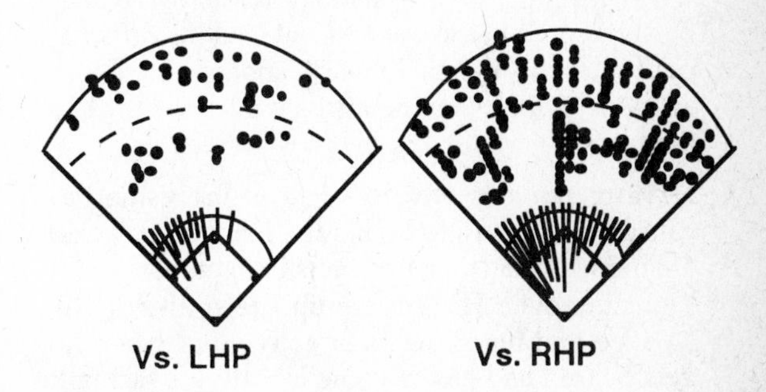

1992 Situational Stats

	AB	H	HR	RBI	AVG		AB	H	HR	RBI	AVG
Home	286	87	4	36	.304	LHP	132	56	6	32	.424
Road	323	108	8	53	.334	RHP	477	139	6	57	.291
Day	200	62	5	35	.310	Sc Pos	164	53	3	75	.323
Night	409	133	7	54	.325	Clutch	87	28	1	12	.322

1992 Rankings (American League)

- 1st in batting average vs. left-handed pitchers (.424), batting average on an 0-2 count (.360) and slugging percentage vs. left-handed pitchers (.659)
- 3rd in hits (195), on-base percentage vs. left-handed pitchers (.464), batting average on the road (.334) and batting average with 2 strikes (.266)
- Led the Brewers in batting average (.320), at-bats (609), hits, triples (7), total bases (281), RBI (89), walks (73), intentionals walks (12), times on base (271), plate appearances (701), games played (158), slugging percentage (.461), on-base percentage (.389), stolen base percentage (83.8%) and batting average vs. left-handed pitchers

PITCHING:

In 1992, Jaime Navarro lowered his ERA for the second year in a row and won a career-high 17 games, leading the Brewers in victories for the second straight year as well. Navarro was outstanding during the heat of the pennant race, going 8-5 with a 2.64 ERA after the All-Star break.

Only 26, Navarro continues to mature as a major league starter. His improvements last year were small but across the board. He lowered his opponents batting average and cut his gopher ball total, while maintaining the workhorse innings and starts totals of 1991. Though he had only five complete games after tossing 10 in 1991, he threw more innings in the same number of starts. Navarro does not show noticeable signs of tiring until after the 100-pitch mark, and no significant drop in effectiveness until he's close to 120 pitches.

Navarro remains effective late in the game because he's willing to let his fielders do the work. He induces many ground balls but gets relatively few strikeouts. His change-up keeps hitters off-balance and his slider is effective, but when he gets behind and has to come in with his fastball, hitters can drive the ball. He gave up 42 doubles and six triples, both high totals. The Brewers scored just 10 runs in his 11 losses over the season.

HOLDING RUNNERS AND FIELDING:

Navarro doesn't help his own groundball strategy much; he committed 4 errors last year. He doesn't have great reactions coming off the mound. Basestealers also took advantage of him to the tune of 17 swipes in 1992. It's an improvement over the 23 he allowed in 1991, but he needs to improve further.

OVERALL:

Navarro, Bill Wegman, and Chris Bosio finished six-seven-eight in the league in baserunners allowed per nine innings and on-base average allowed. Together with Cal Eldred, they make a formidable rotation. Of the four, Navarro may be the most dependable. He may not be the one most likely to win 20 games, but he is probably the least likely to be a sub-.500 pitcher. He should be back in the 15-18 win range in 1993.

JAIME NAVARRO

Position: SP
Bats: R **Throws:** R
Ht: 6' 4" **Wt:** 210

Opening Day Age: 26
Born: 3/27/67 in Bayamon, Puerto Rico
ML Seasons: 4

Overall Statistics

	W	L	ERA	G	GS	Sv	IP	H	R	BB	SO	HR
1992	17	11	3.33	34	34	0	246.0	224	98	64	100	14
Career	47	38	3.71	119	107	1	739.0	756	345	210	345	49

How Often He Throws Strikes

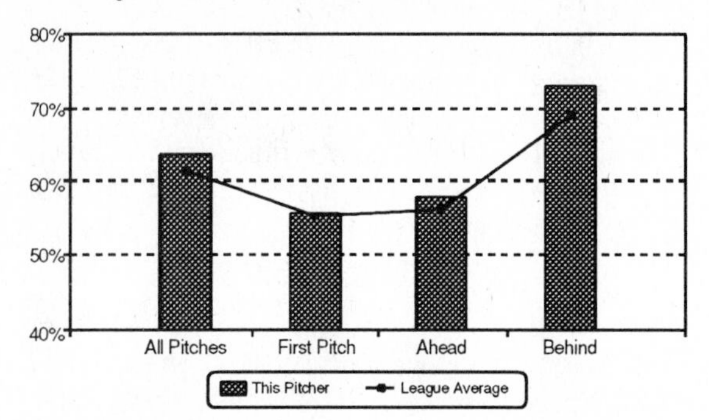

1992 Situational Stats

	W	L	ERA	Sv	IP		AB	H	HR	RBI	AVG
Home	9	4	3.29	0	109.1	LHB	435	112	6	41	.257
Road	8	7	3.36	0	136.2	RHB	477	112	8	38	.235
Day	6	3	3.25	0	72.0	Sc Pos	180	45	2	65	.250
Night	11	8	3.36	0	174.0	Clutch	102	27	1	7	.265

1992 Rankings (American League)

- 4th in shutouts (3) and least strikeouts per 9 innings (3.7)
- 5th in least pitches thrown per batter (3.46)
- 6th in wins (17)
- Led the Brewers in wins, shutouts, walks allowed (64), runners caught stealing (11), lowest batting average allowed (.246), lowest slugging percentage allowed (.351), lowest stolen base percentage allowed (60.7%), least home runs allowed per 9 innings (.51), lowest ERA on the road (3.36) and lowest batting average allowed vs. right-handed batters (.235)

PITCHING:

When Cleveland decided to rebuild last year without any old left-handed bricks, Jesse Orosco was dealt to the Brewers for the legendary "player to be named later." Orosco wasn't terrible in three seasons with the Indians, but they never seemed to trust him in the clutch: he converted five Indian saves in only 10 opportunities. The Brewers were looking for someone to spot against lefties, and they took a chance. Orosco's work against lefty swingers was hardly stellar (.273), but he survived by showing a new ability to get out righties (.207). As a result, he wound up with a fine 3.23 ERA, his best mark since 1989.

Last year Orosco accepted the fact that his best pitch, his slider, was no longer all he needed. He put his other talents, mainly a still-respectable fastball, to work. Though Orosco will probably never be as tough as he was a few years ago, he did regain a measure of his ability to pitch in tight spots. He was excellent with runners on, and allowed just 14 of 64 inherited runners to score. He also boosted his strikeout rate back up to one per inning. Orosco continues to exhibit excellent control, but pitching so much in the strike zone means giving up too many extra-base hits (five homers).

Very much a specialist, Orosco came in to pitch to a single hitter 19 times, and retired that hitter 15 times with five strikeouts. When the Brewers were gaining ground on Toronto and every game counted, Orosco pitched every day from September 16-21.

HOLDING RUNNERS AND FIELDING:

Orosco made no errors in 1992, and has committed just three in his long career. He handled the running game well, holding the opposition to just three steals, picking off two runners. He definitely helps himself as a fielder.

OVERALL:

Orosco was a free agent at season's end, and the Brewers figured to be among the bidders. He revived his career last year, but he still needs to regain some of his effectiveness against lefthanders.

JESSE OROSCO

Position: RP
Bats: R **Throws:** L
Ht: 6' 2" **Wt:** 185

Opening Day Age: 35
Born: 4/21/57 in Santa Barbara, CA
ML Seasons: 13

Overall Statistics

	W	L	ERA	G	GS	Sv	IP	H	R	BB	SO	HR
1992	3	1	3.23	59	0	1	39.0	33	15	13	40	5
Career	63	58	2.84	657	4	122	875.2	718	315	362	759	69

How Often He Throws Strikes

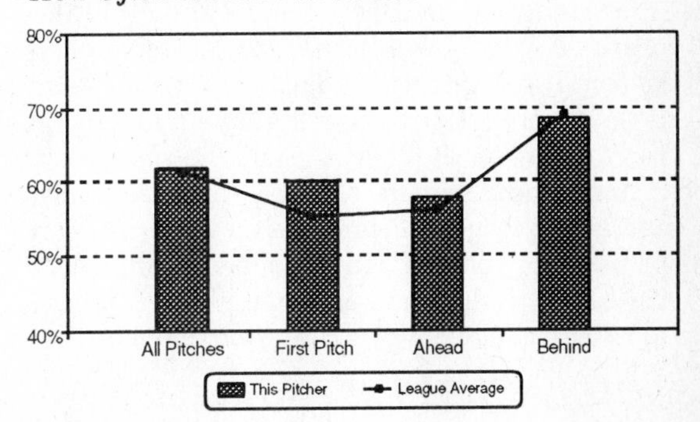

1992 Situational Stats

	W	L	ERA	Sv	IP		AB	H	HR	RBI	AVG
Home	3	1	3.52	0	23.0	LHB	55	15	2	10	.273
Road	0	0	2.81	1	16.0	RHB	87	18	3	14	.207
Day	2	0	2.40	1	15.0	Sc Pos	43	12	2	19	.279
Night	1	1	3.75	0	24.0	Clutch	52	10	1	6	.192

1992 Rankings (American League)

- 10th in lowest percentage of inherited runners scored (21.9%)
- Led the Brewers in holds (11)

PITCHING:

If the Brewers learned one thing in 1992, it was this: Dan Plesac is not a starter. The Brewers had tried their ex-relief ace in a starting role late in 1991, and wanted to put him in the rotation full-time last year. But Plesac's four-start trial in early 1992 was about three starts too many (5.14 ERA). Milwaukee was forced to move the struggling lefty back to the pen, and wonder of wonders, Plesac regained much of his effectiveness. He posted a 2.17 ERA as a reliever, working mostly in middle relief, and reined in the right-handed hitters who had been plaguing him since 1990. His second-half ERA was just 1.55.

Plesac struggled during the early going last year, often going deep into the count. After the All-Star break he worked with somewhat greater aggressiveness, and seemed to adjust to his role. Plesac is now more effective coming in with no one on base, as he has difficulty against the first batter. Garner learned where to use him successfully, and late in the year Plesac was an important part of the AL's most effective bullpen. Still a fastball/slider pitcher, he wasn't the old overpowering Plesac. But he was plenty good enough.

HOLDING RUNNERS AND FIELDING:

Plesac keeps an eye on basestealers and limits the running game. He also has a good move to first and picked off a couple of runners. He doesn't finish his motion in a good position to field and gets to very few balls, but he handles what he can reach.

OVERALL:

Plesac's long career as the Brewer closer makes it difficult to grasp that he's just 31 years old. Left-handed relievers never go out of style; just look at Plesac's portside pen pal, Jesse Orosco, still very effective and 36 years old. A free agent, Plesac will get some offers; since Orosco is also a free agent, the Brewers will probably opt to go after one but not the other.

DAN PLESAC

Position: RP/SP
Bats: L **Throws:** L
Ht: 6' 5" **Wt:** 215

Opening Day Age: 31
Born: 2/4/62 in Gary, IN
ML Seasons: 7

Overall Statistics

	W	L	ERA	G	GS	Sv	IP	H	R	BB	SO	HR
1992	5	4	2.96	44	4	1	79.0	64	28	35	54	5
Career	29	37	3.21	365	14	133	524.1	460	207	186	448	43

How Often He Throws Strikes

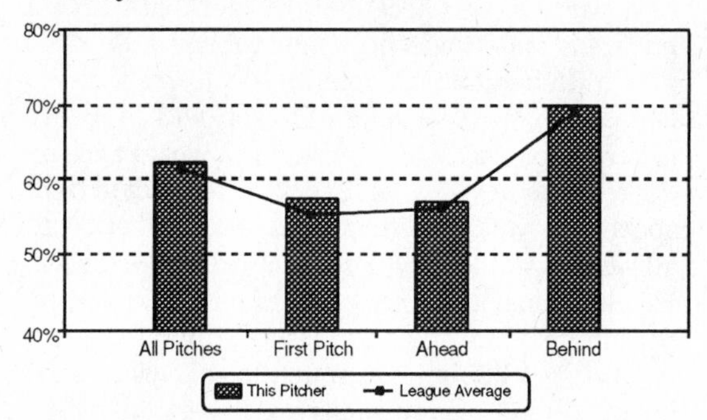

1992 Situational Stats

	W	L	ERA	Sv	IP		AB	H	HR	RBI	AVG
Home	2	2	2.48	0	29.0	LHB	67	17	2	11	.254
Road	3	2	3.24	1	50.0	RHB	213	47	3	27	.221
Day	1	2	2.70	0	23.1	Sc Pos	90	26	4	36	.289
Night	4	2	3.07	1	55.2	Clutch	51	14	1	7	.275

1992 Rankings (American League)

➡ 2nd in worst first batter efficiency (.417)

HITTING:

A major surprise when he hit 20 homers and drove in 69 runs in only 394 at-bats in 1991, Kevin Reimer couldn't match those totals in 1992. Reimer recorded 16 four-baggers with 58 RBI last year while logging 100 more at-bats. By comparison, his '92 season was disappointing, but nevertheless it was pretty solid.

Reimer, who utilizes a leg kick, is a good fastball hitter, and he loves to jump on the first-pitch heater. In 1991 he batted an unreal .458 (33-for-72) with seven homers on first pitches, but he wasn't going to keep doing that forever. Last year the pitchers respected him more and didn't challenge him quite as much. Reimer still whacked the first pitch at a .316 pace (three homers), but that's not .458.

Pitchers will still tease Reimer with the fastball, but these days it's apt to be high and outside. They'll also give him outside breaking stuff, knowing he likes to use the whole field. One difference in Reimer's production last year was that he batted only .211 with men in scoring position, a drop from his .284 mark in 1991. He wasn't getting as many good pitches to hit, and swung at too many bad ones (103 strikeouts, 42 walks).

BASERUNNING:

After entering the season without a major league stolen base, Reimer swiped two last year. It took him six attempts, making him 2-for-10 in his career. He's an aggressive baserunner, though, hustling out 32 doubles.

FIELDING:

One of Reimer's nicknames is "Canuck," an approximate description of the sound of the ball bouncing off his glove. His 11 errors led major league left fielders, and his range and arm are both unexceptional. Often criticized for his defense, he never stops hustling.

OVERALL:

Reimer lost his left field job late last year when the Rangers moved Juan Gonzalez to left and inserted David Hulse in center, prompting the Rangers to leave him unprotected for expansion. Colorado chose him and promptly traded him to the Brewers. He'll step in as a needed lefty DH.

KEVIN REIMER

Position: LF/DH
Bats: L **Throws:** R
Ht: 6' 2" **Wt:** 230

Opening Day Age: 28
Born: 6/28/64 in Macon, GA
ML Seasons: 5

Overall Statistics

	G	AB	R	H	D	T	HR	RBI	SB	BB	SO	AVG
1992	148	494	56	132	32	2	16	58	2	42	103	.267
Career	363	1018	109	267	63	3	39	144	2	85	225	.262

Where He Hits the Ball

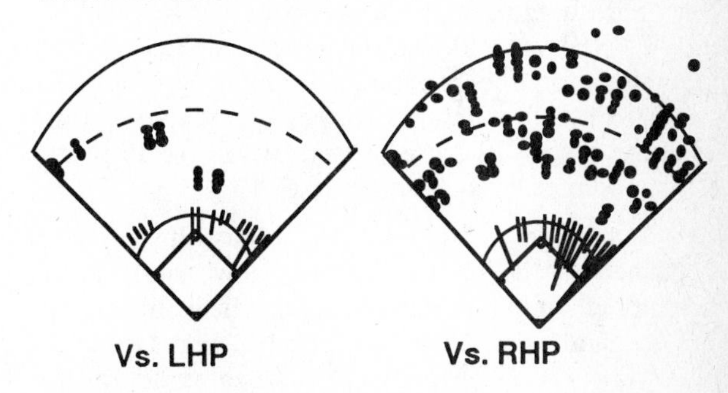

1992 Situational Stats

	AB	H	HR	RBI	AVG		AB	H	HR	RBI	AVG
Home	239	68	10	34	.285	LHP	89	22	2	8	.247
Road	255	64	6	24	.251	RHP	405	110	14	50	.272
Day	103	27	6	14	.262	Sc Pos	123	26	1	35	.211
Night	391	105	10	44	.269	Clutch	83	24	3	11	.289

1992 Rankings (American League)

- 6th in hit by pitch (10) and lowest percentage of swings put into play (36.5%)
- 10th in lowest groundball/flyball ratio (.83)
- Led the Rangers in doubles (32), hit by pitch, batting average vs. right-handed pitchers (.272), batting average at home (.285) and outfield assists (7)
- Led AL left fielders in errors (11)

HITTING:

A late-spring addition to the Brewer roster, Kevin Seitzer burst out of the box last year. He led the league in hitting and on-base average for a few weeks, and got a lot of press. Seitzer had a good May, too, at .339, but thereafter blew hot-and-cold. Still, the Brewers could point out that Seitzer's .270 average, 74 runs scored and 71 RBI were a lot more than they'd been receiving at third base from Gary Sheffield.

Seitzer had been released by the Royals before the season began, and it's worth noting that his overall 1992 numbers -- .270 average, .337 on-base percentage, .367 slugging -- were about the same as his .265 average, .350 on-base percentage and .350 slugging percentage for the '91 Royals. His 71 RBI were the second-most in his career, and his 35 doubles were a career high. But Seitzer's still a marginal on-base type hitter with no power and his walks have slipped. It's tough to find a good place to put a hitter like that.

Seitzer works the count, and he can hit when he's ahead of the pitcher. Pitchers know that, and lead with their best stuff, figuring that he won't be able to handle the best heaters and the sharpest-breaking curves. Seitzer hit .333 when ahead on the count last year, .228 when behind.

FIELDING:

Seitzer is a steady hand at third. He has below-average range, but is sure-handed and makes few errors. His arm is a little weak for third, but he won't kill a team there.

BASERUNNING:

Seitzer didn't run much during his last few years as a Royal, and maybe that was a good idea, given his 13-for-24 success rate in 1992. He did hit 35 doubles, and he runs decently. He just isn't a basestealer.

OVERALL:

Seitzer did okay as the Brewers' regular third baseman, and they might want to bring the free agent back. But Milwaukee lacks power, and third base is a logical place to look for some. Seitzer's no slugger, so he's far from a lock to keep his job, or even return to the Brewers.

KEVIN SEITZER

Position: 3B
Bats: R **Throws:** R
Ht: 5'11" **Wt:** 190

Opening Day Age: 31
Born: 3/26/62 in Springfield, IL
ML Seasons: 7

Overall Statistics

	G	AB	R	H	D	T	HR	RBI	SB	BB	SO	AVG
1992	148	540	74	146	35	1	5	71	13	57	44	.270
Career	889	3289	482	955	163	25	38	336	63	426	370	.290

Where He Hits the Ball

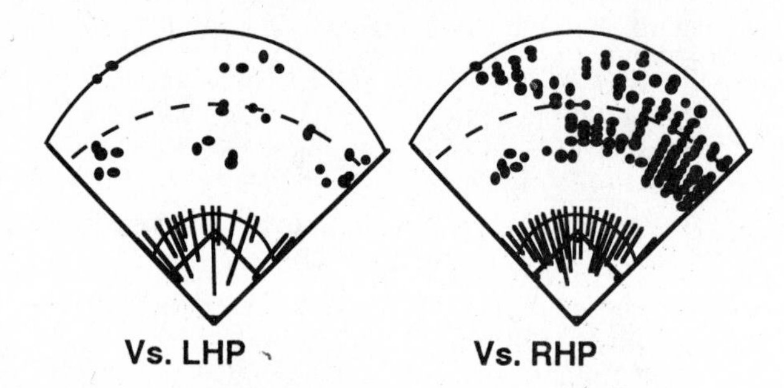

1992 Situational Stats

	AB	H	HR	RBI	AVG		AB	H	HR	RBI	AVG
Home	259	61	2	32	.236	LHP	128	40	2	17	.313
Road	281	85	3	39	.302	RHP	412	106	3	54	.257
Day	176	46	0	22	.261	Sc Pos	150	43	0	64	.287
Night	364	100	5	49	.275	Clutch	86	30	1	16	.349

1992 Rankings (American League)

- 3rd in lowest stolen base percentage (54.2%)
- 8th in batting average in the clutch (.349), lowest slugging percentage vs. right-handed pitchers (.340) and lowest batting average at home (.235)
- 9th in sacrifice flies (9)
- Led the Brewers in GDPs (16)
- Led AL third basemen in sacrifice flies, caught stealing (11) and fielding percentage (.969)

HITTING:

At first glance, 1992 looked like a giant step backward for B.J. Surhoff, who ended a three-year streak of improved batting averages with a 37-point slide. Surhoff's slugging percentage, weak at .372 in 1991, fell to .321, which is about the same as the slugging percentage of Jose Lind. Still, Surhoff's season wasn't as bad as it looked. His run production was fine, as he set career highs in runs scored and walks and didn't lose much in his RBI total. As in 1991, he started slowly but came on to have a good second half (.274).

Surhoff is an extreme groundball hitter who almost never strikes out since he rarely swings and misses. He has good speed for a catcher, so he legs out some infield hits, but his lack of power allows the opposition to cheat in. He grew more patient as the 1992 season went on, drawing some walks and forcing pitchers to throw strikes. He was then able to swing with more authority, and in the second half he pulled his average up from just .234 at the break.

BASERUNNING:

A former shortstop, Surhoff has always run better than the average catcher, and 1992 was no exception. His 14-for-22 success stealing bases was about his career average. He hit into just nine double plays after wiping out the inning a whopping 21 times in 1991.

FIELDING:

Surhoff had his best year behind the plate. Brewer pitchers had an ERA of 3.16 with Surhoff catching, easily the best among regular American League catchers. He also tossed out 35 of 92 baserunners, good for fourth in the league and a big departure from his usual weak performance. It was a group effort, as Brewer pitchers worked harder at keeping the runners close.

OVERALL:

His good year behind the plate hasn't silenced the talk of moving Surhoff to third or the outfield. At 28 it may be too late, but he hit .304 when he didn't catch, and .236 when he did. He'll probably remain the Brewers' primary backstop and one of the better catchers in the league.

B.J. SURHOFF

Position: C/1B
Bats: L **Throws:** R
Ht: 6' 1" **Wt:** 200

Opening Day Age: 28
Born: 8/4/64 in Bronx, NY
ML Seasons: 6

Overall Statistics

	G	AB	R	H	D	T	HR	RBI	SB	BB	SO	AVG
1992	139	480	63	121	19	1	4	62	14	46	41	.252
Career	797	2783	314	745	119	16	32	350	83	205	219	.268

Where He Hits the Ball

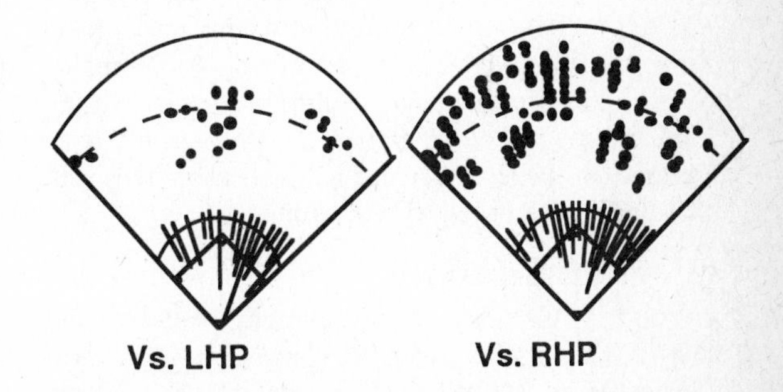

1992 Situational Stats

	AB	H	HR	RBI	AVG		AB	H	HR	RBI	AVG
Home	243	68	3	29	.280	LHP	126	34	2	20	.270
Road	237	53	1	33	.224	RHP	354	87	2	42	.246
Day	147	39	0	20	.265	Sc Pos	134	40	2	57	.299
Night	333	82	4	42	.246	Clutch	93	23	2	13	.247

1992 Rankings (American League)

- 3rd in lowest slugging percentage vs. right-handed pitchers (.308)
- 5th in lowest slugging percentage (.321) and highest batting average on an 0-2 count (.320)
- 6th in sacrifice flies (10)
- Led the Brewers in lowest percentage of swings that missed (9.1%) and highest percentage of swings put into play (56.7%)
- Led AL catchers in sacrifice flies, stolen bases (14), caught stealing (8), highest groundball/flyball ratio (1.8), highest stolen base percentage, batting average on an 0-2 count (.320), lowest percentage of swings that missed and highest percentage of swings put into play

GREG VAUGHN

Position: LF
Bats: R **Throws:** R
Ht: 6' 0" **Wt:** 193

Opening Day Age: 27
Born: 7/3/65 in Sacramento, CA
ML Seasons: 4

Overall Statistics

	G	AB	R	H	D	T	HR	RBI	SB	BB	SO	AVG
1992	141	501	77	114	18	2	23	78	15	60	123	.228
Career	444	1538	227	360	71	9	72	260	28	168	362	.234

Where He Hits the Ball

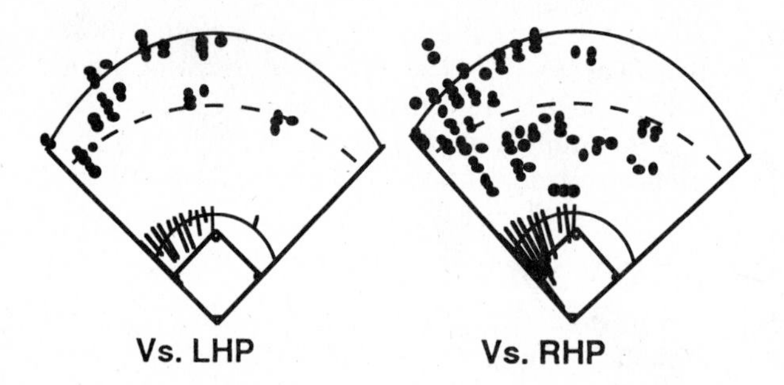

1992 Situational Stats

	AB	H	HR	RBI	AVG		AB	H	HR	RBI	AVG
Home	244	57	11	42	.234	LHP	105	26	6	23	.248
Road	257	57	12	36	.222	RHP	396	88	17	55	.222
Day	148	32	8	21	.216	Sc Pos	144	36	8	58	.250
Night	353	82	15	57	.232	Clutch	81	17	2	6	.210

1992 Rankings (American League)

- 1st in lowest stolen base percentage (50.0%)
- 2nd in lowest batting average (.228)
- 3rd in lowest batting average vs. right-handed pitchers (.222) and most runs scored per time reached base (.43)
- 5th in caught stealing (15), lowest batting average at home (.234) and lowest percentage of swings put into play (36.4%)
- Led the Brewers in home runs (23) and HR frequency (21.8 ABs per HR)
- Led AL left fielders in home runs, strikeouts (123) and HR frequency

HITTING:

After a fine 1991 campaign (27 homers, 98 RBI), Greg Vaughn seemed ready to win recognition as one of the American League's top sluggers. Instead, he had a terrible '92 season. Bothered by a back problem, Vaughn batted only .156 during May and June. He didn't get it all together until September, when he hit .306 with six homers and 22 RBI. His overall figures -- .228 average, 23 HR, 78 RBI -- were hardly what one expects from a club's featured power hitter.

Vaughn has always been prone to long slumps. His career pattern has been to hit in April (.270) and September/October (.267), but not during the other months; his lifetime average in each month from May through August is below .225. Though he's hit .281 over his career with runners in scoring position, he's had clutch hitting problems as well: .210 lifetime as a cleanup hitter, .205 in the late innings of close games. Those patterns continued in 1992 and were a big reason why the Brewers scrambled to score runs.

BASERUNNING:

With Phil Garner's encouragement, Vaughn tried to live up to his minor league reputation as a basestealer last year. He made 30 stolen base attempts, but he turned up the worst success ratio in the league, getting caught half the time. He should go back to his customary five or 10 attempts a year to not hurt the team.

FIELDING:

Vaughn may have taken his hitting woes with him to the field, because he didn't duplicate his fine season in left field. Still, though he doesn't have blazing speed, he's a pretty decent outfielder and covers quite a bit of ground. He has a left fielder's arm, so don't expect a move to any other outfield position.

OVERALL:

Vaughn is an explosive offensive force, but his powder tends to get damp for long stretches. The positive side is that the Brewers have probably seen the low side of his abilities. If he can avoid his annual mid-year slump, he could put up All-Star numbers. As it is, he's good for about 25 homers, power figures no other Brewer can match.

PITCHING:

Bill Wegman threw a lot of baseballs in 1992. Unfortunately, though, a lot of batters sent those baseballs a long way. Try 50 doubles and 28 home runs surrendered; or 251 hits allowed, second-most in the majors to Kevin Brown. Add to that a .286 batting average allowed to right-handed hitters, and you have to wonder how Wegman could have been highly successful.

Since he was only 13-14, highly successful may not be the best term. But his high innings totals reduce some of the impact of the extra-base hit totals. Only Brown faced more batters, and only Jack McDowell threw more pitches. And Wegman's strengths are obvious; he held lefties to a .209 average, kept the leadoff hitter off base, issued just 55 walks, and posted a 3.20 ERA to finish ninth in the league. That is surely success.

Wegman's slider moves, but his fastball isn't that fast, though his change-up disguises it. Naturally, batters try to tee off on his heater, as the 80 extra-base hits he allowed demonstrate. Wegman tries to hit back -- he plunked nine hitters -- but with too little effect. The extra-base hits are undermining his otherwise fine pitching. He was durable, going at least seven innings in 25 of his 35 starts, but allowed 10 or more baserunners 16 times.

HOLDING RUNNERS AND FIELDING:

Wegman induces a lot of ground balls, and helps himself with his excellent fielding. Runners love to run on him, and in 1992 he must have been tipping his pickoff move. Last year 18 of 24 runners stole against him despite 235 pickoff throws, sixth in the league. This should be correctable, as Wegman controlled the running game in 1991.

OVERALL

The oft-injured Wegman, who could barely throw a tantrum two years ago, is now the workhorse of a potentially lethal rotation. Will he stay a .500 pitcher, or make the adjustments that can lift him to a new level? He is a valuable pitcher now; if he cuts down on the extra-base hits he allows, he can be a winning pitcher, too.

BILL WEGMAN

Position: SP
Bats: R **Throws:** R
Ht: 6' 5" **Wt:** 220

Opening Day Age: 30
Born: 12/19/62 in Cincinnati, OH
ML Seasons: 8

Overall Statistics

	W	L	ERA	G	GS	Sv	IP	H	R	BB	SO	HR
1992	13	14	3.20	35	35	0	261.2	251	104	55	127	28
Career	64	65	4.02	186	175	0	1175.2	1203	590	271	537	146

How Often He Throws Strikes

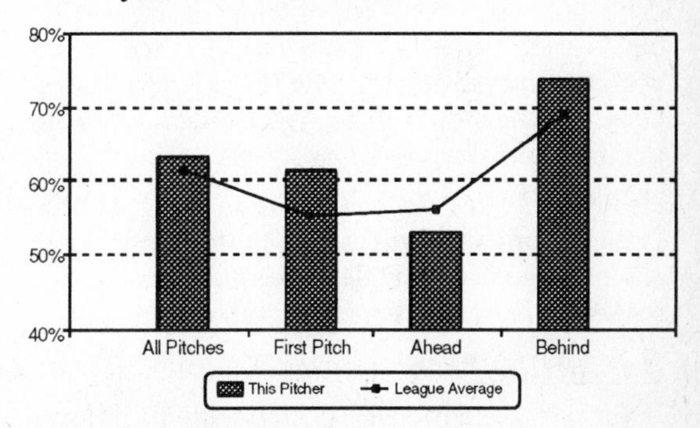

1992 Situational Stats

	W	L	ERA	Sv	IP		AB	H	HR	RBI	AVG
Home	9	5	2.26	0	143.2	LHB	469	98	7	30	.209
Road	4	9	4.35	0	118.0	RHB	535	153	21	63	.286
Day	4	5	3.46	0	78.0	Sc Pos	204	52	5	62	.255
Night	9	9	3.09	0	183.2	Clutch	128	36	3	15	.281

1992 Rankings (American League)

- 1st in ERA at home (2.26)
- 2nd in innings pitched (261.2), hits allowed (251), batters faced (1,079) and most pitches thrown (3,876)
- 3rd in games started (35)
- 4th in home runs allowed (28) and highest batting average allowed vs. right-handed batters (.286)
- Led the Brewers in ERA (3.20), losses (14), games started, complete games (7), innings pitched, hits allowed, batters faced, home runs allowed, hit batsmen (9), strikeouts (127), balks (2), pitches thrown, pickoff throws (235), stolen bases allowed (18) and ERA at home

HITTING:

Robin Yount punched his ticket to the Hall of Fame -- or perhaps merely upgraded it to express class -- when he popped his 3,000th hit last September 9th. Reaching the milestone in 1992 was in question after Yount batted .192 in July and then started August with a 5-for-48 slump. But from August 20 to the end of the season, Yount hit .333 with power, had 31 RBI and 23 runs scored, drew 18 walks, and was 7-of-9 as a basestealer.

Glimpses of the old Yount have occurred in each of the last three seasons. But at 37, he's not the player he was in the 1980s. Yount's home run power has deserted him, and last year he had his fewest round-trippers since 1979. He can still drive the ball, but not out of the park. His strikeout-to-walk ratio slipped a bit in 1991, and stayed at that same level in 1992. He still hits lefties okay, but his ability to hit righthanders has been in precipitate decline for two years.

Health problems dogged Yount in 1991, but his 1992 performance was more a function of his age and mileage. He struggles when pitchers get two strikes on him, which happens often.

BASERUNNING:

Yount only attempted 10 steals in his injury-marred 1991 season, but he was 15-for-21 in 1992. He still runs the bases beautifully, ranking third in the American League last year with 40 doubles.

FIELDING:

Yount made a fine conversion to center field from shortstop in 1985. Now very old for the position, he is a little below average in the field, though he made just two errors. He still has a good arm, but doesn't move quick enough to get to the shallow hits that lead to assists.

OVERALL:

Yount was a free agent after the 1992 season. It seemed impossible that he would play for anyone but the Brewers, and he was expected to re-sign with them. During each of the last three seasons, Yount has driven in exactly 77 runs -- not the old Robin, but good enough to remain a productive player.

ROBIN YOUNT

Position: CF/DH
Bats: R **Throws:** R
Ht: 6' 0" **Wt:** 180

Opening Day Age: 37
Born: 9/16/55 in Danville, IL
ML Seasons: 19

Overall Statistics

	G	AB	R	H	D	T	HR	RBI	SB	BB	SO	AVG
1992	150	557	71	147	40	3	8	77	15	53	81	.264
Career	2729	10554	1570	3025	558	123	243	1355	262	922	1257	.287

Where He Hits the Ball

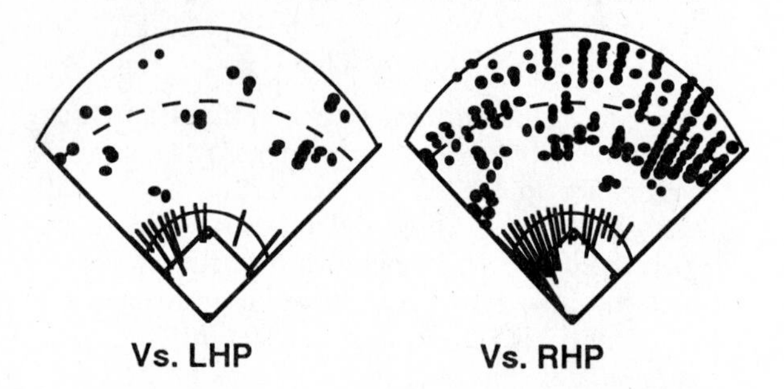

1992 Situational Stats

	AB	H	HR	RBI	AVG		AB	H	HR	RBI	AVG
Home	269	72	3	35	.268	LHP	125	35	2	18	.280
Road	288	75	5	42	.260	RHP	432	112	6	59	.259
Day	160	51	3	27	.319	Sc Pos	157	45	1	62	.287
Night	397	96	5	50	.242	Clutch	74	19	1	8	.257

1992 Rankings (American League)

- 2nd in sacrifice flies (12)
- 3rd in doubles (40)
- Led the Brewers in doubles and sacrifice flies
- Led AL center fielders in doubles and sacrifice flies

JIM GANTNER

Position: 2B/3B
Bats: L **Throws:** R
Ht: 5'11" **Wt:** 175

Opening Day Age: 39
Born: 1/5/54 in Eden, WI
ML Seasons: 17

Overall Statistics

	G	AB	R	H	D	T	HR	RBI	SB	BB	SO	AVG
1992	101	256	22	63	12	1	1	18	6	12	17	.246
Career	1801	6189	726	1696	262	38	47	568	137	383	501	.274

HITTING, FIELDING, BASERUNNING:

In 1992 Jim Gantner and teammates Paul Molitor and Robin Yount set the record for most lifetime hits by a trio of teammates, and Gantner himself became the Brewers' all-time assist leader. That's most of the good news. Bothered by injuries, Gantner notched only 256 at-bats, his lowest total since 1979. His .246 average was the second-lowest of his 17-year career.

After a good start, Gantner slumped badly, went on the disabled list with a bruised right hand, and lost the second base job to Scott Fletcher. He stopped hitting lefthanders, a traditional strength. Gantner had his moments, however. His only home run of the year was a game-winning solo shot against the Red Sox in the 13th inning. He finished the season with a jammed shoulder and played little during the final weeks. Gantner's fielding has slipped further, so unlike Fletcher, he is not an option as a defensive replacement. He still has a little speed, with six steals in eight attempts.

OVERALL:

Gantner has always done two things on the field: hit .270-.280, and play a solid second base. He couldn't do those things in 1992, and at 39 he may not get another chance. Gantner may be done with his on-field bit in Milwaukee, but a coaching position is his for the taking. Without him on the field, though, a Brewer era has passed.

DAVE NILSSON

Position: C
Bats: L **Throws:** R
Ht: 6' 3" **Wt:** 185

Opening Day Age: 23
Born: 12/14/69 in Brisbane, Queensland, Australia
ML Seasons: 1

Overall Statistics

	G	AB	R	H	D	T	HR	RBI	SB	BB	SO	AVG
1992	51	164	15	38	8	0	4	25	2	17	18	.232
Career	51	164	15	38	8	0	4	25	2	17	18	.232

HITTING, FIELDING, BASERUNNING:

Australian native Dave Nilsson made steady progress through the Brewer system after being signed as a non-drafted free agent in 1987. Nilsson's career really took off in 1991, when he batted an unreal .418 in 66 games at AA El Paso. Understandably, expectations were high when the young catcher broke in with the Brewers last year. Nilsson didn't quite measure up, but he showed some promise while batting .232.

Nilsson is a bat-control specialist who seldom strikes out, can hit for average and takes a walk. Shoulder surgery held him back for a while late in 1991, and he started the '92 season at AAA Denver. Recalled on May 18, he whacked a three-run double for his first major league hit. The rest of the year was a learning experience, and the kid learned fast. He sprained his wrist in July, was back in August, and hit .311 in September.

Nilsson's defense improved steadily through the minors. He did a decent job for the Brewers, throwing out 36 percent of attempted stealers and handling pitchers well. For a catcher, he can run a little, with 10 steals in 65 games at Denver last year.

OVERALL:

Nilsson was a switch-hitter for most of his minor-league career, but he's moved now to pure lefty swinging, a valuable trait for a catcher. He'll get work with the Brewers in 1993, especially after they made him one of their 15 expansion protections.

BILL SPIERS

Position: SS
Bats: L **Throws:** R
Ht: 6' 2" **Wt:** 190

Opening Day Age: 26
Born: 6/5/66 in Orangeburg, SC
ML Seasons: 4

Overall Statistics

	G	AB	R	H	D	T	HR	RBI	SB	BB	SO	AVG
1992	12	16	2	5	2	0	0	2	1	1	4	.313
Career	371	1138	161	298	39	12	14	125	36	72	167	.262

HITTING, FIELDING, BASERUNNING:

Back surgery stole the 1992 season from Bill Spiers, and along with it a chance to establish himself as one of the top American League shortstops. Spiers had logged 414 at-bats in 1991 and hit a solid .283. But he underwent off-season surgery to remove a herniated disk, and the recovery process was slow.

After hitting just .136 in 22 spring at-bats, Spiers was placed on the disabled list, opening the door for Pat Listach's sensational debut. Spiers took a rehab stint at Class A Beloit and didn't report to the Brewers until September 2. He logged 16 at-bats during the Brewer's gallant late season charge, hitting .313 with a couple of doubles. He got all five of his hits against Oakland and Baltimore, two contending clubs.

Spiers may have lost his shortstop job to Pat Listach, and thus second base could be his regular position in 1993. Before the surgery, Spiers was a solid-fielding shortstop with a strong arm that sometimes betrayed him, so the shift might be beneficial. He stole 14 bases in 1991, and figures to better that total under Phil Garner if he's healthy.

OVERALL:

A former number-one draft choice, Spiers can be a very good hitter. But question marks remain about his ability to hit lefties, and, of course, his durability. If he's back from his injuries, the Brewers will be tough in the middle infield. They expect his recovery.

FRANKLIN STUBBS

Position: 1B/DH
Bats: L **Throws:** L
Ht: 6' 2" **Wt:** 208

Opening Day Age: 32
Born: 10/21/60 in Laurinburg, NC
ML Seasons: 9

Overall Statistics

	G	AB	R	H	D	T	HR	RBI	SB	BB	SO	AVG
1992	92	288	37	66	11	1	9	42	11	27	68	.229
Career	883	2475	310	573	98	12	102	329	74	241	599	.232

HITTING, FIELDING, BASERUNNING:

The Brewers put on big smiles last season when they reunited first baseman Franklin Stubbs with new manager Phil Garner. Garner had coached for Houston during Stubbs' big 1990 season with the Astros, and they thought that Garner might be able to help Stubbs bring back the magic. He couldn't, and Stubbs suffered through another long season. After starting the campaign as the regular first baseman, Stubbs lost the job and batted only 82 times during the second half. For the year he hit just .229 with nine homers.

Though Stubbs has a career average of .232 after nine seasons, he does have a few virtues. When he gets hold of a ball, it goes out of any park in the league. He especially likes hitting against righties. He hit pretty well as a DH last year (.278), and he was 3-for-10 as a pinch hitter. But Stubbs' baserunning, a former strength, went south in 1992, with an 11-for-19 stolen base mark. He's one of the worst first basemen in the league, committing eight errors in limited chances.

OVERALL:

Stubbs' batting average just destroys his value, and he doesn't walk a lot, so it's tough to put him out there and wait for the homers. He will probably sit on the bench while John Jaha or someone plays this year. The Brewers will sit drumming their fingers, waiting for his big contract to run out after 1993.

ORGANIZATION OVERVIEW:

Out of necessity the small-market Brewers have always had a commitment to their player development program. However, things have not always worked out for them. Though highly regarded, a lot of Milwaukee prospects -- Glenn Braggs, Joey Meyer, B.J. Surhoff, to name three -- never became major-league stars. And whatever happened to Ramser Correa? Rather than abandon player development for free agency, the Brewers decided to work even harder. Last year Milwaukee had two impact rookies -- Pat Listach and Cal Eldred -- along with several other ex-farmhands who played a key role on their contending team. This club knows how to produce and nurture talent.

MIKE FARRELL

Position: P **Opening Day Age:** 24
Bats: L **Throws:** L **Born:** 1/28/69 in
Ht: 6' 2" **Wt:** 187 Logansport, IN

Recent Statistics

	W	L	ERA	G	GS	Sv	IP	H	R	BB	SO	HR
91 R Brewers	2	1	4.64	6	2	0	21.1	25	15	3	17	1
91 R Helena	4	0	0.84	5	3	0	32.0	17	5	8	22	2
91 A Beloit	2	3	1.98	6	5	0	36.1	33	13	8	38	2
92 A Stockton	8	4	2.33	13	13	0	92.2	82	28	21	67	6
92 AA El Paso	7	6	2.62	14	14	0	106.1	95	42	25	66	5

An undrafted free agent who was signed in June of 1991, Farrell has moved through the system at breakneck speed. In '91 he pitched for three Brewer farm clubs, finishing at Class A Beloit. Last year he split time at Class A Stockton and AA El Paso. He's starred at every level, with a two-year record of 23-14 and a 2.40 ERA. Farrell does not possess a blazing fastball, but he's recorded good strikeout totals and shown excellent control. Figure him for AAA this year. If he wins, he may move up again.

TY HILL

Position: P **Opening Day Age:** 21
Bats: L **Throws:** L **Born:** 3/7/72 in
Ht: 6' 7" **Wt:** 200 Fontana, CA

Recent Statistics

	W	L	ERA	G	GS	Sv	IP	H	R	BB	SO	HR
91 R Helena	4	2	3.15	11	11	0	60.0	43	27	35	76	2
92 A Beloit	9	5	3.25	20	19	0	113.2	76	51	74	133	4

Unlike Farrell, the 6-foot-6 Hill was considered a top prospect from day one. A first-round draft pick in 1991, Hill was outstanding that year in rookie ball. Last year he was 9-5 with a 3.25 ERA and 133 strikeouts in 113.2 innings at Beloit. Shoulder tendinitis ended his season early, but it did not appear to be a serious problem. In size and pitching repertoire, scouts are calling him a young John Candelaria.

MARK A. KIEFER

Position: P **Opening Day Age:** 24
Bats: R **Throws:** R **Born:** 11/13/68 in
Ht: 6' 3" **Wt:** 185 Orange, CA

Recent Statistics

	W	L	ERA	G	GS	Sv	IP	H	R	BB	SO	HR
91 AA El Paso	7	1	3.33	12	12	0	75.2	62	33	43	72	4
91 AAA Denver	9	5	4.62	17	17	0	101.1	104	55	41	68	7
92 AAA Denver	7	13	4.59	27	26	0	162.2	168	95	65	145	25

Rated the Brewers' number-five prospect a year ago, Kiefer went 16-6 in 1991 at AA El Paso and AAA Denver. But he had a miserable 1992 with a 7-13 record and a 4.59 ERA while spending the whole season at Denver. The Brewers were only slightly discouraged, however. They noted his 145 strikeouts in 162.2 innings and still feel his stuff is among the best in their system. He was protected from expansion, as the team feels that Kiefer is a possibility for their rotation this season.

MATT MIESKE

Position: OF **Opening Day Age:** 25
Bats: R **Throws:** R **Born:** 2/13/68 in
Ht: 6' 0" **Wt:** 185 Midland, MI

Recent Statistics

	G	AB	R	H	D	T	HR	RBI	SB	BB	SO	AVG
91 A High Desert	133	492	108	168	36	6	15	119	39	94	82	.341
92 AAA Denver	134	524	80	140	29	11	19	77	13	39	90	.267
92 MLE	134	499	59	115	24	6	13	56	9	28	94	.230

As part of the package the Brewers received for Gary Sheffield, Mieske had a lot of pressure placed on him last year. Moved from A ball in '91 all the way to AAA Denver in '92, he was supposed to develop quickly and justify the deal. He did develop, but not quickly, and suffered through a difficult first half. Mieske came on strong thereafter, though, finishing with 19 homers and a .267 average. He's also a good outfielder with excellent speed (11 triples last year). Chances are he'll start the season at AAA again, but may be brought up before too long.

TROY F. O'LEARY

Position: OF **Opening Day Age:** 23
Bats: L **Throws:** L **Born:** 8/4/69 in
Ht: 6' 0" **Wt:** 175 Compton, CA

Recent Statistics

	G	AB	R	H	D	T	HR	RBI	SB	BB	SO	AVG
91 A Stockton	126	418	63	110	20	4	5	46	4	73	96	.263
92 AA El Paso	135	506	92	169	27	8	5	79	28	59	87	.334
92 MLE	135	469	61	132	22	4	3	52	18	33	93	.281

A 13th-round pick in 1987, O'Leary had a big year at AA El Paso, winning the Texas League batting title with a .334 average and stealing 28 bases. Hitters often go crazy at El Paso, but O'Leary's batted over .330 twice before. He doesn't have much power and he's not supposed to be a great defensive player, so he'll have to hit his way to the majors.

STOPPER

PITCHING:

The Twins converted Rick Aguilera from starter to closer before the 1990 season, and it's been baseball's best role-change this side of Dennis Eckersley. Aguilera had been a decent starter, but since the change only Eckersley has had better late-relief numbers over the past three seasons. Aguilera saved 41 games in 1992, giving him a three-year save total of 115. He has blown only 23 saves in the past three seasons, including seven last year.

When Aguilera was good last season -- which was most of the time -- he was superb. When he was bad, however, he was downright horrendous. In his seven blown saves, the righthander was 2-5 with a 21.60 ERA (16 earned runs, 6.2 innings). In his other 57 appearances, he was 0-1 with a 0.75 ERA (five earned runs, 60 innings). Most of his problems can be traced to late-inning home runs; he gave up seven homers in 66.2 innings last season, compared to just three homers in 69 IP in 1991.

Aguilera's best pitches remain a 90-MPH fastball that tends to rise and a sharp-breaking split-fingered fastball. He also has a decent slider and curve. Aguilera was hampered by a mysterious knee ailment in late July and early August. The injury sidelined him nine days and came in between two costly long balls -- a three-run homer by Oakland's Eric Fox in a 5-4 loss on July 29 and a three-run blast by Texas' Juan Gonzalez in a 5-3 defeat on August 12.

HOLDING RUNNERS AND FIELDING:

Aguilera hasn't made an error in 183 appearances as a Twins reliever since 1990, and the streak is hardly a fluke. The former college third baseman (Brigham Young University) has plenty of quickness to get to bunts and cover first base when needed. He has a decent move to first, but is still prone to stolen bases.

OVERALL:

For the first time since becoming a closer, Aguilera had problems with the home run ball last year. He will have to reverse that trend. But two straight seasons of 40-plus saves stamp the righthander as one of the game's best short men.

RICK AGUILERA

Position: RP
Bats: R **Throws:** R
Ht: 6' 5" **Wt:** 203

Opening Day Age: 31
Born: 12/31/61 in San Gabriel, CA
ML Seasons: 8

Overall Statistics

	W	L	ERA	G	GS	Sv	IP	H	R	BB	SO	HR
1992	2	6	2.84	64	0	41	66.2	60	28	17	52	7
Career	51	46	3.29	308	70	122	749.2	705	318	220	582	60

How Often He Throws Strikes

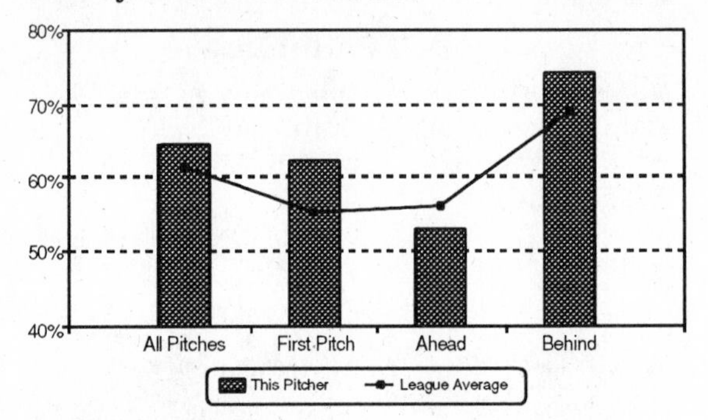

1992 Situational Stats

	W	L	ERA	Sv	IP		AB	H	HR	RBI	AVG
Home	1	3	4.25	17	29.2	LHB	129	32	3	17	.248
Road	1	3	1.70	24	37.0	RHB	123	28	4	15	.228
Day	1	0	0.96	17	28.0	Sc Pos	85	18	5	30	.212
Night	1	6	4.19	24	38.2	Clutch	173	37	5	27	.214

1992 Rankings (American League)

- → 2nd in saves (41) and save opportunities (48)
- → 4th in games finished (61)
- → 5th in relief losses (6)
- → 6th in save percentage (85.4%) and blown saves (7)
- → Led the Twins in games pitched (64), saves, games finished, save opportunities, save percentage, blown saves and relief losses

HITTING:

Randy Bush has been a productive platoon player and pinch hitter since joining the Twins in 1982. But his future -- at least with Minnesota -- appeared to be in jeopardy after 1992. The veteran batted just .214 with two home runs (both career lows) and only 22 RBI in 182 at-bats.

Bush has been a streaky hitter throughout his career. In 1991 he was batting .173 (9-for-52) on June 3, then hit .363 (41-for-113) through the remainder of the season. Last year there was no hot streak. Bush was 5-for-36 (.139) in his last 23 games and was 15-for-81 (.185) in his last 45.

Bush had been a pull hitter who could always handle hard-throwing righthanders throughout his career, but he didn't display his usual quick bat in 1992. After batting .307 against righties in 1991, he dipped to .224 last year. He also batted only .220 with runners in scoring position. Bush has always been a hitter who looks inept on one swing, then lines the next pitch into right field. Last year, however, the ineptitude dominated. He was fooled too many times by good curves, and failed to feast on even mediocre fastball pitchers.

BASERUNNING:

Bush amazed everyone last year by stealing his first base since 1989. He is 1-for-7 over the past three seasons. Though slow, Bush has always been a good baserunner, relying on intelligence and experience to know when to take the extra base and when to play it safe.

FIELDING:

Hours of hard work early in his career have made Bush a sure-handed fielder, though one with very limited range. Playing 24 games in the outfield and eight at first base last year, he played errorless ball.

OVERALL:

Bush turned 34 last season, and it was natural to wonder whether time had taken its toll. The free agent expressed a desire to return to the Twins -- the only organization for whom he has played -- but that prospect appeared to be no better than 50-50. It's possible that the dearth of left-handed power hitters in baseball could earn him a spring look, either with the Twins or somebody else.

RANDY BUSH

Position: DH/RF
Bats: L **Throws:** L
Ht: 6' 1" **Wt:** 190

Opening Day Age: 34
Born: 10/5/58 in Dover, DE
ML Seasons: 11

Overall Statistics

	G	AB	R	H	D	T	HR	RBI	SB	BB	SO	AVG
1992	100	182	14	39	8	1	2	22	1	11	37	.214
Career	1184	3000	387	756	152	26	96	406	33	341	492	.252

Where He Hits the Ball

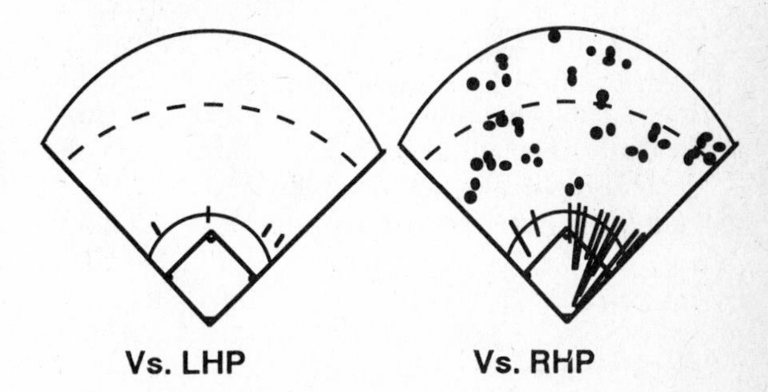

1992 Situational Stats

	AB	H	HR	RBI	AVG		AB	H	HR	RBI	AVG
Home	83	18	0	7	.217	LHP	8	0	0	0	.000
Road	99	21	2	15	.212	RHP	174	39	2	22	.224
Day	62	15	1	8	.242	Sc Pos	59	13	0	20	.220
Night	120	24	1	14	.200	Clutch	48	9	0	3	.188

1992 Rankings (American League)

- Did not rank near the top or bottom in any category

CHILI DAVIS

Position: DH
Bats: B **Throws:** R
Ht: 6' 3" **Wt:** 217

Opening Day Age: 33
Born: 1/17/60 in Kingston, Jamaica
ML Seasons: 12

Overall Statistics

	G	AB	R	H	D	T	HR	RBI	SB	BB	SO	AVG
1992	138	444	63	128	27	2	12	66	4	73	76	.288
Career	1590	5698	799	1538	275	28	197	818	117	707	1087	.270

Where He Hits the Ball

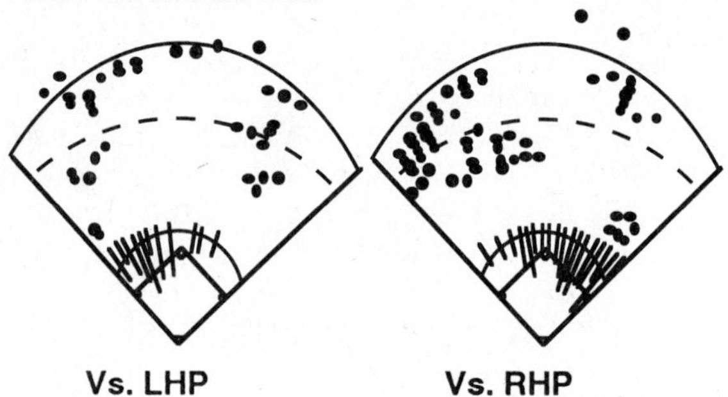

1992 Situational Stats

	AB	H	HR	RBI	AVG		AB	H	HR	RBI	AVG
Home	245	67	6	40	.273	LHP	121	31	4	22	.256
Road	199	61	6	26	.307	RHP	323	97	8	44	.300
Day	124	35	3	22	.282	Sc Pos	133	35	1	49	.263
Night	320	93	9	44	.291	Clutch	81	24	2	16	.296

1992 Rankings (American League)

- 2nd in batting average with the bases loaded (.625) and on-base percentage vs. right-handed pitchers (.408)
- 9th in sacrifice flies (9) and on-base percentage (.386)
- Led the Twins in most pitches seen per plate appearance (3.75), batting average with the bases loaded, batting average on a 3-1 count (.500) and on-base percentage vs. right-handed pitchers
- Led designated hitters in batting average with the bases loaded, batting average vs. right-handed pitchers (.300) and on-base percentage vs. right-handed pitchers

HITTING:

When the finger-pointing began last season over the Twins' second-half collapse, veteran designated hitter Chili Davis was one of those blamed. General manager Andy MacPhail believed that the club's biggest weakness last year was a lack of left-handed power. Davis, a switch-hitter, had come through with 29 homers and 93 RBI during his first season with the Twins in 1991. But he slumped to 12 home runs and 66 RBI last year. Three of those home runs came in the season's final four games, long after the Twins' fate had been decided.

Davis has developed into playing in a good-year/bad-year cycle the past four seasons. During that time, his home run totals have been 22, 12, 29, 12; his RBI counts were 90, 58, 93, 66. Last season Davis' swing appeared slower, making him more vulnerable to his achilles heel: high fastballs. Though Davis' .288 average was the second-highest of his career, he batted .263 with runners in scoring position, with just one home run in 133 at-bats. As usual, he was an excellent low-ball hitter, and better from the left side.

BASERUNNING:

There was a time when Davis was a stolen base threat, but age and back problems have slowed him considerably. He stole four bases in nine attempts last year and hasn't stolen in double figures since 1987. He made one of the worst slides in Twins history August 18 at Cleveland, coming to a stop before reaching home plate as Indians catcher Junior Ortiz applied the tag.

FIELDING:

Davis is now used almost exclusively as a designated hitter. He played only five games in the field last year, and though he played errorless ball, he is a very bad defensive player.

OVERALL:

Davis was in a salary bracket last year at which the Twins felt cheated by his power numbers. He was a free agent over the winter, and although he expressed a desire to return to Minnesota, the feeling did not appear to be mutual. If Davis returns, it will be for a low base salary, heavy on incentives.

PITCHING:

Scott Erickson was the league's most dominating pitcher in early 1991, winning 12 consecutive games with a naturally-sinking fastball that regularly was clocked in at 90-MPH plus. But Erickson suffered elbow problems in '91, and Twins coaches attempted to convince him that he needed to be more of a pitcher, and less of a thrower, if he desired a lengthy major league career. In that sense, 1992 was a season of transition for the righthander. While Erickson's record slipped from 20-8 to 13-12, his ERA rose only a little, from 3.18 to 3.40.

Erickson is a stubborn sort and did not embrace the suggestions of his coaches. But in the latter half of 1992 he appeared to make progress, even earning praise from manager Tom Kelly. Erickson's out pitch remained the hard sinking fastball, but he spotted his curveball and change-up effectively.

When his sinker is darting and he's throwing his curve and change-up for strikes, Erickson is capable of recording 15 to 20 groundball outs per game. But despite being a groundball pitcher, he surrendered 18 homers. Seven of them came on first pitches, which were a problem for him all year. Opposing hitters batted .361 against Erickson when they put the first pitch in play. Erickson may need to make the first offering a little less tempting.

HOLDING RUNNERS AND FIELDING:

Manager Tom Kelly expressed his displeasure several times with Erickson's defensive nonchalance as a 1990 rookie, but the righthander has taken strides toward becoming a complete pitcher. Erickson led Twins pitchers in total chances (52), putouts (18) and double plays (3) while committing just one error. He's also improved his move to first, but still yields too many stolen bases (23 in 30 attempts last year).

OVERALL:

Erickson's biggest obstacle to major-league stardom may be himself. He has frequently feuded with Kelly and pitching coach Dick Such over pitching philosophy, and the righthander needs to be more receptive to instruction. If he can couple his natural ability with pitching savvy, he should become a consistent 15-to-18 game winner.

SCOTT ERICKSON

Position: SP
Bats: R **Throws:** R
Ht: 6' 4" **Wt:** 224

Opening Day Age: 25
Born: 2/2/68 in Long Beach, CA
ML Seasons: 3

Overall Statistics

	W	L	ERA	G	GS	Sv	IP	H	R	BB	SO	HR
1992	13	12	3.40	32	32	0	212.0	197	86	83	101	18
Career	41	24	3.20	83	81	0	529.0	494	215	205	262	40

How Often He Throws Strikes

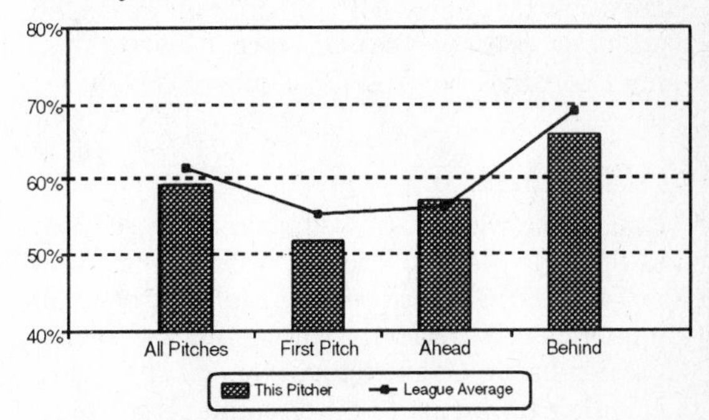

1992 Situational Stats

	W	L	ERA	Sv	IP		AB	H	HR	RBI	AVG
Home	8	6	3.43	0	123.1	LHB	410	99	7	39	.241
Road	5	6	3.35	0	88.2	RHB	371	98	11	39	.264
Day	9	5	2.45	0	110.0	Sc Pos	184	41	6	62	.223
Night	4	7	4.41	0	102.0	Clutch	91	28	3	9	.308

1992 Rankings (American League)

- 1st in most GDPs induced per 9 innings (1.3)
- 2nd in most GDPs induced (31) and highest groundball/flyball ratio (2.5)
- 4th in shutouts (3)
- Led the Twins in losses (12), complete games (5), shutouts, home runs allowed (18), walks allowed (83), hit batsmen (8), balks (1), GDPs induced, highest groundball/flyball ratio, least pitches thrown per batter (3.50), most GDPs induced per 9 innings, ERA on the road (3.35), lowest batting average allowed vs. left-handed hitters (.242) and lowest batting average allowed with runners in scoring position (.223)

HITTING:

In 1991, Greg Gagne hit .265, the second-highest average of his career. He also struck out a career-low 72 times while working for the first time with Twins' hitting coach Terry Crowley. Minnesota naturally hoped that the improvement would continue in 1992. Instead, Gagne batted only .246 and struck out 83 times in 439 at-bats last year.

Manager Tom Kelly was of the opinion that Gagne let his impending free agency status get to him. Gagne had worked hard trying to be more selective in 1991, but last season he walked only 19 times and once again was too often an easy target for low, outside sliders. The book on pitching to Gagne is simple: get ahead in the count, and then throw the slider on the outside corner. Gagne had his worst power season since 1985, totaling only 30 extra-base hits (23 doubles, seven homers).

BASERUNNING:

Gagne has always possessed plenty of speed, but has failed to develop into the basestealing threat the Twins once envisioned. He stole six bases in 13 attempts last season, equalling his career low in stolen bases. Gagne remains an excellent runner going from first-to-third, combining intelligence with speed.

FIELDING:

Kelly's criticism about Gagne's free agent status was most apparent in the field. Gagne was the glue that held the Twins defense together during the World Series championship season of 1991. He committed only nine errors that season, and went a club-record 76 games without a miscue. He had 18 errors last year, although he remained one of the league's best-fielding shortstops. He again had a 53-game errorless streak from June 9 through Aug. 10.

OVERALL:

Gagne's defense might have slipped a notch last season, but he's still an asset to any team even when hitting .240. He has better-than-average range, and when he's in the midst of one of his streaks there isn't a more sure-handed shortstop around. At the age of 31, he could be one of the bargains in the year's free agent market.

GREG GAGNE

Position: SS
Bats: R **Throws:** R
Ht: 5'11" **Wt:** 173

Opening Day Age: 31
Born: 11/12/61 in Fall River, MA
ML Seasons: 10

Overall Statistics

	G	AB	R	H	D	T	HR	RBI	SB	BB	SO	AVG
1992	146	439	53	108	23	0	7	39	6	19	83	.246
Career	1140	3386	452	844	183	35	69	335	79	188	676	.249

Where He Hits the Ball

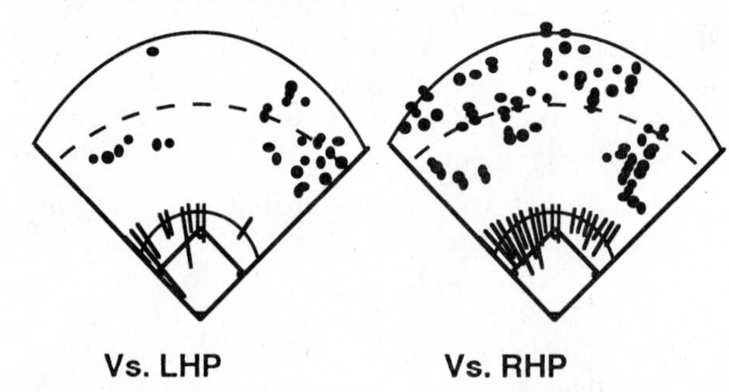

Vs. LHP   Vs. RHP

1992 Situational Stats

	AB	H	HR	RBI	AVG		AB	H	HR	RBI	AVG
Home	219	50	1	18	.228	LHP	105	19	1	6	.181
Road	220	58	6	21	.264	RHP	334	89	6	33	.266
Day	144	38	1	10	.264	Sc Pos	100	28	2	31	.280
Night	295	70	6	29	.237	Clutch	75	20	1	4	.267

1992 Rankings (American League)

- 4th in sacrifice bunts (12)
- 9th in bunts in play (24)
- Led the Twins in sacrifice bunts and bunts in play
- Led AL shortstops in sacrifice bunts

PITCHING:

It is probably accurate to say that Mark Guthrie is a victim of his own success as a left-handed reliever. Guthrie came to the Twins in 1989 as a starter, a role he would still prefer. But he was so effective in the role of set-up man for Rick Aguilera last season that the Twins are reluctant to consider shifting him from the bullpen.

Guthrie's 1992 success -- a 2.88 ERA in 75 innings and an opponents' batting average of .215 -- traces to his ability to pitch ahead in the count. His out pitch remains an excellent forkball, but he's improved his breaking pitch enough to compliment an average major league fastball. The results: In 1991 righthanders batted .293 against Guthrie and lefthanders .337; last season lefties batted .205 and righties .220.

Guthrie's success against righthanders afforded manager Tom Kelly the luxury of using him for longer periods of time as a reliever. In 1991, he was called out of the bullpen primarily to face left-handed batters, often without a great deal of success. Guthrie's biggest problem was that he surrendered seven home runs in 186 at-bats to right-handed batters, compared to no homers in 88 at-bats to left-handed batters. But he walked only 23 while striking out 76.

HOLDING RUNNERS AND FIELDING:

Guthrie arrived in the major leagues with one of baseball's best pickoff moves -- he fell one short of Jerry Koosman's club record of 14 pickoffs in 1990 -- and nothing has changed. He keeps runners close, making him tough to steal against. Basestealers were 6-for-8 against him last year, but the Twins' catchers had a lot to do with that low percentage. He's a fine fielder, making just one error in his 54 appearances.

OVERALL:

Though Guthrie has found success as a reliever, it's tempting for the Twins to wonder whether the lefthander might be just as effective in the starting rotation. His future job status with Minnesota appears to hinge on free-agent lefty John Smiley. If Smiley leaves, Guthrie would probably be moved to the rotation; if Smiley remains, Guthrie is back as set-up man. Either way, he's a big part of the Twins' 1993 plans.

MARK GUTHRIE

Position: RP
Bats: B **Throws:** L
Ht: 6' 4" **Wt:** 200

Opening Day Age: 27
Born: 9/22/65 in Buffalo, NY
ML Seasons: 4

Overall Statistics

	W	L	ERA	G	GS	Sv	IP	H	R	BB	SO	HR
1992	2	3	2.88	54	0	5	75.0	59	27	23	76	7
Career	18	21	3.86	132	41	7	375.0	395	176	124	287	33

How Often He Throws Strikes

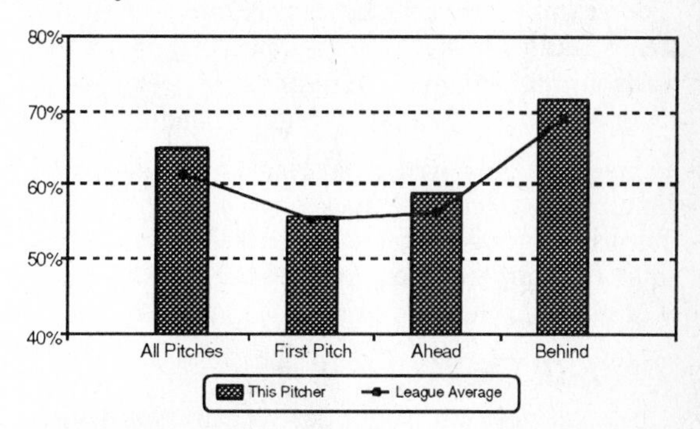

1992 Situational Stats

	W	L	ERA	Sv	IP		AB	H	HR	RBI	AVG
Home	2	0	2.02	3	35.2	LHB	88	18	0	6	.205
Road	0	3	3.66	2	39.1	RHB	186	41	7	17	.220
Day	2	1	1.59	2	28.1	Sc Pos	83	13	1	16	.157
Night	0	2	3.66	3	46.2	Clutch	96	20	1	9	.208

1992 Rankings (American League)

- 2nd in holds (19)
- 3rd in most strikeouts per 9 innings in relief (9.1)
- 4th in lowest percentage of inherited runners scored (15.8%)
- 7th in least baserunners allowed per 9 innings in relief (9.8)
- 8th in first batter efficiency (.173)
- Led the Twins in holds, first batter efficiency, lowest percentage of inherited runners scored, lowest batting average allowed in relief (.215) and most strikeouts per 9 innings in relief

HITTING:

There's not a more consistent-hitting catcher in baseball than Brian Harper. The 33-year-old has a .307 average since coming to the Twins in 1988. He equalled that .307 average last summer, the third time in the last four years he has hit at least that high. The other year, 1990, Harper batted .294.

Harper is one of the game's best contact hitters; he struck out just 22 times last year and only 99 times in his five seasons with Minnesota. He is a line drive hitter who uses all fields. Harper feasts on fastballs, and although some scouts believe he is vulnerable to breaking balls, there's little proof in the numbers. He has only moderate home run power (nine last year), but is generally among the team leaders in doubles. He had 25 doubles last season, and has averaged almost 30 per year in four seasons as the Twins' regular catcher.

About the only weakness Harper displays as a hitter is a reluctance to accept walks, not that surprising for someone who strikes out so infrequently. Harper walked only 26 times last season, but it was his high as a major leaguer.

BASERUNNING:

Speed is not one of Harper's attributes, which makes his doubles total all the more impressive. None of them are leg hits. Harper failed to steal a base in one attempt last year, making him 1-for-4 the past two seasons.

FIELDING:

Harper has long felt he has been unfairly typecast as a poor defensive catcher. However, Twins' pitchers had a 3.85 ERA with Harper catching last year, 3.31 with Lenny Webster. Harper threw out only 23 percent (36-of-154) of would-be basestealers last year, a poor average.

OVERALL:

Harper's bat makes him one of the league's best catchers. He's not the greatest defensively, but he plays well enough to keep his position as long as he hits. The Twins have been a winning team with Harper behind the plate and see no reason to make a change.

BRIAN HARPER

Position: C
Bats: R **Throws:** R
Ht: 6' 2" **Wt:** 205

Opening Day Age: 33
Born: 10/16/59 in Los Angeles, CA
ML Seasons: 13

Overall Statistics

	G	AB	R	H	D	T	HR	RBI	SB	BB	SO	AVG
1992	140	502	58	154	25	0	9	73	0	26	22	.307
Career	788	2363	264	697	145	6	47	323	7	95	140	.295

Where He Hits the Ball

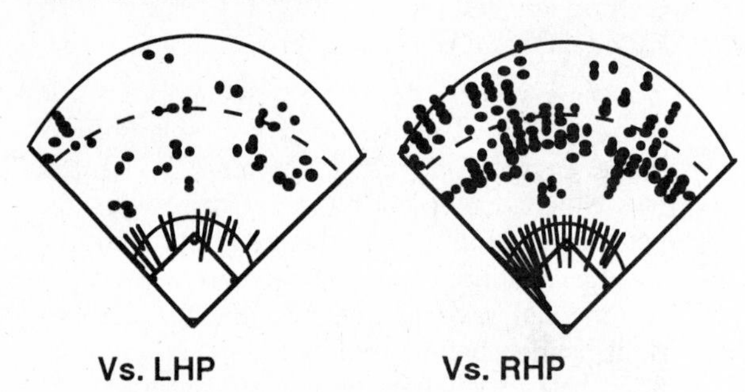

Vs. LHP Vs. RHP

1992 Situational Stats

	AB	H	HR	RBI	AVG		AB	H	HR	RBI	AVG
Home	241	78	3	31	.324	LHP	109	30	1	13	.275
Road	261	76	6	42	.291	RHP	393	124	8	60	.316
Day	141	47	3	26	.333	Sc Pos	147	42	1	61	.286
Night	361	107	6	47	.296	Clutch	84	25	1	9	.298

1992 Rankings (American League)

- 1st in batting average with 2 strikes (.289)
- 3rd in batting average with the bases loaded (.571)
- 4th in batting average vs. right-handed pitchers (.316) and batting average at home (.324)
- 6th in sacrifice flies (10)
- 9th in batting average (.307)
- Led the Twins in batting average with 2 strikes
- Led AL catchers in batting average, hits (154), singles (120), sacrifice flies, batting average with the bases loaded, batting average vs. right-handed pitchers, batting average at home and batting average with 2 strikes

HITTING:

It was proven once again last season that as Kent Hrbek goes, so go the Twins. Hrbek started the season on the disabled list, and the Twins started 6-9. Hrbek returned to the lineup, pushing his average to .274, and the Twins won 54 of 83 (.651), stamping them as baseball's best team. Then Hrbek went into a horrendous slump, hitting .172 after the All-Star break, and the Twins followed, going 30-34 from July 27 on.

The Twins count on Hrbek for left-handed power, and last year the big first baseman had career lows in average (.244), home runs (15) and RBI (58). Hrbek's season ended Sept. 6, and he underwent shoulder surgery two weeks before the season ended. Many of his woes were certainly traced to aching shoulders, but Twins coaches have grown weary of watching Hrbek's weight balloon annually.

Manager Tom Kelly said Hrbek will have to become serious about year-round conditioning if he wants to remain central to the team's plans. Hrbek appeared to lack bat speed last season, and was too often unable to get around on inside fastballs. He remains a good low-ball hitter, but the player who once feasted on righthanders batted only .238 against them last season.

BASERUNNING:

The extra poundage has reduced Hrbek's speed on the bases. Still, he's an intelligent runner, and managed to steal five bases in seven attempts last year. He takes all the extra bases his speed allows.

FIELDING:

Hrbek was steady defensively last year, but not spectacular. He committed only three errors in 104 games, but appeared a step slow on several occasions. Several times hard-hit balls that Hrbek once would have caught found their way into right field.

OVERALL:

Hrbek will be 33 in May, and his future is up to him. If he can get himself into good physical shape and rehabilitate his shoulders (he has separated both since 1989), he could be a productive power hitter for several more seasons. If he gains more weight during the off-season, then the Twins are in big trouble in 1993.

KENT HRBEK

Position: 1B
Bats: L **Throws:** R
Ht: 6' 4" **Wt:** 245

Opening Day Age: 32
Born: 5/21/60 in Minneapolis, MN
ML Seasons: 12

Overall Statistics

	G	AB	R	H	D	T	HR	RBI	SB	BB	SO	AVG
1992	112	394	52	96	20	0	15	58	5	71	56	.244
Career	1543	5526	809	1580	290	17	258	950	33	730	713	.286

Where He Hits the Ball

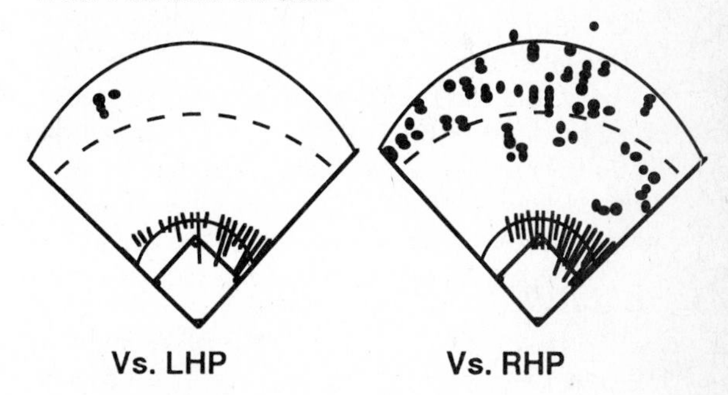

1992 Situational Stats

	AB	H	HR	RBI	AVG		AB	H	HR	RBI	AVG
Home	193	50	10	29	.259	LHP	83	22	1	9	.265
Road	201	46	5	29	.229	RHP	311	74	14	49	.238
Day	129	28	3	15	.217	Sc Pos	124	26	3	42	.210
Night	265	68	12	43	.257	Clutch	64	16	1	8	.250

1992 Rankings (American League)

- 8th in lowest batting average vs. right-handed pitchers (.238)
- Led AL first basemen in fielding percentage (.997)

HITTING:

Sophomore jinx? Chuck Knoblauch never gave it any thought, proving that his 1991 Rookie of the Year award was no fluke. The second baseman improved in batting average (.281 to .297), walks (59 to 88) and runs scored (78 to 104).

Knoblauch batted second in the Twins batting order through the All-Star break, then switched to leadoff when the Twins decided Shane Mack was striking out too often in the first position. Knoblauch was consistent at both spots -- hitting at least .296 in both positions -- and only an 0-for-10 streak in the season's final week prevented him from hitting .300.

Knoblauch is the son of a legendary Texas high school coach, and he is obviously well-schooled at the plate. He still has a tendency to chase high fastballs, but it's hardly a major fault. He lacks home run power (three major league home runs in 1,165 at-bats), but has 43 career doubles (19 last year) and 12 triples (six last season), evidence that he has the power to find the outfield gaps.

BASERUNNING:

On the bases, Knoblauch combines better-than-average speed and the intelligence of a coach's son. He led the Twins with 34 stolen bases in 47 attempts last season. Knoblauch did commit several baserunning blunders during the Twins' second-half slump, but club officials believe it was due to his trying too hard to ignite the floundering offense.

FIELDING:

As a rookie in 1991 Knoblauch committed 18 errors, but only three in the final 45 games. He continued his steady play in the field in 1992, making only six errors. He made the transition from college shortstop to second baseman in the minors, and turns the double play very well for someone still learning his new position.

OVERALL:

The organization that sifted through Tommy Herr, Wally Backman, Fred Manrique and Nelson Liriano from 1988 through 1990 in search of a second baseman is now set for years to come at the position. Knoblauch is everything a team wants in a second sacker, a fiery, intense competitor who can make those around him better.

CHUCK KNOBLAUCH

Position: 2B
Bats: R **Throws:** R
Ht: 5' 9" **Wt:** 179

Opening Day Age: 24
Born: 7/7/68 in Houston, TX
ML Seasons: 2

Overall Statistics

	G	AB	R	H	D	T	HR	RBI	SB	BB	SO	AVG
1992	155	600	104	178	19	6	2	56	34	88	60	.297
Career	306	1165	182	337	43	12	3	106	59	147	100	.289

Where He Hits the Ball

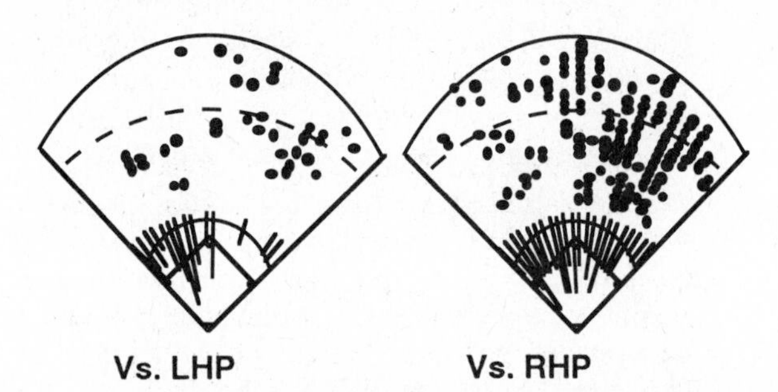

1992 Situational Stats

	AB	H	HR	RBI	AVG		AB	H	HR	RBI	AVG
Home	289	83	0	23	.287	LHP	124	39	1	9	.315
Road	311	95	2	33	.305	RHP	476	139	1	47	.292
Day	185	59	0	17	.319	Sc Pos	145	38	0	52	.262
Night	415	119	2	39	.287	Clutch	95	26	0	14	.274

1992 Rankings (American League)

- 2nd in singles (151), sacrifice flies (12) and batting average on an 0-2 count (.351)
- 4th in runs scored (104), times on base (271) and lowest HR frequency (300 ABs per HR)
- Led the Twins in runs scored, singles, triples (6), sacrifice flies, stolen bases (34), walks (88), times on base, pitches seen (2,618), plate appearances (707), stolen base percentage (72.3%), least GDPs per GDP situation (6.5%), batting average on an 0-2 count, on-base percentage vs. left-handed pitchers (.401), batting average on a 3-2 count (.326), highest percentage of pitches taken (61.0%), lowest percentage of swings that missed (9.0%), highest percentage of swings put into play (54.1%) and steals of third (4)

HITTING:

It's pretty certain that Gene Larkin will never shine over a full season the way he did the one moment when he drove in the winning run in Game 7 of the 1991 World Series. Larkin has been a solid role player since Chili Davis replaced him as the Twins' designated-hitter in 1991, and the role-player job status appears to fit his talents.

Larkin lacks the kind of power that teams like in full-time designated-hitters. But he's a good line drive hitter with enough power to find the gaps. His career-low .246 average last season was largely due to his struggles against left-handed pitchers. A switch-hitter, Larkin batted just .218 from the right side of the plate. He's been consistently better as a right-handed batter throughout his career.

Larkin jams the plate from both sides, and is annually among the team leaders in being hit by pitches. The negative to his style is that he sometimes has problems with inside fastballs. Larkin generally has a good eye, but he walked a career-low 28 times last season and struck out 43 times. The walk-strikeout ratio was the worst of his career.

BASERUNNING:

Larkin has only marginal speed, but is an intelligent baserunner who knows when to take the extra base. He stole a career-high seven bases in nine attempts last season, a noticeable improvement over 1991, when he was 2-for-5.

FIELDING:

Larkin plays a respectable first base and right field for the Twins, although as an outfielder his lack of speed is limiting. He has improved steadily as a first baseman, especially in his ability to dig low throws out of the dirt. He has a decent arm, as evidenced by his five outfield assists.

OVERALL:

Larkin remains a useful player, but at 30, his career is headed the wrong way. Minnesota will likely bring him back, and if so, Larkin figures to be a solid contributor off the bench.

GENE LARKIN

Position: 1B/RF
Bats: B **Throws:** R
Ht: 6' 3" **Wt:** 207

Opening Day Age: 30
Born: 10/24/62 in Astoria, NY
ML Seasons: 6

Overall Statistics

	G	AB	R	H	D	T	HR	RBI	SB	BB	SO	AVG
1992	115	337	38	83	18	1	6	42	7	28	43	.246
Career	702	2177	258	580	124	11	31	247	23	247	262	.266

Where He Hits the Ball

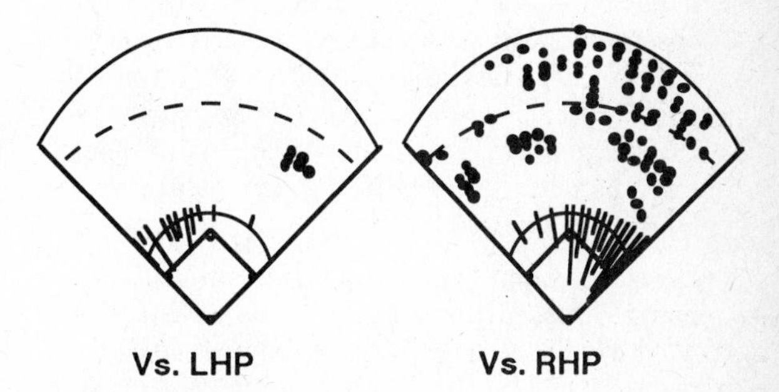

1992 Situational Stats

	AB	H	HR	RBI	AVG		AB	H	HR	RBI	AVG
Home	153	40	5	20	.261	LHP	55	12	0	5	.218
Road	184	43	1	22	.234	RHP	282	71	6	37	.252
Day	95	24	3	12	.253	Sc Pos	95	27	1	32	.284
Night	242	59	3	30	.244	Clutch	63	19	0	10	.302

1992 Rankings (American League)

- 2nd in lowest batting average on a 3-2 count (.043)

SCOTT LEIUS

Position: 3B
Bats: R **Throws:** R
Ht: 6' 3" **Wt:** 190

Opening Day Age: 27
Born: 9/24/65 in Yonkers, NY
ML Seasons: 3

Overall Statistics

	G	AB	R	H	D	T	HR	RBI	SB	BB	SO	AVG
1992	129	409	50	102	18	2	2	35	6	34	61	.249
Career	252	633	89	165	26	4	8	59	11	66	98	.261

Where He Hits the Ball

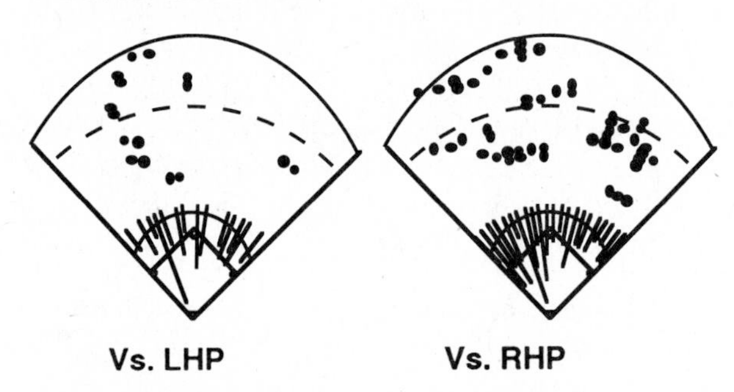

1992 Situational Stats

	AB	H	HR	RBI	AVG		AB	H	HR	RBI	AVG
Home	221	57	2	24	.258	LHP	118	37	0	10	.314
Road	188	45	0	11	.239	RHP	291	65	2	25	.223
Day	126	28	1	11	.222	Sc Pos	126	30	0	33	.238
Night	283	74	1	24	.261	Clutch	67	15	0	6	.224

1992 Rankings (American League)

- Did not rank near the top or bottom in any category

HITTING:

Scott Leius was an effective platoon player in 1991 when he shared third base with left-handed hitting Mike Pagliarulo. A series of injuries ruined Pagliarulo's 1992 season, leaving Leius as the Twins' everyday third baseman. Club officials believe fatigue was a factor in Leius' decline from a .286 average in '91 to .249 last season. Leius was hitting over .290 in May and still carried a .275 average at the All-Star break. But over his last 29 games, he was only 14-for-89 (.157).

All of which raises the obvious question: Can Leius ever be an everyday player in the majors? He might have a better chance as a shortstop, his minor league position, because he doesn't appear to have the power usually associated with at third baseman. Leius had just two home runs and 35 RBI in 129 games last season. The other troubling sign for Leius was his .223 average against right-handed pitchers. Leius hit .314 against lefthanders, a pattern similar to 1991 when he hit .305 vs. lefties, .254 vs. righties.

Leius is a decent fastball hitter, but still chases too many offspeed breaking balls out of the strike zone. He batted only .238 with runners in scoring position, and hit just .182 with runners in scoring position and two out.

BASERUNNING:

Leius has only average speed but is a heady runner who knows when to take the extra base. He is not a good basestealer, however, and is only 11-for-21 in his career.

FIELDING:

Leius' errors at third base increased from seven in 1991 to 15 last season, but he also handled more than twice as many chances -- up from 148 to 330. He's a steady fielder with quick hands that enabled him to make a number of outstanding backhand stops. He also has a respectable arm.

OVERALL:

If the Twins lose Greg Gagne to free agency over the winter, Leius is expected to get a long look at shortstop. Considering his lack of power, he might be better suited to play shortstop on an everyday basis. He appears to have the agility and athletic ability to make the switch.

HITTING:

To think that only three seasons ago the San Diego Padres didn't bother to protect Shane Mack on their 40-man major league roster. Mack is now a bona fide star; he batted .315 in 600 at-bats last season, the third straight year he has batted at least .310 for the Twins.

Considered too nervous to succeed by San Diego, Mack has thrived in the looser Twins' clubhouse. His biggest weakness as a hitter remains strikeouts; he fanned 106 times in 1992. The strikeouts prompted the Twins to switch Mack from the leadoff position to number-two in the order just before the All-Star break.

Mack compensated, trying to shorten his swing in the season's second half, and the results were promising. He struck out 63 times in 333 at-bats before the All-Star break, 43 times in 267 at-bats after the break. More impressively, he batted .348 (93-for-267) after the break. Mack did sacrifice some power with the shortened swing, homering just six times after the break. But the Twins will gladly take the near-.350 average. He was also solid in the clutch, batting .298 with runners in scoring position.

BASERUNNING:

Mack has excellent speed, but needs to refine his basestealing mechanics. He stole 26 bases last season, but was also thrown out 14 times. He was just 13-for-22 in stolen bases in 1991. He's among the Twins' most aggressive players, fearless when it comes to breaking up a double play.

FIELDING:

Mack's natural athletic talents make him one of the league's best left fielders. He covers more territory than most and is adept at the sliding basket catch. Mack made just four errors in 335 chances last season and had nine assists, tying him with Kirby Puckett for the team lead among outfielders.

OVERALL:

You don't have to look any further than Mack to realize that even in the computer age of judging talent, teams are still capable of making huge mistakes. Mack should be a star in the majors for years to come, a .300 hitter with power and an excellent outfielder to boot.

SHANE MACK

Position: LF
Bats: R **Throws:** R
Ht: 6' 0" **Wt:** 185

Opening Day Age: 29
Born: 12/7/63 in Los Angeles, CA
ML Seasons: 5

Overall Statistics

	G	AB	R	H	D	T	HR	RBI	SB	BB	SO	AVG
1992	156	600	101	189	31	6	16	75	26	64	106	.315
Career	585	1712	271	514	82	21	46	230	61	159	322	.300

Where He Hits the Ball

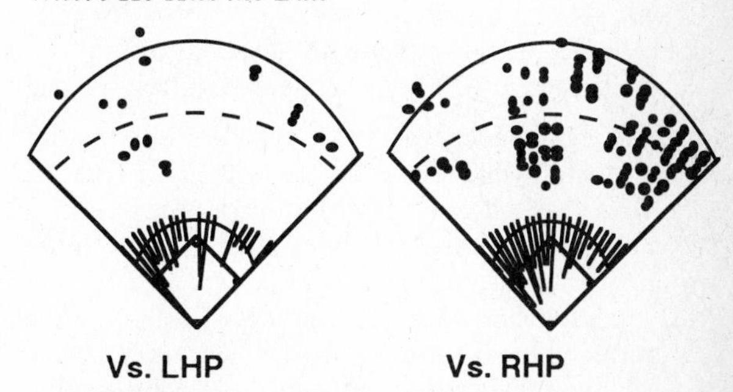

1992 Situational Stats

	AB	H	HR	RBI	AVG		AB	H	HR	RBI	AVG
Home	286	87	10	41	.304	LHP	128	38	4	24	.297
Road	314	102	6	34	.325	RHP	472	151	12	51	.320
Day	186	57	7	23	.306	Sc Pos	141	42	3	56	.298
Night	414	132	9	52	.319	Clutch	94	26	0	6	.277

1992 Rankings (American League)

- 1st in hit by pitch (15)
- 3rd in batting average vs. right-handed pitchers (.320) and on-base percentage vs. right-handed pitchers (.403)
- 4th in hits (189) and highest groundball/flyball ratio (2.3)
- 5th in batting average (.315), on-base percentage (.394) and batting average on the road (.325)
- Led the Twins in triples (6), caught stealing (14), hit by pitch, strikeouts (106), on-base percentage, highest groundball/flyball ratio, slugging percentage vs. left-handed pitchers (.516) and batting average on the road

PITCHING:

The Twins opted for Pat Mahomes as their fifth starter out of spring training last year, and the rookie righthander showed flashes of brilliance. He also showed too much inconsistency to suit manager Tom Kelly, who dispatched Mahomes to the minors in early June. The change didn't help much. Mahomes was 3-2 with a 5.23 ERA before his demotion, 0-2 with a 4.76 ERA after rejoining the Twins in September.

Mahomes has the tools -- a 90-MPH fastball and a hard-breaking slider. But like most young pitchers, he needs to refine his offspeed assortment to be a consistent major-league starter. Mahomes had big problems when he got behind in the count last season, allowing batters to wait on his fastball. Despite his excellent physical tools, opposing batters hit .279 against Mahomes last season.

The righthander was hurt by the big inning after his recall, which drew the ire of Kelly. Example: Mahomes pitched five shutout innings against California in late September, then failed to retire a batter in the sixth. Kelly wondered aloud how a young pitcher could run out of gas so early into a starting assignment. Kelly had criticized Mahomes' approach early in the season, saying the righthander needed to be more consistent in his routine between assignments to be effective.

HOLDING RUNNERS AND FIELDING:

The 22 year old is a splendid natural athlete who turned down a chance to play basketball at Arkansas to sign with the Twins out of high school. He is a decent fielder and will get better with experience. He controlled the running game very well as a rookie, allowing only nine steals in 17 attempts.

OVERALL:

The only question with Mahomes is when the mental portion of his game will catch up with his physical ability. Mahomes needs to learn the basics of pitching, namely how to stay ahead in the count consistently. When he does that, he has a chance to be one of the league's top starting pitchers for years to come. That's why the Twins took no chances with him by protecting him from expansion.

PAT MAHOMES

Position: SP
Bats: R **Throws:** R
Ht: 6' 1" **Wt:** 175

Opening Day Age: 22
Born: 8/9/70 in Bryan, TX
ML Seasons: 1

Overall Statistics

	W	L	ERA	G	GS	Sv	IP	H	R	BB	SO	HR
1992	3	4	5.04	14	13	0	69.2	73	41	37	44	5
Career	3	4	5.04	14	13	0	69.2	73	41	37	44	5

How Often He Throws Strikes

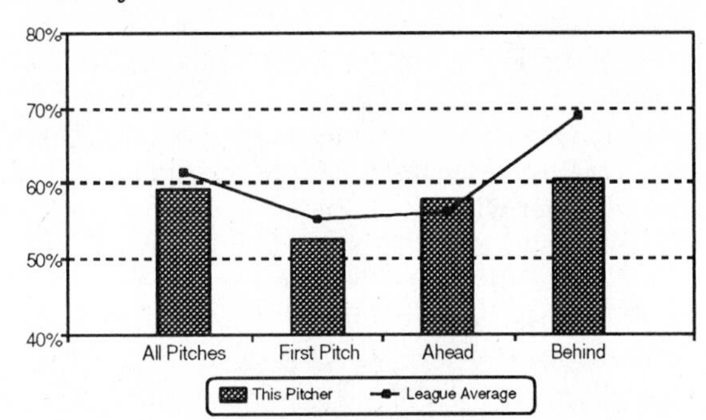

1992 Situational Stats

	W	L	ERA	Sv	IP		AB	H	HR	RBI	AVG
Home	1	2	7.02	0	33.1	LHB	135	38	3	20	.281
Road	2	2	3.22	0	36.1	RHB	127	35	2	19	.276
Day	1	0	5.27	0	13.2	Sc Pos	75	20	3	34	.267
Night	2	4	4.98	0	56.0	Clutch	6	1	0	0	.167

1992 Rankings (American League)

- Did not rank near the top or bottom in any category

PEDRO MUNOZ

Position: RF
Bats: R **Throws:** R
Ht: 5'10" **Wt:** 205

Opening Day Age: 24
Born: 9/19/68 in Ponce, Puerto Rico
ML Seasons: 3

Overall Statistics

	G	AB	R	H	D	T	HR	RBI	SB	BB	SO	AVG
1992	127	418	44	113	16	3	12	71	4	17	90	.270
Career	200	641	72	175	27	5	19	102	10	28	137	.273

Where He Hits the Ball

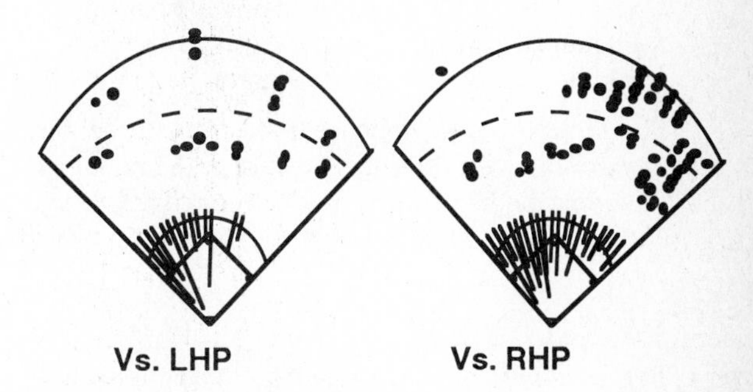

1992 Situational Stats

	AB	H	HR	RBI	AVG		AB	H	HR	RBI	AVG
Home	193	53	8	36	.275	LHP	122	36	3	21	.295
Road	225	60	4	35	.267	RHP	296	77	9	50	.260
Day	134	28	7	27	.209	Sc Pos	121	39	6	62	.322
Night	284	85	5	44	.299	Clutch	53	17	2	8	.321

1992 Rankings (American League)

- 3rd in most GDPs per GDP situation (22.5%)
- 5th in lowest percentage of pitches taken (44.9%)
- 9th in GDPs (18)
- Led the Twins in GDPs and batting average in the clutch (.321)
- Led AL right fielders in GDPs and batting average with runners in scoring position (.322)

HITTING:

A strange thing happened to Pedro Munoz on the way to a productive season: he found himself sitting on the bench for extended periods in August. Twins officials explained the move by saying that with Kent Hrbek and Chili Davis struggling, they felt the need to get another left-handed bat -- Randy Bush or Gene Larkin -- into the lineup against right-handed pitchers.

The numbers say the Twins would have been better off sticking with Munoz. The right fielder batted .322 with runners in scoring position, the second-best average on the team behind Kirby Puckett. His overall numbers -- .270 average, 12 homers and 71 RBI in 418 at-bats -- were solid. And he was by no means an easy out against right-handed pitchers, batting .260 with nine homers and 50 RBI in 296 at-bats.

Twins manager Tom Kelly, however, believed that Munoz' long swing made him too-easy an out against hard-throwing righthanders. Kelly reasoned that Munoz's final stats were the result of knowing when it was prudent to remove the youngster from the starting lineup. The theory was not without merit, because there were many times that Munoz looked overmatched against fastballing righthanders. But there were also plenty of times when Munoz would bounce back to even the score.

BASERUNNING:

The stockily-built Munoz has decent speed, but nothing more. He stole four bases in nine attempts last season. He should improve on that figure with experience; he stole 16 bases in only 86 games at Class AAA Syracuse in 1990.

FIELDING:

Once considered a poor fielder, Munoz appears on his way to proving the early reports false. He's not graceful, but he is steady, making just three errors in 122 games last season. His arm was better than advertised; he recorded eight assists.

OVERALL:

The Twins obtained Munoz and Nelson Liriano from Toronto in late July, 1991 for John Candelaria. Score a big victory for the Twins in this swap, because Munoz looks to be a solid major-league player with big-year potential.

MIKE PAGLIARULO

Position: 3B
Bats: L **Throws:** R
Ht: 6' 2" **Wt:** 201

Opening Day Age: 33
Born: 3/15/60 in Medford, MA
ML Seasons: 9

HITTING:

Mike Pagliarulo appeared to have revived his career in 1991 when he batted a career-high .279 for the Twins. But thanks to a pair of freak injuries, Pagliarulo's major-league future is again in doubt. As a result of his mishaps, Pagliarulo batted only .200 last year and had almost no power. He managed just four doubles (no homers or triples) in 105 at-bats.

The third baseman's woes began in a spring intrasquad game, when he was struck on the side of his head by a pitch from teammate David West. Pagliarulo suffered a perforated ear drum and began the season on the disabled list. He had batted just 17 times (two hits) after returning when he suffered a broken hamate bone in his right hand swinging a bat. Pagliarulo didn't return until late July. Pags never got untracked in 1992.

Pagliarulo likes low pitches in the strike zone, but has trouble with offerings that are high and away. Last year he had trouble with almost everything, and the Twins must ask themselves if Pagliarulo can come back once again.

BASERUNNING:

Pagliarulo has not had more than two stolen bases in a year since swiping three with the Yankees and Padres in 1989. The numbers don't lie: he has minimal speed. But Pagliarulo is not a dumb player, and he is an aggressive baserunner.

FIELDING:

Pagliarulo was reputed to have poor range and a weak arm at third when the Twins signed him as a free agent before the 1991 season. Pagliarulo proved that scouting report wrong, making numerous diving stops and showing a strong, accurate arm. He was steady last year, making three errors in 37 games.

OVERALL:

Pagliarulo was a free agent after the 1992 season, but his age (33 on Opening Day), injuries and up-and-down career made interest from other teams unlikely. It seemed logical that Pagliarulo would be invited to spring training with the Twins as a non-roster player, and the rest would be up to him.

Overall Statistics

	G	AB	R	H	D	T	HR	RBI	SB	BB	SO	AVG
1992	42	105	10	21	4	0	0	9	1	1	17	.200
Career	1044	3290	380	774	165	14	121	434	12	302	687	.235

Where He Hits the Ball

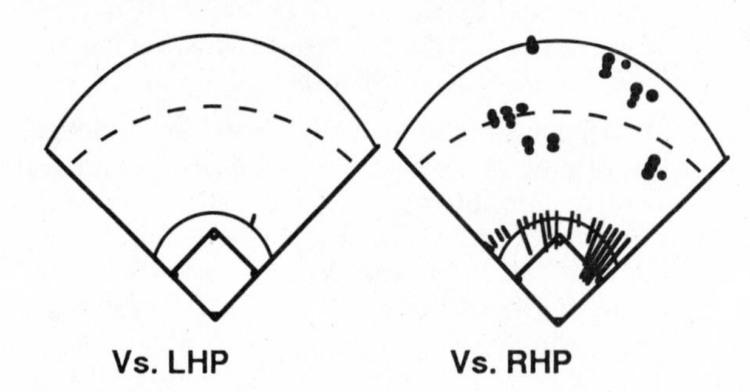

1992 Situational Stats

	AB	H	HR	RBI	AVG		AB	H	HR	RBI	AVG
Home	46	10	0	5	.217	LHP	6	1	0	0	.167
Road	59	11	0	4	.186	RHP	99	20	0	9	.202
Day	26	9	0	4	.346	Sc Pos	26	6	0	9	.231
Night	79	12	0	5	.152	Clutch	14	2	0	0	.143

1992 Rankings (American League)

- Did not rank near the top or bottom in any category

KIRBY PUCKETT

Position: CF
Bats: R **Throws:** R
Ht: 5' 8" **Wt:** 215

Opening Day Age: 32
Born: 3/14/61 in Chicago, IL
ML Seasons: 9

HITTING:

What is there left to say about Kirby Puckett? The center fielder is simply one of -- if not the -- best all-around players in the major leagues. Puckett batted .329 last season with 210 hits, 110 RBI and 104 runs scored. It was the sixth time in the last seven seasons he had hit at least .319, and it raised his career batting average to .321. If Puckett can keep similar pace into his late thirties, he should collect 3,000 hits.

Puckett is a free-swinger, as liable to hit a high, outside pitch for a base hit as he is one down the middle. His strikeouts are generally double his walks, and last season was no exception with 97 whiffs and 44 walks. But all his other numbers are outstanding. Puckett batted .329 against right-handed pitchers and .328 against lefties. He batted .346 with runners in scoring position. His numbers are usually best at the Metrodome, and last year was no exception: a .348 average at home, .309 on the road.

BASERUNNING:

The years have robbed Puckett of some speed but he remains a basestealing threat. He swiped 17 bases in 24 attempts last season, his most stolen bases since 1986. He's an extremely knowledgeable player who seldom makes a mistake on the bases.

FIELDING:

The rap on Puckett has long been that he plays too deep, which has enhanced his ability to make leaping catches over the centerfield fence at the expense of Texas League singles. Perhaps, but at age 32 he still covers plenty of ground and is a steadying influence defensively. He made just three errors in 406 chances last season and had nine assists.

OVERALL:

Puckett tested the free agent market after the season, but his heart was always with the Twins. When they made a competitive offer, he signed a contract which should keep him in Minnesota 'til he's in his late thirties. Twins fans couldn't be happier.

Overall Statistics

	G	AB	R	H	D	T	HR	RBI	SB	BB	SO	AVG
1992	160	639	104	210	38	4	19	110	17	44	97	.329
Career	1382	5645	820	1812	304	51	142	785	117	319	736	.321

Where He Hits the Ball

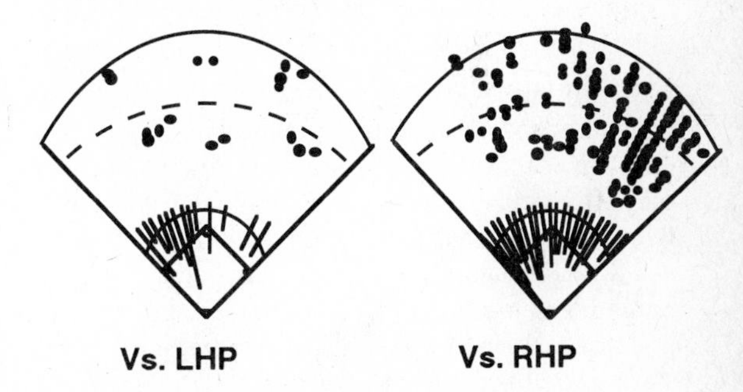

1992 Situational Stats

	AB	H	HR	RBI	AVG		AB	H	HR	RBI	AVG
Home	325	113	9	54	.348	LHP	125	41	3	22	.328
Road	314	97	10	56	.309	RHP	514	169	16	88	.329
Day	200	61	5	35	.305	Sc Pos	188	65	6	87	.346
Night	439	149	14	75	.339	Clutch	104	33	1	14	.317

1992 Rankings (American League)

- 1st in hits (210) and total bases (313)
- 2nd in batting average (.329) and batting average vs. right-handed pitchers (.329)
- 3rd in singles (149), least pitches seen per plate appearance (3.18) and batting average at home (.348)
- Led the Twins in batting average, home runs (19), at-bats (639), runs scored (104), hits, doubles (38), total bases, RBI (110), intentional walks (13), games played (160), slugging percentage (.490), HR frequency (33.6 ABs per HR) and batting average with runners in scoring position (.346),

PITCHING:

The Twins obtained John Smiley from Pittsburgh last spring after losing Jack Morris to free agency. After a slow start (6.84 ERA in April), Smiley established himself as the team's top pitcher, going 16-9 with a 3.21 ERA in 241 innings. He then departed for Cincinnati and free agent millions.

The lefthander has all the tools. He's a power pitcher with a fastball frequently clocked around 90 MPH and a decent slider. What makes facing Smiley so difficult is that he can be as effective pitching with finesse as with power. He has a superb change-up and an improving curveball. Opposing batters had just a .231 average against Smiley, and he walked only 65 men while striking out 163.

The only rap against Smiley is that he has yet to prove himself a big-game pitcher. He did not get past the second inning for the Pirates in two playoff starts in 1991, and failed to quiet his detractors last season. Smiley was only 3-5 with a 5.20 ERA against the other American League contenders -- Oakland, Toronto, Baltimore and Milwaukee. He also lost his first three September starts at a time the Twins were still in the AL West race. Smiley finished strongly -- only one run in his final 27 innings -- after the Twins were eliminated from the division race.

HOLDING RUNNERS AND FIELDING:

Smiley has developed a good pickoff move and has worked hard at shortening his leg kick with runners aboard. But there were times last season, especially early, when Smiley appeared to regress in the attention he afforded baserunners. He is not as natural an athlete as many Twins pitchers, but has worked hard to make himself a decent fielder.

OVERALL:

Minnesota General Manager Andy MacPhail was pleased with Smiley, feeling he gave the Twins everything they could have hoped for. Minnesota would have liked to re-sign the free agent lefty, but felt they couldn't afford both Smiley and Kirby Puckett. He'll take Greg Swindell's place on Cincinnati.

JOHN SMILEY

Position: SP
Bats: L **Throws:** L
Ht: 6' 4" **Wt:** 200

Opening Day Age: 28
Born: 3/17/65 in Phoenixville, PA
ML Seasons: 7

Overall Statistics

	W	L	ERA	G	GS	Sv	IP	H	R	BB	SO	HR
1992	16	9	3.21	34	34	0	241.0	205	93	65	163	17
Career	76	51	3.49	230	151	4	1095.0	992	468	294	697	95

How Often He Throws Strikes

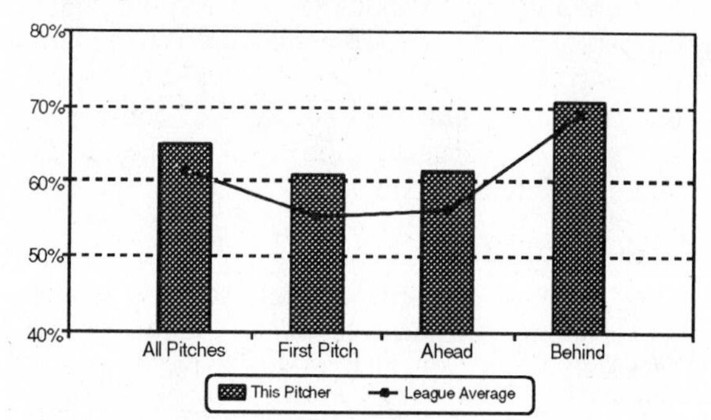

1992 Situational Stats

	W	L	ERA	Sv	IP		AB	H	HR	RBI	AVG
Home	10	4	2.83	0	136.2	LHB	139	36	1	12	.259
Road	6	5	3.71	0	104.1	RHB	747	169	16	72	.226
Day	5	4	4.22	0	74.2	Sc Pos	193	52	3	66	.269
Night	11	5	2.76	0	166.1	Clutch	81	15	1	1	.185

1992 Rankings (American League)

- 2nd in runners picked off (10)
- 3rd in runners caught stealing (16)
- 4th in lowest on-base percentage allowed (.286) and least baserunners allowed per 9 innings (10.3)
- Led the Twins in ERA (3.21), wins (16), games started (34), complete games (5), innings pitched (241), batters faced (970), strikeouts (163), pitches thrown (3,548), runners caught stealing, winning percentage (.640), lowest batting average allowed (.231), lowest slugging percentage allowed (.356), lowest on-base percentage allowed, lowest stolen base percentage allowed (61.0%) and least baserunners allowed per 9 innings

KEVIN TAPANI

Position: SP
Bats: R **Throws:** R
Ht: 6' 0" **Wt:** 183

Opening Day Age: 29
Born: 2/18/64 in Des Moines, IA
ML Seasons: 4

Overall Statistics

	W	L	ERA	G	GS	Sv	IP	H	R	BB	SO	HR
1992	16	11	3.97	34	34	0	220.0	226	103	48	138	17
Career	46	30	3.62	104	101	0	663.1	654	280	129	397	55

How Often He Throws Strikes

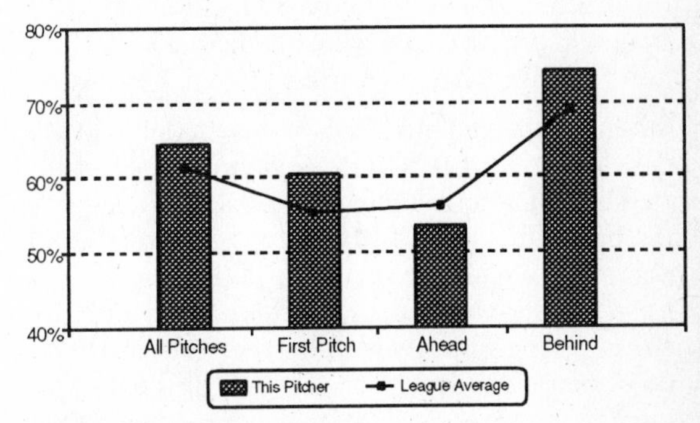

1992 Situational Stats

	W	L	ERA	Sv	IP		AB	H	HR	RBI	AVG
Home	11	4	3.48	0	126.2	LHB	434	121	12	56	.279
Road	5	7	4.63	0	93.1	RHB	405	105	5	38	.259
Day	6	1	3.99	0	58.2	Sc Pos	191	54	2	71	.283
Night	10	10	3.96	0	161.1	Clutch	65	13	2	6	.200

1992 Rankings (American League)

- 2nd in highest run support per 9 innings (6.1)
- 3rd in highest strikeout/walk ratio (2.9)
- 6th in most stolen bases allowed (26)
- 7th in games started (34) and highest batting average allowed (.269)
- 8th in highest slugging percentage allowed (.405)
- Led the Twins in wins (16), games started, hits allowed (226), stolen bases allowed, highest strikeout/walk ratio and highest run support per 9 innings

PITCHING:

Kevin Tapani doesn't dazzle many people, which only proves that appearances can be deceiving. Tapani has won 16 games each of the past two seasons and is 44-28 since moving into the Twins' starting rotation in 1990.

Tapani's ERA rose from 2.99 in 1991 to 3.97 last season, a jump the righthander traced to control problems. Understand that we're speaking in relative terms here, since Tapani walked only 48 batters last season in 220 innings. But the righthander didn't feel he had the complete control he exhibited in 1991, when he walked only 40 in 244 innings. That year he didn't walk a batter in 13 of his 34 starts. Last season Tapani failed to issue a walk in only eight of 34 starts, and six of those eight starts were six innings or less in duration. He walked at least one batter in 12 of his final 13 starts. He found himself pitching behind in counts in key situations too often last season, which was one reason opponents batted .269 (lefthanders .279, righthanders .259).

Tapani's success hinges on his ability to control each of his four pitches -- fastball, slider, change-up and forkball. Even when he fails to live up to personal expectations, his control is still better than most. Tapani has an extremely fluid motion, and although he doesn't appear to be throwing hard, he is routinely clocked near 90 MPH. He reduced his home runs allowed from 23 in 1991 to 17 last year.

HOLDING RUNNERS AND FIELDING:

Tapani is a consummate pitcher. He has developed an adequate pickoff move and a short leg kick, though he did permit 26 steals last year. He's a steady fielder, although he did commit two errors last season.

OVERALL:

Tapani's personality -- low-key, soft-spoken -- has been a perfect fit for his role as number-two starter the past two summers in the Twins' rotation. Tapani pitches without a lot of fanfare, but when the season has ended, he's had 16 victories and at least 220 innings for two straight seasons. At the age of 29, those results should continue for several more seasons.

PITCHING:

After showing up in spring training with a new pitching delivery, Gary Wayne got off to a rough start. Gone was the herky-jerky style of past years; in its place was a smoother, more traditional motion. At first the change didn't sit well with manager Tom Kelly, who saw Wayne's unconventional motion as an aid against left-handed batters. But Wayne slowly won Kelly over, earning him a spot on the roster in spring training. He went on to have a consistent season in the bullpen (2.63 ERA).

Wayne worked in 41 games for the Twins despite being dispatched to the minors for six weeks in midseason. The demotion had more to do with a surplus of lefthanders in the Twins' bullpen than Wayne's performance, since he had a 2.25 ERA in 36 innings when he was sent to AAA Portland.

Wayne appeared justified in his belief that he didn't need his herky-jerky style to be successful as a major-league reliever. He has an adequate fastball (upper 80's-MPH), a good overhand curve and excellent change-up. Wayne's success hinges on his ability to mix up his pitches and stay ahead of the hitter, which he was able to do on most occasions last year. Though he's a flyball pitcher, he gave up just two home runs in 48 innings.

HOLDING RUNNERS AND FIELDING:

Wayne has always had a good pickoff move, and his change in delivery styles has sped up his motion toward the plate. Nonetheless, he permitted five steals in five attempts last year. He's a dependable fielder, not making an error in 41 appearances last year.

OVERALL:

Wayne had pitched just eight games above the Class AA level when the Twins selected him from Montreal in the 1988 major league draft. He has proven that he can pitch at the major-league level. With the loss of Tom Edens, he'll probably be in line for an expanded role with the Twins in '93.

GARY WAYNE

Position: RP
Bats: L **Throws:** L
Ht: 6' 3" **Wt:** 195

Opening Day Age: 30
Born: 11/30/62 in Dearborn, MI
ML Seasons: 4

Overall Statistics

	W	L	ERA	G	GS	Sv	IP	H	R	BB	SO	HR
1992	3	3	2.63	41	0	0	48.0	46	18	19	29	2
Career	8	8	3.44	147	0	3	170.0	150	72	72	105	12

How Often He Throws Strikes

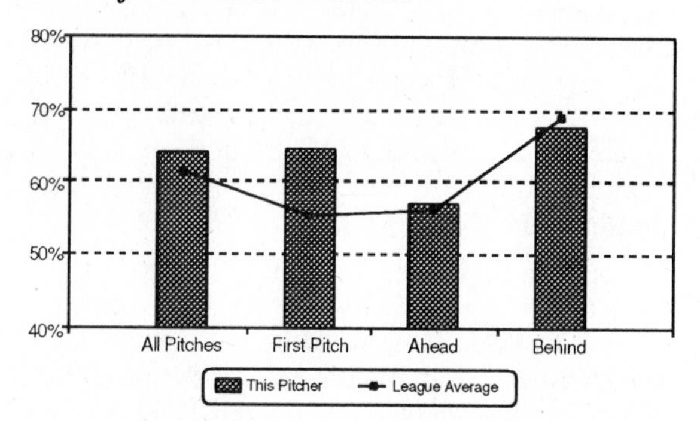

1992 Situational Stats

	W	L	ERA	Sv	IP		AB	H	HR	RBI	AVG
Home	1	2	2.70	0	26.2	LHB	48	12	1	8	.250
Road	2	1	2.53	0	21.1	RHB	129	34	1	15	.264
Day	1	1	2.93	0	15.1	Sc Pos	49	14	1	21	.286
Night	2	2	2.48	0	32.2	Clutch	95	24	1	10	.253

1992 Rankings (American League)

- Did not rank near the top or bottom in any category

CARL WILLIS

Position: RP
Bats: L **Throws:** R
Ht: 6' 4" **Wt:** 213

Opening Day Age: 32
Born: 12/28/60 in Danville, VA
ML Seasons: 6

PITCHING:

The Twins' biggest pitching surprise of 1991, Carl Willis appeared headed for a crash landing early last season. But Willis, a long-time journeyman, righted himself and finished strongly to post his second straight solid season. Willis was 1-2 with a 5.96 ERA after his first 21 appearances last year. But from June 8 on he was 6-1 with a 1.43 ERA in 38 games. The righthander's final figure -- a 2.72 ERA over 79.1 innings -- was only slightly higher than the 2.63 mark he'd recorded for the champion Twins in 1991.

Willis did have some problems last year. The main one was that he allowed 42 percent (21 of 50) of his inherited baserunners to score, the worst figure among Minnesota relievers. In part because of that, Willis, who was the Twins' top middle reliever in 1991, relinquished his role to Tom Edens last season.

Willis relies on a split-fingered fastball that some opposing hitters have accused of being a spitter. He also has a decent fastball, but needs a better change-up if he's to improve his performance with men on base. Willis' key is his ability to throw his split-fingered pitch for strikes; he walked only 11 men (one intentional) in 79.1 innings last season and just 19 in 89 innings in 1991. The splitter gets him lots of groundball outs, and last year he had almost a two-to-one groundball/flyball ratio.

HOLDING RUNNERS AND FIELDING:

Willis has an adequate pickoff move. He needs it, because his height -- 6-foot-4 -- and preference for breaking pitches make him an inviting target for basestealers. He permitted only two steals in three attempts last year. Willis is not blessed with natural quickness, but is adequate in the field.

OVERALL:

Willis slipped a notch in the bullpen last year, and may have a difficult time reclaiming his 1991 status as the Twins' top middle reliever. He needs to keep a few more inherited baserunners from scoring to fit prominently in the Twins' future plans. However, his strong finish should keep him in the majors.

Overall Statistics

	W	L	ERA	G	GS	Sv	IP	H	R	BB	SO	HR
1992	7	3	2.72	59	0	1	79.1	73	25	11	45	4
Career	17	12	3.90	162	2	5	272.0	274	132	81	141	20

How Often He Throws Strikes

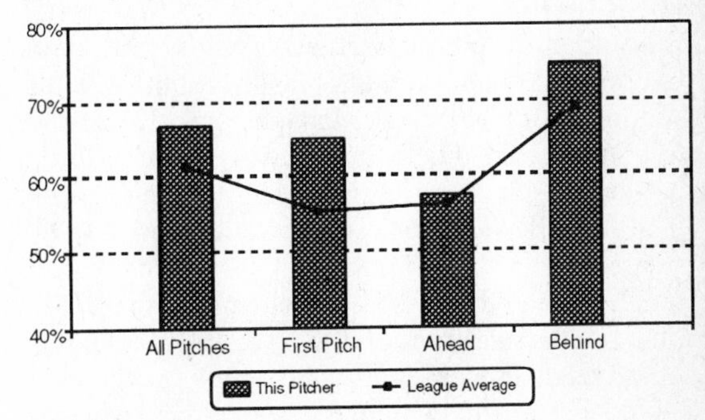

1992 Situational Stats

	W	L	ERA	Sv	IP		AB	H	HR	RBI	AVG
Home	4	2	2.93	1	43.0	LHB	108	25	2	10	.231
Road	3	1	2.48	0	36.1	RHB	189	48	2	27	.254
Day	3	0	2.95	0	21.1	Sc Pos	80	20	0	29	.250
Night	4	3	2.64	1	58.0	Clutch	101	24	1	10	.238

1992 Rankings (American League)

- 4th in least baserunners allowed per 9 innings in relief (9.5)
- 5th in worst first batter efficiency (.346)
- 6th in relief wins (7)
- 7th in most GDPs induced per GDP situation (20.4%) and highest percentage of inherited runners scored (42.0%)
- Led the Twins in balks (1), relief ERA (2.72), relief wins, relief innings (79.1) and least baserunners allowed per 9 innings in relief

PAUL ABBOTT

Position: RP
Bats: R **Throws:** R
Ht: 6' 3" **Wt:** 194

Opening Day Age: 25
Born: 9/15/67 in Van NUys, CA
ML Seasons: 3

Overall Statistics

	W	L	ERA	G	GS	Sv	IP	H	R	BB	SO	HR
1992	0	0	3.27	6	0	0	11.0	12	4	5	13	1
Career	3	6	5.03	28	10	0	93.0	87	55	69	81	6

PITCHING, FIELDING & HOLDING RUNNERS:

Shoulder problems virtually wiped out Paul Abbott's 1992 season and cast a doubt over his future with the Twins. Manager Tom Kelly and pitching coach Dick Such have displayed little patience with injury-prone youngsters in the past, and Abbott's hard-luck story was wearing thin by season's end. The righthander started the season on the disabled list with a shoulder injury suffered in a fall that was rumored to be the result of some ill-advised horseplay. Abbott went on the disabled list again in mid-August with a strained right shoulder.

Twins officials are reluctant to write off Abbott, because he possesses a 90-MPH fastball and a nasty slider. He showed glimpses of his potential at AAA Portland last year, going 4-1 with a 2.33 ERA and striking out 46 in 46.1 innings. But he pitched only six games with the Twins amidst the DL stints. If he can stay healthy and improve his change-up, he has the stuff to be a major-league starter. He's adequate in the field, but has been victimized by basestealers throughout his career.

OVERALL:

Abbott fell behind young Twins pitchers like Pat Mahomes and Mike Trombley in 1992. His name won't be written into the team's 1993 plans this off-season, but he has the stuff to earn a roster spot in spring training.

WILLIE BANKS

Position: SP
Bats: R **Throws:** R
Ht: 6' 1" **Wt:** 195

Opening Day Age: 24
Born: 2/27/69 in Jersey City, NJ
ML Seasons: 2

Overall Statistics

	W	L	ERA	G	GS	Sv	IP	H	R	BB	SO	HR
1992	4	4	5.70	16	12	0	71.0	80	46	37	37	6
Career	5	5	5.71	21	15	0	88.1	101	61	49	53	7

PITCHING, FIELDING & HOLDING RUNNERS:

The one-time phenom of the Twins' farm system, Willie Banks finds himself nearing a make-or-break point in his career. Banks was the third overall selection in the 1987 amateur draft and was heralded by some Twins officials as the second coming of Bob Gibson. But Banks has yet to display that potential in the major leagues.

The righthander has a fastball that approaches 90 MPH and a decent change-up, but he still hasn't mastered control or a breaking pitch. Banks too often worries about falling behind in the count and serves up easy fastballs. One result: opposing hitters devastated Banks on the first pitch last year, going 14-for-31 (.452) with three home runs.

Banks' minor league stats show flashes of his potential. He was 6-1 with a 1.92 ERA at AAA Portland in 11 starts last season, and at Class A Visalia in 1989 he struck out 173 in 174 innings, allowing only 122 hits. Banks is a pretty good fielder, but has had problems holding runners.

OVERALL:

Though Banks is only 24, the Twins are growing a little weary of waiting for him to develop. Defying speculation, however, the Twins protected him from expansion. He'll now be trying to win a starting spot in spring training.

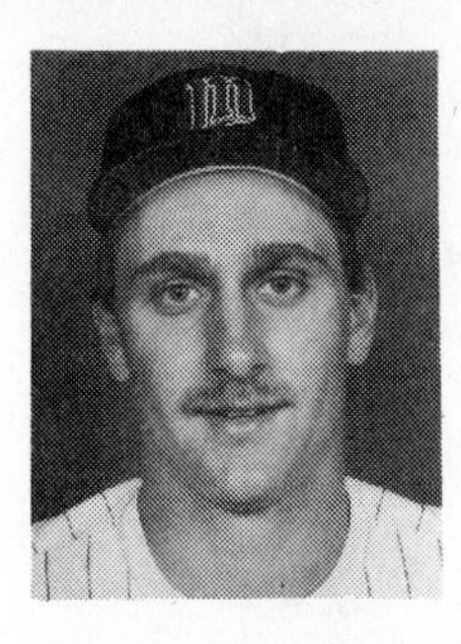

TERRY JORGENSEN

Position: 1B
Bats: R **Throws:** R
Ht: 6' 4" **Wt:** 213

Opening Day Age: 26
Born: 9/2/66 in Kewaunee, WI
ML Seasons: 2

Overall Statistics

	G	AB	R	H	D	T	HR	RBI	SB	BB	SO	AVG
1992	22	58	5	18	1	0	0	5	1	3	11	.310
Career	32	81	6	22	2	0	0	7	1	7	16	.272

HITTING, FIELDING, BASERUNNING:

The Twins got their first look at Terry Jorgensen as a late-season roster addition in 1989 and they weren't overly impressed. The third baseman batted only .174 in 23 at-bats and had just one extra-base hit (a double) among his four hits.

The Twins were much more impressed with their second look at Jorgensen, who batted .310 in 22 games last year. Power was still in question because Jorgensen had just one extra-base hit (a double) among his 18 hits. But he appears to have power potential, thanks to off-season weightlifting that added 20 pounds to his frame since 1989. Jorgensen batted .295 with 32 doubles, two triples and 14 home runs in 505 at-bats at AAA Portland before joining the Twins.

Jorgensen is not blessed with great speed and he has never stolen more than four bases in a professional season. He impressed the Twins by being able to do a decent job at both first and third base. He played errorless ball in 13 games (11 starts) at first base, and committed just one miscue in nine games (five starts) at third base.

OVERALL:

Jorgensen's September performance earned him consideration in the team's plans for 1993. If the Twins lose Greg Gagne to free agency, it's possible that the starters on the left side of the infield could be Scott Leius at shortstop and Jorgensen at third. The Twins like his potential; they protected him in the expansion draft.

JEFF REBOULET

Position: SS/2B/3B
Bats: R **Throws:** R
Ht: 6' 0" **Wt:** 167

Opening Day Age: 28
Born: 4/30/64 in Dayton, OH
ML Seasons: 1

Overall Statistics

	G	AB	R	H	D	T	HR	RBI	SB	BB	SO	AVG
1992	73	137	15	26	7	1	1	16	3	23	26	.190
Career	73	137	15	26	7	1	1	16	3	23	26	.190

HITTING, FIELDING, BASERUNNING:

Jeff Reboulet is the classic story of a player who paid his dues in the minors before even getting a look. The 28-year-old utility infielder spent six full seasons in the minors before being summoned by the Twins last season. Reboulet had a strange season at the plate, batting only .190 overall but .344 (11-for-32) with runners in scoring position. His clutch hitting allowed him to drive in 16 runs in 137 at-bats.

Hitting will be the key to whether Reboulet is able to remain in the major leagues. He struck out 26 times last year, but also showed a good eye, drawing 23 walks. Reboulet has good speed, stealing three bases in five attempts with the Twins. He was in double figures in stolen bases four times in his minor-league career. Reboulet also showed the Twins that he was a dependable fielder, committing one error in 56 chances at second base, four errors in 138 chances at shortstop and handling 43 chances at third base flawlessly. He even saw action in seven games as an outfielder.

OVERALL:

Reboulet looks like he can be a decent major-league utility infielder. He's got the proper temperament -- he's happy just to be in the majors -- and is a solid glove man. If he can hit .230, he should find a reserve job.

MIKE TROMBLEY

Position: SP
Bats: R **Throws:** R
Ht: 6' 2" **Wt:** 200

Opening Day Age: 25
Born: 4/14/67 in Springfield, MA
ML Seasons: 1

Overall Statistics

	W	L	ERA	G	GS	Sv	IP	H	R	BB	SO	HR
1992	3	2	3.30	10	7	0	46.1	43	20	17	38	5
Career	3	2	3.30	10	7	0	46.1	43	20	17	38	5

PITCHING, FIELDING & HOLDING RUNNERS:

As a collegiate player at Duke, Mike Trombley established an NCAA record by hitting 20 batters during the 1989 season. His career record at Duke was 6-22. But Trombley had a major-league fastball, and after his August debut last year, he now has a major league future. The young righthander impressed almost everyone by going 3-2 with a 3.30 ERA in 10 outings.

Considered only a middling prospect, Trombley was selected by the Twins in the 14th round of the 1989 amateur draft. Four seasons in the minor leagues appear to have refined his pitching skills. Trombley still has the excellent fastball, plus a good curve and decent change-up. And he showed the Twins last season that he can control his offerings. He walked 17 and struck out 38 in 46.1 innings.

For a glimpse of Trombley's potential, consider these numbers: 138 strikeouts in 165 innings last season at AAA Portland, 175 strikeouts in 191 innings at AA Orlando in 1991 and 164 strikeouts in 176 innings at Class A Visalia in 1990. He's a good athlete who fields his position well and has a decent pickoff move.

OVERALL:

After his strong finish with the Twins, Trombley will report to spring training pencilled in as one of Minnesota's five starting pitchers. He has surpassed Willie Banks and Pat Mahomes as the young pitcher most likely to win a spot in the 1993 rotation.

LENNY WEBSTER

Position: C
Bats: R **Throws:** R
Ht: 5' 9" **Wt:** 185

Opening Day Age: 28
Born: 2/10/65 in New Orleans, LA
ML Seasons: 4

Overall Statistics

	G	AB	R	H	D	T	HR	RBI	SB	BB	SO	AVG
1992	53	118	10	33	10	1	1	13	0	9	11	.280
Career	87	178	21	51	14	1	4	22	0	19	24	.287

HITTING, FIELDING, BASERUNNING:

Lenny Webster proved himself to be a capable backup catcher in his first full major-league season, batting a solid .280 in 53 games. He showed good power, with 12 extra-base hits (10 doubles, one triple and one home run) among his 33 base hits. Webster finished on a strong note, batting .432 (19-for-44) over his final 22 games. Though the 28-year-old catcher never batted higher than .288 in the minors, his lifetime major-league average for 178 at-bats is now .287.

The bulk of Webster's playing time came from his status as the regular catcher for Scott Erickson. He didn't need to be platooned, batting .267 against righthanders and .321 against lefties. On the negative side, Webster batted only .219 with runners in scoring position and .143 with runners in scoring position and two out. The Twins like his defensive skills, but he threw out only six of 35 (17.1 percent) would-be basestealers. That was probably due more to Erickson's inability to hold baserunners than Webster's throwing liabilities. Stocky at 5'9" and 185 pounds, Webster has little speed. He was thrown out in his only two stolen base attempts last year.

OVERALL:

Webster showed enough last season to stamp himself as a respectable backup major-league catcher. The Twins don't appear sold that he has the potential to be a full-time starter, but they're willing to reserve judgement.

ORGANIZATION OVERVIEW:

The Twins are a much-admired franchise, and not only because they've won two championships in the last six seasons. Minnesota has worked the free agent market beautifully on a restricted budget, made intelligent trades, and brought a steady stream of useful players to the majors. When it comes to developing prospects, Andy MacPhail and Tom Kelly expect them to produce, but they give people more than one chance to screw up. If Willie Banks or David West don't make it, then, it's not because they didn't receive fair opportunities.

MARTIN K. CORDOVA

Position: OF
Bats: R **Throws:** R
Ht: 6' 0" **Wt:** 190
Opening Day Age: 23
Born: 7/10/69 in Las Vegas, NV

Recent Statistics

	G	AB	R	H	D	T	HR	RBI	SB	BB	SO	AVG
91 A Visalia	71	189	31	40	6	1	7	19	2	17	46	.212
92 A Visalia	134	513	103	175	31	6	28	131	13	76	99	.341

A tenth-round draft pick in 1989, Cordova finally got healthy -- and productive -- in 1992. The outfielder tore apart the California League, batting .341 with 28 homers and 131 RBI. Cordova had done little until 1992, but shoulder problems had held him back. Granted that he was playing in the best hitter's park in a good hitter's league, he still had a hell of a year. He and Becker may progress side-by-side from now on.

MIKE MAKSUDIAN

Position: C
Bats: L **Throws:** R
Ht: 5' 11" **Wt:** 220
Opening Day Age: 26
Born: 5/28/66 in Belleville, IL

Recent Statistics

	G	AB	R	H	D	T	HR	RBI	SB	BB	SO	AVG
92 AAA Syracuse	101	339	38	95	17	1	13	58	4	32	63	.280
92 AL Minnesota	3	3	0	0	0	0	0	0	0	0	0	.000
92 MLE	101	326	28	82	14	0	10	43	2	23	66	.252

Probably David Letterman's favorite player, Maksudian is best-known for his ability to eat any kind of creature, the more disgusting the better. Maksudian has also eaten a few pitchers along the way, and last year batted .280 with 13 homers in 339 at-bats for the Blue Jays' AAA farm club at Syracuse. The Twins got him in a postseason deal with catching-rich Toronto, and it could be a big break for him, as Brian Harper can't last forever. Don't try to eat him, Mike.

RICH BECKER

Position: OF
Bats: B **Throws:** L
Ht: 5' 10" **Wt:** 180
Opening Day Age: 21
Born: 2/1/72 in Aurora, IL

Recent Statistics

	G	AB	R	H	D	T	HR	RBI	SB	BB	SO	AVG
91 A Kenosha	130	494	100	132	38	3	13	53	19	72	108	.267
92 A Visalia	136	506	118	160	37	2	15	82	29	114	122	.316

Still only 21 years old, Becker does the little things: he steals bases, draws walks, plays splendid defense. But he also had 54 extra-base hits last year, including 15 homers. The switch-hitter was called the best defensive outfielder in the California League. He bears watching from now on.

DAVE McCARTY

Position: 1B
Bats: R **Throws:** L
Ht: 6' 5" **Wt:** 210
Opening Day Age: 23
Born: 11/23/69 in Houston, TX

Recent Statistics

	G	AB	R	H	D	T	HR	RBI	SB	BB	SO	AVG
91 A Visalia	15	50	16	19	3	0	3	8	3	13	7	.380
91 AA Orlando	28	88	18	23	4	0	3	11	0	10	20	.261
92 AA Orlando	129	456	75	124	16	2	18	79	6	55	89	.272
92 AAA Portland	7	26	7	13	2	0	1	8	1	5	3	.500
92 MLE	137	475	70	129	17	2	15	75	4	45	92	.272

The third player picked in the 1991 draft, McCarty has done little to dissuade the notion that he's going to be in the major leagues very soon. His numbers at AA Orlando last year weren't awesome, but he was playing in a pitcher's park, and he came on after a slow start. McCarty is a hustling player from a bigtime college program at Stanford, and the general consensus is that he will be a major league star.

PAT MEARES

Position: 3B
Bats: R **Throws:** R
Ht: 5' 11" **Wt:** 180
Opening Day Age: 24
Born: 9/6/68 in Salina, KS

Recent Statistics

	G	AB	R	H	D	T	HR	RBI	SB	BB	SO	AVG
91 A Visalia	89	360	53	109	21	4	6	44	15	24	63	.303
92 AA Orlando	81	300	42	76	19	0	3	23	5	11	57	.253
92 MLE	81	296	36	72	19	0	2	20	4	8	54	.243

If Greg Gagne leaves the Twins via free agency, it might open up an opportunity for young Meares, who was a surprise Twin expansion protection. A 15th-round draft pick in 1990, Meares clearly has the defensive goods: he was named the player with the best infield arm in the Southern League. The question is whether he'll hit. After batting .303 at Class A Visalia in 1991, Meares hit only .253 at AA Orlando in 1992. He also walked only 11 times in 300 at-bats. Meares did hit 19 doubles last year, so he has some hitting potential. But he's probably not ready for the majors at this point.

JESSE BARFIELD

Position: RF
Bats: R **Throws:** R
Ht: 6' 1" **Wt:** 201

Opening Day Age: 33
Born: 10/29/59 in Joliet, IL
ML Seasons: 12

Overall Statistics

	G	AB	R	H	D	T	HR	RBI	SB	BB	SO	AVG
1992	30	95	8	13	2	0	2	7	1	9	27	.137
Career	1428	4759	715	1219	216	30	241	716	66	551	1234	.256

Where He Hits the Ball

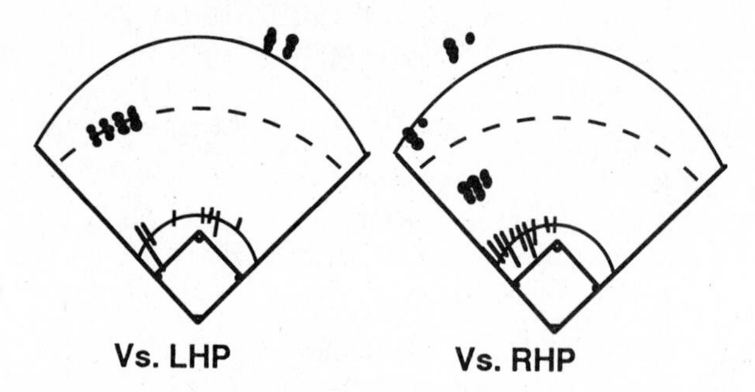

1992 Situational Stats

	AB	H	HR	RBI	AVG		AB	H	HR	RBI	AVG
Home	54	8	2	6	.148	LHP	33	5	1	2	.152
Road	41	5	0	1	.122	RHP	62	8	1	5	.129
Day	27	4	1	1	.148	Sc Pos	29	3	1	6	.103
Night	68	9	1	6	.132	Clutch	17	1	0	1	.059

1992 Rankings (American League)

- Did not rank near the top or bottom in any category

HITTING:

Jesse Barfield's 1992 season was ruined by a fall in his home sauna on May 23, resulting in burns and contusions to his left wrist that required surgery. Before the injury Barfield was having a difficult season, with a .141 average and only two homers in 92 at-bats.

Barfield had fractured the same wrist in 1988, and has often cited its health as the key to regaining the power that brought him 40 home runs in 1986. When healthy, he is a dead pull hitter with tremendous power. As he gets older, however, Barfield has been less able to get around on fastballs and often looks overmatched against hard-throwing righties.

Despite the injuries and aging, Barfield remains dangerous. Like many veterans, he needs to learn a new level of plate discipline. He must lay off more of the high and outside pitches and go to right field more often. If Barfield makes that adjustment, he can be an offensive force again; if he doesn't, he will just be another easy out with some latent home run power.

BASERUNNING:

Barfield still has some of the speed, and all of the intelligence, that helped him to 22 stolen bases eight years ago. That was the only time in his career that he's stolen in double figures. He isn't going to ignite a one-run offense at age 33, but he can help his team by taking an extra base.

FIELDING:

Defense could keep Barfield in the lineup during 1993, even if his hitting is soft. Among all active outfielders he has more career assists than anyone except Dave Winfield. Barfield gets a good jump on the ball because he knows what the pitcher is trying to do.

OVERALL:

The Yankees had a crowded right field at the end of 1992 following the trade for Paul O'Neill. After two seasons wrecked by injuries, Barfield is now face-to-face with the struggle for playing time that reaches every player late in his career. A free agent, he probably will wind up with another club in need of a veteran.

PITCHING:

Tim Burke's career took another turn downward in 1992. The former ace reliever, who recorded 28 saves for the Expos only four years ago, failed to keep his role as set-up man for the Mets and got only limited use in the Yankees' pen. In August he went on the disabled with elbow tendinitis and made only one more appearance in September. Burke's ERA of 4.15 for his two clubs was easily the worst of his eight-year career.

Burke is a sinkerball pitcher with a peculiar hesitation in the middle of his delivery. In addition to the sinking fastball, which has good velocity when he's healthy, Burke also makes extensive use of his slider. His third pitch is a change-up. When his pitches are all working, hitters tend to swing over balls that drop out of the strike zone, missing or producing weak grounders. When he's that sharp, the only way to get a hit is to lay off the low pitches and hope Burke has to come in with something up in the strike zone.

The main problem for Burke in 1992 wasn't hitter discipline; it was simply that his sinker didn't sink enough. He left too many fat pitches up over the plate, allowing the opposition to hit a collective .299 against him. Burke never got on track.

HOLDING RUNNERS AND FIELDING:

Despite a reputation for being good at holding runners, Burke has been relatively easy to run on during the past two years, with 13 of 15 steal attempts succeeding in 1991-1992. He has a respectable pickoff move but hasn't been paying close enough attention. Burke is a solid fielder with steady hands and a good knowledge of situations.

OVERALL:

Burke's problems with elbow and shoulder tendinitis go all the way back to 1986. In the beginning he had spells of inconsistency, separated by long hot streaks. Now the inconsistency lasts all season. A free agent, the 34-year-old Burke will probably be able to find work, but not a lot of money.

TIM BURKE

Position: RP
Bats: R **Throws:** R
Ht: 6' 3" **Wt:** 205

Opening Day Age: 34
Born: 2/19/59 in Omaha, NE
ML Seasons: 8

Overall Statistics

	W	L	ERA	G	GS	Sv	IP	H	R	BB	SO	HR
1992	3	4	4.15	38	0	0	43.1	52	29	18	15	3
Career	49	33	2.72	498	2	102	699.1	624	251	219	444	49

How Often He Throws Strikes

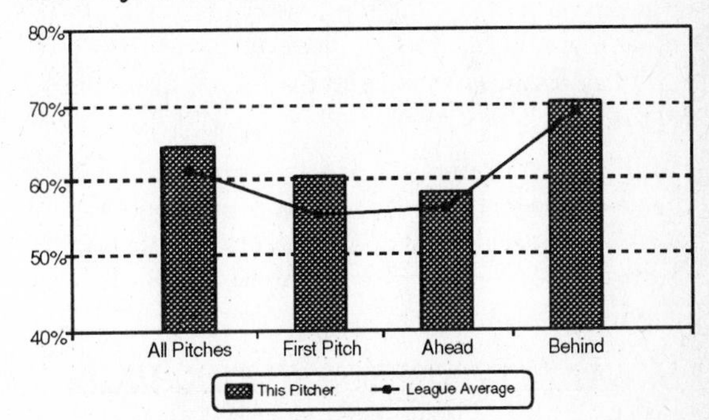

1992 Situational Stats

	W	L	ERA	Sv	IP		AB	H	HR	RBI	AVG
Home	1	1	3.42	0	23.2	LHB	78	17	0	2	.218
Road	2	3	5.03	0	19.2	RHB	96	35	3	25	.365
Day	2	0	0.79	0	11.1	Sc Pos	62	19	0	23	.306
Night	1	4	5.34	0	32.0	Clutch	42	10	0	3	.238

1992 Rankings (American League)

- Did not rank near the top or bottom in any category

STEVE FARR

Position: RP
Bats: R **Throws:** R
Ht: 5'11" **Wt:** 206

Opening Day Age: 36
Born: 12/12/56 in Cheverly, MD
ML Seasons: 9

PITCHING:

At age 36, Steve Farr has finally established himself as one of the game's premier save artists. Farr had been a closer before but never got more than 23 saves in a season. In 1992, although he initially shared the closer duty with Steve Howe and later missed 23 days with a sore back, Farr reached the 30-save plateau which marks the true stoppers.

Farr doesn't have the dominant stuff that often gets relievers promoted to a closer's job. He simply gets the best possible results from his unspectacular repertoire. He has a 90 MPH fastball with which he can hit spots. He also has a good curve and slider. Keeping the ball low and throwing to precise locations are the keys to his success. Farr can use any of his three pitches in any situation, meaning that he doesn't have to give in to any hitter and can always keep the opposition guessing.

With a good bounce-back arm, Farr can handle a heavy workload. While he was finishing the year with a hot streak (just one earned run in his last 14 outings), Farr cited frequent work as the key to staying sharp.

HOLDING RUNNERS AND FIELDING:

Holding runners was the only category in which Farr had a disappointing season in 1992. He yielded seven stolen bases in seven attempts, compared to only two steals in 1991. Farr usually watches runners closely. He is a defensive asset around the mound, covering his position well and always knowing what to do with the ball.

OVERALL:

When the Yankees lost Howe early in 1992, they had no choice but to hand the everyday closer role to Farr. It was a move which worked out well. The more Farr pitched, the better he got. By the end of the year, his confidence and performance were both at career peaks. Though he is at a somewhat precarious age for a late reliever, he seems a good bet to reach 30 saves again. The Yankees left the stopper available to expansion, but he wasn't selected.

Overall Statistics

	W	L	ERA	G	GS	Sv	IP	H	R	BB	SO	HR
1992	2	2	1.56	50	0	30	52.0	34	10	19	37	2
Career	44	42	3.10	430	28	103	749.0	666	283	288	609	57

How Often He Throws Strikes

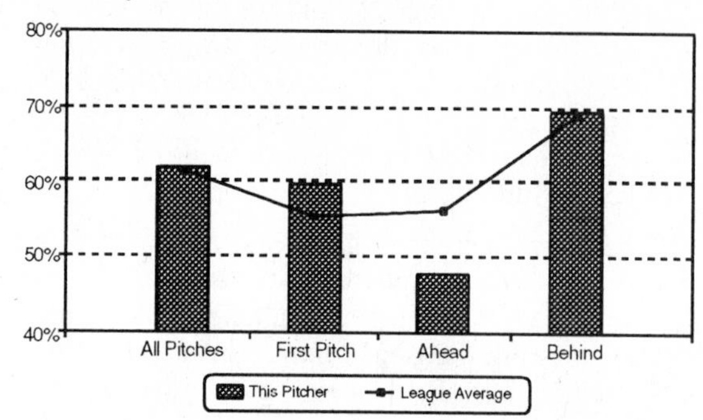

1992 Situational Stats

	W	L	ERA	Sv	IP		AB	H	HR	RBI	AVG
Home	1	1	1.86	18	29.0	LHB	83	18	1	6	.217
Road	1	1	1.17	12	23.0	RHB	100	16	1	10	.160
Day	1	1	2.92	9	12.1	Sc Pos	35	7	1	15	.200
Night	1	1	1.13	21	39.2	Clutch	125	23	2	15	.184

1992 Rankings (American League)

- 6th in saves (30)
- 7th in save opportunities (36)
- 10th in games finished (42) and blown saves (6)
- Led the Yankees in saves, games finished, save opportunities, save percentage (83.3%), blown saves and first batter efficiency (.222)

HITTING:

After a big 1991 season with unprecedented power (12 homers) and a 41-point jump in his batting average (to .247), Oakland's Mike Gallego cashed in by signing a lucrative free agent contract with the Yankees. Gallego came into 1992 expecting to consolidate these gains, but his hopes were undone by injuries.

Gallego was on the disabled list from late-March to mid-May with a strained tendon in his heel, and then on July 6 a Willie Banks pitch broke a bone in his right wrist. Gallego had a cast on the arm until late August. Reduced to 53 games after playing in 159 in 1991, Gallego did lift his average to .254, but belted only three homers.

Gallego's strength is getting on base. He gets respect for his line drive power, but he's usually just trying to work the count and get one good pitch he can drive. He is a spray-type hitter who uses the entire field, and he's happy to take a walk when he doesn't see a pitch he likes. His on-base percentage can be as high as his slugging percentage.

BASERUNNING:

Gallego is extremely aggressive on the bases, but not terribly fast. The Yankees did not use him to steal bases. For breaking up a double play, however, there is no one better.

FIELDING:

Gallego can play second, short or third, but his arm strength is a slight limitation at shortstop and even more of one at third. He is nonetheless fine at both middle infield positions, displaying above-average range. He is sure-handed and turns the double play well.

OVERALL:

With the emergence of Andy Stankiewicz and the improvement of Randy Velarde, the Yankees would have had some trouble keeping Gallego in the lineup even if he had been healthy during 1992. Like many veteran infielders, Gallego is capable of playing every day if a team has a vacancy. But he is more likely to find work as a utility player or in a platoon role against lefty pitching.

MIKE GALLEGO

Position: 2B/SS
Bats: R **Throws:** R
Ht: 5' 8" **Wt:** 160

Opening Day Age: 32
Born: 10/31/60 in Whittier, CA
ML Seasons: 8

Overall Statistics

	G	AB	R	H	D	T	HR	RBI	SB	BB	SO	AVG
1992	53	173	24	44	7	1	3	14	0	20	22	.254
Career	782	1916	243	448	70	10	26	174	21	216	293	.234

Where He Hits the Ball

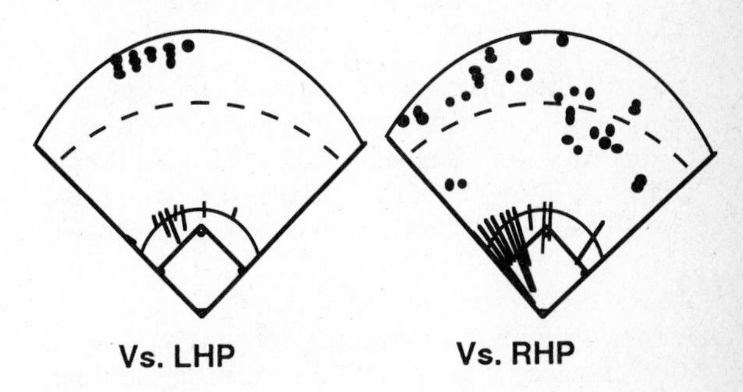

1992 Situational Stats

	AB	H	HR	RBI	AVG		AB	H	HR	RBI	AVG
Home	77	17	1	8	.221	LHP	38	9	0	4	.237
Road	96	27	2	6	.281	RHP	135	35	3	10	.259
Day	52	13	1	7	.250	Sc Pos	33	8	0	9	.242
Night	121	31	2	7	.256	Clutch	39	16	1	3	.410

1992 Rankings (American League)

- 2nd in batting average on a 3-2 count (.438)
- Led the Yankees in batting average on a 3-2 count
- Led AL second basemen in batting average on a 3-2 count

JOHN HABYAN

Position: RP
Bats: R **Throws:** R
Ht: 6' 2" **Wt:** 191

Opening Day Age: 29
Born: 1/29/64 in Bayshore, NY
ML Seasons: 7

PITCHING:

With 56 appearances in 1992, John Habyan became the workhorse of the Yankee bullpen, performing as the set-up man for Steve Farr. Habyan also rose to the occasion by getting five saves in nine days during July when Farr was out with a sore back. Usually Habyan pitched to just a few batters, but worked up to three innings on occasions when the pen was spread thin.

Habyan is a sinker/slider pitcher who relies on control to be successful. He is a direct worker who doesn't like to waste time or pitches. When he's going well he moves the ball around, hitting spots and keeping it low. He is a smart pitcher who understands the relationship between pitching and fielding and who uses his defense effectively.

Short relief pitchers all know that a few bad outings can impair full-year stats disproportionately. Habyan proved that point to the extreme in 1992. Of the 31 earned runs he gave up all year, almost one third of those runs came in just two of his 56 games; more than half of his earned runs were yielded in five appearances totaling six innings. As the numbers imply, Habyan had his good stuff about 90 percent of the time, but when he didn't have his good stuff he was quite hittable.

HOLDING RUNNERS AND FIELDING:

Although Habyan yielded five stolen bases in five attempts last year, he is known for watching runners closely. He doesn't have a good move to first base so he needs to pay attention. As a fielder he is above average in all aspects.

OVERALL:

Habyan is a former starter who failed in repeated trials with Baltimore. The Yankees resurrected Habyan's career when they discovered that he was better suited to short relief work. Habyan likes to work frequently, believing that it helps him stay sharp. But giving him a little breather is not a bad idea; in his eight appearances with no days' rest last year his ERA was 8.59.

Overall Statistics

	W	L	ERA	G	GS	Sv	IP	H	R	BB	SO	HR
1992	5	6	3.84	56	0	7	72.2	84	32	21	44	6
Career	18	18	3.75	170	18	10	331.1	326	157	105	202	33

How Often He Throws Strikes

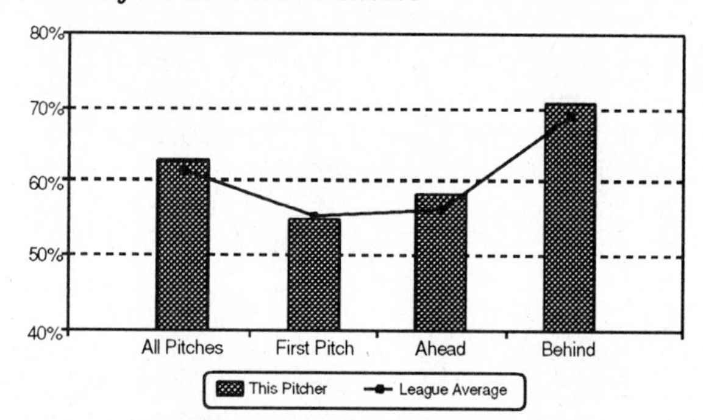

1992 Situational Stats

	W	L	ERA	Sv	IP		AB	H	HR	RBI	AVG
Home	5	3	4.17	3	36.2	LHB	118	40	2	15	.339
Road	0	3	3.50	4	36.0	RHB	167	44	4	27	.263
Day	2	3	5.67	3	27.0	Sc Pos	84	24	3	38	.286
Night	3	3	2.76	4	45.2	Clutch	189	56	4	29	.296

1992 Rankings (American League)

- 1st in highest batting average allowed in relief (.295)
- 2nd in highest percentage of inherited runners scored (47.2%)
- 4th in highest batting average allowed vs. left-handed batters (.339)
- 5th in relief losses (6)
- 6th in holds (16) and worst first batter efficiency (.333)
- Led the Yankees in games pitched (56), holds and relief losses

PITCHING:

After back pain ended his 1991 season, Scott Kamieniecki had surgery to fix a cervical disc. The operation was successful and Kamieniecki worked pain-free through 1992. Problems of a different kind arose, however. In the first half he was simply mediocre, carrying a 2-6 record with a 4.64 ERA at the All-Star break. By mid-August his ERA was up to 4.80, and manager Buck Showalter was being asked how much longer Kamieniecki could remain in the Yankee rotation. Showalter showed just enough patience and the young righty improved, though his final record (6-14) still looked pretty bad.

After mid-August, Kamieniecki became a different pitcher. In his final nine starts he was 4-4 with a 3.47 ERA, yielding just 56 hits in 62.1 innings. What changed? Kamieniecki simply regained his confidence. Given some rare opportunities to pitch with a lead, Kamieniecki quit tinkering and just threw his stuff over the plate. Success led to more confidence and more success.

Kamieniecki has a fastball that clocks over 90 MPH. His repertoire also includes a curve, slider, and change-up. Kamieniecki needs all his pitches to be successful, working in and out and changing speeds. Never noted for great stamina, Kamieniecki usually works about seven innings. Although he had 4 complete games in 1992, they were all in road losses where he didn't have to get the home team out in the ninth inning.

HOLDING RUNNERS AND FIELDING:

Kamieniecki gave up a whopping 29 stolen bases in 35 attempts in 1992. He doesn't have a great move to first and needs to watch runners more closely. A shortstop as a youth, he is a good fielder with quick moves and sharp instincts. He often helps himself on defense.

OVERALL:

When people talk about the Yankees' great young pitchers they are not including Kamieniecki, who was 27 before he reached the major leagues. Although he will never be a star, Kamieniecki has proven himself as a capable major-league starter. On a team that needs innings, he is an asset.

SCOTT KAMIENIECKI

Position: SP
Bats: R **Throws:** R
Ht: 6' 0" **Wt:** 197

Opening Day Age: 28
Born: 4/19/64 in Mt. Clemens, MI
ML Seasons: 2

Overall Statistics

	W	L	ERA	G	GS	Sv	IP	H	R	BB	SO	HR
1992	6	14	4.36	28	28	0	188.0	193	100	74	88	13
Career	10	18	4.25	37	37	0	243.1	247	124	96	122	21

How Often He Throws Strikes

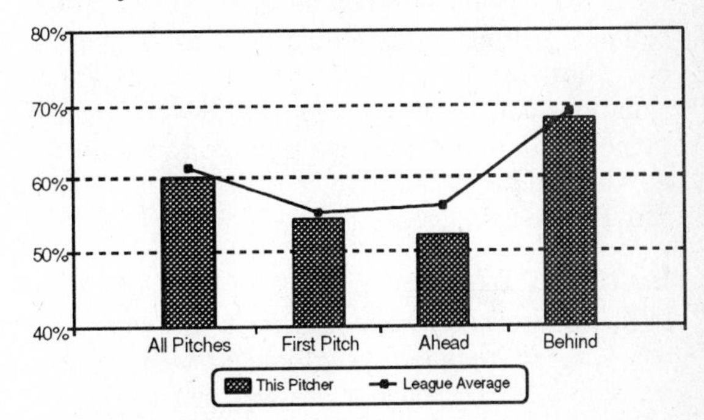

1992 Situational Stats

	W	L	ERA	Sv	IP		AB	H	HR	RBI	AVG
Home	6	4	4.03	0	96.0	LHB	337	94	5	35	.279
Road	0	10	4.70	0	92.0	RHB	380	99	8	46	.261
Day	1	4	4.68	0	59.2	Sc Pos	181	51	3	67	.282
Night	5	10	4.21	0	128.1	Clutch	68	27	1	13	.397

1992 Rankings (American League)

- 2nd in most stolen bases allowed (29) and lowest winning percentage (.300)
- 4th in highest stolen base percentage allowed (82.9%)
- 6th in losses (14) and lowest strikeout/walk ratio (1.2)
- 7th in least strikeouts per 9 innings (4.2)
- 8th in highest batting average allowed (.269) and highest on-base percentage allowed (.340)
- Led the Yankees in hit batsmen (5), stolen bases allowed, GDPs induced (19), highest groundball/flyball ratio allowed (1.3) and most GDPs induced per 9 innings (.91)

HITTING:

The Yankees expected Pat Kelly to improve as a hitter in 1992, and he did. His batting average was down a little compared to his 1991 rookie season, but Kelly was up in almost every other offensive category: doubles, home runs, RBI, walks, on-base percentage, and slugging percentage. Kelly even led the team in hit-by-pitches with 10, getting nailed more than any pinstriped player since Don Baylor in 1985 (24). Though Kelly wound up hitting only .226, he batted .254 after the All-Star break. During the first half, the youngster had hit only .195.

Kelly is a work-the-count, use-all-fields type of hitter. He is always a threat to bunt for a single, which he did eight times in 1992. He is much better at getting on base than he is at driving in runs, however. He is still too eager in pressure situations, and smart pitchers can take advantage by getting him to chase bad pitches. Kelly needs to work on his knowledge of the strike zone and show more patience.

BASERUNNING:

In the minors and as a rookie when he swiped 12 bases in 13 attempts, Kelly looked like he would become a big basestealer. He was bothered by a sore knee at times during 1992 and was only 8-for-13. Kelly is a heads-up runner with good instincts.

FIELDING:

Kelly was moved from second base to third base as a rookie in 1991, but in 1992 he returned full-time to second. A classic, cat-like middle infielder with outstanding athletic ability, Kelly is still learning the finer points of his position, but he is already above-average.

OVERALL:

Like many players who get full-time major-league jobs at age 24 or younger, Kelly has had a few problems, but he hasn't yet tapped his full potential. He isn't ever going to be an All-Star, but in 1993 he could be one of the most improved players, especially in terms of hitting for higher average and stealing more bases.

PAT KELLY

Position: 2B
Bats: R **Throws:** R
Ht: 6' 0" **Wt:** 180

Opening Day Age: 25
Born: 10/14/67 in Philadelphia, PA
ML Seasons: 2

Overall Statistics

	G	AB	R	H	D	T	HR	RBI	SB	BB	SO	AVG
1992	106	318	38	72	22	2	7	27	8	25	72	.226
Career	202	616	73	144	34	6	10	50	20	40	124	.234

Where He Hits the Ball

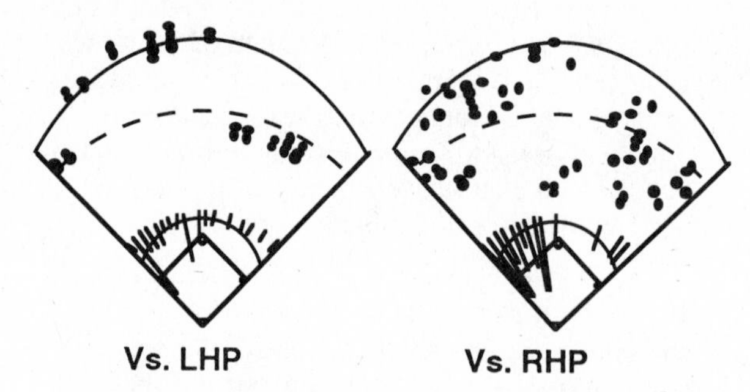

1992 Situational Stats

	AB	H	HR	RBI	AVG		AB	H	HR	RBI	AVG
Home	176	39	3	17	.222	LHP	114	26	3	7	.228
Road	142	33	4	10	.232	RHP	204	46	4	20	.225
Day	100	23	3	13	.230	Sc Pos	62	12	1	17	.194
Night	218	49	4	14	.225	Clutch	50	9	0	5	.180

1992 Rankings (American League)

- 6th in hit by pitch (10) and bunts in play (28)
- 7th in lowest batting average in the clutch (.180) and lowest batting average vs. left-handed pitchers (.228)
- 10th in lowest on-base percentage vs. left-handed pitchers (.288)
- Led the Yankees in hit by pitch and bunts in play
- Led AL second basemen in bunts in play

KEVIN MAAS

Position: DH/1B
Bats: L **Throws:** L
Ht: 6' 3" **Wt:** 209

Opening Day Age: 28
Born: 1/20/65 in Castro Valley, CA
ML Seasons: 3

Overall Statistics

	G	AB	R	H	D	T	HR	RBI	SB	BB	SO	AVG
1992	98	286	35	71	12	0	11	35	3	25	63	.248
Career	325	1040	146	245	35	1	55	139	9	151	267	.236

Where He Hits the Ball

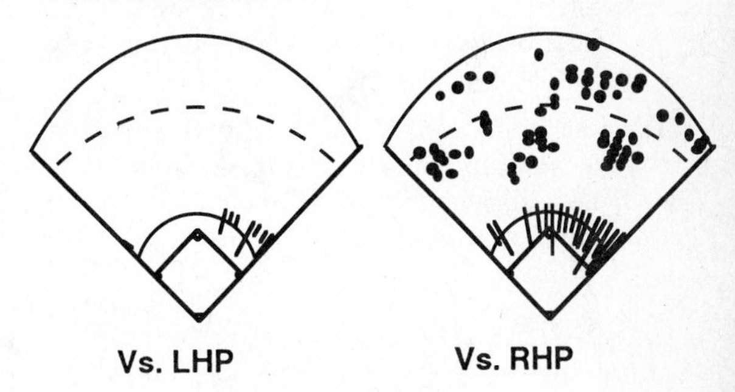

1992 Situational Stats

	AB	H	HR	RBI	AVG		AB	H	HR	RBI	AVG
Home	128	27	7	15	.211	LHP	54	10	1	4	.185
Road	158	44	4	20	.278	RHP	232	61	10	31	.263
Day	79	13	4	11	.165	Sc Pos	60	11	2	22	.183
Night	207	58	7	24	.280	Clutch	66	13	2	7	.197

1992 Rankings (American League)

- 1st in least GDPs per GDP situation (1.9%)
- 5th in batting average on a 3-2 count (.378)
- Led the Yankees in least GDPs per GDP situation and batting average on a 3-2 count
- Led designated hitters in least GDPs per GDP situation and batting average on a 3-2 count

HITTING:

For someone with a 5.3 percent career home run ratio -- higher than sluggers like Andre Dawson, George Bell, and Joe Carter -- Kevin Maas sure doesn't get much playing time. In 1990, Maas raised high expectations by accumulating 15 home runs faster than any rookie ever. But last year Maas managed only 11 homers all season and drove in just 35 runs.

Maas is a killer of fastballs. In batting practice at Yankee Stadium, he can reach the upper deck in right field as easily as most other Yankee hitters can reach the warning track. Unfortunately, Maas doesn't get BP pitching in real games. He rarely sees a fastball in a critical situation, and as a result he has batted just .180 with runners in scoring position over the past two years.

Serious about calisthenics and muscle-building, Maas still gets his share of home runs. But he needs to show more patience and walk more to be a positive force in the batting order. Maas was visibly pressing during 1992. His strikeout/walk ratio rose alarmingly from 1991 to 1992, rising from 1.5 to 2.5.

BASERUNNING:

In 1989 Maas suffered a knee injury that took away much of his speed. He is still aggressive, however, and will steal a few bases every year, just to give the opposition a reason to pay attention. He is nine-for-13 lifetime, and was three-of-four in 1992.

FIELDING:

Playing behind Don Mattingly, Maas looks like a defensive liability by comparison. But so does every other first baseman in the league. Maas is a competent fielder with quick hands; he just doesn't get much opportunity. In 1992 he got into only 22 games in the field.

OVERALL:

Maas had an opportunity to become one of the top power hitters of the 1990's, but that chance is eluding him. Given a full-time job in 1991, he didn't hit for enough average, and since then he's been just a part-timer. A fresh start with a new team is probably his best hope now to advance his career any further.

HITTING:

Still playing with a back ailment, Don Mattingly had his best year since 1989. He hit as many home runs in 1992 as he had in 1990 and 1991 combined. At times when he turned on a pitch, he looked like the same hitter who produced 145 RBI in 1985 and a .352 batting average in 1986. That kind of everyday consistency is behind him now. But Mattingly had a fine season in 1992. He drove in 86 runs, scored 89, and belted 40 doubles, the third-highest total in the American League.

Mattingly today is a crafty batsman with fast hands, a sharp eye, and an outstanding knowledge of the strike zone. He knows the opposition pitchers well enough to give them fits. Mattingly uses the whole ballpark and tailors his swing in every situation, on every pitch.

The consummate professional hitter, Mattingly is always working on something: experimenting with new stances, trying different bats, or just watching opposition pitchers and looking for an edge. He never just sits and rests.

BASERUNNING:

Mattingly has no speed. His biggest assets on the basepaths are intensity, alertness, and a superior knowledge of situations. These are big assets, however. Mattingly is not one of those baserunners who simply "won't hurt his team" or "won't make a mistake." He can actually win a game with a surprising jump or a tricky slide. Since 1988, he is a perfect 10-for-10 on steal attempts.

FIELDING:

If Mattingly couldn't hit, he would be a perfect late-inning defensive replacement. Rarely does a ball get by him, whether it's been hit or thrown. He made only one error before August in 1992. He has soft hands, and his knowledge of positioning is second to no one.

OVERALL:

Everyone in New York was rooting for Mattingly to hit .300 again in 1992. It was a fine year even though he fell short. Over a full season, Mattingly may be less than what he was five years ago; but in any game in any critical situation, he is as dangerous as any hitter in baseball.

DON MATTINGLY

Position: 1B/DH
Bats: L **Throws:** L
Ht: 6' 0" **Wt:** 192

Opening Day Age: 31
Born: 4/20/61 in Evansville, IN
ML Seasons: 11

Overall Statistics

	G	AB	R	H	D	T	HR	RBI	SB	BB	SO	AVG
1992	157	640	89	184	40	0	14	86	3	39	43	.287
Career	1426	5643	808	1754	363	15	192	913	14	427	343	.311

Where He Hits the Ball

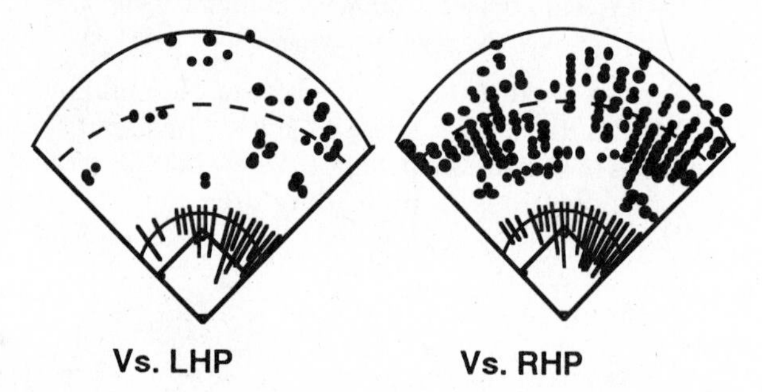

Vs. LHP Vs. RHP

1992 Situational Stats

	AB	H	HR	RBI	AVG		AB	H	HR	RBI	AVG
Home	303	96	6	42	.317	LHP	204	58	2	32	.284
Road	337	88	8	44	.261	RHP	436	126	12	54	.289
Day	204	61	5	29	.299	Sc Pos	160	50	4	69	.313
Night	436	123	9	57	.282	Clutch	114	30	5	19	.263

1992 Rankings (American League)

- 3rd in doubles (40)
- 5th in at-bats (640) and least pitches seen per plate appearance (3.26)
- 6th in hits (184)
- Led the Yankees in batting average (.287), at-bats, runs scored (89), hits, singles (130), doubles, total bases (266), RBI (86), times on base (224), most pitches seen (2,238), plate appearances (686), games played (157), batting average with runners in scoring position (.313), on-base percentage vs. right-handed pitchers (.331), batting average at home (.317), lowest percentage of swings that missed (9.9%) and highest percentage of swings put into play (55.6%)

PITCHING:

In a farm system full of power pitchers, Sam Militello didn't attract much attention before 1992. Although he led all Yankee farmhands in ERA, wins, winning percentage, and strikeouts in 1991, he wasn't on the team's 40-man roster and wasn't invited to spring training in 1992. Militello proved that people simply weren't paying attention. After going 12-2 with a 2.29 ERA at AAA Columbus -- typical numbers for him -- he was 3-3 with a 3.45 ERA with the Yankees.

Though his fastball tops out at about 87 MPH, Militello fanned over a man an inning at each of his minor-league stops. At Columbus, he amassed 152 strikeouts in 141.1 innings. Militello is "sneaky-fast," hiding the ball well and showing the hitter a flurry of knees and elbows when he delivers. His slider breaks so sharply that many broadcasters call it a curveball. He also throws a slower-breaking pitch for a change of pace. Hitters swing at many pitches that drop far below the strike zone.

Although he didn't get much credit as a minor leaguer, Militello excited everyone in New York immediately with his first two starts. In 15 innings, he yielded only seven hits and two runs. He wasn't dominant after that, but he was good. Overall, he held the opposition to a .195 batting average.

HOLDING RUNNERS AND FIELDING:

Like most crafty pitchers, Militello watches runners closely, but he wasn't successful preventing steals in 1992. The same pronounced arm and leg motions that give hitters trouble also give baserunners clues to pick up his delivery and get a good jump. As a fielder, Militello is adequate but improving.

OVERALL:

Militello finished the 1992 season with two problems: a tender elbow and a tendency to issue walks. Time should mend the elbow, but the walks will need further attention in 1993. Militello is the type of pitcher who succeeds when hitters are too eager, or when they haven't seen him enough to know that his breaking pitches usually drop out of the strike zone. He hasn't yet had his toughest tests.

SAM MILITELLO

Position: SP
Bats: R **Throws:** R
Ht: 6' 3" **Wt:** 200

Opening Day Age: 23
Born: 11/26/69 in Tampa, FL
ML Seasons: 1

Overall Statistics

	W	L	ERA	G	GS	Sv	IP	H	R	BB	SO	HR
1992	3	3	3.45	9	9	0	60.0	43	24	32	42	6
Career	3	3	3.45	9	9	0	60.0	43	24	32	42	6

How Often He Throws Strikes

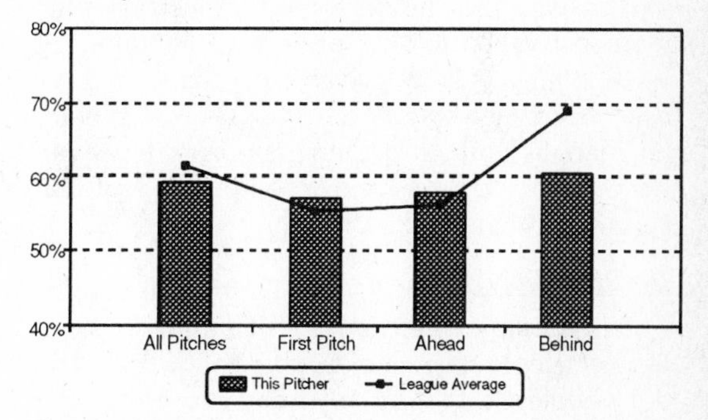

1992 Situational Stats

	W	L	ERA	Sv	IP		AB	H	HR	RBI	AVG
Home	2	1	2.50	0	39.2	LHB	107	28	5	13	.262
Road	1	2	5.31	0	20.1	RHB	114	15	1	7	.132
Day	1	2	3.42	0	23.2	Sc Pos	58	11	1	13	.190
Night	2	1	3.47	0	36.1	Clutch	24	5	2	3	.208

1992 Rankings (American League)

- Did not rank near the top or bottom in any category

HITTING:

The Yankees gave Matt Nokes a strict platoon role early in 1992, hoping he would excel against right-handed pitchers. It didn't happen. Nokes had to produce a strong finish to avoid having an overall embarrassing year at the plate. He hit .289 after August 27, and produced nine home runs and 24 RBI in his final 122 at-bats.

Nokes has come to love hitting at Yankee Stadium, where his natural pull swing was tailored to take advantage of the short right field line. The league's pitchers have respected him ever since he hit 32 home runs as a rookie in 1987, but especially since he became a Yankee. They try to keep everything away from him. Not giving in to Nokes was the theme for 1992; usually that method worked. Nokes drew a career high 37 walks while his batting average dropped. His on-base percentage was a career low. Nokes still got his share of Yankee Stadium home runs, however, with 82 percent of his HR output (18 of 22) coming at home in the Bronx.

BASERUNNING:

Nokes is a slow runner who isn't a threat to steal. He just tries to stay out of trouble on the bases. He did not steal a base in 1992 and has only eight steals in 15 attempts in his eight-year career.

FIELDING

Nokes was rated the "worst pure catcher" in a recent poll of American League umpires, yet the Yankees give him credit for making big advances in his defense since coming to New York in 1990. His throwing arm remains weak, but he has improved as a handler of pitchers. If Nokes isn't the greatest catcher, you can't blame his work ethic.

OVERALL:

The emergence of Mike Stanley as an offensive contributor helped to keep Nokes in a platoon role throughout 1992. Nokes is good enough to play five or six games a week, and will be given that opportunity again if the alternatives in 1993 are not more attractive.

MATT NOKES

Position: C
Bats: L **Throws:** R
Ht: 6' 1" **Wt:** 198

Opening Day Age: 29
Born: 10/31/63 in San Diego, CA
ML Seasons: 8

Overall Statistics

	G	AB	R	H	D	T	HR	RBI	SB	BB	SO	AVG
1992	121	384	42	86	9	1	22	59	0	37	62	.224
Career	762	2379	269	610	83	4	117	362	8	174	333	.256

Where He Hits the Ball

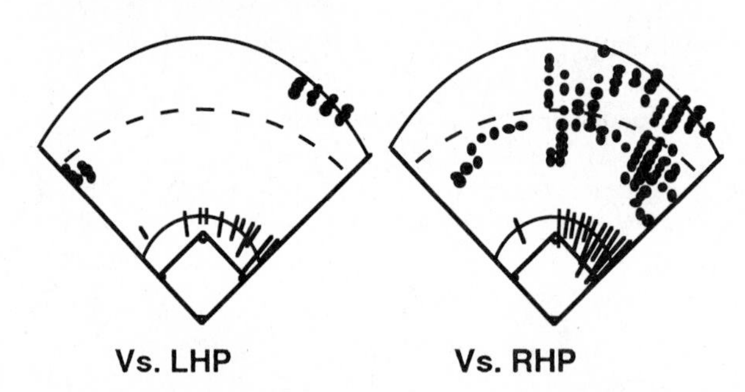

1992 Situational Stats

	AB	H	HR	RBI	AVG		AB	H	HR	RBI	AVG
Home	177	47	18	41	.266	LHP	71	14	5	15	.197
Road	207	39	4	18	.188	RHP	313	72	17	44	.230
Day	121	32	9	22	.264	Sc Pos	90	17	6	37	.189
Night	263	54	13	37	.205	Clutch	72	14	6	11	.194

1992 Rankings (American League)

- 5th in lowest batting average with runners in scoring position (.189)

HITTING:

A chronic wrist injury that he tried to play with all season made 1992 a frustrating year for Paul O'Neill. O'Neill, who hit 28 homers in 1991, fell to 14 last season with his RBI and average also skidding backward. At year's end the Reds gave up on the outfielder, trading him to the New York Yankees in a deal for Roberto Kelly.

The Yankees hope they'll be getting a healthy player. O'Neill's wrist problem prevented him from generating power and also affected his bat speed. A notorious fastball hitter, O'Neill found himself overpowered by the same hard stuff that he used to turn around with power. As he did in his big 1991 season, O'Neill generated virtually all of his homers against right-handed pitching, with only two of his dingers coming against southpaws. Lefthanders, who used to get O'Neill by mixing speeds and throwing breaking balls, also went after him with hard stuff when it was evident he was not pulling the ball.

O'Neill also continues to be his own worst enemy. He had run-ins with Lou Piniella and his temper was always a problem with NL umpires. At least now he has a new manager and a new set of umps to deal with.

BASERUNNING:

O'Neill can steal a base in some situations but is very reluctant to run. His success ratio is the reason. Over the last three seasons he has 31 steals but has been caught 21 times.

FIELDING:

There are few better right fielders in baseball than O'Neill, who has decent range, a strong arm and an aggressiveness that puts him in throwing position as quickly as any outfielder around. Few third-base coaches challenge O'Neill.

OVERALL:

If he returns to full health and finally grows up at 30 years old, there's no reason why O'Neill can't be a power source in the middle of the Yankee lineup. But along with everything else, the short-fused outfielder will have to show he can deal with New York-style pressure.

PAUL O'NEILL

Position: RF
Bats: L **Throws:** L
Ht: 6' 4" **Wt:** 215

Opening Day Age: 30
Born: 2/25/63 in Columbus, OH
ML Seasons: 8

Overall Statistics

	G	AB	R	H	D	T	HR	RBI	SB	BB	SO	AVG
1992	148	496	59	122	19	1	14	66	6	77	85	.246
Career	799	2618	321	679	147	7	96	411	61	306	456	.259

Where He Hits the Ball

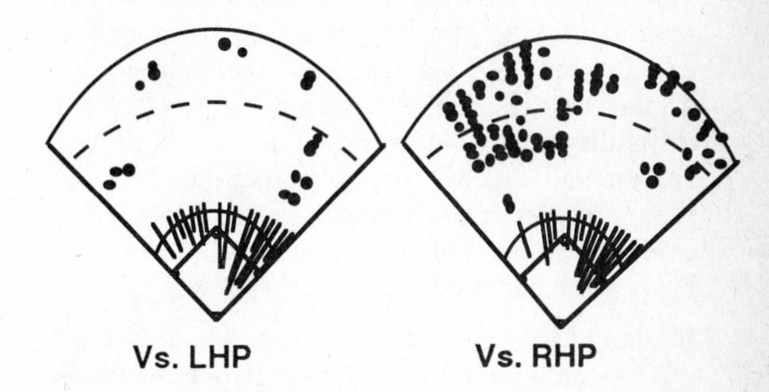

1992 Situational Stats

	AB	H	HR	RBI	AVG		AB	H	HR	RBI	AVG
Home	245	58	6	33	.237	LHP	173	39	2	26	.225
Road	251	64	8	33	.255	RHP	323	83	12	40	.257
Day	175	45	4	24	.257	Sc Pos	141	31	0	47	.220
Night	321	77	10	42	.240	Clutch	81	18	3	13	.222

1992 Rankings (National League)

- 3rd in lowest cleanup slugging percentage (.406)
- 4th in lowest batting average with the bases loaded (.091)
- 5th in intentional walks (15)
- Led the Reds in home runs (14), walks (77), games played (148) and HR frequency (35.4 ABs per HR)
- Led NL right fielders in intentional walks, plate appearances (584), games played, batting average vs. right-handed pitchers, on-base percentage vs. right-handed pitchers (.379), fielding percentage (.997) and highest percentage of pitches taken (58.0%)

OVERLOOKED

MELIDO PEREZ

Position: SP
Bats: R **Throws:** R
Ht: 6' 4" **Wt:** 180

Opening Day Age: 27
Born: 2/15/66 in San Cristobal, Dominican Republic
ML Seasons: 6

PITCHING:

When the Yankees traded Steve Sax to the White Sox for a package including Melido Perez, many fans in New York cried. By the end of 1992, it was the Chicago fans who were shedding tears. After four mediocre seasons in which Perez eventually found himself unable to keep a spot in the White Sox rotation, he immediately became the ace of the staff in New York. Though Perez had a 13-16 record, his 2.87 ERA was the sixth-best in the American League, and he was second in the league in strikeouts.

Perez has a simple yet effective approach to pitching. Basically, he throws fastballs until he gets ahead in the count, and then he throws forkballs until the batter is out. This method usually works. Perez held the opposition to a .235 batting average and his ERA was easily the best among the Yankee starters. If Perez has any weakness it is a difficulty getting settled down in the first inning. He yielded a .287 batting average in his first inning pitched over 33 games, and allowed a .314 average on his first fifteen pitches. After that, however, he cruised.

Pitching for another team, Perez could have been a 20-game winner in 1992. Even when he was at his best, often he didn't win with the Yankees. In his 10 complete games, he was 2-8; he had a classic hard luck season.

HOLDING RUNNERS AND FIELDING:

With a good move to first and keen attention, Perez is adept at holding runners. In 1992, he held the opposition to 18 steals with 18 others getting caught. As a fielder, Perez has good instincts and knows his position well, but he isn't especially quick.

OVERALL:

When Perez got removed from the White Sox rotation in 1991, there was talk about him being too anxious on days he was scheduled to pitch, even losing sleep the nights before his starts. The White Sox solved that problem by giving him unscheduled work in the bullpen. The Yankees found a better answer: giving him more self-confidence. He's now the team's ace.

Overall Statistics

	W	L	ERA	G	GS	Sv	IP	H	R	BB	SO	HR
1992	13	16	2.87	33	33	0	247.2	212	94	93	218	16
Career	58	62	3.90	183	142	1	971.0	891	477	398	791	96

How Often He Throws Strikes

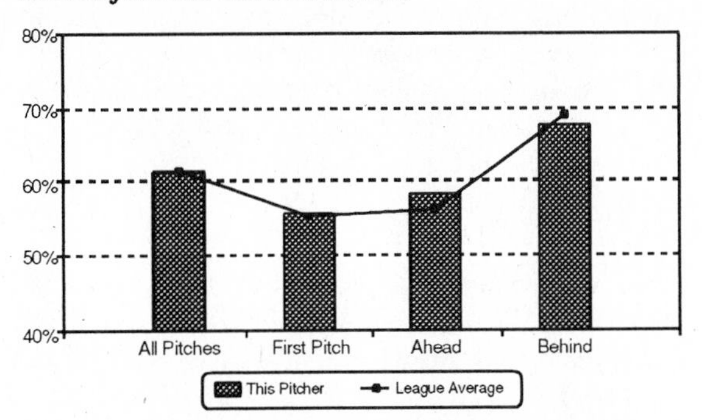

1992 Situational Stats

	W	L	ERA	Sv	IP		AB	H	HR	RBI	AVG
Home	5	6	3.01	0	98.2	LHB	430	106	8	37	.247
Road	8	10	2.78	0	149.0	RHB	471	106	8	51	.225
Day	3	6	3.18	0	70.2	Sc Pos	200	42	3	67	.210
Night	10	10	2.75	0	177.0	Clutch	87	23	1	10	.264

1992 Rankings (American League)

- 1st in runners caught stealing (18), errors by a pitcher (10) and lowest fielding percentage as a pitcher (.811)
- 2nd in losses (16) and strikeouts (218)
- 3rd in wild pitches (13) and most strikeouts per 9 innings (7.9)
- Led the Yankees in ERA (2.87), wins (13), losses, games started (33), complete games (10), shutouts (1), innings pitched (247.2), batters faced (1,013), walks allowed (93), hit batsmen (5), strikeouts, wild pitches, most pitches thrown (3,699), pickoff throws (250), runners caught stealing, GDPs induced (19) and highest strikeout/walk ratio (2.3)

PITCHING:

A 15-year veteran, Scott Sanderson long ago lost the ability to blow his fastball past anyone. On a radar gun he has dropped from 93 MPH down to the mid-80's, and he can't throw as many fastballs in each game. Sanderson now relies on hitting spots and changing speeds. He has a big curve, a forkball, and a change-up. And the fastball can still sneak past hitters who aren't looking for it. In 1992 Sanderson was sneaky enough to go 12-11 for a bad Yankee team, even though his ERA was the second-worst of his career (4.93).

As the ERA attests, all was not well with Sanderson last year. The main problem was that his usually pinpoint control let him down. He didn't walk too many batters (64), but, even so, his walk total more than doubled from 1991. Worse, he had to use his mediocre fastball in far too many situations, a major factor in the 28 home runs that he yielded.

Serious about physical conditioning, Sanderson has reached an age where stamina becomes critical. The Oakland A's made a big winner of Sanderson in 1990 by using him in short outings (typically five or six innings), and the Yankees did the same with him in 1991. Last year, Sanderson was bombed in his final two starts, yielding 13 earned runs without getting through the fifth inning in either. "The season is a marathon with aches and pains," he said. "It's not just the arm; it's the whole body."

HOLDING RUNNERS AND FIELDING:

Once noted for a high leg kick that let runners get a huge jump, Sanderson still isn't adept at holding runners. In 1992 he yielded 18 stolen bases and a 69 percent success rate by the opposition. He is a good fielder, however.

OVERALL:

A crafty righty with 45 victories over the last three years (by far the winningest stretch of his career), Sanderson can still be a big asset on any pitching staff. He has overcome all sorts of physical adversity and just keeps coming back. A free agent, he may find a couple of clubs interested in his veretan presence.

SCOTT SANDERSON

Position: SP
Bats: R **Throws:** R
Ht: 6' 5" **Wt:** 192

Opening Day Age: 36
Born: 7/22/56 in Dearborn, MI
ML Seasons: 15

Overall Statistics

	W	L	ERA	G	GS	Sv	IP	H	R	BB	SO	HR
1992	12	11	4.93	33	33	0	193.1	220	116	64	104	28
Career	143	121	3.72	410	353	5	2227.2	2192	1011	571	1443	239

How Often He Throws Strikes

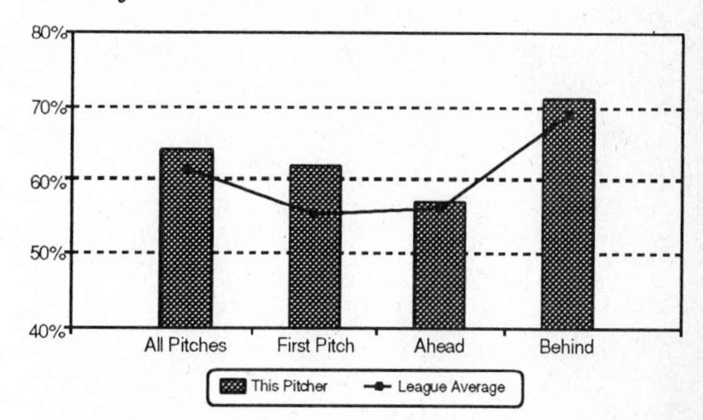

1992 Situational Stats

	W	L	ERA	Sv	IP		AB	H	HR	RBI	AVG
Home	5	6	5.47	0	97.0	LHB	367	110	13	50	.300
Road	7	5	4.39	0	96.1	RHB	402	110	15	54	.274
Day	4	2	6.07	0	59.1	Sc Pos	162	50	5	72	.309
Night	8	9	4.43	0	134.0	Clutch	17	5	0	1	.294

1992 Rankings (American League)

- 1st in highest ERA (4.94), highest slugging percentage allowed (.464), most run support per 9 innings (6.2) and highest ERA at home (5.48)
- 2nd highest batting average allowed (.286) and lowest groundball/flyball ratio (.86)
- 3rd most home runs allowed per 9 innings (1.3)
- 4th most home runs allowed (28) and highest batting average allowed with runners in scoring position (.309)
- Led the Yankees in games started (33), shutouts (1), hits allowed (220), home runs allowed, winning percentage (.522) and most run support per 9 innings

HITTING:

Andy Stankiewicz burst on the New York scene last year with a scrappy style and an appearance that reminded people of Phil Rizzuto. Stankiewicz had only a .269 career average after six minor-league seasons, but he took to major-league pitching immediately. The rookie cooled off during the second half of the year but still wound up hitting .268.

The Yankees made Stankiewicz their leadoff hitter when they saw what he could do: draw a walk, bunt, beat out an infield single, or go to the opposite field. Stankiewicz went one-for-three in his first start, two-for-four in his second start, and finished April with a .308 batting average and a glittering .438 on-base percentage. At the All-Star break, he was still hitting .290. However, he batted only .239 the rest of the way.

Stankiewicz is a spray hitter who uses all fields. He likes to work the count and look for one pitch he can punch through the infield. Stankiewicz' ability to hit the ball hard on the ground is visible in his .340 batting average on artificial turf. He led the Yankees in infield hits in 1992 and beat out five bunts.

BASERUNNING:

Stankiewicz does not possess great speed, but he stole as many as 41 bases in a minor league season. He was only nine for 14 with the Yankees last year, and needs to pick his spots more carefully. Stankiewicz is always alert and aggressive and will often take an extra base or break up a double play.

FIELDING:

The similarity to Rizzuto includes smooth defense. Stankiewicz is sure-handed with good range and he moves well around second base. A versatile athlete, Stankiewicz can play all three of the infield skill positions.

OVERALL:

Stankiewicz was supposed to be a career minor leaguer, biding his time at AAA Columbus in 1992. He made a strong initial impression last year, but by the end of the season New York felt it had too many infielders. Stankiewicz will have to both hustle and hit to remain a regular.

ANDY STANKIEWICZ

Position: SS/2B
Bats: R **Throws:** R
Ht: 5' 9" **Wt:** 165

Opening Day Age: 28
Born: 8/10/64 in Inglewood, CA
ML Seasons: 1

Overall Statistics

	G	AB	R	H	D	T	HR	RBI	SB	BB	SO	AVG
1992	116	400	52	107	22	2	2	25	9	38	42	.268
Career	116	400	52	107	22	2	2	25	9	38	42	.268

Where He Hits the Ball

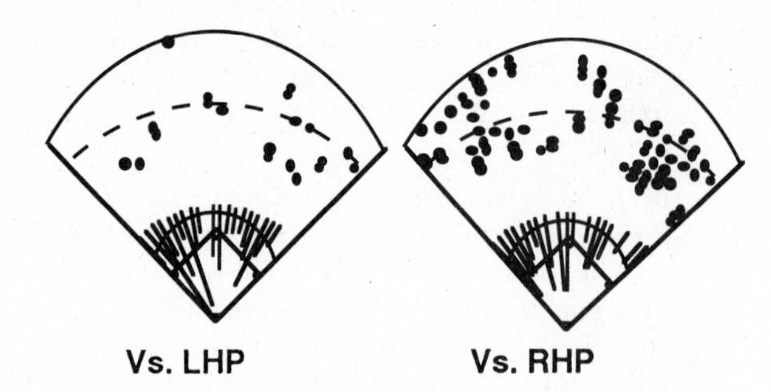

1992 Situational Stats

	AB	H	HR	RBI	AVG		AB	H	HR	RBI	AVG
Home	207	61	2	15	.295	LHP	136	37	0	10	.272
Road	193	46	0	10	.238	RHP	264	70	2	15	.265
Day	132	39	1	6	.295	Sc Pos	69	21	0	21	.304
Night	268	68	1	19	.254	Clutch	71	18	0	6	.254

1992 Rankings (American League)

- 8th in batting average on a 3-2 count (.361)
- 10th in lowest slugging percentage vs. left-handed pitchers (.324)
- Led the Yankees in sacrifice bunts (7)

DANNY TARTABULL

Position: RF/DH
Bats: R **Throws:** R
Ht: 6' 1" **Wt:** 210

Opening Day Age: 30
Born: 10/30/62 in Miami, FL
ML Seasons: 9

Overall Statistics

	G	AB	R	H	D	T	HR	RBI	SB	BB	SO	AVG
1992	123	421	72	112	19	0	25	85	2	103	115	.266
Career	946	3340	507	950	193	16	177	620	35	499	881	.284

Where He Hits the Ball

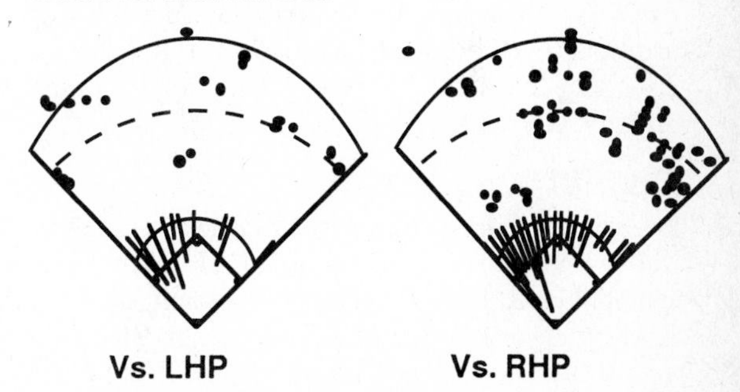

1992 Situational Stats

	AB	H	HR	RBI	AVG		AB	H	HR	RBI	AVG
Home	204	59	11	48	.289	LHP	119	34	11	35	.286
Road	217	53	14	37	.244	RHP	302	78	14	50	.258
Day	133	27	4	18	.203	Sc Pos	118	35	12	67	.297
Night	288	85	21	67	.295	Clutch	84	22	4	15	.262

1992 Rankings (American League)

- 1st in on-base percentage vs. left-handed pitchers (.494)
- 2nd in on-base percentage (.409) and lowest percentage of swings put into play (33.7%)
- 3rd in most pitches seen per plate appearance (4.14)
- Led the Yankees in home runs (25), walks (103), intentional walks (14), strikeouts (115), slugging percentage (.489), on-base percentage, HR frequency (16.8 ABs per HR), highest groundball/flyball ratio (1.5), most pitches seen per plate appearance, slugging percentage vs. left-handed pitchers, on-base percentage vs. left-handed pitchers and highest percentage of pitches taken (58.3%)

HITTING:

The Yankees had high expectations for free agent Danny Tartabull, who'd had his career year for Kansas City in 1991. Tartabull gave New York the quality run-producer they wanted, but they didn't get enough of him. Tartabull missed 39 games with various ailments, including a strained back. His 85 RBI left him just one behind team leader Don Mattingly. Optimists said, "In 162 games Tartabull would have produced 112 RBI," but Tartabull never stays that healthy. He hasn't had a 500 at-bat season since 1988.

Tartabull is an always-dangerous hitter with power to all fields. He will jump on anything up and out over the plate, eager to drive the ball over the right field fence instead of pulling it. The safest approach is to keep the ball down, hoping to induce a grounder. Tartabull's uppercut swing produces rising line drives whenever he gets behind the ball.

A pitcher needs good breaking stuff to succeed against Tartabull. The sinker/slider pitchers and junkballers who can keep their stuff low have the best luck against him. Fastball pitchers who are too optimistic, or who fall behind in the count, are in trouble with Tartabull at bat.

BASERUNNING:

Tartabull has never been a basestealer. His career high in steals is nine, and his lifetime success rate is 58 percent. He was 2-for-4 last year. As a baserunner he is just competent.

FIELDING:

Tartabull is not a good fielder. He has a strong arm, but doesn't get a good jump and doesn't cover territory quickly. As a left fielder, he could hold his own in the American League, but in right field he is below average. Tartabull's future will likely include more DH duty.

OVERALL:

One famous slugger available to expansion was Tartabull, but he wasn't selected. He produced when he played last year, including nine RBI in one game -- more than any Yankee since Tony Lazzeri's AL record of 11 in 1936. The problem was that, as usual, he didn't play enough. The biggest shock may have been that the Yankees seemed so surprised to discover this about him.

HITTING:

For the first time in his career, Randy Velarde became a major-league regular. He responded by hitting .302 with 33 RBI and 41 runs scored in 255 at-bats after the All-Star break. Overall Velarde batted .272 while reaching career highs in almost every offensive category. The veteran utility man became a New York version of Tony Phillips, filling in virtually everywhere.

Velarde is an aggressive, first-pitch hitter. He also loves to swing on 1-0 counts. For a hitter with little power, he strikes out too much. His aim is to hit line drives, using the whole field. A good fastball hitter, Velarde thrives on pitchers who are careless or over-optimistic. In tough situations, however, Velarde is not a very dangerous hitter if cautiously approached. Given a respectful diet of breaking stuff and offspeed pitches he becomes much less selective.

BASERUNNING:

Velarde stole more bases in 1992 (seven) than in five previous seasons combined. He isn't a big speed threat, but after finding himself on base more than ever before he made the most of his opportunities and used them wisely. His confidence and judgement are visibly elevated now.

FIELDING:

Throughout his career Velarde has been error-prone. His positioning and range are good, but he has never had a regular position to master. Velarde was definitely the jack of all trades for manager Buck Showalter, appearing at six positions (three infield and three outfield), the most for any Yankee since Paul Blair played the same six positions in 1978.

OVERALL:

Velarde is more than adequate as a utility infielder, and in 1992 he showed he could play the outfield, too. On a team plagued with injuries, and with a manager who liked to load his lineup with righty hitters against all southpaw pitchers, Velarde was in the perfect situation to bring out his talents. In 1993 he will take the first crack at the starting third baseman's job after Charlie Hayes went west with expansion.

RANDY VELARDE

Position: SS/3B/LF
Bats: R **Throws:** R
Ht: 6' 0" **Wt:** 190

Opening Day Age: 30
Born: 11/24/62 in Midland, TX
ML Seasons: 6

Overall Statistics

	G	AB	R	H	D	T	HR	RBI	SB	BB	SO	AVG
1992	121	412	57	112	24	1	7	46	7	38	78	.272
Career	385	1062	128	263	51	6	20	104	11	91	218	.248

Where He Hits the Ball

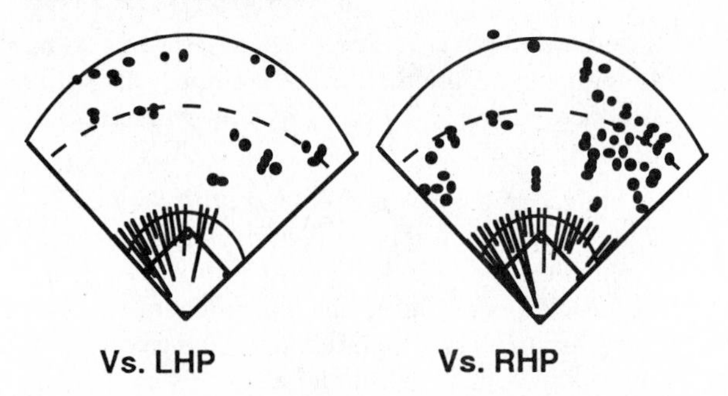

1992 Situational Stats

	AB	H	HR	RBI	AVG		AB	H	HR	RBI	AVG
Home	198	55	2	24	.278	LHP	140	43	4	22	.307
Road	214	57	5	22	.266	RHP	272	69	3	24	.254
Day	132	42	4	14	.318	Sc Pos	91	26	3	40	.286
Night	280	70	3	32	.250	Clutch	76	20	2	8	.263

1992 Rankings (American League)

- 1st in lowest batting average on an 0-2 count (.000)
- Led the Yankees in batting average vs. left-handed pitchers (.307)

FUTURE ALL-STAR

HITTING:

Bernie Williams first came up to the Yankees in midseason 1991, and while he showed promise, his .238 average indicated some difficulties. Sent back to AAA Columbus last year, Williams was again recalled in mid-year. This time he was better: Williams batted .280 and showed off a multi-faceted game.

Williams has the tools to be a top offensive player: speed, power, and a good eye. With his superior knowledge of the strike zone, he can work the count, draw a walk, or pick a pitch to drive. He can also hit with power. Although not noted as a home run hitter, Williams can connect with the best of them. He hit the longest homer in the American League during the month of August in 1992.

Usually Williams just tries to make contact, but the switch-hitter's left-handed swing is just right for power at Yankee Stadium. Most teams pitch Williams up and in or low and away with lots of breaking stuff. He's learning to look for the curveball, however, and will be a tougher out in 1993.

BASERUNNING:

Williams has very good speed and scouts expect him to steal 30 bases a year. Thus far, however, he has been held back by a tentative approach. He is visibly confused by "in-between" situations and occasionally causes a slower runner to hold up behind him. Williams must learn to trust his instincts and watch his coaches.

FIELDING:

The Yankees have twice installed Williams in center field, displacing Roberto Kelly in recognition of his great tools. But the problem of occasional disorientation affects Williams' fielding as well as his running. Except for those lapses, Williams is a defensive gem. He gets a good jump and covers ground rapidly. His arm is good enough for the big Yankee pasture.

OVERALL:

Williams is at the beginning of a what should be a fine major league career, especially with Kelly out of the way. It was a surprise when he went back to AAA Columbus in early 1992; in 1993 the center field job should be his to lose.

BERNIE WILLIAMS

Position: CF
Bats: B **Throws:** R
Ht: 6' 2" **Wt:** 196

Opening Day Age: 24
Born: 9/13/68 in San Juan, Puerto Rico
ML Seasons: 2

Overall Statistics

	G	AB	R	H	D	T	HR	RBI	SB	BB	SO	AVG
1992	62	261	39	73	14	2	5	26	7	29	36	.280
Career	147	581	82	149	33	6	8	60	17	77	93	.256

Where He Hits the Ball

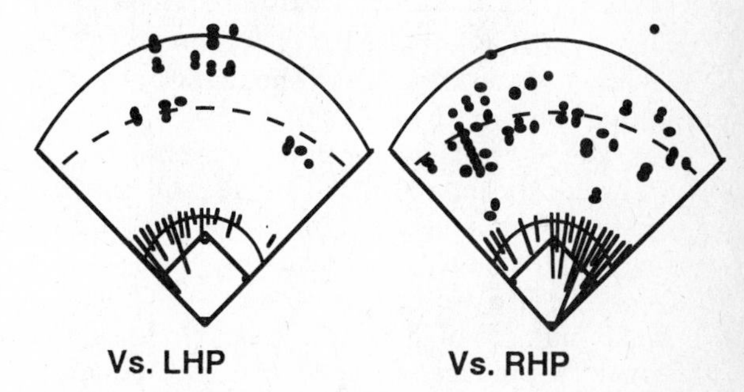

1992 Situational Stats

	AB	H	HR	RBI	AVG		AB	H	HR	RBI	AVG
Home	134	39	3	13	.291	LHP	84	25	1	9	.298
Road	127	34	2	13	.268	RHP	177	48	4	17	.271
Day	77	26	0	10	.338	Sc Pos	65	15	1	20	.231
Night	184	47	5	16	.255	Clutch	46	9	0	5	.196

1992 Rankings (American League)

- Led the Yankees in caught stealing (6)

HENSLEY MEULENS

Position: 3B
Bats: R **Throws:** R
Ht: 6' 3" **Wt:** 212

Opening Day Age: 25
Born: 6/23/67 in Curacao, Netherlands Antilles
ML Seasons: 4

Overall Statistics

	G	AB	R	H	D	T	HR	RBI	SB	BB	SO	AVG
1992	2	5	1	3	0	0	1	1	0	1	0	.600
Career	129	404	52	92	15	1	10	41	4	30	130	.228

HITTING, FIELDING, BASERUNNING:

Once considered the Yankees' top prospect, Hensley Meulens was good enough to be handed a "full-time" role by the Yankees in 1991. He was considered a disappointment when he batted only .222 with six homers in 288 at-bats, and last year other players squeezed him out of the picture. Sent back to AAA Columbus in 1992, a place where he had won much of his fame, Meulens didn't sulk. Though the Yankees didn't seem to notice, he produced 26 home runs and 100 RBI.

Extremely strong at 6'3" and 212 pounds, Meulens is a dangerous power hitter. He feasts on fastballs and is always aggressive. Meulens strikes out too frequently and can be fooled by breaking stuff, but he can still be a big asset to any lineup.

Meulens' career-high 15 stolen bases in 1992 shows that he is adding a knowledge of pitchers and situations to go with his natural speed. He isn't really a big threat to run in the majors, however. Meulens is just adequate as a third baseman.

OVERALL:

Meulens is ready to play big league ball now, though probably not in New York. He told *The Scouting Report* he didn't want to be protected in the expansion draft, saying, "It's time to move on." The Yankees seemed to agree, but Meulens wasn't selected. Meulens should be somewhere in the majors this year, perhaps even as the Yankees' staring third baseman.

RICH MONTELEONE

Position: RP
Bats: R **Throws:** R
Ht: 6' 3" **Wt:** 236

Opening Day Age: 30
Born: 3/22/63 in Tampa, FL
ML Seasons: 6

Overall Statistics

	W	L	ERA	G	GS	Sv	IP	H	R	BB	SO	HR
1992	7	3	3.30	47	0	0	92.2	82	35	27	62	7
Career	12	7	3.50	108	0	0	198.0	185	87	66	136	17

PITCHING, FIELDING & HOLDING RUNNERS:

Rich Monteleone mentions his 10 years of professional experience as his biggest asset on the mound. And this man has vast experience. The Tigers' number-one draft choice in 1982, Monteleone was considered a "wasted pick" and drifted through the Detroit, Seattle and California organizations before landing in New York. At last he may have found success.

Monteleone has a good fastball which he moves in and out, a slider, and a change-up. He isn't overpowering, and needs command of all three pitches to be effective. Many of his strikeouts come on the change-up. Monteleone is a direct worker who doesn't waste pitches. He led the Yankee bullpen in 1-2-3 innings with 38 last year.

Because he doesn't move quickly off the mound, Monteleone is only a fair fielder. He has sure hands and a cool head, however. He has always been good at holding runners; in 1992 five of eight steal attempts against him were snuffed out.

OVERALL:

After a long apprenticeship that included being released by the last-place Mariners in 1988, Monteleone posted his career bests in ERA, wins, innings pitched, strikeouts, strikeout-to-walk ratio, and numerous esoteric pitching stats in 1992. The numbers didn't lie. Monteleone has become an effective and reliable middle reliever.

RUSS SPRINGER

Position: RP
Bats: R **Throws:** R
Ht: 6' 4" **Wt:** 195

Opening Day Age: 24
Born: 11/7/68 in Alexandria, LA
ML Seasons: 1

Overall Statistics

	W	L	ERA	G	GS	Sv	IP	H	R	BB	SO	HR
1992	0	0	6.19	14	0	0	16.0	18	11	10	12	0
Career	0	0	6.19	14	0	0	16.0	18	11	10	12	0

PITCHING, FIELDING & HOLDING RUNNERS:

Russ Springer has always had a big fastball and a small repertoire. He throws a 93 MPH heater with good late movement, complemented by a curve and a change-up. Until his late August recall by the Yankees last year, Springer had been used exclusively as a starter during his professional career. But the Yankees tried Springer in the bullpen, and that's where his future may lie.

Although he was making good progress as a starter -- he was 8-5 with a 2.69 ERA at AAA Columbus before his recall -- Springer responded well to relief work after a rough beginning. In short situations he can rely on his number-one pitch and not have to worry about getting beat with his second-best or third-best pitch.

Springer got clobbered in his first three major-league outings, producing some bad full-year stats. But in his final nine games he had a 1.23 ERA. As a hard thrower he needs to pay more attention to baserunners, and he's just a fair fielder.

OVERALL:

Springer will begin 1993 as a middle reliever and set-up man, sharing the work that was performed by John Habyan and Rich Monteleone last year. His role could enlarge during the season. "He can be a closer," says pitching coach Mark Connor. "He's got that kind of arm." He was on the protected list of 15 Yankee players for the expansion draft.

MIKE STANLEY

Position: C
Bats: R **Throws:** R
Ht: 6' 0" **Wt:** 190

Opening Day Age: 29
Born: 6/25/63 in Ft. Lauderdale, FL
ML Seasons: 7

Overall Statistics

	G	AB	R	H	D	T	HR	RBI	SB	BB	SO	AVG
1992	68	173	24	43	7	0	8	27	0	33	45	.249
Career	520	1160	138	291	50	4	24	147	6	180	260	.251

HITTING, FIELDING, BASERUNNING:

A journeyman catcher who hasn't had 200 at-bats since 1988, Mike Stanley functioned well under the platoon management of Buck Showalter. Getting all but eight of his starts against left-handed pitching, Stanley produced a career-high eight home runs. His batting average was on the low side at .249, but the Yankees probably expected it. A lifetime .251 hitter, Stanley has hit exactly .249 each of the last three seasons.

Stanley is a good fastball hitter who can punish most pitchers when they have to give in to him. He strikes out frequently but compensates for the low batting average by drawing a good number of walks. His on-base percentage in both 1991 and 1992 was a fine .372.

Stanley is a good handler of pitchers and game-caller, but is just adequate in other defensive aspects. Although his arm is below average, he cut down six of 13 attempted steals in his final 12 starts as opposition managers tested him to see what they should expect in 1993. On the bases Stanley is very cautious, as he should be.

OVERALL:

Not outstanding in any aspect of his game, Stanley isn't going to be a major factor anywhere in 1993. But he offers a combination of acceptable offense and steady defense. Most pitchers like throwing to Stanley; that's a big asset when it comes time to deciding playing time.

BOB WICKMAN

Position: SP
Bats: R **Throws:** R
Ht: 6' 1" **Wt:** 207

Opening Day Age: 24
Born: 2/6/69 in Green Bay, WI
ML Seasons: 1

Overall Statistics

	W	L	ERA	G	GS	Sv	IP	H	R	BB	SO	HR
1992	6	1	4.11	8	8	0	50.1	51	25	20	21	2
Career	6	1	4.11	8	8	0	50.1	51	25	20	21	2

PITCHING, FIELDING & HOLDING RUNNERS:

Bob Wickman is used to battling the odds. As a youngster, the righthander lost the tip of his index finger in a farming accident. But just like Three-Finger Brown, Wickman found that the injury gave his pitches a better break. The White Sox made him their second-round draft pick in 1990 and reluctantly included him in the Steve Sax deal with the Yankees two years later. After a stint at AAA Columbus, Wickman arrived in New York last summer. He created a stir by going 6-1 in eight starts.

In college, Wickman was a 90 MPH fastball pitcher, but he made it to the major leagues by adding a two-seam sinker, a slider, and (most recently) a change-up. The change is now his out pitch. He doesn't blow people away, but mixes locations and speeds and throws a lot of low sinkers. Wickman had problems holding runners last year, allowing eight steals in nine attempts. As a fielder, he needs to work on getting off the mound quicker.

OVERALL:

Wickman's 6-1 record raised high expectations for 1993, but he isn't yet ready to dominate. For example, he needs to visualize a smaller strike zone when facing disciplined major-league hitters. Wickman has a good repertoire, though, and he is one of the brighter prospects who came up in 1992. The Yankees made him one of their 15 protected players, seven of whom were pitchers.

GERALD WILLIAMS

Position: RF
Bats: R **Throws:** R
Ht: 6' 2" **Wt:** 185

Opening Day Age: 26
Born: 8/10/66 in New Orleans, LA
ML Seasons: 1

Overall Statistics

	G	AB	R	H	D	T	HR	RBI	SB	BB	SO	AVG
1992	15	27	7	8	2	0	3	6	2	0	3	.296
Career	15	27	7	8	2	0	3	6	2	0	3	.296

HITTING, FIELDING, BASERUNNING:

Gerald Williams developed patiently, spending six years in the Yankee farm system before finally getting a September call-up in 1992. Williams singled in his first major league at-bat, and began appearing regularly in right field. Though he had only 27 at-bats for the Yankees, he impressed all the right people.

Williams spent most of the year at AAA Columbus, where he batted .285 with 31 doubles, six triples, 16 home runs, 86 RBI and 36 stolen bases. Obviously he uses both speed and power as offensive weapons. He is a good, aggressive fastball hitter. Williams' knowledge of the strike zone improved in 1992 as he drew more walks (38) than in 1991. He still strikes out too much.

Manager Buck Showalter was most impressed with Williams' defense: "He makes plays not many in this league can make." Williams has good range and gets a quick jump. On the bases, he is always a threat to steal.

OVERALL

Nicknamed "Ice" for his cool demeanor and slick moves, Williams is one of the good Yankee farmhands who didn't get away during the youth-for-age trades of the 1980s. At the end of 1992 it looked like he had a tentative hold on the third outfield spot with O'Neill and Bernie Williams, with Danny Tartabull moving to DH. But the Yanks were looking at the free agent market as well.

ORGANIZATION OVERVIEW:

Oh, no, he's back! During the pre-banishment George Steinbrenner years, the Yankees had a great reputation for developing prospects . . . for other teams. The notoriously impatient George would be screaming "Get rid of this guy" after a rookie's first error, which is a great way to build a guy's confidence. Then there were those great Yankee deals, like Fred McGriff for Dale Murray. While George was away, however, the Yankees quietly changed their philosophy, rebuilding their system and holding on to their quality youngsters. No American League club had better top prospects than the Yanks last year. Will George gum up the works again?

RUSSELL S. DAVIS

Position: 3B **Opening Day Age:** 23
Bats: R **Throws:** R **Born:** 9/13/69 in Birmingham, AL
Ht: 6' 0" **Wt:** 170

Recent Statistics

	G	AB	R	H	D	T	HR	RBI	SB	BB	SO	AVG
91 AA Albany	135	473	57	103	23	3	8	58	3	50	102	.218
92 AA Albany	132	491	77	140	23	4	22	71	3	49	93	.285
92 MLE	132	473	63	122	20	2	17	58	2	34	99	.258

A 29th-round draft pick in 1988, Davis has shown power potential for several years. But he really blossomed in 1992, belting 22 homers at AA Albany while raising his average 67 points to .285. Davis is also an excellent defensive player and was rated the best fielding third baseman in the Eastern League by Baseball America. He's also played some second base, but his future appears to be at third, especially with Charlie Hayes' departure.

STERLING HITCHCOCK

Position: P **Opening Day Age:** 21
Bats: L **Throws:** L **Born:** 4/29/71 in Fayetteville, NC
Ht: 6' 1" **Wt:** 195

Recent Statistics

	W	L	ERA	G	GS	Sv	IP	H	R	BB	SO	HR
92 AA Albany	6	9	2.58	24	24	0	146.2	116	51	42	155	6
92 AL New York	0	2	8.31	3	3	0	13.0	23	12	6	6	2

Lefty Hitchcock has come on strong the last three seasons, posting ERAs under 3.00 at three different levels. He wound up making three starts for the Yankees; he got hammered, but hopefully that won't be enough to convince George he's no good. Hitchcock is not overpowering, but his curve and fastball are both quality pitches, and he has unusual poise for someone not yet 22. Hitchcock wound up with a tired arm last year, and the Yanks will be watching him carefully.

DAVE SILVESTRI

Position: SS **Opening Day Age:** 25
Bats: R **Throws:** R **Born:** 9/29/67 in St. Louis, MO
Ht: 6' 0" **Wt:** 180

Recent Statistics

	G	AB	R	H	D	T	HR	RBI	SB	BB	SO	AVG
92 AAA Columbus	118	420	83	117	25	5	13	73	19	58	110	.279
92 AL New York	7	13	3	4	0	2	0	1	0	0	3	.308
92 MLE	118	403	66	100	22	2	9	58	13	46	115	.248

The Yankees have yearned for a top-quality shortstop, and they've carefully watched the development of Silvestri and Robert Eenhoorn as the pair has moved up their system. Silvesti, the more advanced of the two, was the shortstop on the gold-medal winning 1988 Olympic team, and has unusual power for the position, with 32 homers the last two seasons. He has a strong arm, but some consider his glove a little shaky. As long as he never makes an error, George will be happy.

J.T. SNOW

Position: 1B **Opening Day Age:** 25
Bats: B **Throws:** L **Born:** 2/26/68 in Long Beach, CA
Ht: 6' 2" **Wt:** 200

Recent Statistics

	G	AB	R	H	D	T	HR	RBI	SB	BB	SO	AVG
92 AAA Columbus	135	492	81	154	26	4	15	78	3	70	65	.313
92 AL New York	7	14	1	2	1	0	0	2	0	5	5	.143
92 MLE	135	470	64	132	23	2	12	62	2	55	68	.281

No Snow job -- this fellow has the goods. J.T. has a slick glove and a nice switch-hitting stroke, though he's considered better from his natural left side. Snow had a big year at AAA Columbus in 1992, showing patience and extra-base power, and Baseball America rated him the number-two prospect in the International League. Only one thing stands in his way: Don Mattingly.

BRIEN M. TAYLOR

Position: P **Opening Day Age:** 21
Bats: L **Throws:** L **Born:** 12/26/71 in Beaufort, NC
Ht: 6' 3" **Wt:** 195

Recent Statistics

	W	L	ERA	G	GS	Sv	IP	H	R	BB	SO	HR
92 A Ft. Laud	6	8	2.57	27	27	0	161.1	121	60	66	187	3

Brien Taylor is 12 years old. He's eight feet, six inches tall. His fastball has been routinely clocked at 300 MPH. The fact that he has two heads makes his delivery . . . sorry, we've been reading the New York tabloids again. But how much more can one say about the awesome Taylor, who broke into professional ball at a tough level (the Florida State League) last year and posted a 2.57 ERA, with 187 strikeouts in 161 innings? Taylor's fastball has been called "otherworldly," and he figures to make a rapid ascent through the New York system. Let's hope his arm stays healthy, and that he can handle all that hype.

HAROLD BAINES

Position: DH/RF
Bats: L **Throws:** L
Ht: 6' 2" **Wt:** 195

Opening Day Age: 34
Born: 3/15/59 in Easton, MD
ML Seasons: 13

HITTING:

Although Harold Baines' 1992 average was the lowest of his career (.253), he remained a dangerous hitter. The A's primary designated hitter totaled 76 RBI, second on the team to Mark McGwire, and clubbed 16 homers. Following the regular season, Baines was a tower of strength in the postseason. He batted .440 in the championship series against Toronto, winning Game 1 with a ninth-inning homer off Jack Morris.

A very unique hitter, Baines uses the whole field when he hits the ball in the air but is a dead-pull hitter if he hits it on the ground. For this reason, many teams play their outfielders straightaway against him but overshift their infielders, moving three of them to the right of second. A line drive hitter, Baines still gets his hits consistently from left center to the right field line. Baines' danger zone is out over the plate and down. Right-handed pitchers should jam him with a fastball; once behind in the count, Baines is vulnerable to sliders down and in. He dives into the ball at the plate, beginning with a pronounced right leg-raise.

BASERUNNING:

Baines is very slow. He stole one base last season, his first since 1986, but it took him four tries. Knee surgery has limited his mobility, yet Baines is smart and won't hurt a team on the basepaths.

FIELDING:

Baines made 19 starts in the outfield last year, his most since 1989. Surgery on his right knee following the 1986 season, and again in 1987, has limited him to the DH role. He made one error, and did not have an assist, but showed he can be a fill-in if needed.

OVERALL:

One of the 15 free agents on the Oakland roster, Baines will most assuredly sign with an American League team in need of a solid designated hitter. The cost-cutting A's were not expected to re-sign him, even though he remains a favorite of Tony La Russa.

Overall Statistics

	G	AB	R	H	D	T	HR	RBI	SB	BB	SO	AVG
1992	140	478	58	121	18	0	16	76	1	59	61	.253
Career	1844	6744	865	1930	334	46	241	1066	30	647	1017	.286

Where He Hits the Ball

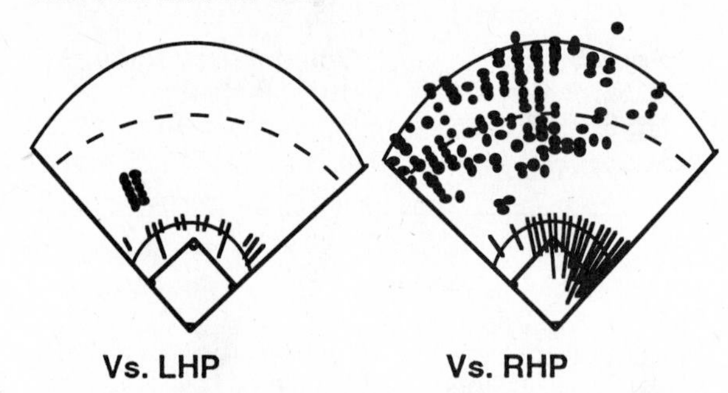

1992 Situational Stats

	AB	H	HR	RBI	AVG		AB	H	HR	RBI	AVG
Home	231	64	10	46	.277	LHP	53	13	1	8	.245
Road	247	57	6	30	.231	RHP	425	108	15	68	.254
Day	187	54	7	27	.289	Sc Pos	121	33	6	57	.273
Night	291	67	9	49	.230	Clutch	63	13	2	6	.206

1992 Rankings (American League)

- 10th in lowest batting average on the road (.231)
- Led designated hitters in highest percentage of swings put into play (50.0%)

HITTING:

Lance Blankenship may have surprised even himself last season. After failing to impress the A's in 1991 while filling in at second, Blankenship found himself pressed into duty last year because of Walt Weiss' injury in spring training. This time, Blankenship showed some maturity and discipline, and stayed in the lineup. Though his batting average slipped eight points to .241, he reached career highs in most offensive categories.

Blankenship started at second base in the season opener, and wound up playing 78 games there. He also filled in at all three outfield positions, making 33 starts, and even started four games at first base when Mark McGwire was sidelined. Blankenship's season was interrupted July 7 when he suffered a broken right hand courtesy of a Kevin Ritz pitch. But he returned quickly.

Always a fairly patient hitter, Blankenship became a veritable walking machine last year. Though he had fewer than 450 plate appearances, he drew 82 walks; as a result his on-base percentage was a hefty .393. At the same time he struck out only 57 times. As usual, he was susceptible to fastballs in, or sliders down and away. He struggled with runners in scoring position (.193).

BASERUNNING:

Though he possesses only above-average speed, Blankenship is a very aggressive baserunner. He had a career-high 21 stolen bases last year and was caught stealing only seven times. Sometimes he's a little over-aggressive and runs himself into outs.

FIELDING:

Blankenship played well defensively. In his first full major-league season, he did not make an error at second base until May 30, a stretch of 41 starts and 221 total chances. He committed just three errors all season for a .992 fielding percentage.

OVERALL:

Blankenship showed the A's he could play last year. With the departure of Walt Weiss, Mike Bordick will take over shortstop shile Blankenship claims second base. Blankenship's ability to play other positions provides the A's with more value and versatility than simply a starting second baseman.

LANCE BLANKENSHIP

Position: 2B/LF/CF/RF
Bats: R **Throws:** R
Ht: 6' 0" **Wt:** 185

Opening Day Age: 29
Born: 12/6/63 in Portland, OR
ML Seasons: 5

Overall Statistics

	G	AB	R	H	D	T	HR	RBI	SB	BB	SO	AVG
1992	123	349	59	84	24	1	3	34	21	82	57	.241
Career	367	798	133	185	40	2	7	69	41	133	154	.232

Where He Hits the Ball

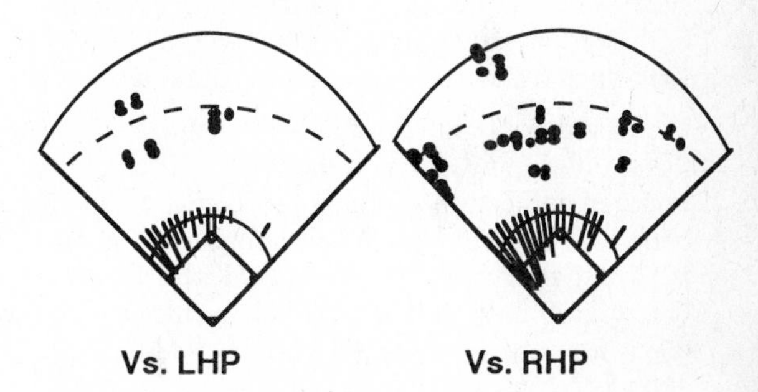

1992 Situational Stats

	AB	H	HR	RBI	AVG		AB	H	HR	RBI	AVG
Home	167	43	1	19	.257	LHP	89	22	0	5	.247
Road	182	41	2	15	.225	RHP	260	62	3	29	.238
Day	136	32	1	12	.235	Sc Pos	88	17	0	24	.193
Night	213	52	2	22	.244	Clutch	66	19	1	7	.288

1992 Rankings (American League)

- 1st in highest percentage of pitches taken (69.3%)
- 6th in lowest batting average with runners in scoring position (.193) and lowest batting average on an 0-2 count (.048)
- 8th in on-base percentage vs. left-handed pitchers (.455)
- Led the A's in on-base percentage vs. left-handed pitchers and highest percentage of pitches taken
- Led AL second basemen in on-base percentage vs. left-handed pitchers and highest percentage of pitches taken

GREAT RANGE

MIKE BORDICK

Position: 2B/SS
Bats: R **Throws:** R
Ht: 5'11" **Wt:** 175

Opening Day Age: 27
Born: 7/21/65 in Marquette, MI
ML Seasons: 3

HITTING:

During the American League Championship Series, Manager Tony La Russa was asked to name his Most Valuable Player during the season. La Russa readily awarded the honors to Mike Bordick. Bordick led the A's with a .300 average, 151 hits, 41 multiple hit games and 154 games played. He was only the second infielder in Oakland history to bat .300 or better -- only Carney Lansford had accomplished that feat. Bordick did it in a rather unorthodox way.

After batting .272 at AAA Tacoma but just .238 in 90 games with the Athletics in 1991, Oakland hitting coach Doug Radar asked Bordick to explain the difference. Bordick said it was the stance he used. So Radar -- a fine hitting coach -- told Bordick to go back to that open, awkward-looking and successful approach. And it worked.

On Opening Night, Bordick's two-run single in the eighth inning drove in the tying and winning runs, an indication of things to come. Bordick batted .355 in April and led the American League in batting from May 25 to June 1. He did not drop below .300 until July 8. Bordick won't be mistaken for Jose Canseco, though. He had only 26 extra-base hits, but 14 sacrifice hits.

BASERUNNING:

An average runner, Bordick will only get better on the basepaths with more experience. He had 12 steals in 18 attempts last year, a professional high for him.

FIELDING:

Moved into the lineup due to Walt Weiss' injury, Bordick wound up starting 66 games at shortstop and 83 at second when Weiss returned. It was his best year in the field. Bordick understands the mental game well, and his ability to anticipate hitters' tendencies is among the best in the league. He has great range and good first-step quickness. An acrobatic infielder, Bordick dazzled the A's with his mid-air moves.

OVERALL:

A smart player, Bordick has won not only La Russa's MVP vote but also a full-time job with the A's. Now that Walt Weiss is in Florida, Bordick will be the regular shortstop. His stance may appear awkward, but it works.

Overall Statistics

	G	AB	R	H	D	T	HR	RBI	SB	BB	SO	AVG
1992	154	504	62	151	19	4	3	48	12	40	59	.300
Career	269	753	83	208	24	5	3	69	15	55	100	.276

Where He Hits the Ball

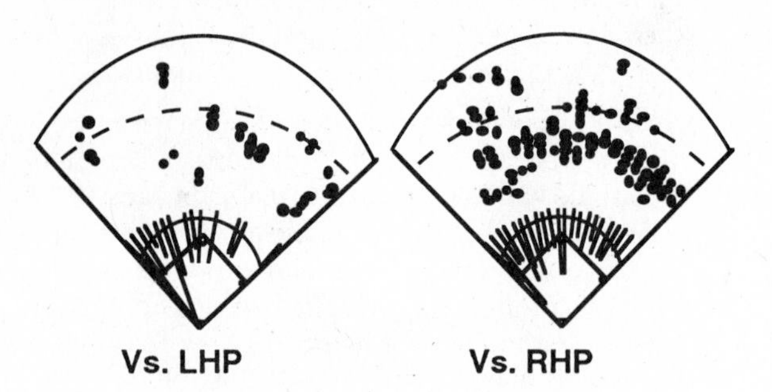

1992 Situational Stats

	AB	H	HR	RBI	AVG		AB	H	HR	RBI	AVG
Home	240	71	3	25	.296	LHP	131	44	1	15	.336
Road	264	80	0	23	.303	RHP	373	107	2	33	.287
Day	205	65	3	20	.317	Sc Pos	154	42	1	45	.273
Night	299	86	0	28	.288	Clutch	69	18	0	10	.261

1992 Rankings (American League)

- 2nd in sacrifice bunts (14)
- 8th in lowest HR frequency (168 ABs per HR) and highest percentage of swings put into play (57.2%)
- 9th in hit by pitch (9)
- Led the A's in batting average (.300), at-bats (504), hits (151), singles (125), hit by pitch, plate appearances (572), games played (154), highest groundball/flyball ratio (1.5), most pitches seen per plate appearance (3.72), highest batting average vs. left-handed pitchers (.336), highest batting average vs. right-handed pitchers (.287), highest batting average at home (.296) and highest percentage of swings put into play

JERRY BROWNE

Position: 3B/2B/LF/CF
Bats: B **Throws:** R
Ht: 5'10" **Wt:** 170

Opening Day Age: 27
Born: 2/13/66 in St. Croix, Virgin Islands
ML Seasons: 7

HITTING:

The Cleveland Indians must be wondering which Jerry Browne they'd had on their roster. Was this Jerry Browne the same player who hit .228 for Cleveland in 1991 now starring for Oakland with a .287 average? Was this the Browne who'd fielded .948 in his last year with the Indians now filling in everywhere and helping the A's with his glove? Yes, it was the man they call "The Governor," showing the form of his best days with Texas and Cleveland.

Browne's .287 batting average not only was second-best on the A's but set an Oakland club record for batting average by a switch-hitter. An efficient bunter, he led the American League in sacrifice hits with 16. Browne was the A's best hitter after the All-Star break with a .308 average, and one of the best in the clutch with a .321 mark with runners in scoring position. Browne is a smart hitter, and pitchers can ill afford to get behind in the count against him. He is dangerous with the count in his favor.

BASERUNNING:

Browne did not pose a stolen base threat for the A's, swiping just three bases -- one more than he totaled in 1991, and well off his rookie year total of 27 swipes in 1987. He has decent speed but is known for making too many mistakes.

FIELDING:

Browne played everywhere for Oakland. He started seven games at second base, 38 at third base and 37 in the outfield, played all three outfield positions and notched one game at shortstop. Despite having to juggle his gloves, Browne made only five errors for the season. He doesn't have a rifle arm and is best suited for infield duties.

OVERALL:

With the retirement of Carney Lansford, Browne could be the A's starting third baseman in '93. His patience is well suited to batting second behind Rickey Henderson. With both the Rangers and Indians, Browne had strong first years, then ran into problems. The A's hope he can avoid a falloff this time, especially after they protected him from expansion.

Overall Statistics

	G	AB	R	H	D	T	HR	RBI	SB	BB	SO	AVG
1992	111	324	43	93	12	2	3	40	3	40	40	.287
Career	728	2417	341	657	101	21	17	222	65	294	265	.272

Where He Hits the Ball

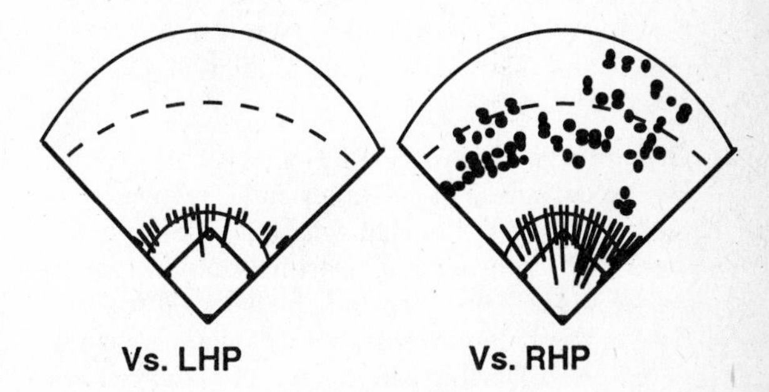

1992 Situational Stats

	AB	H	HR	RBI	AVG		AB	H	HR	RBI	AVG
Home	146	41	1	17	.281	LHP	49	9	0	5	.184
Road	178	52	2	23	.292	RHP	275	84	3	35	.305
Day	139	41	1	14	.295	Sc Pos	78	25	2	37	.321
Night	185	52	2	26	.281	Clutch	43	20	1	9	.465

1992 Rankings (American League)

- 1st in sacrifice bunts (16) and batting average in the clutch (.465)
- 3rd in batting average on an 0-2 count (.333)
- 4th in batting average with the bases loaded (.556)
- 8th in bunts in play (26)
- Led the A's in sacrifice bunts, batting average in the clutch, batting average on an 0-2 count and bunts in play
- Led AL third basemen in sacrifice bunts, batting average in the clutch, batting average with the bases loaded, batting average on an 0-2 count and bunts in play

RON DARLING

Position: SP
Bats: R **Throws:** R
Ht: 6' 3" **Wt:** 195

Opening Day Age: 32
Born: 8/19/60 in Honolulu, HI
ML Seasons: 10

PITCHING:

Ron Darling fit Manager Tony La Russa's scheme perfectly. Darling only needed to pitch six innings before handing the ball over to the Athletics' bullpen. It was that simple. Only Mike Moore's 17 victories were more than Darling's 15 on the Oakland staff in 1992. Darling's four complete games and 206.1 innings in 1992, his first full season in the A's rotation, marked the most since '89 when he also went the distance four times and totaled 217.1 innings for the Mets.

Darling, who did not miss a start in Oakland's injury-riddled year, carried a no-hitter into the sixth inning of a game five times, and twice he went as far as the eighth inning. He threw three two-hit shutouts for the season, setting a career best for low-hit games; they were the only complete-game shutouts by an Oakland starter in 1992.

Darling won't overpower hitters with his fastball. He looked strong in the American League Championship Series, but that was because he had a week off. These days, Darling couldn't overpower Ross Perot. Instead, he will outfox and out-finesse batters. Possessor of a nasty split-fingered pitch, Darling can make it break two ways. Plus, Darling will mix in a cut fastball. To be successful -- and use his forkball to his advantage -- he must get ahead of hitters. If not, Darling forces La Russa to call upon his relief corps earlier than he'd like.

HOLDING RUNNERS AND FIELDING:

Ask American League managers to name a pitcher who deserves a Gold Glove and the majority will pick Darling, one of the best athletes on the Oakland staff. Darling has improved his ability to hold runners. In 1991, 24 of 27 basestealers were successful; in 1992, it was 10 of 23.

OVERALL:

Darling proved to be very valuable to the injury-riddled A's rotation, but he might not have been as successful anywhere else. Not every team has a bullpen like Oakland's. The A's were expected to try to keep Darling, but at a cost within their tight budget.

Overall Statistics

	W	L	ERA	G	GS	Sv	IP	H	R	BB	SO	HR
1992	15	10	3.66	33	33	0	206.1	198	98	72	99	15
Career	117	89	3.57	305	289	0	1918.1	1760	864	729	1318	183

How Often He Throws Strikes

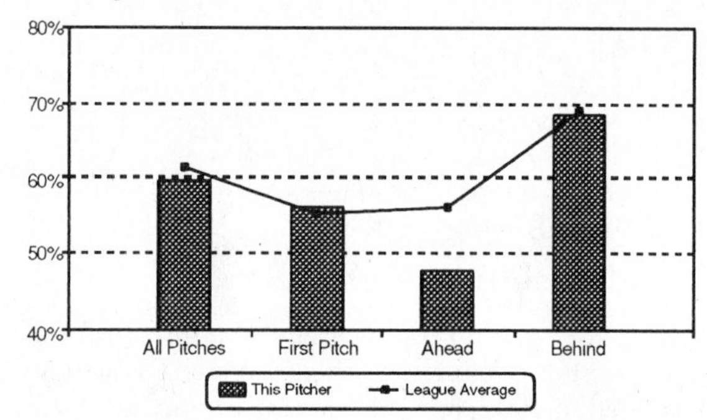

1992 Situational Stats

	W	L	ERA	Sv	IP		AB	H	HR	RBI	AVG
Home	8	6	3.57	0	106.0	LHB	371	100	6	37	.270
Road	7	4	3.77	0	100.1	RHB	412	98	9	46	.238
Day	8	4	2.90	0	93.0	Sc Pos	178	47	3	66	.264
Night	7	6	4.29	0	113.1	Clutch	44	6	0	0	.136

1992 Rankings (American League)

- 2nd in lowest stolen base percentage allowed (43.5%)
- 3rd in wild pitches (13)
- 4th in shutouts (3)
- 9th in least strikeouts per 9 innings (4.3)
- 10th in runners caught stealing (13)
- Led the A's in complete games (4), shutouts, runners caught stealing, lowest slugging percentage allowed (.379), lowest stolen base percentage allowed, least pitches thrown per batter (3.74) and least home runs allowed per 9 innings (.65)

KELLY DOWNS

Position: SP/RP
Bats: R **Throws:** R
Ht: 6' 4" **Wt:** 200

Opening Day Age: 32
Born: 10/25/60 in Ogden, UT
ML Seasons: 7

PITCHING:

Kelly Downs didn't impress the San Francisco Giants with a 1-2 record and 3.47 ERA in 19 games at the beginning of the 1992 season, neither as a starter or out of the bullpen. So Downs moved across the Bay June 30, signed by Oakland six days after the Giants released him. With the A's Downs also shifted between a starting and relief role, but his work was a little better. He was 5-5 with a 3.29 ERA in his first taste of American League action.

Though Downs didn't overwhelm anyone, Oakland was grateful to get him: the Athletics needed anyone with a healthy arm. A smart pitcher, he was well-suited to Tony La Russa's situation pitching. Downs was reasonably effective in a starter's role for the Athletics; he worked six innings or more in six of his 13 starts, and gave up three or fewer earned runs in eight of them. However, he seemed to find his niche when he went back to the bullpen following the late-August acquisition of Bobby Witt. In his last six appearances, which included one start, Downs was 2-0 and gave up just 10 hits and three earned runs in his final 20.2 innings (1.31 ERA).

Downs relies on a strong forkball, similar to Ron Darling's, but has a better slider and fastball than Darling. His arm is still questionable following rotator cuff surgery in early April 1990, but his 144.1 innings pitched last year were his highest total since 1988.

HOLDING RUNNERS AND FIELDING:

In addition to reviving his arm, Downs' surgery in 1990 made him change his delivery. His finish is much more balanced, which helps his fielding. Of 25 runners attempting steals in Downs' 37 appearances, only eight were caught. He just doesn't get rid of the ball quickly enough.

OVERALL:

Downs did a decent job with Oakland, but the A's were not expected to re-sign him. He's been somewhat effective throughout most of his career, with a lifetime won-lost record of 52-43; his problem has always been staying healthy. Whoever signs him will be taking a chance.

Overall Statistics

	W	L	ERA	G	GS	Sv	IP	H	R	BB	SO	HR
1992	6	7	3.37	37	20	0	144.1	137	63	70	71	8
Career	52	43	3.60	195	123	1	844.0	777	374	313	532	59

How Often He Throws Strikes

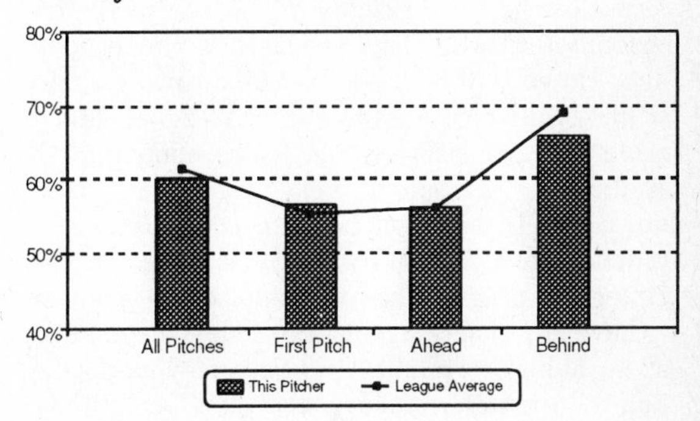

1992 Situational Stats

	W	L	ERA	Sv	IP		AB	H	HR	RBI	AVG
Home	4	2	3.23	0	64.0	LHB	263	72	1	24	.274
Road	2	5	3.47	0	80.1	RHB	277	65	7	30	.235
Day	2	3	3.58	0	50.1	Sc Pos	136	24	2	43	.176
Night	4	4	3.26	0	94.0	Clutch	38	11	0	5	.289

1992 Rankings (American League)

- Led the A's in balks (1) and lowest batting average allowed vs. left-handed batters (.250)

STOPPER

DENNIS ECKERSLEY

Position: RP
Bats: R **Throws:** R
Ht: 6' 2" **Wt:** 195

Opening Day Age: 38
Born: 10/3/54 in Oakland, CA
ML Seasons: 18

PITCHING:

Despite a sour performance in the playoffs, Dennis Eckersley had another brilliant season in 1992, capped by his winning both the American League Most Valuable Player and Cy Young Awards. Eighth all-time with 239 saves though he's been a reliever for only six seasons, Eckersley became only the second major league pitcher to total 50 saves in a season. Consider that 22 major league teams -- 11 in each league -- failed to total 50 saves last year. The A's ace was successful in 51 of 54 save situations last season. He is the leader in save percentage since 1988 with an .887 percentage (220 out of 248 opportunities).

How does he do it? Eckersley's fastball has better velocity than when he was a starting pitcher long ago. However, his key is that he throws so hard while hardly ever missing the strike zone. He did issue 11 walks last year, but six were intentional. At the end of the season, Eckersley seemed fascinated with how few pitches he needed to throw to pluck a save. What Toronto discovered in the American League Championship Series was that to have any chance against Eckersley, they had to swing at his first pitch. After Eckersley works the count, a hitter's chance fades. The strategy worked for Toronto in this case. Despite the nightmarish ALCS, there is no doubt the mustachioed side-armer is still one of the best in the clutch.

HOLDING RUNNERS AND FIELDING:

Eckersley usually doesn't have too many baserunners to concern himself with -- opponents batted .211 against him. He prefers to focus on the batter, and thus nine of 10 basestealers were successful against him. He is not a very good defensive player.

OVERALL:

Eckersley should be able to enjoy this off-season, working on his tan and basking in the post-season accolades -- as long as he doesn't remember the horrendous American League Championship Series. His post season performance (eight hits, two runs, two strikeouts in three innings over three games) was very un-Eck like. The A's probably aren't concerned. Eckersley got them there more than anyone.

Overall Statistics

	W	L	ERA	G	GS	Sv	IP	H	R	BB	SO	HR
1992	7	1	1.91	69	0	51	80.0	62	17	11	93	5
Career	181	145	3.43	740	361	239	2971.1	2747	1224	679	2118	307

How Often He Throws Strikes

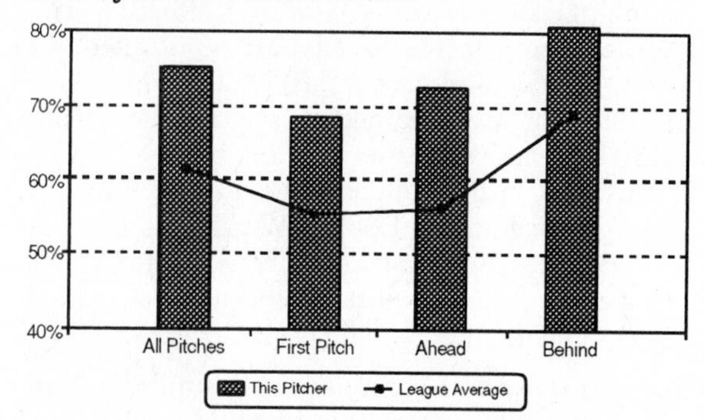

1992 Situational Stats

	W	L	ERA	Sv	IP		AB	H	HR	RBI	AVG
Home	7	0	2.76	21	42.1	LHB	149	39	3	11	.262
Road	0	1	0.96	30	37.2	RHB	145	23	2	7	.159
Day	3	0	1.99	16	22.2	Sc Pos	76	12	1	14	.158
Night	4	1	1.88	35	57.1	Clutch	227	39	1	12	.172

1992 Rankings (American League)

- 1st in saves (51), games finished (65), save opportunities (54), save percentage (94.4%), lowest percentage of inherited runners scored (6.4%), least baserunners allowed per 9 innings in relief (8.3) and most strikeouts per 9 innings in relief (10.5)
- 6th in games pitched (69) and relief wins (7)
- 7th in relief ERA (1.91)
- Led the A's in games pitched, saves, games finished, save opportunities, save percentage, lowest percentage of inherited runners scored, relief ERA, lowest batting average allowed in relief (.211), least baserunners allowed per 9 innings in relief and most strikeouts per 9 innings in relief

HITTING:

Rickey Henderson is still the consummate leadoff hitter. Despite missing 45 games last year because of an assortment of injuries, Henderson raised his batting average 15 points to .283 over his 1991 mark. He also posted a .426 on-base percentage, the second-highest of his 14-year career. The on-base figure would have ranked second in the American League except that he was two plate appearances short of qualifying for the title.

However, Henderson's season was far from satisfying. He had two stints on the disabled list with a pulled left hamstring, and his 396 at-bats, 112 hits, 46 RBI and 77 runs scored were among the lowest totals of his career. And Henderson had a tough playoff series. Previously a .377 hitter in postseason play, he batted .261 in the LCS against Toronto and made three costly errors.

Henderson makes pitchers work. He will shrink at the plate, crouching lower and lower as the count progresses. With each non-strike, he transforms himself into Eddie Gaedel. If he gets ahead 3-1 in the count, Henderson will swing only if he sees a fastball in his zone. Defenses should play him straightaway.

BASERUNNING:

Last season marked only the second time since 1980 that Henderson, baseball's all-time stolen base king, did not lead the league in steals. The hamstring injury was the problem; Henderson's success rate (48 of 59, 81 percent) was as good as ever. Henderson can still get from first to third as well as anybody.

FIELDING:

As talented as Henderson is on the bases, he still has problems in the field. His slip on the turf at SkyDome in Game 6 of the ALCS resulted in a two-base error and ignited a crucial Toronto rally. His range is still good, but his arm has always been on the weak side.

OVERALL:

Often criticized for being selfish, Henderson appeared to be concerned with the team last season, helping the A's stay in contention with a hot August (.309, 15 RBI, 14 stolen bases). He may be one of the few veterans left once Oakland finishes its cost-cutting roster maneuvers.

RICKEY HENDERSON

Position: LF
Bats: R **Throws:** L
Ht: 5'10" **Wt:** 190

Opening Day Age: 34
Born: 12/25/58 in Chicago, IL
ML Seasons: 14

Overall Statistics

	G	AB	R	H	D	T	HR	RBI	SB	BB	SO	AVG
1992	117	396	77	112	18	3	15	46	48	95	56	.283
Career	1859	6879	1472	2000	329	54	199	725	1042	1286	925	.291

Where He Hits the Ball

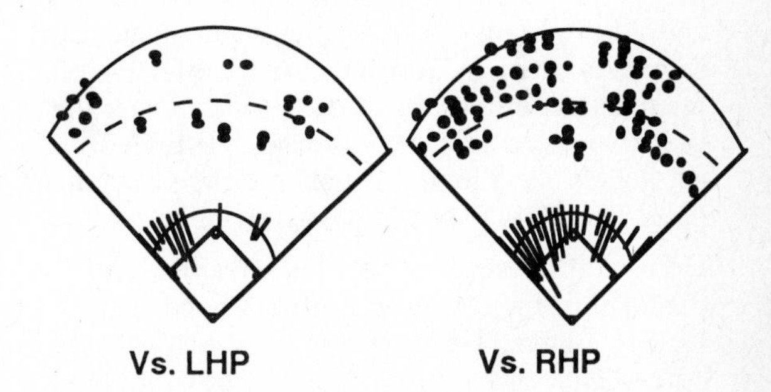

1992 Situational Stats

	AB	H	HR	RBI	AVG		AB	H	HR	RBI	AVG
Home	200	59	10	27	.295	LHP	105	28	5	13	.267
Road	196	53	5	19	.270	RHP	291	84	10	33	.289
Day	149	38	4	16	.255	Sc Pos	89	23	2	28	.258
Night	247	74	11	30	.300	Clutch	50	14	2	13	.280

1992 Rankings (American League)

- → 1st in on-base percentage for a leadoff hitter (.426)
- → 2nd in highest percentage of pitches taken (69.1%)
- → 3rd in steals of third (9)
- → 6th in stolen bases (48)
- → 7th in walks (95)
- → Led the A's in stolen bases, caught stealing (11), walks, most pitches seen (2,261), stolen base percentage (81.4%), least GDPs per GDP situation (6.7%), slugging percentage vs. left-handed pitchers (.476), lowest percentage of swings that missed (10.4%) and steals of third

PITCHING:

After undergoing shoulder surgery in March 1991, Rick Honeycutt was expected to be fully recovered by the start of last season. Unfortunately, Honeycutt was on Oakland's long list of walking wounded at the end of the season. A strained muscle in his right side limited him to one appearance after Sept. 6. In that outing, he faced only one batter.

That one-batter outing symbolizes Honeycutt's role on the A's. For the fifth straight year, he was the A's southpaw set-up man. Over that time, left-handed hitters have batted just .198 against him. In 1992, lefties hit .258 vs. Honeycutt, but he pitched well while he was healthy. The set-up man recorded 18 holds, fifth best in the league, and allowed only 14 of 48 inherited runners to score. As usual, he was much more effective on his own turf at the Oakland Coliseum. Over the past five years, Honeycutt has a 2.40 ERA with six home runs allowed at home; on the road, he has a 3.69 ERA with 12 homers given up.

Honeycutt's best pitches are his sinker and slider, the latter being particularly effective against left-handed hitters. He also throws a fastball and curve. Though he strikes out an above-average number of hitters, Honeycutt needs pinpoint control to be effective. When he was ahead on the count last year, he held the opposition to a .191 average. When he was behind, they lit him up at a .429 clip. Those figures are fairly typical for him. Fortunately for Honeycutt, his control was usually good in 1992. He struck out 32 men last year and walked only 10, three intentional.

HOLDING RUNNERS AND FIELDING:

An average fielder, Honeycutt isn't particularly nimble off the mound. But Honeycutt is very good at keeping runners close. His moves are so deceptive that runners rarely challenge him.

OVERALL:

One of the 15 free agents on the A's club, Honeycutt was not expected to be re-signed. Age, injuries and ineffectiveness have reduced his value. However, lefty relievers have a long shelf life, and though he's nearly 39, he should be able to find work.

RICK HONEYCUTT

Position: RP
Bats: L **Throws:** L
Ht: 6' 1" **Wt:** 191

Opening Day Age: 38
Born: 6/29/54 in Chattanooga, TN
ML Seasons: 16

Overall Statistics

	W	L	ERA	G	GS	Sv	IP	H	R	BB	SO	HR
1992	1	4	3.69	54	0	3	39.0	41	19	10	32	2
Career	100	135	3.73	588	268	30	1998.0	2030	961	610	946	170

How Often He Throws Strikes

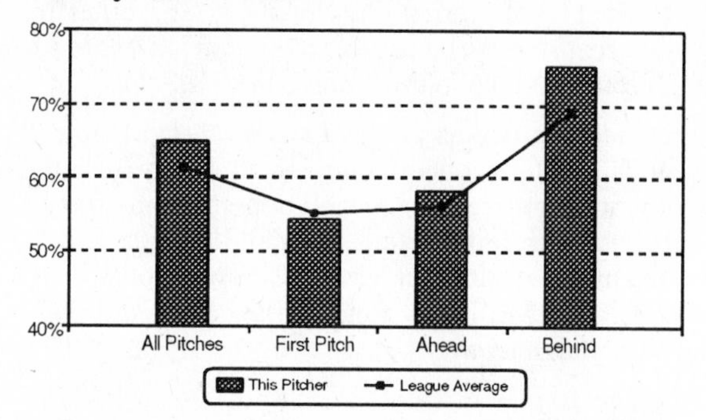

1992 Situational Stats

	W	L	ERA	Sv	IP		AB	H	HR	RBI	AVG
Home	1	2	3.06	2	17.2	LHB	62	16	1	9	.258
Road	0	2	4.22	1	21.1	RHB	89	25	1	17	.281
Day	0	2	2.45	2	14.2	Sc Pos	51	13	1	24	.255
Night	1	2	4.44	1	24.1	Clutch	88	23	2	17	.261

1992 Rankings (American League)

- 5th in holds (18)
- Led the A's in blown saves (4)

HITTING:

What a turnaround for Mark McGwire in 1992. After batting .201 with 22 homers in 1991, Mark McGwire regained his power stroke last year. There's no telling how many home runs he could have clubbed if he was healthy the entire season. A muscle strain in August forced him to miss 20 games and may have cost him the home run title. As it was he belted 42, missing the major-league crown by only one. It was the second-highest total of McGwire's career.

Credit both McGwire and hitting coach Doug Rader with the change. Rader, a power hitter as a player, encouraged McGwire to adopt a pigeon-toed, knock-kneed stance that made him look like a golfer at the plate. McGwire would shift his lower body weight like Fred Couples during his swing, and that shift -- as any duffer will tell you -- gave him more power. With his new, short swing, the ball jumped off his bat. He improved his 1991 average by 67 points, and topped his previous career average by 24.

McGwire likes the ball in the middle of the plate from his knees to his belt, where he can use his great bat extension. Right-handed pitchers took advantage of McGwire by throwing breaking balls right at him or sliders down and away.

BASERUNNING:

McGwire is no threat on the basepaths. He is one of the slowest players in baseball. He was caught stealing in his sole attempt. For him it's much easier to hit the ball out of the park than it is to steal a base.

FIELDING:

A Gold Glove-caliber fielder, McGwire ranked third in the American League among first basemen with a .995 fielding percentage, committing just six errors in 1,195 total chances. As usual, he handled the expansive foul territory at Oakland Coliseum extremely well.

OVERALL:

McGwire put up numbers that should draw plenty of interest. McGwire can control a ballgame with one swing just as Jose Canseco can, and was said to be demanding a similar $5 million a year contract. The A's wanted to keep him, but at that price it was a stretch.

MARK McGWIRE

Position: 1B
Bats: R **Throws:** R
Ht: 6' 5" **Wt:** 225

Opening Day Age: 29
Born: 10/1/63 in Pomona, CA
ML Seasons: 7

Overall Statistics

	G	AB	R	H	D	T	HR	RBI	SB	BB	SO	AVG
1992	139	467	87	125	22	0	42	104	0	90	105	.268
Career	916	3123	504	772	128	5	220	608	6	527	697	.247

Where He Hits the Ball

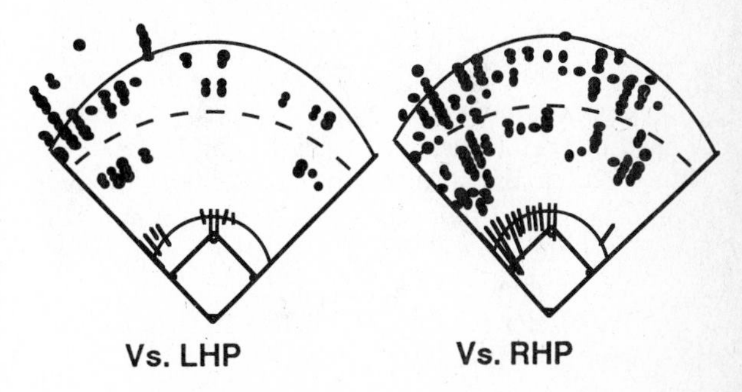

1992 Situational Stats

	AB	H	HR	RBI	AVG		AB	H	HR	RBI	AVG
Home	218	55	24	52	.252	LHP	97	32	14	27	.330
Road	249	70	18	52	.281	RHP	370	93	28	77	.251
Day	180	52	20	46	.289	Sc Pos	107	30	7	61	.280
Night	287	73	22	58	.254	Clutch	59	14	5	14	.237

1992 Rankings (American League)

- 1st in slugging percentage (.585), HR frequency (11.1 ABs per HR) and lowest groundball/flyball ratio (.39)
- 2nd in home runs (42)
- 3rd in slugging percentage vs. right-handed pitchers (.527)
- Led the A's in home runs, runs scored (87), total bases (273), RBI (104), sacrifice flies (9), intentional walks (12), times on base (220), strikeouts (105), slugging percentage, on-base percentage (.385), HR frequency, slugging percentage vs. right-handed pitchers and on-base percentage vs. right-handed pitchers

PITCHING:

Some day Mike Moore will get the recognition he deserves. Forget Game 6 of the American League Championship Series -- Moore hopes to. Six runs on seven hits in less than three innings is not a typical Moore outing, he had a 5-1 record in six career starts at SkyDome prior to that ill-fated start. The righthander has pitched in the shadow of Oakland aces Dave Stewart and Bob Welch, yet if one compares the number of wins, Moore is comparable. In the last six years, Stewart has won 107 games, Welch 99 and Moore 84 to rank second, fourth and 10th of current American League pitchers. In the last 10 years, Welch has 148 wins, Stewart 133 and Moore 125. Not a bad triumvirate.

Last year Moore led the team in wins (17), starts (36) and innings pitched (223). It was his second straight season with 17 wins, and third year in the last four that he has won at least 17 and pitched at least 200 innings. Although consistent in victories and innings, Moore had anything but a smooth season. He was 4-0 with a 1.51 ERA in April, but was a combined 3-7 in May and June with a 6.52 ERA. After a 3-2 July record, Moore finished the season 7-3 with a 3.01 ERA.

Moore throws a fastball, slider, curve, change-up and forkball, but only his curve and change are above-average. The third time through the batting order, opponents start to figure him out. His 22 wild pitches -- most in the league -- don't help either, nor does his extremely slow working pace.

HOLDING RUNNERS AND FIELDING:

An agile athlete, Moore fields his position well, and some even consider him Gold Glove caliber. He keeps runners from getting too good a jump; last year he permitted 19 steals in 32 attempts.

OVERALL:

In their endless effort to reduce the payroll, the A's were not expected to hinder Moore from testing the free agent market. Unless he takes a pay cut, he would likely be too expensive for Oakland in 1993. He'll be an asset to any pitching staff.

MIKE MOORE

Position: SP
Bats: R **Throws:** R
Ht: 6' 4" **Wt:** 205

Opening Day Age: 33
Born: 11/26/59 in Eakly, OK
ML Seasons: 11

Overall Statistics

	W	L	ERA	G	GS	Sv	IP	H	R	BB	SO	HR
1992	17	12	4.12	36	36	0	223.0	229	113	103	117	20
Career	132	142	4.07	364	354	2	2331.0	2300	1166	910	1452	205

How Often He Throws Strikes

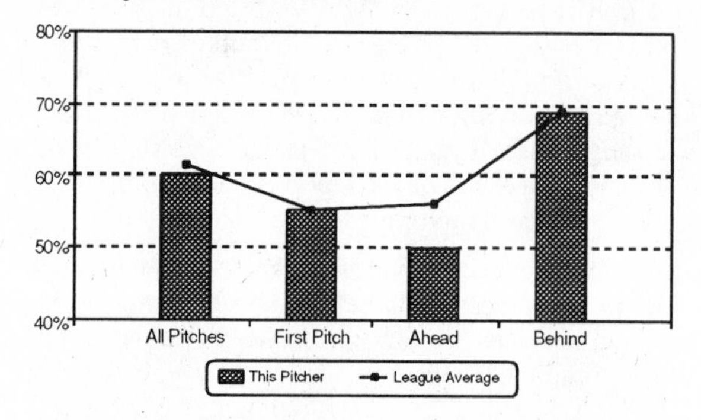

1992 Situational Stats

	W	L	ERA	Sv	IP		AB	H	HR	RBI	AVG
Home	7	4	3.55	0	104.0	LHB	445	116	8	51	.261
Road	10	8	4.61	0	119.0	RHB	407	113	12	51	.278
Day	9	7	3.54	0	122.0	Sc Pos	202	54	3	80	.267
Night	8	5	4.81	0	101.0	Clutch	63	15	2	6	.238

1992 Rankings (American League)

- 1st in games started (36) and wild pitches (22)
- 3rd in walks allowed (103) and lowest strikeout/walk ratio (1.1)
- 4th in highest on-base percentage allowed (.349) and most baserunners allowed per 9 innings (13.7)
- Led the A's in wins (17), losses (12), games started, innings pitched (223), hits allowed (229), batters faced (982), walks allowed, hit batsmen (8), wild pitches, pitches thrown (3,766), pickoff throws (199), stolen bases allowed (19), runners caught stealing (13), GDPs induced (26), highest groundball/flyball ratio allowed (1.5), most run support per 9 innings (5.0) and ERA at home (3.55)

JEFF PARRETT

Position: RP
Bats: R **Throws:** R
Ht: 6' 3" **Wt:** 195

Opening Day Age: 31
Born: 8/26/61 in Indianapolis, IN
ML Seasons: 7

PITCHING:

Just before spring training began, Jeff Parrett signed a minor-league contract with the Oakland Athletics. Parrett had appeared in 18 games for Atlanta in 1991, splitting the season between the major league team and the Braves' Triple-A club in Richmond. A 1-2 record and 6.33 ERA didn't give Atlanta any reason to keep him, so he went looking elsewhere. He found the A's, and they're glad he did. Parrett went 9-1 for Oakland last year and filled the vital righty set-up slot left vacant by the decline of Gene Nelson.

If people were astonished by Parrett's success, maybe they shouldn't have been. Though he struggled with Atlanta in 1991, he'd worked 60-plus games for the Expos, Phillies and Braves each year from 1988 to 1990, and was very effective through 1989. Parrett's 1992 season, in fact, wasn't all that different from his 1988 and 1989 numbers: heavy workloads each season (61, 72, 66 games), good ERAs (2.65, 2.98, 3.02), excellent won-loss records (12-4, 12-6, 9-1).

Decidedly a power pitcher, Parrett relies on a 90 MPH fastball, a pretty good slider, and a split-fingered fastball that he uses as his offspeed pitch. He works up in the strike zone for the most part, getting a lot of fly balls and getting hurt on occasion by the longball. Control is a key for him; Parrett's best seasons have been the ones in which he was able to throw strikes with regularity. When he's on his game, he can be extremely tough on right-handed hitters, and that was the case last year: he held righties to a .192 average.

HOLDING RUNNERS AND FIELDING:

Parrett needs work at holding runners. Only four of 18 basestealers were caught during Parrett's outings last year. He's considered an adequate fielder.

OVERALL:

Give Dave Duncan a full spring with Parrett and he could blossom into an even more useful set-up pitcher than he was in 1992. With all the players expected to leave Oakland over the winter, Parrett could be one busy guy this year.

Overall Statistics

	W	L	ERA	G	GS	Sv	IP	H	R	BB	SO	HR
1992	9	1	3.02	66	0	0	98.1	81	35	42	78	7
Career	46	30	3.65	341	5	21	508.0	459	231	241	415	45

How Often He Throws Strikes

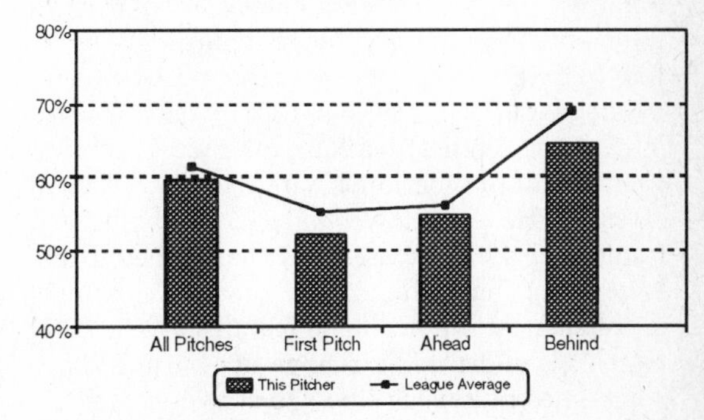

1992 Situational Stats

	W	L	ERA	Sv	IP		AB	H	HR	RBI	AVG
Home	4	0	3.29	0	52.0	LHB	144	40	2	24	.278
Road	5	1	2.72	0	46.1	RHB	214	41	5	23	.192
Day	3	0	3.74	0	33.2	Sc Pos	110	29	1	37	.264
Night	6	1	2.64	0	64.2	Clutch	145	31	2	13	.214

1992 Rankings (American League)

- 2nd in holds (19) and relief wins (9)
- 3rd in wild pitches (13)
- 4th in first batter efficiency (.145)
- 5th in relief innings (98.1)
- 9th in games pitched (66)
- Led the A's in holds, first batter efficiency, relief wins and relief innings

PITCHING:

The A's had hoped that the acquisition of Jeff Russell from Texas would give them a bullpen corps comparable to the 1990 Reds' nasty combination of Norm Charlton and Rob Dibble. Maybe if Russell had been 100 percent healthy it would have worked. Acquired August 31, Russell made eight appearances with the A's, then nursed a sore right elbow for the final two and a half weeks of the season. He pitched just once after Sept. 16, on the final day of the regular season. Russell made a game effort to help the club in the playoffs, but he was cuffed around for a 9.00 ERA.

The hard-throwing righthander and long-time Rangers' closer was successful in two save situations for the A's. He also plucked two wins in relief and pitched 9.2 scoreless innings, giving up four hits and striking out five, so he was dominant in stretches. For the season, Russell had 30 saves in 39 opportunities, marking the second straight year and third time in his career he had reached 30 saves. He also allowed only 12 of 43 inherited runners to score. Russell has the pitches to get batters out, but suffers from occasional control problems. At full health he features a 90+ MPH fastball, a slider and a change-up, but the slider sometimes causes his elbow to ache.

HOLDING RUNNERS AND FIELDING:

Russell thwarted base stealers in 1992, although probably because he was aided by the rifle arm of Texas catcher Ivan Rodriguez most of the season. Of the four base runners who tried to steal on Russell, three were thrown out. He's also a good fielder.

OVERALL:

A free agent, Russell's stay in Oakland was expected to be short-lived. He would have to adjust to being a set-up pitcher as long as Dennis Eckersley is in the A's pen, and that should be for a while. He needs to overcome elbow problems as well as improve his strike zone command, but a number of clubs -- including the Rangers -- figured to be interested in his talents.

JEFF RUSSELL

Position: RP
Bats: R **Throws:** R
Ht: 6' 3" **Wt:** 205

Opening Day Age: 31
Born: 9/2/61 in Cincinnati, OH
ML Seasons: 10

Overall Statistics

	W	L	ERA	G	GS	Sv	IP	H	R	BB	SO	HR
1992	4	3	1.63	59	0	30	66.1	55	14	25	48	3
Career	50	60	3.79	404	79	113	923.2	889	450	354	576	86

How Often He Throws Strikes

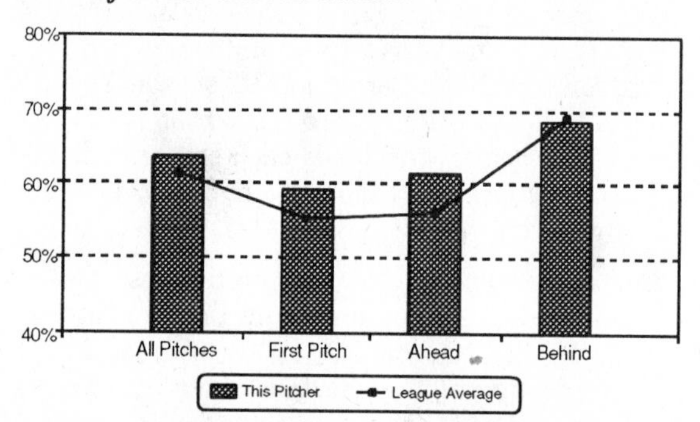

1992 Situational Stats

	W	L	ERA	Sv	IP		AB	H	HR	RBI	AVG
Home	2	1	0.94	16	38.1	LHB	110	27	1	8	.245
Road	2	2	2.57	14	28.0	RHB	136	28	2	14	.206
Day	1	2	2.84	7	19.0	Sc Pos	80	15	1	19	.188
Night	3	1	1.14	23	47.1	Clutch	191	44	2	19	.230

1992 Rankings (American League)

- 1st in blown saves (9) and relief ERA (1.63)
- 3rd lowest save percentage (76.9%)
- 5th in save opportunities (39)
- 6th in saves (30)
- 9th in games finished (46)

IN HIS PRIME

RUBEN SIERRA

Position: RF
Bats: B **Throws:** R
Ht: 6' 1" **Wt:** 200

Opening Day Age: 27
Born: 10/6/65 in Rio Piedras, Puerto Rico
ML Seasons: 7

HITTING:

Ruben Sierra is no Jose Canseco . . . he just might be better. The Athletics acquired Sierra in a blockbuster trade with Texas on August 31 along with Jeff Russell and Bobby Witt for the volatile Canseco. Although Sierra will probably never be a 40-40 player, his career batting average is higher than Canseco's, and his .470 career slugging percentage is not too shabby either.

Sierra made a good impression in his first game for Oakland when he scored the winning run in the 10th inning, scoring from first base on a single and an error. The A's loved his play in his month-plus with them; the big question is whether he'll stick around.

As he has done throughout his career, the switch-hitting Sierra was stronger from the right side. For the season he batted .339 from the right with five homers and a .520 slugging percentage, and .253 from the left with 12 homers in many more at-bats. He has a classic switch-hitter's swing. When batting left-handed, Sierra loves the ball down. When batting right-handed, he thrives on balls up. If a pitcher gets two strikes on him using fastballs, he's susceptible to being fooled by the curve. Pitchers can also work Sierra up the ladder in the strike zone.

BASERUNNING:

Sierra became a much more aggressive baserunner when he joined the Athletics. His ability to stretch hits and advance really helped Oakland. He finished the year with 14 steals in 18 attempts, and over the past five years he has stolen 65 bases in 79 attempts for an 82 percent success rate.

FIELDING:

Sierra also seemed to return to his defensive form of two years ago. He boasted an above average arm in the outfield. His throws weren't as accurate as before, but the change of scenery definitely helped his defensive attitude.

OVERALL:

Sierra would do well to move permanently to the Bay Area, but the A's may not be able to afford him. The trade gave his career a boost, giving him a chance to display his talents in the AL Championship Series. Sierra batted .333, with two doubles, a triple, a home run and seven RBI.

Overall Statistics

	G	AB	R	H	D	T	HR	RBI	SB	BB	SO	AVG
1992	151	601	83	167	34	7	17	87	14	45	68	.278
Career	1060	4144	588	1160	230	44	156	673	88	298	597	.280

Where He Hits the Ball

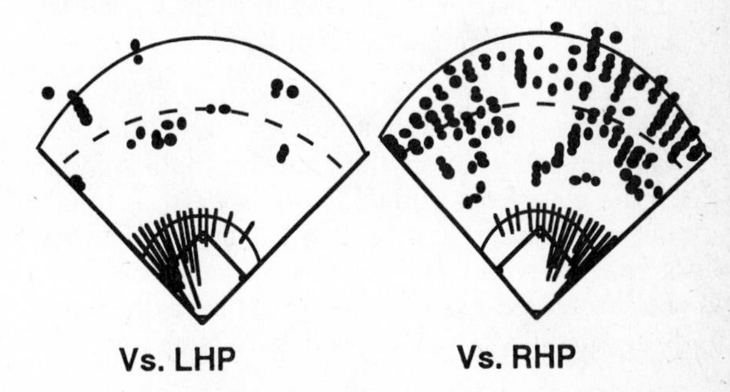

1992 Situational Stats

	AB	H	HR	RBI	AVG		AB	H	HR	RBI	AVG
Home	294	71	10	40	.241	LHP	171	58	5	33	.339
Road	307	96	7	47	.313	RHP	430	109	12	54	.253
Day	131	35	4	22	.267	Sc Pos	156	44	5	63	.282
Night	470	132	13	65	.281	Clutch	97	21	2	14	.216

1992 Rankings (American League)

- 6th in sacrifice flies (10)
- 7th in triples (7) and batting average on the road (.313)
- 8th in intentional walks (12)
- 10th in batting average vs. left-handed pitchers (.339), slugging percentage vs. left-handed pitchers (.521), lowest on-base percentage vs. right-handed pitchers (.299) and lowest batting average at home (.242)
- Led AL right fielders in hits (167), singles (109), doubles (34), triples, batting average vs. left-handed pitchers and batting average on the road (.313)

TERRY STEINBACH

Position: C
Bats: R **Throws:** R
Ht: 6' 1" **Wt:** 195

Opening Day Age: 31
Born: 3/2/62 in New Ulm, MN
ML Seasons: 7

HITTING:

Though he won no national awards, Terry Steinbach had an MVP season in 1992 . . . at least where Oakland was concerned. Steinbach's .279 average was his best since he batted .284 in his rookie year. He doubled his '91 home run total (from six to 12), despite missing 14 games with a hairline fracture on his left wrist. Steinbach also reached a career high in walks with 45, and his on-base and slugging averages were the second-highest of his career.

As a hitter, Steinbach uses his experience from behind the plate. He anticipates what pitchers are going to throw, and as a result he's not fooled very often. He's also become a much more disciplined hitter. Steinbach more than doubled his walk total last year while reducing his strikeouts.

Steinbach's power is to right-center field, and pitchers need to get their pitches in on him. He'll take advantage of anything thrown to the middle of the plate from mid-thigh to his waist. A tough out with men in scoring position, and sometimes compared with former Athletic great Sal Bando, Steinbach led the A's and ranked seventh in the league with a .340 average in such situations.

BASERUNNING:

Steinbach doesn't have much speed on the bases but he is smart in one respect. For his career, he's been caught stealing 10 times, and been successful on only nine tries. In other words, he's smart enough not to try stealing too often.

FIELDING:

Steinbach is a terrific defensive catcher. He threw out 50 of 118 potential base stealers last year for a 42 percent success rate. Only the Rangers' Ivan Rodriguez threw out more, and only Rodriguez (49 percent) and San Francisco's Kirt Manwaring (44 percent) had higher percentages among regulars. Oakland pitchers had a team ERA of 3.50 with Steinbach behind the plate, the third-best catcher ERA for any regular receiver in the AL.

OVERALL:

Steinbach was another of Oakland's many free agents, and has indicated he would test the market. Of all the players Oakland stood to lose, he was one they could least afford. They were expected to make a major effort to try to re-sign him.

Overall Statistics

	G	AB	R	H	D	T	HR	RBI	SB	BB	SO	AVG
1992	128	438	48	122	20	1	12	53	2	45	58	.279
Career	733	2484	278	675	114	9	61	330	9	182	373	.272

Where He Hits the Ball

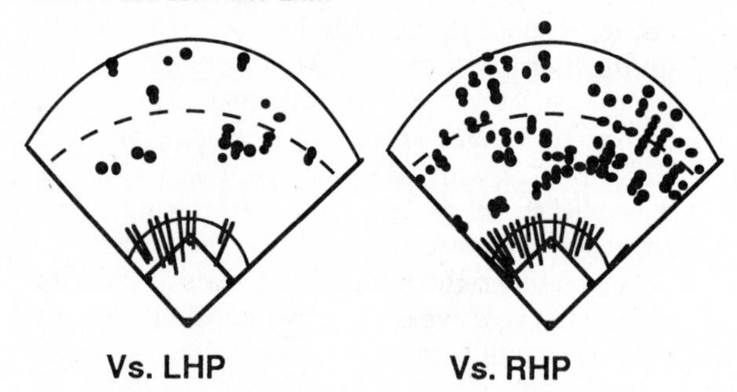

1992 Situational Stats

	AB	H	HR	RBI	AVG		AB	H	HR	RBI	AVG
Home	214	49	3	19	.229	LHP	110	33	5	18	.300
Road	224	73	9	34	.326	RHP	328	89	7	35	.271
Day	154	39	2	14	.253	Sc Pos	97	33	3	42	.340
Night	284	83	10	39	.292	Clutch	50	9	0	5	.180

1992 Rankings (American League)

- → 4th in GDPs (20), lowest batting average with the bases loaded (.071) and highest batting average on the road (.326)
- → 7th in batting average with runners in scoring position (.340)
- → 9th in lowest batting average in the clutch (.180)
- → Led the A's in GDPs, batting average with runners in scoring position and batting average on the road
- → Led AL catchers in GDPs, batting average with runners in scoring position and batting average on the road

DAVE STEWART

Position: SP
Bats: R **Throws:** R
Ht: 6' 2" **Wt:** 200

Opening Day Age: 36
Born: 2/19/57 in Oakland, CA
ML Seasons: 13

PITCHING:

Both Dave Stewart's glare and his pitch command returned last season. After his first sub-20 win season in five seasons in 1991 (11-11), Stewart's 12 wins last season raised his total for the last six years to 107. Only Roger Clemens has more victories (112) over that span. Stewart didn't run out of energy in his bid for a sixth straight 200-inning season -- Oakland Coliseum did. A power outage in the eighth inning of his last start on October 1 knocked Stewart out and left him within 199.1 innings for the year.

Stewart lowered his ERA by more than a run and a half from the 5.18 he recorded in 1991, even though he missed nearly four weeks due to elbow stiffness. It was only his second career stint on the DL. Stewart came back to win four of his last six decisions, posting a 2.72 ERA. As usual, he was plagued by gopher balls (25), a standard problem throughout his career.

Stewart, who possesses an above-average slider and one of the nastiest forkballs around, worked six or more innings in 22 of his 31 starts, and allowed three or fewer runs in 20 of them. And he did get his 20 wins -- sort of. The A's were 20-11 in his 31 starts. He showed signs of the dominating Dave Stewart in Game 5 of the American League Championship Series, glaring menacingly from under his pulled-down cap and postponing Toronto's eventual pennant clinching by one day. Stewart's seven-hit, complete game effort gave the A's hope. Too bad for the A's that he couldn't have pitched every day.

HOLDING RUNNERS AND FIELDING:

Stewart has a quick throw to first, helping keep runners close so that his catchers could throw out 10 of the 25 baserunners who attempted to steal against him. A great athlete, Stewart was hampered on defense last year by the elbow problems.

OVERALL:

The A's were expected to make a priority of re-sign Stewart, one of the 15 free agents on the roster as well as one of the classiest veterans around. If healthy -- and in playoff Game 5 form -- Stewart can win 20 games again, but this time all by himself.

Overall Statistics

	W	L	ERA	G	GS	Sv	IP	H	R	BB	SO	HR
1992	12	10	3.66	31	31	0	199.1	175	96	79	130	25
Career	146	106	3.70	459	284	19	2253.0	2101	1019	861	1476	204

How Often He Throws Strikes

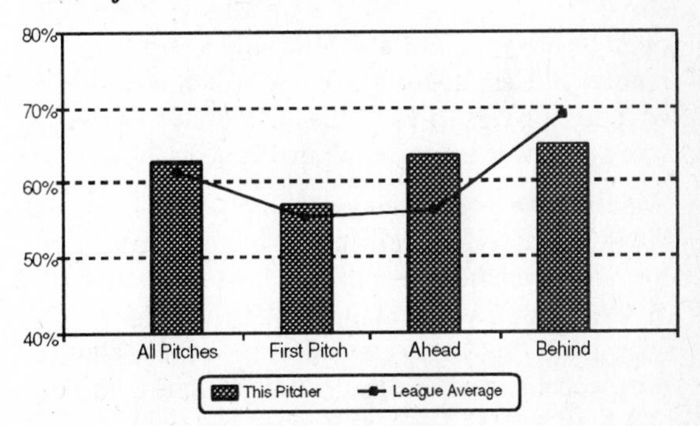

1992 Situational Stats

	W	L	ERA	Sv	IP		AB	H	HR	RBI	AVG
Home	4	5	3.73	0	101.1	LHB	340	89	11	39	.262
Road	8	5	3.58	0	98.0	RHB	397	86	14	44	.217
Day	4	4	4.18	0	64.2	Sc Pos	149	38	6	57	.255
Night	8	6	3.41	0	134.2	Clutch	69	21	4	8	.304

1992 Rankings (American League)

- 1st in lowest groundball/flyball ratio allowed (.70)
- 3rd in lowest batting average allowed vs. right-handed batters (.217)
- Led the A's in ERA (3.66), home runs allowed (25), hit batsmen (8), strikeouts (130), balks (1), strikeout/walk ratio (1.6), lowest batting average allowed (.237), lowest on-base percentage allowed (.315), least baserunners allowed per 9 innings (11.8), most strikeouts per 9 innings (5.9), ERA on the road (3.58), lowest batting average allowed vs. right-handed batters (.217) and lowest batting average allowed with runners in scoring position (.255)

PITCHING:

Bob Welch had a tough 1992 season. He spent three different stints on the disabled list, battling right shoulder tendinitis, a strained back and a sore left knee which flared up after two spring training starts. Still, Welch made 20 starts and won in double figures for the sixth straight year and the 11th time in his career. His 3.27 ERA matched his career percentage and was a big improvement over his 1991 figure of 4.58.

Starting the year on the disabled list, Welch was placed on the active roster May 2, made five starts, and was sidelined again with knee problems. He returned June 14 and finished the first half of the season with a four-game winning streak. But his elbow flared up after five starts to open the second half and he went back on the DL August 8. Despite the ailments, Welch worked six or more innings in 14 of his 20 starts and gave up three or fewer earned runs in 14 of his 20 starts.

Welch has a good change-up and slider and will throw a nasty forkball to left-handed batters. A big game pitcher, he ranks fourth on Oakland's all-time list in wins behind Catfish Hunter (131), Vida Blue (124) and Dave Stewart (116). There's no place like the Coliseum for Welch, who was 4-3 with a 2.94 ERA at home, 7-4 on the road. Since 1988, Welch is 49-18 in Oakland with a 2.74 ERA; on the road, he's 35-25, 4.38.

HOLDING RUNNERS AND FIELDING:

Welch has a quick move to first but he occasionally becomes preoccupied with the runner and loses concentration on the batter. He will aggressively defend his position -- sometimes too aggressively. He sometimes goes for a low-risk play on a lead runner rather than taking the safe out.

OVERALL:

Welch has had a brilliant career and his next victory is his 200th. He was one of the few Athletics who was not a free agent, having two years to go on a four-year contract. If Dave Stewart, Ron Darling and/or Mike Moore don't return, Welch will be counted upon heavily. The A's can only hope he's healthy when they break camp.

BOB WELCH

Position: SP
Bats: R **Throws:** R
Ht: 6' 3" **Wt:** 198

Opening Day Age: 36
Born: 11/3/56 in Detroit, MI
ML Seasons: 15

Overall Statistics

	W	L	ERA	G	GS	Sv	IP	H	R	BB	SO	HR
1992	11	7	3.27	20	20	0	123.2	114	47	43	47	13
Career	199	129	3.27	451	426	8	2856.0	2607	1152	935	1862	232

How Often He Throws Strikes

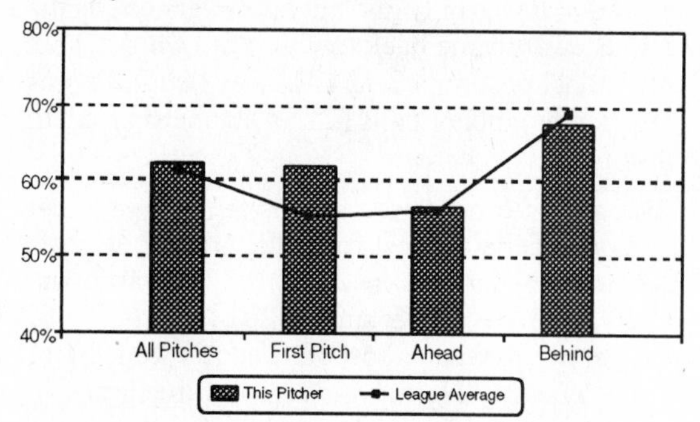

1992 Situational Stats

	W	L	ERA	Sv	IP		AB	H	HR	RBI	AVG
Home	4	3	2.94	0	52.0	LHB	241	64	6	18	.266
Road	7	4	3.52	0	71.2	RHB	220	50	7	22	.227
Day	3	1	2.78	0	35.2	Sc Pos	87	24	3	29	.276
Night	8	6	3.48	0	88.0	Clutch	22	3	0	1	.136

1992 Rankings (American League)

- Led the A's in winning percentage (.611)

HITTING:

Willie Wilson must have tapped into a Fountain of Youth. Looked on strictly as a reserve before the 1992 season began, Wilson wound up starting 98 games in center field because of injuries to Dave Henderson. The ageless Wilson batted .315 in April with seven extra-base hits and 14 RBI in 19 games and was a key factor in Oakland's strong start. He slumped in May, hitting .203, but rallied with a .288 mark for the second half of the season. Overall Wilson batted .270, a 32-point improvement over 1991, while getting his most playing time since 1988.

Though he is now 37 years old, Wilson still relies heavily on his great speed to succeed as a hitter. He doesn't bunt much (just five bunt hits all season), but he loves to hit the ball on the ground and motor down the line. He legged out five triples last season, and leads all active players with 142 in his career. Still a very good fastball hitter, Wilson loves to jump on the first pitch heater (24-for-72, .333, last year) and is most effective when he's ahead in the count and can look for the hard stuff.

BASERUNNING:

Wilson's legs hardly show their age. Wilson stole at least 20 bases for the 15th straight year, tying him with Lou Brock and Ozzie Smith for the second longest all-time streak. He now has 660 career thefts to rank him third among active players (behind Rickey Henderson and Tim Raines), and 13th all-time.

FIELDING:

Wilson doesn't show his age in the outfield either. He still has tremendous range and led all major-league center fielders in chances per game by a good margin. Wilson has always had a weak arm, though, and recorded only two assists last year.

OVERALL:

A free agent, Wilson will probably not get many offers because of his age (he'll be 38 in July). Oakland may try to re-sign him to protect themselves if Dave Henderson does not return. As long as he can run, he should be able to find work.

WILLIE WILSON

Position: CF
Bats: B **Throws:** R
Ht: 6' 3" **Wt:** 200

Opening Day Age: 37
Born: 7/9/55 in Montgomery, AL
ML Seasons: 17

Overall Statistics

	G	AB	R	H	D	T	HR	RBI	SB	BB	SO	AVG
1992	132	396	38	107	15	5	0	37	28	35	65	.270
Career	2032	7489	1136	2145	270	142	40	574	660	413	1098	.286

Where He Hits the Ball

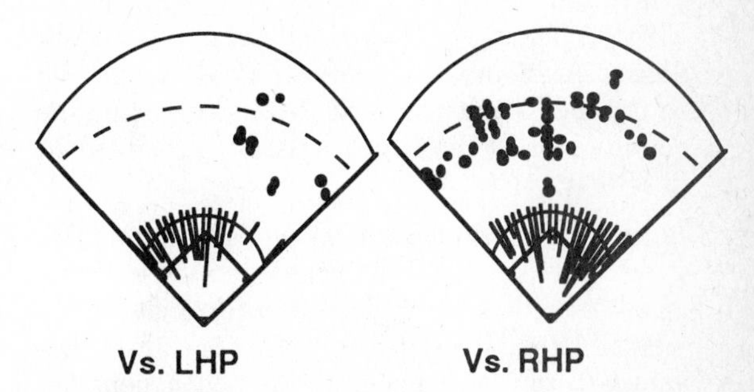

1992 Situational Stats

	AB	H	HR	RBI	AVG		AB	H	HR	RBI	AVG
Home	199	54	0	13	.271	LHP	121	30	0	14	.248
Road	197	53	0	24	.269	RHP	275	77	0	23	.280
Day	136	30	0	12	.221	Sc Pos	97	23	0	34	.237
Night	260	77	0	25	.296	Clutch	63	18	0	5	.286

1992 Rankings (American League)

- 5th in batting average on a 3-1 count (.600)
- 7th in lowest batting average with the bases loaded (.083), lowest slugging percentage vs. left-handed pitchers (.306) and steals of third (7)
- 10th in stolen base percentage (77.8%)
- Led the A's in triples (5) and batting average on a 3-1 count
- Led AL center fielders in batting average on a 3-1 count

PITCHING:

If Oakland does not re-sign free agents Ruben Sierra and Jeff Russell, then all the A's will have received for Jose Canseco apart from draft choices will be Bobby Witt. Maybe after Witt has spent some time with pitching coach Dave Duncan the trade won't look quite so lop-sided. Though Witt won only one game in an Oakland uniform, the A's like his potential.

Possessor of a great arm, Witt has continually struggled with control problems. He was the main reason Bobby Valentine instituted his "two and you're through" exercise in spring training in which the then-Texas manager pulled a pitcher if he walked two straight batters. The Spring exercise didn't help Witt, as he went 9-13 with a 4.46 ERA for Texas. For the year he issued 114 walks, second-most in the American League and the sixth time in seven seasons that he surpassed the century mark. (The time he missed, he walked 74 in 88.2 IP.)

Immediately inserted in Oakland's rotation after the August 31 trade, Witt went 1-1 in six starts for the A's with a 3.41 ERA. Unfortunately, he walked 19 and gave up 31 hits in 31.2 innings. His sole win on September 16 snapped a personal six-game losing streak extending back to July 31. Witt did strike out at least 100 batters for the sixth time in his career. He enjoyed success at the Coliseum as an Athletic, going 1-0 in four starts with a 2.16 ERA.

HOLDING RUNNERS AND FIELDING:

Runners tend to take advantage of Witt's high leg kick and poor control. Not even Ivan Rodriguez could stop them. Of the 32 potential base stealers in Witt's starts, only 10 were caught. He's a real project for the A's in this area. He's no great shakes as a fielder, either.

OVERALL:

The change of scenery -- and some work with ace pitching coach Duncan -- should help Witt. Three years ago his fastball was clocked at 97 MPH. That's the kind of an arm pitching coaches dream about. However, better control is a necessity for Witt no matter how good the arm. The A's didn't protect him from expansion, but he wasn't selected.

BOBBY WITT

Position: SP
Bats: R **Throws:** R
Ht: 6' 2" **Wt:** 205

Opening Day Age: 28
Born: 5/11/64 in Arlington, VA
ML Seasons: 7

Overall Statistics

	W	L	ERA	G	GS	Sv	IP	H	R	BB	SO	HR
1992	10	14	4.29	31	31	0	193.0	183	99	114	125	16
Career	69	73	4.57	191	188	0	1173.0	1024	655	796	1076	87

How Often He Throws Strikes

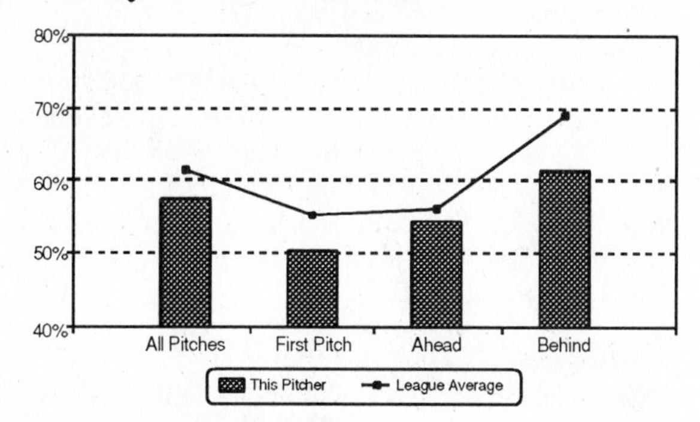

1992 Situational Stats

	W	L	ERA	Sv	IP		AB	H	HR	RBI	AVG
Home	7	8	3.76	0	124.1	LHB	292	71	4	38	.243
Road	3	6	5.24	0	68.2	RHB	423	112	12	41	.265
Day	3	2	4.23	0	38.1	Sc Pos	165	36	2	59	.218
Night	7	12	4.31	0	154.2	Clutch	59	14	2	5	.237

1992 Rankings (American League)

- 1st in most baserunners allowed per 9 innings (13.9)
- 2nd in walks allowed (114), lowest strikeout/walk ratio (1.1) and highest on-base percentage allowed (.356)
- 6th in losses (14)
- 7th in most GDPs induced per 9 innings (1.0)
- 9th in lowest batting average allowed with runners in scoring position (.218)

SCOTT BROSIUS

Position: RF/3B
Bats: R **Throws:** R
Ht: 6' 1" **Wt:** 185

Opening Day Age: 26
Born: 8/15/66 in Hillsboro, OR
ML Seasons: 2

Overall Statistics

	G	AB	R	H	D	T	HR	RBI	SB	BB	SO	AVG
1992	38	87	13	19	2	0	4	13	3	3	13	.218
Career	74	155	22	35	7	0	6	17	6	6	24	.226

HITTING, FIELDING, BASERUNNING:

Utility infielder Scott Brosius made the A's Opening Day roster last year, but appeared in just seven games before he was placed on the disabled list April 18 with a bruised left hip. It was that kind of season for Brosius, who shuttled between Oakland and AAA Tacoma and spent more time on the disabled list. Brosius batted only .218 in 38 games for the A's, but he had his moments. His most memorable game was a four-hit night against Cleveland that included two homers.

As that night suggests, Brosius has some power. He's hit as many as 23 homers in a minor-league season, with good RBI totals and a fine batting eye. He also has good running speed, with potential to steal in double figures, and can play both the infield and outfield. His glove has been a problem: he's committed as many as 61 errors in a season (1988 at Madison).

OVERALL:

Because he's young and has a light contract, Brosius has a good chance to make the A's roster. He was used at several different positions in '92, starting 11 games in the outfield, seven at third base and three at first. Another strong spring -- he led the team with a .360 mark in 1992 -- could lead to more regular playing time. He'll probably be in the A's third base derby, but a utility role is more likely. The A's made him one of their 15 chosen protections from expansion, indicating their interest in him.

KEVIN CAMPBELL

Position: RP/SP
Bats: R **Throws:** R
Ht: 6' 2" **Wt:** 225

Opening Day Age: 28
Born: 12/6/64 in Marianna, AR
ML Seasons: 2

Overall Statistics

	W	L	ERA	G	GS	Sv	IP	H	R	BB	SO	HR
1992	2	3	5.12	32	5	1	65.0	66	39	45	38	4
Career	3	3	4.50	46	5	1	88.0	79	46	59	54	8

PITCHING, FIELDING & HOLDING RUNNERS:

Former Dodger farmhand Kevin Campbell has been in organized ball since 1986, usually posting good ERAs and impressive strikeout-to-walk ratios. Campbell got his first major league shot with the A's in 1991 thanks to an injury to Todd Burns. He pitched pretty well (2.74 ERA in 14 games), but opened the 1992 campaign at AAA Tacoma for the second straight season.

Campbell was recalled on May 5 and from then on was a sort of insurance policy for the Oakland staff. Given two starts against the Brewers in June when Bob Welch was injured, he pitched well enough for Oakland to win both games. Thereafter he was primarily used in relief for the injury-riddled Oakland staff. Campbell kept his ERA around 4.00 for most of the year until his final three outings, when he gave up eight earned runs over four innings to finish the season with a 5.12 mark. Campbell is a good fielder and quite adept at holding runners -- five of seven who tried to steal off him last year were tossed out.

OVERALL:

A sinker-slider pitcher, Campbell does not look like a major-league star; his control, in particular, has been a problem. He is expected to start '93 in the minors unless he has a strong spring, but he is likely to be recalled before long.

ERIC FOX

Position: LF/CF/RF
Bats: B **Throws:** L
Ht: 5'10" **Wt:** 180

Opening Day Age: 29
Born: 8/15/63 in LeMoore, CA
ML Seasons: 1

Overall Statistics

	G	AB	R	H	D	T	HR	RBI	SB	BB	SO	AVG
1992	51	143	24	34	5	2	3	13	3	13	29	.238
Career	51	143	24	34	5	2	3	13	3	13	29	.238

HITTING, FIELDING, BASERUNNING:

Eric Fox had a roller-coaster 1992 season. Fox went from Triple A Tacoma, to Huntsville of the Southern League, to big league Oakland, and back to Tacoma. He had one of the biggest hits of Oakland's season on July 29, hitting a game-winning three-run homer in the ninth inning off Minnesota's Rick Aguilera. The victory put Oakland into a tie for first, and was a visible turning point on their way to the division crown. On the flip side, Fox was the goat in Game 4 of the American League Championship Series when he was out trying to score from third on an infield grounder by Terry Steinbach in the ninth. All tolled Fox hit .238 for the A's, but showed some power with 10 extra-base hits.

One of the final spring training cuts, Fox did not handle the demotion well, batting .198 at Tacoma. He was dropped a notch to Huntsville, then recalled to the majors on July 6. He would make one more trip to Tacoma before spending the last month with the A's. Fox is considered a good defensive outfielder with a fine arm; as his playoff experience shows, he's an aggressive, but not always wise, baserunner.

OVERALL:

Manager Tony La Russa blasted Fox after his baserunning gaffe but will likely give him another chance because of possible openings in center and right. More than likely, Fox will wind up as a reserve.

DAVE HENDERSON

Position: CF
Bats: R **Throws:** R
Ht: 6' 2" **Wt:** 220

Opening Day Age: 34
Born: 7/21/58 in Dos Palos, CA
ML Seasons: 12

Overall Statistics

	G	AB	R	H	D	T	HR	RBI	SB	BB	SO	AVG
1992	20	63	1	9	1	0	0	2	0	2	16	.143
Career	1375	4550	646	1191	253	16	172	624	48	417	964	.262

HITTING, FIELDING, BASERUNNING:

One of Oakland's most respected veterans, Dave Henderson is now battling to save his career. Plagued by injuries, Henderson got into only 20 games last season, hitting .143. He batted just 63 times and produced exactly one extra-base hit, a double.

Henderson's problems began in spring training with a strained right calf. In his first game of the Spring, he pulled his right hamstring running out a ground ball. He started the season on the disabled list, and did not return until April 30. But after just three games, including two starts in right field, Henderson was sidelined again with the hamstring problem. His leg problems kept him out of the next 104 games, and he did not return until September 1.

Henderson loves to play the game and everyone around him benefits from his positive attitude. A good fastball hitter, he has a short quick swing with 20-plus home run power. Henderson is not much of a threat to steal even when healthy, but he's a very fine outfielder.

OVERALL:

If his legs don't recover during the off-season, Henderson could announce his retirement. He does have one year remaining on his three-year contract, and the A's would love to have him back. But he has to be 100 percent.

VINCE HORSMAN

Position: RP
Bats: R **Throws:** L
Ht: 6' 2" **Wt:** 180

Opening Day Age: 26
Born: 3/9/67 in Halifax, Nova Scotia, Canada
ML Seasons: 2

Overall Statistics

	W	L	ERA	G	GS	Sv	IP	H	R	BB	SO	HR
1992	2	1	2.49	58	0	1	43.1	39	13	21	18	3
Career	2	1	2.28	62	0	1	47.1	41	13	24	20	3

PITCHING, FIELDING & HOLDING RUNNERS:

Vince Horsman was claimed off the waiver wire from Toronto on March 20 and took over the short-inning, one-batter type of left-handed relief role that Manager Tony La Russa loves. All La Russa wanted Horsman to do was get lefthanders out, and he responded well in his first major league season. Lefthanders hit just .203 against Horsman, while righthanders batted .296. The southpaw wound up working in 58 games but pitching only 43.1 innings, while turning in a very fine 2.49 ERA. He did not allow a run in his first 16 appearances, covering 14.2 innings.

Possessing a good curve and average fastball, Horsman isn't going to overpower too many hitters. He struck only 18 men in his 43.1 innings, and had more walks (21) than strikeouts. He's tough to take out of the yard, however; he allowed only three homers last year. He also did a very nice job of pitching out of jams: of his 48 inherited runners, he permitted only 11 to score. Horsman appears to hold runners very well, not allowing a stolen base in 1992, and he also looked like a good defensive player.

OVERALL:

Horsman seems to be in a good spot with the Athletics, who are likely to lose numerous free agents. If Rick Honeycutt departs, Horsman will inherit Honeycutt's lefty set-up role. Even if Honeycutt returns, Horsman should see plenty of action as he did in 1992. The lefty was protected by the A's in the expansion draft.

JOE SLUSARSKI

Position: SP
Bats: R **Throws:** R
Ht: 6' 4" **Wt:** 195

Opening Day Age: 26
Born: 12/19/66 in Indianapolis, IN
ML Seasons: 2

Overall Statistics

	W	L	ERA	G	GS	Sv	IP	H	R	BB	SO	HR
1992	5	5	5.45	15	14	0	76.0	85	52	27	38	15
Career	10	12	5.34	35	33	0	185.1	206	121	79	98	29

PITCHING, FIELDING & HOLDING RUNNERS:

Joe Slusarski started 19 games for the Athletics in 1991, the most by an Oakland rookie since Tim Birtsas started 25 in 1985. His record wasn't pretty -- 5-7 with a 5.27 ERA -- but Oakland considered him promising, and Slusarski opened the 1992 season in the Oakland rotation.

Slusarski's pitching, unfortunately, was no better than in 1991. By June 24, he was 5-4 with a 5.58 ERA in 13 starts. He had given up 81 hits in 71 innings. Optioned back to AAA Tacoma, Slusarski wasn't recalled until September 1 and made only one more start.

Slusarski's fastball continues to be impressive, which is why Oakland has been patient with him. He is still trying to develop a complementary off-speed pitch, however, and he's served up numerous fat pitches in an effort to throw strikes. Slusarski has yielded 29 homers in 185.1 major league innings, and last year hitters raked him at a .426 pace on his first pitch. Slusarski's a fine fielder and very good at holding runners.

OVERALL:

Slusarski has shuttled back and forth from the big league club to Tacoma the last two seasons. A second-round selection in the June 1988 draft, Slusarski will likely be needed in the A's rotation this year because of the realities of free agency. He'll have to pitch a lot better if he wants to stay in it, though.

OAKLAND ATHLETICS MINOR LEAGUE PROSPECTS

ORGANIZATION OVERVIEW:

Having won four division titles, three pennants and a world championship over the last five years, the A's ended the 1992 season with 15 free agents, most of whom were not expected to be back. That turns full attention to the Oakland farm system, and it's a mixed bag. The A's have produced a number of good pitching prospects over the last few years, but most of them seem to have come down with sore arms. And most of the hitting prospects seemed to be duds, yet they received terrific contributions last year from Bordick and Blankenship. The A's know how to get the most out of what they have; they'll have to use all their wits this time if they want to remain on top.

TROY NEEL

Position: 1B **Opening Day Age:** 27
Bats: L **Throws:** R **Born:** 9/14/65 in
Ht: 6' 4" **Wt:** 210 Freeport, TX

Recent Statistics

	G	AB	R	H	D	T	HR	RBI	SB	BB	SO	AVG
92 AAA Tacoma	112	396	61	139	36	3	17	74	2	60	84	.351
92 AL Oakland	24	53	8	14	3	0	3	9	0	5	15	.264
92 MLE	112	370	47	113	29	1	11	57	1	46	89	.305

A former Texas A&M football player, Troy Neel, with that name, seems to be a man trapped in the wrong sport. But Neel can play baseball, and last year he won the Pacific Coast League batting championship while somehow not making the list of the league's top ten prospects. No kid at 27, Neel has never hit this high before but he's had two 20-plus home run seasons and has consistently shown extra-base power and patience at the plate. He looks good, and he may have to be, considering that he could be the replacement for both Jose Canseco and Ruben Sierra.

CRAIG H. PAQUETTE

Position: DH **Opening Day Age:** 24
Bats: R **Throws:** R **Born:** 3/28/69 in Long
Ht: 6' 1" **Wt:** 190 Beach, CA

Recent Statistics

	G	AB	R	H	D	T	HR	RBI	SB	BB	SO	AVG
91 AA Huntsville	102	378	50	99	18	1	8	60	0	28	87	.262
92 AA Huntsville	115	450	59	116	25	4	17	71	13	29	118	.258
92 AAA Tacoma	17	66	10	18	7	0	2	11	3	2	16	.273
92 MLE	132	494	57	112	26	2	13	68	12	22	143	.227

Carney Lansford's retirement opens up Oakland's third base position, and that could give Paquette an opportunity. Potentially an outstanding third sacker until shoulder surgery set him back, Paquette has the tools for the position if he can regain throwing strength. He's always had a powerful bat, with 19 homers and 82 RBI last year at AA and AAA. He had 134 strikeouts and only 31 walks last year, so you still have to consider him a long-shot.

STEVE PHOENIX

Position: P **Opening Day Age:** 25
Bats: R **Throws:** R **Born:** 1/31/68 in
Ht: 6' 3" **Wt:** 183 Phoenix, AZ

Recent Statistics

	W	L	ERA	G	GS	Sv	IP	H	R	BB	SO	HR
91 AA Huntsville	0	0	6.00	2	0	0	3.0	7	3	1	3	1
91 A Madison	3	0	2.95	7	2	2	21.1	26	8	10	19	0
91 A Modesto	5	2	3.74	27	3	2	84.1	87	44	33	65	13
92 AA Huntsville	11	5	2.79	32	24	0	174.0	179	68	36	124	8

While other Oakland pitching prospects have either been ineffective or come down with sore arms, Phoenix has quietly been staying healthy and winning games. Last year the righthander went 11-5 with a 2.79 ERA and 124 strikeouts and only 36 walks in 174 innings at AA Huntsville. Phoenix was an undrafted free agent and not considered a hard thrower, but there are any number of good pitchers in the major leagues with stuff like his. Besides, he studied "wildlife management" at Grand Canyon College, and that sounds like perfect preparation for the bigs.

TODD REVENIG

Position: P **Opening Day Age:** 23
Bats: R **Throws:** R **Born:** 6/28/69 in
Ht: 6' 1" **Wt:** 185 Brainerd, MN

Recent Statistics

	W	L	ERA	G	GS	Sv	IP	H	R	BB	SO	HR
92 AA Huntsville	1	1	1.70	53	0	33	63.2	33	14	11	49	8
92 AL Oakland	0	0	0.00	2	0	0	2.0	2	0	0	1	0

Like Phoenix, Revenig is a long-shot. He was a 37th round draft choice in 1991, but let's just look as his record. In 1990, Revenig had an 0.81 ERA in rookie ball. In 1990, splitting the season between two clubs, he had an 0.94 ERA at Class A Madison and an 0.98 ERA at AA Huntsville. In 1992, he worked in 53 games at Huntsville, with a 1.70 mark and 33 saves. In 63.2 innings last year, he allowed 32 hits and 11 walks, with 49 strikeouts. He finished the year with two scoreless innings for the A's. Either he's holding mirrors in guys' faces, or he can pitch.

TODD VAN POPPEL

Position: P **Opening Day Age:** 21
Bats: R **Throws:** R **Born:** 12/9/71 in
Ht: 6' 5" **Wt:** 210 Hinsdale, IL

Recent Statistics

	W	L	ERA	G	GS	Sv	IP	H	R	BB	SO	HR
91 AA Huntsville	6	13	3.47	24	24	0	132.1	118	69	90	115	2
92 AAA Tacoma	4	2	3.97	9	9	0	45.1	44	22	35	29	1

Brien Taylor, beware. You can be the greatest pitching prospect in the world when you're 17, but if your arm starts hurting it doesn't matter much. In three seasons of pro baseball, Van Poppel has displayed a fragile million dollar arm, and control problems. If healthy, there's little doubt he can make it. In 215 minor-league innings, he has 193 strikeouts and a 3.34 ERA. But will he stay healthy?

TOP PROSPECT

BRET BOONE

Position: 2B
Bats: R **Throws:** R
Ht: 5'10" **Wt:** 175

Opening Day Age: 24
Born: 4/6/69 in El Cajon, CA
ML Seasons: 1

Overall Statistics

	G	AB	R	H	D	T	HR	RBI	SB	BB	SO	AVG
1992	33	129	15	25	4	0	4	15	1	4	34	.194
Career	33	129	15	25	4	0	4	15	1	4	34	.194

Where He Hits the Ball

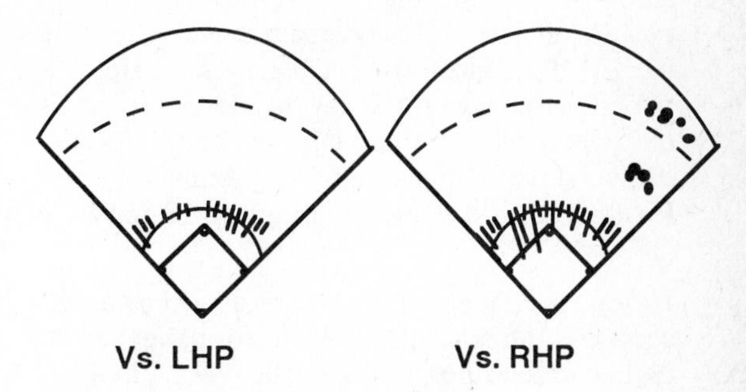

1992 Situational Stats

	AB	H	HR	RBI	AVG		AB	H	HR	RBI	AVG
Home	56	14	2	8	.250	LHP	40	6	0	1	.150
Road	73	11	2	7	.151	RHP	89	19	4	14	.213
Day	30	4	1	2	.133	Sc Pos	34	7	1	11	.206
Night	99	21	3	13	.212	Clutch	26	2	0	0	.077

1992 Rankings (American League)

- Did not rank near the top or bottom in any category

HITTING:

The Mariners made history by promoting Bret Boone to the majors for his major-league debut last August 19 at Baltimore. That night was the first time that a third-generation player played in the major leagues. The move also took the role of everyday second baseman away from Harold Reynolds as part of the Seattle youth movement.

Boone -- son of Bob, grandson of Ray -- wasted no time as he singled and drove in a run in his first major-league at-bat off Arthur Rhodes. But Boone's inaugural success did not last. His swing was quick, but he had trouble adjusting to the majors. Boone struck out 34 times in 129 at-bats in his first look at major league fastballs; he also lost his good minor-league discipline and drew only four walks. Over-eager to get off to a good start, he swung at too many pitches outside of the strike zone and missed too many hittable ones. He did show his power potential by hitting four homers.

Boone's first showing in the majors ended with a .194 average. The Mariners weren't discouraged; they even benched Boone late in the season to keep him eligible for the 1993 Rookie of the Year award.

BASERUNNING:

Boone may have slightly above-average speed, but little more than that. He's a very aggressive runner but not a good basestealer thus far. He stole 17 bases at AAA Calgary, but it took him 29 tries.

FIELDING:

Boone is not the smoothest second baseman around, but his glove work is considered more than acceptable. He has a good arm for second base, good range to his left, and can turn the double play. He's good now, and should get better with experience.

OVERALL:

Boone has the skills to play well in the majors for a long time. The Mariners are still a few years away from contending, unless their pitching makes a dramatic turnaround. That makes Boone a very valuable find, and means they'll probably be patient with him.

HITTING:

Greg Briley is a left-handed batting platoon outfielder who has been used almost exclusively against righthanders throughout his career with the Mariners. Over time his batting average against them has improved consistently. In 1990 he hit for a .250 average against righties; in 1991, .263; in 1992, .282. As a result of that improvement, Briley hit a career-high .275 overall in 1992.

Although Briley's final figure was okay, it came almost exclusively from a late-season hot streak. During April, May and June of '92 Briley's average hovered around .240, a bit below his career .258 average. Then a strained ligament in his right elbow forced him onto the 15-day disabled list twice -- in early July and again in early September. At the end of August his average stood at .242. Up to that point Briley had done duty in the outfield, but beginning in late August he was used exclusively as a pinch hitter or designated hitter. He thrived in that new role, going 18-for-47, a .383 pace, from September 1 on.

Briley is a singles hitter, but can occasionally surprise with a long ball. He is not patient at the plate and does not work the count -- he had just four walks all year. He prefers to put his bat on the ball and take his chances. He's a low-ball hitter who has learned to go with the pitch and hit to all fields.

BASERUNNING:

Briley is a fine basestealer. He swiped nine bases in 11 tries in 1992 and has a 72 percent success rate for his career. He's an intelligent runner, not making many mistakes.

FIELDING:

Converted infielder Briley has played all three outfield positions. His range is good enough for left, but he's a lot less comfortable in center and right. His arm is definitely below average.

OVERALL:

Briley has adjusted well to the role of platoon outfielder. He proved late in the year that he could come off the bench and retain his hitting stroke. He should continue to be a useful reserve outfielder this year.

GREG BRILEY

Position: LF/CF/DH
Bats: L **Throws:** R
Ht: 5' 9" **Wt:** 170
Opening Day Age: 27
Born: 5/24/65 in Greenville, NC
ML Seasons: 5

Overall Statistics

	G	AB	R	H	D	T	HR	RBI	SB	BB	SO	AVG
1992	86	200	18	55	10	0	5	12	9	4	31	.275
Career	478	1348	155	351	69	9	26	123	59	112	218	.260

Where He Hits the Ball

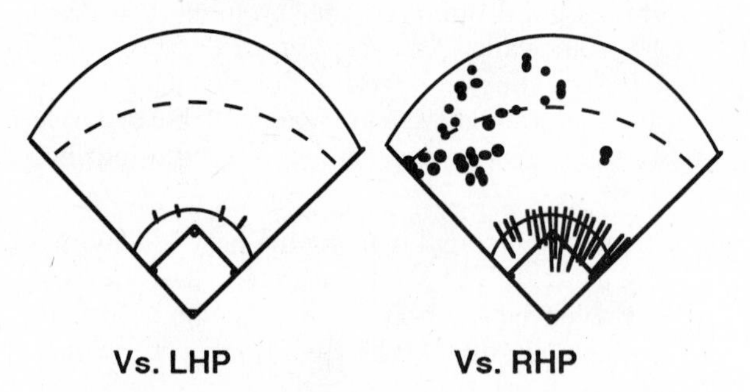

1992 Situational Stats

	AB	H	HR	RBI	AVG		AB	H	HR	RBI	AVG
Home	95	29	1	4	.305	LHP	5	0	0	0	.000
Road	105	26	4	8	.248	RHP	195	55	5	12	.282
Day	67	15	1	3	.224	Sc Pos	46	9	0	7	.196
Night	133	40	4	9	.301	Clutch	37	13	0	4	.351

1992 Rankings (American League)

- Did not rank near the top or bottom in any category

STRONG ARM

HITTING:

With 27 home runs in 1991 and 25 in '92, Jay Buhner became the second Mariner ever to post back-to-back 25-home run seasons (Jim Presley did it in 1985-86). Buhner, who had 77 RBI in 1991, drove in a career-high 79 runs in '92. But the righty slugger wasn't nearly as effective as in 1991, when he posted those similar power numbers in 137 fewer at-bats.

Buhner hit in the .270s in 1989 and 1990, but the last two years his average dipped to the .240 level as he made a more conscious effort to hit for power. During the last two years, Buhner always seemed to be stroking for the fences. He seldom shortened his swing with a two-strike count. The righty slugger fanned a career-high 146 times last year.

Buhner actually has pretty good strike zone judgement and drew 71 walks, another career best, last season. But he feels the Mariners need power from him, so he whales away. An excellent low-ball hitter, Buhner has problems with pitchers who work him carefully with fastballs and breaking stuff away.

BASERUNNING:

Baserunning remains by far the weakest part of Buhner's game. In six attempts to steal last year, he was tossed out every time. For his career he's 4-for-18 (22 percent). Somebody give this guy the stop sign.

FIELDING:

Buhner prides himself on his fielding ability. He had only two errors all season, the last on April 24, and ended the season with a streak of 134 games without an error. That streak is all the more amazing because Buhner does not loaf at all in right field. He doesn't hesitate to use his strong arm to challenge runners on base. He had 14 assists last year, third among all major-league outfielders.

OVERALL

His outfield play makes Buhner arguably the best defensive right fielder in the American League, true Gold Glove caliber, a real pleasure to watch. Plus he brings a bat with crushing power to the plate. Those tools should guarantee him regular duty with the Mariners again this year.

JAY BUHNER

Position: RF
Bats: R **Throws:** R
Ht: 6' 3" **Wt:** 205

Opening Day Age: 28
Born: 8/13/64 in Louisville, KY
ML Seasons: 6

Overall Statistics

	G	AB	R	H	D	T	HR	RBI	SB	BB	SO	AVG
1992	152	543	69	132	16	3	25	79	0	71	146	.243
Career	490	1599	212	393	72	9	81	261	4	189	467	.246

Where He Hits the Ball

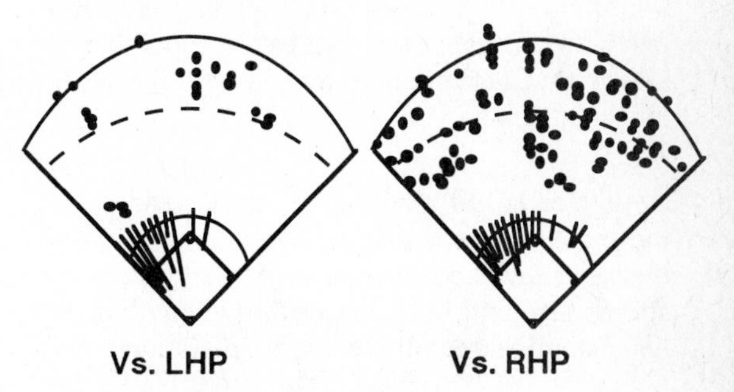

1992 Situational Stats

	AB	H	HR	RBI	AVG		AB	H	HR	RBI	AVG
Home	263	68	9	39	.259	LHP	148	34	10	25	.230
Road	280	64	16	40	.229	RHP	395	98	15	54	.248
Day	159	47	12	29	.296	Sc Pos	135	40	8	59	.296
Night	384	85	13	50	.221	Clutch	98	22	5	14	.224

1992 Rankings (American League)

- 1st in highest percentage of swings that missed (32.2%)
- 3rd in strikeouts (146)
- 8th in lowest batting average (.243)
- 9th in lowest groundball/flyball ratio (.82), lowest batting average vs. left-handed pitchers (.230), lowest batting average on the road (.229) and lowest percentage of swings put into play (37.3%)
- Led the Mariners in sacrifice flies (8), walks (71), strikeouts, most pitches seen (2,388), plate appearances (629) and games played (152)
- Led AL right fielders in strikeouts and fielding percentage (.994)

PITCHING:

After a fast start -- he was baseball's best reliever for the season's first six weeks -- Norm Charlton was one of the reasons why the Reds would eventually blow a whopping 23 save opportunities over the course of the season. Charlton did end up with 26 saves. But he also had eight blown saves, and his 77 percent conversion rate ranked a mediocre seventh among National League closers. The Reds eventually gave the closer's role back to Rob Dibble, and Charlton recorded only one save in the season's final six weeks.

Charlton did wind up with a 2.99 ERA, a normal figure for him, but some of his other numbers were disturbing. He permitted seven home runs, a high number for any short reliever, especially one with his stuff. Opposing batters hit .262 overall against Charlton; even more alarming was that left-handed hitters hit .296.

One problem is that Charlton does not rely enough on his 90-plus fastball and instead throws too many sliders and split-fingered pitches. As a National League manager said, "His slider and splitter are good, but when he throws anything but his fastball, especially to left-handed hitters, he's doing the batter a favor." The slider is effective against right-handed hitters. When Charlton is behind in the count, he becomes too predictable in trying to throw inside fastballs past whoever is hitting.

HOLDING RUNNERS, FIELDING, HITTING:

While Charlton's pickoff move is average, his delivery is slow, so basestealers have a high degree of success against him. He allowed 15 steals in 19 attempts last year, a very high total for a closer. Charlton doesn't hurt himself defensively.

OVERALL:

The days of the Reds' Nasty Boys are now forgotten with only Dibble remaining after Charlton's trade to Seattle on expansion draft eve. Charlton remains an imposing pitcher, and Seattle will bank on him as their full-time stopper. The Mariners will have to hope that he will establish himself, and his fastball, more consistently as a closer than he did in 1992.

NORM CHARLTON

Position: RP
Bats: B **Throws:** L
Ht: 6' 3" **Wt:** 205

Opening Day Age: 30
Born: 1/6/63 in Fort Polk, LA
ML Seasons: 5

Overall Statistics

	W	L	ERA	G	GS	Sv	IP	H	R	BB	SO	HR
1992	4	2	2.99	64	0	26	81.1	79	39	26	90	7
Career	31	24	3.00	238	37	29	500.2	429	194	190	421	34

How Often He Throws Strikes

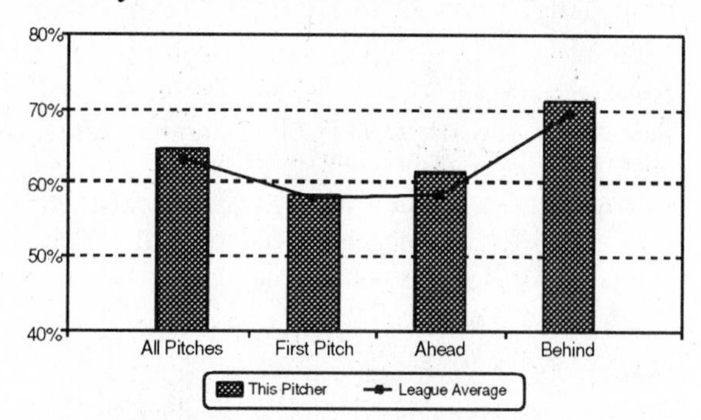

1992 Situational Stats

	W	L	ERA	Sv	IP		AB	H	HR	RBI	AVG
Home	2	1	2.27	13	39.2	LHB	71	21	2	10	.296
Road	2	1	3.67	13	41.2	RHB	231	58	5	31	.251
Day	2	0	3.86	7	25.2	Sc Pos	95	26	3	36	.274
Night	2	2	2.59	19	55.2	Clutch	189	47	4	28	.249

1992 Rankings (National League)

- 2nd in blown saves (8)
- 3rd in most strikeouts per 9 innings in relief (10.0)
- 5th in worst first batter efficiency (.321)
- 6th in saves (26) and save opportunities (34)
- 7th in games finished (46)
- Led the Reds in games pitched (64), saves, hit batsmen (3), save opportunities and blown saves

HENRY COTTO

Position: LF/CF
Bats: R **Throws:** R
Ht: 6' 2" **Wt:** 178

Opening Day Age: 32
Born: 1/5/61 in Bronx, NY
ML Seasons: 9

HITTING:

After a career .305 season in 1991, Henry Cotto reverted back to a more normal .259 last year. As usual, Cotto filled a reserve/part-time role for Seattle, often pinch hitting or being used as a late-inning outfielder. He was deadly as a pinch hitter, batting .500 (9-for-18). Cotto proved he had completely recovered from surgery in 1991 to repair a torn rotator cuff.

As the pinch-hitting mark suggests, Cotto's hits last year were often clutch blows. He always brings a positive attitude to the plate and seems to have an uncanny ability to hit when called upon. He batted .297 with runners in scoring position last year.

There's not much mystery to Cotto as a hitter. He loves the fastball, particularly downstairs; as a result he's much more effective when ahead in the count (.360 over the last five years) -- situations where he can look for a fastball -- than he is when behind it (.215). Looking for the heater, he jumps on the first pitch a lot (14-for-43, .326, last year), and that's one reason he seldom walks. Cotto drew only 14 bases on balls in 294 at-bats last year with 49 strikeouts. His drop in average last season was due to a falloff against right-handed pitchers; after hitting .284 against righties in '91, he batted .175 against them in '92. He continued to pound lefties (.321).

BASERUNNING:

A terrific basestealer, Cotto seems to get better with age. Last year he swiped 23 steals in 25 attempts, an outstanding 92% success rate, and his 84.4% career rate ranks fourth among active players. Cotto has richly earned his nickname, "Turbo".

FIELDING:

Cotto is also an outstanding defensive outfielder. He uses his speed to track down everything he sees, and he can handle all three spots. He was error free in 173 chances in 92 games played. His arm is below-average, however.

OVERALL:

A free agent, Cotto has been a Mariner mainstay. Seattle would love to have him back, but he may entertain offers from other clubs -- particularly from those that can offer him more playing time.

Overall Statistics

	G	AB	R	H	D	T	HR	RBI	SB	BB	SO	AVG
1992	108	294	42	76	11	1	5	27	23	14	49	.259
Career	776	1938	271	509	79	9	39	189	114	102	312	.263

Where He Hits the Ball

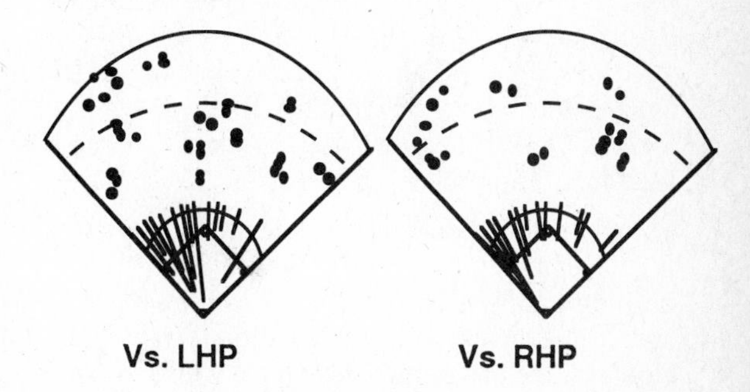

1992 Situational Stats

	AB	H	HR	RBI	AVG		AB	H	HR	RBI	AVG
Home	117	29	2	14	.248	LHP	168	54	4	21	.321
Road	177	47	3	13	.266	RHP	126	22	1	6	.175
Day	99	23	2	10	.232	Sc Pos	64	19	1	22	.297
Night	195	53	3	17	.272	Clutch	51	11	1	5	.216

1992 Rankings (American League)

- 1st in stolen base percentage (92.0%)
- 7th in steals of third (7)
- Led the Mariners in stolen bases (23), stolen base percentage and steals of third
- Led AL left fielders in stolen base percentage

PITCHING:

The Mariners' desperate search for pitching reached new heights last July when they took a chance on 30-year-old righthander Brian Fisher. The former Yankee, Pirate and Astro pitcher hadn't pitched in the majors since 1990, when he'd worked in four games with Houston. Fisher hadn't won a major-league game since 1988, when he was with the Pirates.

Fisher's first outing, on July 7 against the Blue Jays, was hardly promising: four hits and three earned runs allowed in 1.2 innings. But Fisher pitched better after that, and was finally moved into the starting rotation. On July 29 he pitched seven shutout innings against the Angels and was rewarded with his first major-league win since September 14, 1988. Fisher would eventually win three more games, all as a starter, including one against the White Sox on the final day of the season. Overall he went 4-3 but his ERA was a less-than- impressive 4.53.

Fisher actually posted some decent numbers last year. He held opposing hitters to a .234 average, limiting both lefties and righties to the same figure. Eight of his 14 starts were quality outings. However, he had control problems with 47 walks in 91.1 innings, and he was bothered by the home run ball, allowing nine dingers. As in the past, Fisher relied mostly on his good fastball; his breaking stuff isn't much. He pitches up in the strike zone, so when his location is off, he gets hurt.

HOLDING RUNNERS AND FIELDING:

Fisher has a big motion and he's always been notoriously easy to run on. Last year he allowed six steals in nine attempts, a pretty good mark for him. He is not considered a very good defensive player though he committed only one error last year.

OVERALL:

The Mariners probably aren't going to jump all over themselves trying to re-sign Fisher, who struck out only 26 men in 91.1 innings last year. He hasn't had a major league ERA below 4.50 since 1985, his rookie year. But you never know.

BRIAN FISHER

Position: SP/RP
Bats: R **Throws:** R
Ht: 6' 4" **Wt:** 210

Opening Day Age: 31
Born: 3/18/62 in Honolulu, HI
ML Seasons: 7

Overall Statistics

	W	L	ERA	G	GS	Sv	IP	H	R	BB	SO	HR
1992	4	3	4.53	22	14	1	91.1	80	49	47	26	9
Career	36	34	4.39	222	65	23	640.0	638	341	252	370	70

How Often He Throws Strikes

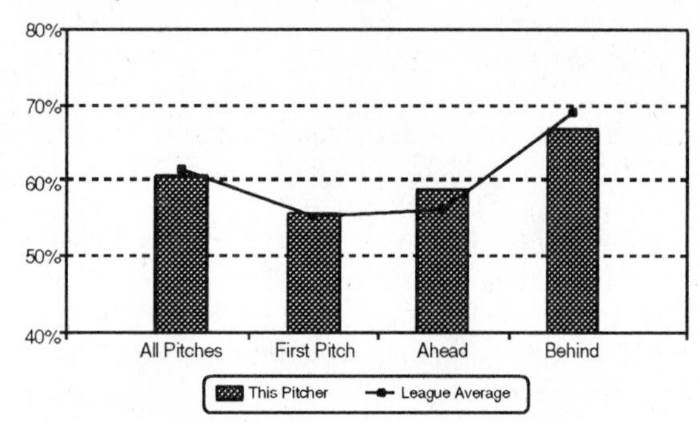

1992 Situational Stats

	W	L	ERA	Sv	IP		AB	H	HR	RBI	AVG
Home	2	2	6.34	0	44.0	LHB	167	39	2	13	.234
Road	2	1	2.85	1	47.1	RHB	175	41	7	26	.234
Day	1	0	3.62	0	27.1	Sc Pos	77	15	4	31	.195
Night	3	3	4.92	1	64.0	Clutch	39	9	0	4	.231

1992 Rankings (American League)

- Led the Mariners in lowest batting average vs. left-handed batters (.234)

PITCHING:

Dave Fleming has a repertoire of pitches that includes a fastball, a sweeping curve, a slider and a change-up. He throws them all with purpose. His pitches are not overpowering; he simply mixes them well. Lance Parrish, who joined the Mariners late in the season, said after catching Fleming, "You stand on the sideline, and its pretty obvious he doesn't have a great fastball, or a great curve, or a great slider, but he knows what he's doing. He knows when to throw strikes, and he knows when to go outside the strike zone. He knows when to throw a hard curve, and when to throw a soft curve."

Fleming ended the year 17-10 on a losing team. Most of the wins came because Fleming could get the key outs when he needed them -- witness his .232 opponent batting average with runners in scoring position. His ability to stifle the opposition had an uplifting effect on the team. Through August they supported him with almost five runs a game.

In late August Fleming's record reached 15-5, but he needed a couple of extra days rest between starts to rest a tired and tender elbow. Then for almost a month, both Fleming and the Mariner offense broke down. Fleming suffered through five losses in a row, pitching without a lead in even one inning. So when Fleming tired a bit and needed some run support, he didn't get it.

HOLDING RUNNERS AND FIELDING:

Fleming has a nifty pickoff move. Of 32 runners who tried to steal on him, 14 were caught -- five on Fleming pickoffs. He is a good fielder, committing only one error last year and starting four double plays.

OVERALL:

A very intelligent pitcher, Fleming mixes his pitches extremely well and uses his brains and skill to confound opposing batters. He may have trouble going 17-10 for a losing team again, but he should continue to be a good pitcher.

DAVE FLEMING

Position: SP
Bats: L **Throws:** L
Ht: 6' 3" **Wt:** 200

Opening Day Age: 23
Born: 11/7/69 in Queens, NY
ML Seasons: 2

Overall Statistics

	W	L	ERA	G	GS	Sv	IP	H	R	BB	SO	HR
1992	17	10	3.39	33	33	0	228.1	225	95	60	112	13
Career	18	10	3.62	42	36	0	246.0	244	108	63	123	16

How Often He Throws Strikes

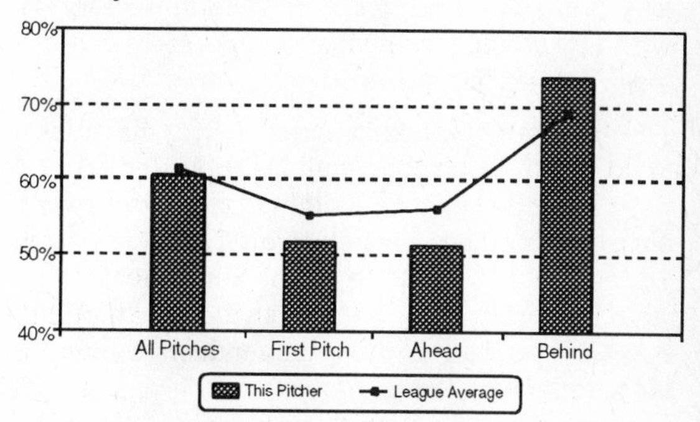

1992 Situational Stats

	W	L	ERA	Sv	IP		AB	H	HR	RBI	AVG
Home	7	5	3.53	0	112.1	LHB	141	35	2	12	.248
Road	10	5	3.26	0	116.0	RHB	736	190	11	69	.258
Day	2	5	5.64	0	52.2	Sc Pos	211	49	1	59	.232
Night	15	5	2.72	0	175.2	Clutch	78	20	2	5	.256

1992 Rankings (American League)

- → 2nd in shutouts (4)
- → 6th in wins (17)
- → 8th in complete games (7)
- → Led the Mariners in ERA (3.39), wins, games started (33), complete games, shutouts, innings pitched (228.1), hits allowed (225), batters faced (946), pickoff throws (183), winning percentage (.630), lowest on-base percentage allowed (.306), lowest stolen base percentage allowed (56.3%), least baserunners allowed per 9 innings (11.4), most run support per 9 innings (4.3), least home runs allowed per 9 innings (.51) and lowest ERA on the road (3.26)

FUTURE MVP?

KEN GRIFFEY JR

Position: CF
Bats: L **Throws:** L
Ht: 6' 3" **Wt:** 195
Opening Day Age: 23
Born: 11/21/69 in Donora, PA
ML Seasons: 4

HITTING:

Is Ken Griffey Jr. washed up? To read some of Griffey's negative press, one might think so. Last year, at age 22, young Griffey belted 27 homers, drove in 103 runs, produced 302 total bases, and had a slugging average of .535 -- all career highs, and all among the best figures ever compiled by someone so young. The problem is that some people think Griffey should be doing even better. Others wonder if his nonchalant attitude is sending the wrong message to the other Mariners.

But even if all true, how about the message Griffey keeps sending to American League pitchers? Last year the youngster batted .333 with runners in scoring position. He also hit .333 in the late innings of close games. He continued to hit with power while seldom striking out -- a career-low 67 times last season.

The negative comments about Griffey have less to do with his play than with his supposed failure to be a team leader. One night Griffey was overheard saying he'd be sick two days later, when Nolan Ryan was due to pitch. Sure enough, he was "ill" that Sunday when Ryan took the mound. It wasn't the sort of thing that endears a man to his teammates.

BASERUNNING:

Griffey stole a career-low 10 bases last season, after swiping 18 in 1991. A sprained right wrist suffered early in the season might have made him reluctant to slide. Certainly, he's capable of doing better.

FIELDING:

There are no complaints about Griffey in the field; he's won three straight Gold Gloves. Among his specialties are perfectly-timed catches in shallow left center, gracefully avoiding collisions with other fielders. His throwing arm is good, but not great.

OVERALL:

Like any great player toiling for a bad team, Griffey catches some heat, as though it's his fault the club isn't winning. Young superstars are often held to unreasonable standards -- Joe DiMaggio, Ted Williams and Mickey Mantle heard the same things early in their careers. There are a lot of clubs who would love a "problem" like Griffey.

Overall Statistics

	G	AB	R	H	D	T	HR	RBI	SB	BB	SO	AVG
1992	142	565	83	174	39	4	27	103	10	44	67	.308
Career	578	2165	311	652	132	12	87	344	60	222	313	.301

Where He Hits the Ball

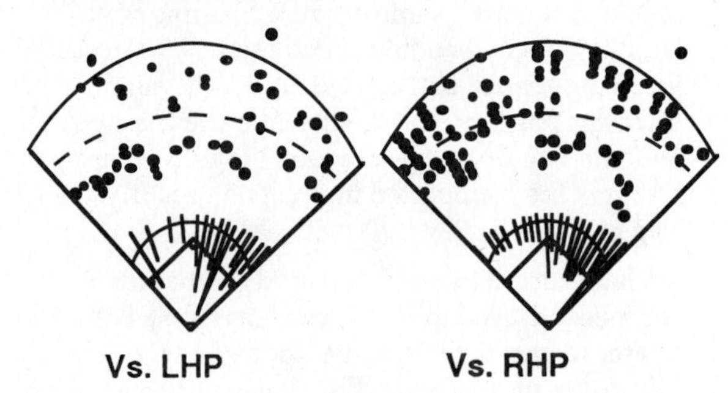

1992 Situational Stats

	AB	H	HR	RBI	AVG		AB	H	HR	RBI	AVG
Home	277	87	16	51	.314	LHP	173	62	12	35	.358
Road	288	87	11	52	.302	RHP	392	112	15	68	.286
Day	152	54	4	25	.355	Sc Pos	150	50	10	76	.333
Night	413	120	23	78	.291	Clutch	81	27	3	12	.333

1992 Rankings (American League)

- 3rd in intentional walks (15) and slugging percentage vs. left-handed pitchers (.624)
- 4th in slugging percentage (.535)
- 5th in doubles (39) and batting average vs. left-handed pitchers (.358)
- 6th in total bases (302) and slugging percentage vs. right-handed pitchers (.495)
- Led the Mariners in home runs (27), at-bats (565), triples (4), total bases, RBI (103), intentional walks, HR frequency (20.9 ABs per HR), batting average with runners in scoring position (.333), batting average with the bases loaded (.364), slugging percentage vs. left-handed pitchers and batting average at home (.314)

PITCHING:

To say Erik Hanson's career is heading in reverse would be putting it mildly. In 1990, Hanson was the toast of the Northwest with an 18-9 record. Two seasons later his record was nearly the opposite -- 8-17. Hanson's 17 losses last year led the majors, and his 4.82 ERA was the second-worst for any major league ERA qualifier.

Over the past three seasons, Hanson has seen his strikeout total decline from 211 to 143 to 112. He insisted he had no arm trouble in '92, but the usual high-80s, low-90s speed on his fastball was missing. Radar guns clocked his top speed at 84 miles per hour. Last season Hanson seemed to be converting himself into a groundball, finesse-type pitcher. Indeed, his 2.19 groundball-to-flyball ratio was one of the highest in the league. Hanson had all kinds of problems with right-handed hitters last year, allowing a .333 average and nine of his 14 homers. Some people claimed he wasn't pitching inside enough, but he plunked a career-high seven batters.

In late August Hanson succumbed to back trouble, which resulted in a spot on the 15-day disabled list. This came after a stretch of four starts in which he had given up 28 hits and posted an ERA of 15.92 over 13 innings. Hanson didn't win another game all season, going 0-2 with an ERA of 4.26 after September 1.

HOLDING RUNNERS & FIELDING:

Hanson did a nice job controlling the running game in 1991, but last year he regressed: He permitted 15 steals in 19 attempts. He remains a good defensive player, committing only one error last year.

OVERALL:

Hanson has become an enigma. The hope is that rest over the winter will let him regain his arm strength and cure his back problems as well. He's still only 27, and with full health there's no reason he can't be a winning pitcher again. Seattle's protection of him from expansion indicates that they sure think so. The problem is that Hanson has been insisting he's healthy and is still getting cuffed around.

ERIK HANSON

Position: SP
Bats: R **Throws:** R
Ht: 6' 6" **Wt:** 210

Opening Day Age: 27
Born: 5/18/65 in Kinnelon, NJ
ML Seasons: 5

Overall Statistics

	W	L	ERA	G	GS	Sv	IP	H	R	BB	SO	HR
1992	8	17	4.82	31	30	0	186.2	209	110	57	112	14
Career	45	42	3.76	114	113	0	752.1	734	341	225	577	56

How Often He Throws Strikes

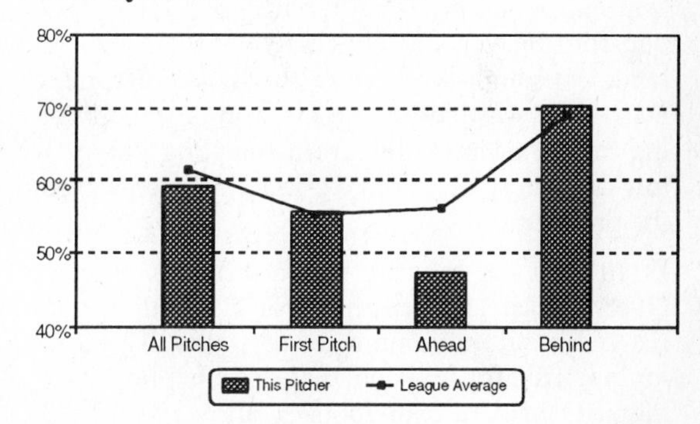

1992 Situational Stats

	W	L	ERA	Sv	IP		AB	H	HR	RBI	AVG
Home	6	6	4.78	0	90.1	LHB	365	88	5	45	.241
Road	2	11	4.86	0	96.1	RHB	363	121	9	54	.333
Day	4	3	3.99	0	49.2	Sc Pos	148	55	5	83	.372
Night	4	14	5.12	0	137.0	Clutch	53	15	2	6	.283

1992 Rankings (American League)

- 1st in losses (17), highest batting average allowed (.287), highest batting average allowed vs. right-handed batters (.333) and highest batting average allowed with runners in scoring position (.372)
- 2nd in highest ERA (4.82)
- 4th in lowest winning percentage (.320), most GDPs induced per 9 innings (1.2) and highest ERA at home (4.78)
- Led the Mariners in losses, home runs allowed (14), GDPs induced (25), highest strikeout/walk ratio (2.0), highest groundball/flyball ratio (2.2), least pitches thrown per batter (3.55) and most GDPs induced per 9 innings

PITCHING:

We've heard this sort of talk before, but Randy Johnson may have turned his career around last year. Johnson, as most know, throws the ball uncommonly hard -- as fast as 102 MPH on one radar gun last year. He has an excellent curve, and a very useful change-up. He struck out 241 hitters last year, most in the American League and second in the majors to David Cone. But controlling those pitches has been enormously difficult for Johnson. Last year he walked 144 men, the third straight year he's led the American League in walks.

Late in the year, though, Johnson began putting his pitching game together. A long losing streak sent him searching for some insights. He sought out Tom Seaver and Nolan Ryan about how to control his high-powered fastball. From Ryan he learned he was landing on his front heel and not his foot. That kept him from finishing properly toward home plate. With work, Johnson corrected the problem.

From then on, Johnson was a different pitcher. Over his last 11 starts, he went 5-2 with a 2.65 ERA. He still gave up a lot of walks (47 in 85 innings), but for Johnson, that was a big improvement. Over that span Johnson allowed only 48 hits, and struck out 117! During one three-start stretch he fanned 45 batters and allowed only seven walks in 25 innings. The last game was Johnson's 18 strikeout gem versus Texas in only eight innings.

HOLDING RUNNERS AND FIELDING:

No progress here. The huge, high-kicking Johnson is about as easy to run on as any pitcher in the majors. Last year he allowed a whopping 42 steals, though he also picked off eight runners. Usually landing in an awkward fielding position, he's terrible defensively (.893 fielding average in '92).

OVERALL:

Johnson's willingness to seek out advice gives evidence that he's developing the maturity that the Mariners have long awaited. He'll probably always walk a lot of batters. But if he can keep pitching like he did late in 1992, he's also going to win a lot of games.

RANDY JOHNSON

Position: SP
Bats: R **Throws:** L
Ht: 6'10" **Wt:** 225

Opening Day Age: 29
Born: 9/10/63 in Walnut Creek, CA
ML Seasons: 5

Overall Statistics

	W	L	ERA	G	GS	Sv	IP	H	R	BB	SO	HR
1992	12	14	3.77	31	31	0	210.1	154	104	144	241	13
Career	49	48	3.95	130	129	0	818.0	649	411	519	818	70

How Often He Throws Strikes

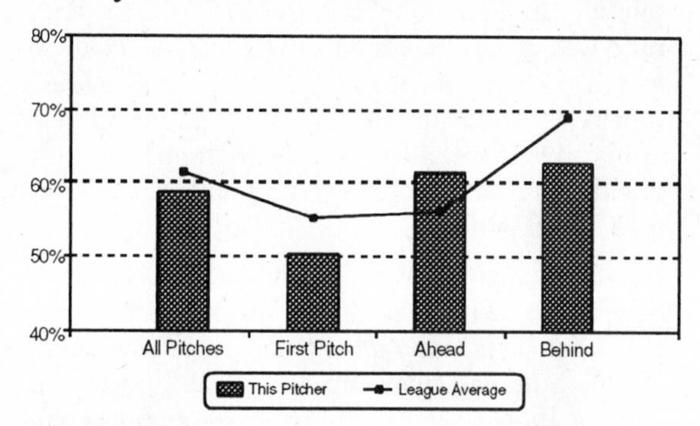

1992 Situational Stats

	W	L	ERA	Sv	IP		AB	H	HR	RBI	AVG
Home	8	6	2.76	0	117.1	LHB	75	14	1	9	.187
Road	4	8	5.03	0	93.0	RHB	674	140	12	81	.208
Day	2	0	2.79	0	38.2	Sc Pos	212	41	5	74	.193
Night	10	14	3.98	0	171.2	Clutch	83	15	2	10	.181

1992 Rankings (American League)

- 1st in walks allowed (144), hit batsmen (18), strikeouts (241), stolen bases allowed (42), lowest batting average allowed (.206), most pitches thrown per batter (4.10), most strikeouts per 9 innings (10.3) and lowest batting average allowed vs. right-handed batters (.208)
- 2nd in lowest slugging percentage allowed (.307)
- 3rd in wild pitches (13) and runners caught stealing (16)
- Led the Mariners in walks allowed, hit batsmen, strikeouts, wild pitches, most pitches thrown (3,776), stolen bases allowed and runners caught stealing

CLUTCH HITTER

HITTING:

A belated star, Edgar Martinez didn't become a major-league regular until he was 27. But after 1992, there's no doubt that Martinez has arrived. The third sacker led the majors in hitting with a .343 average, doing so by improving his batting mark during each of the first five months of the season: .224 April; .340 May; .352 June; a league-leading .388 July; a league-leading .395 August. He earned the league's Player of the Month award in both July and August, joining Don Mattingly and Kirby Puckett as just the third player to win in consecutive months. Remarkably, Martinez accomplished all this while suffering shoulder problems for most of the season. He finally called it quits after 38 September at-bats, undergoing surgery to remove a bone spur from his right shoulder.

Martinez is an extremely smart hitter, and his ability to go with the pitch is what makes him such a threat. He is hard to defense because he sends the ball to all fields. He hits inside pitches to left, outside pitches to right, and over-the-plate pitches to center. He hits them all hard, slugging a career-high 18 homers and a league-leading 46 doubles (tied with Frank Thomas) last year.

BASERUNNING:

A real student of the game, Martinez made remarkable strides as a basestealer last year. After entering the season with only three lifetime steals (0-for-3 in 1991), he was 14-for-18 last year. His hustle on the bases is partially shown by his high doubles total.

FIELDING:

Hampered by his shoulder problem, Martinez posted 17 errors last year. But his range remained better than average and he started 23 double plays despite playing only 103 games in the field. He's a good defensive player.

OVERALL

Martinez is now one of the league's premier players, with a solid bat and an ability to make the tough plays at third base. The new Mariner management demonstrated they are serious about building a contending team by signing him to a lucrative three-year contract with an option for a fourth year.

EDGAR MARTINEZ

Position: 3B/DH
Bats: R **Throws:** R
Ht: 5'11" **Wt:** 175

Opening Day Age: 30
Born: 1/2/63 in New York, NY
ML Seasons: 6

Overall Statistics

	G	AB	R	H	D	T	HR	RBI	SB	BB	SO	AVG
1992	135	528	100	181	46	3	18	73	14	54	61	.343
Career	521	1805	295	561	122	8	45	204	17	235	233	.311

Where He Hits the Ball

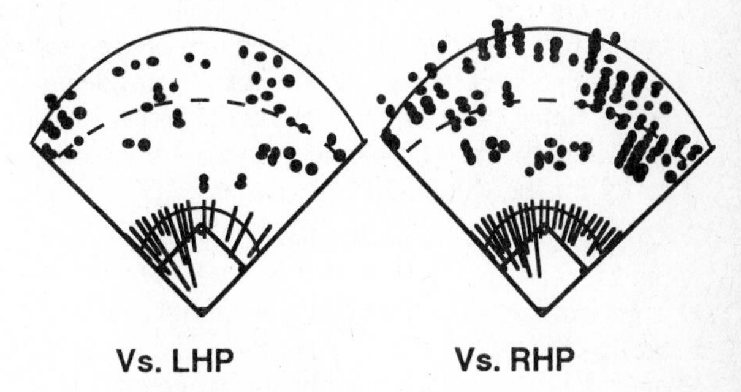

1992 Situational Stats

	AB	H	HR	RBI	AVG		AB	H	HR	RBI	AVG
Home	268	84	11	39	.313	LHP	141	53	4	17	.376
Road	260	97	7	34	.373	RHP	387	128	14	56	.331
Day	139	54	6	20	.388	Sc Pos	133	41	8	62	.308
Night	389	127	12	53	.326	Clutch	82	32	2	10	.390

1992 Rankings (American League)

- 1st in batting average (.343), doubles (46), batting average vs. right-handed pitchers (.331) and batting average on the road (.373)
- 2nd in slugging percentage (.544), batting average vs. left-handed pitchers (.376), slugging percentage vs. right-handed pitchers (.532) and batting average with 2 strikes (.279)
- 3rd in batting average in the clutch (.390)
- Led the Mariners in batting average, runs scored (100), hits (181), doubles, times on base (239), slugging percentage, on-base percentage (.404), most pitches seen per plate appearance (4.03) and batting average in the clutch

TINO MARTINEZ

Position: 1B/DH
Bats: L **Throws:** R
Ht: 6' 2" **Wt:** 205

Opening Day Age: 25
Born: 12/7/67 in Tampa, FL
ML Seasons: 3

HITTING:

After two seasons in which he starred at AAA Calgary while waiting for his major league chance, Tino Martinez finally got his opportunity last year. For a while, it looked like he was going to blow it: a .154 July left Martinez' average at .242 with only eight homers. But the young first baseman finally got it together over the last two months. After August 1 he batted a solid .281 with eight homers and 26 RBI over 167 at-bats. His strong finish and final power numbers -- 16 homers and 66 RBI in only 460 at-bats -- showed that Martinez can play in the majors.

If Martinez was a confused young man for much of the season, you could hardly blame him. The Mariners had another left-handed hitting first baseman, Pete O'Brien, and for much of the year the pair rotated between the first base and designated hitter positions, often taking turns every other day. It was an awkward arrangement, especially for the youngster.

Martinez can hit it out to either corner of the park, but most of his power is to right field. He has an excellent ability to hit the inside pitch. For example, on September 1, Greg Harris of the Red Sox placed a curve ball right where he wanted it -- low and inside. Martinez surprised Harris, homering into the right field seats.

BASERUNNING:

Martinez does not have much speed. He stole only two bases last year and never reached double figures in his minor-league career. He grounded into more double plays (24) than any other Mariner.

FIELDING:

Though not quite in O'Brien's class, Martinez is a good first baseman. He committed only four errors last year and showed good range around the bag. All his defensive mechanics are sound.

OVERALL:

Martinez is still in an awkward situation with Seattle. He should be established as the Mariner first baseman of the future, and his play last year justified that sort of commitment. The problem is that O'Brien has one year left on his lucrative contract.

Overall Statistics

	G	AB	R	H	D	T	HR	RBI	SB	BB	SO	AVG
1992	136	460	53	118	19	2	16	66	2	42	77	.257
Career	196	640	68	156	25	2	20	80	2	62	110	.244

Where He Hits the Ball

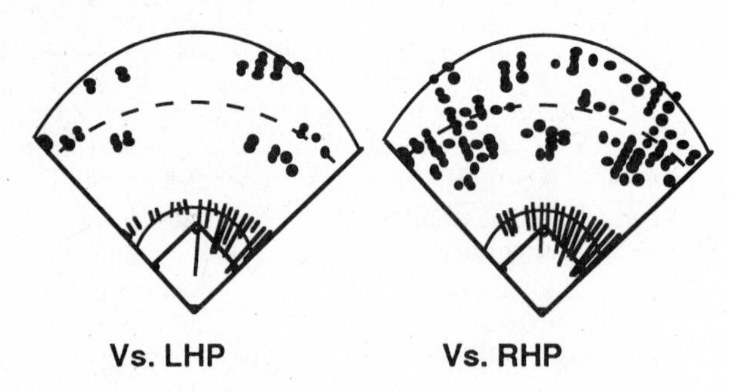

1992 Situational Stats

	AB	H	HR	RBI	AVG		AB	H	HR	RBI	AVG
Home	232	62	10	40	.267	LHP	101	23	3	19	.228
Road	228	56	6	26	.246	RHP	359	95	13	47	.265
Day	130	34	3	16	.262	Sc Pos	117	32	3	52	.274
Night	330	84	13	50	.255	Clutch	90	25	2	13	.278

1992 Rankings (American League)

- 2nd in most GDPs (24) and most GDPs per GDP situation (22.9%)
- 9th in lowest batting average on an 0-2 count (.069)
- Led the Mariners in sacrifice flies (8) and GDPs
- Led AL first basemen in GDPs

PITCHING:

Jeff Nelson's resume must have appealed to the Seattle Mariners. This is a club which has seen some adversity, and Nelson could tell a few tales of his own in that regard. The former Dodger farmhand broke into baseball in 1984. When the 1987 season started, Nelson was still looking for his first professional win. His career record to that point was 0-12. Nelson recovered from that experience, and he'll probably recover from pitching for the 1992 Mariners. The righthander posted a fine 3.44 ERA in 66 appearances, but his win-loss record was 1-7.

One of the biggest players in baseball at 6'8" and 225 pounds, Nelson has always been able to throw hard. Where the ball ends up is another matter. It took him three years to get out of rookie ball, and even then he went through a three-year stretch where he dished out 49 wild pitches. Over the course of time he's learned to take something off his fastball, getting fewer strikeouts but improving his control. Nelson's still not Dennis Eckersley -- he yielded 32 unintentional walks last year in 81 innings -- but he can get by because he's tough to hit.

With the Mariners last year, Nelson worked mostly in middle relief, and he did a nice job. He permitted only 18 of 63 inherited runners to score and he held righties to a .220 average. Late in the season the Mariners used him as their closer and he recorded six saves. After the All-Star break, his earned run average was 2.70.

HOLDING RUNNERS AND FIELDING:

Nelson appears to be an average fielder. He committed two errors in 17 chances, but the handful of opportunities didn't really test him. He did a nice job of holding runners, allowing only four steals in seven attempts.

OVERALL:

Still only 26 after nine professional seasons, Nelson appears to have cemented a spot for himself in the Mariners' bullpen. He probably lacks the stuff of a dominating closer, but he looks like he can be a useful middle reliever. The Mariners made him one of their initial 15 protected players in the expansion proceedings.

JEFF NELSON

Position: RP
Bats: R **Throws:** R
Ht: 6' 8" **Wt:** 225

Opening Day Age: 26
Born: 11/17/66 in Baltimore, MD
ML Seasons: 1

Overall Statistics

	W	L	ERA	G	GS	Sv	IP	H	R	BB	SO	HR
1992	1	7	3.44	66	0	6	81.0	71	34	44	46	7
Career	1	7	3.44	66	0	6	81.0	71	34	44	46	7

How Often He Throws Strikes

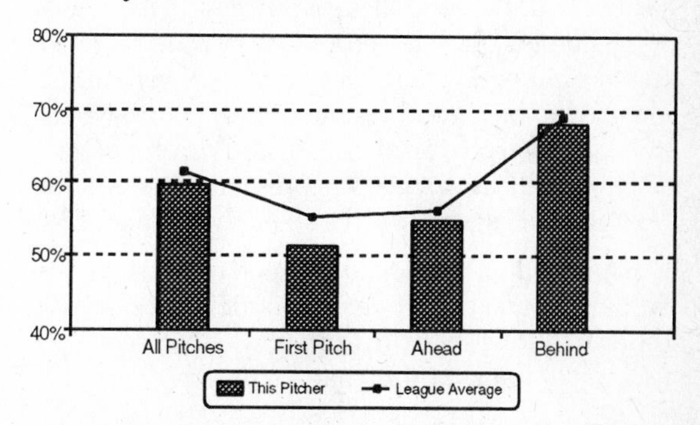

1992 Situational Stats

	W	L	ERA	Sv	IP		AB	H	HR	RBI	AVG
Home	1	2	3.46	5	41.2	LHB	108	31	2	10	.287
Road	0	5	3.43	1	39.1	RHB	182	40	5	30	.220
Day	1	2	2.48	2	36.1	Sc Pos	103	22	1	33	.214
Night	0	5	4.23	4	44.2	Clutch	127	31	3	22	.244

1992 Rankings (American League)

- 2nd in blown saves (8) and relief losses (7)
- 7th in most baserunners allowed per 9 innings in relief (13.4)
- 9th in games pitched (66)
- Led the Mariners in games pitched, blown saves, relief ERA (3.44), relief losses and innings pitched in relief (81)

HITTING:

Early in the 1992 season, Pete O'Brien seemed like he was finally going to erase the bitter memories of the four year, $7.6 million contract Seattle had given him before the 1990 season. Though O'Brien was batting only .213 after two months, he was hitting with great power -- 11 home runs and 27 RBI in 160 at-bats. More than half of his hits had gone for extra bases. But before people could start calling him the Seattle Slugger, O'Brien fell into another long slump. He managed only three homers the rest of the way, and only a .333 September lifted his final average to .222.

In three seasons with the Mariners, O'Brien has yet to hit .250. He did have a power surge in 1991 -- 17 homers, 88 RBI -- but last year he resorted to his old low-average, occasional power habits. He used to be a good fastball hitter, but now he's getting overpowered more and more often. O'Brien still shows good power on occasion, but only in streaks, and mostly on pitchers' mistakes.

One thing O'Brien can do, in good times and bad, is make contact. Last year he struck out only 27 times in 396 at-bats. In 11 major-league seasons, he's never fanned more than 73 times.

BASERUNNING:

Even though O'Brien is not much of a threat to steal, he is a smart baserunner who won't get caught in a rundown or take one extra base too many. He swiped two bases in three attempts last year -- his first steals since 1989.

FIELDING:

O'Brien continues to play good defense, with just three errors last year. His range may have diminished a little, but he still has soft hands and saves his fielders a lot of errors.

OVERALL:

If he didn't have a year left on his big contract, O'Brien would surely be gone from Seattle by now. As it is, he's standing in the way of Tino Martinez, another lefty-hitting first baseman who's a whole lot younger. O'Brien will have to struggle for playing time this year.

PETE O'BRIEN

Position: 1B/DH
Bats: L **Throws:** L
Ht: 6' 2" **Wt:** 195

Opening Day Age: 35
Born: 2/9/58 in Santa Monica, CA
ML Seasons: 11

Overall Statistics

	G	AB	R	H	D	T	HR	RBI	SB	BB	SO	AVG
1992	134	396	40	88	15	1	14	52	2	40	27	.222
Career	1495	5227	624	1367	247	21	162	709	24	615	542	.262

Where He Hits the Ball

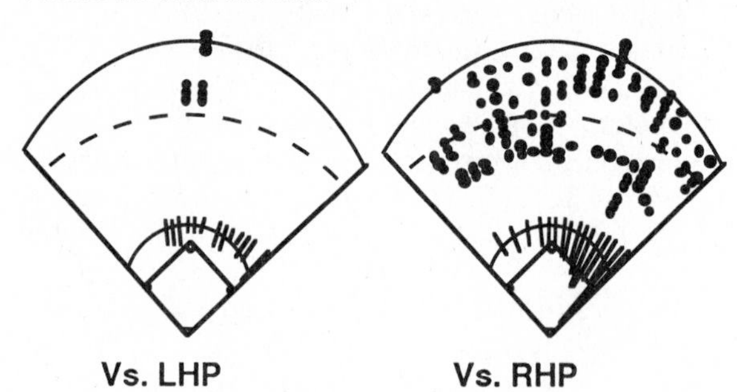

1992 Situational Stats

	AB	H	HR	RBI	AVG		AB	H	HR	RBI	AVG
Home	188	41	6	27	.218	LHP	56	12	1	8	.214
Road	208	47	8	25	.226	RHP	340	76	13	44	.224
Day	106	21	1	7	.198	Sc Pos	85	22	4	39	.259
Night	290	67	13	45	.231	Clutch	76	23	5	18	.303

1992 Rankings (American League)

- 4th in lowest batting average vs. right-handed pitchers (.224)
- 5th in lowest on-base percentage vs. right-handed pitchers (.289)
- 9th in highest percentage of swings put into play (57.2%)
- Led AL first basemen in highest percentage of swings put into play

LANCE PARRISH

Position: C/1B/DH
Bats: R **Throws:** R
Ht: 6' 3" **Wt:** 224

Opening Day Age: 36
Born: 6/15/56 in Clairton, PA
ML Seasons: 16

HITTING:

Cut loose by the Angels last June, Lance Parrish hoped he could catch on with a contending team and go out with a blaze of glory. But the best offer he received was from the lowly Mariners. At 36, not a good age for catchers or chorus girls, Parrish wasn't about to turn up his nose. The veteran proved to be a useful pickup for the M's; though Parrish batted only .234 for Seattle, 20 of his 45 hits were for extra bases.

Even at his advanced age, Parrish still possesses a nice power stroke. He belted a dozen homers last year and he's been in double figures for each of his 15 full seasons. But his 32 RBI were a career low, and he batted only .194 with runners in scoring position. As usual, Parrish struck out much more often than he walked (70 strikeouts, 24 walks). Because he reaches base so infrequently, Parrish needs to produce power numbers to be a useful hitter.

Parrish still loves the fastball, and he does his best work when Number One is headed his way. He batted .375 on the first pitch and .367 when ahead in the count last year. But when behind in the count he hit .175, and with two strikes, it was all over -- his average was .106.

BASERUNNING:

Not exactly Seattle Slew, Parrish has 26 steals in 16 years at a 42 percent success rate. He can seldom leg out a double any more; his most effective bit of running has long been the home run trot.

FIELDING:

Parrish has a wealth of knowledge which can help pitchers develop. Last year Seattle pitchers had an excellent 3.50 ERA with Parrish behind the plate. His arm appears to be weakening, however. Last year he threw out fewer than 30 percent of his opposing basestealers.

OVERALL:

Parrish is eligible for free agency, but says he would like to return to the Mariners next season. They'd like to have him back; so might some of those contending clubs he'd like to play for.

Overall Statistics

	G	AB	R	H	D	T	HR	RBI	SB	BB	SO	AVG
1992	93	275	26	64	13	1	12	32	1	24	70	.233
Career	1868	6743	829	1708	290	27	316	1030	26	575	1442	.253

Where He Hits the Ball

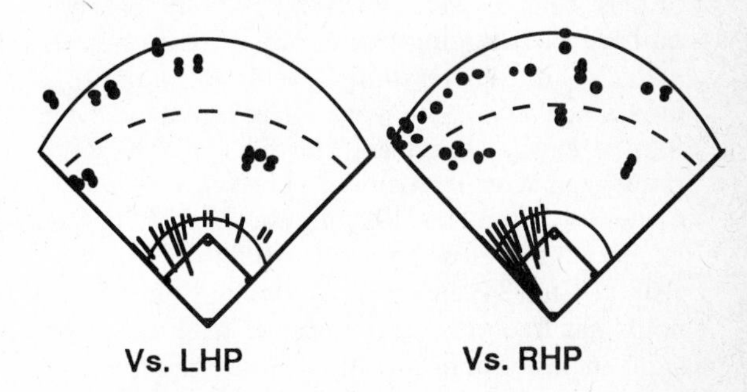

1992 Situational Stats

	AB	H	HR	RBI	AVG		AB	H	HR	RBI	AVG
Home	135	31	7	19	.230	LHP	95	22	4	10	.232
Road	140	33	5	13	.236	RHP	180	42	8	22	.233
Day	101	23	4	14	.228	Sc Pos	72	14	3	21	.194
Night	174	41	8	18	.236	Clutch	62	9	1	4	.145

1992 Rankings (American League)

- 1st in lowest batting average with 2 strikes (.106)
- 3rd in lowest batting average in the clutch (.145), lowest batting average on a 0-2 count (.042) and lowest percentage of runners caught stealing as a catcher (28.0%)

HITTING:

A fine player and a pillar of the Seattle community for his charitable work, Harold Reynolds may have played his last game in a Mariner uniform. The long-time Mariner favorite was relegated to a role on the bench when Brett Boone was promoted from the minors last August. The change was difficult for him to deal with after ten seasons in Seattle. As a consummate professional, Reynolds rose to the challenge and helped Boone get adjusted to the majors. But at year's end he was a free agent, and unlikely to come back to the Mariners.

If 1992 was Reynolds' last Mariner season, it was a sad way for him to exit. Almost every measure of performance went down in 1992. His batting, on-base and slugging averages, runs scored, RBI, walks -- almost everything -- were his worst figures since 1986, the year he became the M's regular second baseman. He did bat .280 with runners in scoring position, but even that was a comedown from his 1991 figure of .322. In the late innings of close games, Reynolds batted only .167 (14-for-84) last year. A switch-hitter, Reynolds has traditionally been better from the right side, but last year he hit only .250 as a righty (.246 lefty). Usually a good low-ball hitter, he didn't show his normal strength last year.

BASERUNNING:

Loss of leg speed has affected Reynolds' baserunning. After stealing 28 bases in 36 attempts in 1991, a career-best 78 percent success rate, he was just 15 for 27 (56 percent) last year.

FIELDING:

A three-time Gold Glove winner, Reynolds is still a fine fielder. His once-wondrous range has diminished, but it remains very good. He is excellent at turning the double play and his .982 fielding average last year was a career best.

OVERALL:

Reynolds ended last year with three games worth of standing ovations from the fans who enjoyed his long contribution to the club. A natural leader and still a fine performer, he should have little trouble finding a team willing to make him their regular second baseman.

HAROLD REYNOLDS

Position: 2B
Bats: B **Throws:** R
Ht: 5'11" **Wt:** 165

Opening Day Age: 32
Born: 11/26/60 in Eugene, OR
ML Seasons: 10

Overall Statistics

	G	AB	R	H	D	T	HR	RBI	SB	BB	SO	AVG
1992	140	458	55	113	23	3	3	33	15	45	41	.247
Career	1155	4090	543	1063	200	48	17	295	228	391	352	.260

Where He Hits the Ball

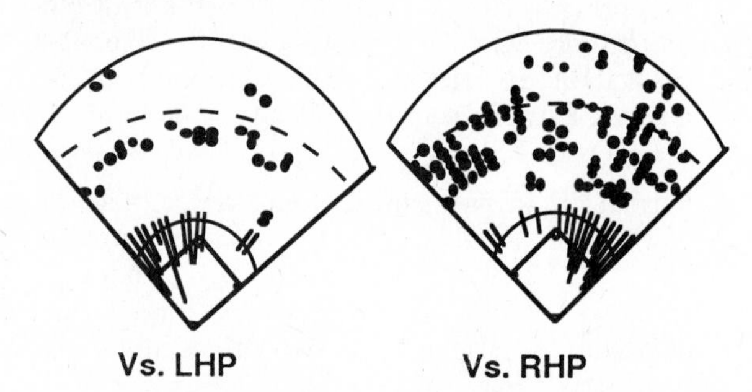

1992 Situational Stats

	AB	H	HR	RBI	AVG		AB	H	HR	RBI	AVG
Home	237	62	2	17	.262	LHP	116	29	0	12	.250
Road	221	51	1	16	.231	RHP	342	84	3	21	.246
Day	129	33	1	12	.256	Sc Pos	107	30	1	30	.280
Night	329	80	2	21	.243	Clutch	84	14	1	7	.167

1992 Rankings (American League)

- → 5th in lowest stolen base percentage (55.6%), lowest batting average in the clutch (.167) and lowest slugging percentage vs. left-handed pitchers (.302)
- → 6th in lowest percentage of swings that missed (8.0%)
- → 7th in sacrifice bunts (11), lowest slugging percentage (.330), lowest slugging percentage vs. right- handed pitchers (.339), bunts in play (27) and highest percentage of swings put into play (57.8%)
- → Led the Mariners in sacrifice bunts, batting average on a 3-1 count (.526), bunts in play and highest percentage of swings put into play

PITCHING:

Only recently regarded as one of the top young closers in baseball, Mike Schooler continues to struggle from a shoulder injury he suffered in 1991. In 1990 Schooler recorded his second straight 30-save season, and his ERA was a glittering 2.25. But last year the big righty could post only 13 saves, all of them before the All-Star break. Schooler's 4.70 ERA was more than double his 1990 mark.

Schooler's 1992 season was one sad litany. In the spring he had tendinitis to deal with. He recovered well enough to resume his closer's role, and he made a workhorse total of 37 appearances before the All-Star break. But Schooler wasn't pitching effectively; though he had 13 saves, his first-half ERA was 4.84. Then in early July, a strained right bicep muscle put him on the disabled list. He rested for about a month, then in mid-August he was re-activated after a rehab assignment. The rest didn't seem to help.

All season long, Schooler appeared timid about letting loose. He never showed his full arm speed, and that led to a lazy fastball that hitters pasted. It also caused a late-breaking slider that tumbled more than it broke, or else just failed to drop, ending high in the strike zone and easy to hit. Schooler set a major league record last year by permitting four grand slam homers. Outgoing manager Bill Plummer put it succinctly: "He has trouble with four-run leads."

HOLDING RUNNERS & FIELDING:

Schooler works at holding runners and has a fairly quick move to first. But as a power pitcher he's easy to run on, and last year he permitted eight steals in nine attempts. He's always been a fine fielder, playing errorless ball last year.

OVERALL:

Schooler is now 30 and is no longer a "great young reliever." He'll enter 1993 still trying to convince people he's recovered from his arm and shoulder problems. Since the Mariners desperately need pitching, he'll get a full shot. But considering the fact that he wasn't protected from expansion just two years since his last 30-save season, the prognosis isn't too promising.

MIKE SCHOOLER

Position: RP
Bats: R **Throws:** R
Ht: 6' 3" **Wt:** 220

Opening Day Age: 30
Born: 8/10/62 in Anaheim, CA
ML Seasons: 5

Overall Statistics

	W	L	ERA	G	GS	Sv	IP	H	R	BB	SO	HR
1992	2	7	4.70	53	0	13	51.2	55	29	24	33	7
Career	12	29	3.30	243	0	98	267.1	253	109	93	232	20

How Often He Throws Strikes

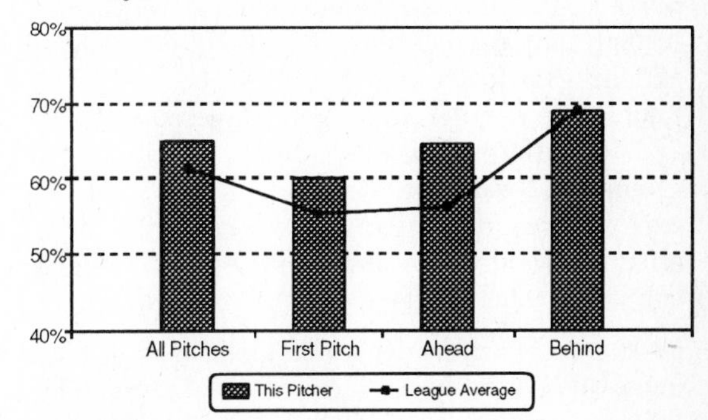

1992 Situational Stats

	W	L	ERA	Sv	IP		AB	H	HR	RBI	AVG
Home	1	4	4.55	6	27.2	LHB	79	22	3	19	.278
Road	1	3	4.88	7	24.0	RHB	121	33	4	26	.273
Day	0	2	4.58	6	17.2	Sc Pos	64	26	6	44	.406
Night	2	5	4.76	7	34.0	Clutch	110	36	6	34	.327

1992 Rankings (American League)

- 2nd in relief losses (7)
- 3rd in highest batting average allowed in relief with runners in scoring position (.406)
- 4th in highest batting average allowed with runners on base (.333)
- 6th in highest percentage of inherited runners scored (42.5%)
- Led the Mariners in saves (13), games finished (36), save opportunities (18) and relief losses

PITCHING:

A successful reliever with a 3.43 ERA over 63 appearances in 1991, Russ Swan began last season as a starter, the role he had held throughout his minor-league career. The switch was anything but successful. After nine starts his record was 2-5 and his ERA was 6.14. Even on the Mariners, those weren't good numbers, and Swan was returned to the bullpen. Once more he pitched effectively. Swan's relief ERA last year was a solid 3.40, and he permitted only 11 of 44 inherited runners to score. The M's even used him as a closer from time to time, and he was probably the best finisher on their shaky staff. Swan converted nine of his 11 save opportunities.

Swan's stuff is well-suited to relief work. His fastball only reaches about 85 MPH, but it sinks, and he gets lots of groundball outs. His other pitches are a slider and a split-fingered fastball, and both offerings also help produce those useful grounders. Swan works the corners well and he is one of those rare righties who's consistently more effective against left-handed hitters (.198 average last year).

Swan's major shortcoming as a closer is that he lacks the velocity to blow away hitters. His pitches also frequently dip out of the strike zone, and control can be a problem for him. Forced to throw a strike, he can get hurt by the longball. Swan permitted eight home runs last year in 104.1 innings.

HOLDING RUNNERS AND FIELDING:

Swan is a very capable fielder and comes off the mound quickly with the best range on the Mariner staff. He committed just one error last year. However, he is not particularly good at holding baserunners. Last year he permitted five steals in seven attempts.

OVERALL:

After two years of success as a reliever, Swan seems to have found his niche with the Mariners. He's the kind of guy who's not intimidated by pressure situations, and he might once again be used as an emergency closer. But most likely Swan will be a middle reliever in 1993; he was an expansion protection and fits solidly in their '93 plans.

RUSS SWAN

Position: RP/SP
Bats: L **Throws:** L
Ht: 6' 4" **Wt:** 215

Opening Day Age: 29
Born: 1/3/64 in Fremont, CA
ML Seasons: 4

Overall Statistics

	W	L	ERA	G	GS	Sv	IP	H	R	BB	SO	HR
1992	3	10	4.74	55	9	9	104.1	104	60	45	45	8
Career	11	18	4.26	133	20	11	239.0	244	131	99	96	23

How Often He Throws Strikes

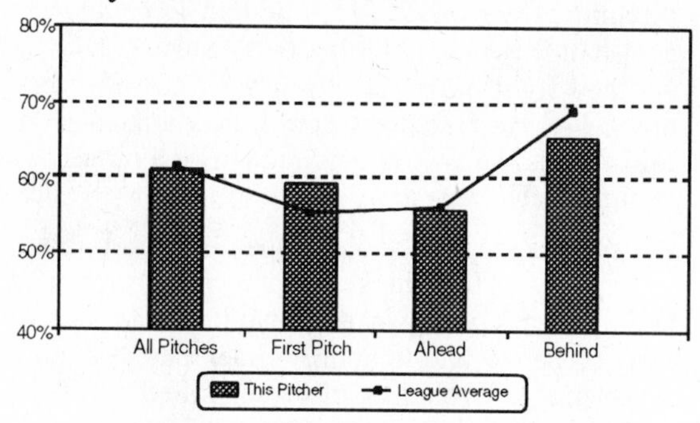

1992 Situational Stats

	W	L	ERA	Sv	IP		AB	H	HR	RBI	AVG
Home	1	6	6.44	4	43.1	LHB	81	16	0	6	.198
Road	2	4	3.54	5	61.0	RHB	316	88	8	53	.278
Day	3	4	2.91	2	43.1	Sc Pos	115	30	2	47	.261
Night	0	6	6.05	7	61.0	Clutch	142	34	4	18	.239

1992 Rankings (American League)

- Led the Mariners in holds (7)

HITTING:

Dave Valle learned the art of catching as a minor leaguer under manager Bill Plummer. Valle was probably one of the happiest Mariners last season, when Plummer became manager of the Mariners. Showing new confidence at the plate, he batted .240, his best season in six years. Now Valle will have to show he can continue to hit under Lou Piniella, as Plummer lasted only one season as the M's manager.

When you hit .240 and people consider it a good year, you're obviously lacking in batting skills. That's the case with Valle. His swing has a pronounced hitch, and as a result he has problems with righthanders' breaking pitches. Valle has always been much more effective against lefties than righties: last year he hit .283 vs. southpaws, .219 vs. righthanders. Valle stands close to the plate, gets hit frequently by pitches, and can occasionally go deep. He's belted between seven and 12 homers every season since 1987 even though he's never batted more than 367 times.

Of course, Valle didn't exactly turn into Johnny Bench last year. He drove in only 30 runs, his lowest total since becoming a regular in 1987. He also batted only .195 with runners in scoring position.

BASERUNNING:

Valle was smart enough not to attempt a steal in 1992. He has only three steals in nine seasons, his last swipe coming in 1990. However, he got out of the box much more quickly last season. After grounding into 19 double plays in 1991, he had only seven GDPs in '92.

FIELDING:

Valle has a strong arm and prides himself on his defense and his ability to handle pitchers. However, his handling of pitchers in '92 was suspect. Last year Mariner pitchers had a 3.50 ERA with Lance Parrish catching, 4.68 with Valle. He's been much better in this category in past seasons.

OVERALL:

With his offensive improvement, Valle seems secure as the regular Mariner catcher this year. Piniella will watch his work with pitchers this year, but the new Mariner slogan seems to fit him: like them, he seems "safe at home."

DAVE VALLE

Position: C
Bats: R **Throws:** R
Ht: 6' 2" **Wt:** 200

Opening Day Age: 32
Born: 10/30/60 in Bayside, NY
ML Seasons: 9

Overall Statistics

	G	AB	R	H	D	T	HR	RBI	SB	BB	SO	AVG
1992	124	367	39	88	16	1	9	30	0	27	58	.240
Career	711	2079	231	479	85	10	59	255	3	177	300	.230

Where He Hits the Ball

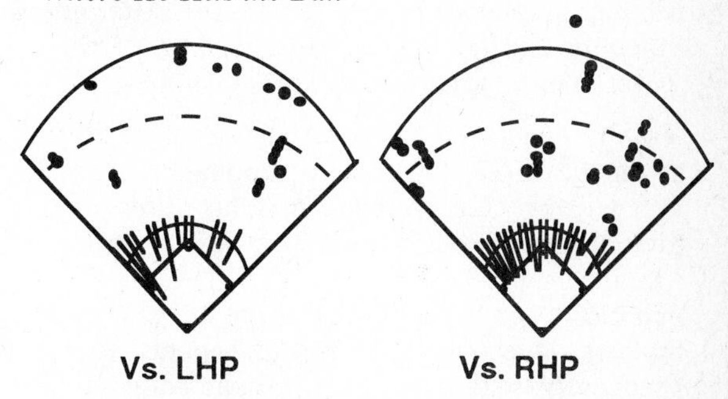

1992 Situational Stats

	AB	H	HR	RBI	AVG		AB	H	HR	RBI	AVG
Home	198	49	7	19	.247	LHP	120	34	4	11	.283
Road	169	39	2	11	.231	RHP	247	54	5	19	.219
Day	94	19	3	6	.202	Sc Pos	87	17	0	20	.195
Night	273	69	6	24	.253	Clutch	47	10	0	3	.213

1992 Rankings (American League)

- Led the Mariners in hit by pitch (8) and batting average on an 0-2 count (.261)
- Led AL catchers in batting average vs. lefthanded pitchers (.283)

GREAT RANGE

OMAR VIZQUEL

Position: SS
Bats: B **Throws:** R
Ht: 5' 9" **Wt:** 165

Opening Day Age: 25
Born: 4/24/67 in Caracas, Venezuela
ML Seasons: 4

Overall Statistics

	G	AB	R	H	D	T	HR	RBI	SB	BB	SO	AVG
1992	136	483	49	142	20	4	0	21	15	32	38	.294
Career	502	1551	155	388	46	13	4	100	27	123	137	.250

Where He Hits the Ball

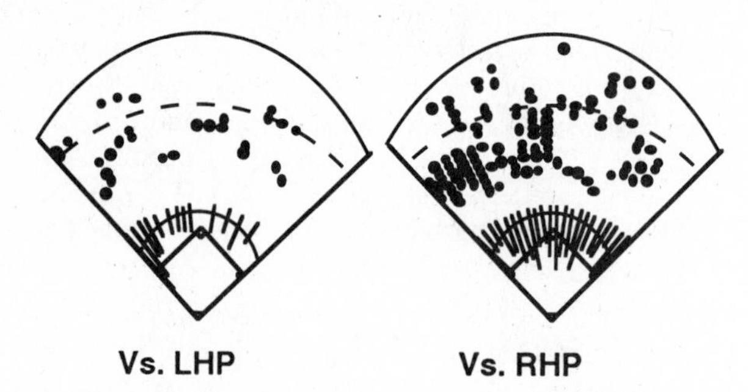

1992 Situational Stats

	AB	H	HR	RBI	AVG		AB	H	HR	RBI	AVG
Home	241	69	0	12	.286	LHP	105	24	0	5	.229
Road	242	73	0	9	.302	RHP	378	118	0	16	.312
Day	134	37	0	11	.276	Sc Pos	101	31	0	20	.307
Night	349	105	0	10	.301	Clutch	87	25	0	4	.287

1992 Rankings (American League)

- 2nd in lowest HR frequency (483 ABs with 0 HR) and lowest stolen base percentage (53.6%)
- 4th in lowest percentage of swings that missed (7.9%)
- 5th in highest batting average vs. right-handed pitchers (.312)
- Led the Mariners in singles (118), triples (4), caught stealing (13), highest groundball/fly-ball ratio (1.4) and lowest percentage of swings that missed
- Led AL shortstops in batting average (.294), batting average vs. right-handed pitchers, on-base percentage vs. right-handed pitchers (.356) and fielding percentage (.989)

HITTING:

No longer "Omar the Out-Maker," Omar Vizquel amazed Seattle with his batting improvement in 1992. A .230 lifetime hitter entering the season, Vizquel batted .294 last year -- a career high by 47 points. Only a dip in September (.223) prevented him from reaching the .300 mark. Prior to 1992, Vizquel had recorded nine three-hit games in his entire career. In 1992 he had 16 of them.

What happened? Vizquel worked hard to improve, mostly. In the past, fastballers were usually capable of overpowering the 5'9" shortstop. After some experimentation, Vizquel finally settled on a lighter bat, and it gave him much better bat speed. The switch-hitter's improvement was especially pronounced from the left side. After hitting only .230 as a lefty in 1991, he batted .312 in 1992. Vizquel continued to struggle as a righty.

Vizquel was also a much more aggressive swinger in 1992, in particular jumping on a lot of first pitches (.328 average). As a result his walk total declined from 45 to 32; even so, his on-base average rose 38 points to .340. Vizquel's RBI count dropped almost in half, from 41 to 21, but that was due mainly to lack of opportunities. Frequently used as a leadoff man, he batted .307 with runners in scoring position.

BASERUNNING:

Vizquel's new aggressiveness showed on the bases as well last year. After stealing seven bases in 1991, he swiped a career-high 15 in '92. But he was probably overly aggressive last year. He was caught stealing twice in 1991, 13 times in '92.

FIELDING:

Vizquel has always been an ace in the field. He committed only seven errors last year and his .989 fielding average was tops among major-league shortstops. He has excellent hands and the ability to make both the soft toss and the hard throw. His range is excellent, and he's very good on the double play.

OVERALL:

Vizquel was one of the most improved offensive players in baseball last season. This year, pitchers figure to give him fewer fastballs. Even if his average slides, Vizquel's defensive excellence should keep him in the lineup.

DAVE COCHRANE

Position: C/LF
Bats: B **Throws:** R
Ht: 6' 2" **Wt:** 180

Opening Day Age: 30
Born: 1/31/63 in Riverside, CA
ML Seasons: 5

Overall Statistics

	G	AB	R	H	D	T	HR	RBI	SB	BB	SO	AVG
1992	65	152	10	38	5	0	2	12	1	12	34	.250
Career	218	514	43	121	24	1	8	43	1	40	129	.235

HITTING, FIELDING, BASERUNNING:

Versatile Dave Cochrane may have dreams of being a regular, but the Mariners consider him one of the best utility players around. In 1992, Cochrane, who adds to his usefulness by being a switch-hitter, batted .250 while playing seven different positions -- all except pitcher and center field -- to set a Mariner team record. Amazingly, he did it while playing part of the year with a broken sesamoid bone in his right foot. Cochrane finally had to go on the disabled list July 31, ending his season.

Though Cochrane's .250 average last year was a career high, it wasn't as good a year for him as 1991 when he'd shown some extra-base power while batting .247. Last year Cochrane had only seven extra-base blows, including two homers. As usual, he didn't walk much (12 times), and strikeouts (34 in 152 at-bats) were a problem.

Though Cochrane can play any position -- he's even pitched in the minors -- he's not really a great fielder. He does have a good arm, but his range is nothing special. He won't embarrass you, though. He has little running speed and has stolen only one base in the majors.

OVERALL

Cochrane's versatility makes him a valuable utility player. He should be fully recovered from his injury this year and figures to see his usual 150-200 at-bats.

RICH DeLUCIA

Position: RP/SP
Bats: R **Throws:** R
Ht: 6' 0" **Wt:** 180

Opening Day Age: 28
Born: 10/7/64 in Wyomissing, PA
ML Seasons: 3

Overall Statistics

	W	L	ERA	G	GS	Sv	IP	H	R	BB	SO	HR
1992	3	6	5.49	30	11	1	83.2	100	55	35	66	13
Career	16	21	4.83	67	47	1	301.2	306	171	122	184	46

PITCHING, FIELDING & HOLDING RUNNERS:

Rich DeLucia had a promising rookie season for the Mariners in 1991, pitching well for most of the year before fading to a 12-13 record. He began last year in the Mariner rotation, but didn't last long. The righthander was eventually shifted to the bullpen, where he pitched a little better. DeLucia still wound up with an ERA above 5.00 for the second consecutive season.

As a major leaguer, DeLucia's problem has been simple: he can't avoid the home run ball. His fastball is only about 85 MPH, so he balances it with a slider, curve and change, none of which are outstanding pitches. When he gets behind and has to throw the fastball, he gets hurt but good -- 46 home runs allowed in 301.2 lifetime innings. DeLucia was also bothered by an inflamed elbow last year, spent time on the disabled list, and had a stint at AAA Calgary. He was finally healthy in September, and worked effectively in the bullpen, with a 2.65 ERA. DeLucia holds runners pretty well, and he's a decent fielder.

OVERALL:

In two-plus seasons with the M's, DeLucia has had only intermittent success. If he can keep the ball in the park, he's effective, but he's never been able to do that on a consistent basis. He'll have to struggle to win a job this season. The fact that he made the Mariners' protected list says more about the organization than it does about him.

TIM LEARY

Position: SP
Bats: R **Throws:** R
Ht: 6' 3" **Wt:** 218

Opening Day Age: 34
Born: 12/23/58 in Santa Monica, CA
ML Seasons: 11

Overall Statistics

	W	L	ERA	G	GS	Sv	IP	H	R	BB	SO	HR
1992	8	10	5.36	26	23	0	141.0	131	89	87	46	12
Career	66	95	4.21	253	194	1	1301.0	1342	669	466	811	122

PITCHING, FIELDING & HOLDING RUNNERS:

The Mariners' search for pitching knew no bounds last year -- just about anyone with a warm body seemed to get a chance. Thus they took a flyer last August on veteran righthander Tim Leary. At the time, Leary was a little-used mop-up man for the Yankees, a club which needed pitching about as much as the M's did.

Leary joined the Mariners on August 22, and while he won three of his eight Seattle starts, he was very fortunate to do so. He barely averaged over five innings an outing and his Mariner ERA was 4.91. Leary once had a pretty good fastball, but in recent years he's relied mainly on his split-fingered fastball. It can be a good pitch, but Leary can't seem to get it over the plate any more. While he had a decent opponents' batting average of .256, he gave up 87 walks in only 141 innings. He had almost twice as walks as strikeouts (46), and that's no way to stay in the majors. It doesn't help that Leary is totally inept at holding runners, allowing 27 steals in 32 attempts last year. He remains a good fielder.

OVERALL:

Given the need for pitchers, one hesitates to say that Leary is through. But at 34, he's got about one and a half feet out the door. He did provide one noted highlight for television viewers when a camera seemed to spot something suspicious in his glove one night. Call it veteran savvy.

DENNIS POWELL

Position: RP
Bats: R **Throws:** L
Ht: 6' 3" **Wt:** 200

Opening Day Age: 29
Born: 8/13/63 in Moultrie, GA
ML Seasons: 7

Overall Statistics

	W	L	ERA	G	GS	Sv	IP	H	R	BB	SO	HR
1992	4	2	4.58	49	0	0	57.0	49	30	29	35	5
Career	11	22	5.09	174	21	3	292.0	318	179	135	167	28

PITCHING, FIELDING & HOLDING RUNNERS:

Lefthander Dennis Powell has become something of an insurance policy for the Mariner bullpen in recent seasons. Except for a brief side trip to Milwaukee in 1990, Powell could usually be found at the M's AAA Calgary farm club, ready to answer the call. The call came early in 1992, on April 8, and Powell wound up appearing in a career-high 49 games.

As usual, he didn't pitch all that well. After seven seasons and 174 major-league games, his lifetime ERA is 5.09. He was only slightly better than that last year (4.58). His one positive figure was that he was the Mariners' most effective pitcher at stranding baserunners in place, allowing only six of 50 inherited runners to score.

Powell has a good major-league fastball along with a serviceable slider and curve, but he's never been able to work effectively once falling behind the hitter. Last year his opponents' batting average when ahead on the count was a meager .149; when pitching from behind, however, the average was .407. He has a good pickoff move, and he's always been a fine fielder.

OVERALL:

With a battered pitching staff, the Mariners will take any kind of help they can get. Powell's good work at stranding inherited runners might be just enough for the M's to extend that insurance policy one more year.

SEATTLE MARINERS MINOR LEAGUE PROSPECTS

ORGANIZATION OVERVIEW:

The old Mariners used to be known as a club which would develop good prospects, then have to let them go at the time when they were starting to get good. The Mariners of more recent vintage have been smart enough to hang onto Junior Griffey and Edgar Martinez, but they're still in last place. What the new ownership will do with the franchise is anyone's guess at this point. Seattle still seems to be cursed with bad luck -- the best Mariner prospect, Roger Salkeld, will miss his second straight season in 1993 -- but they're trying.

JIM CONVERSE

Position: P
Bats: L **Throws:** R
Ht: 5' 9" **Wt:** 180
Opening Day Age: 21
Born: 8/17/71 in San Francisco, CA

Recent Statistics

	W	L	ERA	G	GS	Sv	IP	H	R	BB	SO	HR
91 A Peninsula	6	15	4.97	26	26	0	137.2	143	90	97	137	12
92 AA Jacksnville	12	7	2.66	27	26	0	159.0	134	61	82	157	9

With Salkeld's at-least temporary demise, the Mariners are even hungrier for pitchers than ever, and that's a blessing for guys like Converse. A 16th-round draft choice in 1990, Converse has a 92-95 MPH fastball despite his size and has consistently struck out a batter an inning or better during his career. His problem thus far has been control; walks have plagued him throughout his career. He has a long way to go, but the road will be easier if he can get the ball over the plate.

MIKE HAMPTON

Position: P
Bats: R **Throws:** L
Ht: 5' 10" **Wt:** 180
Opening Day Age: 20
Born: 9/9/72 in Brooksville, FL

Recent Statistics

	W	L	ERA	G	GS	Sv	IP	H	R	BB	SO	HR
91 A San Berndno	1	7	5.25	18	15	0	73.2	71	58	47	57	3
91 A Bellingham	5	2	1.58	9	9	0	57.0	32	15	26	65	0
92 A San Berndno	13	8	3.12	25	25	0	170.0	163	75	66	132	8
92 AA Jacksnville	0	1	4.35	2	2	0	10.1	13	5	1	6	0

Everyone knows the Mariners need pitching, and though Hampton is still a long ways away, his development thus far has given them hope. Whitey Ford-sized at 5'10" (a full inch taller than Converse), Hampton throws harder than many people think, but his main asset has been his tenacity; he has the confidence to use his breaking pitches in tough situations. "He attacks hitters," suggests one report, and that's the key to his success. Still only 20 years old, Hampton had moved to the AA level by the end of last season. He should be heard from soon.

MARC A. NEWFIELD

Position: OF
Bats: R **Throws:** R
Ht: 6' 4" **Wt:** 205
Opening Day Age: 20
Born: 10/19/72 in Sacramento, CA

Recent Statistics

	G	AB	R	H	D	T	HR	RBI	SB	BB	SO	AVG
91 A San Berndno	125	440	64	132	22	3	11	68	12	59	90	.300
91 AA Jacksnville	6	26	4	6	3	0	0	2	0	0	8	.231
92 AA Jacksnville	45	162	15	40	12	0	4	19	1	12	34	.247

Routinely projected to be the Mariners' future cleanup hitter a year ago, Newfield suffered through an injury-riddled 1992 campaign which ended after only 45 games. Newfield has had problems with the big toe on his left foot and needed surgery last year for the second time to align it. He is expected to be ready by spring training; the Mariners will be keeping both their fingers and toes crossed, because Newfield is an outstanding prospect.

BUBBA SMITH

Position: 1B
Bats: R **Throws:** R
Ht: 6' 2" **Wt:** 230
Opening Day Age: 23
Born: 12/18/69 in Riverside, CA

Recent Statistics

	G	AB	R	H	D	T	HR	RBI	SB	BB	SO	AVG
91 A Bellingham	66	253	28	66	14	2	10	43	0	13	47	.261
92 A Peninsula	137	482	70	126	22	1	32	93	4	65	138	.261

"Kill, Bubba, kill" was an affectionate chant which rose through East Lansing, Michigan when fearsome defensive end Bubba Smith was starring for Michigan State. The Mariners have their own Bubba Smith; this one went to the University of Illinois, and he spent the 1992 season terrorizing Carolina League pitchers. In his first full professional season, Bubba II led the league in home runs (32), total bases (246) and extra-base hits (55). This Bubba batted only .261 last year and struck out 138 times, but if he fails, he's big enough at 225 pounds to star for the NFL Seahawks.

KERRY WOODSON

Position: P
Bats: R **Throws:** R
Ht: 6' 2" **Wt:** 190
Opening Day Age: 23
Born: 5/18/69 in Jacksonville, FL

Recent Statistics

	W	L	ERA	G	GS	Sv	IP	H	R	BB	SO	HR
92 AA Jacksnville	5	4	3.57	11	11	0	68.0	74	31	36	55	4
92 AAA Calgary	1	4	3.43	10	0	2	21.0	20	15	12	9	1
92 AL Seattle	0	1	3.29	8	1	0	13.2	12	7	11	6	0

Not the hardest thrower in the Mariner system, Woodson has a nice sinking fastball which got him as far as the major leagues last year. Major-league hitters didn't phase him much, as Woodson posted a 3.29 ERA in eight Seattle appearances. A teammate of the Twins' Scott Erickson at San Jose City College, Woodson lacks his ex-teammate's stuff. But he has a lot of smarts, and that's a good part of the battle.

PITCHING:

If there were such a thing as the "Disabled List Hall of Fame," Ranger lefthander Brian Bohanon would be well on his way to Cooperstown by now. The former number-one draft pick had his usual stint on the shelf last year -- this time for an inflamed left biceps -- while working with both the Rangers and AAA Oklahoma City last year. Bohanon did get into 18 games with Texas, a major league career high, but all he produced was a single victory, and his ERA was an inflated 6.31.

Bohanon has a talented left arm, and that's the main reason the Rangers have been reluctant to give up on him. However, he's had one injury problem after another. Only five games into his 1987 rookie league debut, he broke down with a tired arm. Ever since then, Bohanon has had elbow and shoulder injuries in a never-ending stream. One year he was healthy, made the club . . . and then got whacked in the shoulder with a line drive, tearing some cartilage. Now 24, he's never made it through a season without breaking down.

At the height of his game, Bohanon had a 90 MPH fastball, though his constant arm problems have reduced his velocity. He also has a pretty good overhand curve, a slider and a change-up. Last year his stuff was effective against the few lefties who faced him (.235 opponents' average), but righties cuffed Bohanon around for a .310 average. Control was a problem for him last year, partially due to his sporadic workload.

HOLDING RUNNERS AND FIELDING:

Bohanon has worked on holding runners, and last year he did not allow a steal in three attempts. He's a good enough fielder, and his one error last year was the first of his major league career.

OVERALL:

The Rangers have been waiting on Bohanon for several years, and their patience has about run out. If healthy, he has the talent to make it in the majors, but that's a mighty big if.

BRIAN BOHANON

Position: RP/SP
Bats: L **Throws:** L
Ht: 6' 2" **Wt:** 220

Opening Day Age: 24
Born: 8/1/68 in Denton, TX
ML Seasons: 3

Overall Statistics

	W	L	ERA	G	GS	Sv	IP	H	R	BB	SO	HR
1992	1	1	6.31	18	7	0	45.2	57	38	25	29	7
Career	5	7	5.74	40	24	0	141.0	163	103	66	78	17

How Often He Throws Strikes

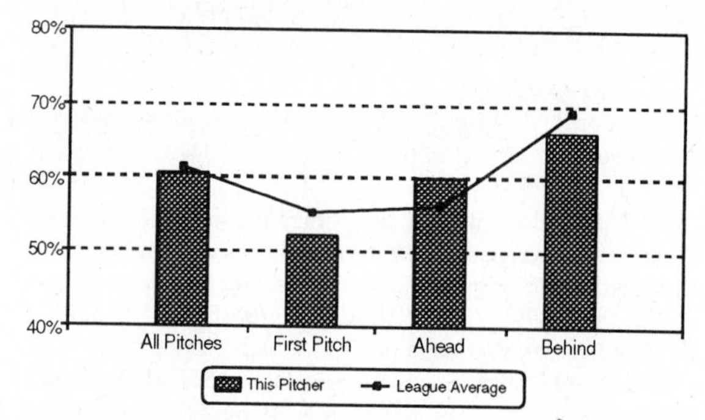

1992 Situational Stats

	W	L	ERA	Sv	IP		AB	H	HR	RBI	AVG
Home	1	1	4.94	0	27.1	LHB	34	8	1	11	.235
Road	0	0	8.35	0	18.1	RHB	158	49	6	27	.310
Day	0	0	7.36	0	7.1	Sc Pos	53	15	1	27	.283
Night	1	1	6.10	0	38.1	Clutch	11	2	0	0	.182

1992 Rankings (American League)

→ Did not rank near the top or bottom in any category

PITCHING:

After years of being cursed as a pitcher with "untapped potential," Kevin Brown finally put it all together in 1992. One season after going 9-12 with a 4.40 ERA (1991), Brown tied for the American League lead in wins with a 21-11 record. He became only the second Texas Ranger pitcher to win 20 games, joining Ferguson Jenkins who won 25 in 1974. The workhorse righty also led the American League in innings pitched with 265.2.

While Brown has always had a world of stuff, he was known to get down on himself, especially in tough situations. Some visits with a sports psychologist helped Brown's confidence last year, and may have been a key to his sudden ability to challenge hitters and stay in the strike zone. In 1991, Brown walked 90 men and fanned only 96 while working 210.2 innings. In '92 he hurled 55 more innings, but nonetheless reduced his walks to 76 while nearly doubling his strikeout total to 173.

Brown's showcase pitch is a hard, two-seam fastball which breaks downward and gets him lots of groundball outs. He also throws a four-seam fastball which is more straight and very explosive, a very hard slider, and a fine change-up. What sets Brown apart from other sinkerballers is the velocity on his pitches: he's been clocked as high as 97 MPH. He's not afraid to pitch inside (he ranked third in the AL in hit batsmen), and while alternating the sinker and slider, he "widens the plate," in effect making all his pitches work better.

HOLDING RUNNERS AND FIELDING:

Brown has a great pickoff move for a righthander. Last year he allowed only seven steals in 19 attempts, the best ratio for any American League pitcher. Usually a very good fielder, he slipped in 1992, committing eight errors.

OVERALL:

Can Brown repeat his outstanding 1992 performance? He cooled off after a sensational start last season, finishing only 7-7 with a 3.71 ERA after the All-Star break. But he's only 28, and appears to have finally matured into one of baseball's best starting pitchers.

KEVIN BROWN

Position: SP
Bats: R **Throws:** R
Ht: 6' 4" **Wt:** 195

Opening Day Age: 28
Born: 3/14/65 in McIntyre, GA
ML Seasons: 6

Overall Statistics

	W	L	ERA	G	GS	Sv	IP	H	R	BB	SO	HR
1992	21	11	3.32	35	35	0	265.2	262	117	76	173	11
Career	56	43	3.67	127	127	0	875.2	876	415	304	477	53

How Often He Throws Strikes

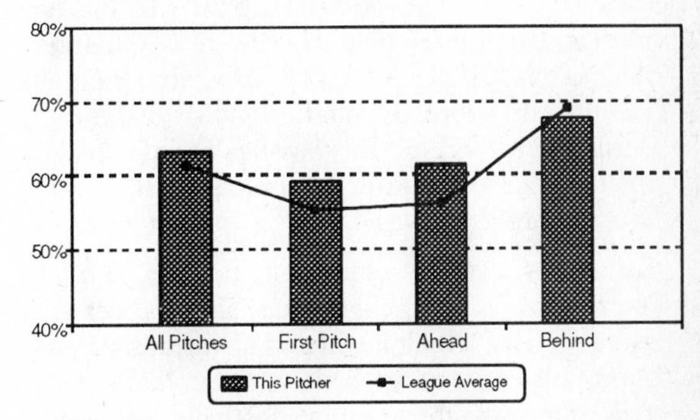

1992 Situational Stats

	W	L	ERA	Sv	IP		AB	H	HR	RBI	AVG
Home	11	4	2.71	0	123.0	LHB	488	131	7	46	.268
Road	10	7	3.85	0	142.2	RHB	519	131	4	58	.252
Day	1	4	5.53	0	42.1	Sc Pos	246	65	5	90	.264
Night	20	7	2.90	0	223.1	Clutch	133	43	1	19	.323

1992 Rankings (American League)

- 1st in wins (21), innings pitched (265.2), hits allowed (262), batters faced (1,108) and lowest stolen base percentage allowed (.368)
- 2nd in complete games (11) and least home runs allowed per 9 innings (.37)
- 3rd in games started (35) and hit batsmen (10)
- Led the Rangers in ERA (3.32), wins, games started, complete games, shutouts (1), innings pitched, hits allowed, batters faced, balks (2), pitches thrown (3,776), pickoff throws (218), GDPs induced (28), winning percentage (.656), lowest batting average allowed (.260), lowest slugging percentage allowed (.335), lowest on-base percentage allowed (.316) and highest grounball/flyball ratio (2.4)

PITCHING:

In need of a pitcher, the Rangers signed former Athletic Todd Burns -- the man with the "shaky cap" -- before the start of the 1992 season. Burns absolutely refuses to touch the bill of his cap, and he has this ritual before each pitch in which he maniacally tugs, twists and adjusts the sides and top of his headgear. Maybe it distracts the hitters, because Burns posted a 3.84 ERA last year, one of the lowest on the beleaguered Texas pitching staff.

When he was with Oakland, Burns' longsuit was versatility, an ability to do a good job as both a starter and a reliever. The Rangers used him in both roles last year, with mixed results. As a starter he was fine, posting a 3.20 ERA in ten outings. But though he pitched well as a member of the rotation in June and July, the Rangers needed him more in relief. Shifted to the pen, Burns did a good job for a while. Then he faded, posting a 5.27 ERA after September 1. His overall ERA as a reliever was 4.93.

Burns uses a variety of pitches, including a high-80s fastball, a good change-up, and a slider and curve, both of which he throws at various speeds. In fact his curve is often slower than his change. As a reliever he throws more fastballs; his varied repertoire, particularly since suffering shoulder problems in 1991, may be better suited for a starting role.

HOLDING RUNNERS AND FIELDING:

Burns is very good at holding runners. Last year runners stole only one base with him on the mound, while being tossed out seven times. He does the basics on defense, but has never been an exceptional fielder.

OVERALL:

Burns presents the Rangers with something of a dilemma. He appears more effective in a starter's role, but the Rangers need bullpen help. Thus he seems likely to open the year as a middle reliever. However, he'll have to prove that he can still handle relief work as effectively as he once did for Oakland.

TODD BURNS

Position: RP/SP
Bats: R **Throws:** R
Ht: 6' 2" **Wt:** 195

Opening Day Age: 29
Born: 7/6/63 in Maywood, CA
ML Seasons: 5

Overall Statistics

	W	L	ERA	G	GS	Sv	IP	H	R	BB	SO	HR
1992	3	5	3.84	35	10	1	103.0	97	54	32	55	8
Career	21	15	3.08	154	28	13	394.0	344	152	134	207	29

How Often He Throws Strikes

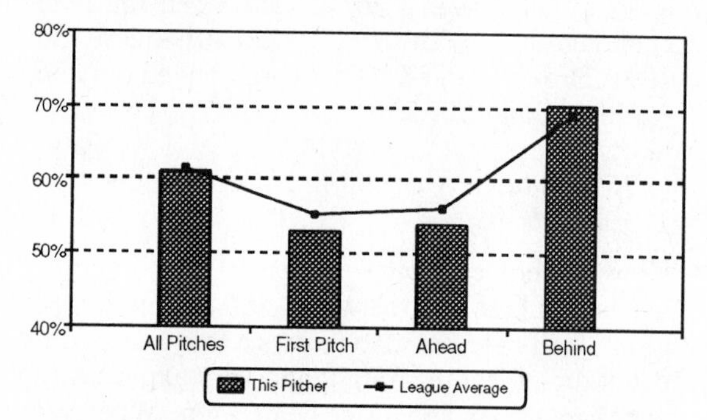

1992 Situational Stats

	W	L	ERA	Sv	IP		AB	H	HR	RBI	AVG
Home	1	1	1.85	1	48.2	LHB	166	39	2	9	.235
Road	2	4	5.63	0	54.1	RHB	224	58	6	30	.259
Day	0	0	4.20	0	15.0	Sc Pos	93	23	1	28	.247
Night	3	5	3.78	1	88.0	Clutch	88	26	3	11	.295

1992 Rankings (American League)

- Led the Rangers in lowest batting average allowed vs. left-handed batters (.235)

HITTING:

After joining the Rangers in a shocking late-season trade with perennial power Oakland, Jose Canseco spent much of the last month trading insults with his former manager Tony La Russa. Though he insisted he was happy in his new surroundings, Canseco batted only .233 in a Texas uniform, with four homers in 73 at-bats.

If Canseco stays with the Rangers, he figures to do a lot better than that. The slugger loves the Texas heat, and Arlington Stadium is a lot better park for him than the cold, massive Oakland Coliseum. Canseco hits them out to all fields, and he should form a devastating one-two power punch with Juan Gonzalez, who belted 43 for the Rangers last year.

Canseco had only 26 homers in 1992, but a shoulder injury which limited him to 119 games had a lot to do with that. The shoulder should benefit from a winter's rest, and so should the bad back which has plagued him on and off for several seasons. Canseco has developed a better batting eye, but he'll still chase a lot of the change-ups and bad breaking stuff pitchers feed him.

BASERUNNING:

Baseball's first and only 40/40 man, Canseco stole only six bases last year. The back and shoulder problems forced him to basically shut down that part of his game, perhaps for good. His caution on the bases is reflected in the fact that he legged out only 15 doubles and no triples.

FIELDING:

Canseco can be a fine outfielder if he's healthy and hustling. Despite his injuries he had a good year with the glove in 1992, and the Rangers were pleased with his effort. His arm remains strong.

OVERALL:

Canseco had the right to demand a trade at season's end, and players will sometimes invoke this right to wrangle a better contract from their current club. However, the Rangers have told Canseco that if he demands a trade, he'll get one. Whatever uniform he's wearing, he should continue to be one of baseball's greatest sluggers . . . when healthy.

JOSE CANSECO

Position: RF/DH
Bats: R **Throws:** R
Ht: 6' 4" **Wt:** 240

Opening Day Age: 28
Born: 7/2/64 in Havana, Cuba
ML Seasons: 8

Overall Statistics

	G	AB	R	H	D	T	HR	RBI	SB	BB	SO	AVG
1992	119	439	74	107	15	0	26	87	6	63	128	.244
Career	972	3655	614	974	171	8	235	734	128	433	998	.266

Where He Hits the Ball

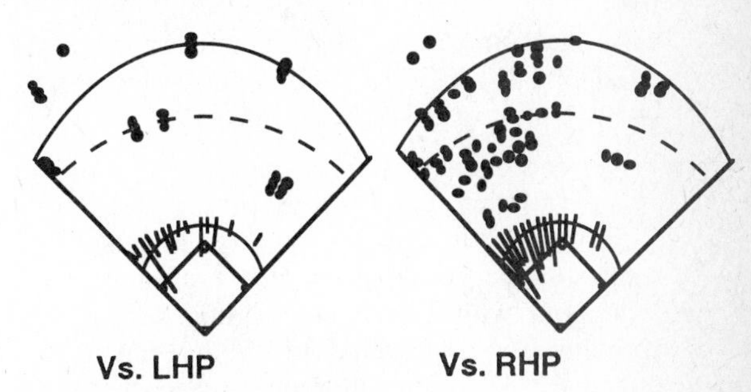

Vs. LHP Vs. RHP

1992 Situational Stats

	AB	H	HR	RBI	AVG		AB	H	HR	RBI	AVG
Home	204	52	15	39	.255	LHP	94	24	7	16	.255
Road	235	55	11	48	.234	RHP	345	83	19	71	.241
Day	158	44	12	37	.278	Sc Pos	146	40	7	63	.274
Night	281	63	14	50	.224	Clutch	70	20	6	19	.286

1992 Rankings (American League)

- 2nd in most pitches seen per plate appearance (4.19)
- 4th in most runs scored per time reached base (.42)
- 5th in HR frequency (16.9 ABs per HR)
- 6th in lowest batting average with 2 strikes (.133)
- 7th in highest percentage of swings that missed (28.2%)
- 9th in lowest batting average (.244), home runs (26) and strikeouts (128)
- Led AL right fielders in most pitches seen per plate appearance

HITTING:

After winning the American League batting title with a .341 mark in 1991, Julio Franco was looking forward to a strong follow-up in '92. It wasn't to be. Tendon problems in his right knee kept Franco on the shelf for most of the 1992 season, and he eventually underwent surgery. He wound up playing only 35 games, none after the All-Star break, while batting a career-low .234. Prior to 1992, Franco had never batted lower than .273 in the majors, even during partial seasons.

Franco made a game effort to play in 1992, but found he couldn't produce. One stat shows how much he was hurting. In '91 he batted .332 vs. right-handed pitching; in '92 he hit only .176 (12 for 68) against righties. Franco was less physically burdened against lefties, and did his usual good job (13-for-39, .333). Eventually, though, he had to shut himself down for the year.

When completely healthy, Franco is one of the very best hitters in the game. He has fine power to all fields, but often prefers to go to center and right. Franco has always been a great fastball hitter, but with his physical problems, he was sometimes overpowered in 1992. Franco was only 3-for-22 (.136) with runners in scoring position last year, a very atypical performance for him. In 1991, he batted .322 with men in scoring position.

BASERUNNING:

Before he was hurt, Franco was an excellent base stealer. In 1991 he reached a career high in steals (36). This part of his game might have to be curtailed in '93.

FIELDING:

At shortstop and more recently second base, Franco has had major defensive problems. He seems to have the talent for the position, but not necessarily the desire. With his physical problems, he might well become a full-time DH.

OVERALL:

Franco is expected to recover from his knee surgery, but the Rangers don't yet know how long it will take. He's signed through 1993, and the Rangers, like everyone, respect him as one of the best hitters in baseball . . . assuming no lingering effects continue to carry over.

JULIO FRANCO

Position: DH
Bats: R **Throws:** R
Ht: 6' 1" **Wt:** 190

Opening Day Age: 31
Born: 8/23/61 in San Pedro de Macoris, Dominican Republic
ML Seasons: 11

Overall Statistics

	G	AB	R	H	D	T	HR	RBI	SB	BB	SO	AVG
1992	35	107	19	25	7	0	2	8	1	15	17	.234
Career	1402	5416	807	1630	249	40	86	679	220	499	637	.301

Where He Hits the Ball

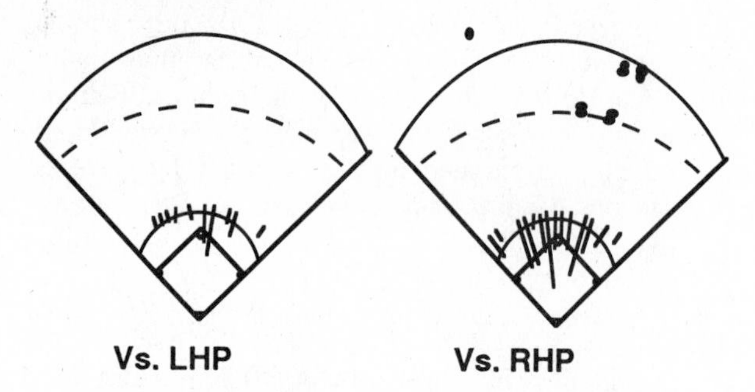

1992 Situational Stats

	AB	H	HR	RBI	AVG		AB	H	HR	RBI	AVG
Home	64	20	2	7	.313	LHP	39	13	1	3	.333
Road	43	5	0	1	.116	RHP	68	12	1	5	.176
Day	16	0	0	0	.000	Sc Pos	22	3	1	6	.136
Night	91	25	2	8	.275	Clutch	16	2	0	1	.125

1992 Rankings (American League)

→ Did not rank near the top or bottom in any category

HITTING:

A former 30th round draft pick, Jeff Frye has been surprising people throughout his athletic career. The 5'9, 165 pound infielder made a good impression in his Ranger debut last year, finishing strongly to wind up hitting .256. He worked his way into the Rangers' 1993 plans by batting a solid .292 after September 1.

Frye began last season at AAA Oklahoma City, hitting .300 in 337 at-bats. When it became obvious that Julio Franco wasn't healthy enough to handle second base, they recalled Frye shortly before the All-Star break. The second sacker had batted over .300 three times in five minor league seasons, and the Rangers figured he could handle major league pitching. They appear to have been right.

Frye is primarily a groundball hitter, and, not surprisingly considering his size, he doesn't have much home run power. He's hardly just a singles hitter, however, as he amassed 47 extra-base hits at AA Tulsa in 1991. In the minors he showed a good eye, walking 70-80 times a season, and he was a good contact hitter. Pitchers tended to work him with fastballs up in the strike zone last year, but Frye looked like he could handle major league hard stuff.

BASERUNNING:

Frye stole only one base in 4 attempts with the Rangers, but he's capable of doing a lot better than that. He stole as many as 33 bases in a season in the minors with some good percentages.

FIELDING:

A major Ranger problem has been poor glove work from their middle infielders. Frye could be one part of a solution. Chosen as the best defensive second baseman in the American Association, he is quick, has good range, and has led two minor leagues in fielding.

OVERALL:

Frye is a scrappy type, the kind managers love. With his speed and good glove, he won't have to hit a ton to stick in the majors. But if his hitting is as good as it's looked thus far, he's capable of nailing down a regular position.

JEFF FRYE

Position: 2B
Bats: R **Throws:** R
Ht: 5' 9" **Wt:** 165

Opening Day Age: 26
Born: 8/31/66 in Oakland, CA
ML Seasons: 1

Overall Statistics

	G	AB	R	H	D	T	HR	RBI	SB	BB	SO	AVG
1992	67	199	24	51	9	1	1	12	1	16	27	.256
Career	67	199	24	51	9	1	1	12	1	16	27	.256

Where He Hits the Ball

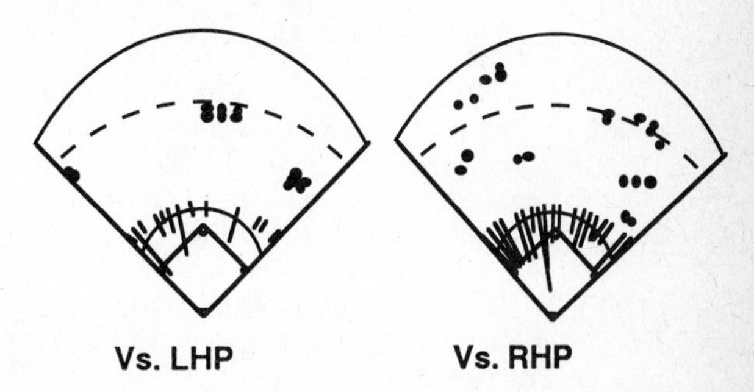

1992 Situational Stats

	AB	H	HR	RBI	AVG		AB	H	HR	RBI	AVG
Home	104	27	0	5	.260	LHP	68	21	1	6	.309
Road	95	24	1	7	.253	RHP	131	30	0	6	.229
Day	32	6	0	2	.188	Sc Pos	40	7	0	8	.175
Night	167	45	1	10	.269	Clutch	26	7	0	3	.269

1992 Rankings (American League)

- 7th in sacrifice bunts (11)
- Led the Rangers in sacrifice bunts

FUTURE MVP?

JUAN GONZALEZ

Position: CF/LF
Bats: R **Throws:** R
Ht: 6' 3" **Wt:** 210

Opening Day Age: 23
Born: 10/16/69 in Vega Baja, Puerto Rico
ML Seasons: 4

HITTING:

Last year at age 22, Juan Gonzalez led the American League in homers with 43, and ranked near the top in RBI with 109. His totals had historians combing the books to find the best seasons ever by a 22-year old. It turned out that Gonzalez' numbers didn't look out of place on a list which included Joe DiMaggio, Johnny Bench, Eddie Mathews, Jimmie Foxx and Ted Williams, all of whom had monster seasons at age 22. This youngster is already in some pretty fast company.

When he is in a groove, Gonzalez can do some truly amazing things. During the months of June, July and August, he got into 79 games, almost exactly half a season. Over that span, he belted 31 homers and drove in 70 runs in 295 at-bats. Imagine how good he'll be when he grows up.

Of course, Gonzalez isn't perfect as a hitter. He batted only .260 last year while drawing only 35 walks and ranking among the league leaders with 143 strikeouts. Pitchers have learned not to throw Gonzalez strikes unless they have to. Generally they try to tease him with shoulder-high fastballs, then try to get him to chase breaking stuff in the dirt. He'll often comply, but if they make a mistake, look out.

BASERUNNING:

A big man at 6-3 and 210 pounds, Gonzalez has a long, loping stride and is faster than he looks. He's no base stealer, however. He tried only one stolen base attempt last year and was thrown out.

FIELDING:

Gonzalez broke in as a center fielder, but didn't really have the range needed for the position. Dave Hulse's arrival last summer pushed him to left field, which was a more comfortable fit. His arm is strong, but he's slow getting rid of the ball and thus is better suited to left field than right.

OVERALL:

Gonzalez is already a major star at an age when most players are just breaking into organized baseball. Though it's possible to build up unrealistic expectations about him, the Rangers have to love his future chances.

Overall Statistics

	G	AB	R	H	D	T	HR	RBI	SB	BB	SO	AVG
1992	155	584	77	152	24	2	43	109	0	35	143	.260
Career	346	1279	172	331	68	4	75	230	4	85	296	.259

Where He Hits the Ball

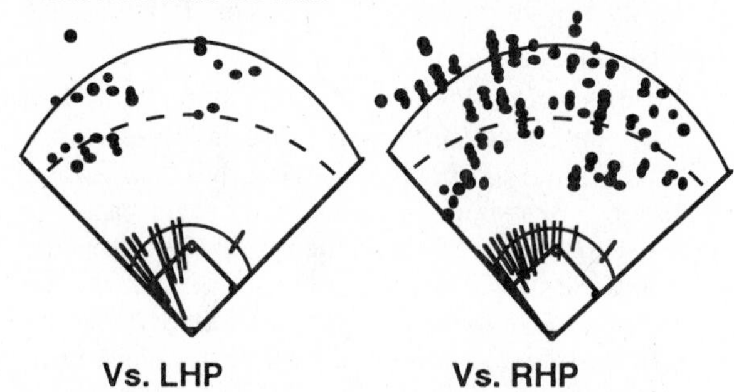

1992 Situational Stats

	AB	H	HR	RBI	AVG		AB	H	HR	RBI	AVG
Home	294	78	19	50	.265	LHP	158	40	8	28	.253
Road	290	74	24	59	.255	RHP	426	112	35	81	.263
Day	99	29	8	23	.293	Sc Pos	177	45	10	69	.254
Night	485	123	35	86	.254	Clutch	93	24	6	12	.258

1992 Rankings (American League)

- 1st in home runs (43) and slugging percentage vs. right-handed pitchers (.561)
- 2nd in HR frequency (13.6 ABs per HR) and slugging percentage at cleanup (.546)
- 3rd in total bases (309)
- 5th in strikeouts (143) and slugging percentage (.529)
- Led the Rangers in home runs, total bases, RBI (109), sacrifice flies (8), GDPs (16), slugging percentage, HR frequency, batting average with the bases loaded (.400) and slugging percentage vs. right-handed pitchers
- Led AL center fielders in home runs, strikeouts, HR frequency, slugging percentage vs. right-handed pitchers and errors (8)

PITCHING:

One year after coming back from the dead, in a baseball sense, Jose Guzman followed up his remarkable 1991 comeback with a season that in many ways was even better. Guzman, who had missed both the 1989 and 1990 seasons with serious shoulder problems, pitched so well that he wound up signing a big free-agent contract with the Cubs.

Few people expected Guzman to match his 1991 record of 13-7, let alone top it. But the righthander proved his comeback was no fluke by going 16-11 with a 3.66 ERA in '92. Guzman was the Rangers' top starter down the stretch, posting an 8-3 mark with a 2.97 ERA after August 1. What made the latter figure so impressive was that it indicated that Guzman's arm was holding up under heavy usage. His 33 starts and 224 innings were both career highs.

Guzman has always been a hard thrower, fanning a team-high 179 batters last year (another career best). His fastball can top 90 MPH, and it sinks, making it even more effective. Guzman has also developed a nasty split-fingered pitch which works very well in conjunction with the fastball. His curve and slider are both decent weapons, and he has nice arm action on his change-up. One major advancement he made last year was his greatly improved control. In 1991, Guzman yielded nearly one walk for every two innings pitched (84 BB in 169.2 IP). In 1992, he reduced the ratio to less than one walk per three innings (73 BB in 224.0 IP).

HOLDING RUNNERS AND FIELDING:

Guzman has always been a good fielder, setting himself up in proper position to handle balls hit back through the box. He's a high leg-kicker, so runners will take off on him, but he keeps them close to the bag. Last year runners stole 16 bases off him, but were also tossed out 15 times.

OVERALL:

Though Guzman will be under pressure with the Cubs, he's probably come too far to feel intimidated. He may not be a Greg Maddux, but the Cubs have bought themselves a pretty good pitcher -- as long as his arm stays healthy.

JOSE GUZMAN

Position: SP
Bats: R **Throws:** R
Ht: 6' 3" **Wt:** 195

Opening Day Age: 30
Born: 4/9/63 in Santa Isabel, Puerto Rico
ML Seasons: 6

Overall Statistics

	W	L	ERA	G	GS	Sv	IP	H	R	BB	SO	HR
1992	16	11	3.66	33	33	0	224.0	229	103	73	179	17
Career	66	62	3.90	159	152	0	1013.2	983	498	395	715	103

How Often He Throws Strikes

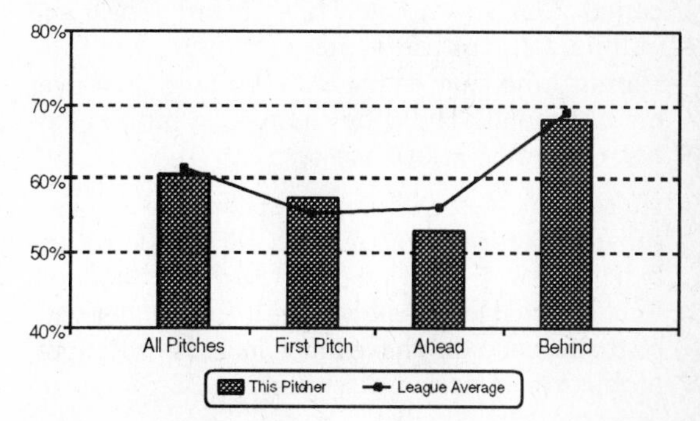

1992 Situational Stats

	W	L	ERA	Sv	IP		AB	H	HR	RBI	AVG
Home	6	7	4.28	0	103.0	LHB	399	111	6	44	.278
Road	10	4	3.12	0	121.0	RHB	454	118	11	42	.260
Day	3	1	3.98	0	43.0	Sc Pos	209	51	1	64	.244
Night	13	10	3.58	0	181.0	Clutch	80	25	0	8	.313

1992 Rankings (American League)

- 4th in strikeouts (179)
- 5th in most run support per 9 innings (5.5) and most strikeouts per 9 innings (7.2)
- 6th in hits allowed (229) and lowest stolen base percentage allowed (51.6%)
- 7th in runners caught stealing (15), highest strikeout/walk ratio (2.5) and highest ERA at home (4.28)
- 8th in lowest ERA on the road (3.12)
- Led the Rangers in home runs allowed (17), strikeouts, runners caught stealing, highest strikeout/walk ratio, most run support per 9 innings, most strikeouts per 9 innings and lowest ERA on the road

HITTING:

David Hulse didn't make an overwhelming impression when he batted .277 at the Rangers' Class A Charlotte farm club in 1991. He wasn't rated one of the Florida State League's top prospects, nor did the Rangers number him among their own top ten. Yet a year later, Hulse was hitting .304 for Texas and looking very much like he might solve the Rangers' need for a legitimate center fielder. No wonder they were calling him "The Incredible" Hulse.

Hulse didn't arrive in Arlington until July, but he quickly established himself. The lefty swinger wound up hitting better than he had for either AA Tulsa (.285) or AAA Oklahoma City, where he'd batted .233 in 30 at-bats. Hulse's fearlessness and enthusiastic attitude pleased manager Toby Harrah, who gave him a lot of playing time over the last month. Hulse never stopped hitting, batting .329 after September 1.

Hulse is blessed with terrific speed, and he takes full advantage of it as a hitter. He tries to hit the ball on the ground and motor down the line. Pitchers tried to overpower the 170-pounder with fastballs, but didn't have much luck. Hulse's main problem was lack of discipline. In 32 games, he drew only three walks.

BASERUNNING:

Hulse can move. In spring training, Hulse beat Donald Harris, thought to be the fastest man in the Texas organization, in a foot race. He stole only three bases with the Rangers, but figures to swipe a lot more once he learns the pitchers.

FIELDING:

Though not a career center fielder, Hulse did a fine job at the position for the Rangers. His arm is not strong, however, and he did not record an assist for Texas.

OVERALL:

Is Hulse for real? He had only 92 at-bats with the Rangers, so he'll have to prove himself over a longer haul. He has weaknesses -- lack of power and discipline, his arm -- and he'll have to show he can hit lefties. The Rangers have liked what they've seen thus far, and he's a front-runner for a starting outfield spot with the departure of Kevin Reimer.

DAVID HULSE

Position: CF
Bats: L **Throws:** L
Ht: 5'11" **Wt:** 170

Opening Day Age: 25
Born: 2/25/68 in San Angelo, TX
ML Seasons: 1

Overall Statistics

	G	AB	R	H	D	T	HR	RBI	SB	BB	SO	AVG
1992	32	92	14	28	4	0	0	2	3	3	18	.304
Career	32	92	14	28	4	0	0	2	3	3	18	.304

Where He Hits the Ball

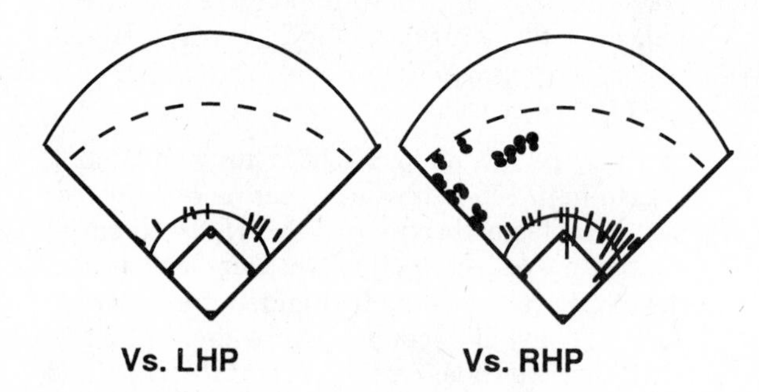

1992 Situational Stats

	AB	H	HR	RBI	AVG		AB	H	HR	RBI	AVG
Home	43	14	0	1	.326	LHP	21	6	0	1	.286
Road	49	14	0	1	.286	RHP	71	22	0	1	.310
Day	26	11	0	1	.423	Sc Pos	13	1	0	2	.077
Night	66	17	0	1	.258	Clutch	14	3	0	0	.214

1992 Rankings (American League)

→ Did not rank near the top or bottom in any category

JEFF HUSON

Position: SS/2B
Bats: L **Throws:** R
Ht: 6' 3" **Wt:** 180

Opening Day Age: 28
Born: 8/15/64 in Scottsdale, AZ
ML Seasons: 5

HITTING:

After Jeff Huson hit a weak .213 in 1991, the Rangers spent the '91-'92 off season actively looking for a shortstop. They didn't find one, and Huson once more wound up as a semi-regular, sharing the position with Dickie Thon and several others. He also logged some time at second, proving to be a very pleasant surprise. The lefty swinger batted a respectable .261, a major improvement over his .227 lifetime average going into the season.

That's not to say that Huson suddenly turned into a star. For one thing, he was benched against lefties. He did hit .281 against southpaws, but that was in only 32 at-bats; he's always shown a career weakness vs. lefthanders. Huson also had problems maintaining a consistent stroke, batting as high as .326 in one month and as low as .220 in another. He also couldn't stay healthy, missing most of the last month with a sore left shoulder.

But for the most part, Huson had a very satisfying year. After entering the season with only two home runs, he belted four in 1992. He showed excellent patience, with 41 walks in his limited action. He continued to be a fine fastball hitter. As usual, pitchers worked Huson mostly with breaking stuff, and he had problems laying off pitches low and away.

BASERUNNING:

Huson has good, but not blinding speed. He makes up for it by being a very smart baserunner. He stole a career-high 18 bases last year, and posted his usual excellent success rate (75 percent).

FIELDING:

Shaky with the glove prior to 1992, Huson had a very fine year on defense. At shortstop he did his best work since joining the Rangers. At second, considered his best position, he was even better, going without an error in over 300 innings of play.

OVERALL:

Huson made great strides in '92 and proved without much question that he's a valuable major-league player. As usual, the Rangers will be looking to replace him as their regular shortstop; as usual, Huson figures to get a lot of playing time.

Overall Statistics

	G	AB	R	H	D	T	HR	RBI	SB	BB	SO	AVG
1992	123	318	49	83	14	3	4	24	18	41	43	.261
Career	439	1098	150	260	41	8	6	83	43	136	138	.237

Where He Hits the Ball

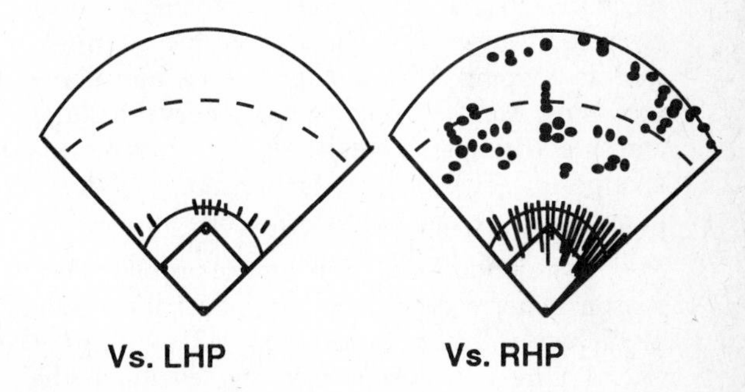

1992 Situational Stats

	AB	H	HR	RBI	AVG		AB	H	HR	RBI	AVG
Home	149	38	0	12	.255	LHP	32	9	1	3	.281
Road	169	45	4	12	.266	RHP	286	74	3	21	.259
Day	77	18	1	3	.234	Sc Pos	64	11	0	18	.172
Night	241	65	3	21	.270	Clutch	54	8	0	1	.148

1992 Rankings (American League)

- 4th in lowest batting average in the clutch (.148)
- Led the Rangers in stolen bases (18), caught stealing (6) and stolen base percentage (75.0%)

TERRY MATHEWS

Position: RP
Bats: L **Throws:** R
Ht: 6' 2" **Wt:** 225

Opening Day Age: 28
Born: 10/5/64 in Alexandria, LA
ML Seasons: 2

PITCHING:

After enjoying success as a Ranger reliever during the second half of 1991, Terry Mathews was expected to pick up where he left off in 1992. Instead, the young righty suffered through a miserable, injury-riddled season. Mathews' ERA was over 6.00 when he went on the disabled list in July with a sore right elbow. He returned toward the end of the season, pitching scoreless ball in three games to reduce his final mark to a still distressing 5.95.

What made the season so frustrating is that Mathews has the stuff to be a very effective reliever. On a club with some very hard throwers he has one of the more impressive fastballs, which reaches 94 MPH. The problem last year was that his velocity was very inconsistent. He often had trouble topping 87, possibly due to his elbow problems. Mathews also throws a curve, a slider and a split-fingered pitch which serves as his change-up. The fastball is his make-or-break pitch, however, and last year it broke him.

Mathews also suffered from control problems last season. After walking 18 men in 57.1 innings in 1991, he yielded 31 walks in only 42.1 innings in '92. Trying to throw strikes and establish the fastball when entering ballgames, he often got lit up: in the first innings of his appearances, opponents hit him at a .325 clip.

HOLDING RUNNERS AND FIELDING:

One of the few areas where Mathews improved last year was in holding baserunners. After permitting eight steals in 11 attempts in 1991, he allowed none in 4 attempts in '92. He's a pretty good fielder, playing errorless ball last year. Of course, the way hitters were teeing off on him, he wasn't getting a lot of easy fielding chances.

OVERALL:

The Rangers dropped Mathews from their 40-man roster after the season, meaning that he was eligible to be drafted by another team. He was put on their Oklahoma City roster, however, and could still return to Texas. Only 28, he can help a major league club if his elbow is sound.

Overall Statistics

	W	L	ERA	G	GS	Sv	IP	H	R	BB	SO	HR
1992	2	4	5.95	40	0	0	42.1	48	29	31	26	4
Career	6	4	4.61	74	2	1	99.2	102	53	49	77	9

How Often He Throws Strikes

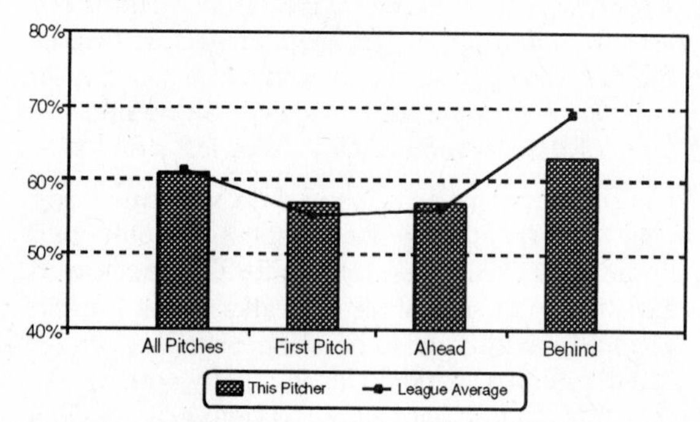

1992 Situational Stats

	W	L	ERA	Sv	IP		AB	H	HR	RBI	AVG
Home	0	2	5.59	0	19.1	LHB	61	20	2	10	.328
Road	2	2	6.26	0	23.0	RHB	102	28	2	18	.275
Day	1	1	22.09	0	3.2	Sc Pos	58	19	2	25	.328
Night	1	3	4.42	0	38.2	Clutch	56	22	3	11	.393

1992 Rankings (American League)

- 3rd in highest percentage of inherited runners scored (45.2%)

EDWIN NUNEZ

Position: RP
Bats: R **Throws:** R
Ht: 6' 5" **Wt:** 240

Opening Day Age: 29
Born: 5/27/63 in Humacao, Puerto Rico
ML Seasons: 11

PITCHING:

Desperate for relief help, the Rangers took a chance last year on oft-injured Edwin Nunez. Texas picked up the big righthander in a late-May deal with the Milwaukee Brewers. For once Nunez stayed relatively healthy and he wound up pitching in 49 games, the second-highest total of his career. Unfortunately, good health did not translate into good results. Nunez' 5.52 Ranger ERA (4.85 overall) only added to the club's season-long relief problems.

One explanation for Nunez' difficulties may lie in the way the Rangers used him. Worked very hard as a teenager coming up through the Seattle system, he developed a tender arm. Since then he has had problems remaining effective over a long season of work. Last year his monthly ERAs were either great or horrible: April 5.40, May 1.64, June 8.74, July 1.35, August 2.70, September 16.88. The Rangers didn't baby Nunez, often working him in long relief stints of 35 pitches or more. His arm simply couldn't seem to handle that kind of usage.

At his best, Nunez possesses some very imposing stuff. He has a good, hard fastball, and balances it very well with an effective split-fingered pitch. Nunez needs both pitches to be effective. Last year most of his problems came in tight situations where he felt he had to come in and throw the fastball. He pitched far better with the bases empty (.211 opponents' average) than with men on (.330).

HOLDING RUNNERS AND FIELDING:

Like most of the Ranger pitchers, Nunez benefitted greatly from having rifle-armed Pudge Rodriguez behind the plate. His stolen base record (one steal allowed in three attempts) was more a credit to Rodriguez than to himself. He is a slow-moving fielder and doesn't help himself with the glove.

OVERALL:

Nunez was a free agent at season's end, and his work last year won't make the Rangers eager to re-sign him. When used more carefully, he can help a team, but he can hardly be counted on as a main facet of any team's bullpen.

Overall Statistics

	W	L	ERA	G	GS	Sv	IP	H	R	BB	SO	HR
1992	1	3	4.85	49	0	3	59.1	63	34	22	49	6
Career	25	30	4.04	356	14	53	561.2	551	289	241	435	70

How Often He Throws Strikes

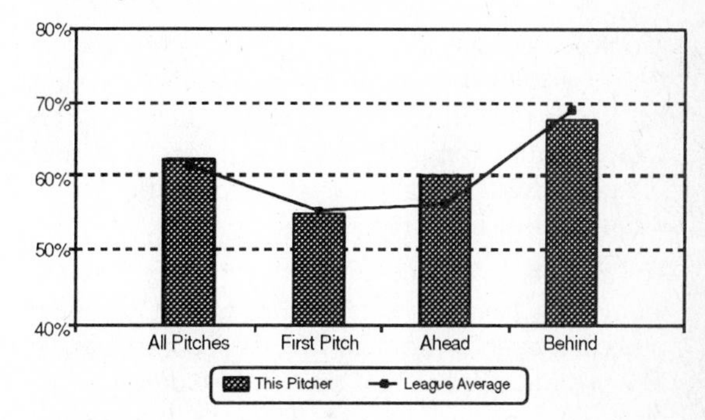

1992 Situational Stats

	W	L	ERA	Sv	IP		AB	H	HR	RBI	AVG
Home	0	2	5.40	1	25.0	LHB	87	20	3	17	.230
Road	1	1	4.46	2	34.1	RHB	148	43	3	23	.291
Day	0	1	10.61	1	9.1	Sc Pos	68	23	2	33	.338
Night	1	2	3.78	2	50.0	Clutch	87	25	3	16	.287

1992 Rankings (American League)

- 1st in least GDPs per GDP situation (1.9%)
- 5th in highest relief ERA (4.85)
- 7th in worst first batter efficiency (.317) and highest batting average allowed in relief (.268)
- 10th in most baserunners allowed per 9 innings in relief (13.2) and most strikeouts per 9 innings in relief (7.4)

HITTING:

Coming off two excellent seasons in which he'd batted .319 and .322, Rafael Palmeiro had every reason to expect a big year in 1992. He'd had his best power numbers in 1991 (26 homers, 49 doubles), and at 27, he was at an age in which many hitters have their best seasons. But Palmeiro had a tough time last year. He did fairly well in the power department with 22 homers and 85 RBI, but his average tumbled all the way to .268 -- his worst figure since his .247 debut over 73 at-bats in 1986.

Palmeiro had a difficult time finding consistency last year. All season long, he alternated good and bad months: .235 April, .305 May, .218 June, .303 July, .230 August, .325 September. The problem seemed to be mechanical. For long stretches of the year, Palmeiro got into a bad habit of moving his hands toward the ball. Pitchers picked up on this, jamming him a lot with inside fastballs and breaking stuff. Palmeiro wound up getting hit by 10 pitches, easily a career high.

His season was hardly a disaster, however. Once labeled by the Cubs as a singles hitter, Palmeiro recorded over 20 homers for the second straight season, and 85-plus RBI for the third consecutive time. He continued to develop into a very patient hitter, recording a career-high 72 walks.

BASERUNNING:

Palmeiro will never set any speed records. He had only two steals in five attempts last year, and has stolen over four only once in his seven-year career. He's earnest enough, just slow.

FIELDING:

Once a below-average first baseman, Palmeiro has improved this part of his game. He led the American League with 143 assists, and reduced his error total from 12 to 7. He's now a little above average, but reports of him as a slick glove man are vastly overstated.

OVERALL:

Palmeiro is a smart, talented hitter, the kind who can learn from a disappointing season. Even while batting .268 last year, he had a lot of virtues at the plate. Palmeiro figures to raise his game a notch higher in 1993.

RAFAEL PALMEIRO

Position: 1B
Bats: L **Throws:** L
Ht: 6' 0" **Wt:** 188

Opening Day Age: 28
Born: 9/24/64 in Havana, Cuba
ML Seasons: 7

Overall Statistics

	G	AB	R	H	D	T	HR	RBI	SB	BB	SO	AVG
1992	159	608	84	163	27	4	22	85	2	72	83	.268
Career	886	3270	463	968	194	23	95	421	28	305	328	.296

Where He Hits the Ball

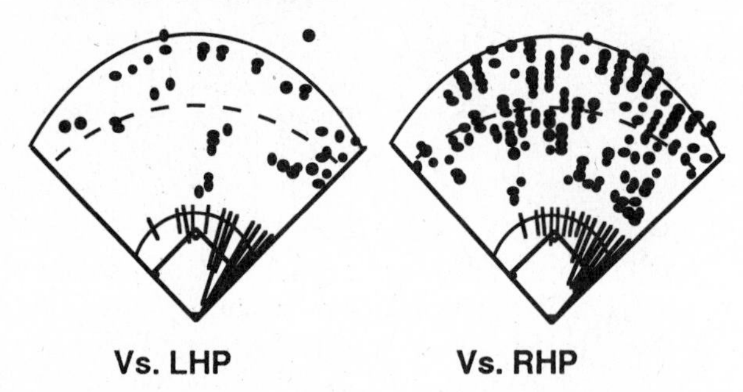

1992 Situational Stats

	AB	H	HR	RBI	AVG		AB	H	HR	RBI	AVG
Home	297	78	8	33	.263	LHP	178	50	5	27	.281
Road	311	85	14	52	.273	RHP	430	113	17	58	.263
Day	116	31	3	20	.267	Sc Pos	148	40	4	60	.270
Night	492	132	19	65	.268	Clutch	97	19	3	11	.196

1992 Rankings (American League)

- 6th in hit by pitch (10) and games played (159)
- Led the Rangers in at-bats (608), runs scored (84), hits (163), singles (110), walks (72), intentional walks (8), hit by pitch, times on base (245), most pitches seen (2,646), plate appearances (701), games played, on-base percentage (.352), batting average with runners in scoring position (.270), batting average on an 0-2 count (.186) and on-base percentage vs. right-handed pitchers (.347)
- Led AL first basemen in triples (4), sacrifice bunts (5), hit by pitch and batting average on a 3-2 count (.273)

HITTING:

Regarded as a top prospect after hitting 15 homers in a half season in 1991, Dean Palmer did little to disprove the notion of his ability in 1992. Though the youngster batted only .229, it represented a major improvement over his rookie figure of .187. More importantly, Palmer proved that his first-year power numbers were no fluke by belting 26 homers and driving home 72 runs.

Palmer is the type of hitter who's always going to have trouble hitting for a high average. Even in the minors, he batted over .266 only once. He has a short stroke and a nice, quick bat, but he loves the challenge of the inside fastball and has a lot of trouble laying off it. Pitchers will also tease Palmer endlessly with breaking stuff outside, but he's learning a little more discipline. He drew 62 walks last year, a figure which should increase even further.

Palmer's numbers would have been a lot better last year if he hadn't had a very poor second half. After hitting .253 with 16 homers and 53 RBI before the All-Star break, his post-break figures were .197-10-19. The problem seemed to be that Palmer simply hadn't played as much at the major league level before; he grew mentally tired as the season wore on. He's the type who should learn from the experience.

BASERUNNING:

No speed burner but fast enough, Palmer pleased the Rangers by swiping 10 bases in 14 attempts last year. He's capable of doing a little better than that, but probably not much.

FIELDING:

Palmer needs to improve at third base, but he has the raw skills. He covers quite a bit of ground, but still commits too many errors. Many of his miscues are the result of poor timing on his throws. He will get better with experience.

OVERALL:

Though Palmer has a great future, the comparisons between him and the early Mike Schmidt have probably been a little premature. It's important to note that he's still only 24, an age at which a lot of players haven't yet reached the majors. He's well on his way into developing into a top power hitter.

DEAN PALMER

Position: 3B
Bats: R **Throws:** R
Ht: 6' 2" **Wt:** 195

Opening Day Age: 24
Born: 12/27/68 in Tallahassee, FL
ML Seasons: 3

Overall Statistics

	G	AB	R	H	D	T	HR	RBI	SB	BB	SO	AVG
1992	152	541	74	124	25	0	26	72	10	62	154	.229
Career	249	828	112	176	36	2	41	110	10	94	264	.213

Where He Hits the Ball

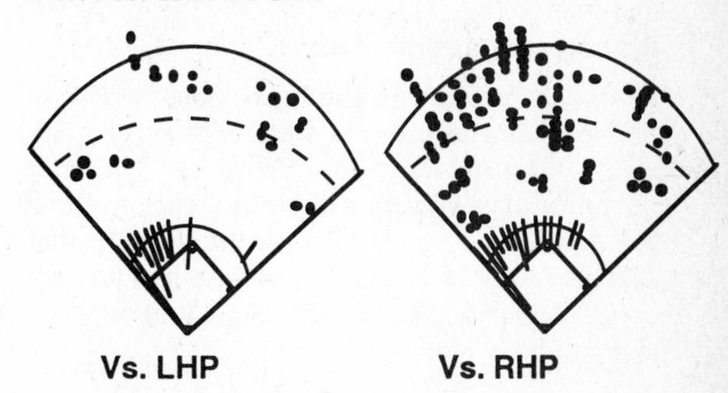

Vs. LHP Vs. RHP

1992 Situational Stats

	AB	H	HR	RBI	AVG		AB	H	HR	RBI	AVG
Home	264	64	11	34	.242	LHP	143	36	8	20	.252
Road	277	60	15	38	.217	RHP	398	88	18	52	.221
Day	113	23	4	11	.204	Sc Pos	124	23	3	37	.185
Night	428	101	22	61	.236	Clutch	95	21	5	11	.221

1992 Rankings (American League)

- 1st in strikeouts (154)
- 2nd in lowest batting average vs right-handed pitchers (.221)
- 3rd in lowest batting average (.229) and lowest percentage of swings put into play (34.3%)
- Led the Rangers in strikeouts and most pitches seen per plate appearance (4.04)
- Led AL third basemen in home runs (26), strikeouts, HR frequency (20.8 ABs per HR), most pitches seen per plate appearance and least GDPs per GDP situation (6.7%)

PITCHING:

On a club desperate for pitching help, Roger Pavlik's performance last year was a major sign of hope. The young righty went only 4-4, and his ERA was middling at 4.21. But Pavlik had enough good outings to indicate that he can be a solid rotation member in the future.

Pavlik showed off some impressive stuff last year. He has a nice, easy, three-quarters motion, and his fastball can reach 89-90 MPH without a lot of effort; he could probably use it more than he does, which is about 60 percent of the time. Like most pitchers he throws both a slider and a curve, but probably needs to pick which one of the two offerings is better in a particular outing and stick with it. He also throws a change-up, but it's not really a major pitch for him yet.

Pavlik's repertoire is a plus but he does have some drawbacks. The minuses were evident last season: control and durability. He walked 34 men in 62 innings last year, and that's too much even for the indulgent Rangers. Pavlik threw more than 110 pitches only once last year, and had just one complete game. He'll need to go longer in his starts to be successful.

HOLDING RUNNERS AND FIELDING:

Pavlik has the athletic ability to be a good fielder, and he holds runners very well for a power pitcher. Last year Pavlik allowed only three steals in 11 attempts.

OVERALL:

Though his record hasn't been overwhelming either in the minors or majors, Pavlik has made a strong impression on the Rangers. They protected him from expansion, and exposed other players such as Kevin Reimer and Scott Chiamparino instead. "Nothing rattles him," said his manager, Toby Harrah, last year. "He's got all the pitches." With a little better control -- and more ability to last into the later innings -- he could be outstanding.

ROGER PAVLIK

Position: SP
Bats: R **Throws:** R
Ht: 6' 2" **Wt:** 220

Opening Day Age: 25
Born: 10/4/67 in Houston, TX
ML Seasons: 1

Overall Statistics

	W	L	ERA	G	GS	Sv	IP	H	R	BB	SO	HR
1992	4	4	4.21	13	12	0	62.0	66	32	34	45	3
Career	4	4	4.21	13	12	0	62.0	66	32	34	45	3

How Often He Throws Strikes

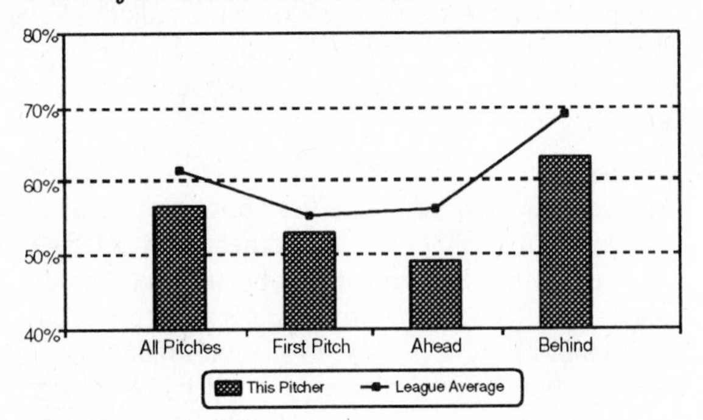

1992 Situational Stats

	W	L	ERA	Sv	IP		AB	H	HR	RBI	AVG
Home	2	2	6.95	0	22.0	LHB	133	36	1	16	.271
Road	2	2	2.70	0	40.0	RHB	103	30	2	7	.291
Day	2	0	0.81	0	22.1	Sc Pos	52	16	1	18	.308
Night	2	4	6.13	0	39.2	Clutch	16	5	0	1	.313

1992 Rankings (American League)

- Led the Rangers in wild pitches (9)

HITTING:

A veteran professional hitter who entered 1992 with a .278 lifetime average, Geno Petralli didn't look like the same player last year. Petralli batted only .198, a career low by a whopping 57 points. He hit only a single home run and notched just 18 RBI, his lowest figure since 1986. Petralli never got untracked at all, batting .226 or lower in five of the season's six months.

The idea that Petralli "didn't look like the same guy last year," is meant quite literally. Ordinarily a lefty swinger, Petralli has had problems hitting left-handed pitchers throughout his career. In 1992, things got so bad that he resorted to switch-hitting on occasion -- an experiment he tried several years ago, with dismal results. It didn't help last year, either; Petralli was 3-for-22 vs. lefties (.136), and stopped hitting righthanders as well (.206).

Petralli has always been known as a good fastball hitter, particularly fastballs low in the strike zone. Pitchers will usually tease him with high heat or breaking stuff, but Petralli has good discipline and ordinarily lays off pitches that aren't strikes. He was still fairly patient last year, but pitchers nonetheless didn't have much trouble getting him out.

BASERUNNING:

After a "career year" on the bases in 1991 -- two steals in three attempts -- the slow-footed Petralli rested on his laurels last year. He didn't venture an attempt last year, which was probably just as well.

FIELDING:

Considered a good handler of pitchers, Petralli seemed to take his hitting problems behind the plate with him last year. Texas hurlers had a 4.63 ERA with him catching, a 3.81 mark with Pudge Rodriguez. Petralli needs to effectively handle the pitching staff, because his other defensive skills (throwing, range, quickness) are below average.

OVERALL:

At 33, Petralli is at the age where players begin to lose their batting skills. As a lefty swinger (usually), he'll get every chance to prove he can still hit. If he can't, he won't last in the majors.

GENO PETRALLI

Position: C
Bats: L **Throws:** R
Ht: 6' 1" **Wt:** 200

Opening Day Age: 33
Born: 9/25/59 in Sacramento, CA
ML Seasons: 11

Overall Statistics

	G	AB	R	H	D	T	HR	RBI	SB	BB	SO	AVG
1992	94	192	11	38	12	0	1	18	0	20	34	.198
Career	750	1741	168	469	78	9	23	179	6	194	246	.269

Where He Hits the Ball

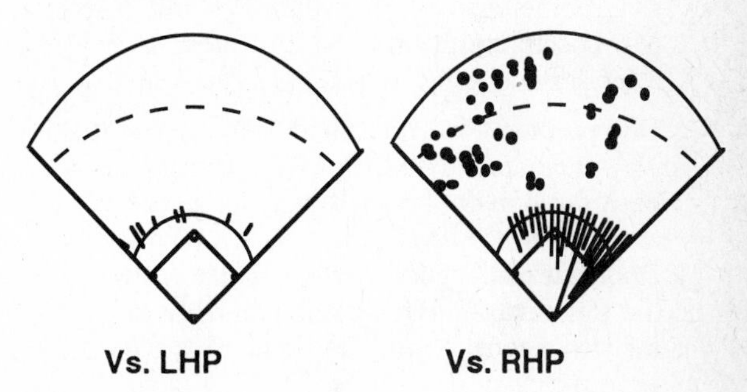

1992 Situational Stats

	AB	H	HR	RBI	AVG		AB	H	HR	RBI	AVG
Home	100	22	0	9	.220	LHP	22	3	0	0	.136
Road	92	16	1	9	.174	RHP	170	35	1	18	.206
Day	47	10	0	7	.213	Sc Pos	46	12	1	18	.261
Night	145	28	1	11	.193	Clutch	50	9	1	5	.180

1992 Rankings (American League)

- 5th in lowest batting average on a 3-2 count (.063)
- 7th in lowest batting average in the clutch (.180)

STRONG ARM

IVAN RODRIGUEZ

Position: C
Bats: R **Throws:** R
Ht: 5' 9" **Wt:** 205

Opening Day Age: 21
Born: 11/30/71 in Vega Baja, Puerto Rico
ML Seasons: 2

HITTING:

When a teenager reaches the majors and immediately performs like a veteran, the tendency is to think that he'll improve year by year. In that sense, Ivan Rodriguez' sophomore season was a disappointment. But taken in context among all major league catchers, his season was strong. Rodriguez continued to do amazing things in 1992, at the ripe old age of 20.

Most of those amazing things were done on defense, not when Rodriguez was swinging a bat. He batted .260 last year, four points lower than in his rookie season. However, he showed improvement in some areas. Rodriguez hit eight homers last year, after belting three (in 140 fewer at-bats) as a rookie. And while he didn't exactly turn into Mr. Discipline, he walked 24 times last season, after drawing only five bases on balls in 1991.

One problem Rodriguez had last year was that he wasn't completely healthy. A stress fracture in his back put him on the shelf in June; he batted only .242 after the All-Star break (.278 before). Rodriguez is a good lowball hitter, particularly the low fastball. Pitchers like to work him up in the strike zone, hoping he'll get impatient.

BASERUNNING:

"Pudge" is faster than the average catcher, but mostly because he's younger. At 5-9 and 205 pounds (Roy Campanella-size), he won't be fast for very long. He did not attempt a steal last year.

FIELDING:

Is Ivan Rodriguez washed up? You might think so, reading reviews of his defensive work last year. His 15 errors led major-league catchers; some were due to poor mechanics, some to careless pickoff throws. But Rodriguez' 52 percent caught-stealing rate on basestealers was the best in baseball. It was awesome considering Texas' high-leg-kicking, throw-it-anywhere pitching staff.

OVERALL:

Will Rodriguez improve? He had problems last year, but many were due to youthful exuberance. On the other hand, there were also signs of laziness (like the failure to run out a last-week fly ball) in his play last year. He has the talent; it's up to him.

Overall Statistics

	G	AB	R	H	D	T	HR	RBI	SB	BB	SO	AVG
1992	123	420	39	109	16	1	8	37	0	24	73	.260
Career	211	700	63	183	32	1	11	64	0	29	115	.261

Where He Hits the Ball

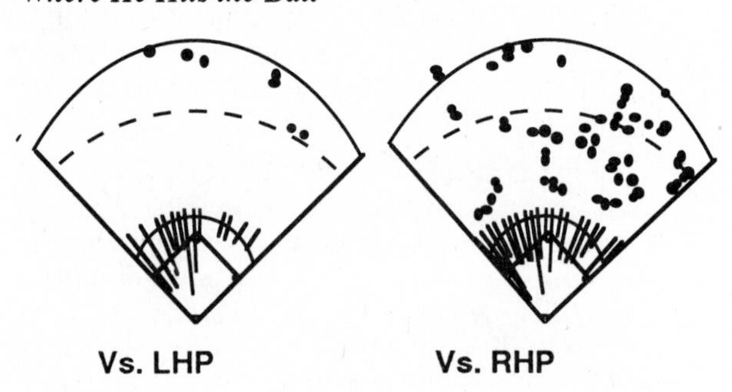

1992 Situational Stats

	AB	H	HR	RBI	AVG		AB	H	HR	RBI	AVG
Home	211	50	4	19	.237	LHP	105	29	2	9	.276
Road	209	59	4	18	.282	RHP	315	80	6	28	.254
Day	83	23	2	9	.277	Sc Pos	102	24	2	28	.235
Night	337	86	6	28	.255	Clutch	82	26	1	9	.317

1992 Rankings (American League)

- 2nd in least pitches taken (42.6%)
- 7th in most GDPs per GDP situation (19.0%)
- Led the Rangers in highest batting average in the clutch (.317)
- Led AL catchers in highest batting average in the clutch, errors (15) and highest percentage of baserunners thrown out as a catcher (51.8%)

PITCHING:

After an unsuccessful attempt to convert him into a starting pitcher in '91, the Rangers kept Kenny Rogers in his familiar bullpen role throughout 1992. He was certainly needed there. One of the few Texas relievers who could consistently get hitters out, Rogers appeared in 81 games, the most in the majors along with Houston's Joe Boever. The heavy workload didn't seem to bother him; in 39 games after the All-Star break, his ERA was an outstanding 2.48. Overall, Rogers' 3.09 ERA was a big improvement over his 1991 mark of 5.42.

Rogers has a variety of stuff, which is one reason why he has been a candidate for a starter's role. He has an excellent fastball, and even with heavy usage, he can consistently top the 90 MPH mark. His curveball has a sweeping break, and he often uses it to "back-door" right-handed hitters, getting it to break over the outside corner. He also has a good straight change, one which he turns over slightly. In '91 he had problems controlling his pitches, yielding 61 walks in 109.2 innings pitched. In 1992, his control was a lot sharper. Rogers yielded only 18 unintentional walks in 78.2 innings last year, while striking out 70 -- an outstanding ratio.

Unlike Bobby Valentine, who often used Rogers for long outings, replacement manager Toby Harrah kept the lefty's stints short last year. In 41 appearances under Harrah, Rogers worked only 35 innings. That may have been a key to his strong second half.

HOLDING RUNNERS AND FIELDING:

Rogers has a good move to first and holds runners well. Last year he permitted only two steals in five attempts. He is not a good defensive player, with a lifetime fielding percentage of only .929.

OVERALL:

Rogers is an ideal reliever -- an effective lefty who can handle a lot of work. If the Rangers don't obtain a big-name closer in the off-season, he might get a chance to be the Texas finisher this year. It's more likely he'll remain in a set-up role where he's one of the good ones.

KENNY ROGERS

Position: RP
Bats: L **Throws:** L
Ht: 6' 1" **Wt:** 205

Opening Day Age: 28
Born: 11/10/64 in Savannah, GA
ML Seasons: 4

Overall Statistics

	W	L	ERA	G	GS	Sv	IP	H	R	BB	SO	HR
1992	3	6	3.09	81	0	6	78.2	80	32	26	70	7
Career	26	26	3.78	286	12	28	359.2	354	180	171	280	29

How Often He Throws Strikes

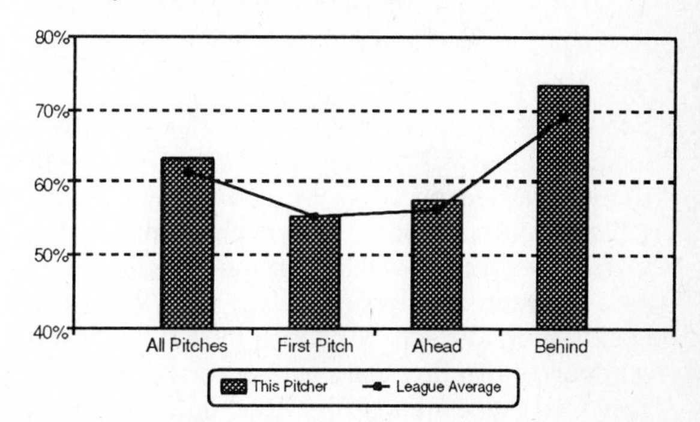

1992 Situational Stats

	W	L	ERA	Sv	IP		AB	H	HR	RBI	AVG
Home	1	4	3.53	2	43.1	LHB	92	24	1	12	.261
Road	2	2	2.55	4	35.1	RHB	214	56	6	38	.262
Day	1	1	3.32	2	19.0	Sc Pos	94	29	5	48	.309
Night	2	5	3.02	4	59.2	Clutch	180	52	4	36	.289

1992 Rankings (American League)

- 1st in games pitched (81)
- 4th in highest percentage of inherited runners scored (43.9%)
- 5th in relief losses (6)
- 6th in holds (16)
- Led the Rangers in games pitched, holds, first batter efficiency (.241), relief losses, relief innings (78.2) and most strikeouts per 9 innings in relief (8.0)

PITCHING:

A Texas institution perhaps second only to the Alamo in longevity, Nolan Ryan suffered through a difficult 1992 season. The 45-year old had to go on the disabled list after his Opening Day start with a strain of his left calf muscle and right achilles tendon. Ryan didn't return until the end of April, and didn't post his first victory until June 28, when the season was nearly half over. He went down again in September with a strained hip muscle.

Ryan finished the year with only five victories, his lowest total since his 0-1, two-game debut in 1966. His 5-9 record was the second worst of his career, and his first losing season since 1987. His 3.72 ERA was his highest since 1985. All in all, if Ryan had decided it was time to call it a career, no one would have blamed him.

So why is Ryan returning for a 26th season, a record which will match the major league mark shared by Deacon McGuire and Tommy John? It's not vanity; it's because he pitched much better than his record showed last season. Ryan got 4.12 runs per game in support last year, but the figure is extremely deceptive, padded by 14- and 8-run outpourings by his teammates. Those were the only two times all year that Ryan got more than five runs to work with. In his last 10 starts the Rangers scored more than two runs exactly once -- they exploded for three that time -- and were shutout five times. In four September starts, Ryan's ERA was 0.99; his record was 0-1.

HOLDING RUNNERS AND FIELDING:

In holding runners, Ryan is almost hopeless. Even Pudge Rodriguez couldn't stop the high-kicking Ryan from allowing 26 steals in 27 starts last year. After playing errorless ball for two years, he returned to his usual (.897 career fielding average) self.

OVERALL:

Can Ryan be effective at age 46? Even last year, he was throwing 94-95 mph. Aches and pains are a concern, and he didn't bounce back well from consecutive 127-pitch starts last year. All in all, though, his problems are nothing a little offense wouldn't cure.

NOLAN RYAN

Position: SP
Bats: R **Throws:** R
Ht: 6' 2" **Wt:** 212

Opening Day Age: 46
Born: 1/31/47 in Refugio, TX
ML Seasons: 26

Overall Statistics

	W	L	ERA	G	GS	Sv	IP	H	R	BB	SO	HR
1992	5	9	3.72	27	27	0	157.1	138	75	69	157	9
Career	319	287	3.17	794	760	3	5320.1	3869	2131	2755	5668	316

How Often He Throws Strikes

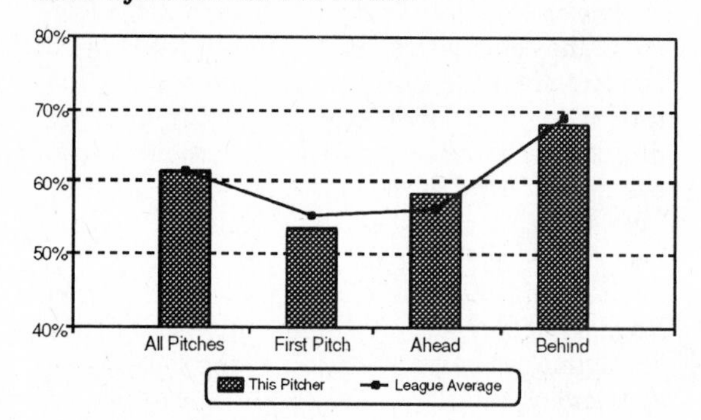

1992 Situational Stats

	W	L	ERA	Sv	IP		AB	H	HR	RBI	AVG
Home	3	6	3.40	0	92.2	LHB	294	72	5	30	.245
Road	2	3	4.18	0	64.2	RHB	286	66	4	30	.231
Day	2	0	2.17	0	29.0	Sc Pos	152	34	3	51	.224
Night	3	9	4.07	0	128.1	Clutch	34	10	0	4	.294

1992 Rankings (American League)

- 2nd in hit batsmen (12)
- 6th in stolen bases allowed (26)
- Led the Rangers in hit batsmen, wild pitches (9) and stolen bases allowed

MATT WHITESIDE

Position: RP
Bats: R **Throws:** R
Ht: 6' 0" **Wt:** 185

Opening Day Age: 25
Born: 8/8/67 in Sikeston, MO
ML Seasons: 1

PITCHING:

Talk about coming out of nowhere. A lightly-regarded 25th-round draft pick in 1990, Matt Whiteside spent 1991 in the Class A South Atlantic League, toiling for the Rangers' Gastonia farm club. By the end of 1992, Whiteside was starring in the Rangers' bullpen, and was considered a strong candidate to replace Jeff Russell as the Texas closer. Whiteside made only 20 appearances for the Rangers last year, but impressed everyone with his 1.93 ERA. He converted all four of his save opportunities.

Judging by the way he pitched last year, the 25-year-old righty should be around to stay. He began the year at AA Tulsa, where he recorded 21 saves and a 2.41 ERA in only 33 appearances. Moved up to the AAA level at Oklahoma City, he posted eight more saves and an ERA of 0.79 in 12 games. All in all, Whiteside totaled 33 saves in his whirlwind season.

A power -- though perhaps not a strikeout -- pitcher, Whiteside displayed a good sinking fastball in his Texas appearances last season. He throws as hard as 92 MPH, though his velocity isn't always quite that high. Whiteside's slider is also a good pitch; it has a nice downward break, and he's confident enough to throw it 30-35 percent of the time. He hasn't had much need for an offspeed pitch yet. Whiteside allowed only one home run last year, but he had a few problems with left-handed hitters (15-51, .294 in the majors).

HOLDING RUNNERS AND FIELDING:

Whiteside has a decent move to first. He permitted only one stolen base in his Texas appearances last year in the only attempt against him. He made one error in six fielding chances last year.

OVERALL:

Whiteside has come a long way in the past year. He appears to have a good closer's profile for the future; the question is whether the Rangers are confident enough to hand the job to him, or whether they'll bring in a veteran. In either case, Whiteside figures to play a major role in the Texas bullpen this year.

Overall Statistics

	W	L	ERA	G	GS	Sv	IP	H	R	BB	SO	HR
1992	1	1	1.93	20	0	4	28.0	26	8	11	13	1
Career	1	1	1.93	20	0	4	28.0	26	8	11	13	1

How Often He Throws Strikes

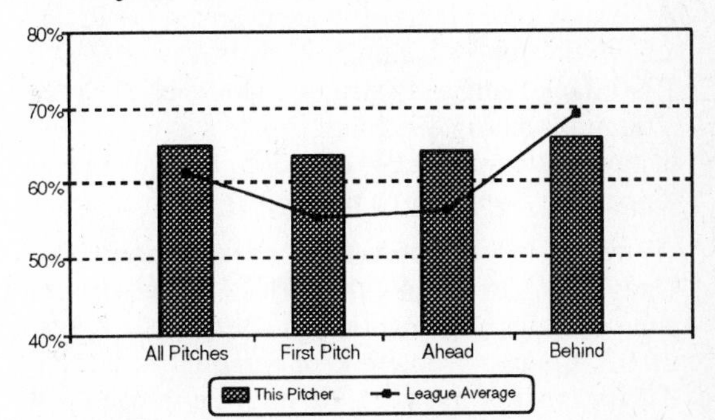

1992 Situational Stats

	W	L	ERA	Sv	IP		AB	H	HR	RBI	AVG
Home	1	0	1.10	0	16.1	LHB	51	15	1	6	.294
Road	0	1	3.09	4	11.2	RHB	55	11	0	4	.200
Day	1	1	0.00	1	4.0	Sc Pos	33	6	0	8	.182
Night	0	0	2.25	3	24.0	Clutch	41	8	0	2	.195

1992 Rankings (American League)

- Did not rank near the top or bottom in any category

JACK DAUGHERTY

Position: LF/RF/DH
Bats: B **Throws:** L
Ht: 6' 0" **Wt:** 190

Opening Day Age: 32
Born: 7/3/60 in Hialeah, FL
ML Seasons: 5

Overall Statistics

	G	AB	R	H	D	T	HR	RBI	SB	BB	SO	AVG
1992	59	127	13	26	9	0	0	9	2	16	21	.205
Career	305	697	73	180	37	6	8	78	5	65	117	.258

HITTING, FIELDING, BASERUNNING:

A veteran minor leaguer who surprised the Rangers with back-to-back .300 years in 1989 and 1990, Jack Daugherty struggled to reach even the .200 mark during 1991 and '92. His averages the last two years were .194 and .205 -- numbers that jeopardize Daugherty's major league future.

Injuries have been the main reason for Daugherty's problems. In 1991, he suffered from strained finger ligaments, and later, appendicitis; in '92, a thumb problem kept him on the disabled list for most of the year. He didn't approach full health until last September, when he showed a few of his skills were still intact by batting .268.

Daugherty's history suggests he's a much better hitter than that. A switch-hitter who has done good work from each side of the plate, he has a nice line drive stroke, and he'll use the whole ballpark. He doesn't have much patience or home run power, though, and he's no longer a fast runner. Daugherty's best defensive position is first base, but mostly he's played the outfield, where his weak arm and lack of range are liabilities.

OVERALL:

Daugherty will be 33 before the 1993 season is half over, and that means he's not going to get many more chances. He has the tools to help a club as a bench player and pinch hitter; the first thing he'll need to do, though, is prove that he's healthy again.

DONALD HARRIS

Position: CF
Bats: R **Throws:** R
Ht: 6' 1" **Wt:** 185

Opening Day Age: 25
Born: 11/12/67 in Waco, TX
ML Seasons: 2

Overall Statistics

	G	AB	R	H	D	T	HR	RBI	SB	BB	SO	AVG
1992	24	33	3	6	1	0	0	1	1	0	15	.182
Career	42	41	7	9	1	0	1	3	2	1	18	.220

HITTING, FIELDING, BASERUNNING:

Another one of those two-sport stars, Donald Harris excelled at both baseball (outfield) and football (free safety) at Texas Tech University. Unlike Deion Sanders and Bo Jackson, he's yet to succeed at the professional level. Harris hasn't hit with the Rangers, and he flunked a trial with the NFL Cowboys.

Harris has spent three seasons at AA Tulsa, raising his average each year from .160 to .227 to his 1992 figure of .254. He's shown power potential as well, with 11 homers in 303 at-bats last year. But Harris continued to show terrible strike zone judgement, walking only nine times while striking out 85 times. In his late-season trial with the Rangers, he fanned 15 times in 33 at bats -- with no walks.

While Harris is raw (to say the least) as a hitter, he's already fully developed as a fielder. He plays shallow and tracks down fly balls beautifully; one Ranger source has described him as "better than Gary Pettis at his best" in center field. Despite his great speed, Harris has shown only marginal ability to steal bases thus far.

OVERALL:

Harris didn't endear himself to the Rangers last spring, when, rather than accept a demotion to the minors, he left to try out for the Cowboys. They love his glove and his athletic skills, but they question his dedication to baseball -- and his ability to hit one.

AL NEWMAN

Position: 2B/3B/SS
Bats: B **Throws:** R
Ht: 5' 9" **Wt:** 212

Opening Day Age: 32
Born: 6/30/60 in Kansas City, MO
ML Seasons: 8

Overall Statistics

	G	AB	R	H	D	T	HR	RBI	SB	BB	SO	AVG
1992	116	246	25	54	5	0	0	12	9	34	26	.220
Career	854	2107	264	476	68	7	1	156	91	236	212	.226

HITTING, FIELDING, BASERUNNING:

The Rangers picked up veteran utility man Al Newman before the start of the 1992 season, looking for a guy who could do a competent job at several positions. The switch-hitter performed about as expected: he displayed a consistently good glove, and a consistently weak bat.

As a hitter, Newman is best known for futility. In eight seasons he's hit exactly one major league homer, off a suitably-embarrassed Zane Smith way back on July 6, 1986. In fact, Newman hasn't hit anything better than a double since the '89 season. Obviously a slap hitter, he goes the other way most of the time. He usually makes contact, and he draws an above-average number of walks. He'll steal some bases, but his recent success rates (9-for-15 last year) have been very mediocre.

So why is Newman still in the majors? Because he does the job in the field at almost any position he's asked to play. Newman has good range at second, plays well at third, and is a capable fill-in at shortstop or even left field. He studies opposing hitters and positions himself well.

OVERALL:

Newman is usually the 24th or 25th man on a roster, and keeping the free agent was not a top Ranger priority. His speed and glove will undoubtedly earn him a job someplace.

DICKIE THON

Position: SS
Bats: R **Throws:** R
Ht: 5'11" **Wt:** 178

Opening Day Age: 34
Born: 6/20/58 in South Bend, IN
ML Seasons: 14

Overall Statistics

	G	AB	R	H	D	T	HR	RBI	SB	BB	SO	AVG
1992	95	275	30	68	15	3	4	37	12	20	40	.247
Career	1302	4204	473	1110	183	41	70	402	161	326	619	.264

HITTING, FIELDING, BASERUNNING:

Hurting for a dependable shortstop, the Rangers took a chance by signing veteran free agent Dickie Thon before the start of the 1992 season. Thon did a so-so job, hitting better than expected but fielding worse. Then a shoulder injury forced him on the shelf in August. Late in the year, Thon felt he was ready to play and left the team when he wasn't used. This move by Thon prompted the Rangers to release him.

Thon batted only .247 for Texas, but that number understated his value. He proved to be a very dependable clutch hitter, batting .288 with runners in scoring position. He drove in 37 runs in only 275 at-bats, and nearly a third of his hits went for extra bases. He was especially dangerous against lefties, batting .293 with a .495 slugging average. As usual, he was an impatient hitter, drawing only 20 walks.

Though he turned 34 shortly after the season started, Thon displayed excellent speed and stole 12 bases in 14 attempts. His defensive work was definitely below expectations, however. Thon's range was nothing special, and he committed 15 errors while starting only 75 games.

OVERALL:

Thon burned his bridges with the Rangers, but he probably played just well enough last year to interest a club looking for a veteran shortstop. Even though his leaving the team raised a few eyebrows, he's a respected player.

ORGANIZATION OVERVIEW:

The Rangers can produce prospects. Much of their current roster, including Juan Gonzalez, Dean Palmer, Kevin Brown, Ivan Rodriguez, and Matt Whiteside -- the backbone of their future -- is home-grown. But Texas has struggled, in good part, because a lot of their best pitching prospects have come down with sore arms. And most of the rest had trouble getting the ball over the plate. The Rangers stuck with pitching coach Tom House for years, even after disastrous experiences with one hurler after another. House is gone now; whether he was the problem or not, the Rangers have a long way to go.

TERRY D. BURROWS

Position: P **Opening Day Age:** 24
Bats: L **Throws:** L **Born:** 11/28/68 in Lake Charles, LA
Ht: 6' 1" **Wt:** 185

Recent Statistics

	W	L	ERA	G	GS	Sv	IP	H	R	BB	SO	HR
91 A Gastonia	12	8	4.45	27	26	0	147.2	107	79	78	151	11
92 A Charlotte	4	2	2.03	14	14	0	80.0	71	22	25	66	2
92 AA Tulsa	6	3	2.13	14	13	0	76.0	66	22	35	59	3
92 AAA Okla City	1	0	1.13	1	1	0	8.0	3	1	5	0	1

The Rangers are desperate for pitching, and they have to be pretty excited about the development of Burrows. The lefthander moved from Class A Charlotte to AA Tulsa to AAA Oklahoma City last year, going a combined 11-5 with a 2.03 ERA. The ERA was a big improvement from 1990 and '91 when Burrows was over the 4.00 mark each year. A power pitcher, he led the Ranger minor-league system in strikeouts in '91. He could well be in the Texas rotation this year.

ROB MAURER

Position: 1B **Opening Day Age:** 26
Bats: L **Throws:** L **Born:** 1/7/67 in Evansville, IN
Ht: 6' 3" **Wt:** 210

Recent Statistics

	G	AB	R	H	D	T	HR	RBI	SB	BB	SO	AVG
92 AAA Okla City	135	493	76	142	34	2	10	82	1	75	117	.288
92 AL Texas	8	9	1	2	0	0	0	1	0	1	2	.222
92 MLE	135	474	60	123	29	1	7	64	0	58	141	.259

A lefty swinger with a nice stroke, Maurer has spent the last two years at AAA Oklahoma City ready in case something happened to Ranger first baseman Rafael Palmeiro. So far nothing has and, perhaps discouraged, Maurer hit only 10 homers last year after belting at least 20 each of the previous two years. Maurer still batted .288, drove in 82 runs, and showed his usual patience with 75 walks. He also struck out 117 times, a normal total for him. Maurer has hit consistently well at the minor-league level and is anxious for a full shot in the majors.

KURT E. MILLER

Position: P **Opening Day Age:** 20
Bats: R **Throws:** R **Born:** 8/24/72 in Tucson, AZ
Ht: 6' 5" **Wt:** 200

Recent Statistics

	W	L	ERA	G	GS	Sv	IP	H	R	BB	SO	HR
91 A Augusta	6	7	2.50	21	21	0	115.1	89	49	57	103	6
92 A Charlotte	5	4	2.39	12	12	0	75.1	51	23	29	58	2
92 AA Tulsa	7	5	3.68	16	15	0	88.0	82	42	35	73	9

The other half of the package the Rangers received in the Buechele deal, Miller is considered an even better prospect than Fajardo and was rated number-one in the Ranger system a year ago by Baseball America. Miller has a fastball which can reach 90 MPH, a good curve, and a lot of poise. He went 12-9 at two levels last year with a slight falloff when he moved to AA Tulsa. Given their history, the Rangers are being very cautious with Miller's arm.

JOSE OLIVA

Position: 3B **Opening Day Age:** 22
Bats: R **Throws:** R **Born:** 3/3/71 in San Pedro De Macoris, DR
Ht: 6' 1" **Wt:** 160

Recent Statistics

	G	AB	R	H	D	T	HR	RBI	SB	BB	SO	AVG
91 R Rangers	3	11	0	1	1	0	0	1	0	2	3	.091
91 A Charlotte	108	384	55	92	17	4	14	59	9	44	107	.240
92 AA Tulsa	124	445	57	120	28	6	16	75	4	40	135	.270
92 MLE	124	439	53	114	26	5	14	69	2	31	167	.260

A self-confident Dominican who said "I can hit the devil himself" before he'd ever played professionally, Oliva started proving himself last year. The third baseman hit .270 at AA Tulsa, his first season above .240, and showed lots of power potential with 50 extra-base hits. He also struck out 136 times, but it was still his best season. Oliva seems to be able to handle third base adequately, but he's hot-tempered and has had weight problems. If he can hit, Texas will be understanding, and they expect he will based on their expansion protection of him.

DAN SMITH

Position: P **Opening Day Age:** 23
Bats: L **Throws:** L **Born:** 8/20/69 in St. Paul, MN
Ht: 6' 5" **Wt:** 190

Recent Statistics

	W	L	ERA	G	GS	Sv	IP	H	R	BB	SO	HR
92 AA Tulsa	11	7	2.52	24	23	0	146.1	110	48	34	122	4
92 AL Texas	0	3	5.02	4	2	0	14.1	18	8	8	5	1

The Rangers' first-round pick in 1990, Smith moved up quickly but had a disastrous year at AAA Oklahoma City in 1991, going 4-17 with a 5.52 ERA. Smith benefitted from a demotion to AA Tulsa, going 11-7 with a 2.52 mark and striking out nearly four times as many batters as he walked. "He looked like Cy Young against us," said one Texas League manager. The Rangers will settle for a successful Smith, especially since they need a lefty starter.

CLUTCH HITTER

ROBERTO ALOMAR

Position: 2B
Bats: B **Throws:** R
Ht: 6' 0" **Wt:** 185

Opening Day Age: 25
Born: 2/5/68 in Ponce, Puerto Rico
ML Seasons: 5

HITTING:

The first thing Roberto Alomar did when he came to Toronto before the 1991 season was establish himself as one of the most popular players ever to wear Blue Jay colors. After two seasons, he's shown that he's also one of the best. Last year Alomar batted over .300 for the first time in his career and drew a career-high 87 walks. In fact, he broke his previous high by 30, showing his increasing maturity at the plate. Getting on base that often made it easier for Carter, Winfield and others to pump up their statistics.

About the only knock on Alomar's game as he came up with the Padres had been that he wasn't a very effective hitter from the right side of the plate. Last season, though, he batted .308 from that side and .311 from the left. He's a spray hitter who can take the ball down the lines or in the gaps -- and pitchers can't blow a fastball by him because he can pull the ball when the situation calls for it.

BASERUNNING:

Alomar stole 40-plus bases for the third time in his career and he's always had a good steal percentage. He stole third base 12 times, and stole both second and third in the same inning six times. He works the bases with speed and intelligence.

FIELDING:

Alomar made only five errors last season, an incredible figure considering that his range allows him to get to balls at which other players can only wave. He'd had high error totals earlier in his career because he'd make a nice stop and a bad throw. No more. Already a two-time Gold Glove winner, he should earn many more.

OVERALL:

Alomar is a considerable MVP candidate because he does everything so well and plays for a team that should continue to contend for championships. Joe Carter had the bigger name when the Jays acquired the duo from San Diego; Alomar is now the guy who'd be the hardest Blue Jay to replace.

Overall Statistics

	G	AB	R	H	D	T	HR	RBI	SB	BB	SO	AVG
1992	152	571	105	177	27	8	8	76	49	87	52	.310
Career	761	2962	439	862	146	31	39	302	192	292	369	.291

Where He Hits the Ball

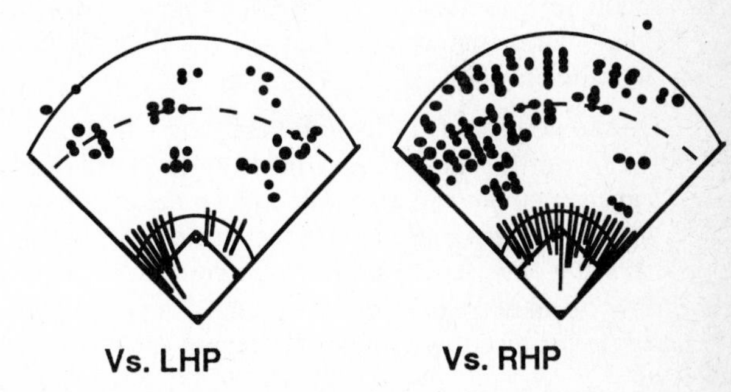

1992 Situational Stats

	AB	H	HR	RBI	AVG		AB	H	HR	RBI	AVG
Home	268	95	5	49	.354	LHP	156	48	5	23	.308
Road	303	82	3	27	.271	RHP	415	129	3	53	.311
Day	185	58	2	25	.314	Sc Pos	147	52	4	68	.354
Night	386	119	6	51	.308	Clutch	79	34	1	16	.430

1992 Rankings (American League)

- 1st in batting average at home (.354) and steals of third (12)
- 2nd in batting average in the clutch (.430)
- 3rd in runs scored (105) and on-base percentage (.405)
- Led the Blue Jays in batting average (.310), runs scored, hits (177), singles (134), triples (8), stolen bases (49), caught stealing (9), walks (87), times on base (269), on-base percentage, highest groundball/flyball ratio (1.7), most pitches seen per plate appearance (3.94), batting average with runners in scoring position (.354), batting average in the clutch, batting average at home, bunts in play (21) and steals of third

HITTING:

The Jays were all set to give Derek Bell a serious shot at being their starting left fielder last season, but he broke a bone in his left hand on the second day of the season and spent about a month on the sidelines before returning to the Jays. In the meantime, veteran Candy Maldonado regained his position in the outfield. Bell was reduced to being the fourth man behind three very solid starters.

Bell has average power and better-than-average speed, and was judged ready for the majors on the basis of the .346 average and 93 RBI he compiled at AAA Syracuse during 1991. Last season, in 161 at-bats, his numbers were understandably much more modest. But being in the environment of a championship team had to be a help to the 24-year-old Bell.

He showed some ability to hit the long ball, tying Joe Carter for the longest home run at SkyDome last season, but can also take a pitch the opposite way. The Jays would like to see him cut down on his strikeouts. Always hustling, a couple of times he took an extra base on what would have been a single for just about any other player.

BASERUNNING:

Bell stole seven bases in nine attempts last year, and appeared to steal more on sheer speed than technique. He could stand to improve that part of his game, especially if he aspires to bat at the top of the order.

FIELDING:

The Jays used Bell to spell Devon White in center field, and he didn't disappoint. He handled 109 chances over all three outfield spots without making an error and threw out four runners. He has good range and gets a good jump on the ball.

OVERALL:

The Jays still have high hopes for Bell, a second-round draft pick who was named Minor League Player of the Year by one major baseball newspaper in 1991. It would not be a surprise if he moved into the lineup on an everyday basis this season.

DEREK BELL

Position: LF/CF/RF
Bats: R Throws: R
Ht: 6' 2" Wt: 200

Opening Day Age: 24
Born: 12/11/68 in Tampa, Fl
ML Seasons: 2

Overall Statistics

	G	AB	R	H	D	T	HR	RBI	SB	BB	SO	AVG
1992	61	161	23	39	6	3	2	15	7	15	34	.242
Career	79	189	28	43	6	3	2	16	10	21	39	.228

Where He Hits the Ball

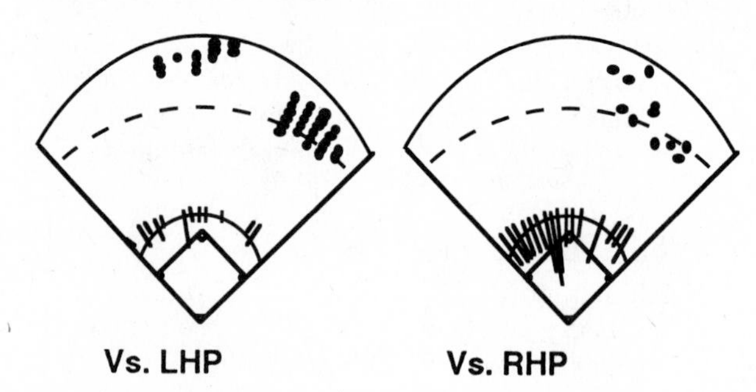

1992 Situational Stats

	AB	H	HR	RBI	AVG		AB	H	HR	RBI	AVG
Home	84	14	2	5	.167	LHP	47	12	2	6	.255
Road	77	25	0	10	.325	RHP	114	27	0	9	.237
Day	61	14	0	4	.230	Sc Pos	38	10	0	12	.263
Night	100	25	2	11	.250	Clutch	21	6	1	2	.286

1992 Rankings (American League)

- Did not rank near the top or bottom in any category

HITTING:

About two-thirds of the way through last season, the Jays signalled to Pat Borders that he was -- finally -- their full-time catcher. They traded Greg Myers, the player he'd often been platooned with, and Borders could finally stop looking over his shoulder. The change seemed to do him good. He finished the season strongly with the second-highest home run total of his career and a confident air that didn't seem to be a part of his game in years past. That confidence showed under the glare of World Series pressure, as Borders batted .450 and was chosen Most Valuable Player of the series.

Borders has outgrown the need to be platooned. During the past two seasons he's hit better against righties than vs. lefties, and last year all 13 of his homers came against righthanders. In 1991 Borders hit only five homers, four of them off righthanders. He still has some bad habits at the plate, like chasing sliders in the dirt and trying to pull everything. But he has developed a little better eye at the plate and has become a killer against fastballs on the inside half of the plate.

BASERUNNING:

Borders stole a base last season! That was one more than his 1991 total and brought his career mark to three. (The other two were in 1989). In other words, Borders is slow. His job is to keep other teams from stealing, not to imitate Robby Alomar and Devon White.

FIELDING:

Borders is especially good at blocking balls in the dirt, which really helps some of the hard-throwing Toronto pitchers stay confident in their good sliders and forkballs. They give him a pretty good workout from time to time. He also is pretty good at throwing out runners, owing to his quick release. He could stand to improve his plate-blocking skills.

OVERALL:

After his World Series performance, Borders has raised the Jays' expectations for this season. Sometimes catchers go from being workman-like to standouts with little notice, and that could be what's happened with him.

PAT BORDERS

Position: C
Bats: R **Throws:** R
Ht: 6' 2" **Wt:** 200

Opening Day Age: 29
Born: 5/14/63 in Columbus, OH
ML Seasons: 5

Overall Statistics

	G	AB	R	H	D	T	HR	RBI	SB	BB	SO	AVG
1992	138	480	47	116	26	2	13	53	1	33	75	.242
Career	518	1512	142	390	84	8	41	188	3	76	246	.258

Where He Hits the Ball

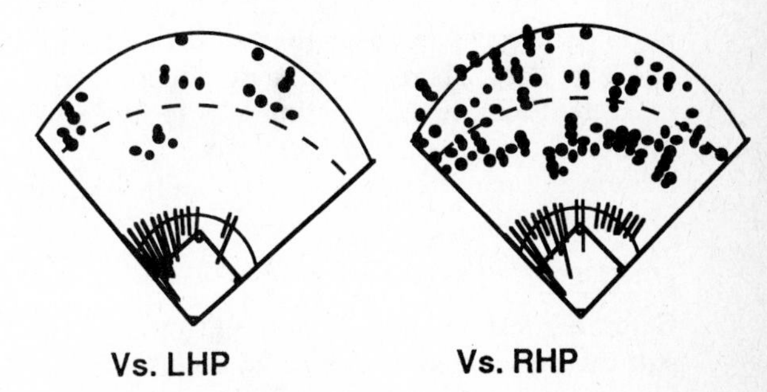

1992 Situational Stats

	AB	H	HR	RBI	AVG		AB	H	HR	RBI	AVG
Home	231	56	7	27	.242	LHP	120	28	0	9	.233
Road	249	60	6	26	.241	RHP	360	88	13	44	.244
Day	148	30	4	12	.203	Sc Pos	107	21	2	39	.196
Night	332	86	9	41	.259	Clutch	82	18	2	3	.220

1992 Rankings (American League)

- 1st in lowest on-base percentage vs. right-handed pitchers (.274)
- 4th in lowest slugging percentage vs. left-handed pitchers (.300)
- 5th in lowest on-base percentage (.290)
- 7th in lowest batting average (.242)
- 8th in lowest batting average with runners in scoring position (.196)

HITTING:

The knock on Joe Carter has always been that he runs up good statistics but doesn't do much when the pressure's on. Well, think back to Game 6 of the 1992 American League Championship Series when Carter told the Jays that they could ride his shoulders to the pennant. He went out and homered his first time up to pace the Jays to their first league title. It was the obvious high point to one of Carter's most productive seasons in the majors, during which he was fourth in the league in homers and second in RBI.

Unlike 1991, Carter's production didn't tail off toward the end of the season; he hit 13 homers in the final two months. There still were some skids when he'd strike out a lot, but that's to be expected of a guy who takes the ball deep as often as Carter does. There are some righthanders who make him look bad by getting him to lunge for outside pitches, but you can't work Carter the same way time after time because he makes adjustments well.

BASERUNNING:

Carter has lost some speed in recent years but he still can be counted on to steal in double figures. He can go from first to third fairly well and he's tough on middle infielders when it comes to breaking up the double play.

FIELDING:

Carter's not a great defensive player. His range is limited and he has trouble hitting cutoff men. Other teams will run on him, which accounts for his 10 assists. The Jays used him at first base during some of the World Series games and he did okay at this position.

OVERALL:

The thing that separates Carter from the greatest players is that he doesn't have a quality on-base percentage to go with his homers and RBI. But he's still a solid star-level player who finally has a World Series ring to quiet the skeptics that doubted if he'd ever contribute to a title-winning squad. The free agent may have ended his stay in Toronto on a very high note.

JOE CARTER

Position: RF/DH
Bats: R **Throws:** R
Ht: 6' 3" **Wt:** 225

Opening Day Age: 33
Born: 3/7/60 in Oklahoma City, OK
ML Seasons: 10

Overall Statistics

	G	AB	R	H	D	T	HR	RBI	SB	BB	SO	AVG
1992	158	622	97	164	30	7	34	119	12	36	109	.264
Career	1344	5201	727	1370	264	34	242	873	181	302	851	.263

Where He Hits the Ball

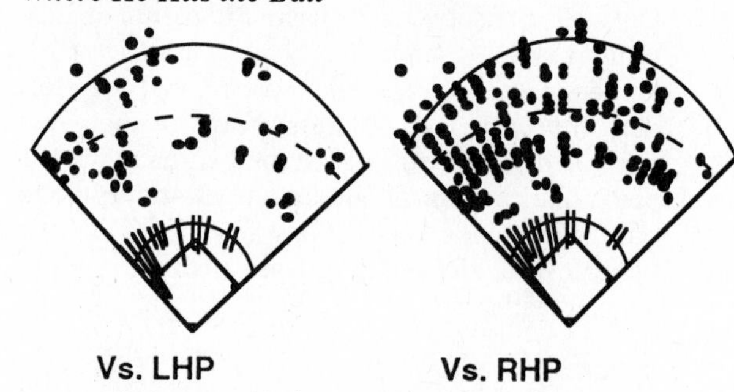

Vs. LHP Vs. RHP

1992 Situational Stats

	AB	H	HR	RBI	AVG		AB	H	HR	RBI	AVG
Home	301	78	21	65	.259	LHP	157	49	7	20	.312
Road	321	86	13	54	.268	RHP	465	115	27	99	.247
Day	194	50	12	40	.258	Sc Pos	179	50	10	83	.279
Night	428	114	22	79	.266	Clutch	86	20	3	16	.233

1992 Rankings (American League)

- 1st in sacrifice flies (13)
- 2nd in total bases (310), RBI (119) and lowest groundball/flyball ratio (.55)
- 3rd in lowest percentage of pitches taken (43.6%)
- 4th in home runs (34)
- 5th in hit by pitch (11)
- Led the Blue Jays in home runs, total bases, RBI, sacrifice flies, hit by pitch, games played (158), slugging percentage (.498), HR frequency (18.3 ABs per HR), batting average vs. left-handed pitchers (.312), slugging percentage vs. left-handed pitchers (.535) and slugging percentage vs. right-handed pitchers (.486)

DAVID CONE

Position: SP
Bats: L **Throws:** R
Ht: 6' 1" **Wt:** 190

Opening Day Age: 30
Born: 1/2/63 in Kansas City, MO
ML Seasons: 7

PITCHING:

For the second straight season the Jays swung a midseason deal to pick up a front-line pitcher to improve their title chances. This second time, it worked. David Cone had seven regular season starts for Toronto after being acquired from the Mets in late August, and he went on to pitch pretty well in the postseason. His six innings of four-hit ball in Game 6 of the Series were an important part of Toronto's clinching victory.

Cone was yet another hard thrower for the Jays staff. He has a fastball, slider and split-fingered pitch that can either blow away opponents or keep them off balance. Having three effective pitches is one of the reasons Cone is one of the toughest pitchers in baseball. He also throws a curve that's better than average, but for him it's just a good fourth pitch.

The interesting thing about Cone is that, while leading the majors in strikeouts for the third straight season (he tied with Roger Clemens in 1991), he's at his best when mixing up his pitches instead of trying to blow away opponents with the fastball. There was some suspicion that the Mets overused him, particularly during a stretch of five outings in which he threw more than 130 pitches each time out (one of them a 166-pitch effort). But he came back strong, yielding only four runs in his final regular season 40.1 innings.

HOLDING RUNNERS AND FIELDING:

Runners steal bases against Cone with ease -- 49 in 59 attempts last year, the highest number of opposing steals in baseball. He makes more than a token number of throws to first, but opposing runners can take advantage of his slow motion to the plate. He does field his position well.

OVERALL:

If Cone can keep his emotions under control and maintain his best stuff, a season like 1988 (when he went 20-3 with a 2.22 ERA) isn't out of reach. However, the free agent's asking price may be out of reach for the Blue Jays and a lot of other clubs.

Overall Statistics

	W	L	ERA	G	GS	Sv	IP	H	R	BB	SO	HR
1992	17	10	2.81	35	34	0	249.2	201	91	111	261	15
Career	84	51	3.10	201	172	1	1267.0	1059	489	460	1227	92

How Often He Throws Strikes

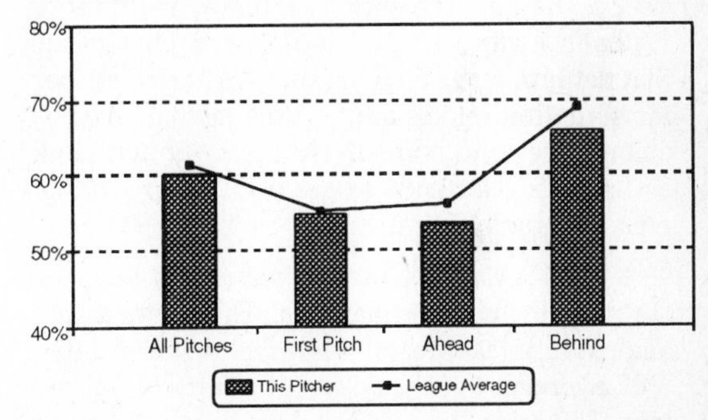

1992 Situational Stats

	W	L	ERA	Sv	IP		AB	H	HR	RBI	AVG
Home	8	6	3.38	0	122.1	LHB	505	116	10	48	.230
Road	9	4	2.26	0	127.1	RHB	411	85	5	33	.207
Day	6	5	3.56	0	93.2	Sc Pos	238	43	4	65	.181
Night	11	5	2.37	0	156.0	Clutch	83	18	1	5	.217

1992 Rankings (American League)

- 3rd in least GDPs induced per GDP situation (2.7%)

MARK EICHHORN

Position: RP
Bats: R **Throws:** R
Ht: 6' 3" **Wt:** 210

Opening Day Age: 32
Born: 11/21/60 in San Jose, CA
ML Seasons: 8

Overall Statistics

	W	L	ERA	G	GS	Sv	IP	H	R	BB	SO	HR
1992	4	4	3.08	65	0	2	87.2	86	34	25	61	3
Career	38	35	3.02	442	7	31	711.2	651	266	218	534	42

How Often He Throws Strikes

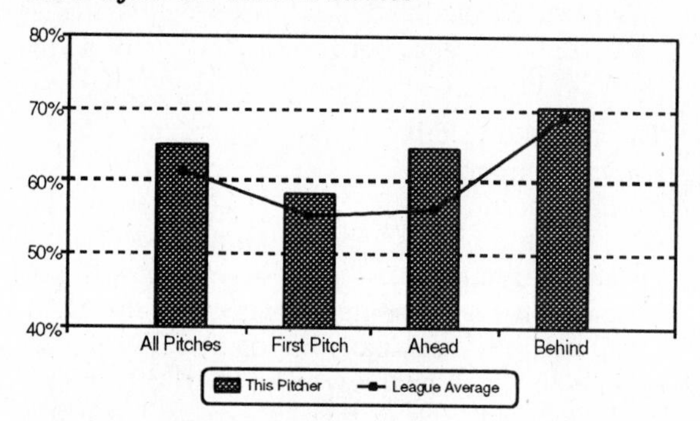

1992 Situational Stats

	W	L	ERA	Sv	IP		AB	H	HR	RBI	AVG
Home	3	0	3.79	2	40.1	LHB	129	44	2	20	.341
Road	1	4	2.47	0	47.1	RHB	208	42	1	23	.202
Day	3	3	2.92	0	37.0	Sc Pos	106	27	1	40	.255
Night	1	1	3.20	2	50.2	Clutch	136	42	2	15	.309

1992 Rankings (American League)

- 3rd in highest batting average allowed vs. left-handed batters (.341)
- 5th in highest percentage of inherited runners scored (43.2%)
- 10th in relief innings (87.2)

PITCHING:

A Blue Jay hero in the mid-to-late 1980s, Mark Eichhorn returned to Toronto last July 31 in a trade with the Angels for catcher Greg Myers and outfielder Rob Ducey. Eichhorn's timing was impeccable; he arrived just in time to help the drive which resulted in Toronto's first championship. Eichhorn's ERA with the Jays was a so-so 4.35, but he was a useful middle reliever.

Few pitchers in the game have a delivery like the soft-throwing righty. In his younger years, Eichhorn threw almost straight underhand. Now, his delivery is between sidearm and three-quarters, which seems to give his pitches more movement -- and movement is what Eichhorn needs. He keeps the ball around the plate, relying on fastballs away to righthanders and change-ups that net him more than his share of called strikes. He sometimes takes a bit off his fastball, and his change seems to come in slow, slower and slowest models. He tends to get a lot of groundball outs, especially against righthanders.

The big flaw in Eichhorn's game has been his inability to retire lefthanders. They batted .341 against him last season while righties had only a .202 average, a continuation of a career-long pattern. He doesn't give up many longballs, but a lefty with some discipline can look at a couple of Eichhorn's pitches and figure him out.

HOLDING RUNNERS AND FIELDING:

Eichhorn made an error last season, only his second in 188 career chances. He has soft hands and is agile around the mound. Holding runners has never been one of Eichhorn's strengths even though he's shown some improvement, mostly by trying to keep them close to first base with frequent pickoff throws.

OVERALL:

If Eichhorn only had to face righthanders, he'd be one of the great relievers in baseball. But he hasn't figured out how to retire lefties during his eight seasons in the majors, and that will always limit his value. Used carefully, the free agent should be an asset to someone's pitching staff this year.

HITTING:

A couple of years ago, Kelly Gruber was on the verge of being recognized as one of the game's best third basemen -- and maybe even one of the most potent offensive players in the American League. Yet he'll enter 1993 coming off two straight substandard years and with a growing list of questions about his ability following his non-protection in the expansion draft.

In 1990 Gruber had 31 homers and 118 RBI. But last season he batted only .229, and his 11 home runs were his lowest total since becoming a regular in 1987. He missed games with minor injuries which caused no shortage of comment among the Toronto media and fans. Then, though he had two key postseason homers, he batted .091 in the playoffs and .105 in the World Series, including a record 0-for-23 at one point. The question seemed to become, "How badly does Kelly want it?"

Gruber is a high fastball hitter, but there were times last season when he was flat-out overpowered. He has never drawn many walks even when he was having his best seasons, but last year he was worse than ever, with only 26 bases-on-balls. Opposing moundsmen could get ahead in the count and then get Gruber to chase their pitch.

BASERUNNING:

Gruber has the tools to be a solid baserunner. He has pretty good speed and has never been one to back away from a collision. He'll take the extra base when he gets the chance. However, he'll never be confused with the guys at the top of the order.

FIELDING:

Gruber makes some excellent plays, but there have been times during his career when his glove work has been too weak and his arm too erratic. The end result is that he can make big plays but miss the little ones.

OVERALL:

Can the old Gruber reemerge? If so, he'd be back at the level of a player who threatens 30 homers and 100 RBI seasons. Though 1992's poor performance was blamed on injuries, the skepticism runs deeper than that.

KELLY GRUBER

Position: 3B
Bats: R **Throws:** R
Ht: 6' 0" **Wt:** 185

Opening Day Age: 31
Born: 2/26/62 in Bellaire, TX
ML Seasons: 9

Overall Statistics

	G	AB	R	H	D	T	HR	RBI	SB	BB	SO	AVG
1992	120	446	42	102	16	3	11	43	7	26	72	.229
Career	921	3094	421	800	145	24	114	434	80	195	493	.259

Where He Hits the Ball

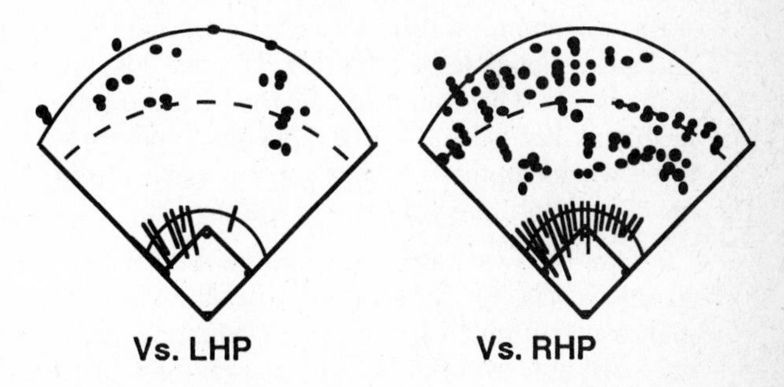

1992 Situational Stats

	AB	H	HR	RBI	AVG		AB	H	HR	RBI	AVG
Home	211	51	7	28	.242	LHP	107	26	3	10	.243
Road	235	51	4	15	.217	RHP	339	76	8	33	.224
Day	130	25	1	10	.192	Sc Pos	113	27	3	30	.239
Night	316	77	10	33	.244	Clutch	72	17	1	8	.236

1992 Rankings (American League)

- 5th in lowest batting average on the road (.217)
- 6th in lowest percentage of pitches taken (45.5%)

CY YOUNG STUFF

PITCHING:

For the second straight season, Juan Guzman had one of the highest winning percentages in baseball and continued to establish himself as one of the best pitchers in the game. The two don't always go hand-in-hand. A young pitcher might look good most of the time, pitch in tough luck, finish barely above .500 -- and everyone raves about him. Well, Guzman is 26-8 in two seasons and the dominating record isn't deceptive.

Guzman doesn't have many secrets. Basically, he goes all out until there's nothing left. He completed only one of 28 starts in 1992, averaging less than seven innings per start. He relies mostly on a blazing fastball which has been clocked in the mid-90s and a hard slider. He cut down on his walks per inning a little bit last season, but he's still wild enough to be effective. The one concern is his health. Guzman broke down with shoulder problems last year after his 12-2 start and spent three weeks on the disabled list. He wasn't fully recovered until the very end of the season.

Guzman throws hard enough that his fastball seems to rise, giving a little hop at the end that makes it that much harder to hit. Opponents hit only six homers off him and he was almost as hard on lefties as right-handed batters.

HOLDING RUNNERS AND FIELDING:

Guzman didn't make any errors last season, but that doesn't mean he's a classic fielder. His motion leaves him out of position to make many plays. Though being a flyball pitcher reduces his chances, Guzman's assist total was still uncommonly low (eight). His move to first base is adequate; he allowed 27 steals in 35 attempts last year.

OVERALL:

Remembering that Guzman wasn't on a major league roster after the 1990 season, his success is pretty surprising. But he's established himself as one of the elite pitchers in the game. The one question that remains is whether his hard-throwing style will leave him vulnerable to injury.

JUAN GUZMAN

Position: SP
Bats: R **Throws:** R
Ht: 5'11" **Wt:** 195

Opening Day Age: 26
Born: 10/28/66 in Santo Domingo, Dominican Republic
ML Seasons: 2

Overall Statistics

	W	L	ERA	G	GS	Sv	IP	H	R	BB	SO	HR
1992	16	5	2.64	28	28	0	180.2	135	56	72	165	6
Career	26	8	2.79	51	51	0	319.1	233	109	138	288	12

How Often He Throws Strikes

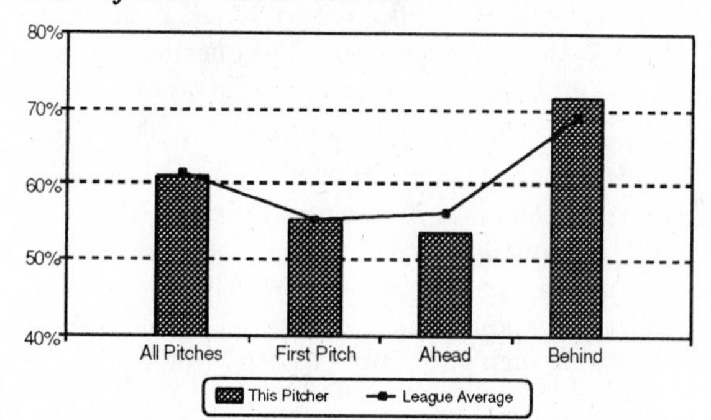

1992 Situational Stats

	W	L	ERA	Sv	IP		AB	H	HR	RBI	AVG
Home	7	2	2.89	0	84.0	LHB	323	69	1	16	.214
Road	9	3	2.42	0	96.2	RHB	329	66	5	32	.201
Day	4	3	3.07	0	67.1	Sc Pos	156	31	2	39	.199
Night	12	2	2.38	0	113.1	Clutch	41	5	0	2	.122

1992 Rankings (American League)

- 1st in lowest slugging percentage allowed (.275), least home runs allowed per 9 innings (.30) and least GDPs induced per 9 innings (.35)
- 2nd in wild pitches (14), lowest batting average allowed (.207), most pitches thrown per batter (4.07) and most strikeouts per 9 innings (8.2)
- 3rd in winning percentage (.762)
- Led the Blue Jays in ERA (2.64), strikeouts (165), wild pitches, balks (2), highest strikeout/walk ratio (2.3), lowest batting average allowed, lowest slugging percentage allowed and lowest on-base percentage allowed (.286)

STOPPER

TOM HENKE

Position: RP
Bats: R **Throws:** R
Ht: 6' 5" **Wt:** 225

Opening Day Age: 35
Born: 12/21/57 in Kansas City, MO
ML Seasons: 11

PITCHING:

For seven straight seasons Tom Henke has saved at least 20 games, and he was again the main contributor to the deepest bullpen in baseball last season. He blew only three save opportunities all year. Manager Cito Gaston used Henke very consistently, having him pitch exactly one inning in all but six of his appearances. His strikeouts were down a bit last season but he still averaged almost 7.5 per nine innings. He also stayed healthy for the entire season, which allowed his main bullpen co-worker, Duane Ward, to play a consistent role as well.

Henke doesn't make it easy for a batter. He'll climb the ladder, throwing a series of fastballs, each slightly higher than the previous one, and then throw a split-fingered fastball that will drop out of the strike zone while the batter swings above it. He doesn't use the split-fingered pitch often, making it very difficult for a batter to recognize and lay off it. Henke has enough discipline to mix up his pitches, working in a slider just to show off a breaking pitch from time to time. Henke's control slipped a bit last season, more noticeably against lefties, but most of the time he'll get ahead of the hitter and leave him with little idea of what's coming next.

HOLDING RUNNERS AND FIELDING:

Henke doesn't have a good pickoff move or a quick delivery, but he's usually pitching in close games when opponents aren't likely to steal. His hard fastball also keeps them from getting a huge jump. Because most of his outs are strikeouts and fly balls, he doesn't get many fielding chances.

OVERALL:

A free agent at the end of last season, Henke seemed unlikely to return to the Jays, who have another potentially great closer in Ward. Wherever Henke ends up, he seems a good bet for 30-plus saves. However, he's at a dangerous age (35).

Overall Statistics

	W	L	ERA	G	GS	Sv	IP	H	R	BB	SO	HR
1992	3	2	2.26	57	0	34	55.2	40	19	22	46	5
Career	32	30	2.64	487	0	220	623.0	477	200	198	695	49

How Often He Throws Strikes

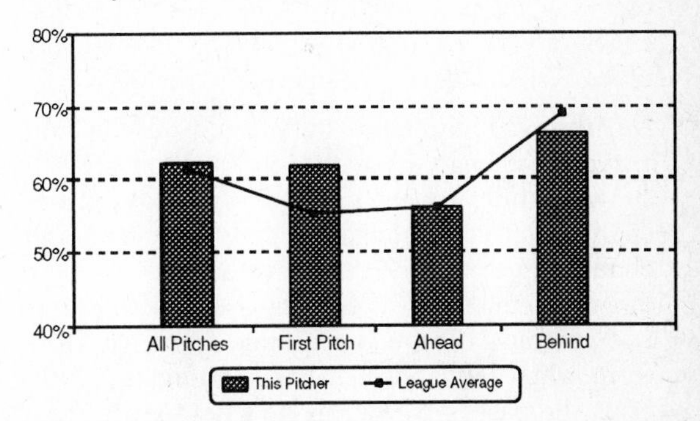

1992 Situational Stats

	W	L	ERA	Sv	IP		AB	H	HR	RBI	AVG
Home	2	0	2.48	19	29.0	LHB	105	20	2	13	.190
Road	1	2	2.03	15	26.2	RHB	98	20	3	6	.204
Day	1	1	2.25	8	20.0	Sc Pos	53	12	2	16	.226
Night	2	1	2.27	26	35.2	Clutch	126	28	4	14	.222

1992 Rankings (American League)

- 2nd in save percentage (91.9%)
- 5th in saves (34) and lowest batting average allowed in relief (.197)
- 6th in save opportunities (37)
- 8th in games finished (50)
- 9th in most strikeouts per 9 innings in relief (7.4)
- Led the Blue Jays in saves, games finished, save opportunities, save percentage, lowest batting average allowed in relief and least baserunners allowed per 9 innings in relief (10.0)

TOUGH ON LEFTIES

JIMMY KEY

Position: SP
Bats: R **Throws:** L
Ht: 6' 1" **Wt:** 185

Opening Day Age: 31
Born: 4/22/61 in Huntsville, AL
ML Seasons: 9

PITCHING:

Jimmy Key had another pretty good season in 1992, but it wasn't enough to keep him among the Big Three in the Jays postseason rotation. Key had been pitching very well (5-1 in September), but David Cone's arrival did him in. Key bided his time and wound up as one of Toronto's stars in the World Series. The lefty took Game 4 as a starter, then won the clincher, Game 6, in relief.

With 13 wins last year, Key has a streak of eight straight seasons with a dozen or more victories. He can be counted on to pitch every fifth day and provide a look that's different from the standard fare. He's a finesse pitcher who can push a batter off the plate with an inside fastball, then throw a breaking pitch that will nip the outside corner. He'll rarely work an opponent the same way twice.

Key throws four pitches, but his mid-80s fastball, curve and change-up are the important ones. He'll show a slider to get a batter off balance, and changes speeds enough so that the curve and change-up don't look the same each time he throws them. Key was especially tough on lefties last season (.176), a big change from his 1991 form when lefthanders batted .286 against him. Over the past five seasons, he's held lefties to a .209 mark.

HOLDING RUNNERS AND FIELDING:

Key keeps runners close by making them know he's watching. His numerous throws to first help make up for an ordinary pickoff move. Key fields his position very well, with a follow-through that leaves him in position for hard grounders and bunts down the baselines.

OVERALL:

If Cone stays with the Jays, Key is probably limited to the Jays' number-four starter in 1993. That would make him one of the best number-four starters in the game. However, Key, like Cone, is a free agent who might not return. The Blue Jays were expected to make a big effort to retain him.

Overall Statistics

	W	L	ERA	G	GS	Sv	IP	H	R	BB	SO	HR
1992	13	13	3.53	33	33	0	216.2	205	88	59	117	24
Career	116	81	3.42	317	250	10	1695.2	1624	710	404	944	165

How Often He Throws Strikes

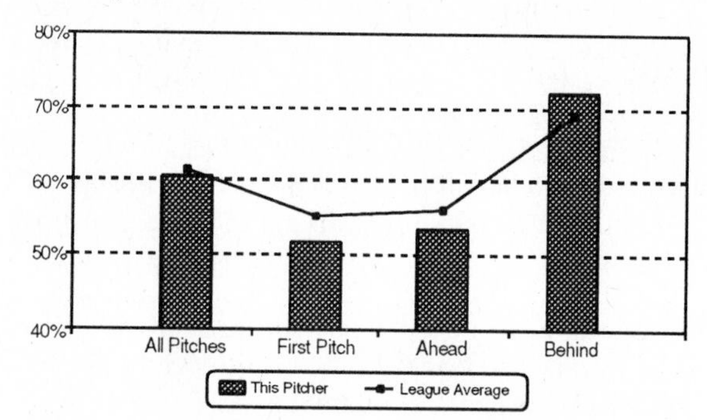

1992 Situational Stats

	W	L	ERA	Sv	IP		AB	H	HR	RBI	AVG
Home	7	5	3.35	0	104.2	LHB	131	23	2	8	.176
Road	6	8	3.70	0	112.0	RHB	697	182	22	73	.261
Day	1	3	3.83	0	56.1	Sc Pos	155	41	6	56	.265
Night	12	10	3.42	0	160.1	Clutch	57	18	4	5	.316

1992 Rankings (American League)

- → 1st in lowest batting average allowed vs. left-handed batters (.176)
- → 5th in least GDPs induced per 9 innings (.46)
- → 7th in most run support per 9 innings (5.4)
- → 8th in shutouts (2) and home runs allowed (24)
- → 9th in lowest on-base percentage allowed (.298)
- → 10th in least baserunners allowed per 9 innings (11.1)
- → Led the Blue Jays in losses (13), shutouts, home runs allowed and lowest batting average allowed vs. left-handed batters

HITTING:

One reason that Manny Lee's position in the lineup had been tenuous until last year was his inability to get on base. The Jays didn't have him in the lineup for his offensive skills, but Lee had the untenable combination of a low average and a poor eye at the plate. Was it too much to ask him to reach base, somehow, 30 percent of the time?

Lee showed marked improvement in this area last season, raising his average from .234 in 1991 to .263 in '92. Despite having about 50 fewer at-bats, he more than doubled his walk total -- from 24 to 50. In fact, he was fifth on the team in walks. Lee showed more discipline at the plate and seemed to understand that everyone was better off if he slapped the ball instead of hitting lazy fly balls.

A switch-hitter, Lee has hit better against lefties throughout his career -- until 1992. when he batted .284 against righthanders and only .212 against lefties. This improvement bodes well for his career because the Jays face righthanders much of the time. Lee is an opposite-field hitter from both sides of the plate; the little power that he does show tends to be generated from the right side.

BASERUNNING:

Lee has some speed but has never put it to use as a basestealer. Maybe he should; over the last three years, he's 16-for-21 (76 percent). He's pretty good at going from first to third.

FIELDING:

Lee cut down his error total markedly last season and seems especially at home playing on artificial turf. He has good range and a good arm, though sometimes he takes his throws for granted and makes life difficult for the first baseman.

OVERALL:

The Jays aren't talking as much about Eddie Zosky these days. Though Lee was a free agent, Toronto seemed very anxious to keep him around. He's made improvements in his game, and it'll be interesting to see if he keeps getting better at the plate. Whatever improvement he makes is a plus for the Jays -- or for a new team.

MANUEL LEE

Position: SS
Bats: B **Throws:** R
Ht: 5' 9" **Wt:** 166

Opening Day Age: 27
Born: 6/17/65 in San Pedro de Macoris, Dominican Republic
ML Seasons: 8

Overall Statistics

	G	AB	R	H	D	T	HR	RBI	SB	BB	SO	AVG
1992	128	396	49	104	10	1	3	39	6	50	73	.263
Career	753	2152	231	547	67	17	16	199	26	158	426	.254

Where He Hits the Ball

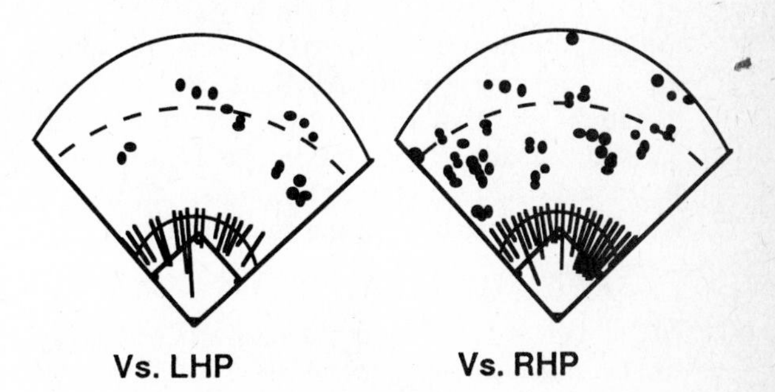

1992 Situational Stats

	AB	H	HR	RBI	AVG		AB	H	HR	RBI	AVG
Home	184	41	1	18	.223	LHP	118	25	0	12	.212
Road	212	63	2	21	.297	RHP	278	79	3	27	.284
Day	114	26	0	7	.228	Sc Pos	94	31	1	37	.330
Night	282	78	3	32	.277	Clutch	62	13	0	3	.210

1992 Rankings (American League)

- 1st in lowest batting average vs. left-handed pitchers (.212) and lowest slugging percentage vs. left-handed pitchers (.246)
- 10th in batting average with runners in scoring position (.330)
- Led the Blue Jays in sacrifice bunts (8) and batting average on a 3-1 count (.500)
- Led AL shortstops in batting average with runners in scoring position

HITTING:

The Jays thought about easing Candy Maldonado out of the lineup when the 1992 season started, but he put together one of his best campaigns since breaking into the majors in 1981. Maldonado wound up playing on his sixth division winner over the past 10 seasons, and his first world champion. He's now helped the Dodgers, Giants and Blue Jays win two division crowns each.

Maldonado is a low-ball hitter who can be fooled by breaking pitches and blown away with high heat. Still, it takes better-than-average stuff to quiet his bat, and he can be especially tough during hot streaks that he tends to have once or twice during his good seasons. Last year, for example, he batted over .350 in July and followed that by hitting eight of his 20 homers in August. His strong pace after the All-Star Game was one of the reasons that Toronto was able to hold off Milwaukee and Baltimore in the final weeks. Maldonado had a career high in walks last season and also a career-best hitting steak of 15 games.

BASERUNNING:

Maldonado's never been much of a basestealing threat, with a career average barely better than 50 percent. He went 2-for-4 last season. Maldonado isn't quick out of the batters box, and the thing that keeps him from grounding into more double plays is his propensity to strike out instead.

FIELDING:

Teams run on Maldonado because they know his arm isn't accurate. He had 13 assists but contributed to only two double plays. He sometimes has trouble going back for balls, and -- as in Game 6 of the World Series -- will make a spectacular-looking play that would be routine for someone with a more polished glove.

OVERALL:

The Jays are a team with talented young outfield prospects, so if free agent Maldonado stays with them, it's likely there will be someone nipping at his heels for playing time. He may hook up with another club who wants a guy with a reputation as a winner.

CANDY MALDONADO

Position: LF
Bats: R **Throws:** R
Ht: 6' 0" **Wt:** 195

Opening Day Age: 32
Born: 9/5/60 in Humacao, Puerto Rico
ML Seasons: 12

Overall Statistics

	G	AB	R	H	D	T	HR	RBI	SB	BB	SO	AVG
1992	137	489	64	133	25	4	20	66	2	59	112	.272
Career	1196	3603	437	928	199	16	124	541	32	316	725	.258

Where He Hits the Ball

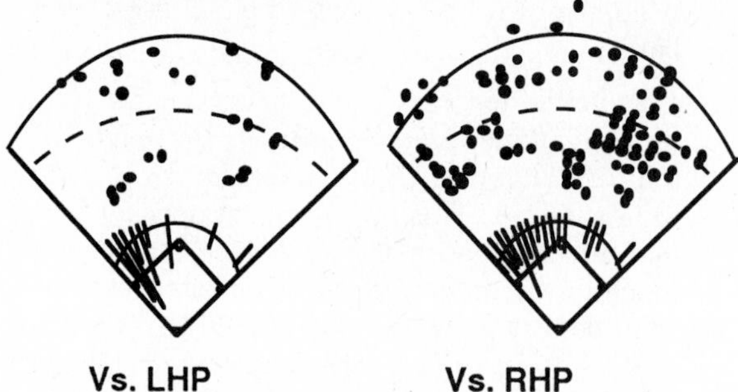

1992 Situational Stats

	AB	H	HR	RBI	AVG		AB	H	HR	RBI	AVG
Home	219	55	8	32	.251	LHP	117	34	4	16	.291
Road	270	78	12	34	.289	RHP	372	99	16	50	.266
Day	151	33	3	14	.219	Sc Pos	115	29	2	33	.252
Night	338	100	17	52	.296	Clutch	67	19	2	9	.284

1992 Rankings (American League)

- Did not rank near the top or bottom in any category

WORKHORSE

PITCHING:

In recent years the Blue Jays needed a full-fledged staff leader, someone who could win a bunch of games and set an example for his teammates with ferocity and talent. That's why they broke the bank to sign Jack Morris when he became a free agent. Morris didn't disappoint. You could point to his 4.04 ERA and say that Morris got a lot of run support from his teammates to make his 21-6 record possible. But the truth is that Morris was as nasty as he needed to be. He was at his best during the final two months, going 9-2 as the division race tightened. He surprisingly went winless in postseason play, but by then he'd clearly earned his keep.

Morris will be 38 years old before the 1993 season is six weeks old, but he has been able to win with some of the same stuff that made him the most consistent starting pitcher of the 1980s. He has a good fastball and a better split-fingered pitch. He throws two kinds of change-ups: a palm ball that has the same action as the splitter except at a slower speed, and a very slow change that he sometimes lobs to the plate to set up his other pitches. At his best, Morris makes quick work of opponents, getting them to go after his first or second pitch. Likewise, deep counts tend to be a sign of trouble.

HOLDING RUNNERS AND FIELDING:

Morris has a high leg kick and has been pretty easy to steal against over the years. Although he allowed 22 steals last year, 16 others were caught -- a fine ratio. He's always been a nimble fielder, with only one error in 95 chances over the past two seasons.

OVERALL:

Morris took another big step last season toward establishing himself as a Hall of Famer. He needs 63 more victories to reach the 300 mark, which might be beyond his grasp. But you can bet that Morris is looking at that magic number, with two straight World Series rings on his hand.

JACK MORRIS

Position: SP
Bats: R **Throws:** R
Ht: 6' 3" **Wt:** 200

Opening Day Age: 37
Born: 5/16/55 in St. Paul, MN
ML Seasons: 16

Overall Statistics

	W	L	ERA	G	GS	Sv	IP	H	R	BB	SO	HR
1992	21	6	4.04	34	34	0	240.2	222	114	80	132	18
Career	237	168	3.73	499	477	0	3530.2	3215	1603	1258	2275	357

How Often He Throws Strikes

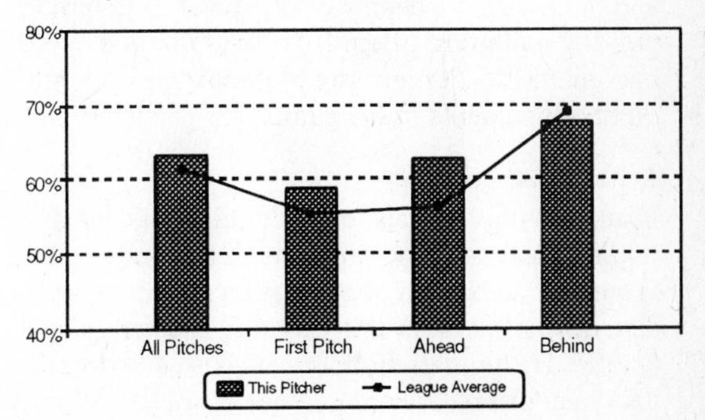

1992 Situational Stats

	W	L	ERA	Sv	IP		AB	H	HR	RBI	AVG
Home	11	2	3.09	0	128.0	LHB	460	121	10	57	.263
Road	10	4	5.11	0	112.2	RHB	442	101	8	50	.229
Day	7	3	4.18	0	92.2	Sc Pos	201	52	2	77	.259
Night	14	3	3.95	0	148.0	Clutch	106	22	2	12	.208

1992 Rankings (American League)

- 1st in wins (21)
- 2nd in winning percentage (.778)
- 3rd in hit batsmen (10), runners caught stealing (16), most run support per 9 innings (6.0) and highest ERA on the road (5.11)
- Led the Blue Jays in wins, games started (34), complete games (6), innings pitched (240.2), hits allowed (222), batters faced (1,005), walks allowed (80), hit batsmen, most pitches thrown (3,566), runners caught stealing, GDPs induced (15), winning percentage, highest groundball/flyball ratio (1.4), lowest stolen base percentage allowed (57.9%), least pitches thrown per batter (3.55) and most run support per 9 innings

HITTING:

The numbers didn't look much different, but John Olerud showed some improvement last season. In 1991, Olerud cracked 30 doubles, hit 17 homers, scored 64 runs, drove in 68, and drew 68 walks over 454 at-bats. In 1992, he batted four more times, and the totals were 28 doubles, 16 homers, 68 runs, 66 RBI, 70 BB. But after striking out 84 times in 1991, Olerud reduced his strikeout total to 61. Largely as a result of making better contact, he improved his batting average from .256 to .284.

Olerud is a pure hitter in the sense that he can spray line drives to all parts of the field and make it look very easy. He can go deep to left or right, and the Jays have been working on getting him to pull the ball more often. If he does that, he could become a 25-homer guy without making any other adjustments in his game.

BASERUNNING:

You draw the conclusion: Olerud didn't hit any triples last season. He bats left-handed. He grounded into more double plays than anyone else on the team. Is this guy a speedster? Not a chance. He lumbers from base to base and doesn't take many risks. He did get his first major-league stolen base last year.

FIELDING:

Olerud has average range and pretty good hands. He's been tested over the past couple of years by Manny Lee and Kelly Gruber at shortstop and third, and has probably saved a couple of errors with his glove. He's not Don Mattingly, but he doesn't cost the Jays in the field.

OVERALL:

It would be nice to see Olerud as an automatic entry in the Jays lineup; that would be a sure sign that he's become invaluable to the team. However, Toronto still seems inclined to rest him against the tough lefties. Still, he's a fine player who makes a solid contribution to winning. He hasn't put up the numbers of his predecessor, Fred McGriff, but the Jays are pleased with his progress.

JOHN OLERUD

Position: 1B
Bats: L **Throws:** L
Ht: 6' 5" **Wt:** 218

Opening Day Age: 24
Born: 8/5/68 in Seattle, WA
ML Seasons: 4

Overall Statistics

	G	AB	R	H	D	T	HR	RBI	SB	BB	SO	AVG
1992	138	458	68	130	28	0	16	66	1	70	61	.284
Career	394	1278	177	344	73	2	47	182	1	195	221	.269

Where He Hits the Ball

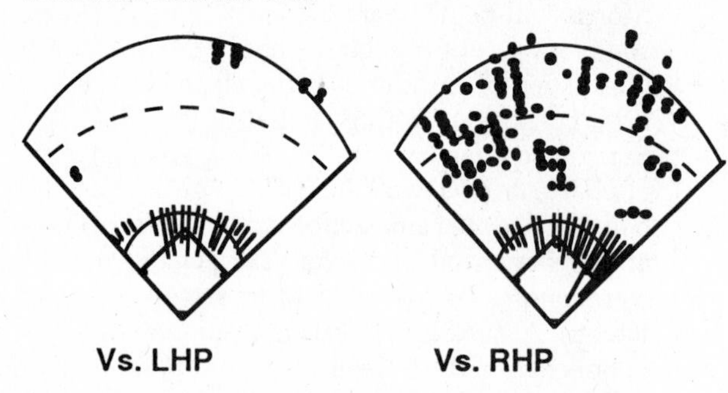

1992 Situational Stats

	AB	H	HR	RBI	AVG		AB	H	HR	RBI	AVG
Home	231	61	4	28	.264	LHP	97	25	3	15	.258
Road	227	69	12	38	.304	RHP	361	105	13	51	.291
Day	134	43	4	20	.321	Sc Pos	120	26	3	48	.217
Night	324	87	12	46	.269	Clutch	72	26	3	14	.361

1992 Rankings (American League)

- 5th in batting average in the clutch (.361)
- Led the Blue Jays in intentional walks (11), GDPs (15), batting average on the road (.304) and highest percentage of swings put into play (50.0%)
- Led AL first basemen in highest groundball/flyball ratio (1.5) and batting average in the clutch

PITCHING:

Whether Dave Stieb can ever regain his form after the back and shoulder problems that have hampered him in recent seasons is an interesting question. The Jays seem to have so much pitching that his comeback isn't vital to their current fortunes. But Stieb meant so much to the team in its early years of contention that many folks would like to see him thrive again.

Stieb was in the Toronto rotation for part of last season and worked out of the bullpen from time to time, starting 14 games and relieving in seven. No matter what the situation -- home or away, left or right -- his statistics were rather ordinary. His strikeout and walk totals were about the same and he allowed more than one hit per inning. His slider no longer has the sharp bite of previous years and his fastball has lost some zip. Opponents tended to figure out Stieb rather easily the second or third time through the order.

Here's an interesting statistical comparison: Reliever Duane Ward pitched five more innings than Stieb in 1992. Yet Stieb yielded 32 extra-base hits to Ward's 17. You can make the argument that it's unfair to compare a swingman to a short reliever, but the fact is that Stieb just didn't have much to show for 1992.

HOLDING RUNNERS AND FIELDING:

Stieb's always been a pretty good fielder dating back to his college days when he was an outfielder at Southern Illinois. His move to first has never been considered especially good but runners seldom get a good jump on him. Last year he allowed only three stolen bases with six caught stealing.

OVERALL:

It would be a surprise if free agent Stieb plays a major role for the Jays in '93. But he's won 174 games in his career and, even if it doesn't happen in Toronto, you have to assume that Stieb will get a couple of chances to prove that he still has what it takes.

DAVE STIEB

Position: SP/RP
Bats: R **Throws:** R
Ht: 6' 1" **Wt:** 195

Opening Day Age: 35
Born: 7/22/57 in Santa Ana, CA
ML Seasons: 14

Overall Statistics

	W	L	ERA	G	GS	Sv	IP	H	R	BB	SO	HR
1992	4	6	5.04	21	14	0	96.1	98	58	43	45	9
Career	174	132	3.39	420	405	1	2823.0	2487	1177	1003	1631	218

How Often He Throws Strikes

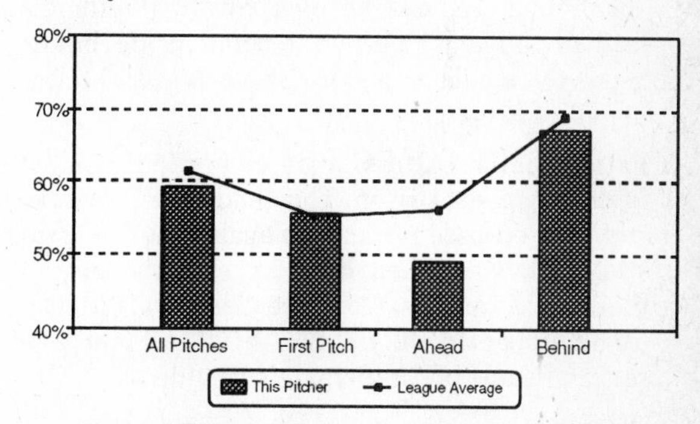

1992 Situational Stats

	W	L	ERA	Sv	IP		AB	H	HR	RBI	AVG
Home	2	4	5.53	0	57.0	LHB	172	48	4	34	.279
Road	2	2	4.35	0	39.1	RHB	185	50	5	24	.270
Day	1	1	5.87	0	23.0	Sc Pos	90	29	2	48	.322
Night	3	5	4.79	0	73.1	Clutch	22	5	2	6	.227

1992 Rankings (American League)

- Led Blue Jays in most GDPs induced per GDP situation (13.3%)

PITCHING:

Just when people were starting to say nice things about how Todd Stottlemyre had arrived on the scene as a front-line pitcher, he took a step backward with a rather ordinary 1992. He posted a winning record for the second time in his career (12-11), but put together a batch of rather ordinary statistics -- 4.50 ERA, 20 homers allowed in 174 innings, 32 walks and only 21 strikeouts in 284 at-bats facing left-handed batters.

Stottlemyre is at his best when he's using all three of his pitches -- fastball, curve and slider -- but the knock on him is that he sometimes relies on his fastball too much. If one of the other pitches isn't working at the start of the game, he seems to abandon it. He can be overpowering with the fastball and he isn't afraid to come inside, but he needs to be encouraged to keep using, and refining all of his pitches.

Patient lefty batters were rewarded against Stottlemyre last season. They had a .282 average and .355 on-base percentage against him. Meanwhile, he was taken deep by righthanders 14 times in 385 at-bats. Compare that to Jack Morris (eight homers in 442 righty at-bats) and you get a sense of some of Stottlemyre's troubles.

HOLDING RUNNERS AND FIELDING:

Opponents have felt that they can run on Stottlemyre; he permitted 17 steals last year in 20 attempts. He needs to do a better job of fielding bunts and grounders. These are two areas where he could show some improvement.

OVERALL:

Like Jimmy Key, Stottlemyre was exiled from the rotation during the Toronto postseason. Though his fine job in relief (one run in 7.1 innings) confirmed his talents, he's probably the one incumbent pitcher that Jays newcomers will challenge for a starting spot. Nevertheless, at age 27 he still has to be considered a pitcher who could put together some excellent seasons.

TODD STOTTLEMYRE

Position: SP
Bats: L **Throws:** R
Ht: 6' 3" **Wt:** 195

Opening Day Age: 27
Born: 5/20/65 in Yakima, WA
ML Seasons: 5

Overall Statistics

	W	L	ERA	G	GS	Sv	IP	H	R	BB	SO	HR
1992	12	11	4.50	28	27	0	174.0	175	99	63	98	20
Career	51	51	4.32	150	128	0	821.2	829	423	297	459	85

How Often He Throws Strikes

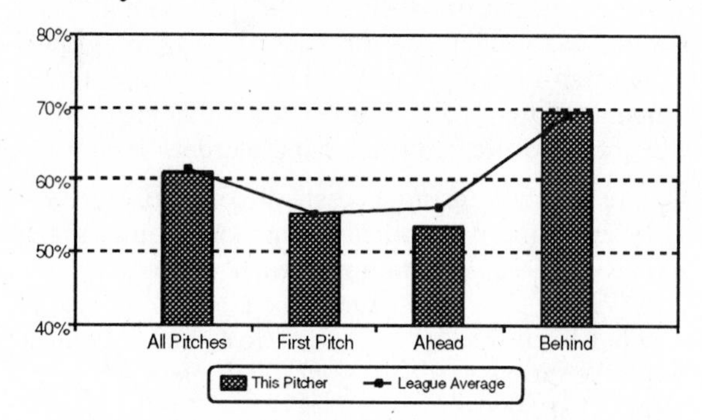

1992 Situational Stats

	W	L	ERA	Sv	IP		AB	H	HR	RBI	AVG
Home	7	5	4.79	0	82.2	LHB	284	80	6	34	.282
Road	5	6	4.24	0	91.1	RHB	385	95	14	54	.247
Day	3	3	5.31	0	39.0	Sc Pos	151	47	6	67	.311
Night	9	8	4.27	0	135.0	Clutch	43	9	1	4	.209

1992 Rankings (American League)

- 2nd in least GDPs induced per 9 innings (.41)
- 3rd in hit batsmen (10), highest stolen base percentage allowed (85.0%), highest ERA at home (4.79) and highest batting average allowed with runners in scoring position (.311)
- 4th in most run support per 9 innings (5.9)
- 5th in highest ERA (4.50)
- 8th in shutouts (2)
- 9th in most home runs allowed per 9 innings (1.0)
- Led the Blue Jays in complete games (6), shutouts and hit batsmen

PITCHING:

Mike Timlin missed the first two months of last season while recovering from elbow surgery and ended the year by fielding Otis Nixon's bunt for the final out of the World Series. That he was out there pitching in that situation meant two things: Toronto had used up its front-line relievers and Timlin had rallied well from some pretty rough times. He was a closer in the low minor leagues who found that position taken in '91 when he broke into the majors. He became a spot starter and middle reliever, the latter role the one in which the Blue Jays used him last season.

Timlin throws a nasty fastball that can shatter bats when it breaks in on the fists of right-handed hitters. One of his problems is that the same pitch looks pretty good to lefties, who had a .407 on-base percentage against him last season. He still needs to develop a better offspeed pitch; doing that would probably allow him to be more effective against lefties. He seems to have the appropriate stuff to pitch to a couple of batters at a time, but it isn't likely that he'll get much more of a chance because of the current depth of the Jays bullpen.

HOLDING RUNNERS AND FIELDING:

"Competent at handling bunts" was the way we described Timlin in last year's edition and the Atlanta Braves certainly learned that the painful way last October. Timlin is an adequate fielder who is athletic enough to spring off the mound and get after balls that are hit near him, which makes up for the fact that he doesn't always finish his delivery in good position. He's only so-so at holding runners.

OVERALL:

Timlin is another one of the players that Toronto has developed without having any open positions in prominent roles. A Blue Jay protected player from expansion, he'll remain with the Jays, but he'll need to come up with another addition to his repertoire to become an effective middleman/spot starter. It wouldn't be a huge surprise to see Timlin flourish if he gets a chance.

MIKE TIMLIN

Position: RP
Bats: R **Throws:** R
Ht: 6' 4" **Wt:** 205

Opening Day Age: 27
Born: 3/10/66 in Midland, TX
ML Seasons: 2

Overall Statistics

	W	L	ERA	G	GS	Sv	IP	H	R	BB	SO	HR
1992	0	2	4.12	26	0	1	43.2	45	23	20	35	0
Career	11	8	3.43	89	3	4	152.0	139	66	70	120	6

How Often He Throws Strikes

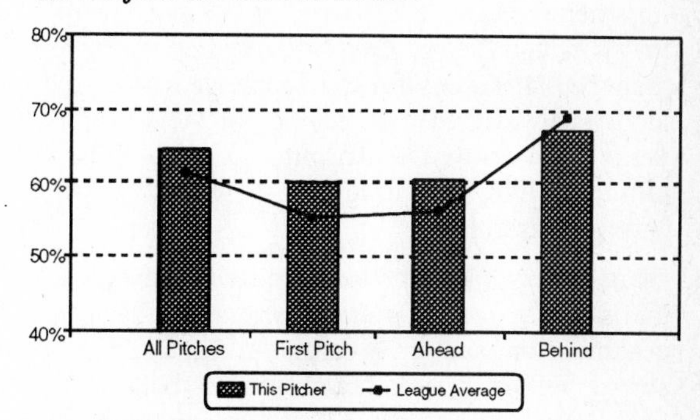

1992 Situational Stats

	W	L	ERA	Sv	IP		AB	H	HR	RBI	AVG
Home	0	2	5.84	1	24.2	LHB	74	23	0	17	.311
Road	0	0	1.89	0	19.0	RHB	92	22	0	12	.239
Day	0	1	1.35	1	13.1	Sc Pos	61	16	0	29	.262
Night	0	1	5.34	0	30.1	Clutch	23	7	0	4	.304

1992 Rankings (American League)

- Did not rank near the top or bottom in any category

PITCHING:

The Blue Jays know by now how lucky they are to have Duane Ward. He's a hard thrower who can pitch in consecutive games without showing any wear on his arm. Ward led the Jays with 79 appearances last season -- 14 more than anyone else on the team -- and he pitched more than 100 innings in relief for the fifth straight season. There aren't too many relievers who can do that kind of work while sporting a 1.95 ERA, which is what Ward did in 1992.

Ward sucked up the seventh and eighth innings of numerous games, marking the transition between the starters and closer Tom Henke. And when Henke needed a break, Ward was able to finish off opponents. He had 12 saves, including the one that clinched the AL East title. He also had more than 100 strikeouts for the fourth year in a row. He's received more accolades from peers over the years than from the Toronto fans, who have turned on him from time to time when he hasn't been successful.

Ward has two overpowering pitches: a fastball that's in the mid-90s and a wicked slider. The combination can be overpowering, especially against lefties. Check this out: lefties batted only .197 against him with a .322 slugging percentage. Meanwhile, they struck out against Ward a third of the time (61 in 183 at-bats). That's pretty powerful stuff, even though Ward allowed all five of his homers to lefties. About the only time that Ward gets into trouble is when his control takes a holiday.

HOLDING RUNNERS AND FIELDING:

Ward has a high leg kick and therefore is pretty easy to steal against. Runners were 14-for-18 against Ward last year. His move to first isn't much better than average. Ward handles the balls he can reach but his follow-through puts him in worse position than most.

OVERALL:

On most teams, Ward would probably be the closer, and the early thinking last winter was that the Jays would let Henke go and promote Ward to the top job. Whether set-up man or closer, he's an extremely valuable reliever.

DUANE WARD

Position: RP
Bats: R **Throws:** R
Ht: 6' 4" **Wt:** 215

Opening Day Age: 28
Born: 5/28/64 in Parkview, NM
ML Seasons: 7

Overall Statistics

	W	L	ERA	G	GS	Sv	IP	H	R	BB	SO	HR
1992	7	4	1.95	79	0	12	101.1	76	27	39	103	5
Career	30	33	3.31	387	2	76	592.1	491	241	256	579	28

How Often He Throws Strikes

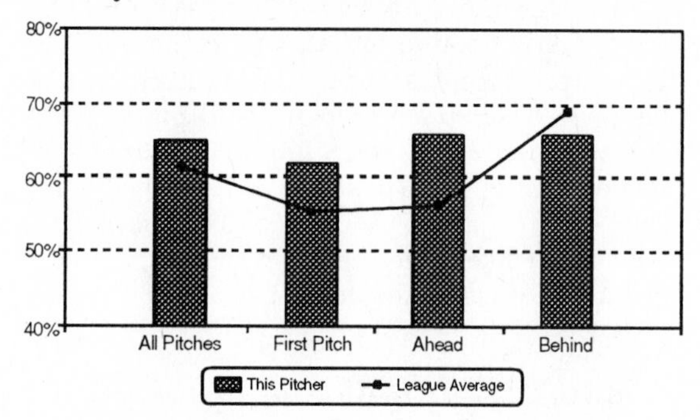

1992 Situational Stats

	W	L	ERA	Sv	IP		AB	H	HR	RBI	AVG
Home	6	1	1.57	6	51.2	LHB	183	36	5	20	.197
Road	1	3	2.36	6	49.2	RHB	184	40	0	12	.217
Day	3	2	2.06	8	35.0	Sc Pos	101	18	3	29	.178
Night	4	2	1.90	4	66.1	Clutch	231	46	4	21	.199

1992 Rankings (American League)

- 1st in holds (25)
- 2nd in games pitched (79) and most strikeouts per 9 innings in relief (9.1)
- 3rd in relief innings (101.1)
- 4th in lowest batting average allowed vs. left-handed batters (.197)
- 6th in relief wins (7)
- Led the Blue Jays in games pitched, holds, blown saves (4), first batter efficiency (.236), lowest batting average allowed in relief with runners on base (.182), lowest percentage of inherited runners scored (30.0%), relief ERA (1.95), relief wins, relief innings and most strikeouts per 9 innings in relief

PITCHING:

The question about David Wells used to be whether to use him out of the bullpen or as a starter. In 1992 the answer seemed to be definitive: Wells belongs in the pen. Used in both roles last year, Wells had a 6.39 ERA for 14 starts and a 3.68 mark for 27 relief appearances. He underscored the fact that he can be a useful reliever with his brilliant work in the World Series -- 4.1 innings of scoreless, one-hit ball, usually in high-pressure situations.

Wells used to be considered a power pitcher, but last year he had barely more than one strikeout every two innings. Once again, the contrast between his starting and relief work was obvious. As a starter Wells seemed intent on pacing himself and averaged only 4.0 strikeouts per nine innings. In relief he cut loose a little more and fanned 5.7 per nine. He often grooved the ball as a starter, permitting 12 of his 16 homers allowed while in a starting role.

Batters who are patient with Wells tend to get a good pitch to hit, and he seemed especially prone to the big inning last season in the games he started. Wells isn't afraid to pitch inside, but he doesn't always take advantage of those purpose pitches. In other words, he'll bust one inside but then come back with a fat pitch out over the plate.

HOLDING RUNNERS AND FIELDING:

Wells has become fairly adept at holding runners, although one could argue that he had a lot of practice in 1992. He gives his catchers a chance by holding the opposition close. He's sometimes a step slow at getting to first base, but otherwise he fields his position pretty well.

OVERALL:

Though he was 14-10 as a starter in 1991, Wells' chances of getting back into the Toronto rotation are now pretty slim. His fine World Series work may have indicated he'll begin this year in the bullpen; it certainly indicated that he can be very effective there, as Toronto's protection of him in the expansion draft clearly showed.

DAVID WELLS

Position: RP/SP
Bats: L **Throws:** L
Ht: 6' 4" **Wt:** 225

Opening Day Age: 29
Born: 5/20/63 in Torrance, CA
ML Seasons: 6

Overall Statistics

	W	L	ERA	G	GS	Sv	IP	H	R	BB	SO	HR
1992	7	9	5.40	41	14	2	120.0	138	84	36	62	16
Career	47	37	3.78	237	69	13	687.1	659	319	201	449	71

How Often He Throws Strikes

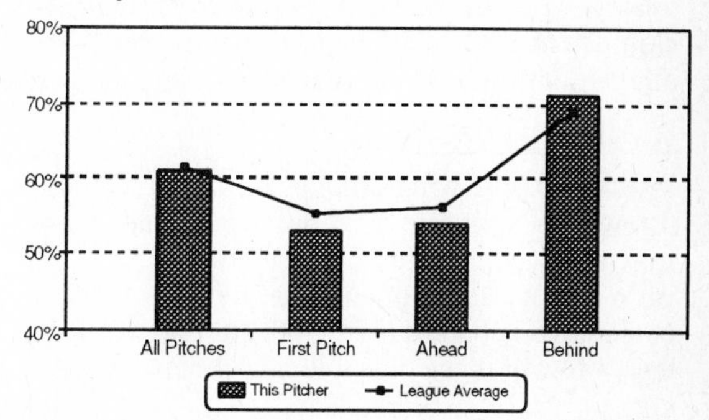

1992 Situational Stats

	W	L	ERA	Sv	IP		AB	H	HR	RBI	AVG
Home	4	3	3.60	1	60.0	LHB	92	27	3	16	.293
Road	3	6	7.20	1	60.0	RHB	386	111	13	60	.288
Day	4	3	6.22	0	46.1	Sc Pos	119	41	2	58	.345
Night	3	6	4.89	2	73.2	Clutch	67	21	1	7	.313

1992 Rankings (American League)

- 3rd in highest batting average allowed vs. right-handed batters (.288)

GREAT RANGE

HITTING:

Devon White brings an odd combination of quality and questions to the top of the Toronto batting order. He had 17 homers and 60 RBIs for the second straight season, but his average slipped from .282 to .248. White had to bat .319 in the final month of the season to even bring his batting mark up that far. He continued to strike out way too often -- 133 times. The Jays keep him as their leadoff batter because he has so much speed.

Speed might not be enough after 1992. White had 14 fewer doubles in 1992 than the previous season and three fewer triples. The switch-hitter struggled terribly from the right side, hitting only .212 with 10 extra-base hits and a .272 on-base average. He batted .348 in the playoffs, but then slumped to a .231 mark in the World Series. All in all, he made his 1991 numbers seem like a fluke.

BASERUNNING:

White can still whiz around the bases. He was thrown out trying to steal only four times in 41 tries and he's hard to double up on the bases. It isn't easy to score 98 runs when your on-base percentage is barely over .300. He created more than a few of those runs with his blazing speed.

FIELDING:

The image of White crashing into SkyDome's center field wall while making a stunning catch and starting what should have been a triple play will be one of the lasting images from last year's World Series. White gets as good a jump as anyone in baseball and doesn't think that a ball can possibly land beyond his reach. He can throw, too. White has won four Gold Gloves in five years; more are on the way.

OVERALL:

The Jays are hoping that White can re-establish himself as more of an offensive weapon -- if not quite like 1991, then at least better than '92. Whether he improves or not, his speed, glove and range in the field will go a long way toward keeping him steadily employed.

DEVON WHITE

Position: CF
Bats: B **Throws:** R
Ht: 6' 2" **Wt:** 182

Opening Day Age: 30
Born: 12/29/62 in Kingston, Jamaica
ML Seasons: 8

Overall Statistics

	G	AB	R	H	D	T	HR	RBI	SB	BB	SO	AVG
1992	153	641	98	159	26	7	17	60	37	47	133	.248
Career	921	3514	545	891	157	41	93	361	193	246	743	.254

Where He Hits the Ball

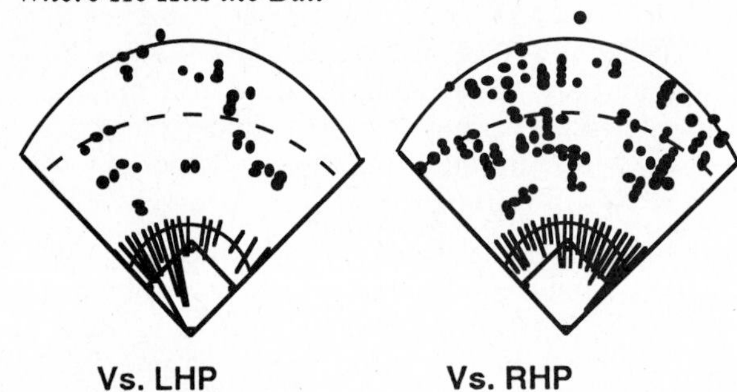

1992 Situational Stats

	AB	H	HR	RBI	AVG		AB	H	HR	RBI	AVG
Home	306	81	7	34	.265	LHP	179	38	5	19	.212
Road	335	78	10	26	.233	RHP	462	121	12	41	.262
Day	193	50	2	13	.259	Sc Pos	136	31	2	39	.228
Night	448	109	15	47	.243	Clutch	90	20	3	11	.222

1992 Rankings (American League)

- 2nd in stolen base percentage (90.2%), lowest batting average vs. left-handed pitchers (.212) and lowest on-base percentage vs. left-handed pitchers (.272)
- 4th in at-bats (641)
- 6th in steals of third (8)
- 7th in triples (7), strikeouts (133) and most pitches seen (2,699)
- 8th in lowest on-base percentage (.303)
- Led the Blue Jays in at-bats, strikeouts, most pitches seen, plate appearances (696) and stolen base percentage
- Led AL center fielders in stolen base percentage

HALL OF FAMER

DAVE WINFIELD

Position: DH/RF
Bats: R **Throws:** R
Ht: 6' 6" **Wt:** 245

Opening Day Age: 41
Born: 10/3/51 in St. Paul, MN
ML Seasons: 19

HITTING:

Toronto picked up 40-year-old Dave Winfield before the 1992 season as a full-time designated hitter and all-around good influence. It was a worthwhile investment from every standpoint they could have imagined. Winfield was second on the club behind Joe Carter in homers and RBI and second to Robby Alomar in average. He became the oldest man ever to drive in 100 runs. The more one saw Winfield play, the more astonishing it was that he missed all of 1989 with a back injury.

Winfield's game improved last season in several areas beyond his increased power numbers. He cut down on his strikeouts and had his highest walk total since playing for the San Diego Padres in 1979. A lot of veterans refuse to acknowledge shortcomings brought on by age. Winfield has learned to adjust. Opposing pitchers know that Winfield doesn't have the bat speed of his younger years and Winfield knows it too. As a result, he seems to be more intent on getting his pitch rather than trying to do too much with the down-and-in fastballs which can put him away.

BASERUNNING:

Though no basestealer, Winfield has good speed. However, it takes him a stride or two longer to reach his top speed, one of the hazards of older age. If you're a second baseman or a shortstop, he's still not a guy that you want to see coming in to break up a double play.

FIELDING:

Winfield used to have excellent range and a fine arm. The range disappeared, and then the arm. Now he's viewed as an offensive weapon who can play passable defense, a DH who plays the outfield only when needed.

OVERALL:

Winfield seems to relish the challenge of performing well at an age when most of his peers have retired. He's one of the few true leaders in baseball, a guy who isn't afraid to share his experiences and always has something to offer -- like an extra-inning double in the final game of the World Series.

Overall Statistics

	G	AB	R	H	D	T	HR	RBI	SB	BB	SO	AVG
1992	156	583	92	169	33	3	26	108	2	82	89	.290
Career	2707	10047	1551	2866	493	83	432	1710	218	1126	1503	.285

Where He Hits the Ball

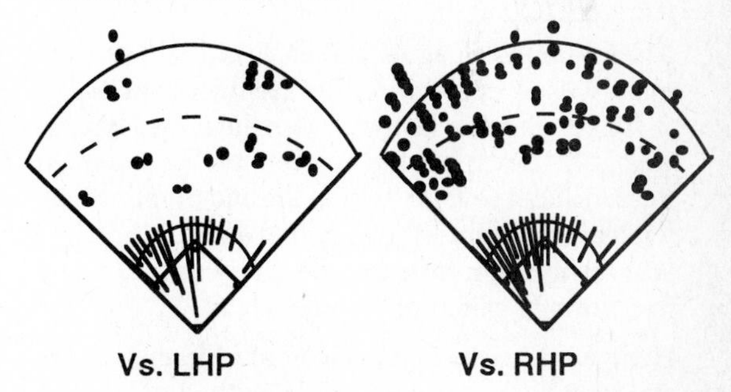

1992 Situational Stats

	AB	H	HR	RBI	AVG		AB	H	HR	RBI	AVG
Home	268	81	13	47	.302	LHP	146	44	8	28	.301
Road	315	88	13	61	.279	RHP	437	125	18	80	.286
Day	175	50	8	27	.286	Sc Pos	165	50	9	82	.303
Night	408	119	18	81	.292	Clutch	70	17	4	12	.243

1992 Rankings (American League)

- 7th in slugging percentage (.491)
- 8th in RBI (108)
- 9th in home runs (26), total bases (286), slugging percentage vs. left-handed pitchers (.527) and slugging percentage vs. right-handed pitchers (.478)
- Led the Blue Jays in doubles (33) and batting average with the bases loaded (.454)
- Led designated hitters in runs scored (92), total bases, walks (82), most pitches seen (2,526), slugging percentage, highest groundball/flyball ratio (1.4), most pitches seen per plate appearance (3.77), slugging percentage vs. right-handed pitchers and highest percentage of pitches taken (58.2%)

PAT HENTGEN

Position: RP
Bats: R **Throws:** R
Ht: 6' 2" **Wt:** 200

Opening Day Age: 24
Born: 11/13/68 in Detroit, Mi
ML Seasons: 2

Overall Statistics

	W	L	ERA	G	GS	Sv	IP	H	R	BB	SO	HR
1992	5	2	5.36	28	2	0	50.1	49	30	32	39	7
Career	5	2	4.99	31	3	0	57.2	54	32	35	42	8

PITCHING, FIELDING & HOLDING RUNNERS:

After a minor-league career in which he was mainly used as a starter, Pat Hentgen was asked to fill a swing role last year with the Blue Jays. He was sent down to the minors twice and then missed about seven weeks at the end of the season with a sore right elbow. In between he pitched acceptably from time to time, but wasn't the guy that Toronto called on to hold a lead.

Hentgen never had pinpoint control in the minors and got himself into trouble with the Jays by throwing too many pitches. One time he needed 50 pitches to get through a two-inning relief stint. A couple of weeks later he threw 63 in two innings. For every six batters he struck out, Hentgen walked five. He'll need to improve those numbers if he wants to be a factor in the majors. He'll also need to improve his ability to hold runners; basestealers were 5-for-5 against him. He played errorless ball last year.

OVERALL:

If Hentgen wants to be more than a solid Triple-A pitcher, he'll need to make some adjustments, particularly with his control. Though he is highly regarded as a prospect, and was thus protected on their 15-man list, the Jays have so many pitchers that you wonder how much patience management will have with him.

BOB MacDONALD

Position: RP
Bats: L **Throws:** L
Ht: 6' 3" **Wt:** 208

Opening Day Age: 27
Born: 4/27/65 in East Orange, NJ
ML Seasons: 3

Overall Statistics

	W	L	ERA	G	GS	Sv	IP	H	R	BB	SO	HR
1992	1	0	4.37	27	0	0	47.1	50	24	16	26	4
Career	4	3	3.48	76	0	0	103.1	101	43	43	50	9

PITCHING, FIELDING & HOLDING RUNNERS:

The Jays didn't have a lot for Bob MacDonald to do last season, so he worked most of his innings in middle relief when the outcome was pretty much decided. He had only one decision and no saves to show for his 27 appearances.

MacDonald is another pitcher who suffers against batters from the opposite side. The southpaw was death on lefties last year, holding them to a .143 average. But the 137 righties he faced batted .336 and pounded him for 16 extra-base hits. By comparison, righthander Juan Guzman faced 357 left-handed batters and allowed only eight extra-base hits. From that it's easy to see why Guzman is a young star and MacDonald is struggling to keep his place in the majors.

MacDonald isn't a hard thrower and needs to have pinpoint control to be useful. He has a pretty good move to first base and pays close attention to runners. He appears to have the makings of a solid defensive player, but hasn't had too much work fielding in the majors.

OVERALL:

Additions to the Jays pitching staff last year pushed MacDonald even further down the pecking order; it didn't seem like he was being groomed to play a big role in their future. But pitching is a funny game, and MacDonald shouldn't be counted out entirely.

ED SPRAGUE

Position: C
Bats: R **Throws:** R
Ht: 6' 2" **Wt:** 215

Opening Day Age: 25
Born: 7/25/67 in Castro Valley, CA
ML Seasons: 2

Overall Statistics

	G	AB	R	H	D	T	HR	RBI	SB	BB	SO	AVG
1992	22	47	6	11	2	0	1	7	0	3	7	.234
Career	83	207	23	55	9	0	5	27	0	22	50	.266

HITTING, FIELDING, BASERUNNING:

If Ed Sprague never gets another hit in a Blue Jay uniform, his Toronto career will be a success. Sprague's two-run, ninth inning pinch hit homer off Jeff Reardon won Game 2 of the World Series and sent the Jays on their way to a World Championship. You could say it was another "gold medal performance" by a Sprague -- but this time for Canada. During the Barcelona Olympics Sprague's wife, American swimmer Kristin Babb-Sprague, won a controversial gold medal in synchronized swimming over Canada's Sylvie Frechette.

Before that big home run, Sprague had a pretty quiet season in a Toronto uniform. The young catcher had spent most of the season at AAA Syracuse and his Toronto action was limited to only 47 at-bats. Sprague finished the season with a .234 average for the Jays, serving primarily as a backup receiver. Sprague has some power potential, but he's not much of a runner and isn't a polished defensive player. His catching skills aren't far below average and will probably improve with time.

OVERALL:

The Jays seem to think that Randy Knorr may be ready to be Pat Borders' backup this year, and have other catching hopefuls like Carlos Delgado. Sprague played only one game at third base in '93, but may get an opportunity there in '93. He was protected in the expansion draft. As the Series homer showed, he has some pop in his bat. Teams will usually make a place for a player like Sprague who can hit.

PAT TABLER

Position: 1B
Bats: R **Throws:** R
Ht: 6' 2" **Wt:** 200

Opening Day Age: 35
Born: 2/2/58 in Hamilton, OH
ML Seasons: 12

Overall Statistics

	G	AB	R	H	D	T	HR	RBI	SB	BB	SO	AVG
1992	49	135	11	34	5	0	0	16	0	11	14	.252
Career	1202	3911	454	1101	190	25	47	512	16	375	559	.282

HITTING, FIELDING, BASERUNNING:

The Jays used Pat Tabler to fill in at four positions last season -- first base, third base, left field and right field -- and he played error-free defense while providing a reasonable amount of offense. In other words, he did the same things that have kept him in the major leagues for 12 seasons.

Tabler is a spray hitter who doesn't have much power or speed. He has limited range in the field and doesn't use his glove as well as he handles the bat. Because of Dave Winfield's arrival, Tabler didn't see much time as the club's DH, which was the main role he filled in the previous season.

Tabler also lost a significant number of the pinch-hit at-bats he'd been receiving. He slipped from 9-for-21 (.429) in 1991 to being hitless in seven pinch-hitting tries last year. Tabler has never had a lot of speed and extended his streak of seasons without a steal to four.

OVERALL:

It's doubtful whether free agent Tabler will get many more chances in the majors. Still, he can hit and he's versatile, so he might be able to last another year or so. The one statistic that Tabler always will be remembered for was his ability to hit with the bases loaded. His career average in those situations is .489 (43 for 88) with 108 RBI.

ORGANIZATION OVERVIEW:

After years of struggle, the Jays won their first World Championship last year. Toronto-developed talent could take a lot of credit -- and not just players like John Olerud and Jimmy Key who have spent their entire careers in the Jay system. General manager Pat Gillick has always had a special gift for spotting good young players in other systems like Juan Guzman and Duane Ward. But last year Toronto brought in some veterans to nail down that title. Does that mark a change in Toronto's philosophy? Probably not; the Jays' system is loaded, and they still seem committed to their young talent.

JUAN de la ROSA

Position: OF **Opening Day Age:** 24
Bats: R **Throws:** R **Born:** 12/1/68 in La Romana, DR
Ht: 6' 1" **Wt:** 168

Recent Statistics

	G	AB	R	H	D	T	HR	RBI	SB	BB	SO	AVG
91 AA Knoxville	122	382	37	82	11	1	4	33	17	17	95	.215
92 AA Knoxville	136	508	68	167	32	12	12	53	16	15	94	.329
92 MLE	136	499	61	158	30	9	11	47	12	11	100	.317

De la Rosa has taken a while to develop. Now 24, he didn't reach the AA level until 1991, and then he batted .215. But in his second year at Knoxville, he caught fire, batting .329 with 56 extra-base hits. De la Rosa has always been a splendid center fielder with great speed, so all he needed to do was start hitting. His walk-strikeout ratio (15 BB, 94 SO) continues to be a matter of concern, however, and he'll have to prove that he wasn't just a one-year wonder.

CARLOS J. DELGADO

Position: C **Opening Day Age:** 20
Bats: L **Throws:** R **Born:** 6/25/72 in Aguadilla, PR
Ht: 6' 3" **Wt:** 206

Recent Statistics

	G	AB	R	H	D	T	HR	RBI	SB	BB	SO	AVG
91 A Myrtle Bch	132	441	72	126	18	2	18	71	9	74	97	.286
91 AAA Syracuse	1	3	0	0	0	0	0	0	0	0	2	.000
92 A Dunedin	133	485	83	157	30	2	30	100	2	59	91	.324

Named Minor League Player of the Year by more than one publication, Delgado destroyed the pitcher-dominated Florida State League (league average .245) last season. He batted .324 with 100 RBI and his 30 homers were more than the entire Miami Miracle club could manage. The league's managers rated him an even better prospect than the Yankees' Brien Taylor, and that's saying something. So why was this man still in Class A? Because his defense still needs work and because the Jays have plenty of catchers at the moment. Delgado has a strong arm, though, and shouldn't take too long to reach the majors.

RANDY KNORR

Position: C **Opening Day Age:** 24
Bats: R **Throws:** R **Born:** 11/12/68 in San Gabriel, CA
Ht: 6' 2" **Wt:** 205

Recent Statistics

	G	AB	R	H	D	T	HR	RBI	SB	BB	SO	AVG
92 AAA Syracuse	61	228	27	62	13	1	11	27	1	17	38	.272
92 AL Toronto	8	19	1	5	0	0	1	2	0	1	5	.263
92 MLE	61	219	20	53	11	0	8	20	0	12	39	.242

Poor Randy Knorr. Last summer the Jays called him up to be their backup catcher, but he promptly got hurt. While recovering, Knorr could monitor Delgado's progress behind the plate, and watch Pat Borders and Ed Sprague starring in the World Series. The Jays definitely like Knorr, who's a fine defensive catcher with some power potential. They just don't have much playing time to offer.

DOMINGO MARTINEZ

Position: 1B **Opening Day Age:** 25
Bats: R **Throws:** R **Born:** 8/4/67 in Santo Domingo, DR
Ht: 6' 2" **Wt:** 185

Recent Statistics

	G	AB	R	H	D	T	HR	RBI	SB	BB	SO	AVG
92 AAA Syracuse	116	438	55	120	22	0	21	62	6	33	95	.274
92 AL Toronto	7	8	2	5	0	0	1	3	0	0	1	.625
92 MLE	116	421	40	103	19	0	17	46	4	24	99	.245

A 25-year-old first baseman, Martinez spent three seasons at the AA level, then two more at AAA, patiently waiting his turn while the Jays promoted numerous other prospects. More than a few people were surprised when the Jays protected Martinez in the expansion draft while exposing the more publicized Juan de la Rosa and Nigel Wilson. Martinez can hit; he's had 55 minor-league homers the last three seasons, including 21 last year. He's also 5-for-8 with a home run at the big-league level. But he's been considered only a one-dimensional slugger, and John Olerud is in his way. Could the Jays be remembering Cecil Fielder when they decided to protect Martinez?

EDDIE ZOSKY

Position: SS **Opening Day Age:** 25
Bats: R **Throws:** R **Born:** 2/10/68 in Whittier, CA
Ht: 6' 0" **Wt:** 170

Recent Statistics

	G	AB	R	H	D	T	HR	RBI	SB	BB	SO	AVG
92 AAA Syracuse	96	342	31	79	11	6	4	38	3	19	53	.231
92 AL Toronto	8	7	1	2	0	1	0	1	0	0	2	.286
92 MLE	96	330	23	67	9	3	3	28	2	14	55	.203

For what seems like forever, the Jays have been expecting Eddie Zosky to push Manuel Lee out of the way and become their regular shortstop. They're still waiting, and with each year Zosky appears to be a bit less of a prospect. He batted only .231 at AAA Syracuse last year, though injuries had a lot to do with that. He has the glove, but it's getting to be make-or-break time.

National League Players

PITCHING:

Most of Steve Avery's "off year" last season was mostly due to illusion, just like his "big year" in 1991. The Cy Young Award winner's annual best friend, run support, had a fickle romance with Avery the past two years. Why would an ERA of 3.38 in 210.1 innings produce an 18-8 record one year and an ERA of 3.20 in 233.2 innings produce a record of 11-11 the next? How about 5.3 runs per game (suspiciously the same as Cy Young candidate and teammate Tom Glavine's 5.3 mark this past year) and 3.9 runs per game the next? And just for good measure, that 3.9 figure includes a game in which the Braves scored 16 runs in the first six innings on September 20.

Though his 1992 postseason (1-2, 5.85) couldn't match 1991's (2-0, 1.53), Avery is a general manager's dream. The former first-round pick has a great fastball, and it's decidedly his favorite pitch. Avery also commands a good curve and change. He'll figure out either when warming up or early in the game which of his breakers is sharpest. When the curve is working best, the change becomes pitch number three. When his change is on, he uses it more than the curve.

A three-season veteran at an age (22) when many hurlers are ready for their first taste of AA, Avery is a prankster in the Atlanta clubhouse. But he puts on his game face on pitching days. His friendly rivalry with fellow aces Glavine and John Smoltz is well-publicized.

HOLDING RUNNERS, FIELDING, HITTING:

Holding runners was a problem for Avery early on last year, and he worked to improve. He'll need to work some more; though he picked off six runners, he permitted a league worst 42 steals. He is a great overall athlete, which shows in his fine hitting and fielding.

OVERALL:

The sky's the limit for Avery. Though the Braves are pretty careful with him, you have to worry about his arm. He's still very young, and heavy usage (233.2 innings for Avery in 1992) is always a concern with a pitcher under 25 years old.

STEVE AVERY

Position: SP
Bats: L **Throws:** L
Ht: 6' 4" **Wt:** 180

Opening Day Age: 22
Born: 4/14/70 in Trenton, MI
ML Seasons: 3

Overall Statistics

	W	L	ERA	G	GS	Sv	IP	H	R	BB	SO	HR
1992	11	11	3.20	35	35	0	233.2	216	95	71	129	14
Career	32	30	3.71	91	90	0	543.0	526	263	181	341	42

How Often He Throws Strikes

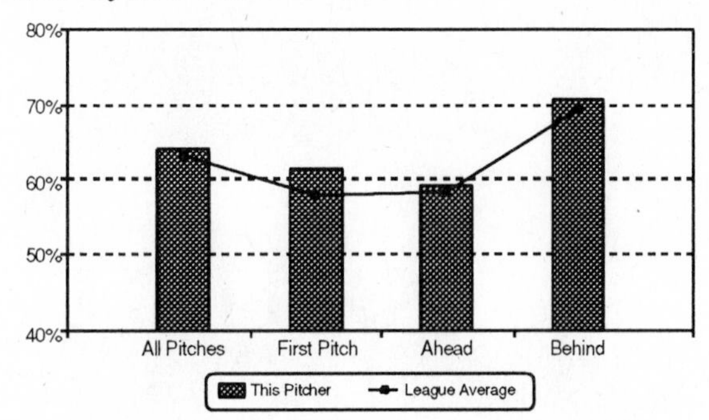

1992 Situational Stats

	W	L	ERA	Sv	IP		AB	H	HR	RBI	AVG
Home	6	4	2.51	0	107.2	LHB	155	40	3	18	.258
Road	5	7	3.79	0	126.0	RHB	723	176	11	61	.243
Day	3	1	1.77	0	35.2	Sc Pos	199	46	2	60	.231
Night	8	10	3.45	0	198.0	Clutch	94	27	1	12	.287

1992 Rankings (National League)

- → 1st in games started (35) and stolen bases allowed (42)
- → 4th in batters faced (969) and runners caught stealing (14)
- → 5th in innings pitched (233.2)
- → 6th in balks (3)
- → 7th in hits allowed (216), most pitches thrown (3,416), lowest strikeout/walk ratio (1.8) and highest stolen base percentage allowed (75.0%)
- → Led the Braves in games started, hits allowed, balks, stolen bases allowed and least pitches thrown per batter (3.53)

HITTING:

The highlight of Rafael Belliard's hitting career was undoubtedly the 1991 World Series when he hit a mighty .375 with a double and four RBI. Belliard's 1991 was entirely a highlight, in fact. It was the first time in his career he had hit for an average respectable enough (.249) to keep his superior glove in the lineup. While Jeff Blauser stalled, Belliard appeared to snatch the everyday shortstop job away.

Unfortunately for Belliard, his bat reverted back to career form last year. The shortstop, who used to battle Sammy Khalifa for Pirate playing time, finds himself back in the role of late-inning defensive sub. Blauser's defense improved so much in Bobby Cox's eyes that he no longer felt the need to sacrifice the offense.

Belliard hits with almost equal ineptitude against pitchers of either hand -- .232 versus lefties and .220 versus righties since 1988. His only appealing split is his average when he swings at the first pitch: .282 last year and .298 over the past five years. But even that is below average. Belliard is a free swinger who is prone to bite on the high fastball. He has developed into a groundball hitter, which one would think would be to his advantage, and is a good bunter.

BASERUNNING:

Belliard is fast and a good baserunner, yet the stolen base has never been a big part of his game. He was unsuccessful in his only attempt of the '92 season, but is 38-for-49 in his career.

FIELDING:

This is Belliard's forte. Nevertheless, while Blauser's fielding improved last season, Belliard's seemed to drop just slightly. His range was not quite up to his usual standard and he committed 14 errors in 860-plus defensive innings at shortstop, below average.

OVERALL:

The smart money says this is Belliard's last year for a full page report in this publication. He turned 31 as the Braves concluded their second straight World Series, and the skills he offers are not the kind that improve with age. Look for a big step forward from co-shortstop Blauser, but nothing more than a spot role for Belliard.

RAFAEL BELLIARD

Position: SS
Bats: R **Throws:** R
Ht: 5' 6" **Wt:** 160

Opening Day Age: 31
Born: 10/24/61 in Pueblo Nuevo, Dominican Republic
ML Seasons: 11

Overall Statistics

	G	AB	R	H	D	T	HR	RBI	SB	BB	SO	AVG
1992	144	285	20	60	6	1	0	14	0	14	43	.211
Career	777	1689	171	377	31	12	1	113	38	121	274	.223

Where He Hits the Ball

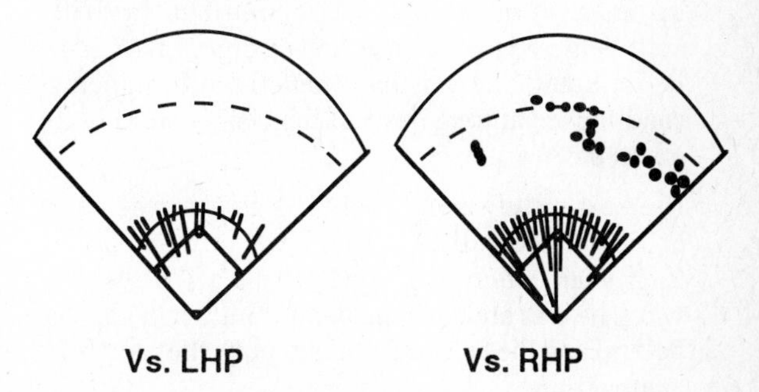

1992 Situational Stats

	AB	H	HR	RBI	AVG		AB	H	HR	RBI	AVG
Home	125	25	0	5	.200	LHP	61	12	0	3	.197
Road	160	35	0	9	.219	RHP	224	48	0	11	.214
Day	90	16	0	5	.178	Sc Pos	67	12	0	14	.179
Night	195	44	0	9	.226	Clutch	35	8	0	2	.229

1992 Rankings (National League)

- 4th in sacrifice bunts (13)
- Led the Braves in sacrifice bunts

PITCHING:

After a late-season trade to the Braves near the end of the 1991 schedule, Mike Bielecki's Atlanta role was up in the air in spring training. He was battling Pete Smith for the number-five spot in the rotation, and going into the final couple of weeks, he was losing. As it turned out, Bielecki cranked it up a notch, made the staff, sent Pete Smith to the minors, and won the battle. But after Bielecki tore a ligament in his right elbow shortly after the All-Star break, Smith came back and went 7-0 in his absence. So Bielecki might have lost the war.

Pitching out of the pen only five times in 1992, Bielecki was a regular in the Braves' rotation and was throwing possibly the best ball of his career, including his 18-7 year in 1989. Bielecki serves up an assortment of junk: a mid-80s fastball, split-fingered pitch, curve and change. Like Charlie Leibrandt, he may have benefitted from being sandwiched among three of the best power pitchers in baseball.

Bielecki's stuff is not such that he can rear back and blow the ball by a batter when he needs to. Last year, hitters managed only a .169 average when he was ahead in the count. But when he was behind and the ball was put into play, they hit .377 against him.

HOLDING RUNNERS, FIELDING, HITTING:

Bielecki's control of the running game is usually good, but he gave up 10 stolen bases in 12 tries in 1992. He is a better-than-average fielder overall. He's one of the worst hitting pitchers in baseball as evidenced by his .079 (21-for-267) career average with no extra-base hits and 135 whiffs.

OVERALL:

When the Braves and other free agent suitors make their plans for 1993, Bielecki's good half-season must be weighed against his elbow trouble and previous record. Bielecki is the kind of pitcher who can look very good on a very good team. Signing with a bad team could make for a long season.

MIKE BIELECKI

Position: SP/RP
Bats: R **Throws:** R
Ht: 6' 3" **Wt:** 195

Opening Day Age: 33
Born: 7/31/59 in Baltimore, MD
ML Seasons: 9

Overall Statistics

	W	L	ERA	G	GS	Sv	IP	H	R	BB	SO	HR
1992	2	4	2.57	19	14	0	80.2	77	27	27	62	2
Career	53	52	4.05	203	148	1	927.1	919	461	376	551	74

How Often He Throws Strikes

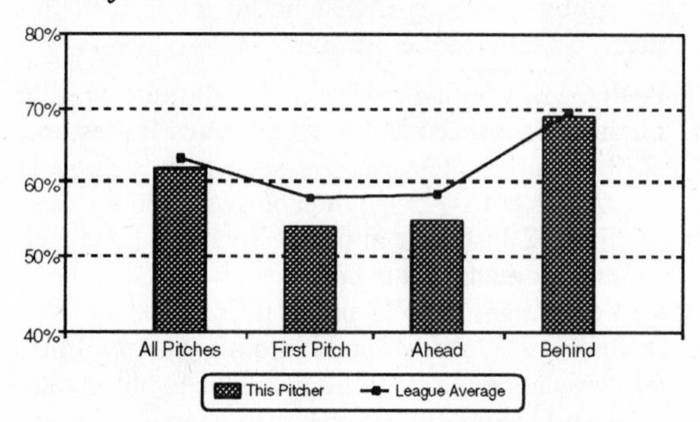

1992 Situational Stats

	W	L	ERA	Sv	IP		AB	H	HR	RBI	AVG
Home	1	2	2.54	0	39.0	LHB	177	48	0	13	.271
Road	1	2	2.59	0	41.2	RHB	126	29	2	10	.230
Day	1	0	2.30	0	31.1	Sc Pos	72	18	0	18	.250
Night	1	4	2.74	0	49.1	Clutch	18	2	0	0	.111

1992 Rankings (National League)

➡ Did not rank near the top or bottom in any category

IN HIS PRIME

JEFF BLAUSER

Position: SS/2B
Bats: R **Throws:** R
Ht: 6' 1" **Wt:** 180

Opening Day Age: 27
Born: 11/8/65 in Los Gatos, CA
ML Seasons: 6

HITTING:

As the 1992 season entered its last two months, the picture seemed dark for Jeff Blauser. Once a prospect with great potential, Blauser's inferior defense had turned him into a part-time shortstop. But with a sizzling bat (a .319 average with .531 slugging after August 1) and improved fielding, Blauser forced his way back into the lineup. This time he figures to stay.

Amazingly, though he's been with the Braves for six seasons Blauser is still just 27. Probably the best fastball hitter on the team, he credited his late-season surge on a slight stance adjustment which allowed him to get his swing started more quickly. Regular playing time did not hurt, either.

A patient hitter with lots of power for a middle infielder, Blauser's season was highlighted by a three-homer game July 12th at Wrigley Field. He pasted lefties for a .585 slugging percentage and is one of the toughest players in the National League to double up. A good hitter to all fields, he is adept at bunting and slapping the ball to the right side to advance a runner.

BASERUNNING:

Although speed was a major part of his offensive arsenal early in his career, Blauser now seems content to focus on his patience-and-power one-two punch. He has been caught stealing more often than he's been successful the last three seasons, so this appears to be a wise decision.

FIELDING:

His fielding has always been the catch. Inferior range and an erratic arm have kept Blauser from holding a full-time shortstop job. But last year he began to cut loose rather than throwing tentatively, and his overall play reflected his increased confidence. However, Rafael Belliard will usually replace Blauser with Atlanta leading in the late innings.

OVERALL:

Blauser is one Brave to keep an eye on for 1993. At 27, the age when so many players turn in career years, he's a prime candidate for his best season yet. No longer the constant subject of trade rumors and a Brave protection from the expansion draft, Blauser may finally have gotten his promising career untracked.

Overall Statistics

	G	AB	R	H	D	T	HR	RBI	SB	BB	SO	AVG
1992	123	343	61	90	19	3	14	46	5	46	82	.262
Career	578	1769	237	464	90	15	49	207	25	193	357	.262

Where He Hits the Ball

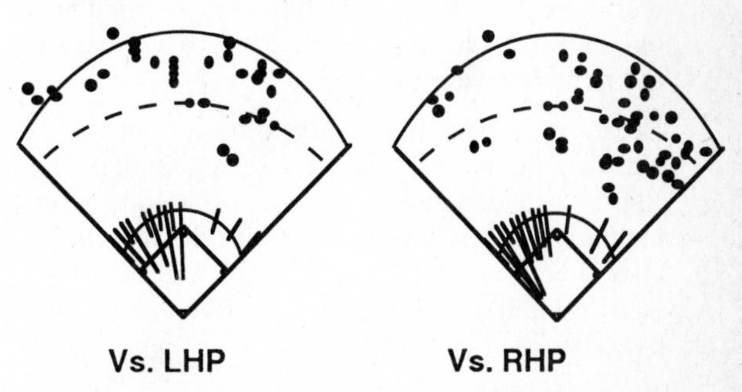

1992 Situational Stats

	AB	H	HR	RBI	AVG		AB	H	HR	RBI	AVG
Home	162	46	5	19	.284	LHP	142	43	9	24	.303
Road	181	44	9	27	.243	RHP	201	47	5	22	.234
Day	94	24	5	15	.255	Sc Pos	75	22	3	31	.293
Night	249	66	9	31	.265	Clutch	61	10	3	8	.164

1992 Rankings (National League)

- 4th in least GDPs per GDP situation (3.0%)
- 5th in slugging percentage vs. left-handed pitchers (.585)
- 7th in lowest percentage of swings put into play (40.0%)
- 8th in on-base percentage vs. left-handed pitchers (.402)
- Led the Braves in slugging percentage vs. left-handed pitchers, on-base percentage vs. left-handed pitchers and highest percentage of pitches taken (58.1%)
- Led NL shortstops in home runs (14) and least GDPs per GDP situation

SID BREAM

Position: 1B
Bats: L **Throws:** L
Ht: 6' 4" **Wt:** 220

Opening Day Age: 32
Born: 8/3/60 in Carlisle, PA
ML Seasons: 10

Overall Statistics

	G	AB	R	H	D	T	HR	RBI	SB	BB	SO	AVG
1992	125	372	30	97	25	1	10	61	6	46	51	.261
Career	925	2770	311	726	172	11	81	413	46	313	398	.262

Where He Hits the Ball

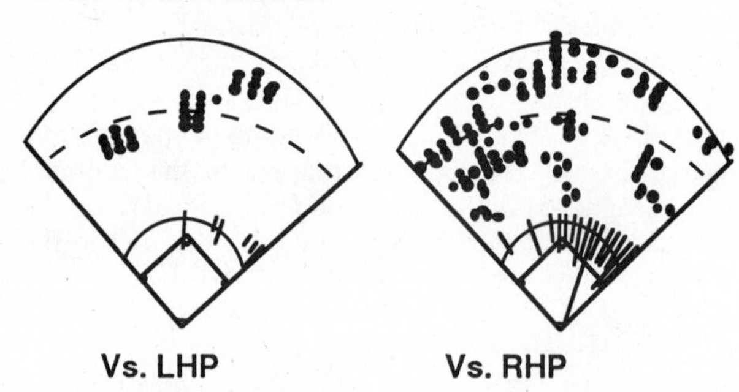

1992 Situational Stats

	AB	H	HR	RBI	AVG		AB	H	HR	RBI	AVG
Home	178	47	4	32	.264	LHP	33	8	1	7	.242
Road	194	50	6	29	.258	RHP	339	89	9	54	.263
Day	113	34	1	22	.301	Sc Pos	107	32	0	45	.299
Night	259	63	9	39	.243	Clutch	52	11	1	7	.212

1992 Rankings (National League)

- ➡ 5th in least GDPs per GDP situation (4.1%) and batting average with the bases loaded (.500)
- ➡ 8th in lowest batting average vs. right-handed pitchers (.263)
- ➡ 10th in lowest on-base percentage vs. right-handed pitchers (.347)
- ➡ Led the Braves in batting average with the bases loaded
- ➡ Led NL first basemen in sacrifice bunts (3), least GDPs per GDP situation, and bunts in play (4)

HITTING:

No one who watched it will ever forget it: Cabrera singles, Justice scores, and here comes Sid Bream with the winning run. This seems to take about five minutes: Bream rounds third, heading for home with the proverbial piano on his back, and then slides oh-so-slowly into the plate, just barely beating the tag from Mike Lavalliere. Pennant. Pandemonium.

That was a great moment for the popular veteran, but the truth is that at age 32 Bream is an unexceptional offensive player -- especially for his position. He hardly ever plays against lefthanders, and even as a platoon man he has trouble hitting above .260. He has a little power, but it's below average for a first baseman, particularly one that plays in Atlanta. He draws a few walks, but not a huge number.

Bream does have the ability to hit a high strike. He likes the ball up from both righthanders and lefthanders, and most of his extra-base hits come on high pitches. He's also tough in the clutch: .299 with runners in scoring position last year (.261 overall), .284 over the last five years (.262 overall).

BASERUNNING:

Well, you saw him run. Although Bream's surgically rebuilt knee has healed, he is still the slowest man on the Braves. He does run the bases intelligently and managed to swipe six bases without being caught in 1992.

FIELDING:

In the field is where Bream shines. He has good range and is adept at turning the 3-6-3 double play. He is renowned as one of the best fielding first baseman in the league although he did make quite a few errors for a platoon first baseman last season (10).

OVERALL:

Highly respected, Bream is a leader and a positive influence. In 1990, Jim Leyland screamed when the veteran left Pittsburgh. And Bobby Cox has stuck with him even though he has other first basemen with good offensive potential. Still, it's doubtful Bream can last much longer as a regular, even in a platoon role. Leadership is important, but it's no match for production.

PITCHING:

The first righthander out of the Atlanta bullpen last year, Marvin Freeman must have been a menacing sight to National League hitters. At 6'7", Freeman looks more like a closer than the middle man he's become. Some say he'd do well as a stopper, and he did record a career-high in saves in '92, converting three out of six opportunities. He also collected 16 holds, leading the Braves and tying for third in the National League in "middle-man saves." However, he finished second-worst in the NL in percentage of inherited runners scored, allowing almost half (20-of-42) to cross the plate.

Freeman throws a fastball, slider and a split-fingered fastball. The fastball is his best pitch, and he's finally learned to harness it. As Braves' pitching coach Leo Mazzone said of Freeman, "He used to be a thrower, trying to macho his way through. When he threw his fastball, he'd give 100 percent effort, but the extra effort was wasted. It took some of the movement off the ball. He still has good life on his fastball, it's got a natural action, but he's learned it isn't necessary for him to try and overpower everybody."

Freeman has been best over the last five years when worked frequently. He sports a 2.03 ERA in 26.2 innings when working on no-days rest, a 2.64 ERA in 75.0 innings on one- or two-days rest, but his ERA balloons to 4.73 in 45.2 innings on three-plus days rest.

HOLDING RUNNERS, FIELDING, HITTING:

Catchers have caught seven of 16 potential base stealers over the past two years with Freeman pitching. That's an indication that he holds baserunners at first fairly well. He is error-prone in the field. He is a not a stick man, either, with five hits in 40 career at-bats, no walks and 25 whiffs.

OVERALL:

Freeman has pitched very well since coming to Atlanta, working almost exclusively in middle relief. Since the Braves ended last season with no established closer, they might be tempted to try Freeman in that role. Then again, they might not want to tamper with success.

MARVIN FREEMAN

Position: RP
Bats: R **Throws:** R
Ht: 6' 7" **Wt:** 222

Opening Day Age: 30
Born: 4/10/63 in Chicago, IL
ML Seasons: 6

Overall Statistics

	W	L	ERA	G	GS	Sv	IP	H	R	BB	SO	HR
1992	7	5	3.22	58	0	3	64.1	61	26	29	41	7
Career	13	10	4.01	132	18	5	231.0	202	111	117	158	16

How Often He Throws Strikes

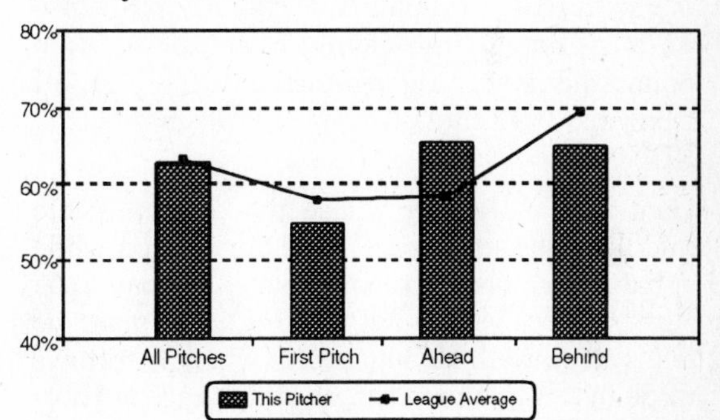

1992 Situational Stats

	W	L	ERA	Sv	IP		AB	H	HR	RBI	AVG
Home	4	3	2.50	1	36.0	LHB	114	28	5	17	.246
Road	3	2	4.13	2	28.1	RHB	129	33	2	24	.256
Day	2	0	3.20	1	19.2	Sc Pos	85	19	0	32	.224
Night	5	5	3.22	2	44.2	Clutch	119	27	3	15	.227

1992 Rankings (National League)

- 2nd in highest percentage of inherited runners scored (47.6%)
- 3rd in holds (16)
- 6th in relief wins (7)
- Led the Braves in holds, blown saves (3), relief ERA (3.22) and relief wins

RON GANT

Position: LF/CF
Bats: R **Throws:** R
Ht: 6' 0" **Wt:** 175

Opening Day Age: 28
Born: 3/2/65 in Victoria, TX
ML Seasons: 6

Overall Statistics

	G	AB	R	H	D	T	HR	RBI	SB	BB	SO	AVG
1992	153	544	74	141	22	6	17	80	32	45	101	.259
Career	701	2586	402	670	131	23	111	363	131	233	483	.259

Where He Hits the Ball

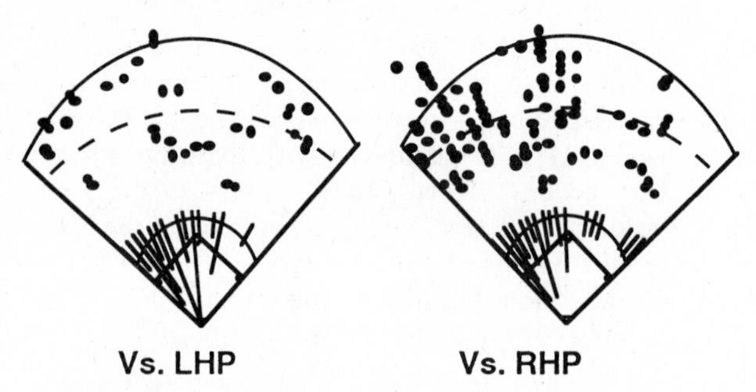

1992 Situational Stats

	AB	H	HR	RBI	AVG		AB	H	HR	RBI	AVG
Home	257	71	10	45	.276	LHP	177	45	5	32	.254
Road	287	70	7	35	.244	RHP	367	96	12	48	.262
Day	141	31	6	17	.220	Sc Pos	152	39	3	63	.257
Night	403	110	11	63	.273	Clutch	85	22	1	6	.259

1992 Rankings (National League)

- 5th in lowest on-base percentage vs. right-handed pitchers (.320)
- 7th in lowest batting average vs. right-handed pitchers (.262)
- 8th in hit by pitch (7)
- 10th in lowest batting average on the road (.244)
- Led the Braves in hit by pitch, strikeouts (101) and stolen base percentage (76.2%)
- Led NL left fielders in triples (6), hit by pitch and games played (153)

HITTING:

From the beginning, the 1992 season was a weird one for Ron Gant. Known for his slow starts, Gant entered the year with a .191 lifetime average for April with just nine home runs and 33 RBI in five previous Aprils. In '92, he finally broke the jinx, going .273-5-19. When he followed with a .291 average in May, a career year appeared a good possibility.

Things didn't work out that way. Gant soon went into a power outage, hitting no home runs and managing a mere four doubles between June 17 and July 20. In August, the slump continued, as Gant batted only .203 with a single home run. He needed a big September/October (.280, five homers, 18 RBI) to get his final figures up to .259-17-80. Though his average was up by eight points, his power figures marked a big dropoff from his 1991 numbers of 32 homers and 105 RBI.

Gant is a pull hitter whose power area is the middle of the strike zone. His body motion while at bat is such that he needs to attack the ball to be successful. When he fall towards home plate, he tends to do well. He hits poorly when he follows through toward third base, as often happened during his long slump.

BASERUNNING:

Due to the home run drop, Gant missed his chance for a record third straight 30 homer/30 steal season. But he probably had his best year as a basestealer. He was two short of his career-high 34 steals in 1991, but his success rate of 76 percent was his best ever. Gant's other baserunning skills are excellent.

FIELDING:

Gant has been better off since Otis Nixon and Deion Sanders took over in center, a position that was a little too demanding for him. His range is good for a left fielder, although his arm is subpar.

OVERALL:

Gant needs to combine his April of '92 with his traditional rest of the season. His five dingers after August 31 suggest there's a good chance he'll return to the 30-30 level in 1993. He's only 28, still in the prime of his career.

STAFF ACE

TOM GLAVINE

Position: SP
Bats: L **Throws:** L
Ht: 6' 1" **Wt:** 190

Opening Day Age: 27
Born: 3/25/66 in Concord, MA
ML Seasons: 6

PITCHING:

Tom Glavine just missed his second straight National League Cy Young Award in 1992, but the lefty had another outstanding season. Glavine was 19-3 in late August and seemed a cinch to repeat as the award winner, but he went 1-5 the rest of the way while being hampered by a rib injury. Glavine didn't seem completely recovered until the World Series, when he rebounded from a miserable playoff series to go 1-1 with a 1.59 ERA.

A fastball, change, curve, and slider round out Glavine's arsenal of pitches. His fastball hits 90 MPH and he'll feed batters a steady diet of circle changes and fastballs away. He stays away from right-handed batters and will try not to throw strikes to anyone on the inside part of the plate. His early-inning troubles are well known and documented. Amazingly, although batters have hit only .249 overall off Glavine over the last five years, in the first inning he's allowed a .285 average, .305 (39-for-128) in 1992.

Glavine is the most aggressive of Atlanta's "Young Guns" and won't give in to a single batter. He put together an astounding period of pitching from May 27 through August 24 in which he failed to lose a game. In 16 outings, he was 13-0 with a 2.13 ERA. Though he didn't need a lot of help, Glavine got great support from the Atlanta batters on the way to his 20-8 record. He led NL starters in run support with an average of 5.3 runs per game, the only starter getting more than five runs.

HOLDING RUNNERS, FIELDING, HITTING:

Glavine throws to first often and has induced 15 pitcher caught stealings over the past three years. He is also a good fielder and bunter. He is becoming a downright dangerous hitter, batting .247 (19-for-77) last year with seven RBI.

OVERALL:

Glavine has emerged as the National League's premier lefthander, and probably the best in baseball. His performance in last year's World Series may have finally put to rest the notion that he folds under postseason pressure -- the only remaining reservation about him.

Overall Statistics

	W	L	ERA	G	GS	Sv	IP	H	R	BB	SO	HR
1992	20	8	2.76	33	33	0	225.0	197	81	70	129	6
Career	73	60	3.60	172	172	0	1117.1	1058	508	353	644	78

How Often He Throws Strikes

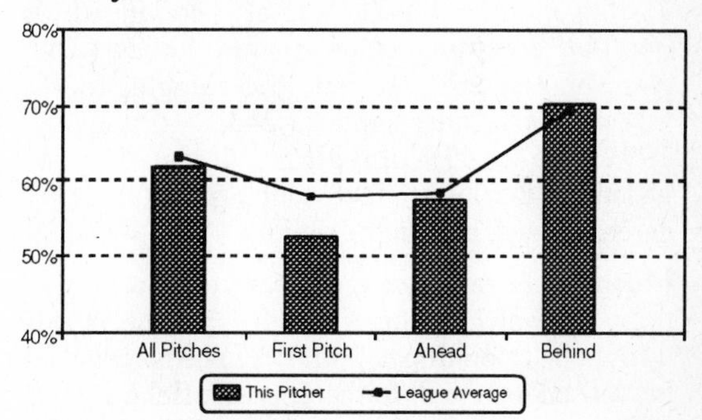

1992 Situational Stats

	W	L	ERA	Sv	IP		AB	H	HR	RBI	AVG
Home	13	4	2.31	0	140.0	LHB	176	48	1	17	.273
Road	7	4	3.49	0	85.0	RHB	663	149	5	53	.225
Day	5	4	3.82	0	66.0	Sc Pos	172	44	2	63	.256
Night	15	4	2.32	0	159.0	Clutch	107	24	0	7	.224

1992 Rankings (National League)

- 1st in wins (20), shutouts (5) and most run support per 9 innings (5.3)
- 2nd in winning percentage (.714) and least home runs allowed per 9 innings (.24)
- 3rd in pickoff throws (247)
- Led the Braves in ERA (2.76), wins, shutouts, GDPs induced (18), winning percentage, lowest slugging percentage allowed (.310), highest groundball/flyball ratio allowed (1.5), lowest stolen base percentage allowed (56.5%), most run support per 9 innings, least home runs allowed per 9 innings, most GDPs induced per 9 innings (.72) and ERA at home (2.31)

IN HIS PRIME

HITTING:

The 1992 season began as a dark cloud for David Justice, but the silver lining showed through in the end. Plagued by back problems, booing fans who pelted him with peanut shells, and a well-publicized fielding misunderstanding with Mark Lemke, Justice's 1992 got off to a rocky start. In fact, he began the year going 1-for-17, then took two weeks off to give his back some needed rest. It wasn't until an eight-homer September/October, during which he slugged a torrid .607, that the Braves' cleanup hitter was again back in the fans' favor.

The last-month home run barrage has become the norm for Justice. He has now hit 43 of his career 71 dingers after July 31. He also continued his tradition of hitting better against lefties (.283, .447 slugging in 1992; .301, .505 slugging for his career) than against righties (.243, .446 slugging, 1992; .254, .479 slugging, career). He has grounded into only eight double plays in 1,370 career at-bats, best in the majors.

Much can be revealed about Justice's plate intentions by watching his stance. When he stands upright he is looking to pull. When he is crouched he will take the ball to the opposite field. Justice will also only open up his stance against lefties.

BASERUNNING:

A fast runner, Justice is neither a frequent nor proficient basestealer. On a team with plenty of other offensive weapons, he is content to be a speedy, intelligent baserunner and leave the thievery to Otis and Deion.

FIELDING:

Speed, great range and an arm good enough for nine outfield assists (tied for tenth best in the National League) make up Justice's defensive portfolio. He does have a tendency toward careless errors, having led all NL right fielders in that dubious distinction with eight in 1992 and seven in 1991.

OVERALL:

When Justice came up in 1990, expectations were low. He delivered 28 home runs in about two-thirds of a season. Now, anything less than 30 seems a disappointment. But as another 27-year-old 1993 Brave, he could be poised to explode.

DAVE JUSTICE

Position: RF
Bats: L **Throws:** L
Ht: 6' 3" **Wt:** 200

Opening Day Age: 26
Born: 4/14/66 in Cincinnati, OH
ML Seasons: 4

Overall Statistics

	G	AB	R	H	D	T	HR	RBI	SB	BB	SO	AVG
1992	144	484	78	124	19	5	21	72	2	79	85	.256
Career	396	1370	228	369	70	8	71	240	23	211	267	.269

Where He Hits the Ball

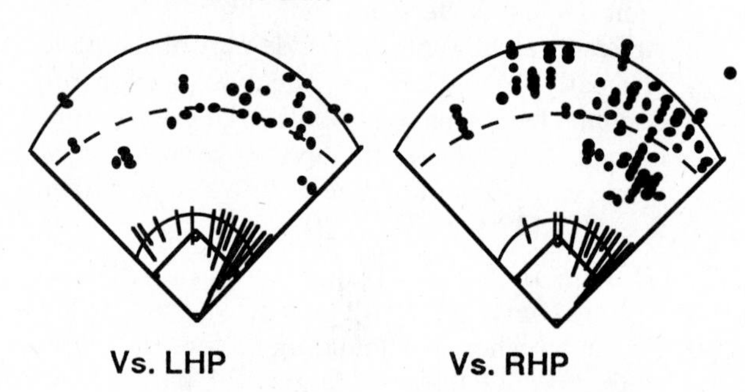

1992 Situational Stats

	AB	H	HR	RBI	AVG		AB	H	HR	RBI	AVG
Home	245	56	10	35	.229	LHP	159	45	5	17	.283
Road	239	68	11	37	.285	RHP	325	79	16	55	.243
Day	140	36	3	20	.257	Sc Pos	126	29	7	50	.230
Night	344	88	18	52	.256	Clutch	77	19	3	8	.247

1992 Rankings (National League)

- 1st in least GDPs per GDP situation (0.9%)
- 3rd in lowest batting average at home (.229)
- 5th in lowest batting average vs. right-handed pitchers (.243)
- 7th in HR frequency (23.1 ABs per HR) and most pitches seen per plate appearance (3.89)
- 8th in walks (79), lowest groundball/flyball ratio (.93) and lowest percentage of swings put into play (40.1%)
- Led the Braves in home runs, walks, on-base percentage (.359), HR frequency, most pitches seen per plate appearance, least GDPs per GDP situation and on-base percentage vs. right-handed pitchers (.362)

PITCHING:

Like the pink rabbit with the bass drum, Charlie Leibrandt just keeps going, and going, and going. Leibrandt bounced back in a big way from the nightmare of the 1991 World Series with the best winning percentage of his 13-year career (15-7, .682). Unfortunately, the hard-luck lefty had yet another nightmare waiting for him in Game 6 of the World Series.

Leibrandt throws four pitches (fastball, change, curve and slider) and is a finesse pitcher all the way. He won't throw too many fastballs and curves, relying predominantly on sliders on the corner and his big change-up. Leibrandt's herky-jerky motion makes his change most effective. He coils up and almost stops in the middle of his delivery before serving up his low-80s fare. Leibrandt gets in trouble when he comes down the middle, but has never been afraid to pitch inside throughout his career.

Atlanta bullpen coach Leo Mazzone has said that Leibrandt's control is the best on the Atlanta staff. His strikeout-to-walk ratio improved to almost 2.5 to one in 1992 (104/42), an improvement from the early and mid-1980's when his control wasn't quite as sharp. When he's on, Leibrandt can mess hitters up pretty badly, as illustrated by his three seven-strikeout outings in 1992. He is undoubtedly helped by his contrast to the other Braves' power-pitching starters.

HOLDING RUNNERS, HITTING, FIELDING:

Leibrandt's move to first is top-notch. He has picked off seven and initiated 21 other pitcher caught-stealings in the past two years. However, he's easy to steal a base against if the pickoff is avoided. Leibrandt is an average fielder and slightly below-average hitter.

OVERALL:

Until he's forced to move elsewhere by Atlanta's endless supply of phenom starters, Leibrandt will continue to take the ball every fifth day and win more often than not. He's shown time and again that he can come back from the kind of adversity he suffered (again) in the Series. With his age a prohibitive factor, even though he wasn't expansion-protected, expect Leibrandt to be back with the Braves in 1993.

CHARLIE LEIBRANDT

Position: SP
Bats: R **Throws:** L
Ht: 6' 3" **Wt:** 200

Opening Day Age: 36
Born: 10/4/56 in Chicago, IL
ML Seasons: 13

Overall Statistics

	W	L	ERA	G	GS	Sv	IP	H	R	BB	SO	HR
1992	15	7	3.36	32	31	0	193.0	191	78	42	104	9
Career	131	109	3.65	368	320	2	2157.2	2221	984	611	1032	157

How Often He Throws Strikes

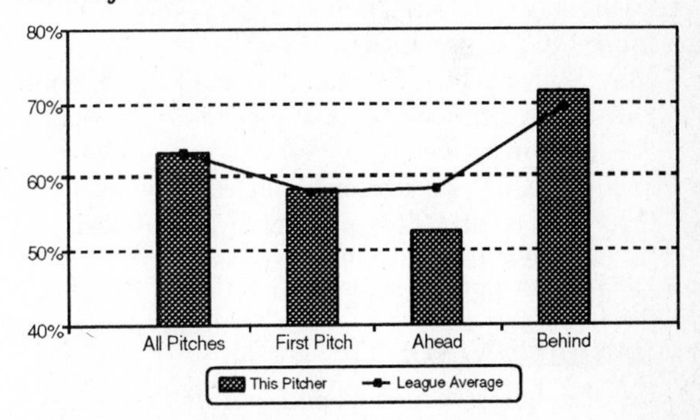

1992 Situational Stats

	W	L	ERA	Sv	IP		AB	H	HR	RBI	AVG
Home	9	4	3.76	0	110.0	LHB	171	39	1	13	.228
Road	6	3	2.82	0	83.0	RHB	570	152	8	53	.267
Day	3	3	4.86	0	46.1	Sc Pos	154	37	1	49	.240
Night	12	4	2.88	0	146.2	Clutch	45	10	0	2	.222

1992 Rankings (National League)

- 1st in pickoff throws (257)
- 2nd in runners caught stealing (16)
- 3rd in winning percentage (.682)
- 4th in least GDPs induced per 9 innings (.28)
- 5th in least home runs allowed per 9 innings (.42)
- 6th in stolen bases allowed (28) and ERA on the road (2.82)
- 7th in wins (15)
- 8th in least strikeouts per 9 innings (4.9)
- Led the Braves in hit batsmen (5), pickoff throws, runners caught stealing, ERA on the road and lowest batting average allowed vs left-handed batters (.228)

MARK LEMKE

Position: 2B/3B
Bats: B **Throws:** R
Ht: 5' 9" **Wt:** 167

Opening Day Age: 27
Born: 8/13/65 in Utica, NY
ML Seasons: 5

Overall Statistics

	G	AB	R	H	D	T	HR	RBI	SB	BB	SO	AVG
1992	155	427	38	97	7	4	6	26	0	50	39	.227
Career	423	1048	108	237	37	7	10	82	1	109	100	.226

Where He Hits the Ball

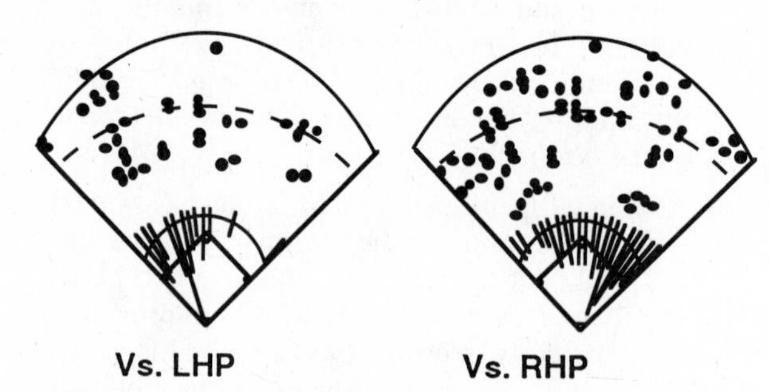

1992 Situational Stats

	AB	H	HR	RBI	AVG		AB	H	HR	RBI	AVG
Home	222	50	4	13	.225	LHP	145	33	5	14	.228
Road	205	47	2	13	.229	RHP	282	64	1	12	.227
Day	119	34	1	9	.286	Sc Pos	105	22	0	19	.210
Night	308	63	5	17	.205	Clutch	69	14	1	7	.203

1992 Rankings (National League)

- 1st in lowest batting average at home (.225)
- 2nd in highest percentage of swings put into play (60.0%)
- 6th in sacrifice bunts (12)
- 8th in bunts in play (20)
- Led the Braves in intentional walks (11) and highest percentage of swings put into play
- Led NL second basemen in sacrifice bunts and highest percentage of swings put into play

HITTING:

The stage was set last year for Mark Lemke to become the ballplayer that Braves' management had always envisioned. A scrappy switch-hitter with too much pop for his 5'9" frame and the possessor of excellent defensive skills, Lemke was ready for his big move forward. With Jeff Treadway unable to begin the season after preseason hand surgery, absolutely nothing stood in Lemke's way. Unfortunately, Lemke never got untracked offensively, although his defensive prowess kept him in the starting lineup almost all of the season.

Lemke's 1992 offensive highlights were few and far between. He did have a tendency to be a hot swinger in certain games, with seven three-or more-hit performances, including a 4-for-5 on May 30th at Shea Stadium against David Cone and an assortment of relievers. But too many "oh-fers" in between dragged his average down to a paltry .227. Lemke suffered equally in 1992 from the right (.228) and left (.227) sides, although he's generally hit better as a righty (.246 vs .214 left in his career).

BASERUNNING:

Lemke has average speed but is a horrible basestealer. In 1992 his three caught stealings with no successes drove his lifetime major-league totals to one steal in ten attempts. He would do best to stay put.

FIELDING:

Only those baseball fans who have been vacationing in other solar systems need to be told of Lemke's wonderful defensive talents. He is unequalled at turning the double play and is the possessor of excellent range. Despite his failings at the plate, Bobby Cox knows Lemke's contribution to the Braves' outstanding infield and up-the-middle defense is worth the offensive sacrifice.

OVERALL:

Like his part-time keystone mate Jeff Blauser, Lemke is at the age at which most players reach their prime, 27. One of these seasons he will manage to hit .260 or so, and he'll be one of the most valuable Braves when it happens. Whatever he does with the bat, though, the stubble-bearded second baseman will see plenty of playing time.

KENT MERCKER

Position: RP
Bats: L **Throws:** L
Ht: 6' 2" **Wt:** 195

Opening Day Age: 25
Born: 2/1/68 in Dublin, OH
ML Seasons: 4

PITCHING:

As has been the case during most of his young major-league career, Kent Mercker's 1992 season ended in uncertainty. After a string of four decent starts near the end of the 1991 season, he seemed headed for a possible rotation spot. But Mike Bielecki's acquisition (and his good pitching) ended that idea. In 1992, Mercker assumed the closer role in late June when the Braves' bullpen suffered a home run barrage. He threw scoreless ball in 13.2 innings and gathered five saves in five opportunities through July 25, but a couple of rough outings sent him back to middle relief.

Mercker, who breezed through the minors, may have become frustrated after losing the stopper role. He was quoted as saying "I think I did a pretty good job as the closer. . . and now what's happened? It's hard enough going out there with the pressure of losing the game, but it makes it a whole lot harder to go out and worry that if I'm not perfect, I might not get out there again very soon." Mercker's season fell apart from there on, his ERA rising from 2.15 on August 1 to its final mark of 3.42.

The coup de grace was Mercker's removal from the World Series roster after the playoffs in favor of young righty Dave Nied. The Braves said it was due to a rib-muscle problem, inhibiting his 90-plus fastball and curve, but Mercker publicly did not agree with that assessment.

HOLDING RUNNERS, FIELDING, HITTING:

Mercker is easy pickings for thieving baserunners. They've succeeded 27 out of 33 times over the past three years. He is a decent fielder but a poor hitter, although he rarely gets to hit at all (1-for-19 career, .053).

OVERALL:

Mercker should try not to be too hard on himself. The Braves did not protect him in the expansion draft, indicating that they had some concerns about him. But if Atlanta doesn't want Mercker, there are a lot of teams who would find him very desirable.

Overall Statistics

	W	L	ERA	G	GS	Sv	IP	H	R	BB	SO	HR
1992	3	2	3.42	53	0	6	68.1	51	27	35	49	4
Career	12	12	3.24	141	5	19	194.1	158	78	100	154	15

How Often He Throws Strikes

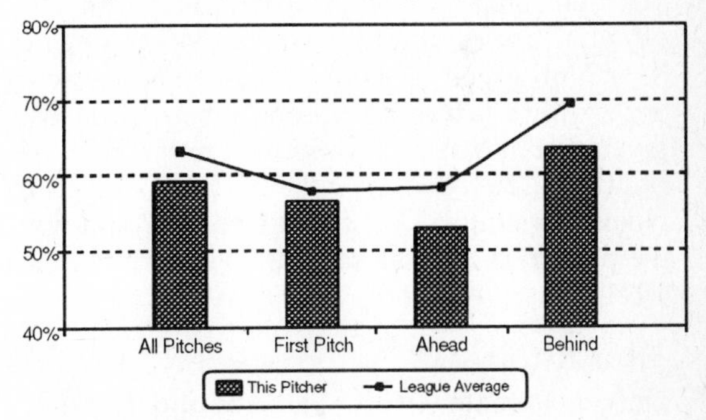

1992 Situational Stats

	W	L	ERA	Sv	IP		AB	H	HR	RBI	AVG
Home	2	1	4.35	4	41.1	LHB	73	19	1	11	.260
Road	1	1	2.00	2	27.0	RHB	173	32	3	21	.185
Day	1	0	1.50	2	18.0	Sc Pos	71	23	3	31	.324
Night	2	2	4.11	4	50.1	Clutch	99	20	0	9	.202

1992 Rankings (National League)

- 4th in first batter efficiency (.152)
- 7th in lowest batting average allowed in relief (.207)
- 9th in highest batting average allowed in relief with runners in scoring position (.324)
- Led the Braves in blown saves (3), first batter efficiency, relief innings (68.1), lowest batting average allowed in relief and most strikeouts per 9 innings in relief (6.5)

GREAT SPEED

OTIS NIXON

Position: CF/RF
Bats: B **Throws:** R
Ht: 6' 2" **Wt:** 180

Opening Day Age: 34
Born: 1/9/59 in Evergreen, NC
ML Seasons: 10

HITTING:

After Otis Nixon's storybook 1991 season had an unhappy ending due to a drug suspension, the doubters lined up. His season had relied heavily on a great first half, and there was talk that Nixon would end up playing elsewhere, if at all. Well, Nixon got off to another fast start and managed to fend off a platoon with Deion Sanders. Even though his season did not start until April 24, by the Fourth of July he was once again firmly entrenched as the Braves' everyday center fielder.

Nixon is strictly a slap hitter. His main weapons are chopping the ball into the ground -- he was second in the league in groundball-to-flyball ratio -- and the bunt. He was second in the league in bunts put in play with 45 and had 17 bunt singles. Nixon's Series-ending bunt to Mike Timlin, though criticized by some, was a typical maneuver by him. It was a high-percentage play, too, given that he was a much weaker hitter from the right side (.263) than from the left (.343) last year. Nixon's walk total fell slightly in 1992 and was the primary reason he scored fewer runs than in 1991.

BASERUNNING:

Only teammate Deion Sanders and Marquis Grissom finished ahead of Nixon in the Baseball America poll of National League managers for fastest baserunner. He dropped from 72 steals to 41, and his stolen base percentage was down last season to 69 percent after four straight seasons above 75. But not many would say Nixon has "lost a step" quite yet.

FIELDING:

Nixon flies in center, exhibiting superior range and almost errorless play. His only weakness is a lackluster arm. No one will forget his reach over the fence to pull back an Andy Van Slyke homer to save a victory on July 25th.

OVERALL:

While brother Donnell toils in the minor leagues, the elder Nixon has secured a spot in the majors as an old man (34) with young man's skills. He has turned his one weapon into a career, something many would not have believed possible.

Overall Statistics

	G	AB	R	H	D	T	HR	RBI	SB	BB	SO	AVG
1992	120	456	79	134	14	2	2	22	41	39	54	.294
Career	869	1996	381	513	53	10	6	123	305	208	264	.257

Where He Hits the Ball

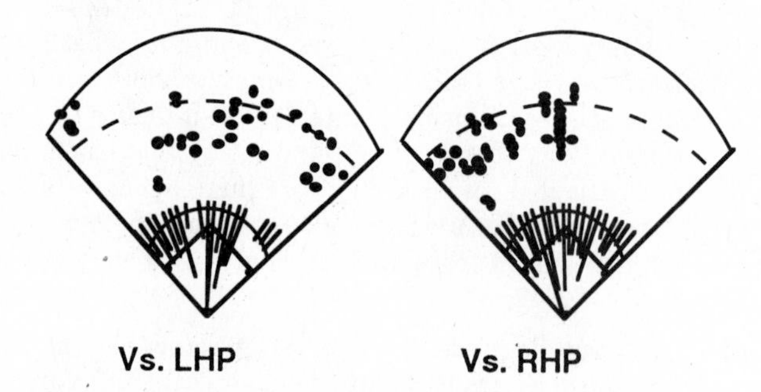

1992 Situational Stats

	AB	H	HR	RBI	AVG		AB	H	HR	RBI	AVG
Home	221	66	1	11	.299	LHP	178	61	2	16	.343
Road	235	68	1	11	.289	RHP	278	73	0	6	.263
Day	134	46	1	8	.343	Sc Pos	86	21	1	20	.244
Night	322	88	1	14	.273	Clutch	73	21	0	9	.288

1992 Rankings (National League)

- 2nd in highest groundball/flyball ratio (3.0) and bunts in play (45)
- 4th in caught stealing (18)
- 5th in lowest slugging percentage (.347), lowest HR frequency (228.0 ABs per HR) and highest percentage of swings put into play (55.2%)
- 7th in stolen bases (41), highest batting average vs. left-handed pitchers (.343) and lowest batting average on an 0-2 count (.091)
- Led the Braves in stolen bases, caught stealing, highest groundball/flyball ratio, batting average on a 3-2 count (.300), bunts in play and steals of third (5)

GREG OLSON

Position: C
Bats: R **Throws:** R
Ht: 6' 0" **Wt:** 200

Opening Day Age: 32
Born: 9/6/60 in Marshall, MN
ML Seasons: 4

Overall Statistics

	G	AB	R	H	D	T	HR	RBI	SB	BB	SO	AVG
1992	95	302	27	72	14	2	3	27	2	34	31	.238
Career	331	1013	109	250	51	3	16	107	4	108	130	.247

Where He Hits the Ball

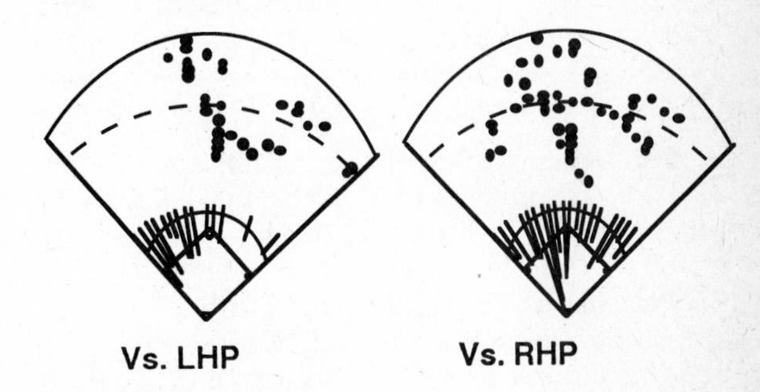

1992 Situational Stats

	AB	H	HR	RBI	AVG		AB	H	HR	RBI	AVG
Home	135	32	0	11	.237	LHP	117	30	1	10	.256
Road	167	40	3	16	.240	RHP	185	42	2	17	.227
Day	85	27	2	13	.318	Sc Pos	80	15	0	20	.188
Night	217	45	1	14	.207	Clutch	51	11	3	8	.216

1992 Rankings (National League)

- 3rd in highest percentage of runners caught stealing as a catcher (39.1%)
- 9th in most GDPs per GDP situation (15.4%)

HITTING:

Greg Olson may have encountered the worst "break" of his career on September 18, 1992. When he sustained a fractured right fibula and torn ligaments in his ankle in a home plate collision with Houston's Ken Caminiti, Olson lost his chance for postseason play . . . and maybe more. The catcher had surgery and was expected to need six to eight months to recover, meaning that he might not be ready by the start of the 1993 season. Olson, who is 32, must be a little nervous about his major-league future.

Olson came out of nowhere in 1990. He had never hit for either much average or power in the minors. When he fought off oldsters Ernie Whitt and Mike Heath to turn in a solid, if unspectacular, 1991, it was hard to believe this undistinguished scrapper had become the main receiver on the super-talented Atlanta squad. The defensive-minded Bobby Cox took a liking to Olson, however, and there was little doubt that Olson was his favorite catcher.

Olson never got untracked with the bat in 1992. He was hitting only .238 with three home runs before the collision. Olson had been particularly struggling since the All-Star break, managing only a .216 average without a round-tripper.

BASERUNNING:

Speedy catchers are few and Olson is no exception. The type of injury he sustained may cut down his speed even further. Olson stole two bases in three attempts in 1992, making him 4-for-7 in his career.

FIELDING:

Olson has a fine reputation for calling a game. John Smoltz especially likes working with him and it showed again in 1992 (2.53 ERA with Olson in 124.2 IP, 3.17 ERA in 122.0 innings with Berryhill). Olson's throwing arm is not exceptional, but good enough.

OVERALL:

A late bloomer, Olson has proven beyond question that he's a major league catcher. His defensive skills are important enough that, even if he hits .238 again, a good-hitting club wouldn't worry about his bat. Neither would a lot of bad-hitting clubs. But he'll have to prove he's healthy.

ALEJANDRO PENA

Position: RP
Bats: R **Throws:** R
Ht: 6' 1" **Wt:** 203

Opening Day Age: 33
Born: 6/25/59 in Cambiaso, Dominican Republic
ML Seasons: 12

PITCHING:

Following a stellar 1991 campaign, 1992 was quite a letdown for Alejandro Pena. In a 21-day period from July 5th until July 25th, though, Pena put together quite a streak of pitching. He got his only victory of the year, piled up eight saves in eight opportunities (he finished with only 15), and pitched 13.1 innings of four-hit, scoreless baseball.

The rest of Pena's season was not nearly as rosy. He experienced migraine headaches in the spring, but it was his right elbow that was to be Pena's biggest headache. It put him on the DL from May 31 until June 18. Then, it put him on again from August 21 until September 5. And finally, it shut him down for good after September 30, causing him to miss the Braves' second consecutive playoffs and World Series. Whether rest or surgery is the answer remains to be seen.

Pena relies on a fastball that can still reach the low 90's. He mixes in an occasional slider and change-up. In his career, he has been equally effective against righties (.240) and lefties (.229). Pena has been a strong finisher, with a 2.13 post-All-Star ERA and a 0.79 ERA after August 31 over the last five years. His career ERA for 15 postseason games is 2.25, another reason why Atlanta missed him late last year.

HOLDING RUNNERS, HITTING, FIELDING:

Pena has been easy to steal upon since he's been with the Braves (six steals, one caught). He is a decent fielder. Pena handles the bat about as well as most pitchers with a .112 career average (20-for-179), three doubles, one homer and seven RBI.

OVERALL:

At age 33, Pena is an old horse among the young colts of the Atlanta staff. The prognosis on his ailing right elbow will surely be a big factor in determining if the Braves' re-sign Pena for their run at a third pennant. He certainly still showed flashes of the kind of pitching that helped take Atlanta there for the first time.

Overall Statistics

	W	L	ERA	G	GS	Sv	IP	H	R	BB	SO	HR
1992	1	6	4.07	41	0	15	42.0	40	19	13	34	7
Career	50	48	2.95	433	72	67	969.1	878	374	301	743	61

How Often He Throws Strikes

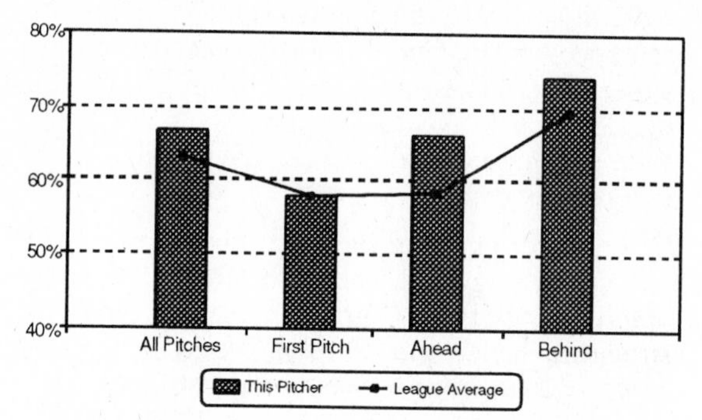

1992 Situational Stats

	W	L	ERA	Sv	IP		AB	H	HR	RBI	AVG
Home	0	2	4.42	5	18.1	LHB	78	16	5	11	.205
Road	1	4	3.80	10	23.2	RHB	79	24	2	10	.304
Day	0	2	2.93	6	15.1	Sc Pos	35	10	1	13	.286
Night	1	4	4.72	9	26.2	Clutch	105	28	4	16	.267

1992 Rankings (National League)

- 6th in first batter efficiency (.158)
- 10th in saves (15) and highest batting average allowed in relief with runners on base (.310)
- Led the Braves in saves, games finished (31), save opportunities (18), blown saves (3), most GDPs induced per GDP situation (16.1%) and relief losses (6)

CLUTCH HITTER

TERRY PENDLETON

Position: 3B
Bats: B **Throws:** R
Ht: 5' 9" **Wt:** 195

Opening Day Age: 32
Born: 7/16/60 in Los Angeles, CA
ML Seasons: 9

Overall Statistics

	G	AB	R	H	D	T	HR	RBI	SB	BB	SO	AVG
1992	160	640	98	199	39	1	21	105	5	37	67	.311
Career	1240	4659	596	1274	228	33	87	633	114	332	567	.273

Where He Hits the Ball

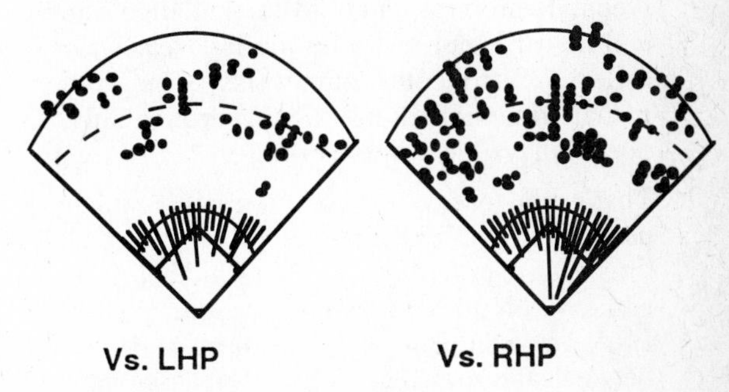

1992 Situational Stats

	AB	H	HR	RBI	AVG		AB	H	HR	RBI	AVG
Home	306	94	13	56	.307	LHP	207	74	8	41	.357
Road	334	105	8	49	.314	RHP	433	125	13	64	.289
Day	183	60	8	33	.328	Sc Pos	161	63	8	86	.391
Night	457	139	13	72	.304	Clutch	91	26	5	14	.286

1992 Rankings (National League)

- 1st in hits (199) and batting average with runners in scoring position (.391)
- 2nd in at-bats (640), singles (138) and RBI (105)
- Led the Braves in batting average (.311), home runs (21), at-bats, runs scored (98), hits, singles, doubles (39), total bases (303), RBI, times on base (236), GDPs (16), most pitches seen (2,341), plate appearances (689), games played (16), slugging percentage (.473), batting average with runners in scoring position, batting average vs. left-handed pitchers (.357), batting average vs. right-handed pitchers (.289), slugging percentage vs. right-handed pitchers (.448) and batting average with 2 strikes (.263)

HITTING:

Just when it seemed safe to write off Terry Pendleton's MVP 1991 season as a fluke, along came 1992. The offensive heights that Pendleton has achieved the past two years cannot simply be attributed to park factors. For Terry Pendleton, life began at 30. He has been dubbed the "best free agent acquisition in baseball history" by Braves' management, and that title is hard to argue with. Pendleton backs up his numbers with high marks for attitude and intangibles. His clubhouse get-togethers and general demeanor have helped lead the young Braves to the World Series two straight years.

Last season Pendleton amassed over 20 home runs for the second straight year after never having hit more than 13 in seven seasons with the Cardinals. He led the major leagues in hitting with runners in scoring position (.391, with a .615 slugging percentage). Pendleton likes to turn on low, inside fastballs and generates most of his power in this fashion. A switch-hitter, he tends to pull the ball against righties much more often than against lefties. He is not a particularly patient hitter and can be susceptible to the double play.

BASERUNNING:

No speed burner, Pendleton has traded his early days of 20-plus steals for his current 20 homers. He has also traded horrible caught stealing percentages for good ones and is 15-for-19 in his two years with the Braves.

FIELDING:

A three-time Gold Glove winner, Pendleton is fun to watch. He plays way up in front of the third base bag and way off the line, almost in shortstop territory. This allows him to cut off many balls hit into the hole. His line coverage may suffer somewhat, but it's hard to notice.

OVERALL:

Otis Nixon said of Pendleton, "Whether he's limping, whether he's injured in any way, he's out there and gives you 100 percent. That is a class act out there, that is a guy that rises to the occasion when you need it most." Though Pendleton did not have a good postseason, most people would second Nixon's words.

PITCHING:

Without question one of the great relievers of all time, Jeff Reardon is the all-time save king with 357 career saves. After joining the Braves late last season, Reardon closed out the year with three victories, three saves and a 1.15 ERA during the crucial stretch drive in for Atlanta. Yet as his World Series performance showed, Reardon is no longer the kind of top closer who can be counted on in a crucial, life-and-death situation.

Reardon's problem is simple: he's become too easy to hit. Last year he allowed 67 hits in 58 innings for a .291 opponents' batting average. It was the first time in his 14-year career that he's permitted more hits than innings pitched. To his credit, Reardon is unafraid to challenge hitters, and his strikeout-to-walk ratio last year was excellent (39 strikeouts, nine walks). The problem is that while he still has the power mentality, he doesn't have the power anymore.

That's not to say that Reardon can't still be a useful reliever. One obvious problem is that he tires easily these days. Working in back-to-back games -- on no days' rest -- last year, Reardon's ERA was 5.84. But given one or more day's rest between appearances, his ERA was less than half that, 2.76. Of course, closers can't be given a day or so's rest; they need to be ready every day. Reardon still throws only two pitches, a fastball and a curve which is really a slider/curve combination, or "slurve."

HOLDING RUNNERS, HITTING, FIELDING:

Reardon has always been easy to run on. Over the last five years he's permitted 24 steals in 27 attempts. Of course, as a closer he is tested infrequently. His delivery leaves him in awkward fielding position and he's not a good defensive player.

OVERALL:

Reardon is a free agent and his World Series disaster had to be devastating to his market value. If he comes back with anyone, it might have to be as a middle reliever. The end is near.

JEFF REARDON

Position: RP
Bats: R **Throws:** R
Ht: 6' 0" **Wt:** 205

Opening Day Age: 37
Born: 10/1/55 in Dalton, MA
ML Seasons: 14

Overall Statistics

	W	L	ERA	G	GS	Sv	IP	H	R	BB	SO	HR
1992	5	2	3.41	60	0	30	58.0	67	22	9	39	6
Career	68	71	3.05	811	0	357	1061.0	917	383	345	838	102

How Often He Throws Strikes

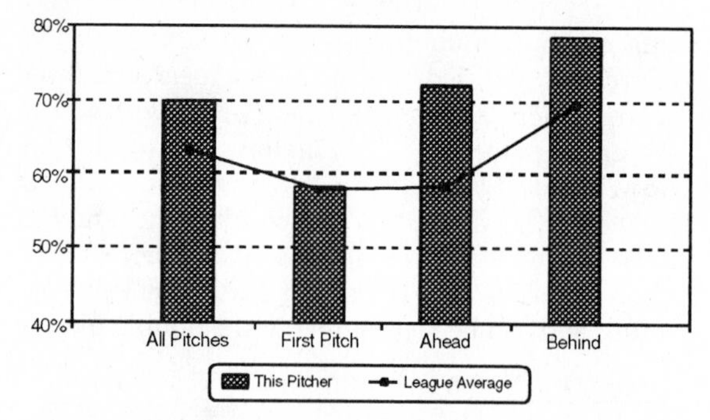

1992 Situational Stats

	W	L	ERA	Sv	IP		AB	H	HR	RBI	AVG
Home	3	1	3.60	19	35.0	LHB	108	33	5	15	.306
Road	2	1	3.13	11	23.0	RHB	122	34	1	22	.279
Day	2	0	2.70	8	20.0	Sc Pos	61	21	2	32	.344
Night	3	2	3.79	22	38.0	Clutch	167	47	5	33	.281

1992 Rankings (National League)

- Did not rank near the top or bottom in any category

GREAT SPEED

DEION SANDERS

Position: CF/LF
Bats: L **Throws:** L
Ht: 6' 1" **Wt:** 195

Opening Day Age: 25
Born: 8/9/67 in Ft. Myers, FL
ML Seasons: 4

HITTING:

The love/hate relationship with "Neon" Deion (or is it "Ice Man"?) Sanders climaxed during the postseason, when baseball fans got about two shots of Sanders sitting in the dugout to each one of his on-field action. Prior to 1992, Deion seemed little more than a circus sideshow attraction whose baseball talents were considered suspect.

Last season, however, Sanders finally proved he could play. After batting .234, .158 and .191 in his first three seasons, he hit .304. His knack for the most exciting play in baseball, the triple, turned on even marginal fans. Sanders had six triples in April alone and wound up with 14 three-baggers, the most in baseball, in only 303 at-bats.

Sanders was used as a platoon player for most of the year, but that was for the benefit of Otis Nixon. His performance against lefties -- .271 average, .583 slugging in 48 at-bats -- indicated pretty strongly that he can play every day. A very aggressive hitter, Sanders loves the fastball and will jump on the first pitch (.354 in 64 at-bats last year).

BASERUNNING:

Sanders is universally acknowledged as the fastest man in baseball. He steals a high number of bases (26 in 1992, 46 career) and doesn't get caught too often. As his triples total suggests, Sanders rarely stops at second on a gap hit.

FIELDING:

Blazing speed never hurts afield, either. The Nixon/Sanders combo graces the Braves with two center fielders who are better than most teams' best. When Sanders goes into the game defensively as a late inning left fielder, there's not too much that can fall in between those two.

OVERALL:

Since the Braves seem to be tolerating Sanders' two-sport ways -- they didn't discipline him for playing football during the NLCS and then protected him in the expansion draft -- he will probably continue to be a part-time baseball player in 1993. "He'd be a helluva player if he just played baseball," said Bobby Cox of Sanders early in the 1992 season. The evidence indicates that he's one already.

Overall Statistics

	G	AB	R	H	D	T	HR	RBI	SB	BB	SO	AVG
1992	97	303	54	92	6	14	8	28	26	18	52	.304
Career	222	593	101	145	11	18	17	57	46	46	110	.245

Where He Hits the Ball

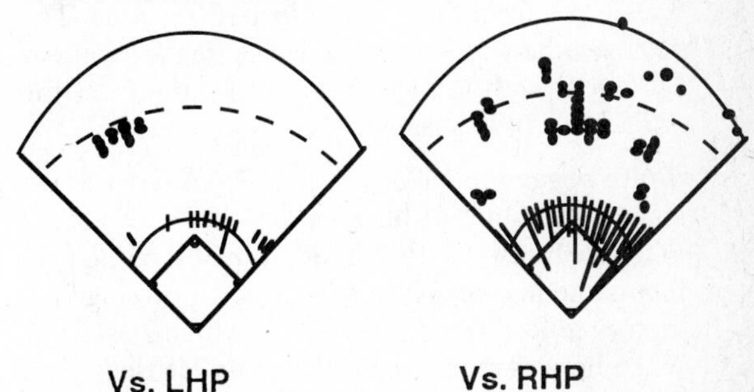

1992 Situational Stats

	AB	H	HR	RBI	AVG		AB	H	HR	RBI	AVG
Home	138	36	5	14	.261	LHP	48	13	2	5	.271
Road	165	56	3	14	.339	RHP	255	79	6	23	.310
Day	80	24	2	7	.300	Sc Pos	64	17	0	19	.266
Night	223	68	6	21	.305	Clutch	44	13	3	8	.295

1992 Rankings (National League)

- 1st in triples (14)
- Led the Braves in triples, batting average in the clutch (.296) and batting average on a 3-1 count (.500)
- Led NL center fielders in triples

PETE SMITH

Position: SP
Bats: R **Throws:** R
Ht: 6' 2" **Wt:** 200

Opening Day Age: 27
Born: 2/27/66 in Weymouth, MA
ML Seasons: 6

PITCHING:

Pete Smith finally had a taste of the "best of times" in 1992. He had certainly been through the "worst of times" from 1987 through 1991. Plagued by arm problems, Smith entered '92 with a career record of 19-40, and had a four-season run in which his ERAs had been 3.69, 4.75, 4.79 and 5.06. Recalled in midseason, Smith finally showed what he could do when completely healthy. In 12 games (11 starts), he went 7-0 with a 2.05 ERA.

Smith had been expected to pitch like this since 1985, when the Braves obtained the former first-round draft choice from Philadelphia. He arrived in Atlanta to stay in 1988, going 7-15 despite a 3.69 ERA for a club which lost 106 games. The next year he was 5-14, and then came the shoulder problems with led to rotator cuff surgery at the end of the 1990 season.

Smith began the 1992 season at AAA Richmond, and the first hint of his recovery came on May 2 when he threw the first International League perfect game in over 17 seasons, a seven-inning, 1-0 victory at Rochester. He was 7-4 with a 2.14 ERA when he was recalled on July 29th. He displayed his usual repertoire upon his return: fastball, slider, curve and circle change. Apparently, the surgery has revived Smith's 90-MPH fastball and hard slider, by far his two best pitches. He can dominate right-handed batters, as evidenced by their .219 average over the past five years, .161 in 1992.

HOLDING RUNNERS, FIELDING, HITTING:

The new Pete Smith looked the same as the old version to baserunners. Only two of ten who challenged Smith's catchers were caught. He is a good fielder, but would do best to stay out of the much-publicized Avery-Glavine-Smoltz hitting contests.

OVERALL:

Smith closed out his comeback season by posting a 2.45 ERA in two playoff appearances, then hurling three scoreless innings in Game 6 of the World Series. He clearly is all the way back, and figures to be a rotation starter in 1993 -- if not for pitching-rich Atlanta, then for someone else.

Overall Statistics

	W	L	ERA	G	GS	Sv	IP	H	R	BB	SO	HR
1992	7	0	2.05	12	11	0	79.0	63	19	28	43	3
Career	26	40	4.05	105	99	0	573.0	554	290	233	378	50

How Often He Throws Strikes

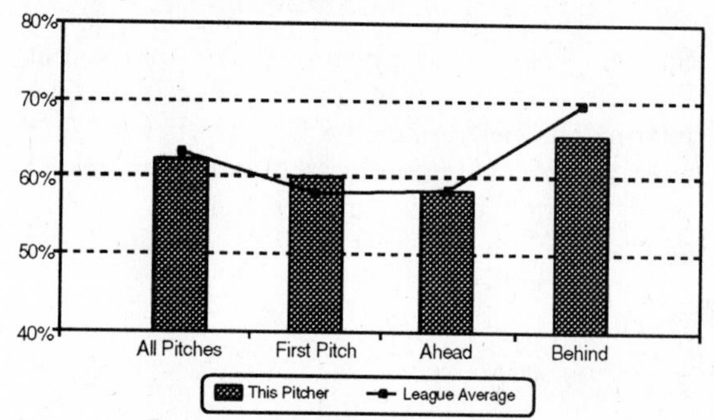

1992 Situational Stats

	W	L	ERA	Sv	IP		AB	H	HR	RBI	AVG
Home	3	0	2.28	0	27.2	LHB	178	45	1	10	.253
Road	4	0	1.93	0	51.1	RHB	112	18	2	6	.161
Day	2	0	1.77	0	20.1	Sc Pos	61	8	0	11	.131
Night	5	0	2.15	0	58.2	Clutch	30	5	0	0	.167

1992 Rankings (National League)

- 2nd in least GDPs induced per GDP situation (2.3%)

WORKHORSE

PITCHING:

The question of who is the ace of the Atlanta staff was answered by Bobby Cox last October. In the National League playoffs, the series Atlanta **had** to win, Cox chose John Smoltz to start Games 1, 4 and 7. As usual, Smoltz came through; Atlanta won all three contests, with Smoltz getting the victory in the first two. He was almost as good in the World Series. Jeff Reardon blew a seemingly-certain win for Smoltz in Game 2; then, with Atlanta down three games to one, he came through with a victory in Game 5. In nine postseason starts over the last two years, Smoltz is 5-0 with a 2.13 ERA. That's what you call an ace.

There's not much that Smoltz can't throw and throw well. His fastball is 90-plus and of the rising variety. He throws a good curveball and one of the best sliders in the business. Smoltz uses both a circle and regular change to keep hitters off-balance. (He had experimented with a split-fingered offspeed pitch, but abandoned it partway into the year.) When he has problems, they stem from lack of control, Smoltz's hitch since early in his career. He tied for third in the National League in walks allowed with 80 and led in wild pitches with 17.

HOLDING RUNNERS, FIELDING, HITTING:

Smoltz is a good athlete with sound mound fundamentals. He controlled the running game well; Brave catchers caught seven baserunners in 18 attempts with Smoltz on the mound. His defense is good (five double plays in 1992). Not an automatic out at the plate, he has shown some muscle with two career homers and 17 RBI.

OVERALL:

It is hard to believe that Smoltz won't turn 26 until the 1993 season is a month old. He seems to be -- and pitches like -- a grizzled veteran. One of these years he'll either: a) manage to keep his postseason pitching intensity through an entire regular season, or b) receive Cy Young run support and join Tom Glavine as a decorated "Young Gun."

JOHN SMOLTZ

Position: SP
Bats: R **Throws:** R
Ht: 6' 3" **Wt:** 185

Opening Day Age: 25
Born: 5/15/67 in Warren, MI
ML Seasons: 5

Overall Statistics

	W	L	ERA	G	GS	Sv	IP	H	R	BB	SO	HR
1992	15	12	2.85	35	35	0	246.2	206	90	80	215	17
Career	57	54	3.50	146	146	0	979.2	852	419	352	738	78

How Often He Throws Strikes

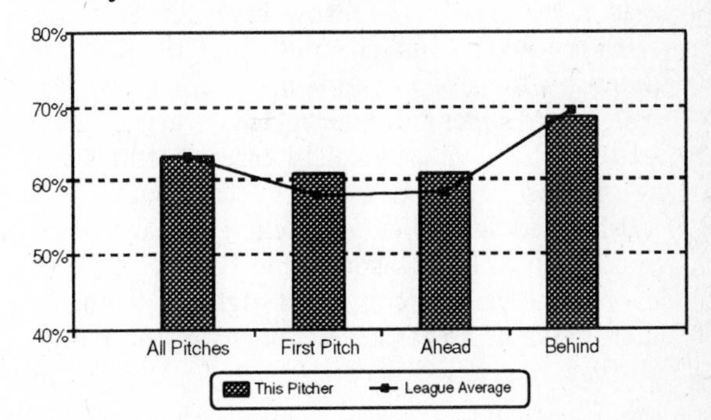

1992 Situational Stats

	W	L	ERA	Sv	IP		AB	H	HR	RBI	AVG
Home	5	6	2.87	0	103.1	LHB	544	134	9	38	.246
Road	10	6	2.83	0	143.1	RHB	377	72	8	34	.191
Day	7	4	2.36	0	87.2	Sc Pos	199	38	5	54	.191
Night	8	8	3.11	0	159.0	Clutch	110	20	3	5	.182

1992 Rankings (National League)

- 1st in games started (35), strikeouts (215), wild pitches (17) and pitches thrown (3,768)
- 2nd in batters faced (1,021)
- 3rd in innings pitched (246.2), walks allowed (80), most strikeouts per 9 innings (7.8) and lowest batting average allowed vs. right-handed batters (.191)
- Led the Braves in losses (12), games started, complete games (9), innings pitched, batters faced, home runs allowed (17), walks allowed, hit batsmen (5), strikeouts, wild pitches, pitches thrown, highest strikeout/walk ratio (2.7), lowest batting average allowed (.224) and lowest on-base percentage allowed (.287)

PITCHING:

Watch out for Mike Stanton in 1993. Last season looked like a washout year for the 25-year-old lefty. But Stanton was shelled in a three-outing stretch between May 23 and June 1. Throw out those bad 10 days and his ERA melts from 4.10 to 3.34. Late in the year he put together a masterful string of pitching, one which showed what he's capable of doing. From August 30 through October 2 he compiled a 20.1 inning string of no earned runs, 14 strikeouts and 1 walk. Then Stanton was awesome in the playoffs and World Series, not allowing a run in nine appearances.

Stanton's delivery, which features what must be the highest leg kick in the major leagues, is the reason he appears to throw so hard. His knee almost touches his chest during his delivery. Stanton's tools of the trade are a 90+ MPH fastball, a hard slider and a curve. He is very tough on lefties, who have only a .214 career batting average against him, as is usually the case with a good left-handed fastball/slider pitcher. He had 11 save opportunities last season in the Braves' bullpen-by-committee and converted eight of them. He didn't give up an earned run in any of those eight outings.

Stanton has always been a second-half pitcher, and 1992 was no exception. He had a 6.10 ERA before the All-Star break, 2.20 ERA afterwards. For his career, Stanton has a 5.86 ERA pre-All Star, 2.29 post-All Star.

HOLDING RUNNERS, FIELDING, HITTING:

Stanton holds runners well. He picked off two last year and had but one steal against him in three tries. He is a surprisingly adept fielder for a pitcher with an awkward motion. His .500 (4-for-8) career batting average was maintained as he singled in two 1992 at-bats.

OVERALL:

Jeff Reardon's free agency, Alejandro Pena's injuries and Mark Wohlers' inability to stick thus far leave the Braves' stopper job wide open for 1993. Stanton figures to be in the hunt; if he's not the closer, he's sure to get plenty of work.

MIKE STANTON

Position: RP
Bats: L **Throws:** L
Ht: 6' 1" **Wt:** 190

Opening Day Age: 25
Born: 6/2/67 in Houston, TX
ML Seasons: 4

Overall Statistics

	W	L	ERA	G	GS	Sv	IP	H	R	BB	SO	HR
1992	5	4	4.10	65	0	8	63.2	59	32	20	44	6
Career	10	13	3.75	166	0	24	172.2	154	79	53	132	13

How Often He Throws Strikes

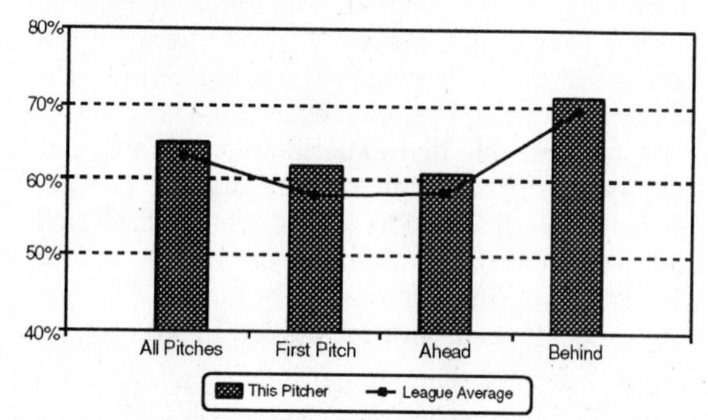

1992 Situational Stats

	W	L	ERA	Sv	IP		AB	H	HR	RBI	AVG
Home	2	1	3.00	3	30.0	LHB	76	18	4	9	.237
Road	3	3	5.08	5	33.2	RHB	163	41	2	18	.252
Day	0	1	5.87	1	15.1	Sc Pos	61	13	1	21	.213
Night	5	3	3.54	7	48.1	Clutch	139	34	4	18	.245

1992 Rankings (National League)

- 5th in holds (15)
- 8th in highest relief ERA (4.10)
- Led the Braves in games pitched (65), blown saves (3), lowest percentage of inherited runners scored (25.0%) and least baserunners allowed per 9 innings in relief (11.5)

DAMON BERRYHILL

Position: C
Bats: B **Throws:** R
Ht: 6' 0" **Wt:** 205

Opening Day Age: 29
Born: 12/3/63 in South Laguna, CA
ML Seasons: 6

Overall Statistics

	G	AB	R	H	D	T	HR	RBI	SB	BB	SO	AVG
1992	101	307	21	70	16	1	10	43	0	17	67	.228
Career	379	1191	98	281	60	2	28	146	3	69	238	.236

HITTING, FIELDING, BASERUNNING:

In the late-1980s, the major leagues were full of feeble-hitting catchers, and the promising Damon Berryhill looked like he would provide the Cubs with a rare commodity. Berryhill's career was just getting untracked when he suffered a rotator cuff injury in 1989. With Joe Girardi and Rick Wilkins now filling the Cubs' catching needs, Berryhill was shipped to Georgia for a new start.

Berryhill flashed a glimpse of his occasional power on a Jack Morris hanging forkball and pulled out a World Series Game 1 victory for Atlanta. The switch-hitter has not hit very well from either side so far in his career (.248 as a righty, .233 as a lefty), but he's finally fully healthy.

Berryhill's defensive talents will both benefit and suffer by working with the Braves' pitchers. His ability to call a game, always top-notch, will appear even better than usual. But his once-heralded throwing arm will look weak supporting the slow-winding Atlanta power-pitchers. He's no running threat, with only three career stolen bases.

OVERALL:

The questionable status of Greg Olson might provide a golden opportunity for Berryhill. Unless Javy Lopez is ready for a big-league platoon job, he should see plenty of playing time in 1993. The Braves are no doubt glad they decided to take a chance on him.

MARK DAVIS

Position: RP/SP
Bats: L **Throws:** L
Ht: 6' 4" **Wt:** 210

Opening Day Age: 32
Born: 10/19/60 in Livermore, CA
ML Seasons: 12

Overall Statistics

	W	L	ERA	G	GS	Sv	IP	H	R	BB	SO	HR
1992	2	3	7.13	27	6	0	53.0	64	44	41	34	9
Career	50	78	4.07	525	85	92	1042.2	948	517	472	908	111

PITCHING, FIELDING, HITTING & HOLDING RUNNERS:

Does a 37-year-old middle reliever (Juan Berenguer) in exchange for a 31-year-old former Cy Young Award winner (Mark Davis) seem like a fair trade? Maybe it does, considering the way Mark Davis has pitched the last three years. Braves' GM John Schuerholz, the man who signed the lefthander for the Royals, proved that it's possible to make the same mistake twice. Last year Davis had a 7.18 ERA in 13 games for Kansas City, 7.02 in 14 games for Atlanta.

The unhittable curveball of 1989 has become just a plain ball in recent years. Davis has an average major league fastball, but without the bender he's been lost. His strikeout to walk ratio has disintegrated from 92/31 in '89, to 73/52 in '90, to 47/34 in '91 to 34/41 in '92. He's been tried as a middle man, a starter, and even at times as a closer again over the past couple of years, all to no avail.

Davis is poor at stopping the running game, too. He is a good fielder and pretty descent hitter, but no one will care if his pitching never returns.

OVERALL:

There's not much room in the Atlanta bullpen or their starting rotation for pitchers who need a break to get back on track. Yet the Braves haven't made too many bad moves lately, either. Davis certainly can't get any worse.

BRIAN HUNTER

Position: 1B
Bats: R **Throws:** L
Ht: 6' 0" **Wt:** 195

Opening Day Age: 25
Born: 3/4/68 in Torrance, CA
ML Seasons: 2

Overall Statistics

	G	AB	R	H	D	T	HR	RBI	SB	BB	SO	AVG
1992	102	238	34	57	13	2	14	41	1	21	50	.239
Career	199	509	66	125	29	3	26	91	1	38	98	.246

HITTING, FIELDING, BASERUNNING:

Brian "Big Game" Hunter has, hopefully, begun figuring out the big game of life. Rising out of the minors to post some impressive numbers, Hunter encountered plenty of off-season trouble. He was twice convicted of driving under the influence, underwent a long process of alcoholism counseling and spent two days in jail before spring training began last year.

Don't expect a high batting average from Hunter. He has never hit higher than .260 in more than 50 at-bats at any level above single-A. Power is how this dead pull hitter makes his living. Last year, in a strict platoon role, he struggled versus righties (.181, 15-for-83). In 1991, when he played more regularly, he hit .233 (35-for-150) with six homers vs. righthanders. A chance to play full-time might improve his ability to hit vs. righties.

Hunter was a good defensive first baseman as an amateur. The minor-league outfielder relearned the position quickly in the bigs. He has good speed for a big man and gets down the line in a hurry. He's hasn't done well as a basestealer, though, with only one steal in five career tries.

OVERALL:

As long as Sid Bream is still around, Hunter will probably have to live with his current platoon situation. It's a shame, because he has intriguing power potential. In his major-league career, he has 26 homers and 91 RBI in 509 at-bats.

LONNIE SMITH

Position: LF
Bats: R **Throws:** R
Ht: 5' 9" **Wt:** 190

Opening Day Age: 37
Born: 12/22/55 in Chicago, IL
ML Seasons: 15

Overall Statistics

	G	AB	R	H	D	T	HR	RBI	SB	BB	SO	AVG
1992	84	158	23	39	8	2	6	33	4	17	37	.247
Career	1475	4888	853	1414	264	54	90	504	360	561	779	.289

HITTING, FIELDING, BASERUNNING:

Do they still call him "Skates"? It's a shame that Lonnie Smith may leave memories of horrendous fielding and his baserunning error in the '91 World Series, because he could always hit. From the speedy high-average high-order kid to the recent, more muscled, patient vet with quite a bit of pop, pitchers will be pleased when Smith calls it quits.

In the Braves' talent-heavy 1992 outfield, Smith found his lightest duty in a full season yet with only 158 at-bats. Luckily he got some usage in the postseason and erased some of those '91 nightmares with his grand slam homer off Jack Morris. Smith likes to jump on the first-pitch fastball, but if he doesn't get it, he'll work the count to his favor. He likes the ball waist-high from pitchers of either hand.

As his 15-year career winds down, Smith's poor fielding will be exposed less and less. He still can move on the basepaths. He managed to add four steals without being caught to give him 360 career thefts and increase his superior percentage to 73 percent.

OVERALL:

Smith was a free agent after the 1992 season. He can help any team in need of a spare bat with a few big hits still left in it. Maybe, as was his role in the World Series, a DH spot looms on the horizon.

JEFF TREADWAY

Position: 2B
Bats: L **Throws:** R
Ht: 5'11" **Wt:** 170

Opening Day Age: 30
Born: 1/22/63 in Columbus, GA
ML Seasons: 6

Overall Statistics

	G	AB	R	H	D	T	HR	RBI	SB	BB	SO	AVG
1992	61	126	5	28	6	1	0	5	1	9	16	.222
Career	555	1764	199	495	84	12	26	163	12	116	151	.281

HITTING, FIELDING, BASERUNNING:

Even though Mark Lemke couldn't carry his 1991 postseason heroics into 1992, Jeff Treadway was unable to take advantage. Treadway underwent hand surgery in the spring and wasn't able to come off the disabled list until late June. When he did return, Lemke was hitting poorly. Although Treadway was given a crack at the platoon arrangement that worked successfully during 1991, he failed to hit and Bobby Cox soon went back to his defensive whiz, Lemke, on a full-time basis.

Treadway batted a career-low .222, a drop of 98 points from his 1991 figure of .320. Treadway must hit .280 or better to be a valuable commodity. He has decent power for a middle infielder, but is not a patient hitter. He can pull a righthander's inside fastball well. Also, he's a good bunter. His bat work hasn't kept him on the bench with the Braves.

But Treadway's fielding is no match for Lemke. He is competent, while Lemke excels. He has average speed and has never been a threat to steal.

OVERALL:

The Braves apparently felt Treadway has slipped pretty badly because they released him after the season. While he's not the greatest fielder in the world, he's a .281 lifetime hitter, and he bats lefty. That should be enough to interest somebody.

MARK WOHLERS

Position: RP
Bats: R **Throws:** R
Ht: 6' 4" **Wt:** 207

Opening Day Age: 23
Born: 1/23/70 in Holyoke, MA
ML Seasons: 2

Overall Statistics

	W	L	ERA	G	GS	Sv	IP	H	R	BB	SO	HR
1992	1	2	2.55	32	0	4	35.1	28	11	14	17	0
Career	4	3	2.78	49	0	6	55.0	45	18	27	30	1

PITCHING, FIELDING, HITTING & HOLDING RUNNERS:

The baseball world still anxiously awaits the true arrival of Baseball America's lucky Number 13 prospect, Mark Wohlers. The much heralded fireballer was supposed to make his move last season. But he struggled with his control in the spring and was demoted to AAA Richmond instead. Wohlers returned late in the year and showed flashes of brilliance, but was then pushed aside in favor of newly-acquired Jeff Reardon.

There's hardly need to mention Wohlers' legendary triple-digit fastball. He abandoned a cut fastball and now complements the blazer with a slider and change-up. His effortless motion is amazing considering the incredible heat he generates. Chuck LaMar, Braves director of player development and scouting was quoted as saying, "Mark's mechanics are such that he has a chance to throw night after night with that velocity and hopefully stay healthy."

Most pitchers who throw smoke are easy to steal on, and Wohlers is no exception. He is a good fielder and batting is not a big concern for this future closer.

OVERALL:

Wohlers must have been a little frustrated by Reardon's arrival. But if he can get his control working more consistently this spring, there's a great chance we'll see a lot of him in 1992. Unless Atlanta picks up a free agent stopper, the door should be open.

ORGANIZATION OVERVIEW:

The rich get richer. The two-time defending National League champions Braves have a roster loaded with good players, most of them fairly young. The bad news for the rest of the league is that Atlanta has just as many good ones -- maybe more -- in their well-stocked farm system. Finishing last several years in a row gave the Braves some outstanding draft picks, and the organization didn't make very many mistakes. Duane Ward (now with Toronto), Tommy Greene (Phillies), Kent Mercker, Steve Avery, Chipper Jones and Mike Kelly were all Atlanta Number One picks over the last decade. With a keen eye for talent, Atlanta figures to have a steady stream of talent coming up for a few more years, at least.

DON ELLIOTT

Position: P **Opening Day Age:** 24
Bats: R **Throws:** R **Born:** 9/20/68 in Pasadena, TX
Ht: 6' 4" **Wt:** 190

Recent Statistics

	W	L	ERA	G	GS	Sv	IP	H	R	BB	SO	HR
92 A Clearwater	1	1	3.00	3	3	0	18.0	12	6	8	12	1
92 AA Reading	3	3	2.52	6	6	0	35.2	37	10	11	23	2
92 AA Greenville	7	2	2.08	19	17	0	103.2	76	28	35	100	8

Righthander Elliott labored for years in the Philadelphia system, usually compiling excellent strikeout totals and low ERAs. The Braves obtained him in midseason last year. Though they have plenty of home-grown prospects, the Braves were very impressed with the tall, thin righthander's work last year. Elliott was 7-2, 2.08 at AA Greenville, and had his usual superior strikeout-to-walk ratio. He'll most likely be in AAA ball this year.

CHIPPER JONES

Position: SS **Opening Day Age:** 20
Bats: B **Throws:** R **Born:** 4/24/72 in Deland, FL
Ht: 6' 3" **Wt:** 185

Recent Statistics

	G	AB	R	H	D	T	HR	RBI	SB	BB	SO	AVG
91 A Macon	136	473	104	153	24	11	15	98	39	69	70	.323
92 A Durham	70	264	43	73	22	1	4	31	10	31	34	.277
92 AA Greenville	67	266	43	92	17	11	9	42	14	11	32	.346
92 MLE	67	258	35	84	15	5	9	35	9	7	33	.326

How good a prospect is Chipper Jones? Well, he split last season between two leagues, the Class A Carolina League and the AA Southern League, and the managers of BOTH leagues chose Jones as the number-one prospect in Baseball America. Most players need to adjust to moving up to the AA level, but Jones got better: he batted .346 and slugged .594 in 67 games. His ability to play big-league shortstop has been questioned, but his defense has been improving. He'll play a position in the majors very soon.

RYAN KLESKO

Position: 1B **Opening Day Age:** 21
Bats: L **Throws:** L **Born:** 6/12/71 in Westminster, CA
Ht: 6' 3" **Wt:** 220

Recent Statistics

	G	AB	R	H	D	T	HR	RBI	SB	BB	SO	AVG
92 AAA Richmond	123	418	63	105	22	2	17	59	3	41	72	.251
92 NL Atlanta	13	14	0	0	0	0	0	1	0	0	5	.000
92 MLE	123	409	50	96	19	1	15	47	2	31	74	.235

Don't look back, Sid Bream, someone's gaining on you -- it's Ryan Klesko. Not yet 22, the big first baseman reached the AAA level last year and had a tough time in the early going. But he finished strongly and wound up with 17 homers. A gung-ho type, Klesko might need another year at AAA. His defense is shaky, and some question his motivation to improve it. Klesko looked a little overawed in a late-season trial with Atlanta, going hitless in 14 at-bats. The Braves will be patient with him.

JAVIER LOPEZ

Position: C **Opening Day Age:** 22
Bats: R **Throws:** R **Born:** 11/5/70 in Ponce, PR
Ht: 6' 3" **Wt:** 210

Recent Statistics

	G	AB	R	H	D	T	HR	RBI	SB	BB	SO	AVG
92 AA Greenville	115	442	63	142	28	3	16	60	7	24	47	.321
92 NL Atlanta	9	16	3	6	2	0	0	2	0	0	1	.375
92 MLE	115	432	53	132	25	1	15	50	4	16	49	.306

When the 1992 season ended, some wags suggested that the Braves' AA farm club at Greenville was better than the Seattle Mariners. That's a slight exaggeration, but Greenville went 100-43 and their catcher, Lopez, was one of the reasons. Lopez, just 22, batted .321 with 16 homers at Greenville and then hit .375 in nine games for Atlanta. His arm came under some scrutiny last year, but he's improving his defensive mechanics. The Braves need a catcher; Lopez could be their man before the '93 season is out.

MELVIN NIEVES

Position: OF **Opening Day Age:** 21
Bats: B **Throws:** R **Born:** 12/28/71 in San Juan, PR
Ht: 6' 2" **Wt:** 200

Recent Statistics

	G	AB	R	H	D	T	HR	RBI	SB	BB	SO	AVG
92 A Durham	31	106	18	32	9	1	8	32	4	17	33	.302
92 AA Greenville	100	350	61	99	23	5	18	76	6	52	98	.283
92 NL Atlanta	12	19	0	4	1	0	0	1	0	2	7	.211
92 MLE	100	343	50	92	21	2	18	63	3	33	103	.268

Ted Turner, this isn't fair: you've got Jane Fonda, three TV networks, Dominique Wilkins, the Braves, Neon Deion . . . and all these great prospects. Nieves, another star from that juggernaut at Greenville, was rated the Southern League's number-two prospect. The switch-hitting outfielder has great power, plays good defense and reminds people of Ruben Sierra.

PITCHING:

Normally one of the few dependables in the Cub bullpen, Paul Assenmacher had a difficult season in 1992. After posting a 2.87 ERA before the All-Star break, the lefty had a 5.64 mark in the second half. Assenmacher's overall ERA of 4.10 was the second-worst of his seven-year career.

The defining workhorse of the team, Assenmacher has pitched in at least 70 games during each of his three full seasons with the Cubs. He worked over 100 innings in both 1990 and 1991, but his 1992 stints were far shorter. Despite the shorter appearances, Assenmacher was still warmed up in almost any conceivable game situation, as he has been throughout his Cub career. His ugly second-half numbers make it conceivable that his arm is losing its resiliency.

Assenmacher's career has relied on a nasty, quick-breaking overhand curve that he uses both to set up the count and to get the hook. As last season wore on his curve was staying up, and his 88 MPH fastball was too hittable. Usually untouchable versus lefty swingers, Assenmacher allowed three homers to lefties last season. He was also too predictable; hitters were sitting and waiting on his first-pitch fastball, on which he allowed a .333 opposing average and four of his six home runs. His curve is still punishing when down in the strike zone, however, and he posted his customarily excellent strikeout numbers.

HOLDING RUNNERS, FIELDING, HITTING:

The big overhand delivery that Assenmacher employs has always made him easy to run against, but last year his pickoff move was being read too easily also. Opposing runners stole 9 of 11 bases off the lefty, who worked with two above-average catchers. His fielding is very solid. Assenmacher's an .059 lifetime hitter, but doesn't bat enough to make it a problem.

OVERALL:

The Cub pitching staff in September was a sorry sight. That definitely included Assenmacher, whose last-month ERA was 7.36. The shaky finish was a big reason the Cubs surprisingly left him unprotected in the expansion draft. Assenmacher's hefty contract contributed to the decision.

PAUL ASSENMACHER

Position: RP
Bats: L **Throws:** L
Ht: 6' 3" **Wt:** 200

Opening Day Age: 32
Born: 12/10/60 in Detroit, MI
ML Seasons: 7

Overall Statistics

	W	L	ERA	G	GS	Sv	IP	H	R	BB	SO	HR
1992	4	4	4.10	70	0	8	68.0	72	32	26	67	6
Career	37	29	3.44	459	1	47	552.2	512	235	203	524	46

How Often He Throws Strikes

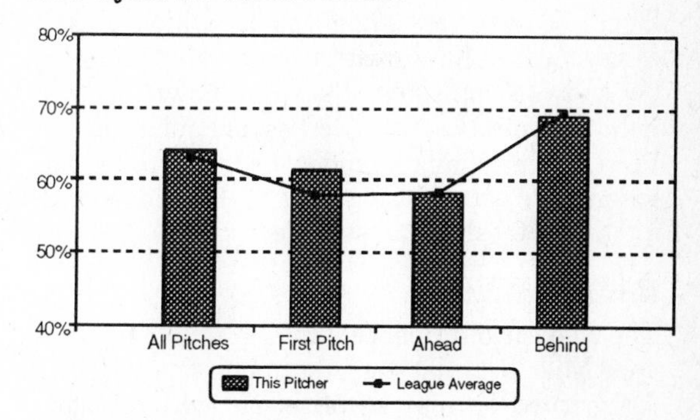

1992 Situational Stats

	W	L	ERA	Sv	IP		AB	H	HR	RBI	AVG
Home	2	3	4.15	5	39.0	LHB	91	20	3	11	.220
Road	2	1	4.03	3	29.0	RHB	175	52	3	28	.297
Day	3	3	3.70	6	41.1	Sc Pos	94	20	2	35	.213
Night	1	1	4.72	2	26.2	Clutch	176	42	2	23	.239

1992 Rankings (National League)

- 2nd in holds (20)
- 3rd in first batter efficiency (.143)
- 5th in lowest percentage of inherited runners scored (21.0%)
- 7th in highest relief ERA (4.10) and most strikeouts per 9 innings pitched in relief (8.9)
- 8th in highest batting average allowed in relief (.271) and most baserunners allowed per 9 innings in relief (13.4)
- 9th in games pitched (70)
- Led the Cubs in holds, blown saves (5), first batter efficiency and lowest percentage of inherited runners scored

STEVE BUECHELE

Position: 3B
Bats: R **Throws:** R
Ht: 6' 2" **Wt:** 200

Opening Day Age: 31
Born: 9/26/61 in Lancaster, CA
ML Seasons: 8

HITTING:

It wasn't Steve Buechele's fault that he hit just one homer in 65 games for the Cubs. Ask Gary Scott -- it's the Curse of Ron Santo. The Cubs finally figured they'd put an end to their everlasting lack of offensive production at third base by sending malcontent Danny Jackson, their only left-handed starter, to the Pirates for Buechele in early July.

What looked like the perfect solution, even a pennant-race solidifier at the time, didn't turn out that way. For the Cubs, Buechele batted .276, but had just 13 extra-base hits in 239 at-bats. Overall, Buechele smacked only nine homers, far less than the 22 he had hit in 1991.

Buechele has a very straight stance which doesn't always afford him great plate coverage, and his bat shows some signs of slowing down. He will help the Cubs beat up on lefties, but at his current level of play against righties, he needs to be platooned. He batted just .233 vs. righthanders with a pitiful .309 slugging average.

BASERUNNING:

The 31-year-old Buechele runs a lot like middle-aged Mike Schmidt -- not fast, but if you take him for granted he may surprise. He will not steal bases and is slow out of the batter's box, but once he gets going he's okay.

FIELDING:

Buechele was valued as much for his defense as anything on a staff so heavily groundball-oriented. Touted as a Gold Glove candidate in the American League, Buechele has good lateral range to either side and a fine arm. His errors come on slow choppers and errant throws, and the slow grass at Wrigley may cause him to play more shallow than he cares to.

OVERALL:

Barring some real curse, Buechele should rebound to do damage in the lower part of the Cub order. At worst, Buechele is a solid defender who can hit lefties consistently, but he needs to improve versus righties to make a bigger impact.

Overall Statistics

	G	AB	R	H	D	T	HR	RBI	SB	BB	SO	AVG
1992	145	524	52	137	23	4	9	64	1	52	105	.261
Career	1056	3337	405	816	143	18	107	421	15	306	653	.245

Where He Hits the Ball

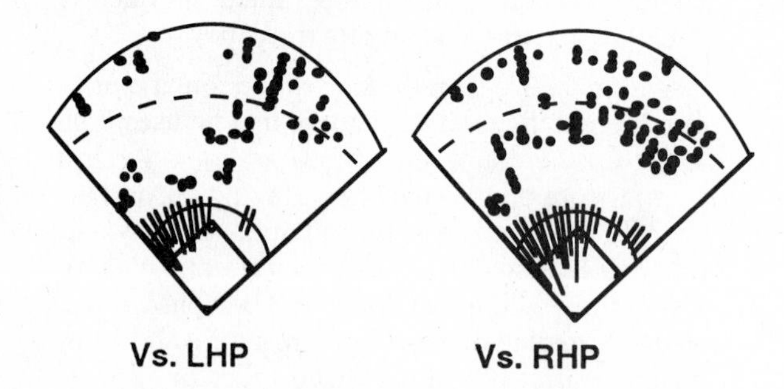

1992 Situational Stats

	AB	H	HR	RBI	AVG		AB	H	HR	RBI	AVG
Home	276	68	4	32	.246	LHP	207	63	5	26	.304
Road	248	69	5	32	.278	RHP	317	74	4	38	.233
Day	188	49	3	21	.261	Sc Pos	146	41	0	51	.281
Night	336	88	6	43	.262	Clutch	105	22	0	6	.210

1992 Rankings (National League)

- 6th in most pitches seen per plate appearance (3.89)
- 8th in hit by pitch (7) and strikeouts (105)
- 9th in lowest batting average at home (.246)
- Led the Cubs in hit by pitch (5)

PITCHING:

It's normally not a good sign for a team when the best midseason pitching help it can find is a converted shortstop like Jim Bullinger. But such was the case for the Cubs, whose top pitching prospects hurt their arms and allowed Bullinger his route to Wrigley and protection among the Cubs 15.

Bullinger was leading the American Association in saves at the time of his recall. Things started grandly for the rookie. Between June 8 and June 26 he converted seven straight save opportunities, won National League Player of the Week honors, and had a 2.53 ERA with seven hits allowed in 10.2 innings. Strangely, after one bad outing on July 1st, he was yanked from the closer's role and shifted to middle relief. Eventually he landed a tryout in the rotation. He threw the first Cub one-hitter since 1983 in his third start -- another strong beginning, but it would be his only win in nine starts. He was 1-6 with a 5.15 ERA as a starter.

Bullinger's stuff is not very impressive. He throws over the top with a good, big-breaking curve and has an assortment of offspeed pitches to complement a 87-89 MPH fastball, which the Cubs encourage him to use more. Bullinger's main problem, which may keep him from much of a career, is that he has no command of the strike zone; he walked 54 batters in 85 innings and whiffed only 36.

HOLDING RUNNERS, FIELDING, HITTING:

Trick question: Which Cubs shortstop or converted shortstop hit the most home runs in 1992: Dunston, Sanchez, Vizcaino, Arias, or Bullinger? Answer: Bullinger tied for the lead with one. He homered on the first major league pitch he faced, another bit of personal glory. He fields his position well, but his junkball repertoire makes him very easy to steal upon.

OVERALL:

The Cubs saw something in either Bullinger's 7-for-7 save streak or his one-hitter that led them to believe that this 27-year-old rookie was a major league pitcher. They're betting against a ton of evidence that suggests he is not.

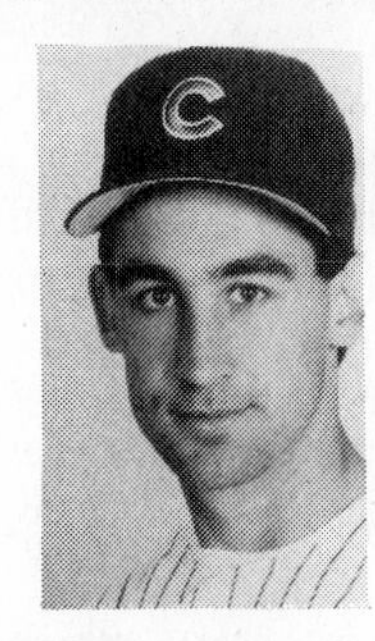

JIM BULLINGER

Position: RP/SP
Bats: R **Throws:** R
Ht: 6' 2" **Wt:** 185

Opening Day Age: 27
Born: 8/21/65 in New Orleans, LA
ML Seasons: 1

Overall Statistics

	W	L	ERA	G	GS	Sv	IP	H	R	BB	SO	HR
1992	2	8	4.66	39	9	7	85.0	72	49	54	36	9
Career	2	8	4.66	39	9	7	85.0	72	49	54	36	9

How Often He Throws Strikes

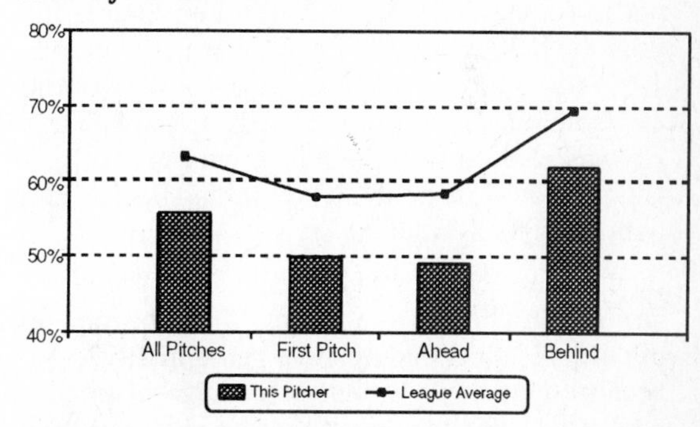

1992 Situational Stats

	W	L	ERA	Sv	IP		AB	H	HR	RBI	AVG
Home	2	6	3.48	4	54.1	LHB	170	36	6	27	.212
Road	0	2	6.75	3	30.2	RHB	139	36	3	17	.259
Day	2	5	3.64	3	54.1	Sc Pos	74	20	3	35	.270
Night	0	3	6.46	4	30.2	Clutch	90	18	1	9	.200

1992 Rankings (National League)

- Led the Cubs in lowest batting average allowed vs. left-handed batters (.212)

PITCHING:

The one thing that Frank Castillo hasn't done so far in his career is win games. For many folks, the win column alone is enough to praise or condemn, but in Castillo's case it is particularly misleading. Castillo won his 10th game (in just 21 decisions out of 33 starts) on the final day of the season, but "pitched better than a ten-game winner."

Castillo is not a hard thrower, with a fastball in the mid-80s, but the pitch has good downward movement. He uses an excellent straight change to ring up strikeouts, and mixes in a slider and curve. Castillo's keys are his ability to effectively change speeds and his fine control in the bottom portion of the strike zone. He gets into trouble any time the ball gets high above the waist, which in 1992 was a bit too many times. Castillo allowed 19 home runs, fifth-most in the National League. He was also third in the NL in wild pitches and had precious few double plays turned behind him with his flyball-inducing style.

Castillo tires easily and his ball begins to rise, so he shouldn't be allowed to work much beyond 90 pitches. He didn't complete a game in 1992, and because he throws a high percentage of pitches per batter, it has been rare to see him pitching well even in the seventh or eighth inning.

HOLDING RUNNERS, FIELDING, HITTING:

Castillo keeps runners close with a preponderance of pickoff throws, which is necessary due to the fact that he doesn't usually give catchers an easy ball to throw. He is athletic in the field but needs about three months in the batting cage with Ted Williams.

OVERALL:

Castillo is a classically anonymous pretty good number-three starter. He isn't flashy and doesn't overpower anyone, but doesn't walk batters and strikes out more than his share. One caveat: Jim Lefebvre and the Cubs should worry about Castillo at home. Flyball pitchers and Wrigley Field don't mix.

FRANK CASTILLO

Position: SP
Bats: R **Throws:** R
Ht: 6' 1" **Wt:** 180

Opening Day Age: 24
Born: 4/1/69 in El Paso, TX
ML Seasons: 2

Overall Statistics

	W	L	ERA	G	GS	Sv	IP	H	R	BB	SO	HR
1992	10	11	3.46	33	33	0	205.1	179	91	63	135	19
Career	16	18	3.78	51	51	0	317.0	286	147	96	208	24

How Often He Throws Strikes

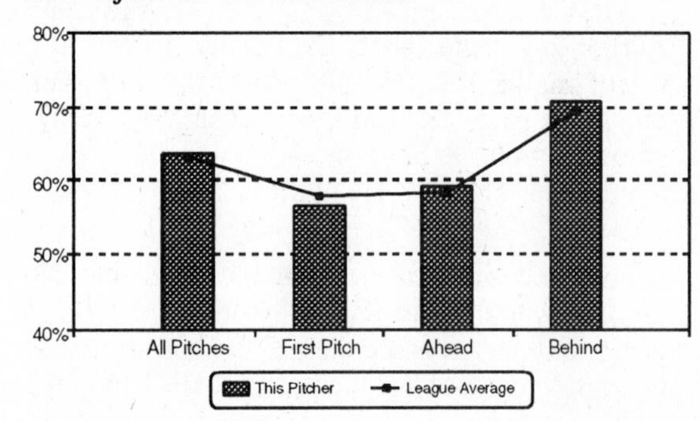

1992 Situational Stats

	W	L	ERA	Sv	IP		AB	H	HR	RBI	AVG
Home	6	7	3.63	0	121.1	LHB	451	103	11	43	.228
Road	4	4	3.21	0	84.0	RHB	319	76	8	26	.238
Day	6	5	3.57	0	108.1	Sc Pos	145	33	3	47	.228
Night	4	6	3.34	0	97.0	Clutch	55	18	1	6	.327

1992 Rankings (National League)

- 3rd in wild pitches (11) and least GDPs induced per 9 innings (.26)
- 5th in home runs allowed (19)
- 6th in hit batsmen (6) and most home runs allowed per 9 innings (.83)
- 7th in least run support per 9 innings (3.5)
- 9th in lowest batting average allowed (.233)
- 10th in games started (33), lowest groundball/flyball ratio (1.2) and most pitches thrown per batter (3.68)
- Led the Cubs in losses (11), home runs allowed and wild pitches

HITTING:

Doug Dascenzo has always been a player for the normal Cub fan to identify with. His stature, demeanor, hustling play, and desire to both be on the field and win make him a popular player whose contributions are magnified. His mistakes usually get the "well, it's only Dascenzo" treatment. In Chicago sports terms, he's a sort of Lilliputian Will Perdue.

One thing this 26th man has is a consistent batting average: .255 last year, .255 in 1991, and .253 in 1990. Even assuming that kind of consistency is positive, beyond that the pickings are mighty slim to try to find a winning player. Many of Dascenzo's past positives became negatives in 1992, not a good sign for an already-limited player. He had some small success against lefties in the past (a .277 career average, .299 in 1991) but in 1992 he slumped to .243 vs. southpaws with a .275 on-base average.

Always in dire straits for a leadoff hitter, Cub skipper Jim Lefebvre couldn't rely on Dascenzo's slap-and-dash to manifest itself on base. Batting leadoff for the Cubs more times than any other player (185 plate appearances), Dascenzo compiled a .285 on-base average in the number-one hole. He said he preferred batting second after one good day, but batted .202 in that slot, too.

BASERUNNING:

Dascenzo has functional speed, but in '92 it functioned well for the opposition. He was nabbed eight times in 14 attempts, including a 2-for-6 success ratio out of the leadoff hole.

FIELDING:

Dascenzo earlier in his career had run up an impressive 442-chance errorless streak, but in 1992 he committed five errors on assorted bobbles and drops. His arm is weak, and his range is good as left fielders go, but very mediocre for a center fielder.

OVERALL:

Well, it's only Dascenzo. But a baseball exec needing a telling stat on the Cubs could begin here: Doug Dascenzo had 81 starts in the Cubs' outfield. At age 28, he offers the Cubs the Four Bottoms: no power, no batting average, no basestealing and no walks.

DOUG DASCENZO

Position: CF/LF/RF
Bats: B **Throws:** L
Ht: 5' 8" **Wt:** 160

Opening Day Age: 28
Born: 6/30/64 in Cleveland, OH
ML Seasons: 5

Overall Statistics

	G	AB	R	H	D	T	HR	RBI	SB	BB	SO	AVG
1992	139	376	37	96	13	4	0	20	6	27	32	.255
Career	443	1070	133	257	37	9	3	80	47	94	93	.240

Where He Hits the Ball

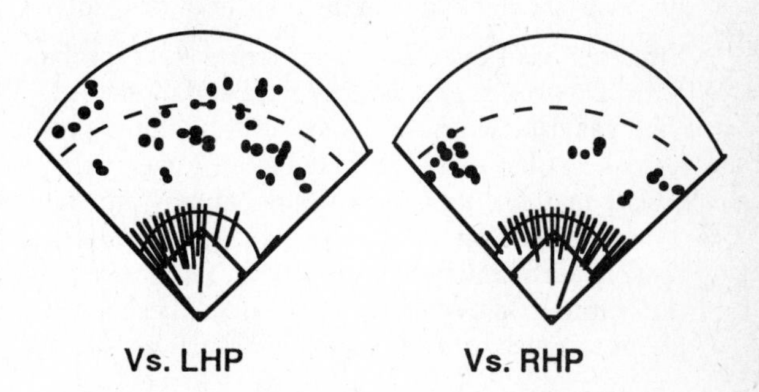

1992 Situational Stats

	AB	H	HR	RBI	AVG		AB	H	HR	RBI	AVG
Home	202	51	0	11	.252	LHP	169	41	0	10	.243
Road	174	45	0	9	.259	RHP	207	55	0	10	.266
Day	199	50	0	10	.251	Sc Pos	78	20	0	19	.256
Night	177	46	0	10	.260	Clutch	81	21	0	3	.259

1992 Rankings (National League)

- 2nd in lowest on-base percentage as a leadoff batter (.285)
- 6th in lowest on-base percentage vs. left-handed pitchers (.275)
- 7th in lowest slugging percentage vs. left-handed pitchers (.296)
- 8th in least GDPs per GDP situation (5.4%)
- Led the Cubs in caught stealing (8) and least GDPs per GDP situation

STRONG ARM

HITTING:

As he nears his 39th birthday, Andre Dawson continues to be a remarkably steady run producer. Since 1977, his first full season, Dawson has averaged 25 homers and 89 RBI per year; his 1992 figures were 22 and 90. Last season was Dawson's 16th straight with 45 or more extra-base hits, a streak surpassed in history only by Henry Aaron's 18.

Dawson continues to treat each pitch as his final opportunity to unleash his 35-inch, 34-ounce club. He recorded his first non-intentional walk of the season on June 7, and it's getting harder for him to be the impact cleanup hitter the Cubs need. When he doesn't connect for extra bases, his .316 on-base is a black hole in the middle of the order.

Streakier than ever due to recurring knee problems, Dawson is getting beat more and more with high gas. But he's a deadly knee-high hitter when he can get bat extension. He batted lower when ahead in the count than when behind, and he worked a pitcher to a 3-1 count 12 times this season, each time failing to get a hit. Pitchers used the common knowledge that Dawson likes a walk about as much as he likes artificial turf: rarely.

BASERUNNING:

Dawson runs the bags hard and can still muster enough acceleration to get the extra base. He used better judgment in his basestealing attempts than in 1991, and was successful on six of eight attempts.

FIELDING:

While his outfield range continues to deteriorate, the former Gold Glover is still worth a good right-field bleacher seat, thanks to his arm. Dawson recorded 11 assists in 1992, and no one was running unduly on him. He is worse than ever, though, on balls over his head and those hit to his left.

OVERALL:

Dawson's 399th home run left Wrigley Field in the last game of 1992, and Chicagoans worried it was his last as a Cub. General manager Larry Himes said he wanted to re-sign Dawson, but let him become a free agent to save a spot in the expansion draft. Himes will be roasted if the Cub hero leaves town.

ANDRE DAWSON

Position: RF
Bats: R **Throws:** R
Ht: 6' 3" **Wt:** 197

Opening Day Age: 38
Born: 7/10/54 in Miami, FL
ML Seasons: 17

Overall Statistics

	G	AB	R	H	D	T	HR	RBI	SB	BB	SO	AVG
1992	143	542	60	150	27	2	22	90	6	30	70	.277
Career	2310	8890	1259	2504	444	94	399	1425	310	552	1349	.282

Where He Hits the Ball

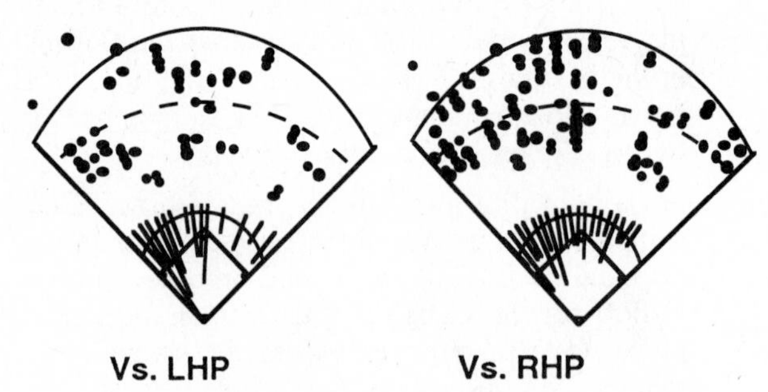

1992 Situational Stats

	AB	H	HR	RBI	AVG		AB	H	HR	RBI	AVG
Home	252	77	13	48	.306	LHP	195	56	7	35	.287
Road	290	73	9	42	.252	RHP	347	94	15	55	.271
Day	286	88	14	58	.308	Sc Pos	145	41	2	59	.283
Night	256	62	8	32	.242	Clutch	113	38	6	16	.336

1992 Rankings (National League)

- 1st in lowest batting average on a 3-1 count (.000) and lowest percentage of pitches taken (42.8%)
- 7th in least pitches seen per plate appearance (3.36)
- 8th in home runs (22) and batting average on an 0-2 count (.289)
- 9th in batting average in the clutch (.336)
- 10th in RBI (90), lowest on-base percentage (.316) and HR frequency (24.6 ABs per HR)
- Led the Cubs in RBI and intentional walks (8)
- Led NL right fielders in at-bats (542) and GDPs (13)

SHAWON DUNSTON

Position: SS
Bats: R **Throws:** R
Ht: 6' 1" **Wt:** 175

Opening Day Age: 30
Born: 3/21/63 in Brooklyn, NY
ML Seasons: 8

HITTING:

The biggest blow to the Cubs' 1992 chances happened in early May, when shortstop Shawon Dunston underwent back surgery after playing just 18 games and was lost for the year. Dunston offered the lineup genuine speed and another productive bat, two items that the team's offense couldn't cope without.

The big change for Dunston before his injury was a trial as the Cubs' leadoff hitter. While most thought the move would flop due to Dunston's impatient style, the Cubs had no other real option. He started out well, batting .313 as a leadoff hitter, but managed just three walks in 70 plate appearances. He promised to become more selective in his new role, but to Dunston this meant letting one pitch go by rather than none.

There may be something to the notion that Dunston will be a better player in his thirties than he was in his twenties. He now gets fooled less often on bad outside breaking stuff, and still pounds anything hard, especially up and in. He is potent against lefthanders, and he maintains a healthy, coachable attitude. Dunston is a terrific bunter and should use that weapon more often.

BASERUNNING:

National League fans should hope that one of the league's electric baserunners is not slowed too much by the back condition. Dunston's basestealing percentages had improved dramatically the last couple of years and around the bags he's a blur.

FIELDING:

To help his back, the Cubs have asked Dunston to work out as a center fielder. His range and cannon arm were fine before the injury, and he has always been terrific on outfield pops. Robin Yount made a successful move from shortstop to center field at approximately the same age (29).

OVERALL:

Dunston's back was still sore after the season, so the Cubs decided to leave him unprotected in the expansion draft. His worrisome injury leaves his 1993 team in a quandary over whether he'll be able to handle the long haul at shortstop or require a move to a new position.

Overall Statistics

	G	AB	R	H	D	T	HR	RBI	SB	BB	SO	AVG
1992	18	73	8	23	3	1	0	2	2	3	13	.315
Career	918	3333	407	863	157	38	73	342	133	137	582	.259

Where He Hits the Ball

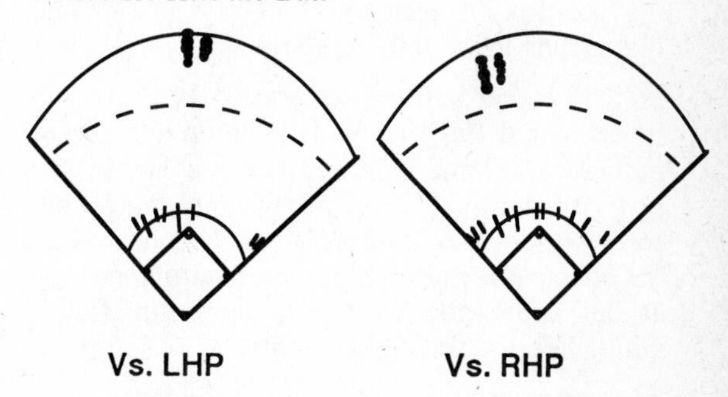

1992 Situational Stats

	AB	H	HR	RBI	AVG		AB	H	HR	RBI	AVG
Home	28	9	0	1	.321	LHP	24	10	0	0	.417
Road	45	14	0	1	.311	RHP	49	13	0	2	.265
Day	42	16	0	2	.381	Sc Pos	10	1	0	1	.100
Night	31	7	0	0	.226	Clutch	14	4	0	0	.286

1992 Rankings (National League)

- Did not rank near the top or bottom in any category

MARK GRACE

Position: 1B
Bats: L **Throws:** L
Ht: 6' 2" **Wt:** 190

Opening Day Age: 28
Born: 6/28/64 in Winston-Salem, NC
ML Seasons: 5

Overall Statistics

	G	AB	R	H	D	T	HR	RBI	SB	BB	SO	AVG
1992	158	603	72	185	37	5	9	79	6	72	36	.307
Career	751	2807	370	840	148	18	46	355	41	341	228	.299

Where He Hits the Ball

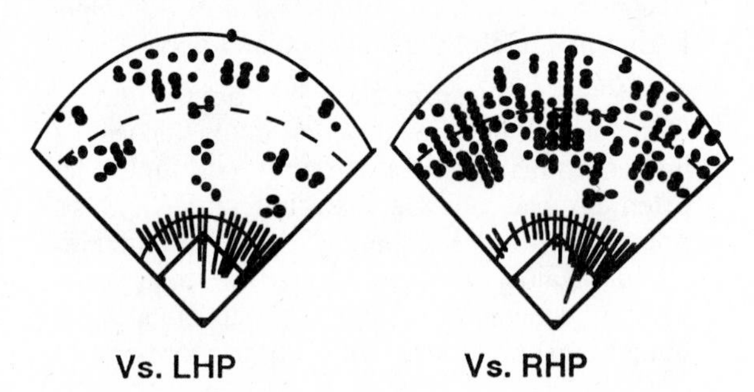

1992 Situational Stats

	AB	H	HR	RBI	AVG		AB	H	HR	RBI	AVG
Home	285	80	5	40	.281	LHP	225	63	3	29	.280
Road	318	105	4	39	.330	RHP	378	122	6	50	.323
Day	314	93	8	45	.296	Sc Pos	138	45	1	65	.326
Night	289	92	1	34	.318	Clutch	108	37	2	18	.343

1992 Rankings (National League)

- 2nd in batting average on the road (.330)
- 3rd in singles (134), batting average vs. right-handed pitchers (.323) and highest percentage of swings put into play (57.2%)
- Led the Cubs in batting average (.307), singles, doubles (37), sacrifice flies (8), walks (72), intentional walks (8), times on base (261), GDPs (14), plate appearances (689), games played (158), on-base percentage (.380), batting average with runners in scoring position (.326), batting average in the clutch (.343), batting average vs. right-handed pitchers, on-base percentage vs. right-handed pitchers (.409), batting average on the road and batting average with 2 strikes (.263)

HITTING:

Rebounding as anticipated from his worst year, Mark Grace took aim at his critics and ripped off a 1992 season much more in line with his ability. After batting .273 with 58 RBI in 1991, Grace hit .307 with 79 ribbies in '92. His 185 hits and 37 doubles were both career highs, his 36 strikeouts a career low.

Grace was at his sweet-swinging best in the first half, working the count until either he saw right-handed heat to pound into either gap or received a free pass. He took a more aggressive approach vs. lefties than he had in 1991, but still had mixed success, particularly with low offspeed stuff. Grace did a tremendous job with runners in scoring position all year (.326), taking pitches and then rifling the ball the opposite way.

In the second half, Grace started to press and revert to bad 1991 habits. In a slump he looks to pull too much and loses his patience. He walked just 22 times post-break after compiling 50 before. Wrigley is not Grace's best friend. He had the league's second-highest road batting average at .330 and batted .351 on the larger turf fields, where he stays within his ability.

BASERUNNING:

While Grace is not extremely fast, he is athletic and fluid on the bases. He knows the pitchers around the league well and could steal a few more bases than the 6-of-7 he nabbed in 1992.

FIELDING:

Grace won his first Gold Glove in 1992 and has no weakness as a fielder. His range is as good as any and he is perfect with the double-play throw. His heavy fielding numbers -- he led the NL in putouts, assists and double plays -- are helped by a groundball staff.

OVERALL:

Grace has become one of the most popular Cub players in recent times. Lacking the power of a classic first baseman, he is just below a star-level player, but a winner. He would be even better if he wasn't asked to carry the Cubs' entire left-handed offensive load.

PITCHING:

Once one of the White Sox' brightest young pitchers, Greg Hibbard has had a tough time the last two seasons. Though Hibbard posted a winning record at 10-7 in 1992, his ERA was a shaky 4.40. The Sox eventually soured on Hibbard, and at year's end they made him available in the expansion draft. He was picked up by Florida, then was immediately dealt to the Cubs.

Strictly a finesse pitcher, Hibbard is not the type who is going to dominate hitters. His best pitch is good sinking fastball, and he also has a nice three-quarter-arm curve and a decent slider. His change-up fades away from a right-handed hitter, and like all his pitches, it breaks down. Hibbard's groundball-to-flyball ratio of 2.5 was the highest in the American League last year. His style should be well suited for the long grass at Wrigley Field, where groundballers like Greg Maddux and Mike Morgan have found success.

Though he'll never set any speed gun records, Hibbard relies a lot on his fastball. He needs to throw it hard enough to set up his offspeed pitches; he also needs to keep it inside, driving hitters off the plate. He was effective in that regard against lefties last year, holding them to a .224 average and one home run. But righties got a good look at Hibbard's stuff, hitting him for a .285 mark with 16 homers.

HOLDING RUNNERS, FIELDING, HITTING:

A pitcher like Hibbard needs to control the running game, and he does. He allowed only nine steals in 15 attempts last year. He's just an average fielder, and would help himself with better glove work. The new National Leaguer will need to work on his hitting.

OVERALL:

The White Sox, with several pitchers who were passable but not dominating, left Hibbard unprotected. The Marlins snatched him up in the first round as part of a pre-arranged deal orchestrated by Cubs GM Larry Himes who needed a lefty starter, and dealt him immediately to the Cubs for Alex Arias and Gary Scott, players who were not integral to the Cubs' future. Hibbard could have a fine season with the crosstown team.

GREG HIBBARD

Position: SP
Bats: L **Throws:** L
Ht: 6' 0" **Wt:** 190

Opening Day Age: 28
Born: 9/13/64 in New Orleans, LA
ML Seasons: 4

Overall Statistics

	W	L	ERA	G	GS	Sv	IP	H	R	BB	SO	HR
1992	10	7	4.40	31	28	1	176.0	187	92	57	69	17
Career	41	34	3.78	119	113	1	718.1	727	337	210	287	56

How Often He Throws Strikes

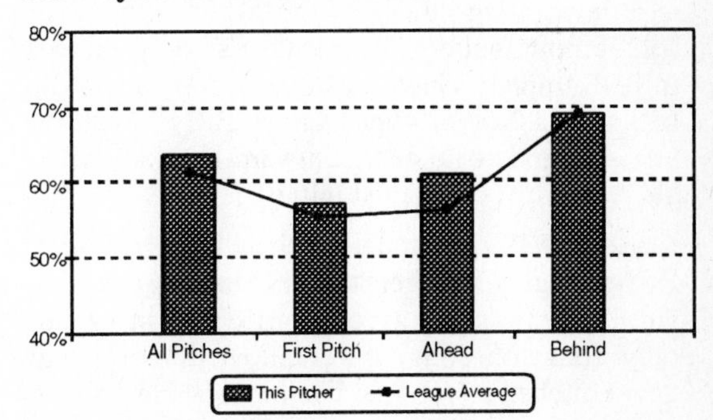

1992 Situational Stats

	W	L	ERA	Sv	IP		AB	H	HR	RBI	AVG
Home	7	3	3.44	1	96.2	LHB	85	19	1	7	.224
Road	3	4	5.56	0	79.1	RHB	590	168	16	75	.285
Day	4	1	5.87	0	38.1	Sc Pos	144	39	2	61	.271
Night	6	6	3.99	1	137.2	Clutch	70	21	2	6	.300

1992 Rankings (American League)

- 1st in highest groundball/flyball ratio (2.5)
- 2nd in least pitches thrown per batter (3.33) and least strikeouts per 9 innings (3.5)
- 4th highest batting average allowed (.277)
- 5th highest batting average allowed vs. right-handed batters (.285)
- Led the White Sox in GDPs induced (20), highest groundball/flyball ratio, least pitches thrown per batter and GDPs induced per 9 innings (1.0)

STAFF ACE

GREG MADDUX

Position: SP
Bats: R **Throws:** R
Ht: 6' 0" **Wt:** 175

Opening Day Age: 26
Born: 4/14/66 in San Angelo, TX
ML Seasons: 7

PITCHING:

Last September 11, Greg Maddux had only one thing left to prove. Maddux hunted down the injured Tom Glavine, who already had 20 wins, by winning four out of his final five starts. The righthander finished at 20-11, beating out Glavine to win his first Cy Young Award.

The award was the culmination of an inexorable effort by Maddux to improve his pitching technique. He throws the four basic pitches, including a sinking fastball that ranges from 83 to 89 MPH. All four have been refined to the point that Maddux makes almost no mistakes and has the utmost confidence in each. And all four are always down in the zone, usually on the paint. His big out pitch is a devastating circle change, which rates with John Smoltz's slider as the league's best producer of half-empty swings. Maddux added a cut fastball to his bag of tricks under Billy Connors' tutelage, and he made that inward-breaking pitch his extra weapon against lefties.

Maddux's 1992 numbers were all phenomenal. He held righty swingers to a .176 batting average. He allowed as many as four earned runs in a game only four times; he never allowed more, and never pitched fewer than five innings. He was the second-most prolific groundball pitcher in the league. A fearsome competitor, he demonstrated ownership of the inner portion of the plate by hitting 14 batters, many in the first two innings.

HOLDING RUNNERS, FIELDING, HITTING:

Three-time Gold Glove winner Maddux made three errors in 1992, but remains the quickest pitcher around the mound in the NL. The few runners that got aboard on Maddux ran frequently, and were successful two-thirds of the time. His hitting is very solid (.184 career) and he is a terrific bunter.

OVERALL:

Maddux turns 27 in April, and spent the period after the season in a dream scenario as perhaps the most complete pitcher to ever enter free agency. Meanwhile the Cubs and their fans lived with a nightmare -- the prospect of losing the best pitcher in the league as he heads into his prime.

Overall Statistics

	W	L	ERA	G	GS	Sv	IP	H	R	BB	SO	HR
1992	20	11	2.18	35	35	0	268.0	201	68	70	199	7
Career	95	75	3.35	212	208	0	1442.0	1352	615	455	937	82

How Often He Throws Strikes

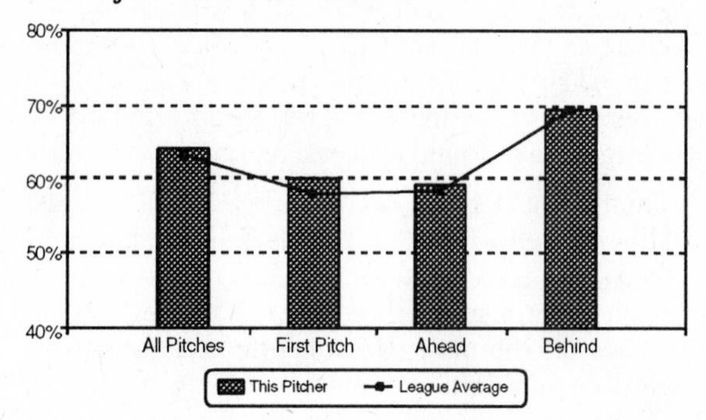

1992 Situational Stats

	W	L	ERA	Sv	IP		AB	H	HR	RBI	AVG
Home	12	4	1.91	0	137.0	LHB	566	132	6	41	.233
Road	8	7	2.47	0	131.0	RHB	393	69	1	23	.176
Day	8	5	2.12	0	106.0	Sc Pos	211	43	0	50	.204
Night	12	6	2.22	0	162.0	Clutch	124	26	0	6	.210

1992 Rankings (National League)

- 1st in wins (20), games started (35), innings pitched (268), batters faced (1,061), hit batsmen (14), lowest slugging percentage allowed (.280), least home runs allowed per 9 innings (.24) and lowest batting average allowed vs. right-handed batters (.176)
- 2nd in most pitches thrown (3,726), lowest batting average allowed (.210) and highest groundball/flyball ratio allowed (2.6)
- 3rd in ERA (2.18), shutouts (4), strikeouts (199), least baserunners allowed per 9 innings (9.6), ERA at home (1.91) and ERA on the road (2.47)
- Led the Cubs in sacrifice bunts as a hitter (13) and almost every starting pitcher category

HITTING:

Through the disarray that plagued the Cubs outfield all season, the progress of Derrick May was one of the year's highlights. May, a semi-hot prospect for the past few seasons, treated his demotion on April 1 as no Fool's Day joke and earned a trip back to stay just three weeks later.

The left-handed hitting outfielder's biggest shortcoming has been his lack of longball power on a team that cries out for a lefty bopper. He didn't show much in April in a semi-platoon arrangement, but later demonstrated a more flexed stance, blasting three homers during June. He finished the year strongly by hitting .303 in his last 44 starts (53-175), with three more homers in September.

May has a long, level swing which has some trouble adjusting to offspeed offerings. He rips fastballs from both sides. While he has been a line drive/groundball hitter throughout, he developed more of an uppercut through work with Billy Williams, increasing his power and flyball tendency. He joins many of the Cubs as holdovers of the Dawson/Dunston School of Many Swings, with just 14 walks and a .306 on-base percentage.

BASERUNNING:

The 6-foot-4 May has decent athleticism and moves around the bases fairly well. He is not much of a basestealing threat (5-for-8 last year). He needs to work on getting out of the box better, with nine double-play grounders last year.

FIELDING:

Work, work, and more work is what May desperately needs defensively. He is tentative on his approach to balls hit on the ground and has a lot of trouble with both lazy pops and the outfield walls. At least his range exceeded that of George Bell.

OVERALL:

May has become a complete player for the Cubs -- completely average. They protected him over Dwight Smith and will give him the left field job to lose. As to questions of his success in this role, there are signs that May may (his increased power), and others that May may not (no patience.)

DERRICK MAY

Position: LF/RF
Bats: L **Throws:** R
Ht: 6' 4" **Wt:** 205

Opening Day Age: 24
Born: 7/14/68 in Rochester, NY
ML Seasons: 3

Overall Statistics

	G	AB	R	H	D	T	HR	RBI	SB	BB	SO	AVG
1992	124	351	33	96	11	0	8	45	5	14	40	.274
Career	156	434	45	116	16	0	10	59	6	18	48	.267

Where He Hits the Ball

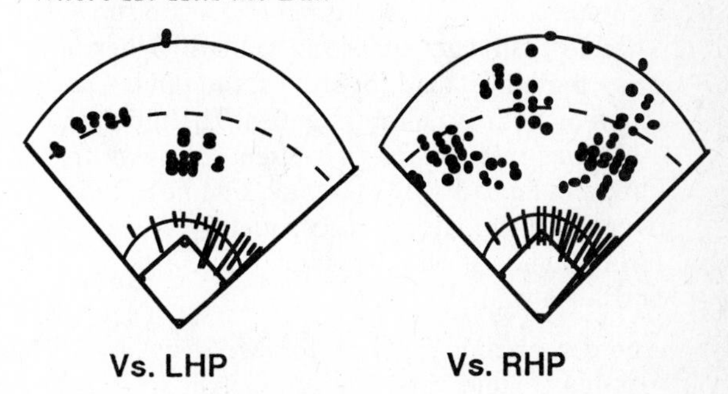

1992 Situational Stats

	AB	H	HR	RBI	AVG		AB	H	HR	RBI	AVG
Home	202	59	3	28	.292	LHP	76	19	2	9	.250
Road	149	37	5	17	.248	RHP	275	77	6	36	.280
Day	201	49	3	24	.244	Sc Pos	92	26	4	38	.283
Night	150	47	5	21	.313	Clutch	64	16	3	9	.250

1992 Rankings (National League)

- Led NL left fielders in errors (5)

CHUCK McELROY

Position: RP
Bats: L **Throws:** L
Ht: 6' 0" **Wt:** 180

Opening Day Age: 25
Born: 10/1/67 in Galveston, TX
ML Seasons: 4

PITCHING:

Fireballing Chuck McElroy came smoking out of the chute in 1992, looking like the next Cub closer. There was Chicago precedent. He was a somewhat wild, hard-throwing lefthander, just like another ex-Cub stopper. McElroy even wears glasses like the real "Wild Thing." But by the end of the season, Cub fans knew there was still only one Mitch Williams.

McElroy was effective early last year because he had rare command of his three pitches. At such times he is virtually unhittable. But as the season wore on, his command eroded to the point where, in September, he allowed 17 hits and 14 walks in his last 16 innings pitched. The 25-year-old uses a compact, three-quarter arm delivery to fire a 91 MPH fastball, tight slider and forkball. When he's throwing his fastball for strikes, the pitch is very tough on both lefties and righties. The problem in 1992 was that the forkball often got away from him, and he had only one pitch that he could get over the plate. Hitters who patiently laid off his forkball and sat on his fastball either ripped him or drew a walk.

Another glaring problem for McElroy in 1992 was his trouble versus lefty swingers. He completely stifled lefties in 1991, but in '92 they batted .275 with a .422 slugging percentage, again by knocking around his fastball. With runners in scoring position McElroy allowed a .398 on-base percentage, not closer-level numbers.

HOLDING RUNNERS, FIELDING, HITTING:

McElroy is strong in performing the little parts of his job. He holds runners very well with a quick spin-move, and few dare to run on him. His fielding is smooth and he is a terror with the bat, knocking out two doubles and a triple in six at-bats last year.

OVERALL:

The prescription is back to the drawing board for McElroy and pitching coach Billy Connors. Developing a reliable pitch to complement his forkball and better location on all pitches should put his lively arm back in prominence in the Cub bullpen.

Overall Statistics

	W	L	ERA	G	GS	Sv	IP	H	R	BB	SO	HR
1992	4	7	3.55	72	0	6	83.2	73	40	51	83	5
Career	10	10	2.97	170	0	9	209.1	182	88	122	199	13

How Often He Throws Strikes

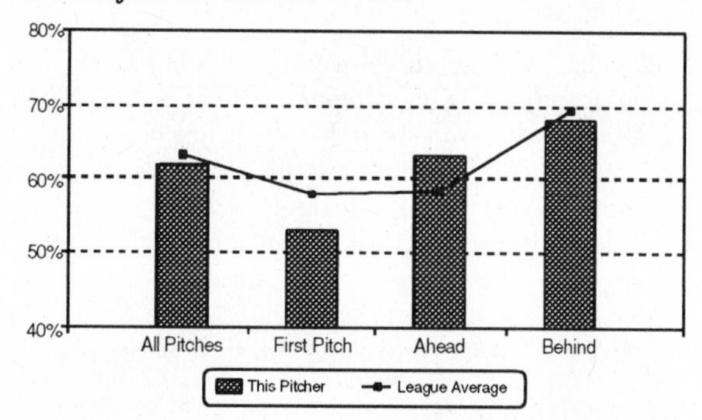

1992 Situational Stats

	W	L	ERA	Sv	IP		AB	H	HR	RBI	AVG
Home	3	4	3.64	1	42.0	LHB	102	28	2	16	.275
Road	1	3	3.46	5	41.2	RHB	206	45	3	26	.218
Day	3	2	3.59	5	47.2	Sc Pos	96	24	1	37	.250
Night	1	5	3.50	1	36.0	Clutch	166	42	1	21	.253

1992 Rankings (National League)

- 6th in least GDPs per GDP situation (2.9%), relief losses (7) and most strikeouts per 9 innings in relief (8.9)
- 7th in games pitched (72)
- 9th in most baserunners allowed per 9 innings in relief (13.3)
- Led the Cubs in games pitched, blown saves (5), relief losses and most strikeouts per 9 innings in relief

PITCHING:

If anyone other than Larry Himes thought that Mike Morgan would be a successful pitcher for the Cubs in 1992, he didn't speak very loudly. Himes made signing Morgan his first move after becoming the Cubs' general manager in November of 1991, and more than one publication predicted that Morgan would be the free agent flop of the year. While the righthander had enjoyed some success working in pitcher-friendly Dodger Stadium, his career record was 67-104, with a 4.10 ERA.

Himes wanted durability and innings from Morgan, and Morgan gave that to the Cubs in spades. He finished with career highs in wins, starts, and innings pitched. The Cubs won 21 of the 34 starts Morgan pitched.

The idea of cozy Wrigley Field wreaking havoc on Morgan couldn't have been further from the truth. The high grass and his heavy, downward-moving ball were a perfect combination, as Morgan stormed to a 9-2 record with a 1.38 ERA at Wrigley. He displayed command of his two fastballs, and his slider was continually beaten into the ground, making Morgan the third most frequent groundball pitcher in the league behind teammate Maddux and the Giants' Bill Swift. The two-seam fastball that he has used to great success the last three seasons was moving well all year, and Morgan held righties to a meager .215 batting average.

HOLDING RUNNERS, FIELDING, HITTING:

Morgan's pickoff move is nothing special. But he keeps baserunners off their rhythm so expertly with head bobs and the like that he takes away the opposition running game almost completely (just six steals allowed in 15 attempts). He is a good-fielding pitcher, a notch below the best, and knows how to bunt well.

OVERALL:

With Morgan's banner year -- one of the top five starters in the league -- the Cubs had the most potent one-two starting combo in baseball. They still finished six games under .500. But as long as Morgan remains the number-two starter on the team, not the ace, Larry Himes can take credit for finding a big piece toward building a contender.

MIKE MORGAN

Position: SP
Bats: R **Throws:** R
Ht: 6' 2" **Wt:** 210
Opening Day Age: 33
Born: 10/8/59 in Tulare, CA
ML Seasons: 12

Overall Statistics

	W	L	ERA	G	GS	Sv	IP	H	R	BB	SO	HR
1992	16	8	2.55	34	34	0	240.0	203	80	79	123	14
Career	83	112	3.87	298	238	3	1625.1	1651	780	546	783	137

How Often He Throws Strikes

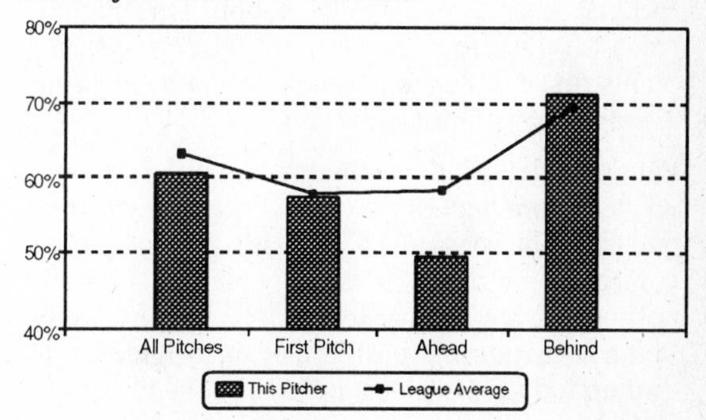

1992 Situational Stats

	W	L	ERA	Sv	IP		AB	H	HR	RBI	AVG
Home	9	2	1.38	0	130.1	LHB	491	122	8	35	.248
Road	7	6	3.94	0	109.2	RHB	377	81	6	35	.215
Day	12	3	2.02	0	164.2	Sc Pos	174	39	3	47	.224
Night	4	5	3.70	0	75.1	Clutch	57	13	0	3	.228

1992 Rankings (National League)

- 1st in GDPs induced (29) and ERA at home (1.38)
- 3rd in wins (16), wild pitches (11), highest groundball/flyball ratio allowed (2.5) and most GDPs induced per 9 innings (1.1)
- Led the Cubs in hits allowed (203), walks allowed (79), wild pitches, most GDPs induced, winning percentage (.667), lowest stolen base percentage allowed (40.0%), most run support per 9 innings (4.1), most GDPs induced per 9 innings, most GDPs induced per GDP situation (17.3%) and ERA at home (1.38)

PITCHING:

Ken Patterson came to the Cubs as the third wheel in the George Bell-Sammy Sosa deal. The idea was to have Patterson as a third lefthander in the bullpen to give manager Jim Lefebvre some flexibility in his matchups. Instead, he was more like a third wheel there, too.

The 28-year-old Patterson was nondescript in an undemanding role and spent some time on the disabled list. Unfortunately, he discontinued what had been a pattern of general improvement each season. Patterson uses a 88 MPH fastball, forkball, slider and curve which are often too polite to the batter. His most common approach is to throw the fastball to get a quick strike, then go to the forkball once ahead in the count. This pattern wasn't fooling too many hitters, who batted .381 on his first offering and .268 with a .490 slugging average against him overall.

Patterson doesn't have much strikeout ability and walked more batters than he whiffed for the second straight season. He doesn't possess sharp control of his slider or curve, which gets him in hot water even against lefties. His slider usually keeps lefthanders honest, but against righties it is cannon fodder. He gets it up in the zone too often, and the result was seven home runs allowed to righthanders. Scouts say he needs more frequent work to stay sharp, but that's a vicious circle.

HOLDING RUNNERS, FIELDING, HITTING:

The bad news is that Patterson is an awful fielder, with no natural instincts and bad hands. The good news is that Patterson holds runners pretty well, but more because of his short, quick delivery than with a great pickoff move.

OVERALL:

Patterson will have to pitch better than he did in 1992 to stay with the Cubs. Moving up in responsibility is not in the picture barring a major new development, like a new arm. But the baseball world often needs a third lefty, and when it does, Ken Patterson will be ready to take the challenge.

KEN PATTERSON

Position: RP
Bats: L **Throws:** L
Ht: 6' 4" **Wt:** 210

Opening Day Age: 28
Born: 7/8/64 in Costa Mesa, CA
ML Seasons: 5

Overall Statistics

	W	L	ERA	G	GS	Sv	IP	H	R	BB	SO	HR
1992	2	3	3.89	32	1	0	41.2	41	25	27	23	7
Career	13	7	3.73	177	4	4	258.0	236	122	131	146	31

How Often He Throws Strikes

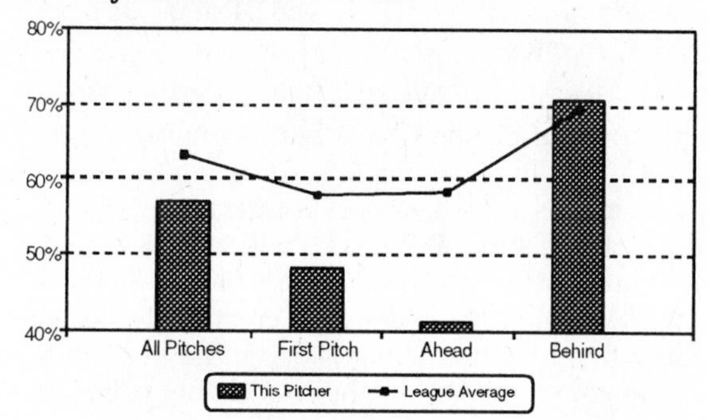

1992 Situational Stats

	W	L	ERA	Sv	IP		AB	H	HR	RBI	AVG
Home	0	1	3.38	0	16.0	LHB	64	17	0	4	.266
Road	2	2	4.21	0	25.2	RHB	89	24	7	21	.270
Day	0	1	3.52	0	15.1	Sc Pos	42	9	1	16	.214
Night	2	2	4.10	0	26.1	Clutch	21	6	1	3	.286

1992 Rankings (National League)

- Did not rank near the top or bottom in any category

PITCHING:

Every team likes to have a few unexpected sources of good production, and for the 1992 Cubs, the pitching of veteran Jeff Robinson certainly qualified as both unexpected and good. After bouncing around the majors since 1984 with four different clubs (mostly Pittsburgh and San Francisco), Robinson tried to win a job with the Cubs in spring training. Despite a 1.98 ERA, the Cubs sent him to Iowa after he had no other offers.

Robinson hung on at Iowa, pitched well, and came back to the club on May 4th permanently. He filled the staff handyman role very well; in the span of one week at the end of July, he picked up a save, pitched in mop-up relief for two innings, and then started two games due to injuries. His versatility was sorely needed on a staff that often had no defined bullpen roles from one month to the next.

In the past, Robinson had been a premier set-up man and workhorse, but those days of heavy usage are over. He still relies on a split-finger pitch taught to him long ago by Roger Craig, and it is by far his most effective pitch. When he is throwing it well, it still gets quite a bit of downward movement inside the strike zone. He completes his pitch array with a below-par fastball and slow curve. As usual, he got lots of groundball outs in 1992.

HOLDING RUNNERS, FIELDING, HITTING:

Robinson has a deliberate delivery to the plate, but has worked on his pickoff move somewhat to try to cut down on opposition running. Last year, Cub catchers gunned down 8 out of 17 who tried to run on Robinson. His fielding ability is decent.

OVERALL:

There is never room to rest for a man in Robinson's position. He'll have to earn a spot on the team again, or find another home. But the fine job he performed in mainly unnoticed roles in 1992 will give him a leg up on his younger, less experienced competition.

JEFF ROBINSON

Position: RP/SP
Bats: R **Throws:** R
Ht: 6' 4" **Wt:** 200

Opening Day Age: 32
Born: 12/13/60 in Santa Ana, CA
ML Seasons: 9

Overall Statistics

	W	L	ERA	G	GS	Sv	IP	H	R	BB	SO	HR
1992	4	3	3.00	49	5	1	78.0	76	29	40	46	5
Career	46	57	3.79	454	62	39	901.1	880	433	349	629	75

How Often He Throws Strikes

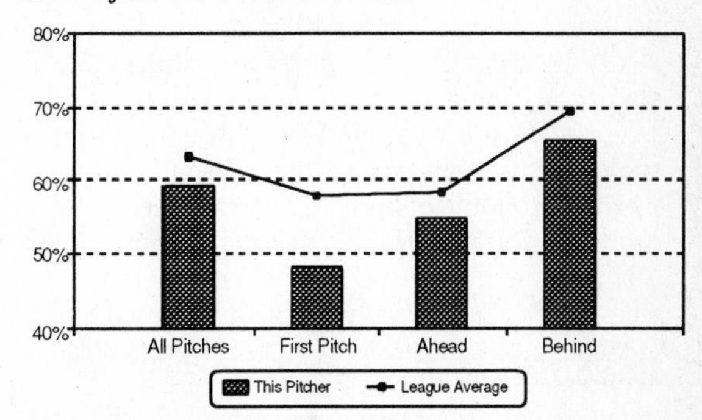

1992 Situational Stats

	W	L	ERA	Sv	IP		AB	H	HR	RBI	AVG
Home	1	2	3.25	1	36.0	LHB	155	45	2	16	.290
Road	3	1	2.79	0	42.0	RHB	134	31	3	14	.231
Day	1	2	2.88	0	34.1	Sc Pos	82	16	0	21	.195
Night	3	1	3.09	1	43.2	Clutch	106	28	2	14	.264

1992 Rankings (National League)

- 9th in first batter efficiency (.175)
- 10th in lowest batting average allowed in relief with runners in scoring position (.195)
- Led the Cubs in lowest batting average allowed in relief with runners in scoring position and relief ERA (2.54)

REY SANCHEZ

Position: SS
Bats: R **Throws:** R
Ht: 5'10" **Wt:** 180

Opening Day Age: 25
Born: 10/5/67 in Rio Piedras, Puerto Rico
ML Seasons: 2

Overall Statistics

	G	AB	R	H	D	T	HR	RBI	SB	BB	SO	AVG
1992	74	255	24	64	14	3	1	19	2	10	17	.251
Career	87	278	25	70	14	3	1	21	2	14	20	.252

Where He Hits the Ball

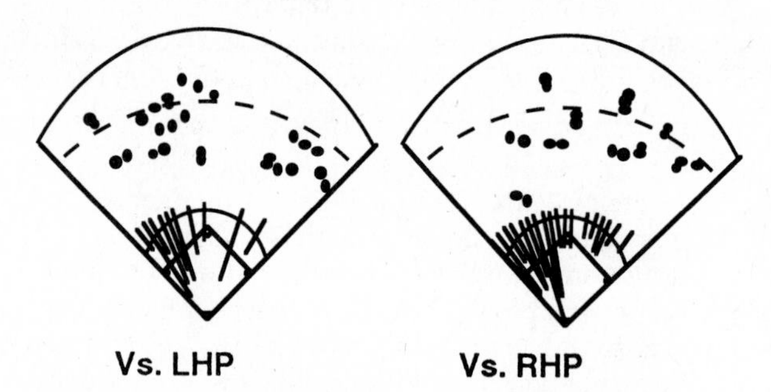

1992 Situational Stats

	AB	H	HR	RBI	AVG		AB	H	HR	RBI	AVG
Home	130	39	1	11	.300	LHP	106	30	0	8	.283
Road	125	25	0	8	.200	RHP	149	34	1	11	.228
Day	131	36	1	12	.275	Sc Pos	48	12	0	16	.250
Night	124	28	0	7	.226	Clutch	54	10	0	3	.185

1992 Rankings (National League)

- Did not rank near the top or bottom in any category

HITTING:

One of the three Cub shortstops asked to fill the 1992 Shawon Dunston injury void, along with Jose Vizcaino and Alex Arias, was 25-year-old Rey Sanchez. Sanchez fought off a variety of ailments throughout the season to notch 255 at-bats, hit .251, and win the first crack at the starting shortstop job in 1993.

Sanchez is the most solid all-around shortstop of the trio behind Dunston. His bat is little more than pesky. Sanchez sprays the ball sharply the opposite way and likes to go down the line; when successful, he has enough speed to garner his share of triples.

Out of his right-handed crouch, Sanchez wastes no time looking to draw walks, and can be fooled easily by right-handed curves and sliders. He'll slap at anything close, but has a better handle on left-handed pitching. He went through a typical rookie adjustment period, but after slumping towards the middle of his campaign he started to get more comfortable. He was on a real tear in August (.311 average, .422 slugging) when a troublesome sign for the Cubs, a bulging disc, sidelined him.

BASERUNNING:

Sanchez has some speed, but not of the blazing variety that would make him a major basestealing threat. However, he stole as many as 29 bases in the minors. He has a thorough knowledge of how to run the bases.

FIELDING:

Sanchez is a solid if not always spectacular fielder -- the opposite of the man he replaced. Sanchez has a very strong arm, but it can be erratic, and he and Ryne Sandberg need more time to develop some rapport on the pivot. His range, particularly in roving behind the bag, is extremely good.

OVERALL:

Sanchez showed enough to nail down a great shot at the 1993 starting shortstop job despite missing time with chicken pox, flu, and the serious back problem last year. He will have competition in the spring, however, possibly from Dunston if his back is okay. Sanchez will need to prove he is fully recovered and improving offensively.

HALL OF FAMER

RYNE SANDBERG

Position: 2B
Bats: R **Throws:** R
Ht: 6' 2" **Wt:** 185

Opening Day Age: 33
Born: 9/18/59 in Spokane, WA
ML Seasons: 12

HITTING:

Ryne Sandberg signed a multi-year, $28.4 million deal with the Cubs just before the start of the 1992 season, but there were no doubts as to whether he would use his newfound security to relax a little. Sandberg batted .304, hit 26 homers, and played his usual brilliant all-around game.

There is never an off year for the National League's most consistently valuable player. Sandberg's 1992 tendency was to take righties deep (22 homers in 406 at-bats), while hitting more for average against lefties (.340, but only four homers in 206 AB). The result was one of the best seasons in his 12-year Hall of Fame-caliber career, including his fourth straight season with 100 or more runs scored.

Sandberg affirmed the success vs. southpaws he had enjoyed in 1991 by remaining less of a dead pull hitter, often taking offspeed pitches the other way. Against righthanders, especially with Mark Grace swinging well, Sandberg started seeing more of his favorite juicy pitches on the inner half. Up or down, Sandberg still can't be beaten with inside heat. He remained the most reluctant first-pitch swinger in the league for the second straight season, a habit the rest of the team would do well to imitate.

BASERUNNING:

Little nicks here and there don't keep Sandberg out of the lineup. But they have cut down on his once-luminous basestealing ability to the point where 20 steals is a reach. He is as heady a baserunner as exists.

FIELDING:

Sandberg hasn't made a throwing error since July 4, 1990, which is not normal for most humans. His failure to win a tenth straight Gold Glove was not caused by any lapse in his unreal consistency. His range is now surpassed by a few other second sackers, like Jose Lind.

OVERALL:

Sandberg is now so taken for granted that Cub fans didn't even think he's the team's most valuable everyday player, selecting Grace instead. But for the leading All-Star vote getter, local glory is a small honor to forego for year-in, year-out excellence.

Overall Statistics

	G	AB	R	H	D	T	HR	RBI	SB	BB	SO	AVG
1992	158	612	100	186	32	8	26	87	17	68	73	.304
Career	1705	6705	1076	1939	320	67	231	836	314	619	948	.289

Where He Hits the Ball

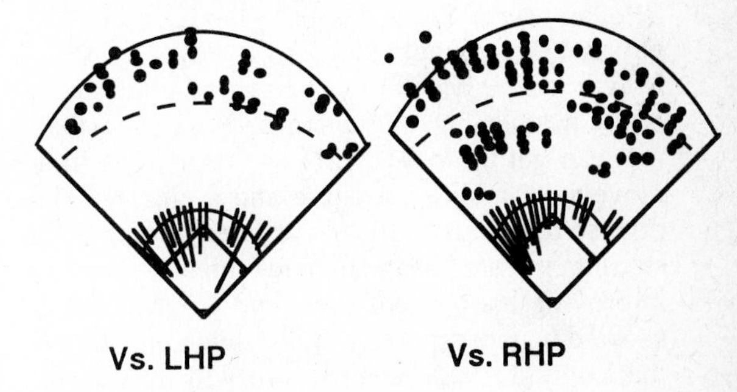

1992 Situational Stats

	AB	H	HR	RBI	AVG		AB	H	HR	RBI	AVG
Home	300	92	16	46	.307	LHP	206	70	4	24	.340
Road	312	94	10	41	.301	RHP	406	116	22	63	.286
Day	314	103	17	52	.328	Sc Pos	125	37	7	54	.296
Night	298	83	9	35	.279	Clutch	109	34	4	15	.312

1992 Rankings (National League)

- 2nd in total bases (312)
- 3rd in hits (186)
- 4th in runs scored (100)
- 5th in slugging percentage (.510) and slugging percentage vs. right-handed pitchers (.515)
- Led the Cubs in home runs (26), at-bats (612), runs scored, hits, triples (8), total bases, stolen bases (17), strikeouts (73), most pitches seen (2,644), games played (158), slugging percentage, HR frequency (23.5 ABs per HR), highest groundball/flyball ratio (1.3), stolen base percentage (73.9%) and most pitches seen per plate appearance (3.85)

PITCHING:

Bob Scanlan was the closest thing to an actual closer in the Cubs' employ in 1992. As the season began his mates were failing to be effective finishers; Scanlan quietly went about compiling a 2.25 ERA before the All-Star break in a setup role.

After the break, Scanlan was given more of an active role as the Cubs' stopper, and in August he was brilliant, recording six saves in as many opportunities with an 0.66 ERA. In September, however, Scanlan was hit hard (17 innings, 30 hits, 7.41 ERA) as part of an overall Cub staff malaise. His overall numbers looked worse than they had all season.

Scanlan was effective thanks to the Cub philosophy that the groundball is their buddy. He leaned heavily on the use of a split-fingered pitch to get out of trouble; his other pitches include a fastball that can get up to 91 MPH but which has little movement, a slider, a curve and a change. The diverse repertoire befits his prior experience as a starting pitcher. Scanlan made great strides in improving his concentration and control, and it showed up most strongly in his clutch numbers -- the league hit .208 against him with runners in scoring position. Still, he is not a strikeout pitcher, which may make it very hard for him to be a full-time closer.

HOLDING RUNNERS, FIELDING, HITTING:

The 6'8" Scanlan takes a while to deliver the ball with his overhand, wristy delivery, and he offers just an average move in compensation. His opposition didn't attempt to steal that often against him (just nine times). Scanlan has trouble getting off the mound and will make mental mistakes in the field. He has only one major league hit in 28 at-bats.

OVERALL:

Scanlan took a large step in 1992 toward a career as a useful reliever. If his true level of pitching was as it appeared for most of the season, he will continue as an effective set-up man. Another good April could quell doubts about him carrying an even larger load.

BOB SCANLAN

Position: RP
Bats: R **Throws:** R
Ht: 6' 8" **Wt:** 215

Opening Day Age: 26
Born: 8/9/66 in Los Angeles, CA
ML Seasons: 2

Overall Statistics

	W	L	ERA	G	GS	Sv	IP	H	R	BB	SO	HR
1992	3	6	2.89	69	0	14	87.1	76	32	30	42	4
Career	10	14	3.45	109	13	15	198.1	190	92	70	86	9

How Often He Throws Strikes

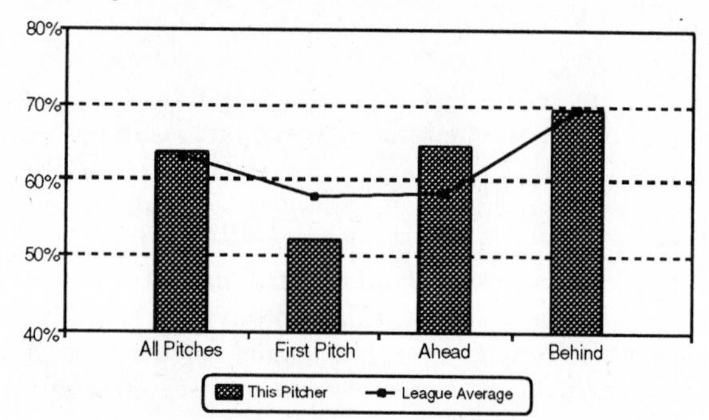

1992 Situational Stats

	W	L	ERA	Sv	IP		AB	H	HR	RBI	AVG
Home	1	2	2.66	3	40.2	LHB	160	37	3	22	.231
Road	2	4	3.09	11	46.2	RHB	163	39	1	11	.239
Day	1	2	3.00	6	42.0	Sc Pos	101	21	0	27	.208
Night	2	4	2.78	8	45.1	Clutch	197	49	2	21	.249

1992 Rankings (National League)

- 3rd in balks (4)
- 5th in least strikeouts per 9 innings in relief (4.3)
- 10th in games finished (41)
- Led the Cubs in saves (14), games finished, balks, save opportunities (18), lowest batting average allowed in relief (.219), relief innings (87.1), lowest batting average allowed in relief (.235) and least baserunners allowed per 9 innings in relief (11.0)

DWIGHT SMITH

Position: CF/LF/RF
Bats: L **Throws:** R
Ht: 5'11" **Wt:** 175

Opening Day Age: 29
Born: 11/8/63 in Tallahassee, FL
ML Seasons: 4

HITTING:

It all depends on perspective when one examines the resume of Dwight Smith. Good solid left-handed stick (.284 vs. righties with a .396 slugging), great hitter with men on base (.312 with runners on base), stolen base speed, good attitude, can play center field. . . sounds like a heck of a role-player. The only problem is that the expectations were so much greater just two seasons ago. Whatever Smith now produces as a pinch-hitting specialist and spot starter, still leaves a nagging feeling that there's something missing.

For much of last season Smith was the club's top lefty pinch hitter, and he did this job well, with 14 hits and a .429 slugging percentage. He is suited to the bench role because of the devastating way he treats fastballs. He batted .364 with two outs and men in scoring position and is now sixth all-time on the Cubs pinch hit list. Smith should be fed a steady diet of breaking balls, but he'll murder them above the waist.

BASERUNNING:

Smith was one the faster players on a very slow team, so he looked better running the bases than he really was. In truth, he's a basestealing threat to both his team and the opponents, swiping nine in 17 tries. Smith is aggressive and will try to take the extra base.

FIELDING:

It was said in these pages last year that the center field experiment with Smith would not be repeated. It was repeated, however, with not-too-horrendous results. He can't play center field regularly, but is okay in a pinch, and in left or right he is a viable player with decent range, except for his rag arm.

OVERALL:

Smith is now 29, so he was not even a young prospect in his rookie year of 1989 when he batted .324. At this stage, he is not too old to have a couple of excellent seasons with someone -- if he has the aggressiveness to seek a big role instead of continuing as the new Greg Gross.

Overall Statistics

	G	AB	R	H	D	T	HR	RBI	SB	BB	SO	AVG
1992	109	217	28	60	10	3	3	24	9	13	40	.276
Career	425	1017	130	285	51	11	21	124	31	83	169	.280

Where He Hits the Ball

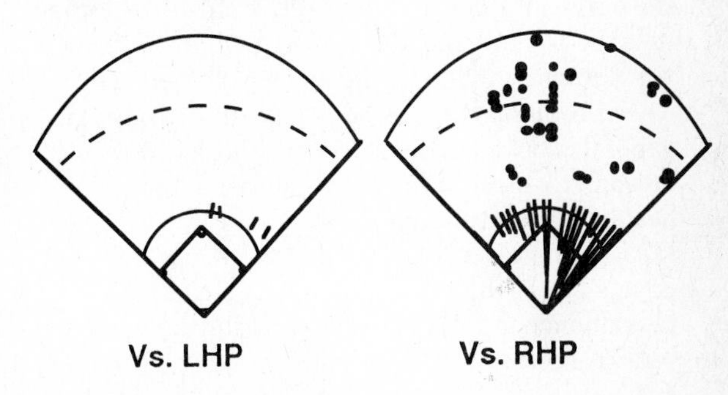

1992 Situational Stats

	AB	H	HR	RBI	AVG		AB	H	HR	RBI	AVG
Home	100	29	3	13	.290	LHP	20	4	1	4	.200
Road	117	31	0	11	.265	RHP	197	56	2	20	.284
Day	122	36	3	14	.295	Sc Pos	49	17	0	17	.347
Night	95	24	0	10	.253	Clutch	64	16	1	4	.250

1992 Rankings (National League)

- Led the Cubs in caught stealing (8) and batting average on a 3-2 count (.353)

SAMMY SOSA

Position: CF
Bats: R **Throws:** R
Ht: 6' 0" **Wt:** 175

Opening Day Age: 24
Born: 11/12/68 in San Pedro de Macoris, Dominican Republic
ML Seasons: 4

HITTING:

Acquired from the crosstown White Sox last March 30, Sammy Sosa was viewed by new general manager Larry Himes -- who has now traded for Sosa on two occasions, once for the Sox -- as the on-field embodiment of a new club direction. It worked, while Sosa was on the field. The young outfielder suffered two big injuries, a broken finger in June and a broken ankle in August. That limited this future Cub weapon to only 67 games on the year.

Sosa was tried for a while as the Cub leadoff hitter after the injury to Shawon Dunston, but both he and the Cubs seem to prefer him batting lower in the lineup. He had success in the number-five and six holes in 1992, batting .298 with three home runs in 47 at-bats. Sosa struggled mightily in April after switching leagues and showed significant problems with good offspeed pitching. He generates awesome bat speed and power, and beware to those who try to sneak a first pitch heater in on him -- he hit the first offering for a .395 average with five of his eight home runs. Sosa's big swing creates too many strikeouts, but his patience at the plate was a bit improved over past seasons.

BASERUNNING:

Not only can Sosa fly, but he improved his reads on pitcher moves and started to get better jumps. He is capable of 40 steals and will leg out many extra bases.

FIELDING:

Cutting off or catching balls hit into the gap is another area the Cubs looked for Sosa to improve the team. He brings to the field one of the game's great arms, giving the Cub outfield two bazookas. He should become a standout.

OVERALL:

While still a raw talent, the 24-year-old Sosa bears true resemblance to Andre Dawson at the same age. It would not be surprising to see him continue to develop into a true all-around force within the next few seasons. Good health will make the path easier.

Overall Statistics

	G	AB	R	H	D	T	HR	RBI	SB	BB	SO	AVG
1992	67	262	41	68	7	2	8	25	15	19	63	.260
Career	394	1293	179	303	51	13	37	141	67	77	358	.234

Where He Hits the Ball

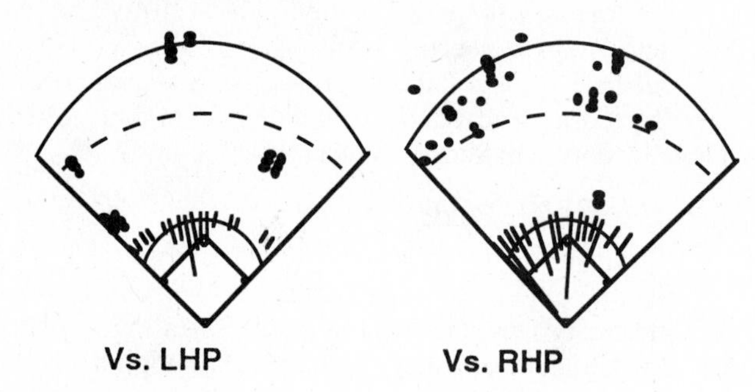

1992 Situational Stats

	AB	H	HR	RBI	AVG		AB	H	HR	RBI	AVG
Home	116	31	4	10	.267	LHP	75	21	0	5	.280
Road	146	37	4	15	.253	RHP	187	47	8	20	.251
Day	134	31	2	9	.231	Sc Pos	48	11	2	16	.229
Night	128	37	6	16	.289	Clutch	51	11	1	4	.216

1992 Rankings (National League)

- 9th in lowest stolen base percentage (68.2%)

JOSE VIZCAINO

Position: SS/3B
Bats: B **Throws:** R
Ht: 6' 1" **Wt:** 180

Opening Day Age: 25
Born: 3/26/68 in Palenque de San Cristobal, Dominican Republic
ML Seasons: 4

HITTING:

Jose Vizcaino had a big chance to take the Cubs shortstop job in 1992. Too bad his own big shots were too few and far between. The puny offensive numbers Vizcaino produced in 285 at-bats (.225 average, .260 on-base average, .298 slugging) indicated that he is far from a major league regular.

The advantage Vizcaino holds over his Cub middle-infield competitors is that he is a switch-hitter. But use the "hitter" part loosely. All three in search of the Cub shortstop job in 1992 (along with Rey Sanchez and Alex Arias) were seemingly in a contest to see who could slap the ball the hardest down the opposite field line.

The 6'1" Vizcaino chokes up on the bat and swats away indiscriminately at most offerings, intending to loop a ball in front of the outfielders or line a shot past the infield. Instead, due to his plate indiscretion, he gets far too many weak dribblers. If Vizcaino could manage some success against righthanders he might have a chance to earn some playing time. But while he did do slightly better batting lefty than right (.228 vs. 216), his numbers were still too weak to allow him in the lineup. Vizcaino needs more strength to be able to handle major league fastballs and needs to work on more plate recognition and discipline.

BASERUNNING:

Nothing special on the basepaths, Vizcaino can be used as a pinch runner without shame. His basestealing skills (3-for-3 in '92) are good.

FIELDING:

Vizcaino will be able to stay in the big leagues in a reserve capacity thanks to his solid defense. He can play all three infield positions very well and possesses a strong enough arm at third to warrant defensive replacement consideration. He has a smooth, strong release moving to his left.

OVERALL:

Despite his complete lack of offensive value, the Cubs protected Vizcaino, obviously fearing a sudden dearth of slick-fielding, no-hit utility infielders. He'll go into 1993 as insurance for the Cubs at shortstop and third base.

Overall Statistics

	G	AB	R	H	D	T	HR	RBI	SB	BB	SO	AVG
1992	86	285	25	64	10	4	1	17	3	14	35	.225
Career	223	491	37	118	16	5	1	29	6	23	62	.240

Where He Hits the Ball

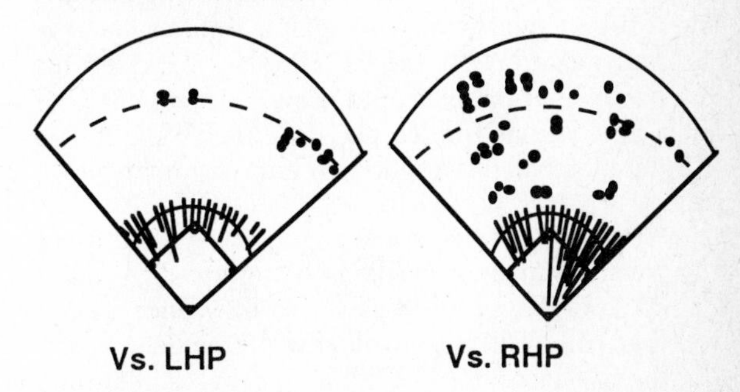

1992 Situational Stats

	AB	H	HR	RBI	AVG		AB	H	HR	RBI	AVG
Home	126	29	0	3	.230	LHP	88	19	0	5	.216
Road	159	35	1	14	.220	RHP	197	45	1	12	.228
Day	152	38	0	8	.250	Sc Pos	56	15	0	14	.268
Night	133	26	1	9	.195	Clutch	52	13	0	7	.250

1992 Rankings (National League)

- 1st in lowest on-base percentage as a leadoff batter (.233)
- 7th in lowest batting average on an 0-2 count (.091)

RICK WILKINS

Position: C
Bats: L **Throws:** R
Ht: 6' 2" **Wt:** 210

Opening Day Age: 25
Born: 6/4/67 in Jacksonville, FL
ML Seasons: 2

Overall Statistics

	G	AB	R	H	D	T	HR	RBI	SB	BB	SO	AVG
1992	83	244	20	66	9	1	8	22	0	28	53	.270
Career	169	447	41	111	18	1	14	44	3	47	109	.248

Where He Hits the Ball

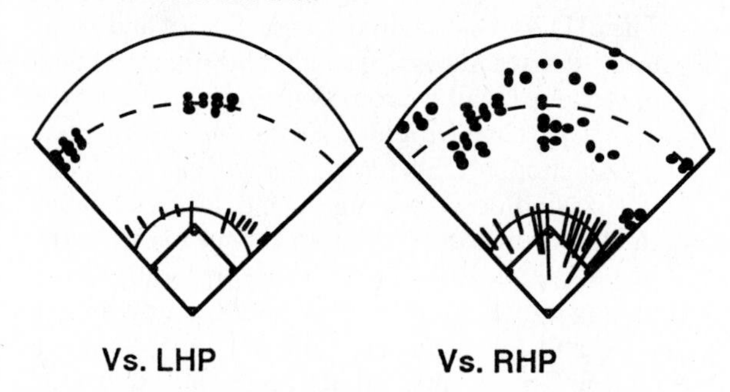

1992 Situational Stats

	AB	H	HR	RBI	AVG		AB	H	HR	RBI	AVG
Home	129	34	3	9	.264	LHP	50	14	0	1	.280
Road	115	32	5	13	.278	RHP	194	52	8	21	.268
Day	139	36	4	15	.259	Sc Pos	53	13	2	16	.245
Night	105	30	4	7	.286	Clutch	49	11	2	4	.224

1992 Rankings (National League)

- Led the Cubs in batting average on a 3-1 count (.500)

HITTING:

Thought to be the Cubs' catcher of the future, Rick Wilkins surprisingly was sent to AAA Iowa after just three weeks of the 1992 season. Ostensibly, Wilkins was to use some time on the farm to work on his pitch calling while the Cubs gave Hector Villanueva a chance.

The demotion seemed to do Wilkins some good, and upon his return, he went about the business of taking the regular catching job. Wilkins will probably never hit in the majors for a higher average than he did in 244 at-bats in 1992 (.270), but he has decent power (14 homers in 447 major league at-bats) and on-base ability (.344 OBP last year).

Wilkins made obvious strides in two of his weak areas during his demotion. He changed his approach to lefties to a more reduced swing than the full-bore cut he employs against righties, helping him make better contact. He also increased his patience at the plate and drew a decent share of walks for his limited playing time. Wilkins is a pure fastball hitter who will murder high heat.

BASERUNNING:

Much is made of Wilkins being a college linebacker. His speed is closer to Lawrence Taylor than Mike Ditka, so in other words he gets around the bags acceptably. Wilkins is capable of around five steals in a good year; he was 0-for-2 in 1992.

FIELDING:

Wilkins came to the majors with enough defensive ability to play right away. He threw out over 34 percent of the runners who tried to steal against him, a fine rate. He is mobile behind the plate and his arm is strong with a great release, although needing work with accuracy.

OVERALL:

In September Wilkins was catching full-time for the Cubs and playing like he intended to stay there, batting .269 with an impressive 15 walks and nine extra-base hits. If he continues to improve as he did in the past year, the 25-year old may have a chance to be one of the better National League catchers.

SHAWN BOSKIE

Position: SP/RP
Bats: R **Throws:** R
Ht: 6' 3" **Wt:** 205

Opening Day Age: 26
Born: 3/28/67 in Hawthorne, NV
ML Seasons: 3

Overall Statistics

	W	L	ERA	G	GS	Sv	IP	H	R	BB	SO	HR
1992	5	11	5.01	23	18	0	91.2	96	55	36	39	14
Career	14	26	4.69	66	53	0	318.1	345	175	119	150	36

PITCHING, FIELDING, HITTING & HOLDING RUNNERS:

Locked in a battle for an opening in the Cubs' starting rotation last spring, Shawn Boskie showed the mettle that has always led them to believe he could be a quality major leaguer. He won the job and started the year in the rotation.

After that, the highlights were few and far between. Boskie struggled almost all season with back spasms and a shoulder ailment which forced him to leave early in three straight June starts, causing manager Jim Lefebvre to rip into him. Boskie spent most of July and August on the disabled list. He returned in September to go 0-5 with a 10.26 ERA, allowing 28 hits and six homers in 16.2 innings.

Boskie had tried to learn a split-fingered pitch in 1991 but didn't have much success. He was also punished with a mistake-prone curveball. He is a flyball pitcher lacking a strikeout pitch, a recipe for doom in the Cozy Confines. Boskie is a decent fielder and has a sharp pickoff move. He can hit (.192 career average.), too.

OVERALL:

Boskie's miserable September may have been his last shot with the Cubs. Still, the 26-year-old shows some moxie and should be able to latch on with a new organization. His stuff is major-league caliber, so with some breaks a good season would not be impossible.

MIKE HARKEY

Position: SP
Bats: R **Throws:** R
Ht: 6' 5" **Wt:** 220

Opening Day Age: 26
Born: 10/25/66 in San Diego, CA
ML Seasons: 4

Overall Statistics

	W	L	ERA	G	GS	Sv	IP	H	R	BB	SO	HR
1992	4	0	1.89	7	7	0	38.0	34	13	15	21	4
Career	16	11	3.12	43	43	0	265.0	241	109	95	148	21

PITCHING, FIELDING, HITTING & HOLDING RUNNERS:

If only Mike Harkey could stay healthy for more than a month . . . Of course, this familiar litany has been sung yearly around Clark and Addison since the big fellow went 12-6 in his only full season, 1990.

Harkey's career has been an unfunny version of Mr. Magoo. The friendly, popular righthander worked back so diligently after serious cartilage damage was repaired in May, 1991 that the Cubs felt confident enough to deal Danny Jackson. Then a strained groin in August stopped him at 4-0; he returned briefly, but a foolhardy cartwheel in the outfield stopped him for good in September when he ruptured a tendon in his left knee.

Harkey throws a good hard fastball that averages around 90 MPH and has a little wiggle to it. His curve and slider are mediocre. His control was spotty in his seven starts, but he has always had a knack for bearing down in a jam (.210 career opposition average with runners in scoring position). His fielding is smooth, and he has good awareness of baserunners.

OVERALL:

Due to his injuries, Harkey's once-bright promise has lost its luster, and the Cubs left him available to expansion. Even when healthy, Harkey is not a top-flight, number-one or two starter. But his lifetime record is 16-11, with a 3.12 ERA. If only . .

LUIS SALAZAR

Position: 3B/SS/LF
Bats: R **Throws:** R
Ht: 5'10" **Wt:** 190

Opening Day Age: 36
Born: 5/19/56 in Barcelona, Venezuela
ML Seasons: 13

Overall Statistics

	G	AB	R	H	D	T	HR	RBI	SB	BB	SO	AVG
1992	98	255	20	53	7	2	5	25	1	11	34	.208
Career	1302	4101	438	1070	144	33	94	455	117	179	653	.261

HITTING, FIELDING, BASERUNNING:

Though the acquisition of Steve Buechele has put the future of 36-year-old Luis Salazar with the Cubs in jeopardy, the 1992 season was again a testament to the versatility of the veteran -- and to the weaknesses of the club itself.

Salazar found a way to get into 98 games for the Cubs, despite an absolute deterioration of his ability to hit right-handed pitching. There weren't many highlights in 1992 for the 13-year major leaguer. His bat speed slowed measurably, reducing him to a hitter who guessed fastball at all times in order to handle the heat. He batted just .141 against righties in 99 at-bats, with only two extra-base hits. He showed some customary pop vs. lefties (.250, .391 slugging).

Salazar is a below average runner but rarely challenges his legs. Besides getting his normal playing time at third base (defensively ordinary), the Cubs tried him in left field, where he was horrible, as an emergency shortstop, which should be erased from fan memory, and at first base.

OVERALL:

Without a major resuscitation of his bat speed and ability to hit right-handed pitching, Salazar has only one hope: that the disasters that routinely seem to befall the Cub infield occur yet again in 1993. Otherwise, he'll take his role-playing ability and call it a nice, long career.

JEROME WALTON

Position: LF
Bats: R **Throws:** R
Ht: 6' 1" **Wt:** 175

Opening Day Age: 27
Born: 7/8/65 in Newnan, GA
ML Seasons: 4

Overall Statistics

	G	AB	R	H	D	T	HR	RBI	SB	BB	SO	AVG
1992	30	55	7	7	0	1	0	1	1	9	13	.127
Career	370	1192	176	308	52	7	12	85	46	105	215	.258

HITTING, FIELDING, BASERUNNING:

Midway through spring training, the Cubs brass had seemingly decided that Jerome Walton would continue as their center fielder and leadoff hitter. Whether there was a verbal promise to Walton or not, the club surprised Walton by placing him on the disabled list just before Opening Day after acquiring Sammy Sosa.

Walton didn't reemerge until late April, as part of a left field platoon. He grumbled and groused his way to 55 totally ineffective at-bats before being sent to the minors for good. In his major league at-bats, he showed decent patience but not much improvement, his past problems with offspeed pitches continued. Walton batted just .127, about on the level of a National League pitcher, with one triple.

Walton has good speed and has always been a fine base thief. His outfield range is passable at the major league level, but he doesn't always get a proper jump on the ball and has a below-par arm.

OVERALL:

The saga of the 1989 pennant race phenom has likely come to an end in Chicago. One would be hard-pressed to find a talented player more disenchanted and unaggressive than Walton was last year. A new scenario may bring the 27-year old back to life, but it would be a major comeback story.

ORGANIZATION OVERVIEW:

It probably isn't fair to evaluate the current state of the Cub farm system, built as it was by Bozo the Clown, Barney Fife, and other mainstays of the Tribune television network. The recently-hired general manager, Larry Himes, built the crosstown White Sox into a contending team, but he hasn't been on the North Side long enough to produce any results yet. Judging by his past record, Himes will soon have some useful players -- and more than that, some potential stars -- on their way to Wrigley Field. Who knows? One of these years, Luis Salazar might find himself out of a job.

LANCE DICKSON

Position: P **Opening Day Age:** 23
Bats: R **Throws:** L **Born:** 10/19/69 in
Ht: 6' 1" **Wt:** 185 Fullerton, CA

Recent Statistics

	W	L	ERA	G	GS	Sv	IP	H	R	BB	SO	HR
91 AAA Iowa	4	4	3.11	18	18	0	101.1	85	39	57	101	5
92 AAA Iowa	0	1	19.29	1	1	0	2.1	6	5	2	2	1

Lance Dickson has been a "top Cub pitching prospect" so long that he may have learned his curveball from Three-Finger Brown. Surprisingly, Dickson is still only 23, and his left arm ought to be pretty well rested given that he worked only 2.1 innings at AAA Iowa in 1992. There's little question that Dickson can pitch -- his ERA for 180 minor league innings is 2.40 -- but lots of questions about his ability to stay healthy. Arm problems, leg problems, foot problems, shoulder problems, he's had about everything go wrong. It's simple: if he can ever stay healthy, Dickson can be a very good major league pitcher.

JESSIE HOLLINS

Position: P **Opening Day Age:** 23
Bats: R **Throws:** R **Born:** 1/27/70 in
Ht: 6' 3" **Wt:** 200 Conroe, TX

Recent Statistics

	W	L	ERA	G	GS	Sv	IP	H	R	BB	SO	HR
92 AA Charlotte	3	4	3.20	63	0	25	70.1	60	28	32	73	4
92 NL Chicago	0	0	13.50	4	0	0	4.2	8	7	5	0	1

Ever since they traded Lee Smith -- and wouldn't you deal him away if you could get Al Nipper and Calvin Schiraldi? -- the Cubs have looked for a big, hard-throwing right-handed relief ace. Hollins, who physically resembles the young Smith, may be their best hope. Moved full-time to the bullpen last year, Hollins saved 25 games at AA Charlotte and earned a promotion to the big club at year's end. Hollins throws hard, though not as hard as Smith, and the Cubs weren't much discouraged by his 13.50 ERA in four major league games.

HEATHCLIFF SLOCUMB

Position: P **Opening Day Age:** 26
Bats: R **Throws:** R **Born:** 6/7/66 in
Ht: 6' 3" **Wt:** 180 Jamaica, NY

Recent Statistics

	W	L	ERA	G	GS	Sv	IP	H	R	BB	SO	HR
92 AAA Iowa	1	3	2.59	36	1	7	41.2	36	13	16	47	0
92 NL Chicago	0	3	6.50	30	0	1	36.0	52	27	21	27	3

Heathcliff Slocumb has one of the great names in baseball, and one of the better arms as well. What Slocumb doesn't have is a major league job, even after two extended trials (82 games) with the Cubs. Slocumb's 90 MPH fastball, cut fastball and wicked slider have thus far been more effective at AAA than the majors. He's been hampered by control problems and has enormous difficulties with left-handed hitters, who batted .413 against him last year. Still, it's hard to give up on an arm -- and a name -- like that. He should get another chance this year.

MATT WALBECK

Position: C **Opening Day Age:** 23
Bats: B **Throws:** R **Born:** 10/2/69 in
Ht: 6' 0" **Wt:** 192 Sacramento, CA

Recent Statistics

	G	AB	R	H	D	T	HR	RBI	SB	BB	SO	AVG
91 A Winston-sal	91	259	25	70	11	0	3	41	3	20	23	.270
92 AA Charlotte	105	385	48	116	22	1	7	42	0	33	56	.301
92 MLE	105	376	39	107	20	0	7	34	0	21	59	.285

There's this big machine in the basement of the Tribune Tower, and about once a year it stamps out a Cub catching prospect -- Damon Berryhill, Joe Girardi, Rick Wilkins, Hector Villanueva, and now Matt Walbeck. Walbeck was an eighth-round draft choice in 1987, and as recently as 1990 he was batting .227 at Class A. Walbeck has developed since then and last year batted .301 at Charlotte. He appears to have the defensive goods, and should arrive in Chicago in a year or so, as the Cubs thought highly enough of him to protect him in the expansion draft.

TURK WENDELL

Position: P **Opening Day Age:** 25
Bats: B **Throws:** R **Born:** 5/19/67 in
Ht: 6' 2" **Wt:** 175 Pittsfield, MA

Recent Statistics

	W	L	ERA	G	GS	Sv	IP	H	R	BB	SO	HR
91 AA Greenville	11	3	2.56	25	20	0	147.2	130	47	51	122	4
91 AAA Richmond	0	2	3.43	3	3	0	21.0	20	9	16	18	3
92 AAA Iowa	2	0	1.44	4	4	0	25.0	17	7	15	12	3

Last year the Cubs waited for the arrival of the colorful Turk Wendell, the man who chews licorice on the mound and brushes his teeth between innings. The wait was in vain, as Wendell suffered a stress fracture in his right elbow -- brushing too vigorously, perhaps? -- after only four starts. At the time, Wendell had a 1.44 ERA. The Cubs expect him to recover and make an impact.

PITCHING:

Rescued from the baseball scrap heap in one of many shrewd pickups by departed general manager Bob Quinn, Scott Bankhead re-established his once-promising career in 1992. The righthander had been an effective starter for a couple of seasons with Seattle -- he went 14-6 with a 3.34 ERA in 1989 -- but shoulder problems kept putting him on the shelf. In 1990 Bankhead was able to work in only four games, and in '91 he was limited to 60.2 innings. The Reds got him cheap and moved him into a set-up relief role. They discovered that bullpen work was a lot easier on Bankhead's arm.

Last year Bankhead notched 10 wins, the second-highest total of his career. He allowed only four home runs in 70.2 innings and opposing hitters batted only .218 against him. Bankhead stranded nearly 90 percent of his inherited runners. Except for a disastrous August, he maintained a consistent level of performance which indicates that he may have found his niche.

Bankhead spots his sinking fastball well and then mixes in a good slider and excellent change. He usually stays ahead in the count with many of his 29 walks coming in a handful of poor outings when he didn't have his control. Bankhead was rarely asked to go through a lineup more than once -- this kept him fresh and also prevented batters from measuring him. New manager Tony Perez shouldn't have to change a thing.

HOLDING RUNNERS, FIELDING, HITTING:

Bankhead has an average move to first but is fairly quick to home with his delivery, which helps combat basestealers. Bankhead is also a good athlete and fields his position well. He rarely gets a chance to hit but occasionally can help himself.

OVERALL:

Bankhead, a free agent after the season, was invaluable to the Reds in 1992. With much of their starting rotation often injured, they needed solid middle relief to get the game to their closers. Bankhead was a key element. The new Cincinnati front office would be wise to keep him.

SCOTT BANKHEAD

Position: RP
Bats: R **Throws:** R
Ht: 5'10" **Wt:** 185

Opening Day Age: 29
Born: 7/31/63 in Raleigh, NC
ML Seasons: 7

Overall Statistics

	W	L	ERA	G	GS	Sv	IP	H	R	BB	SO	HR
1992	10	4	2.93	54	0	1	70.2	57	26	29	53	4
Career	51	44	4.12	180	109	1	760.0	739	376	232	522	90

How Often He Throws Strikes

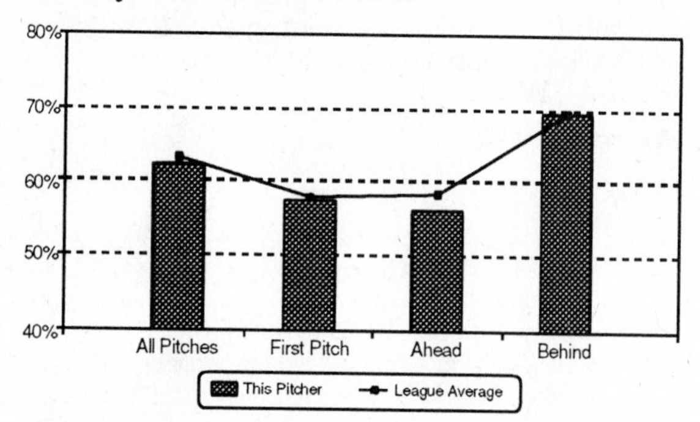

1992 Situational Stats

	W	L	ERA	Sv	IP		AB	H	HR	RBI	AVG
Home	6	0	3.19	0	36.2	LHB	128	29	3	10	.227
Road	4	4	2.65	1	34.0	RHB	133	28	1	13	.211
Day	3	1	2.15	0	29.1	Sc Pos	69	12	1	18	.174
Night	7	3	3.48	1	41.1	Clutch	119	29	3	10	.244

1992 Rankings (National League)

- 2nd in relief wins (10)
- 5th in lowest batting average allowed in relief with runners in scoring position (.174)
- 6th in holds (14)
- 10th in lowest batting average allowed in relief (.218)
- Led the Reds in hit batsmen (3), holds, lowest batting average allowed in relief with runners in scoring position, relief ERA (2.93) and relief wins

PITCHING:

In a 1992 Reds' season riddled with injuries, Tim Belcher was a rock of stability in the Cincinnati rotation. He went to the post every time he was asked, and though he had a rough stretch of 10 starts two-thirds of the way through the season, he battled back to finish strongly. Though his ERA was on the high side at 3.91, Belcher matched his career high with 15 wins.

Belcher's win-loss record actually belies an even stronger performance because he was the victim of several of the Reds' many blown saves. One of the most memorable came late in August at Shea Stadium when Belcher allowed a first-inning run and then retired 23 straight batters to bring the Reds into the ninth inning with a two-run lead. Unfortunately, Rob Dibble blew it.

When Belcher isn't effective, it is usually because he isn't controlling his fastball. His 90-plus heater often gets away from him high in the strike zone and when that happens it causes trouble. Belcher has a wide assortment of pitches, including a hard slider, average curve, split-fingered fastball and an improving change-up. As usual, Belcher was rugged on right-handed hitters, who batted only .178 against him last season. He remains one of the best pitchers in the stretch drive. He was 4-2 last year in September-October, raising his lifetime regular-season record in those months to 16-7.

HOLDING RUNNERS, FIELDING, HITTING:

Belcher would seem fairly easy to run on because of his slow delivery home. However, he has worked at holding runners and last year permitted only six steals in 17 attempts. He is a solid fielder with good instincts and a decent hitter who managed eight hits last year.

OVERALL:

Though he hasn't become the great pitcher some projected when he was the first player picked in the 1983 draft (the Twins couldn't sign him), Belcher has become a very steady starter. He has averaged a dozen wins and 200 innings a year since 1988. Every staff needs a guy like that.

TIM BELCHER

Position: SP
Bats: R **Throws:** R
Ht: 6' 3" **Wt:** 220

Opening Day Age: 31
Born: 10/19/61 in Sparta, OH
ML Seasons: 6

Overall Statistics

	W	L	ERA	G	GS	Sv	IP	H	R	BB	SO	HR
1992	15	14	3.91	35	34	0	227.2	201	104	80	149	17
Career	65	52	3.20	173	153	5	1033.2	881	413	341	782	74

How Often He Throws Strikes

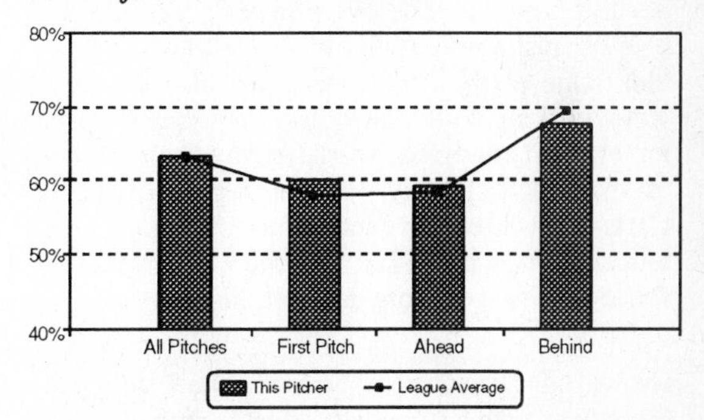

1992 Situational Stats

	W	L	ERA	Sv	IP		AB	H	HR	RBI	AVG
Home	11	7	3.43	0	126.0	LHB	512	142	9	51	.277
Road	4	7	4.51	0	101.2	RHB	331	59	8	39	.178
Day	4	4	3.20	0	70.1	Sc Pos	184	50	5	73	.272
Night	11	10	4.23	0	157.1	Clutch	86	26	2	11	.302

1992 Rankings (National League)

- 3rd in losses (14), walks allowed (80) and lowest stolen base percentage allowed (35.3%)
- 4th in highest ERA (3.91) and games started (34)
- 5th in lowest groundball/flyball ratio (.95)
- Led the Reds in sacrifice bunts as a hitter (7), wins (15), losses, games started, innings pitched (227.2), batters faced (949), home runs allowed (17), walks allowed, hit batsmen (3), most pitches thrown (3,372), lowest batting average allowed (.238), lowest stolen base percentage allowed and bunts in play as a hitter (11)

PITCHING:

When Tom Browning tore up his left knee in a baserunning collision at home plate last July 1, it meant that for only the second time in eight years he would not pitch 200 innings. But Browning's season-ending injury couldn't obscure the fact that before he was hurt, he was getting rocked. Prior to the knee injury, opponents were hitting a whopping .311 against him. His earned run average was over 5.00 and he was able to strikeout only 33 batters in those 87 innings. Those aren't the kind of numbers the Reds wanted out of a staff workhorse like Browning.

Browning, even at his best, has always been what a NL manager termed "a fine-line pitcher. He doesn't have that one overpowering pitch and if he's off just a little with his control, he's in trouble." One problem last year was that the Reds were working with many good starters and trying to get them all regular work. Always better when used more frequently, Browning got only eight starts with three- or four-days rest last year. In those outings his ERA was 3.83. But in eight starts with five or more days off, his ERA shot up to 6.53.

Browning relies on spotting his fastball, which he turns over with a screwball effect to right-handed batters, and on changing speeds. Before his injury last year, his velocity was dropping. It should also be noted that his hits-per-innings ratio has been escalating for the last five years.

HOLDING RUNNERS, FIELDING, HITTING:

Browning is known for his excellent pickoff move and quick delivery to the plate. Perhaps distracted by his pitching problems, he permitted 11 steals in 12 attempts last year. He is a very good fielding pitcher and one of the better hitting pitchers in baseball.

OVERALL:

Browning has been the rock of the Reds' rotation for a long time, averaging 15 wins a year from 1985 to 1991. But his knee injury and the perceptible decline in his ability combine to make his future very murky. Not yet 33, he's young enough to bounce back if he gets a solid chance.

TOM BROWNING

Position: SP
Bats: L **Throws:** L
Ht: 6' 1" **Wt:** 195

Opening Day Age: 32
Born: 4/28/60 in Casper, WY
ML Seasons: 9

Overall Statistics

	W	L	ERA	G	GS	Sv	IP	H	R	BB	SO	HR
1992	6	5	5.07	16	16	0	87.0	108	49	28	33	6
Career	113	80	3.86	272	271	0	1756.1	1725	823	473	922	211

How Often He Throws Strikes

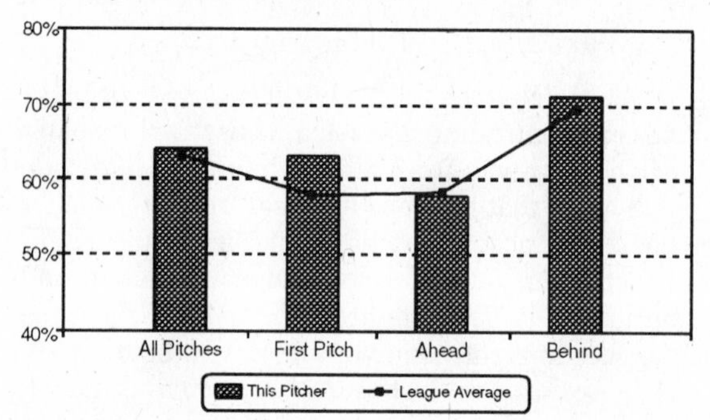

1992 Situational Stats

	W	L	ERA	Sv	IP		AB	H	HR	RBI	AVG
Home	5	1	5.03	0	34.0	LHB	83	27	1	20	.325
Road	1	4	5.09	0	53.0	RHB	264	81	5	25	.307
Day	1	2	7.00	0	18.0	Sc Pos	97	29	1	38	.299
Night	5	3	4.57	0	69.0	Clutch	9	2	0	1	.222

1992 Rankings (National League)

- 9th in most GDPs induced per GDP situation (17.9%)
- Led the Reds in most GDPs induced per GDP situation

PITCHING:

The Yankees installed Greg Cadaret in their starting rotation early in 1992. For a while it looked like Cadaret might finally succeed in that role. In five starts during April he was 2-1 with a 1.86 ERA. But then the old problems returned. Cadaret's established form, proven in four years with New York, is that he is a good reliever and a bad starter. Eventually shifted back to the pen, he wound up with a 4.25 ERA -- 4.57 as a starter, 3.72 in relief.

Cadaret's best pitch is a high-velocity fastball. When he was with Oakland in 1987-1989 he adopted Dave Duncan's philosophy of pitching inside and it has served him well. Cadaret also possesses a curve and occasionally throws a forkball and a straight change, but these pitches are all just supporting cast for the heater. He is traditionally tough on left-handed hitters, holding them to a .227 average last year.

The one problem with Cadaret's style -- and the reason why he has never made it as a starter -- is that he tires early. A small reduction in velocity makes his fastball much more hittable, and he doesn't have enough command of his breaking pitches to rely on them in his second and third time through a batting order. In 1992, Cadaret yielded the opposition a batting average of just .238 on his first 45 pitches and .312 thereafter.

HOLDING RUNNERS AND FIELDING:

With a good pickoff move and a direct approach to the plate, Cadaret has usually enjoyed success at holding runners. But in 1992 the opposition nabbed 19 stolen bases against him at a 73 percent success rate. Cadaret's main problem was simply having too many baserunners. He is a very good fielder who often helps himself.

OVERALL:

With the Yankees, Cadaret was consistently excellent working out of the bullpen. Even during his difficult 1992 season, once Cadaret got back in the pen and regained his best style he posted a 2.22 ERA after July 31. That bodes well for his prospects with his new team -- the Reds figure to keep him in the bullpen.

GREG CADARET

Position: RP/SP
Bats: L **Throws:** L
Ht: 6' 3" **Wt:** 215

Opening Day Age: 31
Born: 2/27/62 in Detroit, MI
ML Seasons: 6

Overall Statistics

	W	L	ERA	G	GS	Sv	IP	H	R	BB	SO	HR
1992	4	8	4.25	46	11	1	103.2	104	53	74	73	12
Career	33	27	3.91	301	35	10	578.0	561	277	314	432	43

How Often He Throws Strikes

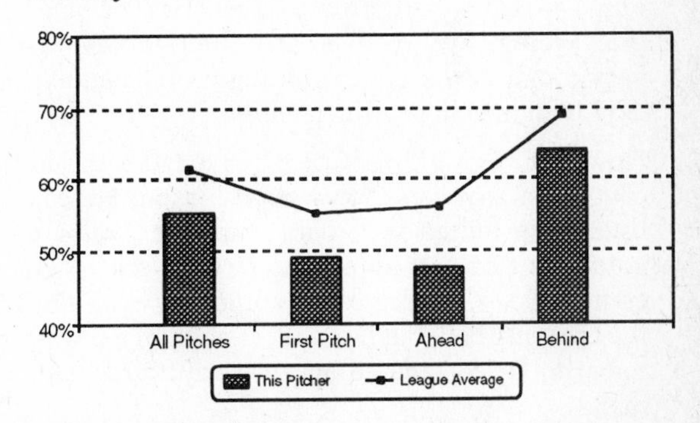

1992 Situational Stats

	W	L	ERA	Sv	IP		AB	H	HR	RBI	AVG
Home	4	3	3.29	0	65.2	LHB	88	20	3	10	.227
Road	0	5	5.92	1	38.0	RHB	301	84	9	46	.279
Day	2	2	4.28	1	33.2	Sc Pos	133	29	4	46	.218
Night	2	6	4.24	0	70.0	Clutch	50	16	1	8	.320

1992 Rankings (American League)

- 8th in lowest batting average allowed with runners in scoring position (.218)
- Led the Yankees in shutouts (1) and lowest percentage of inherited runners scored (33.3%)

DARNELL COLES

Position: 3B/1B
Bats: R **Throws:** R
Ht: 6' 1" **Wt:** 185

Opening Day Age: 30
Born: 6/2/62 in San Bernardino, CA
ML Seasons: 10

HITTING:

A career-long journeyman, Darnell Coles proved to be a valuable fill-in for injured Reds regulars in 1992. Coles had apparently disappeared from the major-league scene after the 1991 season when he was released by the Giants' AAA Phoenix farm club. He signed a contract with the Reds AAA team at Nashville and worked his way back. A .243 lifetime hitter entering the season, Coles batted .312, a career best by 39 points. Unfortunately, he broke an ankle himself and missed the last two months.

For several weeks, Coles picked up the slack left by Chris Sabo's injury. He also chipped in as a pinch hitter. Though he had only three homers, 16 of his 44 hits went for extra bases; his .482 slugging average was another career high. Coles was very tough in the clutch, hitting an outstanding .357 with men in scoring position.

However, as well as Coles played, he hasn't caught on anywhere for a good reason. He can usually be retired with hard stuff. He is also a notorious first-ball hitter who rarely works deep counts. Coles has improved somewhat at hitting the breaking ball, but he is not enough of a power threat to be considered an everyday third baseman.

BASERUNNING:

Coles is an average runner but no basestealing threat. He is aggressive on the bases, as evidenced by his injury which came on a hard-hitting play at the plate.

FIELDING:

Though versatile, Coles has mostly played third base during his career. Though he was a butcher early in his career, he has made himself into a more-than-passable third baseman. He can also fill in at first and in left or right field.

OVERALL:

When there are changes in the offing, as there were for the Reds during the offseason, a utility man like Coles can sometimes fall through the cracks. However, he came through in a big way for Cincinnati at a time when they needed a boost. He also provides some veteran depth in a number of roles. Coles, a free agent, signed with the Toronto Blue Jays during the off-season.

Overall Statistics

	G	AB	R	H	D	T	HR	RBI	SB	BB	SO	AVG
1992	55	141	16	44	11	2	3	18	1	3	15	.312
Career	761	2394	278	592	119	12	63	309	19	195	365	.247

Where He Hits the Ball

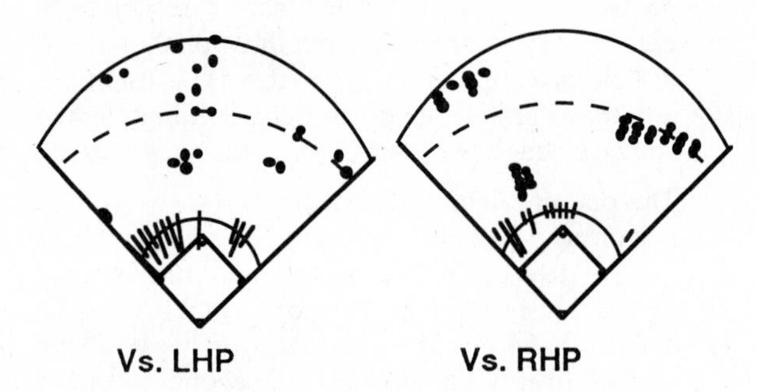

1992 Situational Stats

	AB	H	HR	RBI	AVG		AB	H	HR	RBI	AVG
Home	60	15	1	7	.250	LHP	97	31	1	12	.320
Road	81	29	2	11	.358	RHP	44	13	2	6	.295
Day	35	13	0	5	.371	Sc Pos	28	10	1	16	.357
Night	106	31	3	13	.292	Clutch	27	9	0	3	.333

1992 Rankings (National League)

- Did not rank near the top or bottom in any category

STOPPER

PITCHING:

Rob Dibble is possibly the hardest thrower in baseball, at times hitting 100 MPH with one of the most feared fastballs around. But Dibble also frequently hits 100 MPH on the behavior meter. His history of blow-ups culminated in the bizarre incident late last season in which he became Sergeant Slaughter to Lou Piniella's Hulk Hogan. The incident, once again, obscured some outstanding pitching. Reclaiming his job as the Reds closer, Dibble posted eight saves after September 1. During the second half of last season his ERA was 1.59, and he struck out an amazing 63 men in 34 innings -- an unheard-of rate of nearly two strikeouts per inning.

Dibble opened last season on the disabled list with shoulder trouble and didn't really find a groove until after the All-Star break. He eventually supplanted Norm Charlton as the main closer, earning 25 saves in 30 opportunities. However, Dibble often struggled, especially during the first half of the season. Many of his 31 walks were inexplicable "pitch-arounds" against weak hitters. He got beat far too often with his slider. As a National League pitching coach said, "Dibble's slider can be nasty, but it also can flatten out. And when you can throw 98 miles per hour like he can, anything else you throw is your second-best pitch." All three of the home runs Dibble allowed came on first pitches, and all of them lost games.

HOLDING RUNNERS, FIELDING, HITTING:

Dibble doesn't worry about the non-pitching crafts of his trade. His slow, high leg kick makes him easy pickings for basestealers. Because he falls so far off to the side after throwing a pitch, he is rarely in position to field a ball hit back to the box. He did earn the first two hits of his career in 1992.

OVERALL:

Despite his awesome ability, Dibble has been a constant pain for the Reds' organization with his various transgressions, as well as some contract problems. But how do you give up on an arm like this, even with all the flaws? The Reds didn't, trading Charlton and throwing the closer load full-time on his shoulders.

ROB DIBBLE

Position: RP
Bats: L **Throws:** R
Ht: 6' 4" **Wt:** 230

Opening Day Age: 29
Born: 1/24/64 in Bridgeport, CT
ML Seasons: 5

Overall Statistics

	W	L	ERA	G	GS	Sv	IP	H	R	BB	SO	HR
1992	3	5	3.07	63	0	25	70.1	48	26	31	110	3
Career	25	19	2.35	309	0	69	409.0	282	115	150	570	17

How Often He Throws Strikes

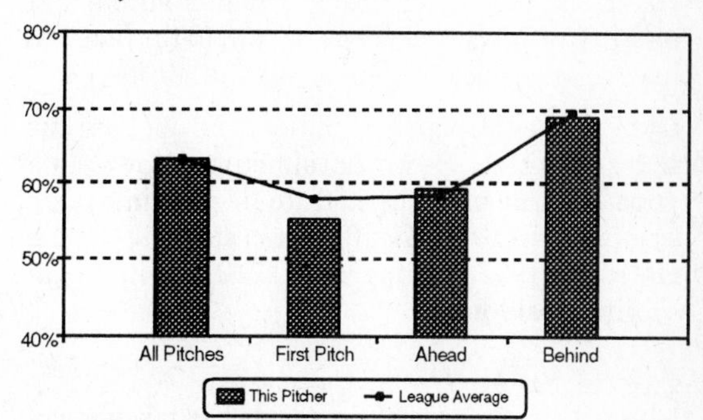

1992 Situational Stats

	W	L	ERA	Sv	IP		AB	H	HR	RBI	AVG
Home	2	1	1.47	16	36.2	LHB	128	23	2	17	.180
Road	1	4	4.81	9	33.2	RHB	121	25	1	17	.207
Day	1	2	3.80	6	21.1	Sc Pos	90	19	2	32	.211
Night	2	3	2.76	19	49.0	Clutch	163	29	3	26	.178

1992 Rankings (National League)

- 1st in most strikeouts per 9 innings in relief (14.1)
- 2nd in lowest batting average allowed in relief (.193)
- 3rd in save percentage (83.3%) and lowest batting average allowed vs. left-handed batters (.180)
- Led the Reds in games finished, save percentage, lowest batting average allowed vs. left-handed batters, first batter efficiency (.167), lowest percentage of inherited runners scored (24.4%), lowest batting average allowed in relief, least baserunners allowed per 9 innings in relief (10.4) and most strikeouts per 9 innings in relief

BILLY DORAN

Position: 2B/1B
Bats: B **Throws:** R
Ht: 6' 0" **Wt:** 180

Opening Day Age: 34
Born: 5/28/58 in Cincinnati, OH
ML Seasons: 11

Overall Statistics

	G	AB	R	H	D	T	HR	RBI	SB	BB	SO	AVG
1992	132	387	48	91	16	2	8	47	7	64	40	.235
Career	1425	5071	720	1353	216	39	84	491	208	703	597	.267

Where He Hits the Ball

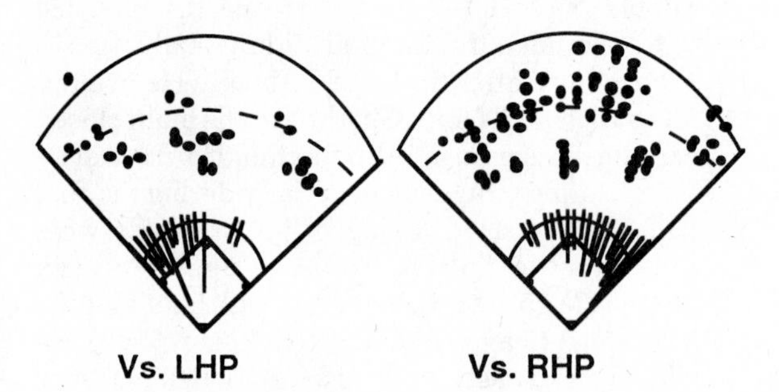

1992 Situational Stats

	AB	H	HR	RBI	AVG		AB	H	HR	RBI	AVG
Home	197	44	6	25	.223	LHP	125	25	2	11	.200
Road	190	47	2	22	.247	RHP	262	66	6	36	.252
Day	126	31	2	16	.246	Sc Pos	105	22	2	38	.210
Night	261	60	6	31	.230	Clutch	68	16	2	17	.235

1992 Rankings (National League)

- 3rd in lowest batting average vs. left-handed pitchers (.200)
- 5th in lowest slugging percentage vs. left-handed pitchers (.288)
- 8th in batting average with the bases loaded (.467)
- 10th in batting average on a 3-1 count (.500)
- Led the Reds in batting average with the bases loaded, batting average on a 3-1 count and lowest percentage of swings that missed (13.5%)

HITTING:

One of the real pros on the Cincinnati club, Billy Doran has seen his performance begin to seriously slip. Doran batted .300 in 1990 and .280 in 1991, his first full year with the Reds. But last year the 11-year veteran hit only .235, a career low. That's not the direction a guy wants his career to be headed in, especially with his 35th birthday about to arrive.

Doran is at the point where if he's going to be in the lineup at all, it might have to be as a platoon player. Though a switch-hitter, he batted only .200 from the right side with a minuscule slugging percentage of .288. He was much more acceptable as a lefty hitter, hitting .252 and belting six of his eight home runs. Doran's strong last month (.317) was due, in good part, to the fact that he was seldom in the lineup against a lefty.

Doran remains a patient hitter who gathers his share of walks. However, although known as a good fastball hitter he had trouble at times last season with the hard stuff. Doran struggled in the clutch in 1992, batting only .210 with men in scoring position.

BASERUNNING:

Doran's history of back problems has taken away much of his basestealing skill. He only attempted 11 steals last year, nabbing seven. However, Doran is still aggressive on the bases. He has good instincts for taking the extra base.

FIELDING:

Doran remains dependable at second base, though his range is now well below average. He's good on the double play and is excellent at positioning himself. He filled in last year at first base also, showing surprising skill at a position he'd hardly played prior to last year.

OVERALL:

Though Cincinnati has several young middle infielders, Doran's veteran stability is a valuable asset. However, the slippage in his production last year could be a sign that he is on the down side of his career. He should still be useful as a platoon/utility player.

PITCHING:

When they were hit by various injuries to their starting rotation, the Reds turned last year to Chris Hammond, a young lefthander who had won seven games while battling elbow problems in 1991. Hammond had posted some eye-popping numbers in the minors, especially in 1990 when he'd gone 15-1 with a league-leading 2.17 ERA at AAA Nashville. But last year Hammond didn't do much in his 26 starts to ensure his future with the Reds.

Hammond's stock might be helped by the departure of Lou Piniella, who did not have the patience for Hammond's nibbling style of pitching. Piniella's dislike of Hammond was well known among the Reds. Once when Hammond was scheduled to pitch in a late-August game, a member of the club was heard to say, "It's a long day for the bullpen because with Hammond pitching Lou will have a reliever up every time there's a three-ball count."

Hammond relies on changing speeds, especially since his arm problems seem to have affected the velocity of his fastball. He has an average curve and slider and runs far too many deep counts for a pitcher who doesn't strike out many batters. He does not challenge left-handed hitters, who batted .291 against him last year. Nor does he seem to be a pitcher who will give a staff a lot of innings -- he doesn't have a complete game in his 47 major-league starts and averaged less than six innings per start.

HOLDING RUNNERS, FIELDING, HITTING:

Hammond has a fairly quick delivery home, but his pickoff move is below average for a left-hander. He is an unsteady fielder with poor instincts. Hammond is a factor as a hitter. Though his hit total fell from 12 in 1991 to six last year, he did hit a home run.

OVERALL:

Hammond has been a disappointment to the Reds, especially considering his minor-league record. With all the Reds' good arms, Hammond could end up in long relief or in another organization.

CHRIS HAMMOND

Position: SP
Bats: L **Throws:** L
Ht: 6' 1" **Wt:** 190

Opening Day Age: 27
Born: 1/21/66 in Atlanta, GA
ML Seasons: 3

Overall Statistics

	W	L	ERA	G	GS	Sv	IP	H	R	BB	SO	HR
1992	7	10	4.21	28	26	0	147.1	149	75	55	79	13
Career	14	19	4.25	51	47	0	258.1	254	135	115	133	19

How Often He Throws Strikes

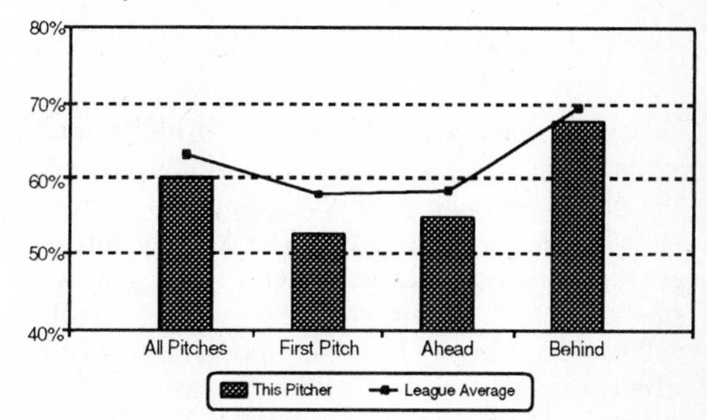

1992 Situational Stats

	W	L	ERA	Sv	IP		AB	H	HR	RBI	AVG
Home	5	4	3.92	0	82.2	LHB	117	34	5	17	.291
Road	2	6	4.59	0	64.2	RHB	444	115	8	45	.259
Day	4	4	3.66	0	66.1	Sc Pos	106	31	4	42	.292
Night	3	6	4.67	0	81.0	Clutch	24	9	0	1	.375

1992 Rankings (National League)

- 8th in highest ERA at home (3.92)
- Led the Reds in hit batsmen (3) and lowest batting average allowed vs. right-handed batters (.259)

PITCHING:

Well-traveled righthander Dwayne Henry has a world of stuff. He averaged nearly a strikeout per inning pitched last season, his first with Cincinnati. Opponents hit only .199 off him (he allowed only 59 hits in 83.2 innings), showing he has the potential to be a quality short reliever. Henry didn't record a save last year, but his 60 games pitched were a career high and his 3.33 ERA was very respectable.

However, Henry is also inconsistent with his control, which is one reason he's modeled a different uniform during each of the last three seasons. He walked 44 batters in those 83.2 innings in 1992. And when he did give up a hit, it usually came at a bad time, costing a run. Over the last two years, Henry has allowed over 40 percent of his inherited runners to score (31 of 72).

Henry routinely tops 90 MPH with his fastball and can throw his slider in the high 80s. He will also throw an occasional change-up, but it is obviously his third-best pitch. The key for him is getting ahead of hitters. When Henry got two strikes on a hitter last year, they were basically defenseless, hitting .128. But in other situations, when he couldn't spot his slider, he was much less effective. Henry is prone to stretches of wildness in which he can't find the plate with any of his pitches.

HOLDING RUNNERS, FIELDING, HITTING:

Henry has no move to first to speak of and is thus easy to run on. In his limited action last year he permitted six steals in eight attempts. He is a decent fielder and no factor as a hitter.

OVERALL:

At the least, Henry can be better than most middle relievers simply because he throws so hard. If he could ever achieve consistent control, he could be a real sleeper. But it's getting pretty late into his career, at age 31, to keep wishing for a significant breakthrough in his pitching style.

DWAYNE HENRY

Position: RP
Bats: R **Throws:** R
Ht: 6' 3" **Wt:** 230
Opening Day Age: 31
Born: 2/16/62 in Elkton, MD
ML Seasons: 9

Overall Statistics

	W	L	ERA	G	GS	Sv	IP	H	R	BB	SO	HR
1992	3	3	3.33	60	0	0	83.2	59	31	44	72	4
Career	11	13	4.21	212	0	7	267.1	225	130	167	229	20

How Often He Throws Strikes

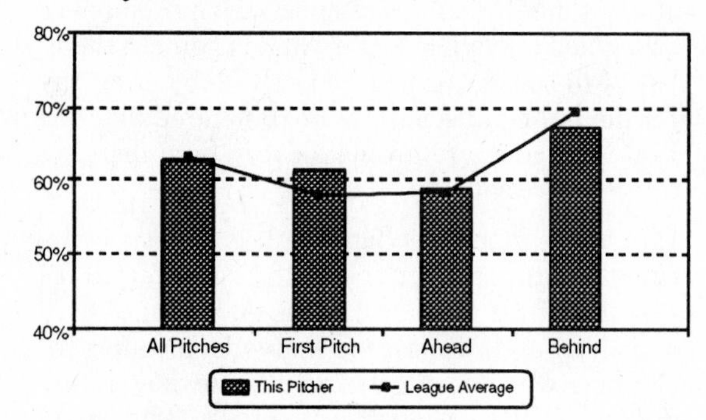

1992 Situational Stats

	W	L	ERA	Sv	IP		AB	H	HR	RBI	AVG
Home	2	1	2.47	0	43.2	LHB	130	27	3	15	.208
Road	1	2	4.28	0	40.0	RHB	167	32	1	17	.192
Day	1	1	1.74	0	20.2	Sc Pos	75	19	1	25	.253
Night	2	2	3.86	0	63.0	Clutch	73	11	0	4	.151

1992 Rankings (National League)

- 2nd in wild pitches (12)
- 4th in lowest batting average allowed in relief (.199)
- 8th in highest percentage of inherited runners scored (37.8%)
- 10th in lowest batting average allowed vs. left-handed batters (.208)
- Led the Reds in wild pitches and relief innings (83.2)

ROBERTO KELLY

Position: CF/LF
Bats: R **Throws:** R
Ht: 6' 2" **Wt:** 192

Opening Day Age: 28
Born: 10/1/64 in Panama City, Panama
ML Seasons: 6

HITTING:

Roberto Kelly was supposed to blossom into a superstar in 1992, but it didn't happen. By most measures, he went the wrong way. His walks went down. His strikeouts went up. And he had his lowest home run total (10) since 1989. He had only 22 RBI after the All-Star break. Over the last three seasons, Kelly has driven in 61, 69 and 66 runs -- not exactly the numbers of an impact player. At the end of the year, the Yankees gave up on him, dealing him to the Cincinnati Reds for Paul O'Neill.

Kelly hasn't changed his approach at the plate. A man who has always had his own personal strike zone, he jumps on any fastball near the middle of the plate. The New York media raised questions about Kelly's motivation, especially after he surrendered the center field job to Bernie Williams. Indeed, Kelly enlarged his already liberal idea of the strike zone and was visibly prone to swing in situations when taking a pitch could have been better for the team. Whether it was an attitude problem or just a simple slump, Kelly wasn't playing at full potential in late 1992 and sat watching a number of games in September.

BASERUNNING:

Kelly's stolen base total was down a little in 1992 (from 32 to 28), but his speed is still intact. There is plenty of hustle in his stride whenever he is racing a catcher's throw. With a career-high success rate of 85 percent on his steal attempts, Kelly showed that he knew the league's pitchers well. He gets a good jump.

FIELDING:

A success as a center fielder, Kelly is truly outstanding in left field. He has tremendous range and should thrive in the larger National League ballparks. His arm is good but not exceptional.

OVERALL:

Kelly's 1992 season was actually within a normal range based on past performance. The biggest disappointment was that he didn't improve. At 28, he gets a new team and another chance to prove he can be a great player.

Overall Statistics

	G	AB	R	H	D	T	HR	RBI	SB	BB	SO	AVG
1992	152	580	81	158	31	2	10	66	28	41	96	.272
Career	638	2277	320	637	110	12	56	258	151	168	440	.280

Where He Hits the Ball

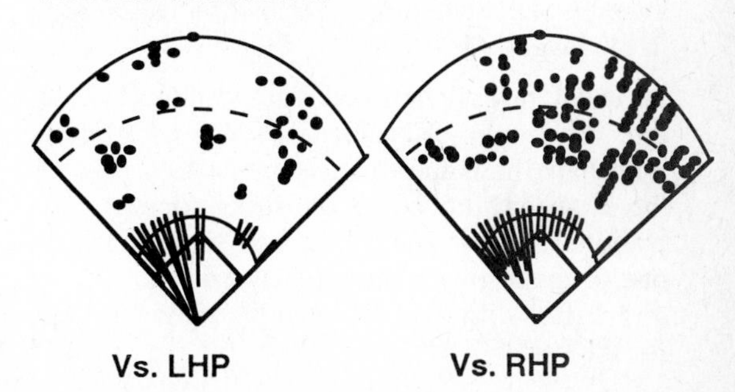

1992 Situational Stats

	AB	H	HR	RBI	AVG		AB	H	HR	RBI	AVG
Home	296	76	6	37	.257	LHP	184	51	4	21	.277
Road	284	82	4	29	.289	RHP	396	107	6	45	.270
Day	171	52	5	34	.304	Sc Pos	145	38	1	51	.262
Night	409	106	5	32	.259	Clutch	106	25	2	15	.236

1992 Rankings (American League)

- 4th in stolen base percentage (84.9%)
- 6th in GDPs (19)
- Led the Yankees in stolen bases (28), GDPs, stolen base percentage and steals of third (4)

GREAT RANGE

HITTING:

One of these years, Barry Larkin will put together the injury-free, breakthrough season that will certify him in everyone's mind as one of the game's greatest players. Even so, a lot of people would put Larkin in that category right now.

Larkin again missed significant playing time due to injuries in 1992. The time off, plus the time he needed to regain his groove, probably cost him a chance at a monster season. Though Larkin had another excellent year, he dropped off in home runs from 20 to 12. He still reached a career high with 78 RBI. All tolled, Larkin continued to be one of the best all-around hitters in the league. He added a new skill, hitting in the clutch. His .340 average with men in scoring position was second in the league.

As usual, few pitchers could get fastballs by Larkin. While a lot of teams now try to get him out with junk, he is increasingly prone to laying off the offspeed stuff out of the strike zone. As one National League pitching coach said, "Larkin's one of those guys who you just tell your pitcher to go after with his best pitch that day and hope for the best."

BASERUNNING:

Larkin dropped off to 15 stolen bases last year, an indication of the hamstring troubles that he had for much of the season. When he needs to steal a base, Larkin is a high-percentage performer who will challenge anybody.

FIELDING:

Ozzie Smith keeps winning Gold Gloves, but there are few better shortstops than Larkin. His range is tremendous and he has a strong throwing arm which he can use even from off-balance positions. He made only 11 errors while ranking among the league leaders in total chances for shortstops.

OVERALL:

Marge Schott complains about her payroll. Here's one of her investments about which there can be little argument. If you put together a list of the game's best 10 players, it would be difficult to leave off the name of Barry Larkin.

BARRY LARKIN

Position: SS
Bats: R **Throws:** R
Ht: 6' 0" **Wt:** 190

Opening Day Age: 28
Born: 4/28/64 in Cincinnati, OH
ML Seasons: 7

Overall Statistics

	G	AB	R	H	D	T	HR	RBI	SB	BB	SO	AVG
1992	140	533	76	162	32	6	12	78	15	63	58	.304
Career	835	3122	478	924	150	30	70	368	148	273	291	.296

Where He Hits the Ball

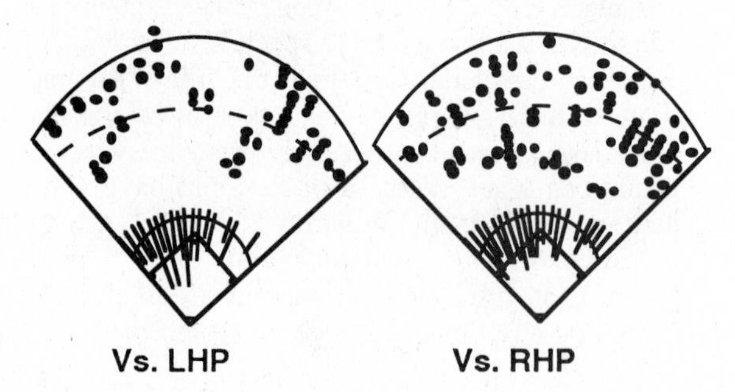

Vs. LHP | Vs. RHP

1992 Situational Stats

	AB	H	HR	RBI	AVG		AB	H	HR	RBI	AVG
Home	254	78	8	53	.307	LHP	200	71	6	29	.355
Road	279	84	4	25	.301	RHP	333	91	6	49	.273
Day	169	43	4	25	.254	Sc Pos	144	49	2	65	.340
Night	364	119	8	53	.327	Clutch	79	23	0	11	.291

1992 Rankings (National League)

- 2nd in batting average with runners in scoring position (.340) and on-base percentage vs. left-handed pitchers (.443)
- Led the Reds in at-bats (533), triples (6), total bases (242), RBI (78), sacrifice flies (7), hit by pitch (4), GDPs (13), most pitches seen (2,206), plate appearances (609), slugging percentage (.454), most pitches seen per plate appearance (3.62), batting average with runners in scoring position, batting average vs. left-handed pitchers (.355), slugging percentage vs. left-handed pitchers (.585), on-base percentage vs. left-handed pitchers, batting average on the road (.301) and highest percentage of swings put into play (51.2%)

HITTING:

Counted on to be a consistent .290-type hitter in a platoon role, Dave Martinez turned out to be one of the Reds' biggest 1992 disappointments. His average fell 41 points from 1991. His home runs and RBI plummeted. Even his stolen base total suffered a decline. Long considered a very underrated clutch hitter, Martinez also had an off-year with men in scoring position, batting only .207.

After three seasons in Montreal in which Martinez had batted .274, .279 and .295, the Reds had expected much more than what they got. Martinez was acquired to be a platoon player vs. righties, easing the way for talented rookie Reggie Sanders. Ironically, he batted 20 points higher against left-handed pitching than right, though he only had 59 at-bats against southpaws. Martinez really didn't add much to the Reds' mix, especially when Sanders came back from injuries and proved to be the real thing.

Martinez has always been known as a hitter who takes too many pitches. While there's nothing inherently wrong with that, he often works deep counts that don't translate into enough walks. Instead, they end with him becoming overanxious and swinging at pitches he can't handle. A good fastball hitter, Martinez has a tendency to be overly intense which takes away from his aggressiveness at bat.

BASERUNNING:

Going way back to when he was a member of the Cubs, Martinez has frustrated managers with his cautiousness. He has the tools to be a 30-steal guy but his stolen bases numbers continue to decline instead. He had a terrible 12-for-20 stolen base success ratio in 1992.

FIELDING:

Martinez can play all three outfield positions with good range and instincts. However, his average throwing arm needs to be accurate; his throws are often erratic.

OVERALL:

Martinez has long been viewed as a platoon player. But if he stays in Cincinnati's well-stocked outfield, he could become even more of a part-time player than he was in 1992. A free agent, he will likely find it better to move on.

DAVE MARTINEZ

Position: CF/1B
Bats: L **Throws:** L
Ht: 5'10" **Wt:** 175

Opening Day Age: 28
Born: 9/26/64 in New York, NY
ML Seasons: 7

Overall Statistics

	G	AB	R	H	D	T	HR	RBI	SB	BB	SO	AVG
1992	135	393	47	100	20	5	3	31	12	42	54	.254
Career	836	2555	329	688	99	37	39	228	107	214	425	.269

Where He Hits the Ball

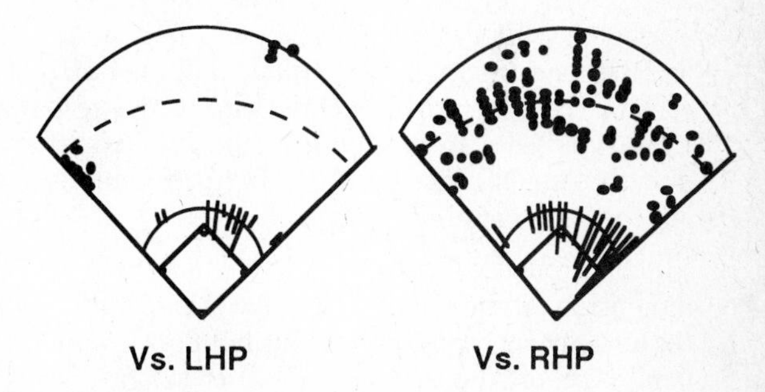

1992 Situational Stats

	AB	H	HR	RBI	AVG		AB	H	HR	RBI	AVG
Home	196	57	3	20	.291	LHP	59	16	0	8	.271
Road	197	43	0	11	.218	RHP	334	84	3	23	.251
Day	131	32	3	13	.244	Sc Pos	111	23	1	28	.207
Night	262	68	0	18	.260	Clutch	52	3	0	2	.058

1992 Rankings (National League)

- 1st in lowest batting average in the clutch (.058)
- 4th in lowest stolen base percentage (60.0%)
- 7th in lowest batting average on a 3-2 count (.091)
- 9th in lowest batting average with runners in scoring position (.207)
- 10th in highest percentage of pitches taken (58.6%)
- Led the Reds in highest percentage of pitches taken

HITTING:

When the Mariners traded for Kevin Mitchell before the start of the 1992 season, many people suggested that he would hit 50 homers or more in the Kingdome -- Babe Ruth-type numbers, or at least Cecil Fielder. Mitchell may have taken that too much to heart; he reported to spring training looking like he'd been on the "Babe/Cecil Diet." But while Mitchell was hefty, his home run numbers were not. Three seasons after he'd hit 47 homers for the Giants, Mitchell hit only nine for the M's.

The big slugger had a curious season all around. He didn't homer until May 6, and through May 31, he was hitting .222, with only two homers and 20 RBI. But from June 1 on, Mitchell batted .337. Though he still wasn't hitting homers, he became an RBI machine, plating 47 runners in only 202 at-bats. Even then, Mitchell ran into other problems. A pulled ribcage put him on the disabled list in early August, and then a stress fracture in his left foot put him out for the year.

Mitchell found out, as others have, that the new dimensions at the Kingdome make it no paradise for a righty slugger. But only his home run numbers were off: he drove in 67 runs in only 99 games, had 24 doubles, and posted a fine .286 average. However, Seattle obviously regretted all the pitchers they lost when they acquired him, and dealt him for Norm Charlton last fall.

BASERUNNING:

Mitchell is now very slow and did not steal a base last year. However, he is a hard-charging baserunner despite his girth.

FIELDING:

Even when he's in shape, Mitchell is not very good in left field. He lacks range and his arm has always been weak. Cincinnati will have to put up with his defensive liabilities.

OVERALL:

Despite his disappointing home run numbers, Mitchell showed that he's still a feared hitter with power and a good batting eye. His physical condition is a problem, but he didn't seem happy in Seattle and should thrive back in the National League.

KEVIN MITCHELL

Position: LF/DH
Bats: R **Throws:** R
Ht: 5'11" **Wt:** 210

Opening Day Age: 31
Born: 1/13/62 in San Diego, CA
ML Seasons: 8

Overall Statistics

	G	AB	R	H	D	T	HR	RBI	SB	BB	SO	AVG
1992	99	360	48	103	24	0	9	67	0	35	46	.286
Career	900	3109	469	859	162	20	171	548	26	352	542	.276

Where He Hits the Ball

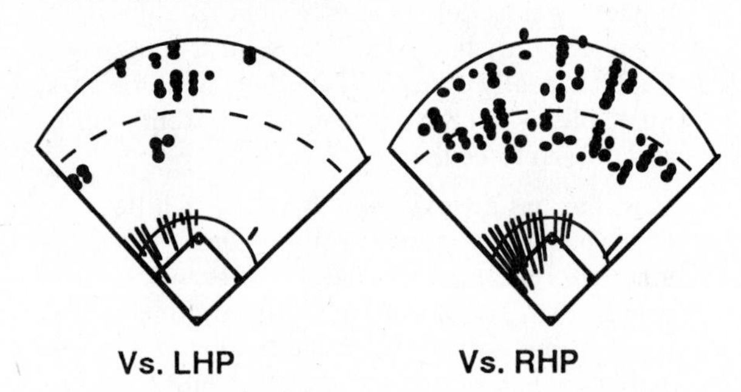

1992 Situational Stats

	AB	H	HR	RBI	AVG		AB	H	HR	RBI	AVG
Home	207	66	5	41	.319	LHP	92	35	5	27	.380
Road	153	37	4	26	.242	RHP	268	68	4	40	.254
Day	96	30	5	22	.313	Sc Pos	113	33	3	54	.292
Night	264	73	4	45	.277	Clutch	58	17	0	5	.293

1992 Rankings (American League)

- → 6th in batting average with 2 strikes (.259)
- → 9th in least GDPs per GDP situation (4.9%)
- → Led the Mariners in least GDPs per GDP situation
- → Led AL left fielders in batting average with 2 strikes

HITTING:

Hal Morris was expected to challenge for a batting title in 1992, but his season proved to be a washout. Morris missed one-fourth of the campaign with injuries and never totally regained the sweet stroke which had produced a .320 lifetime batting average prior to last season. The first sacker wound up batting only .271 -- a number that didn't seem to fit his ability.

However, 1992 was not a totally lost cause for Morris. Despite a drop in home run production, he had a solid RBI season in which he batted .300 with men in scoring position. The Reds found out once and for all what he meant to their lineup, since they were never able to adequately fill the void left by his long absences.

Morris seemed to have slightly reduced bat speed at times in 1992, most likely due to the injuries. He had occasional trouble turning on inside hard stuff, something he did with frequency in 1991. As a result, he reverted back to taking pitches to the opposite field. This kept Morris' average at a decent level, but it was a big reason his slugging average tumbled 96 points to .385. Morris is an excellent fastball hitter, but teams are likely to keep trying to bury him inside until he proves he is once again quick enough to pull some of those pitches with power.

BASERUNNING:

Morris is a below-average runner, last year managing only six steals in 12 attempts. He is also very slow out of the batter's box and not adept at taking the extra base.

FIELDING:

Though possessing limited skills, Morris has worked hard to improve his defense around first base. It started showing last year; he made only one error and was much better at digging throws out of the dirt.

OVERALL:

Morris has had frequent injuries the last two seasons. The 1993 season could be the time for him to put it all together and be the complete hitter a lot of people think he's capable of being. Good health would certainly help.

HAL MORRIS

Position: 1B
Bats: L **Throws:** L
Ht: 6' 4" **Wt:** 215

Opening Day Age: 28
Born: 4/9/65 in Fort Rucker, AL
ML Seasons: 5

Overall Statistics

	G	AB	R	H	D	T	HR	RBI	SB	BB	SO	AVG
1992	115	395	41	107	21	3	6	53	6	45	53	.271
Career	388	1220	166	371	76	7	27	152	25	113	159	.304

Where He Hits the Ball

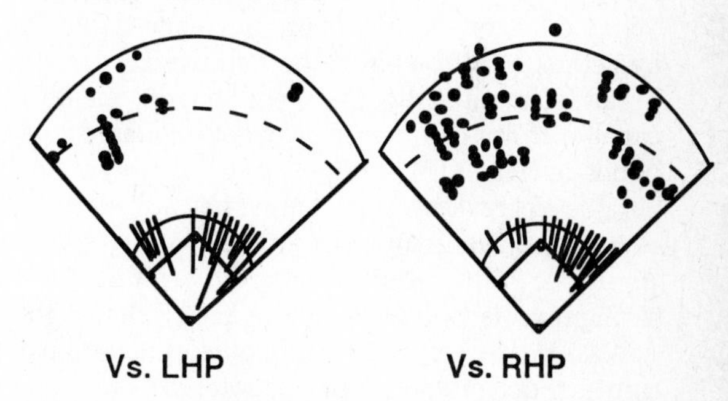

1992 Situational Stats

	AB	H	HR	RBI	AVG		AB	H	HR	RBI	AVG
Home	198	54	3	29	.273	LHP	139	35	1	11	.252
Road	197	53	3	24	.269	RHP	256	72	5	42	.281
Day	135	35	3	21	.259	Sc Pos	110	33	2	48	.300
Night	260	72	3	32	.277	Clutch	62	18	1	5	.290

1992 Rankings (National League)

- 9th in lowest slugging percentage vs. left-handed pitchers (.309)
- Led the Reds in batting average on a 3-2 count (.265)
- Led NL first basemen in fielding percentage (.999) and bunts in play (4)

JOE OLIVER

Position: C
Bats: R **Throws:** R
Ht: 6' 3" **Wt:** 210

Opening Day Age: 27
Born: 7/24/65 in Memphis, TN
ML Seasons: 4

HITTING:

In a season when so many key Cincinnati players were injured or otherwise ineffective, Joe Oliver was one of the few Reds who exceeded expectations. Oliver's performance, the best all-around season of his career, was particularly gratifying because it came on the heels of a 1991 campaign in which serious shoulder problems raised questions about his future.

With a big finish in which he batted .302 after the All-Star break, Oliver batted .270 with a career-best 57 RBI. He appeared in 143 games, another career high. The only down side was his .172 average with men in scoring position, one of the lowest in baseball.

When pitchers retired Oliver, they usually did so by getting inside on him. If he's allowed to extend his arms, he can pull the ball with power, and he's capable of driving pitches out over the plate to the opposite field. Oliver has always been very vulnerable to breaking balls, but he has adjusted his stance by opening up and going the opposite way. As has been his career pattern, Oliver was much stronger vs. left-handed pitching (.307) than right (.249). However, he hit six home runs against right-handed pitching, the best total of his career.

BASERUNNING:

Oliver is one of the slower runners in the National League. He did steal two bases last year, doubling his previous career total. He was also caught three times. All five situations came on blown hit-and-run plays.

FIELDING:

With his shoulder sound, Oliver improved as the season progressed to the point where he was throwing out 40 percent of enemy basestealers over the last two months. However, he has only average agility behind the plate.

OVERALL:

When spring training began, Lou Piniella was asked about Oliver's future and answered, "He better keep an eye over his shoulder for who's coming." That was a reference to Dan Wilson, Cincinnati's blue-chip catching prospect. However, Oliver answered the challenge in 1992 and remains the Reds' number one catcher until further notice.

Overall Statistics

	G	AB	R	H	D	T	HR	RBI	SB	BB	SO	AVG
1992	143	485	42	131	25	1	10	57	2	35	75	.270
Career	407	1269	110	314	67	1	32	173	3	96	231	.247

Where He Hits the Ball

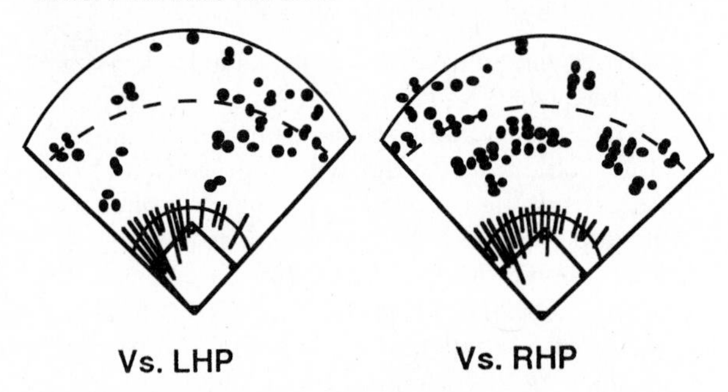

1992 Situational Stats

	AB	H	HR	RBI	AVG		AB	H	HR	RBI	AVG
Home	245	68	7	36	.278	LHP	176	54	4	24	.307
Road	240	63	3	21	.262	RHP	309	77	6	33	.249
Day	143	37	1	17	.259	Sc Pos	122	21	4	45	.172
Night	342	94	9	40	.275	Clutch	79	20	0	5	.253

1992 Rankings (National League)

- 2nd in lowest batting average with runners in scoring position (.172)
- 3rd in lowest percentage of pitches taken (43.8%)
- 4th in intentional walks (19)
- 5th in lowest batting average on an 0-2 count (.083)
- Led the Reds in sacrifice flies (7), intentional walks and bunts in play (11)
- Led NL catchers in at-bats (485), hits (131), singles (95), sacrifice flies, intentional walks, batting average on the road (.262) and highest percentage of swings that missed (18.1%)

CY YOUNG STUFF

PITCHING:

Though again plagued by physical problems and occasionally distracted by disagreements with his manager, Jose Rijo reaffirmed his status as one of the premier pitchers in the National League last year. For a second straight season he was a 15-game winner and again among the league leaders in ERA (2.56) and strikeouts (171). His strikeout-to-walk ratio was spectacular (only 44 walks). Always tough to hit, he held the opposition to a .238 average. Rijo was victimized in several games by either lack of run support or by blown saves from his bullpen. With better support, he could have been a 20-game winner.

Rijo had to labor through a half-dozen starts in which he was recovering from a sore shoulder and held to a pitch-count limit, a restriction which was irritating to the highly competitive righthander. However, once healthy, nothing affected his array of devastating pitching weapons. They include a riding fastball that is consistently in the 90s, a hard slider, a forkball which he is able to throw at different speeds and a straight change that is one of the best in the league. Rijo has also refined his pitching style, staying with his fastball and mixing it more with the change than with the slider. His control is excellent, although always being around the plate was a reason he got touched for 15 home runs last year.

HOLDING RUNNERS, FIELDING, HITTING:

Rijo has worked hard to improve at holding runners, and though it is not a strong part of his game, he's getting better. He is an excellent fielder who can make the tough play on bunts as well as any pitcher. He can also help himself with the bat. Rijo had 14 hits, six RBI and six sacrifices in 1992.

OVERALL:

With his success over the last three years, it should be noted that Rijo is just entering what should be his prime. If he stays healthy, he will be one of the league's dominant pitchers for the next several years.

JOSE RIJO

Position: SP
Bats: R **Throws:** R
Ht: 6' 2" **Wt:** 210

Opening Day Age: 27
Born: 5/13/65 in San Cristobal, Dominican Republic
ML Seasons: 9

Overall Statistics

	W	L	ERA	G	GS	Sv	IP	H	R	BB	SO	HR
1992	15	10	2.56	33	33	0	211.0	185	67	44	171	15
Career	83	68	3.26	256	184	3	1287.1	1131	536	498	1096	91

How Often He Throws Strikes

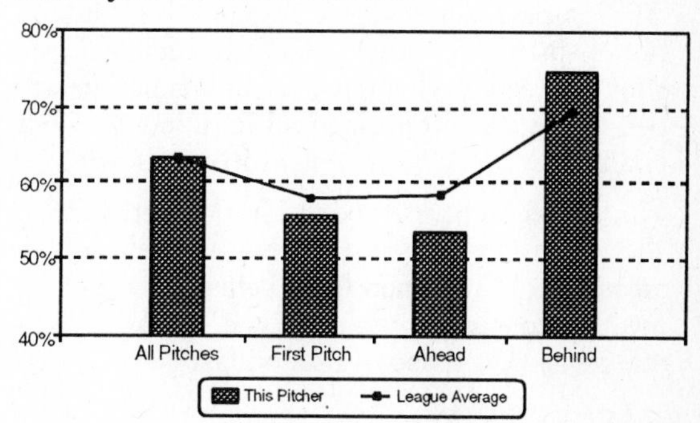

1992 Situational Stats

	W	L	ERA	Sv	IP		AB	H	HR	RBI	AVG
Home	6	4	2.74	0	88.2	LHB	429	114	6	33	.266
Road	9	6	2.43	0	122.1	RHB	347	71	9	28	.205
Day	7	5	2.43	0	103.2	Sc Pos	158	32	0	38	.203
Night	8	5	2.68	0	107.1	Clutch	62	16	5	8	.258

1992 Rankings (National League)

- 2nd in highest strikeout/walk ratio (3.9) and lowest ERA on the road (2.43)
- 4th in highest groundball/flyball ratio (2.0) and strikeouts per 9 innings (7.3)
- Led the Reds in ERA (2.56), wins (15), hit batsmen (3), strikeouts (171), pickoff throws (166), most stolen bases allowed (17), most runners caught stealing (12), most GDPs induced (16), winning percentage (.600), highest strikeout/walk ratio, lowest on-base percentage allowed (.280), highest groundball/flyball ratio, most strikeouts per 9 innings, ERA on the road and lowest batting average allowed with runners in scoring position (.203)

HITTING:

Manager Lou Piniella said it best when he commented late in the season, "We've had a lot of ups and downs, but the one constant we've had all year is Bip Roberts. He's been our best player, day in and day out."

Roberts was everything the Reds had hoped he would be and more after they acquired him from San Diego for malcontent reliever Randy Myers. Everyone knew that the versatile Roberts would provide a one-man source of depth with his ability to play second, third and left field. But he was also the consummate leadoff man, providing Cincinnati with consistent top-of-the-order production. Roberts finished among the league leaders with a .323 average. He scored 92 runs. He had a .393 on-base percentage. He had 44 extra-base blows among his total of 172 hits, which included a league-record tying ten straight hits in September. Roberts also managed 45 RBI and 44 steals and batted .337 with men in scoring position.

The switch-hitting Roberts hit .340 left-handed and .292 right-handed. His improvement in both areas largely stemmed from better plate discipline. He consistently laid off the breaking balls that he used to chase and sat on fastballs.

BASERUNNING:

Roberts was caught stealing 16 times in 60 attempts, an indication that he needs a big jump to be successful; though he's very quick, he simply doesn't have the great speed of the top basestealers. He does have the intelligence, though, and is always looking to take the extra base.

FIELDING:

Roberts has become defensively solid at the three positions he can play, though he is likely most comfortable at second base where he will end up playing full time this year. His lack of arm strength hampers him both in left field and at third base.

OVERALL:

Few trades work as well as this one did for the Reds. Roberts blossomed into a star and was one of the 10 most valuable players in the league. He should be a catalyst for Cincinnati for years to come.

BIP ROBERTS

Position: LF/2B/3B/CF
Bats: B **Throws:** R
Ht: 5' 7" **Wt:** 165

Opening Day Age: 29
Born: 10/27/63 in Berkeley, CA
ML Seasons: 6

Overall Statistics

	G	AB	R	H	D	T	HR	RBI	SB	BB	SO	AVG
1992	147	532	92	172	34	6	4	45	44	62	54	.323
Career	636	2091	378	626	103	22	20	158	151	218	266	.299

Where He Hits the Ball

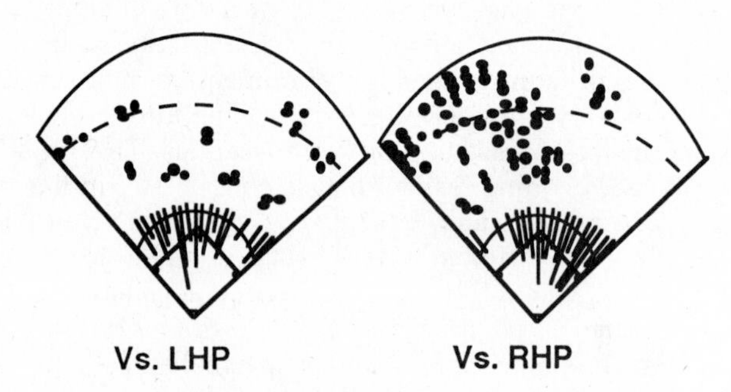

1992 Situational Stats

	AB	H	HR	RBI	AVG		AB	H	HR	RBI	AVG
Home	252	89	3	23	.353	LHP	185	54	3	15	.292
Road	280	83	1	22	.296	RHP	347	118	1	30	.340
Day	163	56	1	13	.344	Sc Pos	98	33	1	40	.337
Night	369	116	3	32	.314	Clutch	84	26	1	9	.310

1992 Rankings (National League)

- 1st in leadoff on-base percentage (.396)
- 2nd in batting average vs. right-handed pitchers (.340), on-base percentage vs. right-handed pitchers (.416) and batting average at home (.353)
- 3rd in stolen bases (44)
- Led the Reds in batting average (.323), runs scored (92), hits (172), singles (128), doubles (34), triples (6), stolen bases, caught stealing (16), times on base (236), on-base percentage (.393), highest groundball/flyball ratio (2.3), stolen base percentage (73.3%), batting average vs. right-handed pitchers, slugging percentage vs. right-handed pitchers (.461) and on-base percentage vs. right-handed pitchers

SCOTT RUSKIN

Position: RP
Bats: R **Throws:** L
Ht: 6' 2" **Wt:** 195

Opening Day Age: 29
Born: 6/8/63 in Jacksonville, FL
ML Seasons: 3

PITCHING:

Last year Cincinnati hoped that Scott Ruskin, who came to the Reds with Dave Martinez and Willie Greene in an off-season deal for John Wetteland and Bill Risley, could fill the role of the situational lefthander which had previously been held by Norm Charlton. The idea was that Ruskin would help set up the late-inning tandem of Charlton, who was moving up to replace the traded Randy Myers, and Rob Dibble. The plan didn't work, as Ruskin was largely a bust for the Reds.

Ruskin could not consistently retire left-handed batters, who hit .250 against him. Since lefties are the hitters Ruskin is specifically supposed to get out to make a living, the figure was disappointing. His high 5.03 ERA was an indication of even worse problems with righties: .287 opposing average, five home runs. By midseason Ruskin had largely been reduced to mop-up duty.

Ruskin's problem is that he is basically a two-pitch pitcher. His curve is his best pitch, but since he has trouble controlling it the pitch becomes a liability as often as it is an asset. His fastball does not have the velocity or movement necessary to be effective after Ruskin falls behind with the breaking stuff. Until Ruskin can throw the curve consistently for strikes, or until he finds another pitch, he's going to have trouble being a reliable reliever.

HOLDING RUNNERS, FIELDING, HITTING:

A former outfielder, Ruskin has the athletic ability to be a good fielding pitcher. He has worked on improving a pickoff move that is still below average. He is an excellent hitter for a pitcher but in his middle-relief role rarely gets the chance to show his stuff. In his five plate appearances last year he fanned three times and sacrificed twice.

OVERALL:

The Reds had hoped they worked a steal with Ruskin when he was included in the deal with Montreal. However, Ruskin has now had two straight disappointing seasons. Unless he shows a lot of improvement in the spring, he'll have trouble holding a job.

Overall Statistics

	W	L	ERA	G	GS	Sv	IP	H	R	BB	SO	HR
1992	4	3	5.03	57	0	0	53.2	56	31	20	43	6
Career	11	9	3.88	188	0	8	192.2	188	90	88	146	14

How Often He Throws Strikes

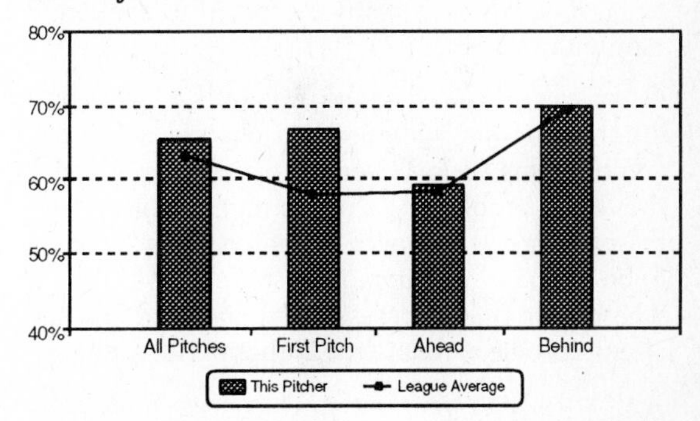

1992 Situational Stats

	W	L	ERA	Sv	IP		AB	H	HR	RBI	AVG
Home	2	2	4.10	0	26.1	LHB	68	17	1	14	.250
Road	2	1	5.93	0	27.1	RHB	136	39	5	22	.287
Day	1	1	3.51	0	25.2	Sc Pos	60	21	3	31	.350
Night	3	2	6.43	0	28.0	Clutch	77	23	3	17	.299

1992 Rankings (National League)

- 2nd in worst first batter efficiency (.346)
- 5th in highest batting average allowed in relief with runners on base (.344) and highest percentage of inherited runners scored (40.5%)
- 8th in highest batting average allowed in relief with runners in scoring position (.350)

HITTING:

Hobbled by serious ankle and foot problems, Chris Sabo had his worst major league season in 1992. He managed to appear in only 96 games and finished the season amid speculation that the Reds might not even protect him in the expansion draft. The Reds ultimately did protect Sabo, figuring that he would be an attractive pick despite all his health problems.

Sabo was so banged up last year that an assessment of his numbers seems unfair. Yet even with problems that rendered him almost immobile for much of the year, he managed 12 home runs and 43 RBI in only 344 at-bats. Though his injuries affected his swing and bat speed, he was still dangerous when teams were forced to challenge him with fastballs.

Even when injured, Sabo was still a dead pull hitter who was vulnerable to change of speeds and breaking balls. However, the Reds worry that the ankle problem is chronic and might require major surgery. It would be unfortunate because Sabo is one of the more underrated power hitters when he is right, possessing a quick bat and the strength to be a consistent 25-home run man.

BASERUNNING:

There's nothing wrong with Sabo's aggressiveness. But when you're walking like Walter Brennan, it's hard to be a factor on the bases. After averaging 26 steals in his career prior to last season, Sabo managed only four steals in nine attempts in 1992.

FIELDING:

When he is healthy, Sabo has good range and outstanding instincts to go along with an accurate arm. Last year he had virtually no range because of his injuries and he made nine errors, most of them on hurried throws.

OVERALL:

Sabo's status is one of the Reds' major questions. There was some thought at first that he might lose his job to young Willie Greene. However, talk of discarding Sabo may be premature. He can be a pain to be around, but if his ankle allows him to, Sabo can resume his status as one of the league's best third basemen.

CHRIS SABO

Position: 3B
Bats: R **Throws:** R
Ht: 6' 0" **Wt:** 185

Opening Day Age: 31
Born: 1/19/62 in Detroit, MI
ML Seasons: 5

Overall Statistics

	G	AB	R	H	D	T	HR	RBI	SB	BB	SO	AVG
1992	96	344	42	84	19	3	12	43	4	30	54	.244
Career	616	2335	342	637	153	11	80	275	108	189	276	.273

Where He Hits the Ball

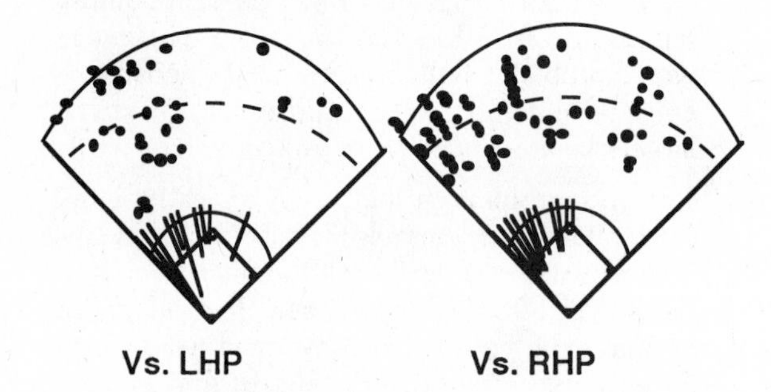

1992 Situational Stats

	AB	H	HR	RBI	AVG		AB	H	HR	RBI	AVG
Home	148	35	8	22	.236	LHP	146	36	6	21	.247
Road	196	49	4	21	.250	RHP	198	48	6	22	.242
Day	110	30	3	12	.273	Sc Pos	107	23	4	33	.215
Night	234	54	9	31	.231	Clutch	42	11	0	4	.262

1992 Rankings (National League)

- 5th in lowest batting average on a 3-2 count (.074)
- 8th in most GDPs per GDP situation (15.6%)
- 9th in lowest batting average with 2 strikes (.135)

REGGIE SANDERS

Position: CF/LF
Bats: R **Throws:** R
Ht: 6' 1" **Wt:** 180

Opening Day Age: 25
Born: 12/1/67 in Florence, SC
ML Seasons: 2

Overall Statistics

	G	AB	R	H	D	T	HR	RBI	SB	BB	SO	AVG
1992	116	385	62	104	26	6	12	36	16	48	98	.270
Career	125	425	68	112	26	6	13	39	17	48	107	.264

Where He Hits the Ball

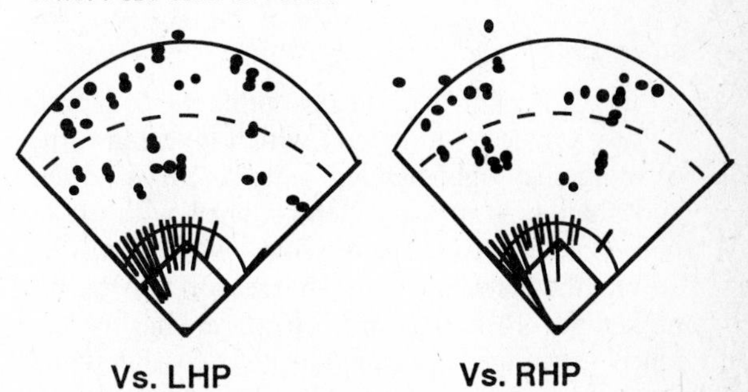

1992 Situational Stats

	AB	H	HR	RBI	AVG		AB	H	HR	RBI	AVG
Home	205	50	6	22	.244	LHP	175	55	7	18	.314
Road	180	54	6	14	.300	RHP	210	49	5	18	.233
Day	119	30	2	12	.252	Sc Pos	98	18	0	19	.184
Night	266	74	10	24	.278	Clutch	65	20	2	8	.308

1992 Rankings (National League)

- 1st in lowest percentage of swings put into play (36.5%)
- 3rd in lowest batting average with runners in scoring position (.184), lowest batting average with the bases loaded (.083) and highest percentage of swings that missed (25.7%)
- 7th in slugging percentage vs. left-handed pitchers (.566)
- Led the Reds in triples (6), hit by pitch (4), strikeouts (98) and least GDPs per GDP situation (6.7%)
- Led NL center fielders in slugging percentage vs. left-handed pitchers

HITTING:

Injuries limited his playing time, but the National League saw enough of Reggie Sanders last year to find out that he has the potential to be a star. As one National League manager said, "We've only seen a glimpse of his talent. Once this guy gets comfortable, he can be really something."

Sanders was set back by leg injuries and a shoulder problem. But he still managed 12 home runs in only 385 at-bats. Said one scout, "His bat speed is really special, and it's going to show up as he learns what pitches to hit." Indeed, Sanders struck out 98 times as he was often fooled by offspeed breaking stuff. He was also vulnerable to hard stuff up and in. But pitchers quickly learned that if they came inside, they had better not leave the ball over the plate; Sanders can turn around any pitch he can reach.

Predictably, Sanders pressed at times as a rookie trying to come back from injuries. He hit only .184 with men in scoring position. He batted nearly 80 points better (.314 to .233) against left-handed pitching than right. However, he showed excellent patience for a rookie, drawing 48 walks and posting a fine .356 on-base average.

BASERUNNING:

Sanders has the potential to be a big-time basestealer once he learns the league's pitchers. He stole 16 last year though often plagued by injuries. In time he should be a 30-to-40 steal man. He showed excellent aggressiveness on the bases, as evidenced by his six triples.

FIELDING:

Sanders still relies heavily on natural instincts to out-run balls he might initially misjudge. However, the potential is there for him to be a solid major-league center fielder. His arm is average.

OVERALL:

Don't forget that Sanders played only 86 games at the Double-A level before making the jump last year to the majors. He needs to play, he needs experience and he needs to be healthy. With last year's troubles behind him, he could start blossoming into a star.

PINPOINT CONTROL

GREG SWINDELL

Position: SP
Bats: R **Throws:** L
Ht: 6' 3" **Wt:** 225

Opening Day Age: 28
Born: 1/2/65 in Fort Worth, TX
ML Seasons: 7

PITCHING:

Back problems caused him to have a poor finish, but until September there were few better left-handers in the National League than Greg Swindell. He made the Reds' big trade with Cleveland (for Jack Armstrong, Scott Scudder and Joe Turek) look good. And Swindell enhanced his free-agent value, before returning home to Texas to sign with the Astros.

Swindell ended up with only 12 victories, a total that could have easily been in the 18-20 range with better support and a healthier finish. His ERA of 2.70 was among the league's finest. So was his strikeout-walk ratio of 138-41. With 213.2 innings, he continued to show his durability. Swindell has averaged 219 innings per year since 1988.

Swindell is one of those rare pitchers with four quality pitches -- a fastball which he often turns over against right-handed batters, curve, slider and change -- and excellent control with all of them. Batters always know that Swindell will be around the plate, and that's one reason why he got nicked for 14 home runs. However, he has the kind of stuff that can quiet any club. Swindell had three shutouts last year and led the Reds with five complete games.

HOLDING RUNNERS, FIELDING AND HITTING:

Swindell has one of the better pickoff moves in the league and further helps himself with what is a quick delivery home for a big man. He is not blessed with exceptional agility but he makes all the routine plays in the field. A hitter for the first time professionally in 1992, Swindell managed 10 hits and four RBI and showed that he can occasionally help himself by at least making contact.

OVERALL:

The Astros are not alone in thinking that Swindell is at the stage of his career where he's ready to break through and be a regular 18- to 20-game winner. He is over the arm problems that he had for years in Cleveland and has one of the best-controlled repertoires in baseball. Swindell is an ace waiting to happen.

Overall Statistics

	W	L	ERA	G	GS	Sv	IP	H	R	BB	SO	HR
1992	12	8	2.70	31	30	0	213.2	210	72	41	138	14
Career	72	63	3.60	184	182	0	1256.2	1269	559	267	894	123

How Often He Throws Strikes

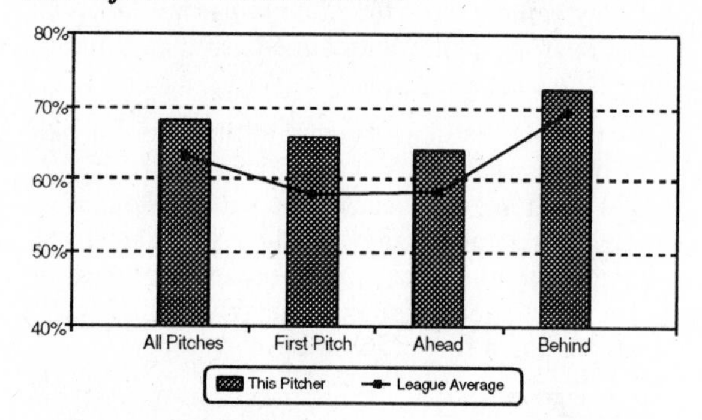

1992 Situational Stats

	W	L	ERA	Sv	IP		AB	H	HR	RBI	AVG
Home	7	2	2.31	0	109.0	LHB	165	40	2	11	.242
Road	5	6	3.10	0	104.2	RHB	643	170	12	52	.264
Day	1	1	4.23	0	27.2	Sc Pos	154	41	2	47	.266
Night	11	7	2.47	0	186.0	Clutch	65	19	3	7	.292

1992 Rankings (National League)

- 3rd in lowest groundball/flyball ratio (.89) and most run support per 9 innings (4.9)
- 4th in highest strikeout/walk ratio (3.4)
- 7th in ERA at home (2.31)
- 8th in shutouts (3)
- 9th in ERA (2.70) and hits allowed (210)
- Led the Reds in complete games (5), shutouts, hits allowed, balks (2), most stolen bases allowed (17), least pitches thrown per batter (3.53), most run support per 9 innings, least home runs allowed per 9 innings (.59) and ERA at home

JEFF BRANSON

Position: 2B
Bats: L **Throws:** R
Ht: 6' 0" **Wt:** 180

Opening Day Age: 26
Born: 1/26/67 in Waynesboro, MS
ML Seasons: 1

Overall Statistics

	G	AB	R	H	D	T	HR	RBI	SB	BB	SO	AVG
1992	72	115	12	34	7	1	0	15	0	5	16	.296
Career	72	115	12	34	7	1	0	15	0	5	16	.296

HITTING, FIELDING, BASERUNNING:

A former second-round draft choice, Jeff Branson is a valuable commodity, a lefty-swinging middle infielder who looks like he can hit. After batting .296 for the Reds last year in limited duty, Branson was slated for a bigger role in 1993. But then disaster struck. Branson suffered tears of the anterior cruciate ligament and medial collateral ligament on a double play takeout slide by the Dodgers' Eric Young on September 30. The immediate prognosis was that he would miss six to nine months, and perhaps the entire 1993 season.

Until the injury, Branson's career was progressing nicely. He had struggled with the bat in the low minors, but last year he hit .325 at AAA Nashville. Recalled by the Reds, he responded to a platoon role against righties. He didn't show much home run power, however.

Signed as a shortstop, Branson showed last year that he can play the position in the majors. He also has good skill at second, but made seven errors in his limited time, some of them the result of rushing routine plays. He was not much of a basestealing threat even before his injury.

OVERALL:

Branson's injury clouds his immediate future. The Reds liked what little they saw of him last year, and will be patient with his recovery. Hopefully, he'll be able to play sometime this season, as the Reds lost their other utility infielder Benavides to expansion.

STEVE FOSTER

Position: RP
Bats: R **Throws:** R
Ht: 6' 0" **Wt:** 180

Opening Day Age: 26
Born: 8/16/66 in Dallas, TX
ML Seasons: 2

Overall Statistics

	W	L	ERA	G	GS	Sv	IP	H	R	BB	SO	HR
1992	1	1	2.88	31	1	2	50.0	52	16	13	34	4
Career	1	1	2.67	42	1	2	64.0	59	21	17	45	5

PITCHING, FIELDING, HITTING & HOLDING RUNNERS:

A bulldog type, Steve Foster had a strong final month with the Reds that greatly upped his stock in the organization. One of his two saves will forever be remembered, since it came against Atlanta on the night when Rob Dibble and Lou Piniella had their clubhouse wrestling match. The brawl stemmed from Piniella not using Dibble because of Dibble's supposed sore arm.

Foster has a live fastball in the 88-90 MPH range and an improving split-fingered pitch that could help make him a quality reliever. He also mixes in an occasional curve. Over the last month, he posted a 0.63 ERA with 11 strikeouts in 14.1 innings. For a young reliever, Foster also demonstrated better-than-average control with all his pitches. He had some problems with lefties, who batted .300 against him.

Like many pitchers schooled in the minors as short relievers, Foster does not have much of a pickoff move; however, he allowed only one stolen base last year. He is also just an average fielder. He has only five at-bats in his career, managing his first hit last season.

OVERALL:

With Dibble around, Foster will probably not be a closer. But with Charlton now gone, Foster showed enough last year to warrant a long look as a set-up man. He figures to get plenty of work this season.

CESAR HERNANDEZ

Position: LF
Bats: R **Throws:** R
Ht: 6' 0" **Wt:** 160

Opening Day Age: 26
Born: 9/28/66 in Yamasa, Dominican Republic
ML Seasons: 1

Overall Statistics

	G	AB	R	H	D	T	HR	RBI	SB	BB	SO	AVG
1992	34	51	6	14	4	0	0	4	3	0	10	.275
Career	34	51	6	14	4	0	0	4	3	0	10	.275

HITTING, FIELDING, BASERUNNING:

A waiver pickup out of the talent-rich Montreal organization, Cesar Hernandez has a lot of offensive skills which could land him a job as a backup outfielder with the Reds this year. Hernandez has shown power in the minor leagues, hitting 19 homers in 1988 in Class A and hitting 10 and 13 in Double-A in 1990 and 1991 respectively. Strangely, he hit only three last year in Double-A and none in his brief trial with the Reds. But he has the potential.

Like many Dominican players, Hernandez is a free swinger who hates to take a walk. He did not have a single free pass for the Reds in his 51 at-bats while striking out 10 times. He had trouble hitting breaking balls and was also vulnerable to hard stuff inside. He had particular problems with righthanders, managing only one hit in 13 at-bats.

Hernandez is an excellent outfielder with a better-than-average arm. He also has good speed, swiping 34 bases at AA Harrisburg in 1991. He managed 12 last year in the minors and stole three in four attempts for the Reds.

OVERALL:

With several changes made in the Reds' roster, Hernandez will likely get a shot to win a reserve job in spring training. Give him enough at-bats and he might draw that first major-league walk.

TIM PUGH

Position: SP
Bats: R **Throws:** R
Ht: 6' 6" **Wt:** 225

Opening Day Age: 26
Born: 1/26/67 in Lake Tahoe, CA
ML Seasons: 1

Overall Statistics

	W	L	ERA	G	GS	Sv	IP	H	R	BB	SO	HR
1992	4	2	2.58	7	7	0	45.1	47	15	13	18	2
Career	4	2	2.58	7	7	0	45.1	47	15	13	18	2

PITCHING, FIELDING, HITTING & HOLDING RUNNERS:

After looking impressive in a late-season trial, Tim Pugh will be given a chance to win a job in the Reds' 1993 starting rotation. The young righthander went 12-9 last year at AAA Nashville, then posted a 4-2 record for Cincinnati after making his debut on September 1. Five of his seven outings were quality starts, and he yielded only two home runs. His ERA was an excellent 2.58.

Pugh is not an overpowering pitcher, but he has good control with a sinking fastball, slider and change-up. When Pugh is throwing well, he will not strike out a lot of batters but instead induce frequent groundballs. He fanned only 18 batters in his 45.1 innings last year, but he also walked only 13 while allowing 47 hits.

Pugh didn't look like he had a very slick pickoff move, but he permitted only one steal in two attempts with the Reds last year. He is a decent fielder but no threat yet as a hitter, going 1-for-13 in his first major-league at-bats.

OVERALL:

Pugh is one of several young Reds pitchers who could win a job in the rotation, depending on such variables as Tom Browning's health and whether Greg Swindell is re-signed or lost as a free agent. His lack of overpowering stuff is another obstacle that stands in his way to making the rotation.

CINCINNATI REDS MINOR LEAGUE PROSPECTS

ORGANIZATION OVERVIEW:

You have to admire the Reds organization. Even though the club is seemingly being run by a St. Bernard, it won the World Championship in 1990 and 90 games in 1992. The Reds system is in such disarray these days that it's impossible to tell who's in charge (though we're pretty certain it's a dog-lover). The future is thus impossible to fathom, but for now, at least, the Reds have some good prospects who could make an impact as early as this season. That dog, and maybe its owner, must be doing something right.

TIM COSTO

Position: 1B
Bats: R **Throws:** R
Ht: 6' 5" **Wt:** 225
Opening Day Age: 24
Born: 2/16/69 in Glen Ellyn, IL

Recent Statistics

	G	AB	R	H	D	T	HR	RBI	SB	BB	SO	AVG
92 AA Chattanooga	121	424	63	102	18	2	28	71	4	48	128	.241
92 NL Cincinnati	12	36	3	8	2	0	0	2	0	5	6	.222
92 MLE	121	417	52	95	16	1	28	58	2	35	132	.228

This is the Reds' luck for you. In 1991, Cincinnati was forced to trade away its top prospect, Reggie Jefferson, because the club botched a complicated waiver procedure. So who did they end up getting in that forced trade? Tim Costo, who might turn out to be a better player than Jefferson. Tremendously powerful at 6'5" and 220 pounds, Costo finally harnessed that power last year at AA Chattanooga, belting 28 homers in only 424 at-bats. A good athlete, he can play both first and third. There are some definite holes in Costo's game -- he batted .241 last year -- but he's a definite major-league power prospect.

WILLIE GREENE

Position: 3B
Bats: L **Throws:** R
Ht: 5' 11" **Wt:** 165
Opening Day Age: 21
Born: 9/23/71 in Milledgeville, GA

Recent Statistics

	G	AB	R	H	D	T	HR	RBI	SB	BB	SO	AVG
92 A Cedar Rapds	34	120	26	34	8	2	12	40	3	18	27	.283
92 AA Chattanooga	96	349	47	97	19	2	15	66	9	46	90	.278
92 NL Cincinnati	29	93	10	25	5	2	2	13	0	10	23	.269
92 MLE	96	340	38	88	17	1	15	54	5	34	93	.259

More Reds luck . . . or maybe something more than that. A former number-one choice of the Pirates, Greene moved on to the Montreal system in the Zane Smith deal; the Reds obtained him last spring with Dave Martinez and Scott Ruskin, for John Wetteland and Bill Risley. Despite the trades, Greene has always been highly regarded, and he's still only 21. He had 27 homers and 106 RBI for two Reds farm clubs last year, then had two more homers and 13 ribbies for Cincinnati. He could be the Reds third baseman this year and has been working out in left field.

JOHN C. ROPER

Position: P
Bats: R **Throws:** R
Ht: 6' 0" **Wt:** 170
Opening Day Age: 21
Born: 11/21/71 in Moore County, NC

Recent Statistics

	W	L	ERA	G	GS	Sv	IP	H	R	BB	SO	HR
91 A Chston-wv	14	9	2.31	27	27	0	186.2	133	59	67	189	5
92 AA Chattanooga	10	9	4.10	20	20	0	120.2	115	57	37	99	11

Another 21-year-old like Greene, Roper only weighs 170 pounds but he throws hard and has a nasty curveball -- the best breaking pitch in the Southern League, according to a Baseball America survey. Roper was only 10-9 with a 4.03 ERA at Chattanooga, but he fanned 99 men in 120.2 innings. He's still pretty raw, and he's been a little less impressive at each succeeding minor league level. Roper should be in AAA ball this year.

SCOTT SERVICE

Position: P
Bats: R **Throws:** R
Ht: 6' 6" **Wt:** 240
Opening Day Age: 26
Born: 2/26/67 in Cincinnati, OH

Recent Statistics

	W	L	ERA	G	GS	Sv	IP	H	R	BB	SO	HR
92 AAA Indianapols	2	0	0.74	13	0	2	24.1	12	3	9	25	0
92 AAA Nashville	6	2	2.29	39	2	4	70.2	54	22	35	87	2
92 NL Cincinnati	0	0	14.14	5	0	0	7.0	15	11	5	11	1

Scott Service, the Cincinnati pitcher, is often confused with Scott Servais, the Houston catcher, and it doesn't help that they were born less than two months apart in 1967. The pitching Service is a 6'6", 240-pound giant who came to the Reds' system from Montreal last year. Originally in the Phillies' system, Service has been around since 1986. Last year he had an overwhelming season at AAA, striking out 112 men and giving up only 66 hits in 95 innings. The Reds, who could use some middle relief help, might give Service a long look this spring.

DAN WILSON

Position: C
Bats: R **Throws:** R
Ht: 6' 3" **Wt:** 190
Opening Day Age: 24
Born: 3/25/69 in Arlington Heights, IL

Recent Statistics

	G	AB	R	H	D	T	HR	RBI	SB	BB	SO	AVG
92 AAA Nashville	106	366	27	92	16	1	4	34	1	31	58	.251
92 NL Cincinnati	12	25	2	9	1	0	0	3	0	3	8	.360
92 MLE	106	354	21	80	14	0	3	27	0	26	59	.226

Lou Piniella wasn't always enamored with Joe Oliver's work behind the plate, and thus the Reds have closely monitored Dan Wilson's development. Now Piniella's gone and Oliver's coming off a good season, so the Reds can afford to be a little more patient with Wilson. The young catcher appears to be very sound defensively, but he's only hit around .250 at AA and AAA with little power. Unless his hitting takes an upward trend, he'll have to be one heck of a defensive catcher to make it in the majors.

PITCHING:

In a 1992 season full of Philadelphia disappointments, Andy Ashby was one of the major ones. He was ticketed to be an up-and-coming part of the Phillies' rotation, one of the better prospects to emerge in years from one of baseball's most downtrodden minor-league systems. But Ashby broke a thumb in the first month and it took until mid-August for him to return. When he did resume pitching, Ashby appeared tentative and was pounded in a series of late-season appearances. At season's end the Phillies made him available in the expansion draft, and Colorado chose Ashby with their final pick in the first round.

If Ashby's going to make it in Colorado, the first thing he'll need is better control. When the tall righthander gets ahead of hitters, he can use a better-than-average fastball and decent slider to be a strikeout-type pitcher. But when he's behind in counts, he often loses his aggressiveness. He gave up six homers in only 37 innings last year while opponents hit him at a .290 clip. The Phillies felt Ashby's stuff was too good for that, but obviously there was a problem somewhere.

Ashby has yet to pick up a reliable offspeed pitch, which is strange since teaching the change-up was the specialty of Phils' pitching coach Johnny Podres. Hopefully for Ashby the Colorado coaches will have better success.

HOLDING RUNNERS, FIELDING, HITTING:

Ashby does not hold runners well since he is slow to the plate with his delivery. He is thus susceptible to the stolen base. He is also no more than an average fielder. The young pitcher is yet another good argument for the designated hitter with only two hits in 23 career at-bats.

OVERALL:

Ashby had dropped significantly in the Phillies' pecking order and he wasn't exactly numero uno for the two expansion teams, either -- Phillie players were among the last picked in every round of the draft. But in an organization starved for pitching, the Phillies hope Ashby doesn't turn the corner better than Juan Bell or Kim Batiste. Ashby is still young (25), and he has that talented arm. This is his big chance to prove himself as a probable member of the Rockies' rotation.

ANDY ASHBY

Position: SP
Bats: R **Throws:** R
Ht: 6' 5" **Wt:** 180

Opening Day Age: 25
Born: 7/11/67 in Kansas City, MO
ML Seasons: 2

Overall Statistics

	W	L	ERA	G	GS	Sv	IP	H	R	BB	SO	HR
1992	1	3	7.54	10	8	0	37.0	42	31	21	24	6
Career	2	8	6.72	18	16	0	79.0	83	59	40	50	11

How Often He Throws Strikes

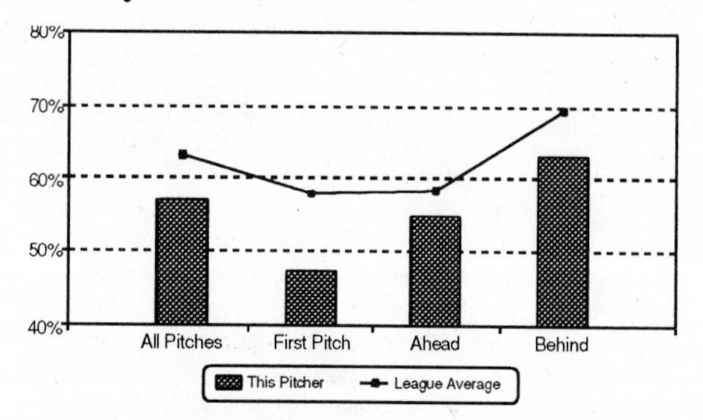

1992 Situational Stats

	W	L	ERA	Sv	IP		AB	H	HR	RBI	AVG
Home	1	1	6.00	0	21.0	LHB	85	27	4	15	.318
Road	0	2	9.56	0	16.0	RHB	60	15	2	11	.250
Day	0	0	8.71	0	10.1	Sc Pos	37	10	2	22	.270
?											

1992 Rankings (National League)

- Did not rank near the top or bottom in any category

FREDDIE BENAVIDES

Position: 2B/SS
Bats: R **Throws:** R
Ht: 6' 2" **Wt:** 185

Opening Day Age: 27
Born: 4/7/66 in Laredo, TX
ML Seasons: 2

Overall Statistics

	G	AB	R	H	D	T	HR	RBI	SB	BB	SO	AVG
1992	74	173	14	40	10	1	1	17	0	10	34	.231
Career	98	236	25	58	11	1	1	20	1	11	49	.246

Where He Hits the Ball

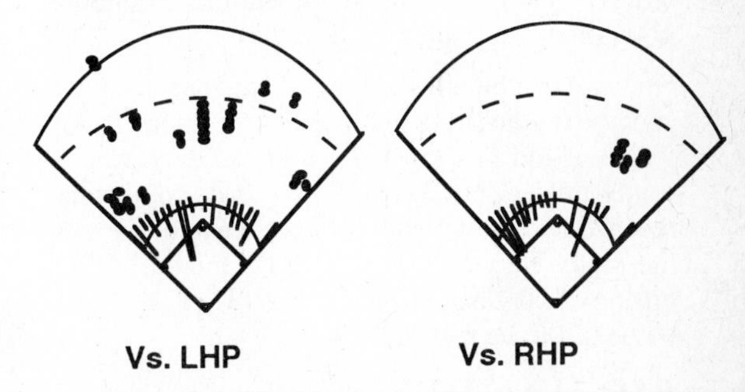

1992 Situational Stats

	AB	H	HR	RBI	AVG		AB	H	HR	RBI	AVG
Home	75	17	1	7	.227	LHP	90	23	1	15	.256
Road	98	23	0	10	.235	RHP	83	17	0	2	.205
Day	61	15	0	6	.246	Sc Pos	51	13	0	14	.255
Night	112	25	1	11	.223	Clutch	29	8	0	8	.276

1992 Rankings (National League)

- 1st in lowest batting average on an 0-2 count (.053)

HITTING:

In two seasons with the Reds, Freddie Benavides has proved a useful utility player. The Rockies, who chose Benavides as the first pick in the second round of the expansion draft, figure he can do more: they project him to be their everyday shortstop this year.

Most observers think that Benavides can handle the defensive load. The question is whether he'll hit enough. After raising Cincinnati hopes by batting .286 in 63 at-bats as a rookie in 1991, Benavides batted .231 over 173 at-bats in '92. Even in the minors, he never hit higher than .259. Thus far in his major-league career, he's shown himself to be easily overpowered by hard stuff.

Benavides managed 10 doubles last year, showing he can sting a pitcher who hangs a breaking ball or takes him for granted. He hits the ball on the ground most of the time and hopes it finds a hole. Benavides figures to strike out over 100 times a year as a regular and he walks infrequently. In 1992 he walked 10 times -- four of them were intentional.

BASERUNNING:

For someone with decent speed, Benavides has never been much of a basestealer. He once stole 18 in a minor-league season but has never stolen more than seven in any year since. Last year he didn't steal a base all season.

FIELDING:

Benavides played as much at second base as at shortstop last season, and he was actually a bit better at second. In about the same number of innings he made six errors at short but none at second, where he showed good range as well. He has a fine arm for short, however, and starts and turns the double play very well.

OVERALL:

The Rockies aren't expecting miracles from Benavides; they'll be happy with good, solid shortstop play. The other shortstop the team chose in the expansion draft, Vinny Castilla, is a slightly more promising hitter, but he lacks Benavides' experience. Meanwhile, Benavides will hold the fort, and if he can hit .250 with 40 walks the Rockies should be okay.

STRONG ARM

DANTE BICHETTE

Position: RF
Bats: R **Throws:** R
Ht: 6' 3" **Wt:** 225

Opening Day Age: 29
Born: 11/18/63 in West Palm Beach, FL
ML Seasons: 5

Overall Statistics

	G	AB	R	H	D	T	HR	RBI	SB	BB	SO	AVG
1992	112	387	37	111	27	2	5	41	18	16	74	.287
Career	424	1365	144	347	69	6	38	176	40	60	291	.254

Where He Hits the Ball

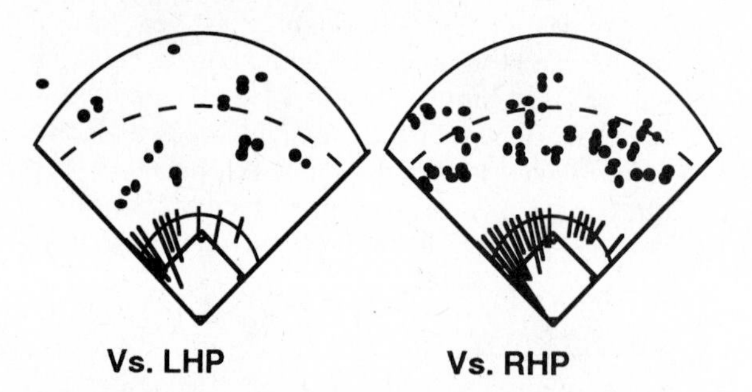

1992 Situational Stats

	AB	H	HR	RBI	AVG		AB	H	HR	RBI	AVG
Home	170	41	3	22	.241	LHP	119	34	2	23	.286
Road	217	70	2	19	.323	RHP	268	77	3	18	.287
Day	149	50	4	21	.336	Sc Pos	99	23	1	32	.232
Night	238	61	1	20	.256	Clutch	66	17	0	3	.258

1992 Rankings (American League)

- 2nd in highest fielding percentage in right field (.990)
- 10th in lowest batting average with the bases loaded (.100)

HITTING:

Expected to be the Rockies' first right fielder, Dante Bichette had a maddeningly unpredictable 1992 season for Milwaukee. After he'd posted consecutive 15-homer seasons while batting .255 and .238 in 1990 and '91, the Brewers counted on him to supply a little power last year, but not average. But in just the reverse, Bichette managed only five dingers . . . and hit a career-high .287.

A man who had always had a platoon split wider than Moon River, Bichette batted .286 against lefties and .287 against righties last year. He did live up to his reputation in one regard, not that it was a blessing. With a career pattern of striking out about five times as often as he walked, he was almost right on the money in '92 (74 strikeouts, 16 walks).

Bichette can hit a fastball strike and has excellent success on the first pitch when pitchers are trying to get ahead of him. He's a guess-hitter who is easily misled, but has had periods during his career when he's shown both patience and brains at the plate. He was in a groove for most of 1992, hitting .326 through August 2. Then poof, he batted .206 the rest of the way.

BASERUNNING:

The Brewers wanted everyone to run in 1992, and Bichette benefitted from the strategy. He was 18-for-25 in stolen base attempts, easily the best performance of his career. After the All-Star break he stole 11 bases in 12 tries. His 27 doubles in just 387 at-bats illustrate his functional speed.

FIELDING:

Bichette had one of the best arms in baseball and runners are leery to challenge him. He didn't display the same range last year as in 1991, when he was among the AL's best, but the Brewers were very happy with his glove work.

OVERALL:

Which Dante Bichette will show up in Colorado in 1993? The slugger who hits .240, or the guy who hits for decent average but can't drive in runs? He should hit more homers in Colorado, and can run, field, and throw. He will certainly bat in the meat of the Rockies' order. Not a bad package for the Rockies for the price of their #5 selection in Round One, Kevin Reimer.

WILLIE BLAIR

Position: RP/SP
Bats: R **Throws:** R
Ht: 6' 1" **Wt:** 185

Opening Day Age: 27
Born: 12/18/65 in Paintsville, KY
ML Seasons: 3

PITCHING:

One of the pleasant surprises of Houston's 1992 season, Willie Blair handled a variety of assignments, displaying good composure and a strong arm. The righthander did a fine job out of the Astro bullpen and the Rockies made him a first-round selection in the expansion draft.

Blair had previously pitched for the Blue Jays and Indians without much success. While his 4.00 ERA last year wasn't much, he had a 4-2 record and 2.68 ERA in 21 middle relief appearances; as a starter, he was 1-5, 5.40. Since the Rockies project Blair as a set-up man, they weren't concerned with the starting numbers. One hopeful sign with Blair was that the velocity of his fastball improved dramatically as the season wore on. He threw around 84 MPH in spring training, but radar guns were catching him in the low 90s late in the year.

Much of Blair's improvement last year resulted from his ability to stay ahead of the hitters and make them hit his pitch. Once he started throwing his fastball, curve and change-up for strikes, he experienced more success. The former American Leaguer rarely walked himself into trouble. "Willie uses his pitches wisely," said Houston pitching coach Bobby Cluck. "He doesn't overthrow the ball when he doesn't have to, and when he needs a little velocity, he can reach back and get it."

HOLDING RUNNERS, BASERUNNING, HITTING:

Blair has a good move to first base and permitted only six steals in ten attempts last year. Runners took few liberties with him. He made only two errors in 29 games covering 78.2 innings. With the bat, he got one more hit than a dead man. He went 1-for-17 and went down swinging on 14 of those plate appearances.

OVERALL:

Blair's stock rose considerably last year, which is why the Rockies made him their 11th pick. While he's yet to post an ERA under 4.00, he's always had a good arm and his relief numbers were very good last year. He could very well be Colorado's main set-up man this year.

Overall Statistics

	W	L	ERA	G	GS	Sv	IP	H	R	BB	SO	HR
1992	5	7	4.00	29	8	0	78.2	74	47	25	48	5
Career	10	15	4.57	67	19	0	183.1	198	107	63	104	16

How Often He Throws Strikes

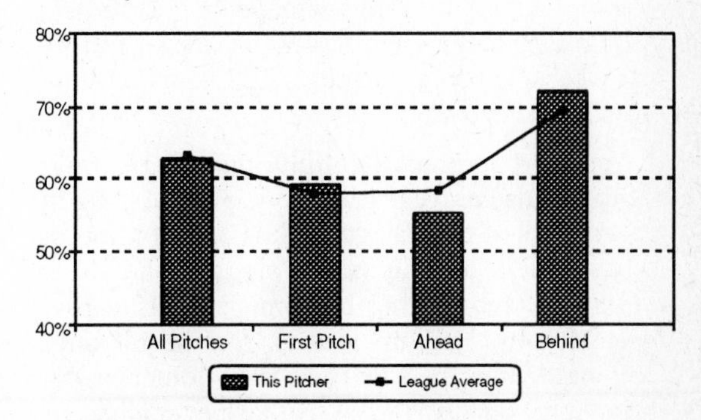

1992 Situational Stats

	W	L	ERA	Sv	IP		AB	H	HR	RBI	AVG
Home	3	2	2.48	0	36.1	LHB	156	39	1	17	.250
Road	2	5	5.31	0	42.1	RHB	141	35	4	29	.248
Day	0	4	5.33	0	27.0	Sc Pos	68	22	2	40	.324
Night	5	3	3.31	0	51.2	Clutch	31	7	1	4	.226

1992 Rankings (National League)

- Did not rank near the top or bottom in any category

HITTING:

In a move that surprised more than a few observers, the Rockies made Jerald their fourth pick in the first round of the expansion draft. A righty swinger with a little bit of power, Clark is expected to take advantage of the chummy left field power alleys at Mile High Stadium. The Rockies are undoubtedly thinking of Clark's 1989 season with Las Vegas of the AAA Pacific Coast League. That year, he enjoyed the high-altitude PCL to the tune of 22 homers, 83 RBI and a .313 average.

Clark has yet to approach those kinds of figures in the majors, but 1992 was really his first season as an everyday player. His figures last year were unspectacular: 12 homers, 58 ribbies, and a .242 average. He did do some damage against lefties, hitting .276 and slugging .480 vs. them. But he was weak against righthanders (.227) and he drew only 22 walks overall.

It would be optimistic to think that Clark could approach his Las Vegas numbers, even playing in Colorado. The San Diego park is one of the best in baseball for a righty power slugger, and Clark took advantage, belting 20 homers in 512 career Jack Murphy Stadium at-bats. But he hit only .229 there. Plus, he's hit only eight homers away from San Diego in 510 AB. He has never adjusted to the high hard stuff National League pitchers have thrown him. He is not a good breaking ball hitter, either, and swings at numerous bad pitches.

BASERUNNING:

Clark is not a good runner, though he did have three stolen bases in as many attempts last season. However, his six triples show that he is willing to go for the extra base.

FIELDING:

Clark is only a very good left fielder. He has fine range, although occasionally has trouble getting a quick jump on the ball. His arm is not the strongest but it is easily good enough for left field.

OVERALL:

Clark is penciled in as the Rockies' starting left fielder. The evidence suggests that his production has a chance to be pretty decent, especially in the power area, and he'll likely bat either 3rd or 5th. Clark would be better off in a platoon role, but hey, we're talking expansion here.

JERALD CLARK

Position: LF/1B/RF
Bats: R **Throws:** R
Ht: 6' 4" **Wt:** 205

Opening Day Age: 29
Born: 8/10/63 in Crockett, TX
ML Seasons: 5

Overall Statistics

	G	AB	R	H	D	T	HR	RBI	SB	BB	SO	AVG
1992	146	496	45	120	22	6	12	58	3	22	97	.242
Career	339	1022	88	242	45	7	28	126	5	61	224	.237

Where He Hits the Ball

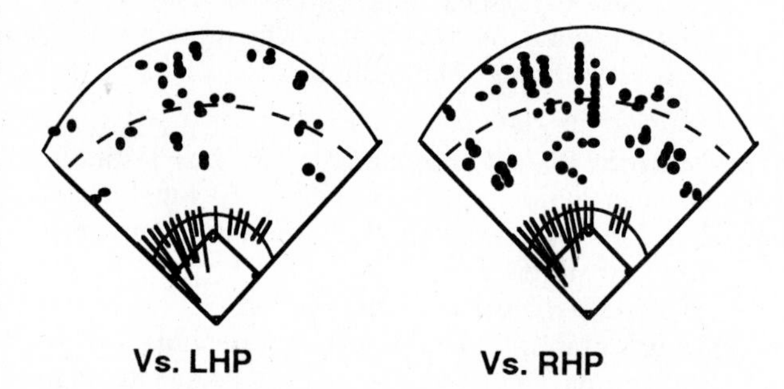

1992 Situational Stats

	AB	H	HR	RBI	AVG		AB	H	HR	RBI	AVG
Home	247	63	9	34	.255	LHP	152	42	6	20	.276
Road	249	57	3	24	.229	RHP	344	78	6	38	.227
Day	148	37	4	15	.250	Sc Pos	118	31	4	45	.263
Night	348	83	8	43	.239	Clutch	95	20	3	17	.211

1992 Rankings (National League)

- 3rd in lowest on-base percentage (.278)
- 5th in lowest batting average (.242)
- 7th in lowest percentage of pitches taken (45.1%)
- 9th in lowest batting average on the road (.229)
- 10th in lowest percentage of swings put into play (40.7%)
- Led the Padres in triples (6)
- Led NL left fielders in triples

HITTING:

Alex Cole must wonder what he has to do to hold a job. In midseason 1990 Cole made a sensational major-league debut with the Indians, batting .300 and stealing 40 bases in only 63 games. But by midyear 1991 he was riding the bench. In '92 the Indians got Kenny Lofton to take Cole's place, then dealt Cole to the Pirates in July. Though Cole helped the Bucs to a division title, his reward was to be left unprotected in the expansion draft. The Rockies picked him as their ninth choice in the first round, and Cole is projected as their starting center fielder. He'll understandably only believe it when he sees his name on the lineup card.

The speedy Cole is primarily a singles hitter. He has yet to hit a home run in 916 major-league at-bats. However, he can drive a bad pitch into the gap and leg it into a triple. Cole didn't show much patience with the Pirates but he drew a respectable number of walks with Cleveland. He'll need to be patient if he wants to be the Colorado leadoff man.

Though the lefty-swinging Cole played almost exclusively against righthanders after coming to Pittsburgh, past history indicates he can handle lefties. He's batted higher against lefties in his major-league career (.313) than he has against righties (.276).

BASERUNNING:

Cole can fly and is quick out of the batters' box. He has become a bit tentative as a basestealer, though; after stealing those 40 bases as a rookie, he has stolen only 43 in 227 games since. Colorado will expect him to run more.

FIELDING:

If speed is Cole's strength, fielding is certainly a weakness. He shows poor instincts and has too many mental lapses. He has an adequate arm and makes up for some mistakes with his speed.

OVERALL:

Cole looked to be on the brink of stardom following his rookie season. He is still young enough to become a star and could be in the right situation. The Rockies figure to stick with him longer than the Indians and Pirates did. Or so he hopes.

ALEX COLE

Position: RF/LF
Bats: L **Throws:** L
Ht: 6' 0" **Wt:** 170
Opening Day Age: 27
Born: 8/17/65 in Fayetteville, NC
ML Seasons: 3

Overall Statistics

	G	AB	R	H	D	T	HR	RBI	SB	BB	SO	AVG
1992	105	302	44	77	4	7	0	15	16	28	67	.255
Career	290	916	145	259	26	14	0	49	83	114	152	.283

Where He Hits the Ball

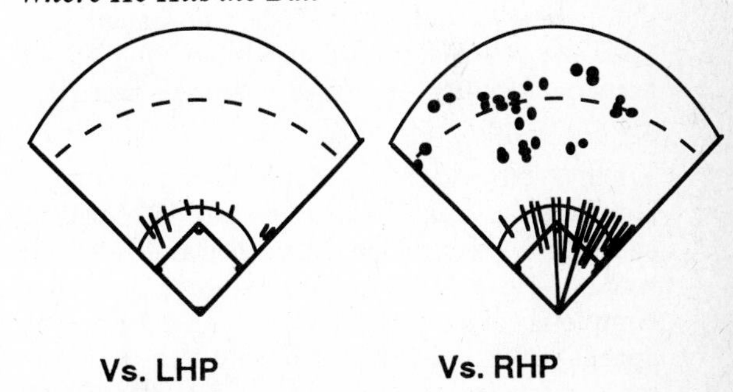

1992 Situational Stats

	AB	H	HR	RBI	AVG		AB	H	HR	RBI	AVG
Home	137	41	0	13	.299	LHP	49	14	0	3	.286
Road	165	36	0	2	.218	RHP	253	63	0	12	.249
Day	83	21	0	4	.253	Sc Pos	55	12	0	14	.218
Night	219	56	0	11	.256	Clutch	60	13	0	5	.217

1992 Rankings (National League)

- 10th in triples (7) and lowest batting average on a 3-2 count (.107)
- Led NL right fielders in triples and steals of third (2)

HITTING:

After hitting the skids with Montreal, Andres Galarraga got a second chance last year with the Cardinals. He batted only .243 but made a good impression on one St. Louis observer: Cardinals batting coach Don Baylor. When Baylor became the first manager of the Rockies last fall, he recommended that Colorado take a chance on "The Big Cat" and sign him as a free agent. Now Galarraga gets a third chance -- probably his last.

The Cardinals' 1991 trade of Ken Hill for Galarraga was widely second-guessed, but the results of the deal were skewed due to Galarraga's wrist injury. Early in the year he was plunked on the wrist by the Mets' Wally Whitehurst and he didn't recover until July. Galarraga batted .296 after the All Star break and hit all ten of his homers after July 1st for a .497 second-half slugging average.

When it comes to free swinging, Galarraga makes Hugh Hefner look like the Pope, and 1992 was no exception -- he struck out six times as often as he walked. He will swing at anything, but when completely at his best he's a .280 -.290 hitter with decent power. Most of his second-half improvement came from a rebound against lefthanders. He batted .320 against southpaws with a .536 slugging average for the year. However, he hit only .195 against righties.

BASERUNNING:

It seems clear that Galarraga's 1991 knee injury has hurt his running speed. During 1988-90 he was 35-of-45 as a base thief; since then, he has been 10-of-20. He scored only 38 runs last year and did not look quick.

FIELDING:

Galarraga is still a good fielder with the smoothness, if not quite the range, that helped him earn his nickname. He made eight errors for the Cardinals but had to contend with a variety of second and third basemen.

OVERALL:

Galarraga will be expected to deliver 20 homers and a good average in Colorado, and he'll try to keep his average up against righties. He'll always have a job as long as he hits lefties like he did in 1992.

ANDRES GALARRAGA

Position: 1B
Bats: R **Throws:** R
Ht: 6' 3" **Wt:** 235

Opening Day Age: 31
Born: 6/18/61 in Caracas, Venezuela
ML Seasons: 8

Overall Statistics

	G	AB	R	H	D	T	HR	RBI	SB	BB	SO	AVG
1992	95	325	38	79	14	2	10	39	5	11	69	.243
Career	942	3407	432	909	182	16	116	472	59	235	859	.267

Where He Hits the Ball

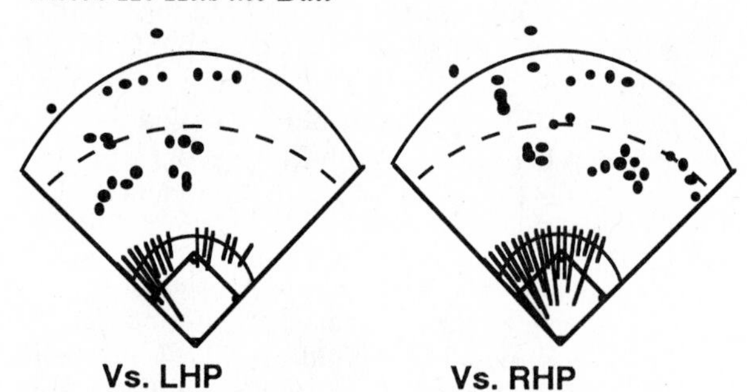

1992 Situational Stats

	AB	H	HR	RBI	AVG		AB	H	HR	RBI	AVG
Home	159	42	4	16	.264	LHP	125	40	6	19	.320
Road	166	37	6	23	.223	RHP	200	39	4	20	.195
Day	84	17	3	7	.202	Sc Pos	94	18	1	27	.191
Night	241	62	7	32	.257	Clutch	72	17	2	9	.236

1992 Rankings (National League)

- 1st in lowest batting average with 2 strikes (.107)
- 4th in hit by pitch (8)
- 5th in lowest batting average with runners in scoring position (.191)
- 10th in slugging percentage vs. left-handed pitchers (.536)
- Led the Cardinals in hit by pitch

HITTING:

Joe Girardi battled back from a terrible back problem in 1991 and settled in as the Chicago Cubs' semi-regular catcher in 1992. Girardi batted .270, tieing his career-high, so it looked like a successful comeback. But looking a little deeper, it was anything but that. Nevertheless, the Rockies selected him from the Cubs in the first round.

In terms of slugging, Girardi almost gave The Mendoza Line a counterpart last year. As of September 15, the world was about to coin the Girardi Line -- .300 slugging percentage -- which the catcher had just fallen below at .299. Girardi rallied and made it an even .300 before a broken bone in his hand was discovered, shelving him for the last two weeks. The injury froze him with a horrifying 5 extra-base hits in 270 at-bats.

With Girardi, the term "offensive presence" can be pronounced two ways. All of Girardi's value is in his batting average, which against lefties in 1992 wasn't bad at .299. Against righties he struggled. He handles mediocre fastballs, but a good heater or any kind of decent offspeed pitch permits Girardi just a little harmless wood on the ball. To his credit, he usually tried to just make contact, making him a hit-and-run favorite.

BASERUNNING:

Despite his back, Girardi is still pretty mobile. But he's no longer a basestealer. After swiping eight bases in 11 attempts in 1990, he didn't make an attempt in '91 and was 0-for-2 in '92.

FIELDING:

He can't hit, but Girardi really deserves acknowledgment for his defensive improvement. Much was made of the Cubs high passed ball total, with Girardi committing eight. But he cut down a fabulous 41 percent of runners trying to steal, 2nd best in the NL, and works very well with the staff.

OVERALL:

Girardi was a highly praised selection by the Rockies because of his great defensive ability and his handling of a pitching staff. But the fact is that Girardi was one of the worst offensive players in baseball last year, catcher or not. There is no way his defensive ability can possibly be worth the vacuum his bat provided in '92, yet he enters the spring as the Rockies' starter.

JOE GIRARDI

Position: C
Bats: R **Throws:** R
Ht: 5'11" **Wt:** 195

Opening Day Age: 28
Born: 10/14/64 in Peoria, IL
ML Seasons: 4

Overall Statistics

	G	AB	R	H	D	T	HR	RBI	SB	BB	SO	AVG
1992	91	270	19	73	3	1	1	12	0	19	38	.270
Career	304	893	73	234	39	3	3	70	10	53	120	.262

Where He Hits the Ball

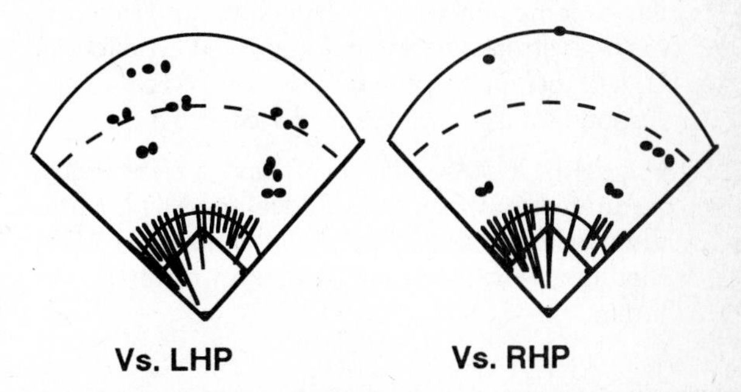

1992 Situational Stats

	AB	H	HR	RBI	AVG		AB	H	HR	RBI	AVG
Home	128	39	1	7	.305	LHP	137	41	0	5	.299
Road	142	34	0	5	.239	RHP	133	32	1	7	.241
Day	144	42	1	7	.292	Sc Pos	51	12	0	11	.235
Night	126	31	0	5	.246	Clutch	62	16	0	3	.258

1992 Rankings (National League)

- 1st in lowest batting average on a 3-1 count (.000)
- 2nd in highest percentage of runners caught stealing as a catcher (41.0%)

CHARLIE HAYES

Position: 3B
Bats: R **Throws:** R
Ht: 6' 0" **Wt:** 205

Opening Day Age: 27
Born: 5/29/65 in Hattiesburg, MS
ML Seasons: 5

HITTING:

Of all the decisions made before the expansion draft, the Yankees' choice to expose Charlie Hayes may have been the most widely second-guessed. New York still hasn't recovered from the loss of Graig Nettles, and Hayes seemed to be the answer, if not the second coming.

Hayes made numerous advances as a hitter in 1992, with career bests in home runs, RBI, slugging percentage, and on-base percentage. What changed? First, he got out of Philadelphia, where he had the impossible mission of competing with Dave Hollins. Second, Hayes learned how to look for the breaking ball and adjust to the fastball, an essential skill in the American League. Overall he has become a more aggressive hitter, reflected in his high strikeout total and improved production. It will be interesting to see how NL pitchers respond to his new style, and vice-versa.

Hayes' best power is to left and center fields, meaning his swing was not ideal for Yankee Stadium. He should do a lot better in Mile High Stadium, which is made to order for righty power hitters.

BASERUNNING:

Hayes has fair speed and will try to steal a base occasionally. That might not be such a great idea, given his dismal career success rate of 50 percent. His main job on the bases is to stay out of trouble, which he usually does.

FIELDING:

Defense was the reason the Yankees acquired Hayes, and he will stabilize the young Rockies infield. He has good range and one of the strongest arms of anyone playing third base. His knowledge of NL hitters is still current and he should be one of the best in the league.

OVERALL:

At this point the availability of Hayes seems like a boneheaded move by the restructuring Yankees, but a vital one for the Rockies. They will need Hayes as an infield coach and semi-big bopper. He could have his finest offensive season in Colorado, though the weakness of the lineup will hurt him. But don't get too carried away: Hayes is no offensive star and has a career on-base average of .282.

Overall Statistics

	G	AB	R	H	D	T	HR	RBI	SB	BB	SO	AVG
1992	142	509	52	131	19	2	18	66	3	28	100	.257
Career	530	1845	168	461	77	4	48	219	13	83	319	.250

Where He Hits the Ball

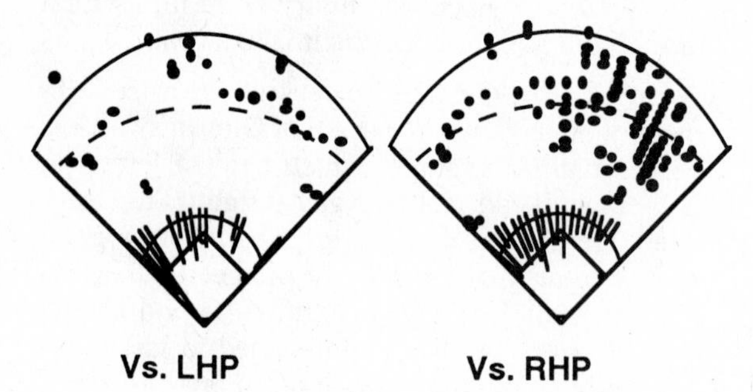

1992 Situational Stats

	AB	H	HR	RBI	AVG		AB	H	HR	RBI	AVG
Home	245	54	7	30	.220	LHP	150	32	6	18	.213
Road	264	77	11	36	.292	RHP	359	99	12	48	.276
Day	162	45	4	16	.278	Sc Pos	108	28	2	41	.259
Night	347	86	14	50	.248	Clutch	91	22	3	7	.242

1992 Rankings (American League)

- 1st in lowest on-base percentage vs. left-handed pitchers (.262) and lowest batting average on a 3-1 count (.000)
- 2nd in lowest batting average at home (.220)
- 3rd in lowest batting average vs. left-handed pitchers (.213)
- 7th in lowest on-base percentage (.297)

BUTCH HENRY

Position: SP
Bats: L **Throws:** L
Ht: 6' 1" **Wt:** 195

Opening Day Age: 24
Born: 10/7/68 in El Paso, TX
ML Seasons: 1

PITCHING:

When Butch Henry reported to spring training a year ago, the Houston Astros did not include him in their pitching plans. Henry forced them to alter their thinking, and he pitched so well that he forced his way into the Houston starting rotation. While his overall record was nothing special, Henry's late improvement was shown in a 3-1 record and 2.65 ERA after August 15, until he was shelved with tendinitis. That impressed the Rockies, who chose Henry in the second round of the expansion draft.

A number of baseball people have likened Henry's style to Tom Glavine, Atlanta's 20-game winner. Astros pitching coach Bob Cluck agreed: "Glavine pitches real aggressively and that's what Butch has to do, pitch inside, change speeds and throw the ball over the plate. Glavine is just a better pitcher right now because he has the experience and success. In time, Henry can be a real winner in this league, too." Obviously if the Astros really thought Henry would be the next Glavine, they would have protected him. But the quote indicates that Henry has potential.

Like Glavine, Henry has an outstanding changeup. He works the hitters smartly, blending in his curveball and slider with a sinking fastball. A finesse pitcher, he won't overpower anyone, so he must be consistent in staying ahead in the count. He issued 41 walks while striking out 96, a decent ratio.

HOLDING RUNNERS, FIELDING, HITTING:

It's a bit unusual for a lefty, but Henry lacks the quick move to first base in holding runners close to the bag. He fields his position well and shows a knack at the plate with a nice stroke, producing eight hits and seven RBI in '92.

OVERALL:

Henry worked 165.2 innings last year, second-most on the Houston staff, and looms as a significant contributor to the Colorado starting rotation in '93 as one of only four left-handed pitchers selected by Colorado. His control must be razor-sharp for him to be effective. By staying ahead in the count and pitching inside fearlessly, he could be one of the Rockies' better pitchers.

Overall Statistics

	W	L	ERA	G	GS	Sv	IP	H	R	BB	SO	HR
1992	6	9	4.02	28	28	0	165.2	185	81	41	96	16
Career	6	9	4.02	28	28	0	165.2	185	81	41	96	16

How Often He Throws Strikes

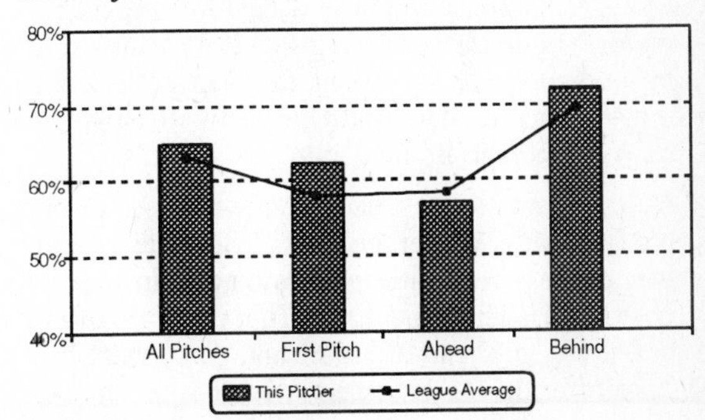

1992 Situational Stats

	W	L	ERA	Sv	IP		AB	H	HR	RBI	AVG
Home	3	3	3.27	0	88.0	LHB	141	42	2	13	.298
Road	3	6	4.87	0	77.2	RHB	508	143	14	56	.281
Day	5	1	2.45	0	69.2	Sc Pos	129	32	4	48	.248
Night	1	8	5.16	0	96.0	Clutch	42	11	1	2	.262

1992 Rankings (National League)

- 1st in highest batting average allowed (.285) and highest slugging percentage allowed (.433)
- 2nd in highest ERA (4.02)
- 3rd in highest on-base percentage allowed (.325) and highest batting average allowed vs. right-handed batters (.282)
- Led the Astros in complete games (2), shutouts (1), hits allowed (185), runners caught stealing (7), highest groundball/flyball ratio (1.3), lowest stolen base percentage allowed (58.8%), least pitches thrown per batter (3.4) and most GDPs induced per 9 innings (.54)

DARREN HOLMES

Position: RP
Bats: R **Throws:** R
Ht: 6' 0" **Wt:** 199

Opening Day Age: 26
Born: 4/25/66 in Asheville, NC
ML Seasons: 3

Overall Statistics

	W	L	ERA	G	GS	Sv	IP	H	R	BB	SO	HR
1992	4	4	2.55	41	0	6	42.1	35	12	11	31	1
Career	5	9	4.10	95	0	9	136.0	140	65	49	109	8

How Often He Throws Strikes

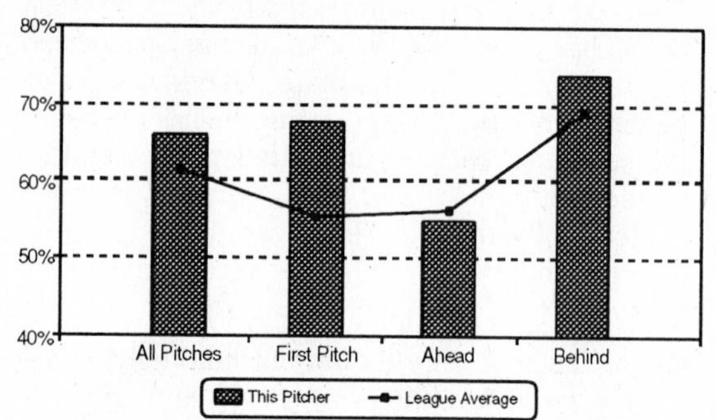

1992 Situational Stats

	W	L	ERA	Sv	IP		AB	H	HR	RBI	AVG
Home	3	2	3.26	3	19.1	LHB	67	15	0	5	.224
Road	1	2	1.96	3	23.0	RHB	89	20	1	6	.225
Day	1	1	1.20	2	15.0	Sc Pos	50	7	0	9	.140
Night	3	3	3.29	4	27.1	Clutch	80	19	0	5	.237

1992 Rankings (American League)

- 4th in lowest batting average allowed in relief with runners on base (.169) and lowest batting average allowed in relief with runners in scoring position (.140)
- 6th in first batter efficiency (.171) and lowest percentage of inherited runners scored (17.1%)
- Led the Brewers in lowest percentage of inherited runners scored, lowest batting average allowed in relief with runners on base and lowest batting average allowed in relief with runners in scoring position

PITCHING:

Darren Holmes is a product of the Dodger system and was the toast of Albuquerque in 1990 with 12 wins and 13 saves in 56 games. He came to the Brewers (for catcher Bert Heffernan) in December of 1990 as a strikeout pitcher with a future as a closer after being primarily a starter prior to then. A bright future seems a lot nearer after 1992, a season in which Holmes had six saves and a 2.55 ERA for the Brewers. Now with the Rockies, Holmes is the clear frontrunner for the closer's job.

Holmes was easy to overlook after 1991. He posted a 4.72 ERA out of the Brewers' terrible bullpen, though he showed some promise early in the year. Holmes acquired a healthy respect for major-league hitters during his 1991 baptism of fire, when the first hitter he faced in each outing hit .400 and he often found himself with a man on base and behind in the count.

Holmes came to the mound ready in 1992; he cut his first batter's average to .171 and was among the league's best with runners on and in scoring position. He still grooves the first pitch too often, but now gets ahead of hitters and gives them less easy offerings to hit. He cut his home runs allowed from six to one and walked only 11 hitters all season. Holmes throws a fastball, curve and slider, and as one scout put it, his heater has "A-plus velocity."

HOLDING RUNNERS, FIELDING, HITTING:

Holmes has good range around the mound and made only one error last year. He didn't have to contend much with basestealers, but of the five who ran, only one was caught. He came up in the National League so he has some experience with the bat.

OVERALL:

Holmes matured last year and helped the Brewers post the best bullpen ERA in the American League. He was at his best in 1992 in closer situations: with runners on and against the first hitter. He may join John Franco and John Wetteland to haunt the save-starved Dodgers.

CALVIN JONES

Position: RP
Bats: R **Throws:** R
Ht: 6' 3" **Wt:** 185

Opening Day Age: 29
Born: 9/26/63 in Compton, CA
ML Seasons: 2

PITCHING:

When Calvin Jones came up to the Mariners late in 1991, he was nearly 28 years old and knew how to pitch. Sporting a newly-developed split-fingered fastball, he posted a 2.53 ERA and allowed only 33 hits in 46.1 innings. His strong work was one reason why the Mariners risked trading three pitchers to get Kevin Mitchell. When the '92 season began, Jones was in the middle relief role formerly occupied by Mike Jackson. Now the Mariners are down another pitcher as Jones heads to the Rockies.

Jones began last year strongly, allowing only a single earned run in his first eight appearances. But then he fell apart, permitting at least one earned run in 16 of his final 29 appearances. In May and June combined Jones allowed 19 earned runs in just 21.1 innings pitched for an 8.02 ERA. He was eventually sent to AAA Calgary to try and straighten himself out. Jones ended the year with a 5.69 ERA in 38 games -- more than doubling his 1991 mark.

Jones wasn't a total disaster last year. For one thing, he allowed only four of 25 inherited runners to score. He continued to throw the splitter and it was still effective -- he had an opponents batting average of only .226. But he couldn't throw it consistently for strikes. Jones gave up 47 walks in 61.2 innings and yielded eight homers, usually when he was forced to groove a fastball. At times during the year he challenged Randy Johnson for the team lead in wild pitches.

HOLDING RUNNERS, FIELDING, HITTING:

Jones is nothing special at holding runners. He allowed six steals in nine attempts last year -- not that bad considering all the runners he put on base. However, his defensive work was horrible with three errors in only 13 chances. His hitting skills are untested.

OVERALL:

Jones will get a chance to bounce back in Colorado. He was tough to hit, even while struggling, and if he can regain the kind of control he had in 1991 the Rockies will have a steal. He is very likely to be in their bullpen in 1993.

Overall Statistics

	W	L	ERA	G	GS	Sv	IP	H	R	BB	SO	HR
1992	3	5	5.69	38	1	0	61.2	50	39	47	49	8
Career	5	7	4.33	65	1	2	108.0	83	53	76	91	8

How Often He Throws Strikes

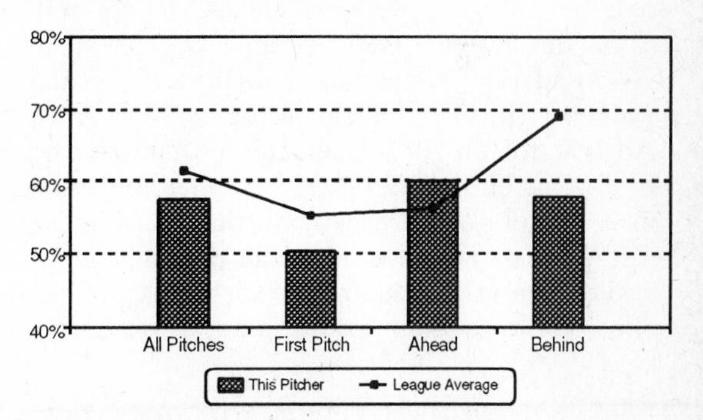

1992 Situational Stats

	W	L	ERA	Sv	IP		AB	H	HR	RBI	AVG
Home	2	2	4.22	0	32.0	LHB	84	21	2	12	.250
Road	1	3	7.28	0	29.2	RHB	137	29	6	18	.212
Day	2	1	7.94	0	11.1	Sc Pos	60	12	1	19	.200
Night	1	4	5.19	0	50.1	Clutch	41	11	1	8	.268

1992 Rankings (American League)

- 2nd highest relief ERA (5.88)
- 3rd most baserunners allowed per 9 innings in relief (14.3)
- 10th in wild pitches (10)
- Led the Mariners in lowest batting average allowed in relief with runners on base (.200), lowest batting average allowed in relief with runners in scoring position (.200), lowest batting average allowed in relief (.233) and most strikeouts per 9 innings in relief (7.3)

TOP PROSPECT

PITCHING:

David Nied got the call last September as the Braves drove toward their second straight pennant, and the rookie was up to the task. Nied went 3-0 with a 1.17 ERA in two starts and four relief appearances. He captured the imagination of baseball fans along with the imagination of the Rockies, who made Nied the overall first pick in the expansion draft.

Nied's trademark is his outstanding control. He not only throws strikes at will but moves his pitches around the strike zone, racking up high strikeout totals. His fastball hits 90 MPH, and his change-up is described as "big league." Nied has perfect confidence in his own ability. "In my opinion, I've got three good pitches," he has said. "I can throw any of them any time for strikes." In 1991 and 1992 in the minors he fanned 337 and walked 87 in 338.1 innings; he was voted a AAA All-Star for the 1992 campaign. After walking four in his big-league debut, he walked only one in five more appearances covering 16 innings. The problem with his continual pitching in the strike zone is obvious with a glance at his hits allowed: he gave up just 10, but five were doubles.

Has Nied proven everything at AAA? Aside from his September call-up, he had a 1.50 ERA in spring training in 1992, and obviously inspired confidence from Bobby Cox.

HOLDING RUNNERS, FIELDING, HITTING:

Nied is a good athlete and fields his position well. He also swings the bat, notching a pair of hits in his seven at-bats with two strikeouts. He allowed only 15 baserunners with the Braves; two of the runners stole without being caught, so it's uncertain if he has a problem there.

OVERALL:

Nied will probably open the 1993 season in the Rockies rotation, probably as the staff ace. His challenge will be to use his exceptional control to keep the ball down and in the park. As the first pick, he will have instant fame and crowd-drawing ability if he can follow up on his early success.

DAVE NIED

Position: RP
Bats: R **Throws:** R
Ht: 6' 2" **Wt:** 185

Opening Day Age: 24
Born: 12/22/68 in Dallas, TX
ML Seasons: 1

Overall Statistics

	W	L	ERA	G	GS	Sv	IP	H	R	BB	SO	HR
1992	3	0	1.17	6	2	0	23.0	10	3	5	19	0
Career	3	0	1.17	6	2	0	23.0	10	3	5	19	0

How Often He Throws Strikes

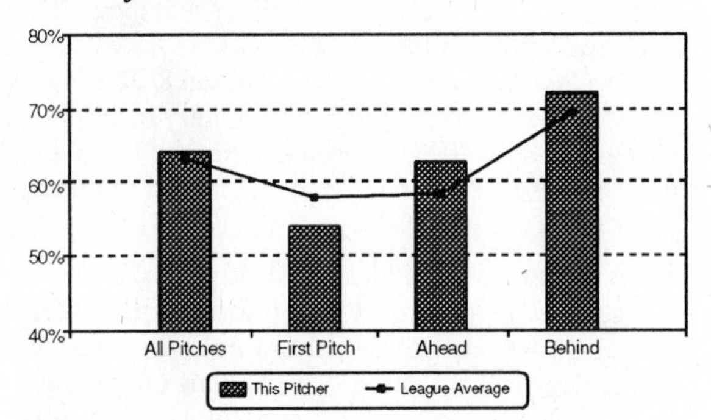

1992 Situational Stats

	W	L	ERA	Sv	IP		AB	H	HR	RBI	AVG
Home	1	0	1.64	0	11.0	LHB	42	8	0	3	.190
Road	2	0	0.75	0	12.0	RHB	35	2	0	0	.057
Day	0	0	0.00	0	4.0	Sc Pos	18	2	0	3	.111
Night	3	0	1.42	0	19.0	Clutch	12	0	0	0	.000

1992 Rankings (National League)

→ Did not rank near the top or bottom in any category

PITCHING:

Steve Reed had a great 1992 season at three levels. He finished third in the league in saves at AA Shreveport despite spending just half a season there, and he was voted the league's best reliever. He was all but perfect; earning 23 saves and a win in 27 games; he also struck out 33 men in 29 innings and didn't walk a single hitter! He was nearly as dominating at AAA Phoenix, where his 20 saves pushed his total to a single-season minor-league record of 43. He was called up to San Francisco and retired Ryne Sandberg with a runner on second in his first major-league appearance. With the Giants he was equally terrific, allowing just 17 baserunners in 15.2 innings while fanning 11.

So why was Reed available to the Rockies in the third round of the expansion draft? Because he doesn't throw hard. Reed is a submarine pitcher and could be the first since Dan Quisenberry to have a big impact in the majors. When he throws 80 MPH he's hitting his top speed, but his control is so good that hitters are forced to swing at pitches they have difficulty picking up and they generally beat the ball into the ground. In the minors Reed dominated lefties and righties alike, but in the National League left-handed hitters had better luck seeing the ball and had some success against him.

HOLDING RUNNERS, FIELDING, HITTING:

Reed didn't bat with the Giants and isn't likely to hit much in Colorado. He does field well which contributes to his success as a groundball pitcher. His motion leaves him more heads-up than a traditional pitcher, helping his fielding and allows him to keep an eye on baserunners.

OVERALL:

Reed's competition for the closer role with Colorado is probably Darren Holmes, who has much more big-league experience -- in the American League -- and excellent closer credentials though he has been in middle relief until now. Reed will be on the big club in 1993, should have success, and will probably get some important relief duties. The Giants will hope he fails, after all, they protected 21 players ahead of him, including Mike Benjamin.

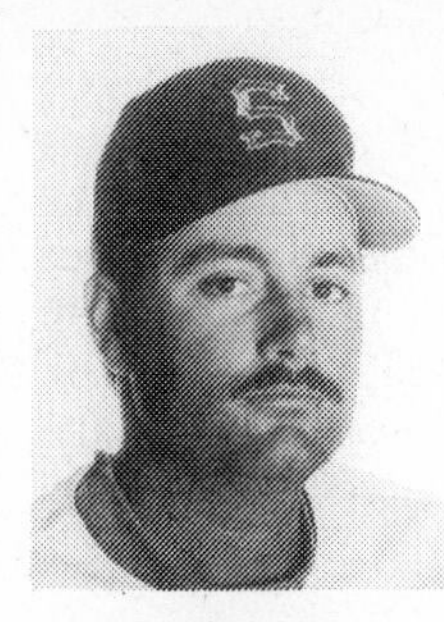

STEVE REED

Position: RP
Bats: R **Throws:** R
Ht: 6' 2" **Wt:** 195

Opening Day Age: 27
Born: 3/11/66 in Los Angeles, CA
ML Seasons: 1

Overall Statistics

	W	L	ERA	G	GS	Sv	IP	H	R	BB	SO	HR
1992	1	0	2.30	18	0	0	15.2	13	5	3	11	2
Career	1	0	2.30	18	0	0	15.2	13	5	3	11	2

How Often He Throws Strikes

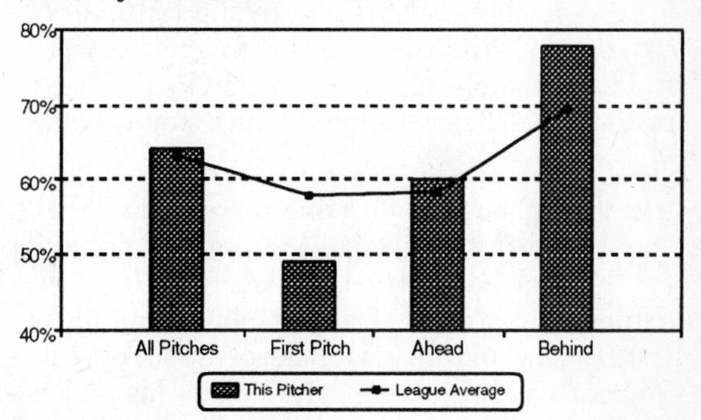

1992 Situational Stats

	W	L	ERA	Sv	IP		AB	H	HR	RBI	AVG
Home	0	0	2.35	0	7.2	LHB	22	6	0	5	.273
Road	1	0	2.25	0	8.0	RHB	37	7	2	7	.189
Day	0	0	0.00	0	1.2	Sc Pos	25	7	2	12	.280
Night	1	0	2.57	0	14.0	Clutch	19	6	1	4	.316

1992 Rankings (National League)

➡ Did not rank near the top or bottom in any category

PITCHING:

Former fourth-round draft pick Kevin Ritz has usually pitched very well at the minor-league level, but in four trials with the pitching-poor Tigers he posted a 6-18 record and an earned run average of 5.85. That record soured Detroit on him and the Tigers made him available into the second round of the expansion draft. Since Ritz is known to have a terrific arm, the Rockies took a chance on him.

Ritz began last season in the Tiger bullpen and finished April with a 3.57 ERA over 17.2 innings -- pretty exciting stuff for a guy whose Detroit ERA had been above 11.00 the previous two seasons. The Tigers finally moved him into their starting rotation, but his first outing lasted all of two innings. Ritz continued to struggle both as a starter and a reliever before finally being placed on the disabled list in August with a strained right elbow.

Ritz has a good fastball, a fine curve, and a decent enough slider and change -- the stuff to succeed at the major-league level. He keeps the ball low, getting a lot of groundball outs, but the problem is that a lot of his pitches dip out of the strike zone. Walks have plagued him throughout his major-league career and he's been hurt when he's had to pitch from behind in the count. Now he also has a sore arm to worry about.

HOLDING RUNNERS, FIELDING, HITTING:

Ritz is a very good fielder, getting off the mound quickly and reacting well to balls hit back to the box. His pickoff move is considered good, but last year runners stole 11 bases in 16 attempts with Ritz on the mound. His next major league at-bat will be his first.

OVERALL:

Ritz is still only 28, and all the expansion picks were gambles in one way or another. The Rockies take a double risk with Ritz because of his elbow tendinitis and his lack of major-league success. Perhaps a new team and a new league will help him.

KEVIN RITZ

Position: RP/SP
Bats: R **Throws:** R
Ht: 6' 4" **Wt:** 220

Opening Day Age: 27
Born: 6/8/65 in Eatonstown, NJ
ML Seasons: 4

Overall Statistics

	W	L	ERA	G	GS	Sv	IP	H	R	BB	SO	HR
1992	2	5	5.60	23	11	0	80.1	88	52	44	57	4
Career	6	18	5.85	50	32	0	177.0	194	127	124	125	7

How Often He Throws Strikes

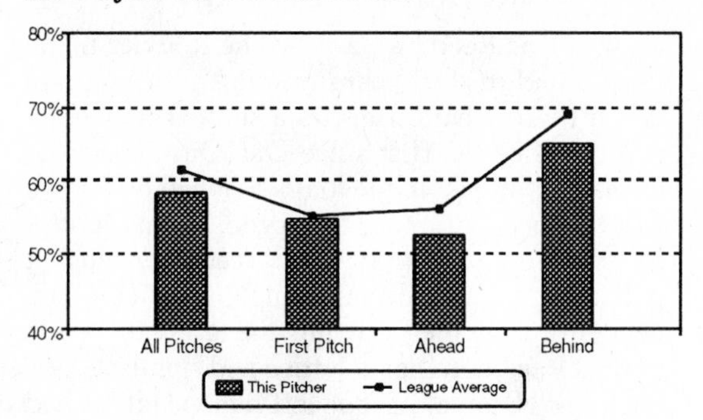

1992 Situational Stats

	W	L	ERA	Sv	IP		AB	H	HR	RBI	AVG
Home	1	1	4.75	0	55.0	LHB	129	38	2	20	.295
Road	1	4	7.46	0	25.1	RHB	187	50	2	22	.267
Day	1	2	6.39	0	25.1	Sc Pos	83	25	1	38	.301
Night	1	3	5.24	0	55.0	Clutch	6	1	1	1	.167

1992 Rankings (American League)

- Led the Tigers in balks (1)

JIMMY TATUM

Position: 3B
Bats: R **Throws:** R
Ht: 6' 2" **Wt:** 200

Opening Day Age: 25
Born: 10/9/67 in San Diego, CA
ML Seasons: 1

HITTING:

A late bloomer, Jimmy Tatum is 25 and has already been released by two major-league systems (the Padres and Indians). His career didn't take off until 1991 when he was an All-Star at AA El Paso, hitting .320 with 18 homers and 128 RBI. In Denver, where he'll get to play his home games, he turned in a .329-19-101 season in 1992 with 36 doubles and just 87 strikeouts. He put up some of the best hitting numbers for a third baseman above A-ball, including the majors.

Caution is a necessity regarding players who put up big numbers in notorious hitters' parks like El Paso and Denver, but Tatum's major-league equivalents stamp him as a definite prospect. He has clutch potential; he won the American Association batting title by a point over Geronimo Berroa by going 4-for-5 with a pair of doubles on the last day of the season.

If Tatum makes it with the Rockies he should get some kind of comeback award. After he was released for the first time by the Padres, he sat out the entire 1989 season. In four stops since his return he's hit .179, .262, .320, and .329.

BASERUNNING:

Tatum has a career high of eight steals and has a 50 percent or worse success rate as a thief in his last four seasons. But his power gives him a chance to stretch for extra bases and he does so very well. He scored only 74 runs in 1992 after scoring 99 the year before.

FIELDING:

Tatum is a good fielder and moved to third base from shortstop in 1992 because of the emergence in Milwaukee of Rookie of the Year Pat Listach. The Brewers organization has played him all over the infield, including at catcher. He can play third, but with Charlie Hayes on the team, he may be see more time at short.

OVERALL:

One guy who is really getting his chance due to expansion, Tatum is an intriguing prospect. He could hit himself into the shortstop job in Colorado, but as a hometown hero to Denver Zephyr fans, he should get a chance to play somewhere.

Overall Statistics

	G	AB	R	H	D	T	HR	RBI	SB	BB	SO	AVG
1992	5	8	0	1	0	0	0	0	0	1	2	.125
Career	5	8	0	1	0	0	0	0	0	1	2	.125

Where He Hits the Ball

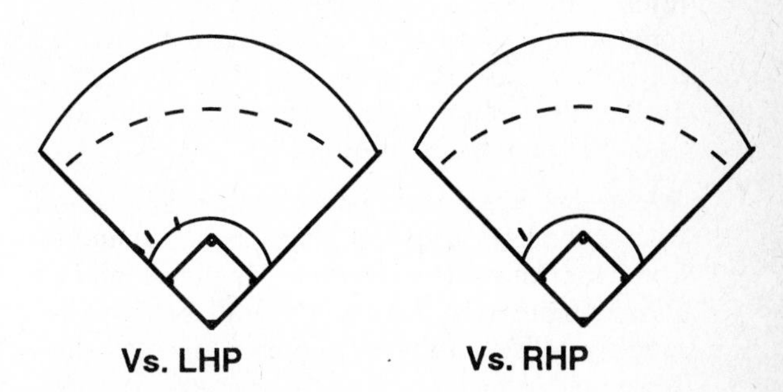

1992 Situational Stats

	AB	H	HR	RBI	AVG		AB	H	HR	RBI	AVG
Home	5	1	0	0	.200	LHP	4	1	0	0	.250
Road	3	0	0	0	.000	RHP	4	0	0	0	.000
Day	6	1	0	0	.167	Sc Pos	3	0	0	0	.000
Night	2	0	0	0	.000	Clutch	1	0	0	0	.000

1992 Rankings (American League)

- Did not rank near the top or bottom in any category

ERIC WEDGE

Position: DH
Bats: R **Throws:** R
Ht: 6' 3" **Wt:** 215

Opening Day Age: 25
Born: 1/27/68 in Fort Wayne, IN
ML Seasons: 2

Overall Statistics

	G	AB	R	H	D	T	HR	RBI	SB	BB	SO	AVG
1992	27	68	11	17	2	0	5	11	0	13	18	.250
Career	28	69	11	18	2	0	5	11	0	13	18	.261

Where He Hits the Ball

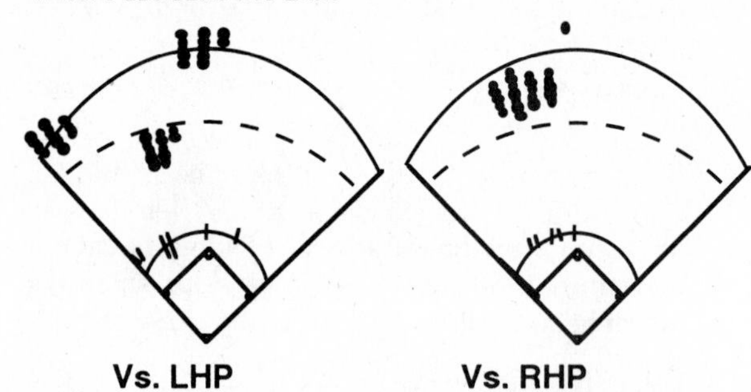

1992 Situational Stats

	AB	H	HR	RBI	AVG		AB	H	HR	RBI	AVG
Home	34	10	3	7	.294	LHP	36	11	4	8	.306
Road	34	7	2	4	.206	RHP	32	6	1	3	.188
Day	21	5	1	2	.238	Sc Pos	17	6	1	5	.353
Night	47	12	4	9	.255	Clutch	16	3	0	1	.188

1992 Rankings (American League)

→ Did not rank near the top or bottom in any category

HITTING:

Eric Wedge is a driven, determined winner and has been known as a comer since he led Wichita State to the NCAA Championship in 1989. It took awhile for his power to emerge as a pro, but in 1992 he hit 11 homers in 211 at-bats in Pawtucket and another five in 27 games with the Red Sox. Since the Sox need power hitters, it was something of a surprise that they made Wedge available into the second round of the expansion draft. The youngster had incurred Boston's ire by undergoing an elbow operation without telling them, and Colorado snagged him.

Wedge says his early struggles were due to adjusting to the pros and to wooden bats. He also had injuries to contend with. He had a strained right forearm muscle in 1991, surgery to remove torn cartilage in his left knee, and then the elbow problem. "I definitely fell behind a little bit . . .," said Wedge of his injuries in 1991.

Wedge has been much better against lefties and has a good eye; his patience against righthanders keeps him valuable as an everyday player, and he should improve against them overall. Some of his long fly balls could turn to homers in Colorado.

BASERUNNING:

Wedge is 4-of-10 in four pro seasons, but that was before his knee surgery; don't look for any speed in the future. He runs like a catcher who's had knee surgery.

FIELDING:

The chronic elbow troubles have seriously clouded Wedge's future as a catcher. He didn't nab any of the four major-league thieves who took off against him. However, he has a catcher's mentality and can help a team behind the plate. Plus, the Rockies have Andres Galarraga at first base, his other possible position.

OVERALL:

Given Tony Pena's age, Boston will need a catcher one of these days. They won't be saying "Hand me my Wedge." The Red Sox protections of Mike Gardiner and Bob Zupcic ahead of Wedge were questionable. Wedge will be teeing off in the thin air of Colorado. He is a valuable hitter and could show enough rapid improvement to take the catching job from Joe Girardi.

GREAT SPEED

HITTING:

Only 26, Eric Young figures to be the Colorado Rockies' second baseman in their debut season. Young broke in with the Dodgers last year and performed decently. But the Dodgers wanted a veteran, so after leaving Young unprotected they went after Jody Reed. Reed, like Young, had been selected by the Rockies in the draft, but a deal was made. Reed was traded, as the Rockies were content with Young.

Young batted only .258 over 132 at-bats in his Dodger debut last year, but he has the potential to do better than that. He hit very well in the minor leagues including a .337 mark for AAA Albuquerque last year before his recall. Young is a contact hitter who slaps the ball to all fields. His diminutive stature and herky-jerky movements are reminiscent of Joe Morgan, though Young hits from the right side. He doesn't have Morgan-type power, however; he's never hit more than four homers in a season.

Young has a good eye but will jump all over a high fastball and drill it back up the middle. It's tough to strike him out; he only had nine Ks in the majors last year. He responds well to pressure, hitting .341 with runners in scoring position last year.

BASERUNNING:

Young has potential to be an outstanding basestealer. He stole 216 bases in three-plus years in the minors, including 71 in 1991 and a 6-for-7 mark with the Dodgers. He has trouble getting out of the batter's box, though, so he doesn't get down to first as quickly as he should.

FIELDING:

A converted outfielder, Young was clumsy around the bag in his Dodger debut. However, he has good range, fair hands and a strong arm. There's no reason he can't become a decent glove man with more experience.

OVERALL:

The last thing the Dodgers needed was a good bat/fair glove second baseman, and that's the big reason they made him available in the expansion draft. Colorado's needs are different, and they figure to be patient with Young's defensive lapses. That may be all he needs.

ERIC YOUNG

Position: 2B
Bats: R **Throws:** R
Ht: 5' 9" **Wt:** 180

Opening Day Age: 26
Born: 11/26/66 in Jacksonville, FL
ML Seasons: 1

Overall Statistics

	G	AB	R	H	D	T	HR	RBI	SB	BB	SO	AVG
1992	49	132	9	34	1	0	1	11	6	8	9	.258
Career	49	132	9	34	1	0	1	11	6	8	9	.258

Where He Hits the Ball

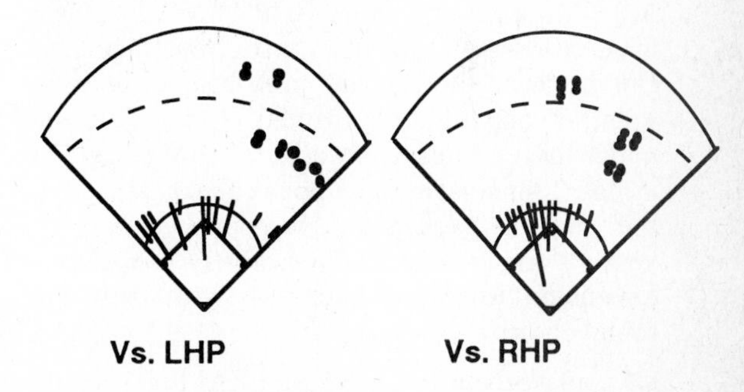

1992 Situational Stats

	AB	H	HR	RBI	AVG		AB	H	HR	RBI	AVG
Home	56	14	0	6	.250	LHP	66	18	1	6	.273
Road	76	20	1	5	.263	RHP	66	16	0	5	.242
Day	34	8	0	1	.235	Sc Pos	41	14	0	9	.341
Night	98	26	1	10	.265	Clutch	22	9	0	2	.409

1992 Rankings (National League)

- 6th in errors at second base (9)

SCOTT ALDRED

Position: SP
Bats: L **Throws:** L
Ht: 6' 4" **Wt:** 215

Opening Day Age: 24
Born: 6/12/68 in Flint, MI
ML Seasons: 3

Overall Statistics

	W	L	ERA	G	GS	Sv	IP	H	R	BB	SO	HR
1992	3	8	6.78	16	13	0	65.0	80	51	33	34	12
Career	6	14	5.80	31	27	0	136.2	151	94	73	76	21

PITCHING, FIELDING, HITTING & HOLDING RUNNERS:

Scott Aldred can throw a 90 MPH fastball, and on the soft-tossing Tiger staff, that looked like 190. But his strikeout-to-walk ratio has never been great; if anything, it's gotten worse. In three major-league stints he's walked 73 and fanned 76 in 136.2 innings, and the poor control has killed him. But the package of his good heat and his youth -- and the fact that he is a lefty -- made the expansion Rockies select him with their 8th round choice.

Of course, there is the matter of Aldred's actual pitching record. After three trials with the Tigers he had a 6-14 record and an ERA of 5.80. He started last year in the Detroit rotation but lasted only 12 starts before being demoted to AAA Toledo. As usual, Aldred's problem was simple: he couldn't get the ball over the plate.

Aldred controlled his numerous baserunners well last year; while seven stole on him, four were caught. He made no errors. He has never to this point dealt with the business end of the bat.

OVERALL:

Aldred showed little in his Detroit trials. However, everyone will take a flyer on a hard-throwing lefty. He has a tremendous amount of work to do and he wasn't getting it done in the Tiger system. He probably won't star for Colorado, but he has no where to go but up.

BRAULIO CASTILLO

Position: RF
Bats: R **Throws:** R
Ht: 6' 0" **Wt:** 160

Opening Day Age: 24
Born: 5/13/68 in Ellas Pina, Dominican Republic
ML Seasons: 2

Overall Statistics

	G	AB	R	H	D	T	HR	RBI	SB	BB	SO	AVG
1992	28	76	12	15	3	1	2	7	1	4	15	.197
Career	56	128	15	24	6	1	2	9	2	5	30	.188

HITTING, FIELDING, BASERUNNING:

Braulio Castillo has needed time at each professional level, but has always managed to progress due to two of the quickest wrists this side of Andre Dawson. However, that progress has not come easily, as Castillo has struggled with various problems, including alcohol-related ones. The Phillies grew weary of waiting for him and chose not to protect him in the expansion draft even into the third round.

Castillo's hitting difficulties are centered in his free swinging. He fanned 96 times in just 386 at-bats at AAA Scranton in 1992, and though his 40 walks were the highest total of his career, he still couldn't solve major-league pitching in his second call up in as many years.

However, Castillo has speed and power and will be an effective offensive player if he hits .250. He's stolen as many as 24 bases in the minors at a decent success rate, but he grounds into too many double plays for a man with his speed. He can play all three outfield positions though he's best in right, and he has a good arm.

OVERALL:

One of the last players chosen in the expansion draft, Castillo is loaded with tools. He may be ready for the bigs now, as a back injury sent him into a terrible tailspin in 1992. He is an interesting gamble for Colorado.

RUDY SEANEZ

Position: RP
Bats: R **Throws:** R
Ht: 5'10" **Wt:** 185

Opening Day Age: 24
Born: 10/20/68 in Brawley, CA
ML Seasons: 3

Overall Statistics

	W	L	ERA	G	GS	Sv	IP	H	R	BB	SO	HR
1992 Did Not Play												
Career	2	1	6.75	34	0	0	37.1	33	31	36	38	4

PITCHING, FIELDING, HITTING & HOLDING RUNNERS:

Still only 24, Rudy Seanez has been throwing top-level heat for six pro seasons. The only trouble is, he's never been able to control that great, 90-plus fastball. But arms like his are in great demand; like the Indians and Dodgers before them, the Rockies wanted to give Seanez a long look, enough so that they dealt Jody Reed plus considerations to get him.

In three stints with the Indians, Seanez struck out 38 hitters in 37.1 innings. But he also walked 36 and allowed 33 hits for a 6.75 ERA. He finally seemed to have mastered some control a year ago after the Dodgers had obtained him from Cleveland. Following some work with the Dodger coaching staff, Seanez was a star in 1991-92 winter ball and the Dodgers' brass figured he'd be a featured member of their bullpen last year. But then he hurt his back hitting in spring training and missed the entire year. Seanez has had back problems in the past, but he's said to be 100 percent now. His non-pitching skills (hitting, holding runners, fielding) are very raw.

OVERALL:

World class heat is precious and Seanez brings it. The Rockies have Darren Holmes and can afford to work with Seanez. The good news is that the mere fact that the Dodgers traded him away almost assures the Rockies that he will emerge as a top closer, given Los Angeles' recent history with guys like John Wetteland.

KEITH SHEPHERD

Position: RP
Bats: R **Throws:** R
Ht: 6' 2" **Wt:** 205

Opening Day Age: 25
Born: 1/21/68 in Wabash, IN
ML Seasons: 1

Overall Statistics

	W	L	ERA	G	GS	Sv	IP	H	R	BB	SO	HR
1992	1	1	3.27	12	0	2	22.0	19	10	6	10	0
Career	1	1	3.27	12	0	2	22.0	19	10	6	10	0

PITCHING, FIELDING, HITTING & HOLDING RUNNERS:

The winner of the 1992 AA All-Star game, Keith Shepherd was traded during the year from the White Sox to the Phillies for Dale Sveum when the Sox were hurting for infielders. Shepherd deserved his All-Star status. Before the trade he had allowed only 70 hits plus walks in 71.1 innings while fanning 64. He had a 2.14 ERA and seven saves.

The Phillies decided to experiment with Shepherd, giving him three starts at AA Reading even though he hadn't started in 114 previous appearances. He did well, posting a 2.78 ERA and moving up to Philadelphia when they had their rash of arm troubles. His ERA was good and he essentially performed as well in the National League as he did in Reading.

Shepherd is not the hardest thrower in the world; if he was, the White Sox wouldn't have traded him for Dale Sveum. Nonetheless he has always had good strikeout totals. He was tested by National League basestealers but caught one himself and allowed only three steals in six chances. He fielded his position well.

OVERALL:

Shepherd seemed unfazed by his three moves in 1992: a fourth would mean he's pitching for Colorado in 1993. But he hasn't yet pitched in AAA and the Rockies may have him prove himself there first, especially if he is to be converted to a starter.

ORGANIZATION OVERVIEW:

The early thinking was that the Marlins would go for instant success, while the Rockies, with the "double honeymoon" of a new team now and a new ballpark a couple of years away, would be the patient ones. But the draft wasn't halfway through the first round before people were saying that Colorado was going for instant respectability. Well if the Rockies had really wanted instant success, they would have picked Danny Tartabull and Bruce Hurst, not Jerald Clark and Willie Blair. The Colorado philosophy, under the well-respected Bob Gebhard, was to draft players with major-league backgrounds in the early rounds, then go for the less experienced prospects.

VINNY CASTILLA

Position: SS **Opening Day Age:** 25
Bats: R **Throws:** R **Born:** 7/4/67 in Oaxaca, Mex
Ht: 6' 1" **Wt:** 175

Recent Statistics

	G	AB	R	H	D	T	HR	RBI	SB	BB	SO	AVG
92 AAA Richmond	127	449	49	113	29	1	7	44	1	21	68	.252
92 NL Atlanta	9	16	1	4	1	0	0	1	0	1	4	.250
92 MLE	127	439	39	103	26	0	6	35	0	16	70	.235

Atlanta has about as many shortstops as they have pitchers, so Vinny Castilla never got a chance with the Braves except for late-season defensive work. Castilla is considered an excellent fielder and he's no automatic out; he had 29 doubles and seven homers in 449 at-bats at AAA Richmond last year. Unfortunately, he hit only .252 with 21 walks. But he has a chance with Colorado if his glove is as good as they say.

RYAN W. HAWBLITZEL

Position: P **Opening Day Age:** 21
Bats: R **Throws:** R **Born:** 4/30/71 in West Palm Beach, FL
Ht: 6' 2" **Wt:** 170

Recent Statistics

	W	L	ERA	G	GS	Sv	IP	H	R	BB	SO	HR
91 A Winston-sal	15	2	2.28	20	20	0	134.0	110	40	47	103	7
91 AA Charlotte	1	2	3.21	5	5	0	33.2	31	14	12	25	2
92 AA Charlotte	12	8	3.76	28	28	0	174.2	180	84	38	119	18

One of the shocks in looking at the 15-man protected lists prior the draft was that the Cubs had not protected Hawblitzel, who'd been considered one of their best prospects. It was hard to figure. Not yet 22, Hawblitzel has a minor league record of 34-17 and was 12-8 at AA Charlotte in 1992. He doesn't have the greatest fastball in the world (around 83 MPH), but it sinks, and he has a nice curve. He can pitch, in other words. Did the Cubs know something the Rockies (and a lot of other people) didn't, or was Jose Vizcaino, a Cubs expansion protection, just too valuable to pass up? We'll see.

LANCE T. PAINTER

Position: P **Opening Day Age:** 25
Bats: L **Throws:** L **Born:** 7/21/67 in Bedford, England
Ht: 6' 1" **Wt:** 195

Recent Statistics

	W	L	ERA	G	GS	Sv	IP	H	R	BB	SO	HR
91 A Waterloo	14	8	2.30	28	28	0	200.0	162	64	57	201	14
92 AA Wichita	10	5	3.53	27	27	0	163.1	138	74	55	137	11

Former Padres draftee Lance Painter has a 31-16 record in three minor-league seasons, a 2.63 ERA, and 442 strikeouts in 435 innings -- very impressive. But San Diego felt his fastball wasn't as good as the record indicated, and left Painter unprotected into round two of the draft. The Rockies hope to be able to disagree. The lefty has excellent control as well as that great strikeout record, so he could be in Mile High Stadium (not a good park for lefties, it would seem) reasonably soon, perhaps in 1993.

ARMANDO REYNOSO

Position: P **Opening Day Age:** 26
Bats: R **Throws:** R **Born:** 5/1/66 in San Luis Potosi, Mex
Ht: 6' 0" **Wt:** 185

Recent Statistics

	W	L	ERA	G	GS	Sv	IP	H	R	BB	SO	HR
92 AAA Richmond	12	9	2.66	28	27	0	169.1	156	65	52	108	12
92 NL Atlanta	1	0	4.70	3	1	1	7.2	11	4	2	2	2

Richmond catchers used to claim that they'd have to give Reynoso signals with both hands since he has so many pitches. He doesn't throw hard but moves the ball around and changes speeds. He won the league ERA title in 1991 in Richmond but was never able to crack the tough Braves pitching staff. He can keep a team in games and should pitch in the National League in '93.

MO SANFORD

Position: P **Opening Day Age:** 26
Bats: R **Throws:** R **Born:** 12/24/66 in Americus, GA
Ht: 6' 6" **Wt:** 220

Recent Statistics

	W	L	ERA	G	GS	Sv	IP	H	R	BB	SO	HR
91 AA Chattanooga	7	4	2.74	16	16	0	95.1	69	37	55	124	7
91 AAA Nashville	3	0	1.60	5	5	0	33.2	19	7	22	38	0
92 AA Chattanooga	4	0	1.35	4	4	0	26.2	13	5	6	28	2
92 AAA Nashville	8	8	5.68	25	25	0	122.0	128	81	65	129	22

One of those guys who might profit from a change of scenery, Sanford got only a five-start trial with the Reds before they gave up on him. He has an extraordinary strikeout record (723 Ks in 642 minor-league innings), but his best pitch is his curveball, not the fastball. Sanford was only 8-8 with a 5.68 ERA at AAA Nashville last year, though he continued to strike people out. Control has always been Sanford's problem and he's also been plagued by too many hanging breaking pitches. With his record, Colorado may have to give him a chance.

HITTING:

Alex Arias entered the 1992 Chicago Cubs shortstop derby as its last entrant, earning full-time consideration due to a back injury to starter Rey Sanchez. In his first full game for the Cubs, he went 5-for-5 with his first 5 major-league hits and wound up hitting a solid .293 in 99 at-bats. His ability impressed the Marlins enough that they arranged a pre-draft trade with Chicago; Florida selected Greg Hibbard in order to deal him to the Cubs for Arias and Gary Scott.

Tall and lanky, Arias has some promise as a hitter. He is a spray hitter who looks to sting the ball hard on the ground but who does have a little power to the gaps. Arias was unique among the Cubs shortstops with his patient eye at the plate; he walked more times than he struck out in his minor-league career, and posted decent on-base averages throughout, including a .375 mark with the Cubs in limited duty.

Although his major-league experience is somewhat limited, Arias has a good knowledge of the strike zone. He'll continue to see a lot of fastballs, his primary diet in the number-eight hole while with the Cubs, until pitchers figure him out. Soon, he'll have to begin the tough adjustment to more offspeed stuff.

BASERUNNING:

Arias is a good baserunner who has stolen as many as 41 bases in a minor-league season. He isn't a blazer but has always had great stolen base success ratios in the minors. He likes to slap the ball down the line and has the speed to take three.

FIELDING:

Although possesing decent range afield, he was not as good as either Jose Vizcaino or Rey Sanchez. His arm is unproven but looks erratic. He was a league-leading fielder while with AA Charlotte in 1991, but one leading publication called him the Fred Gwynne of shortstops.

OVERALL:

Arias has one veteran shortstop standing in his way for a regular shortstop job, injury-riddled Walt Weiss. Arias certainly has the ability to better Weiss offensively, but must work hard in the off-season on defense to gain the Marlins' confidence.

ALEX ARIAS

Position: SS
Bats: R **Throws:** R
Ht: 6' 3" **Wt:** 185

Opening Day Age: 25
Born: 11/20/67 in New York, NY
ML Seasons: 1

Overall Statistics

	G	AB	R	H	D	T	HR	RBI	SB	BB	SO	AVG
1992	32	99	14	29	6	0	0	7	0	11	13	.293
Career	32	99	14	29	6	0	0	7	0	11	13	.293

Where He Hits the Ball

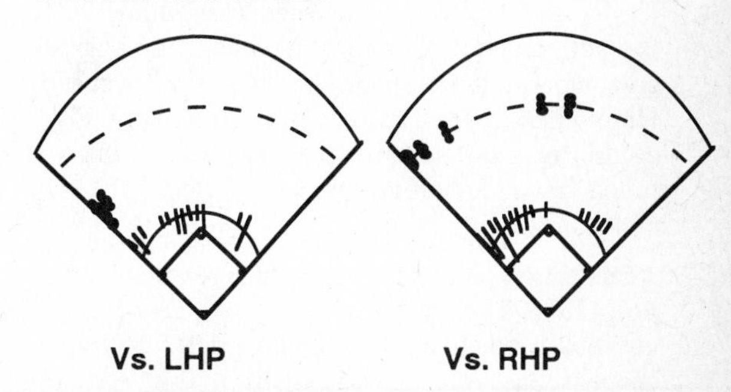

1992 Situational Stats

	AB	H	HR	RBI	AVG		AB	H	HR	RBI	AVG
Home	55	13	0	5	.236	LHP	41	13	0	2	.317
Road	44	16	0	2	.364	RHP	58	16	0	5	.276
Day	59	17	0	5	.288	Sc Pos	21	6	0	6	.286
Night	40	12	0	2	.300	Clutch	15	5	0	0	.333

1992 Rankings (National League)

- Did not rank near the top or bottom in any category

PITCHING:

The Indians had a plan for Jack Armstrong after they acquired him from Cincinnati before the 1992 season. They were going to let Armstrong start every fifth day, apply as little pressure as possible and let him try to pitch his way back to his 1990 form when he started the All-Star game for the National League. The plan didn't work. After 19 starts Armstrong was 2-13 and in danger of losing 20 games. So Armstrong was sent to the bullpen, working four more starts late in the year. He did an outstanding job in relief -- 3-0 with a 1.16 ERA over 31 innings. His move to the Marlins, however, might signal a move back into the rotation.

Hopefully, Armstrong learned something from his bullpen stint. Certainly he was more aggressive, worked more quickly and was very focused. He pitched as hard as he could for as long as he could. As a starter, Armstrong tended to think too much, pace himself and make bad pitches at crucial points of a game.

Armstrong's best pitch is a fastball that sometimes hits 92 MPH. He also throws a sharp slider, curveball and change-up, but his pitch selection is suspect. Last year he continually hurt himself by giving up home runs in close games. He's allowed 48 homers in the last two years.

HOLDING RUNNERS, FIELDING, HITTING:

Armstrong is a fine athlete but led Indians' pitchers with four errors last year. He didn't have much success holding runners, either. Armstrong at times became preoccupied with a baserunner -- often someone who wasn't a threat to steal -- and would throw to first base time and time again. On two occasions he ended up throwing the ball past the first baseman as the runner went to third. He's a poor hitter but can lay down a bunt.

OVERALL:

Armstrong's value lies in his good heat, experience, and major-league success as recently as 1990. But he's still a reclamation project. The Marlins have Bryan Harvey and several good middle relievers, so despite Armstrong's success in the pen last year, a return to the rotation is what the Marlins may have in mind for him.

JACK ARMSTRONG

Position: SP/RP
Bats: R **Throws:** R
Ht: 6' 5" **Wt:** 215

Opening Day Age: 28
Born: 3/7/65 in Englewood, NJ
ML Seasons: 5

Overall Statistics

	W	L	ERA	G	GS	Sv	IP	H	R	BB	SO	HR
1992	6	15	4.64	35	23	0	166.2	176	100	67	114	23
Career	31	47	4.62	114	95	0	580.1	588	330	239	385	70

How Often He Throws Strikes

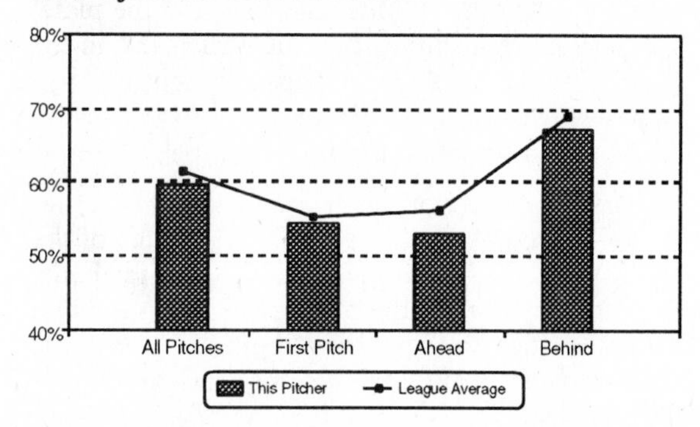

1992 Situational Stats

	W	L	ERA	Sv	IP		AB	H	HR	RBI	AVG
Home	5	5	4.54	0	73.1	LHB	277	76	10	42	.274
Road	1	10	4.72	0	93.1	RHB	377	100	13	50	.265
Day	3	5	4.95	0	40.0	Sc Pos	155	47	5	66	.303
Night	3	10	4.55	0	126.2	Clutch	31	9	0	2	.290

1992 Rankings (American League)

- 1st in lowest winning percentage (.286)
- 2nd in balks (3)
- 3rd in highest ERA (4.64) and losses (15)
- 4th in highest slugging percentage allowed (.430) and least GDPs induced per GDP situation (.43)
- 5th most home runs allowed per 9 innings (1.2) and highest batting average allowed with runners in scoring position (.303)
- 7th in most baserunners allowed per 9 innings (13.3)
- Led the Indians in losses, walks allowed (67), pickoff throws (190), stolen bases allowed (15) and most strikeouts per 9 innings

BRET BARBERIE

Position: 3B/2B
Bats: B **Throws:** R
Ht: 5'11" **Wt:** 180

Opening Day Age: 25
Born: 8/16/67 in Long Beach, CA
ML Seasons: 2

HITTING:

After a 1991 season in which he flashed some exciting numbers, including a .353 average in 57 games, then-Expos manager Tom Runnells felt justified in handing Bret Barberie the third base job and shifting Gold Glove winner and team captain Tim Wallach over to first. Controversy ensued. The normally stoic Wallach was visibly unhappy, both the fans and the media criticized the decision, and Barberie was placed in an awkward position. Literally. Not only was Barberie dreadful at third (.897 fielding average in the first half), he also forgot how to hit. He was so out of synch (his swing was both too long and too slow), that he requested a demotion to AAA. Barberie eventually returned, but at the end of the year the Expos made him available in the expansion draft and Florida selected him with their third pick.

Barberie played better after the All-Star break (.252) until he was disabled with a sprained wrist which prevented him from batting right-handed the rest of the season. Overall the switch-hitter had just 11 hits in 67 at-bats (.164) from the right side of the plate. Despite all his problems, Barberie posted a fine .354 on-base percentage. He is a good low-ball hitter who tends to drop his hands far too early on high pitches.

BASERUNNING:

Barberie hustles around the basepaths with above-average speed. He has the potential to steal in double figures and was good for nine steals in 14 attempts last season.

FIELDING:

At third base, Barberie had numerous problems. At various times, he shifted his feet and broke for the ball poorly, could not catch the ball, or threw wildly. Barberie performed much better at second base, fielding .989 in part time action and displayed good range and a strong arm. Second is where the Marlins plan to play him.

OVERALL:

Being selected in the expansion draft was a great break for Barberie. With his new club he can play second base, his best position, and not be under the pressure he was under in Montreal. He should blossom in his new environment.

Overall Statistics

	G	AB	R	H	D	T	HR	RBI	SB	BB	SO	AVG
1992	111	285	26	66	11	0	1	24	9	47	62	.232
Career	168	421	42	114	23	2	3	42	9	67	84	.271

Where He Hits the Ball

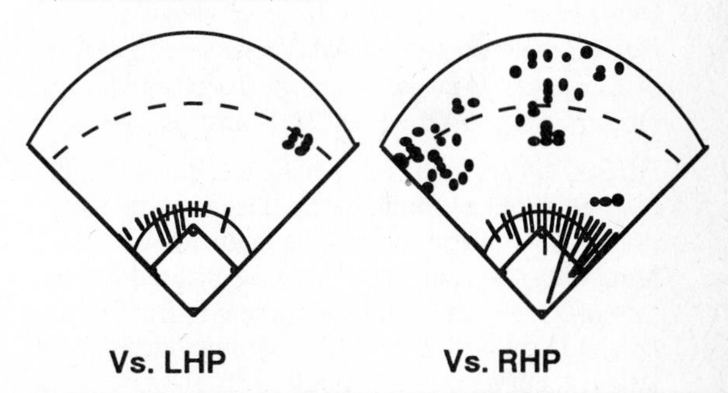

1992 Situational Stats

	AB	H	HR	RBI	AVG		AB	H	HR	RBI	AVG
Home	132	38	0	15	.288	LHP	67	11	0	7	.164
Road	153	28	1	9	.183	RHP	218	55	1	17	.252
Day	112	22	1	9	.196	Sc Pos	75	17	0	23	.227
Night	173	44	0	15	.254	Clutch	62	14	0	7	.226

1992 Rankings (National League)

- 2nd in batting average on a 3-1 count (.750)
- 4th in hit by pitch (8)
- 6th in lowest batting average with 2 strikes (.130)
- Led the Expos in hit by pitch and batting average on a 3-1 count
- Led NL third basemen in batting average on a 3-1 count

PITCHING:

The expansion draft might have been the big break that former number-one draft choice Ryan Bowen needed to finally get his career together. The 13th player chosen in the 1986 amateur draft, Bowen is one of those guys who's known to have a great arm. He hasn't exactly had great results -- especially in 1992, when he was an almost unbelievable 0-7 with a 10.96 ERA in 11 games with Houston.

The Astros always felt Bowen had the pitches to be a winner, and he showed some promise by going 6-4 as a rookie in 1991 though with a pretty high ERA (5.15). Bowen looked good last spring and opened the 1992 season in the Astros' starting rotation, but as his record shows he was a disaster. Bowen went down to AAA Tucson and got himself together. He was 7-6 for the Toros and fanned an impressive 94 men in 122.1 innings.

After six years in the minors, Bowen has probably learned about as much in the bushes as he's ever going to. Control has always been his big problem. With the Astros last year he walked 30 batters in 33.2 innings, hit two others and uncorked five wild pitches. Bowen has an outstanding fastball and curve, but opponents batted .333 against him because he had to take so much off his heater in order to get it over the plate.

HOLDING RUNNERS, FIELDING, HITTING:

Bowen is adequate in the field at best, though he played errorless ball last year. With all his pitching problems, he hasn't devoted much attention to major-league baserunners and it shows: though he's pitched only 105.1 innings, he's permitted 17 steals in 21 attempts. He looks like he'll be an average hitting pitcher (.161 lifetime).

OVERALL:

Bowen was a late expansion selection and should be a major project this spring for Marcel Lachemann and his brother Rene, who are known for their work with pitchers. He can throw in the low 90s and has a good breaking ball; he needs some confidence, but mostly he needs to learn how to get the ball over the plate.

RYAN BOWEN

Position: SP
Bats: R **Throws:** R
Ht: 6' 0" **Wt:** 185

Opening Day Age: 25
Born: 2/10/68 in Hanford, CA
ML Seasons: 2

Overall Statistics

	W	L	ERA	G	GS	Sv	IP	H	R	BB	SO	HR
1992	0	7	10.96	11	9	0	33.2	48	43	30	22	8
Career	6	11	7.01	25	22	0	105.1	121	86	66	71	12

How Often He Throws Strikes

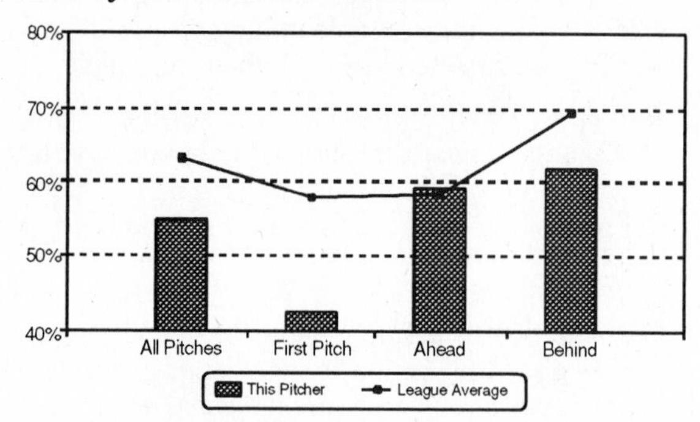

1992 Situational Stats

	W	L	ERA	Sv	IP		AB	H	HR	RBI	AVG
Home	0	4	9.43	0	21.0	LHB	76	30	2	19	.395
Road	0	3	13.50	0	12.2	RHB	68	18	6	16	.265
Day	0	2	14.85	0	6.2	Sc Pos	49	16	3	25	.327

1992 Rankings (National League)

➟ Led the Astros in wild pitches (5)

CRIS CARPENTER

Position: RP
Bats: R **Throws:** R
Ht: 6' 1" **Wt:** 185
Opening Day Age: 28
Born: 4/5/65 in St. Augustine, FL
ML Seasons: 5

PITCHING:

Poor Cris Carpenter. He's so good at his job that the only time he attracts attention is when he makes a mistake. He did that a couple of times in 1992, but for the most part he built on his success of 1991 and continued as one of the most effective middle relievers in the game. The Marlins noticed his sometimes anonymous performance and made him their 19th pick in the expansion draft.

Carpenter throws hard and has his greatest success when he pitches for short stretches. He appeared 73 times last year, sixth in the league, but pitched more than two innings only three times and only once hurled as many as three innings. He was the first pitcher summoned from the pen in about half his appearances, finished 21 games, and generally pitched whenever they needed him. His 10.2 baserunners per nine innings was 10th best in the league for relievers.

What dogged Carpenter's 1992 season were home runs, which are especially rough on middle relievers; he allowed 10 longballs and the Cardinals lost nine of those games, and he gave up 14 of his 29 earned runs from his homers. Carpenter simply made mistakes, giving them up on the first pitch, when ahead in the count and when behind. He gave up four dingers in five games in July. When not allowing homers he allowed runs in only 10 of 63 appearances.

HOLDING RUNNERS, FIELDING, HITTING:

Carpenter fields his position well, committing no errors last year. He repeated his 1991 hitting totals of 1-for-3, but doubled his RBI total to two. Carpenter was vulnerable to the running game, allowing 11 steals, but Tom Pagnozzi had some trouble and could be held to blame partially for this.

OVERALL:

Carpenter is an extremely valuable pitcher, but the home runs simply kill him. In June Carpenter said, "I'm still making stupid pitches with the game on the line." The problem haunted him all season, but the Marlins got a fine pitcher nevertheless. He'll probably find himself setting up a top reliever once again, only Bryan Harvey this time instead of Lee Smith.

Overall Statistics

	W	L	ERA	G	GS	Sv	IP	H	R	BB	SO	HR
1992	5	4	2.97	73	0	1	88.0	69	29	27	46	10
Career	21	15	3.66	180	13	1	277.2	253	121	84	158	25

How Often He Throws Strikes

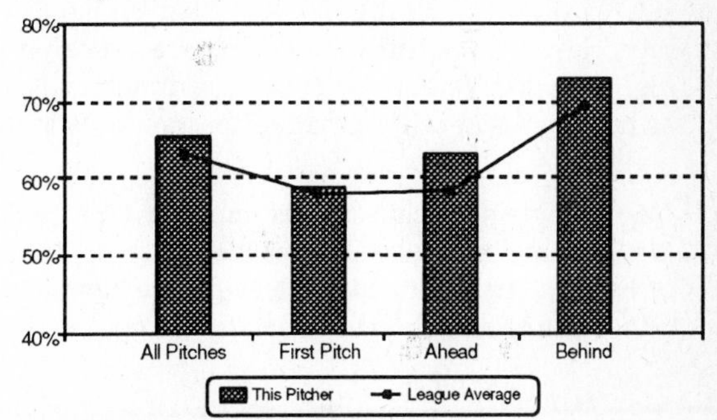

1992 Situational Stats

	W	L	ERA	Sv	IP		AB	H	HR	RBI	AVG
Home	1	1	3.59	1	42.2	LHB	162	36	6	27	.222
Road	4	3	2.38	0	45.1	RHB	151	33	4	18	.219
Day	2	3	3.44	0	18.1	Sc Pos	106	21	2	33	.198
Night	3	1	2.84	1	69.2	Clutch	121	31	6	21	.256

1992 Rankings (National League)

- 6th in games pitched (73) and blown saves (7)
- 7th in relief innings (88) and least strikeouts per 9 innings in relief (4.7)
- 10th in least baserunners allowed per 9 innings in relief (10.2)

GREAT SPEED

CHUCK CARR

Position: CF
Bats: B **Throws:** R
Ht: 5'10" **Wt:** 165

Opening Day Age: 24
Born: 8/10/68 in San Bernardino, CA
ML Seasons: 3

Overall Statistics

	G	AB	R	H	D	T	HR	RBI	SB	BB	SO	AVG
1992	22	64	8	14	3	0	0	3	10	9	6	.219
Career	38	77	9	16	3	0	0	4	12	9	10	.208

Where He Hits the Ball

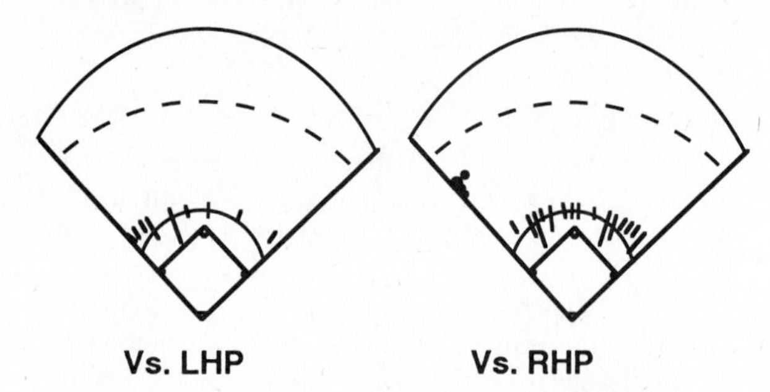

Vs. LHP **Vs. RHP**

1992 Situational Stats

	AB	H	HR	RBI	AVG		AB	H	HR	RBI	AVG
Home	23	6	0	0	.261	LHP	24	6	0	0	.250
Road	41	8	0	3	.195	RHP	40	8	0	3	.200
Day	15	1	0	1	.067	Sc Pos	15	3	0	3	.200
Night	49	13	0	2	.265	Clutch	8	1	0	2	.125

1992 Rankings (National League)

→ Did not rank near the top or bottom in any category

HITTING:

Willie Mays Hayes from the movie "Major League" has nothing on Chuck Carr. A no-hit speed-burner, the switch-hitting Carr bounced from the Reds to the Mariners to the Mets before the candles were cold on his 20th birthday cake. But Carr made some progress with the Mets and even more after coming to the Cardinals. He is now looking at a starting role in the Florida outfield.

In 1990 Carr was voted the most exciting player in the Texas League and even had a couple of call-ups with the Mets. His real break came in 1992. He started the year at AA Arkansas and ended it in St. Louis; in between he hit .308 at AAA Louisville, the first .300 season in his career. Between the three stops Carr drew a career high 48 walks. It increased his value dramatically, as he is a player whose main offensive impact is on the basepaths.

Carr's September call-up was impressive despite his low final numbers. He reached base in eight of his first 16 plate appearances before having a minor slump and showed great discipline.

BASERUNNING:

In his first two pro seasons Carr was 29-of-31 as a basestealer and has never been below 70 percent success. Carr is 12-of-14 in the majors. Voted the fastest baserunner in the International League in 1991, Carr can stretch triples and in 1992 he totaled 93 runs scored. He can burn.

FIELDING:

Carr is a spectacular fielder. He was voted the best outfielder in the Texas League in 1990 and the man with the best outfield arm in 1992 in the American Association. He is sure-handed and can play all three outfield positions, but center is probably his best.

OVERALL:

Carr could open the season in center, but can he get on base? One .308 season doesn't make a hitter, and only twice has his on-base average peeked above .327 in 13 different stops. If he can hit .280 and walk 45 times he'll be a name. If not, he'll be a defensive replacement and a pinch-runner.

PITCHING:

Scott Chiamparino returned to the majors last year after a 15-month absence caused by ligament reconstruction surgery on his elbow in July of 1991. He climbed five levels back to the majors during his 1992 rehabilitation, posting ERAs under 2.87 at four stops before making four starts for Texas in September and October. Despite his 0-4 record and more elbow problems -- he needed another operation after the season to relieve nerve tension -- Chiamparino showed enough to draw the interest of the Marlins, who took him in the middle of the second round.

Florida is the righthander's third organization in four years. Chiamparino was traded to the Rangers in 1990 with Joe Bitker for Harold Baines. Since Baines had come from the White Sox for two of Texas' best prospects, Sammy Sosa and Wilson Alvarez, Chiamparino was expected to provide some return on the two big deals. He couldn't do that for Texas because of his elbow problems.

Chiamparino didn't do a lot of pitching for the Rangers. He totaled just 11 starts for Texas in 1990 and 1991 with a combined 3.15 ERA. He has a 90+ MPH fastball, a pretty good slider, and a change-up. He lost all four of his starts in 1992 but pitched very well in two games and horribly in the other two. He simply had no support in the good starts and not enough support in the bad ones.

HOLDING RUNNERS, FIELDING, HITTING:

Chiamparino is not bad at holding runners, but his defensive work was awful last year with two errors in five chances. He'll have to learn to hit in the majors after having spent his pro career in the American League.

OVERALL:

The Rangers couldn't really afford to lose a starter even one with injury problems. Florida gets another pitcher with major-league experience and some major-league success. In the past Chiamparino has had the reputation of being cocky and immature, but his talent has been unquestioned. Now he has the chance to be a rotation anchor on a young team -- if his arm is sound.

SCOTT CHIAMPARINO

Position: SP
Bats: L **Throws:** R
Ht: 6' 2" **Wt:** 205

Opening Day Age: 26
Born: 8/22/66 in San Mateo, CA
ML Seasons: 3

Overall Statistics

	W	L	ERA	G	GS	Sv	IP	H	R	BB	SO	HR
1992	0	4	3.55	4	4	0	25.1	25	11	5	13	2
Career	2	6	3.27	15	15	0	85.1	87	36	29	40	4

How Often He Throws Strikes

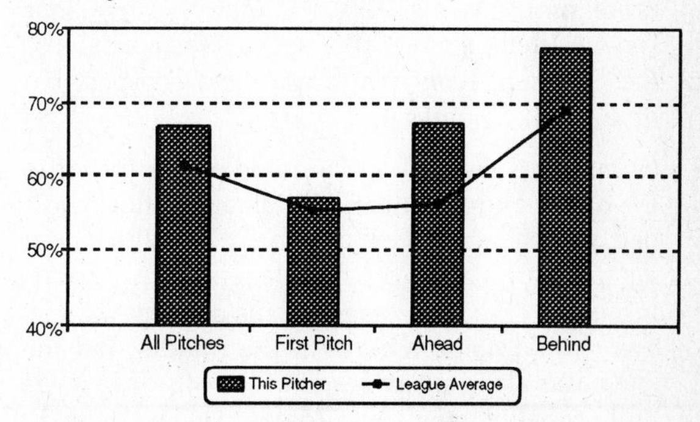

1992 Situational Stats

	W	L	ERA	Sv	IP		AB	H	HR	RBI	AVG
Home	0	1	6.75	0	5.1	LHB	42	13	1	3	.310
Road	0	3	2.70	0	20.0	RHB	54	12	1	6	.222
Day	0	2	1.29	0	14.0	Sc Pos	27	6	1	8	.222
Night	0	2	6.35	0	11.1	Clutch	7	1	0	0	.143

1992 Rankings (American League)

- Did not rank near the top or bottom in any category

JEFF CONINE

Position: LF
Bats: R **Throws:** R
Ht: 6' 1" **Wt:** 220

Opening Day Age: 26
Born: 6/27/66 in Tacoma, WA
ML Seasons: 2

HITTING:

Long considered the Royals' best prospect, first sacker Jeff Conine found himself eligible for the expansion draft in a questionable decision by Kansas City. The Royals elected to protect weak-hitting shortstop David Howard over Conine because they had depth at first base (with Wally Joyner) but not at short. The Marlins were delighted to be able to select him in the first round.

Conine got his first real shot with the Royals last August. He showed little of his minor-league power batting .253 with no homers in 91 at-bats before a mid-September ribcage pull cut his season short. But before being recalled, Conine had batted .302 with 20 homers in AAA Omaha -- quite similar to his .320, 15-homer performance for AA Memphis (1990) when he was considered the Southern League's second-best prospect behind Frank Thomas.

Conine hits the ball up the middle, has power to the alleys and is primarily a fastball hitter who's had trouble with breaking balls. He's hit better against lefties in his brief big-league career, sporting a career .320 average versus southpaws. His eye should come around in the majors, but the .500-plus slugging averages of the minor-leagues will probably translate to 25 doubles and 15 to 20 homers at best in Florida.

BASERUNNING:

Although Conine's been a good basestealer in past seasons, minor-league numbers can be misleading. He runs conservatively. Conine may open up his running game, but at 220 pounds he's no burner.

FIELDING:

Conine was elected the best defensive first baseman in the American Association. Because of Joyner the Royals had to use him in left field and his lack of experience showed. He'll very likely be back at first for the Marlins.

OVERALL:

Conine no longer has to stand in Joyner's shadow and will be called upon to cast his own shadow for the Marlins. They need his power even more than the Royals did. His wrist injury has healed, and this is his big chance. Early projections had him as the Marlins cleanup hitter.

Overall Statistics

	G	AB	R	H	D	T	HR	RBI	SB	BB	SO	AVG
1992	28	91	10	23	5	2	0	9	0	8	23	.253
Career	37	111	13	28	7	2	0	11	0	10	28	.252

Where He Hits the Ball

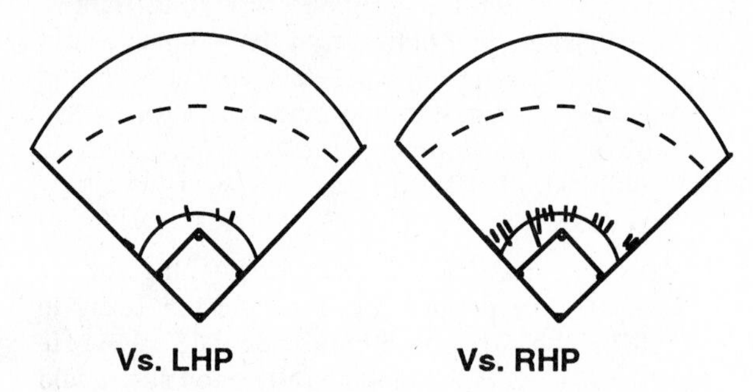

1992 Situational Stats

	AB	H	HR	RBI	AVG		AB	H	HR	RBI	AVG
Home	31	8	0	6	.258	LHP	23	7	0	3	.304
Road	60	15	0	3	.250	RHP	68	16	0	6	.235
Day	25	7	0	2	.280	Sc Pos	23	9	0	9	.391
Night	66	16	0	7	.242	Clutch	14	3	0	0	.214

1992 Rankings (American League)

- Did not rank near the top or bottom in any category

JIM CORSI

Position: RP
Bats: R **Throws:** R
Ht: 6' 1" **Wt:** 220

Opening Day Age: 31
Born: 9/9/61 in Newton, MA
ML Seasons: 4

PITCHING:

The only teams that hit well against Jim Corsi last year were Detroit and American League playoff foe Toronto. Corsi entered the ALCS with a 5.06 career regular season ERA (six earned runs over 10.2 innings) against the Blue Jays. He appeared in three ALCS games totaling two innings, and although he did not give up a run, Toronto collected two hits and three walks against him. So Corsi can see one advantage about being picked up by Florida in the expansion draft: with the Marlins, he doesn't figure to have to worry about the Blue Jays for a while.

Other than Toronto, Corsi seemed to have little problem with the American League in his 32 appearances last year. He was recalled the second time from AAA Tacoma on June 30 and went 3-1 in 27 games after the All-Star break, allowing only three earned runs over 35.2 innings for a 0.76 ERA. By the end of the season he had earned the important set-up job for Dennis Eckersley.

Corsi signed a minor-league contract with the A's late in the spring after being released by Houston in 1991 even though he had delivered a good year for the Astros. His stuff is pretty basic: an 86 MPH fastball, a slider, and a sinker. The sinker is probably his most effective pitch; he gets a huge number of groundball outs and he's very effective at riding it in on right-handed hitters. He's much more effective against righties than lefties.

HOLDING RUNNERS, FIELDING, HITTING:

A big man at 6'1" and 220 pounds, Corsi is a little slow in his defensive reactions though he played errorless ball last year. After having problems holding runners in the past, he improved last year; five of the 10 runners who tried to steal against Corsi were thrown out. He has only one at-bat in the majors, a strikeout.

OVERALL:

Corsi has had success in the National League before and he should again. The Marlins have young or erratic starters, so the relief corps, was looked upon by Dave Dombrowski as especially important. Corsi was one of the veterans selected to stabilize the young staff's development.

Overall Statistics

	W	L	ERA	G	GS	Sv	IP	H	R	BB	SO	HR
1992	4	2	1.43	32	0	0	44.0	44	12	18	19	2
Career	5	10	2.78	112	1	0	181.1	166	67	57	103	11

How Often He Throws Strikes

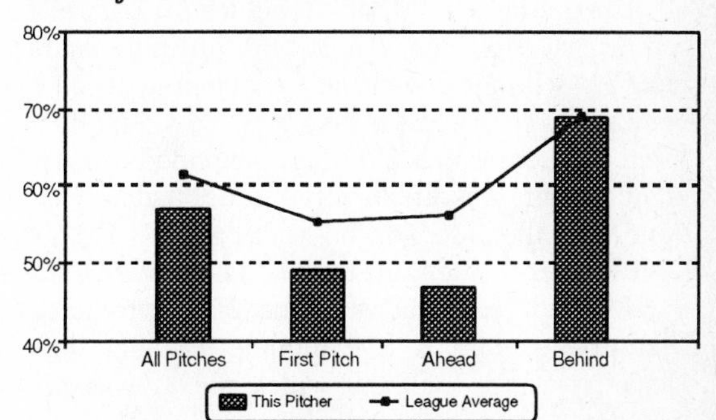

1992 Situational Stats

	W	L	ERA	Sv	IP		AB	H	HR	RBI	AVG
Home	4	1	0.45	0	20.0	LHB	70	25	1	8	.357
Road	0	1	2.25	0	24.0	RHB	90	19	1	10	.211
Day	1	0	1.23	0	7.1	Sc Pos	42	6	0	14	.143
Night	3	2	1.47	0	36.2	Clutch	58	20	2	6	.345

1992 Rankings (American League)

- 5th in lowest batting average allowed in relief with runners in scoring position (.143)
- 6th in lowest batting average allowed in relief with runners on base (.177)
- Led the A's in lowest batting average allowed in relief with runners on base and lowest batting average allowed in relief with runners in scoring position

HITTING:

By now, Steve Decker was supposed to be starring behind the plate for the Giants. In the three years since he hit .296 and slugged .500 in 54 late-season at-bats in 1990, nothing has gone right for Decker. Many blame the Giants for rushing him from AA ball to the majors, then expecting immediate results. The problems started in '91 when Decker choked on the curveball and hit just .206. He had run-ins with the coaches and pitchers over his handling of the staff and lost the starting job. In 1992 he was 26 years old and back at AAA Phoenix, buried behind Kirt Manwaring and eventually left available for Florida in the second round of expansion.

Decker put his swing back together in AAA last season. He started out smoking, hitting around .350 but without power before finishing at .282. He had his moments, hitting a grand slam and a three-run homer in a 15-7 loss; he ended up with eight homers despite cavernous Scottsdale Stadium. But then Decker did nothing in 43 at-bats after his September call-up and has now hit .215 in 330 major league at-bats. The Giants protected Manwaring, who is five months younger than Decker, so time will tell which player was the better risk.

BASERUNNING:

Decker has just 13 minor-league steals and two since 1990. He is 0-for-1 in the pros and has only five career triples. Speed is not part of his game and he is basically a station-to-station man on the bases.

FIELDING:

A converted third baseman, Decker has a good arm but struggles with mechanical problems at times. His reputation as a leader and a good handler of pitchers took a beating in San Francisco, but he was really better than Terry Kennedy and Manwaring in terms of producing good staff ERAs.

OVERALL:

This is a guy who was going to be a big star; it's amazing how quickly and far his star has fallen despite his many positives. In Decker the Marlins got a valuable player with a great chance to improve. He'll probably start ahead of Bob Natal.

STEVE DECKER

Position: C
Bats: R **Throws:** R
Ht: 6' 3" **Wt:** 205

Opening Day Age: 27
Born: 10/25/65 in Rock Island, IL
ML Seasons: 3

Overall Statistics

	G	AB	R	H	D	T	HR	RBI	SB	BB	SO	AVG
1992	15	43	3	7	1	0	0	1	0	6	7	.163
Career	109	330	19	71	10	1	8	33	0	23	61	.215

Where He Hits the Ball

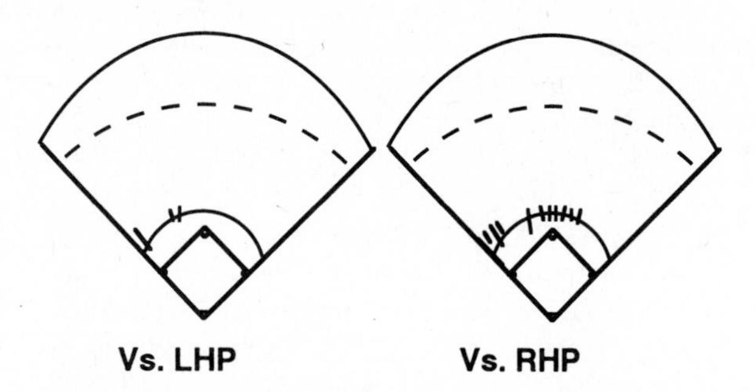

1992 Situational Stats

	AB	H	HR	RBI	AVG		AB	H	HR	RBI	AVG
Home	20	2	0	1	.100	LHP	13	1	0	0	.077
Road	23	5	0	0	.217	RHP	30	6	0	1	.200
Day	9	2	0	0	.222	Sc Pos	8	2	0	1	.250
Night	34	5	0	1	.147	Clutch	7	1	0	1	.143

1992 Rankings (National League)

➡ Did not rank near the top or bottom in any category

CHRIS DONNELS

Position: 3B/2B
Bats: L **Throws:** R
Ht: 6' 0" **Wt:** 185

Opening Day Age: 26
Born: 4/21/66 in Los Angeles, CA
ML Seasons: 2

Overall Statistics

	G	AB	R	H	D	T	HR	RBI	SB	BB	SO	AVG
1992	45	121	8	21	4	0	0	6	1	17	25	.174
Career	82	210	15	41	6	0	0	11	2	31	44	.195

Where He Hits the Ball

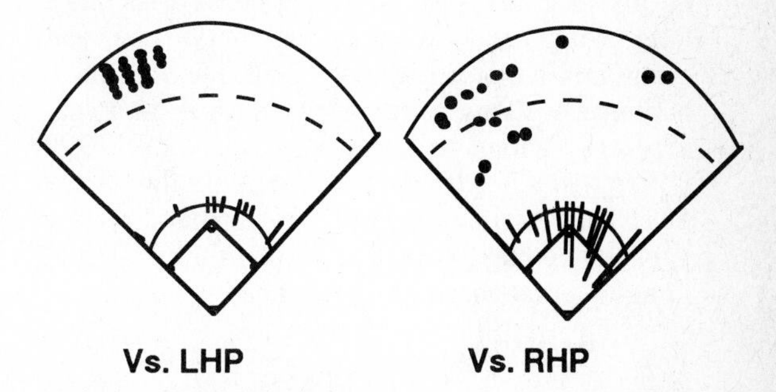

Vs. LHP　　Vs. RHP

1992 Situational Stats

	AB	H	HR	RBI	AVG		AB	H	HR	RBI	AVG
Home	65	9	0	4	.138	LHP	24	4	0	1	.167
Road	56	12	0	2	.214	RHP	97	17	0	5	.175
Day	26	2	0	0	.077	Sc Pos	18	4	0	4	.222
Night	95	19	0	6	.200	Clutch	22	5	0	1	.227

1992 Rankings (National League)

- 1st in lowest batting average on a 3-2 count (.063)

HITTING:

Former Mets prospect Chris Donnels has been a minor-league star, hitting as many as 17 homers and batting over .300 four times. A patient hitter, he's had an on-base average below .370 just once in eight stops and has topped .415 four times. Donnels is primarily a groundball hitter, and his patient eye often gets him into the position of knowing that he's going to get a ball he can drive.

After hitting .303 with 56 RBI in just 287 at-bats for AAA Tidewater in 1991, Donnels had a good chance to make the Mets last year. But he didn't hit in the Spring and was not on the opening day roster. He was soon recalled, didn't play much and got sent down. He again hit .301 with a .419 OBP before being recalled in late July. Donnels ended the year with just a .174 1992 average as a major leaguer, raising questions with the Mets' brass about his true ability. His poor showing in two trials -- .195 in 210 at-bats -- cost him the protection of the Mets but bought him a new chance in Florida.

BASERUNNING:

Donnels is smart and fairly speedy and turned in a perfect 12-for-12 stealing record for Tidewater in 1992. His best season was an 18-for-22 mark in 1989, but stealing will probably not be a major part of his game for the Marlins. He is a good baserunner who will probably deliver around 10 steals.

FIELDING:

Donnels has good range, so much so that the Mets even tried him at second base. He was pretty good there for an inexperienced fielder. He's very good at third and that's where he should play for Florida. He'll most likely battle it out with Gary Scott for regular time.

OVERALL:

Donnels can hit, and his struggles with the Mets seem to be just ill-timed slumps. Donnels and Scott are rather similar in that they have both delivered wonderful minor-league seasons and then been utterly helpless in the majors. Like a prize fight, the first palooka who gets off the canvas wins.

HITTING:

A big-time college star at Oklahoma State, Monty Fariss was the Rangers' number-one draft choice (and the sixth player selected) in the 1988 amateur draft. According to the original plan, Fariss should have been well-established as the Rangers' shortstop by now. That plan went out the window with his draft by the Marlins, his chance to be a local hero has gone. But his chance to be a regular major leaguer is just beginning.

Fariss finally got a chance with the Rangers last year and batted .217 with three homers in 166 at-bats. His main problem was that he continued to strike out at an alarming rate (51 times). He's not a player who chases numerous bad pitches; he'll swing and miss on good ones. Fariss has a long swing and some scouts feel that he can't get around on a major-league fastball. He does have patience, walking as many as 98 times in a season, and his long swing generates power. In 1990 Fariss had 47 extra-base hits and another 55 in 1991. He hits sharp ground balls that find the gaps, so he may have better luck in the National League where there's more turf.

BASERUNNING:

Fariss is 0-for-2 as a major-league thief and has never stolen more than 12 bases in a season. But his speed is adequate; he can stretch for doubles and hit nine triples in Oklahoma City in 1991.

FIELDING:

Fariss has also had numerous defensive problems and isn't a shortstop anymore. He kept making throwing errors on routine throws like Steve Sax did in the mid-1980s. Texas eventually moved him to the outfield and it looks like he'll be able to handle left field.

OVERALL:

Fariss now has to fight it out with half-a-dozen or so other phenoms, but he may emerge as a starter in Florida. He can hit; many of his competitors are merely fast and play good defense. He's still only 25 and could become one of the better hitters on the team.

MONTY FARISS

Position: LF/2B/RF
Bats: R **Throws:** R
Ht: 6' 4" **Wt:** 205

Opening Day Age: 25
Born: 10/13/67 in Cordell, OK
ML Seasons: 2

Overall Statistics

	G	AB	R	H	D	T	HR	RBI	SB	BB	SO	AVG
1992	67	166	13	36	7	1	3	21	0	17	51	.217
Career	86	197	19	44	8	1	4	27	0	24	62	.223

Where He Hits the Ball

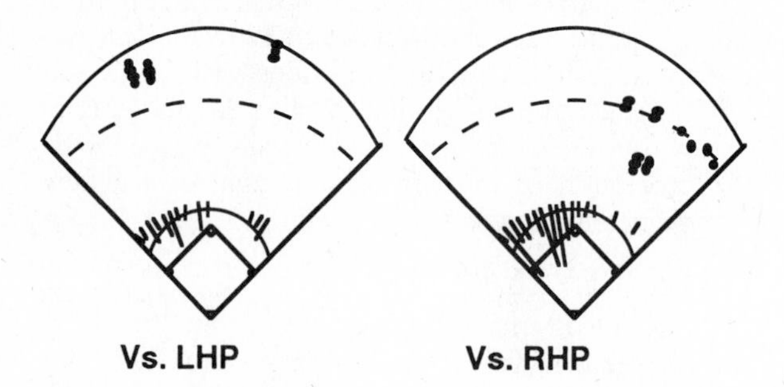

1992 Situational Stats

	AB	H	HR	RBI	AVG		AB	H	HR	RBI	AVG
Home	74	18	0	9	.243	LHP	75	14	2	11	.187
Road	92	18	3	12	.196	RHP	91	22	1	10	.242
Day	28	2	0	0	.071	Sc Pos	47	10	0	14	.213
Night	138	34	3	21	.246	Clutch	33	9	1	3	.273

1992 Rankings (American League)

- 1st in lowest batting average on a 3-2 count (.000)

JUNIOR FELIX

Position: CF
Bats: B **Throws:** R
Ht: 5'11" **Wt:** 165

Opening Day Age: 25
Born: 10/3/67 in Laguna Sabada, Dominican Republic
ML Seasons: 4

HITTING:

Junior Felix could turn out to be the steal of the expansion draft. After batting .283 for the Angels in 1991 despite two stints on the disabled list, Felix slumped to a career-low .246 last year while again spending time on the DL. The Marlins think he can do a lot better than that.

A switch-hitter, Felix has hit as many as 15 home runs in a season but had just nine last year. He likes to pull the ball against lefties but goes the other way against righties. He has respectable power from either side and is always capable of taking a fastball deep. Until 1992, he had hit better from the left side; last year he hit .271 righty, .238 lefty.

Felix drove in 72 runs last year, a career high and easily the best on the Angel club (Gary Gaetti was next with only 48). He also led the club with 22 doubles and five triples. But the 165-pound Felix continued his career trend of wearing down in the second half. He hit .264 with 43 RBI before the All-Star break, .225 with 29 RBI afterward. Lifetime, Felix's figures are .274, 25 HR, 143 RBI before the break, just .237-10-66 after it.

BASERUNNING:

Despite impressive speed, Felix is not an effective baserunner. He has never stolen at higher than a 62 percent clip and last season was merely 8-for-16. He does not get a good jump and is susceptible to being picked off.

FIELDING:

Felix's range in center field is average, but the Marlins are loaded with center fielders. He may therefore move to right, where his strong but erratic arm (nine assists in 1992) will be welcome. He is better going back on the ball than charging it.

OVERALL:

Felix is just 25 (although there are questions in this regard) and is established as a major-league player. He is coming into his prime as an athlete, so a step forward is quite likely. Still, the Angels weren't exactly loaded with offense but nevertheless left him unprotected into the third round of the draft, so there is obviously some room for doubt. With the Marlins Felix will be called upon to supply some sock and RBI production.

Overall Statistics

	G	AB	R	H	D	T	HR	RBI	SB	BB	SO	AVG
1992	139	509	63	125	22	5	9	72	8	33	128	.246
Career	442	1617	230	419	69	22	35	209	46	122	383	.259

Where He Hits the Ball

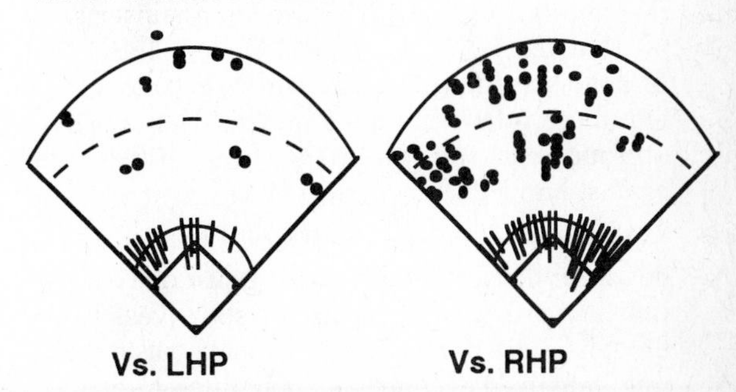

1992 Situational Stats

	AB	H	HR	RBI	AVG		AB	H	HR	RBI	AVG
Home	251	62	5	32	.247	LHP	118	32	3	18	.271
Road	258	63	4	40	.244	RHP	391	93	6	54	.238
Day	164	42	5	31	.256	Sc Pos	141	37	2	59	.262
Night	345	83	4	41	.241	Clutch	81	15	1	3	.185

1992 Rankings (American League)

- 3rd in lowest on-base percentage (.289)
- 6th in lowest on-base percentage vs. right-handed pitchers (.291)
- 7th in lowest batting average vs. right-handed pitchers (.238)
- 8th in highest percentage of swings that missed (28.0%)
- Led the Angels in doubles (22), triples (5), RBI (72), sacrifice flies (9), strikeouts (128), least GDPs per GDP situation (9.3%) and highest batting average vs. left-handed pitchers (.271)

STOPPER

PITCHING:

After a breakthrough year in 1991 (1.60 ERA, a league-leading 46 saves), Angels ace reliever Bryan Harvey found himself on the disabled list in June with a sore right elbow. He never returned to the Anaheim mound. At season's end the Marlins exposed the high-salaried Harvey to the expansion draft, and Florida surprised them by taking a chance on the righty.

Harvey's pitching last year was less effective than in 1991, but that was due primarily to the sore elbow. According to Harvey, the pain made it virtually impossible to throw his forkball, his best pitch and the only one he throws besides his excellent fastball. The difference was apparent in his work against right-handed batters. In 1991 Harvey allowed just a .172 average against righties, but the figure rose to .250 in '92. As the forkball stayed up in the strike zone, batters hurt him more often with the long ball. Harvey gave up four home runs in a total of just 106 at-bats against him.

Not that Harvey was ineffective before going down for the season. He gave up just one earned run in April while picking up six saves. Even though he was pitching hurt, his strikeout-to-walk ratio remained excellent at about three-to-one.

HOLDING RUNNERS, FIELDING, HITTING:

No runner has been caught stealing while Harvey has been on the mound since 1990. However, after allowing 12 steals in 1991, he permitted only two in '92 -- an improvement, even after noting that he pitched about a third as many innings. As a power pitcher, Harvey has a tendency to fall off the mound awkwardly, leading to some problems as a fielder. He'll bat too seldom for hitting to be a concern.

OVERALL:

The Marlins swear he was not acquired as trade bait. "If anything can deflate a team fast, it's losing games late," said GM Dave Dombrowski. There are very few relievers who are as effective as Harvey when healthy, and if he fully recovers, Florida has the ninth inning sewn up.

BRYAN HARVEY

Position: RP
Bats: R **Throws:** R
Ht: 6' 2" **Wt:** 212

Opening Day Age: 29
Born: 6/2/63 in Chattanooga, TN
ML Seasons: 6

Overall Statistics

	W	L	ERA	G	GS	Sv	IP	H	R	BB	SO	HR
1992	0	4	2.83	25	0	13	28.2	22	12	11	34	4
Career	16	20	2.49	250	0	126	307.2	219	99	126	365	24

How Often He Throws Strikes

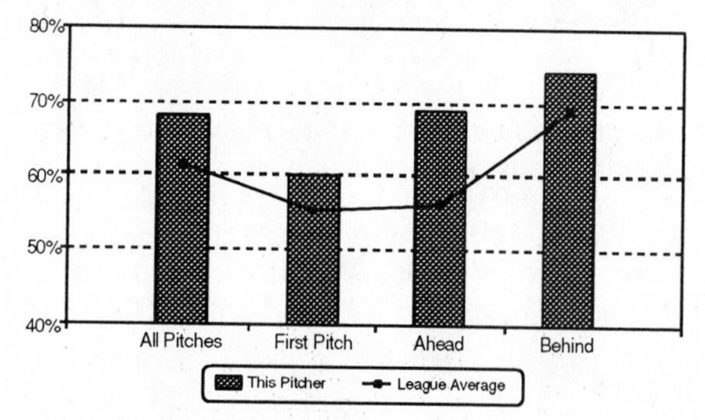

1992 Situational Stats

	W	L	ERA	Sv	IP		AB	H	HR	RBI	AVG
Home	0	3	3.07	6	14.2	LHB	58	10	2	7	.172
Road	0	1	2.57	7	14.0	RHB	48	12	2	5	.250
Day	0	0	2.84	5	6.1	Sc Pos	36	3	0	8	.083
Night	0	4	2.82	8	22.1	Clutch	81	18	2	10	.222

1992 Rankings (American League)

- 1st in lowest batting average allowed in relief with runners in scoring position (.083)
- 3rd in lowest batting average allowed in relief with runners on base (.151)
- Led the Angels in lowest batting average allowed in relief with runners in scoring position and lowest batting average allowed in relief with runners on base

PITCHING:

Pat Rapp had his first taste of the big leagues in 1992 when Francisco Oliveras was hurt and the Giants needed a warm body. He had earned the promotion by posting ERA's of 2.64, 2.50, ad 2.69 in three minor-league stops during 1990 and 1991. At the time of his promotion he had a 2.57 ERA at AAA Phoenix. Rapp had also recorded 50 strikeouts with only 17 walks, an improvement over his usual two-to-one strikeout to walk ratio; it was perhaps a sign that he was ready for the big leagues.

Rapp started out well for the Giants, pitching two scoreless innings in relief. He started next and lost but allowed only five baserunners in 5.2 innings and two runs. In his final outing he was wild, walking five and allowing six runs in just 2.1 innings. He did well against righties but faced stacked lineups and lefties lit him up. He was shipped back to Phoenix, and there was some feeling that he didn't throw quite hard enough to be a top-level prospect. Others, like the Marlins, felt he'd shown plenty of major-league ability. The Giants didn't summon Rapp as a September call-up and perhaps he could see the handwriting on the wall. "It's tough to know exactly where I fit in," he said.

Rapp had been a starter for three years before 1992. But Phoenix gave him just 12 starts and 27 relief appearances, mostly in middle relief. Still, he was expected to start for the Giants as early as 1993, but he was left unprotected and is now a Marlin. Florida selected him high, with their fifth pick, so he obviously impressed them greatly.

HOLDING RUNNERS, FIELDING, HITTING:

Rapp can handle the bat and lay down a bunt but he fanned twice in two at-bats with the Giants. He allowed four steals in five attempts, which is really not bad for a rookie, and he made no errors.

OVERALL:

Rapp's high first-round selection may have been somewhat of a surprise, but he was generally considered one of the Giants' best young prospects. It wasn't like the turmoil-laden Giants made no mistakes in the draft, but Florida wants to prove Rapp was their biggest. He'll get a chance at the Marlins rotation in 1993.

PAT RAPP

Position: SP
Bats: R **Throws:** R
Ht: 6' 3" **Wt:** 195

Opening Day Age: 25
Born: 7/13/67 in Jennings, LA
ML Seasons: 1

Overall Statistics

	W	L	ERA	G	GS	Sv	IP	H	R	BB	SO	HR
1992	0	2	7.20	3	2	0	10.0	8	8	6	3	0
Career	0	2	7.20	3	2	0	10.0	8	8	6	3	0

How Often He Throws Strikes

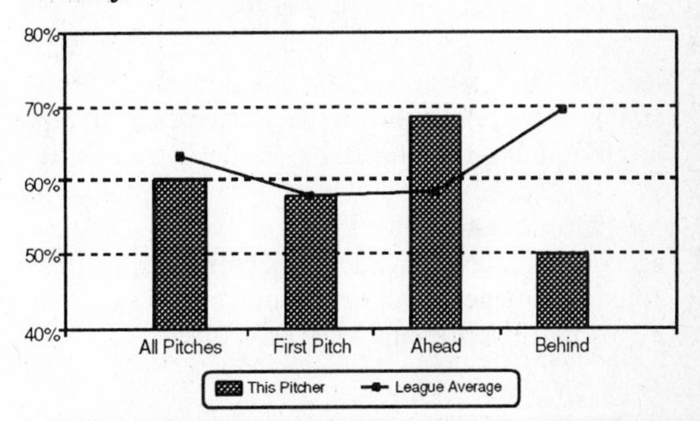

1992 Situational Stats

	W	L	ERA	Sv	IP		AB	H	HR	RBI	AVG
Home	0	0	0.00	0	2.0	LHB	19	6	0	5	.316
Road	0	2	9.00	0	8.0	RHB	15	2	0	2	.133
Day	0	1	23.14	0	2.1	Sc Pos	9	4	0	7	.444
Night	0	1	2.35	0	7.2	Clutch	6	1	0	0	.167

1992 Rankings (National League)

- Did not rank near the top or bottom in any category

HITTING:

The burden of expectation has been placed on Gary Scott like few other prospects in recent seasons. A sore spot for the Cubs since Ron Santo left in 1973, their third base problems looked to be solved in 1991 with the spring training heroics of Scott. Instead he hit .165. Cubs manager Jim Lefebvre thought that Scott was for real after the spring of 1992, too. But Scott hit .156. That made two opening day starts, two disastrous Aprils. His AAA numbers in both seasons were strike three. Scott and Alex Arias were sent to the Marlins in a deal for Greg Hibbard.

Scott can do a little bit of everything but does nothing really well. Throw out his major-league numbers, which all-in-all comprise only 175 at-bats, and Scott still looks like a marginal major leaguer. He stands off the plate with an erect stance but hasn't shown the bat speed to turn around on big-time fastballs. He has some ability to hit offspeed stuff and mediocre heat; he compiled 36 extra-base hits in 354 at-bats at Iowa last season, including 10 homers. He has shown reasonable patience at all levels and is streaky. He is also a hard worker and very coachable.

BASERUNNING:

Scott promised some reasonable basestealing acumen back in 1990 when he swiped 17 of 20 bases at Class A Winston-Salem. But his success planted some bad seeds: since then he has stolen six bases and been caught 13 times in the majors and minors. He is no more than an average runner.

FIELDING:

Scott carried his offensive problems with him to the hot corner. He has good range to his left, strong reflexes, and is mobile on slow choppers; Santo said the kid could play. But he lost confidence and started hitching, making bad throws and bobbling the ball.

OVERALL:

The choice between Chris Donnels and Gary Scott as the Marlins' third baseman is not enticing. The Chicago brass who threw Scott, with 143 at-bats above A ball, into two straight opening day assignments made a big mistake. At age 24 Scott needs to mature beyond his early troubles, but he's in the right place to try again.

GARY SCOTT

Position: 3B
Bats: R **Throws:** R
Ht: 6' 0" **Wt:** 175

Opening Day Age: 24
Born: 8/22/68 in New Rochelle, NY
ML Seasons: 2

Overall Statistics

	G	AB	R	H	D	T	HR	RBI	SB	BB	SO	AVG
1992	36	96	8	15	2	0	2	11	0	5	14	.156
Career	67	175	16	28	5	0	3	16	0	18	28	.160

Where He Hits the Ball

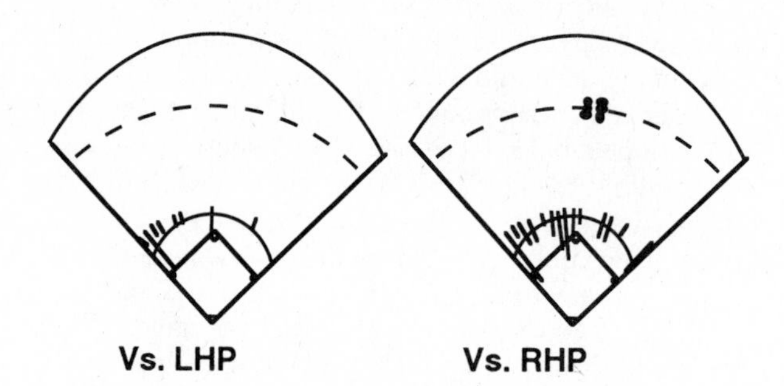

1992 Situational Stats

	AB	H	HR	RBI	AVG		AB	H	HR	RBI	AVG
Home	53	8	1	7	.151	LHP	30	5	1	6	.167
Road	43	7	1	4	.163	RHP	66	10	1	5	.152
Day	45	4	0	1	.089	Sc Pos	27	6	2	10	.222
Night	51	11	2	10	.216	Clutch	15	3	1	2	.200

1992 Rankings (National League)

→ Did not rank near the top or bottom in any category

HITTING:

Even four straight seasons cut short by injury couldn't deter the Marlins from acquiring veteran shortstop Walt Weiss. The latest was a strained ribcage muscle suffered during batting practice in Palm Springs on March 27, and Weiss wasn't activated until June 3. Weiss eventually started 96 games and his .212 average was a career low.

Although he's susceptible to breaking balls, Weiss used to be able to turn on a fastball and hit it over the right field wall. But he hasn't homered since 1990, and some of his batting figures from last year look like those of a National League pitcher. For instance he batted .141 after September 1, he batted only .144 when he was behind in the count, and hit a feeble .138 (12-for-87) with runners in scoring position. A switch-hitter, he was 10-for-74 (.135) as a righty with just one extra-base hit. About the only positives offensively were his 43 walks, the second-highest total of his career, and his 11 sacrifice hits, which were a career high.

BASERUNNING:

Never much of a basestealing threat, Weiss has been slowed by injuries. He had surgery on his right knee in 1989, surgery on his left knee in 1990, and in 1991 tore ligaments in his left ankle. Weiss has lost a half step because of the ailments; he was 6-for-9 as a basestealer last year.

FIELDING:

Weiss covers the gap between shortstop and third very well and he boasts an above-average throwing arm. He comes in aggressively on ground balls and has great leaping ability. Yet the injuries have affected him. He made 19 errors last year, the highest total of his five-year career despite all the missed time.

OVERALL:

The Marlins acquired the possible infield anchor for Marlin expansion selections Eric Helfand (who came from Oakland originally) and Scott Baker. They are taking a chance that Weiss can play regularly. Weiss is a fiery, driven player with tremendous leadership skills. It remains to be seen if his physical skills have survived his four trips to the disabled list; he'll have competition from Alex Arias for the shortstop job.

WALT WEISS

Position: SS
Bats: B **Throws:** R
Ht: 6' 0" **Wt:** 175

Opening Day Age: 29
Born: 11/28/63 in Tuxedo, NY
ML Seasons: 6

Overall Statistics

	G	AB	R	H	D	T	HR	RBI	SB	BB	SO	AVG
1992	103	316	36	67	5	2	0	21	6	43	39	.212
Career	528	1608	178	395	60	7	8	130	32	159	203	.246

Where He Hits the Ball

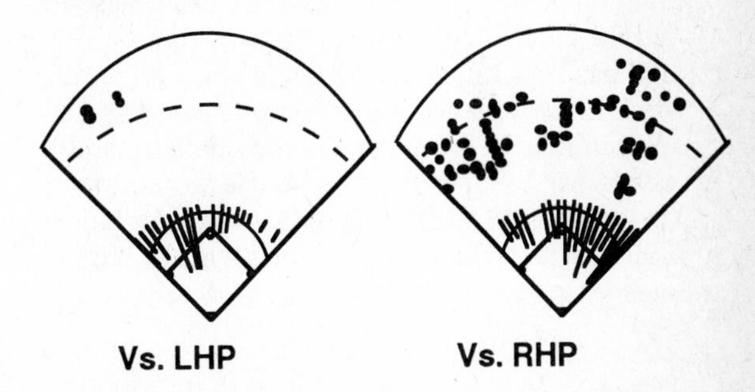

1992 Situational Stats

	AB	H	HR	RBI	AVG		AB	H	HR	RBI	AVG
Home	144	25	0	8	.174	LHP	74	10	0	2	.135
Road	172	42	0	13	.244	RHP	242	57	0	19	.236
Day	118	24	0	7	.203	Sc Pos	87	12	0	20	.138
Night	198	43	0	14	.217	Clutch	40	9	0	3	.225

1992 Rankings (American League)

- → 2nd in lowest batting average with runners in scoring position (.138) and lowest fielding percentage at shortstop (.956)
- → 3rd in batting average on a 3-2 count (.405)
- → 7th in sacrifice bunts (11)
- → Led the A's in batting average on a 3-2 count
- → Led AL shortstops in batting average on a 3-2 count

TOP PROSPECT

HITTING:

The Jays' latest Great Canadian Hope, Nigel Wilson is now as far from Canada as a player can get and still be in major-league baseball. The second player picked overall in the draft and the first by Florida, the 23-year-old has five seasons of pro ball under his belt. Four were in A ball, and he raised his average year by year from .204 to .301 before climbing to AA in 1992.

Wilson busted loose at Knoxville last year with 26 homers and a .274 average. He played the season somewhat in the shadow of talented teammate Juan de la Rosa, but in the end, Wilson had better power stats and scored and drove in more runs. His 67 extra-base hits were second to Tim Salmon's 71 among all AA and AAA hitters. He led the Florida State League in slugging in 1991 and has now raised his slugging percentage four straight seasons to last year's outstanding .516. Wilson may be ready now to provide left-handed power for a major-league club. He would like to continue leading off as he did last year for Knoxville, but he walked only 33 times with 137 strikeouts.

BASERUNNING:

Wilson only scored 85 runs despite leading off and all his extra bases; that total was his career high. He's been a double-figure basestealer for three seasons but has a fluctuating success rate. Speed is part of his game, but he's raw.

FIELDING:

Wilson is considered a good defender. He has all the tools, but an arm injury seriously affected his ability to throw and is probably a big reason why he wasn't protected. But his arm has improved a little, and with his bat skills, he won't have to throw much to stay in left field.

OVERALL:

As the first Marlins pick, there will be some pressure to play Wilson in the majors, and he may very well earn the right in the spring. His performance in 1992 was big league, and it should not be long before he is, too. He will need to learn better plate skills to be a major star, though.

NIGEL WILSON

Position: OF
Bats: L **Throws:** L
Ht: 6' 1" **Wt:** 170

Opening Day Age: 23
Born: 1/12/70 in Oshawa, Ontario, Canada
ML Seasons: 0

Overall Minor League Statistics

	G	AB	R	H	D	T	HR	RBI	SB	BB	SO	AVG
AA '92	137	521	85	143	34	7	26	69	13	33	137	.274
Career	448	1680	255	456	81	33	60	215	77	115	389	.271

Where He Hits the Ball

Did Not Play

1992 Situational Stats

	AB	H	HR	RBI	AVG		AB	H	HR	RBI	AVG
Home	0	0	0	0	.000	LHP	0	0	0	0	.000
Road	0	0	0	0	.000	RHP	0	0	0	0	.000
Day	0	0	0	0	.000	Sc Pos	0	0	0	0	.000
Night	0	0	0	0	.000	Clutch	0	0	0	0	.000

1992 Rankings (National League)

→ Did Not Play

TREVOR HOFFMAN

Position: P
Bats: R **Throws:** R
Ht: 6' 0" **Wt:** 195

Opening Day Age: 25
Born: 10/13/67 in Bellflower, CA
ML Seasons: 0

Overall Minor League Statistics

	W	L	ERA	G	GS	Sv	IP	H	R	BB	SO	HR
AAA '92	4	6	4.27	42	5	6	65.1	57	32	32	63	6
Career	9	7	2.90	89	11	26	142.2	111	50	63	169	7

PITCHING, FIELDING, HITTING & HOLDING RUNNERS:

Righthander Trevor Hoffman made the move from shortstop to the mound before the 1991 season and immediately reeled off ERAs of 1.87 at Class A Cedar Rapids and 1.93 at AA Chattanooga, with 20 saves total, while pitching in the Cincinnati system. He opened 1992 at Chattanooga but was promoted to AAA Nashville after six games. Hoffman's AAA numbers (4.27 ERA) weren't all that impressive, but the Marlins thought enough of him to make him their fourth pick in the first round of the expansion draft.

Hoffman throws a fastball, curve, slider, and change-up, and has fanned 169 hitters in 142.2 minor-league innings. Walks were not a problem until his promotion to AAA. He started out in the rotation but was soon back in the pen with an ERA over 4.00. He walked 32 batters in 65.1 innings, though his strikeout total stayed up. He tried to throw more strikes but surrendered six homers. The Reds were disappointed with his progress, though his transition from shortstop to AAA pitcher seems pretty rapid. As a former infielder, he fields and swings the bat very well.

OVERALL:

Hoffman was drafted rather high by Florida for a raw older pitcher, but his stuff is convincing. As the brother of former Red Sox shortstop Glenn Hoffman, he has baseball in his blood. It may be a year before he is ready to join the Marlins, and they may groom him as the heir apparent to Bryan Harvey at AAA.

JOSE MARTINEZ

Position: P
Bats: R **Throws:** R
Ht: 6' 2" **Wt:** 155

Opening Day Age: 22
Born: 4/1/71 in Guayubin, D.R.
ML Seasons: 0

Overall Minor League Statistics

	W	L	ERA	G	GS	Sv	IP	H	R	BB	SO	HR
AA '92	5	2	1.71	9	8	0	58.0	47	16	13	39	1
Career	40	18	2.01	76	68	0	500.2	438	173	67	423	13

PITCHING, FIELDING, HITTING & HOLDING RUNNERS:

Jose Martinez was buried deep in the Mets system but was hard to hide after being the only 20-game winner in the minor leagues in 1991. Martinez had a wonderful year in '91, leading the Mets' farm clubs in ERA (1.49), strikeouts (158), innings (193.1), and complete games (nine). He walked an amazingly low total of 30 hitters, earning "Pitcher With The Best Control" honors in the South Atlantic League in a thoroughly dominating performance. After another fine year at Class A St. Lucie (6-5, 2.05) and AA Binghamton (5-2, 1.71) in 1992, he was the Marlins' second overall choice and could be their ace of the future.

Martinez has command of a wide variety of pitches but his fastball is the pitch that makes it all work. It's not a top-level, 90-plus MPH type, but his velocity is respectable and the pitch really moves. Martinez is an athletic youngster and a good fielder. He hasn't had much problem with baserunners and is an unknown at the plate.

OVERALL:

Something about Martinez inspires skepticism, since he is rarely mentioned as a top prospect, but is instead called intriguing. Most likely doubts are formed because of his slight stature. However, his pitching speaks for itself, and if it remains true to form, he should be winning for the Marlins by 1994 at the latest. He'd like to be joined by his brother and fellow Marlin selection Ramon, a former Pirate organization shortstop, for what ESPN has called a "Two Martinez Launch."

BOB NATAL

Position: C
Bats: R **Throws:** R
Ht: 5'11" **Wt:** 190

Opening Day Age: 27
Born: 11/13/65 in Long Beach, CA
ML Seasons: 1

Overall Statistics

	G	AB	R	H	D	T	HR	RBI	SB	BB	SO	AVG
1992	5	6	0	0	0	0	0	0	0	1	1	.000
Career	5	6	0	0	0	0	0	0	0	1	1	.000

HITTING, FIELDING, BASERUNNING:

Bob Natal boosted his stock when he hit .317 in a short stint in AAA Indianapolis in 1991 and followed up by leading the league in hitting for a good part of 1992. He was hitting .326 when he was called to Montreal for a cup of coffee in July. He finished back in AAA at .302 with 34 extra-base hits.

Natal is a patient hitter -- he didn't put the first pitch in play in seven major-league plate appearances -- with a compact swing. He chokes up when behind in the count but still generates power. He's fairly quick for a catcher and can steal a base. Natal's also a good handler of pitchers and throws well, though he didn't look so hot in his brief stint in Montreal. He's also a three-time minor-league All-Star. The main negatives surrounding him are his age (27) and the out-of-the-blue nature of his improvement. Can he continue to maintain his 1992 performance?

OVERALL:

Steve Decker has a good reputation and will probably be the Marlins' primary backstop, but Natal could wind up as the number-one man if Decker fails. He's unproven, though, and time is running out if he's going to be a major-league regular. Barring that, he should be a very good backup.

DAVE WEATHERS

Position: RP
Bats: R **Throws:** R
Ht: 6' 3" **Wt:** 205

Opening Day Age: 23
Born: 9/25/69 in Lawrenceburg, TN
ML Seasons: 2

Overall Statistics

	W	L	ERA	G	GS	Sv	IP	H	R	BB	SO	HR
1992	0	0	8.10	2	0	0	3.1	5	3	2	3	1
Career	1	0	5.50	17	0	0	18.0	20	12	19	16	2

PITCHING, FIELDING, HITTING & HOLDING RUNNERS:

Ex-Blue Jay David Weathers earned his first and only major-league victory on the last day of the 1991 season. He'd been called up after turning in the best season among AA Knoxville pitchers with a 2.45 ERA, which was fourth-best in the league. But Weathers was only 10-7 for Knoxville, largely because he issued many walks. In 1992 he posted a single victory again -- but this time it was only for the Jays' AAA Syracuse farm club. That explains why he was available to Florida in the expansion draft.

Weathers gives up quite a few hits, but keeps his home runs allowed under control and makes pitches when he needs to. His fastball, slider and change-up repertoire served him well in the minors but major-league hitters have handed him an ERA of 5.50 in two stints over 18 innings. He only pitched 51.2 innings in 1992 -- 3.1 with Toronto -- after a strained ligament turned out to be more serious than originally thought and then a re-injury of it during a simulated game. He looks like a decent fielder; his other skills are untested.

OVERALL:

Weathers has a great attitude and spent a lot of time observing and talking to Dave Winfield and Jack Morris trying to see what makes a star. But his injuries and control problems need to be ironed out before he can become a star himself with the Marlins.

ORGANIZATION OVERVIEW:

While the Rockies used their early expansion picks on players who could help them now, Florida went out of its way to draft prospects, many of whom were still in Class A. It's a good approach if they stay with it, and the early signs are promising. General Manager Dave Dombrowski had great success at player development with both the White Sox and the Expos. He hired one of the more cerebral men in baseball, Rene Lachemann, as his manager and Lachemann's highly-respected brother, Marcel, as the pitching coach. The Marlins' models are the Royals and Blue Jays, both of whom went with youth and won it all. The Marlins figure to lose for a while, so we'll see how patient their ownership really is.

CARL E. EVERETT

Position: OF
Bats: B **Throws:** R
Ht: 6' 0" **Wt:** 181
Opening Day Age: 22
Born: 6/3/70 in Tampa, FL

Recent Statistics

	G	AB	R	H	D	T	HR	RBI	SB	BB	SO	AVG
91 A Greensboro	123	468	97	127	18	0	4	40	28	57	122	.271
92 A Ft. Laud	46	183	30	42	8	2	2	9	11	12	40	.230
92 A Pr William	6	22	7	7	0	0	4	9	1	5	7	.318

The Yankees were thought to have done one of the worst jobs of any major-league team in terms of protecting themselves in the expansion draft. A good example is Everett, a New York first-round pick in 1990. The youngster spent most of the 1992 season at Class A Ft. Lauderdale where he hit .230 with two homers in 183 at-bats. He then went 7-for-22, with four of the hits homers, at Prince William (also Class A). Everett has great athletic skills, including good speed and one of the best arms around. But he's a long way from the majors.

JOHN W. JOHNSTONE

Position: P
Bats: R **Throws:** R
Ht: 6' 3" **Wt:** 195
Opening Day Age: 24
Born: 11/25/68 in Liverpool, NY

Recent Statistics

	W	L	ERA	G	GS	Sv	IP	H	R	BB	SO	HR
91 AA Williamsprt	7	9	3.97	27	27	0	165.1	159	94	79	99	5
92 AA Binghamton	7	7	3.74	24	24	0	149.1	132	66	36	121	8

The Mets system is said to be loaded with pitchers, which is why John Johnstone was still available in the second round of the expansion draft. The righty has a 44-29 minor-league record, a 3.32 ERA, and excellent strikeout-to-walk ratios. However, most of his success has been at the Class A level; in two seasons at AA he's won only seven games each year with less-than-overwhelming ERAs. Consider him a long shot, especially for 1993.

RICHIE LEWIS

Position: P
Bats: R **Throws:** R
Ht: 5' 10" **Wt:** 175
Opening Day Age: 27
Born: 1/25/66 in Muncie, IN

Recent Statistics

	W	L	ERA	G	GS	Sv	IP	H	R	BB	SO	HR
92 AAA Rochester	10	9	3.28	24	23	0	159.1	136	63	61	154	15
92 AL Baltimore	1	1	10.80	2	2	0	6.2	13	8	7	4	1

By Marlin standards Lewis is ready for his pension; he made two major-league starts for the Orioles. A former Expo prospect, Lewis has an excellent curve, an 85-86 MPH fastball, and a fine minor-league record which featured impressive strikeout totals. However, control has been a problem for him and he's also had some arm troubles. He's 27; if he's healthy, he could be with the Marlins this year.

DARRELL L. WHITMORE

Position: OF
Bats: L **Throws:** R
Ht: 6' 1" **Wt:** 210
Opening Day Age: 24
Born: 11/18/68 in Front Royal, VA

Recent Statistics

	G	AB	R	H	D	T	HR	RBI	SB	BB	SO	AVG
91 A Watertown	6	19	2	7	2	1	0	3	0	3	2	.368
92 A Kinston	121	443	71	124	22	2	10	52	17	56	92	.280

A former football player at West Virginia University, Whitmore has had limited baseball experience; though he was a number-two draft choice in 1990, the '92 season was his first full year in organized ball. Obviously he's still pretty raw, but he had a fine year for the Indians' Class A farm club at Kinston last year, showing some power, speed, discipline and the ability to hit for average. Your typical Marlins pick, he's a long way from the majors, but he has the tools. The Marlins selected him with their eighth choice, the highest player selected with no AA experience.

KIP E. YAUGHN

Position: P
Bats: R **Throws:** R
Ht: 6' 1" **Wt:** 180
Opening Day Age: 23
Born: 7/20/69 in Walnut Creek, CA

Recent Statistics

	W	L	ERA	G	GS	Sv	IP	H	R	BB	SO	HR
91 A Frederick	11	8	3.94	27	27	0	162.0	168	88	76	155	15
92 AA Hagerstown	7	8	3.48	18	18	0	116.1	88	52	33	106	6

The Marlins' 12th pick in the first round of the expansion draft, Yaughn has had a so-so record in organized ball (20-20) but he's said to have a live arm and major-league potential. Yaughn was 7-8 for the Orioles' AA farm club at Hagerstown, but his control was markedly improved and he struck out 106 batters in 116.1 innings. He's a long shot for 1993, but has possibilities for the future.

HITTING:

After long struggling to stay in the big leagues, Eric Anthony finally turned the corner in 1992. When the season began, Pete Incaviglia was the starter in right field and Anthony was the fourth outfielder. Anthony kept pushing his case with strong performance and earned the job as a regular. After three failures, he at last made good on the vast promise of potential and power that greeted his arrival in the majors.

What brought things together for Anthony was a slight leg kick at the plate. It's a timing mechanism which allows him to stay back, use his arms and hands more and not over-commit himself to a pitch. "You've got to have a timing device each time up at the plate." says Astros batting instructor Rudy Jaramillo. "For Eric, it's the leg kick, the element that puts everything in motion. The leg kick keeps his hips in there a little longer and it helps Eric take a consistent approach to each turn at bat."

Although his average faded in the second half to .239, Anthony had never batted over .200 previously. He hammered a team-high 19 homers and drove across 80 runs to provide solid production in Houston's rush to finish at .500 for the season.

BASERUNNING:

He runs hard, but Anthony is not much of a threat on the bases. He stole five bases and was thrown out 4 times, barely breaking even. He is an average baserunner at best.

FIELDING:

Anthony has worked to improve in the field. He needs to concentrate better on recognizing the game situation. He also needs to learn the hitters more to get a better jump on the ball. His arm is best suited to left field, not right.

OVERALL:

Anthony just scratched the surface of his talent in '92. He can be a big run producer for the Astros in the years to come because of his strength and big-hit capabilities. He needs a solid year in '93 to build upon his first year of success.

ERIC ANTHONY

Position: RF
Bats: L **Throws:** L
Ht: 6' 2" **Wt:** 195

Opening Day Age: 25
Born: 11/8/67 in San Diego, CA
ML Seasons: 4

Overall Statistics

	G	AB	R	H	D	T	HR	RBI	SB	BB	SO	AVG
1992	137	440	45	105	15	1	19	80	5	38	98	.239
Career	285	858	89	180	31	1	34	123	11	88	233	.210

Where He Hits the Ball

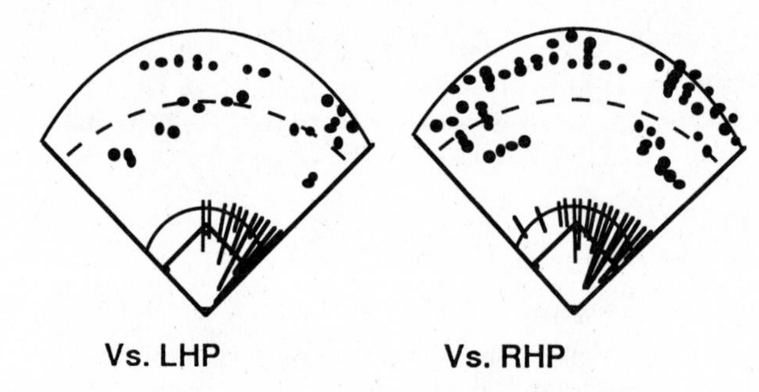

1992 Situational Stats

	AB	H	HR	RBI	AVG		AB	H	HR	RBI	AVG
Home	207	54	9	36	.261	LHP	156	33	5	28	.212
Road	233	51	10	44	.219	RHP	284	72	14	52	.254
Day	138	32	7	23	.232	Sc Pos	139	37	4	56	.266
Night	302	73	12	57	.242	Clutch	89	22	6	22	.247

1992 Rankings (National League)

- 1st in lowest fielding percentage in right field (.973)
- 4th in lowest on-base percentage vs. left-handed pitchers (.269) and highest percentage of swings that missed (25.6%)
- 5th in lowest batting average vs. left-handed pitchers (.212) and lowest batting average on the road (.219)
- Led the Astros in home runs (19), least GDPs per GDP situation (6.3%) and batting average with the bases loaded (.385)

FUTURE ALL-STAR

JEFF BAGWELL

Position: 1B
Bats: R **Throws:** R
Ht: 6' 0" **Wt:** 195

Opening Day Age: 24
Born: 5/27/68 in Boston, MA
ML Seasons: 2

HITTING:

For much of last season, Jeff Bagwell looked like anything but the man who was National League Rookie of the Year in 1991. Bagwell found himself hitting .227 in late-June, an embarrassing level. It took him awhile, but he finished with a closing burst, hitting safely in 19 of the final 21 games (.434) to push his final average to .273. His other numbers were excellent: career highs in home runs (18) and RBI (96). He ranked sixth in the National League in RBI, seventh in walks (84) and first in sacrifice flies (13). He also got plunked by pitches 12 times.

The Astro with the uppercut swing needed to make adjustments in his second year around the league. Pitchers often worked him inside, up and in, then came back with sliders down and away. He tried to level his swing a bit, though not always with good results. But when Bagwell returned to his old ways, he began to rip the ball again. He tagged a ball off Tom Glavine in Atlanta's Fulton County Stadium that traveled an estimated 440 feet. The blast landed in the club (second) level, a height where only six other balls have landed in the ballpark's 27-year history.

BASERUNNING:

Bagwell surprises people with his performance on the basepaths. He scored 87 runs, second only to leadoff man Craig Biggio on the team, and he swiped 10 bases in 16 attempts. He is an aggressive runner and looks to make the first-to-third romp on hits to the outfield.

FIELDING:

Bagwell came up as a third baseman in the Boston system, and he now knows how to handle a first baseman's glove also. He goes well to his left, cutting off balls hit down the line. He made seven errors while handling 1,471 chances at the bag last season.

OVERALL:

Bagwell is a large hunk of the foundation around which the Astros are building for 1993 and beyond. He is the team's leading run producer, averaging 89 RBI a year for the past two seasons. His numbers should grow as he continues to mature.

Overall Statistics

	G	AB	R	H	D	T	HR	RBI	SB	BB	SO	AVG
1992	162	586	87	160	34	6	18	96	10	84	97	.273
Career	318	1140	166	323	60	10	33	178	17	159	213	.283

Where He Hits the Ball

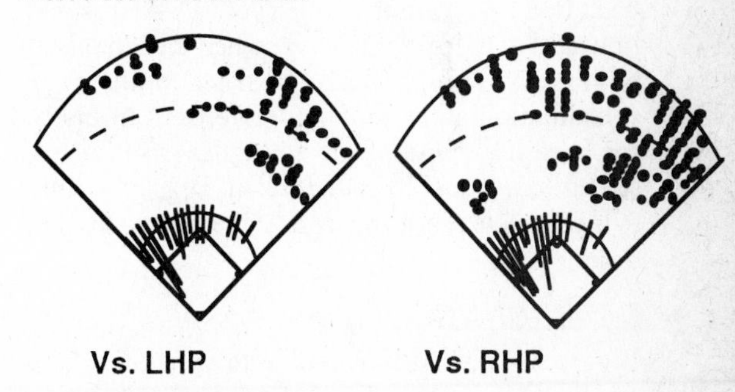

1992 Situational Stats

	AB	H	HR	RBI	AVG		AB	H	HR	RBI	AVG
Home	294	76	8	48	.259	LHP	210	61	10	34	.290
Road	292	84	10	48	.288	RHP	376	99	8	62	.263
Day	160	49	6	27	.306	Sc Pos	177	47	5	78	.266
Night	426	111	12	69	.261	Clutch	99	35	8	28	.354

1992 Rankings (National League)

- 1st in sacrifice flies (13) and games played (162)
- 2nd in hit by pitch (12)
- 3rd in GDPs (17)
- 4th in most pitches seen (2,665) and plate appearances (697)
- 6th in RBI (96) and batting average in the clutch (.354)
- Led the Astros in doubles (34), total bases (260), RBI, sacrifice flies, intentional walks (13), hit by pitch, GDPs, games played, slugging percentage (.444), HR frequency (32.6 ABs per HR), batting average in the clutch, slugging percentage vs. left-handed pitchers (.524) and batting average on the road (.288)

IN HIS PRIME

CRAIG BIGGIO

Position: 2B
Bats: R **Throws:** R
Ht: 5'11" **Wt:** 180

Opening Day Age: 27
Born: 12/14/65 in Smithtown, NY
ML Seasons: 5

HITTING:

An All-Star catcher for Houston, Biggio moved to second base in 1992 and became the first major leaguer to make the All-Star team at each of those two positions. The idea behind the move was that Biggio was athletic enough to handle it and that less wear and tear on his legs would prolong his career. He could play every day; as a catcher, he usually rested once a week and wore down late in the season. This time around, Biggio played in all 162 games and batted .277, a slight dropoff from 1991 (.295). But Biggio ranked among National League leaders with career highs in runs (96), walks (94) and stolen bases (38).

Biggio has a knack for getting on base. Although he batted in the number-one spot, the Astros want him to be more aggressive when he comes up with runners on base. Biggio has good hand-eye coordination and uses the whole field in his bid for base hits. One of his strengths is his mental strength, not just his athleticism. Biggio is quick to make mental adjustments at the plate and in the field.

BASERUNNING:

Biggio is a very talented base runner, aggressively taking the extra base and making things happen. Freed from the grind of catching, he enjoyed his best season yet stealing bases, succeeding 38 times in 53 attempts.

FIELDING:

Not only did he smoothly make the change from catcher to second base, Biggio did it in All-Star fashion. He had only four errors in his first 89 games and finished with 12. He adapted to making the pivot play at the bag much more quickly than anyone thought he would.

OVERALL:

Biggio's switch to second base means that Houston's infield should be set in three spots for years. Biggio is important to the rebuilding process for the improving Astros, both for what he does at the top of the batting order and for what he contributes in the field.

Overall Statistics

	G	AB	R	H	D	T	HR	RBI	SB	BB	SO	AVG
1992	162	613	96	170	32	3	6	39	38	94	95	.277
Career	645	2280	306	624	106	12	30	192	109	256	338	.274

Where He Hits the Ball

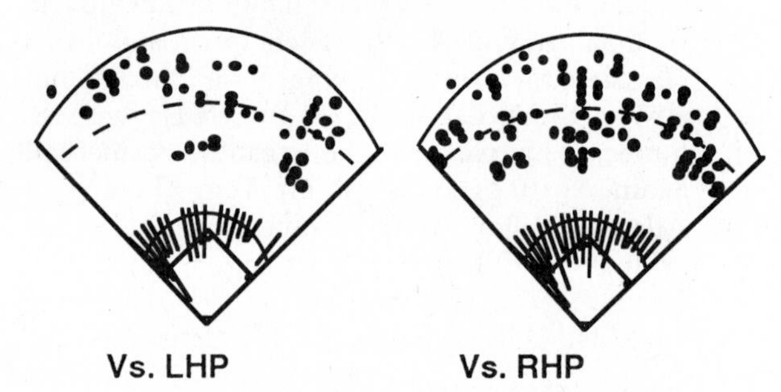

1992 Situational Stats

	AB	H	HR	RBI	AVG		AB	H	HR	RBI	AVG
Home	303	85	3	17	.281	LHP	218	60	3	14	.275
Road	310	85	3	22	.274	RHP	395	110	3	25	.278
Day	168	41	3	10	.244	Sc Pos	104	31	0	32	.298
Night	445	129	3	29	.290	Clutch	95	25	0	5	.263

1992 Rankings (National League)

- 1st in most pitches seen (2,758), plate appearances (721) and games played (162)
- 2nd in times on base (271), on-base percentage batting leadoff (.378) and steals of third (12)
- Led the Astros in at-bats, runs scored (96), caught stealing (15), walks (94), times on base, most pitches seen, plate appearances, games played, on-base percentage (.379), most pitches seen per plate appearance (3.83), batting average with runners in scoring position (.298), batting average on an 0-2 count (.191), on-base percentage vs. left-handed pitchers (.410), highest percentage of pitches taken (60.8%) and steals of third

JOE BOEVER

Position: RP
Bats: R **Throws:** R
Ht: 6' 1" **Wt:** 200

Opening Day Age: 32
Born: 10/4/60 in St. Louis, MO
ML Seasons: 8

PITCHING:

The phrase "tireless worker" was coined for Joe Boever. The veteran righthander appeared in a National League-high 81 games -- one game shy of Juan Agosto's team record -- last year. "I don't feel like I'm being abused," he says. "I love the work." The Astros gave him loads of it, and Boever proved a staff saver. Mister Available throws strikes, keeps his ERA (2.51) low and stays away from the long ball (three homers in 111.1 IP). Only 10 of 61 inherited runners scored on him (16.4 percent), which ranked second in the NL. He has experience and knows how to use it.

In the spring, the Astros' final cut came down to a decision between Boever or Curt Schilling. They dealt Schilling to Philadelphia, where he excelled as a starter. But Boever became a key figure in a revamped bullpen which helped the club play .500 ball for the first time in three years. His frequent outings helped the Astros reach the late innings for closer Doug Jones.

Boever throws a fastball, slider and palmball. He uses the palmball as a change-up, and he throws it frequently. It's effective against all batters since Boever can control it well enough to make it break to the right or to the left. He's perfected the pitch to almost an art form. His record (3-6, two saves) is misleading; Boever played the set-up role very well.

HOLDING RUNNERS, FIELDING, HITTING:

With Boever's slow-breaking pitches, one would think that runners should take advantage of him. But only seven runners stole a base on Boever while five were cut down. He made only two errors in 81 games and went hitless in seven at-bats, striking out three times.

OVERALL:

Boever made the Astros a year ago as a non-roster player. He quickly proved his value as a middle reliever with poise and a rubber arm. His ability to pitch often makes him an ideal set-up man for a Houston team which uses veteran relievers to prop up a young starting staff.

Overall Statistics

	W	L	ERA	G	GS	Sv	IP	H	R	BB	SO	HR
1992	3	6	2.51	81	0	2	111.1	103	38	45	67	3
Career	14	31	3.41	336	0	38	457.0	425	187	212	352	35

How Often He Throws Strikes

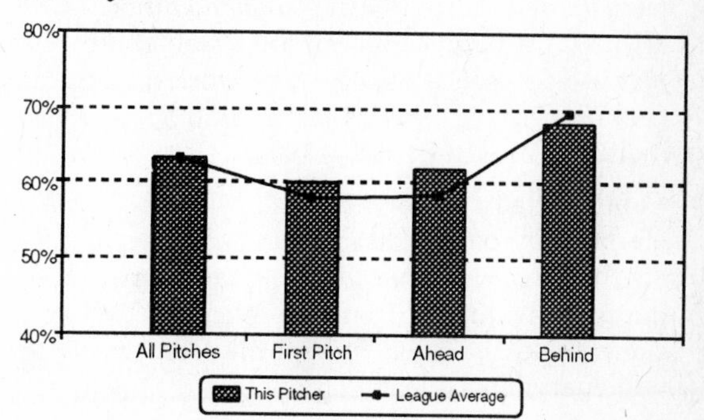

1992 Situational Stats

	W	L	ERA	Sv	IP		AB	H	HR	RBI	AVG
Home	1	2	1.32	1	61.1	LHB	186	45	1	20	.242
Road	2	4	3.96	1	50.0	RHB	230	58	2	21	.252
Day	1	1	2.87	0	31.1	Sc Pos	133	30	0	38	.226
Night	2	5	2.36	2	80.0	Clutch	141	38	1	14	.270

1992 Rankings (National League)

- 1st in games pitched (81)
- 2nd in lowest percentage of inherited runners scored (16.4%) and relief innings (111.1)
- 10th in least strikeouts per 9 innings in relief (5.4)
- Led the Astros in games pitched and first batter efficiency (.206)

STRONG ARM

HITTING:

Ken Caminiti put one old argument to rest in 1992: that he should abandon switch-hitting and go solo as a right-handed swinger. After flirting with a .300 average, Caminiti finished with a team-high .294 mark. It's true that he hit .303 with 7 homers and 35 RBI versus left-handed pitching. But he also batted a solid .289 against righthanders, an overall well-balanced hitting sheet. Going into the 1992 season, Caminiti had batted .285 vs. lefties, .223 vs. righties in his career.

"He's been working for two years to get that left side going," says Astros batting instructor Rudy Jaramillo. "At one time they were saying, 'We need to make this guy a right-handed hitter.' I was against that because he had too much ability. He just had to keep working." The work paid off as Caminiti racked righties for 18 doubles, six homers and 27 RBI in 298 at-bats.

Caminiti tied a career high with 149 hits despite a 23-day stay on the disabled list after separating his shoulder. He thinks his shoulder injury helped improve his hitting from the left side. "When I came back," he says, "it kept me from trying to pull everything. I learned how to hit, how to use more of the field."

BASERUNNING:

Caminiti is not fast by any stretch of the imagination. Still, he has good instincts on the bases and is aggressive. He stole 10 bases in 14 attempts, the first time Caminiti has been in double digits.

FIELDING:

The Astros think Caminiti should have two or three Gold Gloves by now. Though he's yet to win one, he's an outstanding glove man. He makes all the plays, including the diving stop behind the bag. He owns one of the strongest arms in the game.

OVERALL:

Though nearly 30, Caminiti continues to improve. Although rumors of trades occasionally pop up, he has matured as a player and become a team leader. He keeps turning back challenges for his job. Caminiti has made himself a valuable asset to the Astros.

KEN CAMINITI

Position: 3B
Bats: B **Throws:** R
Ht: 6' 0" **Wt:** 200

Opening Day Age: 29
Born: 4/21/63 in Hanford, CA
ML Seasons: 6

Overall Statistics

	G	AB	R	H	D	T	HR	RBI	SB	BB	SO	AVG
1992	135	506	68	149	31	2	13	62	10	44	68	.294
Career	694	2492	271	639	121	11	44	295	27	206	405	.256

Where He Hits the Ball

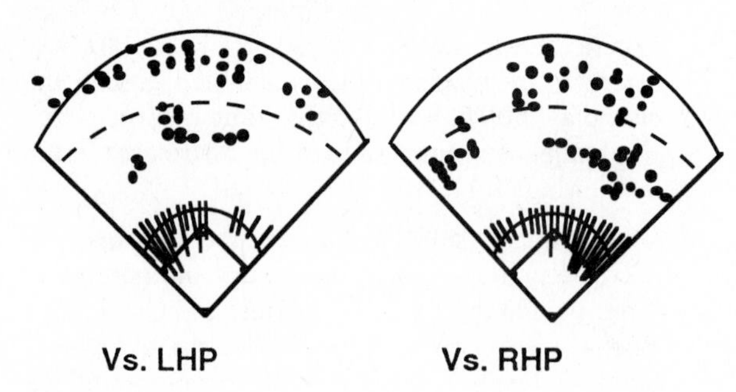

1992 Situational Stats

	AB	H	HR	RBI	AVG		AB	H	HR	RBI	AVG
Home	246	81	7	34	.329	LHP	208	63	7	35	.303
Road	260	68	6	28	.262	RHP	298	86	6	27	.289
Day	156	44	0	9	.282	Sc Pos	136	34	4	45	.250
Night	350	105	13	53	.300	Clutch	92	26	2	11	.283

1992 Rankings (National League)

- → 2nd in fielding percentage at third base (.966)
- → 6th in batting average at home (.329)
- → 7th in intentional walks (13)
- → 9th in GDPs (14)
- → Led the Astros in batting average (.294), intentional walks, batting average vs. left-handed pitchers (.303) and batting average at home
- → Led NL third basemen in intentional walks

HITTING:

Of all the young players promoted to the Houston roster in their rebuilding program, Andujar Cedeno ranks as the biggest disappointment at this stage of his career. In two years, Cedeno has gone from hot prospect to growing suspect. The young shortstop has great hitting tools, and he displays them on occasion. But he lacks consistency, except with his bad habits.

Cedeno slugged nine homers and drove in 36 runs in 67 games his rookie season. Everyone got excited -- over nothing, it turns out. Cedeno opened '92 slowly and was dispatched to AAA Tucson to find himself. Upon his return, he hit for the cycle, the first Astro to do so since Bob Watson in 1977. Cedeno also collected a career-high four hits in one game, but that was the bulk of the fireworks. In a stark contrast to the '91 season, he batted .173 with two homers and 13 RBI in 71 games.

Part of the problem is Cedeno's stubborn approach to making needed adjustments. He has quick bat speed and great wrist action. But he tends to swing hard at every pitch, and the result last year was 71 whiffs in 220 at-bats, way too high for a player trying to win regular playing time.

BASERUNNING:

Cedeno is not a daring baserunner because of his lack of experience. But he runs well and succeeded on his only two stolen base attempts. He seems to possess good instincts on the basepaths, but it's difficult to tell since he so seldom reaches base.

FIELDING:

Cedeno has similar characteristics fielding as hitting. He can pull off spectacular plays in the field, then boot the easy chance. Eleven errors in 71 games were too many. However, he has the ability to make all the plays at shortstop, so it's just a matter of settling down in the field -- if he can.

OVERALL:

Patience is required with Cedeno, with his potential as a future star. It paid off in Eric Anthony's case. The same give-him-time attitude could work wonders with Cedeno. He has "star" written all over him.

ANDUJAR CEDENO

Position: SS
Bats: R **Throws:** R
Ht: 6' 1" **Wt:** 168

Opening Day Age: 23
Born: 8/21/69 in La Romana, Dominican Republic
ML Seasons: 3

Overall Statistics

	G	AB	R	H	D	T	HR	RBI	SB	BB	SO	AVG
1992	71	220	15	38	13	2	2	13	2	14	71	.173
Career	145	479	42	99	26	4	11	49	6	23	150	.207

Where He Hits the Ball

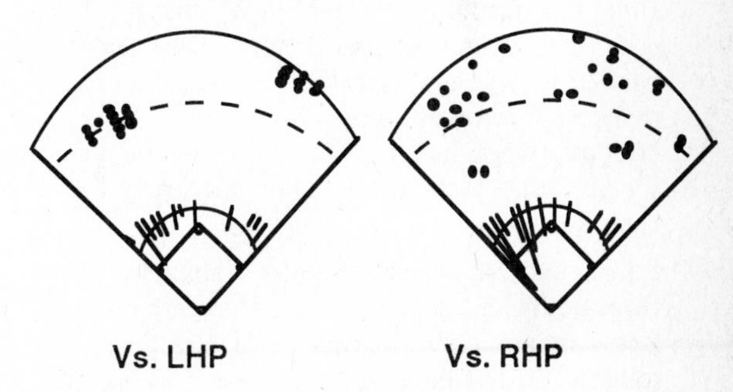

1992 Situational Stats

	AB	H	HR	RBI	AVG		AB	H	HR	RBI	AVG
Home	128	24	2	8	.188	LHP	64	13	0	4	.203
Road	92	14	0	5	.152	RHP	156	25	2	9	.160
Day	56	10	0	4	.179	Sc Pos	52	6	0	9	.115
Night	164	28	2	9	.171	Clutch	32	6	1	2	.188

1992 Rankings (National League)

- 6th in lowest batting average on an 0-2 count (.087) and lowest batting average on a 3-2 count (.077)

PITCHING:

After nine seasons of professional ball, Tom Edens finally spent his first full season in the major leagues in 1992. The righthander blossomed as the Twins' best middle reliever (6-3, 2.83 ERA in 52 games), and was so effective in mid-season that he was employed as a closer on several occasions. Edens did not allow an earned run in 17 appearances between May 19 and July 12, spanning 29.1 innings.

What transformed Edens from a career journeyman (6-7, 4.50 ERA in 45 major league games before last season) to a solid middle reliever? Twins coaches believe an improved change-up allowed Edens more effective use of his fastball and curve. Edens' out pitch has always been a sharp-breaking curve which Twins pitching coach Dick Such claims is among the league's best. But an average fastball allowed Edens no margin for error. He proved last season he can be effective when he's able to throw his change-up for strikes, which was his downfall early in his career.

Edens had respectable numbers against batters from both sides of the plate; lefthanders hit .248, righthanders .229. In many ways, Edens was tougher on left-handed batters. He walked only seven lefties and struck out 29, while walking 29 right-handed batters and striking out 28. A big key to his success was that he allowed just one home run in 76.1 innings. That was proof of Edens' ability to get ahead in the count and make his pitch, rather than being forced to throw his fastball for strikes.

HOLDING RUNNERS AND FIELDING:

Edens is an excellent athlete -- he was an all-state running back as an Idaho high schooler -- and utilizes his quickness on the mound. He didn't make an error in his 52 appearances, but had problems with basestealers last year. Though he worked only 76.1 innings, he allowed 15 steals in 20 attempts.

OVERALL:

Edens was picked up by Florida in the expansion draft, then immediately dealt to Houston. He should be an important middle reliever as the Astros try to move into contention.

TOM EDENS

Position: RP
Bats: R **Throws:** R
Ht: 6' 2" **Wt:** 188

Opening Day Age: 31
Born: 6/9/61 in Ontario, OR
ML Seasons: 4

Overall Statistics

	W	L	ERA	G	GS	Sv	IP	H	R	BB	SO	HR
1992	6	3	2.83	52	0	3	76.1	65	26	36	57	1
Career	12	10	3.88	97	14	5	206.1	203	99	83	120	13

How Often He Throws Strikes

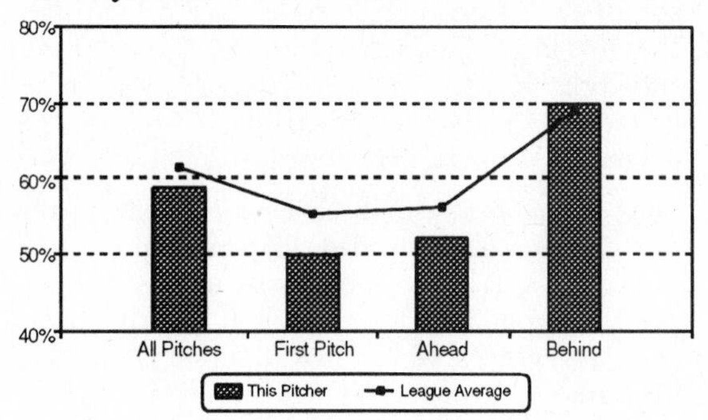

1992 Situational Stats

	W	L	ERA	Sv	IP		AB	H	HR	RBI	AVG
Home	5	1	3.80	2	42.2	LHB	109	27	0	12	.248
Road	1	2	1.60	1	33.2	RHB	166	38	1	14	.229
Day	2	0	1.45	1	31.0	Sc Pos	88	21	0	24	.239
Night	4	3	3.77	2	45.1	Clutch	109	23	1	6	.211

1992 Rankings (American League)

- 4th in worst first batter efficiency (.375)

OVERLOOKED

HITTING:

Steve Finley is a player who is always out to prove a point. In 1991, his first year with Houston, he wanted to prove he was an everyday player, not a reserve outfielder. He made his point. This past season, Finley made it crystal clear that he has become one of the National League's premier center fielders. He cracked out a career-high 177 hits, ranking him in the league's top ten, and he also made the charts in triples (13) and stolen bases (44). When the season ended, Finley showed a total of 47 extra-base hits and 55 RBI.

Nobody predicted this kind of production from Finley when he came from Baltimore in the Glenn Davis swap. He has developed into a solid contact hitter with line-drive skills and a player who uses his speed to full advantage. He struck out only 63 times in 607 at-bats, indicating his ability to put the ball in play. One of three Astros to play in every game in '92, Finley wound up second on the team in total bases (247) to Jeff Bagwell's 260.

BASERUNNING:

Outstanding on the basepaths, Finley's game is built around hustle and leg work. He stole 44 bases (78 in two years) and was flagged down only nine times. He was not thrown out once trying to stretch a double into a three- bagger, and made it to third safely 13 times.

FIELDING:

Finley is a Gold Glove candidate in center field. He is fearless in diving for balls, even on AstroTurf, where he pays the price for such efforts. He will make the sliding catch coming in on a drive or bounce high off the wall to steal away an extra base blow. He made only three errors and had eight assists in the field.

OVERALL:

Along with Craig Biggio, Finley serves as a catalyst for the Houston offense. Each is proficient at getting on base and scoring runs. Finley is continually improving; this season, people around the league should begin recognizing him as one of the NL's best at his position.

STEVE FINLEY

Position: CF
Bats: L **Throws:** L
Ht: 6' 2" **Wt:** 180

Opening Day Age: 28
Born: 3/12/65 in Union City, TN
ML Seasons: 4

Overall Statistics

	G	AB	R	H	D	T	HR	RBI	SB	BB	SO	AVG
1992	162	607	84	177	29	13	5	55	44	58	63	.292
Career	544	1884	249	520	78	29	18	171	117	147	211	.276

Where He Hits the Ball

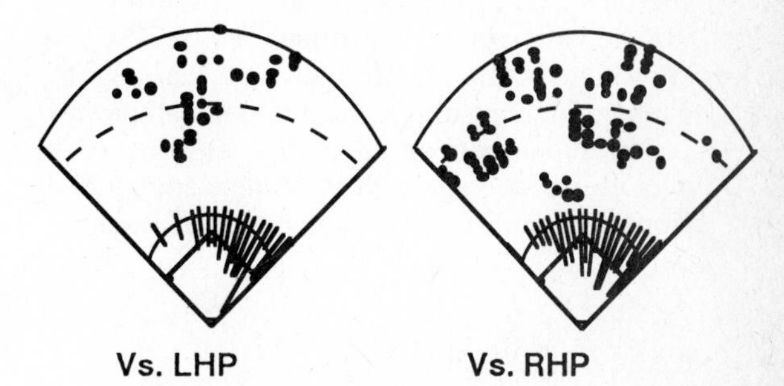

1992 Situational Stats

	AB	H	HR	RBI	AVG		AB	H	HR	RBI	AVG
Home	294	89	5	31	.303	LHP	226	63	1	19	.279
Road	313	88	0	24	.281	RHP	381	114	4	36	.299
Day	179	48	0	13	.268	Sc Pos	141	39	0	40	.277
Night	428	129	5	42	.301	Clutch	102	32	2	12	.314

1992 Rankings (National League)

- 1st in games played (162)
- 2nd in triples (13)
- 3rd in sacrifice bunts (16), stolen bases (44) and bunts in play (40)
- Led the Astros in hits (177), singles (130), triples, sacrifice bunts, stolen bases, games played, highest groundball/flyball ratio (1.9), stolen base percentage (83.0%), batting average vs. right-handed pitchers (.299), slugging percentage vs. right-handed pitchers (.428), on-base percentage vs. right-handed pitchers (.366), batting average on a 3-2 count (.356), batting average with 2 strikes (.259) and bunts in play

LUIS GONZALEZ

Position: LF
Bats: L **Throws:** R
Ht: 6' 2" **Wt:** 180

Opening Day Age: 25
Born: 9/3/67 in Tampa, FL
ML Seasons: 3

Overall Statistics

	G	AB	R	H	D	T	HR	RBI	SB	BB	SO	AVG
1992	122	387	40	94	19	3	10	55	7	24	52	.243
Career	271	881	92	218	49	12	23	124	17	66	158	.247

Where He Hits the Ball

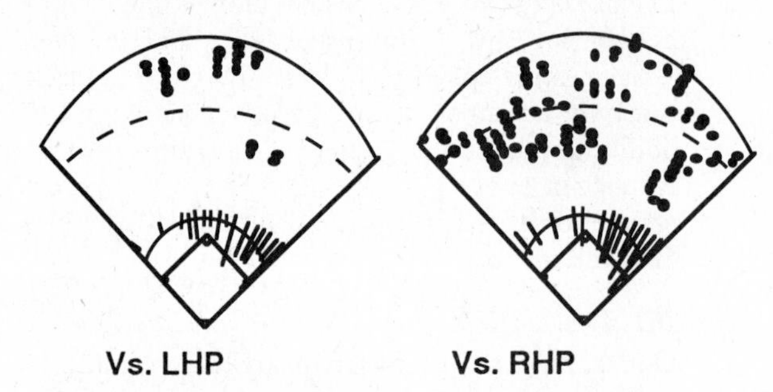

Vs. LHP Vs. RHP

1992 Situational Stats

	AB	H	HR	RBI	AVG		AB	H	HR	RBI	AVG
Home	204	42	4	25	.206	LHP	80	28	1	13	.350
Road	183	52	6	30	.284	RHP	307	66	9	42	.215
Day	112	26	2	12	.232	Sc Pos	108	27	4	45	.250
Night	275	68	8	43	.247	Clutch	71	22	3	15	.310

1992 Rankings (National League)

- Led NL left fielders in least GDPs per GDP situation (6.8%) and fielding percentage (.993)

HITTING:

The big league scout turned the question over in his mind: if you were starting a franchise and could choose one Houston Astro position player, who would it be? Finally, he blurted out, "Luis Gonzalez. I'd take Gonzalez." Not Jeff Bagwell, Craig Biggio or Steve Finley. Not Eric Anthony. Then the scout gave this testimonial: "He's a more complete ballplayer. Gonzalez has a great stroke at the plate, he's got some pop in his bat, he runs well and he plays good defense. He's just a good all-around ballplayer."

Gonzalez' classic left-handed stroke is the first thing baseball people notice about him. He hits the ball to all fields and in 1992 won his case about facing all pitching, not just righthanders. In '91, he batted only .172 versus lefties. Now, he knows his swing better and he's learning the pitchers. As a result, he hammered southpaws at a .350 clip -- best on the club -- en route to an overall .243 average with 10 homers and 55 RBI. Gonzalez hit .271 after his recall from Tucson and only a late slump kept him from finishing in the .260s.

BASERUNNING:

Gonzalez has yet to polish his basestealing talents. He was successful just half of the time (7-of-14) in thefts. But he also hit into only six double plays in almost 400 at-bats. He has the ability to be an aggressive base runner, but he's still learning.

FIELDING:

A former first baseman, Gonzalez plays left field with more confidence after playing two seasons out there. He covers good ground, plays the caroms off the wall well and he has more arm strength than when he first made the switch in spring camp in 1991. He had five assists in the field.

OVERALL:

The Astros outfield is solid for '93; that includes Gonzalez in left field. He has taken hold of the position and now he must refine his skills. With his solid stroke at the plate, Gonzalez should begin making some loud noise this season. A good start could lead to an outstanding season.

PITCHING:

Pete Harnisch walked a fine line as the pitching ace of the Houston Astros in 1992. His wins were down from 12 to nine despite the fact that his team improved considerably; his earned run average was up by a full run to 3.70. Only a strong stretch run enabled Harnisch to avoid a completely disappointing campaign. The righthander won only one game in each of the first five months of the season, but closed with a 4-1 mark and a 3.13 ERA in his final seven starts.

The aggressive Harnisch started out the year throwing too many fastballs and not enough offspeed stuff. The whole league looks for fastballs, so the key for Harnisch in his late comeback was developing a change-up and throwing his slider for strikes. He served up a staff-high 18 home run balls en route to a 9-10 record. Harnisch did keep his team in the game; the Astros rolled up a 20-14 mark in his career-high 34 starts. In 1991, they were 16-17 when he took the mound.

Harnisch also worked more than 200 innings for the second consecutive year. He's decidedly a power pitcher, with over 160 strikeouts during each of his two seasons with Houston. In two seasons he's pitched far better in the spacious Astrodome (14-8, 2.59) than on the road (7-11, 4.11).

HOLDING RUNNERS, FIELDING, HITTING:

Teams stole more bases on Harnisch than any other Astro pitcher, succeeding over 80 percent of the time (27-of-33). He comes off the mound well to take the throw at first base and made only two errors in '92. Harnisch is aggressive at the plate, with five doubles among his 11 hits and eight RBI.

OVERALL:

Harnisch is a workhorse on the mound, and all his effort should pay off with more wins in 1993. He'll have to pitch better on the road, however. With the signing of Doug Drabek, the Astros feel that Drabek and Harnisch give them as good a one-two punch as any other team.

PETE HARNISCH

Position: SP
Bats: R **Throws:** R
Ht: 6' 0" **Wt:** 207

Opening Day Age: 26
Born: 9/23/66 in Commack, NY
ML Seasons: 5

Overall Statistics

	W	L	ERA	G	GS	Sv	IP	H	R	BB	SO	HR
1992	9	10	3.70	34	34	0	206.2	182	92	64	164	18
Career	37	41	3.73	118	117	0	728.1	650	322	306	538	60

How Often He Throws Strikes

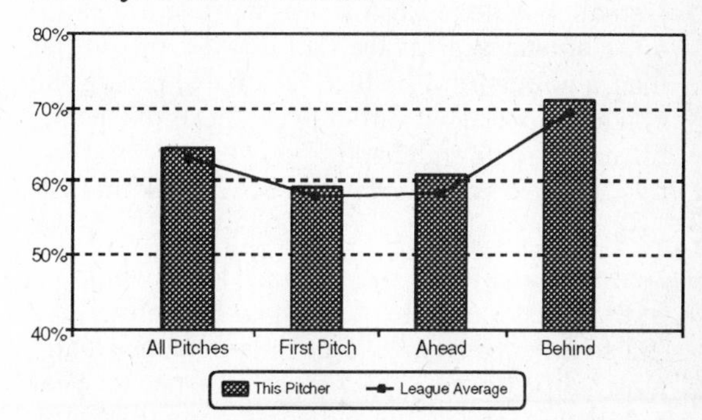

1992 Situational Stats

	W	L	ERA	Sv	IP		AB	H	HR	RBI	AVG
Home	7	4	2.75	0	137.2	LHB	466	109	10	52	.234
Road	2	6	5.61	0	69.0	RHB	313	73	8	33	.233
Day	1	4	4.07	0	48.2	Sc Pos	171	46	4	65	.269
Night	8	6	3.59	0	158.0	Clutch	53	13	1	4	.245

1992 Rankings (National League)

- 2nd in lowest groundball/flyball ratio (.86)
- Led the Astros in ERA (3.70), losses (10), games started (34), innings pitched (206.2), batters faced (859), home runs allowed (18), walks allowed (64), hit batsmen (5), strikeouts (164), most pitches thrown (3,234), pickoff throws (148), stolen bases allowed (27), highest strikeout/walk ratio (2.6), lowest batting average allowed (.234), lowest slugging percentage allowed (.371), lowest on-base percentage allowed (.294), least baserunners allowed per 9 innings (10.9), most run support per 9 innings (4.3), least home runs allowed per 9 innings (.78), most strikeouts per 9 innings (7.1) and ERA at home (2.75)

XAVIER HERNANDEZ

Position: RP
Bats: L **Throws:** R
Ht: 6' 2" **Wt:** 185

Opening Day Age: 27
Born: 8/16/65 in Port Arthur, TX
ML Seasons: 4

PITCHING:

Other than closer Doug Jones, the emergence of Xavier Hernandez proved to be the biggest happening in the Houston bullpen this past season. After struggling in a variety of pitching roles in 1991, he settled into a set-up role for Jones and won nine of 10 decisions. He ranked among National League relief leaders in appearances (with 77) and ERA (2.11) to go with seven saves.

What brought about the change? "He's got the guts of a burglar," says Astros pitching coach Bob Cluck. Hernandez is an aggressive pitcher who will challenge a hitter with his fastball, slider and forkball. The forkball -- Cluck calls it a split-finger -- is his best pitch. Batters used to sit on his fastball, but the forkball acts as more of a change-up. Hernandez grips the ball down a bit further than a splitter and he throws it hard, giving the ball a violent downward movement. It makes the former Toronto righthander's fastball more effective. He gets good movement on his sinking fastball, too.

Hernandez throws with a long-arm, whipping motion that makes his ball alive. He entered the '92 season determined to pitch more consistently after a disastrous (2-7, 4.71) performance the year before that brought him a demotion to the minors. He rebounded (2-1, three saves) that September and has been going strong since.

HOLDING RUNNERS, FIELDING, HITTING:

An improving defensive player, Hernandez made one error in 77 games. However, opposing runners stole 10 bases against him in 14 attempts. He's working on speeding up his leg kick a bit and driving more quickly to home plate. Hernandez has not had a hit since 1990, going 0-for-19 with 12 strikeouts as a batter the last two years.

OVERALL:

The 1993 season should mark the year when Hernandez comes into his own as a reliever. He reached his potential out of the bullpen in 1992 after rotating between starting and relieving earlier in his career. His mental makeup and live arm makes Hernandez a prime candidate to join the league's elite group of firemen.

Overall Statistics

	W	L	ERA	G	GS	Sv	IP	H	R	BB	SO	HR
1992	9	1	2.11	77	0	7	111.0	81	31	42	96	5
Career	14	9	3.58	150	7	10	259.0	232	114	106	182	21

How Often He Throws Strikes

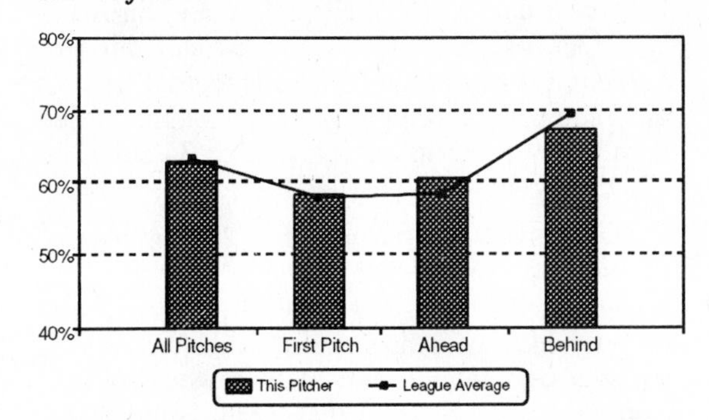

1992 Situational Stats

	W	L	ERA	Sv	IP		AB	H	HR	RBI	AVG
Home	6	1	1.83	5	59.0	LHB	209	44	2	13	.211
Road	3	0	2.42	2	52.0	RHB	195	37	3	22	.190
Day	3	1	3.41	1	29.0	Sc Pos	106	17	2	27	.160
Night	6	0	1.65	6	82.0	Clutch	150	31	1	11	.207

1992 Rankings (National League)

- 3rd in games pitched (77), lowest batting average allowed in relief with runners in scoring position (.160), relief wins (9) and relief innings (111)
- 6th in relief ERA (2.11) and lowest batting average allowed in relief (.200)
- 8th in batting average allowed in relief with runners on base (.206)
- Led the Astros in wild pitches (5), lowest batting average allowed vs. left-handed batters (.211), lowest batting average allowed in relief with runners in scoring position, lowest batting average allowed in relief and most strikeouts per 9 innings in relief (7.8)

PETE INCAVIGLIA

Position: LF/RF
Bats: R **Throws:** R
Ht: 6' 1" **Wt:** 225

Opening Day Age: 29
Born: 4/2/64 in Pebble Beach, CA
ML Seasons: 7

HITTING:

Pete Incaviglia resurrected his career last year in Houston, proving he wasn't finished as a ballplayer. After a disaster of a season in Detroit in '91, Incaviglia became a free agent and hooked up with the Astros and Art Howe, his first batting instructor at Texas. Howe proved a strong influence on Incaviglia. He reported with his weight down by some 30 pounds and hustled his way to open the season in right field. Only the emergence of Eric Anthony kept him from staying there.

Incaviglia hit for a decent average (.266) after three straight years of .236 or under. His 1992 season homer total (11) equalled his '91 output in Detroit, but he was a much more confident hitter. He retains his short, quick swing and outstanding power. His presence also made better players of youngsters Anthony and Luis Gonzalez; he kept them on their toes and also exerted a strong influence in the clubhouse.

Incaviglia had his moments, including a two-homer spree against San Francisco, when he tied the club record for RBI in a game with seven. Another one of his homers beat Pittsburgh. When he gets into a slump, it's usually from overswinging, from trying to muscle up on the ball.

BASERUNNING:

Incaviglia runs well for a man his size, especially since he shed some unnecessary poundage. He seldom steals a base, swiping a pair in four attempts. He runs hard on the basepaths but is adequate at best.

FIELDING:

Incaviglia always hustles in the field, but that doesn't make him a good outfielder. His six errors were the most for an Astro outfielder in 1992. Incaviglia did tie center fielder Steve Finley with eight assists, the most among Astro outfielders. He has a good, strong arm.

OVERALL:

With seven big league seasons behind him, Incaviglia still is only 29 years old. The Astros were reasonably satisfied with his efforts, but let him become a free agent. His talents are better suited for an American League team.

Overall Statistics

	G	AB	R	H	D	T	HR	RBI	SB	BB	SO	AVG
1992	113	349	31	93	22	1	11	44	2	25	99	.266
Career	904	3135	402	772	154	15	146	470	29	280	979	.246

Where He Hits the Ball

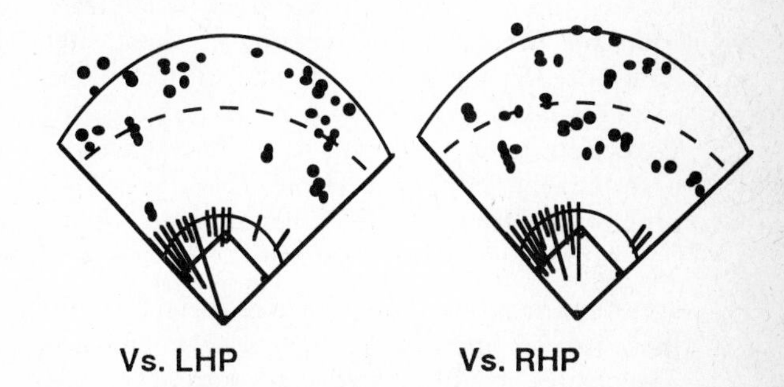

1992 Situational Stats

	AB	H	HR	RBI	AVG		AB	H	HR	RBI	AVG
Home	189	56	6	26	.296	LHP	170	48	7	27	.282
Road	160	37	5	18	.231	RHP	179	45	4	17	.251
Day	95	27	6	20	.284	Sc Pos	92	18	1	25	.196
Night	254	66	5	24	.260	Clutch	65	18	2	7	.277

1992 Rankings (National League)

- 6th in lowest batting average with runners in scoring position (.196)
- Led the Astros in strikeouts (99) and batting average on a 3-1 count (.500)

STOPPER

PITCHING:

Boil down the pitching philosophy of Doug Jones, and it comes out this way: "I've got plenty of muscles to throw slow. I don't have that many to throw hard." Easy does it for the Houston Astros' single season saves record-holder with 36, who was also the team leader in wins (11) last year. Jones is a master at changing speeds with his pitches. Some guys change speeds by throwing harder, but Jones does it by throwing softer. He missed winning the National League Rolaids Relief Man title by one point (103-102) to St. Louis' Lee Smith.

The Astros were able to sign the veteran righthander, formerly a premier reliever with Cleveland, because they offered him a job as their closer. Manager Art Howe got everything he expected and more, as Jones converted all but six of his save opportunities. "Doug's steady, on an even keel. You know what you're getting when you give him the ball," says Howe. "He doesn't get high or low. He makes the other team go out and beat him. He won't beat himself."

Jones has a surprisingly effective fastball which he spots well and three speeds on his change-up. The change acts like a screwball from the way he turns it over. What makes it even tougher is that Jones throws it at slow, slower and slowest speeds. He likes a heavy workload and responded with a 1.85 ERA in 80 games covering 111.2 innings.

HOLDING RUNNERS, FIELDING, HITTING:

Jones uses every skill at his disposal in fielding his position and holding runners. Only nine runners tried to steal a base on him and four didn't make it. As a late-inning man he seldom hits, going 0-for-4 his first year as an Astro.

OVERALL:

Jones deserves much credit for the Astros turnaround in '92. He stopped the team's heavy flow of losses in the eighth and ninth innings. He is a premier closer; the Astros plan on handing him the ball again in the late innings in 1993.

DOUG JONES

Position: RP
Bats: R **Throws:** R
Ht: 6' 2" **Wt:** 195

Opening Day Age: 35
Born: 6/24/57 in Covina, CA
ML Seasons: 8

Overall Statistics

	W	L	ERA	G	GS	Sv	IP	H	R	BB	SO	HR
1992	11	8	1.85	80	0	36	111.2	96	29	17	93	5
Career	37	40	2.82	356	4	164	535.1	518	201	116	433	27

How Often He Throws Strikes

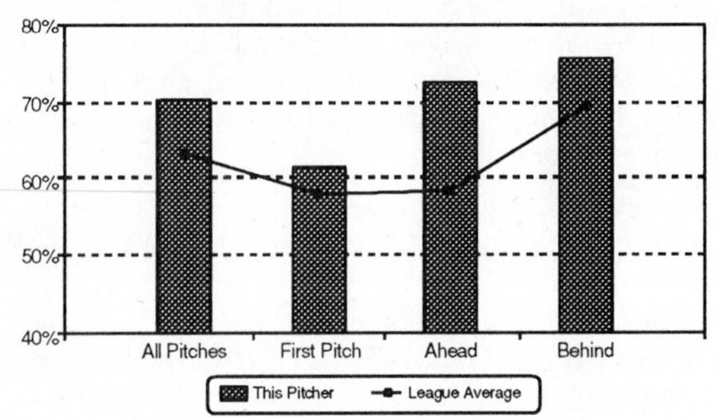

1992 Situational Stats

	W	L	ERA	Sv	IP		AB	H	HR	RBI	AVG
Home	6	5	2.42	17	63.1	LHB	217	55	3	20	.253
Road	5	3	1.12	19	48.1	RHB	192	41	2	17	.214
Day	3	2	0.92	13	29.1	Sc Pos	109	22	0	29	.202
Night	8	6	2.19	23	82.1	Clutch	322	77	5	31	.239

1992 Rankings (National League)

- 1st in games finished (70), save percentage (85.7%), relief wins (11) and relief innings (111.2)
- 2nd in games pitched (80), lowest batting average allowed in relief with runners on base (.175) and least baserunners allowed per 9 innings in relief (9.5)
- Led the Astros in wins, saves (36), games finished, hit batsmen (5), save opportunities (42), save percentage, blown saves (6), lowest batting average allowed in relief with runners on, relief ERA (1.85), relief wins, relief losses (8), relief innings and least baserunners allowed per 9 innings in relief

PITCHING:

All the numbers came up a bit more positive for Jimmy Jones last season. They usually do when the Houston righthander is in the pink of health. He reached double digits in wins (10), compiled his lowest ERA (4.07) and worked over 135 innings for the second straight year.

When sound of arm and body, Jones has been a viable major-league pitcher (39-38 in his career). But something always crops up to put him on the shelf for a spell. He's sprained an ankle, had a bad knee, an overall assortment of ills slowing him down. In 1992, the Astros opened the season without him as he rehabbed from surgery to clean up the clutter in his right elbow. Inflammation in the elbow interrupted his activity late in the season, but he won two games out of the bullpen in the final weeks to finish 10-6, the most victories among the team's starting pitchers.

Jones has sharpened his curveball and now uses his change-up more to keep hitters off-balance. He's added a cut fastball to his repertoire, a pitch that runs away from a right-handed batter like a slider but which breaks across the plate, not down. His is a perfect matchup of pitcher and ballpark. Jones made his major-league debut with the Padres in the Astrodome in 1986 and twirled a one-hitter. In 1991, four of his six wins were rung up in the domed stadium. Last season, he went 5-2 at home with a 3.33 ERA.

HOLDING RUNNERS, FIELDING, HITTING:

Although Jones tries to keep a watchful eye on runners, the opposition stole 20 bases in 25 attempts with him on the mound. He shows quickness at fielding balls hit back to him and made no errors in 25 games. His hitting (.168 lifetime) is acceptable for a pitcher.

OVERALL:

In stretches of the '92 season, Jones was the Astros' best pitcher. But as usual he didn't pitch the whole season. Jones has worked more than 150 innings in a season just once in his career, so the key to his success is staying healthy.

JIMMY JONES

Position: SP
Bats: R **Throws:** R
Ht: 6' 2" **Wt:** 190

Opening Day Age: 28
Born: 4/20/64 in Dallas, TX
ML Seasons: 7

Overall Statistics

	W	L	ERA	G	GS	Sv	IP	H	R	BB	SO	HR
1992	10	6	4.07	25	23	0	139.1	135	64	39	69	13
Career	39	38	4.35	141	112	0	715.1	762	397	230	355	66

How Often He Throws Strikes

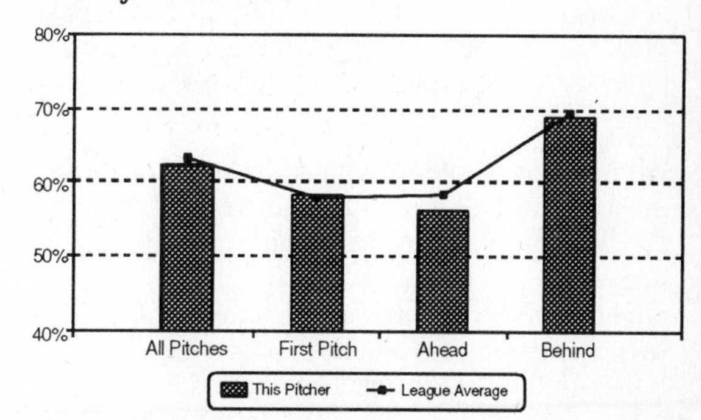

1992 Situational Stats

	W	L	ERA	Sv	IP		AB	H	HR	RBI	AVG
Home	5	2	3.33	0	54.0	LHB	300	85	9	32	.283
Road	5	4	4.54	0	85.1	RHB	224	50	4	20	.223
Day	1	2	3.43	0	39.1	Sc Pos	112	26	2	35	.232
Night	9	4	4.32	0	100.0	Clutch	37	9	0	1	.243

1992 Rankings (National League)

- 6th in highest ERA on the road (4.54)
- 8th in winning percentage (.625)
- Led the Astros in hit batsmen (5), GDPs induced (11) and winning percentage

DARRYL KILE

Position: SP
Bats: R **Throws:** R
Ht: 6' 5" **Wt:** 185

Opening Day Age: 24
Born: 12/2/68 in Garden Grove, CA
ML Seasons: 2

PITCHING:

Darryl Kile had a strong start and a solid finish last season. It's the middle part that created problems and brought his temporary demotion to AAA Tucson to work out his troubles. The tall righthander can look like a world beater when he's on, but when his control is amiss, he struggles to even skim by.

Kile opened the '92 campaign with a 2-2 record and a 1.89 ERA, then went through the throes of an eight-game losing streak -- the team's longest since Nolan Ryan lost that many in a row in 1987. In September, after a tour of Triple-A ball, Kile finished with a 3-1 record capped by a 6-1, 11-strikeout win over Los Angeles. The strikeouts tied his career high and gave him something positive to build on in 1993. But his 5-10 record failed to meet expectations after his promising rookie year.

Kile is a power pitcher with an outstanding curveball. His fastball has a lot of movement, running all over the plate. It is the addition of the split-fingered pitch that makes him a more complete pitcher. "When he throws his pitches for strikes," says teammate Steve Finley, observing from his center field post, "I don't see how anybody hits him." Therein lies the answer to the Kile riddle. He needs to throw his curveball for strikes because it sets up everything else.

HOLDING RUNNERS, FIELDING, HITTING:

Kile is working on all phases of his game. He concentrated on holding runners closer to the bag, with good results -- opponents stole only six bases on him in nine attempts. However, his five errors were tops on the pitching staff. He's not a washout with the stick; his batting average (.156) ranked third among Astro pitchers.

OVERALL:

Kile looms large in the Astros plans in 1993. With only two years' experience under his belt, he is still learning the league. His vast potential offers strong hope that 1993 will be his breakthrough year. With his ability, he should finally begin evening up his 12-21 career record.

Overall Statistics

	W	L	ERA	G	GS	Sv	IP	H	R	BB	SO	HR
1992	5	10	3.95	22	22	0	125.1	124	61	63	90	8
Career	12	21	3.81	59	44	0	279.0	268	142	147	190	24

How Often He Throws Strikes

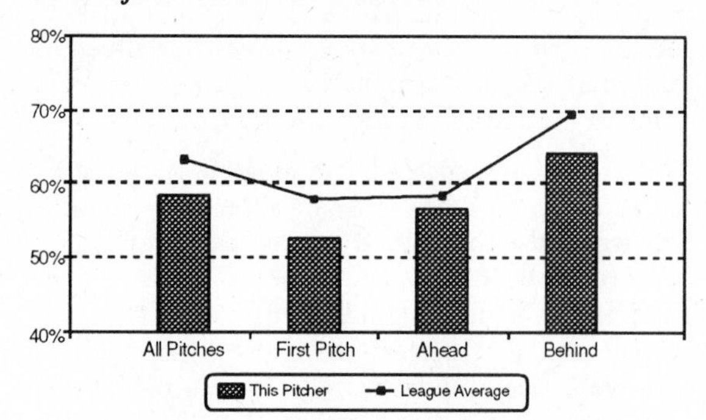

1992 Situational Stats

	W	L	ERA	Sv	IP		AB	H	HR	RBI	AVG
Home	3	5	3.53	0	63.2	LHB	271	69	5	32	.255
Road	2	5	4.38	0	61.2	RHB	205	55	3	17	.268
Day	0	2	5.11	0	24.2	Sc Pos	137	28	2	37	.204
Night	5	8	3.67	0	100.2	Clutch	22	6	0	1	.273

1992 Rankings (National League)

- 3rd in balks (4)
- 4th in lowest winning percentage (.333)
- Led the Astros in losses (10), complete games (2), balks and lowest batting average allowed with runners in scoring position (.204)

PITCHING:

Al Osuna wants to get his pitching career out of reverse. With the arrival of veteran closer Doug Jones, Osuna's role changed last year and he needed some time to make the adjustment to middle relief. His win-loss mark (6-3) was fine, but his ERA (4.23) went up almost a full run and he recorded no saves. Osuna found himself pitching in occasionally meaningless situations, one year after securing a team-leading 12 saves as the closer in 1991.

"It was an off year for him," one Houston insider says of the lanky lefthander. "He was put in a role last year (1991) as a stopper and that was a little tough for him. He wasn't ready to do that." As a result, Osuna developed a style of pitching to corners and was a bit defensive in his approach to hitters. He lost some of his aggressiveness and some of the zip on his fastball; where Osuna's fastball had been clocked in the past at 88 MPH, the radar guns were catching him at 81 last season. Manager Art Howe felt he was dropping down too much, almost side-arming the ball to the plate. The previous year, Osuna whiffed 68 batters in 81.2 innings. In '92, those figures skidded to 37 whiffs in 61.2 IP.

Along with the fastball, Osuna throws a slider and is developing a decent curveball to go with his change-up. Even though he struggled last year, he held opponents to a .236 average.

HOLDING, RUNNERS, FIELDING, HITTING:

Not many opponents chose to run on Osuna, but four of the five who did were successful. He has a good, quick move to the bag. He handled all 13 chances in the field perfectly. His hitting skills remain a mystery since he's had only two major-league at-bats.

OVERALL:

Osuna's primary role with the Astros is to come out of the bullpen and retire left-handed hitters in clutch situations. With righthanders Doug Jones and Xavier Hernandez as the top relief duo, Osuna should become the team's leading lefty in the pen this season.

AL OSUNA

Position: RP
Bats: R **Throws:** L
Ht: 6' 3" **Wt:** 200

Opening Day Age: 27
Born: 8/10/65 in Inglewood, CA
ML Seasons: 3

Overall Statistics

	W	L	ERA	G	GS	Sv	IP	H	R	BB	SO	HR
1992	6	3	4.23	66	0	0	61.2	52	29	38	37	8
Career	15	9	3.84	149	0	12	154.2	121	74	90	111	14

How Often He Throws Strikes

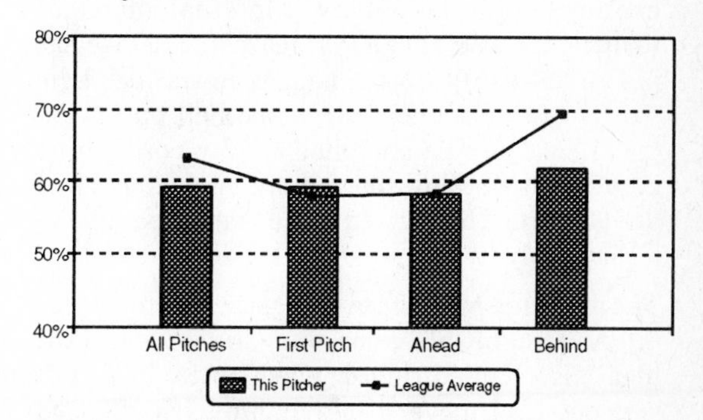

1992 Situational Stats

	W	L	ERA	Sv	IP		AB	H	HR	RBI	AVG
Home	5	1	1.97	0	32.0	LHB	73	18	2	8	.247
Road	1	2	6.67	0	29.2	RHB	147	34	6	18	.231
Day	0	1	4.15	0	26.0	Sc Pos	63	13	2	19	.206
Night	6	2	4.29	0	35.2	Clutch	76	19	4	11	.250

1992 Rankings (National League)

- 1st in lowest percentage of inherited runners scored (15.0%)
- 5th in highest relief ERA (4.23)
- 7th in lowest batting average allowed in relief with runners on base (.205)
- 9th in least strikeouts per 9 innings in relief (5.4)
- 10th in relief wins (6) and most baserunners allowed per 9 innings in relief (13.3)
- Led the Astros in lowest percentage of inherited runners scored

PITCHING:

Mark Portugal has the tenacity of a bulldog. His competitive nature made Portugal Houston's most productive starter before he was forced to the sidelines last July with bone chips in his pitching elbow. After undergoing surgery, he returned the final week of the season for two relief outings and one start, and pitched well. He just managed to crack 100 innings for the season.

When he's healthy, Portugal is a complete pitcher with one of the best change-ups in the game. With a fastball, curve and slider, his offspeed pitch becomes a lethal weapon in his throwing arsenal. Toss in his battling mentality and it's easy to discover what makes him tick: he welcomes a challenge. As testimony, Montreal manager Felipe Alou said after a Portugal shutout, "He has nine lives. Every time I thought he was dead, he would come back and throw the hell out of the ball." Last year he compiled a 6-3 record with a 2.66 ERA, working six or more innings in 12 of his 16 starts. He allowed more than three runs in a game only twice.

The one-time Minnesota Twin is very effective in the Astrodome, where he was 4-0 last year. Portugal also limited right-handed batters to a .171 average. He is never afraid to throw his offspeed pitches when behind in the count. Since joining Houston in 1989, Portugal is 34-26, eight games over .500; over the same period, the Astros are 34 games under.

HOLDING RUNNERS, FIELDING, HITTING:

Portugal is very effective at holding runners, allowing only seven steals in 13 attempts last year. No other Astro pitcher was as close to breaking even on opposing steal attempts, and only two other Astros were under 60 percent. Portugal pounces on ground balls. He had just three hits, probably from spending so much time on the disabled list.

OVERALL:

Until his elbow began barking, Portugal pitched like the ace of the staff. If he ever puts two solid halves together, he can earn that ranking. Portugal is in his prime years and his experience is vital to a young starting staff.

MARK PORTUGAL

Position: SP
Bats: R **Throws:** R
Ht: 6' 0" **Wt:** 190
Opening Day Age: 30
Born: 10/30/62 in Los Angeles, CA
ML Seasons: 8

Overall Statistics

	W	L	ERA	G	GS	Sv	IP	H	R	BB	SO	HR
1992	6	3	2.66	18	16	0	101.1	76	32	41	62	7
Career	45	45	4.01	174	116	5	813.0	771	389	309	542	91

How Often He Throws Strikes

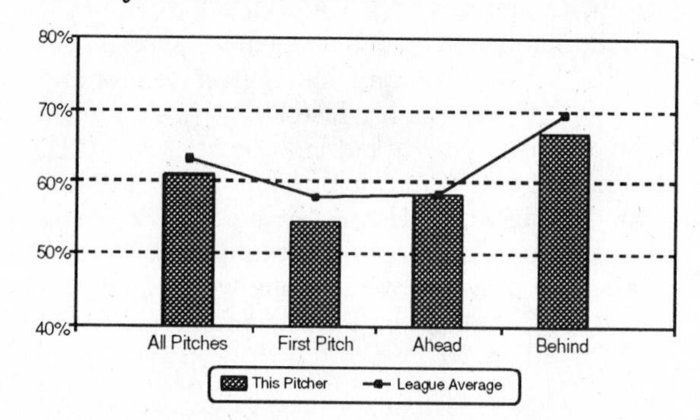

1992 Situational Stats

	W	L	ERA	Sv	IP		AB	H	HR	RBI	AVG
Home	4	0	1.86	0	58.0	LHB	205	50	5	19	.244
Road	2	3	3.74	0	43.1	RHB	152	26	2	8	.171
Day	2	2	4.50	0	30.0	Sc Pos	78	21	1	21	.269
Night	4	1	1.89	0	71.1	Clutch	31	6	2	2	.194

1992 Rankings (National League)

- Led the Astros in shutouts (1) and most GDPs induced per GDP situation (16.9%)

HITTING:

In his first full season with Houston, Scott Servais worked heavily keeping his confidence level high. It was difficult to do, because he split time and shared catching duties with Ed Taubensee. To date, Servais rates as a singles hitter, with nine doubles last year representing his only hits for extra bases. He knocked in 15 runs and batted .239, the top average among the Astros' three catchers in 1992.

Servais is a battler and a hard worker. The former USA Olympian spent only two and a half years in the minors before coming up to the big club in the middle of '91. "Scotty has the bat speed," says team batting instructor Rudy Jaramillo. "But when you're not playing every day, you try to do too much when you get in there. You put a lot of pressure on yourself that way." That tendency showed in 1991 when Servais went 0-for-22 before collecting his first major league hit.

Servais is trying to cut down on his habit of jumping out at the pitch and over-committing himself rather than letting the ball come to him. Most agree he made good progress with his bat in 1992. After starting three consecutive games in midseason, Servais said, "It's nice making adjustments at the plate from at-bat to at-bat, rather than doing it in the batting cage."

BASERUNNING:

Servais runs like your typical catcher. Methodical on the basepaths, he has attempted no steals as an Astro and is 0-for-9 in his professional career.

FIELDING:

Servais' strength at this point is his defensive package. He has an above-average throwing arm and is working to perfect a quick release of the ball. He calls a solid game and is good at blocking the plate. He probably is slightly ahead of Taubensee in all-around abilities behind the plate.

OVERALL:

Servais has improved with big-league exposure. But Taubensee is being groomed as an everyday player, which means that Servais eventually may settle into a spot-starter role with the Astros or another team.

SCOTT SERVAIS

Position: C
Bats: R **Throws:** R
Ht: 6' 2" **Wt:** 195

Opening Day Age: 25
Born: 6/4/67 in LaCrosse, WI
ML Seasons: 2

Overall Statistics

	G	AB	R	H	D	T	HR	RBI	SB	BB	SO	AVG
1992	77	205	12	49	9	0	0	15	0	11	25	.239
Career	93	242	12	55	12	0	0	21	0	15	33	.227

Where He Hits the Ball

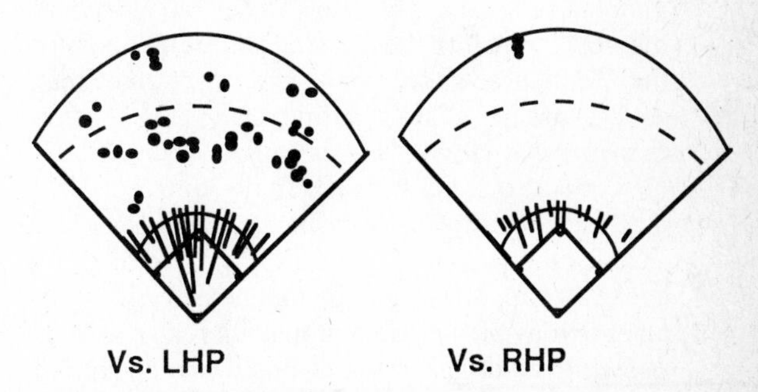

1992 Situational Stats

	AB	H	HR	RBI	AVG		AB	H	HR	RBI	AVG
Home	95	23	0	6	.242	LHP	145	36	0	15	.248
Road	110	26	0	9	.236	RHP	60	13	0	0	.217
Day	74	16	0	4	.216	Sc Pos	54	10	0	15	.185
Night	131	33	0	11	.252	Clutch	43	7	0	1	.163

1992 Rankings (National League)

- 8th in lowest slugging percentage vs. left-handed pitchers (.303)
- 10th in lowest batting average in the clutch (.163)

EDDIE TAUBENSEE

Position: C
Bats: L **Throws:** R
Ht: 6' 4" **Wt:** 205

Opening Day Age: 24
Born: 10/31/68 in Beeville, TX
ML Seasons: 2

HITTING:

Eddie Taubensee took one step backwards to make two big forward strides with Houston in '92. The Astros thought enough of the left-handed hitting Taubensee to deal top prospect Kenny Lofton to Cleveland to get him. Fans expected Taubensee to come in with a bang, as Lofton was doing for the Indians, but it was more like a lightweight firecracker. So in mid-June the tall, solidly-built Astro took a side trip back to AAA Tucson. His orders were to use his hands more and exercise better pitch selection.

Taubensee hit .338 in 20 games at Tucson and returned to Houston a new hitter, the guy they expected all along. After being recalled Taubensee hit at a .269 clip and socked all five of his home runs for the season. His power is such that Taubensee should be a 15-to-20 homer man as he matures. "He's a big, strong kid," says manager Art Howe. "He can juice the ball. He's hit a couple out one-handed. To do something like that tells you how strong he is." Taubensee hit .222 for the season but he hit left-handed pitching at a .234 clip, offering hope that he can emerge as an everyday player. He wrapped up his year on an upswing, batting .300 in the closing seven games.

BASERUNNING:

Taubensee grounded into only four double plays in 104 games and stole two bases in three attempts, so he's not a problem running the bases. For his size he runs decently, but he is not an aggressive runner and won't look for the extra base very often.

FIELDING:

Taubensee is regarded as a good defensive catcher with a strong throwing arm. He is learning the pitchers on the Astro staff and developing a knack for working with them. One needed area of improvement: he had nine passed balls in '92.

OVERALL:

Taubensee is capable of finding his niche and settling in for a long run as the Astros' number-one catcher. He laid the foundation last season and now must build on it.

Overall Statistics

	G	AB	R	H	D	T	HR	RBI	SB	BB	SO	AVG
1992	104	297	23	66	15	0	5	28	2	31	78	.222
Career	130	363	28	82	17	1	5	36	2	36	94	.226

Where He Hits the Ball

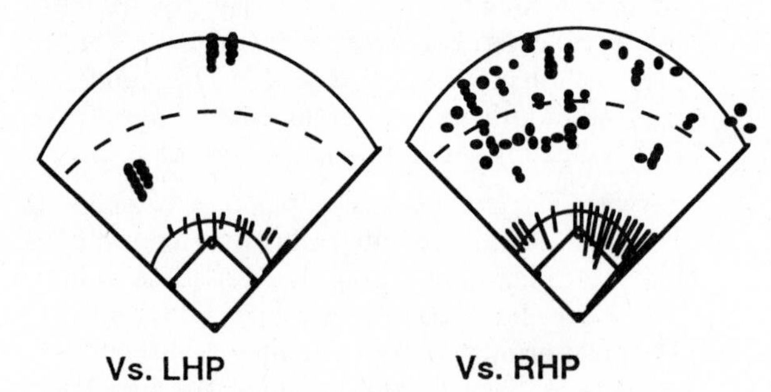

1992 Situational Stats

	AB	H	HR	RBI	AVG		AB	H	HR	RBI	AVG
Home	157	38	2	12	.242	LHP	47	11	2	5	.234
Road	140	28	3	16	.200	RHP	250	55	3	23	.220
Day	69	15	2	9	.217	Sc Pos	73	14	0	18	.192
Night	228	51	3	19	.224	Clutch	53	9	1	7	.170

1992 Rankings (National League)

- Did not rank near the top or bottom in any category

BRIAN WILLIAMS

Position: SP
Bats: R **Throws:** R
Ht: 6' 2" **Wt:** 195

Opening Day Age: 24
Born: 2/15/69 in Lancaster, SC
ML Seasons: 2

PITCHING:

Some young pitchers are the spitting image of former major leaguers. Well, Brian Williams stirs up memories of another Houston whiz, the late Don Wilson, in his pitching style and mannerisms. Now if he can match the success of the former All-Star who twirled two no-hitters, his mark on the game will be notable.

Williams made more progress last season than any of the young pitchers in the Houston starting rotation. He ranked among the team's top starting staff winners, compiling a 7-6 record and a 3.92 ERA. A sprained ankle kept him from improving those totals in the closing weeks. The young righthander expected to make the starting rotation out of spring training, but he pressed and overthrew the ball. The day after the Astros demoted him, he tossed a six-inning no-hitter against a triple-A team. He posted a 6-1 record at Tucson, then staged a successful comeback with the big club.

Williams has the best of both worlds as pitching goes, owning an outstanding arm and good control. It's an unusual combination in someone so young (24). He throws the same pitches as Wilson, who died after the 1974 season in a tragic home accident: fastball, curveball, slider and change-up, though Williams also throws the circle change.

HOLDING RUNNERS, FIELDING, HITTING:

Williams takes a long, hard look at runners at first base, but still had seven bases stolen off him in 16 games. He also made two errors in handling 24 total chances from the mound. As a former outfielder at the University of South Carolina, he is a threat with the bat (4 hits, 4 RBI) and should improve as he learns the league.

OVERALL:

With his raw ability and strong arm, Williams possesses the ingredients to become a dominating pitcher in the National League. He's capable of becoming a number-one type pitcher on the staff once he gains the necessary experience. It seems just a matter of time until he comes into his own as a big winner for the Astros.

Overall Statistics

	W	L	ERA	G	GS	Sv	IP	H	R	BB	SO	HR
1992	7	6	3.92	16	16	0	96.1	92	44	42	54	10
Career	7	7	3.90	18	18	0	108.1	103	49	46	58	12

How Often He Throws Strikes

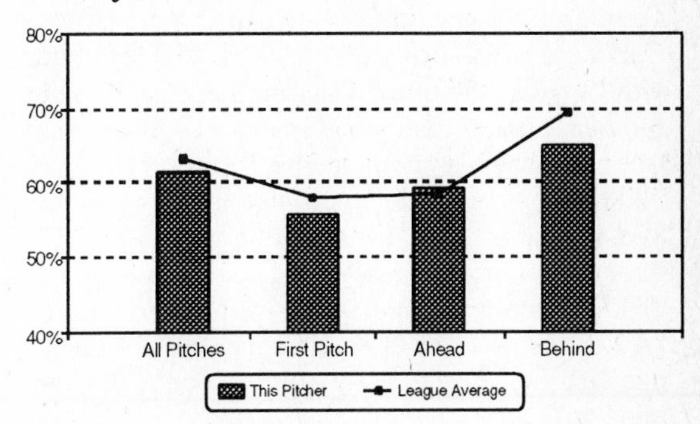

1992 Situational Stats

	W	L	ERA	Sv	IP		AB	H	HR	RBI	AVG
Home	3	3	4.10	0	41.2	LHB	223	60	5	26	.269
Road	4	3	3.79	0	54.2	RHB	138	32	5	16	.232
Day	1	2	4.70	0	15.1	Sc Pos	101	20	2	30	.198
Night	6	4	3.78	0	81.0	Clutch	21	6	0	1	.286

1992 Rankings (National League)

- Did not rank near the top or bottom in any category

CASEY CANDAELE

Position: SS/3B/LF
Bats: B **Throws:** R
Ht: 5' 9" **Wt:** 165

Opening Day Age: 32
Born: 1/12/61 in Lompoc, CA
ML Seasons: 6

Overall Statistics

	G	AB	R	H	D	T	HR	RBI	SB	BB	SO	AVG
1992	135	320	19	68	12	1	1	18	7	24	36	.213
Career	641	1743	175	435	75	20	9	124	34	149	187	.250

HITTING, FIELDING, BASERUNNING:

People sure know how to hurt a guy. When Casey Candaele was growing up, fans in the stands would yell down to him on the field, "Your mother is better than you." In his case, it was half true. Candaele's mom is the former Helen St. Aubin, a center fielder once described as a female Ted Williams. She won a batting title in the All-American Girls Professional Baseball League in 1945, which was popularized by the 1992 movie, "A League of Their Own." Candaele's .213 average last year was equally atypical for both mom and son.

Despite his hitting problems last season, Candaele continued to fill a valuable reserve role for Houston. He started 41 games at shortstop when Andujar Cedeno was demoted, 24 at third base when Ken Caminiti went to the sidelines, and four more filling in for Craig Biggio at second base. It wasn't his best year in the field, either, as he made 11 errors. Candaele is alert on the basepaths, an aggressive runner, and he stole seven bases while being thrown out only once.

OVERALL:

Candaele is a popular player in the Houston clubhouse and an asset to a ballclub even when he's not hitting much. He yearns to be a regular, but those days are probably behind him. But he's a good man coming off the bench and filling in wherever needed.

JUAN GUERRERO

Position: SS/3B
Bats: R **Throws:** R
Ht: 5'11" **Wt:** 160

Opening Day Age: 26
Born: 2/1/67 in Los Llanos, Dominican Republic
ML Seasons: 1

Overall Statistics

	G	AB	R	H	D	T	HR	RBI	SB	BB	SO	AVG
1992	79	125	8	25	4	2	1	14	1	10	32	.200
Career	79	125	8	25	4	2	1	14	1	10	32	.200

HITTING, FIELDING, BASERUNNING:

Juan Guerrero made the big jump from Class AA ball to the major leagues in 1992 after his selection by Houston in the Rule 5 draft. Houston plucked Guerrero from the San Francisco organization after he hit a sizzling .334 with 19 homers and 94 RBI in 128 games at Shreveport in 1991. Under draft rules, he had to stay with the Astros all season or be offered back to the Giants. They held on to him and he responded by squeezing into 79 games, hitting only .200 but showing a little pop with the bat (four doubles, two triples, one homer, 14 RBI).

Guerrero is a line drive hitter and will surprise with his power for someone his size. "There's a certain little click you want to hear from the bat when a hitter makes contact," says batting instructor Rudy Jaramillo. "Juan has that. The ball really jumps off his bat." He's not a speedster, but rather just an average runner. He did good work at four different positions and made only two errors.

OVERALL:

Guerrero is a raw talent who gives positive signs of being able to play at the major-league level. His versatility would make him a valuable player for the Astros. However, since he was mainly on the Houston roster because they were forced to keep him there, there's a good chance he'll go back to AAA this year.

ROB MURPHY

Position: RP
Bats: L **Throws:** L
Ht: 6' 2" **Wt:** 215

Opening Day Age: 32
Born: 5/26/60 in Miami, FL
ML Seasons: 8

Overall Statistics

	W	L	ERA	G	GS	Sv	IP	H	R	BB	SO	HR
1992	3	1	4.04	59	0	0	55.2	56	28	21	42	2
Career	22	26	3.25	457	0	27	504.1	473	203	206	447	34

PITCHING, FIELDING, HITTING & HOLDING RUNNERS:

Rob Murphy is a journeyman pitcher who made Houston his fourth major-league stop in five years. Once a power pitcher, his strikeout ratio declined from a peak of 9.17 whiffs per nine innings with Boston in 1989 to 6.37 with Seattle in 1991. The Astros signed Murphy to a minor league contract and he won a roster spot as expected in spring training. He rebounded nicely during the regular season with a 3-1 record and 42 strikeouts in 55.2 innings (6.79 per 9 innings), displaying a bit of his old fire.

The Astros rebuilt their bullpen with veteran arms and the left-handed Murphy figured in the mix by appearing in 59 games. Murphy throws a fastball, slider and split-fingered pitch. The slider is his big pitch and he uses it often against left-handed batters. Although his ERA (4.04) was up in '92, Murphy allowed only nine of 37 inherited runners to score. He's not agile around the mound, but went errorless in 14 fielding chances. For a lefty, he's poor at holding runners.

OVERALL:

Murphy remains a good spot reliever and is a durable pitcher. With Doug Jones, Xavier Hernandez and Joe Boever, he helped give the Astros their best bullpen performance in years. If Houston doesn't re-sign the free agent, Murphy should be able to help another club. He still has the arm and the pitches to do the job.

RAFAEL RAMIREZ

Position: SS
Bats: R **Throws:** R
Ht: 5'11" **Wt:** 190

Opening Day Age: 34
Born: 2/18/59 in San Pedro de Macoris, Dominican Republic
ML Seasons: 13

Overall Statistics

	G	AB	R	H	D	T	HR	RBI	SB	BB	SO	AVG
1992	73	176	17	44	6	0	1	13	0	7	24	.250
Career	1539	5494	562	1432	224	31	53	484	112	264	621	.261

HITTING, FIELDING, BASERUNNING:

Among the chores Rafael Ramirez handled without any urging in 1992 was taking young shortstop Andujar Cedeno under his wing to help ease the youngster's entry into the big leagues. He did so willingly, although Cedeno was the player taking his job at shortstop. It said a lot about the veteran infielder from the Dominican Republic. He is a backup now, with his best years behind him. But he accepted his role with the Houston Astros in 1992 and remained useful in pinch-hit situations.

Ramirez started 37 games at shortstop when Cedeno was sent to AAA Tucson to pull his game back together. He batted .250 in 73 games. Although the years are taking a toll, he still has good bat speed and is respected for his ability to hit in clutch situations. He can hit-and-run, hit behind the runner, basically whatever the strategy dictates. He committed seven errors in the field, but he doesn't hold back anything in his play. Ramirez did not attempt a steal last year.

OVERALL:

With the tutoring of Cedeno complete, the Astros released Ramirez at the end of the season. Ramirez could still prove valuable to a team seeking a veteran backup. He is not limited to being just a defensive infielder, but can also deliver offense off the bench. This may give him an edge when looking for a job in this expansion year.

HOUSTON ASTROS MINOR LEAGUE PROSPECTS

ORGANIZATION OVERVIEW:

Not expected to do much last year, the young Astros surprised people by playing .500 ball. Now Houston has a new owner, one with some money to spend, and the word was that the 'Stros would be active in the free agent market for the next few years. Hopefully that doesn't mean they're going to start neglecting their player development system. Under general manager Bill Wood, the Astros have been producing some good prospects, and showing some patience with them as well. They've also made astute trades for young players like Steve Finley and Jeff Bagwell. What the Astros haven't produced are impact players (Phil Nevin may change that), which is why they're tempted to go to the free agent route.

TRENT A. HUBBARD

Position: 2B　　**Opening Day Age:** 28
Bats: R **Throws:** R　　**Born:** 5/11/64 in Chicago, IL
Ht: 5' 8" **Wt:** 180

Recent Statistics

	G	AB	R	H	D	T	HR	RBI	SB	BB	SO	AVG
91 AA Jackson	126	455	78	135	21	3	2	41	39	65	81	.297
91 AAA Tucson	2	4	0	0	0	0	0	0	0	0	0	.000
92 AAA Tucson	115	420	69	130	16	4	2	33	34	45	68	.310
92 MLE	115	393	44	103	12	2	1	21	23	29	75	.262

A year ago, the Astros moved catcher Craig Biggio to second base. They may be having a few second thoughts after Trent Hubbard's big season at AAA Tucson last year. Then again, maybe not. Hubbard, nearly 29, is older than Biggio and played in a friendly park that padded his batting average. However, Hubbard has good speed and is considered a solid glove man.

TODD B.G. JONES

Position: P　　**Opening Day Age:** 24
Bats: L **Throws:** R　　**Born:** 4/24/68 in Marietta, GA
Ht: 6' 3" **Wt:** 200

Recent Statistics

	W	L	ERA	G	GS	Sv	IP	H	R	BB	SO	HR
91 A Osceola	4	4	4.35	14	14	0	72.1	68	38	35	52	2
91 AA Jackson	4	3	4.88	10	10	0	55.1	51	37	39	37	2
92 AA Jackson	3	7	3.14	61	0	25	66.0	52	28	44	60	3
92 AAA Tucson	0	1	4.50	3	0	0	4.0	1	2	10	4	0

A former number one draft choice who was selected with the pick Houston received for losing Nolan Ryan, Jones has been expected to do great things. After a move to the bullpen last year, he may be ready to live up to those expectations. Jones is probably the hardest thrower in the Houston system, and he was solid in late relief with 25 saves at AA Jackson. Jones recorded nearly a strikeout an inning, but as usual control was a problem for him. If the control comes along, he could soon be Houston's closer.

JEFF JUDEN

Position: P　　**Opening Day Age:** 22
Bats: R **Throws:** R　　**Born:** 1/19/71 in Salem, MA
Ht: 6' 7" **Wt:** 245

Recent Statistics

	W	L	ERA	G	GS	Sv	IP	H	R	BB	SO	HR
91 AA Jackson	6	3	3.10	16	16	0	95.2	84	43	44	75	4
91 AAA Tucson	3	2	3.18	10	10	0	56.2	56	28	25	51	2
92 AAA Tucson	9	10	4.04	26	26	0	147.0	149	84	71	120	11

"Enigmatic Juden Confounds Astros" was a headline in Baseball America last year, and that about sums up the 1992 season for the former number-one draft choice. In spring training, Juden said he hoped to win 20 games for the Astros, but instead he went 9-10 for AAA Tucson. Juden's weight has been a problem, and he loses velocity on his fastball when he puts on too many pounds. The word is that he's had things too easy and never had to work for success. That's no longer true.

PHIL NEVIN

Position: 3B　　**Opening Day Age:** 22
Bats: R **Throws:** R　　**Born:** 1/19/71 in Fullerton,CA
Ht: 6' 2" **Wt:** 185

College Statistics

	G	AB	R	H	D	T	HR	RBI	SB	BB	SO	AVG
92 Cal State Fullerton	61	200	66	78	18	0	20	75	5	57	32	.390

The overall number-one pick in last year's draft, Nevin came from the baseball factory at Cal State Fullerton and then went on to play in the Olympics. He's not expected to spend much time in the minors. Nevin's athletic skills are so good that the Astros are toying with the idea of moving him from third base to shortstop, a position where they need him more. But before we start preparing Nevin's Hall of Fame plaque, consider that a lot of recent overall number-one picks -- B.J. Surhoff, Jeff King, Andy Benes, Ben McDonald come to mind -- have developed into only good dependable players, not stars. Hopefully Nevin will have a better career than Shawn Abner.

DONNELL L. WALL

Position: P　　**Opening Day Age:** 25
Bats: R **Throws:** R　　**Born:** 7/11/67 in Potosi, MO
Ht: 6' 1" **Wt:** 180

Recent Statistics

	W	L	ERA	G	GS	Sv	IP	H	R	BB	SO	HR
91 A Burlington	7	5	2.03	16	16	0	106.2	73	30	21	102	4
91 A Osceola	6	3	2.09	12	12	0	77.1	55	22	11	62	3
92 A Osceola	3	1	2.63	7	7	0	41.0	37	13	8	30	1
92 AA Jackson	9	6	3.54	18	18	0	114.1	114	51	26	99	6
92 AAA Tucson	0	0	1.13	2	2	0	8.0	11	1	1	2	0

Compared to Nevin, Donnie is sort of a Wal-Mart prospect, an 18th-round draft choice who strikes people out, exhibits great control, and wins -- 38-23 in his minor-league career. By the end of last season, he'd advanced as far as AAA. Soon, the Astros may start noticing him.

PEDRO ASTACIO

Position: SP
Bats: R **Throws:** R
Ht: 6' 2" **Wt:** 174

Opening Day Age: 23
Born: 11/28/69 in Hato Mayor, DR
ML Seasons: 1

PITCHING:

Pedro Astacio's minor-league numbers were not very impressive (4-11, 4.78 ERA in 19 AA starts; 6-6, 5.47 mark in 24 AAA appearances). So when the 22-year-old tossed a three-hit shutout in his major league debut, it was thought to be a fluke. Think again. Astacio made 11 major league starts in '92, 10 of which were quality outings. The only three pitchers to top his four shutouts in '92? Roger Clemens, Tom Glavine and David Cone.

Why the turnaround? For one thing, Astacio's AAA experience was in the hitter-happy Pacific Coast League. Second, pitchers tend to have an advantage the first time around the league. (But when the Reds saw Astacio for the third time, he shut them out -- in Cincinnati.) Third, and most importantly, he had previously relied almost exclusively on a hard sinking fastball. Now he has added a baffling Dominican change and a slow sweeping curveball to his repertoire.

Astacio also threw the ball over the plate. He walked 2.8 batters per nine innings in the minors, 2.2 in the bigs. His strikeouts were down as well (6.2 strikeouts per nine innings in the minors, 4.7 in the majors), but when opponents hit the ball (.255), it was usually on the ground. Astacio's lackluster 5-5 record was largely due to lack of support from his teammates; they fumbled away numerous runs and scored just 2.96 runs per Astacio start.

HOLDING RUNNERS, FIELDING, HITTING:

Potential basestealers were just 5-for-8 with Astacio on the hill as he paid attention to them well. He looks to be an average fielder, but his plate skills leave a lot to be desired. He runs extremely well, both down to first and to the dugout after getting out of a jam.

OVERALL:

A major surprise, Astacio brought some much needed exuberance to the Dodgers and quickly became a fan favorite. There's even talk of making him a closer. Whatever his role, he will enter the '93 season as an important member of the staff.

Overall Statistics

	W	L	ERA	G	GS	Sv	IP	H	R	BB	SO	HR
1992	5	5	1.98	11	11	0	82.0	80	23	20	43	1
Career	5	5	1.98	11	11	0	82.0	80	23	20	43	1

How Often He Throws Strikes

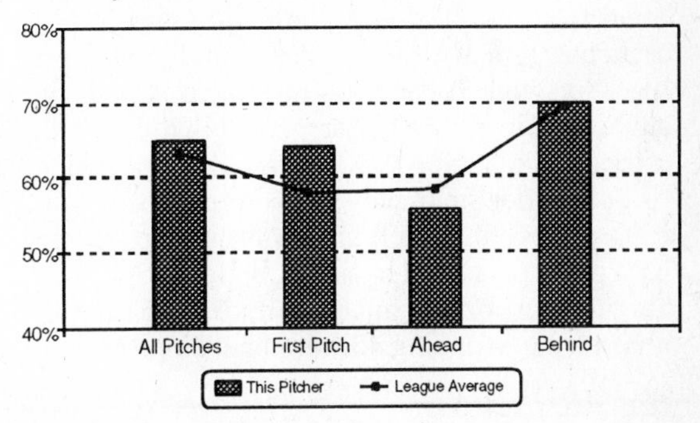

1992 Situational Stats

	W	L	ERA	Sv	IP		AB	H	HR	RBI	AVG
Home	3	3	1.68	0	48.1	LHB	180	44	1	7	.244
Road	2	2	2.41	0	33.2	RHB	134	36	0	11	.269
Day	0	3	3.24	0	25.0	Sc Pos	71	16	0	15	.225
Night	5	2	1.42	0	57.0	Clutch	23	8	1	2	.348

1992 Rankings (National League)

- 3rd in shutouts (4)
- 10th in most GDPs per GDP situation (17.6%)
- Led the Dodgers in shutouts and most GDPs per GDP situation

BRETT BUTLER

Position: CF
Bats: L **Throws:** L
Ht: 5'10" **Wt:** 160

Opening Day Age: 35
Born: 6/15/57 in Los Angeles, CA
ML Seasons: 12

Overall Statistics

	G	AB	R	H	D	T	HR	RBI	SB	BB	SO	AVG
1992	157	553	86	171	14	11	3	39	41	95	67	.309
Career	1678	6169	1048	1777	216	99	44	439	437	857	673	.288

Where He Hits the Ball

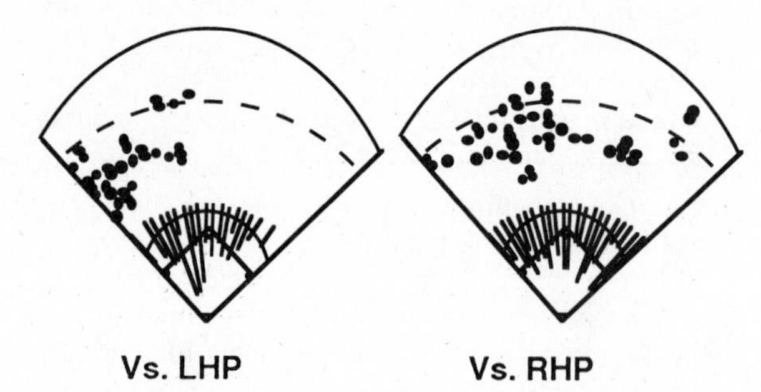

1992 Situational Stats

	AB	H	HR	RBI	AVG		AB	H	HR	RBI	AVG
Home	267	81	1	19	.303	LHP	223	66	1	17	.296
Road	286	90	2	20	.315	RHP	330	105	2	22	.318
Day	166	46	1	10	.277	Sc Pos	126	33	0	34	.262
Night	387	125	2	29	.323	Clutch	92	32	0	1	.348

1992 Rankings (National League)

- 1st in singles (143), sacrifice bunts (24), most pitches seen per plate appearance (4.06), on-base percentage vs. right-handed pitchers (.420) and bunts in play (97)
- 2nd in caught stealing (21) and most pitches seen (2,743)
- 3rd in walks (95), times on base (269), on-base percentage (.413), lowest percentage of swings that missed (8.9%) and steals of third (8)
- Led the Dodgers in batting average (.309), at-bats (553), runs scored (86), hits (171), singles, triples (11), sacrifice bunts, stolen bases (41), caught stealing, walks, times on base and plate appearances (676)

HITTING:

Brett Butler headed into last year's All-Star break a tired and disgruntled ballplayer. He seemed to be taking responsibility for the whole Dodger team's dismal performance. There were a lot of ugly at-bats in his midseason .277 average.

The refreshed guy who returned from the break carried a new pink bat and a lesser burden. Jose Offerman was moved to leadoff and Butler flourished in the number-two spot, hitting .442 in July (.547 on-base average) and .351 (.452 OBP) over the rest of the year. At 35, he wound up hitting .309, which matched the second-highest average of his career.

Butler likes to go deep into the count, and saw over four pitches per plate appearance. He crouches in a wide-open stance and simply refuses to swing at bad offerings, regardless of the situation. He hit .312 after a first pitch ball, .300 after a strike and .346 when he surprised people by going after the first one. When he's going well, Butler peppers the left side with line drives and hard grounders. And he bunts. Butler is still probably the best bunter in baseball; of his 67 infield hits, a league-leading 43 were bunt singles!

BASERUNNING:

Butler's first half lethargy included a 17-for-28 stolen base performance. Coming on the heels of the sub-par 58 percent rate of 1991 (38-for-66), there was true cause for concern. But he rebounded to finish at 41-for-62 (66 percent, 68 percent lifetime). Butler is still a smart and dangerous baserunner.

FIELDING:

Butler is the field captain in center field. He receives hand signals from the club's eye-in-the-sky, then relays the information to his fellow outfielders. He runs down every ball hit anywhere close, and then some. Butler's arm is only fair.

OVERALL:

The fact that his club never gave up can be attributed to Butler's leadership as much as anything. But ironically, unless the Dodgers are willing to spend enough to really improve their team, now would be the time to trade him. However, his hustle and popularity will probably keep him in LA another year.

PITCHING:

The ultimate specialist, John Candelaria has averaged about half an inning per appearance in his two years with the Dodgers. Each year, however, he has worn down in the second half, no doubt a direct result of the number of times the 39 year old has been asked to warm up. His ERA soared to 5.40 after the 1992 break (1.17 before), just like in '91 (1.74 pre-ASB, 6.92 post-ASB). He also had big problems when used two days in a row. Working on no days' rest last year, his ERA was 9.00, and he allowed six of his eight earned runs for the season. But given a day or more off, his mark was 0.93 (two earned runs in 19.1 innings).

The Dodgers bring Candelaria in to get lefthanders out, but lefties hit .269 against him. Ironically, righties hit just .154 in fewer at-bats. He's got a huge wingspan and likes to crossfire with fastballs and sliders away (in on righties). Whether facing a lefty or righty, there's no doubt he had another quality season last year. He converted five of seven save opportunities and permitted only 15 of 64 inherited runners to score (23 percent).

It is crucial that Candelaria get the first pitch in for a strike; batters averaged .125 (with no extra-base hits in 40 AB) when behind in the count, .318 (.636 slugging) when ahead. Opponents hit a paltry .075 (3-for-40) once he got two strikes on them.

HOLDING RUNNERS, FIELDING, HITTING:

Though Candelaria generally keeps his mind on the batter, he will throw over if the situation calls for it. The 18-year veteran still moves well off the mound. He drew a walk in his first plate appearance since 1987, then was promptly picked off.

OVERALL:

At a salary of just under a million bucks, Candelaria earned about twelve thousand per out in '92. If the Dodgers are serious about cutting costs, they cannot afford that kind of luxury in the bullpen. Though he's about ready to hang 'em up, Candelaria's phone will probably ring this winter; after all, he's a lot better than Scott Bailes and Juan Agosto.

JOHN CANDELARIA

Position: RP
Bats: R **Throws:** L
Ht: 6' 6" **Wt:** 225

Opening Day Age: 39
Born: 11/6/53 in Brooklyn, NY
ML Seasons: 18

Overall Statistics

	W	L	ERA	G	GS	Sv	IP	H	R	BB	SO	HR
1992	2	5	2.84	50	0	5	25.1	20	9	13	23	1
Career	177	119	3.29	576	356	28	2506.2	2374	1019	583	1656	243

How Often He Throws Strikes

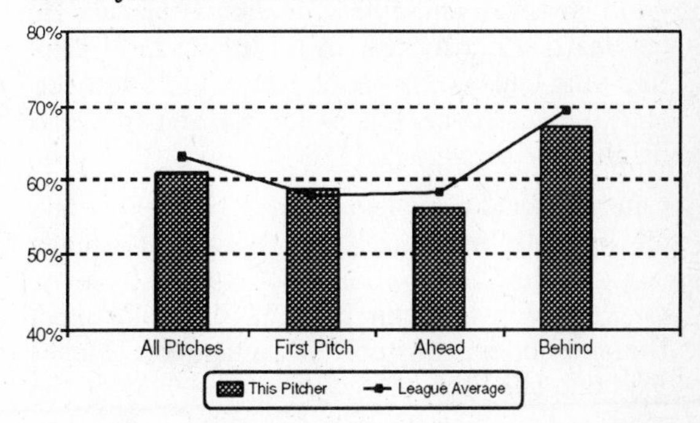

1992 Situational Stats

	W	L	ERA	Sv	IP		AB	H	HR	RBI	AVG
Home	1	3	2.92	2	12.1	LHB	52	14	1	12	.269
Road	1	2	2.77	3	13.0	RHB	39	6	0	4	.154
Day	0	0	0.00	1	9.0	Sc Pos	37	9	1	16	.243
Night	2	5	4.41	4	16.1	Clutch	74	17	0	10	.230

1992 Rankings (National League)

- 1st in worst first batter efficiency (.349)
- 9th in holds (12)
- Led the Dodgers in holds

WORKHORSE

TOM CANDIOTTI

Position: SP
Bats: R **Throws:** R
Ht: 6' 2" **Wt:** 200

Opening Day Age: 35
Born: 8/31/57 in Walnut Creek, CA
ML Seasons: 9

PITCHING:

Considered a free agent bust by some, Tom Candiotti pitched much better than his 11-15 record indicated. Though the Dodger offense was the worst in baseball (26 runs less than their closest competitor), they were especially inept with the veteran knuckleballer on the hill. During one stretch of six Candiotti starts, the Dodgers scored a total of six runs, all in the same game.

Unlike phenom Tim Wakefield, whose knuckler consistently breaks straight down, Candiotti gets great movement both horizontally and vertically. He throws his bread-and-butter pitch at three different speeds, and the fastest one comes in surprisingly hard. Candiotti will also mix in a very good curveball and a very mediocre fastball. He has learned not to give in to hitters; he'll keep throwing junk on any count. He walked a respectable 2.78 batters per nine innings, a bit better than his lifetime average (2.93).

Candiotti held opponents to a .237 average and the knuckler minimizes any platoon advantage (righties hit .227, lefties .246). He was even tougher with men on base (.201). Like most Dodger hurlers, he took advantage of Dodger Stadium. His ERA was 2.33 at home, 3.53 on the road.

HOLDING RUNNERS, FIELDING, HITTING:

Candiotti keeps a close watch on baserunners and has a fair move, but once he delivers the ball to the plate, he's in trouble: runners were 30-for-35 on stolen base attempts. The problem is that his ball gets to the plate too slowly to give his catchers much of a chance. He's a solid defensive player despite being extremely slow afoot. Candiotti held his own in his first year at the plate, especially on bunt attempts. He was second on the team with 12 sacrifices.

OVERALL:

The native Californian fulfilled a lifelong dream when he signed with the Dodgers. After a frustrating year pitching for the current bunch, he may long for Cleveland. Candiotti logged over 200 innings for the seventh straight year and pitched solidly throughout. Thanks to guys like him, starting pitching is the least of the club's worries.

Overall Statistics

	W	L	ERA	G	GS	Sv	IP	H	R	BB	SO	HR
1992	11	15	3.00	32	30	0	203.2	177	78	63	152	13
Career	95	93	3.45	245	235	0	1608.1	1526	704	524	1030	128

How Often He Throws Strikes

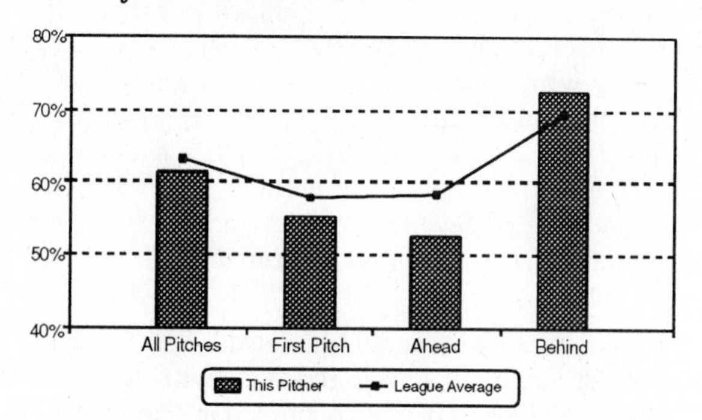

1992 Situational Stats

	W	L	ERA	Sv	IP		AB	H	HR	RBI	AVG
Home	6	6	2.33	0	89.0	LHB	407	100	6	32	.246
Road	5	9	3.53	0	114.2	RHB	339	77	7	38	.227
Day	4	5	4.53	0	55.2	Sc Pos	189	40	6	62	.212
Night	7	10	2.43	0	148.0	Clutch	102	26	3	12	.255

1992 Rankings (National League)

- → 1st in losses (15) and highest stolen base percentage allowed (85.7%)
- → 2nd in least run support per 9 innings (3.2)
- → 3rd in stolen bases allowed (30)
- → 4th in most pitches thrown per batter (3.78)
- → Led the Dodgers in ERA (3.01), wins (11), losses, complete games (6), most pitches thrown (3,168), pickoff throws (172), stolen bases allowed, winning percentage (.423), highest strikeout/walk ratio (2.4), lowest batting average allowed (.237), lowest on-base percentage allowed (.297), least baserunners allowed per 9 innings (10.7), ERA at home (2.33) and lowest batting average allowed with runners in scoring position (.212)

HITTING:

Dodger fans paid $3 million to see Eric Davis hit one home run: an opposite field shot on the 4th of July was his only Dodger Stadium dinger. Davis finished the year with 267 at-bats, five home runs and three surgeries: hand, wrist and shoulder. The damaged left shoulder, separated on a great rolling catch in May, severely hampered his ability to pull the ball the rest of the season.

Davis actually had a great April, hitting .310 with his other 4 home runs, 13 RBI, a .398 on-base average and .521 slugging. But then he batted .199 the rest of the season. Though the team went 11-18 with both Davis and Strawberry together in the lineup, Davis prospered in the number-five spot, hitting .310 with a .524 slugging.

Davis likes the first pitch fastball and has hit .370 on that pitch the last five years. After his first stint on the disabled list, however, he was unable to catch up to the good ones. He has little sense of the outside corner, no matter the pitch. He often swings at balls and is constantly jawing over called strikes that look like like good pitches.

BASERUNNING:

Davis leads all major league players, past or present, in stolen base efficiency (88 percent). Even in another injury-plagued season, he was an incredible 19-for-20 in '92. He is first-step quick, second-step quicker and as aggressive as they come on the basepaths.

FIELDING:

The total disregard that Davis shows for his own well-being when chasing down every ball makes him fun to watch. He gets a good jump and chews up the turf quickly. He also has a great arm. He played all three outfield positions in '92, and all very well.

OVERALL:

Unlike his more celebrated outfield counterpart, Davis gives it all every minute of every game . . . when he's in the lineup. He has stated in print that he owes the Dodgers "a healthy year," but they're looking around for another answer. Wherever free agent Davis ends up, it will be for a lot less money.

ERIC DAVIS

Position: LF
Bats: R **Throws:** R
Ht: 6' 3" **Wt:** 185

Opening Day Age: 30
Born: 5/29/62 in Los Angeles, CA
ML Seasons: 9

Overall Statistics

	G	AB	R	H	D	T	HR	RBI	SB	BB	SO	AVG
1992	76	267	21	61	8	1	5	32	19	36	71	.228
Career	932	3124	575	828	127	19	182	564	266	460	824	.265

Where He Hits the Ball

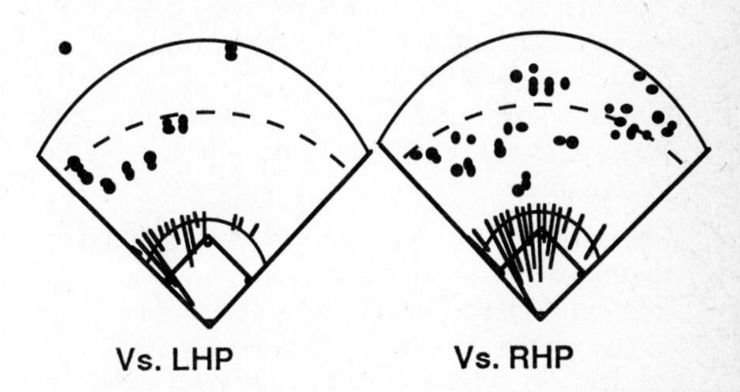

1992 Situational Stats

	AB	H	HR	RBI	AVG		AB	H	HR	RBI	AVG
Home	133	31	1	15	.233	LHP	89	21	4	11	.236
Road	134	30	4	17	.224	RHP	178	40	1	21	.225
Day	92	16	0	8	.174	Sc Pos	80	22	1	26	.275
Night	175	45	5	24	.257	Clutch	45	9	0	6	.200

1992 Rankings (National League)

- 1st in stolen base percentage (95.0%)
- 8th in steals of third (5)
- Led the Dodgers in stolen base percentage
- Led NL left fielders in stolen base percentage

PITCHING:

Though he's obviously a good pitcher, Dodger Stadium has made Jim Gott a better one. Since joining the club in 1990, he has reeled off his three best years in terms of ERA. In '92, he knocked a full half-run off of his '91 ERA thanks to a sparkling 1.79 home mark (3.02 away). Gott goes right after the hitter at home, walking fewer (3.34 walks per nine innings at home, 4.91 on the road) and striking out more (8.70 per nine at home, 6.80 away); on the road, he often tries to be too fine. He has always walked a lot of batters (3.85 walks per nine innings lifetime), and that was true again in '92 (4.19).

Gott has great stuff. He throws hard, especially now that he is fully recovered from 1989 elbow surgery. Since then he has developed a particularly nasty curveball that fools most right-handed hitters, who hit .192 against him (lefties hit .264). When he gets ahead in the count, the curveball is his out pitch.

For some reason, Gott has trouble getting his rhythm early. First batters hit .295 against him (.319 in '91). Fortunately, he is able to bear down in the clutch. Opponents hit exactly .200 with runners on and the same in close-and-late situations. It dropped to .185 with runners in scoring position. He closes out many innings with men left on base.

HOLDING RUNNERS, FIELDING, HITTING:

Gott has worked hard on his pickoff move and it shows; would-be base thieves were just 6-for-11 against him. On fielding chances he moves quickly off the mound, and he handles himself well at the plate also. He has four major league home runs.

OVERALL:

In the first half, Gott was one of the Dodgers' most effective relievers (51 IP, 1.94 ERA), but Roger McDowell remained the closer until he fell apart. By the time Tom Lasorda and Ron Perranoski made the switch, Gott was out of gas. The 33 year old had 34 saves in '88, and the club is toying with making him the full-time closer, but they'll go after Tom Henke or Todd Worrell first.

JIM GOTT

Position: RP
Bats: R **Throws:** R
Ht: 6' 4" **Wt:** 220

Opening Day Age: 33
Born: 8/3/59 in Hollywood, CA
ML Seasons: 11

Overall Statistics

	W	L	ERA	G	GS	Sv	IP	H	R	BB	SO	HR
1992	3	3	2.45	68	0	6	88.0	72	27	41	75	4
Career	45	59	3.84	430	96	61	974.2	926	473	417	722	74

How Often He Throws Strikes

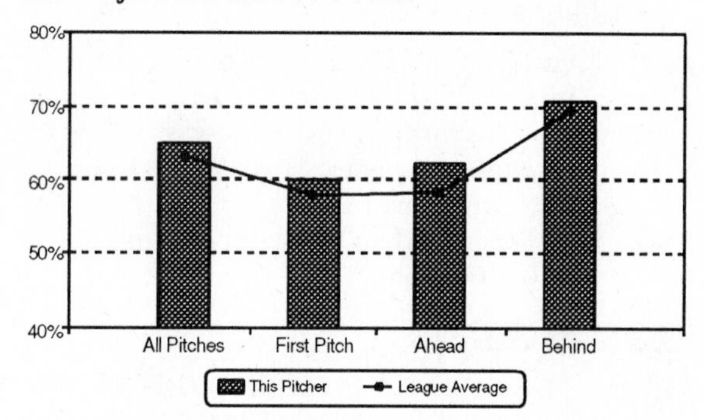

1992 Situational Stats

	W	L	ERA	Sv	IP		AB	H	HR	RBI	AVG
Home	1	1	1.79	2	40.1	LHB	148	39	3	17	.264
Road	2	2	3.02	4	47.2	RHB	172	33	1	9	.192
Day	0	0	2.00	2	27.0	Sc Pos	92	17	0	20	.185
Night	3	3	2.66	4	61.0	Clutch	165	33	3	16	.200

1992 Rankings (National League)

- 5th in lowest batting average allowed in relief with runners on base (.200)
- 6th in balks (3)
- 7th in lowest batting average allowed in relief with runners in scoring position (.185) and relief innings (88)
- Led the Dodgers in games pitched (68), balks, lowest batting average allowed in relief with runners on base, lowest batting average allowed in relief with runners in scoring position, relief ERA (2.45), relief innings, lowest batting average allowed in relief (.225), least baserunners allowed per 9 innings in relief (11.7) and most strikeouts per 9 innings in relief (7.7)

PITCHING:

Kevin Gross threw the only no-hitter in baseball in 1992, and it was no fluke. It came in August during a stretch of 13 starts in which Gross allowed just 23 earned runs (2.30 ERA). In fact, he compiled an overall 2.61 ERA after the All-Star break and his final ERA of 3.17 was almost a run better than his career average. Yet he won only eight ballgames; such is life on the worst team in baseball, though Gross has never been much of a winner (98-114 lifetime).

The difference wasn't Dodger Stadium. Pitching on a staff with a home ERA over a run lower than on the road, Gross actually pitched better on the road (3.35 home, 2.95 away). The secret to his success was simple: Gross threw more strikes than ever before. He walked fewer batters (3.39 walks per nine innings, 3.57 lifetime) and struck out more (6.95 strikeouts per nine, 6.28 lifetime).

With or without sandpaper, Gross carries a full bag of tricks every time he steps onto the mound. He starts with a good hard four-seam fastball, then he'll cut it, make it sink, change speeds, alter his point of delivery, anything to keep the hitter off balance. He also throws two different curve balls: a nasty overhand job that breaks straight downward and a slow sidearm version that sweeps tantalizingly across the hitting zone.

HOLDING RUNNERS, FIELDING, HITTING:

Gross is a big guy with a herky-jerky delivery. It takes him a long time to deliver the ball and he ends up a bit off-balance. As a result, basestealers do well against him (18-of-27 last year) and come-backers will often sneak through. Gross had a bad year at the plate in 1992 (.095), but has been a good hitter in the past.

OVERALL:

Gross was one of the Dodgers' most effective pitchers over the second half and amassed over 200 innings for the sixth time in his career. He did wonders for his overall value, so the Dodgers were strongly considering trading him after protecting him from expansion. Starting pitching is the least of their needs.

KEVIN GROSS

Position: SP
Bats: R **Throws:** R
Ht: 6' 5" **Wt:** 215

Opening Day Age: 31
Born: 6/8/61 in Downey, CA
ML Seasons: 10

Overall Statistics

	W	L	ERA	G	GS	Sv	IP	H	R	BB	SO	HR
1992	8	13	3.17	34	30	0	204.2	182	82	77	158	11
Career	98	114	3.89	345	261	4	1789.2	1752	849	710	1249	154

How Often He Throws Strikes

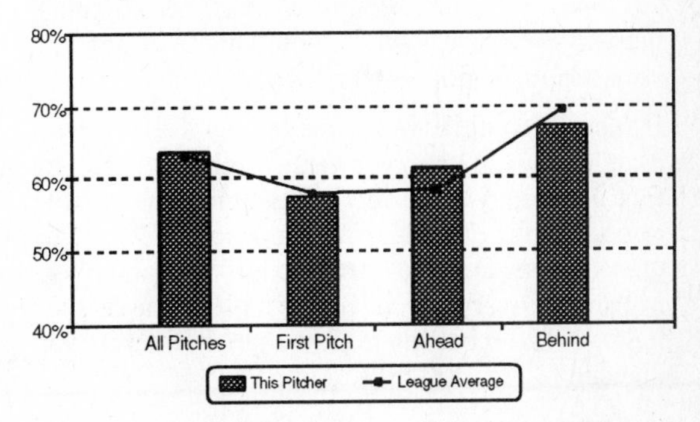

1992 Situational Stats

	W	L	ERA	Sv	IP		AB	H	HR	RBI	AVG
Home	5	9	3.35	0	113.0	LHB	409	113	5	48	.276
Road	3	4	2.95	0	91.2	RHB	347	69	6	23	.199
Day	3	3	2.25	0	52.0	Sc Pos	181	41	3	56	.227
Night	5	10	3.48	0	152.2	Clutch	100	27	1	6	.270

1992 Rankings (National League)

- 4th in lowest batting average allowed vs. right-handed batters (.199)
- 6th in walks allowed (77) and most strikeouts per 9 innings (6.9)
- 7th in lowest winning percentage (.381)
- 8th in losses (13), shutouts (3) and least run support per 9 innings (3.5)
- 9th in strikeouts (158)
- 10th in balks (2) and ERA on the road (2.95)
- Led the Dodgers in strikeouts, lowest slugging percentage allowed (.337), most strikeouts per 9 innings, ERA on the road and lowest batting average allowed vs. right-handed batters

HITTING:

In a year full of Dodger disappointments, Dave Hansen was one of the biggest. After a brief yet promising trial run in 1991 (.268 in 56 at-bats) and two successful years in Triple A, he never got untracked in '92. They platooned him, they sat him down, they played him every day, but nothing worked. Hansen batted only .214 and drove in just 22 men in 341 at-bats.

Hansen is a line drive hitter with the unusual habit of tapping his bat on his shoulder as he awaits the delivery. The patience and ability to make contact he showed as a minor-leaguer (339 walks, 269 strikeouts in six seasons) have not been evident in the bigs. Hansen's 49 strikeouts in '92 (34 walks) are awfully high for a guy with a .299 slugging percentage. Once pitchers noted his over-aggressiveness, they stopped throwing him strikes.

Hansen's inability to hit lefties (.196) was matched by his struggles versus righties (.217). In fact, Hansen was ineffective in almost every situation. He hit .171 with runners on and .145 late in close games. Despite hitting to left field and playing almost every day, he hit just .198 in the second half. And after batting .313 as a pinch hitter in '91, Hansen fell to .200 in '92.

BASERUNNING:

Hansen has below-average speed and will seldom take the extra base. He takes a cautious lead at first, seemingly terrified of being picked off. Like several recent Dodger prospects, he shows an alarming lack of instinct on the basepaths (and elsewhere, for that matter).

FIELDING:

Hansen plays very deep at third; he is susceptible to bunts and slow rollers. He charges hard but is slow afoot, so he often ends up throwing off-balance and late. His hands are average at best.

OVERALL:

Hansen maintains that a sore back, a remnant from a car wreck several years back, hampered his 1992 performance. Promising minor-league numbers and a chronic injury; sounds like Jeff Hamilton, the last failed third base phenom. The Dodgers left Hansen unprotected to expansion, but he wasn't selected. Right now, Hansen's career seems as wrecked as his old car.

DAVE HANSEN

Position: 3B
Bats: L **Throws:** R
Ht: 6' 0" **Wt:** 180

Opening Day Age: 24
Born: 11/24/68 in Long Beach, CA
ML Seasons: 3

Overall Statistics

	G	AB	R	H	D	T	HR	RBI	SB	BB	SO	AVG
1992	132	341	30	73	11	0	6	22	0	34	49	.214
Career	190	404	33	89	15	0	7	28	1	36	64	.220

Where He Hits the Ball

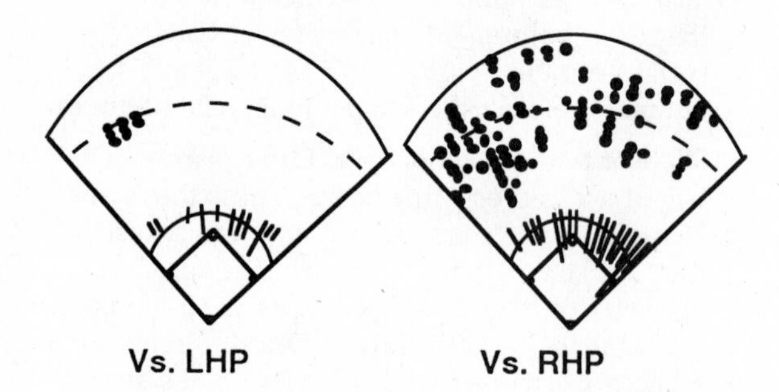

1992 Situational Stats

	AB	H	HR	RBI	AVG		AB	H	HR	RBI	AVG
Home	182	42	1	10	.231	LHP	46	9	0	1	.196
Road	159	31	5	12	.195	RHP	295	64	6	21	.217
Day	117	24	2	12	.205	Sc Pos	70	11	0	13	.157
Night	224	49	4	10	.219	Clutch	69	10	0	3	.145

1992 Rankings (National League)

- 5th in lowest batting average in the clutch (.145)
- 8th in lowest batting average on a 3-1 count (.091)
- Led NL third basemen in fielding percentage (.968)

HITTING:

The chances of Lenny Harris ever becoming an everyday ballplayer lessen with each passing year. After threatening to break out of his platoon role by hitting .241 vs. lefties in 1991, Harris dropped to .139 against southpaws in '92. The lefty swinger continued his good work against righties (.286), but his overall average of .271 looks a lot more well-rounded than it really was.

Harris could learn a lot from Tony Gwynn. A naturally good contact man, Harris too often patty-cakes the pitch to avoid a strikeout when he should be driving the ball up the middle or to the opposite field. He totalled just 11 extra-base hits in 347 at-bats last year, all doubles, for an eye-popping .303 slugging percentage. Futhermore, he drew only 24 walks for a .318 on-base average.

The team's performance (or lack of it) seemed to weigh heavily on Harris' concentration. He did fairly well in key situations, hitting .299 with runners on, .298 with runners in scoring position and .333 with runners in scoring position and two out. But he is not very good coming off the bench: he was just 6-for-29 (.207) as a pinch hitter.

BASERUNNING:

Harris stole 19 bases in '92 (in 26 attempts), setting a new career high. He gets a good jump and masks his intentions pretty well. Harris is quite fast, though he doesn't always run intelligently. He needs constant coaching.

FIELDING:

The versatile Harris played five positions last year (second, third, shortstop, left, right), all of them poorly. His 27 errors were the second-most in the National League, behind teammate Jose Offerman. Most of his time was spent at second base, where he has great range and little else.

OVERALL:

After beginning the year as the starting second sacker, Harris played his way onto the Dodgers' unprotected list. He played much better when the Dodgers were contenders, but that may not help him much in 1993, especially with Jody Reed taking over at second. Though he has the versatility to become the Tony Phillips of the NL, he lacks the power, the walks, the switch-hitting, the defense . . .

LENNY HARRIS

Position: 2B/3B
Bats: L **Throws:** R
Ht: 5'10" **Wt:** 205

Opening Day Age: 28
Born: 10/28/64 in Miami, FL
ML Seasons: 5

Overall Statistics

	G	AB	R	H	D	T	HR	RBI	SB	BB	SO	AVG
1992	135	347	28	94	11	0	0	30	19	24	24	.271
Career	548	1585	191	443	54	6	8	131	64	115	124	.279

Where He Hits the Ball

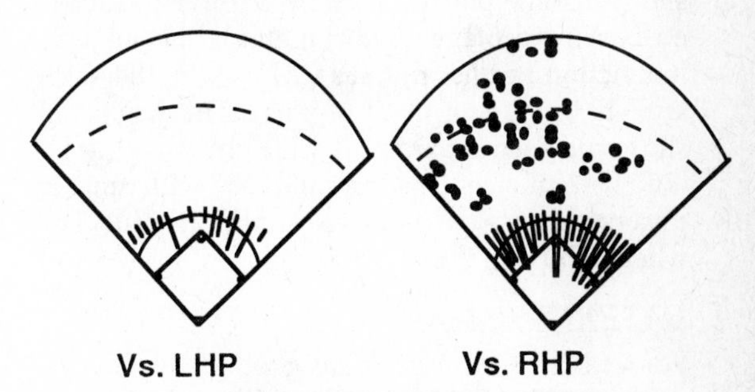

1992 Situational Stats

	AB	H	HR	RBI	AVG		AB	H	HR	RBI	AVG
Home	177	47	0	15	.266	LHP	36	5	0	0	.139
Road	170	47	0	15	.276	RHP	311	89	0	30	.286
Day	119	34	0	12	.286	Sc Pos	84	25	0	30	.298
Night	228	60	0	18	.263	Clutch	60	17	0	5	.283

1992 Rankings (National League)

- 10th in batting average with 2 strikes (.256)
- Led NL second basemen in batting average with 2 strikes

HITTING:

Carlos Hernandez made a good account of himself in his first season in the majors. After receiving just 11 at-bats in April, his playing time increased as Mike Scioscia struggled. He hit .278 and all three of his homers after the break. Since Scioscia was a free agent and a good possibility to leave LA, Hernandez built a good case for his future. The problem is, the Dodgers have an even better catching prospect in Mike Piazza, who also hits from the right side.

Hernandez goes up there hacking: he batted .345 on the first pitch. He has a pretty good eye (11 walks, 21 strikeouts) despite his weakness for high hard stuff and outside breaking balls. He showed some pop vs. lefties (.287 average, .336 on-base percentage, .398 slugging), but saw limited action against righties (.215 with .284 OBP and .231 slugging in 65 at-bats). The youngster shows no fear, regardless of the situation; he hit .260 with runners on and a solid .267 with runners in scoring position and two out. He also hit .267 when behind in the count, hanging in well.

BASERUNNING:

For a catcher, Hernandez has good speed. He gets down the line well and runs intelligently. He was thrown out in his sole stealing attempt, though he's stolen as many as eight in a minor league season.

FIELDING:

Hernandez looks like a real pro behind the plate, handling everyone on the veteran Dodger staff including knuckleballer Tom Candiotti. He shows good footwork on both bunts and balls in the dirt. The only glaring weakness in his defense is throwing. Hernandez often drops his arm and his throws sail off to the second base side of the bag.

OVERALL:

Down the yawning stretch drive, the Dodgers played Scioscia (for the past) and Piazza (for the future). Since Piazza hits with more power than Hernandez, the latter may be gone. The club thinks they can get something for him, maybe in a package deal, which is why they protected him from expansion. He is solid behind and consistent at the plate; the exuberant backstop could help a lot of teams.

CARLOS HERNANDEZ

Position: C
Bats: R **Throws:** R
Ht: 5'11" **Wt:** 185

Opening Day Age: 25
Born: 5/24/67 in San Felix, Bolivar, Venezuela
ML Seasons: 3

Overall Statistics

	G	AB	R	H	D	T	HR	RBI	SB	BB	SO	AVG
1992	69	173	11	45	4	0	3	17	0	11	21	.260
Career	94	207	14	52	6	0	3	19	1	11	28	.251

Where He Hits the Ball

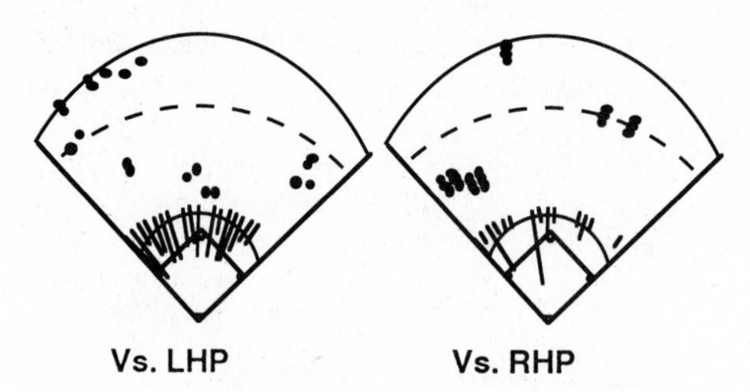

1992 Situational Stats

	AB	H	HR	RBI	AVG		AB	H	HR	RBI	AVG
Home	87	23	1	8	.264	LHP	108	31	3	9	.287
Road	86	22	2	9	.256	RHP	65	14	0	8	.215
Day	70	15	1	10	.214	Sc Pos	37	9	1	14	.243
Night	103	30	2	7	.291	Clutch	37	9	0	2	.243

1992 Rankings (National League)

➡ Led the Dodgers in hit by pitch (4)

PITCHING:

The fact that Orel Hershiser led the Dodger staff in innings pitched in 1992 (210.2) is cause alone for rejoicing. Hershiser averaged 252 innings per year from 1985-89, but that was before shoulder re-construction. He seems to have recovered completely, and showed it at home where he was 7-5 with a very Hershiser-like 2.75 ERA.

On the road, it was a completely different story last year (3-10, 4.86 ERA). He was winless on turf (0-7, 4.98), a sure sign that his sinker was not as devastating as it used to be. Ironically, he may be throwing harder than before but flattening his fastball out. To combat this, Hershiser has added a slow curve and a straight change to his sinker/slider arsenal.

Without the sharp down-and-away action of the sinker, Hershiser had a lot of trouble with lefties (.286 vs. LHP, .221 vs. RHP). It may take longer to loosen up the new shoulder. Batters hit .301 in his first 15 offerings, but their average decreased as the game wore on until Hershiser hit the wall right around 90 pitches. Though his walk totals were up just a little (2.9 walks per nine innings in '92, 2.7 lifetime), he seems to have less control within the strike zone.

HOLDING RUNNERS, FIELDING, HITTING:

Hershiser is a complete baseball player and helps the team whether on the mound, on the bases, or at the plate. He holds runners close and fields his position impeccably. He entered the '92 season with a .193 lifetime average and actually increased it (.221 in '92). He's a master at faking the bunt, then whacking the ball past a charging third baseman.

OVERALL:

It is very possible that Hershiser will improve as he gets accustomed to his new rotator cuff. He is just 34 and was used as a reliever throughout most of his minor-league career, so he might have some fuel left in the tank. Hershiser had 130 strikeouts last year, not a sign that he's merely hanging on as a finesse hurler. Most importantly, he has an incredible work ethic and wants to win every time out.

OREL HERSHISER

Position: SP
Bats: R **Throws:** R
Ht: 6' 3" **Wt:** 192

Opening Day Age: 34
Born: 9/16/58 in Buffalo, NY
ML Seasons: 10

Overall Statistics

	W	L	ERA	G	GS	Sv	IP	H	R	BB	SO	HR
1992	10	15	3.67	33	33	0	210.2	209	101	69	130	15
Career	116	82	2.87	289	249	5	1805.0	1587	664	539	1230	94

How Often He Throws Strikes

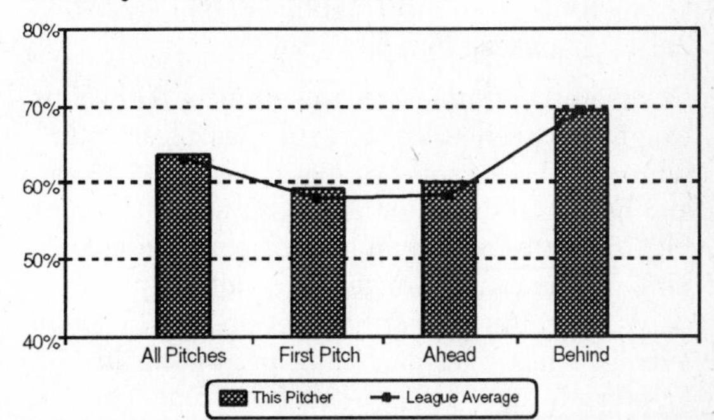

1992 Situational Stats

	W	L	ERA	Sv	IP		AB	H	HR	RBI	AVG
Home	7	5	2.75	0	118.0	LHB	455	130	11	45	.286
Road	3	10	4.86	0	92.2	RHB	357	79	4	34	.221
Day	2	6	4.20	0	64.1	Sc Pos	205	48	1	58	.234
Night	8	9	3.44	0	146.1	Clutch	61	16	2	5	.262

1992 Rankings (National League)

- 1st in losses (15)
- 2nd in highest ERA on the road (4.86)
- 3rd in least pitches thrown per batter (3.33) and least run support per 9 innings (3.3)
- 5th in hit batsmen (8) and most baserunners allowed per 9 innings (12.2)
- 6th in highest groundball/flyball ratio (1.9)
- Led the Dodgers in losses, games started (33), innings pitched (210.2), hits allowed (209), batters faced (910), home runs allowed (15), hit batsmen, wild pitches (10), GDPs induced (19), highest groundball/flyball ratio, least pitches thrown per batter and most GDPs induced per 9 innings (.81)

JAY HOWELL

Position: RP
Bats: R **Throws:** R
Ht: 6' 3" **Wt:** 212

Opening Day Age: 37
Born: 11/26/55 in Miami, FL
ML Seasons: 13

PITCHING:

Jay Howell can still get batters out when he is physically able to pitch. In 1992, he didn't take the mound until mid-May after missing most of spring training with a bad elbow. His left knee hasn't been completely sound since surgery in 1990. Howell's innings have decreased each of the last three years, from 79.2 in 1989 (when he had 28 saves) to just 46.2 last year. But he was plenty good in those limited innings, with a 1.54 ERA that was the lowest of his 13-year career.

Howell is now 37, and his fastball, though still decent, has lost a few feet. To counter that he has improved his change-up. His out pitch is a devastating overhand curveball that gives nightmares (and jelly-legs) to most righthanders; they batted only .218 against him last year.

Despite his "terminator" temperament, Howell is caught between roles. He still has closer stuff, with a .303 opponents on-base average last year, and he doesn't wilt under pressure -- opponents hit .233 with runners in scoring position against him. Yet he can no longer be counted upon on a daily basis. As primarily a set-up man, Howell averaged just over an inning per outing in '92. Opponents' batted .211 in his first 15 pitches, but batted .273 after that.

HOLDING RUNNERS, FIELDING, HITTING:

Howell's below-average move and big leg kick make him easy prey for basestealers, who were 7-for-8 with him on the mound last year. He fields his position just fine. He has not made a plate appearance in the last two years.

OVERALL:

The Dodger bullpen is in shambles and they are looking for a dominant closer. It probably won't be Howell. Though undeniably a good guy to have around, he is one of those free agents who will have to accept a pay cut to keep on playing. He retains the ability to pitch another year or two; it remains to be seen if he also has the desire.

Overall Statistics

	W	L	ERA	G	GS	Sv	IP	H	R	BB	SO	HR
1992	1	3	1.54	41	0	4	46.2	41	9	18	36	2
Career	51	49	3.30	474	21	153	742.2	690	290	259	607	44

How Often He Throws Strikes

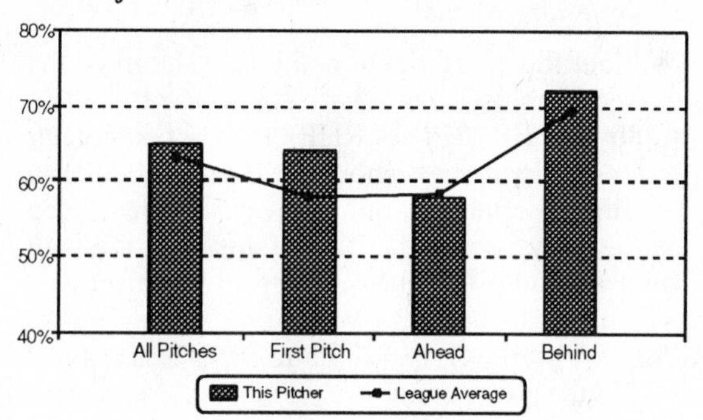

1992 Situational Stats

	W	L	ERA	Sv	IP		AB	H	HR	RBI	AVG
Home	1	2	1.57	0	23.0	LHB	91	22	2	7	.242
Road	0	1	1.52	4	23.2	RHB	87	19	0	7	.218
Day	0	2	1.15	2	15.2	Sc Pos	43	10	0	12	.233
Night	1	1	1.74	2	31.0	Clutch	88	26	0	10	.295

1992 Rankings (National League)

- 4th in least GDPs induced per GDP situation (2.6%)

HITTING:

In retrospect, it is hard to believe that Eric Karros was the last Dodger to make the squad out of spring training last year. By season's end, he had knocked in and/or scored 28 percent of the team's runs and hit 28 percent of their homers, walking away with the National League Rookie of the Year Award. The second-highest Dodger totals behind his team-leading 20 home runs and 88 RBI were six homers (Hansen and Webster) and 39 RBI (Brett Butler)!

Equally impressive was Karros' ability to adjust over the course of the season and during a game. He is a natural pull hitter, but when pitchers began to pitch him away, he began to drive the ball to right-center. His bat control helped him over the long haul; Karros had 55 post All-Star break RBI, highest in the league.

Karros likes the ball up and in and if he gets his arms extended, look out. He is not the most patient hitter (37 walks, 103 strikeouts) and can be fooled with breaking stuff away. Like any young player, he tries to do too much at times; he hit only .234 with runners in scoring position (.174 with two out). Yet eight of his homers either tied the game or gave the team the lead.

BASERUNNING:

Karros is slow. He stole 18 bases in 25 attempts as a minor-leaguer in 1989, but that seems well beyond his capabilities now. He hustles all the time but is strictly a station-to-station guy.

FIELDING:

In the field, Karros needs some work. He handles grounders fairly well, though he often ranges into no-man's land on balls he has no chance to get. He cannot scoop a throw in the dirt to save his life, but he gets lots of practice on the Dodgers.

OVERALL:

Karros looks like the cornerstone for the Dodger future. He is solid and dependable and even handles the media well. Plus, he has big-time power. Despite the fact that only six of his home runs came in notoriously pitcher-friendly Dodger Stadium, he is capable of bettering the power totals of his rookie season.

ERIC KARROS

Position: 1B
Bats: R **Throws:** R
Ht: 6' 4" **Wt:** 205
Opening Day Age: 25
Born: 11/4/67 in Hackensack, NJ
ML Seasons: 2

Overall Statistics

	G	AB	R	H	D	T	HR	RBI	SB	BB	SO	AVG
1992	149	545	63	140	30	1	20	88	2	37	103	.257
Career	163	559	63	141	31	1	20	89	2	38	109	.252

Where He Hits the Ball

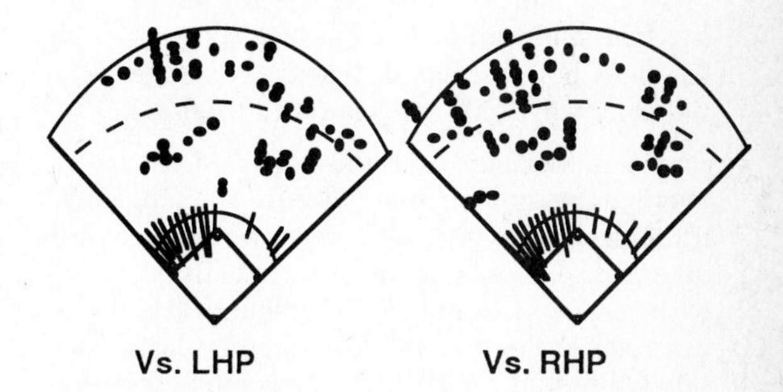

1992 Situational Stats

	AB	H	HR	RBI	AVG		AB	H	HR	RBI	AVG
Home	251	65	6	35	.259	LHP	213	59	8	32	.277
Road	294	75	14	53	.255	RHP	332	81	12	56	.244
Day	174	46	6	25	.264	Sc Pos	171	40	4	65	.234
Night	371	94	14	63	.253	Clutch	98	24	4	16	.245

1992 Rankings (National League)

- 2nd in batting average with the bases loaded (.625)
- 5th in GDPs (15)
- 7th in most GDPs per GDP situation (15.6%)
- 8th in batting average on a 3-1 count (.563)
- 9th in strikeouts (103) and lowest on-base percentage (.304)
- 10th in lowest groundball/flyball ratio (.98)
- Led the Dodgers in home runs (20), doubles (30), total bases (232), RBI (88), sacrifice flies (5), strikeouts, GDPs, slugging percentage (.426), HR frequency (27.3 ABs per HR), batting average with the bases loaded and batting average on a 3-1 count

PITCHING:

Ramon Martinez is 13-21 with a 4.06 ERA since the 1991 All-Star break. He shows occasional flashes of his old brilliance, only to follow with yet another short and trouble-filled outing. Though he insisted time and time again that his arm was fine and the team attributed his problems to mechanics, Martinez' 1992 season ended with "tennis elbow" on August 25th.

At his best, Martinez countered his blistering fastball with a great change-up. When he could get his curveball over, he was unhittable. But now that his heater is just lukewarm, the change of speeds is not as drastic. Losing confidence, Martinez tries to work on the corners. While the hits (8.42 hits per nine innings in '92 vs. 7.64 lifetime) and walks (4.12 per nine last year, 3.26 lifetime) both increased, his strikeout rate went the other way (6.03 last year, 7.13 lifetime).

In 1991, Martinez held the opponent to a .171 average late in the game (.240 from innings one through six). No wonder Lasorda was reluctant to take him out. In '92, he was actually stronger early on (.234 in the first six innings), but was pounded to the tune of .320 when he lasted beyond the sixth. Martinez can no longer finish what he started. Some days, he can barely get through the first.

HOLDING RUNNERS, FIELDING, HITTING:

His gangly frame takes a long time to unwind, and Martinez is terrible at holding runners. He is a fundamentally sound fielder once he gets to the ball. After two years of hitting left-handed exclusively, Martinez is getting comfortable and will occasionally help himself at bat.

OVERALL:

Martinez will be just 25 on Opening Day, but his Jekyll-and-Hyde starts are a potential sign of serious shoulder problems. He threw 234.1 tough innings when he was just 22, then 220.1 more the next year. His physical frame is not the sturdiest, and his mechanics were always odd. Martinez will of course be in the rotation if healthy, but he can no longer be counted upon as the ace of a staff.

RAMON MARTINEZ

Position: SP
Bats: L **Throws:** R
Ht: 6' 4" **Wt:** 173

Opening Day Age: 25
Born: 3/22/68 in Santo Domingo, Dominican Republic
ML Seasons: 5

Overall Statistics

	W	L	ERA	G	GS	Sv	IP	H	R	BB	SO	HR
1992	8	11	4.00	25	25	0	150.2	141	82	69	101	11
Career	52	37	3.32	115	112	0	739.2	628	316	268	586	62

How Often He Throws Strikes

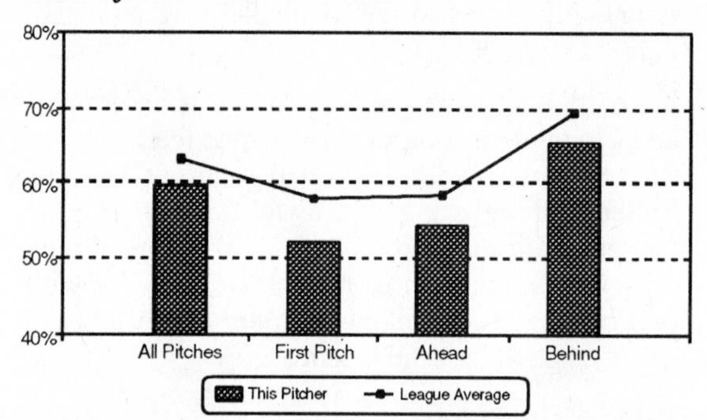

1992 Situational Stats

	W	L	ERA	Sv	IP		AB	H	HR	RBI	AVG
Home	4	7	4.29	0	92.1	LHB	316	81	9	40	.256
Road	4	4	3.55	0	58.1	RHB	259	60	2	28	.232
Day	3	3	3.18	0	39.2	Sc Pos	155	42	4	56	.271
Night	5	8	4.30	0	111.0	Clutch	52	12	0	5	.231

1992 Rankings (National League)

- 3rd in highest ERA at home (4.29)
- 8th in wild pitches (9)
- 9th in highest batting average allowed with runners in scoring position (.271)

PITCHING:

Roger McDowell believes that he has been miscast as a closer and he proved it in 1992. He started out very well, recording a 1.59 ERA in April and five saves in May, but his ERA increased with each passing month. Eventually McDowell completely fell apart; opposing batters hit an astronomical .348 against him after the All-Star break. McDowell finished the year with a 4.09 ERA, the second-highest of his eight-year career. He did record 14 saves, but he also blew eight. His 64 percent conversion rate was the worst of all major league closers.

McDowell has made a career out of just one pitch: his sinker. When it's working, his ball explodes down and in on right-handed batters and sneaks across the inside corner versus lefties. When it's not working, McDowell's sinker is just a mediocre fastball. He threw more curveballs in '92, but it didn't help. Lefties hit .318 against him, righties just behind at .295.

Without his bread-and-butter pitch, McDowell has to nibble more than usual. He walked 4.51 per nine innings, far above his career average of 3.40. Add the walks to the 11.07 hits per nine, and he's closing in on two baserunners allowed per inning. Quite simply, McDowell had no out pitch to go to. Even after a first-pitch strike opponents hit .323.

HOLDING RUNNERS, FIELDING, HITTING:

McDowell keeps a close eye on opposing baserunners, and he had an eyeful in '92. He fields his position relatively well, though he tends to try to do too much with his throws. He has a pretty good hitting stroke but seldom gets a chance to exhibit it in game situations.

OVERALL:

McDowell's wacky personality only plays well when he is getting guys out. He's a free agent, but there can't be much of a market for a two million dollar set-up comedian. The Dodgers are rebuilding; McDowell will probably have to take his act out on the road and accept a substantial pay cut as well.

ROGER McDOWELL

Position: RP
Bats: R **Throws:** R
Ht: 6' 1" **Wt:** 182

Opening Day Age: 32
Born: 12/21/60 in Cincinnati, OH
ML Seasons: 8

Overall Statistics

	W	L	ERA	G	GS	Sv	IP	H	R	BB	SO	HR
1992	6	10	4.09	65	0	14	83.2	103	46	42	50	3
Career	57	59	3.14	532	2	149	796.1	764	326	301	399	33

How Often He Throws Strikes

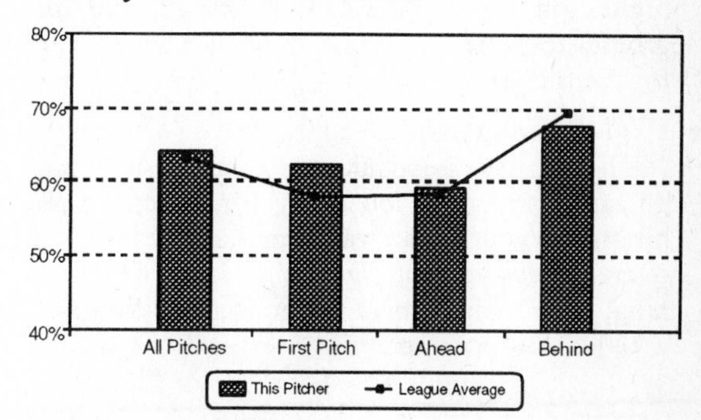

1992 Situational Stats

	W	L	ERA	Sv	IP		AB	H	HR	RBI	AVG
Home	2	2	2.92	8	37.0	LHB	154	49	3	29	.318
Road	4	8	5.01	6	46.2	RHB	183	54	0	16	.295
Day	3	3	4.55	3	29.2	Sc Pos	128	34	2	41	.266
Night	3	7	3.83	11	54.0	Clutch	215	60	2	32	.279

1992 Rankings (National League)

- 1st in lowest save percentage (63.6%) and relief losses (10)
- 2nd in blown saves (8) and most baserunners allowed per 9 innings in relief (15.7)
- 3rd in highest batting average allowed in relief (.306)
- 6th in lowest winning percentage (.375) and worst first batter efficiency (.312)
- 7th in highest batting average allowed vs. left-handed batters (.318)
- Led the Dodgers in saves (14), games finished (39), save opportunities (22), save percentage, blown saves, relief wins (6) and relief losses

GREAT SPEED

HITTING:

Despite the intensely negative media pressure, Jose Offerman did not carry his defensive woes to the plate. After getting off to a slow start (.216 in April), Offerman adopted a crouched stance. The switch-hitter's improvement was instantaneous, especially from the left side (.255; .111 in 1991). Most importantly, his on-base percentage was a respectable .331 overall.

Offerman has a good eye (57 walks) and often goes deep into the count (3.78 pitches per plate appearance). He uses the entire field and shows occasional gap power (20 doubles, eight triples), only getting into real trouble when he swings for the fences. The speedster hit almost thirty points higher on turf (.282, .254 on grass), and his ground-to-flyball ratio of two-to-one bodes well for the future.

Hard-throwing righties can overpower Offerman, and he still has a good number of ugly at-bats. His 98 strikeouts were too many for a non-power hitter. The young man was remarkably consistent overall, however, hitting .267 to lead off an inning, .276 with runners in scoring position and .278 late in the game.

BASERUNNING:

Offerman can really fly and has great instincts on the basepaths. Nobody this side of Deion Sanders makes the turn at first faster. His stolen base success rate was not very good, especially after he was moved to the top of the lineup (11-for-15 pre-All Star break, 12-for-24 post), but that was largely due to the predictability of the manager.

FIELDING:

Needless to say, Offerman has lots to work on in the field. He often catches the ball in poor throwing position, and like many young shortstops, he should eat some balls rather than fire them into the dugout. On the plus side he shows tremendous range and turns the double play quite well.

OVERALL:

Offensively, Offerman was an exciting catalyst, and he's only going to get better. He was clearly in over his head as a 23-year-old infield anchor, but one would expect major improvement now that he's paired with veteran Jody Reed.

JOSE OFFERMAN

Position: SS
Bats: B **Throws:** R
Ht: 6' 0" **Wt:** 160

Opening Day Age: 24
Born: 11/8/68 in San Pedro de Macoris, Dominican Republic
ML Seasons: 3

Overall Statistics

	G	AB	R	H	D	T	HR	RBI	SB	BB	SO	AVG
1992	149	534	67	139	20	8	1	30	23	57	98	.260
Career	230	705	84	170	22	8	2	40	27	86	144	.241

Where He Hits the Ball

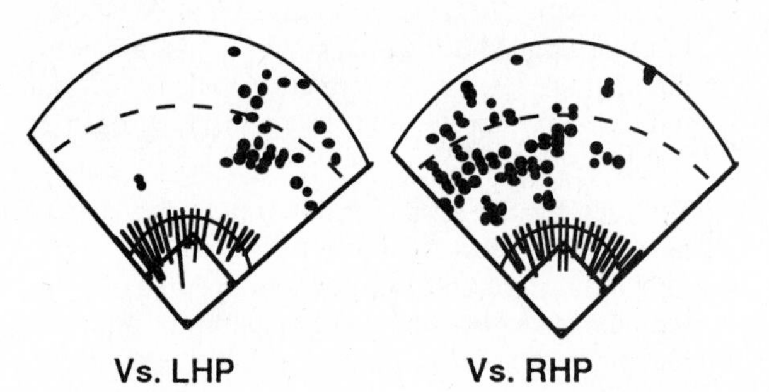

1992 Situational Stats

	AB	H	HR	RBI	AVG		AB	H	HR	RBI	AVG
Home	283	77	1	20	.272	LHP	201	54	1	7	.269
Road	251	62	0	10	.247	RHP	333	85	0	23	.255
Day	159	43	0	5	.270	Sc Pos	98	27	0	26	.276
Night	375	96	1	25	.256	Clutch	105	27	0	6	.257

1992 Rankings (National League)

- 2nd in lowest stolen base percentage (59.0%)
- 3rd in lowest slugging percentage (.333), lowest HR frequency (534 ABs per HR) and steals of third (8)
- 5th in caught stealing (16)
- 6th in triples (8)
- Led the Dodgers in intentional walks (4), batting average with runners in scoring position (.275) and steals of third
- Led NL shortstops in triples, most pitches seen per plate appearance (3.78), batting average on a 3-1 count (.500), errors (42), bunts in play (24) and steals of third

PITCHING:

One must wonder how many years Bobby Ojeda has left as a starter. He has never been the most durable pitcher, with only two years over 200 innings, nor has he ever had overwhelming stuff. Though he entered the 1992 campaign with a fine 107-88 lifetime record, Ojeda was able to coax just six wins out of his 29 starts last year, losing nine.

It wasn't solely due to the sorry club behind him. After averaging 11.7 baserunners per nine innings lifetime, Ojeda put 11.9 guys on in '91 and then 13.5 in '92. That's an alarming trend for a 35 year old in arguably the best pitchers' park in baseball. In fact, Ojeda was quite good in Dodger Stadium, going 4-2 with a 2.40 ERA. On the road, he was a very different, ineffective pitcher: 2-7, 4.84 ERA, 14.31 baserunners per nine innings.

Ojeda has always worked strictly on the outside edge of the plate, with nothing fancy. He has an average fastball, and he'll cut it, and also has great arm motion on his change. He has never given in to hitters, but now appears to lack the ability to put them away. Opponents hit .199 to lead off an inning, but .283 with runners on and .271 when in scoring position. As always, Ojeda hits the wall in the sixth inning; batters hit .298 from the seventh onward.

HOLDING RUNNERS, FIELDING, HITTING:

Ojeda throws over to first a lot using several different moves. He will sometimes freeze his leg in mid-air, hoping to do the same to the runner. It often worked; though runners attempted 35 stolen bases against him in 1992, only 20 succeeded. Ojeda is a good fielder and a real battler at the plate. He rumbled to the first triple of his career in '92.

OVERALL:

Ojeda wants to win badly, not play badly. He lost interest in '92, and when he won exactly zero games in September, a month in which he had been 26-13, 2.62 lifetime, the Dodgers "asked" him to skip his last start for Pedro Martinez' debut. A contending team will snap up the veteran free agent lefty.

BOBBY OJEDA

Position: SP
Bats: L **Throws:** L
Ht: 6' 1" **Wt:** 195

Opening Day Age: 35
Born: 12/17/57 in Los Angeles, CA
ML Seasons: 13

Overall Statistics

	W	L	ERA	G	GS	Sv	IP	H	R	BB	SO	HR
1992	6	9	3.63	29	29	0	166.1	169	80	81	94	8
Career	113	97	3.60	340	282	1	1838.0	1774	826	649	1098	139

How Often He Throws Strikes

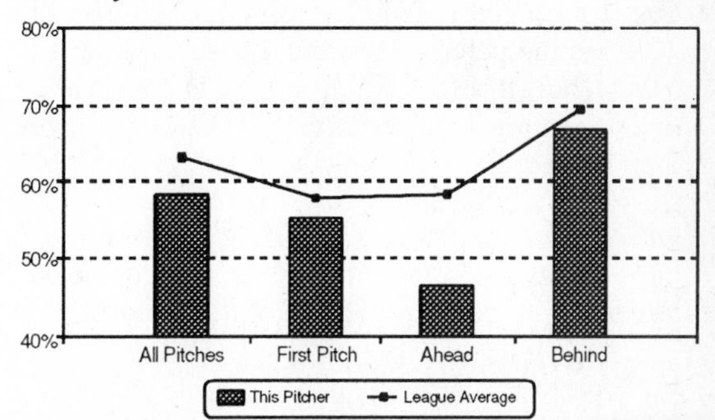

1992 Situational Stats

	W	L	ERA	Sv	IP		AB	H	HR	RBI	AVG
Home	4	2	2.40	0	82.2	LHB	116	25	1	12	.216
Road	2	7	4.84	0	83.2	RHB	515	144	7	64	.280
Day	2	4	3.19	0	67.2	Sc Pos	166	45	1	67	.271
Night	4	5	3.92	0	98.2	Clutch	19	7	1	2	.368

1992 Rankings (National League)

- 1st in lowest strikeout/walk ratio (1.2), highest on-base percentage allowed (.349) and most baserunners allowed per 9 innings (13.6)
- 2nd in walks allowed (81)
- 3rd in most runners caught stealing (15) and highest ERA on the road (4.84)
- 4th in highest batting average allowed vs. right-handed batters (.280)
- Led the Dodgers in walks allowed, runners caught stealing, lowest stolen base percentage allowed (57.1%), most run support per 9 innings (3.9), least home runs allowed per 9 innings (.43) and lowest batting average allowed vs. left-handed batters (.215)

JODY REED

Position: 2B
Bats: R **Throws:** R
Ht: 5' 9" **Wt:** 165

Opening Day Age: 30
Born: 7/26/62 in Tampa, FL
ML Seasons: 6

Overall Statistics

	G	AB	R	H	D	T	HR	RBI	SB	BB	SO	AVG
1992	143	550	64	136	27	1	3	40	7	62	44	.247
Career	715	2658	361	743	180	7	17	227	23	319	227	.280

Where He Hits the Ball

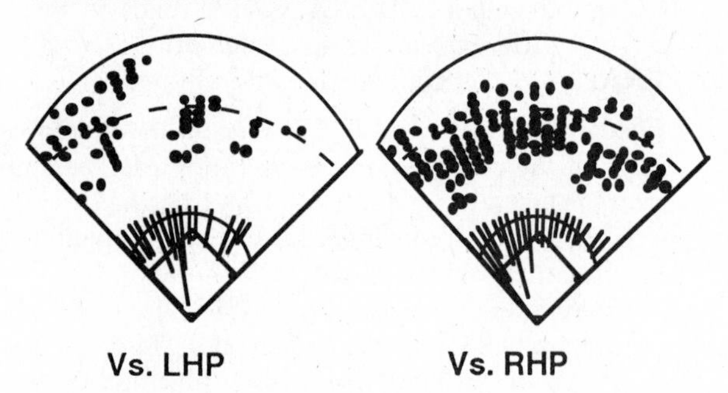

1992 Situational Stats

	AB	H	HR	RBI	AVG		AB	H	HR	RBI	AVG
Home	279	77	2	22	.276	LHP	154	40	1	7	.260
Road	271	59	1	18	.218	RHP	396	96	2	33	.242
Day	192	49	1	14	.255	Sc Pos	101	24	0	36	.238
Night	358	87	2	26	.243	Clutch	107	21	0	7	.196

1992 Rankings (American League)

- 1st in highest percentage of swings put into play (64.4%)
- 2nd in lowest slugging percentage vs. right-handed pitchers (.296)
- Led the Red Sox in at-bats (550), runs scored (64), hits (136), singles (105), stolen bases (7), caught stealing (8), GDPs (17), pitches seen (2,288), plate appearances (626) and games played (143)
- Led AL second basemen in GDPs, lowest percentage of swings that missed (7.6%) and highest percentage of swings put into play

HITTING:

After hitting between .283 and .293 each of his first four full major league seasons, Jody Reed turned 30 last July, and his career hit a wall. He batted a mere .247, he struggled defensively and often seemed completely distracted. At one point in the season, when he failed to advance a runner on second and none out in game Boston eventually lost by a run, Reed said it was not a lack of effort. "I was trying to do the right thing," he said later. "But I'm so messed up, I can't see or play right."

The Dodgers swung a deal for Reed after he'd been picked up by Colorado in the expansion draft, so they obviously feel he has a lot left. But this is a crucial season for Reed as he turns 31. There is the perception around baseball that like Marty Barrett before him, Reed could go fast after overachieving. But Reed is a little different player than Barrett. For one thing, he has a big man's bat speed on a little man's body. He is also blessed with a more lithe body than Barrett, who worked hard for everything. But in 1992, Reed looked like a player on the downside of the curve.

BASERUNNING:

Reed has always been an aggressive baserunner, and it's one reason he's recorded high doubles totals. He is a good basestealer only by his former Red Sox standards: 7-for-15 in 1992, 47 percent success rate for the season and his career.

FIELDING:

It was evident in spring training that Reed had worked so hard on weight training that he had tightened up. One result was that his range suffered at second base. He is still above-average for the position and good on the double play.

OVERALL:

If Reed bounces back physically and mentally, he'll be a solid player for the Dodgers. He's certainly capable of hitting .280 again, and he offers a fairly steady glove -- something which should make him a valuable player for the Dodgers, whatever he hits.

HITTING:

What a difference a year can make. Mike Scioscia entered the 1992 campaign as one of the most consistent players in baseball. He had hit between .250 and .265 for six straight seasons. When he remained mired below the Mendoza Line through May, however, people wondered if Scioscia's many home plate collisions had finally begun to take their toll. Indeed, they may have. Though Scioscia rallied somewhat after the break, he finished the year batting .221.

Scioscia is a contact hitter who uses the entire field. He's always been dangerous on high, inside fastballs, but he appeared to pull off the ball more in '92. To be fair, even when the burly backstop began to hit the ball hard, the hits were just not dropping in. The more he struggled, the more impatient he became. Scioscia owns an excellent .344 lifetime on-base average (567 walks, 307 strikeouts) and has walked more than he has struck out every season of his 13-year career. In 1992, however, he needed four intentional walks to maintain that record (32 BB, 31 Ks). His OBP last year was a career-low .286.

BASERUNNING:

As one might expect of a 220-pound catcher, Scioscia is slow as molasses. He is a cagey baserunner, though, and stole three more bases in '92 to raise his career total to 29. He was caught twice.

FIELDING:

Scioscia calls a great game and frames pitches extremely well. But he couldn't reach second base early on with his throws last year, and garnered nine errors. He recovered to throw out a respectable 27 percent of potential basestealers over the season. As always, if the play at the plate is anywhere close, the runner will not score on Scioscia.

OVERALL:

Scioscia insists that he simply had a bad year and is not ready for the backup role that the Dodgers had in mind for him. Though his work ethic has made him a fan favorite in Los Angeles, the free agent will probably move on to handle a different pitching staff in '93. His new staff will be better for it.

MIKE SCIOSCIA

Position: C
Bats: L **Throws:** R
Ht: 6' 2" **Wt:** 220

Opening Day Age: 34
Born: 11/27/58 in Upper Darby, PA
ML Seasons: 13

Overall Statistics

	G	AB	R	H	D	T	HR	RBI	SB	BB	SO	AVG
1992	117	348	19	77	6	3	3	24	3	32	31	.221
Career	1441	4373	398	1131	198	12	68	446	29	567	307	.259

Where He Hits the Ball

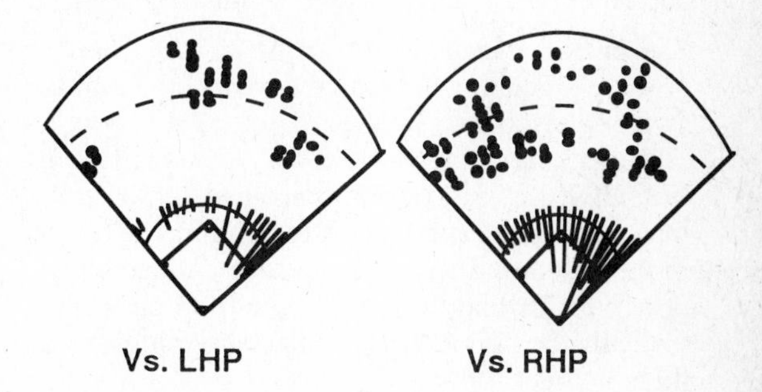

1992 Situational Stats

	AB	H	HR	RBI	AVG		AB	H	HR	RBI	AVG
Home	178	44	1	17	.247	LHP	81	19	1	10	.235
Road	170	33	2	7	.194	RHP	267	58	2	14	.217
Day	92	16	1	4	.174	Sc Pos	76	15	0	19	.197
Night	256	61	2	20	.238	Clutch	68	18	1	5	.265

1992 Rankings (National League)

- 6th in lowest batting average with the bases loaded (.111)
- Led the Dodgers in intentional walks (4) and batting average on an 0-2 count (.263)

HITTING:

Mike Sharperson had a tremendous half of a season. When he went off to collect autographs at the All-Star Game (as the Dodgers' only representative), he was batting .328 and already had 27 of his career-high tying 36 RBI. Sharperson couldn't buy a hit when he returned, unfortunately, and his playing time decreased drastically down the Dodgers' youth-filled stretch. He still batted .300 for the season, a career high.

His success was no fluke. Sharperson hits line drives to all fields. He seldom has a bad at-bat, striking out just 33 times while drawing 47 walks. When he gets behind in the count, Sharperson will shorten up and hit it back through the box; he had an excellent .275 average with two strikes.

Sharperson needs playing time to stay sharp. After platooning the last few years, the righty swinger responded to everyday play by hitting .280 against righthanders; he hit .312 vs lefties in '92, .309 lifetime. He's an excellent hit-and-run man with an uncanny knack for finding the holes in the defense. Sharperson has even added some power as his body matures; he turned on inside fastballs for 21 doubles (another career high) and three homers.

BASERUNNING:

Sharperson was quite the base stealer in his more youthful years and swiped 15 just two years ago. Though he still shows good instincts on the basepaths, his added weight has slowed him down considerably. He was just 2-for-4 in SB attempts in 1992.

FIELDING:

Sharperson is a fine utility infielder who can fill in at both second and third. As his playing time increases, however, his liabilities begin to surface. His range is laughable, his arm mediocre and he tends to duck away from sharply hit grounders.

OVERALL:

Sharperson was exposed to the expansion draft, but his age (31) kept the new clubs from taking him. Though a big league hitter, he lacks the power for third base and the range and wherewithal for second. One suspects that he will regain his utility role for the Dodgers next year.

MIKE SHARPERSON

Position: 2B/3B
Bats: R **Throws:** R
Ht: 6' 3" **Wt:** 190

Opening Day Age: 31
Born: 10/4/61 in Orangeburg, SC
ML Seasons: 6

Overall Statistics

	G	AB	R	H	D	T	HR	RBI	SB	BB	SO	AVG
1992	128	317	48	95	21	0	3	36	2	47	33	.300
Career	477	1106	135	313	56	5	8	111	20	134	135	.283

Where He Hits the Ball

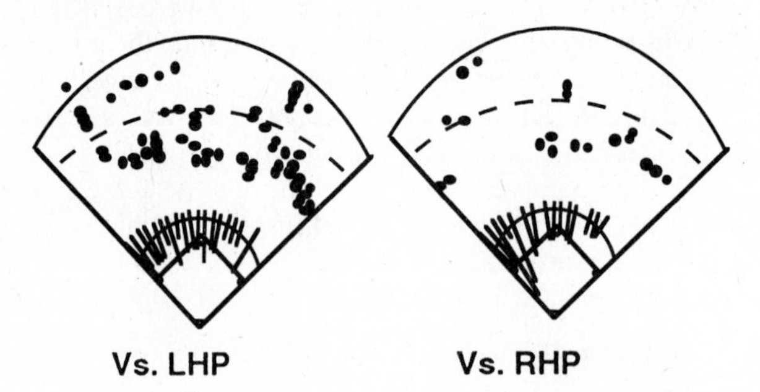

1992 Situational Stats

	AB	H	HR	RBI	AVG		AB	H	HR	RBI	AVG
Home	159	50	2	19	.314	LHP	199	62	3	22	.312
Road	158	45	1	17	.285	RHP	118	33	0	14	.280
Day	94	32	3	11	.340	Sc Pos	90	23	0	30	.256
Night	223	63	0	25	.283	Clutch	75	20	1	12	.267

1992 Rankings (National League)

- 4th in batting average with 2 strikes (.275)
- 8th in batting average on a 3-2 count (.361)
- Led the Dodgers in batting average vs. left-handed pitchers (.312) and batting average with 2 strikes
- Led NL third basemen in batting average on a 3-2 count and batting average with 2 strikes

HITTING:

Darryl Strawberry made only 177 plate appearances in 1992, hardly time for his streaky bat to get warmed up. He hit a respectable .259 in April with 4 homers and 18 RBI; little did he know that his season was about to end. A herniated disk sent Strawberry to the disabled list on May 14th and he was not the same player in two futile comeback attempts.

One wonders if his potent looping stroke will return intact. Strawberry's lanky frame generates a lot of torque when he swings, whether he hits the ball or not, and that has to put pressure on his damaged spinal column.

Strawberry showed evidence of his usual clutch performance in '92. With runners on base, he hit .295 with a .391 on-base average and .526 slugging percentage (he batted .179 with the bases empty). He looks to hammer the first pitch fastball, or any heater for that matter, and will often get fooled by something offspeed. He's got a good eye, though; he owns a .358 lifetime on-base percentage.

BASERUNNING:

Strawberry is no longer the basestealing threat he was in the 1980s. Five years after his only 30/30 season in 1987, he had three stolen bases to go along with his five homers. He still has good speed, especially from first to third, but even before the injury he had become a more cautious player. He only ran hard in September, when he felt he had something to prove.

FIELDING:

Years of coasting have made Strawberry an average outfielder. He has always had trouble going back for balls and now lets sinking liners drop in front of him for hits. His arm remains strong.

OVERALL:

Strawberry has never had to work too hard, at least not on the baseball diamond. Now he is facing an enormous challenge. In addition to recovering from the most serious injury of his career, it's time for the Strawman to show increased maturity. He showed a lack of class in '92 by hiding from a big Camera Day crowd. Nevertheless, Strawberry still has the talent to continue on the path towards a 400-HR (maybe 500) career.

DARRYL STRAWBERRY

Position: RF
Bats: L **Throws:** L
Ht: 6' 6" **Wt:** 200

Opening Day Age: 31
Born: 3/12/62 in Los Angeles, CA
ML Seasons: 10

Overall Statistics

	G	AB	R	H	D	T	HR	RBI	SB	BB	SO	AVG
1992	43	156	20	37	8	0	5	25	3	19	34	.237
Career	1291	4564	768	1196	217	34	285	857	204	674	1119	.262

Where He Hits the Ball

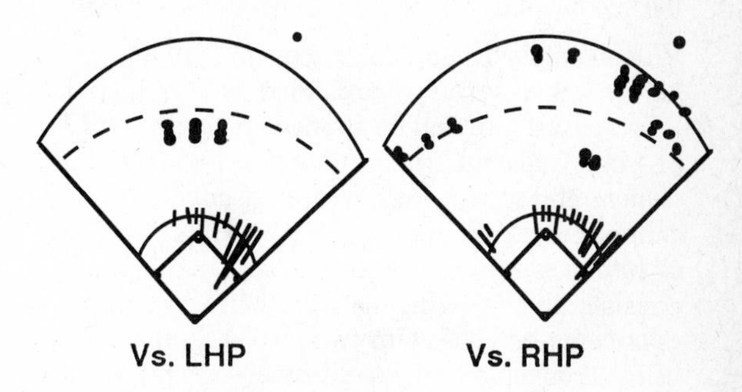

1992 Situational Stats

	AB	H	HR	RBI	AVG		AB	H	HR	RBI	AVG
Home	72	20	3	13	.278	LHP	66	16	2	10	.242
Road	84	17	2	12	.202	RHP	90	21	3	15	.233
Day	44	9	1	7	.205	Sc Pos	49	15	4	22	.306
Night	112	28	4	18	.250	Clutch	25	5	2	5	.200

1992 Rankings (National League)

→ Led the Dodgers in intentional walks (4)

PITCHING:

Steve Wilson sparkled in his Dodger debut at the tail end of 1991. Pitching coach Ron Perranoski moved him from the first to the third base side of the rubber and the results were immediate and dramatic. Though Wilson had never tallied an ERA under 4.20, he allowed nary a run in 11 appearances down the '91 stretch, picking up two saves in the process.

Cut to 1992 and back to reality for the not-so-young journeyman lefthander. Wilson started strongly, posting a 2.53 ERA in April and 2.84 in May, but he was allowing more hits than innings pitched (20 in 17 IP). Wilson couldn't sustain the increasing flow of baserunners and fell apart in the second half; his ERA after the break was 5.40.

Wilson enters the game firing on all cylinders and he throws extremely hard. First batters hit just .176 against him and he stranded 77 percent (37-of-48) of his inherited runners. He has a fair change and is working hard on a curveball, but cannot get them over consistently. He gets ahead of hitters but doesn't know how to get them out consistently. Knowing that a fastball was coming, opponents hit .265 with two strikes in the count last year against him, an extremely high number. Even more disconcerting is his penchant for falling apart in tight ballgames; Wilson allowed a .415 average in close and late situations.

HOLDING RUNNERS, FIELDING, HITTING:

Wilson keeps a close eye on opposing baserunners, though his move is only fair for a lefty. A former hockey player, he fields his position like a goalie, unafraid to stick out any limb to stop the ball. Wilson garnered a hit in three at-bats in '92, but his career average is .138.

OVERALL:

Wilson joins a long tradition of mediocre southpaws in the Dodger bullpen. His numbers against left-handed hitters were nothing special last year (.255 average), but due to a lack of any real competition, Wilson should be able to keep his middle relief job.

STEVE WILSON

Position: RP
Bats: L **Throws:** L
Ht: 6' 4" **Wt:** 195

Opening Day Age: 28
Born: 12/13/64 in Victoria, BC, Canada
ML Seasons: 5

Overall Statistics

	W	L	ERA	G	GS	Sv	IP	H	R	BB	SO	HR
1992	2	5	4.18	60	0	0	66.2	74	37	29	54	6
Career	12	18	4.39	180	23	5	319.2	318	169	116	229	31

How Often He Throws Strikes

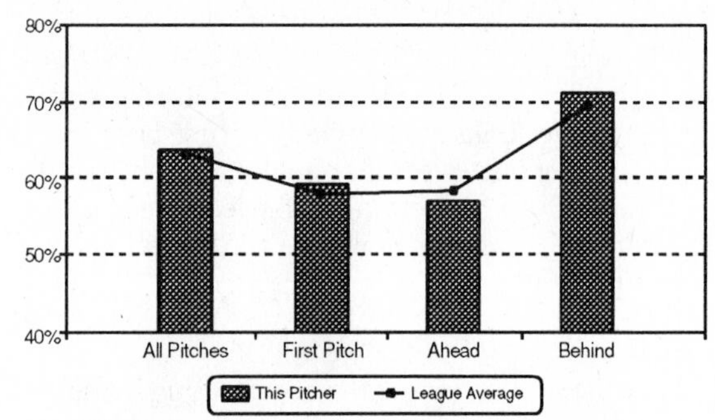

1992 Situational Stats

	W	L	ERA	Sv	IP		AB	H	HR	RBI	AVG
Home	2	2	4.25	0	29.2	LHB	98	25	2	15	.255
Road	0	3	4.14	0	37.0	RHB	164	49	4	24	.299
Day	0	2	3.86	0	16.1	Sc Pos	92	21	1	29	.228
Night	2	3	4.29	0	50.1	Clutch	53	22	1	13	.415

1992 Rankings (National League)

- 4th in most baserunners allowed per 9 innings in relief (14.0)
- 5th in highest batting average allowed in relief (.282)
- 6th in highest relief ERA (4.19)
- 10th in first batter efficiency (.176) and lowest percentage of inherited runners scored (22.9%)
- Led the Dodgers in first batter efficiency and lowest percentage of inherited runners scored

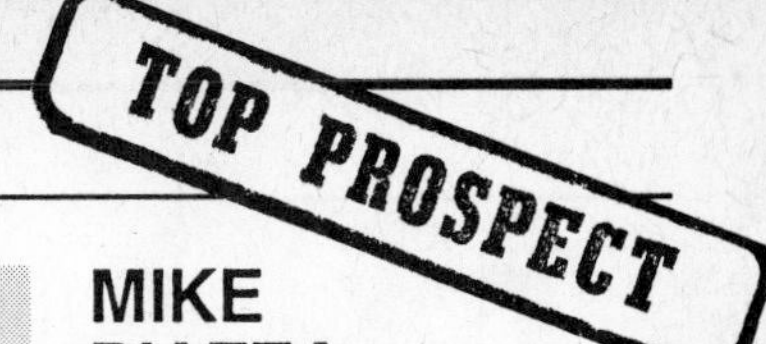

KIP GROSS

Position: RP
Bats: R **Throws:** R
Ht: 6' 2" **Wt:** 190

Opening Day Age: 28
Born: 8/24/64 in Scottsbluff, NE
ML Seasons: 3

Overall Statistics

	W	L	ERA	G	GS	Sv	IP	H	R	BB	SO	HR
1992	1	1	4.18	16	1	0	23.2	32	14	10	14	1
Career	7	5	3.66	50	10	0	115.2	131	60	52	57	9

PITCHING, FIELDING, HITTING & HOLDING RUNNERS:

Acquired by the Dodgers in the Eric Davis deal with Cincinnati, Kip Gross has not yet showed the ability to get guys out at the big-league level. In parts of three seasons he has allowed 14.2 baserunners per nine innings and has walked almost as many as he has struck out (52 walks, 57 strikeouts).

Gross comes to the mound with a wide assortment of pitches, the best of which is a curveball. He's got a mediocre fastball, so he'll mix in a cutter, a sinker and a split-fingered version. None of them worked in 1992 -- opponents hit .323 against him. To enjoy any success, Gross must get ahead in the count; batters went 17-for-33 (.515) after a first pitch ball.

Opponents seldom run on Gross. Why bother when he gives up so many hits? He appears to be an average fielder and was 2-for-2 with an RBI at the plate.

OVERALL:

Trivia question of the future: who did the Dodgers get in exchange for Tim Belcher and John Wetteland? Gross was probably available in all three of the expansion rounds, but neither the Rockies nor Marlins were biting. He had a 5.00 ERA in Dodger Stadium in '92; it might have reached mile-high figures in Colorado.

MIKE PIAZZA

Position: C
Bats: R **Throws:** R
Ht: 6' 3" **Wt:** 200

Opening Day Age: 24
Born: 9/4/68 in Norristown, PA
ML Seasons: 1

Overall Statistics

	G	AB	R	H	D	T	HR	RBI	SB	BB	SO	AVG
1992	21	69	5	16	3	0	1	7	0	4	12	.232
Career	21	69	5	16	3	0	1	7	0	4	12	.232

HITTING, FIELDING, BASERUNNING:

Mike Piazza continued his meteoric rise through the Dodger system in 1992. In his first 31 games at the AA level, he hit .377 with seven homers and 20 RBI at San Antonio. Piazza then hit .341 (16 HR, 69 RBI) when promoted to AAA Albuquerque. He finished the year with 69 AB for the big league club. Though he batted only .232, he didn't do much to harm his reputation.

The 24 year old packs a lot of punch in a compact swing, showing surprising power to right-center. Piazza seldom gets cheated at the plate and hits the ball hard. Surprisingly, most of his shots were on the ground in his brief debut (2.42 groundball-to-flyball ratio).

Piazza moves and runs well, but is not a basestealing threat. Tommy Lasorda claims to have suggested his godson's late conversion to catcher. With just four seasons under his chest protector, catching mechanics are the weakest part of his game. He has a strong arm and should improve.

OVERALL:

Piazza agreed to play in the Arizona Fall League to work on his defense. He is slated to be the starting catcher in '93 and looks ready. The club would like to retain Scioscia as a left-handed back-up and mentor, but the veteran still wants to play full-time. Piazza may be a solo number-one this year.

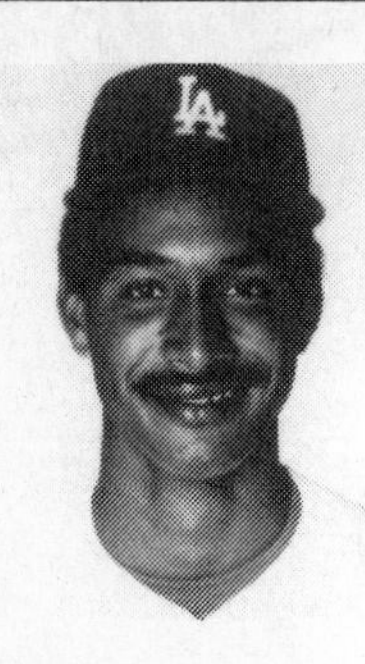

HENRY RODRIGUEZ

Position: RF/LF
Bats: L **Throws:** L
Ht: 6' 1" **Wt:** 180

Opening Day Age: 25
Born: 11/8/67 in Santo Domingo, DR
ML Seasons: 1

Overall Statistics

	G	AB	R	H	D	T	HR	RBI	SB	BB	SO	AVG
1992	53	146	11	32	7	0	3	14	0	8	30	.219
Career	53	146	11	32	7	0	3	14	0	8	30	.219

HITTING, FIELDING, BASERUNNING:

Henry Rodriguez is a powerfully built left-handed hitter who was described as "a man among boys" when he was in the minors. Called up to the Dodgers in July, he looked more like a boy amongst men for a time, getting off to an 0-for-15 start before finally managing a bloop single. Rodriguez had a good August (.282, 3 HR, 11 RBI), but could not sustain it.

Rodriguez showed good power to all fields, though the club wants him to pull the ball more. He has a big swing and pitchers often let him get himself out. He struck out 23 times in the 66 at-bats that began with a first-pitch strike. Ironically, though he was used almost exclusively against right-handed pitching, he was 6-for-15 (.400) vs. southpaws.

Rodriguez is not a basestealer but he has above-average speed. A converted first baseman, he has turned into a good outfielder. He gets a good jump and has an extremely strong arm.

OVERALL:

Rodriguez has not developed as quickly as the Dodgers had hoped after his breakthrough 1990 season in AA San Antonio (.291, 28 HR, 109 RBI). Yet he's only 25 and seems to have both the tools and the attitude to make it in the bigs. The question is whether the Dodgers will be the club; they left him unprotected for expansion, although he was not selected.

MITCH WEBSTER

Position: RF/LF
Bats: B **Throws:** L
Ht: 6' 1" **Wt:** 185

Opening Day Age: 33
Born: 5/16/59 in Larned, KS
ML Seasons: 10

Overall Statistics

	G	AB	R	H	D	T	HR	RBI	SB	BB	SO	AVG
1992	135	262	33	70	12	5	6	35	11	27	49	.267
Career	1041	3107	456	825	139	52	63	313	155	302	527	.266

HITTING, FIELDING, BASERUNNING:

Nearly 34, Mitch Webster is a valuable veteran who comes to the park ready to play every day. He broke the all-time Dodger record for pinch-hits in a season in '92, going 17-for-47 (.362, .418 on-base average, .489 slugging) off the bench. Webster comes out swinging and hit .360 on the first pitch.

A switch-hitter, Webster is much stronger from the right side (.292, .242 as a lefty); over the past five seasons, he's .272 righty, .240 lefty. He hit .324 on the turf last year and is 45 points better on turf fields since 1988, so Dodger Stadium is not doing him any favors. Webster is a solid performer in the clutch; he hit .297 late in the game and .318 if it was close.

Webster has stolen as many as 36 bases in one year and was 11-for-16 in '92. He may have lost a step, but makes up for it with savvy. He is a very good outfielder, able to play anywhere needed. His throws are on target if not the most powerful.

OVERALL:

Webster took a big pay cut to play another year in LA, and had a good season. His professional approach to the game could prove to be a valuable influence on a young club, which the Dodgers are quickly becoming. He will be the number-four or five outfielder somewhere in the majors.

ORGANIZATION OVERVIEW:

Through most of the Tommy Lasorda era, the Dodger philosophy was sort of the hippie era in reverse: never trust anyone under 30. Last year's shocking last-place finish seems to have convinced the Dodgers that signing free agents and trading for veterans is no longer the way to go. LA's Eric Karros won the Rookie of the Year award in '92, and he may be the first of many Dodger youngsters to win a spot in the lineup. The system is supposed to be well-stocked; now we'll see.

BILLY ASHLEY

Position: OF **Opening Day Age:** 22
Bats: R **Throws:** R **Born:** 7/11/70 in Taylor, MI
Ht: 6' 7" **Wt:** 220

Recent Statistics

	G	AB	R	H	D	T	HR	RBI	SB	BB	SO	AVG
92 AAA Albuquerque	25	95	11	20	7	0	2	10	1	6	42	.211
92 AA San Antonio	101	380	60	106	23	1	24	66	13	16	111	.279
92 NL Los Angeles	29	95	6	21	5	0	2	6	0	5	34	.221
92 MLE	126	446	46	97	20	0	16	50	8	12	164	.217

If the Dodgers had known Billy Ashley would turn out like this, maybe they wouldn't have been so hot to get Eric Davis. In 1991 Ashley batted .252 at Class A Vero Beach, and that figure was a career high. Considered the Dodgers' best power prospect at 6'7" and 220 pounds, he'd never hit more than nine homers. But in 1992 Ashley finally got it together. He belted 24 homers at AA San Antonio, two at AAA Albuquerque, and two more with the Dodgers. With his size, Ashley is sometimes called a "young Dave Kingman," but he shouldn't consider it a compliment. Last year he had a Kingman-like 186 strikeouts at his three levels and only 27 walks.

RAFAEL BOURNIGAL

Position: SS **Opening Day Age:** 26
Bats: R **Throws:** R **Born:** 5/12/66 in Azua, DR
Ht: 5' 11" **Wt:** 160

Recent Statistics

	G	AB	R	H	D	T	HR	RBI	SB	BB	SO	AVG
92 AAA Albuquerque	122	395	47	128	18	1	0	34	5	22	7	.324
92 NL Los Angeles	10	20	1	3	1	0	0	0	0	1	2	.150
92 MLE	122	365	28	98	12	0	0	20	3	13	7	.268

Not even considered one of the Dodgers' top ten prospects a year ago, Bournigal could be their shortstop this year if Jose Offerman stumbles. Bournigal is considered much more sure-handed than Offerman (only nine errors last year), and his hitting has improved greatly over the last couple of seasons. He's also bilingual, very intelligent and considered a future coach or manager. Offerman may be getting a little worried about this guy.

GREG HANSELL

Position: P **Opening Day Age:** 22
Bats: R **Throws:** R **Born:** 3/12/71 in Bellflower, CA
Ht: 6' 5" **Wt:** 215

Recent Statistics

	W	L	ERA	G	GS	Sv	IP	H	R	BB	SO	HR
91 A Bakersfield	14	5	2.87	25	25	0	150.2	142	56	42	132	5
92 AAA Albuquerque	1	5	5.24	13	13	0	68.2	84	46	35	38	9
92 AA San Antonio	6	4	2.83	14	14	0	92.1	80	40	33	64	6

At 22, Greg Hansell has already pitched for three good organizations -- the Red Sox, Mets and now Dodgers. When a guy gets dealt that much, there's usually a reason, and with Hansell, it's probably because he lacks the velocity a man of his size is expected to have. However, Hansell has a good arm and has posted good ERAs at every stop except for a brief stint at Albuquerque last year. The Dodgers consider him one of their top pitching prospects and protected him in the expansion draft.

PEDRO MARTINEZ

Position: P **Opening Day Age:** 21
Bats: R **Throws:** R **Born:** 10/25/71 in Manoguayabo, DR
Ht: 5' 11" **Wt:** 150

Recent Statistics

	W	L	ERA	G	GS	Sv	IP	H	R	BB	SO	HR
92 AAA Albuquerque	7	6	3.81	20	20	0	125.1	104	57	57	124	10
92 NL Los Angeles	0	1	2.25	2	1	0	8.0	6	2	1	8	0

Pedro Martinez came up to the Dodgers late last year and appears ready to take his place beside his brother Ramon in the L.A. rotation -- that is if Ramon, who seems washed up at 25 after a few years of Lasorda-type usage, is still around. The younger Martinez (there's a third brother, Jesus, in the Dodger system) is shorter and slighter than Ramon, so hopefully the Dodgers will be gentler with his arm . . . he's already had some shoulder problems.

RAUL R. MONDESI

Position: OF **Opening Day Age:** 22
Bats: R **Throws:** R **Born:** 3/12/71 in San Cristobal, DR
Ht: 5' 11" **Wt:** 150

Recent Statistics

	G	AB	R	H	D	T	HR	RBI	SB	BB	SO	AVG
91 A Bakersfield	28	106	23	30	7	2	3	13	9	5	21	.283
91 AA San Antonio	53	213	32	58	10	5	5	26	7	8	47	.272
91 AAA Albuquerque	2	9	3	3	0	1	0	0	1	0	1	.333
92 AAA Albuquerque	35	138	23	43	4	7	4	15	2	9	35	.312
92 AA San Antonio	18	68	8	18	2	2	2	14	3	1	24	.265

If Ashley's the next Dave Kingman, than Mondesi's the next Roberto Clemente, or so he's been described. Despite hand and knee injuries, Mondesi played very well at both San Antonio and Albuquerque last year, especially in the field. It's really his arm that draws the Clemente comparisons; Mondesi, who doesn't have much power and who has logged only 709 minor-league at-bats while fighting injuries, has a long way to go as a hitter.

MOISES ALOU

Position: LF/CF/RF
Bats: R **Throws:** R
Ht: 6' 3" **Wt:** 190

Opening Day Age: 26
Born: 7/3/66 in Atlanta, GA
ML Seasons: 2

Overall Statistics

	G	AB	R	H	D	T	HR	RBI	SB	BB	SO	AVG
1992	115	341	53	96	28	2	9	56	16	25	46	.282
Career	131	361	57	100	28	3	9	56	16	25	49	.277

Where He Hits the Ball

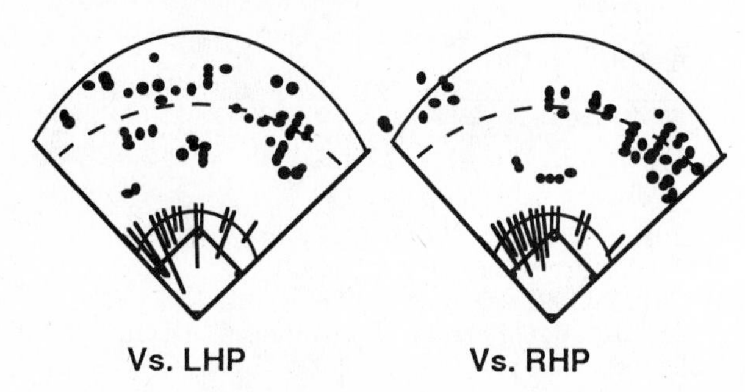

1992 Situational Stats

	AB	H	HR	RBI	AVG		AB	H	HR	RBI	AVG
Home	143	48	6	35	.336	LHP	136	40	2	14	.294
Road	198	48	3	21	.242	RHP	205	56	7	42	.273
Day	113	38	3	16	.336	Sc Pos	113	33	5	47	.292
Night	228	58	6	40	.254	Clutch	66	18	3	14	.273

1992 Rankings (National League)

- Led the Expos in batting average with 2 strikes (.247)
- Led NL left fielders in sacrifice bunts (5)

HITTING:

Not even the most optimistic observers in the Expos' organization could predict Moises Alou's emergence as one of the league's potential bright stars. The "other" prospect, along with Willie Greene (and Scott Ruskin) in the deal that sent Zane Smith to the Pirates, Alou took his time moving up the minor-league ladder. On top of that, surgery to repair a rotator cuff tear forced him to sit out all of the 1991 season. However, the latest in a long line of major-league Alous quickly proved himself.

If not for an injured left hamstring suffered in July, Alou might have captured Rookie of the Year honors. At the time of the injury, Alou was batting a hearty .316 with a .509 slugging average and 31 RBI in just 171 at-bats. Alou returned from the disabled list prematurely, sliding into a .184 funk for the next three weeks. He recovered to finish with some terrific numbers for someone with less than 350 at-bats.

Lean and muscular, Alou possesses incredibly quick hands and a strong upper body, enabling him to turn on any fastball (including a Rob Dibble 99 MPH heater that became a game-winning homer). Alou is a line drive/contact hitter who will sometimes try to put more muscle on the ball early in the count and will take the occasional walk.

BASERUNNING:

Not surprisingly, Alou is an excellent baserunner. He chooses his spots to display his aggressiveness and does not fail often. He had 16 steals in only 18 tries and is capable of 30 or more.

FIELDING:

Alou has the ability to play all three outfield positions. Because of the arm surgery which wiped out his 1991 season, Alou is better suited for left. He reacts well on the ball and moves quickly. Even his questionable arm improved as the season progressed.

OVERALL:

The Expos, convinced that Alou is capable of becoming a consistent contributor, will try their best to trade Ivan Calderon to allow Alou free reign next season. The manager's son is growing up in a hurry.

PITCHING:

For the second straight season, Brian Barnes failed in an extended trial at establishing himself as one of the Expos' starting five. He started the year at AAA Indianapolis after a poor spring. Immediately following his mid-June call-up, he strung a few quality starts together, but by mid-September he was working out of the pen.

Despite sporting solid numbers (6-6 2.97 ERA) at the time of the move, Barnes failed to gain Felipe Alou's confidence for several reasons. Foremost among them was his lack of stamina. As was the case in 1991, Barnes rarely pitched six innings (he failed to do that in his last seven starts last season) and had trouble the second time through the batting order, running out of good stuff after 55 pitches or so. Barnes also had problems when pitching out of the stretch position. In an effort to keep runners close, he sped up his motion; as a result his pitches were less effective.

When Barnes is on, he has no problem retiring batters. Last season he held the opposition to a paltry .213 batting average (in 1991, the figure was .233). Barnes has a great change-up and a sharp curveball but has problems spotting his 87 MPH fastball. That combination produced almost the same results as in '91: one walk every two innings, one homer every 10, and frequent multi-run innings.

HOLDING RUNNERS, FIELDING, HITTING:

Barnes improved greatly as a hitter with eight singles in 29 at-bats (a .276 average) and six sacrifices. As mentioned, he sped up his delivery from the stretch and was more difficult to run against last season (14 steals in 21 tries). He is an average defensive player.

OVERALL:

A former college and minor-league standout with huge strikeout totals, Barnes has had difficulty adjusting to his failure to attain consistent success as a major-league starter. He needs to be less delicate during moments of adversity if he wants to be a consistent winner and avoid a transfer to the bullpen. The talent is there.

BRIAN BARNES

Position: SP
Bats: L **Throws:** L
Ht: 5' 9" **Wt:** 170

Opening Day Age: 26
Born: 3/25/67 in Roanoke Rapids, NC
ML Seasons: 3

Overall Statistics

	W	L	ERA	G	GS	Sv	IP	H	R	BB	SO	HR
1992	6	6	2.97	21	17	0	100.0	77	34	46	65	9
Career	12	15	3.66	53	48	0	288.0	237	126	137	205	27

How Often He Throws Strikes

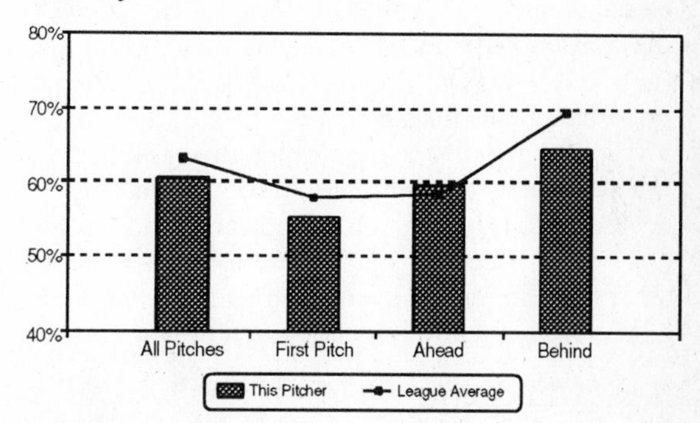

1992 Situational Stats

	W	L	ERA	Sv	IP		AB	H	HR	RBI	AVG
Home	4	3	2.47	0	58.1	LHB	60	14	2	7	.233
Road	2	3	3.67	0	41.2	RHB	302	63	7	22	.209
Day	2	1	1.45	0	37.1	Sc Pos	77	15	3	20	.195
Night	4	5	3.88	0	62.2	Clutch	10	1	0	0	.100

1992 Rankings (National League)

- 10th in balks (2)

HITTING:

The Expos, confident about their success with entry-level major leaguers, took a chance on 26-year-old Sean Berry, obtaining him from the Royals late last season. Berry had enjoyed a solid season in AAA Omaha, batting .287 with an eye-catching 21 homers and 77 RBI in 439 at-bats. The Royals had given Berry an opportunity in 1991, calling him up three different times. The result was a meager .133 batting average and a strikeout in 38 percent of his trips.

Berry hit for a high average (.333) with Montreal, but showed very little power (two extra-base hits in 57 at-bats). He was also incredibly impatient, striking out 11 times with only one walk. Clearly, Berry cannot sustain a major-league career with his present five-to-one lifetime strikeout-walk ratio. He's drawn walks in the minors, so his impatience thus far may have just been a result of a youthful effort to make a quick impression. Jay Ward, the Expos hitting coach, was attempting to get Berry to stay short on the bottom hand during his swing. Because of his strength, Berry can afford to shorten his swing and wait on the pitch a little longer without losing much power.

BASERUNNING:

Despite his bulky 5'11", 210 lb. frame, Berry is a fairly aggressive baserunner who possesses deceptive speed. He has stolen as many as 37 bases in the minors and was 2-for-3 with Montreal.

FIELDING:

Berry came to the Expos with a solid defensive reputation. He had been voted the top fielding third baseman in two different minor leagues, and displayed both quickness and a strong throwing arm in 20 games in Montreal. However, his footwork was shaky at times, and as a result he muffed routine plays and fielded at an atrocious .875 percentage.

OVERALL:

The Expos like Berry's offensive potential. His use will largely depend on both Tim Wallach's performance and the success the Expos have in landing a run-producing first baseman if Greg Colbrunn does not cut it. Since Wallach is getting older (35), Berry should get a chance to show what he can do.

SEAN BERRY

Position: 3B
Bats: R **Throws:** R
Ht: 5'11" **Wt:** 210

Opening Day Age: 27
Born: 3/22/66 in Santa Monica, CA
ML Seasons: 3

Overall Statistics

	G	AB	R	H	D	T	HR	RBI	SB	BB	SO	AVG
1992	24	57	5	19	1	0	1	4	2	1	11	.333
Career	63	140	12	32	5	1	1	9	2	8	39	.229

Where He Hits the Ball

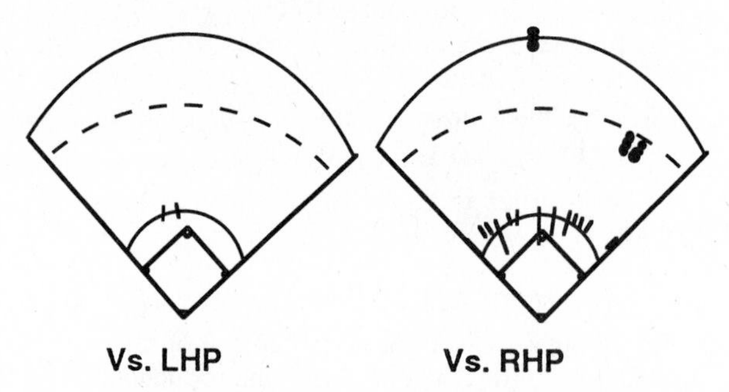

1992 Situational Stats

	AB	H	HR	RBI	AVG		AB	H	HR	RBI	AVG
Home	22	9	0	2	.409	LHP	3	2	0	0	.667
Road	35	10	1	2	.286	RHP	54	17	1	4	.315
Day	21	8	1	2	.381	Sc Pos	14	4	0	2	.286
Night	36	11	0	2	.306	Clutch	14	6	0	0	.429

1992 Rankings (National League)

- Did not rank near the top or bottom in any category

HITTING:

Ivan Calderon spent most of 1992 on the sidelines with an assortment of injuries while watching Moises Alou develop into an everyday player. In just a year, Calderon's value to the Expos plunged from being the team's most productive hitter to an overpriced spare part.

Despite his physical problems, there is no reason to doubt Calderon's hitting ability. In 170 at-bats last season, he produced 19 extra-base hits and drove in 24 runs -- good numbers for someone who spent three different stints on the disabled list and underwent arthroscopic surgery on his left shoulder on June 24. When he finally resumed an everyday schedule, Calderon excelled; he batted .309 in his final 81 at-bats with five doubles, two triples and a home run.

Calderon, a Walt Hriniak student, prides himself as being a business-like hitter. He displays both patience at the plate and the ability to adjust his stroke depending on the pitcher, the game situation, and the ball-strike count. Calderon will try to pull a pitch early in the count but will tend to go with the pitch using a shortened swing when he is behind in the count.

BASERUNNING:

Calderon has put on about 20 pounds in recent seasons and does not run as well as he once did. Coming off a year (1991) in which he stole 31 bases but was caught 16 times, Calderon barely budged from the first base bag in 1992, attempting just three steals. One attempt was successful.

FIELDING:

In the past, Calderon has been a slightly better-than-average left fielder whose hustle has compensated for an ordinary jump on the ball. Now with the added weight and the continual shoulder problems, Calderon has become a more conservative fielder with a questionable throwing arm.

OVERALL:

Calderon's ability to avoid the disabled list has become a question mark. He has always considered himself a complete athlete, but realistically there is no room for him in the Expos outfield. Returning to the American League might help reduce the strain of everyday play.

IVAN CALDERON

Position: LF
Bats: R **Throws:** R
Ht: 6' 1" **Wt:** 221
Opening Day Age: 31
Born: 3/19/62 in Fajardo, Puerto Rico
ML Seasons: 9

Overall Statistics

	G	AB	R	H	D	T	HR	RBI	SB	BB	SO	AVG
1992	48	170	19	45	14	2	3	24	1	14	22	.265
Career	842	3073	444	851	190	23	103	422	93	285	523	.277

Where He Hits the Ball

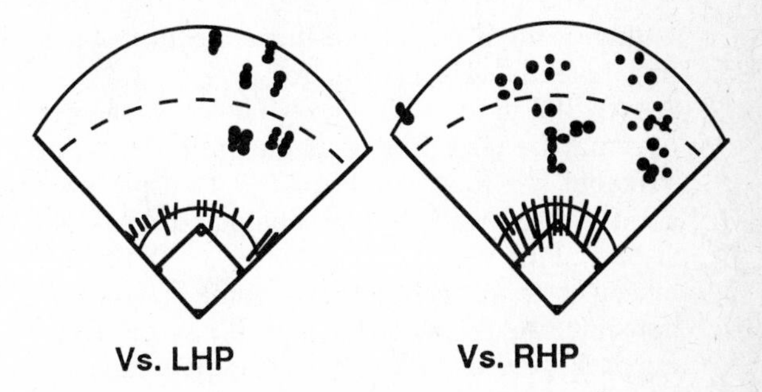

1992 Situational Stats

	AB	H	HR	RBI	AVG		AB	H	HR	RBI	AVG
Home	101	26	2	15	.257	LHP	51	17	0	3	.333
Road	69	19	1	9	.275	RHP	119	28	3	21	.235
Day	61	19	1	12	.311	Sc Pos	43	9	0	17	.209
Night	109	26	2	12	.239	Clutch	29	7	1	4	.241

1992 Rankings (National League)

- Did not rank near the top or bottom in any category

TOP PROSPECT

HITTING:

Wil Cordero had a chance to make the Expos roster on Opening Day last year, less than four years after he signed with the team at the age of 16. But the kid struck out 17 times in 38 spring training at-bats. Cordero bounced back at AAA Indianapolis, however, batting .314 despite missing significant stretches of playing time due to a sprained ankle, a strained middle finger, and a serious case of the chicken pox. He made it to the Expos after the All-Star break, and at 20 years old, went two-for-three in his first big league game.

Like the privileged few who have made it the majors so quickly, Cordero can look great in one at-bat and horrible in the next. The line drive hitting Cordero is an interesting collection of batting potential. He can hit for average (.314 in AAA, .302 in the NL). Though he often seemed overmatched by major-league pitching (one strikeout per four at-bats), he also displayed a good eye (33 walks in 330 combined AAA-NL at-bats). Plus, he showed that his 6'2", 185 pound muscular frame can generate some power (six homers in AAA, two in the NL). It's a very exciting package, but Cordero needs time to temper his aggressiveness and maintain consistent concentration from at-bat to at-bat.

BASERUNNING:

Cordero possesses above-average speed but is still learning how to run the bases. Not much of a threat to run, he did not attempt a stolen base with the Expos.

FIELDING:

Cordero has displayed excellent range, a strong throwing arm and the cool demeanor necessary to make the outstanding play. He looked uncomfortable in the nine games he spent at second and was error-prone at both second base and shortstop.

OVERALL:

Cordero is just a kid, so it might take awhile before he displays consistency both in the field and at the plate. Two things that are certain, however: he possesses a great deal of talent, and the Expos' starting shortstop position is now his to lose.

WIL CORDERO

Position: SS
Bats: R **Throws:** R
Ht: 6' 2" **Wt:** 185

Opening Day Age: 21
Born: 10/3/71 in Mayaguez, PR
ML Seasons: 1

Overall Statistics

	G	AB	R	H	D	T	HR	RBI	SB	BB	SO	AVG
1992	45	126	17	38	4	1	2	8	0	9	31	.302
Career	45	126	17	38	4	1	2	8	0	9	31	.302

Where He Hits the Ball

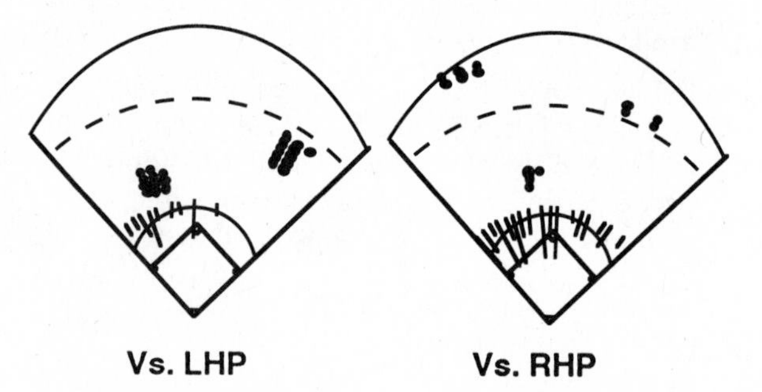

1992 Situational Stats

	AB	H	HR	RBI	AVG		AB	H	HR	RBI	AVG
Home	62	19	1	3	.306	LHP	34	16	0	2	.471
Road	64	19	1	5	.297	RHP	92	22	2	6	.239
Day	31	9	0	0	.290	Sc Pos	21	6	1	7	.286
Night	95	29	2	8	.305	Clutch	25	6	0	1	.240

1992 Rankings (National League)

- Did not rank near the top or bottom in any category

FUTURE ALL-STAR

DELINO DeSHIELDS

Position: 2B
Bats: L **Throws:** R
Ht: 6' 1" **Wt:** 170

Opening Day Age: 24
Born: 1/15/69 in Seaford, DE
ML Seasons: 3

HITTING:

In 1992, his third year in the majors, Delino DeShields matured into an impact player. In retrospect, 1991 was a year of growing pains: a batting slump (.238) produced fielding and basestealing problems, a home run binge began a sequence of overswinging and strikeouts: and the fear of striking out brought about frequent changes in his batting stance and, not surprisingly, a league-leading 151 strikeouts. DeShields seemed equally uncomfortable when last season began and criticized management for demanding too much from the team's young talent.

DeShields flourished, as did the whole team, when Felipe Alou took over. One of Alou's early payoffs was giving the leadoff spot back to DeShields, who hit .400 during the next 32 games. He was the Expos' MVP as the team vaulted into the pennant race. His final stats would be more impressive if not for a strained muscle suffered in the last month, a period in which he managed just six hits in 43 at-bats.

DeShields is very selective at the plate and is unafraid to go deep in the count and risk striking out. Possessing a lightning quick pair of hands, he thrives on fastballs, especially on the inside part of the plate. At his best, DeShields sprays line drives all over the field.

BASERUNNING:

A speedster, DeShields finally evolved into an efficient basestealer (45 steals in his last 55 attempts) by improving his ability to read opposing pitchers and acquire a quick jump. He's only beginning to tap his potential.

FIELDING:

Like other facets of his game, DeShields' fielding improved noticeably as the season wore on. He committed nine errors in the 37 games managed by Tom Runnels, but just six the rest of the way. A gifted athlete, DeShields moves gracefully to either side and possesses a strong, accurate arm.

OVERALL:

Just 24 years old as he enters his fourth season, DeShields has both the talent and the attitude to become one of the league's most valuable players. He matured greatly in 1992, and the best is yet to come.

Overall Statistics

	G	AB	R	H	D	T	HR	RBI	SB	BB	SO	AVG
1992	135	530	82	155	19	8	7	56	46	54	108	.292
Career	415	1592	234	433	62	18	21	152	144	215	355	.272

Where He Hits the Ball

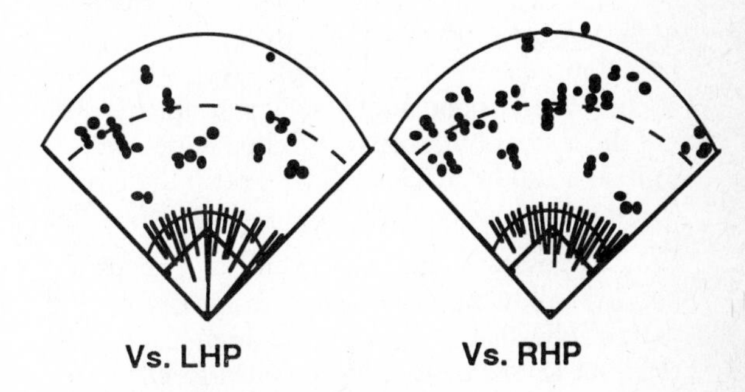

1992 Situational Stats

	AB	H	HR	RBI	AVG		AB	H	HR	RBI	AVG
Home	271	75	1	19	.277	LHP	185	58	2	21	.314
Road	259	80	6	37	.309	RHP	345	97	5	35	.281
Day	155	51	2	18	.329	Sc Pos	115	35	2	47	.304
Night	375	104	5	38	.277	Clutch	82	24	2	19	.293

1992 Rankings (National League)

- 2nd in stolen bases (46) and errors at second base (15)
- 3rd in most pitches seen per plate appearance (3.96)
- 4th in strikeouts (108)
- Led the Expos in singles (121), triples (8), caught stealing (15), walks (54), strikeouts, on-base percentage (.359), highest groundball/flyball ratio (1.9), most pitches seen per plate appearance, batting average with the bases loaded (.500), batting average vs. right-handed pitchers (.281), on-base percentage vs. left-handed pitchers (.389), on-base percentage vs. right-handed pitchers (.343) and bunts in play (26)

JEFF FASSERO

Position: RP
Bats: L **Throws:** L
Ht: 6' 1" **Wt:** 195

Opening Day Age: 30
Born: 1/5/63 in Springfield, IL
ML Seasons: 2

PITCHING:

After riding minor-league buses since 1984, Jeff Fassero got his first taste of major-league action in 1991 at 28 and was a pleasant surprise amidst a terrible Expo bullpen. Last season, Fassero was quietly effective in his role as the team's left-handed set-up man. Among left-handed relievers, Fassero was second in the league in innings pitched, third in appearances and was tied for fourth in holds (12). His 2.84 ERA for 70 appearances was only slightly higher than his rookie figure of 2.44.

As in 1991, Fassero pitched well in the early part of the season. Through June 22nd, he had limited the opposition to just a .199 batting average over 44.2 innings, but was inconsistent the remainder of the way. He posted a 5.40 ERA in July, then did not allow an earned run during 11 August appearances. When he encountered a few problems during the last month, manager Felipe Alou seemed to lose a little confidence in Fassero, though he continued to use the lefty frequently.

Fassero possesses good hard stuff and keeps the ball low, allowing just one homer last season and just one the year before. Even though his fastball tops out at 88 MPH, Fassero likes to challenge hitters and works quickly. His out pitch is a nasty slider which breaks in to a right-handed batter. As a result, Fassero is more effective against opposing righthanders (.241 as opposed to .269 against lefties). In 1991, his numbers were .171 against righties, .243 against lefties.

HOLDING RUNNERS AND FIELDING:

Fassero is a good fielder but has a mediocre move to first. Accordingly, opponents were successful in 12 of 14 stolen base attempts against him last year. He rarely picks up a bat and has just one hit in 10 career at-bats. He is a decent bunter.

OVERALL:

Jeff Fassero has become a reliable left-handed set-up man, something of a rare luxury these days. Despite a few ups and downs over the course of the long season, it's been a role which seems to suit his talents.

Overall Statistics

	W	L	ERA	G	GS	Sv	IP	H	R	BB	SO	HR
1992	8	7	2.84	70	0	1	85.2	81	35	34	63	1
Career	10	12	2.68	121	0	9	141.0	120	52	51	105	2

How Often He Throws Strikes

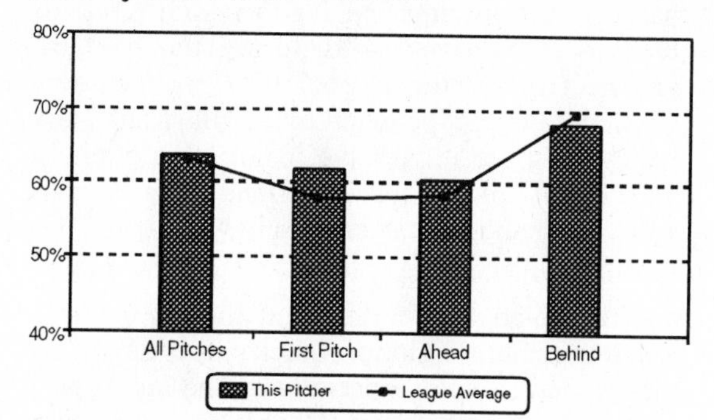

1992 Situational Stats

	W	L	ERA	Sv	IP		AB	H	HR	RBI	AVG
Home	6	3	4.05	0	40.0	LHB	93	25	1	12	.269
Road	2	4	1.77	1	45.2	RHB	232	56	0	20	.241
Day	2	1	3.92	0	20.2	Sc Pos	103	24	1	29	.233
Night	6	6	2.49	1	65.0	Clutch	157	37	1	16	.236

1992 Rankings (National League)

- 5th in relief wins (8)
- 6th in relief losses (7)
- 7th in first batter efficiency (.161)
- 8th in blown saves (6)
- 9th in games pitched (70) and holds (12)
- Led the Expos in games pitched, first batter efficiency, relief wins and relief losses

DARRIN FLETCHER

Position: C
Bats: L **Throws:** R
Ht: 6' 1" **Wt:** 199

Opening Day Age: 26
Born: 10/3/66 in Elmhurst, IL
ML Seasons: 4

HITTING:

The jury is still out on whether Darrin Fletcher can ever be more than a backup catcher in the majors. The player the Expos received in return for dumping Barry Jones onto the Phillies, Fletcher was supposed to handle most of Montreal's catching last year. But he was sidelined for about a month with a severe case of bronchitis. Even worse, he developed a sickly bat, hitting .212 with just three extra-base hits in 99 at-bats before the All-Star break.

Fletcher performed much better after the break following some batting sessions with hitting coach Jay Ward. Fletcher was encouraged to use his legs to a much greater advantage; the advice definitely paid off. Fletcher batted .268 after the break, but the most encouraging sign was that a third of his 33 hits went for extra bases.

Fletcher seems to have become more of a contact hitter and less of a gap hitter since arriving in Montreal. He's also shown more patience at the plate, cutting his strikeout-walk ratio from 3-to-1 to 2-to-1. Considered strictly a platoon player, Fletcher managed to rap out four hits in 14 at-bats against southpaws.

BASERUNNING:

There is very little to say about Fletcher's baserunning. He moves one base at a time and, after 145 games, has yet to successfully steal in the majors.

FIELDING:

Fletcher calls a pretty fair game but is just an adequate receiver. Clearly, he will have to hit to be a starter since his defense is not strong enough to guarantee him regular playing time. Lacking in arm strength, Fletcher's percentage of runners caught stealing (25.5) was significantly lower than the league average of 32.2 percent.

OVERALL:

Though no longer projected as a regular, Fletcher provides the Expos with an additional left-handed bat in games started by tough right-handed pitchers. He also gives Montreal some insurance if Tim Laker, who's expected to be their number-one catcher, needs more seasoning in AAA.

Overall Statistics

	G	AB	R	H	D	T	HR	RBI	SB	BB	SO	AVG
1992	83	222	13	54	10	2	2	26	0	14	28	.243
Career	145	389	22	92	19	2	4	41	0	21	49	.237

Where He Hits the Ball

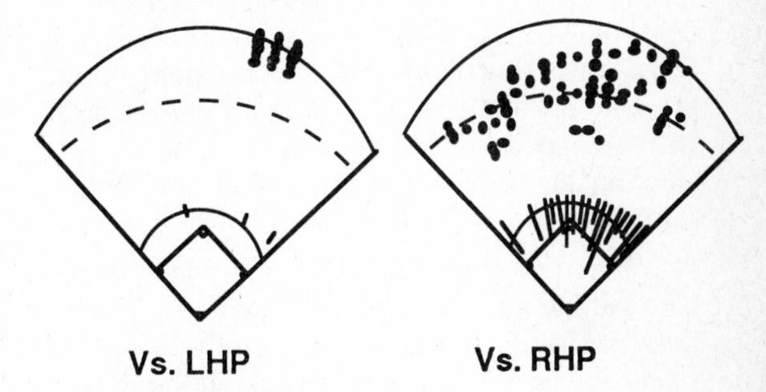

1992 Situational Stats

	AB	H	HR	RBI	AVG		AB	H	HR	RBI	AVG
Home	85	19	0	10	.224	LHP	14	4	0	1	.286
Road	137	35	2	16	.255	RHP	208	50	2	25	.240
Day	64	17	1	11	.266	Sc Pos	58	13	0	21	.224
Night	158	37	1	15	.234	Clutch	43	7	0	1	.163

1992 Rankings (National League)

- 5th in batting average on a 3-2 count (.368)
- Led the Expos in batting average on a 3-2 count
- Led NL catchers in batting average on a 3-2 count

PITCHING:

A pair of nagging injuries (a hip flexor and a bad heel) helped make last season a difficult one for Expo righthander Mark Gardner. But Gardner's problems ran deeper than injuries. For the third straight year, his season turned sour at the end. In 1990, a tired arm kept him from throwing. During the last month of both 1991 and 1992, Gardner relinquished nearly an earned run per inning (7.44 ERA in 1991, 6.85 in '92). Late in the year, he lost his spot in the rotation to journeyman Bill Krueger. Though Gardner posted a career-high 12 wins, he won only four games after the All-Star break and had a 5.53 ERA.

Apart from injuries, Gardner's main problem is an inconsistent fastball. Frequently, the pitch dips from 88 MPH to 84 MPH within a few innings from the start of the game, exerting tremendous pressure on him for success with his nasty curveball. As good as that pitch is, it cannot carry Gardner throughout the game. Opposing hitters can afford to hold back and wait for the fastball.

An obvious sign of trouble was Gardner's opponent batting average, which jumped 29 points to .259 last season. Another problem was that he rarely showed up with his best stuff at the start of the game, allowing 21 first inning runs in 30 starts. With that in mind, pitching coach Joe Kerrigan will try to add a new pitch to Gardner's repertoire, most likely a cut fastball.

HOLDING RUNNERS, FIELDING, HITTING:

Though Gardner has a quick delivery and works hard at holding runners, a mediocre move to first makes him an inviting target for opposing baserunners (29 steals in 40 attempts). Gardner helped himself at the plate last year with seven hits and eight sacrifices in 50 at-bats. His fielding is adequate.

OVERALL:

The Expos remain positive on Gardner despite his mediocre 1992 season, although they left him unprotected for expansion. He can be overwhelming when he shows up with his grade A curveball. In starts where he struggles without it, the Expos hope that the addition of a new pitch will help bail him out.

MARK GARDNER

Position: SP
Bats: R **Throws:** R
Ht: 6' 1" **Wt:** 200

Opening Day Age: 31
Born: 3/1/62 in Los Angeles, CA
ML Seasons: 4

Overall Statistics

	W	L	ERA	G	GS	Sv	IP	H	R	BB	SO	HR
1992	12	10	4.36	33	30	0	179.2	179	91	60	132	15
Career	28	33	3.96	94	87	0	527.0	473	247	207	395	47

How Often He Throws Strikes

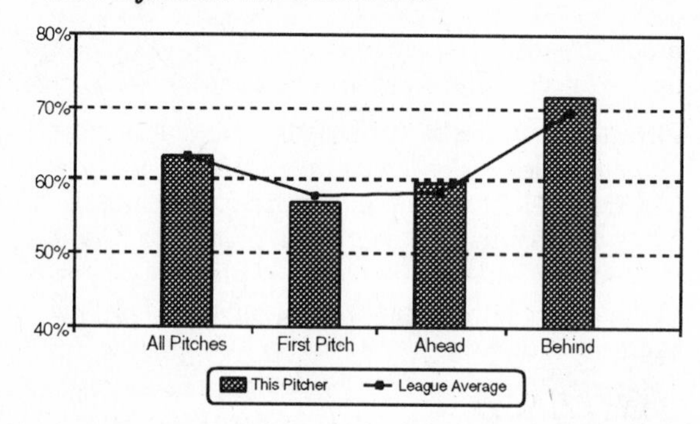

1992 Situational Stats

	W	L	ERA	Sv	IP		AB	H	HR	RBI	AVG
Home	6	5	4.80	0	105.0	LHB	397	108	7	49	.272
Road	6	5	3.74	0	74.2	RHB	293	71	8	30	.242
Day	4	5	3.88	0	65.0	Sc Pos	178	47	3	60	.264
Night	8	5	4.63	0	114.2	Clutch	49	14	1	4	.286

1992 Rankings (National League)

- 1st in highest ERA (4.36), least GDPs induced per 9 innings (0.1), least GDPs induced per GDP situation (1.7%) and highest ERA at home (4.80)
- 2nd in hit batsmen (9)
- 3rd in most pitches thrown per batter (3.85) and most baserunners allowed per 9 innings (12.4)
- 4th in highest on-base percentage allowed (.324) and lowest groundball/flyball ratio (.91)
- 5th in stolen bases allowed (29)
- Led the Expos in home runs allowed (15), hit batsmen and most strikeouts per 9 innings (6.6)

GREAT SPEED

MARQUIS GRISSOM

Position: CF
Bats: R **Throws:** R
Ht: 5'11" **Wt:** 190

Opening Day Age: 25
Born: 4/17/67 in Atlanta, GA
ML Seasons: 4

Overall Statistics

	G	AB	R	H	D	T	HR	RBI	SB	BB	SO	AVG
1992	159	653	99	180	39	6	14	66	78	42	81	.276
Career	431	1573	230	422	78	17	24	136	177	115	231	.268

Where He Hits the Ball

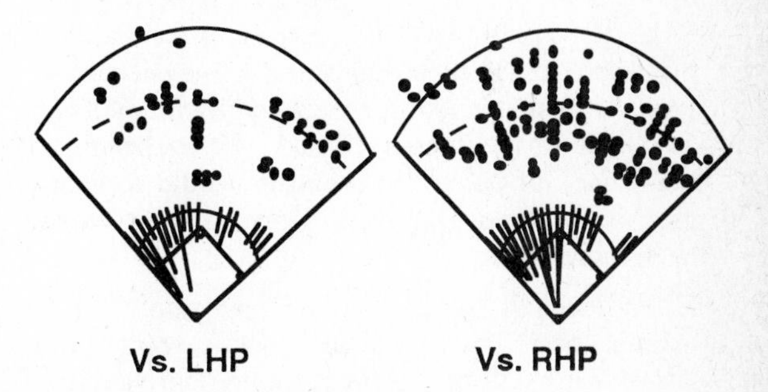

1992 Situational Stats

	AB	H	HR	RBI	AVG		AB	H	HR	RBI	AVG
Home	316	84	8	31	.266	LHP	212	57	6	24	.269
Road	337	96	6	35	.285	RHP	441	123	8	42	.279
Day	199	54	5	21	.271	Sc Pos	154	45	3	50	.292
Night	454	126	9	45	.278	Clutch	109	25	2	10	.229

1992 Rankings (National League)

- 1st in at-bats (653), stolen bases (78) and steals of third (24)
- 3rd in plate appearances (707) and stolen base percentage (85.7%)
- Led the Expos in at-bats, runs scored (99), hits (180), singles (121), doubles (39), total bases (273), stolen bases, times on base (227), GDPs (12), most pitches seen (2,398), plate appearances, games played (159), stolen base percentage, slugging percentage vs. right-handed pitchers (.399) and steals of third
- Led NL center fielders in at-bats, stolen bases, intentional walks (6), hit by pitch (5), plate appearances, stolen base percentage, errors (7) and steals of third

HITTING:

In 1992, just his second year as a regular, Marquis Grissom was probably Montreal's most consistent offensive performer. Improving in almost every category, Grissom took giant strides towards becoming a star. As is the case with many young Expos, the progress was a result of maturity and confidence superimposing themselves on outstanding natural ability.

Grissom attacked the ball with more power in 1992. Following a season in which he produced just 38 extra-base hits, Grissom belted 39 doubles (fifth in the NL), more than doubled his home run total (from six to 14) and finished ninth in the league in extra-base hits with 59. Grissom also made some strides toward becoming a more selective hitter, particularly with runners in scoring position (.292 with 19 walks in 154 at-bats). As a result of his better clutch hitting, Grissom nearly doubled his RBI total from 39 to 66.

Grissom has a long swing and is sometimes late on fastballs, but he has become very adept at handling breaking stuff. He drives the ball into the gaps and might convert some of his doubles into even more homers very soon. His great speed turns a lot of would-be groundouts into singles. He legged out 33 infield hits last season and now has 89 in his two-and-a-half seasons.

BASERUNNING:

In addition to being fast, Grissom runs hard and is unafraid of baserunning collisions. With 154 stolen bases in 184 attempts -- an 84 percent success rate -- over the last two seasons, Grissom must be considered the game's best basestealer. He excels at stealing third, picking his spots depending on the game situation almost perfectly.

FIELDING:

Grissom is an excellent fielder. In addition to his great range, his strong, accurate arm gunned down seven baserunners last season.

OVERALL:

Grissom is an intense competitor who made significant strides at the plate last season. With Delino DeShields firmly fixed in the leadoff spot, Grissom's overall stolen base total may fall but should be more than offset by an increase in run production.

KEN HILL

Position: SP
Bats: R **Throws:** R
Ht: 6' 2" **Wt:** 175

Opening Day Age: 27
Born: 12/14/65 in Lynn, MA
ML Seasons: 5

PITCHING:

In one of the biggest steals in Expos' history, Ken Hill came to Montreal in exchange for Andres Galarraga and quickly emerged as a staff ace. Hill easily set career highs in every category and tied for third in the league in wins (16), was eighth in ERA (2.68), seventh in opponents batting average (.230) and was just two strikeouts shy of the top 10 with 150. Hill set the tone for the season in his first Expos start by defeating Dwight Gooden with a four-hit shutout in which he walked just two batters.

In retrospect, Hill's last season with the Cardinals in 1991, was the year he turned himself around. In that season, he showed that he could get hitters out (.224 opponent batting average), logged 181.1 innings and added an effective forkball to his repertoire. The Cardinals must have chosen to focus on his penchant for walks and wild pitches as well as his mediocre record (11-10) in deciding that a lack of poise and maturity would forever plague Hill's development. They couldn't have been more wrong.

Hill's forkball has developed into one of the league's best. It tails away at the last second from left-handed batters -- one reason he held them to a .222 average. Another reason is an explosive 95 MPH fastball. In addition, his tendency to throw inside combined with more than a touch of wildness (11 wild pitches) has made Hill one of the league's most feared pitchers.

HOLDING RUNNERS, FIELDING, HITTING:

Hill is an excellent athlete who helps himself equally on the field, on the basepaths and at the plate. His final batting average, .177, is misleading. Before hurting his right wrist on July 18th, Hill was batting .314. Despite throwing over to first often, Hill's opponents had no trouble stealing 30 bases in 38 attempts against him.

OVERALL:

Still only 27, Hill made huge strides last season. At this point in his career, with full command of both his fastball and his forkball (which he throws as much as 50 times in a game), no one should be surprised if he comes close to 20 wins next season.

Overall Statistics

	W	L	ERA	G	GS	Sv	IP	H	R	BB	SO	HR
1992	16	9	2.68	33	33	0	218.0	187	76	75	150	13
Career	39	41	3.61	117	111	0	688.2	615	302	280	447	44

How Often He Throws Strikes

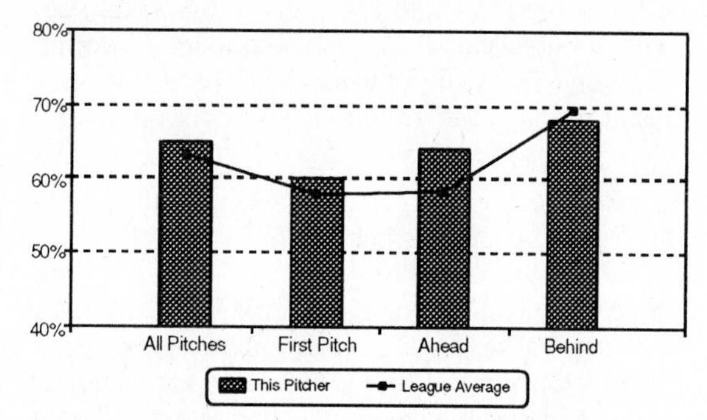

1992 Situational Stats

	W	L	ERA	Sv	IP		AB	H	HR	RBI	AVG
Home	6	6	3.15	0	94.1	LHB	469	104	6	32	.222
Road	10	3	2.33	0	123.2	RHB	343	83	7	35	.242
Day	5	4	2.07	0	82.2	Sc Pos	226	45	3	53	.199
Night	11	5	3.06	0	135.1	Clutch	62	16	4	8	.258

1992 Rankings (National League)

- 1st in ERA on the road (2.33)
- 3rd in wins (16), wild pitches (11), balks (4) and stolen bases allowed (30)
- 4th in pickoff throws (228)
- Led the Expos in sacrifice bunts as a hitter (10), wins, games started (33), shutouts (3), hits allowed (187), batters faced (908), walks allowed (75), strikeouts (150), wild pitches, balks, stolen bases allowed, winning percentage (.640), least pitches thrown per batter (3.47), most run support per 9 innings (4.5), lowest ERA on the road and lowest batting average allowed with runners in scoring position (.199)

PITCHING:

Coming off his best season, when he went 11-8 with a more than respectable 3.60 ERA with the Mariners in 1991, Bill Krueger started '92 in excellent fashion. He won his first five decisions, (including a 4-0, 0.84 April) and helped the Twins win 16 of his first 19 starts. Krueger was 9-2 at the All-Star break, but his season soured after that. On August 31, the Twins sent Krueger to the Expos in exchange for reserve outfielder Darren Reed.

The trade gave the Expos another lefty in the bullpen and some insurance for their starting rotation. The team was hoping Krueger's slump was just a case of fatigue, but rest failed to help. Krueger was hammered, posting a 6.75 ERA in 17.1 innings for Montreal, and allowing the opposition to bat at a .315 clip.

Krueger's repertoire includes the four basic pitches: fastball, slider, curve and change-up. In order to be effective, he has to mix his pitches and keep the ball in the strike zone -- something with which he has struggled throughout his career, including his stint with the Expos (seven walks in 17.1 innings). Good control is essential since Krueger has averaged over a hit allowed per inning lifetime. Not particularly powerful, his fastball depends on movement, something it did not have during last season's slide. According to Krueger, an inconsistent arm angle on his delivery causes his fastball to flatten out.

HOLDING RUNNERS, FIELDING, HITTING:

Krueger's herky-jerky delivery completely negates a good move to first and allows opposing baserunners to steal at will (22 in 26 tries last season). He's a decent fielder. As a veteran American Leaguer, hitting is foreign to him, but he did manage one sacrifice in four plate appearances with the Expos.

OVERALL:

Though not a bad pitcher, Krueger is the type of journeyman left-handed sixth starter who bounces from team to team and occasionally streaks together a good month or two. Chances are that he'll be modeling yet another new uniform this season.

BILL KRUEGER

Position: SP/RP
Bats: L **Throws:** L
Ht: 6' 5" **Wt:** 205

Opening Day Age: 34
Born: 4/24/58 in Waukegan, IL
ML Seasons: 10

Overall Statistics

	W	L	ERA	G	GS	Sv	IP	H	R	BB	SO	HR
1992	10	8	4.53	36	29	0	178.2	189	95	53	99	18
Career	57	57	4.25	233	143	4	1024.0	1097	571	431	516	85

How Often He Throws Strikes

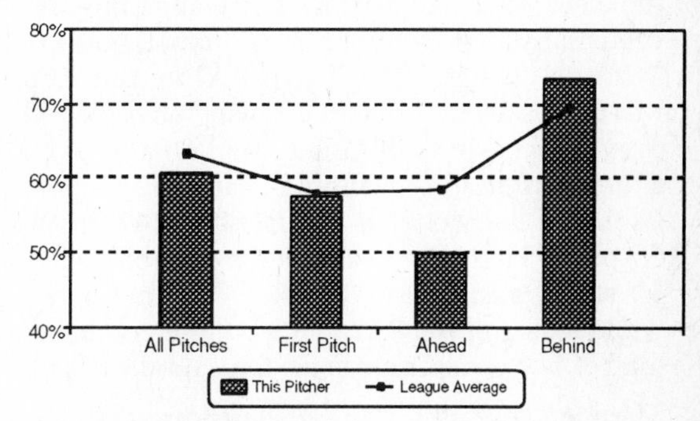

1992 Situational Stats

	W	L	ERA	Sv	IP		AB	H	HR	RBI	AVG
Home	2	4	4.80	0	65.2	LHB	104	32	1	11	.308
Road	8	4	4.38	0	113.0	RHB	599	157	17	63	.262
Day	1	1	4.50	0	30.0	Sc Pos	160	45	7	58	.281
Night	9	7	4.54	0	148.2	Clutch	53	10	1	4	.189

1992 Rankings (National League)

- Did not rank near the top or bottom in any category

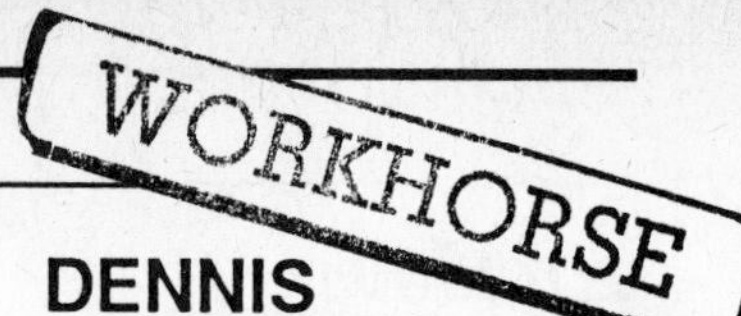

PITCHING:

At 37, Dennis Martinez remains one of the game's most consistently effective pitchers. Last season, he matched his personal best with 16 wins and logged over 220 innings for the fifth straight year. His 2.47 ERA marked his third straight season under 3.00. Martinez has been rewarded with three straight All-Star Game selections -- quite an achievement for someone whose first appearance came at the age of 35.

Possibly as a lesson learned while suffering both physical and alcohol-related problems in Baltimore between 1983 and 1986 -- the prime years that should have been -- Martinez never allows himself to take the game for granted. He approaches each start with intensity and stays exceptionally fit in-between starts. In fact, midway through last season, Felipe Alou reduced Martinez's between-start throwing in order to prevent possible burnout. Martinez peaked shortly after that, winning National League Pitcher of the Month in August (4-0, 1.42 ERA). He pitched through the seventh in each of his last 12 starts, posting a 1.80 ERA, winning seven while losing only two and allowing a combined total of two earned runs in the three no-decisions.

Martinez possesses a varied repertoire that displays both power and smarts. His fastball is delivered at different speeds with an 89 MPH maximum and is generally accompanied with a sharp sink. He also throws one of the sharpest curves in the game and mixes in a split-fingered change-up and the occasional slider. Martinez fights for the inside part of the plate and is not afraid to hit opposing batters (nine last year).

HOLDING RUNNERS, FIELDING, HITTING:

Martinez is an excellent fielder and through hard work has become quite difficult to run against; he picked off three and helped nail 17 of 39 attempted basestealers last year. He also helped himself with the bat, hitting .189 in 74 at-bats with 10 sacrifices.

OVERALL:

Though Martinez will be 38 on May 14, he shows no signs of wearing down. He needs seven victories for 200; his right arm appears to have many more than that left in it.

DENNIS MARTINEZ

Position: SP
Bats: R **Throws:** R
Ht: 6' 1" **Wt:** 180

Opening Day Age: 37
Born: 5/14/55 in Granada, Nicaragua
ML Seasons: 17

Overall Statistics

	W	L	ERA	G	GS	Sv	IP	H	R	BB	SO	HR
1992	16	11	2.47	32	32	0	226.1	172	75	60	147	12
Career	193	156	3.62	523	442	5	3159.2	3050	1417	926	1693	286

How Often He Throws Strikes

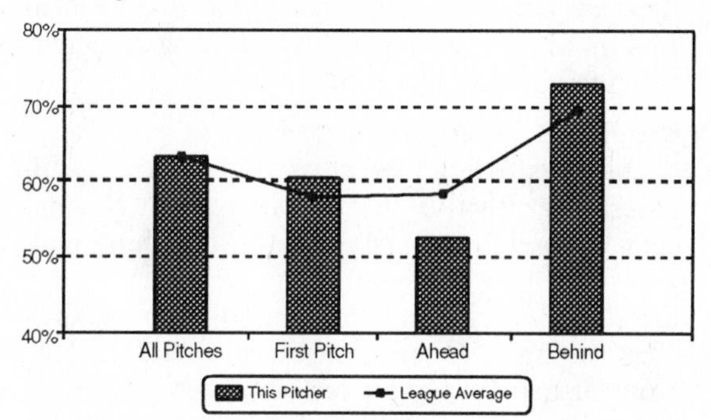

1992 Situational Stats

	W	L	ERA	Sv	IP		AB	H	HR	RBI	AVG
Home	8	4	2.09	0	116.0	LHB	503	106	8	39	.211
Road	8	7	2.85	0	110.1	RHB	311	66	4	25	.212
Day	2	5	4.25	0	55.0	Sc Pos	165	37	2	50	.224
Night	14	6	1.89	0	171.1	Clutch	81	14	3	8	.173

1992 Rankings (National League)

- 1st in most runners caught stealing (17)
- 2nd in hit batsmen (9) and lowest slugging percentage allowed (.287)
- 3rd in wins (16) and lowest on-base percentage allowed (.271)
- Led the Expos in sacrifice bunts as a hitter (10), ERA (2.47), wins, complete games (6), innings pitched (226.1), hit batsmen, most pitches thrown (3,287), runners caught stealing, highest strikeout/walk ratio (2.5), lowest batting average allowed (.211), lowest slugging percentage allowed, lowest on-base percentage allowed, lowest stolen base percentage allowed (56.4%) and least home runs allowed per 9 innings (.48)

CHRIS NABHOLZ

Position: SP
Bats: L **Throws:** L
Ht: 6' 5" **Wt:** 210

Opening Day Age: 26
Born: 1/5/67 in Harrisburg, PA
ML Seasons: 3

PITCHING:

Chris Nabholz is the enigma of the Expos staff. Honored as National League Pitcher of the month in September of 1991 with a 6-0, 2.23 streak, Nabholz was counted on to mature into a 15-game winner last year. Instead he struggled all season to get in sync and finished one game short of .500 at 11-12. Nabholz was far from awful, contributing a 3.32 ERA and 195 innings -- both improvements from the year before. However, considering his quality stuff and his strong 1991 finish, more was expected. In terms of innings pitched per start (6.0), hits allowed (8.1) walks (3.4) and strikeouts (6.0) per nine innings, his performance did not improve.

In many of his starts, Nabholz comes across as a combination of two distinct pitchers. Early on he relies on an 89 MPH fastball, but then he switches almost exclusively to his sinker -- an excellent pitch which tails away from right-handed hitters and produces quite a few double play balls. There is no questioning his stuff. His problems are more a product of immaturity and carelessness. Far too frequently, Nabholz will hand the opposition a lead shortly after acquiring it. He tends to beat himself by walking the inning's leadoff hitter on four pitches, by allowing a hit to the pitcher, or by performing other common acts of self-destruction. Nabholz completed just one game all last year.

HOLDING RUNNERS, FIELDING, HITTING:

Nabholz is an average fielder. He has a good move to first but is often lax with opposing baserunners, and they cashed in with 23 steals in 29 attempts last season. Nabholz is fair at the plate with eight hits and seven sacrifices in 65 at-bats in 1992.

OVERALL:

This season is a pivotal one for Nabholz. It will probably dictate if he is destined to be a perennial 10-game winner or become the solid second or third starter the Expos expect him to become. With his stuff, all he needs to do is to stay focused throughout the game, something he should have learned by now.

Overall Statistics

	W	L	ERA	G	GS	Sv	IP	H	R	BB	SO	HR
1992	11	12	3.32	32	32	0	195.0	176	80	74	130	11
Career	25	21	3.35	67	67	0	418.2	353	169	163	282	22

How Often He Throws Strikes

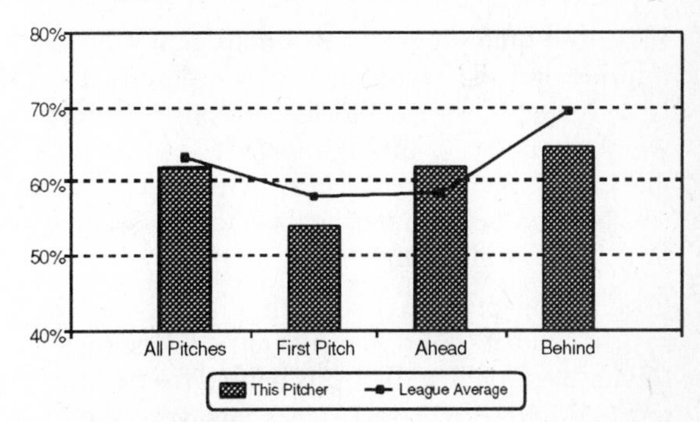

1992 Situational Stats

	W	L	ERA	Sv	IP		AB	H	HR	RBI	AVG
Home	5	7	3.09	0	99.0	LHB	131	35	3	14	.267
Road	6	5	3.56	0	96.0	RHB	591	141	8	49	.239
Day	6	1	1.96	0	59.2	Sc Pos	158	41	1	47	.259
Night	5	11	3.92	0	135.1	Clutch	39	11	1	2	.282

1992 Rankings (National League)

- 2nd in pickoff throws (250)
- 4th in most GDPs induced per 9 innings (.97)
- 5th in GDPs induced (21), lowest strikeout/walk ratio (1.8), highest groundball/flyball ratio (1.9) and highest stolen base percentage allowed (79.3%)
- 9th in walks allowed (74), stolen bases allowed (23) and highest on-base percentage allowed (.317)
- Led the Expos in losses (12), pickoff throws, GDPs induced, highest groundball/flyball ratio, GDPs induced per 9 innings and lowest batting average allowed vs. right-handed batters (.239)

SPIKE OWEN

Position: SS
Bats: B **Throws:** R
Ht: 5'10" **Wt:** 170

Opening Day Age: 31
Born: 4/19/61 in Cleburne, TX
ML Seasons: 10

HITTING:

Last season, super shortstop prospect Wil Cordero finally showed up in Montreal, but the unspectacular Spike Owen did his best to delay the inevitable with the best offensive year of his career. In fact, when Cordero arrived in July it was due to an Owen injury, not his poor performance. Owen picked up where he left off in the latter part of 1991, when he hit .294 and slugged .416 in his last 69 games. In '92 he posted career highs in batting average (.269), home runs (seven) and slugging percentage (.381). In addition, he sported a healthy .348 on-base percentage and performed well in the clutch. Owen batted .319 in 91 at-bats with runners in scoring position and drove in 40 runs in 386 at-bats overall.

Increased time off -- he missed 40 games due to injuries and the emergence of Cordero -- may have helped Owen avoid the prolonged slumps which he suffered through in past seasons with the Expos. As always, the switch-hitting Owen was a much better hitter against southpaws, batting .286 and slugging .447.

Owen is adept at executing the little things: he makes contact (only 30 strikeouts), takes a walk (47 unintentional walks), hits behind the baserunner and lays down sacrifice bunts very intelligently.

BASERUNNING:

Owen's speed is ordinary but he can hustle from first to third on a base hit better than most. Owen was more daring than usual on the basepaths last season, stealing nine bases in 13 attempts. It was his best stolen base total in five seasons.

FIELDING:

Once again, Owen was near the top of the league in fielding percentage last year. However, with limited range and a mediocre arm, he often needs to hustle in order to make less-than-difficult plays.

OVERALL:

Though the chances that Owen will enjoy two successive career seasons are remote, the Yankees signed the respected veteran to a free agent contract. He doesn't figure to be a miracle man, but he should give them steady shortstop work for a couple of seasons.

Overall Statistics

	G	AB	R	H	D	T	HR	RBI	SB	BB	SO	AVG
1992	122	386	52	104	16	3	7	40	9	50	30	.269
Career	1277	4110	499	1000	173	52	40	354	74	473	450	.243

Where He Hits the Ball

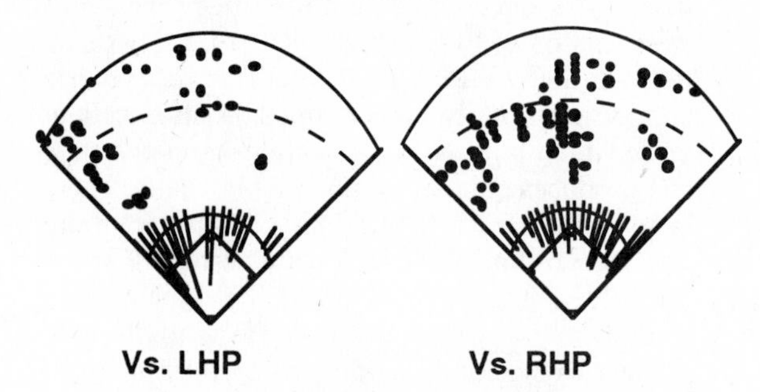

1992 Situational Stats

	AB	H	HR	RBI	AVG		AB	H	HR	RBI	AVG
Home	173	42	3	19	.243	LHP	161	46	4	23	.286
Road	213	62	4	21	.291	RHP	225	58	3	17	.258
Day	123	29	4	14	.236	Sc Pos	91	29	0	28	.319
Night	263	75	3	26	.285	Clutch	57	21	0	8	.368

1992 Rankings (National League)

- 3rd in highest percentage of pitches taken (62.7%)
- 4th in batting average in the clutch (.368) and highest percentage of swings put into play (56.4%)
- 6th in lowest percentage of swings that missed (9.9%)
- Led the Expos in batting average with runners in scoring position (.319), batting average in the clutch, highest percentage of pitches taken, lowest percentage of swings that missed and highest percentage of swings put into play

PITCHING:

Felipe Alou's nephew, 26-year-old Mel Rojas, was nothing short of spectacular last season as the relay man between the Montreal starters and closer John Wetteland. Rojas had shown flashes of brilliance in September of 1991, picking up two wins and five saves with a 1.02 ERA in 13 appearances. But he started last season in the minors, trying to shorten a strained, over-stretched delivery which had caused him to over-throw for most of his career.

When he came back up, the stocky (5'11", 185 lbs) Rojas looked like a pitcher, not a thrower. He immediately began one of the best seasons ever enjoyed by a set-up man in recent memory. Rojas led all National League relievers with a 1.43 ERA, stranded 82.8 percent of his inherited runners (third in the league) and held the opposition to a meager .199 batting average. He was always ready to work, pitching in 64 of Montreal's last 136 games. Rojas held the opposition to just three hits in their final 36 at-bats with runners in scoring position and finished the year with seven straight wins.

Rojas throws a good, moving 94 MPH fastball which handcuffs right-handed hitters and a devastating forkball which Eddie Murray praised as the league's best. Thrown at about 80 MPH, the pitch breaks sharply away from left-handed hitters, whom Rojas limited to just a .196 average. When he misses the plate, Rojas tends to miss low, so the ball doesn't leave the park very often (only two home runs allowed).

HOLDING RUNNERS, FIELDING, HITTING:

Rojas is an awkward fielder who does not pay attention to opposing runners (they stole 12 bases in 15 attempts). He is a no-show at the plate with just one hit and 10 strikeouts in 15 at-bats.

OVERALL:

It will be interesting to see if Rojas, just one year removed from a large number of mechanical problems, can enjoy another superb season. He can afford to slip a little and still remain an excellent set-up man. Uncle Felipe will be counting on him.

MEL ROJAS

Position: RP
Bats: R **Throws:** R
Ht: 5'11" **Wt:** 185

Opening Day Age: 26
Born: 12/10/66 in Haina, Dominican Republic
ML Seasons: 3

Overall Statistics

	W	L	ERA	G	GS	Sv	IP	H	R	BB	SO	HR
1992	7	1	1.43	68	0	10	100.2	71	17	34	70	2
Career	13	5	2.48	128	0	17	188.2	147	55	71	133	11

How Often He Throws Strikes

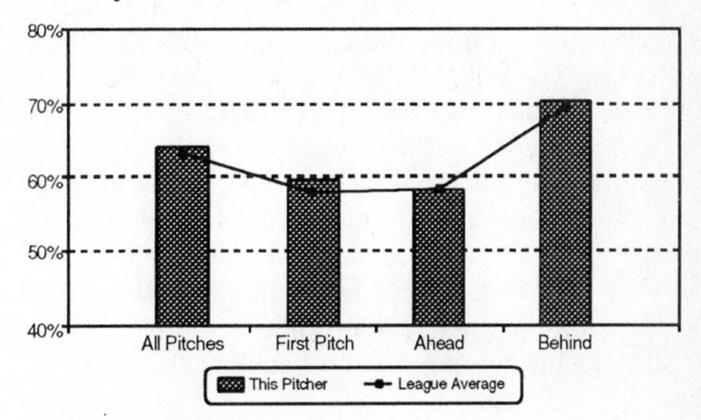

1992 Situational Stats

	W	L	ERA	Sv	IP		AB	H	HR	RBI	AVG
Home	5	0	1.72	3	52.1	LHB	199	39	1	11	.196
Road	2	1	1.12	7	48.1	RHB	158	32	1	11	.203
Day	3	0	0.68	2	26.1	Sc Pos	115	14	0	19	.122
Night	4	1	1.70	8	74.1	Clutch	151	36	0	14	.238

1992 Rankings (National League)

- 1st in lowest batting average allowed in relief with runners on base (.143), lowest batting average allowed in relief with runners in scoring position (.122) and relief ERA (1.43)
- 3rd in lowest percentage of inherited runners scored (17.2%) and least baserunners allowed per 9 innings in relief (9.6)
- 4th in relief innings (100.2)
- Led the Expos in holds (13), lowest batting average allowed vs. left-handed batters (.196), lowest batting average allowed in relief with runners in scoring position, lowest percentage of inherited runners scored, relief ERA and relief innings

JOHN VANDERWAL

Position: LF
Bats: L **Throws:** L
Ht: 6' 2" **Wt:** 190

Opening Day Age: 26
Born: 4/29/66 in Grand Rapids, MI
ML Seasons: 2

HITTING:

A well-seasoned minor-leaguer, 26-year-old John VanderWal cracked the Expos' roster last season after spending five years in the Montreal farm system. VanderWal was used mostly as a backup and did a nice job of filling in, especially when Moises Alou injured his left hamstring in July. During one 21-game stretch, VanderWal batted .344 in 61 at-bats with two doubles, two homers and seven RBI. But his season was a lot like his minor-league days: a collection of hot streaks and slumps.

Overall, VanderWal hit .239. But if you subtract his work as a pinch hitter, a role that he struggled with all season long (six hits in 35 at-bats) his batting average was a more respectable .253. VanderWal, a high-ball hitter, possesses a quick batting stroke. He demonstrated the ability to drive the ball into the gap (14 extra-base hits) as well as a good knowledge of the strike zone (24 walks). He was tentative with runners in scoring position, walking 10 times in 60 at-bats but batting just .217. Last year he seemed to need regular work in order to find his hitting groove, not a surprising problem for a rookie. He'll have to be able to hit coming off the bench if he wants to help the Expos.

BASERUNNING:

VanderWal possesses above-average speed and runs the bases very well. He is not much of a basestealer, however, though he succeeded in all three of his attempts last season.

FIELDING:

VanderWal's best position is left field. He moves well and has a better-than-average arm, and by the end of the year, he was getting a good jump on the ball. VanderWal can also play right field adequately and can fill in at first.

OVERALL:

With more than merely average skills in all facets of the game, VanderWal is a valuable reserve. However, he must adjust to the role of non-starter -- and especially, sharpen his pinch-hitting skills -- in order to maximize his contribution.

Overall Statistics

	G	AB	R	H	D	T	HR	RBI	SB	BB	SO	AVG
1992	105	213	21	51	8	2	4	20	3	24	36	.239
Career	126	274	25	64	12	3	5	28	3	25	54	.234

Where He Hits the Ball

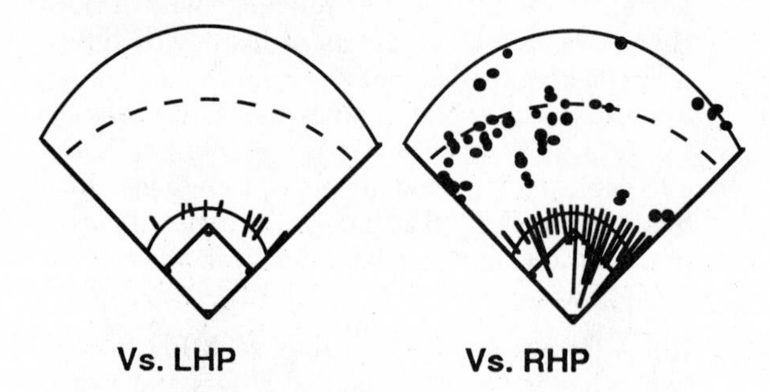

1992 Situational Stats

	AB	H	HR	RBI	AVG		AB	H	HR	RBI	AVG
Home	99	24	2	11	.242	LHP	29	7	0	1	.241
Road	114	27	2	9	.237	RHP	184	44	4	19	.239
Day	80	21	1	7	.262	Sc Pos	60	13	0	13	.217
Night	133	30	3	13	.226	Clutch	46	6	0	4	.130

1992 Rankings (National League)

- 3rd in lowest batting average in the clutch (.130)

STRONG ARM

LARRY WALKER

Position: RF
Bats: L **Throws:** R
Ht: 6' 3" **Wt:** 215

Opening Day Age: 26
Born: 12/1/66 in Maple Ridge, BC, Canada
ML Seasons: 4

Overall Statistics

	G	AB	R	H	D	T	HR	RBI	SB	BB	SO	AVG
1992	143	528	85	159	31	4	23	93	18	41	97	.301
Career	433	1481	207	409	79	9	58	212	54	137	324	.276

Where He Hits the Ball

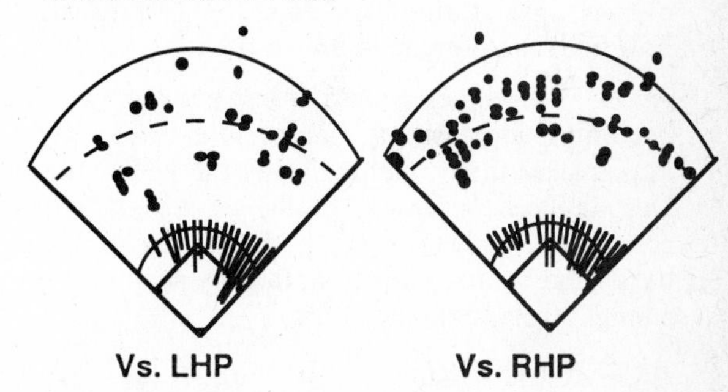

1992 Situational Stats

	AB	H	HR	RBI	AVG		AB	H	HR	RBI	AVG
Home	257	73	13	43	.284	LHP	209	66	10	42	.316
Road	271	86	10	50	.317	RHP	319	93	13	51	.292
Day	169	41	6	27	.243	Sc Pos	158	49	6	68	.310
Night	359	118	17	66	.329	Clutch	89	25	4	15	.281

1992 Rankings (National League)

- 2nd in least pitches seen per plate appearance (3.15), lowest percentage of pitches taken (43.6%) and highest percentage of swings that missed (26.1%)
- 4th in sacrifice flies (8)
- 5th in batting average on the road (.317)
- Led the Expos in batting average (.301), home runs (23), RBI (93), sacrifice flies, intentional walks (10), slugging percentage (.506), HR frequency (23.0 ABs per HR), batting average vs. left-handed pitchers (.316), batting average on an 0-2 count (.200), slugging percentage vs. left-handed pitchers (.517), batting average at home (.284) and batting average on the road

HITTING:

As many expected, Larry Walker established himself as one of the league's premier hitters in 1992. He batted a solid .301, hit 23 homers and drove home 93 runs, all career highs. Walker demonstrated that his post All-Star game excellence in 1991 (.338, 10 homers and 43 RBI) was an indication of his actual performance level and not just an extended hot streak.

Walker's flexible approach to hitting virtually assures him of continued success. When pitchers make an effort to finesse him with breaking stuff, Walker shortens his swing, allowing him to wait the necessary extra time before committing himself. Walker also used his legs more in his swing last year, and at 6'3" 215 lbs, generated tremendous power. Walker had no difficulties against southpaws, batting .316 and slugging .517 -- not bad for someone Buck Rodgers labelled a platoon player just two years ago.

BASERUNNING:

Despite his imposing physique, Walker possesses good speed and runs the bases intelligently. Last year he swiped 18 bases in 24 attempts, including 10 in his last 11 tries. Walker picks his spots; his nagging injuries (groin and quadriceps) prevent him from being more aggressive.

FIELDING:

Walker is a spectacular right fielder. He covers a lot of ground, gets a great jump on the ball, and from time to time will deke the runner out of taking an extra base. He committed just two errors and his powerful, accurate arm allowed him to lead all major-league right fielders in assists with 16. Twice last season he threw the batter out at first on apparent singles (Tim Wakefield and Tony Fernandez). He won his first Gold Glove last year and should win several more.

OVERALL:

Walker is a complete player who may be on the verge of becoming a perennial All-Star. Last season he sometimes tried too hard. As a result, some old habits, such as trying to pull everything in sight, occasionally crept back into his game. Those were the mistakes of a still-improving player; at 26, Walker is just approaching his prime.

HITTING:

Not many players are as likeable, or as respected by his teammates, or as willing to play the game with physical pain, as Tim Wallach. On the other hand not many players hit less than Tim Wallach did last year. In fact, with a .223 average Wallach (along with Brian McRae) was dead last in the majors.

After 1991's disappointing .225 season, Wallach had high hopes heading into 1992. But he started slowly and never put any sort of streak together. Just two years removed from batting .296 with 21 home runs and 98 RBI, Wallach's homer and RBI totals have slid to 13-73 in 1991 and 9-59 in 1992 without a major reduction in playing time. He was useless against righthanders, batting a measly .201 with two homers in 339 at-bats.

At 35, Wallach has a mass of bad habits that are becoming increasingly harder to conceal. He lunges at too many pitches outside the strike zone. Despite working hard in batting practice, he still commits himself too early by both dropping his hands and bobbing his head, thereby sapping the strength from his swing.

BASERUNNING:

Wallach is a slow-poke but does not embarrass himself on the basepaths and does the best he can with his mediocre speed. No basestealer, he was 2-for-4 in 1992 and is under 50 percent for his career (50-for-111).

FIELDING:

The defensive part of Wallach's game remains strong. At third base he possesses good reactions, has soft hands and an accurate arm, and moves well laterally. In addition, Wallach is adept at charging in for both bunts and weak grounders, skills which are especially important at third. He also showed signs of becoming a quality first baseman, a position he originally didn't want to play.

OVERALL:

Both management and Expos' fans have been very patient with Wallach. As he enters the fat part of his contract (over $3 million next season), he desperately needs a good season. If he fails to show up with a revamped hitting approach next spring, the season might be very long for him.

TIM WALLACH

Position: 3B/1B
Bats: R **Throws:** R
Ht: 6' 3" **Wt:** 202

Opening Day Age: 35
Born: 9/14/57 in Huntington Park, CA
ML Seasons: 13

Overall Statistics

	G	AB	R	H	D	T	HR	RBI	SB	BB	SO	AVG
1992	150	537	53	120	29	1	9	59	2	50	90	.223
Career	1767	6529	737	1694	360	31	204	905	50	514	1009	.259

Where He Hits the Ball

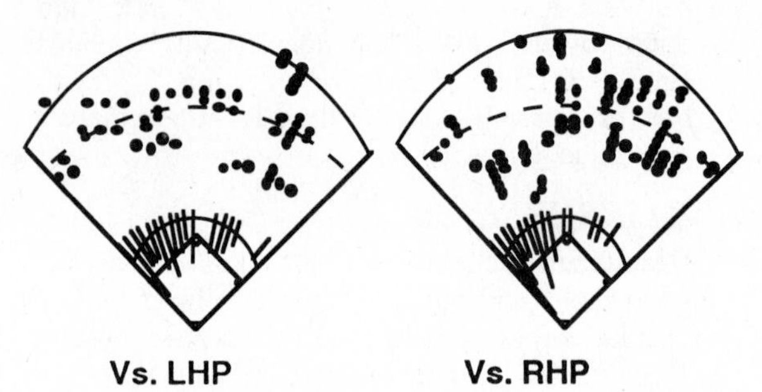

1992 Situational Stats

	AB	H	HR	RBI	AVG		AB	H	HR	RBI	AVG
Home	262	69	5	41	.263	LHP	198	52	7	29	.263
Road	275	51	4	18	.185	RHP	339	68	2	30	.201
Day	159	35	3	16	.220	Sc Pos	132	30	2	45	.227
Night	378	85	6	43	.225	Clutch	98	22	2	10	.224

1992 Rankings (National League)

- 1st in lowest batting average (.223), lowest batting average vs. right-handed pitchers (.201), lowest slugging percentage vs. right-handed pitchers (.271), lowest on-base percentage vs. right-handed pitchers (.276) and lowest batting average on the road (.185)
- 2nd in lowest slugging percentage (.331)
- 4th in hit by pitch (8)
- 8th in sacrifice flies (7) and lowest on-base percentage (.296)
- Led the Expos in hit by pitch
- Led NL third basemen in sacrifice flies

STOPPER

JOHN WETTELAND

Position: RP
Bats: R **Throws:** R
Ht: 6' 2" **Wt:** 195

Opening Day Age: 26
Born: 8/21/66 in San Mateo, CA
ML Seasons: 4

PITCHING:

According to John Wetteland, the Dodgers do not pay attention to AAA stats. Well, maybe they should. In 37 relief appearances with Albuquerque in 1991, Wetteland converted all 20 of his save opportunities. The performance was even more impressive when considering the fact that Wetteland was a career starter in the minors who approached the Dodgers himself to request the stopper role. The Expos, on the other hand, virtually handed him the job during the early days of spring training last year and watched him put an end to their bullpen miseries.

Wetteland finished third in the league in saves (37), sixth in save percentage (80.4 percent) and sixth in stranding inherited runners (78.4 percent). He limited the opposition to a .213 batting average while striking out 10.7 batters per nine innings. Wetteland was more effective as the season progressed -- in his last 40 appearances, he posted a 2.26 ERA, allowing just 39 hits in 51.2 innings while striking out 61. Early in the season, Wetteland too often looked like a Mitch Williams clone, spending too much energy on intimidating the batter and overthrowing his fastball. He mixed it up more as the season went along without suffering a drop in his strikeout frequency.

Wetteland comes straight at the hitter with a moving 97 MPH fastball and a wicked curveball that enables him to hold left-handed hitters in check (.200). Wetteland also throws a slider which tails away from righthanders and is working on a cut fastball, too.

HOLDING RUNNERS, FIELDING, HITTING:

Wetteland has a decent move but his power delivery makes it easy for opposing basestealers, who succeeded in 14 of 17 tries. Wetteland needs to work on his fielding. He showed he could bunt and managed one hit in five at-bats last season.

OVERALL:

In view of last season's strong finish, Wetteland figures to enjoy another productive season in 1993, especially if he learns to set up hitters on the inside and outside part of the plate. He possesses both the fearless demeanor and the intimidating stuff of the ideal stopper.

Overall Statistics

	W	L	ERA	G	GS	Sv	IP	H	R	BB	SO	HR
1992	4	4	2.92	67	0	37	83.1	64	27	36	99	6
Career	12	16	3.52	126	17	38	238.0	194	103	90	240	20

How Often He Throws Strikes

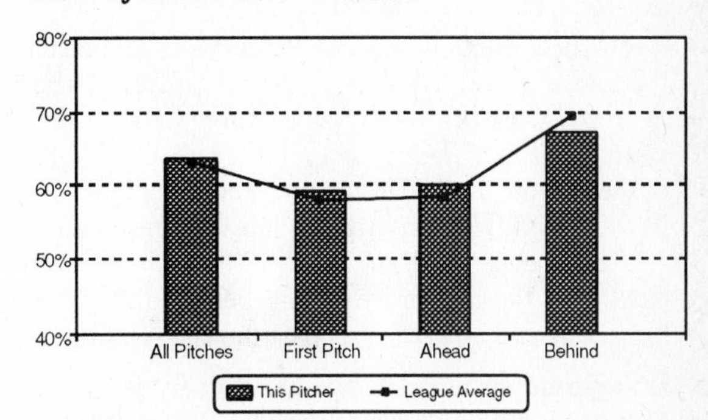

1992 Situational Stats

	W	L	ERA	Sv	IP		AB	H	HR	RBI	AVG
Home	2	3	3.83	21	44.2	LHB	175	35	3	17	.200
Road	2	1	1.86	16	38.2	RHB	126	29	3	14	.230
Day	1	1	3.41	10	29.0	Sc Pos	101	24	3	27	.238
Night	3	3	2.65	27	54.1	Clutch	207	47	6	26	.227

1992 Rankings (National League)

- 1st in blown saves (9)
- 2nd in games finished (58), save opportunities (46) and most strikeouts per 9 innings in relief (10.7)
- 3rd in saves (37)
- 6th in lowest percentage of inherited runners scored (21.6%)
- 9th in lowest batting average allowed vs. left-handed batters (.200) and lowest batting average allowed in relief (.213)
- Led the Expos in saves, games finished, save opportunities, save percentage (80.4%), blown saves and most strikeouts per 9 innings in relief

KENT BOTTENFIELD

Position: RP/SP
Bats: B **Throws:** R
Ht: 6' 3" **Wt:** 225

Opening Day Age: 24
Born: 11/14/68 in Portland, OR
ML Seasons: 1

Overall Statistics

	W	L	ERA	G	GS	Sv	IP	H	R	BB	SO	HR
1992	1	2	2.23	10	4	1	32.1	26	9	11	14	1
Career	1	2	2.23	10	4	1	32.1	26	9	11	14	1

PITCHING, FIELDING, HITTING & HOLDING RUNNERS:

There is nothing fancy about 24-year-old Kent Bottenfield, a trait that seems to impress the Expos. A workhorse-type pitcher with seven years of minor-league experience, Bottenfield comes straight at the hitter and tends to get ahead in the count. His opportunity late last year came at the expense of Brian Barnes -- someone who frustrated the Expos by falling behind hitters in the count and rarely lasted past the fifth inning.

Bottenfield kept the Expos close in three of his four starts and posted a save in his only opportunity. Overall, he posted a 2.23 ERA in 32.1 innings and held the opposition to just a .217 average. He is a control-type pitcher who throws the four basic pitches: fastball, slider, curve and change, keeping them low in the strike zone. He strikes out just a few (3.9 per nine innings), but he will keep the ball in the park (only one home run allowed). Bottenfield is a good fielder with a decent move to first. He helped himself out at the plate with three hits in eight at-bats and a sacrifice.

OVERALL:

Bottenfield has shown steady improvement over the last couple of seasons. The Expos like his no-nonsense approach. They showed how much he's a part of their future plans by protecting him in the expansion draft.

GREG COLBRUNN

Position: 1B
Bats: R **Throws:** R
Ht: 6' 0" **Wt:** 190

Opening Day Age: 23
Born: 7/26/69 in Fontana, CA
ML Seasons: 1

Overall Statistics

	G	AB	R	H	D	T	HR	RBI	SB	BB	SO	AVG
1992	52	168	12	45	8	0	2	18	3	6	34	.268
Career	52	168	12	45	8	0	2	18	3	6	34	.268

HITTING, FIELDING, BASERUNNING:

Greg Colbrunn quickly re-established himself as one of the Expos' bright young talents last year. Considered a premier minor-league catching prospect in 1990, Colbrunn missed the entire 1991 season after undergoing surgery to his right elbow, a Tommy John-type procedure which involved a tendon transfer and ligament reconstruction.

The surgery has momentarily forced Colbrunn to relocate defensively, but it has not hindered his offense. He batted a powerful .306 (.556 slugging) at AAA Indianapolis with 48 RBI in 216 at-bats, and was promoted at midseason. He impressed immediately, hitting his way into the starting lineup at first base by batting .325 in his first 114 at-bats. Then Colbrunn suffered minor elbow problems and an 8-for-54 skid at the end of season. Colbrunn likes fastballs up in the strike zone. He has a long, powerful upswing that produces many flyball outs as well as many strikeouts. A good athlete, the 23-year-old Colbrunn has decent speed and was adjusting to first base quite rapidly, fielding a respectable .992.

OVERALL:

Despite the uncertainty surrounding his future as a catcher, the Expos are very excited about Colbrunn. His elbow still bothers him from time to time -- he had to rest it during the offseason and could not play winter ball -- but with occasional rest, he could be an important figure in the Expos' offense in 1993. They protected him from expansion to prove their expectations.

TIM LAKER

Position: C
Bats: R **Throws:** R
Ht: 6' 2" **Wt:** 175

Opening Day Age: 23
Born: 11/27/69 in Encino, CA
ML Seasons: 1

Overall Statistics

	G	AB	R	H	D	T	HR	RBI	SB	BB	SO	AVG
1992	28	46	8	10	3	0	0	4	1	2	14	.217
Career	28	46	8	10	3	0	0	4	1	2	14	.217

HITTING, FIELDING, BASERUNNING:

Tim Laker had himself quite a season last year. Always considered a good, if not spectacular, defensive catcher, he emerged as an offensive threat, blasting 15 homers and 68 RBI in 409 at-bats at AA Harrisburg. At 23, Laker jumped ahead of strong-hitting Bob Natal on the Expos' depth chart. He was protected from expansion while Natal was off to Florida.

Laker didn't overwhelm anyone in his Expo debut, striking out too frequently (14 times) and walking very little (twice) in 46 at-bats. He did show he could hit breaking stuff and displayed good speed for a catcher.

Laker was promoted mainly for his ability to gun down opposing basestealers -- an area of weakness among Expo catchers. Surprisingly he allowed 13 steals in 15 attempts. He did show off a strong arm, but often, probably due to nervousness, his throws were either too high or wound up in center field. Laker displayed very quick feet, making some terrific plays on both pitches in the dirt and bunt hits in front of the plate.

OVERALL:

Of all the kids brought up by the Expos last season, Laker was ranked by Felipe Alou as the most impressive. Alou, who managed Laker in A ball in 1991, is counting on Laker to be the starter next year, so it seems fitting that Laker pinch ran for Gary Carter after the Kid's final major-league at-bat.

SERGIO VALDEZ

Position: RP
Bats: R **Throws:** R
Ht: 6' 1" **Wt:** 190

Opening Day Age: 27
Born: 9/7/65 in Elias Pina, Dominican Republic
ML Seasons: 5

Overall Statistics

	W	L	ERA	G	GS	Sv	IP	H	R	BB	SO	HR
1992	0	2	2.41	27	0	0	37.1	25	12	12	32	2
Career	8	14	4.89	87	19	0	219.0	225	133	83	155	29

PITCHING, FIELDING, HITTING & HOLDING RUNNERS:

After being invited to camp by the Expos as a non-roster player, Sergio Valdez started last season at AAA Indianapolis. Valdez was finally called up in midseason by Montreal, the team which had originally signed him at the age of 17 back in 1983. The Expos' bullpen was well-stocked and Valdez saw very little action, especially when it counted. His impressive numbers -- 32 strikeouts and just 37 baserunners allowed in 37.1 innings, a .185 opponents batting average -- were mostly achieved in the baseball version of "garbage time." His career stats before last season were ugly: 200 hits allowed and 71 walks in 181.2 innings.

Valdez has a good forkball but has difficulty keeping it around the strike zone. His fastball lacks movement and strays to the top of the strike zone, not what a team looks for in a successful power pitcher.

Valdez is poor both at the plate and in the field. He seems completely oblivious to opposing baserunners, allowing nine steals last season in 10 attempts, a ridiculous figure for someone who allowed so few batters to reach base.

OVERALL:

Despite his excellent numbers last season, Valdez is by no means assured of a spot with the Expos this season. More than anything, he was a body the Expos threw out on the mound when no one else was available.

ORGANIZATION OVERVIEW:

The Expos have yet to win a pennant, but they're getting closer, and the biggest reason is their splendid farm system. Montreal doesn't have free agent money to toss around, and a lot of guys don't want to play there. The Expos have put what money they do have into player development and have paid special attention to black and Latin players -- many of whom like the international flavor of their city and organization. Problems with the city and stadium remain, and it'll be interesting to see if the club can overcome them long enough to win a title. The talent seems to be there, especially at the lower levels of the system.

TAVO ALVAREZ

Position: P **Opening Day Age:** 21
Bats: R **Throws:** R **Born:** 11/25/71 in Obregon Sonora, Mex
Ht: 6' 3" **Wt:** 183

Recent Statistics

	W	L	ERA	G	GS	Sv	IP	H	R	BB	SO	HR
91 A Sumter	12	10	3.24	25	25	0	152.2	152	68	58	158	6
92 A Wst Plm Bch	13	4	1.49	19	19	0	139.0	124	30	24	83	0
92 AA Harrisburg	4	1	2.85	7	7	0	47.1	48	15	9	42	3

Only 21 years old, the Mexican Alvarez looks -- and pitches -- older. He throws consistently in the 90s and has a good curve and circle change to go with his fastball. In three minor-league seasons, Alvarez is 34-17 with a 2.49 ERA, including a 17-5 record at two levels last year. Mexican pitchers are often worked very hard when they're young, but if his arm holds up, Alvarez could be very, very good.

JON HURST

Position: P **Opening Day Age:** 26
Bats: R **Throws:** R **Born:** 10/20/66 in New York, NY
Ht: 6' 2" **Wt:** 175

Recent Statistics

	W	L	ERA	G	GS	Sv	IP	H	R	BB	SO	HR
92 AAA Indianapols	4	8	3.77	23	23	0	119.1	135	59	29	70	7
92 NL Montreal	1	1	5.51	3	3	0	16.1	18	10	7	4	1

One of three good prospects the Expos got from the Rangers in the Oil Can Boyd swindle, Hurst made three starts for the big club last year, going 1-1 with a 5.51 ERA. Hurst was then sent back to AAA Indianapolis, where his final record was only 4-8. Those numbers may make it seem like he's not much of a prospect, but Hurst was 15-3 in 1991. He throws hard, and his pitches have good movement. He should do better when he gets another chance.

MIKE LANSING

Position: SS **Opening Day Age:** 25
Bats: R **Throws:** R **Born:** 4/3/68 in Rawlins, WY
Ht: 6' 0" **Wt:** 175

Recent Statistics

	G	AB	R	H	D	T	HR	RBI	SB	BB	SO	AVG
91 A Miami	103	384	54	110	20	7	6	55	29	40	75	.286
92 AA Harrisburg	128	483	66	135	20	6	6	54	46	52	64	.280
92 MLE	128	464	51	116	17	4	4	42	34	34	69	.250

A slow developer, Lansing suffered back problems in college and was drafted not by a major-league club but by the independent Miami Miracle Class A team. The Expos bought him late in 1991 and last year he hit .280 with 46 stolen bases at AA Harrisburg. He's a scrappy type, and hard work has enabled him to overcome a lack of sheer talent. Beating out Wil Cordero will be difficult, but Lansing figures to make it to the majors soon.

MATT STAIRS

Position: OF **Opening Day Age:** 24
Bats: R **Throws:** R **Born:** 2/27/69 in Saint John, N.B. Canada
Ht: 5' 9" **Wt:** 175

Recent Statistics

	G	AB	R	H	D	T	HR	RBI	SB	BB	SO	AVG
92 AAA Indianapols	110	401	57	107	23	4	11	56	11	49	61	.267
92 NL Montreal	13	30	2	5	2	0	0	5	0	7	7	.167
92 MLE	110	382	41	88	19	2	7	40	8	35	64	.230

The diminutive Stairs made it to Montreal last year and was disappointed when he was sent back after only 18 at-bats. It showed in his play; he batted only .267 at Indianapolis after hitting .333 at AA Harrisburg in 1991. Stairs has good offensive skills, with excellent strike zone judgement and surprising power for his size (11 homers last year). He played second base in 1991, but with Delino DeShields around, he was moved to the outfield last year. He's not a good defensive player, though he has fine speed. It's his bat which will make or break him.

RONDELL B. WHITE

Position: OF **Opening Day Age:** 21
Bats: R **Throws:** R **Born:** 2/23/72 in Baldwin, GA
Ht: 6' 1" **Wt:** 193

Recent Statistics

	G	AB	R	H	D	T	HR	RBI	SB	BB	SO	AVG
91 A Sumter	123	465	80	121	23	6	12	67	51	57	109	.260
92 A Wst Plm Bch	111	450	80	142	10	12	4	41	42	46	78	.316
92 AA Harrisburg	21	89	22	27	7	1	2	7	6	6	14	.303

Probably the crown jewel of Montreal's talent-rich organization, White was chosen the number-three prospect in the star-studded Florida State League -- after Brien Taylor and Carlos Delgado, not bad company. White has been compared with Andre Dawson; he has the potential to hit for average, steal a lot of bases, and be an ace in the field. However, his power and arm are not in the Dawson range. Only 21, White is an outstanding prospect.

KEVIN BASS

Position: LF/RF
Bats: B **Throws:** R
Ht: 6' 0" **Wt:** 180

Opening Day Age: 33
Born: 5/12/59 in Redwood City, CA
ML Seasons: 11

HITTING:

With quick hands, speed and power, Kevin Bass averaged .281 with 17 home runs per year for the Astros from 1985 to 1988. Knee and hamstring injuries have prevented Bass from repeating such numbers in any season since, but he staged a minor comeback in 1992 with his highest totals since 1988 in at-bats, hits, extra-base hits, and his best batting average (.269) since 1989.

Without his old bat speed, Bass has adjusted by becoming more selective. When he sees a pitch he likes, he commits himself just a little earlier than he used to. As a result he is striking out more, but he is also getting around on fastballs better. Bass has always had a good knowledge of the strike zone and he knows the league's pitchers well.

The best way to pitch Bass is to give him plenty of outside breaking balls. When he's looking for a fastball, he has trouble adjusting to curves that break over the outside corner. Bass has power from both sides of the plate, but lefty pitchers, in particular, are wise not to give him anything he can pull.

BASERUNNING:

In his first game as a Met, Bass stole two bases. He showed how glad he was to get away from San Francisco, but he was also showing that his left knee was on the mend. Bass is once again a threat to steal. His 14 steals in 1992 were his highest total since 1988. Bass is above average in all aspects of baserunning.

FIELDING:

Although Bass had numerous injury-related problems in San Francisco, it was concern over his defense that kept him out of the lineup most often. Bass' sore left knee cut down his ability to get to balls quickly. However, in late 1992 he was substantially improved. He has always had a strong, accurate arm.

OVERALL:

If his legs hold up, Bass can be a valuable player in 1993. If he's hobbled, he will just be another former star. He looks better now than he did two years ago, so the outlook is favorable.

Overall Statistics

	G	AB	R	H	D	T	HR	RBI	SB	BB	SO	AVG
1992	135	402	40	108	23	5	9	39	14	23	70	.269
Career	1267	4112	509	1108	203	39	104	507	134	279	566	.269

Where He Hits the Ball

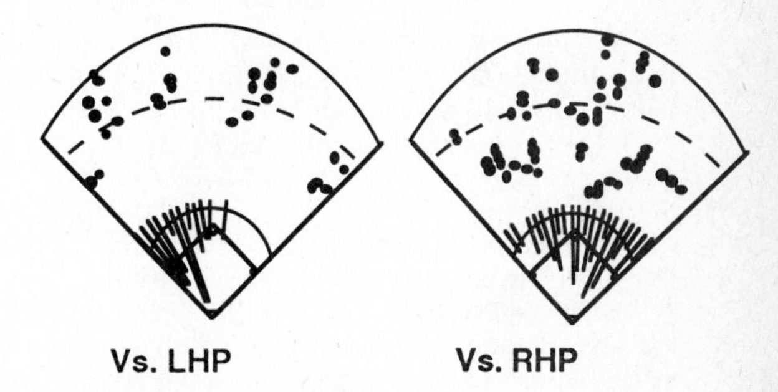

1992 Situational Stats

	AB	H	HR	RBI	AVG		AB	H	HR	RBI	AVG
Home	216	63	7	25	.292	LHP	144	32	4	17	.222
Road	186	45	2	14	.242	RHP	258	76	5	22	.295
Day	150	47	7	24	.313	Sc Pos	117	24	1	28	.205
Night	252	61	2	15	.242	Clutch	99	29	3	11	.293

1992 Rankings (National League)

- 1st in lowest on-base percentage vs. left-handed pitchers (.236)
- 5th in lowest stolen base percentage (60.9%)
- 8th in lowest batting average with runners in scoring position (.205) and lowest batting average vs. left-handed pitchers (.222)
- Led the Mets in triples (2)

HITTING:

Expected to be the Mets' big run-producer after signing a massive free agent contract, Bobby Bonilla was one of the major disappointments of 1992. Bonilla fractured a rib and had shoulder surgery, causing him to miss over 30 games. But even if his season was projected to 162 games, his RBI output would have been just 89. His 1992 batting average (.249) was a career low. He had barely half as many doubles in 1992 as he had in 1991 and no triples.

A big swinger from both sides of the plate, Bonilla is more of a pull hitter against lefty pitching, but he has power to all fields whether he's batting right or left. Bonilla needs discipline to get the most from his talent. In 1992 he was visibly pressing. He had well-publicized problems hitting in front of the Shea Stadium fans; he batted only .214 at home with five homers and 21 RBI. On the road he hit more like Bobby Bonilla (.277, 14, 49).

Bonilla is always aggressive. He looks for a pitch he likes, especially a fastball, and commits himself early. Opposing pitchers simply didn't throw his favorite pitches last year; they didn't need to as he swung at their less generous offerings.

BASERUNNING:

Although he is not a big basestealer (his career-high is eight steals), Bonilla is an aggressive and intelligent runner. He will help his team by taking an extra base whenever possible and by breaking up double plays.

FIELDING:

Bonilla has a strong arm and good range. He learned quickly how to deal with the swirling winds at Shea Stadium. He is not a Gold Glove right fielder, but he is not a defensive liability either.

OVERALL:

At his low point in 1992, Bonilla called the press box during a game to protest an official scorer's ruling. It was a tough year. In a weak lineup with few people getting on base, Bonilla didn't see many good pitches and became overeager. If the Mets lineup is stronger in 1993, it will help Bonilla, but he needs to show more patience and discipline.

BOBBY BONILLA

Position: RF
Bats: B **Throws:** R
Ht: 6' 3" **Wt:** 240

Opening Day Age: 30
Born: 2/23/63 in New York, NY
ML Seasons: 7

Overall Statistics

	G	AB	R	H	D	T	HR	RBI	SB	BB	SO	AVG
1992	128	438	62	109	23	0	19	70	4	66	73	.249
Career	1046	3732	572	1040	224	37	135	596	32	463	570	.279

Where He Hits the Ball

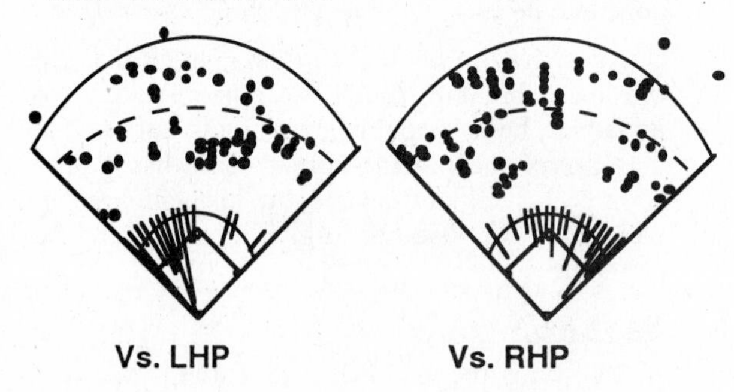

1992 Situational Stats

	AB	H	HR	RBI	AVG		AB	H	HR	RBI	AVG
Home	196	42	5	21	.214	LHP	175	42	4	21	.240
Road	242	67	14	49	.277	RHP	263	67	15	49	.255
Day	148	30	5	19	.203	Sc Pos	117	30	5	51	.256
Night	290	79	14	51	.272	Clutch	74	20	6	15	.270

1992 Rankings (National League)

- 5th in lowest groundball/flyball ratio (.88)
- 8th in HR frequency (23.1 ABs per HR) and lowest batting average (.249)
- Led the Mets in home runs (19), walks (66), intentional walks (10), slugging percentage (.431), on-base percentage (.348) and HR frequency

DARYL BOSTON

Position: LF/CF/RF
Bats: L **Throws:** L
Ht: 6' 3" **Wt:** 210

Opening Day Age: 30
Born: 1/4/63 in Cincinnati, OH
ML Seasons: 9

Overall Statistics

	G	AB	R	H	D	T	HR	RBI	SB	BB	SO	AVG
1992	130	289	37	72	14	2	11	35	12	38	60	.249
Career	882	2261	321	565	114	21	65	224	97	205	392	.250

Where He Hits the Ball

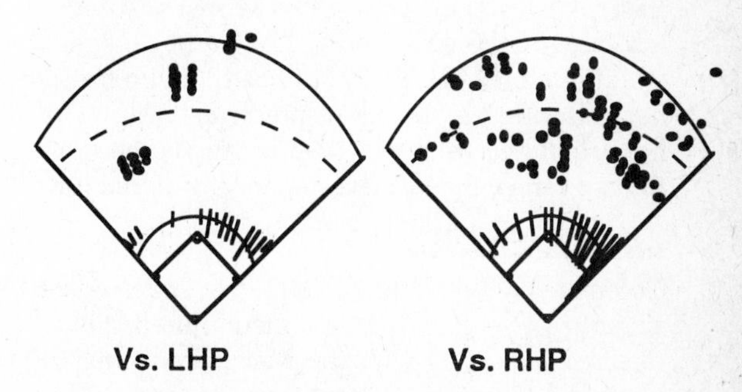

1992 Situational Stats

	AB	H	HR	RBI	AVG		AB	H	HR	RBI	AVG
Home	140	32	5	17	.229	LHP	47	15	1	4	.319
Road	149	40	6	18	.268	RHP	242	57	10	31	.236
Day	90	18	2	11	.200	Sc Pos	54	17	3	27	.315
Night	199	54	9	24	.271	Clutch	61	14	4	9	.230

1992 Rankings (National League)

→ Led the Mets in triples (2)

HITTING:

With injuries to all three of their starting outfielders in 1992, the Mets needed help from Daryl Boston, and as usual, they got it. Boston provided both power and speed in an otherwise anemic lineup. Playing almost exclusively against right-handed pitching, he produced 11 homers in his part-time role.

In just 289 at-bats, Boston drew a career-high 38 walks last year. Once a notorious free swinger, he studied Walt Hriniak's methods and with maturity he has developed more patience. His nature is still free-swinging and aggressive, but he benefits from having a good knowledge of the strike zone and being familiar with the league's pitchers.

Boston has good power. He can pull anything inside, but his longest shots are to right center or left center, depending on where the ball is pitched. Boston is a good clutch performer. He contributed three pinch-hit home runs to the Mets' 1992 campaign.

BASERUNNING:

Boston has good speed and is aggressive as a basestealer. Twice in his professional career he has exceeded 40 steals in a season. He won't put up numbers like that any more, but he bears watching on the basepaths.

FIELDING:

Boston played all three outfield positions for the Mets in 1992. Although he was in the lineup mainly because of injuries, he is a good enough fielder to be a late-inning defensive replacement for any team. He has above-average range, a good arm, and he gets a good jump now that he knows the league's hitters well.

OVERALL:

The Mets could have made Boston a regular player the last two years, but they chose instead to pursue bigger names like Hubie Brooks and Bobby Bonilla. During 1992 it must have occurred to many people that Boston would have been a better choice, and at a lower price. If the free agent returns to the Mets, he'll once again be in a reserve role. But as soon as someone gets hurt, he'll be back in the lineup, and he'll be valuable.

GREAT SPEED

VINCE COLEMAN

Position: LF/CF
Bats: B **Throws:** R
Ht: 6' 1" **Wt:** 185

Opening Day Age: 31
Born: 9/22/61 in Jacksonville, FL
ML Seasons: 8

Overall Statistics

	G	AB	R	H	D	T	HR	RBI	SB	BB	SO	AVG
1992	71	229	37	63	11	1	2	21	24	27	41	.275
Career	1021	4042	648	1071	124	62	18	255	610	380	716	.265

Where He Hits the Ball

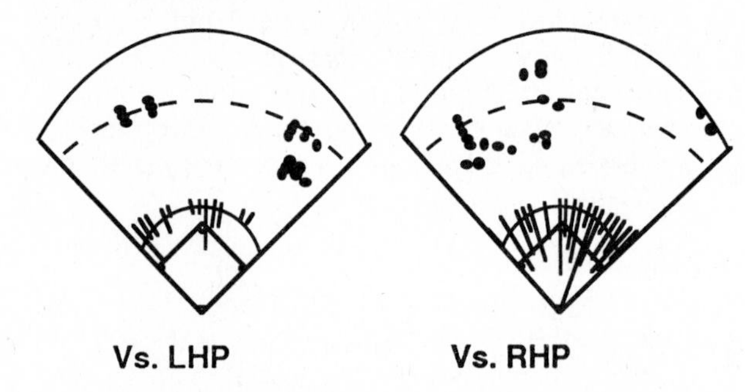

1992 Situational Stats

	AB	H	HR	RBI	AVG		AB	H	HR	RBI	AVG
Home	119	33	2	14	.277	LHP	60	17	1	9	.283
Road	110	30	0	7	.273	RHP	169	46	1	12	.272
Day	44	13	1	6	.295	Sc Pos	45	14	2	21	.311
Night	185	50	1	15	.270	Clutch	41	9	1	6	.220

1992 Rankings (National League)

- Led the Mets in stolen bases (24), caught stealing (9), batting average with 2 strikes (.241) and steals of third (4)
- Led NL left fielders in bunts in play (14)

HITTING:

The only question about Vince Coleman used to be whether he could get on base enough. Now there are two others: can he stay healthy, and can he avoid run-ins with management? Last year, his second with the Mets, Coleman made three separate trips to the disabled list with hamstring and rib injuries. He appeared in only 71 contests, giving him a two-year total of just 143 games in a Met uniform. He also got into an on-field tiff with his manager Jeff Torborg. In '91, he'd tangled with coach Mike Cubbage.

When he's between the lines, Coleman remains a very good offensive player. To his credit, he's improved his once-measly on-base percentage. Last year his OBP was .355, the second-best of his career. He's striking out less these days, and walking more. The grass at Shea Stadium hasn't hurt his offense, as many predicted. His .277 home batting average in 1992 is exactly the same as his average the last five years on artificial turf.

BASERUNNING:

Coleman led the National League in stolen bases six straight years. Although often injured, he has retained his speed with the Mets, producing 61 steals in 143 games. Coleman set a team record in 1992 with four steals in one game. He is beyond the spectrum covered by traditional scouting terms. He gets the most from his speed by running aggressively.

FIELDING:

After beginning the year as a left fielder, a position where his speed makes him well above average, Coleman was pressed into service in center field. His range is terrific at any of the outfield positions, but his arm is not especially strong.

OVERALL:

Coleman has been disabled five times in two years with the Mets. Along with these absences, he added a two-game suspension by management in 1992 for insubordination. Coleman hasn't seemed like a happy ballplayer since coming to New York. It's probably fair to say that New York has been equally unhappy with Coleman.

TOUGH ON LEFTIES

SID FERNANDEZ

Position: SP
Bats: L **Throws:** L
Ht: 6' 1" **Wt:** 215

Opening Day Age: 30
Born: 10/12/62 in Honolulu, HI
ML Seasons: 10

PITCHING:

After making only eight starts in 1991 due to wrist and knee injuries, Sid Fernandez came back strong in 1992. It wasn't just a good comeback year; Fernandez excelled in every category. He posted his career-best ERA, worked his second highest innings total ever, and tied his career mark for games started.

Quietly emerging as the Mets' best starter, Fernandez led the team in ERA, wins, innings, and games started. With a stronger team, 1992 could have been his long-awaited 20-win season.

A fastball/flyball pitcher, Fernandez gets his rising heater past hitters with a combination of velocity and guile. He hides the ball well and hits spots effectively. Fernandez' best pitch is the rising fastball that produces innumerable foul tips and pop-ups. When he is ahead in the count, he can drop his slow curve over the corner of the plate, often for a called third strike. Fernandez also gets strikeouts when hitters are tantalized into chasing the fastball out of the strike zone.

Fernandez is a serious-minded, gritty competitor, tough in clutch situations and big games. He is a smart pitcher who understands game situations; he will often yield a semi-intentional walk rather than give in to a dangerous hitter. His 26 quality starts in 32 appearances demonstrate a high level of consistency.

HOLDING RUNNERS, FIELDING, HITTING:

Never very good at holding runners, Fernandez yielded 17 steals in 26 attempts in 1992. As a fielder he is just fair, but with a bat in his hands he can really help himself.

OVERALL:

Ever since Davey Johnson was the Mets' manager, Fernandez has received less than his fair share of favorable publicity. While opponents have been unanimous in their admiration of Fernandez as a tough competitor, the New York media has perpetuated the image of an overweight, out-of-shape pitcher, wholly inconsistent with his superb track record. With the rest of the Mets' staff collapsing around him, it is now clear to almost everyone that Fernandez is truly a fine pitcher.

Overall Statistics

	W	L	ERA	G	GS	Sv	IP	H	R	BB	SO	HR
1992	14	11	2.73	32	32	0	214.2	162	67	67	193	12
Career	93	73	3.17	239	233	1	1471.0	1092	563	567	1377	121

How Often He Throws Strikes

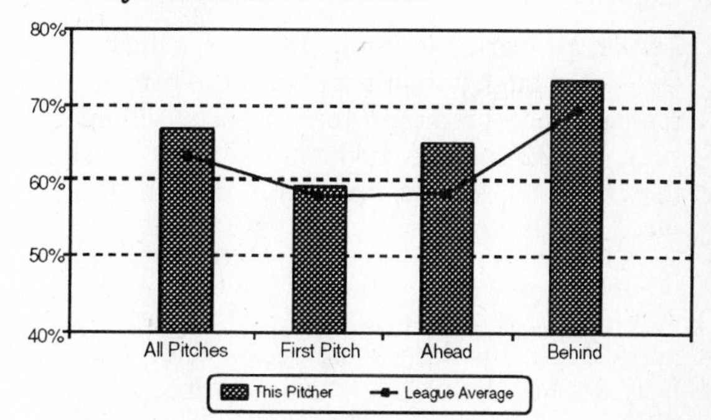

1992 Situational Stats

	W	L	ERA	Sv	IP		AB	H	HR	RBI	AVG
Home	7	4	2.17	0	99.1	LHB	149	28	0	12	.188
Road	7	7	3.20	0	115.1	RHB	622	134	12	48	.215
Day	3	2	2.35	0	53.2	Sc Pos	146	28	1	43	.192
Night	11	9	2.85	0	161.0	Clutch	57	18	1	4	.316

1992 Rankings (National League)

- 1st in lowest groundball/flyball ratio (.50) and most pitches thrown per batter (3.96)
- 2nd in least GDPs induced per 9 innings (.21) and most strikeouts per 9 innings (8.1)
- 3rd in lowest batting average allowed (.210)
- 4th in strikeouts (193)
- Led the Mets in ERA (2.73), wins (14), games started (32), innings pitched (214.2), batters faced (865), home runs allowed (12), most pitches thrown (3,424), highest strikeout/walk ratio (2.9), lowest batting average allowed, lowest on-base percentage allowed (.273), lowest stolen base percentage allowed (65.4%) and ERA at home (2.17)

TONY FERNANDEZ

Position: SS
Bats: B **Throws:** R
Ht: 6' 2" **Wt:** 175

Opening Day Age: 30
Born: 6/30/62 in San Pedro de Macoris, Dominican Republic
ML Seasons: 10

HITTING:

After two seasons, Tony Fernandez' contract was too expensive for the Padres' frugal diet and his production too quiet. So the Padres traded him after the '92 season to the New York Mets, a club desperate for quality shortstop play, for Wally Whitehurst and D.J. Dozier. For Fernandez, it was probably a good career move. In San Diego, he had to listen to people talk about how Joe Carter and Roberto Alomar, the two players the Padres had traded for Fernandez and Fred McGriff, were leading Toronto to a championship. With the Padres Fernandez had been considered a malcontent, one of the guys who'd caused manager Greg Riddoch to be fired. In New York, at least, he'll start with a clean slate.

Fernandez had another solid season for the Padres in 1992, though it didn't approach the batting title plateau once predicted for him. He scored 84 runs, had 32 doubles and he hit .275. Figures like that, considered disappointing in San Diego, would thrill the Mets.

National League pitchers continue to feed Fernandez a diet of hard stuff when he bats right-handed and breaking stuff away when he bats lefty. He has all but given up any hint of trying to hit for power, preferring to take pitches the opposite way instead of looking for anything to drive.

BASERUNNING:

The good news was that Fernandez led the Padres in 1992 with 20 stolen bases. The bad news is that he was also caught stealing 20 times. His career success rate is 67 percent, so he's obviously capable of doing a whole lot better.

FIELDING:

Playing his second year on the San Diego grass, Fernandez was much more consistent. His range may be falling off just a bit but he remains one of baseball's better defensive shortstops.

OVERALL:

Fernandez likely will never be the premier player that people once insisted he'd become. In fact, some scouts view him as a talented but overrated player. That said, Fernandez is definitely among the top echelon at his position. He should be the best Mets shortstop in many years.

Overall Statistics

	G	AB	R	H	D	T	HR	RBI	SB	BB	SO	AVG
1992	155	622	84	171	32	4	4	37	20	56	62	.275
Career	1328	5132	675	1465	251	70	48	479	181	396	480	.285

Where He Hits the Ball

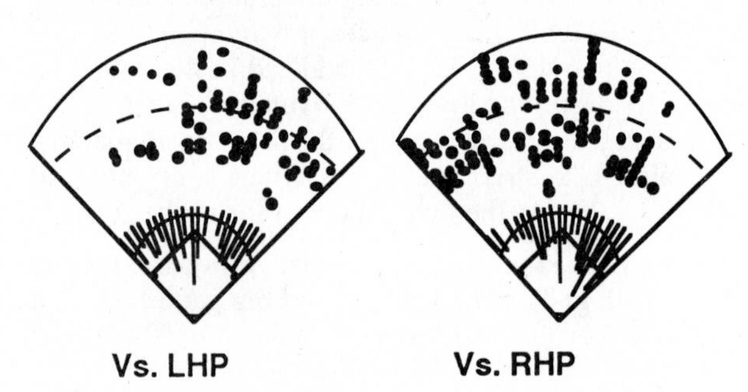

Vs. LHP　　Vs. RHP

1992 Situational Stats

	AB	H	HR	RBI	AVG		AB	H	HR	RBI	AVG
Home	301	85	3	19	.282	LHP	207	58	1	18	.280
Road	321	86	1	18	.268	RHP	415	113	3	19	.272
Day	189	46	1	13	.243	Sc Pos	99	27	1	34	.273
Night	433	125	3	24	.289	Clutch	103	33	0	6	.320

1992 Rankings (National League)

- → 1st in lowest stolen base percentage (50.0%)
- → 3rd in caught stealing (20)
- → 4th in at-bats (622), singles (131) and batting average on an 0-2 count (.310)
- → 5th in plate appearances (694)
- → 6th in lowest slugging percentage vs. right-handed pitchers (.369)
- → Led NL shortstops in hits (171), singles, caught stealing, times on base (231), batting average vs. right-handed pitchers (.272), slugging percentage vs. right-handed pitchers and on-base percentage vs. right-handed pitchers (.331)

PITCHING:

After pitching with pain throughout the summer and missing all of September, John Franco had surgery on his left elbow last September 29. Results were satisfactory. Physicians said Franco should be able to throw again by December. Aside from the injury, Franco had a great season. He held the opposition to a .209 batting average (compared to .271 in 1991), demonstrating that he still has the magic touch of a true stopper. His 1.64 ERA was the second-lowest of his career. Franco's career save total already places him among the all-time great relief aces.

Franco's best pitch is a fade-away change-up. Against right-handed batters, he typically works his fastball and slider in on the hands, inducing weak grounders and fouls down the left side. The change-up may tail away outside of the strike zone or catch the inside corner as the hitter steps back. The slow pitch has such good movement that is has often been called a screwball. Against lefty hitters, Franco simply works inside with fastballs and keeps his slider low.

Like most groundball pitchers, Franco uses his fielders well. He has a fine understanding of the connection between pitch selection, pitch location, and defensive positioning. His knowledge and command of his three pitches often make him look lucky when he gets a groundball for an easy double play. It isn't luck; it's design.

HOLDING RUNNERS, FIELDING, HITTING:

With a quick pickoff move that discourages big leads, Franco is adept at holding runners. Only two of five attempted steals were successful against him in 1992. Franco helps his own groundball defense with good movement and sure hands around the mound. He never comes to bat unless something has gone wrong.

OVERALL:

After a somewhat disappointing 1991 season, Franco needed a sharp performance in 1992 to reestablish himself as the NL's top closer. The sore elbow held him back by limiting his appearances, but Franco was consistently sharp whenever he worked. The elbow should be fine in 1993, and the Mets are counting on him, as evidenced by his surprising expansion protection.

JOHN FRANCO

Position: RP
Bats: L **Throws:** L
Ht: 5'10" **Wt:** 185

Opening Day Age: 32
Born: 9/17/60 in Brooklyn, NY
ML Seasons: 9

Overall Statistics

	W	L	ERA	G	GS	Sv	IP	H	R	BB	SO	HR
1992	6	2	1.64	31	0	15	33.0	24	6	11	20	1
Career	58	44	2.49	531	0	226	684.0	611	229	260	488	34

How Often He Throws Strikes

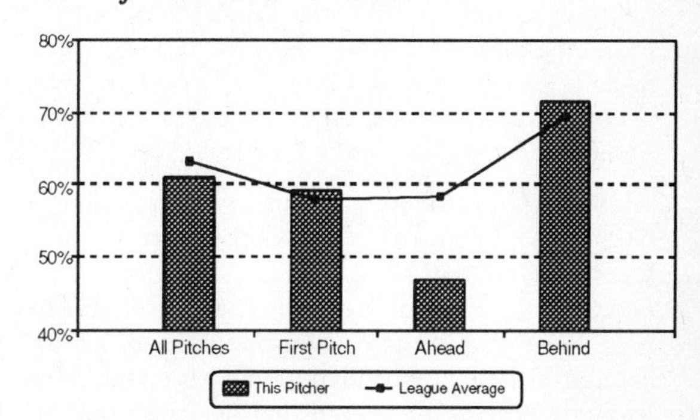

1992 Situational Stats

	W	L	ERA	Sv	IP		AB	H	HR	RBI	AVG
Home	4	1	0.92	8	19.2	LHB	28	7	0	3	.250
Road	2	1	2.70	7	13.1	RHB	87	17	1	7	.195
Day	3	2	2.13	3	12.2	Sc Pos	26	5	0	7	.192
Night	3	0	1.33	12	20.1	Clutch	91	20	0	9	.220

1992 Rankings (National League)

- 9th in lowest batting average allowed in relief with runners in scoring position (.192)
- 10th in saves (15) and relief wins (6)
- Led the Mets in saves, games finished (30), lowest batting average allowed in relief with runners on base (.239), lowest batting average allowed in relief with runners in scoring position and relief wins

PITCHING:

Dwight Gooden is a rare pitcher: although he will pitch two more seasons before reaching age 30, he has already logged nearly 2000 major-league innings, and in them won 142 games. But all those innings pitched at a young age have taken their toll. Gooden had rotator cuff surgery late in 1991, and the '92 season was the first losing campaign of his career (10-13).

While he came back from the surgery to pitch 206 innings, Gooden still had a little soreness in 1992. Nonetheless his fastball had good movement with velocity like he had before the operation. Although he still throws well over 90 MPH, Gooden needs to make more adjustments from power pitching to finesse pitching. In games when he has sharp command of both his curve and fastball, he is a very tough pitcher, but those games are becoming scarce. Even on good days, he isn't the dominant force that people remember.

Although Gooden has tried other pitches at times, he is essentially a two-pitch pitcher. He complements the fastball with a sharp-breaking curve. Gooden can take a little speed off either pitch. He gets the most out of his two-pitch repertoire by changing velocities and pitching to spots. The league's best hitters agree that sharp control is now the key to Gooden's success.

HOLDING RUNNERS, FIELDING, HITTING:

With a high leg kick, Gooden has never held runners well. Paying more attention in 1992, he held the opposition to 22 stolen bases, down from 33 in 1991. But he is still amongst the easiest pitchers to run on. Gooden is a strong fielder, and he is one of the best hitters in the pitching profession.

OVERALL:

Gooden's 1985 season still provides a reference point for people who talk about godlike pitching. Since then he has gradually fallen back into the population of pitching mortals. His career winning percentage dropped below .700 in 1992; his lifetime ERA could easily rise above 3.00 in 1993. To succeed from now on, Gooden needs to stay healthy and come up with another pitch.

DWIGHT GOODEN

Position: SP
Bats: R **Throws:** R
Ht: 6' 3" **Wt:** 210

Opening Day Age: 28
Born: 11/16/64 in Tampa, FL
ML Seasons: 9

Overall Statistics

	W	L	ERA	G	GS	Sv	IP	H	R	BB	SO	HR
1992	10	13	3.67	31	31	0	206.0	197	93	70	145	11
Career	142	66	2.99	269	267	1	1919.2	1664	702	575	1686	98

How Often He Throws Strikes

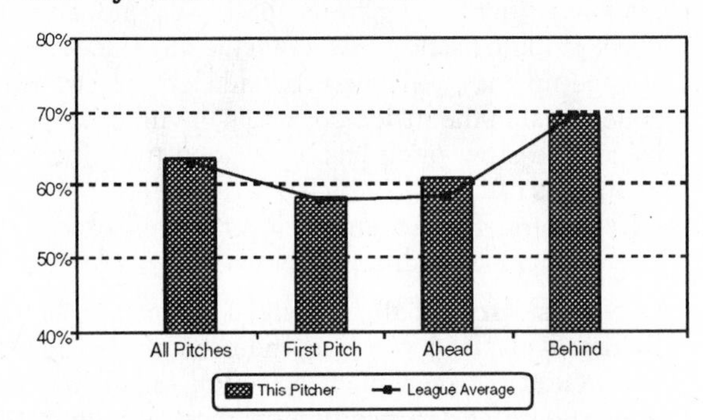

1992 Situational Stats

	W	L	ERA	Sv	IP		AB	H	HR	RBI	AVG
Home	7	5	4.25	0	97.1	LHB	450	120	9	45	.267
Road	3	8	3.15	0	108.2	RHB	323	77	2	41	.238
Day	3	4	3.53	0	66.1	Sc Pos	207	49	2	65	.237
Night	7	9	3.74	0	139.2	Clutch	70	16	2	8	.229

1992 Rankings (National League)

- 4th in highest ERA at home (4.25)
- 6th in GDPs induced (20)
- 8th in losses (13), most pitches thrown per batter (3.70), most baserunners allowed per 9 innings (11.8) and most GDPs induced per 9 innings (.87)
- 9th in least run support per 9 innings (3.6)
- Led the Mets in hits allowed (197), runners caught stealing (11), GDPs induced, highest groundball/flyball ratio (1.6), most pitches thrown per batter, least home runs allowed per 9 innings (.48) and most GDPs induced per 9 innings

PITCHING:

Lee Guetterman would like to forget 1992. Opposition hitters feasted on him, compiling a .335 batting average. In 275 at-bats, they hit 10 home runs and had 54 RBI. His ERA nearly doubled from 3.68 in 1991 to 7.09 in '92. What went wrong? Guetterman simply threw too many fat pitches up in the strike zone. His style is to work directly and throw strikes, but he was too direct in his approach last year.

Like most sinkerball pitchers, Guetterman needs to keep the ball low and get ahead in the count to be successful; his first pitch should be a tough strike. In 1992 the opposition hit .422 (19 for 45) on the first pitch from Guetterman. Batters were often looking for an easy strike and were ready to jump on it.

Guetterman has a large repertoire for a reliever. In addition to the sinker, he can straighten out the fastball, or throw a curve, a slider, or a straight change-up. He uses the sinker most often, however, looking for groundball outs. Guetterman doesn't like to nibble. He has little stamina, generally losing effectiveness after about 15 pitches. Going deep in the count is what he tries to avoid with all hitters. Accordingly, he simply throws strikes and hopes for the best.

HOLDING RUNNERS, FIELDING, HITTING:

Although he has worked on his pickoff move and pays attention well, Guetterman is only fair at holding runners. A former first baseman, he is a good fielder. He rarely comes to bat, but won't embarrass himself at the plate.

OVERALL:

Guetterman faces a chicken-and-egg problem in 1993. He can't get too fancy, because he lacks stamina and isn't overpowering. But he can't keep throwing strikes in the same spots where hitters are always looking for them. His sinker just doesn't sink enough to retire batters who know that it's coming. Within his large repertoire, Guetterman needs to find another pitch that he can mix in extensively with the sinker.

LEE GUETTERMAN

Position: RP
Bats: L **Throws:** L
Ht: 6' 8" **Wt:** 230
Opening Day Age: 34
Born: 11/22/58 in Chattanooga, TN
ML Seasons: 8

Overall Statistics

	W	L	ERA	G	GS	Sv	IP	H	R	BB	SO	HR
1992	4	5	7.09	58	0	2	66.0	92	52	27	20	10
Career	35	31	4.37	345	23	23	584.1	644	312	185	251	50

How Often He Throws Strikes

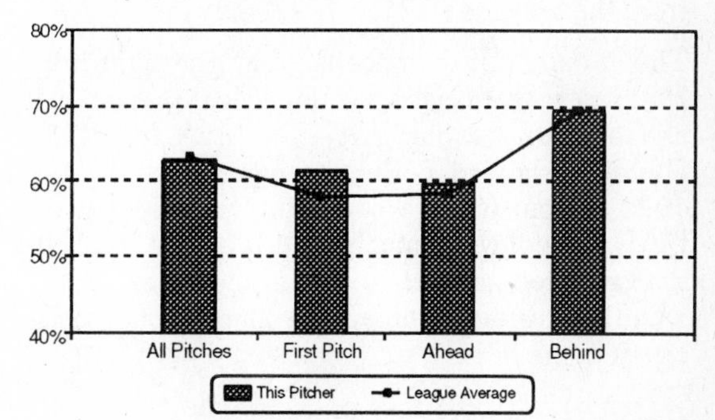

1992 Situational Stats

	W	L	ERA	Sv	IP		AB	H	HR	RBI	AVG
Home	3	4	8.41	1	35.1	LHB	90	25	1	9	.278
Road	1	1	5.58	1	30.2	RHB	185	67	9	45	.362
Day	2	2	4.50	0	20.0	Sc Pos	80	27	3	43	.338
Night	2	3	8.22	2	46.0	Clutch	111	36	7	21	.324

1992 Rankings (National League)

- 8th in most GDPs per GDP situation (17.9%)
- Led the Mets in first batter efficiency (.231)

HITTING:

In a season filled with disappointments for the Mets, Todd Hundley offered a ray of hope. He failed to hit for a high average but he showed good power, and his batting average improved substantially after the All-Star break. The young catcher batted only .186 in the first half, .232 in the second.

Obviously, Hundley still has a long way to come as a hitter. The switch-hitter is especially vulnerable when batting from the right side (.177 last year). He can jack a pitch from a southpaw who is optimistic enough to throw him an inside fastball, but lefties give him fits with outside breaking stuff. Hundley has hit for a better average from the left side (.224 in 1992) thus far.

The most optimistic consideration regarding Hundley is that he is so young. Most players his age are just reaching AA or AAA in 1993. Hundley showed definite progress during the 1992 season, as the Mets tried to use him selectively. Hundley did much better when he stopped swinging too hard. However, in the second half, when his average improved, he hit only one of his seven home runs.

BASERUNNING:

Within the catcher population Hundley is fast. In 1992 he was three-for-three in steal attempts. Working as a catcher will inevitably slow him down in the future, but in 1993, pitchers still have to pay attention to him, and infielders can't be lazy when Hundley is running out a ground ball.

FIELDING:

Defense is Hundley's biggest strength. He is quick and agile around home plate. He can throw out runners. Most importantly, he can handle pitchers like an old pro. The Mets had 13 shutouts in 1992, and Hundley was behind the plate for 12 of them.

OVERALL:

Despite his low average last year Hundley still has the potential to be an All-Star. He can learn hitting with practice and patience, and his power is already good. His biggest gifts are not skills that can be taught: the strong throwing arm and the great instincts behind the plate.

TODD HUNDLEY

Position: C
Bats: B **Throws:** R
Ht: 5'11" **Wt:** 185

Opening Day Age: 23
Born: 5/27/69 in Martinsville, VA
ML Seasons: 3

Overall Statistics

	G	AB	R	H	D	T	HR	RBI	SB	BB	SO	AVG
1992	123	358	32	75	17	0	7	32	3	19	76	.209
Career	180	485	45	97	23	1	8	41	3	31	108	.200

Where He Hits the Ball

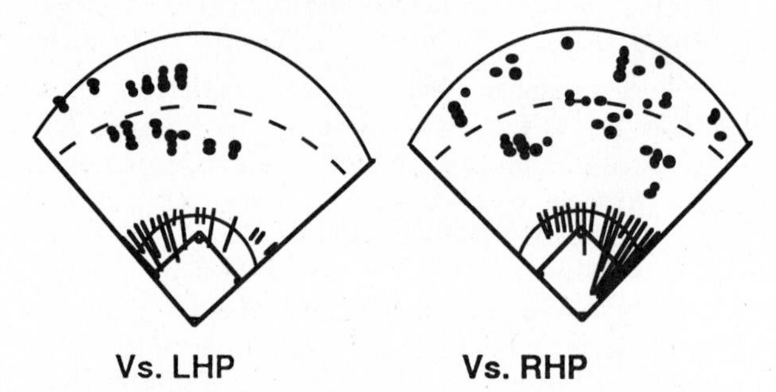

1992 Situational Stats

	AB	H	HR	RBI	AVG		AB	H	HR	RBI	AVG
Home	181	40	2	16	.221	LHP	113	20	4	10	.177
Road	177	35	5	16	.198	RHP	245	55	3	22	.224
Day	98	23	3	7	.235	Sc Pos	83	13	2	26	.157
Night	260	52	4	25	.200	Clutch	76	19	0	3	.250

1992 Rankings (National League)

- → 4th in batting average on a 3-1 count (.625)
- → 10th in lowest batting average with the bases loaded (.154)
- → Led the Mets in batting average on a 3-1 count
- → Led NL catchers in sacrifice bunts (7) and batting average on a 3-1 count

JEFF INNIS

Position: RP
Bats: R **Throws:** R
Ht: 6' 1" **Wt:** 168

Opening Day Age: 30
Born: 7/5/62 in Decatur, IL
ML Seasons: 6

PITCHING:

The workhorse of the Mets bullpen, Jeff Innis appeared in a team-record 76 games in 1992. He typically worked just one inning, setting up for John Franco or Anthony Young to get the last three outs in save situations or pitching in late innings of games when the Mets were tied or down by a run. As usual, Innis remained remarkably consistent. He had a 2.82 ERA before the All-Star break last year, 2.94 afterward. His lifetime ERA is 2.76, and he's usually right around that mark -- 2.66 and 2.86 the last two years.

Innis has the sinker/slider repertoire typical of sidearm pitchers, and he is naturally tougher on right-handed batters. On occasion he will mix in an overhand curve or even a knuckleball, but most of the time he just comes right at the hitter with sinkers and sliders. A direct worker who doesn't like to waste pitches, Innis doesn't overpower anyone. He just throws strikes and relies on his defense to handle the many ground balls that he induces.

Innis' biggest asset is a bounce-back arm that keeps him available day after day. Because he has good control and doesn't nibble, he keeps his pitch counts low and avoids getting overtired in any outing. The Mets only let him throw more than 45 pitches once in 1992.

HOLDING RUNNERS, FIELDING, HITTING:

Scouts have occasionally criticized Innis for lack of attention to runners, but he is at least average when it comes to preventing the stolen base. It is one aspect of his game that he has worked on during the past two seasons. Innis is a fairly good fielder. He rarely comes to bat.

OVERALL:

Because he doesn't strike out many people, Innis can't be an ace reliever like fellow sidearmers Kent Tekulve and Dan Quisenberry. He is a good set-up man, however, and in crucial situations the Mets have often used him against the toughest right-handed hitters rather than going to their stopper.

Overall Statistics

	W	L	ERA	G	GS	Sv	IP	H	R	BB	SO	HR
1992	6	9	2.86	76	0	1	88.0	85	32	36	39	4
Career	8	17	2.76	221	1	2	283.1	256	102	83	156	17

How Often He Throws Strikes

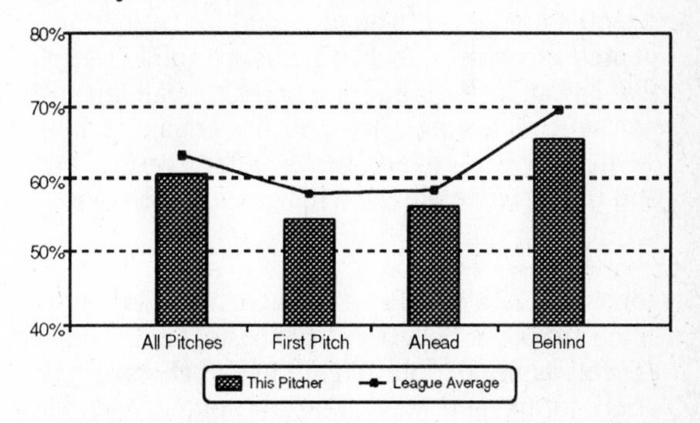

1992 Situational Stats

	W	L	ERA	Sv	IP		AB	H	HR	RBI	AVG
Home	3	5	2.81	1	48.0	LHB	159	46	2	23	.289
Road	3	4	2.92	0	40.0	RHB	160	39	2	12	.244
Day	0	4	3.18	0	22.2	Sc Pos	96	23	1	30	.240
Night	6	5	2.76	1	65.1	Clutch	183	57	2	25	.311

1992 Rankings (National League)

- 2nd in relief losses (9)
- 3rd in holds (16) and least strikeouts per 9 innings in relief (4.0)
- 5th in games pitched (76)
- 6th in hit batsmen (6)
- 7th in most GDPs induced per GDP situation (18.4%) and relief innings (88)
- Led the Mets in games pitched, holds, most GDPs per GDP situation, lowest percentage of inherited runners scored (30.0%), relief ERA (2.86), relief wins (6), relief losses, relief innings, lowest batting average allowed in relief and least baserunners allowed per 9 innings in relief (13.0)

HITTING:

Howard Johnson went on the disabled list last August 2 with a fractured wrist, ending a season he would like to forget. Johnson finished 1992 with career lows in batting average, home runs, and runs batted in. He also failed to make a successful switch to the outfield. Almost everything that could go wrong did go wrong.

When healthy, Johnson is still one of the most dangerous switch-hitters in the game. Against lefty pitching, he is a great pull hitter. Against righties he can also pull anything inside, but he is better at going with the outside pitch when he swings from the left side.

Like most power hitters, Johnson strikes out frequently, but he is not an easy out. He bears down in pressure situations. His hands are quick enough that he can be looking for a breaking ball but still adjust to a fastball. In 1991 he began making written notes on every pitcher after every at-bat, and this practice elevated his game noticeably.

BASERUNNING:

Johnson's 22 steals last year were his lowest total since 1986, but on a per at-bat basis, he did about as well as usual. Johnson studies pitchers, gets a good jump, and has great flat-out speed. He showed better judgment in 1992 as well, improving his success rate to 81 percent.

FIELDING:

Johnson has never been a good fielder. Changing positions frequently has had an adverse impact, but Johnson has also shown a tendency to butcher easy plays. He doesn't get a good jump and doesn't have much lateral quickness. He was handed the center field job at the start of 1992 and proceeded to produce the fewest outs per nine innings (worst range factor) of all major-league regulars at that position.

OVERALL:

After a career year in 1991, Johnson crashed hard in 1992. A mature professional, he has come back from adversity before, and his 1992 stats were so far below his career averages that a comeback in 1993 has to be expected. An expected return to third base, his natural position, should help.

HOWARD JOHNSON

Position: CF/LF
Bats: B **Throws:** R
Ht: 5'10" **Wt:** 195

Opening Day Age: 32
Born: 11/29/60 in Clearwater, FL
ML Seasons: 11

Overall Statistics

	G	AB	R	H	D	T	HR	RBI	SB	BB	SO	AVG
1992	100	350	48	78	19	0	7	43	22	55	79	.223
Career	1279	4309	672	1092	225	17	204	672	213	576	891	.253

Where He Hits the Ball

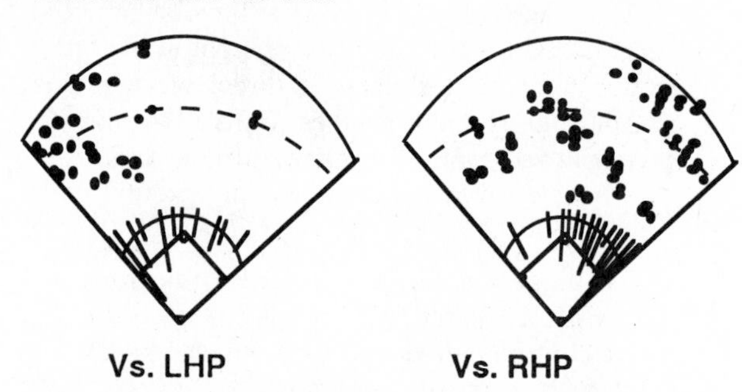

1992 Situational Stats

	AB	H	HR	RBI	AVG		AB	H	HR	RBI	AVG
Home	164	31	2	16	.189	LHP	132	30	4	21	.227
Road	186	47	5	27	.253	RHP	218	48	3	22	.220
Day	111	28	4	21	.252	Sc Pos	95	23	1	35	.242
Night	239	50	3	22	.209	Clutch	49	12	1	8	.245

1992 Rankings (National League)

- → 2nd in lowest percentage of swings put into play (38.2%)
- → 7th in highest percentage of swings that missed (24.8%)
- → 9th in stolen base percentage (81.5%)
- → Led the Mets in stolen base percentage, lowest percentage of GDPs per GDP situation (7.5%), slugging percentage vs. left-handed pitchers (.379) and steals of third (4)
- → Led NL center fielders in batting average with the bases loaded (.300)

DAVE MAGADAN

Position: 3B
Bats: L **Throws:** R
Ht: 6' 3" **Wt:** 205

Opening Day Age: 30
Born: 9/30/62 in Tampa, FL
ML Seasons: 7

Overall Statistics

	G	AB	R	H	D	T	HR	RBI	SB	BB	SO	AVG
1992	99	321	33	91	9	1	3	28	1	56	44	.283
Career	701	2088	275	610	110	11	21	254	5	347	248	.292

Where He Hits the Ball

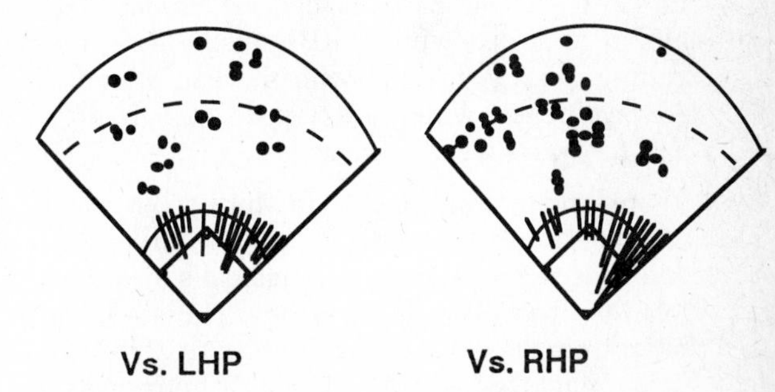

1992 Situational Stats

	AB	H	HR	RBI	AVG		AB	H	HR	RBI	AVG
Home	153	48	2	13	.314	LHP	120	37	0	7	.308
Road	168	43	1	15	.256	RHP	201	54	3	21	.269
Day	106	26	1	8	.245	Sc Pos	69	20	2	26	.290
Night	215	65	2	20	.302	Clutch	47	14	2	6	.298

1992 Rankings (National League)

- 1st in highest percentage of pitches taken (63.5%)
- 5th in lowest percentage of swings that missed (9.5%)
- Led the Mets in batting average vs. left-handed pitchers (.308), highest percentage of pitches taken, lowest percentage of swings that missed and highest percentage of swings put into play (49.3%)
- Led NL third basemen in highest percentage of pitches taken and lowest percentage of swings that missed

HITTING:

Dave Magadan is a patient hitter with excellent knowledge of the strike zone. His career .391 on-base percentage places him among the active leaders. Unfortunately, he doesn't have any speed or power. Since Magadan plays either third or first -- power positions -- and lacks speed, he's always had to fight for playing time. In 1992 Magadan won the fight and the Mets' third base job. But then a broken wrist ended his season on August 9.

While the Mets admire Magadan's skills, they wish he would be more aggressive, especially with men on base. But it just isn't Magadan's nature to swing at pitches he doesn't like. There is no safe way to pitch to him, other than keeping the ball out of the strike zone. In clutch situations, pitching carefully to the point of walking Magadan is a better idea than giving him a pitch he can drive.

One of the bright spots in Magadan's 1992 performance was his .308 batting average against left-handed pitching. He hit just .256 and .245 against lefties in 1990 and 1991 respectively. Magadan believes that increased playing time against southpaws has helped him improve. But it's hard to draw conclusions from just 120 at-bats.

BASERUNNING:

If Magadan had any speed he would be a great leadoff hitter. When he attempts a steal, he uses the element of surprise. But usually Magadan just stays put and moves station-to-station around the bases.

FIELDING:

At third base, Magadan has poor range and just an average arm. In 1992 he had the fewest outs per nine innings and the second-lowest fielding percentage among major-league regulars. At first, he is adequate. His biggest asset is a soft glove.

OVERALL:

Magadan played solidly before his injury last year, but if he returns to the Mets he'll once more have to fight for a job. Their current plan is to return Howard Johnson to third base, and Eddie Murray seems set at first. A free agent, Magadan figured to be shopping for a new club, and could help someone.

HITTING:

Reports of Eddie Murray's demise were once again premature. In 1992 he tied his career-best total in doubles, led his team in runs batted in, and walked almost as often as he struck out. While Murray had only 16 homers, a career low, his 93 RBI were only five less than his career average. In 16 seasons, the remarkable Murray has never driven home fewer than 84 men except in the 1981 strike season, when he had a league-leading 78.

For a power hitter, Murray has astounding discipline. In tight games it often seems that he can foul off pitches indefinitely until he gets the one he wants. He is a pure terror in clutch situations. In 1992 with the bases loaded, he produced 10 hits in 15 at-bats with 27 RBI, raising his career batting average to .424 with the bases loaded. Always treated with great respect, Murray drew half his walks with the sacks full.

There is no safe way to pitch to Murray, other than walking him. He can cover the whole strike zone and is especially deadly with fastballs anywhere from the belt down to the knees. He is a better hitter from the left side; last year he hit .275 lefty, .238 righty, and had 13 of his 16 homers as a left-handed hitter.

BASERUNNING:

Murray doesn't look fast, but he can surprise a sleepy defense with a stolen base or a burst of speed in a crucial situations. He studies pitchers well and knows which catchers have good arms.

FIELDING:

A three-time Gold Glove winner, Murray positions himself well, has great anticipation, and fields with soft hands. He has led both leagues in fielding percentage in his career.

OVERALL:

In one of the most bizarre moments in an unusual season, Murray was ejected from a game during an at-bat in his favorite situation, with the bases loaded. His offense? He wanted the second base umpire to move so he could see the pitches better. Murray probably won't let the umps distract him enough to keep him from his usual 90-plus RBI in 1993.

EDDIE MURRAY

Position: 1B
Bats: B **Throws:** R
Ht: 6' 2" **Wt:** 222

Opening Day Age: 37
Born: 2/24/56 in Los Angeles, CA
ML Seasons: 16

Overall Statistics

	G	AB	R	H	D	T	HR	RBI	SB	BB	SO	AVG
1992	156	551	64	144	37	2	16	93	4	66	74	.261
Career	2444	9124	1343	2646	462	32	414	1562	90	1147	1224	.290

Where He Hits the Ball

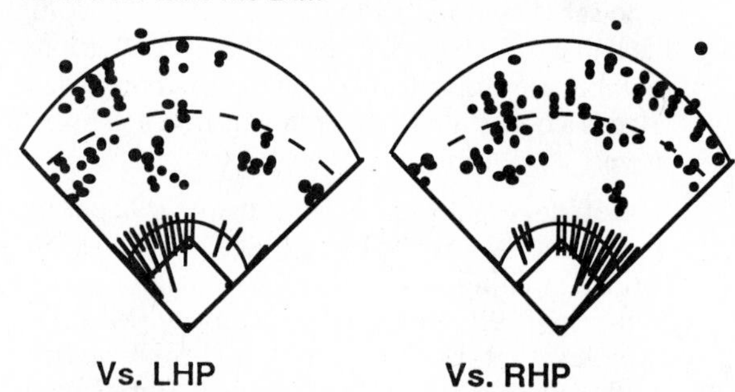

1992 Situational Stats

	AB	H	HR	RBI	AVG		AB	H	HR	RBI	AVG
Home	266	60	7	43	.226	LHP	202	48	3	35	.238
Road	285	84	9	50	.295	RHP	349	96	13	58	.275
Day	155	49	7	24	.316	Sc Pos	141	38	4	76	.270
Night	396	95	9	69	.240	Clutch	91	19	1	19	.209

1992 Rankings (National League)

- 1st in batting average with the bases loaded (.667)
- 2nd in lowest batting average at home (.226)
- 4th in sacrifice flies (8)
- Led the Mets in batting average (.261), at-bats (551), runs scored (64), hits (144), singles (89), doubles (37), triples (2), total bases (233), RBI (93), sacrifice flies, walks (66), times on base (210), GDPs (14), most pitches seen (2,318), plate appearances (625), games played (156), highest groundball/flyball ratio (1.1), most pitches seen per plate appearance (3.71), batting average with runners in scoring position (.270) and batting average with the bases loaded

HITTING:

Nobody thought Bill Pecota could hit until he got a chance to play regularly in 1990. Before that, in three of four trials with Kansas City, Pecota had hit between .205 and .208. When he finally got into the regular lineup he became an offensive asset, and in 1991 produced career highs across the board. With the Mets in 1992, however, Pecota didn't play regularly and regressed. His average tumbled 59 points, from .286 in 1991 to .227.

Pecota has always had trouble with right-handed pitchers, especially hard throwers who work him inside and then hit the outside corners with breaking stuff. Against lefties he does a better job of covering the whole plate. But in 1992 he didn't excel against southpaws, either, hitting only .234. Over the past five seasons Pecota has batted .276 vs. lefties, .228 against righties.

With versatile skills, Pecota is useful in all offensive situations and is a good clutch player. Last year he hit .286 in close and late situations. Although he had only 10 hits with runners in scoring position, he also drew 13 walks. Pecota can hit for power to left and left-center. He is an excellent bunter.

BASERUNNING:

Pecota has good speed and uses it wisely, as indicated by his career stolen base success rate of 72 percent. He learns pitchers' moves quickly and gets a good jump. He is always a threat to take an extra base.

FIELDING:

Versatility helps Pecota in the field. He made 20 or more starts at three infield positions in 1992. He can also play outfield when required. Pecota is sure-handed and has an accurate throwing arm, but his range is only fair.

OVERALL:

Pecota was regarded by many as a throw-in in the Bret Saberhagen trade. However, the Mets wouldn't have made the trade without him. He will never be an everyday starter at any position, but he can platoon against lefties, substitute at any infield position without hurting the defense, and be a helpful off-the-bench role player.

BILL PECOTA

Position: 3B/2B/SS
Bats: R Throws: R
Ht: 6' 2" Wt: 195

Opening Day Age: 33
Born: 2/16/60 in
Redwood City, CA
ML Seasons: 7

Overall Statistics

	G	AB	R	H	D	T	HR	RBI	SB	BB	SO	AVG
1992	117	269	28	61	13	0	2	26	9	25	40	.227
Career	562	1353	195	336	65	10	20	127	50	142	195	.248

Where He Hits the Ball

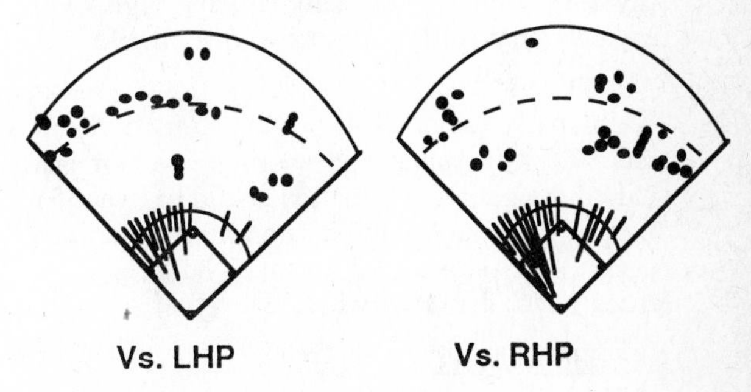

1992 Situational Stats

	AB	H	HR	RBI	AVG		AB	H	HR	RBI	AVG
Home	125	34	1	17	.272	LHP	107	25	2	13	.234
Road	144	27	1	9	.188	RHP	162	36	0	13	.222
Day	95	21	0	6	.221	Sc Pos	54	10	0	21	.185
Night	174	40	2	20	.230	Clutch	49	14	0	4	.286

1992 Rankings (National League)

- 6th in batting average on a 3-1 count (.571)
- Led NL second basemen in batting average on a 3-1 count

HITTING:

After a Cinderella comeback year featuring a career-high batting average in 1991 (.327), Willie Randolph played more like a 37 year old in 1992. He was a steady but unspectacular presence in the Mets lineup until he broke his hand in August. Randolph batted .252 last year, 24 points below his career average.

Randolph is still a fine professional hitter. His knowledge of the strike zone is outstanding and he knows what opposing pitchers can do. Randolph is a master bat-handler with quick hands, especially adept at making contact on breaking balls. Pitchers with a really good fastball can now blow it by him, but they still have to be careful. Anything in the wrong location (waist-high, over the plate) could become a line drive off Randolph's bat.

Traditionally tough in the clutch, Randolph hit just .172 with runners in scoring position last year, although in this situation he did have a .351 on-base percentage. In close and late situations he hit .302. As usual, he hit much better against lefties (.276) than righties (.238).

BASERUNNING:

Fifteen years ago, Randolph would steal 30 to 35 bases in a season. That speed is now eroded. He still has enough baserunning smarts to get the most out of any situation, and the defense needs to watch Randolph at all times.

FIELDING:

Randolph could teach a correspondence course on how to turn the double play. He is still the model to watch for anyone learning the pivot. His range is not what it used to be, but he studies hitters and positions himself perfectly, and thus covers his position adequately. His arm is still quick and accurate.

OVERALL:

Before his big 1991 season, Randolph was talking about retiring. The big resurgence dictated that he play another year, and he remained a quality player through 1992 until his injury. If Randolph wants to play in 1993, there should be a roster slot for him somewhere. If not, he has good credentials to be a future coach or manager.

WILLIE RANDOLPH

Position: 2B
Bats: R **Throws:** R
Ht: 5'11" **Wt:** 170

Opening Day Age: 38
Born: 7/6/54 in Holly Hill, SC
ML Seasons: 18

Overall Statistics

	G	AB	R	H	D	T	HR	RBI	SB	BB	SO	AVG
1992	90	286	29	72	11	1	2	15	1	40	34	.252
Career	2202	8018	1239	2210	316	65	54	687	271	1243	675	.276

Where He Hits the Ball

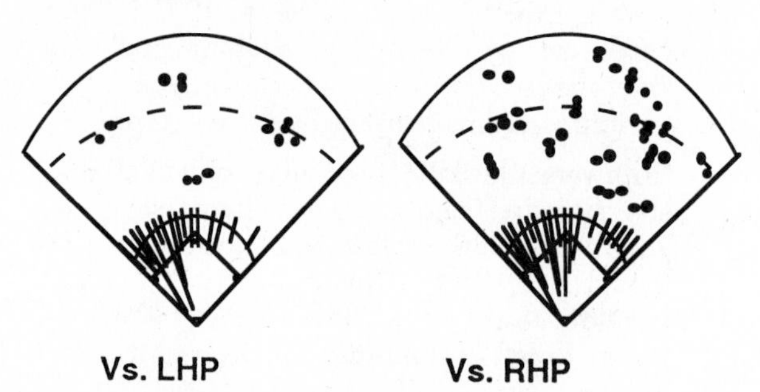

1992 Situational Stats

	AB	H	HR	RBI	AVG		AB	H	HR	RBI	AVG
Home	153	39	2	6	.255	LHP	105	29	2	8	.276
Road	133	33	0	9	.248	RHP	181	43	0	7	.238
Day	65	15	1	2	.231	Sc Pos	58	10	0	11	.172
Night	221	57	1	13	.258	Clutch	43	13	1	2	.302

1992 Rankings (National League)

➡ Led the Mets in batting average in the clutch (.302) and on-base percentage vs. left-handed pitchers (.397)

PITCHING:

When Bret Saberhagen gave up seven runs in 2.1 innings on April 7th last year, it was an omen for a bad season. Saberhagen went on the disabled list twice in 1992, both times with an inflamed tendon in his index finger. Though his ERA was respectable at 3.50, Saberhagen won only three games and worked just 97.2 innings -- both career lows.

Saberhagen still produced several superb outings in 1992. After three bad starts, he found his stride. In five appearances from April 23 through May 15, he yielded only three earned runs in 39 innings (0.69 ERA), and in his final three starts of the year he gave up just four earned runs in 24 innings (1.50 ERA). But except for these two streaks, his season was mediocre.

While he possesses a full assortment of pitches, including a fastball, slider, curve, and change-up, Saberhagen prefers to feature his fastball. His heater has very good movement and he can pitch to spots and change speeds effectively. A durable pitcher with 65 complete games in his career, Saberhagen is a classic staff ace who can usually be expected to stop a losing streak or give the bullpen a day off when required.

HOLDING RUNNERS, FIELDING, HITTING:

A former Gold Glove winner, Saberhagen is a quick and smooth fielder. He is especially impressive when he snares a foul pop, or when he races to pick up a bunt, always throwing flawlessly to the right base. Saberhagen is adept at holding runners; he yielded only six steals in 1992. He is not a good hitter.

OVERALL:

Looking behind the infamous "odd year good, even year bad" track record which continued in 1992, one finds that Saberhagen's good years actually result from spectacular half seasons, when he's untouchable for streaks of 10 to 15 games. Some years he has such a long streak; other years he doesn't. When he's not on a streak, he is just an average pitcher. That inconsistency, not odd/even jinxes, will be the key issue to his future.

BRET SABERHAGEN

Position: SP
Bats: R **Throws:** R
Ht: 6' 1" **Wt:** 200

Opening Day Age: 29
Born: 4/11/64 in Chicago Heights, IL
ML Seasons: 9

Overall Statistics

	W	L	ERA	G	GS	Sv	IP	H	R	BB	SO	HR
1992	3	5	3.50	17	15	0	97.2	84	39	27	81	6
Career	113	83	3.23	269	241	1	1758.0	1635	689	358	1174	132

How Often He Throws Strikes

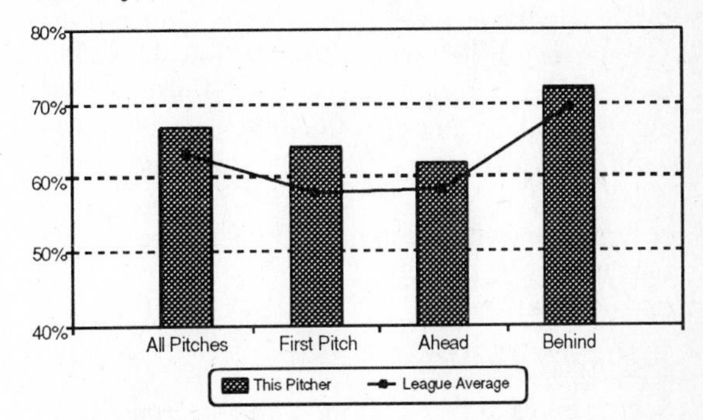

1992 Situational Stats

	W	L	ERA	Sv	IP		AB	H	HR	RBI	AVG
Home	1	2	2.41	0	59.2	LHB	212	48	3	22	.226
Road	2	3	5.21	0	38.0	RHB	148	36	3	14	.243
Day	0	2	3.79	0	35.2	Sc Pos	65	13	1	26	.200
Night	3	3	3.34	0	62.0	Clutch	59	15	2	4	.254

1992 Rankings (National League)

- Led the Mets in balks (2)

MACKEY SASSER

Position: C/1B
Bats: L **Throws:** R
Ht: 6' 1" **Wt:** 210

Opening Day Age: 30
Born: 8/3/62 in Fort Gaines, GA
ML Seasons: 6

Overall Statistics

	G	AB	R	H	D	T	HR	RBI	SB	BB	SO	AVG
1992	92	141	7	34	6	0	2	18	0	3	10	.241
Career	434	971	84	272	58	5	15	135	0	40	74	.280

Where He Hits the Ball

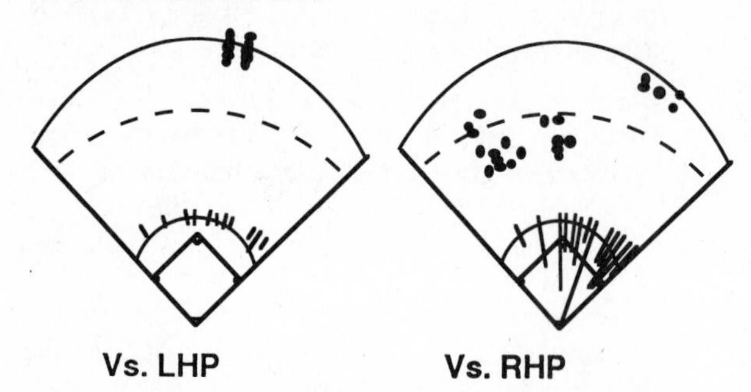

1992 Situational Stats

	AB	H	HR	RBI	AVG		AB	H	HR	RBI	AVG
Home	75	19	1	11	.253	LHP	18	4	0	2	.222
Road	66	15	1	7	.227	RHP	123	30	2	16	.244
Day	32	8	0	3	.250	Sc Pos	45	9	0	15	.200
Night	109	26	2	15	.239	Clutch	43	4	0	5	.093

1992 Rankings (National League)

➡ Did not rank near the top or bottom in any category

HITTING:

Normally one of the Mets' most dependable bats, Mackey Sasser suffered from a lack of playing time in 1992. Throughout his career, he has always been a better hitter when getting regular playing time. But last year Sasser got only 141 at-bats, and the result was a career-low .241 average.

Sasser is an outstanding contact hitter. He doesn't have much discipline at the plate, but that's not a big problem. Sasser can reach almost any pitch he likes and put it in play. There are no holes in his swing, and he can hit to all fields. Sasser rarely strikes out.

Against right-handed pitching, Sasser is a real threat. He has a career .296 average against righties and can hit them with good power whether pulling the ball or going to the opposite field. Against lefties, Sasser is much less effective. If a southpaw just keeps the ball low, Sasser will usually hit a weak ground ball or bouncer. A clutch hitter with a career .293 average with runners in scoring position, Sasser hit just .200 in that situation in 1992.

BASERUNNING:

Sasser gives definition to the phrase "runs like a catcher." He is very slow. Even among the population of major-league backstops, he is at the sluggish end of the spectrum. He does make a good effort in critical situations.

FIELDING:

Sasser is a defensive liability. He fields his position well but is poor at throwing out runners (just four caught stealing in 27 attempts last year). Sasser has also had a problem pumping the ball repeatedly before throwing it back to the pitcher. His biggest problem is that some pitchers simply don't like working with him. Sasser suffers in comparison with the other Mets catchers, and it's hurt his playing time.

OVERALL:

A catcher who can hit .296 against righties should be eminently employable in 1993, but it's not clear what Sasser's role would be with the Mets. He can still help a club given enough at-bats.

HITTING:

Dick Schofield is a naturally aggressive hitter. As a minor-leaguer, he tried to pull everything and had success with that approach. But in the major leagues he had to learn patience. California manager Gene Mauch took a special interest in getting Schofield to use all fields. That resulted in dramatic improvement -- and with no loss of power. But in the years since, Schofield has struggled to remain selective and patient, and often finds himself losing the struggle. Such was definitely the case in 1992, when Schofield came to the Mets from California and hit just .205 (.206 overall).

Eagerness took over in 1992; Schofield produced a career-high 82 strikeouts but didn't generate the kind of power that should come with such free swinging. Part of the problem was getting accustomed to National league pitchers, but his biggest problem was simple pressing. National League pitchers quickly discovered that he likes low fastballs; they started pitching him more up and in, then with fastballs away and breaking balls. His patience soon withered, and he spent the rest of the year chasing the less attractive pitches.

BASERUNNING:

Schofield has good speed, and manager Jeff Torborg let him attempt 15 steals last year at a 73 percent success rate. Schofield is an expert at slides. He is a smart baserunner, always looking for opportunities, and is very quick getting to first base.

FIELDING:

Schofield is an exceptionally steady fielder. He led the American League in fielding percentage in 1987 and '88, and he broke Bud Harrelson's club record for a shortstop with a .988 fielding percentage in 1992. Schofield has good range, and he throws well.

OVERALL:

The Mets were very happy to get Schofield after losing Kevin Elster, and Schofield was happy to leave California, where he had lost out to Gary DiSarcina. But his second chance didn't produce a great comeback story. Tired of weak-hitting shortstops, the Mets pursued and obtained Tony Fernandez as soon as the season ended. A free agent, Schofield will look for a new employer.

DICK SCHOFIELD

Position: SS
Bats: R **Throws:** R
Ht: 5'10" **Wt:** 179

Opening Day Age: 30
Born: 11/21/62 in Springfield, IL
ML Seasons: 10

Overall Statistics

	G	AB	R	H	D	T	HR	RBI	SB	BB	SO	AVG
1992	143	423	52	87	18	2	4	36	11	61	82	.206
Career	1203	3818	452	875	122	29	52	314	109	390	591	.229

Where He Hits the Ball

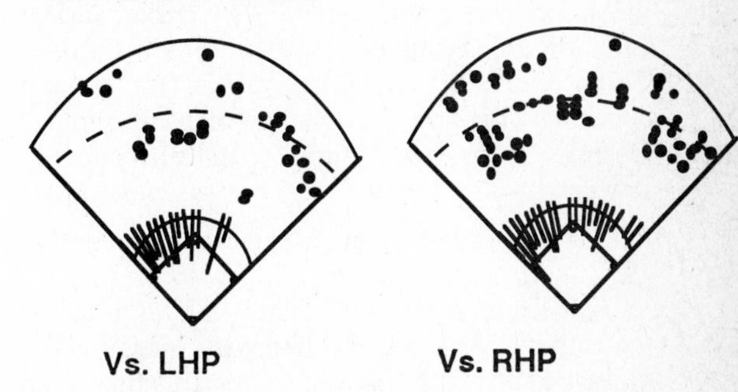

1992 Situational Stats

	AB	H	HR	RBI	AVG		AB	H	HR	RBI	AVG
Home	204	44	3	18	.216	LHP	145	29	2	17	.200
Road	219	43	1	18	.196	RHP	278	58	2	19	.209
Day	122	26	2	15	.213	Sc Pos	100	21	1	29	.210
Night	301	61	2	21	.203	Clutch	81	16	1	7	.198

1992 Rankings (National League)

- 2nd in lowest batting average vs. left-handed pitchers (.200), lowest batting average on an 0-2 count (.064) and lowest batting average on the road (.196)
- 4th in lowest batting average with 2 strikes (.121)
- 9th in bunts in play (19)
- 10th in sacrifice bunts (10) and lowest slugging percentage vs. left-handed pitchers (.310)
- Led the Mets in triples (2), sacrifice bunts, hit by pitch (5), strikeouts (82) and bunts in play
- Led NL shortstops in hit by pitch and fielding percentage (.988)

PITCHING:

In 1992, Anthony Young went from being a good starter, to a bad starter, to a good reliever, to a bad reliever. He started the season auspiciously with a complete game six-hitter. By late June, however, Young was struggling; the bullpen needed help, so his move to relief work solved two problems. Subbing for John Franco, Young recorded eight saves from July 1 to August 1, and pitched 23.2 scoreless innings from July 7 to August 28. But in September he faltered badly, giving up 11 earned runs in his last 10 appearances and recording only three saves in his last eight opportunities.

Young is a classic sinker/slider pitcher. He thrives on ground balls and double plays. In addition to the sinker and slider, he also has a curve, and he can straighten out his fastball. There's more: Young can pull the string on his fastball and curve, giving him two change-of-pace pitches. Despite the large repertoire, Young throws mostly low sinkers.

Opposition hitters had considerable success in 1992 by looking for Mets' pitchers to throw a fat strike with their first pitch. Ironically, the pitchers with the best control suffered the most. Young yielded a .368 batting average when his first pitch was put in play.

HOLDING RUNNERS, FIELDING, HITTING:

Young has a deceptive pickoff move and watches runners closely. He is a good fielder and a solid hitter who will often help himself in both departments.

OVERALL:

Young is a talented pitcher who hasn't yet tapped his full potential. Although he now has a track record as an ace reliever, his arm isn't very resilient. In addition, his pitch assortment isn't well suited to being a stopper; he doesn't have a big fastball and his large repertoire is wasted in that role. Look for him in a role that includes long relief, some set-up work, and some spot starts in 1993.

ANTHONY YOUNG

Position: RP/SP
Bats: R **Throws:** R
Ht: 6' 2" **Wt:** 200

Opening Day Age: 27
Born: 1/19/66 in Houston, TX
ML Seasons: 2

Overall Statistics

	W	L	ERA	G	GS	Sv	IP	H	R	BB	SO	HR
1992	2	14	4.17	52	13	15	121.0	134	66	31	64	8
Career	4	19	3.86	62	21	15	170.1	182	86	43	84	12

How Often He Throws Strikes

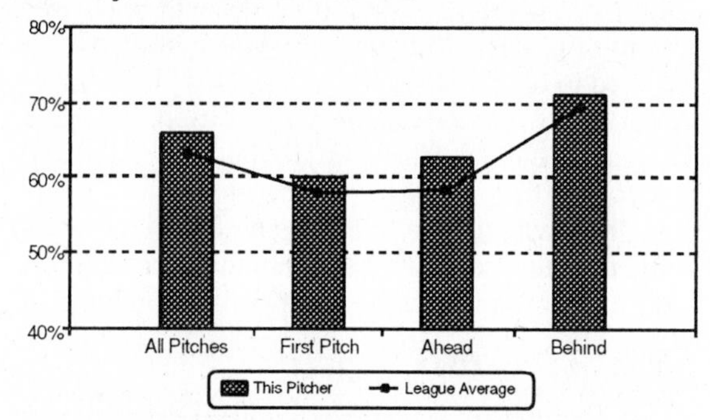

1992 Situational Stats

	W	L	ERA	Sv	IP		AB	H	HR	RBI	AVG
Home	0	7	3.96	8	52.1	LHB	259	84	3	34	.324
Road	2	7	4.33	7	68.2	RHB	211	50	5	24	.237
Day	2	2	3.16	5	31.1	Sc Pos	109	36	5	49	.330
Night	0	12	4.52	10	89.2	Clutch	121	30	3	17	.248

1992 Rankings (National League)

- 2nd in lowest winning percentage (.125)
- 3rd in losses (14)
- 4th in lowest save percentage (75.0%)
- 6th in highest batting average allowed vs. left-handed batters (.324) and relief losses (7)
- 10th in saves (15)
- Led the Mets in losses, saves, save opportunities (20), save percentage and blown saves (5)

DAVE GALLAGHER

Position: RF/LF/CF
Bats: R **Throws:** R
Ht: 6' 0" **Wt:** 184

Opening Day Age: 32
Born: 9/20/60 in Trenton, NJ
ML Seasons: 6

Overall Statistics

	G	AB	R	H	D	T	HR	RBI	SB	BB	SO	AVG
1992	98	175	20	42	11	1	1	21	4	19	16	.240
Career	533	1555	199	422	70	8	8	136	19	127	195	.271

HITTING, FIELDING, BASERUNNING:

Dave Gallagher is a spray-type singles hitter. Although he doesn't swing hard, he is not very selective and likes to put the ball in play. Moving to the National League last year figured to help him, because he generally likes fastballs and has trouble with breaking stuff. But while 1992 was the first year Gallagher ever posted more walks than strikeouts, his batting average tumbled 53 points to a career-low .240.

With fair speed and good bat-handling skills, Gallagher fit well into the Mets' low-power lineup. He had only one homer -- he has only eight four-baggers in his whole career -- but he had 11 doubles in only 175 at-bats. He is aggressive on the bases, but not a good basestealer; he was four-for-nine in 1992, and is under 50 percent for his career. Gallagher played all three outfield positions for the Mets, appearing most frequently in right. He is not a flashy fielder but is sure-handed and throws well.

OVERALL

With their entire starting outfield injured in 1992, the Mets found Gallagher a useful off-the-bench asset. When Jeff Torborg managed the White Sox, he gave Gallagher his only full season, 601 at-bats for Chicago in 1989. If Torborg has a say, Gallagher will be back in New York in 1993.

PAUL GIBSON

Position: RP
Bats: R **Throws:** L
Ht: 6' 1" **Wt:** 185

Opening Day Age: 33
Born: 1/4/60 in Center Moriches, NY
ML Seasons: 5

Overall Statistics

	W	L	ERA	G	GS	Sv	IP	H	R	BB	SO	HR
1992	0	1	5.23	43	1	0	62.0	70	37	25	49	7
Career	18	22	4.06	257	15	11	479.1	493	228	208	284	44

PITCHING, FIELDING, HITTING & HOLDING RUNNERS:

Paul Gibson is a sinker/slider pitcher with a history of success in short relief. He was used marginally as a general set-up reliever, facing mostly righties, in his first season with the Mets after coming over from the Detroit Tigers. It's just as well that he didn't face lots of lefties, as they hit .338 off him for the season. Gibson had some very forgettable outings last year; more than half of his inherited runners scored. His ERA of 5.23 was the worst of his career, and he allowed seven home runs in only 62 innings.

Although he has a decent pickoff move, Gibson is only fair at holding runners. Aggressive National Leaguers often made him look easy to steal upon. Gibson handles himself well in the field; he likes to have the ball hit to him and is good at snagging bunts. He is a weak hitter.

OVERALL:

The Mets would enjoy having a lefty set-up reliever to complement John Franco in 1993, but Gibson simply didn't do the job last year. His game is better suited to the American League, where hitters are less patient and baserunners are less aggressive. Being left-handed, and alive, he'll probably be able to land a job if the Mets don't want him.

BARRY JONES

Position: RP
Bats: R **Throws:** R
Ht: 6' 4" **Wt:** 225

Opening Day Age: 30
Born: 2/15/63 in Centerville, IN
ML Seasons: 7

Overall Statistics

	W	L	ERA	G	GS	Sv	IP	H	R	BB	SO	HR
1992	7	6	5.68	61	0	1	69.2	85	46	35	30	3
Career	33	32	3.57	342	0	23	425.2	401	191	191	243	30

PITCHING, FIELDING, HITTING & HOLDING RUNNERS:

One of many Chicago White Sox alumni on Jeff Torborg's roster, Barry Jones signed with the Mets after being dropped by the Phillies last August. Jones had been highly effective as a set-up reliever in the past, producing 11 wins and a 2.31 ERA in 1990. But his career took a wrong turn when the Expos made Jones their ace reliever in June 1991. Jones didn't want the job, and botched it. His career then went into a spin which produced a career-worst 5.68 ERA last year -- including a 9.39 mark in 17 games with the Mets.

Jones is a hard-throwing, nothing-fancy set-up reliever. He has a fastball, a slider, and a change-up, relying mainly on the fastball and slider. Jones has lost some velocity since his best years, but his main problem is that National League hitters have a finer sense of the strike zone than their American League counterparts. They simply won't swing at Jones' marginal offerings. Jones is not adept at holding runners. He isn't graceful coming off the mound, but is adequate on defense. He is a poor hitter.

OVERALL

Despite Torborg's fondness for Jones, there isn't a huge demand for relievers who don't pursue pressure situations eagerly. He'll have to scramble to land a major-league job this spring.

JEFF KENT

Position: 2B/3B
Bats: R **Throws:** R
Ht: 6' 1" **Wt:** 185

Opening Day Age: 25
Born: 3/7/68 in Bellflower, CA
ML Seasons: 1

Overall Statistics

	G	AB	R	H	D	T	HR	RBI	SB	BB	SO	AVG
1992	102	305	52	73	21	2	11	50	2	27	76	.239
Career	102	305	52	73	21	2	11	50	2	27	76	.239

HITTING, FIELDING, BASERUNNING:

Considered a good prospect by the Blue Jays, Jeff Kent was one of two young players Toronto sent to the Mets in order to obtain David Cone for last year's stretch run. Kent made a good impression in his 37 games with New York and had a fine rookie season after jumping from AA to the majors.

Kent's major asset is that he has good power for a middle infielder. He had 11 homers last year in only 305 major-league at-bats. On the downside, he has compiled high strikeout totals throughout his career. In the minors he also walked frequently; in the majors he hasn't yet. Kent should improve as he learns the strike zone better and has more opportunity to study pitchers.

Kent didn't steal many bases in 1992, but he has good speed. By working on getting better leads, he should steal 10 to 15 bases in 1993. As a fielder Kent is mediocre. He was used mostly at third base by the Blue Jays, but returned to his original position as a second baseman for the Mets. He has a good arm, but his range and positioning are below average.

OVERALL

Going into spring training, Kent was the front-runner for the Mets' second base job in 1993. He is young and talented, and they're eager to show that they received value in return for Cone.

PETE SCHOUREK

Position: SP
Bats: L **Throws:** L
Ht: 6' 5" **Wt:** 205

Opening Day Age: 23
Born: 5/10/69 in Austin, TX
ML Seasons: 2

Overall Statistics

	W	L	ERA	G	GS	Sv	IP	H	R	BB	SO	HR
1992	6	8	3.64	22	21	0	136.0	137	60	44	60	9
Career	11	12	3.89	57	29	2	222.1	219	109	87	127	16

PITCHING, FIELDING, HITTING & HOLDING RUNNERS:

Pete Schourek is a developing talent who made good progress in 1992. Schourek has outstanding minor-league credentials, including a 1990 season in which he was 16-5 with a 2.57 ERA spread over three levels from A to AAA. After breaking in with the Mets in 1991, Schourek got 21 starting assignments last year. He turned in a 6-8 record and a 3.64 ERA, but he was better than his numbers indicated.

Schourek has a sneaky fastball which he complements with a curve and a change-up. He isn't overpowering (86-88 MPH), but he gets good movement on the heater and can hit spots with all his pitches. His success depends on moving the ball around.

A former first baseman, Schourek helps himself with steady fielding around the mound. He needs to work on holding runners, however. The opposition was 15-for-20 in steal attempts against him last year despite his low innings total (136). Schourek is not a good hitter, with a .078 career batting average.

OVERALL:

Schourek has made a good impression on the Mets. He pitches very well at Shea Stadium, and the club can use another solid lefty to complement Sid Fernandez in the rotation in 1993. While it's unlikely that Schourek will develop into a dominant hurler, he should be a valuable number-five type starter.

RYAN THOMPSON

Position: CF
Bats: R **Throws:** R
Ht: 6' 3" **Wt:** 200

Opening Day Age: 25
Born: 11/4/67 in Chestertown, MD
ML Seasons: 1

Overall Statistics

	G	AB	R	H	D	T	HR	RBI	SB	BB	SO	AVG
1992	30	108	15	24	7	1	3	10	2	8	24	.222
Career	30	108	15	24	7	1	3	10	2	8	24	.222

HITTING, FIELDING, BASERUNNING:

One of two young prospects the Mets acquired in last August's "rent-a-pitcher" deal with Toronto for David Cone, Ryan Thompson made great progress as a hitter in 1992. The young outfielder batted .282 for the Blue Jays' Syracuse farm club in his first year at the AAA level. Thompson then showed promise in his 30-game trial with the Mets, though he batted only .222.

Last year Thompson adopted a shorter and more compact swing with more wrist action, and found that he got more power than he had with his old looping swing. Thompson had never hit more than eight home runs before 1992, but hit 17 last year for Syracuse and New York combined. He is learning the strike zone and studying pitchers. He still strikes out a whole lot (138 times last season), but he's beginning to draw some walks (51).

Thompson has good speed and is a definite threat to steal. With increased knowledge of pitchers and situations, he will be a big asset on the bases. He covers ground well in center field and has a good arm.

OVERALL:

New York hasn't had a good center fielder since they traded Lenny Dykstra. Thompson will be given every chance to win that job in 1993. He is a good talent with speed and power, and the club has high hopes for him.

ORGANIZATION OVERVIEW:

The Mets were baseball's best organization for a period of about five years, ending abruptly when -- as heavy favorites -- they lost in the 1988 playoffs to the Dodgers. You could argue that the Mets still haven't recovered from that shocker. Since then they've made a number of deals for aging veterans, hoping for a quick fix while letting go of some very good talent (both young and old). As for the Met farm system, it's been awhile since they've produced an impact player. Last year their top three prospects were Todd Hundley, Jeromy Burnitz and Anthony Young. Where are the Straw-men of yesteryear?

JEROMY N. BURNITZ

Position: OF **Opening Day Age:** 23
Bats: L **Throws:** R **Born:** 4/14/69 in
Ht: 6' 0" **Wt:** 190 Westminster, CA

Recent Statistics

	G	AB	R	H	D	T	HR	RBI	SB	BB	SO	AVG
91 AA Williamsprt	135	457	80	103	16	10	31	85	31	104	127	.225
92 AAA Tidewater	121	445	56	108	21	3	8	40	30	33	84	.243
92 MLE	121	429	43	92	18	2	6	31	22	25	90	.214

The Mets' number-one pick in 1990, Burnitz was a 30-30 man at AA Williamsport in 1991 (31 homers, 31 steals). Moved up to AAA Tidewater last year, he reached the 30s in one category, but the least interesting one, stolen bases. Burnitz hit only eight homers for the Tides and batted just .243. He did cut his strikeout total from 127 to 85, but his walks also dropped from 104 to 33. Burnitz will undoubtedly get another year in AAA to straighten himself out --if he can.

BROOK A. FORDYCE

Position: C **Opening Day Age:** 22
Bats: R **Throws:** R **Born:** 5/7/70 in New
Ht: 6' 1" **Wt:** 185 London, CT

Recent Statistics

	G	AB	R	H	D	T	HR	RBI	SB	BB	SO	AVG
91 A St. Lucie	115	406	42	97	19	3	7	55	4	37	51	.239
92 AA Binghamton	118	425	59	118	30	0	11	61	1	37	78	.278
92 MLE	118	412	49	105	26	0	8	51	0	26	85	.255

Todd Hundley was supposed to be the Mets' catcher of the future, but his tepid performance in 1992 left the door open for Brook Fordyce, who's a year younger. Hundley is probably the better catcher at this point, but that's not much of a knock on the improving Fordyce. The hope is that he'll be a better hitter than Hundley. Fordyce has a .284 career minor-league average, with 11 homers at AA Binghamton last year. He'll probably be at the AAA level this year.

BUTCH HUSKEY

Position: 3B **Opening Day Age:** 21
Bats: R **Throws:** R **Born:** 11/10/71 in
Ht: 6' 3" **Wt:** 240 Anadarko, OK

Recent Statistics

	G	AB	R	H	D	T	HR	RBI	SB	BB	SO	AVG
91 A Columbia	134	492	88	141	27	5	26	99	22	54	90	.287
92 A St. Lucie	134	493	65	125	17	1	18	75	7	33	74	.254

Since all the Mets' power hitters seem to have been around since Casey Stengel was manager, one can understand their excitement about third baseman Butch Huskey. Huskey belted 26 homers for the Mets Class A farm club at Columbia in 1991, and last year he had 18 more for St. Lucie in the Florida State League. A former defensive end prospect, Huskey has weighed as much as 280 pounds, but he has good speed and defensive reactions. He hit only .254 last year, but he's still only 21.

BOBBY JONES

Position: P **Opening Day Age:** 23
Bats: R **Throws:** R **Born:** 2/10/70 in
Ht: 6' 4" **Wt:** 210 Fresno, CA

Recent Statistics

	W	L	ERA	G	GS	Sv	IP	H	R	BB	SO	HR
91 A Columbia	3	1	1.85	5	5	0	24.1	20	5	3	35	2
92 AA Binghamton	12	4	1.88	24	24	0	158.0	118	40	43	143	5

The next Dwight Gooden? No. The next David Cone? Not really. The Mets' number-one pick in 1991, Jones doesn't throw as hard as either of those aces. But he looks awfully good. A college star at Fresno State, Jones has a lifetime minor-league ERA of 1.88, a record of 15-5, 178 strikeouts and only 46 walks allowed in 182.1 innings. He's said to have great command of all his pitches, though none are really overpowering. He should be at AAA this year, possibly not for the whole season.

JOE VITKO

Position: P **Opening Day Age:** 23
Bats: R **Throws:** R **Born:** 2/2/70 in
Ht: 6' 8" **Wt:** 210 Somerville, NJ

Recent Statistics

	W	L	ERA	G	GS	Sv	IP	H	R	BB	SO	HR
92 AA Binghamton	12	8	3.49	26	26	0	165.0	163	76	53	89	11
92 NL New York	0	1	13.50	3	1	0	4.2	12	11	1	6	1

A 6'8" giant who played basketball at St. Francis (PA) College, Vitko had a fine year at AA Binghamton last year, and the Mets used him in three late-season appearances. Vitko has a minor league record of 37-19, and he already has a good repertoire of pitches. He's not as overpowering as he looks, but he can throw in the high 80s and he has good control. The big guy's not afraid to throw inside; he hit 12 batters last year. He'll probably be in AAA this year.

PITCHING:

The nightmare never seemed to end last year for Kyle Abbott. The young lefthander lost seven straight decisions before being mercifully sent to the minors for a much-needed psyche massage. It was a first full major-league season that Abbott will have to forget. But though he was obviously a big disappointment, he did not always pitch as bad as his record indicated.

With a bad team behind him, Abbott was often burned by lack of support. In several of his defeats, he pitched solid baseball but had one bad inning that would end up beating him. Still, the numbers don't all lie. Opponents hit .283 against Abbott, they had a .338 on-base percentage against him, and he allowed a staff-high 20 home runs. The southpaw allowed lefty swingers to shellack him for a .326 average.

The jury thus remains out on the former Angels number-one draft pick. One problem is that Abbott still has not developed a major-league caliber change-up to go along with an average fastball and decent curve. Abbott also continues to pitch too deep into counts. Lacking one overpowering pitch, he's in trouble when he has to pitch from behind. Of course, when a young pitcher loses as much as Abbott did, an organization wonders about whether his mental makeup will suffer irrevocable damage.

HOLDING RUNNERS, FIELDING, HITTING:

Abbott is more than passable at holding runners. He has worked to shorten his stride in his stretch delivery, and it has helped; despite all the baserunners he allowed last year, he permitted only nine steals in 16 attempts. He is an average fielder. Abbott may never help himself with the bat; he put the ball into play on only half his plate appearances, striking out the rest of the time.

OVERALL:

The Phillies gave Abbott every possible chance to nail down a job in the rotation, but he still couldn't do it. He ended the year being used mostly in middle relief; that might be his immediate future with Philadelphia.

KYLE ABBOTT

Position: SP/RP
Bats: L **Throws:** L
Ht: 6' 4" **Wt:** 195

Opening Day Age: 25
Born: 2/18/68 in Newbury Port, MA
ML Seasons: 2

Overall Statistics

	W	L	ERA	G	GS	Sv	IP	H	R	BB	SO	HR
1992	1	14	5.13	31	19	0	133.1	147	80	45	88	20
Career	2	16	5.06	36	22	0	153.0	169	91	58	100	22

How Often He Throws Strikes

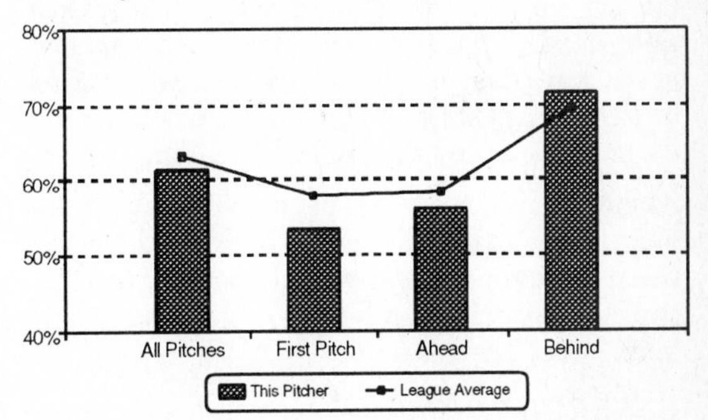

1992 Situational Stats

	W	L	ERA	Sv	IP		AB	H	HR	RBI	AVG
Home	1	7	5.64	0	75.0	LHB	129	42	3	17	.326
Road	0	7	4.47	0	58.1	RHB	391	105	17	55	.269
Day	0	3	4.74	0	38.0	Sc Pos	119	30	4	46	.252
Night	1	11	5.29	0	95.1	Clutch	20	9	2	6	.450

1992 Rankings (National League)

- 1st in lowest winning percentage (.067)
- 3rd in losses (14) and home runs allowed (20)
- 5th in highest batting average allowed vs. left-handed batters (.326)
- 8th in wild pitches (9)
- 9th in highest batting average allowed vs. right-handed batters (.269)
- Led the Phillies in losses, home runs allowed, wild pitches and runners caught stealing

HITTING:

Projected as a fourth or fifth outfielder when the Phillies acquired him from California before last season, Ruben Amaro ended up getting much more playing time than anticipated due to injuries suffered by Lenny Dykstra, Wes Chamberlain and Dale Murphy. Unfortunately, the extra exposure did nothing to alter the impression that Amaro is not a front-line player. After a brief hot spell which included three April homers, Amaro wound up batting only .219 in his rookie season.

Amaro did show some surprising power, especially batting from the left side. However, the switch-hitter batted nearly 60 points higher as a righty and struck out far less often from that side. For the most part he looked overmatched against right-handed pitching, save for the occasional home run (five in 220 at-bats). He was buried inside by hard stuff and then often would go out of the strike zone trying to hit a breaking ball.

Amaro was also very sub-par in the clutch. He hit only .155 with men in scoring position, the worst such mark for players with 100 or more plate appearances. He also hit only .197 in the late innings of close games.

BASERUNNING:

Amaro is a better-than-average runner, one who can steal an occasional base and has solid instincts on the bases. If he is going to stay in the majors, he needs to improve his on-base percentage to better use his decent running ability.

FIELDING:

Amaro's greatest strength at this point is his defense. He has center field ability, possessing excellent range while rarely misjudging balls. He also has a good throwing arm, even when judged as a center fielder.

OVERALL:

The Phillies worry that Amaro's best production came in early April and in September, the two periods which baseball people agree can be the most illusory. Amaro has enough tools to be useful in a reserve role. However, he is not likely to ever be an adequate everyday player.

RUBEN AMARO

Position: RF/LF/CF
Bats: B **Throws:** R
Ht: 5'10" **Wt:** 170

Opening Day Age: 28
Born: 2/12/65 in Philadelphia, PA
ML Seasons: 2

Overall Statistics

	G	AB	R	H	D	T	HR	RBI	SB	BB	SO	AVG
1992	126	374	43	82	15	6	7	34	11	37	54	.219
Career	136	397	43	87	16	6	7	36	11	40	57	.219

Where He Hits the Ball

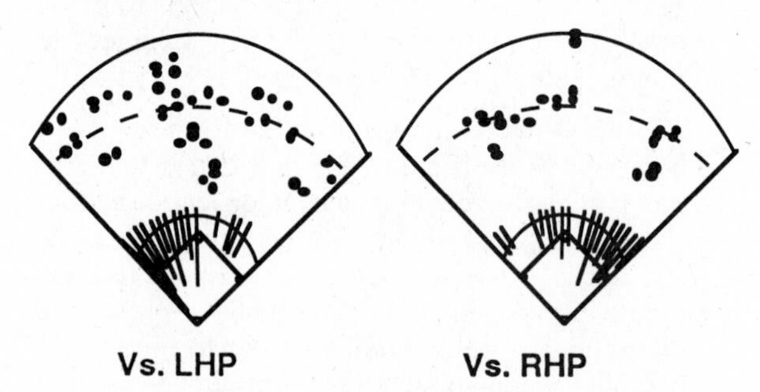

1992 Situational Stats

	AB	H	HR	RBI	AVG		AB	H	HR	RBI	AVG
Home	169	36	5	17	.213	LHP	154	39	2	17	.253
Road	205	46	2	17	.224	RHP	220	43	5	17	.195
Day	123	24	3	11	.195	Sc Pos	84	13	0	24	.155
Night	251	58	4	23	.231	Clutch	66	13	1	3	.197

1992 Rankings (National League)

- 1st in lowest batting average with runners in scoring position (.155)
- 2nd in lowest batting average with the bases loaded (.077)
- 3rd in hit by pitch (9)
- Led the Phillies in lowest percentage of swings that missed (15.6%) and highest percentage of swings put into play (47.9%)
- Led NL right fielders in hit by pitch

JUAN BELL

Position: SS
Bats: B **Throws:** R
Ht: 5'11" **Wt:** 176

Opening Day Age: 25
Born: 3/29/68 in San Pedro de Macoris, Dominican Republic
ML Seasons: 4

Overall Statistics

	G	AB	R	H	D	T	HR	RBI	SB	BB	SO	AVG
1992	46	147	12	30	3	1	1	8	5	18	29	.204
Career	159	362	41	66	12	3	2	23	6	26	82	.182

Where He Hits the Ball

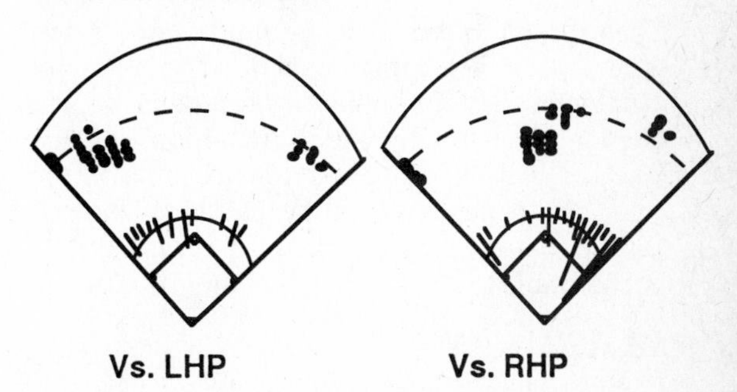

1992 Situational Stats

	AB	H	HR	RBI	AVG		AB	H	HR	RBI	AVG
Home	70	14	1	6	.200	LHP	62	12	0	3	.194
Road	77	16	0	2	.208	RHP	85	18	1	5	.212
Day	36	6	0	1	.167	Sc Pos	27	5	0	7	.185
Night	111	24	1	7	.216	Clutch	23	4	1	2	.174

1992 Rankings (National League)

- Did not rank near the top or bottom in any category

HITTING:

Still only 25, Juan Bell remains an intriguing prospect. However, George Bell's little brother is now playing for his third different organization (the Dodgers and Orioles were the others). The reasons that Bell keeps being dealt are his attitude and poor hitting. He has long been known as a problem player who does not take advice very well. However, Phils general manager Lee Thomas only had to give up journeyman Steve Scarsone for Bell and felt it to be a good gamble because of Bell's physical skills.

Bell seemed to have matured upon joining the Phillies, but the question still remains whether he will ever hit. He tends to overswing and strikes out far too much for someone with so little power. However, he showed improved discipline with the Phillies, drawing 18 walks in 168 plate appearances. He needs to cut down his swing and use the whole field instead of trying to slash every pitch. A switch-hitter, Bell batted only .194 righty, .212 lefty. As one scout said late in the season, "What's the point of switch-hitting if that's all you get out of it?"

BASERUNNING:

Bell has the speed to be a good basestealer. He stole five bases for the Phillies without being caught. But he also has poor instincts and is prone to making mistakes of over-aggressiveness on the bases.

FIELDING:

Bell is a natural shortstop and that's where the Phillies hope he can settle in. No less an authority than Larry Bowa, the former great Philadelphia shortstop, is positive about Bell's defensive skill. "He catches everything and has a good arm. He can play in the field, there's no question about that," said Bowa, now a Phils coach.

OVERALL:

Philadelphia liked what they saw of Bell and protected him in the expansion draft. If their lineup is healthy, they can afford to carry his weak bat in exchange for his defense. If they don't make a move for an established shortstop, the job will likely be Bell's to lose this spring.

HITTING:

Wes Chamberlain was his own worst enemy in a disappointing 1992 season in which he was demoted to the minor leagues. Nevertheless, the campaign could prove to be a turning point for the talented outfielder.

Chamberlain strutted through spring training overweight and arrogant, exuding the unmistakable air of someone who thought he had it made in the majors. But when he played abysmally for the first several weeks of the season, he was summarily dispatched to AAA Scranton. To his credit, Chamberlain eventually stopped sulking, got his swing together and returned to play well until a serious ankle injury ended his season prematurely.

Chamberlain appeared to be much more disciplined after his banishment to Triple-A, not swinging solely for home runs for which he was often guilty, but willing to shorten his swing and take the ball to right field when behind in the count. He remains a good fastball hitter but can still be fooled easily by changing speeds and by pitchers able to mix up their pitching pattern.

BASERUNNING:

Chamberlain's speed is above average but his baserunning instincts are poor. Left to his own devices, he is an accident waiting to happen. He remains a high-percentage basestealer, though one who seldom gets the green light from the coaches. He was 4-for-4 in 1992 and is 17-for-21 in his career.

FIELDING:

Chamberlain fits into the Phillies' left-field tradition of Greg Luzinski, Lonnie Smith and Gary Matthews; namely, someone with serious fundamental flaws. He was averaging a mistake a day early last season.

OVERALL:

The Phillies hope they will see more of the Chamberlain who played well late last season than the immature liability he was for much of the year. No one denies his talent. But until the attitude changes and the ability is harnessed more consistently, the jury will still be out on Chamberlain ever becoming the star some have predicted he would become.

WES CHAMBERLAIN

Position: RF/LF
Bats: R **Throws:** R
Ht: 6' 2" **Wt:** 210

Opening Day Age: 27
Born: 4/13/66 in Chicago, IL
ML Seasons: 3

Overall Statistics

	G	AB	R	H	D	T	HR	RBI	SB	BB	SO	AVG
1992	76	275	26	71	18	0	9	41	4	10	55	.258
Career	195	704	86	176	37	3	24	95	17	42	137	.250

Where He Hits the Ball

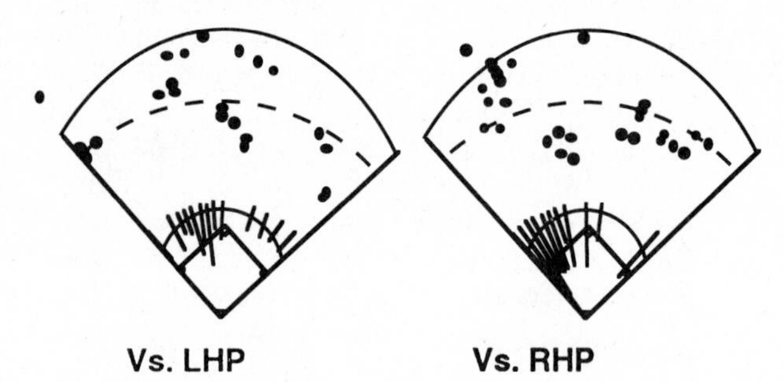

1992 Situational Stats

	AB	H	HR	RBI	AVG		AB	H	HR	RBI	AVG
Home	144	40	3	19	.278	LHP	104	27	3	15	.260
Road	131	31	6	22	.237	RHP	171	44	6	26	.257
Day	88	28	2	12	.318	Sc Pos	76	19	2	31	.250
Night	187	43	7	29	.230	Clutch	48	11	1	5	.229

1992 Rankings (National League)

- Did not rank near the top or bottom in any category

DARREN DAULTON

Position: C
Bats: L **Throws:** R
Ht: 6' 2" **Wt:** 195

Opening Day Age: 31
Born: 1/3/62 in Arkansas City, KS
ML Seasons: 9

HITTING:

It's not enough to say that Darren Daulton had a career season in 1992. The truth is that Daulton had the best offensive year by a National League catcher since the prime of Gary Carter over a decade ago. Since the RBI became an official stat in 1920, only four catchers have ever led the National League: Roy Campanella, Johnny Bench, Carter and now Daulton, with 109 last year.

How did it happen? One factor was health. Consumed by injuries for much of his career, Daulton stayed injury-free and was able to play 145 games. But he changed himself physically as well. Long one of the strongest Phillies and a weight-lifting aficionado, Daulton changed his off-season routine. He worked more on flexibility and light weights, enabling him to take some muscle off his upper body.

The result was better bat speed and the flexibility to turn on the high, inside pitch that used to tie him up. At the same time, Daulton reversed his reputation as a dead pull hitter. He learned to take breaking pitches away and send them to the opposite field instead of trying to pull them. As a result, he became one of the most dangerous hitters in baseball, especially in the clutch. He hit .299 with men in scoring position.

BASERUNNING:

Even after six different surgeries on his knees, Daulton is still one of the better running catchers in the game. He had 11 steals in 13 attempts last season.

FIELDING:

The Phillies staff has been notoriously bad in terms of control and holding runners, factors that make Daulton's defensive statistics worse than he deserves. He is the unquestioned team leader on the field and has become an excellent handler of pitchers.

OVERALL:

Daulton might never again approach his 1992 numbers, but he should remain a potent offensive force, given good health. The Phils are considering having him play some outfield. They want to extend his career and keep his bat in the lineup on days when he isn't catching.

Overall Statistics

	G	AB	R	H	D	T	HR	RBI	SB	BB	SO	AVG
1992	145	485	80	131	32	5	27	109	11	88	103	.270
Career	706	2114	263	492	105	9	75	309	32	341	441	.233

Where He Hits the Ball

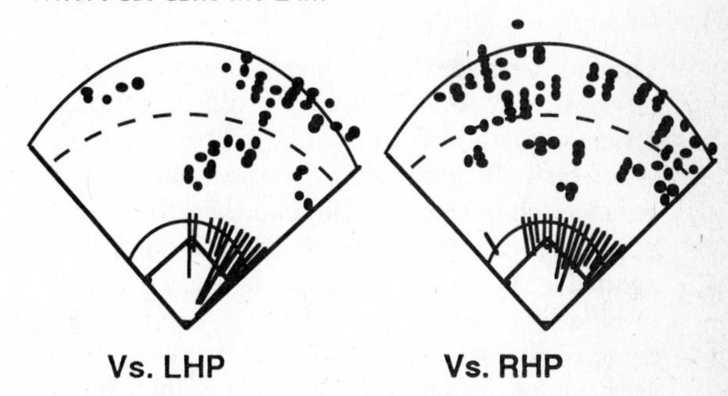

1992 Situational Stats

	AB	H	HR	RBI	AVG		AB	H	HR	RBI	AVG
Home	229	73	17	63	.319	LHP	202	52	11	40	.257
Road	256	58	10	46	.227	RHP	283	79	16	69	.279
Day	113	22	4	13	.195	Sc Pos	134	40	8	72	.299
Night	372	109	23	96	.293	Clutch	94	21	2	13	.223

1992 Rankings (National League)

- 1st in RBI (109)
- 2nd in lowest groundball/flyball ratio (.77)
- 3rd in least GDPs per GDP situation (2.4%)
- Led the Phillies in home runs, RBI, intentional walks (11), slugging percentage, HR frequency (18.0 ABs per HR), least GDPs per GDP situation, batting average at home (.319) and steals of third (3)
- Led NL catchers in batting average (.270), home runs (27), at-bats (485), runs scored (80), hits (131), doubles (32), triples (5), total bases (254), RBI, stolen bases (11), walks (88), times on base (225), strikeouts (103), games played (145), slugging percentage (.524) and on-base percentage (.385)

JOSE DeLEON

Position: SP/RP
Bats: R **Throws:** R
Ht: 6' 3" **Wt:** 226

Opening Day Age: 32
Born: 12/20/60 in Rancho Viejo, La Vega, Dominican Republic
ML Seasons: 10

Overall Statistics

	W	L	ERA	G	GS	Sv	IP	H	R	BB	SO	HR
1992	2	8	4.37	32	18	0	117.1	111	63	48	79	7
Career	75	113	3.73	293	261	4	1697.0	1397	774	745	1422	129

How Often He Throws Strikes

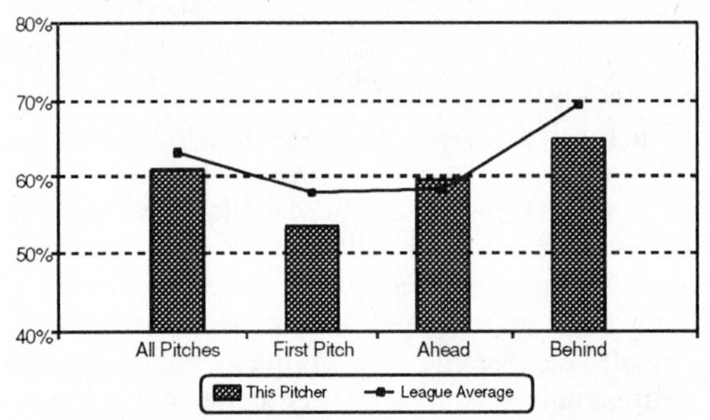

1992 Situational Stats

	W	L	ERA	Sv	IP		AB	H	HR	RBI	AVG
Home	2	3	3.33	0	67.2	LHB	245	69	5	33	.282
Road	0	5	5.80	0	49.2	RHB	199	42	2	20	.211
Day	1	3	5.71	0	34.2	Sc Pos	135	30	3	44	.222
Night	1	5	3.81	0	82.2	Clutch	8	2	0	2	.250

1992 Rankings (National League)

- Did not rank near the top or bottom in any category

PITCHING:

It will now be the Phillies' turn to solve an enigma that has previously frustrated three other organizations. The paradox of Jose DeLeon is well known: he has some of the best pure stuff in baseball, but has a career record 38 games under .500. This mystery has befuddled the Pirates, White Sox and St. Louis.

DeLeon has not always had good luck; he's been plagued throughout his career by lack of support. He has often compiled strong ERAs without them translating into victories. But DeLeon has also hurt himself by not better diversifying his repertoire of pitches. What other hurler could have been called "the best 2-19 pitcher in baseball," as DeLeon was in 1985?

The Phillies hope that Johnny Podres, the change-up guru, can teach DeLeon to mix an effective offspeed pitch into an established repertoire of a solid fastball, good slider, occasional split-fingered pitch and curve. Beyond that, the Phillies hope they can adjust DeLeon's attitude. The rap against him has often been that he's too nice a guy to be a big winner, so the Phils will presumably try to make DeLeon less nice. Perhaps this is one area where the sullen Philadelphia fans can help for a change.

HOLDING RUNNERS, FIELDING, HITTING:

DeLeon's delivery to the plate is slow and he has only an average pickoff move. But he usually does a decent job of holding runners; his work in 1992 (12 steals allowed in 17 attempts) was well below his norm. He is an adequate fielder. As a hitter he is no threat, but he at least can get a sacrifice bunt down on occasion.

OVERALL:

DeLeon's stock has fallen so far that when the Cardinals released him, only the Phillies -- sort of the Bob Vila of baseball, with their fondness for reclamation projects -- were willing to offer him a guaranteed contract for this season. However, there are no guarantees about him finally being a winning pitcher, or even being in the Philadelphia rotation. DeLeon could end up in long relief.

MARIANO DUNCAN

Position: LF/2B/SS
Bats: R **Throws:** R
Ht: 6' 0" **Wt:** 185

Opening Day Age: 30
Born: 3/13/63 in San Pedro de Macoris, Dominican Republic
ML Seasons: 7

HITTING:

Mariano Duncan wore down toward the end of last season, after receiving everyday duty for the first time since his rookie season of 1985. But he nevertheless had a solid year as the Phillies' version of Tony Phillips. Duncan got playing time at four different positions, left field and second base most frequently. Signs point him to opening this season as a platoon second baseman.

Duncan was among league leaders in doubles with 40 and his 50 RBI were the second-best total of his career. Duncan also improved his production against right-handed pitching, against whom he has been notoriously weak. He batted .254 vs. righthanders compared to the .286 mark he had against lefties.

However, Duncan also developed a habit of overswinging. He struck out 108 times, a terribly high total for someone who has never hit more than a dozen home runs in any season. Never a disciplined hitter, Duncan was helpless against breaking stuff low and away. With his once-short stroke becoming longer, he was also vulnerable at times to fastballs up and inside.

BASERUNNING:

Turned loose by manager Jim Fregosi and often batting in the second spot, Duncan stole 23 bases, his best total since he had 48 in 1986. He showed he can be a high-percentage basestealer by being caught only three times. He can be counted on to be a baserunning weapon this year.

FIELDING:

Duncan's never going to be a Gold Glover at any position he plays. He was erratic at second base last season as well as in his several starts at short. His arm is adequate for the infield, though its the cause of many of his errors. In the outfield, his arm is a liability and he has only average range.

OVERALL:

Duncan has a lot of flaws which aren't going to disappear at this stage of his career. However, his various offensive skills and versatility make him a useful commodity. He should get lots of playing time in 1993.

Overall Statistics

	G	AB	R	H	D	T	HR	RBI	SB	BB	SO	AVG
1992	142	574	71	153	40	3	8	50	23	17	108	.267
Career	788	2830	368	722	123	27	53	253	147	146	536	.255

Where He Hits the Ball

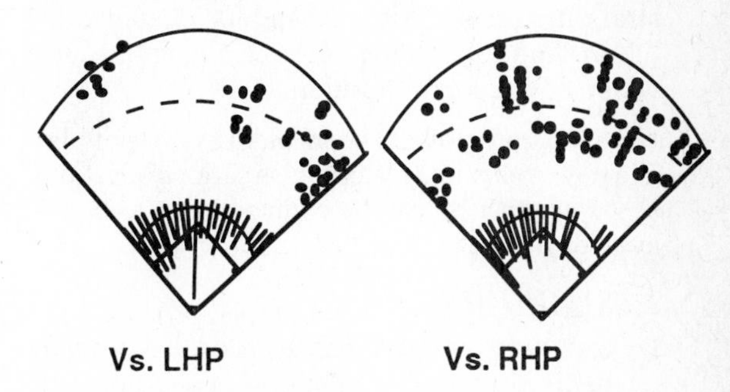

1992 Situational Stats

	AB	H	HR	RBI	AVG		AB	H	HR	RBI	AVG
Home	276	67	3	18	.243	LHP	231	66	4	19	.286
Road	298	86	5	32	.289	RHP	343	87	4	31	.254
Day	151	52	4	16	.344	Sc Pos	122	30	4	44	.246
Night	423	101	4	34	.239	Clutch	90	24	1	8	.267

1992 Rankings (National League)

- → 2nd in doubles (40) and stolen base percentage (88.5%)
- → 4th in strikeouts (108)
- → 5th in GDPs (15)
- → 7th in lowest on-base percentage (.292)
- → 8th in lowest batting average at home (.243)
- → Led the Phillies in doubles, GDPs, stolen base percentage and steals of third (3)
- → Led NL left fielders in at-bats (574), doubles, sacrifice bunts (5), strikeouts, GDPs and batting average on an 0-2 count (.220)

HITTING:

Lenny Dykstra had his thumb broken on the second pitch of the season. He came back too quickly and spent a month slumping. Then when he finally got things going and seemed to be revving up for a run at the batting title, he broke his wrist and missed the last two months. So that's two straight seasons of injuries for Dykstra, without whom the Phillies are nearly 40 games under .500.

There's nothing wrong with Dykstra's baseball skills. In his limited playing time last year he still had the speed to steal 30 bases in 35 attempts. He had a .375 on-base percentage. He was on a pace to drive in around 60 runs, score at least 90, and reach double figures in home runs. For the third straight year he hit lefthanders consistently (.322). And he was great in the clutch, hitting .368 with men in scoring position.

But Dykstra is now 30 years old. His style of play and recent physical history raise serious questions about whether he can be counted upon to be the everyday force the Phillies need him to be.

BASERUNNING:

Dykstra does not have blazing speed, but he reads pitchers exceptionally well and is a very quick starter making him an excellent basestealer. He also has superb baseball instincts that allow him to be an aggressive baserunner adept at taking the extra base.

FIELDING:

Only a handful of center fielders are in Dykstra's class in terms of getting a jump on the ball and aggressively taking chances. His arm is only average at best, but his accuracy, quick release and ability to charge balls still make him a threat to throw out runners.

OVERALL:

Dykstra is one of baseball's best leadoff men, an All-Star caliber player with charisma and a winning attitude. But to help the Phillies he needs to stay in the lineup. This could be a crucial year in his career. Another season of disabled list appearances could make him expendable.

LENNY DYKSTRA

Position: CF
Bats: L **Throws:** L
Ht: 5'10" **Wt:** 180

Opening Day Age: 30
Born: 2/10/63 in Santa Ana, CA
ML Seasons: 8

Overall Statistics

	G	AB	R	H	D	T	HR	RBI	SB	BB	SO	AVG
1992	85	345	53	104	18	0	6	39	30	40	32	.301
Career	931	3219	533	916	190	28	52	283	220	384	342	.285

Where He Hits the Ball

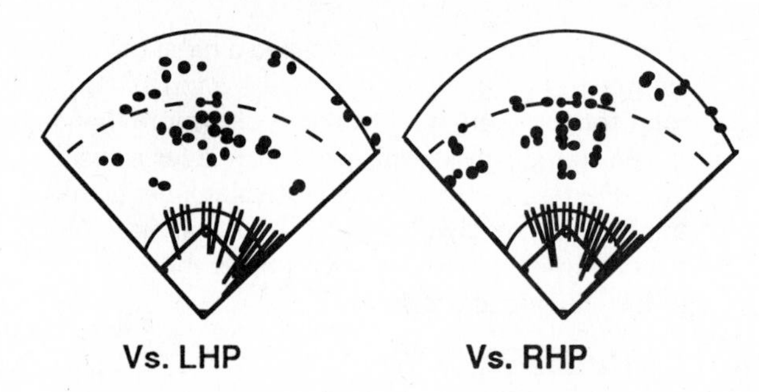

1992 Situational Stats

	AB	H	HR	RBI	AVG		AB	H	HR	RBI	AVG
Home	196	60	5	27	.306	LHP	146	47	4	23	.322
Road	149	44	1	12	.295	RHP	199	57	2	16	.286
Day	86	25	1	11	.291	Sc Pos	68	25	1	31	.368
Night	259	79	5	28	.305	Clutch	58	24	1	15	.414

1992 Rankings (National League)

- 1st in batting average in the clutch (.414)
- 2nd in batting average with 2 strikes (.299)
- 3rd in batting average on a 3-2 count (.389)
- 4th in stolen base percentage (85.7%)
- Led the Phillies in stolen bases (30), batting average in the clutch, batting average on a 3-2 count, batting average with 2 strikes, steals of third (3) and outfield assists (6)
- Led NL center fielders in batting average in the clutch, batting average on a 3-2 count and batting average with 2 strikes

TOMMY GREENE

Position: SP
Bats: R **Throws:** R
Ht: 6' 5" **Wt:** 225

Opening Day Age: 26
Born: 4/6/67 in Lumberton, NC
ML Seasons: 4

PITCHING:

Seemingly on the verge of stardom after a 1991 season which featured a 13-7 record and a no-hitter at Montreal on May 23, Tommy Greene spent most of last season rehabilitating a sore arm. He made only 12 starts and only rarely displayed the overpowering fastball that seemed to promise the Phillies 200-strikeout, 18- to 20-win seasons for years to come.

Greene's ability and 1991 success forced the Phillies to be patient. But they developed some questions about his toughness and willingness to take advice. His fragile psyche needs constant reinforcing. He has required constant instruction aimed at improving his change-up and making his curve a sharper and later-breaking pitch.

Greene did go 3-3 last season, but he allowed opponents to hit him for a .291 average and his ERA was a career-high 5.32. He permitted almost as many walks (34) as he had strikeouts (39). The Phillies weren't too concerned because they knew he was injured. He eased their concern with some decent late-season efforts. However, his velocity must be in the low 90s for him to be effective; for Greene to throw like that, he needs to feel completely healthy.

HOLDING RUNNERS, FIELDING, HITTING:

Two years ago, Greene was among the best hitting pitchers in baseball. However, like his pitching, his hitting deteriorated in '92. Greene managed only three hits and struck out on 12 of his 24 at-bats. He should be better than that. Greene's a solid, athletic fielder but he is very easy to run upon because of his slow delivery and a nondescript move to first. Although he only pitched 64.1 innings, he permitted 13 steals in 14 attempts last year -- a ridiculously high total.

OVERALL:

Like so many other Phillies, Greene enters the 1993 season shrouded in question marks because of injuries. Yes, he must be healthy and if he is, he can be a dominant pitcher. But Greene must answer questions about his attitude that cropped up in Philadelphia as well.

Overall Statistics

	W	L	ERA	G	GS	Sv	IP	H	R	BB	SO	HR
1992	3	3	5.32	13	12	0	64.1	75	39	34	39	5
Career	20	15	4.04	68	52	0	349.2	324	167	132	231	37

How Often He Throws Strikes

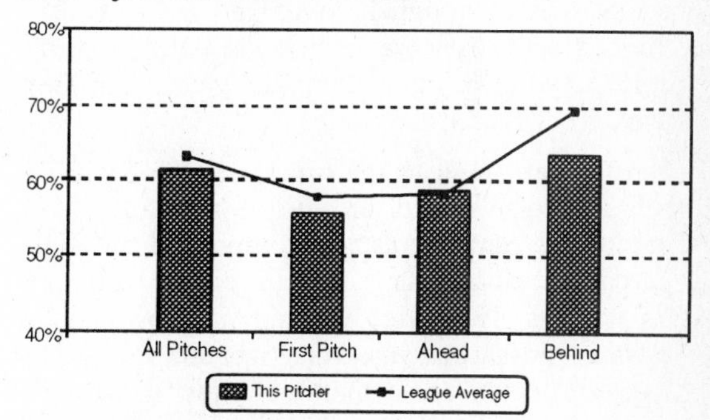

1992 Situational Stats

	W	L	ERA	Sv	IP		AB	H	HR	RBI	AVG
Home	2	0	3.26	0	30.1	LHB	127	47	2	15	.370
Road	1	3	7.15	0	34.0	RHB	131	28	3	16	.214
Day	1	2	8.31	0	13.0	Sc Pos	71	19	2	25	.268
Night	2	1	4.56	0	51.1	Clutch	3	2	0	1	.667

1992 Rankings (National League)

- 1st in highest batting average allowed vs. left-handed batters (.370)
- Led the Phillies in stolen bases allowed (13)

MIKE HARTLEY

Position: RP
Bats: R **Throws:** R
Ht: 6' 1" **Wt:** 197

Opening Day Age: 31
Born: 8/31/61 in Hawthorne, CA
ML Seasons: 4

PITCHING:

Mike Hartley is one of those pitchers who fills a role in workman-like fashion. The righthander was one of the better pitchers on a very shaky Philadelphia staff last year, turning in a 7-6 record and a 3.44 ERA in 46 relief outings. The problem is that Hartley is reaching an age and salary level where the Phillies might decide they could get as much from a younger and cheaper alternative.

Though he has worked almost exclusively as a reliever during his major-league career -- except for six starts with the Dodgers in 1990 -- there's always been suspicion that Hartley might eventually be more successful as a starting pitcher. Indeed, in his six career starts Hartley went 3-2 with a 2.52 ERA, though he averaged less than six innings a start. However, the Phils never really considered that option, even last year when they used 15 different starters.

Hartley remained in the middle and long relief role where he's been for most of his career. And he did a decent job, using an improved split-fingered fastball and curve to strike out 53 batters in 55 innings. However, a string of blown leads toward midseason caused manager Jim Fregosi to lose confidence somewhat in Hartley. In the second half, his work was largely of the mop-up variety.

HOLDING RUNNERS, FIELDING, HITTING:

Hartley has no pickoff move to speak of and his slow delivery makes him easy to run on. Such a flaw hurts him as a middle reliever who are usually in a position to hold his team close and thus can't afford allowing runners to take extra bases. He's an adequate fielder and no threat as a hitter.

OVERALL:

Hartley is the classic journeyman pitcher who can give a club some decent innings but isn't likely to ever break through as a closer or quality starter. In this budget-conscious age, his ability to make the Phillies roster will depend as much on his salary as it does on his pitching.

Overall Statistics

	W	L	ERA	G	GS	Sv	IP	H	R	BB	SO	HR
1992	7	6	3.44	46	0	0	55.0	54	23	23	53	5
Career	17	11	3.50	141	6	3	223.2	188	96	100	196	23

How Often He Throws Strikes

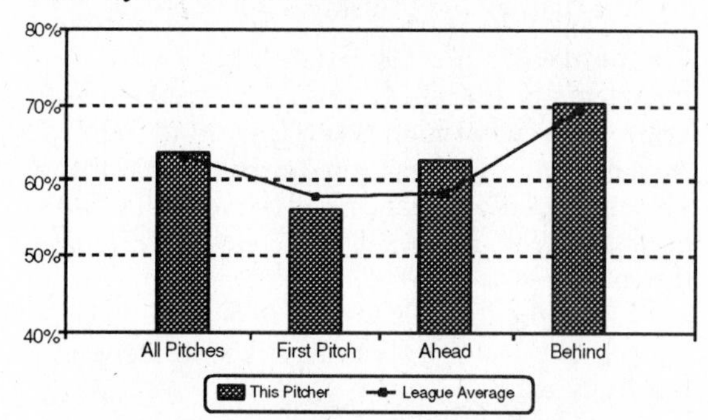

1992 Situational Stats

	W	L	ERA	Sv	IP		AB	H	HR	RBI	AVG
Home	3	2	3.65	0	24.2	LHB	107	27	0	9	.252
Road	4	4	3.26	0	30.1	RHB	105	27	5	17	.257
Day	2	4	4.50	0	16.0	Sc Pos	78	17	2	23	.218
Night	5	2	3.00	0	39.0	Clutch	104	24	2	12	.231

1992 Rankings (National League)

- 6th in relief wins (7)
- 9th in most strikeouts per 9 innings in relief (8.7)
- Led the Phillies in holds (8), relief ERA (3.44), relief wins, least baserunners allowed per 9 innings in relief (12.9) and most strikeouts per 9 innings in relief

FUTURE ALL-STAR

DAVE HOLLINS

Position: 3B
Bats: B **Throws:** R
Ht: 6' 1" **Wt:** 205

Opening Day Age: 26
Born: 5/25/66 in Buffalo, NY
ML Seasons: 3

Overall Statistics

	G	AB	R	H	D	T	HR	RBI	SB	BB	SO	AVG
1992	156	586	104	158	28	4	27	93	9	76	110	.270
Career	284	851	136	224	38	6	38	129	10	103	164	.263

Where He Hits the Ball

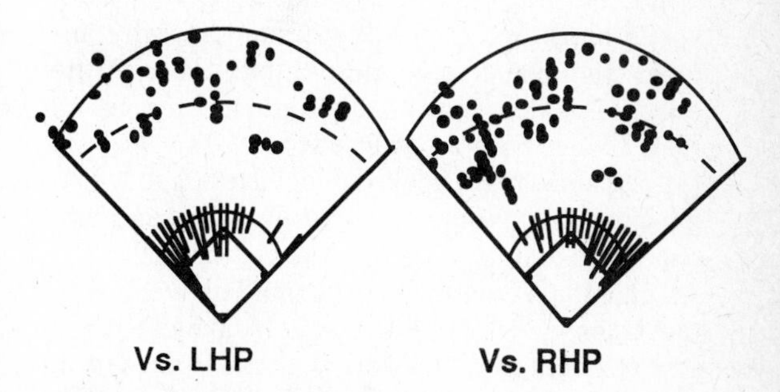

1992 Situational Stats

	AB	H	HR	RBI	AVG		AB	H	HR	RBI	AVG
Home	291	77	14	48	.265	LHP	245	79	17	45	.322
Road	295	81	13	45	.275	RHP	341	79	10	48	.232
Day	159	43	11	35	.270	Sc Pos	164	43	4	55	.262
Night	427	115	16	58	.269	Clutch	97	23	4	16	.237

1992 Rankings (National League)

- 1st in hit by pitch (19)
- 2nd in runs scored (104), strikeouts (110) and slugging percentage vs. left-handed pitchers (.620)
- 4th in home runs (27), batting average with the bases loaded (.500), lowest batting average vs. right-handed pitchers (.232) and lowest slugging percentage vs. right-handed pitchers (.361)
- Led the Phillies in home runs, at-bats (586), runs scored, total bases (275), caught stealing (6), hit by pitch, strikeouts, pitches seen (2,635), plate appearances (685), games played (156) and slugging percentage vs. left-handed pitchers

HITTING:

It was a breakthrough 1992 season for Dave Hollins, who established himself as one of the National League's emerging young stars. Always considered one of the Phillies' strongest players physically, Hollins translated that strength into 27 home runs and a .469 slugging percentage. He finally gave Philadelphia hope that there is life at third base after Mike Schmidt.

And there's still room for improvement. A switch-hitter, Hollins batted 90 points higher batting right-handed than left. He is also more powerful against left-handed pitching, hitting 17 home runs in just 245 at-bats and compiling a whopping .620 slugging percentage against southpaws. If he can quicken his left-handed stroke, Hollins is a potential 30-35 home run man.

While right-handed pitchers can get him out with hard stuff in and breaking balls away, Hollins appears quicker on the inside pitch when he is batting against lefthanders. He crowds the plate from both sides, as evidenced by the league-leading 19 times he was hit by pitches last season. He remains prone to the strikeout but has developed patience at the plate. Hollins had 76 walks last year and should become even more selective as he gains experience.

BASERUNNING:

Hollins has average speed but is an aggressive runner who will try for the extra base and go hard into second to break up double plays. He can also steal an occasional base, though his percentage last year (nine steals in 15 attempts) was among the worst on a Phillies club that led the majors in stolen base percentage (80 percent).

FIELDING:

Hollins has had a history of shoulder problems causing him some throwing difficulties. Those troubles accounted for the majority of his errors. However, he has made himself into an adequate third baseman who should continue to improve.

OVERALL:

Hollins was a steal via the Rule V major-league draft out of the San Diego organization. Barring injuries, he should be the Phillies' third baseman for years to come with a chance to be one of the league's premier players.

PITCHING:

"Have Arm, Will Travel" seems to be Danny Jackson's motto. The veteran lefthander seems intent on making a tour of the National League. In 1990, Jackson worked for the Reds. In 1991, it was the Cubs. In 1992, he outdid himself. After splitting the season between the Cubs and Pirates, Jackson was picked up by the Florida Marlins in the expansion draft. A few hours later, the Marlins had passed him on to the Philadelphia Phillies. Someday Jackson will be able to make his living appearing in a different club's old-timers game each week.

When a guy gets dealt as often as Jackson has been -- he also put in five seasons with the Royals -- it's obvious that he has talent (why a team wants him), and also a few problems (why another team wants to get rid of him). There's little question that Jackson has an arm people covet. He's always been a power pitcher with a 90-mph fastball and a hard, wicked slider. He began working on a change-up last season in Chicago and continued to improve it once he got to the Pirates. As usual, his results were mixed. His work with the Cubs (5-14 in a season and a half) made people doubt him; his work with the Pirates (4-4, 3.36 in 15 starts) raised his stock again, though he was a flop in the playoffs.

HOLDING RUNNERS, FIELDING, HITTING:

Jackson is a one-dimensional pitcher, not doing the "other things" well. For a lefthander he is not very good at holding runners. He is also unsure on bunts and not accurate on throws to bases. Jackson is one of the game's poorest hitters. He struggles to make contact and consistently fails on bunt attempts.

OVERALL:

Jackson gave the Pirates' rotation a boost in the second half of last season. They let him go unprotected in the expansion draft mostly because of his salary. The Phillies pride themselves on reviving careers; Jackson, who's revived himself more than once (including in 1992), might fit in perfectly with them.

DANNY JACKSON

Position: SP
Bats: R **Throws:** L
Ht: 6' 0" **Wt:** 205

Opening Day Age: 31
Born: 1/5/62 in San Antonio, TX
ML Seasons: 10

Overall Statistics

	W	L	ERA	G	GS	Sv	IP	H	R	BB	SO	HR
1992	8	13	3.84	34	34	0	201.1	211	99	77	97	6
Career	81	92	3.83	247	231	1	1478.1	1462	721	598	865	84

How Often He Throws Strikes

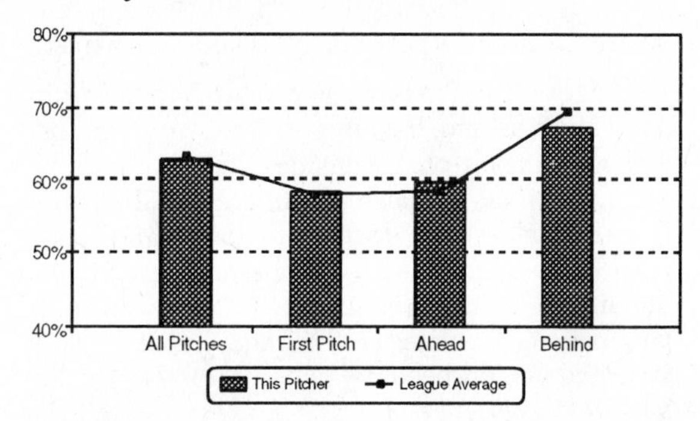

1992 Situational Stats

	W	L	ERA	Sv	IP		AB	H	HR	RBI	AVG
Home	6	4	2.85	0	116.2	LHB	118	29	2	14	.246
Road	2	9	5.21	0	84.2	RHB	657	182	4	66	.277
Day	4	6	3.65	0	81.1	Sc Pos	216	60	0	69	.278
Night	4	7	3.97	0	120.0	Clutch	43	18	1	4	.419

1992 Rankings (National League)

- 1st in highest ERA on the road (5.21), errors by a pitcher (8) and lowest fielding percentage by a pitcher (.840)
- 2nd in lowest strikeout/walk ratio (1.3), highest on-base percentage allowed (.337) and most baserunners allowed per 9 innings (13.1)
- 3rd in least home runs allowed per 9 innings (.27)
- 4th in games started (34)
- 5th in highest batting average allowed (.272), least pitches thrown per batter (3.40), least strikeouts per 9 innings (4.3) and highest batting average allowed vs. right-handed batters (.277)

HITTING:

The Phillies acquired Stan Javier from the Dodgers when they were running out of outfielders due to injuries last summer. Now 29, Javier has fashioned a useful career as a fourth or fifth outfielder whose specialty is speed and defense. The Phillies didn't expect miracles, and he provided none. But Javier played a lot of center field after Lenny Dykstra's season-ending hand injury and batted .261 while flashing his speed and some on-base ability. It was a satisfactory performance, and all the Phils could have expected.

Javier is a switch-hitter who has this problem: he's seldom effective from both sides in the same season. In 1992, he batted .271 lefty and .219 righty, doing almost all his RBI damage from the left side. But in 1991, he hit .152 lefty, .247 righty. In 1990, his best year (.298), Javier hit .286 from the left side, .315 from the right. You figure it out.

Javier has no power and hits the ball on the ground as much as possible, hoping to take advantage of his speed. He can be overpowered with hard stuff, especially when batting right-handed. Except for the years when he can be overpowered by hard stuff when batting left-handed.

BASERUNNING:

Baserunning is one of Javier's greatest strengths. He stole 18 bases last year while being caught only three times, improving his outstanding career percentage to 83-for-99 (84 percent). He also has good instincts in taking the extra base.

FIELDING:

Javier is used so often as a defensive replacement that he's played at least 110 games in each of the last five seasons while never batting even 400 times. He's a natural center fielder with outstanding range and a better-than-average arm, and the Phillies lost little with him replacing Dykstra.

OVERALL:

Javier brings some assets to the table, notably his running and defense. But his inconsistent hitting makes him a spare player. He was a free agent after the '92 season and figured to look for a club which needed a spare outfielder. The Phillies could do worse.

STAN JAVIER

Position: CF/LF/RF
Bats: B **Throws:** R
Ht: 6' 0" **Wt:** 185

Opening Day Age: 29
Born: 1/9/64 in San Francisco de Macoris, Dominican Republic
ML Seasons: 8

Overall Statistics

	G	AB	R	H	D	T	HR	RBI	SB	BB	SO	AVG
1992	130	334	42	83	17	1	1	29	18	37	54	.249
Career	758	1798	250	442	67	17	10	147	83	191	309	.246

Where He Hits the Ball

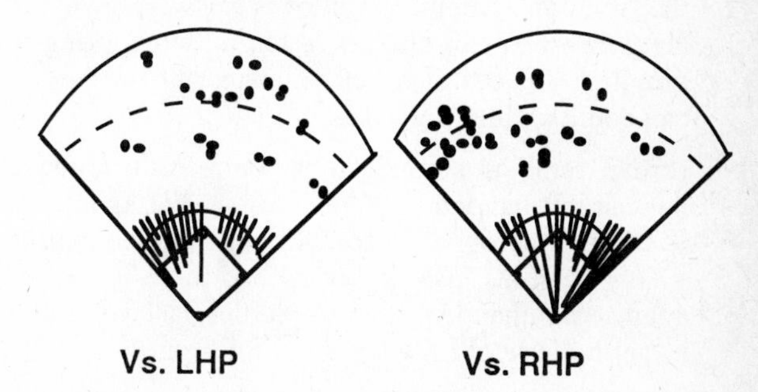

Vs. LHP Vs. RHP

1992 Situational Stats

	AB	H	HR	RBI	AVG		AB	H	HR	RBI	AVG
Home	150	41	1	16	.273	LHP	146	32	0	5	.219
Road	184	42	0	13	.228	RHP	188	51	1	24	.271
Day	94	20	0	4	.213	Sc Pos	79	22	1	27	.278
Night	240	63	1	25	.262	Clutch	64	10	0	5	.156

1992 Rankings (National League)

- 4th in lowest slugging percentage vs. left-handed pitchers (.288)
- 5th in stolen base percentage (85.7%)
- 7th in lowest batting average vs. left-handed pitchers (.219)
- 8th in lowest batting average in the clutch (.156)
- Led the Phillies in batting average on an 0-2 count (.261) and steals of third (3)
- Led NL center fielders in batting average on a 3-1 count (.500)

RICKY JORDAN

Position: 1B/LF
Bats: R **Throws:** R
Ht: 6' 3" **Wt:** 208

Opening Day Age: 27
Born: 5/26/65 in Richmond, CA
ML Seasons: 5

HITTING:

A broken jaw and the presence of John Kruk limited Ricky Jordan's playing time in 1992. But Jordan continued to offer glimpses of being a player who should play more, managing a .304 average with 34 RBI in only 276 at-bats. As usual, Jordan was a second-half terror, hitting .364 after the All-Star break. In his career, he's hit .257 before the break, .302 afterward.

The amazing thing about Jordan's high average was how undisciplined a hitter he continued to be. He walked only five times in those 276 at-bats, giving him 62 bases on balls in 500 major-league games. Jordan is a notorious high-ball hitter; teams stay away from the hard stuff and try to feed him offspeed breaking balls, especially on the first pitch when Jordan loves to swing away. Hard throwers can also retire Jordan by working him high and out of the strike zone, pitches they can count on him to chase.

Jordan remains a much more dangerous hitter against left-handed pitching. He hit .371 against southpaws as opposed to .243 vs. righthanders. That's been his history, but he had more at-bats against righthanders than vs. lefties last year, a rather odd use of his talents by Jim Fregosi.

BASERUNNING:

Jordan has decent speed for a big man and he can steal on rare occasions. He was three-for-three last year. He is also a better-than-average baserunner who has good instincts.

FIELDING:

Ever since coming into the majors, Jordan has been unfortunately known for having a terrible throwing arm. He rarely turns the 3-6-3 double play and is very unlikely to ever knock down the lead runner while fielding a bunt. However, he has good hands and decent range around the bag.

OUTLOOK:

In a perfect world, Jordan would be a platoon player. But his future is intriguing. The Phils protected him in the expansion draft, indicating they want to keep him around. They might even decide to shop John Kruk, thus banking on Jordan to be their everyday first baseman.

Overall Statistics

	G	AB	R	H	D	T	HR	RBI	SB	BB	SO	AVG
1992	94	276	33	84	19	0	4	34	3	5	44	.304
Career	500	1697	207	477	98	7	41	245	10	62	233	.281

Where He Hits the Ball

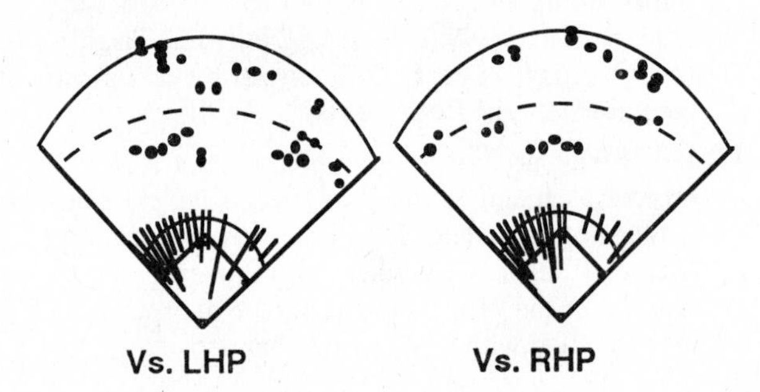

1992 Situational Stats

	AB	H	HR	RBI	AVG		AB	H	HR	RBI	AVG
Home	116	37	2	20	.319	LHP	132	49	3	21	.371
Road	160	47	2	14	.294	RHP	144	35	1	13	.243
Day	81	23	0	7	.284	Sc Pos	79	21	1	27	.266
Night	195	61	4	27	.313	Clutch	56	15	0	5	.268

1992 Rankings (National League)

- 2nd in batting average vs. left-handed pitchers (.371)
- Led the Phillies in batting average vs. left-handed pitchers
- Led NL first basemen in batting average vs. left-handed pitchers

HITTING:

Until wearing down with assorted physical woes, John Kruk was in the hunt for a batting title last year. But though he batted a career-high .323, things were not all positive for Kruk. His power numbers seriously deteriorated from 1991 when he hit 21 homers and drove in 92 runs; he had only 10 homers and 70 ribbies. As one National League pitching coach said, "When he got his average up there, he seemed to go away from the shorter stroke he used to pull balls for power and went back to hitting the opposite way for average."

With all that, Kruk continues to be one of the most solid hitters in the National League. He is difficult to pitch to because he can turn around most fastballs -- but if pitchers try working him away with breaking stuff, they're pitching to his basic strength, hitting to the opposite field. Kruk over the last two years has been nearly as effective against left-handed pitching as against right.

Kruk has also become increasingly disciplined. He cut down his strikeouts last season to 88 while upping his walks to a career-high 92. The combination produced a .423 on-base percentage, another career high.

BASERUNNING:

What with his knee problems and well-documented girth, Kruk is hardly a basestealing threat anymore. He is, however, aggressive on the basepaths, as evidenced by the 10 triples he's had over the last two seasons.

FIELDING:

A rumpled body belies Kruk's athleticism. He is a superb first baseman with excellent range and soft hands. He is also a solid outfielder with surprising range and an accurate arm. However, with his creaky knees and Veteran Stadium's artificial surface, Kruk will likely remain mostly at first.

OVERALL:

As outstanding as Kruk has been with the Phillies, there is concern that his physical problems could escalate as he grows older. There's been talk that Philadelphia would be willing to deal him at the right price. However, bats like Kruk's are hard to find.

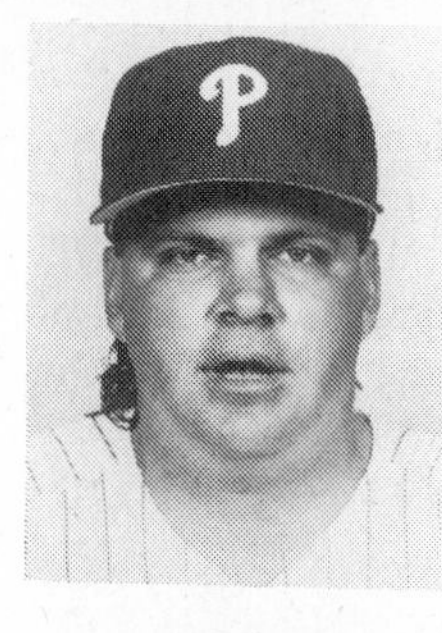

JOHN KRUK

Position: 1B/RF
Bats: L **Throws:** L
Ht: 5'10" **Wt:** 200

Opening Day Age: 32
Born: 2/9/61 in Charleston, WV
ML Seasons: 7

Overall Statistics

	G	AB	R	H	D	T	HR	RBI	SB	BB	SO	AVG
1992	144	507	86	164	30	4	10	70	3	92	88	.323
Career	930	2948	434	875	142	29	79	446	48	470	530	.297

Where He Hits the Ball

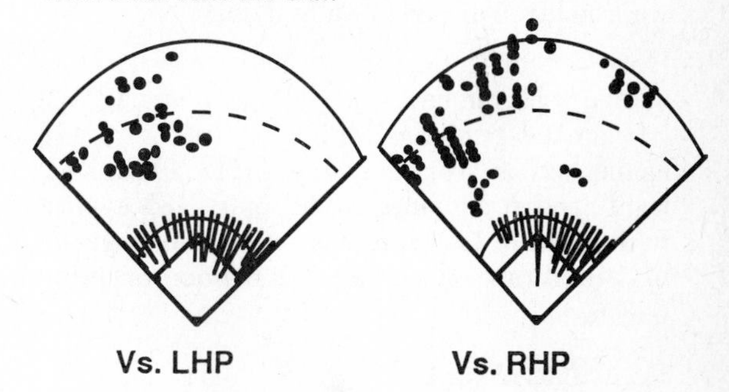

1992 Situational Stats

	AB	H	HR	RBI	AVG		AB	H	HR	RBI	AVG
Home	248	76	7	37	.306	LHP	210	66	1	18	.314
Road	259	88	3	33	.340	RHP	297	98	9	52	.330
Day	130	46	4	22	.354	Sc Pos	135	41	4	60	.304
Night	377	118	6	48	.313	Clutch	87	28	0	5	.322

1992 Rankings (National League)

- 1st in batting average on the road (.340)
- 2nd in on-base percentage (.423)
- 3rd in batting average (.324)
- 4th in highest groundball/flyball ratio (2.4)
- Led the Phillies in batting average, hits (164), singles (120), sacrifice flies (7), walks (92), times on base (257), on-base percentage, highest groundball/flyball ratio, most pitches seen per plate appearance (3.92), batting average with runners in scoring position (.304), batting average on a 3-1 count (.471), on-base percentage vs. left-handed pitchers (.414), batting average on the road and highest percentage of pitches taken (60.2%)

MICKEY MORANDINI

Position: 2B
Bats: L **Throws:** R
Ht: 5'11" **Wt:** 175

Opening Day Age: 26
Born: 4/22/66 in Kittanning, PA
ML Seasons: 3

HITTING:

Rated the Phillies' top prospect only two years go, Mickey Morandini is still trying to establish himself as an everyday player. In both 1991 and 1992, the young second sacker was handed stretches of regular duty but couldn't keep himself in the lineup. In each season, he wound up being benched, then returned later as a platoon player.

So who knows what to expect this year? Morandini adjusted his batting style toward the end of last season and the change seemed to help. He began using a heavier, thick-handled bat and concentrated on spraying the ball to all fields. He closed the year strongly (.283 September/October); the new bat allowed him to fight off the hard stuff inside that used to eat him up.

However, for Morandini to establish himself as an everyday player, he still needs to do better against left-handed pitching. Morandini hit only .198 against lefties last year, as opposed to .292 against right-handed pitching. He hit only .185 against lefthanders in 1991; until he gets that average up, he will always be viewed as a platoon or utility player.

BASERUNNING:

Morandini has decent speed and gets a good jump off first. However, the Phillies did not want him running ahead of John Kruk, preferring to give Kruk the hole on the right side. Thus, Morandini attempted only 11 steals. He is capable of taking the extra base.

FIELDING:

Morandini has made considerable improvement at second base since arriving in the majors. He has better-than-average range and an accurate arm. He is learning to hang in at second base while turning the double play, though that remains the one iffy part of his defense.

OVERALL:

At the least, Morandini is a solid extra infielder who won't hurt his team in the field and can chip in with some offense. If he could ever be just adequate against left-handed pitching, he could be even more valuable. But as of now, he appears likely to platoon at second with Mariano Duncan.

Overall Statistics

	G	AB	R	H	D	T	HR	RBI	SB	BB	SO	AVG
1992	127	422	47	112	8	8	3	30	8	25	64	.265
Career	250	826	94	212	23	12	5	53	24	60	128	.257

Where He Hits the Ball

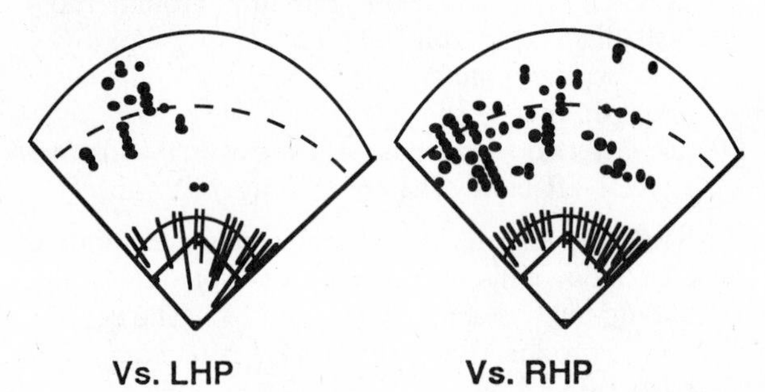

1992 Situational Stats

	AB	H	HR	RBI	AVG		AB	H	HR	RBI	AVG
Home	202	55	2	16	.272	LHP	121	24	1	8	.198
Road	220	57	1	14	.259	RHP	301	88	2	22	.292
Day	114	35	0	6	.307	Sc Pos	101	24	1	25	.238
Night	308	77	3	24	.250	Clutch	74	21	0	5	.284

1992 Rankings (National League)

- 1st in lowest batting average vs left-handed pitchers (.198) and lowest slugging percentage vs. left-handed pitchers (.248)
- 2nd in lowest on-base percentage vs. left-handed pitchers (.240)
- 5th in lowest batting average with the bases loaded (.091)
- 6th in triples (8)
- 10th in least GDPs per GDP situation (5.8%)
- Led the Phillies in triples and bunts in play (10)
- Led NL second basemen in least GDPs per GDP situation and batting average on an 0-2 count (.226)

PINPOINT CONTROL

TERRY MULHOLLAND

Position: SP
Bats: R **Throws:** L
Ht: 6' 3" **Wt:** 208

Opening Day Age: 30
Born: 3/9/63 in Uniontown, PA
ML Seasons: 6

PITCHING:

A chronic knee problem finally ended Terry Mulholland's season last September. But even though he labored at times because of the knee and a sore shoulder, Mulholland still managed to top the Phillies' staff with 229 innings and lead the league with 12 complete games. While pitching for weak clubs the last two years, he's gone 29-24.

Mulholland's 1992 ERA of 3.81 looks high, but it suffered because of a handful of starts in which he was bombed early. The knee was obviously bothering him later in the year; he was only 2-4 with a 5.28 ERA after August 1. But even then, he was consistently able to keep the Phillies in most of the games he started.

Until the knee problems affected his pushoff, Mulholland had the good sinking fastball which has become his out pitch. He mixes in an average slider and an improving change-up that is a key to his repertoire. Although only the best lefty swingers are usually permitted to face him, he held lefties to a lowly .211 batting average. He did have a few problems with righties, however (.272).

Mulholland is also a lefthander with great control, amongst the best southpaws in the league. For the second straight year, he averaged less than two walks per nine innings. His sinker is a big reason why he induced 14 double play grounders.

HOLDING RUNNERS, FIELDING, HITTING:

Mulholland has perhaps the best move to first in the National League. He picked off 16 runners last year. Combining the move with a quick delivery to the plate, he permitted only two steals in his 229 innings last year, an astonishingly low total. Mulholland is not a good fielder, though. Long an automatic out, he did manage eight hits last year.

OVERALL:

With his consistently good work over the last two seasons, Mulholland has established himself as one of the more dependable lefthanders in the league. If his knee responds to off-season surgery, it should be more of the same consistency in 1993.

Overall Statistics

	W	L	ERA	G	GS	Sv	IP	H	R	BB	SO	HR
1992	13	11	3.81	32	32	0	229.0	227	101	46	125	14
Career	45	49	3.87	148	126	0	857.2	868	398	215	453	58

How Often He Throws Strikes

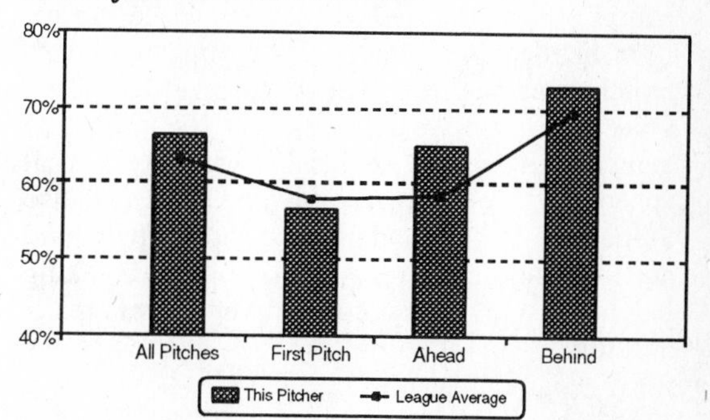

1992 Situational Stats

	W	L	ERA	Sv	IP		AB	H	HR	RBI	AVG
Home	9	6	3.63	0	146.1	LHB	161	34	4	18	.211
Road	4	5	4.14	0	82.2	RHB	710	193	10	73	.272
Day	3	5	4.29	0	65.0	Sc Pos	171	59	3	74	.345
Night	10	6	3.62	0	164.0	Clutch	93	26	1	10	.280

1992 Rankings (National League)

- 1st in complete games (12), lowest stolen base percentage allowed (28.6%), highest batting average allowed with runners in scoring position (.345) and runners picked off (16)
- 2nd in hits allowed (227) and most run support per 9 innings (5.0)
- Led the Phillies in games started (32), complete games, innings pitched (229), hits allowed, batters faced (937), pickoff throws (154), GDPs induced (14), highest strikeout/walk ratio (2.7), highest groundball/flyball ratio (1.4), lowest stolen base percentage allowed, least pitches thrown per batter (3.44), most run support per 9 innings and runners picked off

DALE MURPHY

Position: RF
Bats: R **Throws:** R
Ht: 6' 4" **Wt:** 221

Opening Day Age: 37
Born: 3/12/56 in Portland, OR
ML Seasons: 17

HITTING:

Once one of the premier players in baseball, Dale Murphy is now squarely facing the end of his career. Serious knee injuries ended the two-time MVP's 1992 season after only 62 at-bats. He managed only two home runs, leaving him still two short of 400 for his career. For Murphy, it must be frustrating to watch contemporaries like Dave Winfield, George Brett, Robin Yount and Eddie Murray still going strong. All of them are older than him.

Even before the injury, Murphy had shown signs of slowing down. His 18 homers in 1991 were his lowest total since the strike year of 1981, and he hasn't driven in 85 runs in a season since 1987. Murphy has struggled for quite a while against right-handed pitching and has appeared overmatched against the hardest throwing righties. Over the last five seasons, he's hit only .217 against righties, .274 against lefties. Murphy's bat speed has slowed appreciably and he is now also vulnerable to lefthanders who throw their hard stuff up and in. Murphy has become a breaking ball hitter, a tough way for a power hitter to make a living.

BASERUNNING:

Murphy stole 30 bases back in 1983, but age and his knee woes have turned him into one of the slower runners in all of baseball. He is no longer any basestealing threat; in 1991, his last full year, he made only one attempt. Though he still has aggressive instincts, his lack of speed makes such aggressiveness dangerous.

FIELDING:

Once one of the best outfielders in the game, Murphy's range has deteriorated significantly. He must play deep because of his problem going back on balls; he thus allows a lot of catchable balls to drop. His arm remains above average.

OVERALL:

There seems to be little chance that Murphy will be back in Philadelphia. The question is whether he can rehabilitate his knee and find a club that will be interested in giving him a look in spring training. However, most signs point to a great career at its end.

Overall Statistics

	G	AB	R	H	D	T	HR	RBI	SB	BB	SO	AVG
1992	18	62	5	10	1	0	2	7	0	1	13	.161
Career	2154	7918	1196	2105	349	39	398	1259	161	981	1733	.266

Where He Hits the Ball

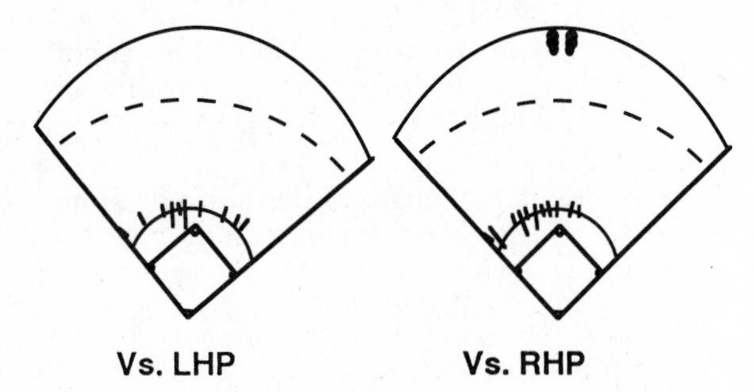

1992 Situational Stats

	AB	H	HR	RBI	AVG		AB	H	HR	RBI	AVG
Home	47	7	2	6	.149	LHP	31	6	1	3	.194
Road	15	3	0	1	.200	RHP	31	4	1	4	.129
Day	13	1	0	0	.077	Sc Pos	15	4	0	4	.267
Night	49	9	2	7	.184	Clutch	13	0	0	0	.000

1992 Rankings (National League)

- Did not rank near the top or bottom in any category

BEN RIVERA

Position: SP/RP
Bats: R **Throws:** R
Ht: 6' 6" **Wt:** 210

Opening Day Age: 24
Born: 1/11/69 in San Pedro De Macoris, Dominican Republic
ML Seasons: 1

PITCHING:

Barely known for anything more than his size and being able to throw hard, Ben Rivera arrived last year from Atlanta, and was made into a starting pitcher. He became one of the Phillies' most pleasant surprises. He made 14 starts for the Phils and was very impressive, going 7-3 with a 2.95 ERA in those outings. For the year opposing hitters batted only .230 against Rivera. He was especially tough on right-handed hitters who batted only .221 against him.

The big righthander has outstanding velocity, being clocked frequently in the 90-92 MPH range. He also has a good slider, but the key to his development was learning to a throw a change-up. He picked up the offspeed pitch very quickly and when he threw it for strikes, it made his imposing fastball even more effective.

Rivera had worked in the pitching-rich Braves system for a number of years, usually turning in good, but not great records. One thing that held him back was spotty control. Working with the Braves earlier last season, he permitted 13 walks in only 15.1 innings. But given regular rotation work by the Phillies, he was able to get the ball over the plate consistently. He had 66 strikeouts and only 32 walks in 102 Philadelphia innings, a solid ratio for a young pitcher with Rivera's stuff.

HOLDING RUNNERS, FIELDING AND HITTING:

Rivera's big, slow delivery makes it easy to run on him, but he began learning to hold runners better toward the end of last season. He still permitted 15 steals in only 117.1 innings, a high ratio. He is a crude fielder and is not a factor as a hitter.

OVERALL:

The Phillies don't think Rivera's impressive showing was a flash in the pan. They are counting on him to progress further and become a big part of their starting rotation. However, the one caution is that he's never made more than 27 starts in a season; he'll be watched for signs of wearing down. But with his size, he might not have any problems.

Overall Statistics

	W	L	ERA	G	GS	Sv	IP	H	R	BB	SO	HR
1992	7	4	3.07	28	14	0	117.1	99	40	45	77	9
Career	7	4	3.07	28	14	0	117.1	99	40	45	77	9

How Often He Throws Strikes

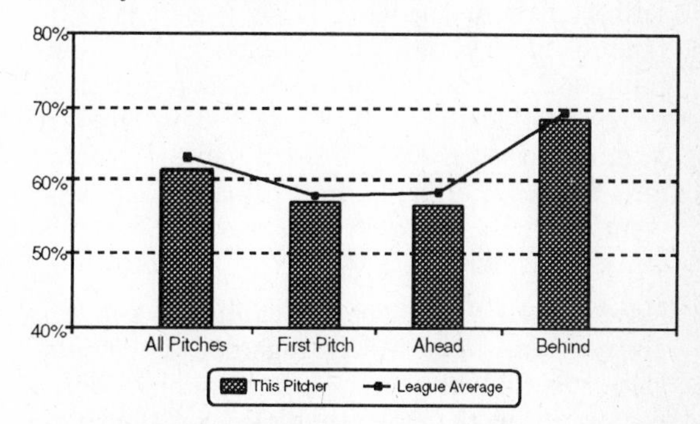

1992 Situational Stats

	W	L	ERA	Sv	IP		AB	H	HR	RBI	AVG
Home	5	0	2.01	0	53.2	LHB	250	59	4	24	.236
Road	2	4	3.96	0	63.2	RHB	181	40	5	18	.221
Day	2	2	3.49	0	38.2	Sc Pos	106	25	2	32	.236
Night	5	2	2.86	0	78.2	Clutch	26	6	1	3	.231

1992 Rankings (National League)

- Led the Phillies in stolen bases allowed (13)

CURT SCHILLING

Position: SP/RP
Bats: R **Throws:** R
Ht: 6' 4" **Wt:** 215

Opening Day Age: 26
Born: 11/14/66 in Anchorage, AK
ML Seasons: 5

PITCHING:

No pitcher in baseball came farther more impressively than did Curt Schilling in 1992. Buried in the Houston Astros bullpen, Schilling was acquired just before the start of the season by Philadelphia. When injuries decimated the Phillies' rotation, he was tried as a starter for the first time since 1989 and was a revelation. Schilling led the Phillies with 14 wins and ranked fourth in the National League with a 2.35 ERA.

Over the second half of last season, there were few better pitchers in the National League than Schilling. For the season, he completed 10 of his 26 starts, and his .201 opponents' batting average was the lowest among major-league starters. He was almost equally tough on righties (.207) and lefties (.197), and he walked only 59 batters while fanning 147. He threw four shutouts while compiling a 2.27 earned run average as a starter. A heavy workload (226.1 innings) didn't bother him; he posted a 2.00 ERA (and an 8-5 record) after the All-Star break. In his final six starts he went 3-2, had a 1.62 ERA and averaged over eight innings an outing.

How did all this happen? Schilling's arm has always been very highly regarded by scouts. However, Phillies pitching coach Johnny Podres was able to work on Schilling's delivery and give him more consistency in being able to spot his 90-plus fastball. The mechanical improvements also helped Schilling's excellent split-fingered pitch and his developing change-up.

HOLDING RUNNERS, FIELDING, HITTING:

Schilling does a solid job of holding runners on base though he has only an average pickoff move. He permitted only seven steals in 14 attempts last year. A good athlete, he is one of the Phillies' better fielding pitchers. He managed 10 hits last season and showed some potential as a hitter.

OVERALL:

Give the Phillies credit for good scouting in picking up arms like Ben Rivera, Tommy Greene, Terry Mulholland and Schilling. Of them all, Schilling could end up as the best. If the second half of '92 is any indication, the Phillies might have found themselves an ace.

Overall Statistics

	W	L	ERA	G	GS	Sv	IP	H	R	BB	SO	HR
1992	14	11	2.35	42	26	2	226.1	165	67	59	147	11
Career	18	22	3.05	142	31	13	371.1	314	140	130	260	19

How Often He Throws Strikes

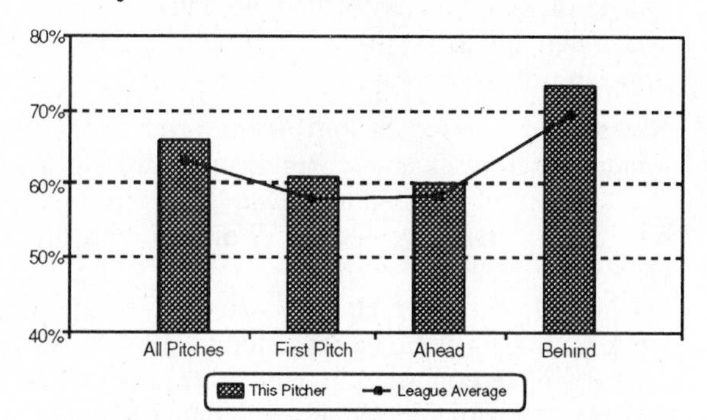

1992 Situational Stats

	W	L	ERA	Sv	IP		AB	H	HR	RBI	AVG
Home	8	6	2.21	0	130.1	LHB	456	90	7	30	.197
Road	6	5	2.53	2	96.0	RHB	363	75	4	31	.207
Day	1	4	3.14	2	57.1	Sc Pos	148	26	1	42	.176
Night	13	7	2.08	0	169.0	Clutch	102	22	3	10	.216

1992 Rankings (National League)

- 1st in lowest batting average allowed (.201), lowest on-base percentage allowed (.254), least baserunners allowed per 9 innings (8.9) and lowest batting average allowed with runners in scoring position (.176)
- 2nd in complete games (10)
- 3rd in shutouts (4) and lowest slugging percentage allowed (.288)
- Led the Phillies in sacrifice bunts as a hitter (8), ERA (2.35), wins (14), shutouts, strikeouts (147), most pitches thrown (3,268), runners caught stealing (7), winning percentage (.560), lowest batting average allowed, lowest slugging percentage allowed and lowest on-base percentage allowed

PITCHING:

All the "Wild Thing" stuff might be amusing. But after a while the Phillies, like the Cubs and Rangers before them, have begun to get frustrated with their unconventional closer, Mitch Williams.

Yes, he did save 29 games. And in his defense, Williams was often distracted by a serious illness in his family. But it was not a good year for him. Williams blew seven save opportunities last year and his earned run average was a lofty 3.78. As usual, his control numbers were horrid. He allowed 64 walks in 81 innings. But what made last year so disquieting was that he also allowed 69 hits. Opposing hitters batted .240 and had a .386 on-base percentage against Williams. In 1991, the figures were .182 average, .330 OBP.

Williams hasn't changed at all. He lives and dies with a 90-plus fastball which is liable to go anywhere. He also has an excellent slider, which also is liable to go anywhere. After all this time, one would think that he would start getting himself under control. But Williams shows no sign of that.

HOLDING RUNNERS, FIELDING, HITTING:

Williams has a good pickoff move and isn't afraid to use it. However, once he comes home, he becomes very easy to steal on. He permitted nine steals in 15 attempts while working only 81 innings last year -- a very high total for a late relief man. His out-of-control delivery leaves him completely out of position; as a result, he is one of the worst-fielding pitchers in baseball. Williams rarely gets to hit.

OVERALL:

General manager Lee Thomas has to be questioning his decision to give Williams a three-year, $9 million contract before the 1992 season. The club made him available in the expansion draft, but neither Colorado nor Florida were interested. Williams' unreliability is difficult to live with, especially if the Phillies think they are close to contending. However, with so many other needs, the Phils will likely have to live with their eccentric closer.

MITCH WILLIAMS

Position: RP
Bats: L **Throws:** L
Ht: 6' 4" **Wt:** 205

Opening Day Age: 28
Born: 11/17/64 in Santa Ana, CA
ML Seasons: 7

Overall Statistics

	W	L	ERA	G	GS	Sv	IP	H	R	BB	SO	HR
1992	5	8	3.78	66	0	29	81.0	69	39	64	74	4
Career	40	44	3.39	502	3	143	592.0	436	252	448	560	39

How Often He Throws Strikes

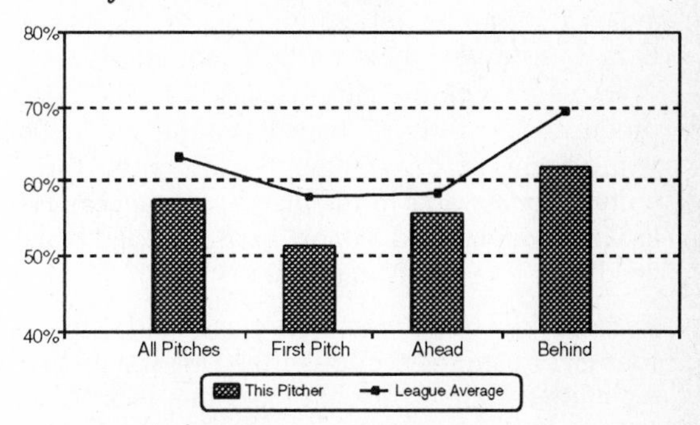

1992 Situational Stats

	W	L	ERA	Sv	IP		AB	H	HR	RBI	AVG
Home	3	5	4.29	16	42.0	LHB	49	13	0	7	.265
Road	2	3	3.23	13	39.0	RHB	238	56	4	31	.235
Day	2	0	3.10	6	20.1	Sc Pos	107	26	2	35	.243
Night	3	8	4.01	23	60.2	Clutch	212	53	3	29	.250

1992 Rankings (National League)

- 3rd in most baserunners allowed per 9 innings in relief (15.4)
- 4th in games finished (56) and relief losses (8)
- 5th in saves (29) and save opportunities (36)
- 6th in hit batsmen (6), balks (3) and blown saves (7)
- Led the Phillies in games pitched (66), saves, games finished, walks allowed (64), hit batsmen, balks, save opportunities, save percentage (80.6%), blown saves, relief losses, relief innings (81) and lowest batting average allowed in relief (.240)

KIM BATISTE

Position: SS
Bats: R **Throws:** R
Ht: 6' 0" **Wt:** 175

Opening Day Age: 25
Born: 3/15/68 in New Orleans, LA
ML Seasons: 2

Overall Statistics

	G	AB	R	H	D	T	HR	RBI	SB	BB	SO	AVG
1992	44	136	9	28	4	0	1	10	0	4	18	.206
Career	54	163	11	34	4	0	1	11	0	5	26	.209

HITTING, FIELDING, BASERUNNING:

When the Phillies left spring training last year, Kim Batiste was their starting shortstop. However, his hold on the job was short-lived. Batiste produced very little offensively, batting only .206 with no power (.257 slugging) or discipline (three unintentional walks in 145 plate appearances). He looked overmatched against hard stuff and managed only five extra-base hits.

In the field, Batiste was erratic at best. He had a four-error game and through the first month had committed eight errors. By that time, there were questions about his attitude as well. Batiste was soon banished to AAA Scranton, from which he would never return. Meanwhile the Phillies went through all sorts of shortstop options through the rest of the season.

Batiste has good athletic skills. He has decent speed and an exceptionally strong arm. However, he did not attempt a major league stolen base last year and he grounded into seven double plays in his limited action. His work habits were widely questioned -- not a good reputation for a marginal player to start developing.

OVERALL:

Batiste was somewhat surprisingly protected for the expansion draft, indicating that the Phillies still have hopes for his future. But as of now, it appears that Juan Bell, whom they also protected, would get first shot at shortstop. Batiste will try to impress in spring training.

CLIFF BRANTLEY

Position: RP/SP
Bats: R **Throws:** R
Ht: 6' 1" **Wt:** 190

Opening Day Age: 25
Born: 4/12/68 in Staten Island, NY
ML Seasons: 2

Overall Statistics

	W	L	ERA	G	GS	Sv	IP	H	R	BB	SO	HR
1992	2	6	4.60	28	9	0	76.1	71	45	58	32	6
Career	4	8	4.25	34	14	0	108.0	97	57	77	57	6

PITCHING, FIELDING, HITTING & HOLDING RUNNERS:

The Phillies have had hopes for Cliff Brantley, their second-round draft pick in 1986, for quite a while. But after an inconsistent 1992 season as both a starter and reliever, his status is now in question.

Brantley has good velocity and can be effective when he keeps the ball down in the strike zone. However, he falls behind too often in the count and does not have a quality second pitch to help him out of trouble when his fastball is wandering. The result last year was 58 walks and six home runs allowed in only 76.1 innings. Brantley gave up almost twice as many walks as he had strikeouts, a devastating ratio. The control problems are especially damaging in the set-up relief role that the Phillies had hoped Brantley might fill.

Defensively, Brantley is just average. He is poor at holding runners (10 opposing steals last year). He does handle the bat fairly well, and was second on the Phillies with seven sacrifice bunts while striking out only four times.

OVERALL:

Brantley will be among a large group of young Philadelphia pitchers who must either impress in spring training or face demotion to the minors and/or an outright release. Put up or shut up, in other words. Brantley will likely get a chance in relief.

PAT COMBS

Position: SP
Bats: L **Throws:** L
Ht: 6' 4" **Wt:** 200

Opening Day Age: 26
Born: 10/29/66 in Newport, RI
ML Seasons: 4

Overall Statistics

	W	L	ERA	G	GS	Sv	IP	H	R	BB	SO	HR
1992	1	1	7.71	4	4	0	18.2	20	16	12	11	0
Career	17	17	4.22	56	54	0	305.0	299	157	147	190	21

PITCHING, FIELDING, HITTING & HOLDING RUNNERS:

Once the crown jewel of the Philadelphia farm system, Pat Combs is now just another disappointment trying to find a job. Combs was hampered in 1992 with a second straight year of shoulder and elbow problems. He made only four starts in the big leagues before spending the rest of the season in the minors.

The lefthander has had two years of control problems and the patience of hard-edged manager Jim Fregosi quickly grew thin with him. Combs was never brought back after his exile to AAA Scranton. When he has control, his fastball and change can be very effective. But his consistency has been missing for two years.

Combs has also become very easy to run upon. With his mechanics fouled up, he has misplaced his pickoff move and become a feast for basestealers. Though he worked only 18.2 innings last year, he permitted four steals in five attempts. He is an average fielder and is not completely helpless as a hitter.

OVERALL:

At 26 years old, Combs finds himself facing release from an organization that once considered him a future star. He would be helped by a change of scenery; perhaps league expansion will help him find another club willing to give him a chance.

JEFF GROTEWOLD

Position: C
Bats: L **Throws:** R
Ht: 6' 0" **Wt:** 215

Opening Day Age: 27
Born: 12/8/65 in Madera, CA
ML Seasons: 1

Overall Statistics

	G	AB	R	H	D	T	HR	RBI	SB	BB	SO	AVG
1992	72	65	7	13	2	0	3	5	0	9	16	.200
Career	72	65	7	13	2	0	3	5	0	9	16	.200

HITTING, FIELDING, BASERUNNING:

Pinch hitting is a specialized niche. At least in 1992, Jeff Grotewold filled this niche fairly well, hitting three pinch-hit homers, including blasts in successive pinch-hit opportunities. It was pretty much an all-or-nothing season for the rookie, who batted only .200.

The question is whether the left-handed hitting Grotewold will have a chance at anything else. He did not have a hit in the season's last four weeks as pitchers quickly learned that they could tie him up inside with hard stuff or get him to reach for outside breaking stuff. If he gets a pitch he can turn on, Grotewold has excellent power. He had two 15-homer seasons in the minors.

Grotewold is a catcher by trade, but the Phillies were reluctant to use him defensively. He is very crude behind the plate and has a poor arm. Philadelphia may try to find him another position, but as one scout said, "His only possible position is DH, and only a platoon one." Grotewold is a below-average runner.

OVERALL:

Grotewold could stick with the Phillies as left-handed pinch hitter and emergency catcher. But he was never considered a prospect in the minors and it seems that his chances of winning a job are slim at best.

ORGANIZATION OVERVIEW:

The current state of the Phillies' farm system might be best shown in the list of players that they protected in the expansion draft. While other clubs were wrestling with the decision, reserving three or so spots for minor league hopefuls while reluctantly exposing several more, the Phillies were protecting guys like Ricky Jordan and the oft-traded Juan Bell. The one prospect they did protect -- shortstop Kim Batiste -- was tried and found wanting in 1992. Lee Thomas and company have a good reputation and have made some good draft picks, but thus far the overall results have been lacking.

BRAD BRINK

Position: P **Opening Day Age:** 28
Bats: R **Throws:** R **Born:** 1/20/65 in
Ht: 6' 2" **Wt:** 195 Roseville, CA

Recent Statistics

	W	L	ERA	G	GS	Sv	IP	H	R	BB	SO	HR
92 AA Reading	1	1	3.29	3	3	0	13.2	14	6	3	12	0
92 AAA Scranton/wb	8	2	3.48	17	17	0	111.1	100	47	34	92	15
92 NL Philadelphia	0	4	4.14	8	7	0	41.1	53	27	13	16	2

The Phillies' first choice in the 1986 draft, Brink didn't reach the majors until last year, when he made seven starts for the Phils. He went 0-4 though his ERA wasn't that bad at 4.14. Brink has some talent, but he's been set back by serious shoulder problems, including rotator cuff surgery. Last year he didn't seem to be throwing as hard as in the past, and he was usually good for only five or six innings a start. He should get another chance this year. Whether he'll produce is the big question.

TYLER S. GREEN

Position: P **Opening Day Age:** 23
Bats: R **Throws:** R **Born:** 2/18/70 in
Ht: 6' 5" **Wt:** 185 Springfield, OH

Recent Statistics

	W	L	ERA	G	GS	Sv	IP	H	R	BB	SO	HR
91 A Batavia	1	0	1.20	3	3	0	15.0	7	2	6	19	0
91 A Clearwater	2	0	1.38	2	2	0	13.0	3	2	8	20	0
92 AA Reading	6	3	1.88	12	12	0	62.1	46	16	20	67	2
92 AAA Scranton/wb	0	1	6.10	2	2	0	10.1	7	7	12	15	1

Along with some bad draft picks in recent years, the Phillies have had some bad luck. Green, their number-one pick in 1991 out of Wichita State, symbolizes that bad luck. The young righty has a world of stuff, and he's been considered a potential staff ace. But Green has had problems with his right shoulder -- in the dreaded rotator cuff area. When he's been healthy, he's been brilliant: a 9-4 minor league record, a 2.15 ERA, and 121 strikeouts in 100.2 innings.

MIKE LIEBERTHAL

Position: C **Opening Day Age:** 21
Bats: R **Throws:** R **Born:** 1/18/72 in
Ht: 6' 0" **Wt:** 170 Glendale, CA

Recent Statistics

	G	AB	R	H	D	T	HR	RBI	SB	BB	SO	AVG
92 AA Reading	86	309	30	88	16	1	2	37	4	19	26	.285
92 AAA Scranton/wb	16	45	4	9	1	0	0	4	0	2	5	.200
92 MLE	102	341	26	84	14	0	1	31	2	13	33	.246

If the Phils have bad luck with Green, they've been fortunate thus far with Lieberthal, their number-one pick in 1990. The young catcher has been everything they've hoped for thus far. Lieberthal is a good defensive catcher and last year was chosen the best fielding catcher in the Eastern League. After a tough year in rookie ball, he's hit .280 or better at three stops, but without power. He's been so good that the Phils have toyed with the idea of moving Darren Daulton to left field, at least on a part-time basis.

TODD PRATT

Position: C **Opening Day Age:** 26
Bats: R **Throws:** R **Born:** 2/9/67 in
Ht: 6' 3" **Wt:** 195 Bellevue, NE

Recent Statistics

	G	AB	R	H	D	T	HR	RBI	SB	BB	SO	AVG
92 AA Reading	41	132	20	44	6	1	6	26	2	24	28	.333
92 AAA Scranton/wb	41	125	20	40	9	1	7	28	1	30	14	.320
92 NL Philadelphia	16	46	6	13	1	0	2	10	0	4	12	.283
92 MLE	82	248	32	75	13	0	10	45	1	43	44	.302

Like Lieberthal, Todd Pratt is a young catcher with an obstacle in front of him -- Darren Daulton. A former Red Sox prospect, Pratt can hit -- .333 at AA Reading last year, .320 at AAA Scranton, .283 in 46 at-bats for the Phillies. He has power, too, with 15 homers at his three levels last season. There are a lot of questions about his defense, but Pratt looked improved last year. He should be in the majors this year, and possibly as a regular if he's with another club than the Phillies (or if Daulton gets hurt).

MIKE WILLIAMS

Position: P **Opening Day Age:** 24
Bats: R **Throws:** R **Born:** 7/29/68 in
Ht: 6' 2" **Wt:** 190 Radford, VA

Recent Statistics

	W	L	ERA	G	GS	Sv	IP	H	R	BB	SO	HR
92 AA Reading	1	2	5.17	3	3	0	15.2	17	10	7	12	1
92 AAA Scranton/wb	9	1	2.43	16	16	0	92.2	84	26	30	59	4
92 NL Philadelphia	1	1	5.34	5	5	0	28.2	29	20	7	5	3

A 14th-round pick in 1990, Mike Williams was one of the numerous pitchers who got a shot in the Philadelphia rotation last year. Williams went 9-1 with a 2.43 ERA at AAA, but in five starts for the Phillies his stuff looked weak. Williams struck out only five men in 28.2 innings and 13 of his 29 hits allowed went for extra bases. Still, Williams will probably get another chance this year.

STAN BELINDA

Position: RP
Bats: R **Throws:** R
Ht: 6' 3" **Wt:** 187

Opening Day Age: 26
Born: 8/6/66 in Huntingdon, PA
ML Seasons: 4

PITCHING:

The Pirates have felt that Stan Belinda could be a dominating closer ever since he broke into the major leagues late in 1989. They are still waiting. Belinda has shown signs of being a top-flight closer the past three years, but he has yet to do it on a consistent basis. In 1992, Belinda led the club with a career-high 18 saves. However, six of the eight homers he allowed either won or tied the game for the opposition, and 18 of his 28 inherited runners scored. He capped the season by blowing the save, and the pennant, in Game 7 of the National League Championship Series.

Belinda, who throws side-armed, relies on a fastball that can reach the 94-MPH range. However, he has yet to develop a dependable second pitch that would induce batters to hit balls on the ground. He throws a forkball as a change of pace but has not mastered it. Too many times, hitters will work Belinda deep in the count then catch up to a belt-high fastball.

Another attribute Belinda must gain before he can become a good closer is durability. Though he is always willing to take the ball, he sometimes struggles when pitching on consecutive days. At times, he has lost as much as 8-10 MPH off his fastball on the second day.

HOLDING RUNNERS, FIELDING, HITTING:

Belinda has a big leg kick, is slow to the plate and has a below-average move to first. Opposing baserunners can take liberties with him. Belinda is an adequate fielder and an improving hitter. He notched his first two career hits last season and both drove in runs.

OVERALL:

With a live fastball and poise, Belinda still has the makings of a closer. He is young (26) but the time is coming for him to prove he can fill the role. One wonders what kind of scars blowing the National League pennant will leave on his psyche.

Overall Statistics

	W	L	ERA	G	GS	Sv	IP	H	R	BB	SO	HR
1992	6	4	3.15	59	0	18	71.1	58	26	29	57	8
Career	16	14	3.50	182	0	42	218.1	169	87	95	193	22

How Often He Throws Strikes

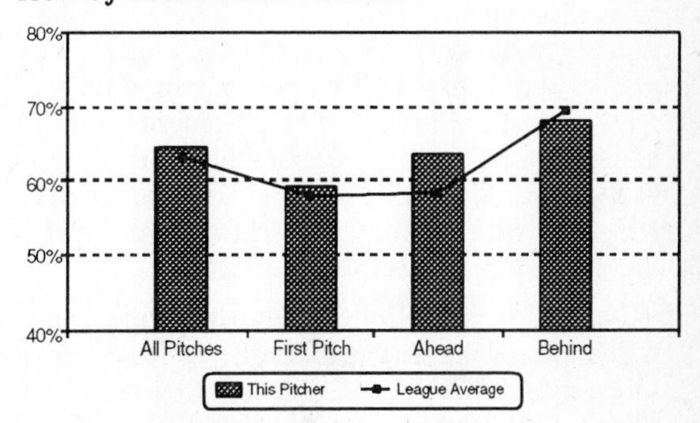

1992 Situational Stats

	W	L	ERA	Sv	IP		AB	H	HR	RBI	AVG
Home	2	1	1.89	8	33.1	LHB	135	26	4	15	.193
Road	4	3	4.26	10	38.0	RHB	125	32	4	26	.256
Day	1	3	4.64	7	21.1	Sc Pos	79	19	6	36	.241
Night	5	1	2.52	11	50.0	Clutch	196	44	6	29	.224

1992 Rankings (National League)

- 3rd in least GDPs induced per GDP situation (2.4%)
- 6th in lowest batting average allowed vs. left-handed batters (.193)
- 8th in saves (18), games finished (42), save opportunities (24) and blown saves (6)
- 10th in relief wins (6)
- Led the Pirates in saves, games finished, save opportunities, save percentage (75.0%), blown saves, lowest batting average allowed vs. left-handed batters, relief wins, lowest batting average allowed in relief (.223) and least baserunners allowed per 9 innings in relief (11.0)

IN HIS PRIME

JAY BELL

Position: SS
Bats: R **Throws:** R
Ht: 6' 0" **Wt:** 185

Opening Day Age: 27
Born: 12/11/65 in Eglin AFB, FL
ML Seasons: 7

HITTING:

Jay Bell's offensive statistics slipped in 1992, but he maintained his reputation as one of baseball's top young shortstops. Through two-thirds of the season, Bell was batting just .246 with five homers and 29 RBI, far below his .270-16-67 season of 1991. However, when the pennant race heated up, so did Bell. He hit .297 with four homers and 26 RBI in the final 54 games to finish with a respectable .264-9-55 season. Included in that stretch was a 22-game hitting streak, the longest in the National League last season.

Bell fell into the same trap that many of the Pirates did at the start of last season. With cleanup hitter Bobby Bonilla gone to the New York Mets as a free agent, many of the Pirates' hitters seemed tentative and unsure. Bell took more pitches in the first half before regaining his aggressiveness in the second half. Sometimes overaggressive, he has fanned more than 100 times in two of his three full seasons. He particularly struggles with outside stuff from righthanders, though he hits lefties extremely well.

With Bonilla gone, Bell did not bunt as much and failed to lead the league in sacrifices for the first time since 1989. He did continue to show good gap power with 51 extra-base hits.

BASERUNNING:

Bell is not exceptionally fast but will steal an occasional base. He is also smart on the basepaths, knowing when he can take the extra base and when he can't. He rarely runs himself into an out.

FIELDING:

Bell's range is only average but he has a good knowledge of the hitters and positions himself well. He occasionally boots the routine ground ball and his hands are a little stiff. He has a very strong arm, though, and that makes up for most shortcomings.

OVERALL:

Bell is a solid major-league shortstop who may be on the brink of stardom. Though there has been talk of trading him, he's a major reason why the Pirates have won three straight National League East titles, after solving their long-standing shortstop problem.

Overall Statistics

	G	AB	R	H	D	T	HR	RBI	SB	BB	SO	AVG
1992	159	632	87	167	36	6	9	55	7	55	103	.264
Career	669	2444	349	627	125	26	39	239	38	222	445	.257

Where He Hits the Ball

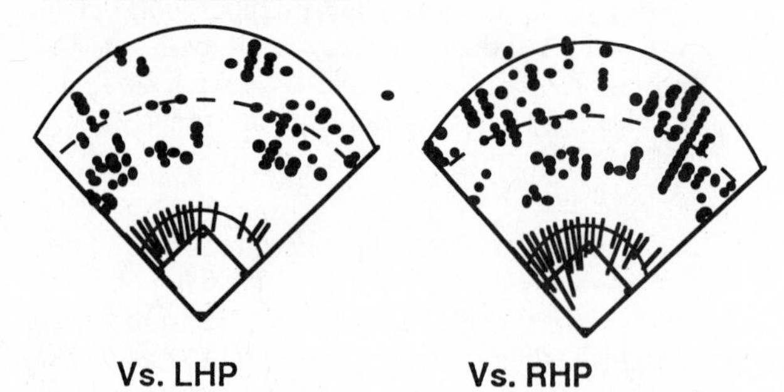

1992 Situational Stats

	AB	H	HR	RBI	AVG		AB	H	HR	RBI	AVG
Home	302	84	5	27	.278	LHP	238	77	1	20	.324
Road	330	83	4	28	.252	RHP	394	90	8	35	.228
Day	176	47	2	17	.267	Sc Pos	120	40	1	41	.333
Night	456	120	7	38	.263	Clutch	115	32	2	11	.278

1992 Rankings (National League)

- → 2nd in sacrifice bunts (19), plate appearances (712), lowest slugging percentage vs. right-handed pitchers (.343) and lowest on-base percentage vs. right-handed pitchers (.282)
- → 3rd in at-bats (632) and lowest batting average vs. right-handed pitchers (.228)
- → 5th in games played (159)
- → Led the Pirates in at-bats, sacrifice bunts, strikeouts (103), plate appearances, games played, batting average vs. left-handed pitchers (.324) and bunts in play (19)
- → Led NL shortstops in at-bats, runs scored (87), doubles (36), total bases (242), sacrifice bunts, strikeouts, most pitches seen, plate appearances and games played

BARRY BONDS

Position: LF
Bats: L **Throws:** L
Ht: 6' 1" **Wt:** 187

Opening Day Age: 28
Born: 7/24/64 in Riverside, CA
ML Seasons: 7

Overall Statistics

	G	AB	R	H	D	T	HR	RBI	SB	BB	SO	AVG
1992	140	473	109	147	36	5	34	103	39	127	69	.311
Career	1010	3584	672	984	220	36	176	556	251	611	590	.275

Where He Hits the Ball

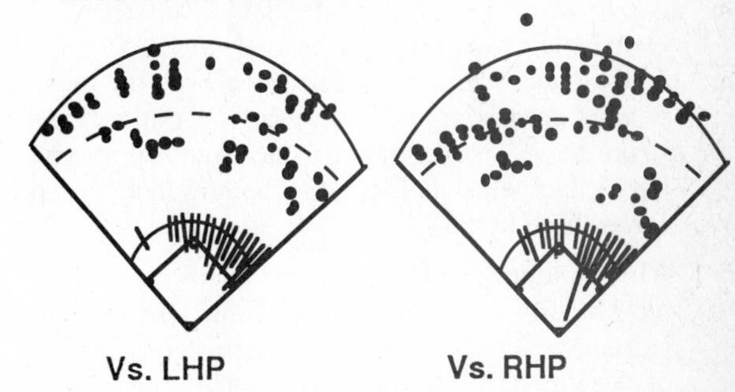

1992 Situational Stats

	AB	H	HR	RBI	AVG		AB	H	HR	RBI	AVG
Home	210	71	15	44	.338	LHP	222	69	13	44	.311
Road	263	76	19	59	.289	RHP	251	78	21	59	.311
Day	131	40	10	32	.305	Sc Pos	118	37	13	71	.314
Night	342	107	24	71	.313	Clutch	91	23	3	10	.253

1992 Rankings (National League)

- 1st in runs scored (109), walks (127), intentional walks (32), times on base (279), slugging percentage (.624), on-base percentage (.456), HR frequency (13.9 ABs per HR), lowest groundball/flyball ratio (.74), cleanup slugging percentage (.684) and on-base percentage vs. left-handed pitchers (.445)
- 2nd in home runs (34) and highest percentage of pitches taken (63.2%)
- 3rd in batting averave on a 3-1 count (.625), slugging percentage vs. left-handed pitchers (.599) and batting average at home (.338)
- Led the Pirates in home runs, runs scored, RBI (103), stolen bases (39), caught stealing (8), walks and many other categories

HITTING:

Barry Bonds did nothing in 1992 to stem the growing consensus that he is the best all-around player in baseball. He capped the year by winning his second National League MVP award in three seasons. The year he missed, 1991, Bonds finished second in a photo-finish with Terry Pendleton. Though Bonds isn't the only five-tool player in baseball, there probably isn't another whose tools are more advanced. With the bat, he is able to do just about anything. He hits for power to all fields and for a high average.

Bonds was forced to make adjustments in 1992 and became more patient in the process. Though he got frustrated, he never lost his composure and refused to chase bad pitches. Already blessed with one of the better eyes in the game, he drew a major-league leading 127 walks. However, he will still swing at the first pitch if it's one he can drive.

A man without a weakness, Bonds is as tough on left-handed pitchers as he is on righthanders. He hits any kind of pitching and hits well in the clutch, evidenced by his .313 (186-for-594) career average with runners in scoring position.

BASERUNNING:

Despite hitting cleanup, Bonds stole 39 bases last year. He has excellent speed and became a smart basestealer with experience. If he didn't hit in the middle of the order, he would likely double his steal total.

FIELDING:

Bonds' goal is to be known as the game's best defensive left fielder in history. That may happen. He goes to the line and into gap to make catches, and he turns doubles into singles better than any left fielder. He is equally adept at coming in or going out on balls. His arm isn't superior but baserunners think twice before taking a chance.

OVERALL:

A man with perfect timing, Bonds was headed for free agency at the end of last season. In a market with many outstanding players, he was clearly the best. While Pittsburgh was out of the running, whichever club could afford the investment could expect a tremendous return.

STAFF ACE

DOUG DRABEK

Position: SP
Bats: R **Throws:** R
Ht: 6' 1" **Wt:** 185

Opening Day Age: 30
Born: 7/25/62 in Victoria, TX
ML Seasons: 7

PITCHING:

Without flash or fanfare, Doug Drabek has become one of baseball's most consistent pitchers. Drabek continually churns out good seasons by relying on intelligence, poise and tenacity. He has had five straight winning seasons and has hit double figures in wins the past six years.

Drabek has four pitches -- fastball, curveball, slider and change-up -- and can throw any of them effectively. He understands early in the game which pitches are working for him and then adjusts accordingly. In recent seasons, the curve has replaced the slider as Drabek's best pitch. After years of working on it, Drabek's curveball now has bite. He enhances the curve by throwing it at two speeds. Drabek's slider lacks the break it once had, but he spots it effectively along with the fastball and change-up. His success with those pitches comes from moving them around in the strike zone. Thanks in good part to the improved curve, Drabek struck out 177 batters last year, a career high by 35.

Always durable, Drabek was even more of a workhorse in 1992. His career-high 10 complete games and 256.2 innings came partially as a result of the Pirates' oft-shaky bullpen. He pitched into the sixth inning in 32 of his 34 starts. In big games he rises to the occasion, and always gets stronger as the season progresses. He was 0-3 in the '92 playoffs, but his teammates cost him what should have been a Game 7 win.

HOLDING RUNNERS, FIELDING, HITTERS:

Drabek always pays attention to finer details like holding runners. He has a quick move to first and keeps runners close very well for a righthander. An outstanding athlete, Drabek fields his position well and is active around the mound. Drabek is an adequate hitter and enjoys taking his turn at bat.

OVERALL:

Drabek was a free agent at the end of last season. The Pirates wanted Drabek back and he seemed interested in staying. But it all came down to money and Pittsburgh didn't have enough. The Houston Astros bought themselves a very good pitcher.

Overall Statistics

	W	L	ERA	G	GS	Sv	IP	H	R	BB	SO	HR
1992	15	11	2.77	34	34	0	256.2	218	84	54	177	17
Career	99	70	3.11	226	217	0	1494.1	1353	570	387	896	125

How Often He Throws Strikes

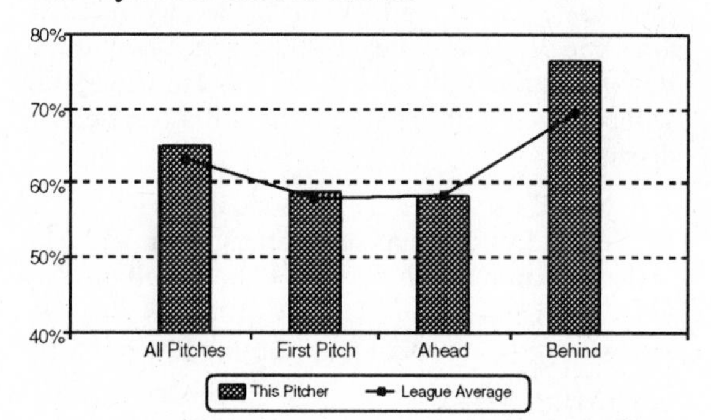

1992 Situational Stats

	W	L	ERA	Sv	IP		AB	H	HR	RBI	AVG
Home	8	3	2.44	0	110.2	LHB	548	143	11	47	.261
Road	7	8	3.02	0	146.0	RHB	397	75	6	28	.189
Day	2	2	2.68	0	40.1	Sc Pos	192	34	4	56	.177
Night	13	9	2.79	0	216.1	Clutch	131	28	0	6	.214

1992 Rankings (National League)

- 2nd in complete games (10), innings pitched (256.2), batters faced (1,021), lowest batting average allowed vs. right-handed batters (.189) and lowest batting average allowed with runners in scoring position (.177)
- 3rd in shutouts (4), wild pitches (11) and most pitches thrown (3,699)
- Led the Pirates in ERA (2.77), wins (15), losses (11), games started (34), complete games, shutouts, innings pitched, batters faced, home runs allowed (17), walks allowed (54), strikeouts (177), wild pitches, pitches thrown, highest strikeout/walk ratio (3.3), lowest batting average allowed (.231), lowest slugging percentage allowed (.330) and lowest on-base percentage allowed (.274)

JEFF KING

Position: 3B/1B/2B
Bats: R **Throws:** R
Ht: 6' 1" **Wt:** 180

Opening Day Age: 28
Born: 12/26/64 in Marion, IN
ML Seasons: 4

HITTING:

In the first half of the 1992 season, Jeff King did nothing to dispel the feeling that he has been a colossal draft bust. But in the second half, he showed why the Pirates used the first pick in the 1986 draft to select him. King, who missed almost all of 1991 and underwent back surgery, batted just .187 before the All-Star break. As a last resort, the Pirates sent him to AAA Buffalo on July 4 to regain his batting stroke. The move apparently worked. King was back 12 days later and went on to be one of the Pirates' top hitters in the second half, hitting .268 with eight homers and 45 RBI. Though his final average was low at .231, he finished with 14 homers and a career-high 65 RBI.

King's biggest problem is confidence. He is his own worst critic and gets down on himself at the slightest sign of failure. Though he will probably never become a great player, he has a chance to be an above-average run producer. He has a decent eye, a quick bat and can murder mistake pitches. However, good breaking balls from righthanders give him trouble.

BASERUNNING:

King is not fast and no stealing threat. He matched his career high with four steals last year, but it took him 10 attempts. He runs the bases intelligently and has an innate ability for knowing when to take the extra base.

FIELDING:

King's primary position is third base, but he also started at first base, second base, shortstop and right field last season. He shows above-average skills at third base with good reflexes and a decent arm. He is adequate at the other positions.

OVERALL:

With the trade of Jose Lind, King may be playing second base full-time this year. And with Barry Bonds not expected back, the Pirates will count on him to become a big run-producer. Those are major responsibilities. King has the ability to handle them; it's a question of whether he has the confidence.

Overall Statistics

	G	AB	R	H	D	T	HR	RBI	SB	BB	SO	AVG
1992	130	480	56	111	21	2	14	65	4	27	56	.231
Career	365	1175	149	270	52	7	37	155	14	82	155	.230

Where He Hits the Ball

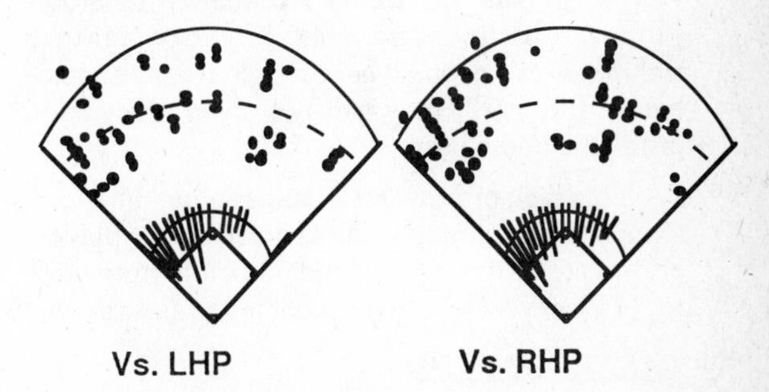

1992 Situational Stats

	AB	H	HR	RBI	AVG		AB	H	HR	RBI	AVG
Home	247	59	6	37	.239	LHP	216	51	6	32	.236
Road	233	52	8	28	.223	RHP	264	60	8	33	.227
Day	141	36	4	23	.255	Sc Pos	149	34	1	45	.228
Night	339	75	10	42	.221	Clutch	93	20	3	14	.215

1992 Rankings (National League)

- 1st in lowest on-base percentage (.272)
- 3rd in lowest batting average (.231) and lowest groundball/flyball ratio (.81)
- 7th in lowest on-base percentage vs. left-handed pitchers (.277), lowest batting average at home (.239) and lowest batting average on the road (.223)
- Led NL third basemen in sacrifice bunts (8), bunts in play (16) and highest percentage of swings put into play (50.8%)

MIKE LaVALLIERE

Position: C
Bats: L **Throws:** R
Ht: 5' 9" **Wt:** 210

Opening Day Age: 32
Born: 8/18/60 in Charlotte, NC
ML Seasons: 9

HITTING:

The book on Mike LaValliere stays the same year after year: Good contact, no power and decent average. LaValliere's main offensive attribute is his ability to make consistent contact. He has a good eye, rarely strikes out and puts the ball in play. His walk-strikeout ratio was 44-21 last season in 293 at-bats. In fact, he has had more walks than strikeouts in each of the past six seasons.

LaValliere goes with the pitch. He occasionally turns on inside pitches but will gladly take the outside offering to the opposite field for a single. This skill makes him a good man on the hit-and-run. Singles are pretty much all LaValliere generates; he has only 118 extra-base hits in 2,134 lifetime at-bats. He has been primarily a platoon player, hitting almost exclusively against righthanders. Though he struggled against lefthanders in 1992, they had not given him major problems in the past.

With his lack of power, LaValliere must hit close to .300 to have much value as an offensive player. However, his average dipped 33 points from .289 to .256 last year and his bat seemed to slow down.

BASERUNNING:

LaValliere is among the slowest players in the game. He takes it one base at a time and a double will hardly ever score him from first base. He is also no threat as a basestealer.

FIELDING:

LaValliere's ability to handle pitchers compensates for his lack of power and speed. He is like having an extra pitching coach; he communicates so well with the pitchers. Knee problems and age have cut down on his mobility and he doesn't block balls as well anymore. However, he still has a quick release and threw out 33 percent of runners trying to steal last season, an average mark.

OVERALL:

LaValliere is getting older and is not in the best physical condition. Though he still has some value, he also has two years and more than $4 million remaining on a three-year contract. The cost-conscious Pirates would like to unload that contract.

Overall Statistics

	G	AB	R	H	D	T	HR	RBI	SB	BB	SO	AVG
1992	95	293	22	75	13	1	2	29	0	44	21	.256
Career	736	2134	166	574	97	5	16	243	5	288	200	.269

Where He Hits the Ball

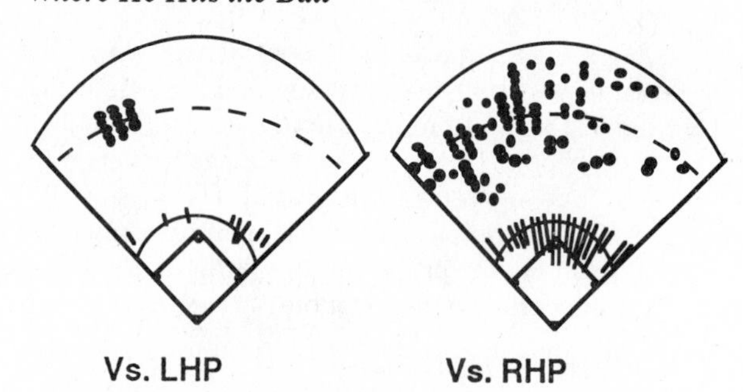

1992 Situational Stats

	AB	H	HR	RBI	AVG		AB	H	HR	RBI	AVG
Home	135	35	1	16	.259	LHP	31	5	0	5	.161
Road	158	40	1	13	.253	RHP	262	70	2	24	.267
Day	87	26	1	12	.299	Sc Pos	71	18	0	25	.254
Night	206	49	1	17	.238	Clutch	47	11	0	5	.234

1992 Rankings (National League)

- 6th in intentional walks (14)

PITCHING:

Roger Mason transformed from minor-league journeyman to postseason star in 1991. In 1992, he was just a mere mortal for the Pittsburgh Pirates. However, the big right-handed reliever finally notched his first full major-league season at age 34; his 65 appearances led the club.

Mason came from nowhere to bolster the Pirates' bullpen in 1991 and saved a 1-0 win over Atlanta in Game 5 of the National League Championship Series. He didn't pitch as well in 1992, but was solid and durable. Mason's turnaround has coincided with the addition of a forkball. Though not his primary pitch, it gives him a change of pace. When it is working right, Mason can get hitters to chase it down in the strike zone. He also throws a fastball and a slider. With his 6-foot-6 frame, Mason can give batters the impression that his fastball is right on top of them. He has some trouble with his slider and hung it with alarming regularity last season. Mason gave up 11 homers in 88 innings last year.

Mason had a chance to become the Pirates' closer last season, as he and Stan Belinda were basically co-closers in the first two months. However, his tendency to allow the long ball caused his removal from that role.

HOLDING RUNNERS, FIELDING, HITTING:

Mason pays very close attention to baserunners and varies his delivery to keep them off balance. Potential basestealers were successful only four times in nine tries with Mason pitching last season. He is an adequate fielder and has quick reflexes for a big man. He is particularly adept at stopping balls hit through the box. He rarely bats and just tries to make contact when he gets the chance.

OVERALL:

Considering that it took him until age 34 to play a full season in the majors, Mason is obviously not a developing prospect. The Pirates confirmed this notion by releasing him after the '92 season. However, he quickly signed with the Mets, who figure to use him for middle relief and occasional closing duties.

ROGER MASON

Position: RP
Bats: R **Throws:** R
Ht: 6' 6" **Wt:** 220

Opening Day Age: 34
Born: 9/18/58 in Bellaire, MI
ML Seasons: 7

Overall Statistics

	W	L	ERA	G	GS	Sv	IP	H	R	BB	SO	HR
1992	5	7	4.09	65	0	8	88.0	80	41	33	56	11
Career	14	18	4.07	117	23	12	256.2	240	129	102	182	24

How Often He Throws Strikes

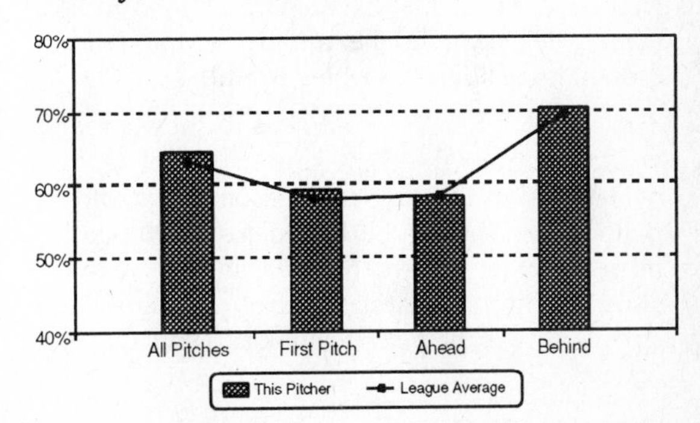

1992 Situational Stats

	W	L	ERA	Sv	IP		AB	H	HR	RBI	AVG
Home	2	1	3.60	4	45.0	LHB	162	35	2	10	.216
Road	3	6	4.60	4	43.0	RHB	163	45	9	31	.276
Day	3	2	2.70	0	26.2	Sc Pos	83	19	4	32	.229
Night	2	5	4.70	8	61.1	Clutch	180	49	7	26	.272

1992 Rankings (National League)

- 4th in lowest percentage of inherited runners scored (20.5%)
- 5th in first batter efficiency (.153)
- 6th in relief losses (7)
- 7th in relief innings (88)
- 9th in highest relief ERA (4.09)
- Led the Pirates in games pitched (65), holds (11), lowest batting average allowed in relief with runners on base (.214), lowest percentage of inherited runners scored, relief losses and relief innings

ORLANDO MERCED

Position: 1B/RF
Bats: B **Throws:** R
Ht: 5'11" **Wt:** 170

Opening Day Age: 26
Born: 11/2/66 in San Juan, Puerto Rico
ML Seasons: 3

Overall Statistics

	G	AB	R	H	D	T	HR	RBI	SB	BB	SO	AVG
1992	134	405	50	100	28	5	6	60	5	52	63	.247
Career	279	840	136	218	46	7	16	110	13	117	153	.260

Where He Hits the Ball

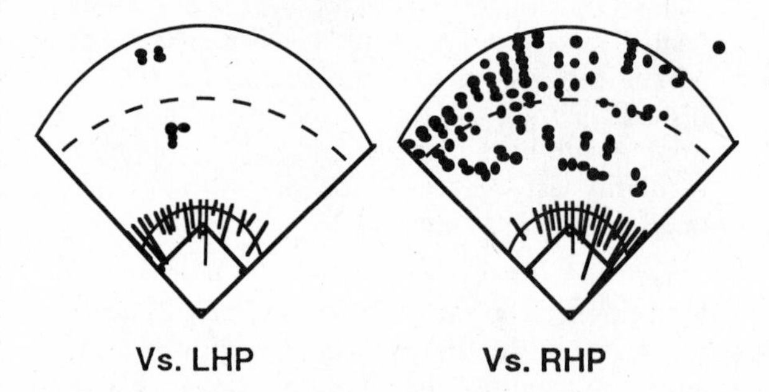

1992 Situational Stats

	AB	H	HR	RBI	AVG		AB	H	HR	RBI	AVG
Home	199	50	4	25	.251	LHP	84	16	0	7	.190
Road	206	50	2	35	.243	RHP	321	84	6	53	.262
Day	115	34	1	21	.296	Sc Pos	121	35	2	53	.289
Night	290	66	5	39	.228	Clutch	86	20	1	14	.233

1992 Rankings (National League)

- 4th in lowest batting average on an 0-2 count (.077)

HITTING:

Orlando Merced went from rising young star in 1991 to question mark in 1992. Merced came from nowhere to finish second in the National League Rookie of the Year voting in 1991, batting .275 with 10 homers and 50 RBI. But last year his average fell to .247 and he hit only six homers. Though he did increase his RBI total by 10, that was mainly due to him being dropped from the leadoff spot that he occupied in '91.

Merced is a dead fastball hitter. Pitchers have caught up with him, throwing him more breaking balls and offspeed pitches. The Pirates were hoping the line-drive hitting Merced would develop into more of a home run threat, but it didn't happen. Five of his six homers came during a three-week span in the middle of the season, though he did hit 28 doubles overall.

The switch-hitter also continues to show a major weakness from the right side of the plate. Expected to play full time last season, he wound up platooning again as he batted just .190 against lefties. Some believe Merced should abandon switch-hitting and bat strictly from his natural left side. However, he plans to stick as a switch-hitter for 1993.

BASERUNNING:

Merced has decent speed but not the kind one looks for in a leadoff hitter, which is why he was dropped in the order after Alex Cole arrived from Cleveland. Merced doesn't steal much but can go from first to third acceptably.

FIELDING:

Merced was a player without a position throughout much of his minor-league career. He has settled in at first base in the majors and become adequate. Last season, the Pirates hoped Merced could replace Bobby Bonilla in right field. However, he was shaky on fly balls and showed only an ordinary arm.

OVERALL:

Merced must prove that last year can be chalked up to the old sophomore jinx. With Barry Bonds expected to leave as a free agent, the Pirates desperately need more power and hope Merced can provide some. He must improve his production from the right side, however.

DENNY NEAGLE

Position: RP/SP
Bats: L **Throws:** L
Ht: 6' 4" **Wt:** 205

Opening Day Age: 24
Born: 9/13/68 in Prince Georges County, MD
ML Seasons: 2

PITCHING:

Denny Neagle came to Pittsburgh trying to replace a 20-game winner. He didn't do that, but still wound up salvaging his 1992 season, his first full year in the majors. Neagle was acquired along with outfield prospect Midre Cummings in the controversial spring training deal that sent John Smiley to the Minnesota Twins. He did some starting work early in the year but bombed, going 1-3 with a 5.40 ERA in six starts. Moved to the bullpen, he started to blossom and show the promise he'd held in Minnesota's organization. He allowed only four of 26 inherited baserunners to score.

The lefthander's fastball gained in velocity, jumping from 84 to 88 MPH regularly in his shorter bullpen stints. Besides working fewer innings as a reliever, a shortened step to the plate aided Neagle's fastball. However, his top pitch is the change-up. Unlike most young pitchers, he does not alter his motion when throwing the change. Batters cannot distinguish it from his fastball until the last moment. He also throws a curveball and slider but both need polish, as does his overall control. Neagle lacked stamina as a starter, consistently tiring around the fifth or sixth inning. A long winter ball season in '91 may have been a factor. Neagle worked long stints as a reliever when necessary.

HOLDING RUNNERS, FIELDING, HITTING:

Like most young pitchers, Neagle is still learning the nuances of holding runners. He is very easy to run against at this stage of his career. Neagle is a good athlete and a solid fielder, quick around the mound and in covering first base. Neagle says he was a home run threat in high school but hasn't shown it in his few major-league opportunities.

OVERALL:

Neagle showed signs of being an effective major-league pitcher last season. A lefthander with the ability to start or relieve, he could become a valuable member of the staff. At age 24, he needs more experience before a final judgment is made. He showed enough last season to still be considered a prospect.

Overall Statistics

	W	L	ERA	G	GS	Sv	IP	H	R	BB	SO	HR
1992	4	6	4.48	55	6	2	86.1	81	46	43	77	9
Career	4	7	4.40	62	9	2	106.1	109	55	50	91	12

How Often He Throws Strikes

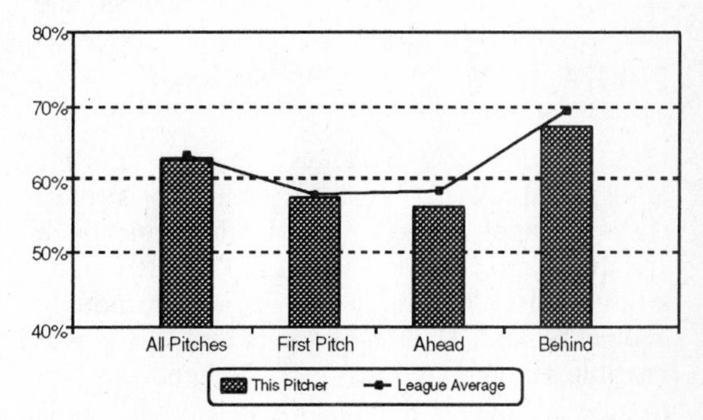

1992 Situational Stats

	W	L	ERA	Sv	IP		AB	H	HR	RBI	AVG
Home	1	5	6.05	0	38.2	LHB	92	21	2	13	.228
Road	3	1	3.21	2	47.2	RHB	236	60	7	26	.254
Day	2	0	3.34	0	29.2	Sc Pos	81	25	4	34	.309
Night	2	6	5.08	2	56.2	Clutch	103	20	3	5	.194

1992 Rankings (National League)

- 2nd in first batter efficiency (.133)
- 4th in most strikeouts per 9 innings in relief (9.1)
- 9th in least GDPs induced per GDP situation (3.2%)
- 10th in balks (2)
- Led the Pirates in balks, first batter efficiency and most strikeouts per 9 innings in relief

PITCHING:

Apart from a nightmarish stretch in early September, Bob Patterson was the most consistent reliever on the Pirates' staff in 1992. That was particularly impressive since consistent performance was rare in the Pirates' 1992 bullpen. The lefthander posted a 2.92 ERA last year, a career low, and his 60 appearances were his most ever.

Patterson's stuff is only ordinary. However, he has become an effective reliever by using his intelligence. He makes few mistakes, has good control and rarely gets rattled in pressure situations. With only an average fastball, Patterson gets hitters out with his good breaking pitches. His curveball ties up righties and causes left-handed batters to chase it as it breaks on the outside corner. He also throws an effective screwball that helped make him equally successful against lefties and righties in 1992.

One of the secrets to Patterson's success is his ability to throw his breaking pitches for strikes. Hitters cannot afford to take his breaking pitch and make him come in with his fastball. Patterson will occasionally hang a curve or slider, though, and get burned. That happened to him during that horrible 10-day stretch in early September when he gave up three home runs which scored 10 runs total. All three of the homers cost the Pirates a game.

HOLDING RUNNERS, FIELDING, HITTING:

Patterson is extremely difficult to run against. He allowed only one steal in four attempts last year, and has permitted only eight -- in 22 attempts -- over the last five campaigns. Patterson does not hurt himself in the field, either. Though not a Gold Glove candidate, he handles bunts well and always covers bases. He has not embarrassed himself at the plate in his limited chances.

OVERALL:

Patterson did not reach the major leagues for good until age 31. However, he has quietly played an important role in the Pirates' success the past three seasons as an effective left-handed reliever. Guys like him have the savvy to stay around for a long time.

BOB PATTERSON

Position: RP
Bats: R **Throws:** L
Ht: 6' 2" **Wt:** 185

Opening Day Age: 33
Born: 5/16/59 in Jacksonville, FL
ML Seasons: 7

Overall Statistics

	W	L	ERA	G	GS	Sv	IP	H	R	BB	SO	HR
1992	6	3	2.92	60	0	9	64.2	59	22	23	43	7
Career	25	21	4.22	210	21	17	335.0	348	165	97	238	33

How Often He Throws Strikes

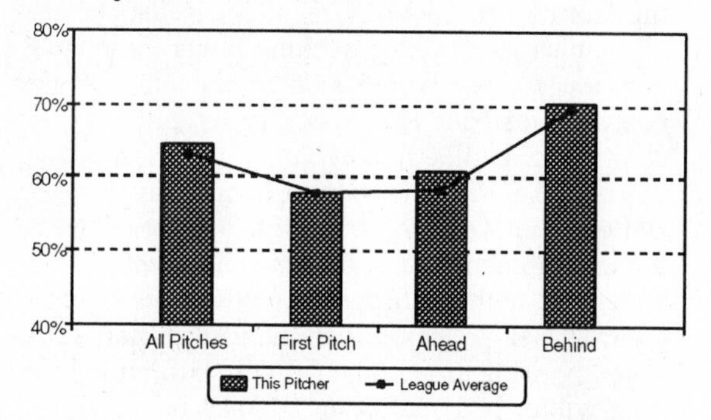

1992 Situational Stats

	W	L	ERA	Sv	IP		AB	H	HR	RBI	AVG
Home	4	2	3.47	6	36.1	LHB	78	20	1	10	.256
Road	2	1	2.22	3	28.1	RHB	162	39	6	20	.241
Day	2	1	4.91	1	14.2	Sc Pos	55	14	5	28	.255
Night	4	2	2.34	8	50.0	Clutch	130	35	6	22	.269

1992 Rankings (National League)

- 7th in worst first batter efficiency (.309)
- 9th in highest percentage of inherited runners scored (36.1%)
- 10th in relief wins (6)
- Led the Pirates in relief ERA (2.92) and relief wins

GARY REDUS

Position: 1B/RF
Bats: R **Throws:** R
Ht: 6' 1" **Wt:** 185

Opening Day Age: 36
Born: 11/1/56 in Tanner, AL
ML Seasons: 11

HITTING:

After looking washed up for most of the year, Gary Redus showed renewed life in the final weeks of the 1992 season. Redus struggled for much of the campaign and his batting average still stood as low as .209 in early September. However, he batted .405 in his final 13 games to raise his final average to .256. Then he went 7-for-16 (.438) with four doubles and a triple in the National League Championship Series.

Despite the strong finish, Redus showed many signs of slowing down last year. He had repeated problems with hamstring pulls and his bat seemed to be considerably late. Pitchers are now able to blow more high fastballs by him. Long a power/speed threat as a role player, Redus lacked both in '92. He hit only three home runs and stole just 11 bases, both the lowest figures of his 10 full major-league seasons.

Though some people have insisted that Redus should hit the ball on the ground to best take advantage of his speed, he has always been a flyball hitter -- a key to his usually-strong extra base numbers. Ironically, he actually hit more ground balls (65) than fly balls (63) last year. With the poorer results, maybe he knew what he was doing all along.

BASERUNNING:

Age and recent leg problems reduced some of Redus' speed. However, he is still an intelligent runner who doesn't cost his team outs. He is a high-percentage basestealer (11-for-15 last year) who knows when he can and can't take an extra base.

FIELDING:

Though he has been playing first base on a platoon basis for four seasons, Redus has never been totally comfortable at the position. He is cautious around the bag and not sure-handed. He is also a below-average outfielder with a poor arm.

OVERALL:

Though Redus showed life in the postseason, he declined noticeably last season overall. The Pirates didn't renew the option year of his three-year contract, making him a free agent. Redus, who wants to end his career in Pittsburgh, will likely retire unless he gets an overwhelming offer.

Overall Statistics

	G	AB	R	H	D	T	HR	RBI	SB	BB	SO	AVG
1992	76	176	26	45	7	3	3	12	11	17	25	.256
Career	1064	3258	561	813	170	47	84	319	318	454	647	.250

Where He Hits the Ball

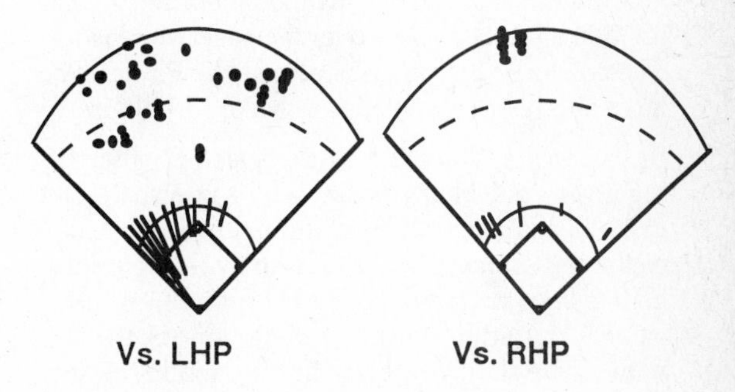

1992 Situational Stats

	AB	H	HR	RBI	AVG		AB	H	HR	RBI	AVG
Home	88	25	1	8	.284	LHP	151	39	2	10	.258
Road	88	20	2	4	.227	RHP	25	6	1	2	.240
Day	56	14	1	4	.250	Sc Pos	30	9	1	10	.300
Night	120	31	2	8	.258	Clutch	25	10	1	4	.400

1992 Rankings (National League)

➟ Did not rank near the top or bottom in any category

HITTING:

The older he gets, the higher Don Slaught's batting average climbs. It jumped all the way to .345 last season, the highest mark of his 11-year career. Always a decent hitter in the American League, Slaught has become a dangerous hitter since coming to the National League three years ago. He has hit .300 in two of his three seasons with the Pirates.

Slaught has good power and makes consistent contact. He will hit only an occasional home run, but he reaches the gaps with some consistency. He has cut down on his strikeouts since coming to the NL and is outstanding on the hit-and-run. Though he is a platoon player, it is not because of a weakness against right-handed pitching. He has hit .366 against righties over the past two seasons. The reason he platoons is because the Pirates also have another good catcher in Mike LaValliere.

In past years, Slaught was inconsistent, alternating a very good half-season with a poor half. But in 1992, his average never fell below .329. Much of the reason has to do with him avoiding injury; he has been on the disabled list nine times in his career. But after starting last season on the DL with a sore shoulder, Slaught returned in the second week and stayed healthy.

BASERUNNING:

Injuries and the physical pounding of catching have robbed Slaught of once-decent speed. However, the opposition can't take him for granted. He had six bunt hits last season and doesn't clog the bases like most catchers.

FIELDING:

Slaught carried the rap of being a poor defensive catcher when he came to the NL. However, he has been more than adequate behind the plate for the Pirates. His throwing has improved and pitchers like working with him.

OVERALL:

Now 34, Slaught gets better with age and shows no signs of slowing down. If the Pirates are successful in dealing LaValliere and his big contract, they have no reservations about making Slaught their number-one catcher in 1993.

DON SLAUGHT

Position: C
Bats: R **Throws:** R
Ht: 6' 1" **Wt:** 190
Opening Day Age: 34
Born: 9/11/58 in Long Beach, CA
ML Seasons: 11

Overall Statistics

	G	AB	R	H	D	T	HR	RBI	SB	BB	SO	AVG
1992	87	255	26	88	17	3	4	37	2	17	23	.345
Career	1004	3071	320	859	193	26	59	351	16	219	438	.280

Where He Hits the Ball

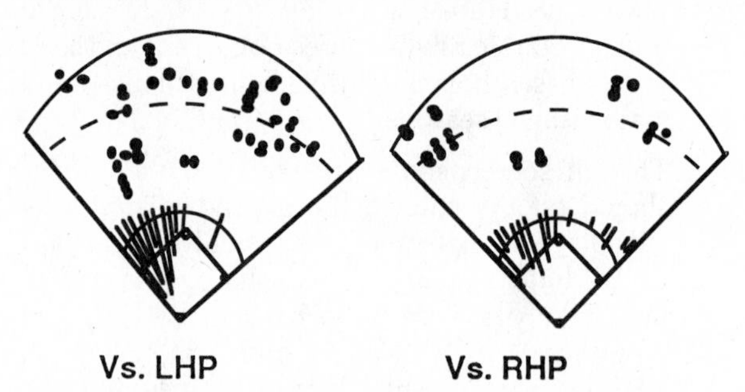

1992 Situational Stats

	AB	H	HR	RBI	AVG		AB	H	HR	RBI	AVG
Home	131	44	2	21	.336	LHP	174	56	3	21	.322
Road	124	44	2	16	.355	RHP	81	32	1	16	.395
Day	61	21	1	9	.344	Sc Pos	71	21	0	27	.296
Night	194	67	3	28	.345	Clutch	52	16	0	9	.308

1992 Rankings (National League)

→ Led NL catchers in batting average in the clutch (.308), batting average vs. left-handed pitchers (.322), batting average with 2 strikes (.250) and bunts in play (15)

ZANE SMITH

Position: SP
Bats: L **Throws:** L
Ht: 6' 1" **Wt:** 205

Opening Day Age: 32
Born: 12/28/60 in Madison, WI
ML Seasons: 9

PITCHING:

Zane Smith seemed poised to have a big second half in 1992 before shoulder tendinitis all but ended his season. Smith was 3-0 with a 0.39 ERA in three July starts. However, the shoulder problems kept him on the disabled list for the majority of the second half. Smith's problems multiplied, as he was discovered to have a slight cartilage tear as well. The lefthander came back to pitch five scoreless inning over two outings in the final weeks of the season. However, the Pirates weren't impressed enough to put him on the postseason roster. He wound up 8-8, his worst year in a Pirate uniform.

Smith's fastball has a heavy sinking action that compensates for the fact that he throws it with only average velocity. By keeping the ball low, Smith gets by with a succession of groundouts. Smith also throws a curveball, slider and change-up, but they are only average; he still gives up nearly a hit an inning. However, Smith survives because his sinker induces so many double play balls and because he has great control of his pitches. Since coming to the Pirates in a trade from Montreal in August, 1990, his control has been sensational. If he walks more than two batters in a game, it is news.

HOLDING RUNNERS, FIELDING, HITTING:

Smith has a good pickoff move and keeps runners honest. He can catch a runner napping and pick him off. As a sinkerballer, Smith understands the value of good defense. He finishes his delivery in good fielding position and helps himself with the glove. He is not an automatic out at bat.

OVERALL:

Smith is a quality major-league starting pitcher who can be counted on for 200 innings and 15 wins if healthy. However, health is an issue with Smith. He had elbow problems earlier in his career and now his shoulder is a question mark. It's hard to predict his future until he proves he can rebound from his latest physical problems.

Overall Statistics

	W	L	ERA	G	GS	Sv	IP	H	R	BB	SO	HR
1992	8	8	3.06	23	22	0	141.0	138	56	19	56	8
Career	75	86	3.53	281	216	3	1485.1	1473	692	483	828	85

How Often He Throws Strikes

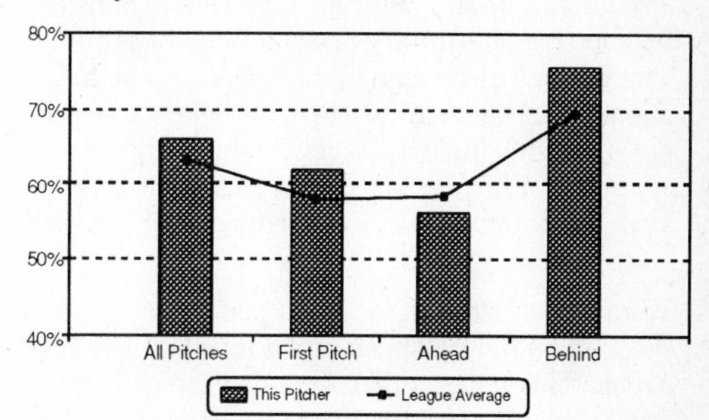

1992 Situational Stats

	W	L	ERA	Sv	IP		AB	H	HR	RBI	AVG
Home	4	4	3.25	0	63.2	LHB	93	20	2	9	.215
Road	4	4	2.91	0	77.1	RHB	436	118	6	41	.271
Day	3	3	2.23	0	44.1	Sc Pos	105	35	4	45	.333
Night	5	5	3.44	0	96.2	Clutch	69	17	1	4	.246

1992 Rankings (National League)

- 2nd in most GDPs induced per GDP situation (23.5%)
- 7th in GDPs induced (19)
- 8th in shutouts (3) and highest batting average allowed vs. right-handed batters (.271)
- Led the Pirates in most GDPs induced per GDP situation

RANDY TOMLIN

Position: SP
Bats: L **Throws:** L
Ht: 5'10" **Wt:** 170

Opening Day Age: 26
Born: 6/14/66 in Bainbridge, MD
ML Seasons: 3

Overall Statistics

	W	L	ERA	G	GS	Sv	IP	H	R	BB	SO	HR
1992	14	9	3.41	35	33	0	208.2	226	85	42	90	11
Career	26	20	3.10	78	72	0	461.1	458	184	108	236	25

How Often He Throws Strikes

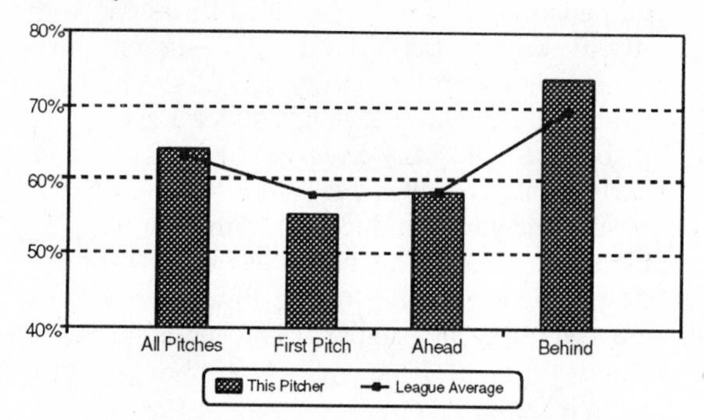

1992 Situational Stats

	W	L	ERA	Sv	IP		AB	H	HR	RBI	AVG
Home	7	3	2.37	0	110.0	LHB	148	37	2	9	.250
Road	7	6	4.56	0	98.2	RHB	653	189	9	66	.289
Day	3	5	4.03	0	76.0	Sc Pos	194	52	3	58	.268
Night	11	4	3.05	0	132.2	Clutch	70	16	1	5	.229

1992 Rankings (National League)

- 2nd in GDPs induced (27), most GDPs induced per 9 innings (1.2), least strikeouts per 9 innings (3.9) and highest batting average allowed vs. right-handed batters (.289)
- 3rd in hits allowed (226) and highest batting average allowed (.282)
- 5th in highest slugging percentage allowed (.397) and highest ERA on the road (4.56)
- Led the Pirates in hits allowed, balks (2), pickoff throws (150), stolen bases allowed (21), GDPs induced, least pitches thrown per batter (3.49), highest run support per 9 innings (4.0), least home runs allowed per 9 innings (.47), most GDPs induced per 9 innings and ERA at home (2.37)

PITCHING:

Randy Tomlin, the epitome of the crafty little lefthander, continued to silence the skeptics in 1992. Since he broke into the major leagues in 1990, there have been suspicions that Tomlin was a fluke. Many felt that the league would catch up to him once it got used to his unorthodox crossfire motion. However, Tomlin had his best season yet in 1992 with a career-high 14 wins.

Tomlin has the normal array of pitches -- fastball, slider, curveball and change-up. Not one particular pitch of his stands out. However, like many Pirates' pitchers, Tomlin succeeds by changing speeds and being consistently around the strike zone. He keeps hitters off balance, more than anything, with his "Vulcan" change. He jams the ball between his middle and ring fingers, reminiscent of the Vulcan sign on Star Trek -- which just happens to be Tomlin's favorite television program. Righthanders are comfortable and dig in against Tomlin (.271 lifetime against him). However, he presents major problems to lefties with his odd delivery (.220 lifetime).

Tomlin was streaky in 1992, putting together a six-game winning streak and a four-game losing streak. The losing streak included seven straight starts without a victory. When he struggled, it was because he started bringing his delivery from more over the top than crossfire. Tomlin still needs to build more arm strength, as he completed just one of 33 starts last season.

HOLDING RUNNERS, FIELDING, HITTING:

Tomlin does not have a great pickoff move and is slow to the plate. His unorthodox delivery throws runners off a little, but he still allowed 21 steals in 29 attempts last year. A good fielder, he has quick reactions on balls hit back through the box. Tomlin also played first base at Liberty University and can handle the bat.

OVERALL:

All Randy Tomlin does is keep quieting his critics. Though he may never be a big winner in the majors, he is good enough to be a third or fourth starter on most clubs and be counted on for double-digit win totals.

HITTING:

Back problems placed Andy Van Slyke's career in jeopardy last spring. But instead his problems turned out to be the best thing that could have happened to him.

Early in spring training, Van Slyke was diagnosed with having three degenerative discs and a bulging disc in his lower back. Many felt his effectiveness would be curtailed by the pain.

Van Slyke compensated for them by cutting down on his swing. Instead of trying to drive the ball out of the park, he just concentrated on making solid contact. As a result, he hit a career-best .324 and challenged Gary Sheffield for the National League batting title. He had never hit higher than .293 in nine previous seasons.

Van Slyke also put to rest concerns that his power would diminish, as he reached double figures in all three extra-base hit categories. He led the league with 45 doubles and had 12 triples and 14 home runs. The most dramatic improvement came in his approach to facing left-handed pitchers. Prior to last season, Van Slyke had a .218 career average against lefties. Last year, he hit .297 against them.

BASERUNNING:

Van Slyke remains an aggressive baserunner despite his back pain. After stealing 30 or more bases three separate times earlier in his career, he has averaged just 13 over the past four seasons. He might have stolen more, but he was hesitant to open up first base with the cleanup hitter at bat.

FIELDING:

Van Slyke is not quite as reckless in the field anymore because of his back. However, he is still one of the top center fielders in the National League, a Gold Glove winner for five straight seasons. He covers both gaps and has no fear of walls. His arm is still among the strongest in the game and no one takes chances against him.

OVERALL:

Van Slyke, despite back problems, had his best season in four years in 1992. Without peer in the field, his new approach to hitting has returned him to his status as one of the game's better all-around players.

ANDY VAN SLYKE

Position: CF
Bats: L **Throws:** R
Ht: 6' 2" **Wt:** 195

Opening Day Age: 32
Born: 12/21/60 in Utica, NY
ML Seasons: 10

Overall Statistics

	G	AB	R	H	D	T	HR	RBI	SB	BB	SO	AVG
1992	154	614	103	199	45	12	14	89	12	58	99	.324
Career	1390	4737	720	1308	251	82	144	688	220	558	895	.276

Where He Hits the Ball

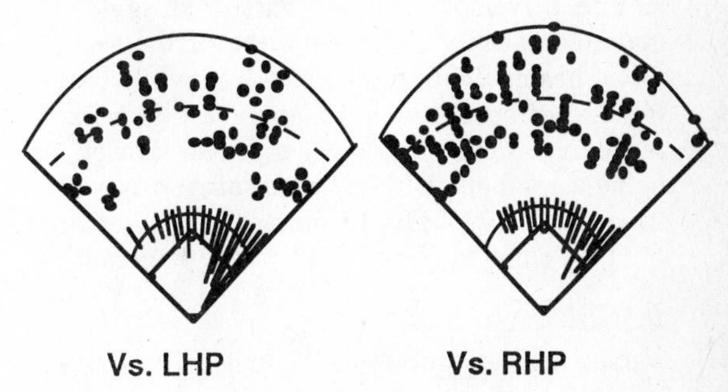

1992 Situational Stats

	AB	H	HR	RBI	AVG		AB	H	HR	RBI	AVG
Home	315	101	6	40	.321	LHP	269	80	4	41	.297
Road	299	98	8	49	.328	RHP	345	119	10	48	.345
Day	176	59	3	22	.335	Sc Pos	145	49	3	64	.338
Night	438	140	11	67	.320	Clutch	111	35	1	13	.315

1992 Rankings (National League)

- 1st in hits (199), doubles (45) and batting average vs. right-handed pitchers (.345)
- 2nd in batting average (.324)
- 3rd in runs scored (103), triples (12), total bases (310), sacrifice flies (9), slugging percentage vs. right-handed pitchers (.545), on-base percentage vs. right-handed pitchers (.411) and batting average on the road (.328)
- Led the Pirates in batting average, hits, singles (128), doubles, triples, total bases, sacrifice flies, most pitches seen (2,662), least GDPs per GDP situation (6.5%), batting average with runners in scoring position (.338), batting average in the clutch (.315) and batting average vs. right-handed pitchers

HITTING:

Gary Varsho was a very pleasant surprise for the Pittsburgh Pirates in 1991, his first year with the club. Last year, he was a disappointment. The Pirates appeared to have stolen Varsho from the Cubs in '91. After spending parts of three seasons with Chicago while being used almost exclusively as a pinch hitter, Varsho became a valuable extra man for the Bucs. He batted .273 with 4 homers and 23 RBI. But last year, Varsho showed why he had failed to spend a full season in the majors until age 30. Though his home run total stayed the same and his RBI count slipped by only one, his batting average plummeted 51 points to .222.

A line drive/spray hitter, Varsho struggled to make contact for a great portion of the season. Good heaters were blown past him while breaking and offspeed pitches also gave him a lot of problems. Varsho has always prided himself on being a good pinch hitter, but he also struggled in that role in 1992. His 13 pinch hits led the club, but they came in 55 at-bats for a .236 average.

BASERUNNING:

Varsho has very good speed and is willing to take risks on the bases. He looks to go from first to third on all singles and usually wins his gambles. He also knows when to steal a base and is an excellent 24-for-28 stealing in his career. He legged out 4 bunt hits last season.

FIELDING:

An infielder in the minor leagues, Varsho has worked very hard on his outfield defense and is now adequate. He can play all three outfield spots, though center field is his weakest spot. His arm is best suited to playing left field.

OVERALL:

With his $332,500 salary and eligibility for arbitration, the likable Varsho proved too rich for the Pirates' blood, and they released him after the season. He was signed by the Reds as a left-handed pinch-hit specialist and reserve outfielder.

GARY VARSHO

Position: RF/LF
Bats: L **Throws:** R
Ht: 5'11" **Wt:** 188

Opening Day Age: 31
Born: 6/20/61 in Marshfield, WI
ML Seasons: 5

Overall Statistics

	G	AB	R	H	D	T	HR	RBI	SB	BB	SO	AVG
1992	103	162	22	36	6	3	4	22	5	10	32	.222
Career	355	557	71	135	28	7	8	57	24	35	91	.242

Where He Hits the Ball

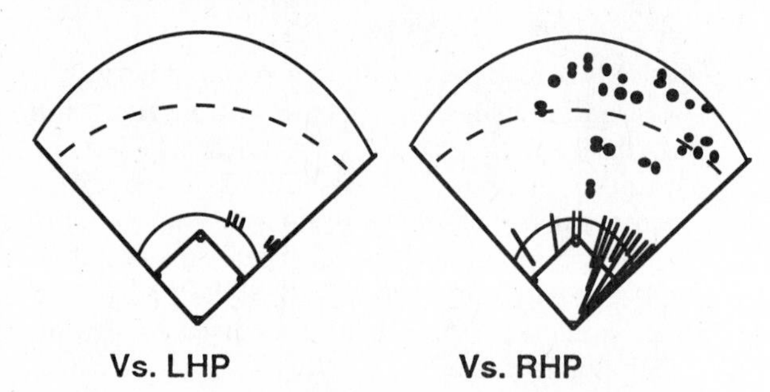

1992 Situational Stats

	AB	H	HR	RBI	AVG		AB	H	HR	RBI	AVG
Home	85	19	3	15	.224	LHP	13	3	1	3	.231
Road	77	17	1	7	.221	RHP	149	33	3	19	.221
Day	62	17	2	13	.274	Sc Pos	48	12	2	18	.250
Night	100	19	2	9	.190	Clutch	48	6	0	2	.125

1992 Rankings (National League)

- 2nd in lowest batting average in the clutch (.125)

TIM WAKEFIELD

Position: SP
Bats: R **Throws:** R
Ht: 6' 2" **Wt:** 195

Opening Day Age: 26
Born: 8/2/66 in Melbourne, FL
ML Seasons: 1

PITCHING:

By the end of last season, Pirates General Manager Ted Simmons referred to Tim Wakefield as simply "The Miracle." The rookie knuckleballer was quite a sensation, helping the Pirates to a third straight National League East title. He went 8-1 and ended the regular season with a five-game winning streak. He impressively allowed more than three runs only once in 13 starts, and was 2-0 in the National League Championship Series. Amazingly, it was only Wakefield's fourth season as a pitcher. He was a power-hitting first base prospect who was converted into a knuckleballer when his career as a position player stalled after one pro season.

Wakefield throws the knuckleball 80 percent of the time. Its path to the plate resembles a slider but the ball darts and dives when it gets to the hitter. Wakefield is able to make the knuckler break both down-and-in and down-and-away. Wakefield also throws a fastball and curveball, but they're mainly for show. His fastball only reaches 80 MPH and is used as a change of pace to offset his 60-MPH knuckler.

The knuckler puts little strain on Wakefield's arm; he is able to throw as many as 150 pitches in a start if needed. He averaged more than seven innings in his 13 regular season starts last season and pitched complete games in both NLCS outings.

HOLDING RUNNERS, FIELDING, HITTING:

Because the knuckler is so slow arriving to the plate, Wakefield compensates with one of the quickest deliveries in the game. Last year he allowed only 4 steals in 13 attempts -- remarkable for any pitcher, let alone a knuckleballer. Wakefield also helps himself in the field. Though he was a noted slugger in college, Wakefield has yet to show his hitting prowess in the major leagues.

OVERALL:

Was Wakefield's rookie season a fluke? Will the National League catch up to him? Keep in mind, Phil Niekro won over 300 games because of the knuckleball. Unless he loses control of the floater, Wakefield should be a consistent winner for many years.

Overall Statistics

	W	L	ERA	G	GS	Sv	IP	H	R	BB	SO	HR
1992	8	1	2.15	13	13	0	92.0	76	26	35	51	3
Career	8	1	2.15	13	13	0	92.0	76	26	35	51	3

How Often He Throws Strikes

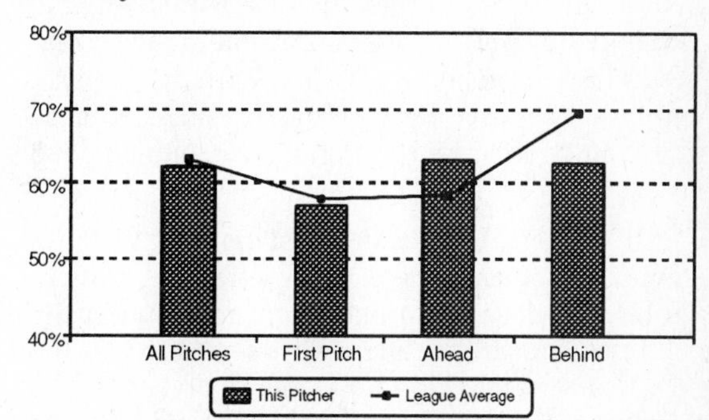

1992 Situational Stats

	W	L	ERA	Sv	IP		AB	H	HR	RBI	AVG
Home	5	0	2.09	0	43.0	LHB	202	43	1	12	.213
Road	3	1	2.20	0	49.0	RHB	125	33	2	13	.264
Day	3	0	2.97	0	30.1	Sc Pos	76	14	1	22	.184
Night	5	1	1.75	0	61.2	Clutch	58	12	0	4	.207

1992 Rankings (National League)

- Did not rank near the top or bottom in any category

BOB WALK

Position: SP/RP
Bats: R **Throws:** R
Ht: 6' 3" **Wt:** 217
Opening Day Age: 36
Born: 11/26/56 in Van Nuys, CA
ML Seasons: 13

PITCHING:

Who has been the most reliably winning pitcher in the National League over the past six years? A case could be made for journeyman Bob Walk. He has posted six consecutive winning seasons -- the only NL pitcher with at least 10 decisions each year to do so -- while going 59-35 for the Pirates in that span. Despite being hampered by nagging groin muscle pulls for the third consecutive season, Walk wound up going 10-6 with two saves in 1992 while splitting the season between the rotation and bullpen.

Walk's success is based on his curveball. In almost any situation, he will start a batter off with the curve in an attempt to get ahead in the count. From there, he comes in with a fastball and change-up. Walk's biggest problem in recent seasons have been injuries. He has been disabled six times in the past three seasons, five times because of groin muscle problems and once with a pulled hamstring.

Last season, Walk made 19 starts and 17 relief appearances and was equally effective in both roles. He does not mind bouncing between the rotation and bullpen and always seems to give the Pirates a boost. Witness Game 5 of last year's National League Championship Series: with the Pirates facing elimination, he went the distance on a three-hitter.

HOLDING RUNNERS, FIELDING, HITTING:

Walk does not have a great move to first. He frequently steps off the rubber in an attempt to disrupt the runner, but still allowed 19 steals in 24 attempts in his limited action last year. He may be the least graceful player in the major leagues, yet Walk manages to get the job done both in the field and at the plate in his own unorthodox way.

OVERALL:

Walk gets hurt a lot and will likely log his share of time on the disabled list. But when healthy, he is still solid as both a starter and reliever. He knows how to win and his versatility makes him a welcome addition to a pitching staff.

Overall Statistics

	W	L	ERA	G	GS	Sv	IP	H	R	BB	SO	HR
1992	10	6	3.20	36	19	2	135.0	132	54	43	60	10
Career	92	67	3.82	318	227	5	1479.0	1457	708	536	768	120

How Often He Throws Strikes

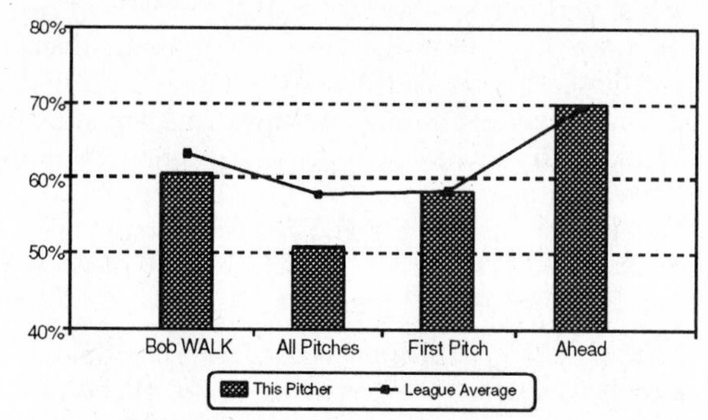

1992 Situational Stats

	W	L	ERA	Sv	IP		AB	H	HR	RBI	AVG
Home	8	3	2.82	1	76.2	LHB	287	83	6	33	.289
Road	2	3	3.70	1	58.1	RHB	225	49	4	17	.218
Day	3	2	2.87	1	47.0	Sc Pos	128	37	2	41	.289
Night	7	4	3.38	1	88.0	Clutch	66	23	1	9	.348

1992 Rankings (National League)

- 4th in highest batting average allowed with runners in scoring position (.289)
- 6th in hit batsmen (6)
- 8th in winning percentage (.625)
- 10th in balks (2)
- Led the Pirates in hit batsmen, balks and winning percentage

JOHN WEHNER

Position: 3B/1B
Bats: R **Throws:** R
Ht: 6' 3" **Wt:** 205

Opening Day Age: 25
Born: 6/29/67 in Pittsburgh, PA
ML Seasons: 2

HITTING:

As many scouts suspected, National League pitchers caught up to John Wehner in 1992. Before undergoing season-ending back surgery, Wehner had come from nowhere to hit .340 in 37 games as a Pirate rookie in 1991. He was given an outside chance at winning the Bucs' third base job last year, but had a bad spring and started last season in the minors. Wehner performed decently for AAA Buffalo, hitting .269 in 60 games. But after being recalled in mid-June, he struggled and finished with a .179 average in 55 games.

Last year, pitchers took advantage of Wehner's unorthodox stance, in which he keeps his hands well in front of his body. They continually busted Wehner with good fastballs inside, and his hands weren't quick enough to get around on them. Even when he moved his hands to a more conventional style, he failed to hit. Wehner had shown some power in his minor-league days, particularly in 1989 when he had 32 doubles and 14 homers at Class A Salem. But he had only six extra-base hits for the Pirates last year, all of them doubles.

BASERUNNING:

Wehner runs exceptionally well for a big man and is aggressive on the bases. He's stolen more than 20 bases in two different minor-league seasons and is a perfect six-for-six in the majors.

FIELDING:

Wehner's primary position is third base, but the Pirates made him a utility man last season. He has a good arm at third, and displayed solid footwork and the ability to start the double play. His range is better than average. He is good at first base but shaky on the pivot at second base and shortstop.

OVERALL:

The luster is off Wehner's star. His best hope for a regular role this year is that Jeff King will be shifted to second and that rookie Kevin Young will flop as his third base replacement. But Wehner himself will also have to make a strong impression. Otherwise, he'll be back in the minors.

Overall Statistics

	G	AB	R	H	D	T	HR	RBI	SB	BB	SO	AVG
1992	55	123	11	22	6	0	0	4	3	12	22	.179
Career	92	229	26	58	13	0	0	11	6	19	39	.253

Where He Hits the Ball

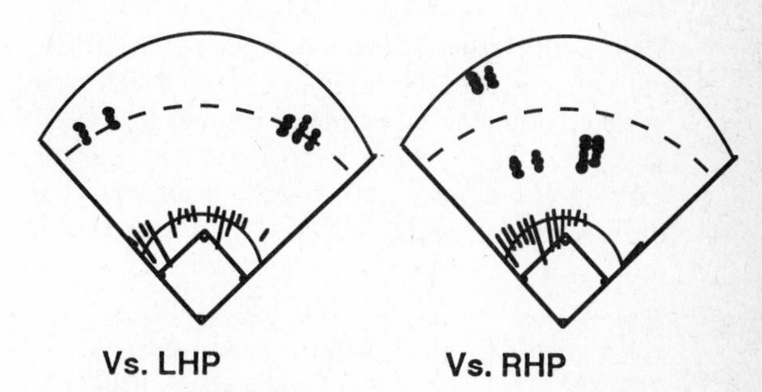

1992 Situational Stats

	AB	H	HR	RBI	AVG		AB	H	HR	RBI	AVG
Home	41	8	0	2	.195	LHP	56	10	0	3	.179
Road	82	14	0	2	.171	RHP	67	12	0	1	.179
Day	49	8	0	2	.163	Sc Pos	32	4	0	3	.125
Night	74	14	0	2	.189	Clutch	27	4	0	1	.148

1992 Rankings (National League)

➡ Did not rank near the top or bottom in any category

TOP PROSPECT

DANNY COX

Position: RP/SP
Bats: R **Throws:** R
Ht: 6' 4" **Wt:** 225

Opening Day Age: 33
Born: 9/21/59 in Northhampton, England
ML Seasons: 8

Overall Statistics

	W	L	ERA	G	GS	Sv	IP	H	R	BB	SO	HR
1992	5	3	4.60	25	7	3	62.2	66	37	27	48	5
Career	65	65	3.57	200	174	3	1150.2	1155	528	363	587	90

PITCHING, FIELDING, HITTING & HOLDING RUNNERS:

Danny Cox' remarkable comeback stalled at first but then resumed better than ever in 1992. Cox, who did not pitch in the major leagues in 1989 or 1990 after undergoing ligament transplant surgery in his elbow, got off to a rough start in Philadelphia in 1992. He was then released after refusing a minor-league assignment.

The Pirates signed the righthander to a Class AAA contract with Buffalo, where he posted a 1.70 ERA in eight minor-league starts. The Bucs promoted him to the majors with six weeks left in the season. Converted from starter to reliever when he got to Pittsburgh, Cox gave the Pirates' sagging bullpen a lift, going 3-1 with his first three major-league saves. After posting a 5.40 ERA in nine games with the Phillies, he had a 3.33 mark in 16 games with the Pirates.

Cox is no longer a power pitcher. However, he keeps his sinker down and throws a big-breaking curveball and an effective change-up. Cox varies his pickoff moves keeping runners off balance. He is an adequate fielder for a big man and takes his cuts at the plate.

OVERALL:

Cox again resurrected his career in Pittsburgh in the final weeks of the 1992 season. He seemed comfortable working in relief, a new role, and fewer innings should lessen the strain on his reconstructed elbow.

CARLOS GARCIA

Position: 2B
Bats: R **Throws:** R
Ht: 6' 1" **Wt:** 185

Opening Day Age: 25
Born: 10/15/67 in Tachira, Venezuela
ML Seasons: 3

Overall Statistics

	G	AB	R	H	D	T	HR	RBI	SB	BB	SO	AVG
1992	22	39	4	8	1	0	0	4	0	0	9	.205
Career	38	67	7	16	1	2	0	5	0	1	19	.239

HITTING, FIELDING, BASERUNNING:

For nearly three seasons, Carlos Garcia has been sitting at the Pirates' AAA Buffalo farm team waiting for his chance to play in the major leagues. Garcia has nothing left to prove in the minors. He had his best season yet at Buffalo in 1992, batting .303 with 13 homers and 70 RBI.

Though he has batted only .239 in 38 major-league games, Garcia is an outstanding hitting prospect. He has quick wrists and hands and whips the bat through the strike zone. Garcia also shows good power to all fields, a particularly rare attribute for a middle infielder. He is still a bit of a free swinger and struggles against good breaking balls.

Garcia has stolen 51 bases over the past two AAA seasons and should be a basestealing threat in the majors. He is an outstanding shortstop with great range and a strong arm. With Jay Bell entrenched at shortstop, the Pirates have looked at Garcia at both second and third base. He is somewhat shaky turning the double play at second, but that is where his future probably lies.

OVERALL:

The Pirates' trade of Jose Lind gives Garcia an opportunity at second base. There was also off-season talk of the Pirates trading Bell, which would hand Garcia the job at his natural position. One thing is clear: Garcia is ready for the major leagues.

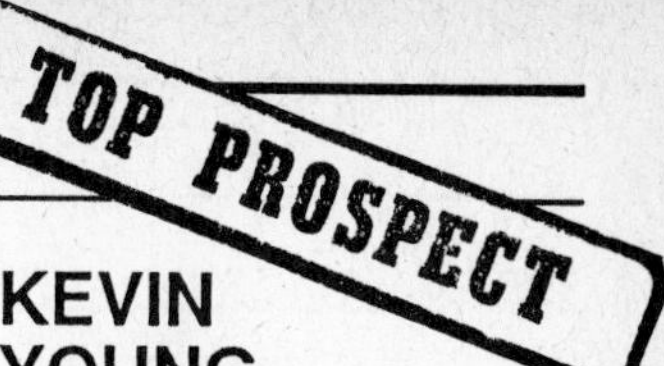

LLOYD McCLENDON

Position: RF/1B
Bats: R **Throws:** R
Ht: 6' 0" **Wt:** 212

Opening Day Age: 34
Born: 1/11/59 in Gary, IN
ML Seasons: 6

Overall Statistics

	G	AB	R	H	D	T	HR	RBI	SB	BB	SO	AVG
1992	84	190	26	48	8	1	3	20	1	28	24	.253
Career	431	931	120	232	39	2	29	123	15	116	137	.249

HITTING, FIELDING, BASERUNNING:

Much like teammate Gary Redus, Lloyd McClendon followed a disappointing regular season with a great postseason for the Pittsburgh Pirates in 1992. McClendon batted just .253 with three homers and 20 RBI in the regular campaign. His performance was a drop from his 1991 figures of .288-7-24, even though he had more at-bats in '92. But McClendon sizzled in the National League Championship Series, going an incredible 8-for-11 (.727).

McClendon, who feasts on lefties but rarely faces righthanders, lost his aggressiveness last season as he slumped. A good first-ball hitter, he took many good pitches and often put himself in a hole. He is a line drive hitter with power; although he had his string of five consecutive seasons with a pinch homer ended in 1992. He retains a short, quick stroke.

McClendon takes it strictly one base a time as a runner and has stolen just 15 bases in his career. He is a versatile player: he can catch, play first and third base, as well as left and right field. He settled in as a platoon right fielder last year but is weak defensively at all positions. His arm is fairly strong, but not particularly accurate.

OVERALL:

McClendon is a useful bench player with good pop. Although a role player, the Pirates made him feel valued after his great postseason with a two-year contract worth $1.3 million. The loss of Gary Varsho and Cecil Espy should ensure McClendon of similar, or even more, duty in '93.

KEVIN YOUNG

Position: 3B
Bats: R **Throws:** R
Ht: 6' 3" **Wt:** 210

Opening Day Age: 23
Born: 6/16/69 in Alpena, MI
ML Seasons: 1

Overall Statistics

	G	AB	R	H	D	T	HR	RBI	SB	BB	SO	AVG
1992	10	7	2	4	0	0	0	4	1	2	0	.571
Career	10	7	2	4	0	0	0	4	1	2	0	.571

HITTING, FIELDING, BASERUNNING:

As free agency takes its toll on the supposedly financially-strapped Pirate organization, the organization continues to spurt out surprising young players (Tim Wakefield in 1992 and Orlando Merced in 1991) who have played key roles in their title runs. If the Pirates are again to be surprise contenders in '93, the latest impact rookie may be Kevin Young.

Basically, the development of Young at AAA Buffalo as an exciting third base prospect enabled the Pirates to deal away incumbent Steve Buechele in midseason to bolster the Pirates rotation without fear for their future. The 23-year-old Young, playing only his third season of pro ball, was voted the best prospect in the American Association after hitting .314 with 43 extra-base hits (8 homers) in 490 at-bats. Athletically-built, Young has decent speed (19 steals in 31 tries last year) and indications of excellent patience; he walked 67 times and compiled a .406 on-base percentage at Buffalo. His fielding is the question. While he has good range, he made 30 errors at AAA last season.

OVERALL:

Young will be pushing for the starting third base job in the spring. The rapid adaptability shown by his meteoric rise to the majors should enable him to work through his fielding problems. He has a good chance at a high on-base, medium power first major-league season.

PITTSBURGH PIRATES MINOR LEAGUE PROSPECTS

ORGANIZATION OVERVIEW:

The Pirates have won three straight division titles on a very tight budget. They must be doing something right. Last year the Pirates survived the loss of Bobby Bonilla and the salary-forced trade of John Smiley in their usual way: they brought in cheap, useful replacements. Kirk Gibson didn't work out as the right fielder, so they imported Alex Cole, who did. When replacing Smiley proved tougher than they thought, they brought up a rookie, Tim Wakefield, who was absolutely brilliant. Can they keep losing talented veterans and still stay in first place? If Barry Bonds departs, it'll be very difficult. But the Bucs, with a sound minor-league system, will try to find a way.

STEVE COOKE

Position: P **Opening Day Age:** 23
Bats: R **Throws:** L **Born:** 1/14/70 in Kanai, HI
Ht: 6' 6" **Wt:** 200

Recent Statistics

	W	L	ERA	G	GS	Sv	IP	H	R	BB	SO	HR
92 AA Carolina	2	2	3.00	6	6	0	36.0	31	13	12	38	1
92 AAA Buffalo	6	3	3.75	13	13	0	74.1	71	35	36	52	2
92 NL Pittsburgh	2	0	3.52	11	0	1	23.0	22	9	4	10	2

Rated the Bucs' number-one prospect a year ago, Cooke pitched at three levels last year, going a combined 10-5. His record included 11 games out of the Pirate bullpen. A big man, Cooke doesn't have a blazing fastball, but his pitches move. His control has sometimes been a problem, though it was excellent in his stint with the Pirates last year. Cooke seems a cinch to make the big club in 1993 and could well crack the starting rotation.

JOEL JOHNSTON

Position: P **Opening Day Age:** 26
Bats: R **Throws:** R **Born:** 3/8/67 in West Chester, PA
Ht: 6' 5" **Wt:** 218

Recent Statistics

	W	L	ERA	G	GS	Sv	IP	H	R	BB	SO	HR
92 AAA Omaha	5	2	6.39	42	0	2	74.2	80	54	45	48	9
92 NL Pittsburgh	0	0	13.50	5	0	0	2.2	3	4	2	0	2

Considered the Royals' top prospect a year ago, Johnston was used for batting practice by both AAA and major-league hitters last year. He had a 6.39 ERA at Omaha and a 13.50 mark for the Royals, though that was in only 2.2 innings. Johnston can throw hard but he doesn't know where the ball is going. Last year he gave up 45 walks in 74.2 innings at Omaha. After five seasons, he hasn't had an ERA lower than 4.88, except for one amazing September with the Royals in '91, when he had an 0.40 mark in 22.1 innings (13 games). The Pirates, who acquired him for Jose Lind, will hope for the best.

AL MARTIN

Position: OF **Opening Day Age:** 25
Bats: L **Throws:** L **Born:** 11/24/67 in West Covina, CA
Ht: 6' 2" **Wt:** 220

Recent Statistics

	G	AB	R	H	D	T	HR	RBI	SB	BB	SO	AVG
92 AAA Buffalo	125	420	85	128	16	15	20	59	20	35	93	.305
92 NL Pittsburgh	12	12	1	2	0	1	0	2	0	0	5	.167
92 MLE	125	400	66	108	14	10	14	45	13	26	98	.270

A six-year minor-league free agent who was buried in the deep Atlanta farm system, Martin took off after signing with the Pirates last winter. The speedy outfielder batted .305 with 20 homers at AAA Buffalo. He also belted 15 triples and stole 20 bases in 25 attempts. American Association managers rated him the league's number-eight prospect and raved about his talent and bat speed.

BRIAN D. SHOUSE

Position: P **Opening Day Age:** 24
Bats: L **Throws:** L **Born:** 9/26/68 in Effingham, IL
Ht: 5' 11" **Wt:** 175

Recent Statistics

	W	L	ERA	G	GS	Sv	IP	H	R	BB	SO	HR
91 A Augusta	2	3	3.19	26	0	8	31.0	22	13	9	32	1
91 A Salem	2	1	2.94	17	0	3	33.2	35	12	15	25	2
92 AA Carolina	5	6	2.44	59	0	4	77.1	71	31	28	79	3

Not considered a top prospect a year ago, Shouse developed so quickly last year that the Pirates wound up protecting him in the expansion draft. The lefty reliever posted a 2.44 ERA in 59 games, striking out over a man an inning. Shouse's control is good and he's allowed only eight homers in 181.2 minor league innings. Shouse will probably pitch in AAA this year, but given Jim Leyland's dissatisfaction with his left-handed relief corps, he could soon be pitching in Pittsburgh.

PAUL WAGNER

Position: P **Opening Day Age:** 25
Bats: R **Throws:** R **Born:** 11/14/67 in Milwaukee, WI
Ht: 6' 3" **Wt:** 205

Recent Statistics

	W	L	ERA	G	GS	Sv	IP	H	R	BB	SO	HR
92 AA Carolina	6	6	3.03	19	19	0	121.2	104	52	47	101	3
92 AAA Buffalo	3	3	5.49	8	8	0	39.1	51	27	14	19	1
92 NL Pittsburgh	2	0	0.69	6	1	0	13.0	9	1	5	5	0

Another Pirate who's come a long way in a short time, Wagner was a 13th-round pick in 1989. His work at AA Carolina and AAA Buffalo wasn't all that great -- a 9-9 record and a 5.49 ERA in eight starts for Buffalo -- but Wagner impressed the Bucs in six outings with them. He had a 2-0 record and an 0.69 ERA over 13 innings, and the Pirates liked his work enough to protect him in the expansion draft. Wagner has always had good strikeout ratios and could make the Pirate roster this year.

LUIS ALICEA

Position: 2B
Bats: B **Throws:** R
Ht: 5' 9" **Wt:** 165
Opening Day Age: 27
Born: 7/29/65 in Santurce, Puerto Rico
ML Seasons: 3

Overall Statistics

	G	AB	R	H	D	T	HR	RBI	SB	BB	SO	AVG
1992	85	265	26	65	9	11	2	32	2	27	40	.245
Career	234	630	51	141	22	15	3	56	3	60	91	.224

Where He Hits the Ball

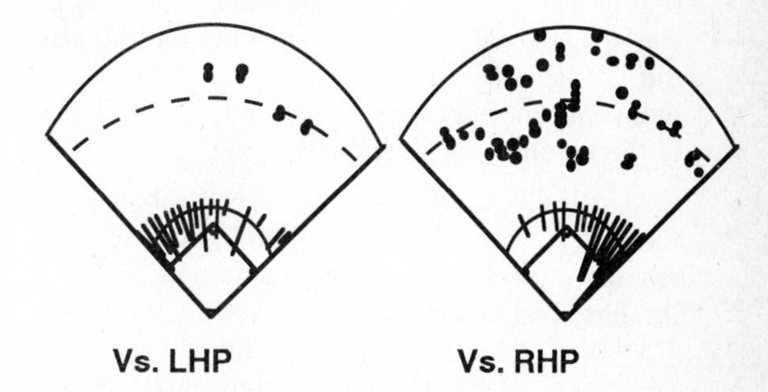

1992 Situational Stats

	AB	H	HR	RBI	AVG		AB	H	HR	RBI	AVG
Home	145	40	2	18	.276	LHP	85	25	0	12	.294
Road	120	25	0	14	.208	RHP	180	40	2	20	.222
Day	74	23	2	12	.311	Sc Pos	71	16	0	25	.225
Night	191	42	0	20	.220	Clutch	63	13	1	6	.206

1992 Rankings (National League)

- 1st in lowest batting average on a 3-1 count (.000)
- 3rd in lowest batting average with 2 strikes (.119)
- 4th in triples (11)
- 8th in lowest batting average on a 3-2 count (.091)
- Led the Cardinals in triples
- Led NL second basemen in triples

HITTING:

Luis Alicea made his first trip to the big club as a heralded prospect in 1988 and bombed out, hitting just .212. It has taken him awhile to get over that and to grow as a hitter. Alicea spent 1989 at Louisville and then was disabled for parts of 1989 and 1990 with a broken bone in his wrist that required surgery. In 1991 he took a big step forward, hitting .393 in 112 minor-league at-bats. He got a brief trial with the Cardinals in 1991 and batted .191, but last year he got a more regular shot and did better, hitting .245.

Alicea got his chance in 1992 when Jose Oquendo was hurt on Opening Day. Geronimo Pena was already disabled so the job was his, but he hit just a buck and change and lost out to Rex Hudler. When Hudler was hurt, Alicea got another chance. This time he hit very well, but he strained a ribcage muscle and when he came back he seemed to have some trouble swinging the bat.

Alicea is a contact hitter with a level swing and the Cards have tried with mixed success to get him to hit the ball more on the ground. He has power to the alleys and hit 11 triples in only 265 at-bats. Though a switch-hitter, he was far superior from the right side last year.

BASERUNNING:

Though Alicea stole as many as 27 bases in the minors, his running game has faded and he was only two-of-seven in 1992. His 11 triples, though, showed that his good speed remains.

FIELDING:

Alicea's fielding made him a number-one draft pick in 1985 and he does have the tools. But he has been merely average in St. Louis, mostly as a backup for Oquendo and Ozzie Smith at shortstop. He made three errors in just 27 innings at short.

OVERALL:

Alicea's role with the Cards, if he can stay healthy, is to play backup at second base and short and hit against lefties. His skills are not broad enough to guarantee a roster spot.

MARK CLARK

Position: SP
Bats: R **Throws:** R
Ht: 6' 5" **Wt:** 225
Opening Day Age: 24
Born: 5/12/68 in Bath, IL
ML Seasons: 2

PITCHING:

After a meteoric rise in 1991, promising righthander Mark Clark had a difficult 1992. Clark went from AA ball to the majors in 1991, not because of his won-loss record but because his abilities were outstanding. Those abilities were still apparent in 1992 but the youngster nonetheless suffered through a 3-10 season.

Clark throws a slider and forkball, but his bread-and-butter is a sinking fastball which hits 90 MPH. None of these pitches were working in the spring -- he turned in an ERA of 9.00 -- and he was shipped to AAA Louisville, where he stumbled to an 0-4 start before gaining a measure of control. Recalled on May 31, he worked in the regular rotation, but the Cards lost 14 of his 20 starts. Clark didn't get much run support but also did not keep St. Louis in the games. Though he had some success early in the year, he unraveled in the second half (1-7, 5.84).

Last year Clark couldn't seem to control his good fastball. He served up a lot of high, hittable heaters and sliders and gave up 12 homers in 113.1 innings. Just trying to get the first pitch over, he got whacked for 32 first-pitch hits (.327 average), 13 of them for extra bases. His high-pitch troubles severely cut into his usually good strikeout totals, though he did keep his walks down.

HOLDING RUNNERS, FIELDING, HITTING:

Clark didn't have much attention to spare for baserunners; they stole him blind at a 17-for-19 pace. The same was true of his fielding, as he turned into a spectator instead of a fifth infielder on ground balls. Experience should improve his performance in these areas.

OVERALL:

Clark has come through tough stretches of pitching before. He is very strong and keeps his velocity up late into the game and throughout the season. He did toss one complete game four-hit shutout. Clark hasn't come close to exhausting the Cards' patience and he'll be back, if not in '93, then in '94.

Overall Statistics

	W	L	ERA	G	GS	Sv	IP	H	R	BB	SO	HR
1992	3	10	4.45	20	20	0	113.1	117	59	36	44	12
Career	4	11	4.38	27	22	0	135.2	134	69	47	57	15

How Often He Throws Strikes

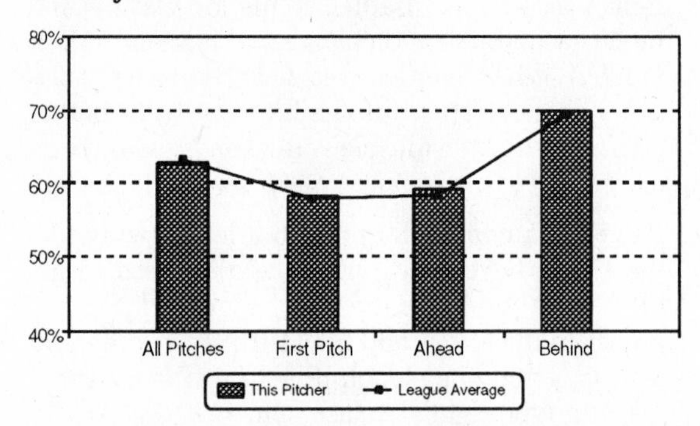

1992 Situational Stats

	W	L	ERA	Sv	IP		AB	H	HR	RBI	AVG
Home	1	6	5.25	0	48.0	LHB	263	70	6	29	.266
Road	2	4	3.86	0	65.1	RHB	178	47	6	17	.264
Day	1	3	3.89	0	39.1	Sc Pos	103	22	2	32	.214
Night	2	7	4.74	0	74.0	Clutch	21	7	0	3	.333

1992 Rankings (National League)

- Led the Cardinals in losses (10), shutouts (1) and stolen bases allowed (17)

RHEAL CORMIER

Position: SP
Bats: L **Throws:** L
Ht: 5'10" **Wt:** 185

Opening Day Age: 25
Born: 4/23/67 in Moneton, NB, Canada
ML Seasons: 2

PITCHING:

A series of physical problems dogged Rheal Cormier for the first few months of 1992. He pitched sparingly and not too well in spring training due to leg troubles and a bout with the flu, and started the year at AAA Louisville. He was recalled, perhaps before he was ready, when Bryn Smith was hurt. For two months he struggled, getting very little support (three runs in his first five losses, and six in his 10 losses for the season). He was walking too many hitters, then began to pitch too much in the strike zone and started giving up hits and home runs. He was sent down May 31, with an 0-5 record and a 6.56 ERA.

Cormier called the demotion "a shot in the chest." He was recalled a week later. From that point on he walked only 17 batters in 138 innings, kept his fastball down, and reaped a crop of groundball outs from the sinker. Cormier could also get a strikeout when he needed one, and his strikeout-to-walk ratio was third in the league. He also coaxed some big double plays (19 in all). Cormier had a 2.88 ERA after the All-Star break and won seven in a row to end the season. The Cards won his last nine starts.

HOLDING RUNNERS, FIELDING, HITTING:

During the first half Cormier was stolen blind, but he then steadied and caught three of five in the second half. The lefthander has a good pickoff move and keeps runners close when he's on his game. He is a fine athlete and committed no errors while doing his share of glovework. His batting ability is also commendable, he had 10 sacrifice hits, one of the league's highest marks.

OVERALL:

Cormier's control is going to make him a winner; he has walked an average of one batter every five innings in just over 700 professional innings. The Cardinals' vaunted defense and cavernous park is suited to his sinker. His second half is his real level of ability, and given some support and some luck, he should win 15 to 18 games in 1993.

Overall Statistics

	W	L	ERA	G	GS	Sv	IP	H	R	BB	SO	HR
1992	10	10	3.68	31	30	0	186.0	194	83	33	117	15
Career	14	15	3.80	42	40	0	253.2	268	118	41	155	20

How Often He Throws Strikes

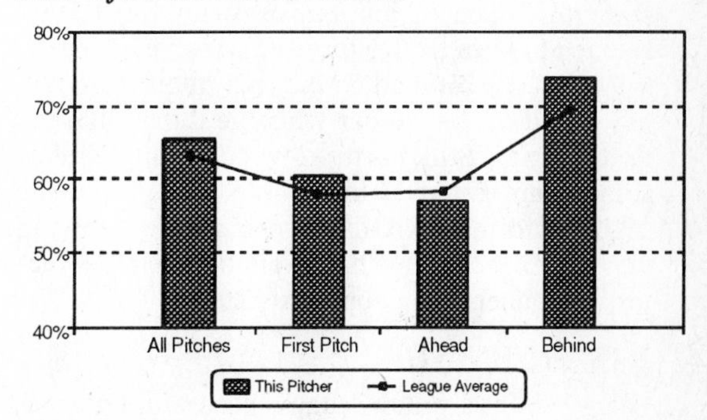

1992 Situational Stats

	W	L	ERA	Sv	IP		AB	H	HR	RBI	AVG
Home	7	4	3.98	0	92.2	LHB	132	38	1	12	.288
Road	3	6	3.38	0	93.1	RHB	588	156	14	58	.265
Day	4	4	3.06	0	64.2	Sc Pos	159	40	5	54	.252
Night	6	6	4.01	0	121.1	Clutch	53	20	1	6	.377

1992 Rankings (National League)

- 3rd in highest strikeout/walk ratio (3.5)
- 4th in least pitches thrown per batter (3.35)
- 6th in highest batting average allowed (.269), most GDPs induced per 9 innings (.92) and highest ERA at home (3.98)
- 7th in GDPs induced (19)
- 8th in highest slugging percentage allowed (.387) and highest stolen base percentage allowed (73.3%)
- 9th in most home runs allowed per 9 innings (.73)
- Led the Cardinals in losses (10), hit batsmen (5) and balks (2)

BERNARD GILKEY

Position: LF
Bats: R **Throws:** R
Ht: 6' 0" **Wt:** 190

Opening Day Age: 26
Born: 9/24/66 in St. Louis, MO
ML Seasons: 3

HITTING:

Young Bernard Gilkey made tremendous strides in the 1992 season, improving his average by 86 points to .302. The righty-swinging Gilkey opened the 1992 season sharing time in left field with Milt Thompson and Brian Jordan. When Jordan slumped and Gilkey showed he could handle righties, he became the starter -- perhaps for good. Gilkey responded to the Cardinals' need for RBI by driving in 30 runs in 234 at-bats after the break with seven home runs. Plus, he showed off his clutch hitting by batting .359 with runners in scoring position for the season.

Gilkey has put on 20 pounds since reaching the majors, so his slugging may be a function of new strength. Much of his improvement from 1991 seemed to stem from a more aggressive approach to hitting. He jumped on the first pitch more and got ahead of the pitcher when he didn't like the first offering. Still, his true level of ability may be somewhere between his rookie season and his 1992 performance. Gilkey seems to be growing into the expectations that awaited him in the majors, just later than people expected.

BASERUNNING:

Gilkey was a minor-league basestealing stud, with 158 thefts during the 1988-90 seasons. But his major-league success rate hasn't been outstanding; at 32-for-52 over the last two years, he hasn't done his team a whole lot of good. The hopeful sign was his second half, when he was 11-of-15.

FIELDING:

Gilkey made five errors in left field last year, but he is a good fielder with fine range. He's a heady outfielder, too, starting three double plays from left, the most in the league and second in the majors to Brady Anderson's four.

OVERALL:

The Cardinals outfield is poised to be one of the best in baseball, and Gilkey brings his share of talent to the table. He'll be the starter in left field in 1993 and perhaps will lead off as well, either against lefties or everyday. He's just 26 and has shown a wide range of major-league skills. The Cardinals are ready for a breakthrough year.

Overall Statistics

	G	AB	R	H	D	T	HR	RBI	SB	BB	SO	AVG
1992	131	384	56	116	19	4	7	43	18	39	52	.302
Career	230	716	95	193	31	8	13	66	38	86	90	.270

Where He Hits the Ball

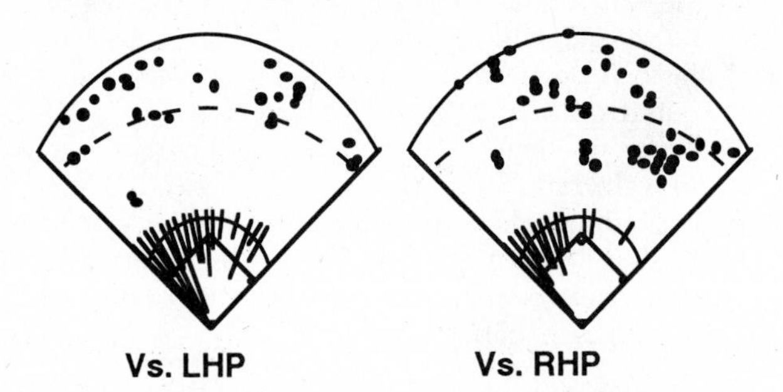

1992 Situational Stats

	AB	H	HR	RBI	AVG		AB	H	HR	RBI	AVG
Home	196	58	3	20	.296	LHP	176	62	2	20	.352
Road	188	58	4	23	.309	RHP	208	54	5	23	.260
Day	94	28	2	10	.298	Sc Pos	78	28	2	35	.359
Night	290	88	5	33	.303	Clutch	94	29	3	11	.309

1992 Rankings (National League)

- 3rd in lowest stolen base percentage (60.0%)
- 6th in batting average vs. left-handed pitchers (.352)
- 9th in on-base percentage vs. left-handed pitchers (.402)
- 10th in caught stealing (12)
- Led NL left fielders in batting average vs. left-handed pitchers and errors (5)

IN HIS PRIME

FELIX JOSE

Position: RF
Bats: B **Throws:** R
Ht: 6' 1" **Wt:** 221

Opening Day Age: 27
Born: 5/8/65 in Santo Domingo, Dominican Republic
ML Seasons: 5

HITTING:

A strained right hamstring forced Felix Jose to the disabled list at the start of last year and kept him there for four weeks. But while the injury hobbled Jose in a number of ways, it didn't prevent him from having another fine season. Jose batted .295, 10 points lower than his .305 average of '91. But he had 75 RBI, only two less than in 1991 when he appeared in 23 more games and had 59 more at-bats. He also had a career-high 14 homers. Jose clearly liked the new dimensions at Busch Stadium, hitting 12 round-trippers there.

When he returned from the DL, Jose sparked the Cardinals to a run at the Pirates with a .346 average and 25 RBI in 27 May games. He was hot-and-cold after that, but generally produced a season that matched his All-Star 1991. In both seasons he was consistent and showed the ability to hit all kinds of pitching. The switch-hitter was especially effective from the right side; he led the league against lefties, hitting .374. Jose did suffer an obvious decline in doubles and triples and scored just 62 runs, so his ability to stretch the long hit may be showing the effects of his hamstring problems.

BASERUNNING:

The hamstring problems didn't hurt Jose's straightaway speed, as he had his best year as a basestealer at 28-for-40. But his drop from 40 doubles, good for second in the league in 1991, to just 22 is troubling. He may recover his extra-base speed, but hamstring injuries can be chronic.

FIELDING:

Jose has an outstanding arm and was among the leaders in assists by right fielders with 11. He has good range but is not much more than an average right fielder.

OVERALL:

The injury did little more than slow Jose, and Torre commented on his new air of confidence. He compared him to the imposing Reggie Smith, without the power but with more speed. He could return to hitting 40 doubles, or he could hit 25 homers, or he could do both and be an MVP candidate.

Overall Statistics

	G	AB	R	H	D	T	HR	RBI	SB	BB	SO	AVG
1992	131	509	62	150	22	3	14	75	28	40	100	.295
Career	439	1566	190	449	81	10	33	210	61	118	308	.287

Where He Hits the Ball

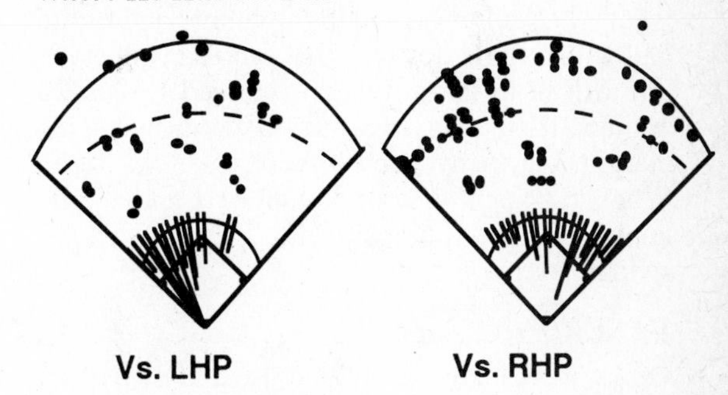

1992 Situational Stats

	AB	H	HR	RBI	AVG		AB	H	HR	RBI	AVG
Home	255	75	12	46	.294	LHP	182	68	6	31	.374
Road	254	75	2	29	.295	RHP	327	82	8	44	.251
Day	130	37	2	21	.285	Sc Pos	153	40	1	56	.261
Night	379	113	12	54	.298	Clutch	113	36	4	20	.319

1992 Rankings (National League)

- 1st in batting average vs. left-handed pitchers (.374)
- 4th in on-base percentage vs. left-handed pitchers (.419)
- 6th in lowest percentage of swings put into play (38.7%)
- Led the Cardinals in batting average in the clutch (.319), batting average with the bases loaded (.467), batting average vs. left-handed pitchers, slugging percentage vs. left-handed pitchers (.555), on-base percentage vs. left-handed pitchers and batting average on the road (.295)

FUTURE ALL-STAR

RAY LANKFORD

Position: CF
Bats: L **Throws:** L
Ht: 5'11" **Wt:** 198

Opening Day Age: 25
Born: 6/5/67 in Modesto, CA
ML Seasons: 3

Overall Statistics

	G	AB	R	H	D	T	HR	RBI	SB	BB	SO	AVG
1992	153	598	87	175	40	6	20	86	42	72	147	.293
Career	343	1290	182	353	73	22	32	167	94	126	288	.274

Where He Hits the Ball

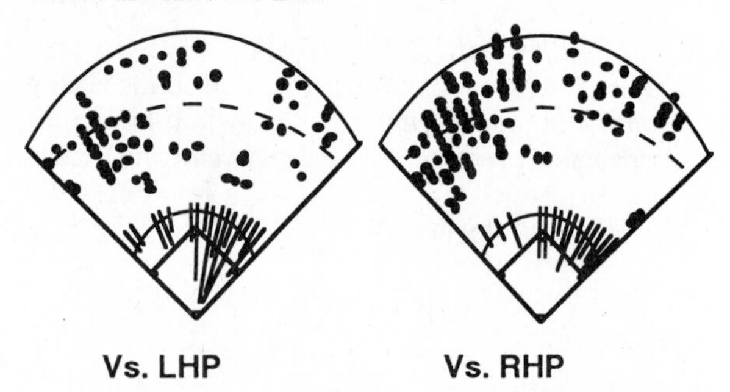

1992 Situational Stats

	AB	H	HR	RBI	AVG		AB	H	HR	RBI	AVG
Home	314	97	13	54	.309	LHP	216	55	4	32	.255
Road	284	78	7	32	.275	RHP	382	120	16	54	.314
Day	162	41	4	18	.253	Sc Pos	162	53	7	67	.327
Night	436	134	16	68	.307	Clutch	131	37	5	18	.282

1992 Rankings (National League)

- 1st in caught stealing (24) and strikeouts (147)
- 2nd in doubles (40)
- 3rd in most pitches seen (2,697)
- Led the Cardinals in home runs (20), at-bats (598), runs scored (87), hits (175), doubles, total bases (287), RBI (86), caught stealing, walks (72), times on base (252), strikeouts, most pitches seen, plate appearances (682), games played (153), slugging percentage (.480), on-base percentage (.371), HR frequency (29.9 ABs per HR), least GDPs per GDP situation (5.8%) and steals of third (5)

HITTING:

Ray Lankford started the 1992 season as the Cardinals' leadoff hitter. He was a good one, compiling an April on-base average of .387 and ranking among the top 10 in the league in runs scored for two months. But since his power was blossoming as well, manager Joe Torre dropped Lankford to the number-three spot on June 12 and watched him take off. The young lefty swinger drove in 51 runs in the second half and slugged .511 while maintaining his high on-base average. He went from 47 extra-base hits in 1991 to 66 in 1992 and raised his batting average 42 points to .293. That's what you call development.

Lankford is an extremely patient, thinking hitter with a great eye that allows him to hit effectively whether ahead or behind in the count. He hits the ball with a slight upswing that causes some of his line drives to take off, as witnessed by his 20 homers. He led the league in strikeouts by a wide margin, but many good hitters strike out often. When not striking out Lankford hit .388; he knows that good things tend to happen when he swings.

BASERUNNING:

Lankford is inconsistent as a thief. He's had 86 steals the last two years, but he's also been caught 44 times. He stole 12 in a row early last season but would sometimes go weeks without a successful swipe. He has great speed and should improve.

FIELDING:

Lankford is a wonderful defender and led the league in putouts by a center fielder. He made just two errors and generally showed the maturity that comes with experience. His arm is not great, but it doesn't significantly limit him.

OVERALL:

Lankford's range of skills present Joe Torre with a pleasant Barry Bonds/Paul Molitor type "number-one or number-three" lineup dilemma. He'll probably bat third; that's where the best hitters usually are and he's one of the best. The next few years should reveal him as one of the game's elite hitters.

BOB McCLURE

Position: RP
Bats: R **Throws:** L
Ht: 5'11" **Wt:** 188

Opening Day Age: 39
Born: 4/29/53 in Oakland, CA
ML Seasons: 18

PITCHING:

The Cardinals opened the 1992 season with a couple of question marks as their left-handed relievers: Juan Agosto and Bob McClure. Agosto, a giant disappointment in 1991, turned out to be the same in '92; though he was in the first year of a three-year, $5 million contract, the Cardinals swallowed it and released him in June. The work of McClure, seemingly washed up after his release by the Angels in June of 1991, helped make that decision easier. McClure appeared in a career-high 71 games, eighth in the NL, and his .180 batting average allowed to the first batter was amongst the best in the league. He permitted only 15 of 67 inherited runners to score and registered 14 holds.

Manager Joe Torre did an outstanding job of spotting his veteran southpaw. McClure found himself facing the lefties he handles so well nearly half the time. He usually went less than a full inning and threw more than 25 pitches only a handful of times. Todd Worrell got the call against lefthanders late in the game, but McClure was terrific in his early to mid-game role.

McClure's curveball is a mystery to lefties, but he's vulnerable to righthanders. He tries to fool them with his change-up but it's not very effective and in 1992 they teed off on it. McClure generally walks too many hitters also.

HOLDING RUNNERS, FIELDING, HITTING:

Like most lefties, McClure can control the running game; only three runners took off for one successful steal. He has one of the best pickoff moves in the game and nailed one runner in 1992. He fields pretty well, but he didn't hit in 1992 and may never swing the bat again.

OVERALL:

McClure will turn 40 during the first month of 1993 and has now spent almost half his life as a professional baseball player with seven different organizations. In his last four seasons he's delivered two of his best years. As long as he can get lefties out, he'll be around, but at his age the free agent could lose it at any time.

Overall Statistics

	W	L	ERA	G	GS	Sv	IP	H	R	BB	SO	HR
1992	2	2	3.17	71	0	0	54.0	52	21	25	24	6
Career	67	56	3.79	684	73	52	1152.1	1112	546	492	695	102

How Often He Throws Strikes

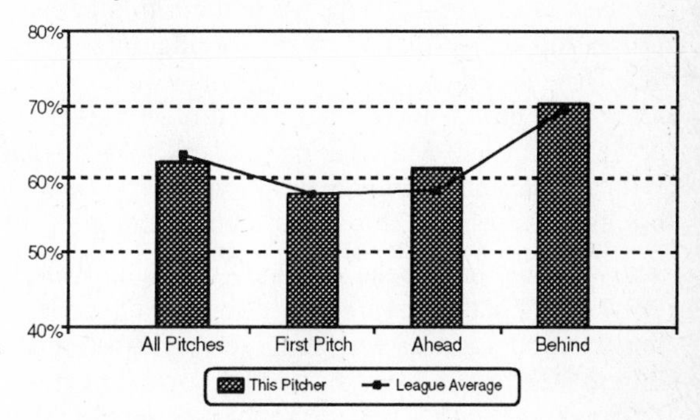

1992 Situational Stats

	W	L	ERA	Sv	IP		AB	H	HR	RBI	AVG
Home	1	0	2.22	0	28.1	LHB	91	18	4	13	.198
Road	1	2	4.21	0	25.2	RHB	108	34	2	16	.315
Day	0	1	2.87	0	15.2	Sc Pos	69	15	1	23	.217
Night	2	1	3.29	0	38.1	Clutch	73	18	1	10	.247

1992 Rankings (National League)

- 4th in least strikeouts per 9 innings in relief (4.0)
- 6th in holds (14)
- 8th in games pitched (71)
- 9th in lowest percentage of inherited runners scored (22.4%)
- Led the Cardinals in first batter efficiency (.180)

OMAR OLIVARES

Position: SP
Bats: R **Throws:** R
Ht: 6' 1" **Wt:** 193

Opening Day Age: 25
Born: 7/6/67 in Mayaguez, Puerto Rico
ML Seasons: 3

PITCHING:

It was a frustrating 1992 season for the Cardinals as they watched Omar Olivares squander his considerable talent. Olivares improved his control while raising his strikeout total, leading the team with 124. But his often poor judgment in pitch selection led to 20 home runs, tying him for third-most in the National League. The young righthander just doesn't pitch intelligently, and it drives his coaches crazy.

Olivares throws 90 MPH and his sinker is as good as they come. But as pitching coach Joe Coleman fretted, "He gets bored throwing it." Olivares has a reputation of not preparing for games, and he has a tendency to challenge hitters with less than his best stuff. He gave up two homers in a game twice and three homers once, forcing manager Joe Torre to take him out. Part of his trouble was a strained groin muscle that put him on the disabled list in late May. He came back to go 4-1 with an ERA of 2.05 in his first seven starts back, but he soon resumed his uninspired pitching.

Things could have been worse. Olivares allowed only a .199 batting average with runners in scoring position. He was very tough on right-handed hitters (.218), but lefties cuffed him around for a .285 average with a .451 slugging percentage.

HOLDING RUNNERS, FIELDING, HITTING:

Good news here: Olivares is among the best in all non-pitching areas. He had 40 assists, 14 putouts and no errors in the field, and runners were only 11-for-24 stealing against him. Best of all was his hitting: .235 with a home run and 4 RBI. He pinch hit three times for Torre, notching one hit. His average was around .270 -.280 all season before a late slump.

OVERALL:

Olivares should listen to his coaches, because what he's doing on his own isn't working. The Cardinals have had repeated sit-down talks with this problem child with no real success. He'll be back in 1993, but the competition for rotation spots will be tougher. If Olivares continues to be Oliv-air-head, he could lose his spot.

Overall Statistics

	W	L	ERA	G	GS	Sv	IP	H	R	BB	SO	HR
1992	9	9	3.84	32	30	0	197.0	189	84	63	124	20
Career	21	17	3.68	69	60	1	413.2	382	173	141	235	35

How Often He Throws Strikes

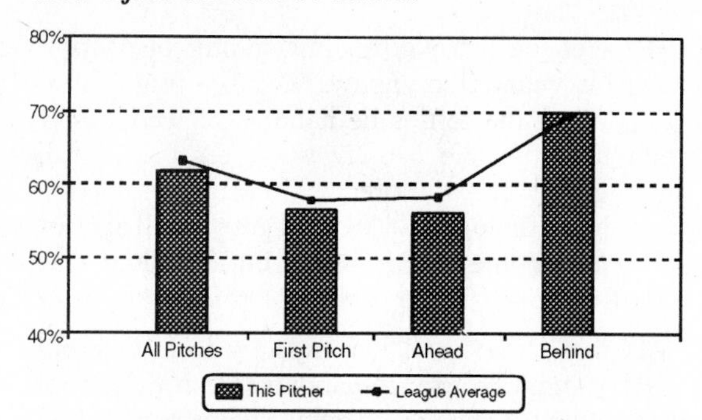

1992 Situational Stats

	W	L	ERA	Sv	IP		AB	H	HR	RBI	AVG
Home	5	6	3.96	0	120.1	LHB	428	122	13	47	.285
Road	4	3	3.64	0	76.2	RHB	308	67	7	27	.218
Day	0	3	4.91	0	55.0	Sc Pos	151	30	5	48	.199
Night	9	6	3.42	0	142.0	Clutch	87	25	2	10	.287

1992 Rankings (National League)

- 2nd in most home runs allowed per 9 innings (.91)
- 3rd in home runs allowed (20)
- 5th in lowest stolen base percentage allowed (45.8%)
- 6th in highest slugging percentage allowed (.394)
- Led the Cardinals in home runs allowed, walks allowed (63), strikeouts (124), most pitches thrown (2,979), pickoff throws (151), runners caught stealing (13), lowest stolen base percentage allowed and most strikeouts per 9 innings (5.7)

JOSE OQUENDO

Position: 2B
Bats: B **Throws:** R
Ht: 5'10" **Wt:** 171

Opening Day Age: 29
Born: 7/4/63 in Rio Piedras, Puerto Rico
ML Seasons: 9

Overall Statistics

	G	AB	R	H	D	T	HR	RBI	SB	BB	SO	AVG
1992	14	35	3	9	3	1	0	3	0	5	3	.257
Career	1001	2780	288	726	94	19	12	224	33	380	331	.261

Where He Hits the Ball

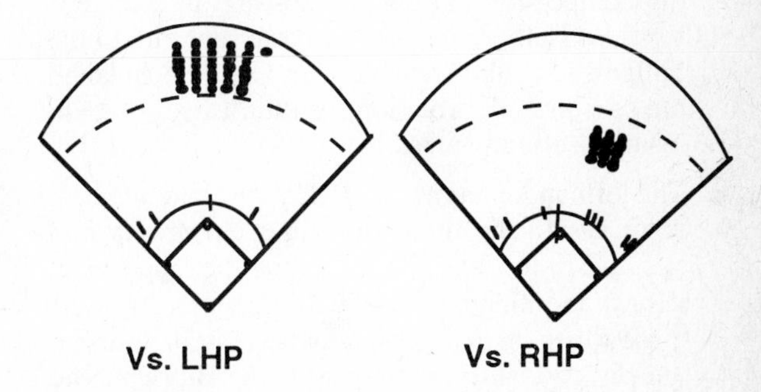

1992 Situational Stats

	AB	H	HR	RBI	AVG		AB	H	HR	RBI	AVG
Home	12	3	0	1	.250	LHP	12	2	0	1	.167
Road	23	6	0	2	.261	RHP	23	7	0	2	.304
Day	8	1	0	0	.125	Sc Pos	8	2	0	3	.250
Night	27	8	0	3	.296	Clutch	6	2	0	1	.333

1992 Rankings (National League)

- Did not rank near the top or bottom in any category

HITTING:

After never being disabled in 12 professional seasons, Jose Oquendo made three trips to the disabled list in 1992. He emerged for 35 at-bats and a few dozen innings at second and shortstop, but it was a lost season for the longtime Cardinal infielder.

Oquendo had a good spring, hitting .295, but on opening day he didn't even get to bat. He dove for a Howard Johnson ground ball and was disabled until May 31. When he came back he strained his foot after getting into just five games, came back July 12, played in five more games, hurt his foot again, and was out until August 31. On this last activation, he finally reached his 1000th career game.

When he did swing the bat, it was pretty much the Oquendo of old: no home runs and a .250-something average. He even had more walks than strikeouts again (five to three) for the sixth straight year. He had four extra-base blows in his nine hits, but it's unlikely that if he gets 150 hits next year he'll lead the league with 50 doubles and 17 triples.

BASERUNNING:

Oquendo didn't even attempt a steal in 1992 and has a career success rate of only 52 percent. He's not a good baserunner but stretches out a few doubles and triples.

FIELDING:

Oquendo made an error in his limited playing time, but he is a fine fielder. He was being pushed at second base by Geronimo Pena and may have spent the year as a fill-in anyway if he hadn't been hurt. He is a decent shortstop and a tremendous second baseman with fantastic range. His arm is good and he can turn the double play.

OVERALL:

Though he's been around since 1983, Oquendo is still only 29, so he's young enough to return as a regular this year. His problem is that the Cardinals have two other second basemen in Pena and Luis Alicea. He'll have to fight for playing time, though he could well be the shortstop if Ozzie Smith doesn't return.

DONOVAN OSBORNE

Position: SP/RP
Bats: B **Throws:** L
Ht: 6' 2" **Wt:** 195

Opening Day Age: 23
Born: 6/21/69 in Roseville, CA
ML Seasons: 1

PITCHING:

Donovan Osborne was the Cardinals' first-round pick in 1990, but he has advanced even faster than his pedigree might have predicted. Osborne made some important adjustments during 1991 and began to overpower AA hitters at Arkansas. He was expected to spend 1992 in AAA, but he pitched well and learned fast in spring training, so he opened the season in St. Louis.

Osborne was the talk of the league early in the year, turning in a 5-2 record in his first 10 starts with a 2.48 ERA. But when he started to get roughed up he tried to make the perfect pitch, and when he missed he began trying to blow his fastball past hitters for strikes. During July he lost his composure completely, posting a 7.20 ERA for the month. Manager Joe Torre sent him to the bullpen for a time, and though Osborne finished the season in the rotation, he didn't really regain his early effectiveness.

The lefthander has a 90 MPH heater, and when he is successful he mixes it with a change-up and slider. Mixing his pitches keeps the opposition honest and makes his fastball more effective. At these times he is a good situation pitcher, inducing big outs and double play balls. But when he loses his confidence, he tends to throw -- and overthrow -- heat in tough situations.

HOLDING RUNNERS, FIELDING, HITTING:

Osborne advanced so rapidly that his ability to hold the running game hasn't really developed. He only prevented three of 18 runners from stealing last year. He's a fair fielder, though he made two errors. He really likes to swing the bat, striking out 21 times in 58 at-bats but rapping out six singles and a triple.

OVERALL:

Osborne has the stuff to pitch in the majors. However, he has yet to develop the mental approach to pitching in the major leagues. When he ran into problems last year, he was unable to relax and to trust what he had learned in the minors. But he can and will learn, and should rebound in 1993.

Overall Statistics

	W	L	ERA	G	GS	Sv	IP	H	R	BB	SO	HR
1992	11	9	3.77	34	29	0	179.0	193	91	38	104	14
Career	11	9	3.77	34	29	0	179.0	193	91	38	104	14

How Often He Throws Strikes

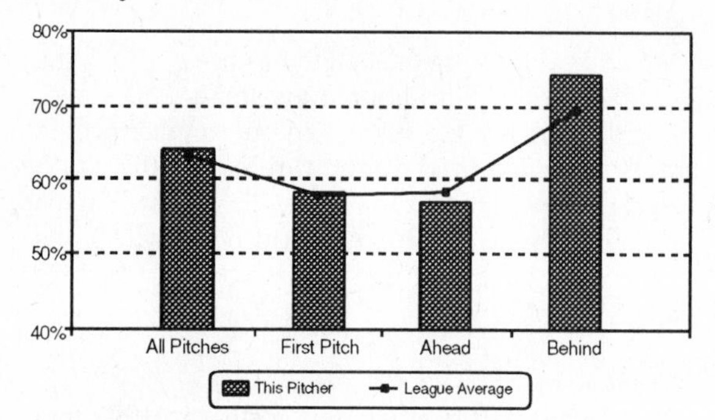

1992 Situational Stats

	W	L	ERA	Sv	IP		AB	H	HR	RBI	AVG
Home	5	3	3.42	0	79.0	LHB	151	48	3	23	.318
Road	6	6	4.05	0	100.0	RHB	552	145	11	53	.263
Day	2	3	4.47	0	56.1	Sc Pos	171	51	2	57	.298
Night	9	6	3.45	0	122.2	Clutch	64	15	1	4	.234

1992 Rankings (National League)

- 3rd in highest stolen base percentage allowed (83.3%) and highest batting average allowed with runners in scoring position (.298)
- 4th in highest batting average allowed (.275) and highest slugging percentage allowed (.404)
- 7th in most GDPs induced per 9 innings (.91)
- 9th in highest strikeout/walk ratio (2.7), highest ERA on the road (4.05) and highest batting average allowed vs. left-handed batters (.318)
- 10th in highest ERA (3.77), least run support per 9 innings (3.6) and most home runs allowed per 9 innings (.70)
- Led the Cardinals in wild pitches (6)

HITTING:

After a wonderful start last year, Tom Pagnozzi cooled off, finishing the season with numbers comparable to his fine 1991 campaign -- a little worse in some areas but a little better in others. Pagnozzi's .282 first half earned him an All-Star selection. Though he batted only .208 after the break, his overall totals of 26 doubles and seven homers were career highs.

Pagnozzi's second-half slump was probably due to the grind of catching so often. He had a nice stretch late in July but still hit just .226 for the month. He failed to score a run in August and had just four runs scored in September. But Pagnozzi has many weaknesses as a hitter that are not related to the nagging injuries which are part of a catcher's job. He can hit a strike when he knows its coming, but otherwise he's not effective. He's extremely impatient, though he doesn't strike out all that much. What he's done over the past two years is probably about what he's capable of. Overall, his production has been pretty good for a catcher.

BASERUNNING:

Pagnozzi is slow. After it took him 22 attempts to get nine steals while going for a Cardinal record in 1991, he tried just seven thefts last year, succeeding twice. His rate of runs scored per times on base was the worst in the league.

FIELDING:

Gold Glover Pagnozzi tied another record in 1992. He made just one error and his .999 fielding percentage matched Wes Westrum's NL record for catchers (New York, 1950). His throwing took a terrible dive from 1991, though. He was catching about a third of opposing runners -- the league average -- for most of the year, but slipped towards the end to 27.5 percent. His handling of the staff is fine.

OVERALL:

Pagnozzi is now a fixture behind the plate for St. Louis since Todd Zeile is not moving back from third. His hitting is average, at times better than that, and he is a good handler of pitchers. But as he continues to catch a tremendous number of innings, he could begin lose effectiveness.

TOM PAGNOZZI

Position: C
Bats: R **Throws:** R
Ht: 6' 1" **Wt:** 190

Opening Day Age: 30
Born: 7/30/62 in Tucson, AZ
ML Seasons: 6

Overall Statistics

	G	AB	R	H	D	T	HR	RBI	SB	BB	SO	AVG
1992	139	485	33	121	26	3	7	44	2	28	64	.249
Career	508	1487	119	379	77	8	13	151	13	99	228	.255

Where He Hits the Ball

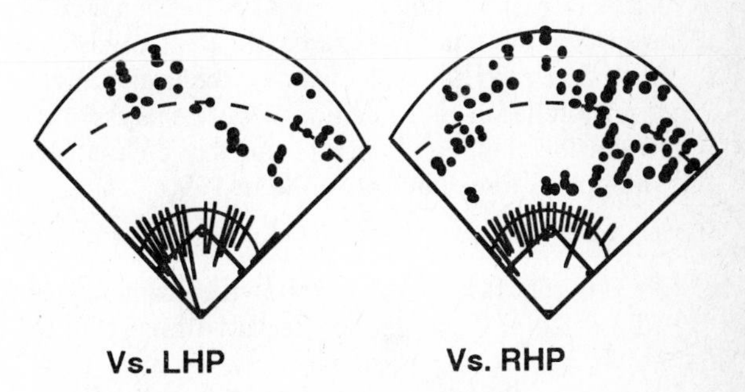

1992 Situational Stats

	AB	H	HR	RBI	AVG		AB	H	HR	RBI	AVG
Home	223	55	3	18	.247	LHP	176	43	5	15	.244
Road	262	66	4	26	.252	RHP	309	78	2	29	.252
Day	123	32	1	15	.260	Sc Pos	128	31	1	32	.242
Night	362	89	6	29	.246	Clutch	111	22	2	7	.198

1992 Rankings (National League)

- 4th in least pitches seen per plate appearance (3.19)
- 5th in GDPs (15)
- 6th in lowest on-base percentage (.290) and most GDPs per GDP situation (16.5%)
- 8th in lowest slugging percentage (.359) and lowest percentage of pitches taken (45.9%)
- Led the Cardinals in intentional walks (9) and GDPs
- Led NL catchers in at-bats (485), caught stealing (5), GDPs, highest groundball/flyball ratio (1.2), fielding percentage (.999) and highest percentage of swings put into play (47.4%)

GERONIMO PENA

Position: 2B
Bats: B **Throws:** R
Ht: 6' 1" **Wt:** 170

Opening Day Age: 26
Born: 3/29/67 in Distrito Nacional, Dominican Republic
ML Seasons: 3

HITTING:

Geronimo Pena had his chance to play regularly at second base for the Cardinals last year and hit a very fine .305, even though injuries sent him to the disabled list twice. In spring training Pena slipped on a glove and broke his clavicle -- really -- and was out until the end of May. Then he had nerve problems in his shoulder that knocked him out for six weeks. But when Pena was healthy, he hit. After a miserable time hitting left-handed in 1990 and 1991 (.194), the switch-hitter improved to .294 left-handed in 1992. Since the 1991 All-Star break, Pena has hit .292 overall, and in 1992 he slugged an amazing .478.

Though Pena has gained 25 pounds, his power is a function of his quick bat; he's always sent about a third of his hits for extra bases. He crowds the plate fearlessly to reach outside pitches and to get more pitches in his wheelhouse, but he pays for it. He has been hit by pitches 11 times in the majors, and got 18 lumps in Louisville in 1990.

BASERUNNING:

Pena is very fast but has not shown consistency as a basestealer. Manager Joe Torre will use him to pinch run but not to come in to steal a base. Pena didn't ground into a major-league double play in the majors until last June.

FIELDING:

Pena shows excellent skills at second with good range, and he turns the double play very well. But he often made boneheaded plays and did not show hustle afield. After the season the Cards sent him to the Instructional league to get his head and glove together.

OVERALL:

Pena has a dark side: his attitude, which is perceived as lackadaisical. But he drove in as many runs as Ozzie Smith in 315 less at-bats, and he seems to be able to play a mean second base when he wants to. He's a valuable player, and even if he slips again as a left-handed hitter, he should have a big year in 1993.

Overall Statistics

	G	AB	R	H	D	T	HR	RBI	SB	BB	SO	AVG
1992	62	203	31	62	12	1	7	31	13	24	37	.305
Career	184	433	74	118	22	4	12	50	29	46	96	.273

Where He Hits the Ball

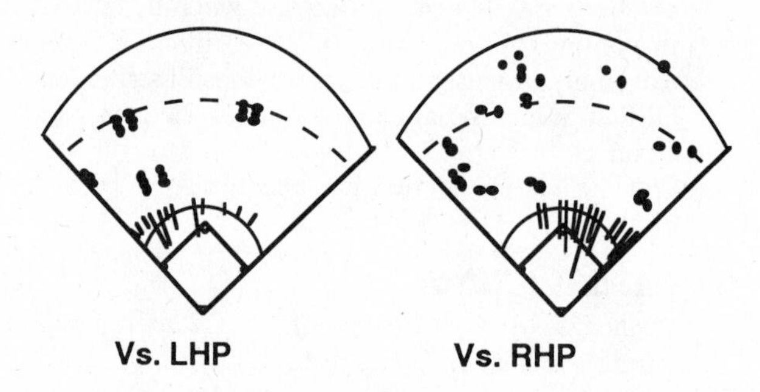

1992 Situational Stats

	AB	H	HR	RBI	AVG		AB	H	HR	RBI	AVG
Home	103	30	4	12	.291	LHP	67	22	3	10	.328
Road	100	32	3	19	.320	RHP	136	40	4	21	.294
Day	54	18	2	15	.333	Sc Pos	48	14	0	20	.292
Night	149	44	5	16	.295	Clutch	44	13	0	2	.295

1992 Rankings (National League)

- 6th in lowest stolen base percentage (61.9%)

MIKE PEREZ

Position: RP
Bats: R **Throws:** R
Ht: 6' 0" **Wt:** 187

Opening Day Age: 28
Born: 10/19/64 in Yauco, Puerto Rico
ML Seasons: 3

Overall Statistics

	W	L	ERA	G	GS	Sv	IP	H	R	BB	SO	HR
1992	9	3	1.84	77	0	0	93.0	70	23	32	46	4
Career	10	5	2.62	104	0	1	123.2	101	40	42	58	5

How Often He Throws Strikes

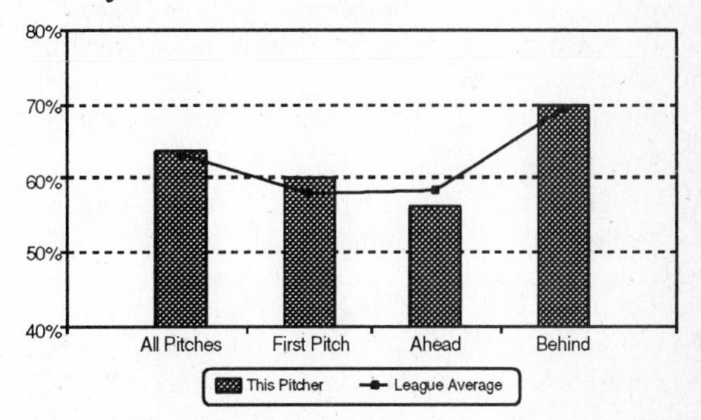

1992 Situational Stats

	W	L	ERA	Sv	IP		AB	H	HR	RBI	AVG
Home	5	1	0.96	0	47.0	LHB	156	38	2	17	.244
Road	4	2	2.74	0	46.0	RHB	177	32	2	9	.181
Day	2	0	3.09	0	32.0	Sc Pos	73	14	1	22	.192
Night	7	3	1.18	0	61.0	Clutch	159	36	2	13	.226

1992 Rankings (National League)

- 3rd in games pitched (77) and relief wins (9)
- 4th in relief ERA (1.84)
- 5th in relief innings (93)
- 6th in least baserunners allowed per 9 innings (10.0) and least strikeouts per 9 innings in relief (4.5)
- 8th in lowest batting average allowed in relief with runners in scoring position (.192), lowest percentage of inherited runners scored (22.2%) and lowest batting average allowed in relief (.210)
- Led the Cardinals in games pitched, lowest percentage of inherited runners scored, relief ERA, relief wins, relief innings and least baserunners allowed per 9 innings in relief

PITCHING:

Mike Perez must be an inspiration to every minor-league star who's been told that he didn't quite have major-league skills. While working his way up the Cardinals' minor-league system, Perez led three leagues in saves and racked up 123 saves in four years. But he came up short in two trials with the Cardinals, and people kept saying he didn't throw hard enough to fool major-league hitters. It's true that Perez doesn't throw hard, but after 1992 no one could say that he doesn't know how to fool hitters. Given a full shot finally, the well-seasoned righty went 9-3 with a 1.84 ERA while working in 77 games.

Perez moves the ball around and changes speeds, getting by without great heat or knee-buckling breaking stuff. Even while recording those spectacular minor-league save totals, his ERAs were never as spectacular as the results. Perez obviously knows how to pitch. His 77 games were a Cardinal record, his nine wins in relief were third in the league, he was fourth in relief ERA, and he allowed opposing hitters a .192 average with runners in scoring position. He did set a major-league record for relief appearances without a save, but that was due mainly to the presence of Lee Smith and Todd Worrell.

HOLDING RUNNERS, FIELDING, HITTING:

Perez has fine fielding range and was involved in three double plays last year. He is about average at controlling the running game and allowed five steals last year while nabbing two. Perez can lay down a bunt but rarely gets to bat and can't hit.

OVERALL:

Perez had a stretch of 27-out-of-28 games when he was unscored upon, including 17 straight. When it was broken, Lee Smith said "Hey, we're all human. I wish I could be as inhuman as he was for that long a time." Perez went from non-roster invitee to being one of the 15 protected players in the expansion draft in just eight months. With Cris Carpenter gone, he will have an even more important role in 1993.

STOPPER

LEE SMITH

Position: RP
Bats: R **Throws:** R
Ht: 6' 6" **Wt:** 269

Opening Day Age: 35
Born: 12/4/57 in Jamestown, LA
ML Seasons: 13

PITCHING:

Big Lee Smith had another great year for the Cardinals in 1992. Smith led the league in saves for the second straight year, despite a cold spell in June when he went almost three weeks without one. He ended up breathing down the neck of the all-time save leader Jeff Reardon, finishing just two behind Reardon's 357 career saves.

Smith slipped slightly in some areas from 1991. He dropped from first to second in save percentage, and his ERA went from 2.34 to 3.12. His walks were up, but they were unnaturally low in '91, and his strikeouts were down for the third year in a row. He also lost nine games, high compared to his recent success, although he'd lost nine or more three times previously in his career. On the other hand, his opposition batting average was .221, down from .249, and he only allowed the first batter a .200 average with no walks.

Smith continues to rely mostly on his 90-plus MPH fastball. In 1991 he added a split-fingered fastball that some hitters think is a slider. The combination sets up doubt in hitters' minds, making his heater more effective. He doesn't ring up the strikeouts he used to get, but it still works. Smith's 70 appearances were his most since 1982 and tied for ninth in the league; he was pretty much the same pitcher in each half, though he lost four games after September 4.

HOLDING RUNNERS, FIELDING, HITTING:

Smith is not much of a defensive factor. He has a deliberate delivery that doesn't discourage runners, 12-of-13 were successful off him last year. He's a big man and doesn't get to very many balls, and he committed one error. He doesn't hit. The only plate he steps up to is the dinner plate.

OVERALL:

Sometime around mid-April, barring injury, Smith will become the all time save leader, and maybe he and Reardon will have a nice battle for a time until Smith pulls away. The Cardinals are very close to gelling into a contender and Smith looks like he'll still be around for some postseason action.

Overall Statistics

	W	L	ERA	G	GS	Sv	IP	H	R	BB	SO	HR
1992	4	9	3.12	70	0	43	75.0	62	28	26	60	4
Career	65	74	2.86	787	6	355	1067.1	919	375	402	1050	63

How Often He Throws Strikes

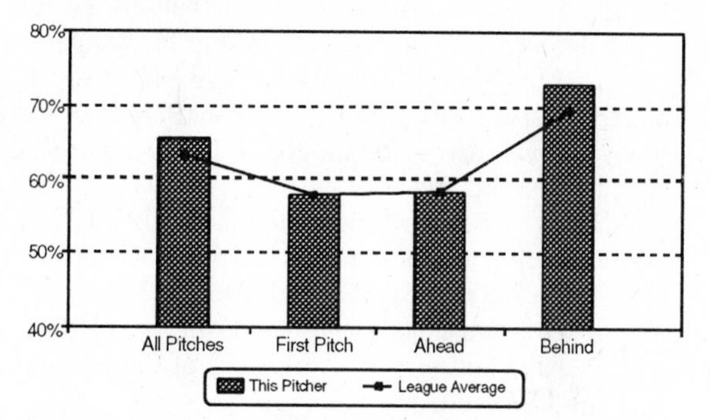

1992 Situational Stats

	W	L	ERA	Sv	IP		AB	H	HR	RBI	AVG
Home	3	8	3.25	18	44.1	LHB	164	36	2	19	.220
Road	1	1	2.93	25	30.2	RHB	117	26	2	12	.222
Day	2	3	3.72	11	19.1	Sc Pos	74	19	1	24	.257
Night	2	6	2.91	32	55.2	Clutch	240	49	2	24	.204

1992 Rankings (National League)

- 1st in saves (43) and save opportunities (51)
- 2nd in save percentage (84.3%), blown saves (8) and relief losses (9)
- 5th in games finished (55)
- 9th in games pitched (70)
- Led the Cardinals in saves, games finished, save opportunities, save percentage, blown saves and relief losses

GREAT RANGE

HITTING:

The 1992 campaign was another stellar season for The Wizard, Ozzie Smith --. a few ups, a few downs, but one that could be compared to his best. Smith raised his batting average for the third straight year to his second-highest ever (.295). His walks and on-base average were down, but his OBP was still a fine .367. Smith was better than his career average in nearly every area. His totals might have been better but he had chicken pox in June and missed some time.

The Cardinals keep getting dividends from the blue chip Smith. His lifetime average in San Diego was .231 with a .295 on-base average. In St. Louis he's hit .272 with a .354 on base average. He can bunt, sacrifice, work the pitcher, and he rarely strikes out. One problem last year was his very low RBI production: Smith's 31 RBI were his lowest total since coming to St. Louis. But as long as he keeps walking, he's an offensive force.

BASERUNNING:

Smith has only twice topped his 43 steals of 1992, and his percentage remains one of baseball's best (83 percent last year). He flew past 500 career steals and now looks ahead to 600. He's one of the smartest baserunners in the league and rarely makes blunders on the bases.

FIELDING:

People say that Barry Larkin is now the best, but Smith had one less putout, more assists, more double plays, and a better fielding percentage in fewer innings. He still exhibits great range, heads-up play and makes very few errors. He was rewarded with a record 13th straight Gold Glove at shortstop.

OVERALL:

Smith is now one of only 12 players in history with 2,000 hits and 500 steals. The free agent has had ongoing contractual spats with the Cardinals for the last few years; they seem worried that he's going to lose it all at once at age 38 and they don't want to be stuck with the bill. He can't play forever, but he's still playing well. Even a gradual slide leaves him a top player for several years.

OZZIE SMITH

Position: SS
Bats: B **Throws:** R
Ht: 5'10" **Wt:** 168

Opening Day Age: 38
Born: 12/26/54 in Mobile, AL
ML Seasons: 15

Overall Statistics

	G	AB	R	H	D	T	HR	RBI	SB	BB	SO	AVG
1992	132	518	73	153	20	2	0	31	43	59	34	.295
Career	2208	8087	1079	2108	347	57	22	681	542	949	524	.261

Where He Hits the Ball

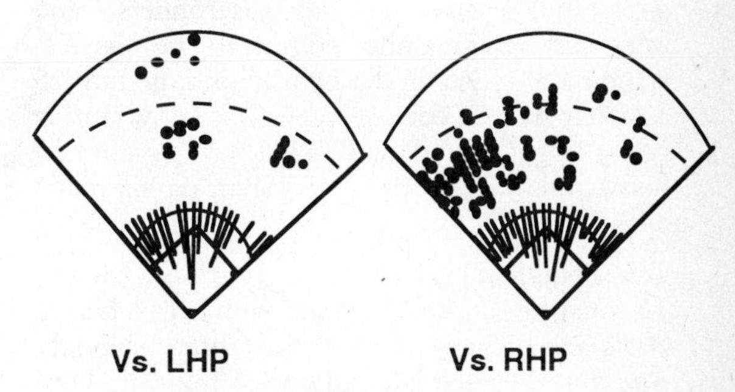

1992 Situational Stats

	AB	H	HR	RBI	AVG		AB	H	HR	RBI	AVG
Home	278	93	0	18	.335	LHP	202	55	0	13	.272
Road	240	60	0	13	.250	RHP	316	98	0	18	.310
Day	112	35	0	4	.313	Sc Pos	110	27	0	29	.245
Night	406	118	0	27	.291	Clutch	113	30	0	11	.265

1992 Rankings (National League)

- 1st in lowest HR frequency (518 ABs with 0 HR) and highest batting average with 2 strikes (.303)
- 2nd in batting average on an 0-2 count (.333) and lowest percentage of swings that missed (8.6%)
- 3rd in highest groundball/flyball ratio (2.5)
- Led the Cardinals in batting average (.295), singles (131), sacrifice bunts (12), stolen bases (43), highest groundball/flyball ratio, stolen base percentage (82.7%), batting average on an 0-2 count, batting average on a 3-2 count (.373), batting average at home (.335), batting average with 2 strikes, bunts in play and steals of third (5)

PINPOINT CONTROL

PITCHING:

Bob Tewksbury has always shown amazing control when he's been healthy, but has paid for his continual pitching in the strike zone by giving up a high number of hits. In 1991 he began to pitch more inside and to use his curve and slider to set up his 84 MPH fastball. The new system paid off in a big way in 1992 as Tewksbury was one of the most effective pitchers in the league.

Tewksbury works quickly, keeping hitters off balance by mixing pitches and getting many easy groundouts. He only walked -- count 'em -- 20 batters in a career high 233 innings, so don't talk to him about Dennis Eckersley. Though he fanned just 91 hitters, he led the league in strikeout-to-walk ratio. When he did allow baserunners -- and only Curt Schilling allowed fewer -- he was outstanding at inducing the twin killing, getting 25 double plays. Of course, some of his slow stuff is going to get tagged, and Tewksbury gave up 15 home runs despite Busch Stadium as his home park.

Tewksbury simply made it tough for his team to lose last year. The Cardinals won 23 of his 32 starts and he gave up more than three runs only five times. He earned one win in relief in April when he was the last of eight pitchers to go to the mound for the Cards; he tossed two innings and drove in the winning run in the 17th.

HOLDING RUNNERS, FIELDING, HITTING:

Tewksbury likes to swing the bat but went 6-for-70 last year, one of the worst performances of the year for any pitcher. He did drive in three runs and had six sacrifice hits. He's a very active and competent fielder and his few baserunners tended to stay put: he allowed only seven steals in 11 attempts.

OVERALL:

Tewksbury seems to have shaken the injuries that robbed him of his twenties and has blossomed in his thirties. In the last three years he's walked 73 hitters in 569.1 innings and lowered his ERA each year. If the Cardinals can get their offense clicking, he could win 20 games.

BOB TEWKSBURY

Position: SP
Bats: R **Throws:** R
Ht: 6' 4" **Wt:** 208

Opening Day Age: 32
Born: 11/30/60 in Concord, NH
ML Seasons: 7

Overall Statistics

	W	L	ERA	G	GS	Sv	IP	H	R	BB	SO	HR
1992	16	5	2.16	33	32	0	233.0	217	63	20	91	15
Career	48	39	3.22	137	116	1	784.1	828	332	136	305	52

How Often He Throws Strikes

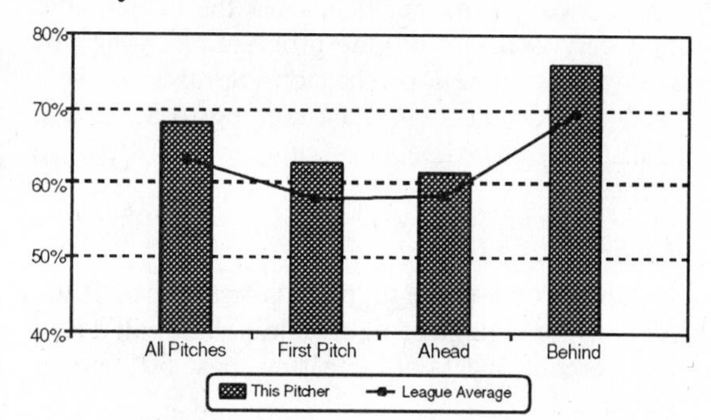

1992 Situational Stats

	W	L	ERA	Sv	IP		AB	H	HR	RBI	AVG
Home	10	2	1.52	0	124.1	LHB	517	125	10	36	.242
Road	6	3	2.90	0	108.2	RHB	359	92	5	22	.256
Day	2	0	3.18	0	34.0	Sc Pos	162	32	3	42	.198
Night	14	5	1.99	0	199.0	Clutch	81	17	2	3	.210

1992 Rankings (National League)

- 1st in winning percentage (.762), highest strikeout/walk ratio (4.6), least pitches thrown per batter (3.14) and least strikeouts per 9 innings (3.5)
- 2nd in ERA (2.16), lowest on-base percentage allowed (.265) and least baserunners allowed per 9 innings (9.3)
- 3rd in wins (16)
- Led the Cardinals in ERA, wins, games started (32), complete games (5), innings pitched (233), hits allowed (217), batters faced (915), GDPs induced (25), winning percentage, highest strikeout/walk ratio and lowest batting average allowed (.248)

MILT THOMPSON

Position: LF/RF
Bats: L **Throws:** R
Ht: 5'11" **Wt:** 200
Opening Day Age: 34
Born: 1/5/59 in Washington, DC
ML Seasons: 9

HITTING:

Bernard Gilkey learned to hit lefties, Ray Lankford became a star, and Felix Jose was terrific when he wasn't injured, so Milt Thompson worked as a substitute and pinch hitter for the Cardinals last year. Manager Joe Torre spotted Thompson -- who has generally had problems with lefties -- against righthanders and Thompson had another decent season, batting .293. In nine seasons, the consistent Thompson has batted between .288 and .307 seven times. But despite his good work last year, the Cardinals released him after the season, making him a free agent.

Even when Thompson bats for a respectable average, he is fairly limited as a hitter. He has good speed and uses it to advantage by hitting the ball on the ground as much as possible. The style produces lots of singles but not a lot of extra-base hits (he does leg out some triples). He's not much of an RBI guy and he's a notorious streak hitter, alternating good and bad months with regularity. He likes the low fastball and is very effective jumping on the first pitch (.364 over the last five years), but the consequence is that he doesn't draw many walks. He also doesn't hit lefties very well.

BASERUNNING:

Thompson is a good baserunner, scoring 86 runs as a part-timer over the last two seasons in 534 at-bats. He is an accomplished basestealer, good for 15 or 20 steals a year, though at age 34 he could begin to slow down.

FIELDING:

Thompson made a couple of errors while playing a little in right field and a little in left. He didn't get nearly as much time in the outfield as he did in 1991 and he was a little rusty. He is still a fair fill-in in left field, though his arm isn't very strong.

OVERALL:

Thompson is reliable and still effective, but limited and he's getting older. He also commanded a good salary, the biggest reason the Cards released him. He should be able to find work if he's willing to take a pay cut.

Overall Statistics

	G	AB	R	H	D	T	HR	RBI	SB	BB	SO	AVG
1992	109	208	31	61	9	1	4	17	18	16	39	.293
Career	980	2982	398	838	124	35	37	258	191	251	498	.281

Where He Hits the Ball

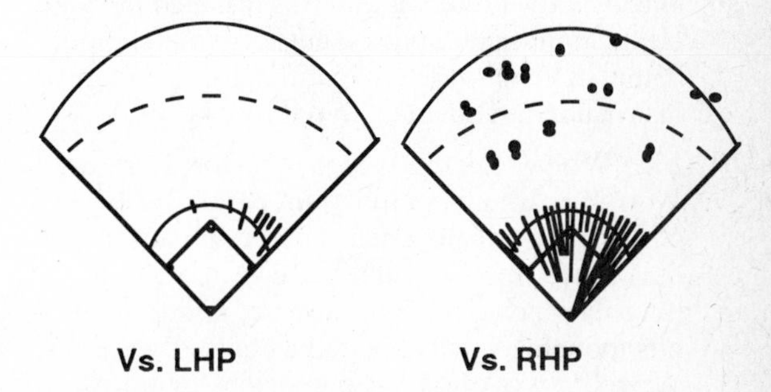

1992 Situational Stats

	AB	H	HR	RBI	AVG		AB	H	HR	RBI	AVG
Home	105	29	1	9	.276	LHP	22	7	0	0	.318
Road	103	32	3	8	.311	RHP	186	54	4	17	.290
Day	77	25	2	7	.325	Sc Pos	40	10	0	13	.250
Night	131	36	2	10	.275	Clutch	69	21	1	4	.304

1992 Rankings (National League)

- 2nd in lowest batting average on a 3-2 count (.067)

TODD WORRELL

Position: RP
Bats: R **Throws:** R
Ht: 6' 5" **Wt:** 222

Opening Day Age: 33
Born: 9/28/59 in Arcadia, CA
ML Seasons: 6

PITCHING:

He's baaack. After two complete seasons without throwing a major-league pitch, Todd Worrell returned to the Cardinals in 1992. He came back throwing hard, the same way he left, and was effective from the start. He had a couple of terrible outings and dozens of good ones; in fact, he allowed runs in only eight of his 67 appearances. His second half ERA was just 0.55 and he led the league with 25 holds. His second save, in September, pushed him past Bruce Sutter as the Cards all time save leader. It was a triumphant return.

Worrell was the National League Rookie of the Year in 1986 and quickly established himself as one of the league's top relievers. But he experienced elbow problems and was disabled in 1989. He had off-season surgery, but nerve and shoulder complications -- including arthroscopic repair of his rotator cuff -- kept him out for two years.

Like Whitey Herzog before him, Joe Torre used Worrell sparingly, pulling him before he ran out of gas. He generally pitched the eighth inning and only three times pitched more than a single inning. He moves the ball around, giving up few hits though he suffers periodic bouts of wildness. Worrell's weakness is his passion for throwing his fastball early in the count. He allowed four homers, two on the first pitch and two after falling behind 1-0, which accounted for seven of the 15 runs he allowed and two of his three losses.

HOLDING RUNNERS, FIELDING, HITTING:

Worrell is poor in all departments. He's a poor fielder and is basically an observer once the ball is hit. He allowed 13 steals without a single runner being caught, the worst ratio in the majors. He didn't bat in 1992 and it's a good thing. Lifetime he's 2-for-25 with 18 strikeouts.

OVERALL:

Worrell wants to resume his career as a closer, and there is no reason to think he wouldn't be effective, assuming his arm holds up. The problem is that the Cardinals already have Lee Smith. So Worrell, a free agent, figured to be shopping for a new employer in 1993. He was sure to attract a lot of attention.

Overall Statistics

	W	L	ERA	G	GS	Sv	IP	H	R	BB	SO	HR
1992	5	3	2.11	67	0	3	64.0	45	15	25	64	4
Career	33	33	2.56	348	0	129	425.2	345	133	167	365	34

How Often He Throws Strikes

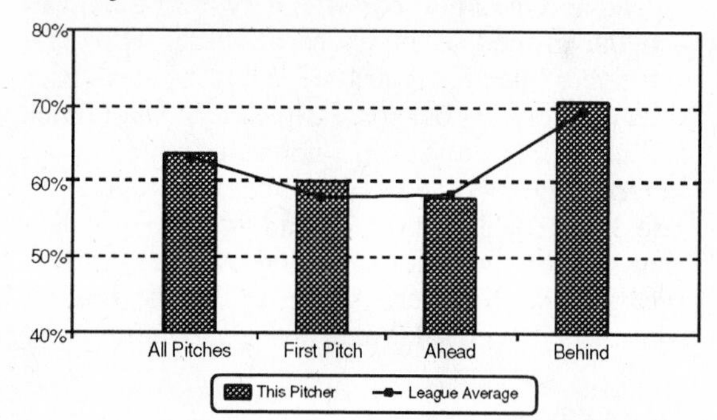

1992 Situational Stats

	W	L	ERA	Sv	IP		AB	H	HR	RBI	AVG
Home	1	0	0.76	2	35.1	LHB	121	21	3	8	.174
Road	4	3	3.77	1	28.2	RHB	106	24	1	4	.226
Day	1	0	1.59	1	17.0	Sc Pos	62	8	1	8	.129
Night	4	3	2.30	2	47.0	Clutch	169	32	3	10	.189

1992 Rankings (National League)

- 1st in holds (25) and lowest batting average allowed vs. left-handed batters (.174)
- 2nd in lowest batting average allowed with runners in scoring position (.129)
- 3rd in lowest batting average allowed in relief (.198)
- 4th in lowest batting average allowed in relief with runners on base (.183)
- 5th in most strikeouts per 9 innings in relief (9.0)
- Led the Cardinals in holds, lowest batting average allowed in relief with runners in scoring position, lowest batting average allowed in relief and most strikeouts per 9 innings in relief

TODD ZEILE

Position: 3B
Bats: R **Throws:** R
Ht: 6' 1" **Wt:** 190

Opening Day Age: 27
Born: 9/9/65 in Van Nuys, CA
ML Seasons: 4

Overall Statistics

	G	AB	R	H	D	T	HR	RBI	SB	BB	SO	AVG
1992	126	439	51	113	18	4	7	48	7	68	70	.257
Career	453	1581	196	413	82	11	34	194	26	206	255	.261

Where He Hits the Ball

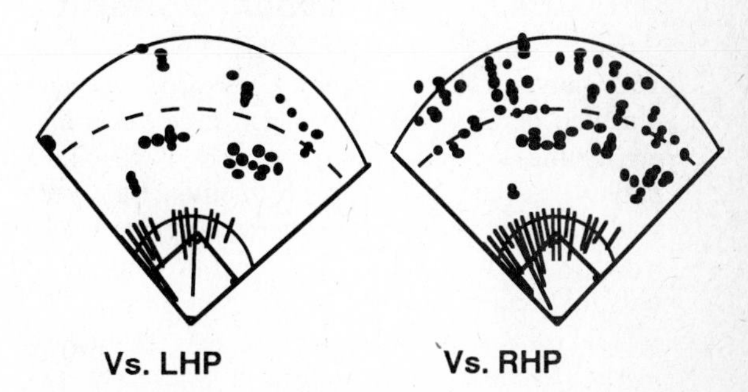

1992 Situational Stats

	AB	H	HR	RBI	AVG		AB	H	HR	RBI	AVG
Home	226	52	4	27	.230	LHP	133	37	1	15	.278
Road	213	61	3	21	.286	RHP	306	76	6	33	.248
Day	120	27	3	10	.225	Sc Pos	131	28	1	39	.214
Night	319	86	4	38	.270	Clutch	99	21	0	5	.212

1992 Rankings (National League)

- 2nd in most pitches seen per plate appearance (3.98)
- 4th in lowest batting average at home (.230) and highest percentage of pitches taken (61.8%)
- 8th in sacrifice flies (7)
- 9th in lowest slugging percentage (.364)
- Led the Cardinals in sacrifice flies, most pitches seen per plate appearance, batting average on a 3-1 count (.333) and highest percentage of pitches taken
- Led NL third basemen in sacrifice flies, caught stealing (10) and most pitches seen per plate appearance

HITTING:

After seemingly reaching stardom with a .280, 81-RBI season in 1991, Todd Zeile had a 1992 season of ups and downs. But the downs were doozies. Zeile finally landed at AAA Louisville in August in a move that stunned and puzzled observers. At the time he was leading the Cards in walks and had hit .291 in June and .297 in July. But between the All-Star break and his demotion he batted only .197, and just .121 in his last 33 at-bats. He also wasn't showing his 1991 power.

Zeile was philosophical about the demotion. "It's not a death sentence." he said. He started out poorly in Louisville but in 21 games he hit .311 with five homers, and when he rejoined the Cards in September he hit .282 with 15 walks. In fact, his good eye never deserted him. His on-base average in his shining 1991 was .353; in his disappointing 1992, it was .352, despite a batting average 23 points lower.

Some feel Zeile is simply too selective, letting RBI opportunities go by. He had problems in the clutch last year, hitting only .214 with runners in scoring position. Ex-hitting Coach Don Baylor felt that Zeile needed the demotion because he didn't take extra hitting on his own. Still, it was hard for an outsider to understand.

BASERUNNING:

Zeile is fast enough to have logged four triples in 1992, but he had a bad year stealing with only seven thefts in 17 attempts. After a decent start he went 0-for-6 and pretty much stopped running, but steals may still be part of his game in the future.

FIELDING:

Zeile led the league in fielding percentage for a good part of last year but ended up at about the average, committing 13 errors. It was an improvement over the 25 he committed in 1991. He is sure-handed, and though a converted catcher, he is a better-than-average fielder.

OVERALL:

Baylor is gone and maybe Zeile's attitude problem has gone with him. His batting eye is fine and his power should return. Zeile should bounce back in 1993 and, hopefully for the Cardinals, become the RBI man they need.

PEDRO GUERRERO

Position: 1B
Bats: R **Throws:** R
Ht: 6' 0" **Wt:** 199

Opening Day Age: 36
Born: 6/29/56 in San Pedro de Macoris, Dominican Republic
ML Seasons: 15

Overall Statistics

	G	AB	R	H	D	T	HR	RBI	SB	BB	SO	AVG
1992	43	146	10	32	6	1	1	16	2	11	25	.219
Career	1536	5392	730	1618	267	29	215	898	97	609	862	.300

HITTING, FIELDING, BASERUNNING:

Since batting .311 with 117 RBI while playing 162 games in 1989, Pedro Guerrero has been disabled during each of the last three years and eight times overall in that span. Each year he's played less and been less productive. Last year was the worst ever for the veteran slugger: a .219 average and a single home run while playing in only 43 games.

Last year the Cardinals obtained Andres Galarraga, and their somewhat dubious plan was to have Guerrero spend time in left field and hit fifth. When Galarraga was hurt, Guerrero went back to first base and batted cleanup, but shoulder troubles and a pinched nerve in his neck affected his hitting and landed him on the DL in June. Arthroscopic surgery was ruled out by Guerrero. "I'm 36 years old," he said. "I'm not 21 or 22." He came back to go 0-for-1 in October and he was wise to stop; an 0-for-3 would have dropped his career average under .300. His defense in left and at first was terrible and he couldn't run a lick.

OVERALL:

Guerrero's 1990 disablement with back spasms seemed to signal the end of his career as an effective hitter. It's unlikely that the free agent will be playing in 1993, and his career totals have been dimmed by injuries and Dodger and Busch Stadiums. But when he was healthy, he was a truly outstanding hitter.

REX HUDLER

Position: 2B
Bats: R **Throws:** R
Ht: 6' 0" **Wt:** 195

Opening Day Age: 32
Born: 9/2/60 in Tempe, AZ
ML Seasons: 8

Overall Statistics

	G	AB	R	H	D	T	HR	RBI	SB	BB	SO	AVG
1992	61	98	17	24	4	0	3	5	2	2	23	.245
Career	467	955	135	239	47	7	21	70	77	42	155	.250

HITTING, FIELDING, BASERUNNING:

Jack-of-all trades Rex Hudler had slipped into a nice niche with the Cardinals in 1990 and 1991. He came off the bench, played a lot of positions, and filled in to the tune of around 100 games and 200 at-bats a year. But after Hudler slumped to a .227 average in '91, he found his role diminished last season. He appeared in only 61 contests and batted just 98 times. Hudler did raise his average to .245 and once again he filled in everywhere.

Last year Hudler played all three outfield positions, first base and second base. His defensive work was fine; he made three errors at second but showed good range. However, Hudler's bat work was very mixed. He batted only .130 against righthanders but he killed lefties to a .346 tune. He was excellent as a pinch hitter, blasting two of his three home runs off the bench. He was disabled for a time in May with a partially torn knee ligament, which may have contributed to his 2-of-8 basestealing record. However, he was not a good basestealer in 1991, either.

OVERALL:

Considering the injury problems that the Cardinals suffered last year, it is telling that Hudler didn't have a greater role. They will have to ask themselves if his excellent hitting against lefthanders, versatility, and gung-ho attitude are enough to keep him around.

JOE MAGRANE

Position: SP
Bats: R **Throws:** L
Ht: 6' 6" **Wt:** 230

Opening Day Age: 28
Born: 7/2/64 in Des Moines, IA
ML Seasons: 5

Overall Statistics

	W	L	ERA	G	GS	Sv	IP	H	R	BB	SO	HR
1992	1	2	4.02	5	5	0	31.1	34	15	15	20	2
Career	43	44	3.11	121	119	0	805.0	747	314	257	448	32

PITCHING, FIELDING, HITTING & HOLDING RUNNERS:

Cardinal manager Joe Torre projected Joe Magrane as the 1992 opening day starter, but Magrane's medial collateral ligament couldn't meet the deadline. Nonetheless Magrane worked his way back to St. Louis in September after missing the entire 1991 season while recovering from elbow surgery. He pitched surprisingly well, though he won only one of five starts.

When healthy Magrane has a great curve, good low heat, and a sinking slider. He seems to have his stuff, and his smarts fairly intact. His stuff was evident in his second start, when he recorded nine strikeouts in 6.2 innings. His "game" ERAs in the five starts were 5.06, 5.40, 4.50, 2.84, and 2.57, though his hits and walks allowed were virtually the same in each outing. Now he has to show that he can combine his talents and resume his past dominant pitching.

Slugging Joe Magrane hit another homer in 1992, giving him four for his career. He also has eight doubles among his 35 career hits. He made no errors and allowed just two steals.

OVERALL:

Magrane is a gamble, finishing only one season without a trip to the disabled list (1990) in his five major-league campaigns. But he will only be 28 when the 1993 season opens, and he has an ERA title and an 18-9 season on his resume. If he's healthy, he can pitch 200 innings and win 15 games. But it's a big if.

BRYN SMITH

Position: RP
Bats: R **Throws:** R
Ht: 6' 2" **Wt:** 205

Opening Day Age: 37
Born: 8/11/55 in Marietta, GA
ML Seasons: 12

Overall Statistics

	W	L	ERA	G	GS	Sv	IP	H	R	BB	SO	HR
1992	4	2	4.64	13	1	0	21.1	20	11	5	9	3
Career	106	90	3.44	354	250	6	1761.2	1678	779	421	1019	138

PITCHING, FIELDING, HITTING & HOLDING RUNNERS:

His second stint on the disabled list in three years was a tough one for Bryn Smith. The veteran righty's first start in 1992 lasted only 2.2 innings before he came out with elbow stiffness. He had to undergo surgery and didn't start again in 1992, though he had 12 relief appearances in September.

Although Smith pitched well initially -- no runs in his first four relief outings -- he tired easily. He was good for about an inning but then weakened, and after about 30 pitches he lost his effectiveness and had some tough outings. His 4.64 ERA was the worst of his 12-year career.

Though he was 0-for-3 last year, Smith has been the Cards' best hitting pitcher in recent years with three lifetime homers. He's a good bunter and a good fielder, though he doesn't control the running game all that well.

OVERALL:

At age 37, Smith will have trouble rebounding from his serious arm troubles. On the plus side, the free agent doesn't need to throw hard to be successful. He throws offspeed stuff (mostly a sinker and palmball) and spots the ball, and he can be rough on right-handed hitters in particular. He may have a fall-back position in long relief if he can't cut it as a starter, but time is not on his side, and he may have to earn a job in Spring training somewhere.

CRAIG WILSON

Position: 3B/2B
Bats: R **Throws:** R
Ht: 5'11" **Wt:** 208

Opening Day Age: 28
Born: 11/28/64 in Anne Arundel County, MD
ML Seasons: 4

Overall Statistics

	G	AB	R	H	D	T	HR	RBI	SB	BB	SO	AVG
1992	61	106	6	33	6	0	0	13	1	10	18	.311
Career	182	313	25	78	10	0	0	34	1	25	44	.249

HITTING, FIELDING, BASERUNNING:

After three seasons with the Cardinals, Craig Wilson has established a role as a seldom-used fill-in around the infield and occasionally the outfield, getting around 100 at-bats a season. It's a dirty job, but someone's got to do it, and in 1992 Wilson did it very well. The righty swinger batted a career high .311, an improvement of exactly 140 points over his 1991 figure of .171.

Whatever his average, Wilson is a slap hitter without power; his extra-base hits total 10 doubles in 313 major-league at-bats. But he hit for a good average in the minors, learned to take a walk, and was a top run scorer. His 1992 figures show that he hasn't lost his stroke. He hit very well with runners in scoring position (.308).

With the Cardinals, Wilson has played first, second, third and the outfield. He was a minor-league All-Star at second base, which is probably his best position. He's not a basestealing threat.

OVERALL:

Wilson has been in the Cardinal system for nine seasons and has barely a half season of major-league at-bats to show for his work. But his 1992 performance was very good, and not out of line with his minor-league promise. He should be back on the bench in 1993.

TRACY WOODSON

Position: 3B
Bats: R **Throws:** R
Ht: 6' 3" **Wt:** 215

Opening Day Age: 30
Born: 10/5/62 in Richmond, VA
ML Seasons: 4

Overall Statistics

	G	AB	R	H	D	T	HR	RBI	SB	BB	SO	AVG
1992	31	114	9	35	8	0	1	22	0	3	10	.307
Career	153	429	38	109	20	2	5	48	2	19	64	.254

HITTING, FIELDING, BASERUNNING:

Minor-league veteran Tracy Woodson has had six seasons of Triple A ball. About all he had to look forward to in 1992 was that his new club, Louisville, was in the American Association, the only AAA league he hadn't yet toured. Signed by the Cardinals as a minor-league free agent, Woodson had a great spring and almost made the big club: he was the last player cut along with Brian Jordan.

Manager Joe Torre remembered Woodson though, and brought him back in August to fill in for the demoted Todd Zeile and add some sock to the Cardinals' lineup. Woodson did just that, driving in 17 runs in 18 August contests. "I'm not saying he's going to be our savior, but he's given us a little bit of life," said Torre. Woodson has a little power but not much speed or patience at the plate. His work at third base is solid and he can play first base, which may be a needed role as the Busch club attempts to break in a Brewer (Rod) at first.

OVERALL:

Woodson could never burst through with the Dodgers, and his chance at being a regular is probably finished. But he may have a couple of good years as a right-handed bat off the bench and backup first baseman/third baseman.

ORGANIZATION OVERVIEW:

The National League's dominant club during the Whitey Herzog years, the Cardinals are now an efficiently-run, above-average club . . . a moderate threat to win a division, but not to dominate it. Under Dal Maxvill the Cards operate on a tight budget, and that hasn't made winning easy. The St. Louis farm system has helped by continually turning out good prospects -- Todd Zeile, Ray Lankford, Donovan Osborne among them. However, the Cardinals seem to need a few impact players, and there aren't many candidates in their system. The best, Dmitri Young, is still a couple of years away from the majors.

RENE AROCHA

Position: P **Opening Day Age:** 27
Bats: R **Throws:** R **Born:** 2/24/66 in Havana, Cuba
Ht: 6' 0" **Wt:** 180

Recent Statistics

	W	L	ERA	G	GS	Sv	IP	H	R	BB	SO	HR
92 AAA Louisville	12	7	2.70	25	25	0	166.2	145	59	65	128	8

After only 25 minor-league starts, Arocha is a good bet to crack the Cardinals' staff this spring. The righthander was a star pitcher on the Cuban national team, and when he defected in 1991 the Cardinals were able to sign him. At 27, Arocha is a polished pitcher, and American Association managers chose him the league's number-three prospect. Not overpowering, he has tricky stuff and fanned 128 men in 166.2 innings last year.

ROD BREWER

Position: 1B **Opening Day Age:** 27
Bats: L **Throws:** L **Born:** 2/24/66 in Eustis, FL
Ht: 6' 3" **Wt:** 208

Recent Statistics

	G	AB	R	H	D	T	HR	RBI	SB	BB	SO	AVG
92 AAA Louisville	120	423	57	122	20	2	18	86	0	49	60	.288
92 NL St. Louis	29	103	11	31	6	0	0	10	0	8	12	.301
92 MLE	120	404	42	103	17	1	13	64	0	37	59	.255

Like Arocha, Brewer is 27 and has been around. Mostly he's been at AAA Louisville, waiting for his major-league chance. After three seasons at the Cardinals' top farm club, Brewer got his break last year: the Cardinals' resident first basemen, Pedro Guerrero and Andres Galarraga, both had terrible seasons while Brewer was having a good one for Louisville. Recalled in September, Brewer batted .301 in 103 at-bats, fielded well, and basically wrapped up the job. Now he'll have to hold it; if Brewer's not ready by now, he never will be.

OZZIE CANSECO

Position: OF **Opening Day Age:** 28
Bats: R **Throws:** R **Born:** 7/2/64 in Havana, Cuba
Ht: 6' 3" **Wt:** 220

Recent Statistics

	G	AB	R	H	D	T	HR	RBI	SB	BB	SO	AVG
92 AAA Louisville	98	308	53	82	19	1	22	57	1	43	96	.266
92 NL St. Louis	9	29	7	8	5	0	0	3	0	7	4	.276
92 MLE	98	295	39	69	16	0	16	42	0	33	95	.234

Yet another guy who's seen the world, Jose Canseco's twin brother Ozzie spent the 1991 season in Japan after he couldn't latch on with a major-league organization. Signed to a minor-league contract by the Cardinals last winter, Canseco was expected to be a useful AAA player but nothing more. Ozzie had other ideas. Looking like a mature hitter at last, he belted 22 homers in 308 at-bats at Louisville, forcing his way onto the Cardinals' expansion protection list. They need a power hitter, and Ozzie, who's had only 48 big-league at-bats, could get his big chance this year.

BRIAN JORDAN

Position: OF **Opening Day Age:** 26
Bats: R **Throws:** R **Born:** 3/29/67 in Baltimore, MD
Ht: 6' 1" **Wt:** 205

Recent Statistics

	G	AB	R	H	D	T	HR	RBI	SB	BB	SO	AVG
92 AAA Louisville	43	155	23	45	3	1	4	16	13	8	21	.290
92 NL St. Louis	55	193	17	40	9	4	5	22	7	10	48	.207

Two-sport star Jordan made up his mind last year -- he was going to be a full-time baseball player. At the time, Jordan was doing some promising work as a Cardinal outfielder, but he soon slumped and had to be sent back to the minors. Jordan hit .290 at Louisville and continued to show his great athletic skills. He has speed, power, defensive ability, you name it. If he is indeed fully committed to baseball, there's still time for him to make it. If not, there's always the NFL.

DMITRI D. YOUNG

Position: SS **Opening Day Age:** 19
Bats: B **Throws:** R **Born:** 10/11/73 in Vicksburg, MS
Ht: 6' 2" **Wt:** 215

Recent Statistics

	G	AB	R	H	D	T	HR	RBI	SB	BB	SO	AVG
91 R Johnson Cty	37	129	22	33	10	0	2	22	2	21	28	.256
92 A Springfield	135	493	74	153	36	6	14	72	14	51	94	.310

Dmitri in St. Louis? It might not be long. Only 18 years old last season, Young batted .310 with 14 homers for Class A Springfield and was chosen the top prospect in the Midwest League. A switch-hitter, he has power from both sides; his defense is still pretty rough. "He's a once-in-a-lifetime guy," said his manager, Rick Colbert. Young should be starring for the Cardinals in two or three years.

PITCHING:

When he was healthy last year, Larry Andersen demonstrated that he could still be an effective middle reliever. He had a 3.34 ERA as a Padres set-up man and his opponents' batting average was a very fine .202. But shoulder and back problems limited him to only 34 appearances; at 39 years old, the free agent will likely be seeking employment elsewhere in 1993.

If he's healthy, Andersen still has the stuff to be effective. He throws one of baseball's best sliders, with which he spots only the most occasional fastball and change. There has been suspicion for years that Andersen's slider is enhanced by his ability to scuff the baseball, a skill he may have learned in his days with Houston as a teammate to such notable suspected scuffers as Mike Scott and Dave Smith. But until he gets caught, it's a really, really good slider.

Even in his limited 1992 duty, Andersen's numbers were typical of his last several seasons. As usual, he had superb control, walking only eight and fanning 35 in 35 innings. As if auditioning for his future, Andersen came back to pitch well in the season's final month. He allowed only four hits and one run after September 1 in 8.1 innings.

HOLDING RUNNERS, FIELDING, HITTING:

Andersen uses a lot of veteran tricks to try to hold runners close, but his high leg kick makes him easy to run on. He is a good fielder who consistently makes all the routine plays. Andersen is one of the worst hitters around, going without a hit in his last three seasons.

OVERALL:

It's certain that Andersen won't be in San Diego, where his age and price tag are no longer wanted. If he can physically hold up, he can still be a very effective set-up man in the right bullpen. With so much bad pitching around, there's got to be a place for Andersen provided he's healthy.

LARRY ANDERSEN

Position: RP
Bats: R **Throws:** R
Ht: 6' 3" **Wt:** 205

Opening Day Age: 39
Born: 5/6/53 in Portland, OR
ML Seasons: 15

Overall Statistics

	W	L	ERA	G	GS	Sv	IP	H	R	BB	SO	HR
1992	1	1	3.34	34	0	2	35.0	26	14	8	35	2
Career	36	35	3.11	606	1	49	901.2	845	360	275	664	52

How Often He Throws Strikes

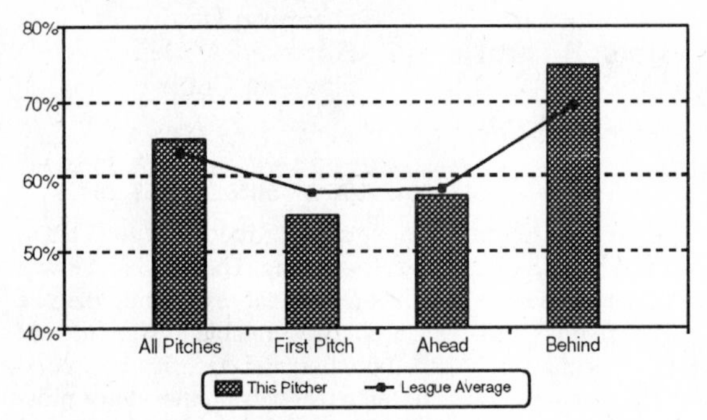

1992 Situational Stats

	W	L	ERA	Sv	IP		AB	H	HR	RBI	AVG
Home	1	0	3.26	2	19.1	LHB	69	14	1	9	.203
Road	0	1	3.45	0	15.2	RHB	60	12	1	8	.200
Day	1	0	1.23	0	7.1	Sc Pos	33	10	0	15	.303
Night	0	1	3.90	2	27.2	Clutch	52	12	1	9	.231

1992 Rankings (National League)

➡ Led the Padres in holds (8)

OSCAR AZOCAR

Position: LF
Bats: L **Throws:** L
Ht: 6' 1" **Wt:** 195

Opening Day Age: 28
Born: 2/21/65 in Soro, Venezuela
ML Seasons: 3

HITTING:

Few major-league hitters have had less productive seasons than Oscar Azocar did in 1992. But at least Azocar had the distinction of having one of the more unique bad seasons.

Usually when a part-time player hits .190, it's because he struggles to make contact and strikes out too much. But Azocar, amazingly, fanned only 12 times in 168 at-bats, meaning that he was putting an awful lot of weakly hit balls into play. The free-swinging Azocar only walked nine times. Furthermore, he managed only six extra-base hits (all doubles) out of his 32 hits for the year. As a pinch hitter, he was completely ineffective (10-for-56, .179) and was one big reason why Padres pinch hitters were among baseball's worst.

Pitchers were able to handle Azocar by feeding him hard stuff up and in or breaking balls out of the strike zone. Azocar is a low-ball, fastball hitter who struggles with anything else, so pitchers never give him a fastball below the belt. He also tries to pull too many pitches, which means a lot of harmless infield ground outs.

BASERUNNING:

Azocar is a below-average runner but quite good at basestealing on those rare occasions when he actually is a baserunner. He's a perfect 10-for-10 in his major-league career.

FIELDING:

Azocar broke in as a pitcher and he was a pretty good one (14-5 in three minor-league years). A strong throwing arm, not surprisingly, is his major defensive asset. But as for his other skills, he looks like a pitcher playing the outfield. Azocar has poor instincts and does not get a good jump on many balls.

OVERALL:

One of the Padres' weakest areas was their bench, where Azocar was one of the key people. It wouldn't be a surprise if Azocar is job-hunting during the off-season, and it also wouldn't be a surprise if he has trouble finding a taker for his limited skills. Maybe he should go back to pitching.

Overall Statistics

	G	AB	R	H	D	T	HR	RBI	SB	BB	SO	AVG
1992	99	168	15	32	6	0	0	8	1	9	12	.190
Career	202	439	38	99	16	0	5	36	10	12	36	.226

Where He Hits the Ball

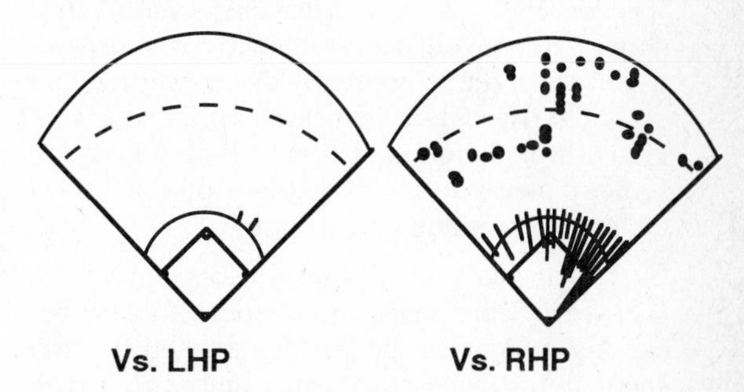

1992 Situational Stats

	AB	H	HR	RBI	AVG		AB	H	HR	RBI	AVG
Home	96	19	0	4	.198	LHP	5	2	0	0	.400
Road	72	13	0	4	.181	RHP	163	30	0	8	.184
Day	44	6	0	3	.136	Sc Pos	41	9	0	7	.220
Night	124	26	0	5	.210	Clutch	41	9	0	5	.220

1992 Rankings (National League)

→ Did not rank near the top or bottom in any category

PITCHING:

After the 11-1 finish to his 1991 season, a lot of people predicted that 1992 would be a break-through season for Andy Benes. But though he was the Padres' workhorse, leading them in innings and strikeouts, Benes was somewhat of a disappointment. He finished below .500 with a 13-14 record; opposing hitters batted .264 against him and he allowed 230 hits. Benes' ERA was decent at 3.35, but even that was worse than his 1991 figure of 3.03.

All in all, it was not a bad season for Benes. But expectations were just higher than a 13-14 record. One reason Benes hasn't yet put it all together is that he still doesn't feel comfortable changing speeds. When he gets in trouble, Benes relies almost exclusively on two pitches: his fastball, which sinks but is not really overpowering, and his slider. He can be predictable, and that's what gets him into trouble. He still needs to mature some; it's easy to forget that he's only 25 years old and just coming into his prime.

Even with his won-loss record less impressive last year, Benes made more strides toward becoming a complete pitcher. He pitched through some minor aches and pains and with Bruce Hurst's future now cloudy, Benes is now looked upon as San Diego's ace.

HOLDING RUNNERS, FIELDING, HITTING:

Benes has a good feel for holding runners, but his rather slow delivery to the plate hinders him. At least he has sorted out the balk problems that plagued him for his first two full seasons. He is a solid fielder and continues to show promise as a hitter. In 1992, he hit the third home run of his career, one of 10 hits he had last season.

OVERALL:

San Diego faces wholesale changes as they try to pinch pennies amid ownership's cash problems. But Benes will be around for a few years. For this club to stay competitive, he needs to take the next step and be the 18-20 game winner he has the potential to become.

ANDY BENES

Position: SP
Bats: R **Throws:** R
Ht: 6' 6" **Wt:** 240

Opening Day Age: 25
Born: 8/20/67 in Evansville, IN
ML Seasons: 4

Overall Statistics

	W	L	ERA	G	GS	Sv	IP	H	R	BB	SO	HR
1992	13	14	3.35	34	34	0	231.1	230	90	61	169	14
Career	44	39	3.33	109	108	0	713.1	652	281	220	542	62

How Often He Throws Strikes

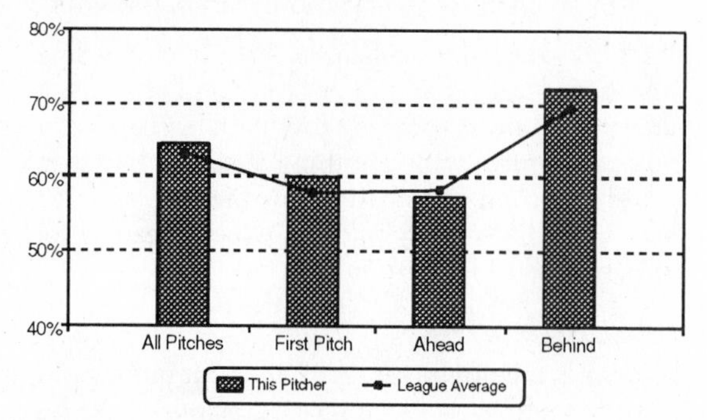

1992 Situational Stats

	W	L	ERA	Sv	IP		AB	H	HR	RBI	AVG
Home	7	6	3.55	0	116.2	LHB	533	147	10	63	.276
Road	6	8	3.14	0	114.2	RHB	337	83	4	21	.246
Day	6	1	2.34	0	73.0	Sc Pos	206	55	2	65	.267
Night	7	13	3.81	0	158.1	Clutch	74	21	1	4	.284

1992 Rankings (National League)

- 1st in hits allowed (230) and least run support per 9 innings (3.0)
- 3rd in losses (14)
- 4th in games started (34) and most pitches thrown (3,471)
- Led the Padres in ERA (3.35), losses, games started, innings pitched (231.1), hits allowed, batters faced (961), walks allowed (61), hit batsmen (5), strikeouts (169), most pitches thrown, stolen bases allowed (20), runners caught stealing (11), highest strikeout/walk ratio (2.8), lowest batting average allowed (.264), lowest slugging percentage allowed (.371), least home runs allowed per 9 innings (.55) and most strikeouts per 9 innings (6.6)

PITCHING:

Cut adrift by Houston and then bounced by Oakland, Jim Deshaies finally hooked on with San Diego and gave the Padres some solid starting efforts during the second half of last year. His 4-7 win-loss record was not good, but he was pitching in a stretch when the Padres were in a team tailspin. More indicative of Deshaies' pitching was the solid 3.28 ERA he compiled in his 15 starts.

As has been true throughout his career, Deshaies' ability to change speeds and turn his fastball over made him more effective against right-handed hitters than left-handed ones last year. In his stint with the Padres, Deshaies held righthanders to a .239 average while left-handed hitters hit him at a .356 clip. Over the past five years his numbers are .281 vs. lefties, .227 vs. righties.

Deshaies doesn't overpower anybody anymore as evidenced by the six home runs he allowed in 96 innings. His fastball, which he tends to throw up in the strike zone, rarely gets beyond the mid 80s. However, with his mechanics improved through work with Padres pitching coach Mike Roarke, Deshaies was able to regain the effectiveness in his change-up, his best pitch. He occasionally throws a slider, but Deshaies basically needs control and to mix up his speeds to have a chance.

HOLDING RUNNERS, FIELDING, HITTING:

Deshaies throws over to first as frequently as any pitcher because he does not have a good pickoff move and his motion to the plate is slow. Last year this tactic worked brilliantly, as he permitted only six steals in 16 attempts. He can handle himself defensively and can occasionally help himself with the bat. Deshaies had six hits last year in 29 at-bats.

OVERALL:

Deshaies showed last year that he still has some life left in his left arm. With Bruce Hurst's status iffy and with Deshaies' price deflated, the Padres might want to keep him around as insurance for their uncertain starting rotation. As a free agent, he could shop around.

JIM DESHAIES

Position: SP
Bats: L **Throws:** L
Ht: 6' 4" **Wt:** 220

Opening Day Age: 32
Born: 6/23/60 in Massena, NY
ML Seasons: 9

Overall Statistics

	W	L	ERA	G	GS	Sv	IP	H	R	BB	SO	HR
1992	4	7	3.28	15	15	0	96.0	92	40	33	46	6
Career	65	67	3.68	198	195	0	1205.0	1066	528	463	782	120

How Often He Throws Strikes

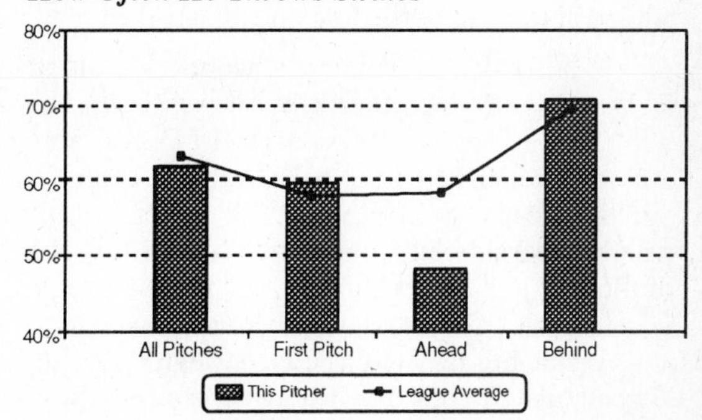

1992 Situational Stats

	W	L	ERA	Sv	IP		AB	H	HR	RBI	AVG
Home	2	4	4.11	0	50.1	LHB	59	21	1	4	.356
Road	2	3	2.36	0	45.2	RHB	297	71	5	24	.239
Day	1	2	4.50	0	24.0	Sc Pos	70	21	1	20	.300
Night	3	5	2.88	0	72.0	Clutch	20	8	0	2	.400

1992 Rankings (National League)

- 10th in balks (2)

TONY GWYNN

Position: RF
Bats: L **Throws:** L
Ht: 5'11" **Wt:** 215

Opening Day Age: 32
Born: 5/9/60 in Los Angeles, CA
ML Seasons: 11

HITTING:

Though he is still one of the game's incomparable hitters, Tony Gwynn has become something of a question mark after another year of injury problems. Gwynn appeared in only 128 contests last year and has reached the 145-game mark only once in the last five seasons. In 1992 Gwynn was out of the lineup for occasional spells throughout the summer, then was sidelined for good in the last three weeks due to knee and hand problems.

The injuries may have slowed his bat a little. Gwynn hit .317 for the second straight season, very good but 10 points below his career average. After a stretch of six seasons without ever going three straight games hitless, Gwynn has had extended slumps in both 1991 and 1992.

That said, Gwynn remains a wonderful hitter. He's still the toughest strikeout in baseball -- he will reach 300 career strikeouts in 1993, the same season in which he passes 6,000 at-bats. As an NL pitching coach said last year, "His knees and his weight have slowed him down, but he still is one of the few guys for whom there is not one single way to pitch." Gwynn is usually pitched with hard stuff inside but he is still quick enough to pull it. He can take pitches over the plate basically anywhere he wants.

BASERUNNING:

Gwynn once stole 56 bases in a season, but those days are long gone. His knees, plus batting ahead of Gary Sheffield, have basically eliminated the threat of Gwynn stealing. He was a terrible 3-for-9 last year.

FIELDING:

Gwynn's arm, knowledge of hitters and baseball instincts still make him a solid right fielder. However, his range has deteriorated noticeably and he is no longer a Gold Glove type.

OVERALL:

A lot of questions are beginning to develop around Gwynn, whose chubby body has always been suspect. He has been the Padres' franchise player for nearly a decade. But with the franchise now looking to cut corners, Gwynn could suddenly become expendable if his availability to play continues to slip.

Overall Statistics

	G	AB	R	H	D	T	HR	RBI	SB	BB	SO	AVG
1992	128	520	77	165	27	3	6	41	3	46	16	.317
Career	1463	5701	842	1864	275	75	59	591	249	506	291	.327

Where He Hits the Ball

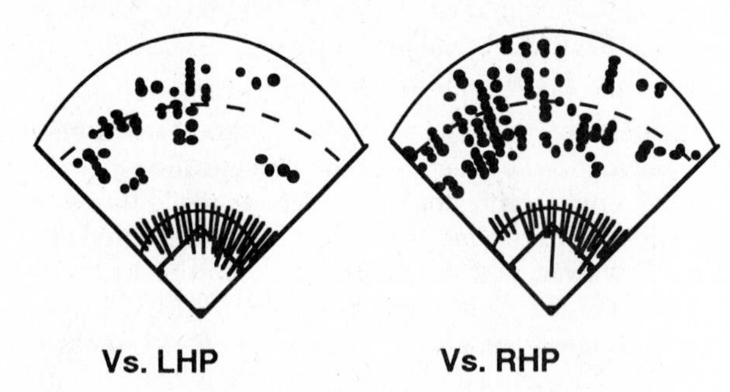

1992 Situational Stats

	AB	H	HR	RBI	AVG		AB	H	HR	RBI	AVG
Home	229	70	4	15	.306	LHP	205	67	3	16	.327
Road	291	95	2	26	.326	RHP	315	98	3	25	.311
Day	161	45	1	10	.280	Sc Pos	90	29	1	32	.322
Night	359	120	5	31	.334	Clutch	75	27	2	8	.360

1992 Rankings (National League)

- 1st in least pitches seen per plate appearance (3.15), batting average on a 3-2 count (.438), lowest percentage of swings that missed (6.5%) and highest percentage of swings put into play (62.3%)
- 3rd in batting average with 2 strikes (.291)
- 4th in batting average on the road (.326)
- 5th in batting average (.317) and batting average in the clutch (.360)
- Led the Padres in highest groundball/flyball ratio (1.7), batting average on a 3-2 count, batting average on the road, batting average with 2 strikes, lowest percentage of swings that missed and highest percentage of swings put into play

PITCHING:

It was another largely lost season for Greg Harris, whose physical problems keep standing in the way of his becoming a solid starting pitcher. Harris missed much of 1992 with a sore back and then a broken middle finger on his pitching hand. The downtime basically short-circuited any chance of him continuing the development that he began in the second half of '91. After going 9-5 with a 2.23 ERA in 1991, Harris was 4-8, 4.12 in '92. He worked in only 20 games, all starts, in each of the past two seasons.

However, Harris did pitch decently over the season's final six weeks to lend hope that he can finally realize his promise. His final start was a seven-inning three-hitter that showed the kind of stuff Harris is capable of throwing. He has always had a good riding fastball and an excellent curveball. His challenge has been to add to those two pitches. He throws occasional sliders, but has particularly worked on learning the change-up to give himself another look.

In a pinch, Harris is usually going to rely on the curve or fastball. That can cause problems, especially with left-handed hitters. Harris will try to challenge lefties with fastballs and often leaves them over the plate. The results are a lot of home runs. In the last two seasons Harris has pitched a total of 251 innings and has allowed 29 home runs, 23 to lefties.

HOLDING RUNNERS, FIELDING, HITTING:

Harris has worked to improve his pickoff move. But last year he permitted 18 steals in 23 attempts, indicating he still needs a lot more work. He is a solid fielder and is not an automatic out when he bats, though he is hardly a dangerous hitter.

OVERALL:

At 29, Harris is no longer a kid, and the Padres need him to realize his considerable promise. They hope he's durable enough to start 32-35 games. But if he keeps breaking down, they may have to return him to the bullpen, where he was effective -- and healthy -- in 1989-90.

GREG W. HARRIS

Position: SP
Bats: R **Throws:** R
Ht: 6' 2" **Wt:** 195

Opening Day Age: 29
Born: 12/1/63 in Greensboro, NC
ML Seasons: 5

Overall Statistics

	W	L	ERA	G	GS	Sv	IP	H	R	BB	SO	HR
1992	4	8	4.12	20	20	0	118.0	113	62	35	66	13
Career	31	30	2.74	172	49	15	521.1	440	185	166	379	43

How Often He Throws Strikes

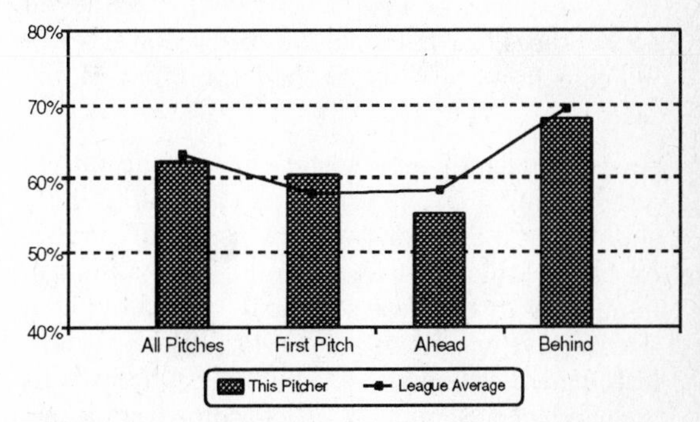

1992 Situational Stats

	W	L	ERA	Sv	IP		AB	H	HR	RBI	AVG
Home	2	3	3.36	0	61.2	LHB	287	80	11	40	.279
Road	2	5	4.95	0	56.1	RHB	161	33	2	15	.205
Day	1	3	5.14	0	35.0	Sc Pos	100	27	5	45	.270
Night	3	5	3.69	0	83.0	Clutch	30	6	1	2	.200

1992 Rankings (National League)

- Did not rank near the top or bottom in any category

PITCHING:

It was stormy, but another effective season was underway for Bruce Hurst until shoulder problems shelved him in the final month. The news was ominous -- the classy lefthander needed surgery for a frayed rotator cuff. Thus the future is suddenly cloudy for one of the most consistent, if underrated, pitchers in baseball. Before the injury, the cash-poor Padres were expected to shop Hurst in order to unload his salary. Now, he will be difficult to move.

Until his shoulder became too painful, Hurst was on his way to another excellent season. He had a shot at 18-to-20 wins with a strong finish, but instead was winless in his last three starts. His ERA went up over a half a run over his last seven appearances, so his final numbers don't really indicate how well he pitched for most of the season.

As usual, Hurst was a master of changing speeds and mixing his sneaky-quick fastball with a slider, curve and forkball. As usual, he had an excellent strikeout-to-walk ratio. And as usual, his ability to be always around the plate meant that he gave up a lot of home runs (22). Curiously, left-handed hitters hit .305 with eight home runs against Hurst. Scouts say he had some trouble last year getting consistent movement on his fastball, which made him easier for left-handed hitters.

HOLDING RUNNERS, FIELDING, HITTING:

Hurst does the little things very well. He has one of the best pickoff moves in baseball and is one of the best fielding pitchers in the National League. He can also help himself with the bat. He had 11 hits and nine sacrifices in 1992.

OVERALL:

Rotator cuff injuries at 35 years old are not the best prescription for any pitcher. In Hurst's favor is the fact that he is not strictly a power pitcher -- if the injury costs him some velocity, it wouldn't be fatal. If he comes back with the Padres, they will again benefit from his professionalism.

BRUCE HURST

Position: SP
Bats: L **Throws:** L
Ht: 6' 3" **Wt:** 220

Opening Day Age: 35
Born: 3/24/58 in St. George, UT
ML Seasons: 13

Overall Statistics

	W	L	ERA	G	GS	Sv	IP	H	R	BB	SO	HR
1992	14	9	3.85	32	32	0	217.1	223	96	51	131	22
Career	143	110	3.84	366	346	0	2366.2	2395	1101	718	1656	249

How Often He Throws Strikes

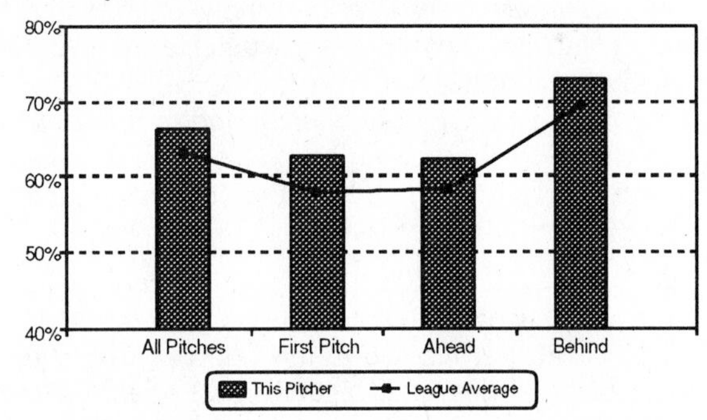

1992 Situational Stats

	W	L	ERA	Sv	IP		AB	H	HR	RBI	AVG
Home	5	4	4.38	0	100.2	LHB	151	46	8	22	.305
Road	9	5	3.39	0	116.2	RHB	684	177	14	63	.259
Day	3	2	3.40	0	50.1	Sc Pos	174	47	1	48	.270
Night	11	7	3.99	0	167.0	Clutch	74	22	2	7	.297

1992 Rankings (National League)

- 2nd in home runs allowed (22) and highest ERA at home (4.38)
- 3rd in shutouts (4) and most home runs allowed per 9 innings (.91)
- 4th in hits allowed (223)
- Led the Padres in sacrifice bunts as a hitter (9), wins (14), complete games (6), shutouts, home runs allowed, balks (3), pickoff throws (183), winning percentage (.609), lowest on-base percentage allowed (.308), highest groundball/flyball ratio (1.5), least baserunners allowed per 9 innings (11.3) and lowest batting average allowed vs. right-handed batters (.259)

DARRIN JACKSON

Position: CF
Bats: R **Throws:** R
Ht: 6' 0" **Wt:** 185

Opening Day Age: 29
Born: 8/22/63 in Los Angeles, CA
ML Seasons: 7

HITTING:

Darrin Jackson came back from a very slow start to salvage a decent season in 1992, proving that his 1991 power burst was not a fluke. However, Jackson's production was down from '91, especially when considering that he was an everyday player for the entire season in 1992.

Jackson's 17 homers were four less than his '91 total even though he had 228 more at-bats. National League pitchers have learned that Jackson can turn around most fastballs, especially those thrown high in the strike zone. So he was fed a steady diet of breaking and offspeed stuff, usually thrown out of the strike zone. A noted free-swinger, Jackson had 106 strikeouts, only 26 walks and a very poor .283 on-base percentage.

However, not all of Jackson's figures were negative. He was very productive from late-May through August and proved to be at his best in the clutch. Jackson batted .301 with men in scoring position to help him to a career-high 70 RBI.

BASERUNNING:

Jackson is a very underrated baserunner. He was one of the few Padres with a good basestealing percentage in 1992, stealing 14 bases in 17 attempts. He is also a very aggressive runner who will break up a double play and take the extra base, as evidenced by his five triples. However, Jackson is very slow out of the batter's box; he grounded into a league-high 21 double plays last year.

FIELDING:

Because of a below-average throwing arm and poor throwing mechanics, Jackson is best suited to play left or center field. He has good range in the outfield and gets the kind of jump that enables him to do a solid job in center.

OVERALL:

He's not a star, but Jackson has made himself into a very productive player whose value is overshadowed by some of his better-known teammates. He is a desirable commodity around baseball who could be made expendable in the Padres' money scheme. He would likely be pursued strongly.

Overall Statistics

	G	AB	R	H	D	T	HR	RBI	SB	BB	SO	AVG
1992	155	587	72	146	23	5	17	70	14	26	106	.249
Career	517	1433	181	361	57	9	51	168	27	76	261	.252

Where He Hits the Ball

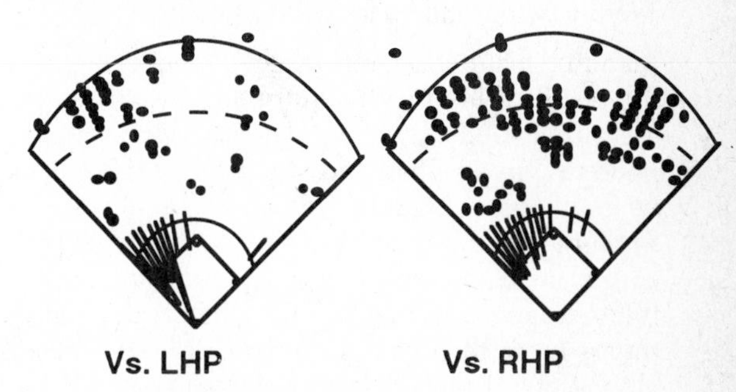

1992 Situational Stats

	AB	H	HR	RBI	AVG		AB	H	HR	RBI	AVG
Home	299	86	11	45	.288	LHP	188	38	7	19	.202
Road	288	60	6	25	.208	RHP	399	108	10	51	.271
Day	165	39	6	22	.236	Sc Pos	136	41	6	57	.301
Night	422	107	11	48	.254	Clutch	92	26	6	16	.283

1992 Rankings (National League)

- → 1st in GDPs (21)
- → 3rd in lowest on-base percentage vs. left-handed pitchers (.242) and lowest batting average on the road (.208)
- → 4th in lowest on-base percentage (.283), lowest batting average vs. left-handed pitchers (.202), lowest on-base percentage vs. right-handed pitchers (.302) and lowest percentage of pitches taken (44.1%)
- → 5th in most GDPs per GDP situation (16.8%) and highest percentage of swings that missed (25.5%)
- → Led the Padres in GDPs and games played (155)
- → Led NL center fielders in GDPs

OVERLOOKED

PITCHING:

For a second straight season, veteran Mike Maddux was a very effective all-purpose pitcher for San Diego. He specialized in middle-relief and set-up work, though he did make one emergency start. Maddux has definitely found his niche in the bullpen after originally being a starter as part of the Philadelphia organization.

Maddux improved upon his ERA from his strong 1991 season, leading the Padres with a 2.37 mark. Opposing hitters batted only .236 against him and his strikeout-to-walk ratio was again excellent (60-24). He allowed only two home runs in 79.2 innings. He was equally tough on lefties (.235) and righties (.237) and held opponents to a .220 average with runners in scoring position.

Maddux' maturation into a solid pitcher is largely the result of improved control and the development of a solid change-up. He has always had a good moving fastball and at times his curve can be unhittable. Maddux' slider is also an out pitch for him. Over the last two years, Maddux has gained the confidence to use any of his pitches in tight situations. Since he rarely has to face any hitters more than once in his middle-relief role, his variety of pitches becomes even more effective.

HOLDING RUNNERS, FIELDING, HITTING:

Maddux has a decent pickoff move and a quick delivery home which can make him tough on basestealers. But after doing good work at holding runners in past seasons, he allowed 15 steals in 18 attempts last year. He is a good athlete. While not in his brother Greg's class as a fielder, he is still excellent defensively. Maddux is no factor as a hitter.

OVERALL:

For a long time scouts said that Greg got all the guts in the Maddux family. But Mike Maddux has proven them wrong by reviving his career in San Diego. With Randy Myers' status in the air, Maddux, who had five saves last year, could become one of the closers in a bullpen by committee.

MIKE MADDUX

Position: RP
Bats: L **Throws:** R
Ht: 6' 2" **Wt:** 190

Opening Day Age: 31
Born: 8/27/61 in Dayton, OH
ML Seasons: 7

Overall Statistics

	W	L	ERA	G	GS	Sv	IP	H	R	BB	SO	HR
1992	2	2	2.37	50	1	5	79.2	71	25	24	60	2
Career	19	18	3.74	189	37	11	426.1	421	201	142	272	24

How Often He Throws Strikes

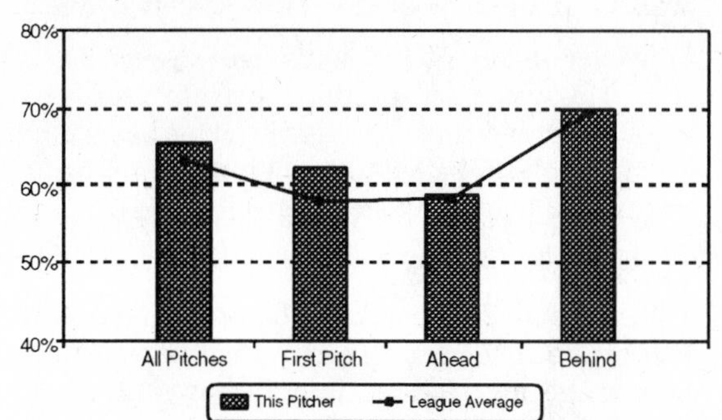

1992 Situational Stats

	W	L	ERA	Sv	IP		AB	H	HR	RBI	AVG
Home	2	0	1.87	2	33.2	LHB	162	38	1	12	.235
Road	0	2	2.74	3	46.0	RHB	139	33	1	14	.237
Day	0	0	2.59	1	24.1	Sc Pos	82	18	0	23	.220
Night	2	2	2.28	4	55.1	Clutch	101	27	1	10	.267

1992 Rankings (National League)

- 9th in lowest batting average allowed in relief with runners on base (.206) and relief ERA (2.41)
- Led the Padres in holds (8), lowest batting average allowed vs. left-handed batters (.235) and lowest batting average allowed in relief with runners on base

FRED McGRIFF

Position: 1B
Bats: L **Throws:** L
Ht: 6' 3" **Wt:** 210

Opening Day Age: 29
Born: 10/31/63 in Tampa, FL
ML Seasons: 7

HITTING:

No one, not even Jose Canseco or Cecil Fielder, has hit more home runs over the last five years than Fred McGriff. But McGriff has become more than just a home run hitter. He's a certified offensive monster who last year produced a galaxy of glittering offensive numbers -- 104 RBI, 30 doubles, 96 walks, a .394 on-base percentage, a .556 slugging percentage, a .286 batting average, and a .298 average with men in scoring position.

McGriff played no favorites between right-handed pitchers and lefties. He hit .283 with 13 homers vs. lefties, .288 with 22 homers vs. righties. He took the challenge of teammate Gary Sheffield's triple crown bid and ended up out-homering and driving in more runs than Sheffield.

As a National League pitching coach said last season, McGriff just keeps getting better. "You used to be able tie him up inside and that's still the best way to pitch him," said the coach. "But he doesn't go out of the strike zone very much anymore. He takes the breaking ball away and hits it a long way to the opposite field. And he's the kind of guy who you can strike out once but later that night, he's still going to get you."

BASERUNNING:

If you overlook him, McGriff will steal a base. He had eight steals last year, though like most of the Padres, his percentage was lousy -- he was caught six times. He is not overly aggressive on the bases, however.

FIELDING:

McGriff committed 12 errors in 1992. Many came on indifferent handling of routine plays. However, McGriff is capable of the outstanding play as well and has become very adept at handling balls in the dirt.

OVERALL:

McGriff was an All-Star for the first time in 1992 and he should repeat the honor for years to come, since there are few more consistent big boppers in all of baseball. Rumors of him being offered in trades could only lead one to wonder why?

Overall Statistics

	G	AB	R	H	D	T	HR	RBI	SB	BB	SO	AVG
1992	152	531	79	152	30	4	35	104	8	96	108	.286
Career	883	3003	511	839	148	13	191	515	33	553	738	.279

Where He Hits the Ball

Vs. LHP

Vs. RHP

1992 Situational Stats

	AB	H	HR	RBI	AVG		AB	H	HR	RBI	AVG
Home	273	83	21	56	.304	LHP	205	58	13	50	.283
Road	258	69	14	48	.267	RHP	326	94	22	54	.288
Day	146	39	9	28	.267	Sc Pos	131	39	7	63	.298
Night	385	113	26	76	.294	Clutch	81	26	2	13	.321

1992 Rankings (National League)

- 1st in home runs (35), batting average on a 3-1 count (.800) and slugging percentage vs. right-handed pitchers (.558)
- 2nd in walks (96), intentional walks (23), cleanup slugging percentage (.557) and HR frequency (15.2 ABs per HR)
- 3rd in RBI (104) and slugging percentage (.556)
- Led the Padres in home runs, RBI, walks, intentional walks, times on base (249), strikeouts (108), on-base percentage (.394), HR frequency, most pitches seen per plate appearance (3.70), slugging percentage vs. right-handed pitchers and on-base percentage vs. right-handed pitchers (.409)

PITCHING:

A versatile and tireless utility pitcher, Jose Melendez joined with Mike Maddux to give the Padres solid right-handed middle-relief depth last year. Along with a fine 2.92 ERA, he displayed superb control as evidenced by his gaudy strikeout-to-walk ratio (82-20), among the best of all NL relievers.

Melendez' success over the last two years with San Diego represents yet another personnel blunder by Woody Woodward and the Seattle Mariners -- an organization now desperate for pitching. Melendez is one of a dozen quality arms let go by the Mariners' organization. He was left out on waivers and the Padres grabbed him with good results.

Though he's obviously a fine pitcher, Melendez has one major problem: the home run ball. He allowed nine last year in 89.1 innings after getting nicked for 11 in 1991. The home run total is indicative of Melendez' control. He will occasionally overuse his slider, which when right has the action of a split-fingered pitch like that of Toronto's Juan Guzman. Sometimes Melendez will hang the slider, which is when he gets hurt. However, he also has a good sinking fastball, a decent curve and is learning how to better change speeds.

HOLDING RUNNERS, FIELDING, HITTING:

With more experience, Melendez is becoming better and better at holding runners close and developing an effective pickoff move. He permitted only three steals in seven attempts last year. Melendez is an athletic fielder who makes the tough play. He struck out on four of his five 1992 at-bats.

OVERALL:

Melendez was a steal for San Diego. He has found a niche in the Padres' bullpen and should keep getting better with more experience. He is 27 years old, so he should be at his physical prime over the next few years. The Padres snuck Melendez and Maddux through expansion. Like Maddux, Melendez could get time as a closer should Myers travel elsewhere.

JOSE MELENDEZ

Position: RP/SP
Bats: R **Throws:** R
Ht: 6' 2" **Wt:** 175

Opening Day Age: 27
Born: 9/2/65 in Naguabo, Puerto Rico
ML Seasons: 3

Overall Statistics

	W	L	ERA	G	GS	Sv	IP	H	R	BB	SO	HR
1992	6	7	2.92	56	3	0	89.1	82	32	20	82	9
Career	14	12	3.35	90	12	3	188.1	167	75	47	149	22

How Often He Throws Strikes

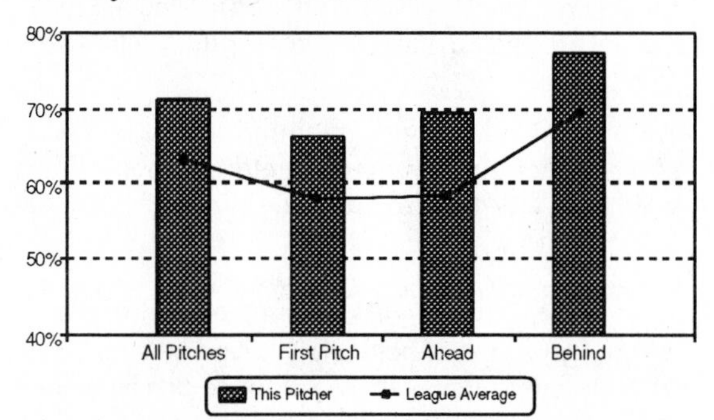

1992 Situational Stats

	W	L	ERA	Sv	IP		AB	H	HR	RBI	AVG
Home	2	4	3.51	0	51.1	LHB	160	45	6	22	.281
Road	4	3	2.13	0	38.0	RHB	169	37	3	20	.219
Day	2	2	3.63	0	17.1	Sc Pos	76	24	0	30	.316
Night	4	5	2.75	0	72.0	Clutch	107	23	0	8	.215

1992 Rankings (National League)

- 3rd in highest percentage of inherited runners scored (42.1%) and relief ERA (1.81)
- 5th in least baserunners allowed per 9 innings in relief (9.9)
- 10th in relief wins (6)
- Led the Padres in relief ERA, relief wins, least baserunners allowed per 9 innings in relief and most strikeouts per 9 innings in relief (8.4)

PITCHING:

It's not often that someone with 38 saves is widely viewed as having a lousy season. But such was the case with Randy Myers, whom a lot of people blamed for the Padres not hanging in contention last year. San Diego seemed unlikely to pursue the free agent lefty over the winter.

When picking through Myers' season, one finds the reasons for this apparent contradiction. For one thing, Myers blew eight saves. For another, his ERA was a horrendous 4.29. For another, several of the saves he did convert were messy episodes in which runs scored and baserunners needed to be stranded before the game ended. Opposing hitters batted .279 against Myers and reached him for seven home runs. After averaging slightly more than a strikeout per inning pitched prior to last year, Myers fanned 66 in 79.2 innings in 1992.

A big reason for all these negatives is that Myers' velocity no longer consistently reaches the low 90s heat that he used to throw in his early days with the New York Mets. Scouts also say that his fastball has straightened out. Myers has a deserved reputation for being headstrong and tough to handle. His inability to develop a decent slider or curve to throw as an alternative to the steady diet of fastballs is an indication of that attitude problem.

HOLDING RUNNERS, FIELDING, HITTING:

Baserunners have to be careful of Myers' pickoff move, which can be deceptive. His slow delivery home usually leaves him in an awkward position to field the ball. He had only one hit in seven at-bats with five strikeouts.

OVERALL:

Myers figured to provide one of the winter's most intriguing free-agent sagas. He is virtually certain not to be back in San Diego, and his checkered resume could result in a surprising lack of interest for someone coming off a 38-save season. His high ERA was no fluke, and neither are concerns about Myers' attitude, which could be brought back to earth this winter.

RANDY MYERS

Position: RP
Bats: L **Throws:** L
Ht: 6' 1" **Wt:** 215

Opening Day Age: 30
Born: 9/19/62 in Vancouver, WA
ML Seasons: 8

Overall Statistics

	W	L	ERA	G	GS	Sv	IP	H	R	BB	SO	HR
1992	3	6	4.29	66	0	38	79.2	84	38	34	66	7
Career	30	38	3.06	375	12	131	538.1	438	202	249	536	37

How Often He Throws Strikes

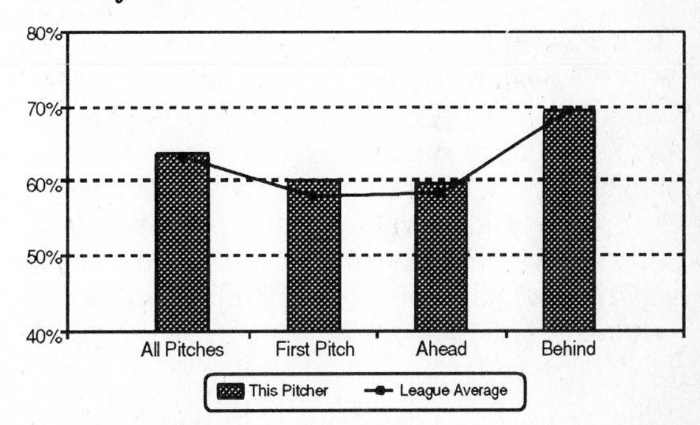

1992 Situational Stats

	W	L	ERA	Sv	IP		AB	H	HR	RBI	AVG
Home	2	3	4.58	20	39.1	LHB	63	17	0	9	.270
Road	1	3	4.02	18	40.1	RHB	238	67	7	44	.282
Day	3	1	3.77	11	28.2	Sc Pos	101	26	0	40	.257
Night	0	5	4.59	27	51.0	Clutch	244	67	6	46	.275

1992 Rankings (National League)

- 2nd in saves (38), save opportunities (46) and blown saves (8)
- 3rd in games finished (57)
- 4th in save percentage (82.6%) and highest relief ERA (4.29)
- 6th in highest percentage of inherited runners scored (40.0%) and highest batting average allowed in relief (.279)
- Led the Padres in games pitched (66), saves, games finished, wild pitches (5), save opportunities, save percentage, blown saves and relief losses (6)

RICH RODRIGUEZ

Position: RP
Bats: R **Throws:** L
Ht: 6' 0" **Wt:** 200

Opening Day Age: 30
Born: 3/1/63 in Downey, CA
ML Seasons: 3

Overall Statistics

	W	L	ERA	G	GS	Sv	IP	H	R	BB	SO	HR
1992	6	3	2.37	61	1	0	91.0	77	28	29	64	4
Career	10	5	2.80	157	2	1	218.2	195	76	89	126	14

How Often He Throws Strikes

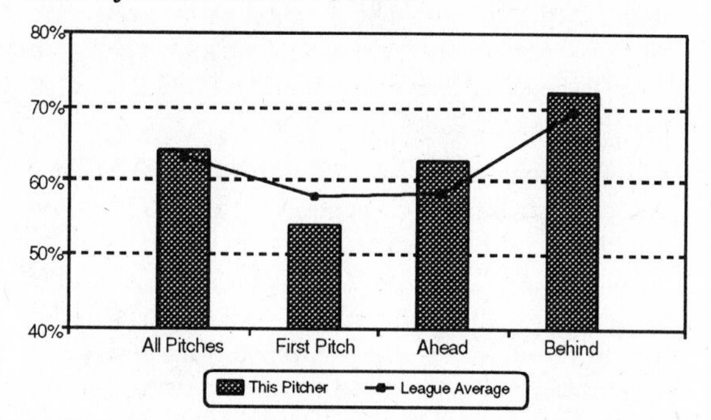

1992 Situational Stats

	W	L	ERA	Sv	IP		AB	H	HR	RBI	AVG
Home	4	1	1.93	0	51.1	LHB	103	24	2	12	.233
Road	2	2	2.95	0	39.2	RHB	233	53	2	21	.227
Day	0	1	2.48	0	29.0	Sc Pos	91	20	1	28	.220
Night	6	2	2.32	0	62.0	Clutch	51	11	0	3	.216

1992 Rankings (National League)

- 8th in relief ERA (2.28) and least baserunners allowed per 9 innings in relief (10.1)
- 10th in relief wins (6)
- Led the Padres in first batter efficiency (.218), lowest percentage of inherited runners scored (30.2%), relief wins, relief innings (87) and lowest batting average allowed in relief (.226)

PITCHING:

What with all the problems suffered by Randy Myers last year, the work of the Padres' set-up men was largely overlooked. Such was the case with Rich Rodriguez, the Padres' left-handed middle reliever who got a lot of work and did a solid job for most of 1992. Appearing in 61 games, second-most on the staff, Rodriguez pitched 91 innings and tied Mike Maddux for the club lead in ERA with a 2.37 mark. It was the third straight solid season put together by the little-noticed lefty.

Rodriguez was tough to hit last year, holding opposing batters to a .229 average. Unlike many left-handed relievers who don't consistently get out the lefthanders they are paid to retire, Rodriguez did his job. Left-handed hitters batted only .233 vs. Rodriguez, and right-handed hitters batted only .227. A groundball pitcher, he allowed only four home runs in his 91 innings. He was tough in the clutch, yielding a lowly .220 average with runners in scoring position and permitting only 13 of 43 inherited runners to score. Rodriguez' strikeout-to-walk ratio improved markedly last year: 40 Ks/44 BBs in 1991, 64 Ks/29 BBs in 1992.

With the use of a funky delivery helping him hide the ball well, Rodriguez uses sliders, change-ups and curves to left-handed hitters and will turn his fastball over to right-handed hitters. His change-up is also effective to righties. Rodriguez' assortment of pitches have had the Padres at least toying with the idea of making him a starter.

HOLDING RUNNERS, FIELDING, HITTING:

Rodriguez has improved his move to first and is thus much improved at holding runners. He permitted only six steals in 11 attempts last year. He handles the routine fielding plays. He is still perfect as a major-league hitter: 0- for-14 lifetime.

OVERALL:

Left-handed relievers are among baseball's most elusive commodities. Though the Padres didn't protect their fine middle-relief corps, including Rodriguez, they are happy to have him in '93. Another of those minor (at the time) acquisitions that have panned out, Rodriguez has become a very nice bargain for the Padres.

HITTING:

As talented a catcher as there is in baseball, Benito Santiago is also one of the game's biggest enigmas. Santiago was a free agent after the 1992 season and the Padres were adamant about cutting him loose. After several disappointing seasons in San Diego, interest in the veteran catcher wasn't anything like it would have been a few years ago.

Santiago was missing for much of last season after breaking a finger. He returned and played well for a period, ending up with 10 homers and 42 RBI in 386 at-bats. Though not spectacular, how many catchers surpassed those numbers in a full season? The Padres, as if to keep Santiago from bettering those numbers, sat him down for much of the last month after telling him they had no interest in retaining him.

There was a lot of excess baggage surrounding the relationship between Santiago and the Padres, including his 1992 refusal to play the outfield in order to get both he and Dan Walters in the lineup. Notoriously lacking in discipline, Santiago has always been vulnerable to high fastballs and breaking balls out of the strike zone. It was more of the same last season.

BASERUNNING:

A better than average runner for a catcher, Santiago used to be a good basestealer. But his success rate has declined every year since 1988 and last year he was only 2-for-7. He is always a big double play guy because of his out-of-control swings.

FIELDING:

Santiago offers a mixed bag defensively. There is hardly a better arm and he retains his ability to throw out runners from his knees. But he tends to overthrow, which results in a lot of errors. The Padres' pitchers disliked how Santiago called a game.

OVERALL:

He's been on his way out of San Diego for two years. Now Santiago will get his chance to play somewhere else. He's only 28 and with a better attitude, he could still re-emerge as one of the game's best catchers.

BENITO SANTIAGO

Position: C
Bats: R **Throws:** R
Ht: 6' 1" **Wt:** 185

Opening Day Age: 28
Born: 3/9/65 in Ponce, Puerto Rico
ML Seasons: 7

Overall Statistics

	G	AB	R	H	D	T	HR	RBI	SB	BB	SO	AVG
1992	106	386	37	97	21	0	10	42	2	21	52	.251
Career	789	2872	312	758	124	15	85	375	62	139	516	.264

Where He Hits the Ball

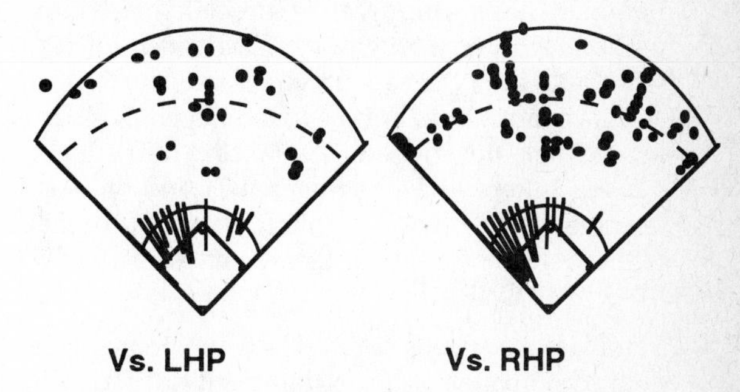

1992 Situational Stats

	AB	H	HR	RBI	AVG		AB	H	HR	RBI	AVG
Home	195	60	8	30	.308	LHP	130	38	7	17	.292
Road	191	37	2	12	.194	RHP	256	59	3	25	.230
Day	86	18	2	8	.209	Sc Pos	103	27	1	30	.262
Night	300	79	8	34	.263	Clutch	66	17	3	8	.258

1992 Rankings (National League)

- 1st in most GDPs per GDP situation (20.3%)
- 9th in GDPs (14)
- 10th in batting average on an 0-2 count (.269)
- Led NL catchers in caught stealing (5), batting average on an 0-2 count, slugging percentage vs. left-handed pitchers (.508) and errors (12)

FRANK SEMINARA

Position: SP
Bats: R **Throws:** R
Ht: 6' 2" **Wt:** 205

Opening Day Age: 25
Born: 5/16/67 in Brooklyn, NY
ML Seasons: 1

PITCHING:

Recalled when injuries to Greg Harris and Bruce Hurst were thinning the Padres' rotation, Frank Seminara gave San Diego some workmanlike efforts on the way to a solid 9-4 record and 3.68 ERA. Originally a Yankee product whom the Padres drafted out of the New York organization, Seminara had won 31 minor-league games in 1990-1991.

The righthander did well in his first major-league shot, finishing strongly by going 3-1 in the season's final month. Many of Seminara's other numbers were similarly impressive: he allowed only five home runs in 100.1 innings, and he allowed fewer hits (98) than innings pitched. Seminara has a whippy, cross-fire delivery which proved to be very tough on right-handed hitters, who batted only .216 with one home run in 176 at-bats against him. Lefties found his pitches easier to pick up and hit .294 versus him. Left-handed hitters had slugging (.407) and on-base averages (.390) that were more than 100 points higher against Seminara than righties had (.273 SLG, .282 OBP).

Seminara also needs to develop better control. He walked 46 batters while striking out only 61, not a good ratio. He has a sinking fastball and a slider, neither of which is overpowering and both of which he needs to throw for strikes. Seminara changes speed well for an inexperienced pitcher; indeed, his feel for pitching and mixing speeds was impressive.

HOLDING RUNNERS, FIELDING, HITTING:

Seminara needs work on his pickoff move. He does have a fairly quick delivery home which helps him against basestealers. He managed only four hits in 34 at-bats but was at least able to make fairly consistent contact with the bat.

OVERALL:

Not the kind of pitcher to knock your eyes out with his stuff, Seminara has a lot of poise for a younger pitcher and a good sense of how to pitch. He did enough in his 18 starts to warrant expansion protection and a solid chance at winning a job in the '93 rotation. In order to succeed, however, he'll need to find a way to neutralize left-handed hitters.

Overall Statistics

	W	L	ERA	G	GS	Sv	IP	H	R	BB	SO	HR
1992	9	4	3.68	19	18	0	100.1	98	46	46	61	5
Career	9	4	3.68	19	18	0	100.1	98	46	46	61	5

How Often He Throws Strikes

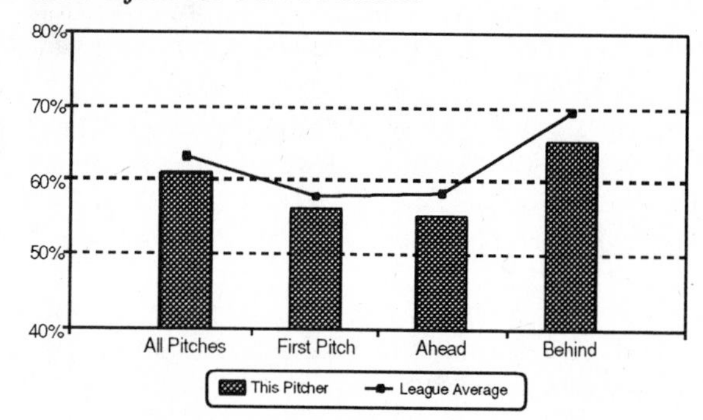

1992 Situational Stats

	W	L	ERA	Sv	IP		AB	H	HR	RBI	AVG
Home	6	1	3.04	0	56.1	LHB	204	60	4	25	.294
Road	3	3	4.50	0	44.0	RHB	176	38	1	13	.216
Day	5	2	3.20	0	45.0	Sc Pos	86	22	1	29	.256
Night	4	2	4.07	0	55.1	Clutch	9	3	0	0	.333

1992 Rankings (National League)

- Led the Padres in most GDPs induced per GDP situation (12.9%)

FUTURE MVP?

GARY SHEFFIELD

Position: 3B
Bats: R **Throws:** R
Ht: 5'11" **Wt:** 190

Opening Day Age: 24
Born: 11/18/68 in Tampa, FL
ML Seasons: 5

HITTING:

There were few more unbelievable stories in 1992 than that of Gary Sheffield, who came to San Diego via a pre-season trade with Milwaukee. Long considered a potential superstar, the young third baseman was healthy for the first time in his career and out of a city in which he never felt comfortable. The result was a possible Triple Crown until a late-season slump, and then a finger injury, cut short his bid.

Sheffield did it all. He batted for average (.330) and power (33 homers and a .580 slugging percentage). He was great in the clutch, driving in 100 runs while batting .339 with men in scoring position. He struck out only 40 times in 557 at-bats. National League scouts and opposition marveled at his skills. Said Braves manager Bobby Cox, "He generates the most awesome bat speed I've ever seen. The guy just doesn't hit balls, he kills them." And said Reds manager Lou Piniella, "I look at him and the guy I think of is a young Jim Rice, who was as strong a hitter as I've ever seen."

NL pitchers learned quickly not to try to get fastballs by Sheffield. They instead served him offspeed stuff and breaking balls away. Sheffield killed anything on the inner half of the plate, and he could go out and drive outside pitches with power to the opposite field.

BASERUNNING:

Sheffield stole 25 bases back in 1990, so the ability is there. However, he did not run much in San Diego (five steals in 11 attempts) largely because he was hitting in front of Fred McGriff.

FIELDING:

Long disparaged in Milwaukee as an erratic and indifferent third baseman, Sheffield did a decent job for the Padres. He made 16 errors, many of them throwing errors, but he showed decent range and fairly good hands.

OVERALL:

At age 23, Sheffield blossomed last year. Some people expect his Milwaukee attitude problems to re-surface, but they haven't yet, and players often outgrow youthful immaturity. Sheffield could be on his way to an awesome career.

Overall Statistics

	G	AB	R	H	D	T	HR	RBI	SB	BB	SO	AVG
1992	146	557	87	184	34	3	33	100	5	48	40	.330
Career	440	1667	225	471	95	6	54	233	48	145	136	.283

Where He Hits the Ball

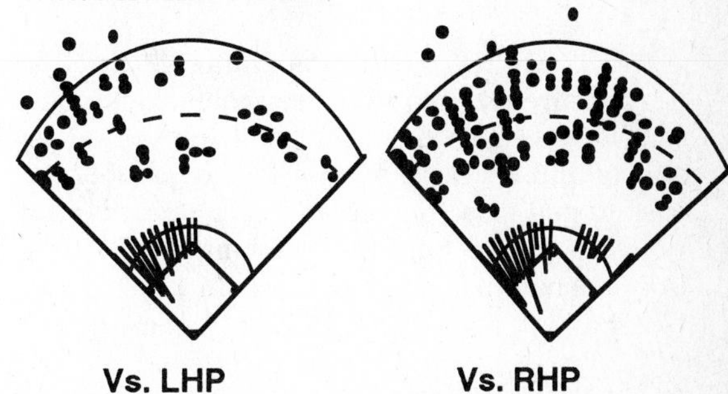

1992 Situational Stats

	AB	H	HR	RBI	AVG		AB	H	HR	RBI	AVG
Home	288	105	23	58	.365	LHP	189	69	13	38	.365
Road	269	79	10	42	.294	RHP	368	115	20	62	.313
Day	163	53	8	21	.325	Sc Pos	127	43	11	71	.339
Night	394	131	25	79	.332	Clutch	78	32	4	15	.410

1992 Rankings (National League)

- 1st in batting average (.330), total bases (323), slugging percentage vs. left-handed pitchers (.640) and batting average at home (.365)
- 2nd in GDPs (19), slugging percentage (.580), batting average in the clutch (.410) and slugging percentage vs. right-handed pitchers (.549)
- 3rd in home runs (33), HR frequency (16.9 ABs per HR), least pitches seen per plate appearance (3.18), batting average with runners in scoring position (.339), batting average vs. left-handed pitchers (.365), batting average on an 0-2 count (.314) and on-base percentage vs. left-handed pitchers (.420)

KURT STILLWELL

Position: 2B
Bats: B **Throws:** R
Ht: 5'11" **Wt:** 185

Opening Day Age: 27
Born: 6/4/65 in Glendale, CA
ML Seasons: 7

HITTING:

After being dumped by Kansas City, Kurt Stillwell hoped to find new life in San Diego last year as the Padres' second baseman. Stillwell got off to a fine start in his return to the National League, posting a .289 average through May 31. But then his bat died; he hit only .198 the rest of the way. He wound up with the worst figures of his career in most categories.

Stillwell is never going to provide power, but the Padres had to hope for more than the .227 average and 24 RBI he produced in 1992. He managed only 20 extra-base hits all year and batted just .184 with runners in scoring position. Plus, he only walked 26 times. The result was a miserable .274 on-base percentage.

A notorious first-pitch fastball hitter, Stillwell is not patient enough to work deep counts. Throughout his career he has been routinely retired by sliders and curves thrown away. Invariably, he tries to pull those pitches and ends up with a lot of weak infield outs. A switch-hitter, Stillwell does not have one dominant side. In 1992 he was better as a righty (.250 vs. .217 left-handed).

BASERUNNING:

Stillwell is a below-average runner who rarely tries to steal. He's made only 14 attempts over the last three years, though last season he was successful on four of five.

FIELDING:

Kansas City dumped Stillwell because they felt that he could not cut it defensively at shortstop. The Padres used him at second but were unhappy with his play. He committed 16 errors and showed very poor range. He was also tentative in turning the double play. Stillwell has a decent arm but has become gun-shy in the field. With Tony Fernandez gone, he could be moving back to shortstop this year.

OVERALL:

The Padres could carry Stillwell's tepid offense if he were more dependable in the field. But his defensive liabilities make him a huge question mark. He could hang on, especially since the Padres are very thin at both middle infield positions.

Overall Statistics

	G	AB	R	H	D	T	HR	RBI	SB	BB	SO	AVG
1992	114	379	35	86	15	3	2	24	4	26	58	.227
Career	873	2866	339	716	141	28	32	292	32	249	411	.250

Where He Hits the Ball

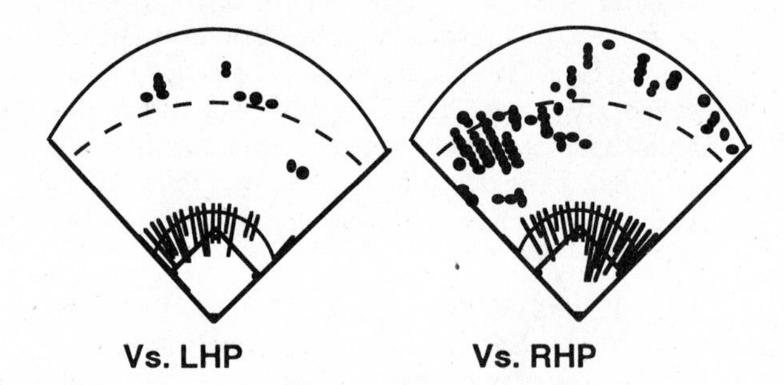

1992 Situational Stats

	AB	H	HR	RBI	AVG		AB	H	HR	RBI	AVG
Home	191	42	1	14	.220	LHP	112	28	1	8	.250
Road	188	44	1	10	.234	RHP	267	58	1	16	.217
Day	119	29	1	9	.244	Sc Pos	87	16	0	20	.184
Night	260	57	1	15	.219	Clutch	71	16	0	3	.225

1992 Rankings (National League)

- 4th in lowest batting average with runners in scoring position (.184)
- 5th in lowest batting average with 2 strikes (.122)
- 9th in lowest batting average on a 3-2 count (.094)
- Led NL second basemen in sacrifice flies (6) and errors (16)

HITTING:

When Kurt Stillwell struggled last year, the Padres turned to veteran Tim Teufel. He did a decent job as a fill-in, especially during the first half of the season. Though Teufel batted only .228, he supplied good power -- a marked contrast with Stillwell. The righty swinger belted 16 extra-base hits, including 6 homers, in only 246 at-bats.

For years Teufel has been used primarily as a platoon player against left-handed pitching. While he hit only .239 against lefthanders last year, his slugging average was an excellent .435. Curiously, deposed manager Greg Riddoch gave Teufel nearly twice as many at-bats against right-handed pitching than left. Teufel hit only .214 with a .279 slugging percentage against righties.

Teufel has always been a good fastball hitter with decent patience. However, his walks dropped some last year and he did not seem to be able to catch up to the fastballs like he used to do in his prime. He's never been a good breaking ball hitter, which is the way most clubs still try to get him out. As a pinch hitter Teufel struggled like most Padres, but his ability to hit the long ball made him a threat in that role.

BASERUNNING:

Teufel is capable of stealing once in a while but is hardly a consistent threat on the bases. He is fairly aggressive in trying to break up double plays.

FIELDING:

A classic utility man, Teufel can play first, second or third. His primary experience is at second, but he does not turn the double play very well and lacks good range. However, he can do an adequate job at any of the three positions.

OVERALL:

It's been said before, but Teufel is the kind of player who is much better on a winning team, where his occasional power and veteran savvy make up for his low average and defensive shortcomings. It's uncertain that he has a useful role in what could be a bargain-basement operation in San Diego.

TIM TEUFEL

Position: 2B/3B
Bats: R **Throws:** R
Ht: 6' 0" **Wt:** 175

Opening Day Age: 34
Born: 7/7/58 in Greenwich, CT
ML Seasons: 10

Overall Statistics

	G	AB	R	H	D	T	HR	RBI	SB	BB	SO	AVG
1992	101	246	23	55	10	0	6	25	2	31	45	.224
Career	977	2912	389	739	174	10	79	348	21	360	492	.254

Where He Hits the Ball

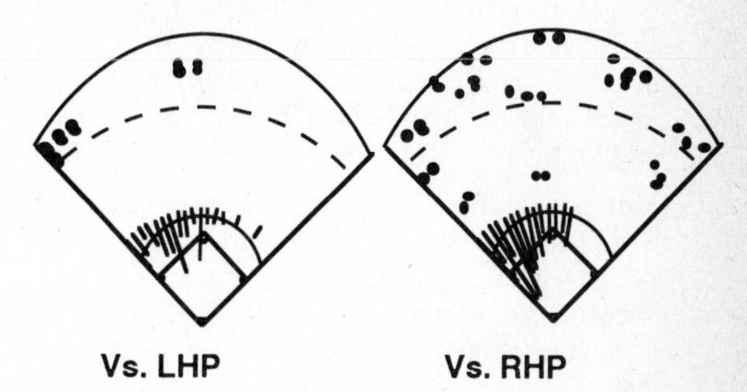

1992 Situational Stats

	AB	H	HR	RBI	AVG		AB	H	HR	RBI	AVG
Home	109	28	2	14	.257	LHP	92	22	4	14	.239
Road	137	27	4	11	.197	RHP	154	33	2	11	.214
Day	82	19	4	12	.232	Sc Pos	59	14	1	17	.237
Night	164	36	2	13	.220	Clutch	55	10	1	4	.182

1992 Rankings (National League)

→ Did not rank near the top or bottom in any category

DAN WALTERS

Position: C
Bats: R **Throws:** R
Ht: 6' 4" **Wt:** 225

Opening Day Age: 26
Born: 8/15/66 in Brunswick, ME
ML Seasons: 1

HITTING:

Heretofore a minor-league journeyman, Dan Walters was hitting .394 at AAA Las Vegas last year when injuries sidelined Padres catcher Benito Santiago. Walters was recalled and went on to do a solid job, hitting .251 and showing good defensive skills. With Santiago scheduled to depart via free agency, Walters will likely get the chance to be an everyday catcher this year.

Walters showed some offense in his limited playing time. Sixteen of his 45 hits went for extra bases and he managed 22 RBI in 179 at-bats. However, the question remains whether Walters can produce on an everyday basis. He started strongly last year, but National League pitchers soon learned that they could tie him up with hard stuff inside and breaking balls away. Walters can hit the fastball, but he does not have the kind of power that makes pitchers hesitant about challenging him.

Perhaps significantly, Walters had only nine hits in his last five weeks and finished the season in a 1-for-18 slump. Walters also struck out nearly three times as much as he walked. At 26 years old, he isn't likely to get a whole lot better than he is now.

BASERUNNING:

Walters is a prototype journeyman catcher who can't run at all. He had one stolen base and that came on a blown hit-and-run. Even in the minors he never swiped more than two bases in a season.

FIELDING:

San Diego pitchers liked throwing to Walters. He has good hands and can block balls in the dirt. He also worked well with the pitching staff, learning quickly how to handle each pitcher's stuff. Though not in Santiago's class as a thrower, Walters has a good arm and can throw out his share of basestealers if his pitchers give him a chance.

OVERALL:

San Diego never envisioned Walters as anything more than a backup. However, unless their budget dramatically changes, he will likely be given the chance to catch every day. Time will tell whether he can handle the load.

Overall Statistics

	G	AB	R	H	D	T	HR	RBI	SB	BB	SO	AVG
1992	57	179	14	45	11	1	4	22	1	10	28	.251
Career	57	179	14	45	11	1	4	22	1	10	28	.251

Where He Hits the Ball

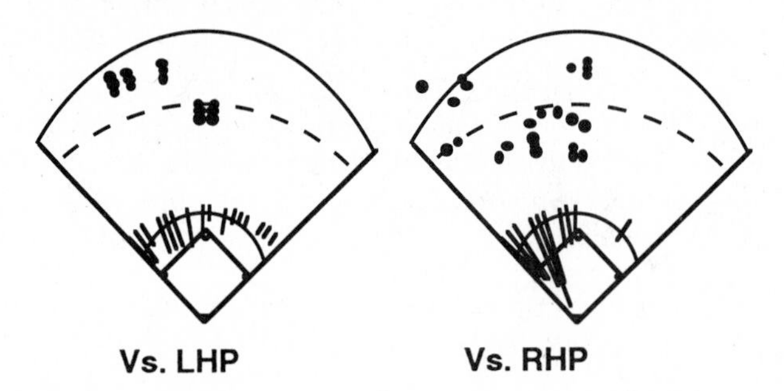

1992 Situational Stats

	AB	H	HR	RBI	AVG		AB	H	HR	RBI	AVG
Home	90	24	3	12	.267	LHP	61	16	1	8	.262
Road	89	21	1	10	.236	RHP	118	29	3	14	.246
Day	72	21	2	11	.292	Sc Pos	49	10	0	16	.204
Night	107	24	2	11	.224	Clutch	24	5	1	6	.208

1992 Rankings (National League)

→ Did not rank near the top or bottom in any category

PITCHING:

The Mets' jack of all trades in 1992, Wally Whitehurst worked as a starter, short reliever, and long reliever. His role was supposed to be long relief, but injuries to the Mets' starters pressed him into the rotation. Always much better as a reliever (5-5 career, 3.13 ERA) than as a starter (6-17, 4.48), Whitehurst was adequate in the rotation last year (3.91 ERA). But he still did better out of the bullpen (3.30). His new club, the Padres, might want to remember that.

Whitehurst's best pitch is a big curveball which he uses extensively. In addition he has a fastball, slider, and change-up. He likes to throw the curve for strike one and then mix in other pitches to keep hitters off balance. Whitehurst is neither overpowering nor especially fine with his locations. He just tries to throw strikes and keep the ball in play. That approach often led to problems during 1992; opposition batters did very well against Mets' pitchers in general by swinging at the first pitch. Against Whitehurst they hit .355 on the first pitch.

Although he doesn't usually show evidence of tiring as he throws more pitches in each game, Whitehurst has a tendency to be less effective later in the season. Throughout his career his performance in the second half of the season has been weaker than in the first half. In 1992 he had a 2.92 ERA before the All-Star break, 4.43 after; his career marks are 2.97 before and 4.72 after.

HOLDING RUNNERS, FIELDING, HITTING:

Whitehurst watches runners closely but doesn't have a good pickoff move. He is adequate in the field, while at bat he can usually put the ball in play.

OVERALL:

A starter in the minor leagues, Whitehurst always wanted to be in the rotation for the Mets. He got his chance and failed in that role in 1991, and in 1992 he did nothing to further his future as a starter with New York. Thus the deal to San Diego. The Padres will likely give him another chance in a rotation beset by injuries and inconsistency.

WALLY WHITEHURST

Position: RP/SP
Bats: R **Throws:** R
Ht: 6' 3" **Wt:** 195

Opening Day Age: 29
Born: 4/11/64 in Shreveport, LA
ML Seasons: 4

Overall Statistics

	W	L	ERA	G	GS	Sv	IP	H	R	BB	SO	HR
1992	3	9	3.62	44	11	0	97.0	99	45	33	70	4
Career	11	22	3.83	127	32	3	310.0	321	146	72	212	23

How Often He Throws Strikes

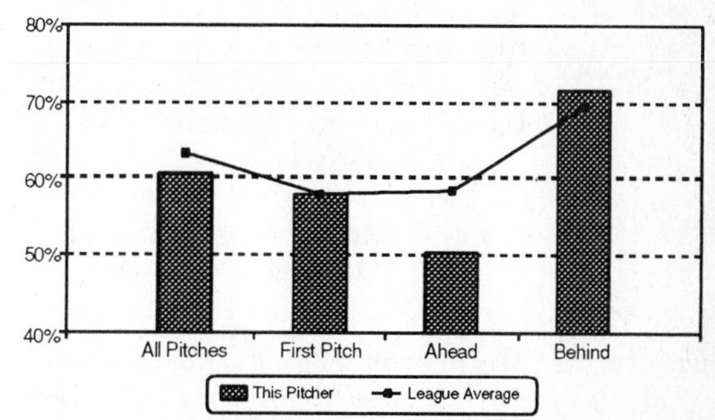

1992 Situational Stats

	W	L	ERA	Sv	IP		AB	H	HR	RBI	AVG
Home	3	4	3.17	0	54.0	LHB	204	53	3	28	.260
Road	0	5	4.19	0	43.0	RHB	171	46	1	22	.269
Day	0	2	4.82	0	18.2	Sc Pos	122	31	2	42	.254
Night	3	7	3.33	0	78.1	Clutch	76	25	1	15	.329

1992 Rankings (National League)

- 7th in highest percentage of inherited runners scored (38.2%)

GENE HARRIS

Position: RP
Bats: R **Throws:** R
Ht: 5'11" **Wt:** 190

Opening Day Age: 28
Born: 12/5/64 in Sebring, FL
ML Seasons: 4

Overall Statistics

	W	L	ERA	G	GS	Sv	IP	H	R	BB	SO	HR
1992	0	2	4.15	22	1	0	30.1	23	15	15	25	3
Career	3	9	5.00	76	7	2	135.0	132	86	80	99	13

PITCHING, FIELDING, HITTING & HOLDING RUNNERS:

When Seattle decided to release talented righthander Gene Harris, it wasn't only due to his 7.00 ERA. Harris had embarrassed the club by announcing he was retiring to pursue a football career. The Padres took a chance by claiming him on waivers -- and if Harris matures a little, San Diego (the Padres, not the Chargers) might have latched onto a steal.

Harris has a world of athletic ability. He throws a moving fastball that consistently is in the 90 MPH range. He also has a hard slider and has begun learning how to throw a change. The Padres liked what they saw of him in a late-season trial. He had a 2.95 ERA in 21.1 innings, striking out 19 and walking only nine. Opposing hitters managed only a .195 average against Harris. His moving fastball was especially tough on left-handed hitters, who managed only a .158 average against him.

A good athlete, Harris must still develop the skill to hold on runners. He is a good fielder. An American Leaguer since 1989, Harris had one hit in three at-bats while with the Padres in 1992.

OVERALL:

Harris could be among a big group of Padre pitchers who get a chance to fill the closer's role. At the least, he has the stuff to do a job in middle relief.

JEREMY HERNANDEZ

Position: RP
Bats: R **Throws:** R
Ht: 6' 6" **Wt:** 205

Opening Day Age: 26
Born: 7/7/66 in Burbank, CA
ML Seasons: 2

Overall Statistics

	W	L	ERA	G	GS	Sv	IP	H	R	BB	SO	HR
1992	1	4	4.17	26	0	1	36.2	39	17	11	25	4
Career	1	4	3.00	35	0	3	51.0	47	18	16	34	4

PITCHING, FIELDING, HITTING & HOLDING RUNNERS:

Well-seasoned prospect Jeremy Hernandez had 11 saves with a 2.91 ERA at AAA Las Vegas last year. His ERA was almost two runs lower than his 1991 figure at Las Vegas (4.74), when he saved 13, and the improvement caused the Padres to recall him for a look late last season. Hernandez pitched somewhat better at the end of the year after an ominous April/May, after which he was sent to the minors. Surprisingly, he was protected from expansion while other more successful bullpen mates were left unprotected.

Hernandez had a high ERA for San Diego (4.17). He also allowed more hits than innings pitched and was touched for four home runs in his 36.2 innings pitched. A forkballer who mixes in a fastball and change, Hernandez had trouble keeping his best pitch down in the strike zone. He was acquired from the St. Louis organization and was originally a starting pitcher after debuting in 1987. He's been a full-time reliever for the last two seasons and the Padres feel that's where his future lies.

Hernandez is a good fielder and has a decent move to first base. He is still looking for his first major-league hit.

OVERALL:

Hernandez is yet another possible option in the crowd seeking work in the wide-open San Diego bullpen. At 26 he is not a kid, but he has as good a shot as any current Padre to pick up significant work in the bullpen.

TIM SCOTT

Position: RP
Bats: R **Throws:** R
Ht: 6' 2" **Wt:** 185

Opening Day Age: 26
Born: 11/16/66 in Hanford, CA
ML Seasons: 2

Overall Statistics

	W	L	ERA	G	GS	Sv	IP	H	R	BB	SO	HR
1992	4	1	5.26	34	0	0	37.2	39	24	21	30	4
Career	4	1	5.35	36	0	0	38.2	41	26	21	31	4

PITCHING, FIELDING, HITTING & HOLDING RUNNERS:

Tim Scott was a successful closer at the Triple-A level for the Padres last year, saving 15 games for Las Vegas in only 24 appearances. However, he was not as successful when he was brought to San Diego. Scott did win four games but otherwise was largely ineffective on the way to a 5.26 ERA. Scott is a long-time minor-leaguer who was signed out of the Dodgers' organization. He's been primarily a reliever since 1988, but last year was the first season he'd compiled saves in double figures.

With the Padres, control was Scott's biggest problem. He walked 21 in 37.2 innings. He throws an average fastball, slider, change and forkball; he was behind in too many counts to exploit the forkball, which has a chance to be his best pitch. Scott's fastball, while in the high 80s, is too straight to throw by most hitters when they know it's coming.

Scott does a decent job of holding runners and is a good fielder. He did not have an at-bat last season.

OVERALL:

Scott is another of the many Padres' fringe pitchers who could get a chance to stick in what will likely be a revamped pitching staff. But he is hardly a big-time prospect. He is likely as good right now as he's ever going to be.

CRAIG SHIPLEY

Position: SS/2B
Bats: R **Throws:** R
Ht: 6' 1" **Wt:** 185

Opening Day Age: 30
Born: 1/7/63 in Sydney, Australia
ML Seasons: 5

Overall Statistics

	G	AB	R	H	D	T	HR	RBI	SB	BB	SO	AVG
1992	52	105	7	26	6	0	0	7	1	2	21	.248
Career	131	265	22	64	11	0	1	19	1	6	47	.242

HITTING, FIELDING, BASERUNNING:

The pride of Sydney, Australia, Craig Shipley is a utility player who can fill in at all infield positions. However, in stops with the Dodgers, Mets and now Padres, he has never stuck for longer than a brief trial. The 105 at-bats he had last year were the most he's ever had in one season. But Shipley, like most of the Padres' bench, did little with his chances. He had only six extra-base hits (all doubles) and just seven RBI. He struck out 21 times while walking just twice, one of them intentionally.

Shipley has shown little major-league power and does not generate enough bat speed to catch up with most good hard stuff. He did have some success against left-handed pitching in limited opportunities, batting .294 (10-for-34).

Shipley has average speed at best, so he is not going to be a factor on the bases. His best position is probably second base though he does not have good range. He can also fill in at first, short and third and does an adequate job at them all.

OVERALL:

San Diego got virtually nothing from their bench in 1992. Shipley was one of the most-used players, and he's 30 years old. His status is in doubt as the Padres are likely to shake up their roster.

SAN DIEGO PADRES MINOR LEAGUE PROSPECTS

ORGANIZATION OVERVIEW:

Last summer's All-Star game in San Diego was definitely a mixed blessing for the host club. The Padres, an organization known for producing talent, could boast about all the San Diego products who were performing in the game. The only trouble was, most of those All-Stars weren't wearing Padre uniforms. Bip Roberts, Roberto Alomar, Carlos Baerga . . . it got a little embarrassing. How could San Diego produce three of the best second basemen in baseball, people wondered, and yet trade them all away? It's the sort of question that defies an answer. General manager Joe McIlvaine has a reputation for building a solid farm system. The trick from now on will be to keep the finished products in San Diego.

RAY A. HOLBERT

Position: SS
Bats: R **Throws:** R
Ht: 6' 0" **Wt:** 165
Opening Day Age: 22
Born: 9/25/70 in Torrance, CA

Recent Statistics

	G	AB	R	H	D	T	HR	RBI	SB	BB	SO	AVG
91 A High Desert	122	386	76	102	14	2	4	51	19	56	83	.264
92 AA Wichita	95	304	46	86	7	3	2	23	26	42	68	.283
92 MLE	95	286	30	68	5	1	1	15	15	23	72	.238

The trading of Tony Fernandez means the Padres will be looking for a shortstop, and Holbert will be one of the leading candidates to fill the position. A third-round pick in 1988, Holbert has steadily been raising his batting average -- .155, .204, .264, .283 -- while moving up the Padre ladder. Holbert has very little power but he does have good speed and plate discipline. He has good range in the field but has been prone to making errors. A jump from AA to the majors this year is possible but unlikely.

SCOTT G. SANDERS

Position: P
Bats: R **Throws:** R
Ht: 6' 4" **Wt:** 210
Opening Day Age: 24
Born: 3/25/69 in Hannibal, MO

Recent Statistics

	W	L	ERA	G	GS	Sv	IP	H	R	BB	SO	HR
92 AA Wichita	7	5	3.49	14	14	0	87.2	85	35	37	95	7
92 AAA Las Vegas	3	6	5.50	14	12	0	72.0	97	49	31	51	7

A bonus first-round pick in 1990 when the Padres lost Mark Davis to free agency, Sanders has developed, but slowly. Some arm problems held him back for a while, but he has moved through the system quickly the past two years, finishing 1992 at AAA Las Vegas. Sanders is a big guy with a major-league fastball, a good slider and an improving change-up. He struggled at AAA last year, so he'll probably be back there at the start of the '93 season. The Padres protected him from expansion, just in case.

DARRELL E. SHERMAN

Position: OF
Bats: L **Throws:** L
Ht: 5' 9" **Wt:** 160
Opening Day Age: 25
Born: 12/4/67 in Los Angeles, CA

Recent Statistics

	G	AB	R	H	D	T	HR	RBI	SB	BB	SO	AVG
91 AA Wichita	131	502	93	148	17	3	3	48	43	74	28	.295
92 AA Wichita	64	220	60	73	11	2	6	25	26	40	25	.332
92 AAA Las Vegas	71	269	48	77	8	1	3	22	26	42	41	.286
92 MLE	135	454	68	115	13	0	6	29	30	47	69	.253

The Padres almost lost Darrell Sherman once, and they don't want it to happen again. Left off their 40-man roster a year ago, Sherman was picked up by Baltimore in the Rule 5 draft, but was returned. After he had an outstanding 1992 season at AA Wichita and AAA Las Vegas (52 steals, 108 runs scored, 82 walks), San Diego took no chances: they protected from expansion. Sherman was rated the best defensive outfielder, best baserunner and most exciting player in the Texas League by Baseball America.

GUILLERMO VELASQUEZ

Position: 1B
Bats: L **Throws:** R
Ht: 6' 0" **Wt:** 170
Opening Day Age: 24
Born: 4/23/68 in Mexicali, Mex

Recent Statistics

	G	AB	R	H	D	T	HR	RBI	SB	BB	SO	AVG
92 AAA Las Vegas	136	512	68	158	44	4	7	99	3	44	94	.309
92 NL San Diego	15	23	1	7	0	0	1	5	0	1	7	.304
92 MLE	136	473	41	119	32	1	4	60	1	26	98	.252

A 25-year-old native of Mexico, Velasquez batted .309 with 99 RBI at Las Vegas, then hit .304 in 23 at-bats for the Padres. Considered a power prospect, he shortened his swing and hit only seven homers for Las Vegas, but he did have 44 doubles. A lefty-hitting first baseman, his path is blocked by Fred McGriff. The Padres protected Velasquez in the expansion draft, but it's possible they'll trade him. There are even whispers that McGriff could be traded.

TIM WORRELL

Position: P
Bats: R **Throws:** R
Ht: 6' 4" **Wt:** 210
Opening Day Age: 25
Born: 7/5/67 in Pasadena, CA

Recent Statistics

	W	L	ERA	G	GS	Sv	IP	H	R	BB	SO	HR
91 A Waterloo	8	4	3.34	14	14	0	86.1	70	36	33	83	5
91 A High Desert	5	2	4.24	11	11	0	63.2	65	32	33	70	2
92 AA Wichita	8	6	2.86	19	19	0	125.2	115	46	32	109	8
92 AAA Las Vegas	4	2	4.26	10	10	0	63.1	61	32	19	32	4

Like his older brother Todd, Tim Worrell is a big, strong, hard-throwing righthander with a 93 MPH fastball. Unlike his brother, the younger Worrell has been a starter throughout his minor-league career. Rated the number-nine prospect in the Texas League last year, he finished the year going 4-2 for Las Vegas. He might be back there this spring, but probably not for too long.

OVERLOOKED

PITCHING:

In yet another season in which the San Francisco pitching staff underwent significant transformation, Rod Beck emerged as the Giants' closer of the future. Working for a bullpen that managed only 30 total saves, Beck was the one success story as he saved 17 and led the club in ERA with a super 1.76 mark.

From day one of 1992 Beck made the most of every opportunity. An aggressive pitcher who comes right at hitters with a nasty sinking fastball, a hard slider and an improving forkball that he uses as an offspeed pitch, Beck was one of the toughest pitchers to hit in all of baseball.

Opposing hitters batted only .190 against Beck. He allowed only four home runs in 92 innings and only 13 of the 62 hits he permitted went for extra bases. Beck has also developed outstanding control. He walked only 15 batters (two of them intentional) while fanning 87, an outstanding ratio. His slider and riding fastball were especially tough on left-handed hitters, who collectively hit only .178 against him. The burly Beck demonstrated that his heavy work load did not wear him down. He did his best pitching in September/October when he went 2-0 with a 0.48 ERA and four saves.

HOLDING RUNNERS, FIELDING, HITTING:

Beck is one of those pitchers who basically doesn't worry about baserunners. He prefers to just go after the hitter, and thus does not have much of a move to first. However, he delivers to the plate quickly and last year permitted only two steals in six attempts. He is not the most agile of fielders and will make mistakes in the field. As a closer, he doesn't get much chance to hit.

OVERALL:

No team entered the off-season with more questions than the Giants. But identifying their bullpen ace wasn't one, because Beck has blossomed into a legitimate late-inning intimidator.

ROD BECK

Position: RP
Bats: R **Throws:** R
Ht: 6' 1" **Wt:** 215

Opening Day Age: 24
Born: 8/3/68 in Burbank, CA
ML Seasons: 2

Overall Statistics

	W	L	ERA	G	GS	Sv	IP	H	R	BB	SO	HR
1992	3	3	1.76	65	0	17	92.0	62	20	15	87	4
Career	4	4	2.49	96	0	18	144.1	115	42	28	125	8

How Often He Throws Strikes

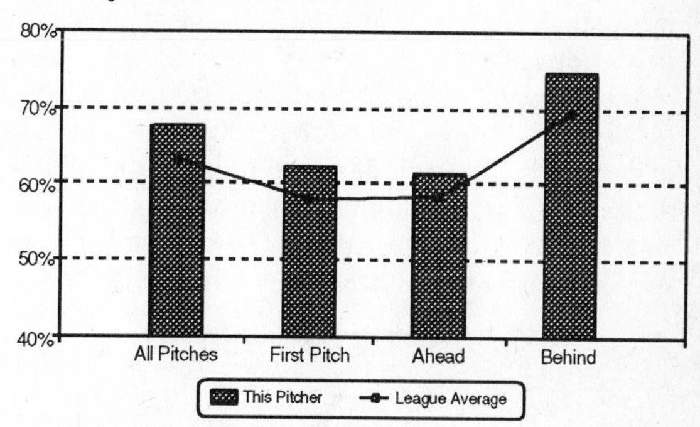

1992 Situational Stats

	W	L	ERA	Sv	IP		AB	H	HR	RBI	AVG
Home	2	3	2.06	9	43.2	LHB	180	32	2	13	.178
Road	1	0	1.49	8	48.1	RHB	147	30	2	12	.204
Day	0	0	1.80	8	35.0	Sc Pos	82	16	0	20	.195
Night	3	3	1.74	9	57.0	Clutch	187	36	2	14	.193

1992 Rankings (National League)

- 1st in lowest batting average allowed in relief (.190) and least baserunners allowed per 9 innings in relief (7.7)
- 2nd in lowest save percentage (73.9%), lowest batting average allowed vs. left-handed batters (.178) and relief ERA (1.76)
- 3rd in lowest batting average allowed in relief with runners on base (.183)
- Led the Giants in saves (17), games finished (42), save opportunities (23), save percentage, blown saves (6), lowest percentage of inherited runners scored (22.0%), relief ERA, relief innings (92), lowest batting average allowed in relief and least baserunners allowed per 9 innings in relief

PITCHING:

At one point in 1992, Bud Black seemed on his way to a solid 15-win season. But then the roof fell in down the stretch. He lost nine of his last 10 decisions to end the year under a mediocre 10-12 cloud. Black lost all six of his September/October starts and compiled an 8.01 ERA.

Black's durability has always been a problem -- he seems to wear down after reaching the 150-inning plateau. Over the last five years he's gone 38-28 through July 31 but 13-26 thereafter. When he tires, Black becomes susceptible to the home run ball. He allowed 23 last season after getting tagged for 25 dingers in 1991.

To be successful, Black needs to be able to spot his fastball and curve and then change speeds. He does not have overpowering stuff, so when he gets behind in counts, as he did too frequently late last season, hitters wait for his average fastball and tee off. The lack of one real quality pitch is evident in Black's numbers against right-handed hitters. They hit him at a .272 clip and were responsible for 19 of the 23 homers he allowed.

HOLDING RUNNERS, FIELDING, HITTING:

Using a variety of pickoff moves, Black is as good as there is at holding runners. He varies his moves, uses a slide-step and quickens his delivery to help out his catchers immensely. Last year he permitted only seven steals in 21 attempts, an outstanding ratio. Black is a decent fielder, though he is prone to mistakes at times on bunt plays. He had a woeful year at bat with only three hits in 54 at-bats.

OVERALL:

One of Black's problems is the four-year free-agent contract he signed before the 1991 season. The money probably led people to expect too much. No star, Black is a pitcher with a career record slightly under .500 who is sometimes inconsistent but usually keeps his team in the game. He might have received an ace's money, but in truth he is a savvy pro who is a complementary member of the starting rotation.

BUD BLACK

Position: SP
Bats: L **Throws:** L
Ht: 6' 2" **Wt:** 185

Opening Day Age: 35
Born: 6/30/57 in San Mateo, CA
ML Seasons: 12

Overall Statistics

	W	L	ERA	G	GS	Sv	IP	H	R	BB	SO	HR
1992	10	12	3.97	28	28	0	177.0	178	88	59	82	23
Career	105	110	3.76	361	260	11	1858.0	1776	865	558	932	187

How Often He Throws Strikes

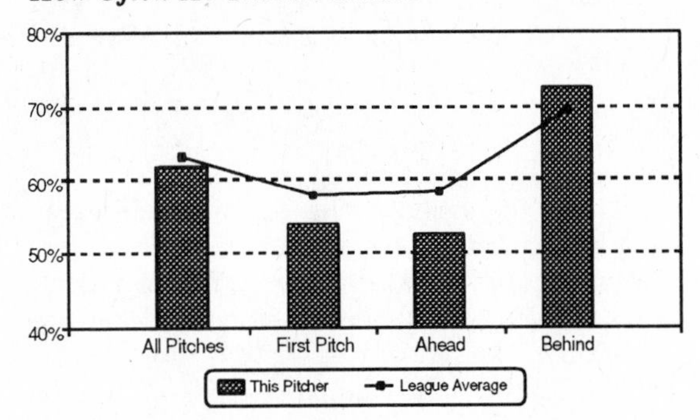

1992 Situational Stats

	W	L	ERA	Sv	IP		AB	H	HR	RBI	AVG
Home	8	5	2.91	0	111.1	LHB	140	32	4	10	.229
Road	2	7	5.76	0	65.2	RHB	537	146	19	57	.272
Day	7	2	2.62	0	75.2	Sc Pos	136	34	3	41	.250
Night	3	10	4.97	0	101.1	Clutch	42	9	3	4	.214

1992 Rankings (National League)

- 1st in home runs allowed (23), balks (7) and most home runs allowed per 9 innings pitched (1.2)
- 2nd in highest slugging percentage allowed (.423) and lowest stolen base percentage allowed (33.3%)
- 3rd in highest ERA (3.97), lowest strikeout/walk ratio (1.4) and least strikeouts per 9 innings (4.2)
- Led the Giants in sacrifice bunts as a batter (10), home runs allowed, balks, runners caught stealing (14), lowest stolen base percentage allowed and lowest batting average allowed with runners in scoring position (.250)

PITCHING:

Jeff Brantley was just another decent relief pitcher who had lost his closer's role when Giants manager Roger Craig decided to give him a look as a starter. The results were stunning as Brantley got four September starts and went 3-0 with a 0.44 ERA. By season's end, Craig was saying that Brantley, one of the Giant manager's favorite pitchers, could become the club's ace down the road. That might be a little premature, but there are signs with Brantley that suggest he has the stuff to be a quality starter.

For one thing, unlike many long-time relievers Brantley is far from being a one- or two-pitch pitcher. He throws a split-fingered fastball that sinks away from left-handed hitters, a second fastball that is a riser and difficult to pull, a hard slider and a very underrated curveball. Brantley has never been afraid to pitch deep into counts in order to set up a hitter. His deep repertoire and pitching mentality are indeed better suited for starting than relieving.

Perenially one of the league leaders in relief innings, Brantley also seems to have the necessary stamina to be a starter. As one NL manager said, "Brantley's a bulldog who works hard. As a reliever, he doesn't have the stuff to blow people away, but as a starter he could be really tough with the way he works hitters."

HOLDING RUNNERS, FIELDING, HITTING:

Brantley works hard to hold baserunners with a variety of pickoff moves. He pays as much attention to runners as any Giant pitcher. He also helps himself defensively with good skills and defensive instincts. He can occasionally handle the bat, though he had only one hit in nine at-bats last year.

OVERALL:

Four starts, averaging five innings each, do not make a career. But Brantley showed the Giants enough to make them think that their endless search for starting pitching might have found at least one solid answer.

JEFF BRANTLEY

Position: RP/SP
Bats: R **Throws:** R
Ht: 5'11" **Wt:** 180

Opening Day Age: 29
Born: 9/5/63 in Florence, AL
ML Seasons: 5

Overall Statistics

	W	L	ERA	G	GS	Sv	IP	H	R	BB	SO	HR
1992	7	7	2.95	56	4	7	91.2	67	32	45	86	8
Career	24	14	2.94	246	6	42	391.2	345	140	173	308	31

How Often He Throws Strikes

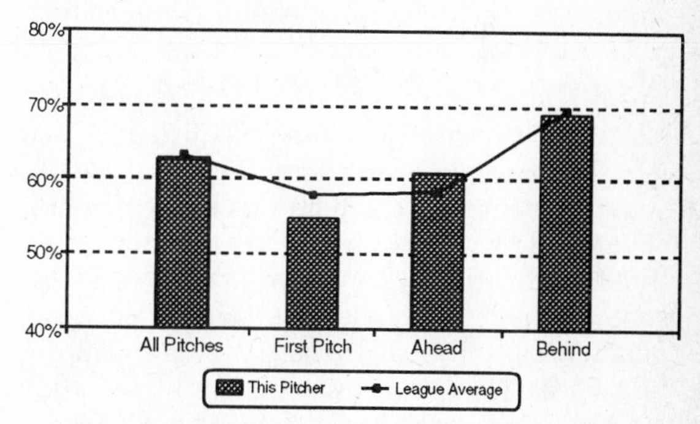

1992 Situational Stats

	W	L	ERA	Sv	IP		AB	H	HR	RBI	AVG
Home	4	3	2.30	3	47.0	LHB	193	35	4	16	.181
Road	3	4	3.63	4	44.2	RHB	130	32	4	24	.246
Day	3	1	1.76	3	46.0	Sc Pos	92	20	3	33	.217
Night	4	6	4.14	4	45.2	Clutch	111	28	3	21	.252

1992 Rankings (National League)

- 4th in lowest batting average allowed vs. left-handed batters (.181)
- 6th in relief losses (7)
- 10th in highest percentage of inherited runners scored (34.4%)
- Led the Giants in relief losses

PITCHING:

Part of the big Kevin Mitchell trade with Seattle, Dave Burba bounced between the minors and the Giants in 1992 with mixed results. He started the season with some promising outings for the Giants, but when he struggled, he returned to the minors and proceeded to continue his difficulties in the Pacific Coast League. Burba was only 5-5 with a 4.72 ERA at AAA Phoenix, hardly encouraging numbers.

Burba's numbers with the Giants weren't eye-popping, either. Opposing batters hit .287 against him while his ERA finished at 4.97. However, switched to pitching in relief, Burba finished the year with some encouraging appearances. He struck out 11 in his last 13.1 innings, an indication of the stuff that still makes the Giants think that he can be a useful major-league pitcher.

Burba is a hard thrower with a fastball that can get into the 90s and a hard slider. He also throws a split-fingered pitch which he uses as an offspeed counter. However, his fastball is too straight at times and he still does not have confidence in the splitter. The result is a lot of sliders, which gets him in trouble. Burba also had problems controlling his stuff last year: he issued 31 walks in 70.2 innings. Burba permitted 20 hits in 44 at-bats on the first pitch (.455 average), when he often just laid one down the middle in an attempt to get ahead.

HOLDING RUNNERS, FIELDING, HITTING:

Burba is very slow to home plate, making him fairly easy to run on by enemy basestealers. However, his four steals allowed in five attempts last year weren't a disaster. Burba is not quick off the mound to field his position. He is no threat whatsoever as a hitter, with only one hit in 15 career at-bats.

OVERALL:

The Giants still like Burba's potential and he will likely get a shot to stick in a starting rotation which in the off-season had very few sure things. But if he wants to stay there, he'll have to pitch a lot better than he did in 1992.

DAVE BURBA

Position: RP/SP
Bats: R **Throws:** R
Ht: 6' 4" **Wt:** 220

Opening Day Age: 26
Born: 7/7/66 in Dayton, OH
ML Seasons: 3

Overall Statistics

	W	L	ERA	G	GS	Sv	IP	H	R	BB	SO	HR
1992	2	7	4.97	23	11	0	70.2	80	43	31	47	4
Career	4	9	4.53	51	13	1	115.1	122	65	47	67	10

How Often He Throws Strikes

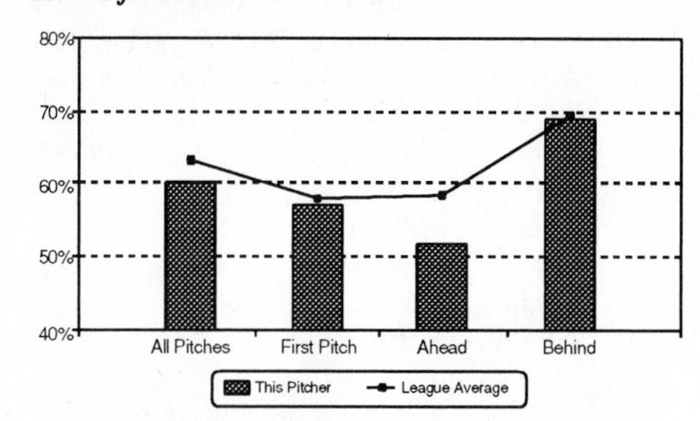

1992 Situational Stats

	W	L	ERA	Sv	IP		AB	H	HR	RBI	AVG
Home	1	2	2.94	0	33.2	LHB	151	48	1	18	.318
Road	1	5	6.81	0	37.0	RHB	128	32	3	26	.250
Day	0	4	7.33	0	23.1	Sc Pos	72	23	1	38	.319
Night	2	3	3.80	0	47.1	Clutch	10	0	0	1	.000

1992 Rankings (National League)

- 8th in highest batting average allowed vs. left-handed batters (.318)

PITCHING:

John Burkett is one of those guys who doesn't knock anyone's eyes out with an abundance of overpowering stuff. But he was the Giants' biggest winner in 1992, again defying assessments that his stuff is too short and that he is not durable enough to go the long haul. Over the last three seasons Burkett has gone 14-7, 12-11 and 13-9 despite the fact that he's usually worked for a struggling club.

In 1992 Burkett led the Giants in innings pitched. Though he allowed nearly 200 hits, he was able to keep his club in most of his starts with good control and the ability to pitch through trouble. His strikeout-to-walk ratio (107-45) was excellent. Burkett was extremely tough on right-handed hitters, holding them to a .208 average and only two home runs in 269 at-bats. However, he had major problems with lefties (.296, 11 homers).

When Burkett is at his best, he will mix a good sinking fastball with a sharp curve and either a change, slider or splitter. He often gets himself in trouble by not challenging hitters and instead trying to finesse himself out of trouble. When Burkett goes after hitters, he can be very effective. As he wears down, however, he often stops throwing the fastball and instead becomes too much of a breaking-ball pitcher.

HOLDING RUNNERS, FIELDING, HITTING:

Burkett will make numerous throws to first and has developed a deceptive pickoff move. But he still had some problems with the stolen base last year, permitting 17 steals in 24 attempts. He is an average fielder at best. Burkett is also one of baseball's worst hitting pitchers. He had all of one hit in 55 at-bats with 24 strikeouts. He did manage eight sacrifices and two RBI.

OVERALL:

Burkett is one of the few starting pitchers whom the Giants can count on. He is not a number-one starter who they can count on for 240 innings. But if they view him as a solid third or fourth starter, he won't disappoint. Unfortunately, the Giants have all third and fourth starters and not much better.

JOHN BURKETT

Position: SP
Bats: R **Throws:** R
Ht: 6' 2" **Wt:** 210

Opening Day Age: 28
Born: 11/28/64 in New Brighton, PA
ML Seasons: 4

Overall Statistics

	W	L	ERA	G	GS	Sv	IP	H	R	BB	SO	HR
1992	13	9	3.84	32	32	0	189.2	194	96	45	107	13
Career	39	27	3.95	104	98	1	606.1	625	295	169	361	52

How Often He Throws Strikes

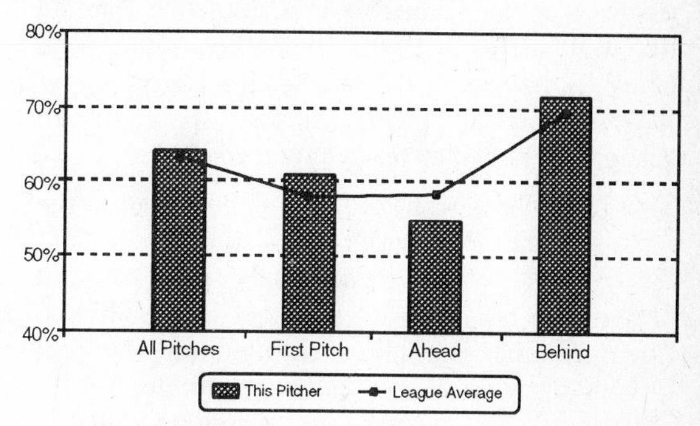

1992 Situational Stats

	W	L	ERA	Sv	IP		AB	H	HR	RBI	AVG
Home	10	2	3.09	0	102.0	LHB	466	138	11	58	.296
Road	3	7	4.72	0	87.2	RHB	269	56	2	25	.208
Day	8	4	3.59	0	87.2	Sc Pos	168	51	3	66	.304
Night	5	5	4.06	0	102.0	Clutch	30	9	2	7	.300

1992 Rankings (National League)

- 2nd in highest batting average allowed with runners in scoring position (.304)
- 4th in highest ERA on the road (4.72)
- 5th in most run support per 9 innings (4.7)
- Led the Giants in wins (13), games started (32), complete games (3), innings pitched (189.2), hits allowed (194), batters faced (799), strikeouts (107), most pitches thrown (2,762), pickoff throws (202), stolen bases allowed (17), winning percentage (.591), highest strikeout/walk ratio (2.4), least pitches thrown per batter (3.46), most run support per 9 innings and most strikeouts per 9 innings (5.1)

CLUTCH HITTER

WILL CLARK

Position: 1B
Bats: L **Throws:** L
Ht: 6' 1" **Wt:** 190

Opening Day Age: 29
Born: 3/13/64 in New Orleans, LA
ML Seasons: 7

HITTING:

By most players' standards, a .300 average with 16 homers and 73 RBI would not be a bad year. But for Will Clark, those 1992 numbers represented the second-worst season of his career. Clark's deflated production seemed to embody the entire Giants season. He missed 18 games with assorted injuries. Clark also seemed visibly affected by the club's second-half swoon and the uncertainty surrounding where it would play its games in '93.

Some people around the Giants also felt Clark's attitude also changed. He's long been known as a fierce competitor, but there were grumblings that he was more of a selfish player last year. Said one member of the Giants' organization, "It seemed like Will was taken with the idea of being Will Clark, Superstar instead of being a tough player like he always had been. And when things started going bad, he never really bounced back."

That said, Clark was still a tough customer in the clutch, hitting .330 with men in scoring position. His low RBI total was due mostly to the fact that he was the only consistent threat in the Giants' lineup. Teams often pitched around him resulting in him drawing more walks (73, including 23 intentional passes) and receiving fewer pitches he could drive with power.

BASERUNNING:

Once a poor baserunner, Clark has improved. His 12 steals last year were a career high. He gambles less than he used to in his earlier years in terms of taking extra bases.

FIELDING:

Clark is one of the best fielding first basemen in the game. Along with all his other 1992 problems he made 10 errors, many of them throwing miscues. He will always try to make the tough play but it will sometimes backfire.

OVERALL:

On the heels of his poor 1992 season, this will be a crossroads season for "The Thrill." There's no reason to believe that he won't make last year just an aberration and bounce back to be one of the game's great hitters. He is still a potential Hall of Fame talent.

Overall Statistics

	G	AB	R	H	D	T	HR	RBI	SB	BB	SO	AVG
1992	144	513	69	154	40	1	16	73	12	73	82	.300
Career	1028	3778	605	1139	222	35	162	636	50	443	676	.301

Where He Hits the Ball

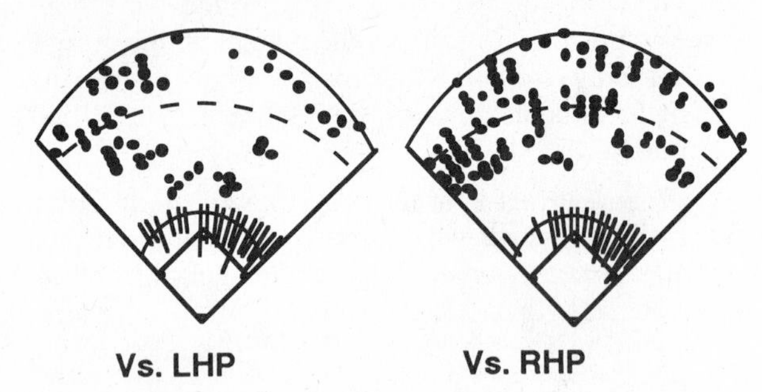

1992 Situational Stats

	AB	H	HR	RBI	AVG		AB	H	HR	RBI	AVG
Home	270	91	11	44	.337	LHP	205	63	2	30	.307
Road	243	63	5	29	.259	RHP	308	91	14	43	.295
Day	212	61	4	19	.288	Sc Pos	112	37	5	55	.330
Night	301	93	12	54	.309	Clutch	87	23	2	12	.264

1992 Rankings (National League)

- 2nd in doubles (40), sacrifice flies (11) and intentional walks (23)
- 4th in batting average at home (.337)
- Led the Giants in batting average (.300), runs scored (69), hits (154), doubles, total bases (244), RBI (73), sacrifice flies, walks (73), intentional walks, times on base (231), most pitches seen (2,111), plate appearances (601), slugging percentage (.476), on-base percentage (.384), least GDPs per GDP situation (4.9%), batting average vs. left-handed pitchers (.307), on-base percentage vs. left-handed pitchers (.366), batting average at home (.337) and lowest percentage of swings that missed (18.9%)

HITTING:

The Giants handed young Royce Clayton the shortstop job coming out of spring training last year. But when he couldn't cut it offensively, they sent him back to Triple-A for a spell, although he returned later in the season. So in a sense it was a disappointing year for the talented 23 year old.

But it was also a learning season for a kid who was trying to make the big jump from Double-A to the majors. Said a National League manager, "That kind of jump is tough on any kid, but especially on a shortstop where there is so much to worry about in the field on top of trying to hit major-league pitching for the first time."

Clayton showed occasional flashes of the offensive potential that so excites the Giants. However, he was also overmatched plenty of other times. He could not handle hard stuff on the inside half of the plate and was often over-anxious trying to catch up with breaking stuff out of the strike zone. Clayton struck out 63 times with only 26 walks in 321 at-bats.

BASERUNNING:

Clayton could soon blossom into a 25-30 stolen base talent. He has good instincts and better-than-average speed and only needs experience to be a good basestealing threat.

FIELDING:

Said Hall of Famer Joe Morgan, who telecasts many Giant home games, "What impressed me most about Clayton is that when he was struggling to hit, he didn't take that with him out on the field like a lot of young players. He played the heck out of shortstop even when he couldn't buy a hit. I like to see that in a young guy." In time, Clayton should be in the elite group of defensive shortstops.

OVERALL:

The Giants only saw the tip of the iceberg with Clayton. He was able to survive some growing pains and should enter 1993 much more relaxed. This year, Clayton has a chance to start blossoming into a star.

ROYCE CLAYTON

Position: SS
Bats: R **Throws:** R
Ht: 6' 0" **Wt:** 175

Opening Day Age: 23
Born: 1/2/70 in Burbank, CA
ML Seasons: 2

Overall Statistics

	G	AB	R	H	D	T	HR	RBI	SB	BB	SO	AVG
1992	98	321	31	72	7	4	4	24	8	26	63	.224
Career	107	347	31	75	8	4	4	26	8	27	69	.216

Where He Hits the Ball

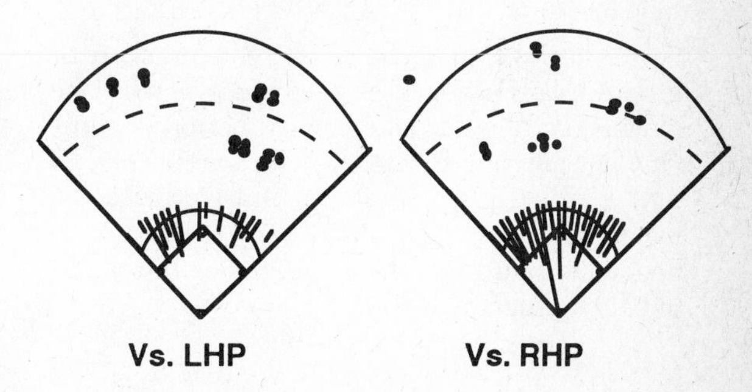

1992 Situational Stats

	AB	H	HR	RBI	AVG		AB	H	HR	RBI	AVG
Home	172	43	3	15	.250	LHP	96	24	0	4	.250
Road	149	29	1	9	.195	RHP	225	48	4	20	.213
Day	132	29	2	12	.220	Sc Pos	82	15	1	20	.183
Night	189	43	2	12	.228	Clutch	61	12	0	2	.197

1992 Rankings (National League)

- 3rd in lowest batting average on an 0-2 count (.071)
- 4th in most GDPs per GDP situation (17.2%)

MIKE FELDER

Position: CF/LF/RF
Bats: B **Throws:** R
Ht: 5' 8" **Wt:** 160

Opening Day Age: 30
Born: 11/18/62 in Vallejo, CA
ML Seasons: 8

HITTING:

Mike Felder remained a good role player in 1992, doing quality work off the bench for the Giants and frequently filling in for injured or slumping players. The veteran got into 145 games but logged only 322 at-bats while batting a career-high .286. At season's end he cashed in, signing a free agent contract with the Mariners.

One of the rare switch-hitters who is almost equally effective from either side of the plate, Felder is a spray hitter who rarely pulls from either side. He is content to fight off hard stuff inside and take pitches he can handle to the opposite field. This doesn't translate into many extra-base hits, yet Felder surprised with four home runs and three triples last year.

Felder is also a good bunter who gets his share of infield hits. However, he wears down when he plays every day for an extended period of time. One tell-tale sign is that when he starts tiring, he will lose his patience at bat and start chasing inside pitches he really isn't quick enough to handle. In addition, Felder takes far too few walks to be a topflight leadoff hitter.

BASERUNNING:

Felder is an aggressive baserunner who has excellent instincts for taking extra bases. He has always been a high-percentage basestealer and last season was successful on 14 of 18 attempts. The steal total was his lowest in four years, however.

FIELDING:

With the ability to play all three outfield positions with competence, Felder is a valuable man to have around. His arm is only fair and he is probably best suited to playing left field. However, he gets an excellent jump on the ball from all positions and has very good range.

OVERALL:

Felder, for all his plusses, didn't really fit in with the Giants' plan to break in some younger outfielders. Seattle, looking for a vet after Henry Cotto turned free agent, signed Felder after the expansion draft. New Mariner Manager Lou Piniella plans to give Felder the opportunity to start in left field and bat leadoff. If he falters, he will probably fill in the fourth or fifth outfielder role he handles so well.

Overall Statistics

	G	AB	R	H	D	T	HR	RBI	SB	BB	SO	AVG
1992	145	322	44	92	13	3	4	23	14	21	29	.286
Career	732	1803	277	464	50	25	13	140	143	142	171	.257

Where He Hits the Ball

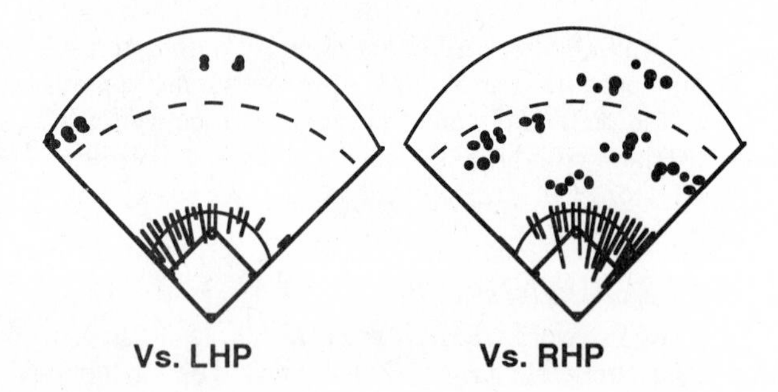

1992 Situational Stats

	AB	H	HR	RBI	AVG		AB	H	HR	RBI	AVG
Home	164	43	1	7	.262	LHP	88	27	1	6	.307
Road	158	49	3	16	.310	RHP	234	65	3	17	.278
Day	146	35	3	14	.240	Sc Pos	54	14	1	19	.259
Night	176	57	1	9	.324	Clutch	90	26	1	9	.289

1992 Rankings (National League)

- 1st in lowest batting average on a 3-1 count (.000)
- 7th in batting average on an 0-2 count (.290)
- Led the Giants in batting average on an 0-2 count and steals of third (3)
- Led NL center fielders in batting average on an 0-2 count

PITCHING:

Bryan Hickerson exceeded expectations in his rookie season by handling one of the most difficult roles in baseball, namely that of the left-handed reliever. Hickerson was a stable and effective performer, rolling up 87.1 innings and compiling a solid ERA of 3.09 in 61 games. Though he didn't post a save he recorded eight holds and permitted only 11 of 39 inherited runners to score.

Hickerson performed his primary job very well -- handling left-handed hitters. He held lefties to a .235 average and only one left-handed hitter hit a home run off him all season. Hickerson also held righties to a .236 mark but was touched for six four-baggers. Twenty of the 50 hits he yielded to righties went for extra bases, a dangerously high total.

Hickerson's main weapon is a good split-fingered pitch which he mixes with a riding fastball and slider. He also has excellent control, walking only 21 batters while fanning 68 in his 87.1 innings last year. He held up over the season despite his 61-game load. Apart from one poor final-week appearance, he was excellent the last month of the season (3.06 ERA) while pitching in the situational roles in which he excelled.

HOLDING RUNNERS, FIELDING, HITTING:

Hickerson has a slow delivery home but does a very good job of holding runners. He permitted only one stolen base last year with six caught stealings. He is an average fielder, though his delivery sometimes leaves him out of position to make a play. He was hitless in four at-bats.

OVERALL:

Finding decent left-handed relievers is sort of like mining for gold. Though Hickerson might not be an overpowering lefthander, he showed last year that he has a solid future in this difficult-to-fill role and the Giants protected him from expansion. He should see lots of action in middle relief this year.

BRYAN HICKERSON

Position: RP
Bats: L **Throws:** L
Ht: 6' 2" **Wt:** 195

Opening Day Age: 29
Born: 10/13/63 in Bemidji, MN
ML Seasons: 2

Overall Statistics

	W	L	ERA	G	GS	Sv	IP	H	R	BB	SO	HR
1992	5	3	3.09	61	1	0	87.1	74	31	21	68	7
Career	7	5	3.28	78	7	0	137.1	127	51	38	111	10

How Often He Throws Strikes

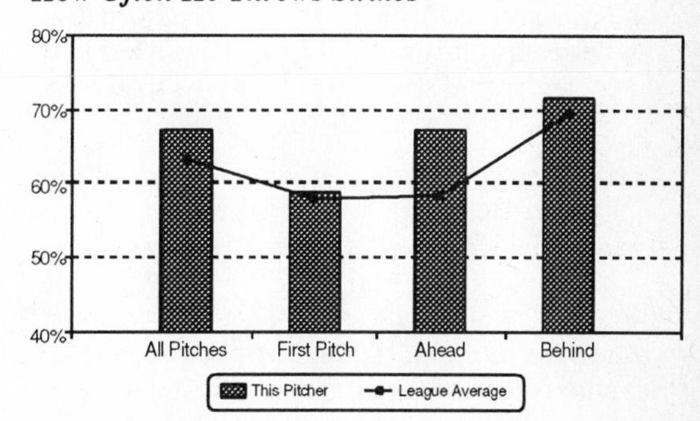

1992 Situational Stats

	W	L	ERA	Sv	IP		AB	H	HR	RBI	AVG
Home	2	3	3.95	0	41.0	LHB	102	24	1	8	.235
Road	3	0	2.33	0	46.1	RHB	212	50	6	27	.236
Day	1	1	4.15	0	34.2	Sc Pos	72	18	3	28	.250
Night	4	2	2.39	0	52.2	Clutch	116	28	3	15	.241

1992 Rankings (National League)

- 1st in first batter efficiency (.113)
- 4th in least baserunners allowed per 9 innings in relief (9.8)
- Led the Giants in first batter efficiency

PITCHING:

Mike Jackson was one of the three good arms acquired by the Giants in the Kevin Mitchell trade with Seattle. If pure stuff were the only barometer, Jackson would be the best of the trio. He throws a fastball that is routinely in the mid 90s. He also has a wicked slider, an improving forkball and dabbles with a change. It is the kind of stuff teams expect from a closer.

However, Jackson has never adapted to that role and instead has settled in as a sometimes inconsistent middle reliever. The righthander led the Giants with 67 appearances last year but had a very shaky second half, posting a 5.57 ERA after the break. As one NL pitching coach said, "Jackson has a great arm and the kind of stuff you love. But he seems like he might be too nice a kid to be a real closer. And sometimes he seems to give the hitters too much credit."

Jackson had spurts last year where he was almost unhittable. But there were also spells like the season's final four weeks when he allowed 18 hits in 9.2 innings and had an ERA of over nine. Jackson also allowed seven home runs in his 82 innings for the year, far too many for a man with his stuff. Jackson did strike out 80 in those 82 innings with only 23 unintentional walks.

HOLDING RUNNERS, FIELDING, HITTING:

Jackson has a decent move to first, but a slow delivery home makes him vulnerable to stolen bases. He played a lot of infield in high school and it shows, because he is an agile defensive player. He had two hitless at-bats last year and is 2-for-19 lifetime.

OVERALL:

Jackson is only 28 years old with the kind of ability that could still allow him to step up and be a big-time reliever. In the meantime, while he remains a talented enigma, he also has a lot of value to the Giants' bullpen.

MIKE JACKSON

Position: RP
Bats: R **Throws:** R
Ht: 6' 0" **Wt:** 200

Opening Day Age: 28
Born: 12/22/64 in Houston, TX
ML Seasons: 7

Overall Statistics

	W	L	ERA	G	GS	Sv	IP	H	R	BB	SO	HR
1992	6	6	3.73	67	0	2	82.0	76	35	33	80	7
Career	31	41	3.56	393	7	31	569.1	459	252	268	489	56

How Often He Throws Strikes

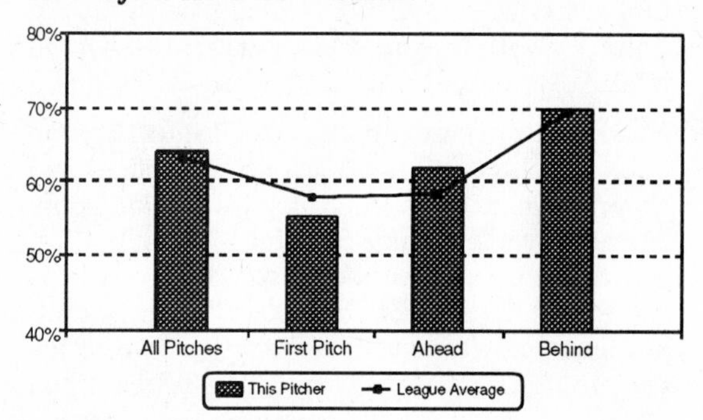

1992 Situational Stats

	W	L	ERA	Sv	IP		AB	H	HR	RBI	AVG
Home	3	0	3.15	1	40.0	LHB	162	43	3	14	.265
Road	3	6	4.29	1	42.0	RHB	140	33	4	20	.236
Day	2	1	2.67	1	33.2	Sc Pos	71	16	0	22	.225
Night	4	5	4.47	1	48.1	Clutch	150	36	5	12	.240

1992 Rankings (National League)

- 8th in most strikeouts per 9 innings in relief (8.8)
- 10th in relief wins (6)
- Led the Giants in games pitched (67), holds (9), relief wins and most strikeouts per 9 innings in relief

HITTING:

There is not a more streaky hitter than Chris James, who lumped together some decent production last year with slumps such as a 2-for-32 spell that plagued him from April 22nd through the end of May. He still managed 32 RBI in his 248 at-bats, many coming in pinch-hitting or late-inning replacement opportunities. James was very effective against left-handed pitching; he had a .302 average vs. lefties but he was buried by righties to the tune of .189.

James is at his best when he thinks opposite field and drives pitches the other way. However, he will too often try to pull; when that happens he gets tied up with hard stuff inside or overswings trying to jerk offspeed stuff out of the strike zone. James is also notorious for pressing when he starts slumping. He can be his own worst enemy because of the way he gets down on himself. In addition, he has never been a disciplined hitter, as shown by his 45 strikeouts and 14 walks last year.

James had to adapt to part-time duty after logging over 400 at-bats for four straight seasons. He adjusted fairly well; 19 of his 60 hits went for extra-bases, as he usually made the most of his limited opportunities.

BASERUNNING:

James has average speed and is no threat to steal a base. However, he has a football background and is an extremely aggressive baserunner when going for extra bases or trying to break up double plays.

FIELDING:

After years of shoulder trouble, James has become something of a liability in the field. He has a very weak throwing arm and can only play left adequately. He gets a decent jump on the ball, however, and will occasionally make a great play.

OVERALL:

James was a free agent and his status with the Giants was very uncertain. His days as a front-line player might be over, but he can still be a solid major-league reserve with his occasional power and hard-nosed approach to the game.

CHRIS JAMES

Position: LF
Bats: R **Throws:** R
Ht: 6' 1" **Wt:** 190

Opening Day Age: 30
Born: 10/4/62 in Rusk, TX
ML Seasons: 7

Overall Statistics

	G	AB	R	H	D	T	HR	RBI	SB	BB	SO	AVG
1992	111	248	25	60	10	4	5	32	2	14	45	.242
Career	779	2665	283	694	122	19	72	333	24	148	398	.260

Where He Hits the Ball

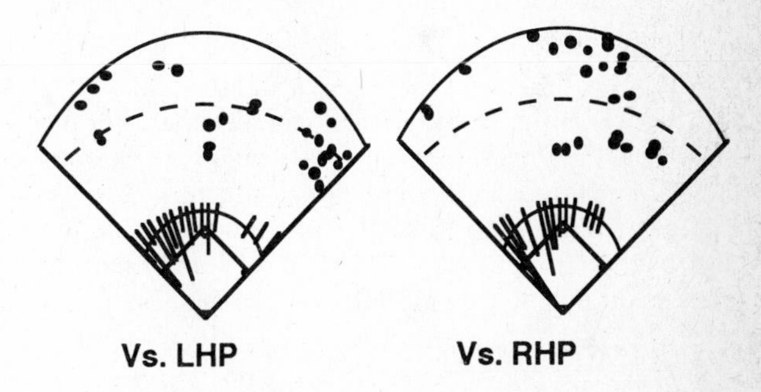

1992 Situational Stats

	AB	H	HR	RBI	AVG		AB	H	HR	RBI	AVG
Home	127	27	3	19	.213	LHP	116	35	2	13	.302
Road	121	33	2	13	.273	RHP	132	25	3	19	.189
Day	99	27	2	16	.273	Sc Pos	66	17	0	23	.258
Night	149	33	3	16	.221	Clutch	41	10	1	2	.244

1992 Rankings (National League)

- → 7th in batting average on a 3-2 count (.364)
- → 10th in lowest batting average with 2 strikes (.140)
- → Led NL left fielders in batting average on a 3-2 count

HITTING:

After several years of wasted opportunities, Kirt Manwaring finally nailed down the Giants' starting catching job last year. He did it by producing enough offensively to justify a lineup spot, something which was previously open to question.

Entering last season Manwaring had hit one home run in 514 career at-bats. Last year, he hit four in 349 at-bats. He had three triples prior to 1992, but last year he had five. He also added 10 doubles to give him 19 extra-base hits for the season after having only 24 lifetime before '92. One reason for the improvement was a quicker bat which allowed Manwaring, who previously had been easily overpowered by fastballs, to occasionally turn around the hard stuff. He also moved up slightly on the plate, giving him better coverage.

Manwaring also makes contact at the plate fairly consistently; he only struck out 42 times. For the first time in his career, he became dangerous against left-handed pitching, hitting .305. Of course, he didn't exactly turn into Gary Carter. Manwaring hit only .214 with runners in scoring position and just .217 after the All-Star break.

BASERUNNING:

Manwaring has decent speed for a catcher. Still, he's no basestealing threat (he matched his career high with two steals last year) and rarely tries to take an extra base.

FIELDING:

The Giants have stuck with Manwaring for so long because of his defensive ability. He blocks balls well and frames the plate with soft hands. He has become an excellent handler of pitchers and a good student of opposing hitters' tendencies. Manwaring has a strong, accurate arm which is one of the best in the game; he gunned down a NL-leading 51 percent of opposing runners.

OVERALL:

With Manwaring, it's always been a question of whether he could hit enough to keep his good glove in the lineup. Finally in 1992 he did just that and the Giants made him their only expansion-protected catcher. If he can keep his offense at this level (his second-half slump opens up questions), he could be the Giants' number-one catcher for the next several years.

KIRT MANWARING

Position: C
Bats: R **Throws:** R
Ht: 5'11" **Wt:** 190

Opening Day Age: 27
Born: 7/15/65 in Elmira, NY
ML Seasons: 6

Overall Statistics

	G	AB	R	H	D	T	HR	RBI	SB	BB	SO	AVG
1992	109	349	24	85	10	5	4	26	2	29	42	.244
Career	315	863	66	199	30	8	5	79	5	51	117	.231

Where He Hits the Ball

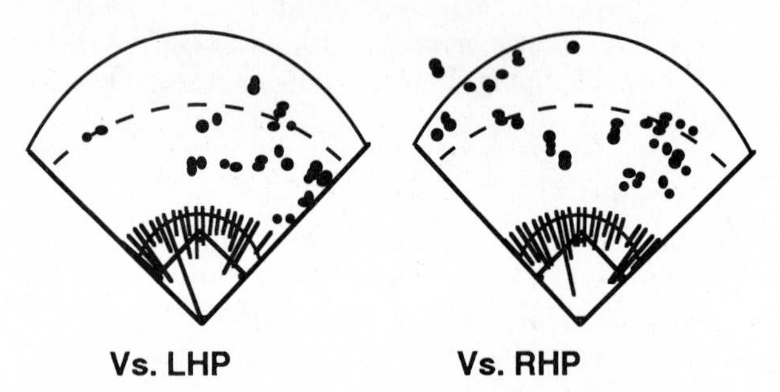

1992 Situational Stats

	AB	H	HR	RBI	AVG		AB	H	HR	RBI	AVG
Home	168	39	1	15	.232	LHP	131	40	0	6	.305
Road	181	46	3	11	.254	RHP	218	45	4	20	.206
Day	154	41	4	18	.266	Sc Pos	84	18	0	22	.214
Night	195	44	0	8	.226	Clutch	70	17	2	6	.243

1992 Rankings (National League)

- 1st in lowest batting average on a 3-1 count (.000)
- 2nd in most GDPs per GDP situation (19.7%)
- Led the Giants in triples (5)
- Led NL catchers in triples and highest percentage of runners caught stealing as a catcher (50.5%)

WILLIE McGEE

Position: RF/CF
Bats: B **Throws:** R
Ht: 6' 1" **Wt:** 195

Opening Day Age: 34
Born: 11/2/58 in San Francisco, CA
ML Seasons: 11

HITTING:

As usual, Willie McGee flirted with the .300 mark all last year. As usual, he also was solid with men in scoring position with a .337 average in those situations. So why did the Giants leave McGee exposed in the expansion draft?

Well, as one member of the Giants organization put it, the numbers don't tell the whole story. Said the Giant, "You watch the guy every day and you come to realize that the .300 he hits is the most meaningless .300 you've ever seen. He doesn't drive in runs. He doesn't run much anymore. He doesn't have power. He doesn't walk. So that .300 is a really soft .300."

Indeed, McGee had only 36 RBI and scored only 56 runs last year. He rarely walks and he strikes out a lot for a singles hitter -- his strikeout-to-walk ratio was an atrocious 88-29. Of his 141 hits, only 23 were for extra bases. Hard stuff inside accounts for most of his strikeouts; that's how pitchers try to work him. If they don't have the stuff to get inside, pitchers try to go away and out of the strike zone because they know McGee won't walk.

BASERUNNING:

Though he still runs well, for some reason McGee stopped trying to steal bases a few years ago and hasn't resumed with the Giants. He attempted only 17 steals in 1992, two less attempts than Will Clark of all people.

FIELDING:

McGee can track the ball with the best center fielders, though you can count on him for his share of mental lapses during the course of any season. He has a below-average throwing arm.

OVERALL:

McGee will still be with the Giants in all probability, but his starter's role could be in jeopardy if younger alternatives arise. He does give the Giants a lot of hits and he is still a pro in center field and in the clubhouse. But he is far from being the impact player he once was in St. Louis.

Overall Statistics

	G	AB	R	H	D	T	HR	RBI	SB	BB	SO	AVG
1992	138	474	56	141	20	2	1	36	13	29	88	.297
Career	1462	5669	773	1689	257	83	57	639	307	315	878	.298

Where He Hits the Ball

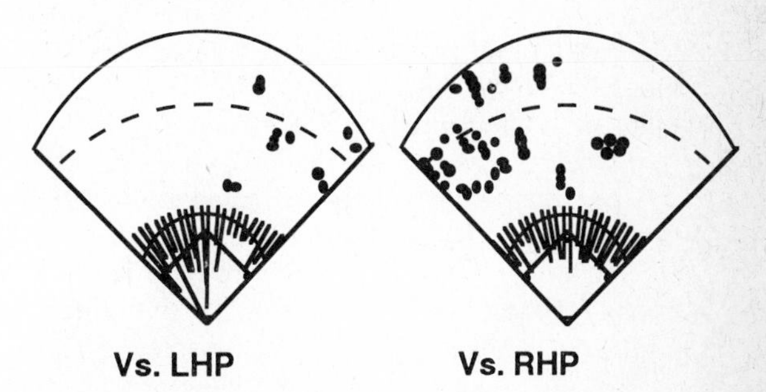

1992 Situational Stats

	AB	H	HR	RBI	AVG		AB	H	HR	RBI	AVG
Home	224	71	0	14	.317	LHP	159	45	1	12	.283
Road	250	70	1	22	.280	RHP	315	96	0	24	.305
Day	182	65	0	17	.357	Sc Pos	101	34	0	29	.337
Night	292	76	1	19	.260	Clutch	95	26	0	11	.274

1992 Rankings (National League)

- 1st in highest groundball/flyball ratio (3.6)
- 2nd in batting average on a 3-2 count (.419)
- 4th in lowest HR frequency (474 ABs per HR)
- 5th in lowest percentage of pitches taken (44.3%) and lowest percentage of swings put into play (38.6%)
- Led the Giants in singles (118), highest groundball/flyball ratio, batting average with runners in scoring position (.337), batting average with the bases loaded (.300), batting average on a 3-1 count (.429), batting average on a 3-2 count and batting average on the road (.280)

PITCHING:

By midseason of 1992, Dave Righetti had become the forgotten man of the Giants' bullpen. He never approached any consistent effectiveness. The Giants even gave Righetti four starts in hopes he would pitch his way out of trouble, but the sad fact is that he might be on an irreversible career slide.

Righetti's 5.06 ERA last year was a career worst by plenty -- in 12 previous seasons, he'd never had a mark higher than 3.79. The sinking fastball which Righetti used to throw in the low 90s was rarely clocked last year above 87. He had trouble throwing his curve for strikes and his slider lacked the sharp break it once had a few years ago.

The result of all this decline in his repertoire was that Righetti was hit very hard. He allowed more hits than innings pitched for only the second time in his career. His strikeout rate was a career-low 5.4 per nine innings. He managed only three saves and was hardly used in the season's final weeks, and only in middle relief or mop-up situations for most of the year. He did seem to throw a little harder near the end of the season.

HOLDING RUNNERS, FIELDING, HITTING:

Righetti has never had a good pickoff move. His high leg kick on his delivery home gives baserunners an advantage. Righetti often lands out of good defensive position but generally does a decent job of making routine fielding plays. He is no factor as a hitter, with four of his seven at-bats last year ending in strikeouts.

OVERALL:

One of baseball's class acts, Righetti faces a very uncertain future. He has lost his closer's role to Rod Beck and is unlikely to be able to return as a starting pitcher. If last year was any indication, his stuff might be sliding to the point where he can't cut it in a set-up role, either. However, the Giants aren't likely to eat his big contract, so he'll probably get the chance to show he has something left, maybe as a lefty specialist.

DAVE RIGHETTI

Position: RP/SP
Bats: L **Throws:** L
Ht: 6' 4" **Wt:** 212

Opening Day Age: 34
Born: 11/28/58 in San Jose, CA
ML Seasons: 13

Overall Statistics

	W	L	ERA	G	GS	Sv	IP	H	R	BB	SO	HR
1992	2	7	5.06	54	4	3	78.1	79	47	36	47	4
Career	78	75	3.25	637	80	251	1286.0	1142	524	537	1038	73

How Often He Throws Strikes

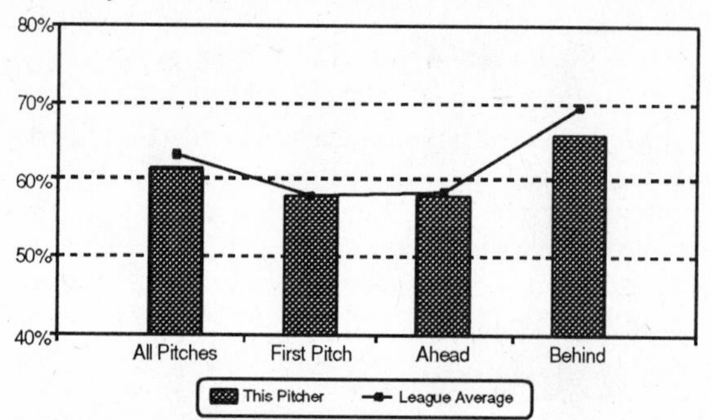

1992 Situational Stats

	W	L	ERA	Sv	IP		AB	H	HR	RBI	AVG
Home	1	3	2.82	3	44.2	LHB	89	21	0	9	.236
Road	1	4	8.02	0	33.2	RHB	205	58	4	22	.283
Day	2	4	5.73	1	33.0	Sc Pos	76	17	1	24	.224
Night	0	3	4.57	2	45.1	Clutch	98	29	1	6	.296

1992 Rankings (National League)

- 10th in balks (2) and highest batting average allowed in relief (.263)
- Led the Giants in wild pitches (6)

CORY SNYDER

Position: RF/1B/3B/LF/CF
Bats: R **Throws:** R
Ht: 6' 3" **Wt:** 185

Opening Day Age: 30
Born: 11/11/62 in Inglewood, CA
ML Seasons: 7

Overall Statistics

	G	AB	R	H	D	T	HR	RBI	SB	BB	SO	AVG
1992	124	390	48	105	22	2	14	57	4	23	96	.269
Career	852	2987	360	729	139	12	132	414	23	165	798	.244

Where He Hits the Ball

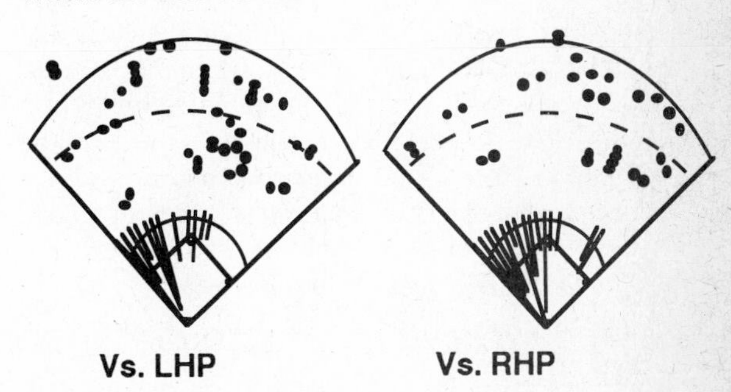

1992 Situational Stats

	AB	H	HR	RBI	AVG		AB	H	HR	RBI	AVG
Home	184	55	8	34	.299	LHP	170	50	6	20	.294
Road	206	50	6	23	.243	RHP	220	55	8	37	.250
Day	152	44	7	33	.289	Sc Pos	118	30	2	41	.254
Night	238	61	7	24	.256	Clutch	79	18	2	10	.228

1992 Rankings (National League)

- 9th in lowest batting average on a 3-1 count (.091)
- Led the Giants in slugging percentage vs. left-handed pitchers (.471)

HITTING:

There was no more pleasant surprise for the Giants in 1992 than Cory Snyder. He had bounced around several organizations before the Giants gave him a spring training look last season. Snyder ended up being one of their most productive players after assuming a regular role six weeks into the season.

Snyder showed he still had power; his 14 homers were surpassed on the Giants only by Will Clark and Matt Williams. Only Clark and Williams had more RBI than Snyder's 57. Only Clark and Robby Thompson had more doubles than Snyder's 22. Snyder was especially potent in June, hitting .372 to win the National League's Player of the Month award.

Always a free swinger, Snyder struck out a lot (96) while walking only 23 times. However, he made some successful adjustments to his hitting style that helped him hit a respectable .269. He moved slightly up on the plate, giving him better plate coverage on the outside breaking balls that always gave him trouble. He also raised his hands slightly and worked on hitting more on top of the ball rather than upper-cutting. The result was much more consistency than Snyder had shown in several years. For the first time in a while, he held his own against right-handed pitching. Snyder managed a decent .250 average against righties with eight of his home runs.

BASERUNNING:

Snyder is an aggressive runner but does not have good speed. He was just four-for-eight in stolen base tries last season. However, he has decent instincts in trying for the extra base and he is rugged in breaking up double plays.

FIELDING:

Snyder can play left or right and can also fill in at first or third in emergencies. However, he has only fair range in the outfield, though his arm remains as powerful as ever.

OVERALL:

The Giants picked Snyder up off the scrap heap and he gave them unexpected numbers. The free agent will likely return to play a variety of roles in what is a very uncertain Giants outfield picture.

BILL SWIFT

Position: SP/RP
Bats: R **Throws:** R
Ht: 6' 0" **Wt:** 180

Opening Day Age: 31
Born: 10/27/61 in South Portland, ME
ML Seasons: 7

Overall Statistics

	W	L	ERA	G	GS	Sv	IP	H	R	BB	SO	HR
1992	10	4	2.08	30	22	1	164.2	144	41	43	77	6
Career	40	44	3.69	283	108	25	923.2	971	436	296	369	43

How Often He Throws Strikes

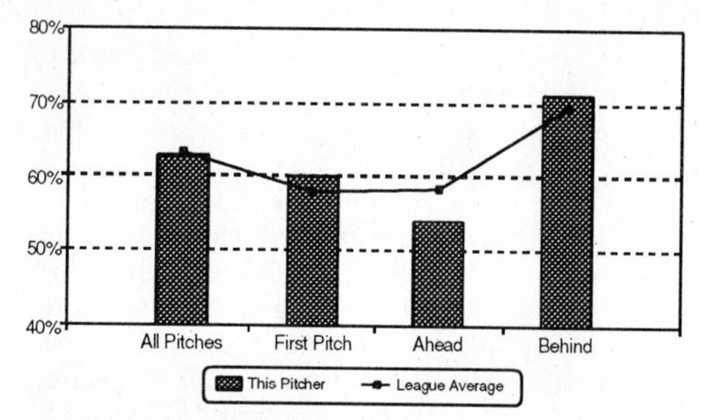

1992 Situational Stats

	W	L	ERA	Sv	IP		AB	H	HR	RBI	AVG
Home	4	3	2.55	1	84.2	LHB	383	101	5	31	.264
Road	6	1	1.58	0	80.0	RHB	219	43	1	9	.196
Day	7	1	1.79	1	80.2	Sc Pos	114	19	2	31	.167
Night	3	3	2.36	0	84.0	Clutch	69	16	2	6	.232

1992 Rankings (National League)

- 1st in ERA (2.08), highest groundball/flyball ratio allowed (2.6) and most GDPs induced per 9 innings (1.4)
- 3rd in GDPs induced (26)
- Led the Giants in ERA, complete games (3), shutouts (2), GDPs induced, lowest batting average allowed (.239), lowest slugging percentage allowed (.314), lowest on-base percentage allowed (.292), highest groundball/flyball ratio allowed, least baserunners allowed per 9 innings (10.4), least home runs allowed per 9 innings (.33), most GDPs induced per 9 innings, most GDPs induced per GDP situation (21.0%) and ERA at home (2.55)

PITCHING:

When all was said and done the Giants had to be pleased with the acquisition of Bill Swift, the key man in the Kevin Mitchell deal with Seattle. Swift came out of the chute as the hottest pitcher in baseball, winning his first six starts. Then, as a lot of people predicted, Swift couldn't handle the rigors of starting and had some shoulder problems. He returned later in the season and pitched superbly out of the bullpen, where he'd had his greatest success in Seattle.

Swift ended up leading the National League in ERA with a 2.08 mark. He allowed just six homers and opponents batted only .239 against him. Over the last three years he's permitted only 13 home runs in nearly 400 innings.

As usual, Swift had the hard, sinking fastball that makes him so tough to hit. Thrown in the low 90s, the heavy sinker is his out pitch helping him induce 26 double play grounders, third in the league in 1992. Swift also throws a good slider, a curve and uses a forkball as an offspeed pitch. He is especially tough on right-handed hitters, who batted only .196 against him last year.

HOLDING RUNNERS, FIELDING, HITTING:

Few pitchers in baseball are better athletes than Swift. He compensates for not having a great move to first with an extremely quick delivery home. The result is that he's one of the toughest pitchers to run on in the majors. Swift is also among the best half-dozen fielding pitchers in the game. In his first year in the NL he managed eight hits, including three doubles and three RBI.

OVERALL:

It is uncertain how the Giants will use Swift this year. He pitched well as a starter, but predictions that his arm couldn't handle the load proved correct. He is a proven reliever who could combine with Rod Beck for a solid one-two bullpen punch. Given his history, the Giants might have little choice except to use him as a reliever.

ROBBY THOMPSON

Position: 2B
Bats: R **Throws:** R
Ht: 5'11" **Wt:** 170

Opening Day Age: 30
Born: 5/10/62 in West Palm Beach, FL
ML Seasons: 7

Overall Statistics

	G	AB	R	H	D	T	HR	RBI	SB	BB	SO	AVG
1992	128	443	54	115	25	1	14	49	5	43	75	.260
Career	983	3426	487	883	174	34	85	342	87	313	713	.258

Where He Hits the Ball

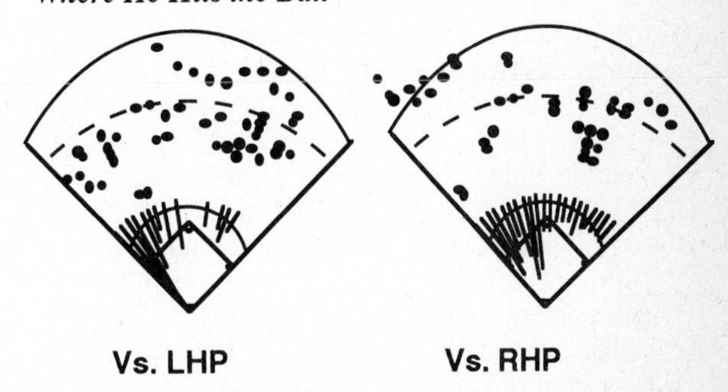

1992 Situational Stats

	AB	H	HR	RBI	AVG		AB	H	HR	RBI	AVG
Home	236	64	8	27	.271	LHP	164	46	1	11	.280
Road	207	51	6	22	.246	RHP	279	69	13	38	.247
Day	170	51	6	21	.300	Sc Pos	88	18	4	35	.205
Night	273	64	8	28	.234	Clutch	86	14	2	10	.163

1992 Rankings (National League)

- 4th in hit by pitch (8)
- 7th in lowest batting average with runners in scoring position (.207)
- 9th in lowest batting average in the clutch (.163)
- Led the Giants in caught stealing (9), hit by pitch, most pitches seen per plate appearance (3.81), highest percentage of pitches taken (55.6%) and highest percentage of swings put into play (44.1%)
- Led NL second basemen in hit by pitch

HITTING:

As usual, back troubles limited Robby Thompson's playing time last year. But while he appeared in only 128 games, Thompson still put together a solid season and remained a reliable part of the Giants' small nucleus. In a year when most Giants had their production drop, Thompson had a decent power season with 14 homers and 25 doubles. The steady second baseman's .260 average was two points higher than his current career average.

Though a valuable middle infielder because of his power, Thompson has his limitations. He's always struggled in clutch situations, batting only .205 with men in scoring position in 1992 and .217 over the last five seasons. He's always hit for a higher average against lefties (.280 last year, .247 vs. righties). But Thompson has begun to hit for more power against righthanders: last year 13 of his 14 homers were off righties.

Once a prolific strikeout man, Thompson has gradually reduced his whiff total from 133 in 1989 to a career-low 75 last year. He has learned to lay off the outside fastballs and breaking balls which have always plagued him. Thompson hits to all fields but remains primarily a pull hitter who crowds the plate, looking for pitches to yank.

BASERUNNING:

Thompson tries to be a basestealer but has always lacked the necessary speed and instincts to be much of a threat. Last year was a good example, as he stole only five bases in 14 attempts. Several of them were pickoffs, to which he has always been vulnerable. However, Thompson is aggressive in taking the extra base.

FIELDING:

Thompson is a heady defensive player who is excellent at turning the double play. However, his range is subpar and he will make his share of errors on balls a lot of second baseman can reach.

OVERALL:

If his back holds up (always a big if with Thompson), he is one of this shaky franchise's few reliable players. Thompson is a leader on and off the field and his value goes far beyond his statistics.

JOSE URIBE

Position: SS
Bats: B **Throws:** R
Ht: 5'10" **Wt:** 165

Opening Day Age: 34
Born: 1/21/59 in San Cristobal, Dominican Republic
ML Seasons: 9

Overall Statistics

	G	AB	R	H	D	T	HR	RBI	SB	BB	SO	AVG
1992	66	162	24	39	9	1	2	13	2	14	25	.241
Career	993	3011	303	725	98	34	19	216	73	248	420	.241

Where He Hits the Ball

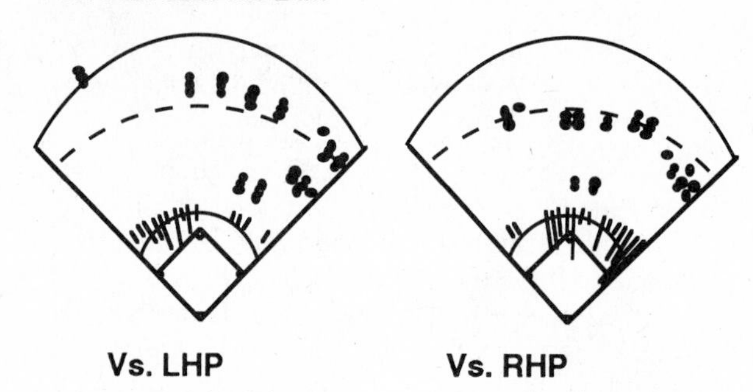

1992 Situational Stats

	AB	H	HR	RBI	AVG		AB	H	HR	RBI	AVG
Home	69	19	0	6	.275	LHP	53	16	1	6	.302
Road	93	20	2	7	.215	RHP	109	23	1	7	.211
Day	80	19	1	8	.237	Sc Pos	31	11	0	11	.355
Night	82	20	1	5	.244	Clutch	39	10	0	2	.256

1992 Rankings (National League)

→ Did not rank near the top or bottom in any category

HITTING:

It was evident in the final days of the '92 season that the San Francisco career of Jose Uribe was coming to an end. Uribe had always been something of an overachiever with the Giants and he had given the club several seasons of solid work. However, Royce Clayton is obviously the club's future shortstop.

Uribe did another adequate job of playing short last year after Clayton was sent to the minors. He led the Giants with a .355 average with men in scoring position, though his at-bats were limited. He got into only 66 games and batted just 162 times -- both were his lowest totals since coming to the Giants in 1985.

The switch-hitting Uribe has always been much more effective as a right-handed hitter -- .302 as a righty last year, .211 as a lefty. Uribe has always struggled trying to hit any kind of breaking ball from the left side. He is much more patient hitting right-handed; if he catches on somewhere else, he might well give up switch-hitting. Though a hitter without power, Uribe has also been a free-swinger who does not take many pitches and walks infrequently. He had only 14 walks last year, three of them intentional, and his lifetime on-base average is a lowly .298.

BASERUNNING:

Though he has good quickness, Uribe has never been much of a basestealing threat. He had only two steals in four attempts last year and hasn't stolen in double figures since 1988. He lacks overall aggressiveness on the bases.

FIELDING:

Uribe's once-good range has deteriorated noticeably in the last three years. He rarely gets to balls in the hole that other shortstops reach. He does have soft hands and a strong accurate arm.

OVERALL:

A free agent, Uribe's hope is to catch on with another club looking for some veteran insurance up the middle. His days with the Giants are probably over, and at 34, it won't be easy for him to find another job.

GREAT RANGE

MATT D. WILLIAMS

Position: 3B
Bats: R **Throws:** R
Ht: 6' 2" **Wt:** 210

Opening Day Age: 27
Born: 11/28/65 in Bishop, CA
ML Seasons: 6

Overall Statistics

	G	AB	R	H	D	T	HR	RBI	SB	BB	SO	AVG
1992	146	529	58	120	13	5	20	66	7	39	109	.227
Career	682	2428	293	586	97	16	121	376	24	143	556	.241

Where He Hits the Ball

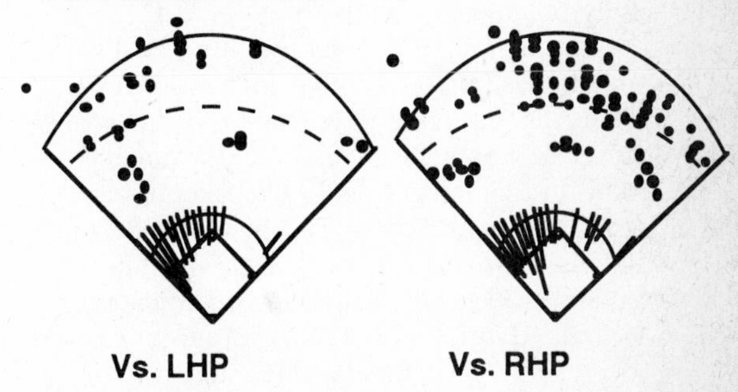

1992 Situational Stats

	AB	H	HR	RBI	AVG		AB	H	HR	RBI	AVG
Home	269	62	9	29	.230	LHP	164	37	10	21	.226
Road	260	58	11	37	.223	RHP	365	83	10	45	.227
Day	213	44	8	24	.207	Sc Pos	149	31	8	49	.208
Night	316	76	12	42	.241	Clutch	107	20	2	13	.187

1992 Rankings (National League)

- 1st in errors at third base (23) and highest percentage of swings that missed (26.6%)
- 2nd in lowest batting average (.227) and lowest batting average vs. right-handed pitchers (.227)
- 3rd in strikeouts (109), lowest slugging percentage vs. right-handed pitchers (.356), lowest on-base percentage vs. right-handed pitchers (.290) and lowest percentage of swings put into play (38.4%)
- Led the Giants in home runs (20), at-bats (529), triples (5), strikeouts, GDPs (15), games played (146) and HR frequency (26.5 ABs per HR)
- Led NL third basemen in triples and errors

HITTING:

There was no more disappointing member of the Giants in 1992 than Matt Williams. Seemingly established as one of the game's premier players, Williams took a sharp skid backward in production. Williams fell from 34 home runs in '91 to 20, from 98 RBI to 66 and from a .268 average to .227.

Williams also hit only .208 with men in scoring position last year. What caused consternation was the impression that as the long season dragged on, Williams lost interest and became a listless player. The Giants had hoped that he was beyond the stage where slumps bothered him. But Williams definitely was not the same player in 1992.

Williams has always lacked discipline at the plate and it was evident again last season when he fanned 109 times while walking only 39 times. For so talented a player, Williams has made remarkably few adjustments. He continues to have trouble with breaking stuff away, which he constantly tries to pull instead of taking to the opposite field. Williams is murder on high fastballs and can also turn on low pitches. But unless he adjusts better to breaking pitches, he'll continue to have some very ugly at-bats.

BASERUNNING:

Williams has decent quickness but he uses poor judgement in trying to steal bases. He was only seven-for-14 in steal attempts last year. Williams will also run into occasional outs on the bases, but he has basically solid instincts.

FIELDING:

Williams has Mike Schmidt-like defensive skills at third. His reactions are as good as those of any third baseman in baseball. However, his concentration seemed to wander at times last year. That tendency, along with a habit of off-balance, misguided throws, contributed to a 23-error season.

OVERALL:

Everybody has their share of off years. But Williams should be at the point in his career where a season full of the abject futility he demonstrated last year would be behind him. Still, he remains one of the franchise's foundation players. At 27, he's at a perfect age to show some maturity and put together a big comeback season.

TREVOR WILSON

Position: SP
Bats: L **Throws:** L
Ht: 6' 0" **Wt:** 195

Opening Day Age: 26
Born: 6/7/66 in Torrance, CA
ML Seasons: 5

PITCHING:

The 1992 season was one that lefthander Trevor Wilson would just as soon forget. He was never the same after undergoing spring surgery for a tumor in his rib. Later in the year, when he was finally getting reasonably healthy, Wilson had a tragedy in his family when his elderly grandmother was beaten in her home. It all added up to an 8-14 record on the heels of Wilson's encouraging 13-win 1991 season when for much of the year he was the Giants' best pitcher. His ERA soared to 4.21 as opposing hitters hit .265 against him and he allowed 18 home runs.

Always an excitable sort who seems to press in difficult situations, Wilson wasn't helped last season by the injuries. It took him much of the year to regain his velocity, which at his best hits 90 with a fastball that rides in on left-handed hitters. Wilson also struggled constantly with his mechanics and as a result pitched too much from behind in the count. His 1992 strikeout-to-walk ratio (88-64) is simply not acceptable for a pitcher with his stuff, especially considering his 1991 numbers (139 strikeouts, 77 walks). Wilson's injuries also largely retarded the progress he was making with a slider and change-up.

HOLDING RUNNERS, FIELDING, HITTING:

Wilson has a deceptive pickoff move which can be quite effective. He is quick to the plate with his delivery, making him one of the tougher pitchers against stolen bases: last year he permitted only six steals in 13 attempts, an excellent record. He is a pretty good athlete who is usually in position to make defensive plays. Wilson had a poor year with the bat in 1992 but he's a very respectable .172 lifetime hitter and a good bunter.

OVERALL:

Wilson has often been an enigma for the Giants, but last year's problems are very understandable considering his physical and personal difficulties. He's only 26 years old and talented enough to mature into a quality member of the Giants' pitching staff.

Overall Statistics

	W	L	ERA	G	GS	Sv	IP	H	R	BB	SO	HR
1992	8	14	4.21	26	26	0	154.0	152	82	64	88	18
Career	31	37	3.92	115	80	0	527.2	465	255	222	330	45

How Often He Throws Strikes

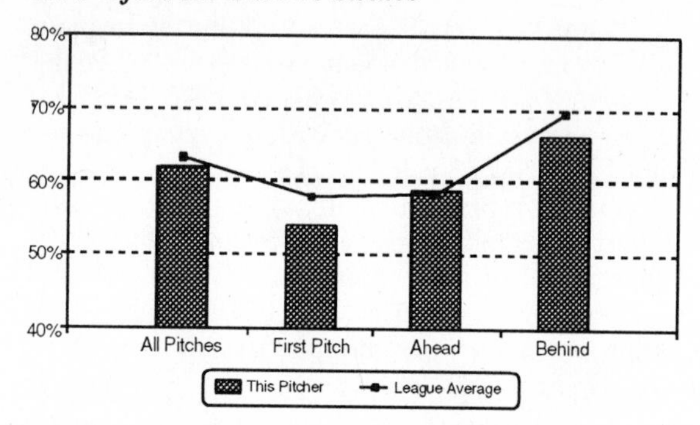

1992 Situational Stats

	W	L	ERA	Sv	IP		AB	H	HR	RBI	AVG
Home	4	9	4.17	0	86.1	LHB	134	35	3	16	.261
Road	4	5	4.26	0	67.2	RHB	440	117	15	56	.266
Day	4	6	3.57	0	68.0	Sc Pos	131	34	6	51	.260
Night	4	8	4.71	0	86.0	Clutch	24	5	0	0	.208

1992 Rankings (National League)

- 1st in balks (7)
- 3rd in losses (14)
- 5th in lowest winning percentage (.364) and highest ERA at home (4.17)
- 6th in home runs allowed (18) and hit batsmen (6)
- 7th in GDPs induced (19)
- 9th in pickoff throws (188)
- Led the Giants in losses, walks allowed (64), hit batsmen, balks, and lowest batting average allowed vs. right-handed batters (.266)

HITTING:

Former Olympic star Ted Wood didn't show much in a brief look last year, but he will likely get a chance to win a job in what is a wide-open Giants outfield situation. Wood certainly has nothing left to prove at the Triple A level. He hit .311 with 109 RBI in 1991 at Phoenix and last year batted .304 there.

The one knock against Wood (pardon the pun) is that he strikes out an awful lot for someone who has never shown power. He is more of a line drive hitter who might hit 10 or so homers but is more likely to hit a double or an occasional triple. Wood fanned 74 times in Triple-A last year and struck out 15 times in only 58 at-bats with the Giants. However, the upside is that he's a very patient hitter who figures to draw an above-average number of walks. In the minors, Wood had consistently excellent on-base averages.

In his brief trials with the Giants, Wood has had trouble catching up with hard stuff. Plus, he's been vulnerable to breaking balls out of the strike zone. However, the left-handed hitter hangs in decently against southpaw pitchers, something many young lefties have trouble doing.

BASERUNNING:

Wood isn't a burner but he is a better-than-average runner who will likely be able steal a dozen or so bases a year. He's stolen as many as 17 in a minor-league season, but his career success rate is a mediocre 61 percent.

FIELDING:

Wood has excellent outfield instincts and shows signs of becoming a good defensive outfielder as he gains more experience. He has fine range and an outstanding throwing arm that could fit nicely in either left or right field.

OVERALL:

With so many questions in the Giants' outfield, Wood should get his chance to win a job this year. The Giants wish he had more power, but he does offer solid defense and the promise of a decent average, discipline, and some extra-base potential.

TED WOOD

Position: RF
Bats: L **Throws:** L
Ht: 6' 2" **Wt:** 178

Opening Day Age: 26
Born: 1/4/67 in Mansfield, OH
ML Seasons: 2

Overall Statistics

	G	AB	R	H	D	T	HR	RBI	SB	BB	SO	AVG
1992	24	58	5	12	2	0	1	3	0	6	15	.207
Career	34	83	5	15	2	0	1	4	0	8	26	.181

Where He Hits the Ball

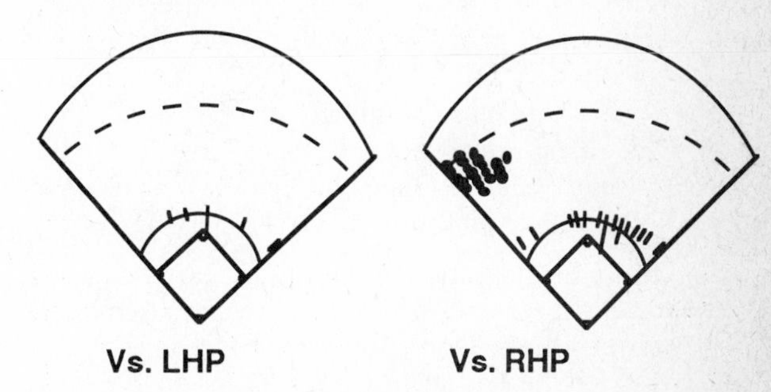

1992 Situational Stats

	AB	H	HR	RBI	AVG		AB	H	HR	RBI	AVG
Home	30	7	0	2	.233	LHP	13	5	0	0	.385
Road	28	5	1	1	.179	RHP	45	7	1	3	.156
Day	32	4	0	1	.125	Sc Pos	10	1	0	2	.100
Night	26	8	1	2	.308	Clutch	12	0	0	0	.000

1992 Rankings (National League)

- Did not rank near the top or bottom in any category

SCOTT GARRELTS

Position: RP/SP
Bats: R **Throws:** R
Ht: 6' 4" **Wt:** 210

Opening Day Age: 31
Born: 10/30/61 in Urbana, IL
ML Seasons: 10

Overall Statistics

	W	L	ERA	G	GS	Sv	IP	H	R	BB	SO	HR
1992				Did Not Play								
Career	69	53	3.29	352	89	48	959.1	815	395	413	703	74

PITCHING, FIELDING, HITTING & HOLDING RUNNERS:

Scott Garrelts has missed the better part of two years with shoulder injuries, but the Giants have some hope that he might be able to return in the '93 season. He did not appear at all last season but by year's end the Giants thought he was close to being able to pitch.

If he's healthy, and that's a big if, Garrelts has an excellent forkball with which he can often over-power hitters. Don't forget that this is a pitcher who led the National League in ERA in 1989 and who won in double figures four times from 1986 to 1990. Garrelts is also a pitcher who has both started and relieved with success, which gives him added value.

Garrelts has never been good at holding runners, though he is fairly quick at delivering the ball home. He is a decent fielder and can help himself at times with his bat.

OVERALL:

On a pitching staff which has some openings, a comeback by the free agent Garrelts would be a welcome surprise for the Giants. However, he has hardly pitched at all for two years and the kind of serious arm troubles that he's had suggest another problem could be just around the corner. It will be tough for the Giants to count on Garrelts, and he may have to win a job in Spring training.

STEVE HOSEY

Position: RF
Bats: R **Throws:** R
Ht: 6' 3" **Wt:** 218

Opening Day Age: 24
Born: 4/2/69 in Oakland, CA
ML Seasons: 1

Overall Statistics

	G	AB	R	H	D	T	HR	RBI	SB	BB	SO	AVG
1992	21	56	6	14	1	0	1	6	1	0	15	.250
Career	21	56	6	14	1	0	1	6	1	0	15	.250

HITTING, FIELDING, BASERUNNING:

The Giants have high hopes that Steve Hosey will become a legit major-league power hitter very soon. He got a 56-at-bat look last year. The good news was that he hit .341 when he made contact. The bad news was that he struck out 15 times without walking for a .241 on-base average.

However, Hosey has hit with power at every level at which he's played. If the development of this former number-one draft pick continues, the Giants would be willing to live with the strikeouts in exchange for some extra-base pop. He is still raw, still vulnerable to offspeed stuff and breaking balls. But he can hit a mistake a long way.

Hosey is a good runner for a big man. He's had good stolen base totals in the minors, but he's also been caught stealing a high number of times (16-for-32 last year). Hosey is a solid outfielder with good range and an above-average throwing arm.

OUTLOOK:

Hosey has been one of the Giant organization's darlings for a while. After a good year at AAA Phoenix, he's at the point where he could be poised for a breakthrough. If it comes, the timing would be perfect because the Giants are dying for an outfielder to take charge of a very unsteady situation. Hosey was the team's only outfielder protected from expansion.

DARREN LEWIS

Position: CF
Bats: R **Throws:** R
Ht: 6' 0" **Wt:** 175

Opening Day Age: 25
Born: 8/28/67 in Berkeley, CA
ML Seasons: 3

Overall Statistics

	G	AB	R	H	D	T	HR	RBI	SB	BB	SO	AVG
1992	100	320	38	74	8	1	1	18	28	29	46	.231
Career	197	577	83	137	13	4	2	34	43	72	80	.237

HITTING, FIELDING, BASERUNNING:

At times, Darren Lewis has shown signs of blossoming as a major-league leadoff hitter. But in each of the last two seasons, he has followed promising stretches with long periods of non-production. Last year Lewis landed back in Triple-A, where he languished for part of the summer.

Lewis' lifetime stats show his potential: 577 at-bats, 72 walks, 43 stolen bases, 83 runs scored. However, his career batting average is only .237. His biggest problem is learning to not try to pull pitches but to simply slap the ball and let his speed take over. While he's become a groundball hitter, Lewis has stretches where he'll try to lift everything, a trait that allows pitchers to bury him with outside breaking balls and hard stuff up and in. When he puts his mind to it, though, Lewis can handle the bat well.

Lewis led the league in stolen bases for a spell last year and finished with 28 steals in 36 attempts. He can run down fly balls in center field with the best of them, though he will occasionally make a mistake of over-aggressiveness. He has a good throwing arm.

OVERALL:

Lewis has too many skills for the Giants to give up on him just yet. He's only 25 years old and he still could be the Giants' center fielder of the future. He wasn't protected by the Giants from expansion, but escaped selection, which may or may not be an indicator of how he is viewed by major-league scouts at this point.

JOHN PATTERSON

Position: 2B
Bats: B **Throws:** R
Ht: 5' 9" **Wt:** 160

Opening Day Age: 26
Born: 2/11/67 in Key West, FL
ML Seasons: 1

Overall Statistics

	G	AB	R	H	D	T	HR	RBI	SB	BB	SO	AVG
1992	32	103	10	19	1	1	0	4	5	5	24	.184
Career	32	103	10	19	1	1	0	4	5	5	24	.184

HITTING, FIELDING, BASERUNNING:

The Giants had hopes of making second baseman John Patterson into an outfielder before the '93 season. However, Patterson needed major surgery to repair a torn rotator cuff in his right shoulder, and as a result his future is up in the air.

If he can make a comeback, Patterson offers a lot of potential. He is a switch-hitter with excellent speed and athletic ability. He was overmatched in most of the major-league action he saw last year, but he showed his talent by hitting .301 with 20 doubles, six triples and 22 steals at AAA Phoenix. Patterson has had three straight solid seasons while moving up the Giants' minor-league ladder, displaying extra-base pop along with the ability to make consistent contact.

Patterson's speed, range and throwing arm made the Giants think he could cut it as an outfielder. If not, he could settle in as a back-up at second base, though he also has the skill to play short or third. He can be an excellent basestealer with the proper experience.

OVERALL:

The Giants felt they had a real sleeper in the talented Patterson, but his shoulder injury means that he will likely be sidelined into the season. He could be back with San Francisco before the campaign ends, but they're not really counting on him.

ORGANIZATION OVERVIEW:

San Francisco is now under new ownership and field leadership; it'll be interesting to see where the franchise is heading. General manager Al Rosen and field manager Roger Craig are both gone. Will the Giants' new GM Bob Quinn move conservatively, staying away from free agents and blending in some youth, or will he try to get competitive more quickly? The Giant farm system has a good reputation, but some of its recent products -- like Steve Decker and Royce Clayton -- haven't lived up to their advance billing. To succeed, the Giants will have to get better performance from their young players. Quinn faces a daunting challenge to rebuild a franchise left in turmoil after some poor signings and shaky expansion protection decisions.

MIKE BENJAMIN

Position: SS **Opening Day Age:** 27
Bats: R **Throws:** R **Born:** 11/22/65 in
Ht: 6' 3" **Wt:** 195 Euclid, OH

Recent Statistics

	G	AB	R	H	D	T	HR	RBI	SB	BB	SO	AVG
92 AAA Phoenix	31	108	15	33	10	2	0	17	4	3	18	.306
92 NL San Francisco	40	75	4	13	2	1	1	3	1	4	15	.173

Probably the biggest shocker on the supposedly-secret "protected list" in last year's expansion draft was shortstop Mike Benjamin. Benjamin has had four separate trials with the Giants, and though he's proven himself to be a defensive ace, his lifetime average is .160 after 243 at-bats. Benjamin has never hit much even in the minors -- his career high is .259 -- so he's probably not going to start now. Just how bad can Royce Clayton (supposedly the number-one prospect in baseball a year ago) be?

RICK HUISMAN

Position: P **Opening Day Age:** 23
Bats: R **Throws:** R **Born:** 5/17/69 in Oak
Ht: 6' 3" **Wt:** 200 Park, IL

Recent Statistics

	W	L	ERA	G	GS	Sv	IP	H	R	BB	SO	HR
91 A San Jose	16	4	1.83	26	26	0	182.1	126	45	73	216	5
92 AA Shreveport	7	4	2.35	17	16	0	103.1	79	33	31	100	3
92 AAA Phoenix	3	2	2.41	9	8	0	56.0	45	16	24	44	3

One of the Giants' most talented minor-league pitchers, Huisman had another outstanding year in 1992. Moved up in midseason, he finished with a 2.41 ERA for 56 innings at Phoenix and seemed a cinch to be one of the club's 15 protected expansion draft players. But then Huisman came down with arm problems and needed surgery on his right bicep muscle, so they took a chance and left him unprotected. If he's healthy, he could be a star.

KEVIN McGEHEE

Position: P **Opening Day Age:** 24
Bats: R **Throws:** R **Born:** 1/18/69 in
Ht: 6' 0" **Wt:** 190 Alexandria, LA

Recent Statistics

	W	L	ERA	G	GS	Sv	IP	H	R	BB	SO	HR
91 A San Jose	13	6	2.33	26	26	0	174.0	129	58	87	171	1
92 AA Shreveport	9	7	2.96	25	24	0	158.1	146	61	42	140	10

A righthander drafted in 1990, McGehee is a take-charge type with a good sinking fastball that has produced excellent strikeout totals in the minors. In two and a half seasons, he's fanned 397 batters in 406 innings while compiling a 3.01 ERA. He also throws a curve and change, and his control was greatly improved last year at AA Shreveport where he went 9-7. The Giants didn't protect McGehee in the first round of the expansion draft, indicating he was no Mike Benjamin in their eyes, but they were relieved when he wasn't taken. He might be with the big club this year.

KEVIN ROGERS

Position: P **Opening Day Age:** 24
Bats: B **Throws:** L **Born:** 8/20/68 in
Ht: 6' 2" **Wt:** 190 Cleveland, MS

Recent Statistics

	W	L	ERA	G	GS	Sv	IP	H	R	BB	SO	HR
92 AA Shreveport	8	5	2.58	16	16	0	101.0	87	34	29	110	3
92 AAA Phoenix	3	3	4.00	11	11	0	69.2	63	34	22	62	0
92 NL San Fran.	0	2	4.24	6	6	0	34.0	37	17	13	26	4

Another Giant on the fast track, Rogers followed the same path as former Giant Steve Reed, moving from Shreveport to Phoenix to San Francisco over the course of the 1992 season. The lefty was rated the number-two prospect in the Texas League where he was 8-5, 2.58. Rogers has a good, moving fastball, excellent slider and great location. He could be in the Giants' rotation this year.

SALOMON TORRES

Position: P **Opening Day Age:** 21
Bats: R **Throws:** R **Born:** 3/11/72 in San
Ht: 5' 11" **Wt:** 150 Pedro De Macoris, DR

Recent Statistics

	W	L	ERA	G	GS	Sv	IP	H	R	BB	SO	HR
91 A Clinton	16	5	1.41	28	28	0	210.2	148	48	47	214	4
92 AA Shreveport	6	10	4.21	25	25	0	162.1	167	93	34	151	10

Shreveport must have had some staff last year, with Huisman, Steve Reed, Rogers and Salomon Torres all working for them at one time during the season. Unlike the others, Torres spent the whole year there and had some problems, going 6-10 with a 4.21 ERA. He was nonetheless picked as the seventh-best prospect in the league. The Dominican righthander was 16-5, 1.41 at Class A Clinton in 1991 and he's only 21 years old. The Giants will take their time with him.

About STATS, Inc.

It all starts with the **system**. The STATS scoring method, which includes pitch-by-pitch information and the direction, distance, and velocity of each ball hit into play, yields an immense amount of information. Sure, we have all the statistics you're used to seeing, but where other statistical sources stop, STATS is just getting started.

Then, there's the **network**. Our information is timely because our game reporters send their information by computer as soon as the game is over. Statistics are checked, rechecked, updated, and are available daily.

Analysis comes next. STATS constantly searches for new ways to use this wealth of information to open windows into the workings of baseball. Accurate numbers, intelligent computer programming, and a large dose of imagination all help coax the most valuable information from its elusive cover.

Finally, distribution!

For 13 years now, STATS has served over a dozen Major League teams. The box scores that STATS provides to the *Associated Press* and *USA Today* have revolutionized what baseball fans expect from a box score. *Baseball Weekly* is chock full of STATS handiwork, while ESPN's nightly baseball coverage is supported by a full-time STATS statistician. We provide statistics for *Strat-O-Matic Baseball, Earl Weaver Baseball, Tony LaRussa Baseball, Rotisserie Baseball* and many other baseball games and fantasy leagues all over the country.

For the baseball fan, STATS publishes monthly and year-end reports on each major-league team. We offer a host of year-end statistical breakdowns on paper or disk that cover hitting, pitching, catching, baserunning, fielding, and more. STATS even produces custom reports on request.

Computer users with modems can access the STATS computer for information with STATS On-Line. If you own a computer with a modem, there is no other source with the scope of baseball information that STATS can offer.

STATS and Bill James enjoy an on-going affiliation that has produced much of the STATS product catalogue. We also administer *Bill James Fantasy Baseball,* the ultimate baseball game, designed by Bill James himself, which allows you to manage your own team and compete with other team owners around the country. Whether you play BJFB or another fantasy game, our new STATSfax report can show you what your players did the previous night as soon as you can get to the fax machine in the morning. STATS also offers a head-to-head fantasy football game *STATS Fantasy Football. BJFB: The Winter Game* is a brand new, totally unique historically-based fantasy baseball game for those who can't wait for Spring.

For more information on any of our products write to:

STATS, Inc.
7366 North Lincoln Ave.
Lincolnwood, IL 60646-1708

. . . or call us at 1-708-676-3322. We can send you a STATS brochure, a free *Bill James Fantasy Baseball, STATS Fantasy Football* or *BJFB: The Winter Game* information kit, and/or information on STATS On-Line or STATSfax.

For the story behind the numbers, check out the other STATS publications. *The STATS 1993 Baseball Scoreboard*: The first edition of this book in 1990 took the nation's baseball fans by storm. The all new 1993 edition, available in book stores or directly from STATS, is back with the same great writing, great graphics and stats you won't find anywhere else. *The STATS 1993 Major League Handbook* and *STATS 1993 Minor League Handbook* will provide a complete 1993 reference library, especially important for the coming expansion season. Last, but certainly not least, the new addition to the STATS Publishing family, the *STATS 1993 Player Profiles Book*, is full of breakdowns and situational stats for every major-league player, for those fans who need more than just wins, losses, home runs and RBI.

A

B

C

D

E

F

G

H

I

J

K

L

M

N

O

P

Q

R

S

T

U

V

W

Y

Z